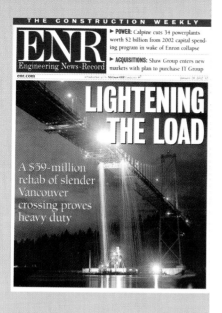

Student

Please enter my subscription for **Engineering News-Record**.

6 months ☐ $29.50 (Domestic)

Name

Address

City State Zip

☐ Payment enclosed ☐ Bill me later

McGraw_Hill CONSTRUCTION ENR

5EN2DMHE

Friendly

Please enter my subscription for **Architectural Record**.

6 months ☐ $19.50 (Domestic)

Name

Address

City State Zip

☐ Payment enclosed ☐ Bill me later

McGraw_Hill CONSTRUCTION Architectural Record 5AR2DMHE

Savings

Please enter my subscription for **Aviation Week & Space Technology**.

6 months ☐ $29.95 (Domestic)

Name

Address

City State Zip

☐ Payment enclosed ☐ Bill me later

CAW34EDU

PASSIVE AND ACTIVE ENVIRONMENTAL CONTROLS

INFORMING THE SCHEMATIC DESIGNING OF BUILDINGS

Dean Heerwagen

University of Washington
Department of Architecture

ILLUSTRATIONS BY

Brendan Connolly, David Hudacek, Lisa Kirkendall, and Kate Sweeney

University of Washington
Department of Architecture

Boston   Burr Ridge, IL   Dubuque, IA   Madison, WI   New York   San Francisco   St. Louis
Bangkok   Bogotá   Caracas   Kuala Lumpur   Lisbon   London   Madrid   Mexico City
Milan   Montreal   New Delhi   Santiago   Seoul   Singapore   Sydney   Taipei   Toronto

Higher Education

PASSIVE AND ACTIVE ENVIRONMENTAL CONTROLS:
INFORMING THE SCHEMATIC DESIGNING OF BUILDINGS

Published by McGraw-Hill, a business unit of The McGraw-Hill Companies, Inc., 1221 Avenue of the Americas, New York, NY 10020.

Some ancillaries, including electronic and print components, may not be available to customers outside the United States.

This book is printed on acid-free paper.

1 2 3 4 5 6 7 8 9 0 CCW/CCW 0 9 8 7 6 5 4 3

ISBN 0–07–250173–1

Publisher: *Elizabeth A. Jones*
Senior sponsoring editor: *Suzanne Jeans*
Developmental editor: *Amanda J. Green*
Marketing manager: *Sarah Martin*
Lead project manager: *Susan J. Brusch*
Senior production supervisor: *Laura Fuller*
Coordinator of freelance design: *Rick D. Noel*
Cover/interior designer: *Amy E. Redmond*
Cover image: *©Getty Images, Digital Vision, Ventilation Pipes #dv199028*
Compositor: *Amy E. Redmond*
Typeface: *10/12 Times Roman*
Printer: *Courier Westford*

The credits section for this book begins on page 927 and is considered an extension of the copyright page.

Library of Congress Cataloging-in-Publication Data

Heerwagen, Dean.
   Passive and active environmental controls : informing the schematic designing of buildings / Dean Heerwagen. — 1st ed.
      p. cm.
   Includes index.
   ISBN 0–07–250173–1
   1. Buildings—Environmental engineering. 2. Human comfort. I. Title.

TH6021.H44   2004
696—dc21   2003046419
                                                                                        CIP

www.mhhe.com

Table of Contents

207   Chapter 6 | THE "PHYSICS" OF LIGHT

245   Chapter 7 | WHAT DO WE SEE?

Preface

APPROACH

The fundamental goal of this text is to present information about environmental controls to use during the early design phases of building creation. Our expectation is that if suitable information about environmental controls can be incorporated during the phases of programming and schematic designing, better buildings and a more efficient design process will result. Consequently, we offer guidelines and approximations that can advise the designer, encouraging her or him to consider and to make early accommodations for environmental controls. We also believe that if these guidelines and approximations are used in schematic designing, then the proposed solutions can readily be "fine tuned" during subsequent design phases.

ORGANIZATION

The text is divided into two parts: the first discusses passive environmental controls, and the second describes active environmental control systems. The environments noted throughout this text include those within buildings as well as those immediately adjacent to building exteriors. Integration of various passive and active environmental controls in buildings will better insure that occupants can live and work comfortably.

PASSIVE ENVIRONMENTAL CONTROLS

The first part of the text—the discussion of passive environmental controls—focuses on the passive management of the thermal, luminous, and acoustic properties of the built environment. The discussion is organized into three *four-chapter units*. Each of these units contain, in order, a *first* chapter that describes the physical principles that characterize heat, light, and sound in natural and built environments; a *second* chapter that identifies the sensory system in the human body that responds to the physical stimulus of heat, light, or sound; a *third* chapter that delineates the properties (or manifestations) of heat, light, or sound, as they appear in the natural (and built) environment(s); and, finally, a *fourth* chapter that catalogs numbers of guidelines—based on the application of passive environmental controls—suggesting how buildings (and adjacent external spaces) can be created to support the sensory needs of occupants.

The *first* chapters of these three units describe heat, light, and sound (i.e., in terms of energy form) and show how each behaves physically. Also, in these first chapters, we have briefly identified how these energy forms are measured. In addition, we explain the unit systems that are applied to characterize the energy forms.

The *second* chapters of the three units describe how the particular human sensory system responds to the physical stimulus (of heat, light, or sound). The discussions of physiology focus particularly on how the information from the physical world is taken in and interpreted by the appropriate sensory system. Then, in these second chapters, we have identified the magnitudes of interpretable physical stimuli and the ranges of these magnitudes that occupants would find comfortable to live and work in.

The *third* chapters of the three four-chapter units describe attributes of the natural and built environments that stimulate our sensory systems. Indeed, these attributes may enable our living, work, and play, or they may exist as challenges to our existence. Subjects addressed in these third chapters include weather and climate, daylight availability, and noise presence. A goal of this text is to encourage the reader to compare the ranges of human sensitivities—to heat, light, and sound—to characteristics of the natural and built environments, thus forcing consideration of the ways in which we are challenged by these environments and how we can respond.

The *fourth* chapters in each of these units identify passive control recommendations whose applications in and around buildings can enhance occupants' living, work, and play. These recommendations, or guidelines, include (a) strategies for siting buildings and using site conditions like vegetation, topography, microclimate, and the presence or absence of adjacent buildings or other built forms; (b) ideas about the internal organizations of buildings such as horizontal and vertical layouts; (c) bases for selecting building envelope compositions (i.e., whether to exclude negative qualities or to introduce positive aspects of the external environment); and (d) suggestions about what internal finishes, furnishings, space divisions, and other like features to apply to acheive satisfactory environmental control.

ACTIVE ENVIRONMENTAL CONTROLS

The second part of the text—six chapters about active environmental controls—discusses HVAC systems (to provide heating, ventilating, and air-conditioning in buildings), electrical systems (to convey electrical energy and operate communication systems in buildings), plumbing systems (to supply water and carry out liquid-borne wastes), fire safety systems and design issues, and human conveyance systems (to move people through buildings). This section describes what these systems do, how they operate, what their primary components are, where these components are commonly placed in buildings, how large the components are, how large the spaces used to house the components need to be, and how the components and spaces may be integrated into building designs. Various rules-of-thumb, design strategies, and other planning short-cuts are also suggested for applications in the early stages of the architectural design process.

Overall, this textbook is the result of collaboration between an author and four graphic artists, all from the University of Washington. My background is in building engineering. Three of the four artists are architects; the fourth is a medical illustrator. I have identified the contents addressed in the text and have suggested—in very approximate manners—the composition of the drawn materials. The four artists have taken these suggestions and have created the artwork that appears throughout the text. So, in the end, this text is the result of the teamwork of five individuals.

DEAN HEERWAGEN
University of Washington, Seattle

Acknowledgements

THE FIVE OF US at the University of Washington wish to offer our gratitude and appreciation to a number of individuals who also are members of the University of Washington community. These people who have enabled our text work include the late Gordon Varey, former Dean of the College of Architecture and Urban Planning; Jeffrey Ochsner, former Chair of the Department of Architecture; Barbara Erwine, Lecturer, Department of Architecture; Ashley Emery and Charles Kippenhan, faculty members in the Department of Mechanical Engineering; Brett Magnuson and Denis Devries, engineers in the Department of Engineering Services; Peter Vickers, fire protection engineer in the Department of Environmental Health and Safety; Thomas Berg, architect in the Department of Engineering Services; Mark Kirschenbaum, Plant Engineer, UW Power Plant; and Terry Holm, Lead Elevator Mechanic, Physical Plant Campus Operations. Similarly, we also wish to acknowledge the guidance of Larry Vogel of the City of Seattle Lighting Department. To all of these people who have offered continuing encouragement and enthusiasm for this text project, we wish to say thank you.

Additionally, comprehensive critiques were offered by the following:

Guy W. Carwile,
Louisiana Technical University

Gary Coates,
Kansas State University

Larry O. Degelman,
Texas A&M University

Walter Grondzik,
Florida A&M University

Melinda La Garce,
Southern Illinois University

Ganapathy Mahalingam,
North Dakota State University

Tahar Messadi,
Georgia Technological University

Carol Prafcke,
North Dakota State University

David Scheatzle,
Arizona State University

CHAPTER ONE

Designing to Control Building Environments

1

THE BASIC REQUIREMENTS for any building are numerous. First, a building should bear evidence of the culture that has created it, and show a link to its historical (or temporal) milieu. Second, the building should control its internal environment well enough to satisfy the occupants' physical and physiological needs. Third, the building should support the psychological state and social activities of each occupant. Fourth, the building should resist the natural forces that act against it (e.g., gravity and seismic loads, weather and climate, and so forth). And, fifth, the building should provide for these first four requirements at a reasonable cost and with an efficient use of resources (e.g., water, fuel, space, occupants' time, etc.). How well any building meets these needs will determine its usefulness and desirability.

The principal responsibility of designers and builders is to create buildings that satisfy these five requirements. How one designs and constructs satisfactory buildings necessarily encompasses the entire study and practice of architecture and building construction. This text will primarily address how to meet the second of these five requirements: how to design and construct buildings to satisfy occupants' physical and physiological needs. Where physical and physiological issues may touch upon working with the other four basic requirements (e.g., how one's state of mind may affect one's physical and physiological needs), then this text will also discuss, at least briefly, interactions between these fundamental requirements.

In any case, the principal topics that will be treated in this book include how to provide the range of environmental services that occupants need and desire. This text will also describe why control of the built environment is necessary and what alternatives exist for achieving adequate environmental control. But, in response to the inevitable question of how much control should be present, we would remind the reader of the story of Goldilocks and The Three Bears. Entering the Bears' home, Goldilocks found that each bear had porridge and that the Papa Bear's was too hot, the Mama Bear's was too cold, and that the Baby Bear's was "just right." Here in this text we will try to identify what environmental controls are "just right," so that these controls will assure *comfortable* internal environments and efficient building operations.

This text will describe how to produce buildings whose internal environments are well-conditioned. As such, a primary focus will be on how various forms of energy are used to manipulate the building interior to suit the occupants' needs and wishes. The text will stress how and why these manipulations are implemented, including discussing the underlying principles that govern the behaviors of the building interior and the devices used to control it. First, *passive* components of buildings will be identified, and strategies for their development will be presented. These passive components are those that are static or relatively immobile (i.e., they move or are moved only when energy is passed on to them by human beings or by natural agents). Such agents may include the wind, solar radiation, and so forth, and are generally said to be renewable or sustainable.

Second, the composition and operation of *active* control systems will be described. The term *active* implies that the system or its components are moved by energy either derived from the consumption of some fuel (i.e., a fossil material or a radioactive element) or powered by electricity. The driving force for active systems generally involves non-renewable energy sources. But note that when the driving force is electricity, the energy can be generated in hydroelectric dams or with photovoltaic cells. For hydroelectric dams water moves under the force of gravity through generators producing electricity. Alternatively, in photovoltaic cells, solar energy bombarding the energy-absorbing materials causes electron flow, also producing electricity. Both hydroelectric and photovoltaic energy productions are basically renewable.

The text will also offer catalogs of guidelines and other approximations to aid the designer and builder in creating buildings that are comfortable for the occupants and that operate with reasonable energy-efficiency. These guidelines and approximations are intended for use in the *programming* and preliminary schematic design phases of the building design process. Our expectation is that if designers and builders know what environmental controls to use and why these applications make sense, they will produce better buildings and serve occupants better.

Section 1.1 | WHAT ARE ENVIRONMENTAL CONTROL DEVICES FOR?

Designers and builders create buildings for a number of reasons. One fundamental reason is that a building provides a means of modifying various elements of the natural environment, which we sample with our five senses (e.g., feeling, seeing, hearing, smelling, and tasting). Our senses enable us to experience heat, light, sound, and odors and thus determine the character of natural and built environments. Our experience of an environment is determined specifically by our capacities to sense the several types of energy that surround us: radiant energy (light); thermal energy (heat); and mechanical energy (sound). And, although odor is not specifically manifested as an energy form, it is affected by thermal — and, possibly, mechanical — energy.

So, why do we use buildings as means for controlling the environment around us? First, because each of our sensing mechanisms can deal with some energy form. Second, because the sensing mechanism perceives a range of energy presence (or intensity) that is either *comfortable* or bearable. (For instance, we are thermally comfortable, generally, when the air temperature is between 20 to 27 °C (68 to 80 °F).) But, third, because the energy presences (or absences) in the natural environment vary over a much greater range than we would find comfortable or even bearable (e.g., in much of northern North America and Europe air temperatures commonly hover below freezing for much of the winter). Because there is a difference between what we find comfortable or bearable and the conditions likely to be present in the natural environment, we create buildings and service systems that enable us to live and work in places that we would otherwise find uncomfortable or unbearable.

Thus, we construct buildings to provide *localized,* enclosed environments that will enable occupants to live and work comfortably. The building includes a physical enclosure and some means for creating a suitable internal environment. This physical enclosure can be as simple as a roof over one's head or can separate us physically from the external environment. Similarly, service systems can be simple or elaborate, providing very modest or comprehensive control of the enclosed environment.

Thus, buildings serve as *modifiers* of the natural environment. When the natural environment is too hot, too noisy, or too bright, we can enter a building looking for shade, a quiet place, or relief from glare since the building and/or its service systems filter out excess heat, noise, and brightness. The building becomes a habitable (acceptable) interior space because the enclosure and the systems provide environmental control. In the subsequent chapters of this text we will discuss two important questions concerning the use of buildings (and building parts) as means of producing a controlled internal environment. The first question asks how much control should be provided for the building occupants. Finding answers to this question will require us to consider what attributes the internal environment should (or must) have for the occupants. This question will also require us to examine the characteristics of the natural environment (at the location where the occupant wishes to work or live). The second question asks about cost: can whatever level of control that is sought be provided at a reasonable expense? This latter question will no doubt be more difficult to answer directly because it forces us to consider the topics of efficiency and, perhaps, the allocation of potentially limited resources. In this introductory chapter, we can state that, regardless of the character of the natural environment, a built environment can be created that occupants will find satisfying in terms of basic physical and physiological needs.

For much of this text, our discussions will be organized to identify what environmental controls should be employed in buildings to provide *shelter,* ensure *comfort,* and foster *efficient operation.* Definitions for these three attributes of an environment can be stated accordingly. Shelter is a device (or a collection of related devices) that sustains human activity. Comfort is the state of pursuing an activity without experiencing environmental stress. And efficiency is achieved when one can pursue an activity with a minimum of waste. Necessarily, these attributes can be regarded as sequential in terms of achievement. Shelter is the basic requirement for someone attempting to exist in an otherwise uninhabitable or unbearable natural environment. Without shelter, a person in an unbearable environment cannot long survive. But once shelter is established, then an occupant can seek to enhance dwelling or work spaces to attain comfort. A comfortable setting therefore is one in which the occupant is freed from the uncertainties and rigors imposed by the natural environment. Application of environmental controls removes occupants from the mutability of the external environment. Finally, when comfortable conditions are assured, then the occupant — or the designer and builder who furnish these controls — should seek to have the controlling device(s) operate as efficiently as possible. If a created (or built) environment can indeed be made to operate comfortably and efficiently, we can be confident that the control device — or a group of devices — is well-selected.

An alternate description of the role of environmental controls revolves about the notion that the built environment (and its components) serves as "lines of defense" for an occupant who seeks relief from a potentially unbearable or uncomfortable natural environment. Suppose, for instance, that you are walking along a snow-covered street on a winter day. The day is sunny and very bright (especially as sunlight reflects off of the surface of the snow). Because of the unusually cold weather a water pipe — laid too close to the street surface — has frozen, ruptured, and now needs to be dug up and replaced. A worker is using a jackhammer to remove the surface layers of the street. Thus, what you experience as you pass along the street is the cold weather, excessively bright light, and too much noise.

There are four lines of defense for each of these three stresses (i.e., the cold, the light, and the noise). To deal with the cold weather, you can gain warmth from the sun, wear a down-filled jacket (using clothing to insulate you from the cold), go into a building whose interior is warmed by the sun, or go into a building heated by a wood-burning stove. Similar treatments against the excessive light and noise can also be pursued. For the very bright light, initially, shading can be gained from a coniferous tree that intercepts the sunlight. Donning dark glasses would create a second line of defense. Entering a building whose glazing faces away from the sun (and the accompanying brightness) could ease visual discomfort. Or closing Venetian blinds and turning on electrically powered lamps could reduce the brightness, while furnishing adequate illumination. And, for the excessive noise, you first could walk away from the jackhammer until you are some distance from the noise source. At this distance you would find that the noise is less intense and bothersome. Second, you could insert noise plugs into your ears. Third, you could enter a building whose thick walls substantially minimize the transmission of the noise through the building envelope. Or, fourth, you could enter a building with a less-noise-limiting envelope and then proceed to turn on your stereo system and raise the intensity of the sounds coming from the stereo system until the sounds override whatever noise enters through the envelope.

In each of these examples four lines of defense are available. The first defense employs a potentially beneficial feature of the natural environment to counter the effect of an unbearable or uncomfortable aspect of the environment. For instance, incident solar radiation can warm you, perhaps chasing away feelings of being cold. The second defense alters the extent to which the environmental burden weighs upon a person, essentially by altering or transforming the nature of the burden (e.g., the down-filled jacket reduces heat lost by the wearer to the natural environment, whereas the dark glasses filter out the excessive brightness of the sunlight and its reflected rays). The third line uses a building as the basis of its defense; this line may also rely on a *passive*-conditioning feature of the building. Finally, the fourth defense implements the use of an active control device that operates through the consumption of a human-generated energy source (e.g., oil or electricity). These four lines of defense can and should be deployed sequentially. Thus, use the first line and, if it is not enough, try the second, and so forth. These lines of defense can also be applied to the creation of buildings. We suggest that active control devices should be relied on principally when the stress from the natural environment exceeds the capability of the passive features of a building to provide shelter and comfort.

The *principle of sequential deployment* is a fundamental notion of this text. We believe that the intelligent application of the first three lines of defense during the designing, constructing, and operating of buildings can often successfully combat the vagaries of the natural environment. Further, when well chosen and employed, these lines will ensure more comfortable and efficient buildings. By manipulating the passive elements of the building, the designer and builder can reduce the dependence on active devices. Alternatively, when the first three lines of defense are well applied and active systems are then employed as both needed and efficient supplements, then there will be a greater likelihood that effective, sensible environmental control is being provided for occupants. The reductions in the time of use and the capacity demanded, when these active systems operate, will save the future occupant both energy and money.

This text will identify how buildings and their passive and active elements can present efficient, comfortable shelters. We will not frequently discuss what first and second line-of-defense strategies should be employed. Instead, we will generally expect the reader to anticipate where or when such devices can be usefully employed. Third lines of defense—passive means of environmental control—will be described in the first part of this text. Within this part there will be explanations of heat, light, and sound affect building use. Guidelines for designing to achieve comfortable and efficient buildings by controlling heat, daylight, and sound will also be presented. In the second part, the fourth line of defense—active control systems—will be discussed. In this part guidelines will also be offered for locating, sizing, and designing the spaces that these active control systems will likely require to be integrated with the rest of the features in buildings.

Section 1.2 | A BRIEF DESCRIPTION OF THE BUILDING DESIGN PROCESS AND HOW INFORMATION ABOUT ENVIRONMENTAL CONTROLS CAN FIT WITHIN IT

In the first main part of this text (Chapters 2–13), physical principles will be described that determine how a building behaves (or should behave) thermally, luminously, and acoustically. The text will also identify numbers of guidelines and approximations that can be used to create buildings. In the second main part of the text (Chapters A–F), common active control systems will be explained, both in terms of how these systems function and what system components are needed for building operation. A variety of guidelines and spatial approximations will be presented so that accommodations for these systems can be made during building designing. Throughout the presentations of these two main parts, the goal is to offer the information so that it can be integrated into the traditional building design process.

The design process is an activity involving a number of steps that are engaged in by individuals working alone or in groups. These steps begin with the gathering of information about the needs of the future occupants and the development of expectations about how the building should support the activities that these occupants will likely pursue. Then, designers commence the creation process by proposing approximate solutions. These approximations will be iteratively fine-tuned and made more definite. Eventually, a final product will be defined and drawn up. This final design will then be passed along to a builder who will transform the design solution into a constructed building.

The process may appear to be organized linearly. But there is much activity within it that occurs along nonsystematic paths. The process necessarily includes (or requires) "feedback loops." Thus, information learned at some later step may cause a designer to return to some aspect of a design generated earlier and re-think and/or modify it. Overall, the process requires intuition and care and encompasses many bits of information that are frequently disparate one from another. The steps in this process cannot be precisely defined because the activities pursued in each step differ from designer to designer. But from a normative viewpoint the following descriptions should be roughly accurate and will hopefully indicate where the information presented throughout this text can be employed.

The principal steps in the building design process generally occur in the following sequence. Note that we will use the word "designer" to encompass all of the several people, with their various skills and knowledge bases, who participate in built space creation. And, in this portrayal of the job sequence, we are concentrating on how and when questions about environmental controls enter into the creation process.

1. *Job acquisition and initiation.* This first step is essential to all the others. Herein, the designer acquires a commission and begins organizing the design (and, sometimes, construction) team.

2. *Programming.* The designer gathers data about the occupants, the services the building is to provide, the characteristics of the natural environment in which the building is to be placed, and so forth. Ultimately, the designer undertakes this phase to determine what the building needs to be and do for the future occupants.

3. *Preliminary schematic designing.* Taking the information gathered in the programming phase, the designer now begins to think conceptually about the building and to define the future form of the building. The designer will draw out approximate floor plans (i.e., how the spaces in the building will relate to one another), elevations (what the building envelopes will look like and roughly consist of), and sections (commonly, how the spaces in the building will be stacked vertically). These schematic drawings are approximate and require much further definition before construction can begin. A designer may produce alternative schematic solutions (rather than a single one), thus permitting the exploration of different concepts of building organization, form, materials, environmental control, or whatever.

4. *Design development.* If the designer produces a number of alternative solutions in the schematic phase, s/he will commonly select one for further work. The basis for this selection frequently will be criteria identified in the programming phase that are deemed important for the future building. If the designer has generated a single schematic solution, then no selection process will be needed. But, in either case, the working design now will be "fine-tuned," during which the various approximations are more closely resolved and the many parts of the building begin to be integrated. At this stage, the components of various systems—both passive and active—are specifically sized and the integration of these systems is resolved.

5. *Preparation of construction documents (including both drawings and specifications).* This phase continues and completes the more precise definition—begun in design development—of the building components and how they relate to one another. Ultimately, the purpose of this phase is to produce a set of documents from which the building can be constructed. Thus, the drawings produced here will need to provide a relatively precise identification of what the building will look like, what it will be built of, and how all the various passive devices and active systems will be integrated into the overall building solution.

6. *Construction oversight.* Once construction of the building has commenced, the designer usually oversees this process to ensure that the building is assembled according to the designer's intentions and what is shown in the construction documents.

7. *Post-occupancy evaluation (and participation in the building commissioning, as appropriate).* This last step in the design process is generally optional. It may be pursued

if specifically defined as a responsibility of the designer, or a designer may perform it as a means for evaluating the building design or the design process itself. A designer may undertake this activity as a means of learning about the product and the process that created it, so that the information gained can be employed in subsequent design projects.

The contents of this text primarily concern the second and third phases of this seven-step process: gathering useful data about a proposed building (and the immediately surrounding built environment) and then using those data to help in defining what the *approximate* form and composition of the building should be. During preliminary schematic designing (the third step in this process), the designer has to consider a complex array of information about such disparate topics as community needs, zoning and building regulations, financial data, and environmental control requirements. Therefore, the amount of detail and the level of precision (for the information used) must be suitably "scaled" to the task. In synthesizing a building solution (or a number of solutions) from all of these data, the designer can scarcely focus on detailed information on any one topic. Thus, approximations or quickly stated guidelines provide the most useful information for the designer.

Later, after the designer has generated one schematic design (or more), then the individual will need criteria for evaluating the solution(s) and information for "fine-tuning" the design. At this design development stage, when the proposed building solution becomes less approximate and more precise, more detailed information is required about how the building should perform. This information can be obtained from systematic analytic techniques and from the attention provided by the specialists in the design team (e.g., the various engineering, construction, and management consultants).

What environmental controls issues are appropriate for consideration, how to gather information about environmental control opportunities, what forms should this information have, and why these controls should be employed are the four topics that will be addressed in this text. Also, design guidelines and approximations will be a central offering. These guidelines will enable the designer and builder to establish the appropriate environmental controls for a specific building and to determine how these controls should be deployed. The text will treat such issues as sizing a window for adequate daylighting and view provision, laying out a floor plan for sufficient occupant cooling and noise separation, choosing a wall assembly that keeps the heat from escaping from the building interior, and placing and sizing spaces for housing HVAC system components. Ultimately, this text will identify what are the primary needs for environmental controls and will suggest rational bases for designing buildings with good environmental controls.

The Basics of Heat Transfer

2

MANAGING ENERGY IN BUILDINGS concerns the creation both of efficient environmental controls and buildings whose internal environments are comfortable. In this chapter and the two succeeding ones we will describe principles that manage the presence of heat in buildings and the surrounding environment. Then, in Chapter 5, we will offer a catalogue of devices that can be employed to control the amount of heat that exists in buildings or that is transferred between the building and its surroundings. One premise of these four chapters is that if a designer or builder wants to know how (thermal) energy can be controlled for the operation of a building, then that individual needs to know how the energy moves or is transferred from one location to another.

Before we begin to explain how heat is transferred in buildings, we should define some terms that will form the basis for this explanation. The term *energy* is applied ubiquitously and is almost indefinable. A dictionary definition suggests that energy is "the capacity of acting" or "the capacity for doing work."[1] A second general term is *system,* which does not necessarily refer to a "hardware" device. Rather, a system can be a single object or a collection of many components. Thus, this book, an automobile, and the sun and the nine known planets are all systems. Similarly, a building can be regarded as a system. But note that a building is also composed of a number of individual systems. Finally, the term *surroundings* includes everything that encompasses a system, except the system itself. An alternative to the term *surroundings* is *environment*.

Heat is *thermal* energy. It is energy that is present in a system or that is being exchanged between a system and its surroundings. Additionally, heat can move from one system to another. *Temperature* is an indication or measure of the density of heat that a system has. In thermodynamics heat is considered to be that form of energy that is transferred from one system at a higher temperature to an adjoining system at a lower temperature.

Section 2.1 | THE FIRST TWO LAWS OF THERMODYNAMICS AND WHAT THEY HAVE TO DO WITH HOW BUILDINGS FUNCTION

The *First Law of Thermodynamics* states that the amount of energy present in a system and its surroundings together is constant. The amount of energy in a system can increase or decrease. But the corresponding change in the amount of energy that the surroundings has must be equal to the energy change experienced by the system. Thus, we can say that energy cannot be "created" or "destroyed." Rather, it is *moved* from a system to its surroundings or between two systems or, simply, from place to place. There may be changes in the *forms* of some of the energy, but the total amount will remain constant.

A wonderful example, suggested by Buckminster Fuller, may demonstrate both the essence and significance of this Law.[2] Consider a tree (see Figure 2.1). The tree takes in water from the ground, carbon dioxide from the air, and sunlight (i.e., solar energy). And, by photosynthesis, the tree produces organic compounds and oxygen. The organic compounds become new cells, and the tree grows in stature and mass. If we come along and cut the tree down and then divide it up into logs that will fit in our fireplace, we can burn these logs. The thermal energy released from these logs will then warm the interior of our building.

But where does this released energy come from? The answer is that the heat we are releasing by burning a log is the solar energy that was taken in during photosynthesis. The solar energy was converted to chemical energy that was stored in the cells of the wood. When the logs are burned, the chemical energy is converted to thermal energy. Thus, the First Law is fulfilled, and energy is neither created nor destroyed. Instead, it simply changes form: from solar (thermal) to chemical to thermal. If you regard the tree as your system, then it has drawn energy from its surroundings (the sun). Subsequently, the stored heat is released to yet other surroundings (i.e., the interior of a building).

The *Second Law of Thermodynamics* describes when thermal energy will be transferred. This Law states that heat will flow from a system with a higher temperature to surroundings that have a lower temperature. An alternative way of saying this is that heat will move from a warmer *source* to a cooler *sink*. So, this transfer of thermal energy will occur because there is a *temperature difference* between the system and its surroundings (see Figure 2.2).

Following the tenets of the Second Law of Thermodynamics, a building that is warmed by the sun during the day will cool off at night. As the sun is hotter—its surface temperature is about 6,000 °C (11,000 °F)—than the building, the building gains heat from the sun. But when the sun sets and the external air temperature falls below the internal air temperature of the building, then the building will lose heat to the air surrounding it.[3] The temperature difference between the sun and the building causes the building to gain heat throughout the day. However, at night, when the building interior is warmer than the exterior, heat will flow from the interior to the exterior.

Figure 2.1 Conserving energy: the transformation of solar energy to thermal energy for heating a home.

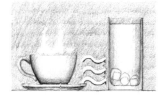

Figure 2.2 Establishing a thermal equilibrium between hot tea and iced tea.

If we do not alter this nighttime heat exchange, then sooner or later the room air and the night air will wind up having the same air temperature and each will be in *equilibrium* with the other (i.e., there will be no heat transfer between the two). Of course, if we want to offset the loss of heat transferred from inside the building to the exterior, then we could provide some sort of a supplemental heat source for the building interior (e.g., a furnace or a wood fire). This source would replace the thermal energy that is being lost through the building envelope and would maintain the building interior at a higher temperature. Alternatively, we can slow down the rate of heat exchange between the warmer building interior and the cooler exterior. Devices that we can supply, during the design and construction of the building, to reduce the rate of this heat loss (or later during the operation of the building) will be discussed in Chapter 5. Using these devices to minimize heat loss to the environment present essential opportunities for improving the thermal performance of buildings.

Section 2.2 | THE TWO FUNDAMENTAL FORMS OF HEAT TRANSFER

The Second Law of Thermodynamics states that heat exchange will occur between two systems or a system and its surroundings when a temperature difference exists between them. Heat transfer can happen in one of two fundamental ways: *by molecular (or atomic) action* or *by electromagnetic radiation.* Heat transfer by molecular activity presumes that the molecules (or atoms) are in close proximity to each other as they are in a solid, liquid, or gas. This molecular activity is manifested as *conductive* or *convective* heat exchange. Heat transfer by electromagnetic radiation can occur across a vacuum (for instance, between the sun and the Earth) or through a gas or liquid. Radiation from some warmer object *can cause* heat transfer to occur in a cooler object (e.g., solar radiation warms up the exterior surface of a brick wall, and then heat captured by the brick at its exterior surface passes inward through the brick). But the transfer in the cooler object—here, the brick—*does not occur* by the radiation passing through the solid: instead, the transfer in the solid will occur by conductive heat transfer.

2.2.1   TRANSFER BY MOLECULAR ACTION

2.2.1.1   Conductive heat transfer   To understand how heat transfer occurs by conductive heat exchange, think about a piece of iron. As with most solids, the iron is composed primarily of atoms linked together in a three-dimensional array. These atoms are essentially fixed in place (i.e., they do not move from place to place as molecules do in air). But, because these atoms have internal energy, they *vibrate in place* without actually switching locations. How fast the atoms vibrate depends primarily on how much thermal energy is present in the iron piece.

If we apply a heat source to one side of the iron (for example, suppose we light a fire under an iron skillet), then the atoms at the outer edge of the array—those exposed to the fire—will begin to vibrate more quickly (see Figure 2.3). Because these outer atoms are *fixed-in-place* and are part of the array, the atoms cannot use the thermal energy, which they gain from the heat source, to move about. As these atoms commence vibrating faster (i.e., have more thermal energy) than the ones in the adjacent internal layer, the atoms in the first (outer) layer pass some of their newly acquired vibrational energy onto those atoms in the second layer. Then, the second-layer atoms, which begin to vibrate faster than

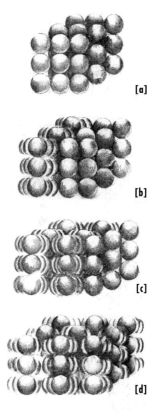

[a]

[b]

[c]

[d]

Figure 2.3 Transferring heat through an array of atoms by thermal conduction (note the movement of the heat across the array as the atoms progressively vibrate faster).

the third-layer atoms, pass some of their incremental thermal energy onto the third-layer atoms, causing these third-layer atoms to vibrate more rapidly than they were before. This process of moving thermal energy added at one side of an atomic array to the other side — by passing incremental quantities of thermal energy from one atomic layer to the next — is *conductive heat transfer.*

SIDEBAR 2.1 Conducting heat through an iron skillet

The rate with which the heat from the fire is conducted through the skillet — the amount of heat transferred per unit time — depends on four parameters. First, what is causing the transfer is the *temperature difference* that exists from one side of the skillet to the other (i.e., from the bottom surface to the top surface). The larger this temperature difference is the faster conductive heat transfer will occur. Second, the *thickness* of the skillet will affect the rate with which heat transfer occurs. So, if we considered several skillets whose thicknesses ranged from thinner to thicker, then we would find that the passage of heat will require more time to flow across the thicker skillets than the thinner ones. Third, the conductive heat transfer rate will depend on the *surface area* of the skillet (top and bottom), with a larger area transferring the heat more slowly than a small area would. And, fourth, the reason why the heat would

be transferred faster through this iron skillet than through a skillet of a different material — say, Pyrex glass — is because of the *thermal conductivity* of each material. The thermal conductivity of iron is substantially greater than the thermal conductivity of glass. This last parameter is a basic property of any material. The first three parameters noted here are *situational* factors: they affect the conductive heat transfer rate through the skillet according to whether the cook used a big or little skillet or built a small or large fire. Alternatively, the thermal conductivity of the iron in the skillet is a fundamental *material* property and is an essential factor to be considered when selecting materials from which something like a building will be constructed. To provide a basis for comparing the thermal conductivity of various materials, we will list below the values for a few building materials.

THERMAL CONDUCTIVITY VALUES FOR SOME COMMON MATERIALS

MATERIAL	THERMAL CONDUCTIVITY	
	IN BTU/HR-FT-°F	IN W/M²-K
Copper	227	392.6
Mild steel	26	45.0
Window glass	0.59	1.02
Concrete, 140 lbs/cu.ft.	0.54	0.93
White oak	0.10	0.17
Fiberglass batt	0.022	0.038

Note that the higher the thermal conductivity, the faster heat will be conducted through the material. The source of these values is the *2001 ASHRAE Handbook of Fundamentals,* (Atlanta: American Society of Heating, Refrigerating, and Air-Conditioning Engineers, Inc., 2001), pages 38.3–38.4.

Returning to our example of placing an iron skillet over a fire, we know that the underside of the skillet will grow hot immediately and that the topside will become hot soon afterwards. The fire imparts heat to the underside of the iron skillet. The thermal energy conducts through the skillet until the heat reaches the other side. If we now place a piece of beefsteak on the hot skillet, the steak will begin to warm up (i.e., cook), as heat is conducted from the topside of the skillet into the steak.

For another example, place your hand against a window. For the average human being under normal conditions, the surface temperature of the palm of one's hand will be about 32 °C (90 °F). If the air temperature outside of the building is less than 32 °C (say, 10 or 20 °C [50 or 68 °F]), then your hand will feel "cool." This feeling is the result of the conduction of thermal energy from your palm to the cooler window surface. Then, as the inner window surface is *comparatively warmer* than the outer window surface, thermal energy will pass through the glass by conductive heat transfer (see Figure 2.4). Suppose, however, that the external air were warmer than 32 °C (90 °F). When you place your hand on the window surface your palm would feel "warm." In this latter case the temperature difference would favor conductive heat transfer from the outer surface through the window to the inner surface and from the inner surface into your hand.

2.2.1.2 Convective heat transfer

In the description of conductive heat transfer we explained how the thermal energy from the heat source passes through the many layers of an array of atoms until at least some incremental amount of heat reached the other side of the array (i.e., the farthest layer of the array). Now, presuming that this other side of the array is warmer than the air surrounding it, there will be heat transfer from the surface to the air. This transfer will occur as follows. First, remember that the atoms in the three-dimensional array are fixed-in-place and cannot change their locations. Instead, as incremental thermal energy is imparted to them, they vibrate more rapidly. Air molecules alongside the surface of this atomic array make contact with the vibrating atoms (at the array surface). Some of the thermal energy from the solid is transferred to the air molecules, giving them more thermal energy. Because these air molecules are not held in place, they can use the newly acquired thermal energy to move about more rapidly. These increased velocities will cause the air molecules to collide more frequently with each other and with the outer surface of the solid. As the air molecules move about more rapidly, *the*

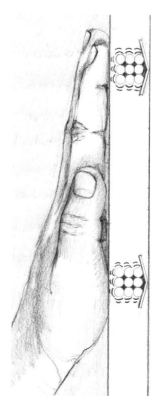

Figure 2.4 Heat transfer through the window glass by thermal conduction: the hand warms the inner surface of the glass, and heat is conducted across the glass to the outer surface.

SIDEBAR 2.2 What parameters affect convective heat transfer?

The rate with which convective heat exchange between a gas and a solid (or a liquid and a solid or a gas and a liquid) occurs is dependent on three parameters. Similar to the parameters that determine the rate of conductive heat exchange, two of these parameters are the *magnitude* of the temperature difference that exists between the two entities and the *surface area* (or area of contact) between them. The third parameter is the *nature of the contact* between the two entities, including such surface characteristics as roughness and whether some force exists other than

that due to the temperature difference between the two entities (e.g., that the air near a building surface was wind-blown). The contact nature is generally described in terms of a *surface convection coefficient* (or, alternatively, a *film conductance*). In contrast to the parameter thermal conductivity that is a fundamental property of any material, this coefficient (or conductance) is a property of the interface between the two entities and any non-thermal energy that is operating over the interface.

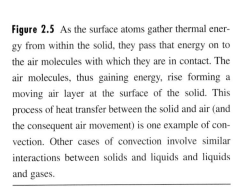
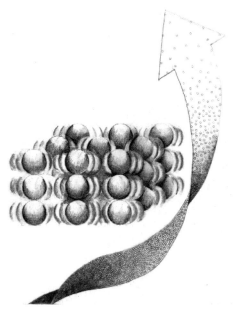

Figure 2.5 As the surface atoms gather thermal energy from within the solid, they pass that energy on to the air molecules with which they are in contact. The air molecules, thus gaining energy, rise forming a moving air layer at the surface of the solid. This process of heat transfer between the solid and air (and the consequent air movement) is one example of convection. Other cases of convection involve similar interactions between solids and liquids and liquids and gases.

numbers of such air molecules in the volume of air near the solid will decrease and the air will become less dense. As the density of the air near the solid decreases, the air becomes more buoyant and rises from the surface of the solid. In response to this apparent creation of a partial vacuum (caused by the rising air molecules), other air molecules with less thermal energy and lower velocities will move closer to the surface of the solid and gain heat from the surface (see Figure 2.5).

The actual heat exchange happening when the air molecules come in contact with the atoms at the surface of the solid is by *conductive heat transfer.* But the overall process of the air molecules gathering the additional thermal energy and rising up and away from the surface atoms is described as *convective heat exchange.* Thus, convection is a process in which conductive heat exchange occurs between the atoms of the solid and the molecules of the air, *and* the resulting buoyancy force causes the warmed, less densely packed air volume to rise and be replaced by a comparatively cooler, more dense air molecule volume which then can be warmed.

Alternatively, if the adjacent air were warmer than the surface of the solid, then the air molecules that come in contact with the atoms of the array would transfer some of their greater thermal energy to the surface of the solid, warming up the atoms. As the air molecules transfer some of their heat to the solid, their velocities will decrease, and the volume of space in which they are present will become denser. This volume will be less buoyant than the ambient air (that is in the vicinity of the solid but is not in contact with the array atoms). This relatively denser, less buoyant air volume will sink down and away from the surface of the solid and will be replaced by ambient air moving in. Thus, convective heat exchange occurs whenever there is a temperature difference between a gas and a solid (or between a gas and a liquid or between a liquid and a solid).

The direction of the heat transfer will dictate the pattern of movement for the convective layer. If, for example, the solid is warmer than the air, then the convective airflow

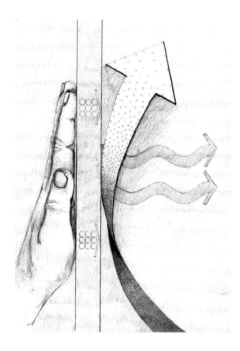

Figure 2.6 As the outer window surface is warmed by the conduction of heat through the glass, a convective heat exchange occurs between the window surface and the external air. The air molecules gain thermal energy from the glass surface. The layer of air containing these warmed molecules becomes less dense, and it rises. Then, air molecules that had been away from the glass surface move toward the surface and gather thermal energy. (Note: also occurring at the outer surface of the glass is radiant heat exchange between the glass surface and objects external to the glass; how this third form of heat exchange occurs will be discussed in subsection 2.2.2).

will be upward. But if the air is warmer than the solid, the convective air movement will be downward.

Reconsider the example of placing one's hand against the window pane. When the palm of the hand is warmer than the inner surface of the glass (and the inner surface of the glass is warmer than the outer surface), thermal energy will be transferred through the glazing by conductive heat transfer, warming the glazing and, subsequently, the outer glazing surface. As this outer surface gains warmth from the heat source (i.e., your hand), the glass will transfer the thermal energy to the air in contact with it. Convection heat exchange will thus be present (see Figure 2.6). We can draw a further distinction to this example by supposing that the interior air temperature (for the room in which you are) is at 20 °C (68 °F) and the exterior air temperature is at 10 °C (50 °F). In addition to the heat transfer occurring when you place your palm (at 32 °C [90 °F]) against the interior glazing surface, there will be a heat transfer path between the internal air and the external air through the glazing. This path will include a convective heat exchange between the internal air and the internal surface of the glass, heat transfer by conduction through the glazing, and a convective heat exchange between the external surface of the glazing and the external air. The internal convective exchange will cause the convective layer near the glass to descend, whereas the external convective layer will ascend. Thus, there will be an apparent matching (or pairing) of the directions of the convective layer movements, one up and one down. Generally, in most building applications where convective layers are present in pairs (e.g., across air-envelope-air heat transfer paths), the convective layers will exhibit opposing directions of movement.

Free and forced convection. Lastly, on the subject of convective heat exchange and the presence of attendant air layers, two types of convective exchange are common in the natural and built environments: *free convection* and *forced convection*. Free convection occurs strictly due to localized temperature differences between surfaces and the gas or

Placing a pot of water over a fire will initiate convective heat exchange between the surface of the pot and the enclosed water. First, the fire will warm the exterior surface of the pot. The heat from the fire will be conducted through the pot envelope to the internal surface of the pot. Then, at this internal surface, water molecules will gather thermal energy from the surface.

Packets of these warmed molecules will grow more buoyant and will rise up and away from the surface, allowing new packets of cooler molecules to replace the warmer, rising molecules. Thus, convective heat exchange occurs at the interior surface of the pot. Subsequently, when enough heat has been added to the water, it will begin to boil.

liquid adjacent to them. Examples of free convection include smoke rising up a chimney, air currents rising off hot asphalt pavement, or drafts flowing downward off of cold window surfaces and cooling occupants' feet and lower legs. A principal heating device used in many buildings is finned-tube radiation (see Figures 2.7 and 2.8). This device is often called "architectural radiation" by the heating industry because its application has permitted use of the largely glazed curtain-wall building envelope that, without this device, would cause cold window surfaces and drafts![4]

In contrast to the circumstance where a temperature difference across the surface-to-air boundary produces free convection, some agent—in addition to the temperature difference—may affect a convective air layer near a surface. This agent, either a natural or artificial one, will thus influence the rate of air movement in the layer. When such an agent does affect the convective air layer, then that convection is described as *forced*. A primary example of forced convection occurs when the wind blows air across a building envelope. Due to the wind the rate of convective heat transfer between the outer surface of the envelope and the ambient air will be increased. An alternative example of forced convection is present in many furnaces. For instance, an oil or gas-fired furnace has a heat exchanger whose surfaces become hot from the combustion of fuel inside the exchanger. Ducted air flows past the surfaces of the heat exchanger, gathering heat. By using a fan to force the ducted air past the exchanger more rapidly, the convective heat transfer to the air is increased, and the heating effectiveness of the furnace increases. A third example of forced convection is present when you pick up a spoonful of hot soup and blow across it. You are hastening the cooling process by increasing the rate of convection heat transfer between the soup and the air. Alternatively, by sticking the spoon into the hot soup and stirring it, you are enhancing the convective exchange (i.e., "forcing" it) between the air and the overturning surface of the soup.

2.2.2   RADIATIVE HEAT TRANSFER

Let's begin by considering an incandescent light bulb. When you turn on the lamp, electrical current flows through the tungsten filament, producing light. If you move your hand near the light bulb, your hand will feel warmth emanating from it. The source of the heat is the filament. The current (or electrical energy), when it passes through the filament, experiences resistance. This resistance impedes the flow of the current and induces some

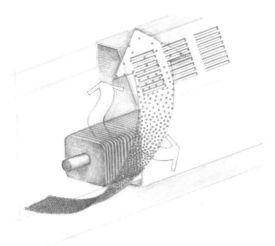

Figure 2.7 The finned-tube "architectural radiation" is composed of one or more metal tubes through which hot water flows. Each tube has a series of metal fins connected to the tube. When the hot water flows through the tube, the thermal energy from the hot water is conducted into the wall of the tube and then out to the fins. The warmed fins thus provide greatly increased surface areas for the promotion of convective heat transfer to the air. The warmed air is useful in heating any window glass surface that is located just above this architectural radiation device. (Radiant heat transfer also occurs — from the fins to the cabinet and then from the cabinet to window surface — but this radiant transfer is less useful in warming the cool glass surface).

Figure 2.8 A finned-tube convector has been installed along the base of these glazing assemblies in a store.

electrical energy to be converted to thermal energy. This thermal energy causes the tungsten filament to glow at a "white heat," providing the useful light we seek when we turn on the light bulb. The thermal energy is perceivable to us as heat. But the filament is present in a vacuum that is maintained within the glass bulb that separates the filament from the ambient air around the bulb.[5] So, if you cannot touch the filament to experience heat transfer by conduction and the filament is present in a vacuum (which means that convective exchange cannot be occurring), then how do you feel the warmth escaping from the filament? The answer is that you are receiving thermal energy from the filament by radiant heat transfer.

A following question then might be, What else gives off thermal energy by radiation? The answer to this question is that virtually everything does. We can refer to *Prevost's Law* as an indicator of what does or does not emit radiation: "All systems with a temperature above absolute zero (i.e., greater than −273 °C [−460 °F]) give off electromagnetic radiation." So, you might ask, if everything gives off radiation, how can thermal energy be exchanged by radiation? Well, the rate by which some object or system emits radiation is, to a major extent, determined by its temperature. An object with a higher surface temperature will give off more radiant energy than an object at a comparatively cooler temperature. If we were to measure the rates of thermal radiation being emitted from these two objects, we would find that there was a *net positive* radiant heat transfer from the warmer object to the cooler one. Indeed, when we write that there is a net positive radiant flow from a warmer object to a cooler one, we mean that more energy will transfer from the warmer object to the cooler object (i.e., so the numerical difference of the two flow rates is *positive,* when we consider the flow moving along the direction *from* the warmer object *to* the cooler one).

That a warmer object will give off more thermal energy than a cooler one and will sustain a net positive flow in the direction from this warmer object to the cooler one is one of the principal corollaries of Prevost's Law. The other major corollary is that if an object is receiving more radiant energy than it is emitting, then its temperature will rise. Thus, as the net positive flow of thermal energy occurs from the warmer object to the cooler one, the cooler object will become warmer (i.e., its temperature will increase). The warmer object will cool down, and its temperature will decrease. So, the two objects will proceed toward an equal temperature, and a thermal energy equilibrium will be established between the objects (i.e., once the equilibrium is present, the *net* radiant exchange between the two objects will be zero).

What is radiation? To answer this question, we need to talk not of arrayed atoms, but instead about what happens within individual atoms. All matter is made up of atoms, and all atoms are composed of a nucleus (of protons and neutrons and some other components) and electrons orbiting the nucleus. Initially, early atomic physicists thought that electrons moved about the nucleus in well-defined rings. But, more recently, physicists have come to believe that the electrons are present in a "cloud" surrounding the nucleus. Within this cloud the electrons revolve around the nucleus in a series of spherical shells or orbits (see Figure 2.9). The electrons also "jump" from one shell to another (i.e., in toward the nucleus or out from the nucleus). As an electron jumps inward to get closer to the nucleus, energy is given off from the atom to the environment around the atom. Alternatively, as an electron jumps outward from a shell near to the nucleus, the atom takes energy in from the environment.

If we consider a clump of atoms together, each with its electron cloud experiencing this jumping behavior, then at some time more electrons within the atomic clump will be moving inward (rather than outward), and a certain net energy will be given off by the

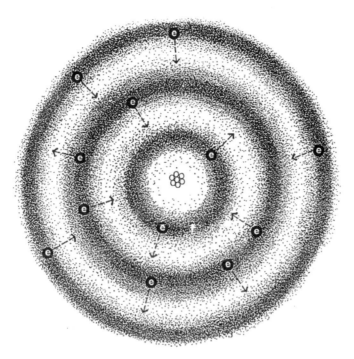

Figure 2.9 In this drawing of an atom of some common element (e.g., iron) the nucleus is shown as a tightly packed mix of protons and neutrons (and some other comparatively much smaller objects). The electrons orbit this nucleus in a "cloud." This cloud is not sharply bounded, and the electrons do not exist at precisely defined distances from the nucleus. Rather, the electrons are present at many alternative positions within the cloud, the identities of which vary with time. In quantum mechanics, a principal topic of study concerns where these electrons are likely to be. The probable positions of the electrons are described statistically (i.e., what is the likelihood of finding electrons at any distance from the nucleus at some moment in time). In this drawing we have shown the cloud as a continuous entity with the darker areas representing locations where electrons are more likely to be and the lighter areas portraying locations where electrons are less likely to be. Necessarily, any static picture of an atom showing electron locations would be valid for only an extremely brief moment in time because the electrons are "jumping" about throughout the cloud, in toward and out from the nucleus.

SIDEBAR 2.4 What causes electromagnetic radiation?

The electrons and protons (in the nucleus) are of opposite charges and are thus attracted to each other. What keeps them apart is the fact that the electrons are revolving rapidly around the nucleus, thus experiencing a *centrifugal* force. This force pulls each electron away from the nucleus. But the difference in charge between the electron and the proton provides an attractive force. Thus, the centrifugal force outward more or less balances the attractive force inward, and the electrons and protons, which are of equal numbers in an atom, are generally in a state of equilibrium. However, when energy from outside the atom is applied to the atom, there is an outward movement of electrons between the clouds. And, when the electrons subsequently "jump" back inwards, then the atom gives off energy.

The amounts of energy given off or taken in occur in multiples of a fundamental increment (or quantum) of energy. The rate with which energy is exchanged at the atomic level is one of the principal areas of study in quantum mechanics.

SIDEBAR 2.5 Characterizing the frequency and wavelength of electromagnetic radiation

We have established that the atom is composed of a nucleus surrounded by a "cloud" of electrons and that these electrons change positions in this cloud, alternatively "jumping" in towards and away from the nucleus. In jumping the overall atom gives off and takes on energy. Now, if we consider a clump of atoms, we can generally reach three observations: the amount of energy that is given off or taken in varies periodically from some maximum amount given off to some maximum amount taken in; the periodicity occurs because the electrons are regularly jumping inwardly and outwardly; and the periodicity is continuous for as long as the electrons jump about in the atom.

We can describe this fundamental behavior in two ways. First, we can consider the amount of energy emitted or taken in by the clump of atoms compared to the time over which this behavior is observed. Second, we can regard the emission of "waves" emanating out from the clump of atoms in terms of the amount of energy emitted and the distance that the waves travel from the atom.

In the first instance — examining the energy emitted or taken in by the atomic clump in terms of time — this behavior occurs periodically and varies regularly between some maximum amount of energy given off (to the environment) and some maximum amount of energy taken in (from the environment). To illustrate this behavior we can draw a graph relating these alternating energy maxima to the duration of time over which this alternating behavior occurs (see Figure 2.10a). We show time along the x-axis and the amount of energy given off or taken in along the y-axis. We define the value of energy along the x-axis as an equilibrium position (i.e., when the clump of atoms is neither giving off nor taking in energy). Above the x-axis we say that the clump of atoms is giving off energy; the area below the x-axis represents the situation when the atom clump is taking in energy from its environment. Now, the amounts of energy given off and taken in are related directly to the manner in which the electrons are jumping inwards and outwards.

After a period of time with the predominant behavior for the atomic clump characterized by the electrons jumping inward, there will be a similar period of time while the electrons jump outward and so forth. Thus, we can observe a regular, gradual variation

between the maximum energy given off to the maximum taken in to the maximum given off and so on. We can define this variation from the maximum energy amount given off to the next maximum amount given off as a *cycle*. Finally, a significant characteristic of this variation in the amount of energy present versus the time taken for this cycle is the rate or frequency with which the variation occurs. Thus, the frequency of variation tells us how often for some unit of time the behavior is observed.

Alternatively, we can consider the emanation of energy outward from the clump of atoms. When energy is being given off by the clump (i.e., when more electrons are jumping inward toward the nucleus), then energy will flow out away from this clump. When more electrons are jumping outward, then energy will be drawn in from the environment. We can say that this energy flow, outwards and back, behaves like ocean waves beating against a beach. And we can portray this behavior graphically (see Figure 2.10b), relating the amount of energy that is being given off or taken in (at some moment in time) versus the distance that the wave (of energy) has moved out from the atom clump. To develop this graph we again plot the amount of energy along the y-axis setting where the x-axis crosses the y-axis as the point at which energy is neither given off nor taken in. The x-axis represents the physical distance from the atom clump. We will show the variation in the amounts of energy that are being imparted to its environment by the atom clump (and to the atom clump by its environment). This variation will progress from a maximum amount of energy output to a maximum amount input to a maximum amount output and so forth. The pulsing of the energy is wave-like as the energy moves outward away from the clump of atoms. Thus, in this graph we are recording the amount of energy that has pulsed outward from the atom clump (at any moment in time) against the distance from the atom clump that the time-specific pulse has moved from the atom clump. When energy is being given off, that quantity is shown above the x-axis. When energy is being taken in, that quantity is shown below the x-axis. The distance that the pulse (or wave) has moved from a moment when the amount of energy given off is maximum to the moment when the amount of energy given off is again maximum is described as one wavelength.

clump. Then, in a subsequent moment, the atomic clump will take on energy from its environment, and more electrons will move outward (than inward). The energy exchange between the clump of atoms and its surroundings — as energy is given off and then taken in — occurs by *electromagnetic radiation*.

Wavelength and frequency. The electron-jumping behavior can be described statistically: the amounts of energy given off and taken in vary continuously over time (i.e., between some maximum and minimum values). The variation is regular and displays a periodicity, having a *frequency* and a *wavelength*. In other words, the amount of energy given off by the clump of matter reaches a maximum value at some moment, decreases over some time period to a minimum value, and then increases again to the maximum

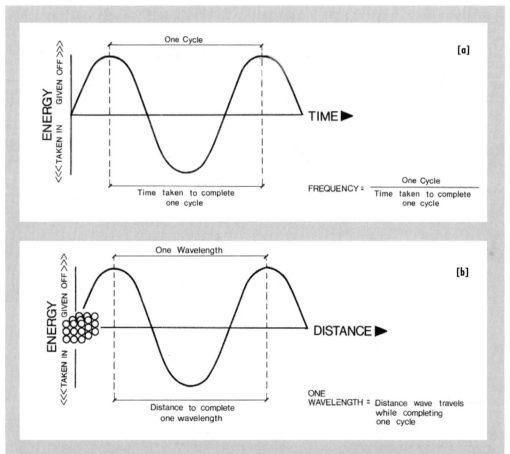

Figure 2.10 (a) The intensity of the thermal radiation emanating from a clump of atoms varies regularly. The character of this variation can be described in terms of the frequency (i.e., how often the cyclically varying energy achieves a maximum (or minimum) value for some unit of time). Frequency is usually described in terms of cycles per second or Hertz (the latter abbreviated as Hz). (b) An alternative means for characterizing the emission of radiation from a source is the wavelength, which is essentially the distance that a ray can move during the time while the intensity of the emission (from the clump of atoms) varies from one maximum value to the next maximum value.

value. This variation from the maximum energy given off to the minimum to the maximum is described as a *cycle*. The number of cycles that occur in one second is the *frequency* of the electromagnetic radiation emitted by the matter. The *wavelength* of the radiation may be visualized by the following model. As the radiation is emitted outward from the clump of matter, the energy pulses in a wave-like fashion. The physical distance between the crest (or maximum energy level) of each wave to the next crest is described as *one wavelength*. The frequency and wavelength of electromagnetic radiation emitted from some source are inversely proportional to each other. Or, as one increases, the other parameter will decrease. Further, the product of the frequency and wavelength of electromagnetic radiation is a constant, having the value of the speed of light.

The electromagnetic radiation emitted from some source can be described by its wavelength (or frequency). Both the wavelength and the frequency are dependent upon the temperature of the source. For instance, when the temperature of a radiating source increases, the characteristic wavelengths of the emitted radiation decrease. Thus, as a range of objects at various temperatures is present in nature (i.e., from the nearly absolute zero temperature found in outer space to the great heat present in stars), so, too, is there a range in the character of the electromagnetic radiation observed. We call this range of electromagnetic radiation the *electromagnetic spectrum.* The types of radiation present in nature vary from the cosmic rays (that have very short wavelengths and are produced by the very hottest stars) to the sub-audio radiation (that has extremely long wavelengths and that has been theorized as coming from the long-cooling remnants of the "Big Bang" that began our universe fourteen billion years ago!) These remnants exist in the virtually empty space between the stars and are thought to have temperatures of only a few degrees above absolute zero.

From the standpoint of heat transfer, we need be concerned about only a very small portion of this electromagnetic spectrum. *Thermal radiation* is present as that part of the spectrum including some of the ultraviolet radiation wavelengths, all of the visible spectrum (i.e., the radiation that we are able to see with our eyes), and a portion of the infrared band of the spectrum (see Figure 2.11).

In subsequent discussions in this text we will make reference to *short* and *long wavelength* thermal radiation. We have previously said that the wavelengths of radiation are inversely proportional to the temperatures of the emitting objects. Warmer objects radiate at comparatively shorter wavelengths than do cooler objects. The primary thermal energy transfer from the sun—with a surface temperature of about 6,000 °C (11,000 °F)—to the surface of the Earth occurs in the wavelength range of 0.3 to 2.0 microns (300 to 2000 nm). Alternatively, objects at temperatures common to people and buildings generally radiate thermal energy in the range of 3 to 50 microns (3000 to 50,000 nm). Therefore, solar energy is described as *shortwave radiation,* and radiant energy exchanged between most terrestial sources and sinks is *longwave radiation.*

Radiation properties. Heat transfer by radiation displays several important properties. First, the radiant transfer of thermal energy *does not occur by means of some kind of matter* (e.g., molecules of a liquid or gas). Radiant energy can be transferred through the near-vacuum of outer space (for example, between the sun and the Earth). It can also be transferred through a liquid or gas. For instance, when you are swimming underwater, you can look up through the water and see the sun. You see the sunlight because visible light—a portion of the radiant spectrum from the sun that passes through the Earth's atmosphere (i.e., a mixture of gases)—also passes through water.

Second, radiant transfer occurs along straight lines. In other words, radiant transfer will exist between two objects only if there is a "line-of-sight" between them. If one object

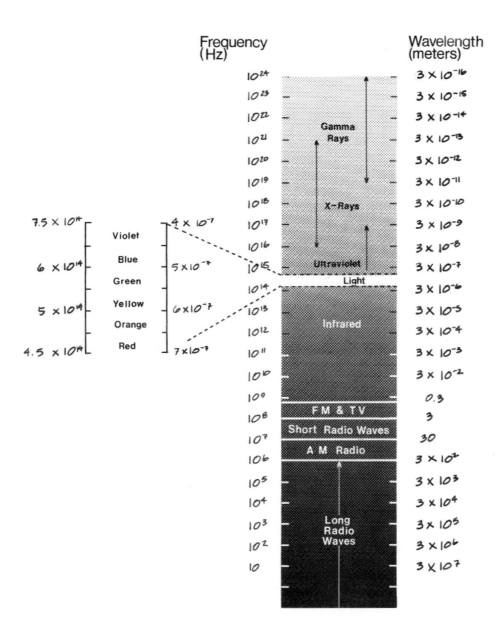

Figure 2.11 A representation of the electromagnetic spectrum identifying the primary forms of radiation. Thermal radiation occurs from over the wavelength range from about 10^{-4} m to 10^{-7} m (thus encompassing the infrared, visible, and ultraviolet radiation forms). This drawing is a reproduction of an illustration shown in a book by Spears, J.D., and D. Zollman, *The Fascination of Physics,* (Menlo Park, California: The Benjamin/Cummings Publishing Company, Inc., 1985), page 338. Permission to reproduce that illustration has been granted by Professor Zollman.

cannot see the other, then no direct transfer can occur between the two. For instance, if a screen is placed between the two objects that have been radiating to each other and if the temperature of the screen is intermediate to the two objects, then each will radiate to the screen. Heat can then be transferred across the screen (presumably, by conduction) and radiant transfer will then occur from the alternate sides of the screen to the objects. The net positive radiation transfer will still occur in the direction from the warmer object toward the cooler object.[6]

Third, radiant heat incident on (or arriving at) a surface will behave in any of three ways: the radiant energy can be reflected by the surface, absorbed by the surface, or transmitted through the material. Examples of each of these three behaviors include light reflecting off of a mirror, an asphalt road surface growing hot during a sunny summer day because of the absorption of solar radiation, and you being able to see the sun when you are swimming underwater (i.e., the sunlight is transmitted through the water). The abilities of a surface to reflect, absorb, and transmit radiant energy are described in terms of the *reflectance, absorptance,* and *transmittance* of the surface.[7] Each term is defined as the ratio of the amount of incident energy that is reflected, absorbed, or transmitted versus the total amount of radiant energy that is incident on the surface. Each term — reflectance, absorptance, and transmittance — will be a decimal fraction having a value between zero and 1.0, and, for any surface, the sum of these three terms will be 1.0. And, excepting transparent and translucent materials, the transmittances for building materials are generally zero (i.e., no thermal radiation will pass through opaque building materials).

For describing radiant heat transfer between building surfaces we must ascertain what the temperature of the radiation source is and, thus, whether the source is emitting shortwave or longwave radiation. The primary source of shortwave radiation is the sun, whereas most terrestial objects (having temperatures less than a few hundred degrees °C) emit longwave radiation. Further, when describing radiation between building surfaces, we must also consider the character of the receiving surface (i.e., how well it absorbs or reflects). Table 2.1 shows absorptance and reflectance values for common building materials. Note that for some building materials substantial differences exist between how they behave toward shortwave and longwave radiation. Most building materials are excellent absorbers of longwave radiation. Alternatively, their abilities to absorb shortwave radiation depend on their surface color and degree of surface roughness. Generally, darker colors and rougher surface textures promote absorption of solar radiation, and smoother, white-colored (or shiny metallic) surfaces have low absorptances.

Finally, let's reconsider the heat transfer mechanisms that are present when you place your hand on the window pane. If the air outside the window glass is colder than your hand, then heat from your hand will be transferred through the glass and expended to the exterior. We have noted previously that the exchanges of heat from your hand to the glass and from the inner surface of the window pane to the outer surface will occur by conduction. Further, because the outer window surface is warmer than the outside air, then there will be convective heat exchange between the surface and the air. As most inanimate objects outside of the building will likely have surface temperatures approximately equal to that of the ambient external air, there will be a net positive longwave radiant exchange from the outer surface of the glass to all of these objects that are in "line-of-sight" with the window pane. Thus, in fact, both convective *and* radiative exchange will be taking place from the outer window pane to the building exterior (see Figure 2.12).

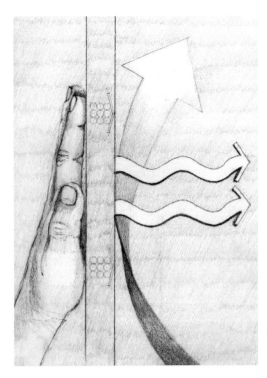

Figure 2.12 In addition to the convective heat exchange that occurs at the outer window surface (made warm by the heat conducted through the glass), a net positive radiative heat transfer will occur between the outer surface and cooler objects that are within line-of-sight of this glass surface.

TABLE 2.1
ABSORPTANCE & REFLECTANCE VALUES FOR SOME COMMON BUILDING MATERIALS

MATERIAL	ABSORPTANCE* Shortwave (solar radiation)	ABSORPTANCE Longwave (terrestial radiation)	REFLECTANCE Longwave (terrestial radiation)
Aluminum, polished	0.15 to 0.25	0.03 to 0.05	0.95 to 0.97
Nonmetallic black surfaces such as asphalt or paint	0.90 to 0.95	0.90 to 0.95	0.10 to 0.05
Red brick	0.70 to 0.80	0.85 to 0.95	0.15 to 0.05
White painted surface	0.10 to 0.20	0.90 to 0.95	0.10 to 0.05
Stainless steel, polished	0.30 to 0.40	0.50 to 0.60	0.50 to 0.40
Copper, polished	0.15 to 0.25	0.05 to 0.10	0.95 to 0.90
Copper, tarnished	0.60 to 0.70	0.70 to 0.80	0.30 to 0.20
Common window glass, clear	0.03 to 0.05	0.90	0.10

*Absorptances for surfaces normal to direct-beam solar radiation

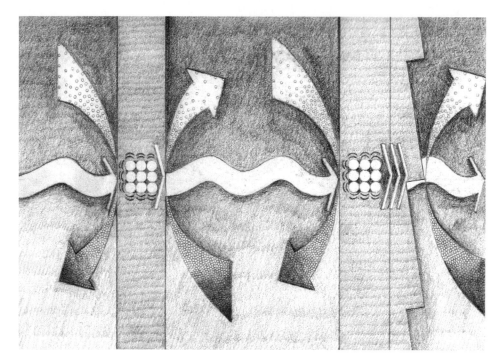

Figure 2.13 Heat transfer mechanisms are present across an uninsulated wood-frame wall (when the air on the left side of the wall is warmer than on the right side). The exchange mechanisms in the room include a convective heat transfer from the room air to the wall surface and radiant transfer from warmer objects in the room (e.g., occupants, a chair, a lamp, and so forth) to the wall surface. Similarly, the exchange mechanisms on the outside of the wall will include a convective heat transfer from the wall surface to the ambient external air and longwave radiant exchange between the wall surface and external objects at temperatures less than the outer wall surface.

2.2.3   A SUMMARY EXAMPLE:
HOW IS HEAT TRANSFERRED THROUGH AN UNINSULATED STUD WALL?

Suppose that you have an older house that is constructed of uninsulated wood-framed (stud) walls and that you have a furnace that allows you to maintain an internal air temperature of 20 °C (68 °F). Let's also suppose that the external air temperature is presently at 10 °C (50 °F). For this situation there is clearly a temperature difference between the inside air and the outside air. Thus, heat transfer will occur across the stud wall. Now, presume that the stud wall is composed of the following materials (moving horizontally from inside the house to outside and choosing a path that misses any of the studs): a layer of gypsum wallboard; a "dead air space" between the studs; a layer of plywood sheathing; and some wood siding.

A summary of the heat transfer mechanisms existing from the inside air to the outside air is shown in Figure 2.13. Heat transfer between the room air and the inside surface of the wallboard will occur by convection.[8] Heat will also be transferred by radiation between any objects in the room — you, a television, or a stove — and the surface of the wallboard. Thus, provided that these interior objects are warmer than the wallboard surface, then a net positive radiant transfer will occur from these objects to the wallboard. Depending on the temperatures of these radiant sources, most (if not all) of the radiant exchange will be by longwave radiation. The heat from inside the room reaching the interior surface of the wallboard will be conducted through the wallboard to the other side. If you placed temperature sensors on the two surfaces of what is called the "dead air space," you would find a temperature difference existent across this space with the surface closer to the room interior warmer than the other surface.[9] The thermal difference across this air space causes heat transfer by radiation and convection, thus warming the outer surface of this air space. The heat collected on this outer surface is then conducted through the plywood and the wood siding. Finally, because the external surface of the siding will be slightly warmer than the ambient external air, heat will be transferred from the siding surface to the air by convection and to surfaces near the building, but not in direct contact with it, by longwave radiation.

Note that to impede the rate of heat transfer across this uninsulated stud wall, we could place some insulating material into the "dead air space." Using conventional insulations we would thus be able to reduce the heat transfer rate across the entire wall assembly by about 70 percent. Controlling heat transfer rates through building envelopes — by these three *sensible* means of heat exchange — will be discussed further in Section 5.3.

Section 2.3 | DIFFERENTIATING BETWEEN SENSIBLE AND LATENT HEAT EXCHANGE

Previously we have stated that heat transfer happens by two fundamental mechanisms: molecular (or atomic) activity and electromagnetic radiation. In both instances these mechanisms occur because of temperature differences that exist between systems or objects. As the temperature of a source is greater than the temperature of a sink, then heat will be exchanged from the source to the sink. As we can generally perceive this exchange — except when the difference is small — by our *sense of feel,* we say that the energy transferred is *sensible heat.* Because sensible heat exchange occurs when a temperature difference is present between objects, sensible heat is thus transferred by conduction, convection, and radiation.

An alternative form of heat transfer is observed between objects (or systems and their surroundings). This other form is called *latent heat* exchange. It is the energy that is taken in or released by some material when it changes *state* (or *phase*). So, when a liquid like water freezes, latent heat is given off to the surroundings. Or, when water boils and turns into steam, latent heat is taken in (presumably, from the heat source that causes the water to boil). Note that the introduction or removal of latent heat does not coincide with a change in temperature of the material. Rather, the state or phase change proceeds as the latent heat is exchanged. In fact, if we placed a container of water over a heat source, allowed the water to boil, and meanwhile recorded the time duration and the temperature of the water, we would obtain a graph like the one in Figure 2.14. You can see that the temperature of the water increases for some period of time until it reaches 100 °C (212 °F). At that point the temperature levels off and remains constant. Even when more heat is added to the water, the temperature of the water does not increase. The reason for this lack of an increase in the temperature of the water is that the energy being supplied by the heat source does not act as sensible heat. Instead the additional energy becomes the *latent heat of vaporization,* which enables the water to boil and change to steam.

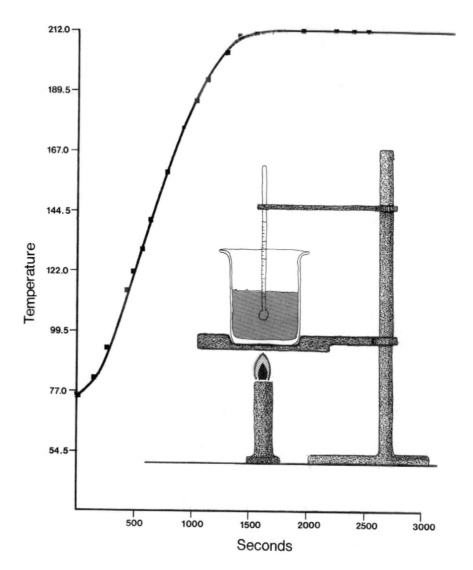

Figure 2.14 A graph of the temperature of water heated to boiling versus the time elapsed during the heating. Here, we begin with the water at a temperature similar to that of the room air and supply sensible heat to the water, causing it to rise in temperature. When the water temperature reaches 212 °F (100 °C), the temperature levels off and does not increase. The leveling-off of the temperature indicates that all the heat we are supplying is then being "consumed" as latent heat, the energy that must be given to the water to cause it to change its phase from liquid to gas (or, here, water to steam). If we were to cover this vessel, thus enclosing the steam and the boiling water, we could subsequently increase the temperature of the steam by adding sensible heat. This hotter steam (at temperatures above 212 °F [100 °C]) is called *superheated steam* and is supplied by municipal utilities for the conditioning of buildings. (Note: if you replicate this demonstration, you will find that bubbles of steam form in the water long before the water temperature reaches 212 °F (100 °C). The presence of these bubbles—usually present near the bottom and lower sides of the container—is the result of a nonuniform distribution of the heat throughout the water. These bubbles also indicate that some of the heat you are supplying to the water is being consumed as latent heat before the thermometer shows a temperature of 212 °F (100 °C). If you stir the water, insuring a more uniform heat distribution in the water, the steam bubbles will not form.

Finally, in more rigorous texts on thermodynamics, you would find that the term *latent heat* is not used. This omission is occasioned by the fact that heat is defined by the thermodynamicist as the thermal energy that is exchanged between a system and its surroundings when a temperature difference exists between them. As we have noted, latent heat exchange occurs independent of a temperature difference. Supplying or taking away latent heat is not strictly a heat exchange process. But, for the sake of simplicity, we shall use the term *latent heat* throughout this text as the description for energy that causes some material to change from one state or phase to another.

Section 2.4 | FURTHER READINGS ABOUT HEAT, THERMODYNAMICS, AND HEAT TRANSFER

There are many fine books on these topics. The subjects of thermodynamics and heat transfer are basic areas of concern for mechanical and other engineers, and textbooks treating these subjects are numerous. We will suggest six books that discuss these subjects.

First, for books that offer more qualitative treatments (and employ nonnumerically-based explanations) of principles and the thermal behaviors of materials, we suggest:

Heschong, L., *Thermal Delight in Architecture,* (Cambridge, Massachusetts: MIT Press, 1979); and

Mott-Smith, M., *The Concept of Heat and Its Workings Simply Explained,* (New York: Dover Publications, Inc., 1962), see Chapters I and XIV–XV, particularly.

And, second, we note four books that consider heat transfer topics relating directly to the thermal behavior of buildings:

Bansal, N.K., G. Hauser, and G. Minke, *Passive Building Design: A Handbook of Natural Climatic Control,* (Amsterdam: Elsevier Science B.V., 1994);

Givoni, B., *Man, Climate, and Architecture* (2nd edition), (London: Applied Science Publishers, Ltd., 1976);

Moss, K., *Heat and Mass Transfer in Building Services Design,* (London: E. & F.N. Spon, 1998); and

Pratt, A.W., *Heat Transmission in Buildings,* (Chichester, England: John Wiley and Sons, Ltd., 1981.

ENDNOTES and SELECTED ADDITIONAL COMMENTS

1. *Webster's Seventh New Collegiate Dictionary,* (Springfield, Massachusetts: G. & C. Merriam Company, 1967), page 247.

2. Kenner, H. "Bucky Fuller and The Final Exam," *The New York Times Magazine,* July 6, 1975, Section VI, pages 10–12ff.

3. The building will likely also lose heat to other surrounding entities (e.g., the night sky, ground surfaces, nearby vegetation, and so forth). This exchange of heat between the probably warmer external building surface and these other entities will occur by radiant transfer (a mechanism that will be described in Section 2.2.3 below).

4. Actually, finned-tube radiation operates more effectively by convection than by radiation.

5. Many incandescent light bulbs now are filled with gases like nitrogen and/or argon, which would permit heat transfer between the filament and the glass bulb by convection. But the primary means of heat transfer between the filament in the gas-filled light bulb and your hand is still by radiation.

6. However, if the two objects and the screen were all at the same temperature, radiant exchange would still occur from the objects to the screen and from the screen to the objects. But the net radiation between either object and the screen would be zero.

7. Alternative terms that are equally acceptable for reflectivity, absorptivity, and transmissivity are *reflectance, absorbance,* and *transmittance.*

8. Although, most precisely, the heat exchange at the air-wallboard interface will really be by conduction.

9. This space is said to be filled with "dead air" because it was thought, in the past, that the air in the stud space would not exchange locations with the inside or outside air. In fact, primarily by infiltration, the air molecules do move from this dead air space to the room interior or the exterior of the building. The process by which air infiltration occurs will be discussed in Section 5.3.

CHAPTER THREE

Establishing Thermal Comfort

IN THE FIRST CHAPTER we stated that a fundamental reason for constructing buildings is to control the immediate environment around people. Such control can be manifested by providing shelter from the external environment, by enabling occupants to live and work comfortably, and by operating controlled environments with reasonable efficiency. We suggested that providing shelter involves meeting basic needs like placing a roof over one's head and insuring the security of the occupant. Alternatively, we defined comfort as "the state of being able to pursue some activity without experiencing environmental stress." In this chapter we will examine what constitutes thermal comfort, describe parameters that affect the maintenance of thermal comfort, and then define the ranges for these parameters, across which thermal comfort is likely to be present.

If we can agree that the maintenance of thermal comfort should be a fundamental attribute for the operation of a building, then identifying what environmental parameters provide thermal comfort will present us with a statement of requirements for how a building interior should be operated. We can then take this statement of requirements and use it as a "benchmark" for establishing how well a building should perform thermally. In Chapter 4 we will describe the various climates that occur worldwide (thus, cataloging the basic characteristics of all the natural environments present on Earth). Then, in Chapter 5,

Figure 3.1 Being outside on a cold day without solar radiation to warm you or adequate clothing to insulate you from the cold would leave you defenseless against the natural environment.

by contrasting these climates and the environmental parameters that constitute thermal comfort, we can identify building design and construction guidelines whose use will ensure and facilitate the provision of thermal comfort in these buildings. Essentially, the guidelines offered in Chapter 5 will be derived from the following conceptual model:

| Climatic conditions of building of the natural environment | − | Thermal comfort needs | = | "Amount" required for the occupant |

Stated verbally, this model specifies that the type and degree of building support needed for a person, who strives to exist in some otherwise natural setting, should be established by comparing thermally comfortable environmental conditions with the attributes of the climate (or weather) present in that setting. By selecting the level of support to match (and not greatly exceed) any deficit between thermal comfort needs and the properties of the natural setting, the designer and the builder should be able to develop a building that will operate efficiently.

In Chapter 1 we introduced the notion that a series of devices could be employed to combat stressful and potentially hostile conditions present in the natural environment (Figure 3.1). These devices would be applied sequentially according to the severity of the conditions and would effectively constitute alternative lines of defense. Thus, which line of defense should be used in some situation would indeed depend upon how adverse the environment was and how much support or control an individual required for establishing shelter or being comfortable. We previously described four lines of defense: first, adapting some thermal attribute of the natural environment to assist a person in establishing comfort; second, modifying the person's state to reduce an environmental stress (e.g., putting on a jacket on a cool day); third, providing a built enclosure to separate the person from the natural environment; and, fourth, employing an active control device to alter the internal environment within the built enclosure.

Figure 3.2 The warming rays from the sun can offset discomfort that could otherwise result on a cool autumn day.

These lines of defense should be deployed as alternative, graduated means for dealing with challenges presented by a climate (or some weather) at some location (i.e., to satisfy this climate-versus-comfort model). For example, on a cool day one can use solar radiation as a heat source (Figure 3.2); or on a warm day one can stand under a tree to find shade and to keep from being overheated by the sun. The solar radiation and the shading tree are integral parts of the natural environment, and each changes the ambient environment around the person. Alternatively, by modifying a clothing ensemble or increasing an activity rate, one can adjust the personal aspect of this model (Figure 3.3). The building envelope, as the third line of defense, creates an enclosed space (Figure 3.4). This built space separates the person from the natural environment and enables the development of an environment that is in many ways independent of the space external to the enclosure. Drawing upon natural sources of energy will further enhance the sheltering features provided by the built space. The final means of responding to the climate-versus-comfort challenge encompasses the addition of some form of active control (Figure 3.5) that enables regulation of a separated, smaller, and more fully managed environment within the building envelope.

Figure 3.3 Warm clothing topped by a down-filled jacket will enable you to feel thermally comfortable and enjoy the winter landscape.

Thus, as long as a primary responsibility for designers and builders is to create environments that provide occupants with thermally comfortable conditions, then these environments can be based selectively on any one or more of these four lines of defense. Which of these alternative strategies should be employed for any given situation will depend upon the extent of support required and the resources available to the designer, builder, and client. Also, a host of other considerations may influence the choice of strategies (e.g., the types of activities requiring support, the physical context surrounding and present at a site, relevant aesthetic traditions, and so forth).

Section 3.1 | FINDING AN UNBIASED VIEW OF WHAT CONSTITUTES THERMAL COMFORT

Our discussion here will focus on the physical and physiological aspects of attaining thermal comfort. We will identify the environmental properties that affect thermal comfort, and we will describe how the human body reacts (or adapts) to the environment. First, we will describe how the human body functions thermally, what parameters affect the thermal performance of the human being, and under what conditions individuals are thermally comfortable. Then, after we have presented the physical and physiological determinants of thermal comfort, we will briefly introduce some qualifications that suggest that thermal comfort and thermal sensation may be affected by one's state-of-mind.

One other important qualification to our description of what constitutes thermal comfort is that we will be presenting a normative view. Scientific research on the physical and physiological parameters of thermal comfort is well-established and has been carefully performed since about 1920. This research has been founded on the testing of many thousands of subjects in the intervening years. The results from these tests have then been used to derive relationships that describe thermally comfortable conditions. Necessarily, though, these relationships concern averaged responses to research tests. Thus, whereas the likelihood is high that the conditions you find to be thermally comfortable will fall within the ranges predicted by these relationships, there can be little assurance that everyone will be satisfied with conditions within these ranges.

Figure 3.4 A greenhouse on a sunny day, even in winter, can be a very pleasant environment to work tending your plants. The warmth from the solar radiation will make the greenhouse into a real "shirt-sleeve" work setting.

Figure 3.5 Sitting by your wood-burning stove on a cold winter night can be a relaxing experience after a long day working outside amid the cold and snow.

SIDEBAR 3.1 Determining thermally comfortable conditions

The principal research procedure employed by most scientists studying the thermal comfort of human beings is performed in a room-sized chamber whose environmental conditions are closely controlled and monitored. Normally, subjects for a specific test will be dressed in a standardized uniform (worn by all the subjects for the test) and then will be admitted to the chamber. The interior of the chamber will be maintained at some set of conditions, and the subjects will be allowed some amount of time to adapt to these conditions. Then, the subjects will be asked to characterize the test conditions, indicating to what extent they feel thermally comfortable. Descriptions of test chambers, uniforms, and test procedures can be found in the following two papers: Nevins, R.G., F.H. Rohles, W. Springer, and A.M. Feyerherm, "Temperature-humidity chart for thermal comfort of seated persons," *ASHRAE Transactions*, 72 (Part I), 1966, pages 283–291; and Kjerulf-Jensen, P., Y. Nishi, P.O. Fanger, and A.P. Gagge, "Investigation on man's thermal comfort & physiological response," *ASHRAE Journal*, 17(1), January 1975, pages 65–68.

Section 3.2 | THERMAL REGULATION IN THE HUMAN BODY: MAINTAINING A THERMAL BALANCE

The human body resembles a simple machine. You eat some food (i.e., the machine takes in fuel). The food is broken down by digestion (or, the fuel is combusted). Useful energy is produced (changed in form so that the chemical energy stored in the food or fuel can be utilized). Some of the energy produced in the human body (or, in the machine) then is employed to perform "useful work." The remaining energy is exhausted to the environment. One significant, but minor, complication in this analogy is that, for the human body, some energy is used involuntarily as various bodily functions occur (e.g., breathing, circulation of the blood, movement of digested materials and wastes through the gastrointestinal tract, the generation (or destruction) of tissue, and so forth). But, otherwise, this simple analogy is a good beginning for explaining how the body processes energy: food is consumed, usable energy is produced for activating the muscles in the body, useful work is performed, and excess heat is exchanged to the environment surrounding the body.

Basically, the human being is a *homeotherm,* or a creature that maintains a nearly constant body temperature while existing within an environment whose physical characteristics vary substantially. This nearly constant body — or, more precisely, deep-body or core — temperature is maintained by a thermal regulation system, which attempts to match the production of heat within the body with the exchange of heat to the environment. Heat regulation in the body is a function of the nervous system. The thermal regulation is composed of both localized sensors and centralized sensors and controllers. What these sensors are able to discern of the environment surrounding the body and what actions the controllers are able to initiate in response to messages from the sensors determine feelings of thermal comfort (or discomfort). Most of the activities directed by the centralized controllers occur involuntarily. However, the feelings that a person experiences from these centralized regulatory activities can lead the individual to undertake voluntary steps to overcome any thermal discomfort.

3.2.1 HEAT PRODUCTION WITHIN THE HUMAN BODY

Heat is generated as a by-product of metabolism, which is the sum total of all the chemical reactions that occur in all the cells that make up one's body. Fundamental to metabolism is the intake of food, which provides energy for living. The food contains quantities of carbohydrates, lipids (fatty substances), and proteins, as well as trace amounts of various vitamins and minerals. These food materials are decomposed into simpler compounds during digestion in the gastrointestinal tract. The most important of the products resulting from this decomposition is the chemical adenosine triphosphate (known as ATP). This chemical is found everywhere in the human body and is the medium that transfers usable energy throughout the body. This substance undergoes a formation and decomposition cycle, with each step involving the acquisition or release of energy.

As the ATP passes to all the bodily systems that carry out the functions of life, thermal energy embodied in the ATP is then exchanged to surrounding tissues. This heat exchange from the ATP to the tissues is the second means by which heat is spread throughout the body (the first means being the decomposition of food and the production of this ATP). The third mechanism for heat production is the performance of basic bodily functions (i.e., the energy remaining in the ATP is consumed by these systems and their components, enabling them to carry out these functions). The essential body functions that use the energy borne by the ATP are the absorption of food decomposition products along the gastrointestinal tract; all muscular contractions; glandular secretions; the generation of cellular substances; and the formation of the electrical impulses which serve as the message units between the many sensors (spread throughout the body), the central nervous system, and the brain.

The rate with which heat is produced within the body is known as the *metabolic rate.* This rate encompasses the total amount of heat given off by all the chemical reactions occurring in the body. Of the five basic body functions identified above, the only one that can be directly affected by voluntary actions is the rate of energy required for muscular contractions. Each person experiences a *basal* metabolic rate, which is the rate of energy produced when the individual is in a quiet, resting state. The basal metabolic rate is the lowest rate of activity that the person can experience. All other activities, excepting normal sleep, will be comparatively more active than this basal state and will produce greater rates of heat production.

Performing these more active endeavors—for example, being seated in a class and taking notes, typing at a word processor, riding a bicycle, sawing a piece of wood with a hand or electric saw, and so forth—still requires that the various involuntary bodily functions continue. Further, each more active endeavor demands the consumption of greater quantities of the ATP for the activity to occur (and, thus, increased heat production will

---

SIDEBAR 3.2 Metabolic rates

Metabolic rates for various activities for an average-sized adult man (i.e., where average-sized is commonly defined as 175 cm of height [69 in] and having a weight of 70 kg [154 lbs]) include the following:

ACTIVITY	NUMBER OF METS*
Sleeping	0.7
Seated, quiet	1.0
Typing w/ electric typewriter (40 wpm)	1.0
Drafting	1.2
Walking @ 2 MPH (3.2 km/hr)	2.0
Walking @ 3 MPH (4.8 km/hr)	2.6
Dancing	2.4–4.4
Tennis, singles	4.6
Squash, singles	7.2
Wrestling	8.7

* The metabolic rates for these activities for the average-sized adult woman (i.e., defined as 163 cm [64 in] in height and weighing 55 kg [120 lbs]) are approximately 85 percent of the amounts reported for the adult man. The source for these values is the book by Fanger, P.O., *Thermal Comfort,* (New York: McGraw-Hill Book Company, 1972), pages 24–26. Note that 1 MET = 18.4 Btu/h-ft^2 (or 58.1 W/m^2). Permission to reproduce the tabular data has been sought from The McGraw-Hill Companies.

result). Conducting any of these endeavors is known generally as "useful work" (i.e., referring to that component of the metabolic heat production that actually results in some endeavor being accomplished). The term includes all the voluntary activities that a person undertakes.

The energy derived from the digestion of food is thus expended in two fashions: about 20 percent of the food energy is employed for useful work, and the remaining 80 percent is exchanged to the surroundings as waste heat. Surprisingly, then, the human body is only about 20 percent efficient in performing its various life activities. In fact, the range of efficiency is thought to vary from about 17 to 23 percent (with the former value observed for the elderly and the infirm, and the latter value seen among some world-class athletes). So, about four-fifths of the potential food energy an individual ingests will ultimately be exchanged to the environment as wasted heat.

3.2.2 MAINTAINING A HEAT BALANCE WITH THE ENVIRONMENT

How do you get rid of waste heat?   Three groups of mechanisms are employed to exchange the unutilized energy (as waste heart) to the environment. All three devices happen involuntarily (i.e., we cannot control their occurrences directly). But, as we will discuss subsequently, there are conditions that an individual can create which will markedly influence the rates with which these mechanisms proceed. The first group of loss mechanisms consists of the three sensible heat exchange devices: *conduction, convection, and (longwave) radiation.* As long as the body surface is warmer than the air surrounding it, some object in contact with it, or some object in line-of-sight with it, then sensible heat transfer from the body to the air and/or from the body to these objects will proceed. Examples of such heat losses are convective exchange from bare skin to the air, conductive exchange experienced between the skin and the surrounding water while swimming, and a net positive radiative transfer from the bare skin of your body toward the cold surface of a window.

The second group of loss mechanisms includes two fundamental body functions: *respiration* and *perspiration.* For respiration, each time you exhale you are sending out from your lungs warm, relatively wet air. For evidence of this fact, think about how you can see your breath on cold winter days. What you are seeing is the crystallizing of the water droplets that are borne in the air as it leaves your lungs. So, generally, when the air around you is cooler than the expelled air, sensible heat transfer occurs. Additionally, when the expelled water vapor condenses and the resulting droplets crystallize, latent heat exchange happens. Because the air around you will commonly be both cooler and drier than your exhaled breath, you will lose both sensible and latent heat to the environment. Alternatively, perspiration—frequently called *insensible* perspiration—is a process in which water in the body diffuses through the skin and evaporates at the skin surface. As evaporation of the perspiration occurs, energy in the form of latent heat leaves the body, cooling the skin. If the ambient air is not too humid, then water from perspiration will evaporate readily, and this process can serve as a useful heat loss mechanism. However, when the air is quite humid, perspired water will evaporate less well and the process becomes a less successful means of shedding excessive heat. The sensation of feeling "clammy" occurs when the ambient air is humid, and evaporation of perspired water proceeds slowly and seems to provide little useful cooling.

These first two groups of loss mechanisms can be characterized as being ever-present, in the sense they occur constantly (although their heat exchange rates may vary from low to rapid depending on the intensity of a person's activity). The third group of loss mechanisms, instead, operates sporadically in response to the existence of certain environmental and personal conditions that we will discuss further on. This third group consists of corrective thermoregulatory devices. *Thermoregulation,* generally, is the overall body process in which the body seeks to maintain a near-constant deep-body (or core) temperature. Under normal circumstances, the rates of the two groups of ever-present heat loss mechanisms will be sufficient to shed the excess heat produced during metabolism. But, for certain conditions (e.g., during rigorous exercise, when feeling ill, when confronting some emotional situation, or, simply, when exposed to particularly warm environmental conditions around the body), the ever-present loss mechanisms will not be able to shed the markedly increased amount of heat that is produced under these conditions. Thus, to maintain the overall heat balance with the environment, the body will activate various corrective thermoregulatory mechanisms.

For instance, when you exercise, you increase your rate of metabolic heat production (i.e., you consume energy much faster). This increased heat production requires that additional heat will need to be given off to the surrounding environment (if a heat balance is to be maintained). The two groups of ever-present heat loss mechanisms together have limits to how much heat they can exchange with the environment. So, if you exercise to the point of (or beyond) "breaking a sweat," then sweating is a further means of losing heat to the surroundings (i.e., the sweat evaporates, taking up heat from the body). In this manner, then, sweating is a corrective thermoregulatory device occurring in response to the increased activity. Sweating thus enables the human body to maintain a heat balance with the environment.

Generally, however, these thermoregulatory devices are not strictly useful in maintaining thermal comfort. An explanation of why this is so will be presented in the next subsection.

How might you gain heat from the environment?   Thermal energy gained from warm (or hot) sources can also affect the tempering of the body. Like the mechanisms that promote heat loss to the surrounding environment, these gain mechanisms happen by sensible heat transfer. For instance, a major source of radiative heat is the sun. If you are exposed to solar radiation directly (i.e., there is a line-of-sight between you and the sun), then a significant amount of thermal energy can be transferred to you. Further, the sun can cause inanimate objects to become warm (as these objects absorb solar radiation). If these objects have surface temperatures exceeding the temperature of your body surface, then there will be a net positive radiative transfer from the object to your body. Heat conduction will occur between an object and you when that object has a higher surface temperature than your body and there is physical contact between the object and you. Alternatively, convective heat transfer will pass from the ambient air to your body when the air is warmer than your skin.

Thus, for instance, a fire is a useful heat gain source. Sitting in front of the fire, you gain radiant heat from the burning coals or the warmed brick surfaces that surround the fire. Also, you experience convective heating from the air that is warmed by the fire. Alternatively, if you sit in a hot bath, you will be gaining heat by conduction. The gain of sensible heat from surrounding objects and materials that are at higher temperatures than the surface of the body can also be characterized as ever-present. Whenever such higher-temperature objects or materials exist in the environment surrounding a person, heat will be transferred to the individual.

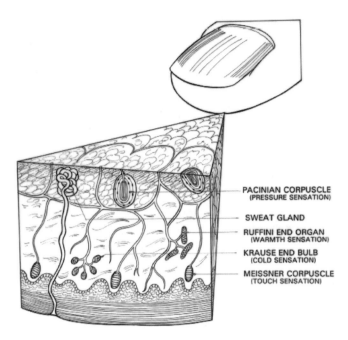

Figure 3.6 The thermoreceptor cells, along with those cells sensing pressure and touch, are located in the dermis and subcutaneous layers of the skin. The Ruffini and Krause receptors sense hot and cold objects, respectively. For further information about the receptor cells in the skin, see the book by Bloch, G., *Body & Self,* (Los Altos, California: William Kaufman, Inc., 1985), Chapter 6 (pages 79–80 and 84–89, especially). Additional illustrations showing the composition of the skin can be found in the book by Schlossberg, L., *The Johns Hopkins Atlas of Human Functional Anatomy* (3rd edition), (Baltimore: The Johns Hopkins University Press, 1986), pages 121–122.

3.2.3   THE THERMOREGULATORY SYSTEM IN THE HUMAN BODY

We have described how heat is produced in the human body and have stated that the human body acts to maintain a heat balance with the surrounding environment. Now, we shall address the question of what is responsible for regulating this thermal balance. Subsequently, we will examine some mechanisms that the body can employ when maintenance of the heat balance is threatened by environmental (or, even, internal) conditions.

Maintaining a heat balance requires, first, the sensing of the presence of heat in and about the body and, second, the regulating of the production of heat within the body and the exchange of heat between the body and the surrounding (or ambient) environment. Three essential structures participate in this sensing and regulation. Generally, the sensing structures are known as *thermoreceptors* and are located in the skin, in the spinal cord, and at the base of the brain in the hypothalamus. These thermoreceptors do not sense levels of temperature (i.e., they cannot enable one to establish the temperature of some object that the individual might touch). Instead, they sense differences between the temperatures of the object that is touched and the body. Thus, you can tell that something is hot or cold and, also, whether it is too hot or cold!

Figure 3.7 Sensing the warmth of the cooking pot commences with the peripheral thermoreceptor cells—the Ruffini end organs—sending electrical messages up the afferent nerve system to the hypothalamus. The emission rate by these thermoreceptor cells indicates to the hypothalamus how much heat is present (i.e., providing information that the hypothalamus can decode, permitting it to determine that the pot is indeed hot). This lower-brain structure then passes additional electrical messages to numerous other brain areas for them to form a response (e.g., pulling your finger away from the pot before your skin is burned!).

The thermoreceptors in the skin are located just below the surface of the skin (Figure 3.6) and are distributed over the entire surface of the body. The receptors are able to sense hot or cold objects (i.e., some receptors detect hot objects and others detect cold objects). These receptors thus operate at the periphery of the body's heat-sensing network. Their initial function is to sense whether an object, a liquid, or air is hot, cold, or some level in-between. Then, the receptors emit an electrical message about the relative warmth of the sensed "thing," which is transmitted along nerves to the spinal cord and on to the hypothalamus. Additionally, the spinal cord also is able to sense heat (or its absence) independently from the peripheral (skin) receptors. Messages from heat sensations started along the spinal cord also proceed to the hypothalamus. The hypothalamus functions as the integrative center, reading the messages sent from thermoreceptors that are present at the skin, along the spinal cord, and in the hypothalamus itself. From these messages, the hypothalamus establishes whether excessive heat loss or gain is present. Then, the hypothalamus directs the various heat production or exchange devices throughout the body to initiate and carry out (sufficient) action to maintain a thermal balance. Much of this maintenance action is involuntary, involving the ever-present and corrective thermoregulatory devices described previously. But messages about the temperature sensations will also be transmitted to the cerebral cortex—a portion of the brain where much conscious thought occurs. There, particularly if the sensations are unpleasant or harmful, the cortex will engage in thinking about the sensations and may direct some appropriate response (e.g., if you touch a very hot object such as a cooking pan (Figure 3.7), the cortex is the body part that directs your hand to remove itself from the pan).

Under ordinary conditions (e.g., the environment around you is neither too warm nor too cold and you feel fit and well), the human body is able to maintain a thermal balance with the ambient environment. Thus, the sum of heat gained from the environment—for instance, from the sun—and heat produced by metabolism will equal the sum of heat lost to the environment and the useful work performed in carrying out everyday life activities. As a thought model, an equation can be written to describe this heat balance:

(heat gained from the environment + metabolic heat production) =
(useful work performed + heat lost to the environment).

This heat balance will be maintained, under ordinary conditions, primarily by the involuntary actions of heat gain and loss (including the ever-present heat exchange mechanisms) and of metabolism. However, when the thermal balance is challenged by some internally or externally motivated condition, then these ordinary heat producing and regulating functions will not be adequate and corrective thermoregulatory functions will have to be activated if the heat balance is to be maintained.

Let's suppose you have been sitting and watching some friends play tennis and you feel thermally comfortable. Now, you get up and join them in playing. After a brief period of time you begin to feel warm, and soon you start to sweat. Or suppose you have been inside a building whose environment you find thermally comfortable (perhaps because its internal conditions are regulated by an air conditioning system) and you walk outside, discovering the external air to be very warm and humid. After a few minutes you begin to notice prickly heat forming on your skin and you feel clammy. Or suppose that you have been relaxing in a warm bath and feeling very comfortable. Then, you stand up and get out of your bath. As you towel off, the water droplets clinging to your body evaporate and you notice goose bumps forming on your skin.

For each of these three scenarios, a thermal imbalance has been established because the ever-present mechanisms by which you lose heat to or gain heat from the environment are not adequate to maintain the balance. Recall that the ever-present means for losing heat to the environment include the sensible exchange of heat and the heat lost by respiration and perspiration. These have limits to the amount of heating or cooling they can provide. For instance, for the tennis-playing scenario, your increased activity rate promotes additional metabolic heat production. If the sum of the heat produced while playing tennis and the heat gained from the environment exceeds the sum of work being done and the heat lost to the environment by these ever-present mechanisms, then this incremental heat increase must be exchanged with the environment if a thermal balance is to be maintained. So, if the ever-present loss mechanisms are inadequate, corrective thermoregulatory devices will begin to function, helping to reestablish the thermal balance.

What happens when one is too hot?   Two corrective thermoregulatory devices promote additional heat loss to the environment. The first device is called *vasodilation*. This mechanism involves an increase in the rate of blood flow near the skin surface (which occurs as a response by the central nervous system to the overheatedness). By being brought closer to the surface the blood cools more easily. Thus, the overheatedness can be reduced, if not removed altogether. However, if vasodilation is not sufficient to promote a thermal balance, then a second corrective thermoregulatory heat loss device—sweating— begins operation. Sweating occurs with the secretion of a solution of salty water from the eccrine sweat glands. These glands are located in the subcutaneous layer of the skin just below the surface. There are approximately two to five million of these sweat glands placed generally over the entire body (although they are concentrated on the forehead, palms of the hands and soles of the feet, along the backbone, and across the chest). The production of sweat has the greatest capacity for exchanging heat to the environment. But it has two limitations: first, there are limits, necessarily, to how fast an individual can sweat; and, second, as one sweats, the person becomes dehydrated and the rate of sweating is gradually reduced (finally, to a cessation of sweating). Ultimately, if the sweating process is incapable of reestablishing the thermal balance, then the last response of the human body is to have the core (or deep-body) temperature increase above that of its healthy state. If the core temperature rises too high, heat stroke will result and death may follow.

Both these vasodilation and sweating responses are initiated and controlled by the hypothalamus as it detects the deep-body temperature state of the individual.

What happens when one is too cold?   In situations when the sum of metabolic heat production and heat gained from the environment is less than the sum of energy expended as useful work and heat lost to the environment, then three corrective thermoregulatory devices can aid in restoring an energy balance. The first two corrective mechanisms reduce the rate of heat being lost to the environment, whereas the third promotes additional heat production. The two corrective thermoregulatory mechanisms that diminish the rate of heat loss from the body are *piloerection* and *vasoconstriction.* In piloerection the skin around hair follicles contracts creating "goose bumps." This corrective mechanism is left over from our evolutionary ancestors whose skin was more greatly covered with hair. For these ancestors, when piloerection occurred, the insulating value of the hair covering would have increased, thereby improving one's resistance against the cold. With our comparatively hairless bodies the effectiveness of piloerection as a defense against the cold is minimal. Vasoconstriction operates somewhat in reverse to vasodilation. For vasoconstriction the blood flow into the capillaries near the skin surface slows. Thus, heat loss from the blood through the skin to the environment will be reduced. But, similar to vasodilation, the capacity of vasoconstriction to reduce any thermal imbalance is relatively small.

If reducing heat loss from the body surface is insufficient to restore a thermal balance, additional heat production can be accomplished by shivering. This action is an involuntary response by the body to being cold and proceeds with the repeated contraction and release of skeletal muscles. As with sweating, the onset of shivering is initiated by signals from the hypothalamus. If shivering is insufficient to add needed heat production, then the last reaction of the body to excessive heat loss is hypothermia, a condition in which the core body temperature will fall below its normal level. Continued or intense hypothermia will end with the death of the individual.

Section 3.3 | WHAT IS THERMAL COMFORT?

A summary of Section 3.2 could be that the human body ingests food, processes it, performs useful work, and sheds heat to the surrounding environment while receiving heat from other elements of the environment. Alternatively, we could say that the human body is exposed, broadly, to a series of heat sinks and sources, all of which operate at various rates of exchange. As heat production, work, and heat exchanges occur, the human body tries to maintain a thermal balance with the environment. Given these statements, a fundamental question for a designer and/or a builder is, What can you do to control heat exchanges so that the occupant of a building will be thermally comfortable? To answer this question we will first define what thermal comfort is, then identify the environmental

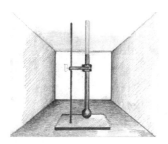

Figure 3.8 The temperature of the air is commonly measured with a dry-bulb thermometer.

Figure 3.9 A globe thermometer integrates both the short and longwave radiation that pass to its globe and the longwave radiation that emanates from the globe. Here, the shortwave radiation from the sun is transmitted through a window, falling on the globe. The walls and other objects in the room radiate, by longwave radiation, to the globe. The globe radiates back to all the surfaces in the room, also by longwave radiation. The difference in the amounts of radiation to and from the globe establishes what the thermometer within the globe will sense.

and personal parameters that affect your ability to be thermally comfortable, and subsequently describe what conditions are required for maintaining thermal comfort.

Numerous definitions for thermal comfort can be found in the professional and scientific literature. For example, Givoni defines thermal comfort, "as the absence of irritation and discomfort due to heat or cold, or in a positive sense, as a state involving pleasantness."[1] Dagostino suggests that thermal comfort "means being able to carry on any desired activity without being either chilly or too hot."[2] Alternatively, Fanger states that thermal comfort is "that condition of mind which expresses satisfaction with the thermal environment."[3] Fanger further notes that, because of "biological variance," establishing a condition that will satisfy everyone is not likely to be achievable.[4] Rather, the designer or the builder should instead seek to create a condition that will satisfy the largest number in a group of probable occupants. A fourth definition of thermal comfort, by Yaglou, says that "comfortable air conditions are those under which a person can maintain a normal balance between production and loss of heat, at normal body temperature and without sweating."[5]

This definition by Yaglou tells us what the two fundamental needs are for establishing thermal comfort. The first of these basic needs is that an individual must be able to maintain a thermal balance between his or her body and the environment. To create this thermal balance, the sum of heat gains from environmental sources and from metabolic processes must be equal to the sum of the useful work performed and the heat lost to the environment.

The second basic requirement for establishing thermal comfort is that the individual must be able to maintain this thermal balance without relying on the action of some corrective thermoregulatory device (e.g., sweating). Restated, this second requirement means that, if the only way for an individual to establish a thermal balance with the environment is by having some corrective thermoregulatory mechanism function, then the conditions affecting the individual are not thermally comfortable.

Section 3.4 | EIGHT PARAMETERS THAT AFFECT HEAT TRANSFER BETWEEN THE HUMAN BODY AND THE ENVIRONMENT

In Sections 3.2 and 3.3 we have considered the physiological mechanisms that control how the human body regulates itself thermally and what thermal comfort is. To understand better what the designer and the builder can do to facilitate maintenance of occupant thermal comfort, we will identify eight parameters that affect heat exchange between the occupant's body and the environment. Four of these parameters are environmental: they are basic properties of the environment surrounding a person. The other four parameters can be described as personal and concern what activity an individual pursues in the environment and the nature of the person's clothing ensemble. The task for the designer and the builder is to anticipate what ranges of these parameters will likely be present in any environment that is being planned. What magnitudes these parameters have will determine how much building (i.e., how much defense against the external environment) needs to be provided if the building interior is to be thermally comfortable.

3.4.1   THE FOUR ENVIRONMENTAL PARAMETERS THAT AFFECT THE MAINTENANCE OF THERMAL COMFORT

The four environmental parameters affecting comfort are the air temperature in the occupied space; the net radiant exchange rate between the person and the environment; the relative humidity of the air in the space; and the rate of air movement around the person (i.e., or, more generally, the relative air velocity in the space).

Air temperature (Figure 3.8). The significant question concerning how air temperature affects thermal comfort is, Is the air temperature less than or greater than the skin temperature? The difference between these two temperatures determines in which direction heat transfer will occur. If the skin temperature is greater, then heat will be lost to the environment by convection (and, possibly, by conduction, if various inanimate objects in the surrounding environment have temperatures similar to or equal to the air temperature and the person is touching those objects). Additionally, if the temperature of the air is less than the temperature of the gases exhaled from the lungs, then heat from respiration will be exchanged to the air. Alternatively, if the air temperature is higher than the temperature of the skin or of the respired gases, heat gain from the surroundings will proceed. Generally, whenever the air temperature exceeds the temperatures of the skin and the respired gases, it is quite difficult to maintain thermal comfort.

Net radiant exchange rate between the body and the environment (Figure 3.9). The direction of the net radiant exchange rate between a person and any object seen by the person depends on the surface temperatures of the person and the object. The warmer surface radiates more energy to the cooler surface. So, if you are sitting by a window and solar radiation falls on you, this radiation will warm you. But sitting near the same window surface on a day when the external air temperature is low and the sky is overcast may cool you.

Relative humidity (Figure 3.10). The amount of moisture in the air affects the rates of evaporation for moisture on the skin (e.g., present from insensible perspiration or sweating) and water droplets amongst respired gases. This evaporation serves as a cooling process. So, in a warm environment, evaporative cooling can be an important means of exchanging heat with the environment. But, if the air is both warm and relatively humid, then water on the skin or in the respired-gas mixture will evaporate less readily, and less cooling will be achieved.

Air movement around a person (Figure 3.11). Moving air increases the heat exchange rates between a person and the environment. Convective transfer becomes greater as the velocity of air movement increases. So, too, does the rate of evaporation increase as the rate of air movement increases. Thus, air movement can be a most useful means for accelerating body cooling in warm and warm-humid climates (as we shall discuss in Chapter 5). But moving air can also pose a liability for maintaining a thermal balance (and, perhaps, thermal comfort), when the air is cool or cold. In those situations moving air will hasten the heat exchange to the environment with potentially harmful results. The interacting effects of cold air temperatures and moving air are recognized by the Wind Chill Index, a scale used by meteorologists to describe the severity of winter weather conditions.[6]

3.4.2   THE FOUR PERSONAL PARAMETERS THAT AFFECT THE MAINTENANCE OF THERMAL COMFORT

The four personal parameters that influence the maintenance of thermal comfort are the activity rate of the individual; the insulation level of the person's clothing ensemble; the moisture permeability of the clothing ensemble; and the compressibility of the clothing ensemble.

Activity level of the person (or, the *metabolic rate*) (Figure 3.12). When a person is more active, the individual uses more energy derived from the consumption of the chemical ATP (adenosine triphosphate). This increase in the metabolic rate causes a concomitant increase in the production of "waste" heat that must be exchanged to the

Figure 3.10 Our mental associations about moisture present in air around us lead to a scene of an antebellum plantation house located somewhere in the American South. The house is surrounded by large trees from which is suspended lots of Spanish moss. The air is hot and very humid. But the air is also redolent, filled with the scents of flowers, grass, crops, and animal life. Animate things move slowly and languidly. It is time to pause and enjoy the environment around us.

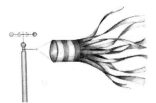

Figure 3.11 Moving air can be as pleasant as a summer breeze or as discomforting as the winter wind. How the moving air will feel depends greatly on the velocity of the air as it moves around us.

Figure 3.12 Standing still, walking slowly or quickly, or running along each presents a different activity rate (and a different level of internal heat production).

SIDEBAR 3.3 Measuring environmental parameters, characterizing radiant exchange rates around a person

One widely applied means for describing the net radiant exchange rate is the *mean radiant temperature* (which is abbreviated as the MRT). The mean radiant temperature is essentially an average of the surface temperatures of the various objects "seen" by a radiation receiver (e.g., a person). This average is weighted in favor of larger surfaces and surfaces closer to the receiver. For example, if you are in a warm room on a cold day and are sitting near a large window, the mean radiant temperature measured at the place where you are sitting will be lower than for other room locations that are more distant from the window. Thus, the mean radiant temperature is a highly location-dependent parameter.

Establishing the mean radiant temperature at some location in or out of a building is approximated most easily with a globe thermometer. The globe thermometer consists of a temperature-sensing device placed inside and at the center of a six-inch diameter hollow copper ball, which is finished with a flat black paint. The temperature-sensing device within the globe can be a standard fluid-filled glass thermometer (or some electrically based thermometer). The globe thermometer can then be read in the same way as one would read a glass thermometer (or an electrical temperature sensor).

In actual practice, the globe thermometer is somewhat sensitive to air movement across the globe. So, if the mean radiant temperature is established with a globe thermometer for conditions where the air is not relatively still, a correction must be made to the observed globe temperature. The equation

$$t_{mrt} = [(t_g + 460)^4 + (4.74 \times 10^7 V_a^{0.6} / (\varepsilon D^{0.4})(t_g - t_a)]^{0.25} - 460$$

where t_{mrt} = mean radiant temperature, °F ε = emissivity (0.95 for a black globe)
          t_g = globe temperature, °F D = globe diameter, ft
          V_a = air velocity, fpm t_a = air temperature, °F

provides the necessary correction for the effects of moving air. This equation and further discussion of the globe thermometer can be found in the *2001 ASHRAE Handbook of Fundamentals,* (Atlanta: American Society of Heating, Refrigerating, and Air-Conditioning Engineers, Inc., 2001), pages 14.28–14.29.

One qualification about the globe thermometer is that, especially when a glass thermometer with a fluid-filled bulb is used as the temperature sensor, the time required for the globe thermometer to reach a stable reading will be at least several minutes. However, globe thermometers with electrically based internal temperature sensors will need less time to arrive at a stable reading (i.e., perhaps five or so minutes).

[The equation for determining mean radiant temperature using S-I units appears below:

$$t_{mrt} = [(t_g + 273)^4 + (1.10 \times 10^8 V_a^{0.6} / \varepsilon D^{0.4})(t_g - t_a)]^{0.25} - 273$$

where t_{mrt} = mean radiant temperature, °C ε = emissivity (0.95 for a black globe)
          t_g = globe temperature, °C D = globe diameter, m
          V_a = air velocity, m/s t_a = air temperature, °C

This equation can be found in the *1997 ASHRAE Handbook of Fundamentals,* (Atlanta: American Society of Heating, Refrigerating, and Air-Conditioning Engineers, Inc., 1997), pages 14–26.]

Measuring relative humidity
Relative humidity essentially compares the amount of water vapor in the air (at some moment) with the amount of water vapor that saturated air at the same air temperature could contain. The formal definition of relative humidity is the water vapor pressure present in the air divided by the partial pressure of water vapor that would

be present in the air (at the same dry-bulb temperature) if the air were saturated. Algebraically, relative humidity (in percent) = 100 times $(p_{vapor})/(p_{saturated})$. Saturation of the air by moisture means that no additional moisture can be maintained as a vapor (i.e., in a gaseous state); the addition of more water vapor would cause that additional vapor to condense out as water droplets. Alternatively, *absolute humidity* is the amount of water vapor (in terms of its mass) that is present in some volume of air (i.e., the units for absolute humidity are either kilograms/cubic meter or pounds/cubic foot).

Relative humidity is readily measured with a sling psychrometer. This device consists of two glass mercury-bulb thermometers, one deployed with a bare (or uncovered) bulb and the other with the bulb covered with a cotton wick (or "sock"), which is wetted (i.e., dipped in water). The uncovered bulb measures the dry-bulb temperature of the air, and the wetted-wick-covered bulb measures the wet-bulb temperature of the air. The readings of the dry and wet-bulb temperatures are established by vigorously swinging them horizontally on an attached handle (held vertically), for a period of time (usually 90 seconds to two minutes). After the thermometers have been slung, the temperatures are read on the side of each thermometer. The wet-bulb thermometer will nearly always show a temperature somewhat below that found on the dry-bulb thermometer. This temperature difference is known as the wet-bulb depression. This depression is present because the moisture in the wetted-wick evaporates while the wet-bulb thermometer is slung: the moving air induces evaporation to occur more rapidly. The drier the air, the greater the wet-bulb depression will be. Once the two temperatures have been noted, you may use a comparison scale—which is frequently placed on the side of the case holding the two thermometers—to determine the relative humidity of the air. Alternatively, you may also employ a psychrometric chart to establish the relative humidity. For further information about describing and measuring the humidity in air, see Chapter 6 ("Psychrometrics") of the *2001 ASHRAE Handbook of Fundamentals*, (Atlanta: American Society of Heating, Refrigerating, and Air-Conditioning Engineers, Inc., 2001); note, particularly, pages 6.1 and 6.13–6.16.

Measuring the velocity of air

Air velocity, particularly when measured within a built environment, is commonly the most difficult of these several environmental parameters to measure accurately. First, the rates of air movement in a building are relatively slow (i.e., less than 1.0 m/s [a few mph]). Second, whether in an enclosed space or outside, air movement tends to be a highly variable phenomenon. Indeed, even in buildings where the principal air movement may be the result of air blown into a space by an air-conditioning or forced ventilation system, such air movement will be affected by a variety of secondary influences like air infiltrating through the building envelope, the convective rise of air through the building (sometimes called the *stack effect*), the movement of people, and the operation of machines (some of which are equipped with cooling fans), and so forth. Thus, air movement patterns within a building space can be complex.

When the air movement is wind-aided (or wind-caused), the presence of gusting and lulls is likely, creating wide variations in observed velocities. A third difficulty in measuring air motion occurs because many readily available sensors have a threshold below which they will not provide accurate readings (e.g., commonly, 1.0 m/s [a few mph]). Fourth, air movement-reading devices that are sufficiently sensitive to detect relatively slow air motion are usually expensive and fragile. Thus, measuring air velocities accurately—particularly, inside buildings—requires comparatively precise equipment, whose costs and difficulties of use often exceed the needs and interests of most designers and builders.

However, a number of devices for measuring air velocities are currently available. Some of these devices offer good accuracy and are useful for taking careful measurements, whereas others can be employed for obtaining approximate results and are quite inexpensive and simple to use. Among the better scientific and technical-grade instruments are the hot-wire anemometer and the air meter. Both can be used as hand-held instruments. The hot-wire anemometer typically has one of the lowest threshold velocities of any of the air motion-measuring devices and offers quite good accuracy. It may be used in buildings and outside. The greatest limitations of this device are its fragility and expense. The air meter has a higher threshold velocity (0.15 to 0.22 m/s [or 0.33 to 0.5 mph]) and provides somewhat less accuracy than the hot-wire anemometer. The air meter is

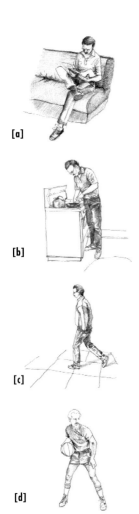

[a]

[b]

[c]

[d]

Figure 3.13 Four different activities, each exhibiting a specific metabolic rate: (a) reading a book, while sitting quietly, 1.0 MET; (b) cooking some scrambled eggs, 1.6–2.0 MET; (c) walking along at about 1.8 m/s (4 mph), 3.8 MET; and (d) playing basketball in a pick-up game, 5.0–7.6 MET. These specific MET ratings have been derived from Table 4 of Chapter 8 of the *2001 ASHRAE Handbook of Fundamentals,* (Atlanta: American Society of Heating, Refrigerating, and Air-Conditioning Engineers, Inc., 2001), page 8.7.

intended for use outdoors and for specific applications within buildings such as for measuring air movement rates in ventilation ducts. It is both less fragile and less expensive than the hot-wire anemometer.

For further information about observing air movement and measuring air flow in and around buildings, see the monograph by Heerwagen, D.R., *Observing air flow in buildings* (prepared for the Vital Signs Project, University of California, Berkeley, March 1996). This monograph may be found at the Web address: http://arch.ced.berkeley.edu/vitalsigns/res/rps.html.

environment. The exchange will initially proceed with increases in the rates of heat loss by the two ever-present mechanisms of heat loss (i.e., by sensible heat transfer and from respiration and perspiration). But, if heat exchange by these two ever-present means is not sufficient, then corrective thermoregulatory mechanisms will commence. Alternatively, if a person is relatively inactive (e.g., passively sitting watching television or standing in line outside of a theater on a cold winter evening), the person may feel cold. This feeling of coldness usually results when a thermal imbalance is present (i.e., the sum of the heat losses to the environment and the work rate together exceeds the sum of heat gains from the environment and energy from the person's metabolism). One way to remedy this imbalance is to have the person increase his/her activity rate (thus generating additional metabolic heat and establishing a thermal balance).

The activity rate for an individual is commonly described in terms of the quantity METs. An activity rate of one MET is approximately equivalent to the amount of energy required to power a 100-watt light bulb for one hour. Or one MET describes the average metabolic heat rate of a sedentary man (Figure 3.13). A table cataloging the metabolic rate for various activities has been included in Sidebar 3.2.

Insulation level of a person's clothing (Figure 3.14). A person's clothing ensemble can markedly affect the rates of heat loss (and heat gain) between the person and the environment. First, the clothing restricts sensible heat transfer from one's body to the surrounding environment (i.e., by any of the three sensible heat transfer mechanisms). Clothing can also modify the ability of the body to exchange heat by perspiration and sweating, particularly, because the clothing will reduce the amount of skin area exposed to the environment. Thus, clothing can be beneficial in maintaining a thermal balance when heat losses to the environment would otherwise be too great. Alternatively, the presence of clothing can hinder the maintenance of a thermal balance when the body is seeking to shed excessive heat. The suggested practice of wearing clothes in layers makes much good sense because this approach allows the wearer easily to alter the rate of heat exchange between one's body and the surrounding environment. The layering of clothing enables the wearer selectively to shed one or more layers (i.e., thus, permitting modification of the insulation value of one's ensemble to suit the environment, the person's activity rate, and other related factors).

The extent to which some ensemble will influence heat exchange is described by the unit CLO. An ensemble rated at 1.0 CLO will keep a person, so clothed, comfortable at an air temperature 8.3°C (15 °F) less than the air temperature required to keep the same person comfortable while nude. For example, an ensemble consisting of the following items — cotton briefs and T-shirt, warm socks, long-sleeved broadcloth dress shirt, cotton twill trousers, low shoes, and a long-sleeved woolen sweater — is rated at 1.0 CLO. Various data about the insulative capabilities of clothing articles and ensembles are shown in Tables 3.1 through 3.3. Also, note Figure 3.14 for the CLO ratings of alternative clothing ensembles.

The CLO ratings for various clothing ensembles are often determined using a copper manikin clothed with the ensemble to be tested (Figure 3.15). By measuring heat transfer rates between the manikin and the test environment, experimenters can establish what the insulative capability of some ensemble would be. For a description of tests with the copper manikin, see the paper by McCullough, E.A., B.W. Jones, and J. Huck, "A comprehensive data base for estimating clothing insulation," *ASHRAE Transactions,* 91(Part II), 1985, pages 29–47. The unit CLO was first suggested in a paper by Gagge, A.P., A.C. Burton, and H.C. Bazett, "A practical system of units for the description of the heat exchange of man with his environment," *Science,* 94(2445), November 7, 1941, pages 428–430.

Figure 3.15 This is a photograph of Fred, a computerized, moveable thermal manikin used to measure the insulation value of clothing systems. Fred is employed as a test subject at the Institute for Environmental Research, Kansas State University, Manhattan, Kansas. This photograph has been provided by Professor E.A. McCullough of the Institute and is printed with her permission.

[a]

[b]

[c]

[d]

The final two of the four personal parameters that affect heat exchange to and from the body are the moisture permeability of the clothing ensemble and the compressibility of the clothing ensemble. The first of these two parameters concerns the ease with which moisture can pass through the clothing. The second parameter accounts for the fact that, when certain insulating materials are compressed (e.g., goose-down jackets and vests), their insulative values will be decidedly less than when these materials are fully lofted (i.e. by fluffing up a material, thus greatly increasing the amount of air trapped amongst insulation particles like goose down). Also, if you wear clothing in layers, the outer layers will generally compress your innermost clothes. So, the overall insulative capability of the ensemble will not be as high as the summed amount of insulation values for the several individual components. These last two parameters are often of comparatively lesser consequence when describing conditions that will promote the maintenance of thermal comfort. Also, these last two parameters are usually relatively difficult to evaluate in practice.

In summary, there are six principal environmental and personal parameters that influence the establishment of a thermal balance between an individual and the environment surrounding this person. The four environmental parameters characterize the external environment in which buildings are designed and constructed. These four environmental parameters also describe the essential thermal qualities the interiors of buildings should have. It is the responsibility of the designer and the builder to provide adequate controls within the building package—whether by means of the building envelope or with active control systems—so that the interiors supply comfortable surroundings. Further, the two

Figure 3.14 Four different clothing ensembles: (a) an informal basketball uniform, rated at about 0.3 CLO; (b) clothes for lounging around on a mild summer day, about 0.6 CLO; (c) clothing to wear at home on a winter night, approximately 0.9–1.1 CLO (depending on whether the sweater is buttoned or open as shown); and (d) an ensemble appropriate for a cold, late autumn day, about 2–3 CLO (depending on the thickness and loft of the down in the outer jacket).

TABLE 3.1
INSULATION RATINGS FOR VARIOUS CLOTHING ARTICLES (IN CLO) [i]

FOR MEN		FOR WOMEN	
CLOTHING ITEM	**CLO**	**CLOTHING ITEM**	**CLO**
UNDERWEAR		UNDERWEAR	
Sleeveless shirt	0.06	Bra & panties	0.05
T-shirt	0.09	Half slip	0.13
Briefs	0.05	Full slip	0.19
Long underwear top	0.35	Long underwear top	0.35
Long underwear bottom	0.35	Long underwear bottom	0.35
TORSO		TORSO	
Shirts		*Blouses*	
Lt, short sleeve	0.14	Light	0.20
Lt, long sleeve	0.22	Heavy	0.29
Hvy short sleeve	0.25	*Dresses*	
Hvy long sleeve	0.29	Light	0.22
(add 5% for tie or turtleneck)		Heavy	0.70
Vest		*Skirt*	
Light	0.15	Light	0.10
Heavy	0.29	Heavy	0.22
TROUSERS		SLACKS	
Light	0.26	Light	0.26
Heavy	0.32	Heavy	0.44
SWEATER		SWEATER	
Light	0.20	Light	0.17
Heavy	0.37	Heavy	0.37
JACKET		JACKET	
Light	0.22	Light	0.17
Heavy	0.49	Heavy	0.37
FOOTWEAR		FOOTWEAR	
Socks		*Stockings*	
Ankle length	0.04	Any length	0.01
Knee-high	0.10	Pantyhose	0.01
Shoes		*Shoes*	
Sandals	0.02	Sandals	0.02
Oxfords	0.04	Pumps	0.04
Boots	0.08	Boots	0.08

i. This table has been reprinted from Chapter 8, "Physiological principles for comfort and health," *1985 ASHRAE Handbook of Fundamentals* (Atlanta: American Society of Heating, Refrigerating, and Air-Conditioning Engineers, Inc., 1985), page 8.5. Permission to reprint this table has been granted by the Society (© American Society of Heating, Refrigerating, and Air-Conditioning Engineers, Inc., www.ashrae.org).

TABLE 3.2
ESTIMATION OF INSULATION VALUES FOR ALTERNATIVE CLOTHING ENSEMBLES[i]

CLOTHING ARTICLE	ENSEMBLE A	ENSEMBLE B
Underwear briefs	0.05 CLO	0.05 CLO
T-shirt	0.09	0.09
Ankle (cotton) socks	0.04	0.04
Cotton, shortsleeve shirt	0.14	—
Wool, longsleeve shirt	—	0.29
Lightweight summer slacks	0.26	—
Heavyweight winter trousers	—	0.32
Wool, longsleeve sweater	—	0.37
Sneakers (low-cut)	0.04	0.04
TOTAL, UNADJUSTED	0.62	1.20
ACTUAL	0.51 CLO	0.99 CLO

i. The ACTUAL amounts include correction factors suggested by Nevins et al. that discount the "unadjusted totals" to account for the overlapping and compression of the underlayers of these ensembles. The correction factors are, for men, multiply the unadjusted total by 0.83 to find the ACTUAL amount, and, for women, multiply the unadjusted total by 0.84 to find the ACTUAL amount. These correction factors and the CLO estimation procedure are described in the paper by Nevins, R.G., P.E. McNall, and J.A.J. Stolwijk, "How to be comfortable at 65 to 68 °F," *ASHRAE Journal*, 16(4), April 1974, pages 41–43. Permission to reproduce this table has been granted by the American Society of Heating, Refrigerating, and Air-Conditioning Engineers, Inc. (ASHRAE Journal 1974. © American Society of Heating, Refrigerating, and Air-Conditioning Engineers, Inc., www.ashrae.org).

TABLE 3.3
INSULATION VALUES NEEDED TO MAINTAIN THERMAL COMFORT[i]

ACTIVITY	THERMAL CONDITIONS	
	18–20 °C (65–68 °F)	21–22 °C (70–72 °F)
Seated, reading with light mental activity	1.8–2.0 CLO	1.2–1.4 CLO
Seated, relaxed; or seated, typing; or drafting; or miscellaneous office work	1.2–1.5 CLO	0.9–1.1 CLO
Cooking; or washing dishes; or shaving; or teaching in school	0.8–1.0 CLO	0.5–0.7 CLO
House cleaning; or walking @ 3 mph; or washing & ironing	0.5–0.7 CLO	0.3–0.5 CLO

i. Reprinted from: Page 42 of Nevins, R.G., P.E. McNall, Jr., and J.A.J. Stolwijk, "How to be comfortable at 65 to 68 degrees F," *ASHRAE Journal*, 16(4), 1974, pages 41–43. Permission to reprint this table has been granted by the American Society of Heating, Refrigerating, and Air-Conditioning Engineers, Inc. (ASHRAE Journal 1974. © American Society of Heating, Refrigerating, and Air-Conditioning Engineers, Inc., www.ashrae.org).

primary personal parameters—activity rate and clothing insulation—offer a means of "fine-tuning" how the environment appears to building occupants. Whereas a designer or builder cannot proscribe magnitudes of activity rate (in METs) and clothing insulation (in CLO), the occupant does have choices about what magnitudes are indeed employed. Thus, flexibility with both the design and the use of the building is available.

3.4.3   TIME AS AN ESSENTIAL PARAMETER AFFECTING ONE'S THERMAL COMFORT

One can argue whether time is indeed a physical attribute of a person's experience. But, necessarily, how long one spends in a space can markedly influence the perception that the person will have of the space. Suppose you enter into a building after being outside in cool autumn air. You are dressed in an ensemble consisting of a series of clothing layers, that has enabled you to feel warm and comfortable in the cool exterior air. You continue to wear this well-insulating clothing indoors (perhaps because you anticipate soon going outside again and it is inconvenient to remove your outer clothing). Initially, you will not feel over-warm. But, gradually with the passage of time, you will begin to feel uncomfortable as the ability of your body to transfer heat to the warmer interior environment is retarded by the insulation of the clothing. Thus, in this manner the duration of time exposed to some set of environmental conditions is an important determinant of how one feels about the environment.

Another aspect of how time can participate in an occupant's assessment of thermal comfort arises in terms of how rapidly or slowly conditions in a space can change over some time period. For instance, if a space warms rapidly (to some temperature level) rather than more slowly (but ultimately reaching the same temperature level), occupants will have less time to adjust and are more likely to feel uncomfortable.

A third aspect of how time influences feelings of thermal comfort involves the potential habituation or adaptation of an individual to conditions that are different from those in which the person previously lived or worked. Brager and de Dear have written about how physiological acclimatization can affect an individual's feelings about a thermal environment.[7] These authors suggest that such acclimatization is more likely to occur when environmental conditions are more extreme than those usually experienced inside well-conditioned buildings. Alternatively, habituation or adaptation may result from psychological influences that also occur across time. We will discuss how an individual's state of mind may offer such influences in Section 3.7.

Section 3.5 | DESCRIBING THERMALLY COMFORTABLE CONDITIONS IN AND OUT OF BUILDINGS

From extensive research conducted during the past 80 years, the conditions required for insuring occupant thermal comfort have been well-established. This research has identified—for the principal environmental and personal parameters specified above—what ranges (of numerical values for these parameters) will create thermally comfortable conditions in and out of buildings. These parametric ranges thus can serve as targets to be sought after by designers and builders, when they plan and operate the built environment. So, comparisons of these comfort conditions to climatic information about a building site will enable determination of the character of the building that needs to be provided (i.e., what level of support must be furnished to match the deficit between thermal comfort needs and the character of the natural environment).

An initial catalogue of what values the six principal parameters should have for the maintenance of thermal comfort includes: an air temperature of between 20 to 27 °C (68 to 80 °F); the mean radiant temperature at the occupant's location equal to the air temperature; a relative humidity somewhere between 25 and 55 percent; the relative air velocity less than or equal to 0.36 m/s (70 feet per minute); an activity rate of 1.0 MET (i.e., that of a sedentary person); and clothing insulation of about 0.6 CLO.

Note, however, that the value(s) for any of these parameters may lie outside of these ranges, and thermal comfort can still be maintained. To explain this statement you might consider that the principal requirement for the maintenance of thermal comfort is that a thermal balance must exist. Thus, if you modify some one parameter that, by itself, would accelerate the rate of heat loss between you and the surrounding environment, and at the same time you alter some other parameter that, by itself, would decrease the heat loss rate, then a balance could likely be sustained. For instance, if the air temperature falls as nighttime approaches and you add clothing (to increase the insulative value of your ensemble), you would probably still be maintaining a thermal balance. An essential problem in the design and construction of buildings then is to find ways to manipulate these six parameters such that comfort can be present and the building can have the form and composition you wish.

Creating thermally comfortable conditions depends primarily on being able to control all six principal parameters. Therefore, anyone wishing to ensure that thermal comfort will be present in a building ultimately must manage these six attributes. A fundamental issue concerning these parameters is determining the nature of the interdependency between them (i.e., establishing how a change in one parameter can be offset by a change in another, so that thermally comfortable conditions will continue to exist). For instance, if the air temperature in a room is reduced below the thermal comfort range, can we ensure that thermal comfort will still be present for an occupant if he or she is wearing a sufficiently well-insulating clothing ensemble? Alternatively, is there a direct correspondence between an air temperature reduction of some number of degrees and an increase in clothing insulation in CLO (i.e., so that a thermal balance and comfort continue to exist for the occupant)? Or, if the air temperature does decrease, can a radiant heat source provide sufficient heat gain to offset the increased rate of heat loss to the air surrounding the person (and, further, how much radiation is needed)?

Therefore, what is needed for creating and operating thermally comfortable buildings is some means for relating these six parameters together. Then, when this relationship is established, we can examine what effect changing one or more of these parameters will have on the maintenance of thermally comfortable conditions. Additionally, we also need some means that will enable us to establish what (and how much) corrective action is needed when the magnitudes of some one (or more) of these parameters deviate from the values of these parameters, which have been identified as providing thermally comfortable conditions.

Perhaps because of the complexity of the physiology of the human body, a somewhat sizeable number of ways have been developed for relating the parametric values required for maintaining thermal comfort. These many relational devices exist in a variety of forms and include indices, envelopes, and charts. Some of the devices relate only one, two, or three of the six parameters: essentially, these relational devices consider the parameters that the inventor of the device believed to be most critical for describing how the body reacts to the thermal environment. Also, some devices have been derived to predict the thermal sensation that one will experience in some thermal environment, rather than to predict thermal comfort, specifically. As such, these thermal sensation devices generally describe conditions under which one would experience thermal stress. They also will forecast the extent of the thermal stress.

Alternatively, the relational devices that focus specifically on comfort normally indicate what combinations of the parameters will provide thermally comfortable conditions. These relational comfort devices often establish the parametric boundaries (e.g., how high or low can the air temperature be; or, for some elevated activity rate, what clothing insulation is appropriate for some set of the four environmental parameters; etc.). No one device or method is without detractions. Generally, those devices that consider only a few of the six parameters necessarily have limited accuracy, but are easier to use and understand. Instead, the most comprehensive (and, frequently, the most accurate) methods are the most difficult and time-consuming to use.

Among the simplest devices are various one-number indices. These indices generally are based on some algebraic relationship between two (or more) of the six environmental and personal parameters (e.g., an index might be an average value between two parameters or a number derived by plotting two parameters against each other). The principal feature of these indices is that they are expressed as single numbers (and, thus, are easy to use as "quick-and-dirty" references). Many of these single-number indices employ a pseudo-temperature scale. So, for such indices, the result of combining the parameters becomes a "temperature." With each of these "temperature" scales some range of values will portray conditions which occupants would find thermally comfortable. Alternatively, when environmental conditions fall outside of these ranges, people will likely be excessively stressed by thermal attributes of the environment and feel uncomfortable. A large number of these indices are in existence (although many enjoy only limited usage). Here, we will present a few of the most commonly used indices.

The most common single-number thermal index is the air (or dry-bulb) temperature, which is widely used to characterize climates and weather and to predict how people will feel about surrounding environments. The obvious limitation to this index is that it fails to acknowledge the important effects that the other five parameters have on the maintenance of thermal comfort. A second single-number index employs an averaging of the air temperature and the mean radiant temperature measured at some place within the

---

SIDEBAR 3.5 Distinguishing between thermal comfort and thermal sensation

The distinction between thermal *sensation* and thermal *comfort* arises from the fact that sensation is basically the response to a stimulus, whereas comfort is a feeling derived from the integration of the initial sensation with an interpretation arrived at by the brain. Thus, for example, for any combination of these six parameters a body is thermally stimulated and some response ensues, such as having a thermal balance maintained by the ever-present loss mechanisms or by having sweating begin. The sensing of the thermal environment occurs with the thermoreceptors present in a person's skin (see Section 3.2.3). Messages from these receptors then are passed by the nervous system to the hypothalamus where the interpretation of the message commences. Sensation thus precedes a developing awareness of the thermal environment. Indeed, establishing whether the thermal environment is comfortable or not derives from the integration of the initial sensation and some additional series of brain functions. For more discussion of this distinction, see the paper by Auliciems, A., "Towards a psycho-physiological model of thermal perception," *International Journal of Biometeorology*, 25(2), 1981, pages 109–122.

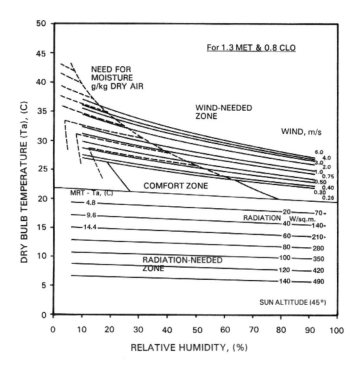

Figure 3.16 The Arens et al. Bioclimatic Chart. This illustration has previously been published in a paper by Arens, E.A., R. R. Gonzalez, L.G. Berglund, P.E. McNall, and L. Zeren, "A new bioclimatic chart for passive solar design," *Proceedings of the 5th National Passive Solar Conference* (edited by J. Hayes and R. Snyder), (Newark, Delaware: American Solar Energy Society, 1980), pages 1202–1206. Permission to reproduce this illustration has been granted by the American Solar Energy Society.

environment. This average is known as the *adjusted dry-bulb temperature* (abbreviated as the ADBT). Its strength is that it incorporates the two parameters that generally have the greatest impact on establishing a thermally comfortable environment. As long as the other parameters are within reasonable ranges and are otherwise unknown, the ADBT can be a useful index of comfort. But, if any or all of the other parameters vary outside of reasonable ranges (e.g., in a warm, humid climate), then the ADBT is not an accurate means of evaluating thermal comfort. The third of these indices is a more complex device known as the *Effective Temperature* (abbreviated as ET). This term is a weighted composite of the dry-bulb temperature, the wet-bulb temperature, and the relative air velocity. The ET index has been derived for two situations: for people wearing a 1.0 CLO ensemble and at rest, or for people "stripped to the waist" and at rest. The ET index can be established—when the dry-bulb and wet-bulb temperatures and the air velocity around a person are known—by employing a nomograph. This index has been modified several times since its inception. The most recent version of this index is known as the *New Effective Temperature* (ET*). The ET* is defined as "the dry-bulb temperature of a uniform enclosure at 50 percent relative humidity in which people have the same net heat exchange by radiation, convection, and evaporation as they do in varying humidities of the test environment."[8]

A second group of devices that are available for describing thermally comfortable environments employs graphs to portray comfort envelopes (or zones). The best-known and most widely used of these graphs was developed by Olgyay and is called the *Biocli-matic Chart.*[9] This graph relates dry-bulb temperature and relative humidity for the specific conditions of a sedentary occupant, wearing ordinary indoor clothing, in still air, and not affected by a net positive radiant exchange toward the occupant (i.e., thus accounting for all six of the environmental and personal parameters that principally define conditions required for maintaining thermal comfort). The Bioclimatic Chart shows a comfort zone existing for air temperatures between approximately 20 to 26.7 °C (68 and 80 °F) and relative humidities between about 20 and 80 percent. A series of modified versions of this graph (see Figure 3.16 for one example) has since been offered by Arens et al.[10] These modified Bioclimatic Charts are similar in form to Olgyay's graph and specifically address various MET and CLO combinations. One particular utility of the Bioclimatic Chart (and its several modified versions) is that it permits the user to see — for air temperature and relative humidity combinations beyond the customary comfort zone — what changes to the environment would need to be implemented to reestablish thermal comfort. For instance, we can see (from Figure 3.16) that the combination of 22 °C (72 °F) and 50 percent RH is within the comfort zone. But a combination of 28 °C (83 °F) and 50 percent RH is not. However, if we provide supplemental air movement in the environment (say, about 1 m/s (200 fpm), then a thermally comfortable condition will be present. Alternatively, for a combination of 18.3 °C (65 °F) and 50 percent RH, the provision of some radiant heating (i.e., from the sun or from architectural radiation) will sustain thermal comfort. The opportunity supplied the user of this graph is that an overall interrelationship between the six parameters begins to be defined. Using other graphs in this series by Arens et al., it is possible to examine further the nature of the interrelationship between these parameters.

Several scientists working at Kansas State University have developed a third type of device that can be used to relate the parametric values that define thermally comfortable environments.[11] A chief product of this research is a *Comfort Equation,* in which the six parameters (and other variables) have been rationally organized. This Comfort Equation includes as variables the several rates with which heat is exchanged between the body and the surrounding environment (noting the insulation value of a person's clothing ensemble), the rate of metabolism, and the energy expended doing useful work (that is accounted for by a term describing the "efficiency" of the body). This equation has then been solved iteratively — using a computer — to predict combinations of parametric values for which thermal comfort will exist. Additionally, the results of these computer-generated solutions have been summarized in a series of *Comfort Diagrams* that show the interrelationship between these parameters. Six of these diagrams are shown in Figure 3.17. The lines on these diagrams represent combinations of parametric values for which thermal comfort will be present. A user of these diagrams can thus examine whether an environment having some set of values for the environmental and personal parameters will be thermally

Figure 3.17 Six graphs demonstrating the relationships between the six primary environmental and personal parameters that affect the establishing of occupant thermal comfort. The graphs have been derived by the repeated solving of the Fanger Comfort Equation. These graphs are taken from the *1985 ASHRAE Handbook of Fundamentals,* (Atlanta: American Society of Heating, Refrigerating, and Air-Conditioning Engineers, Inc., 1985), page 8.21, and have been reproduced with the permission of the Society. (© American Society of Heating, Refrigerating, and Air-Conditioning Engineers, Inc., www.ashrae.org).

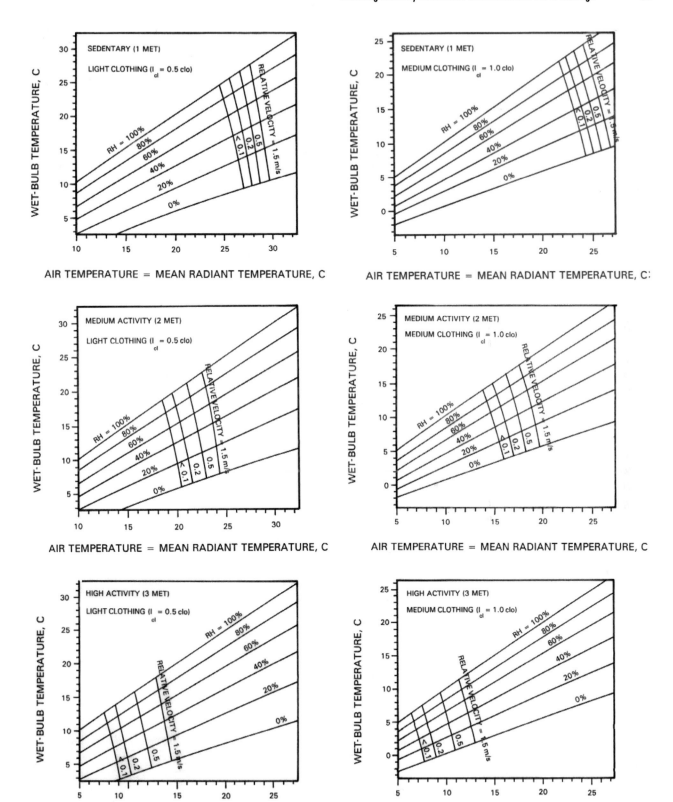

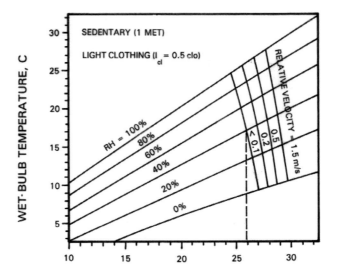

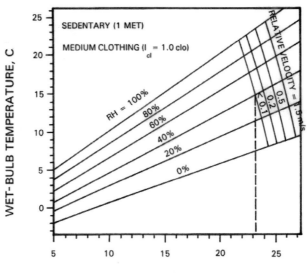

Figure 3.18 In Figure 3.13(a) the subject is sitting on his couch reading a novel. His metabolic rate for this activity is about 1 MET. If we presume that his clothing ensemble has an insulation value of about 0.5–0.6 CLO, we can use the Comfort Diagram in the upper lefthand corner of Figure 3.17 (i.e., for the conditions where the subject is sedentary and is dressed in light clothing.) According to this diagram, if the temperature of the air around this subject is equal to the mean radiant temperature at the subject's location, the air around the occupant is quite still (< 0.1 m/s or < 20 fpm), and the relative humidity of the air is 40 percent, then the air temperature at which the subject would be thermally comfortable is 26 °C (79 °F). If the subject were to change his clothing, adding a long-sleeved shirt and a heavy sweater, his new clothing insulation value would be about 1.0 CLO. Then, the air temperature for a thermally comfortable condition could be reduced to 23 °C (73 °F). This latter temperature has been found from the diagram in the upper righthand corner of Figure 3.17.

comfortable. Further, if the environment is shown by these diagrams to be uncomfortable, the user can also determine what changes amongst the environmental and personal parameters would be necessary to establish a thermally comfortable setting (Figure 3.18).

A final benefit of the Comfort Equation is that it can be used in conjunction with computer programs that simulate — predict — the thermal performance of a building. A designer or a builder can take a set of design drawings for a building and, using suitable computer programs, analyze the proposed building design. This analysis will indicate how the building will behave thermally for some weather conditions and will also predict whether the proposed building will be thermally comfortable for the future occupants. Thus, the designer and the builder can determine how well a building is likely to perform thermally before the building has left the designer's drafting table![12]

Section 3.6 | TWO SUMMARY EXAMPLES CONSIDERING THE ATTAINMENT OF THERMAL COMFORT

3.6.1   WHY IS THE CHAIRMAN "COLD"?

Several recent occupants of the chairman's office in our department have described the chairman's office as "cold" and have wondered why the room made them feel that way (Figure 3.19). After all, the air temperature in the room is maintained at 20 °C (68 °F) with relative humidities well within comfort ranges, as required by university regulations. Additionally, three of the four walls, the floor, and the ceiling all adjoin other interior spaces. The fourth wall, however, is part of the envelope of the building (and is, in fact, along the north elevation). Seventy percent, by area, of this fourth side is glazed with single-pane plate glass and the remainder of the wall is 15.2 cm (6 in) thick poured-in-place heavyweight concrete. There is some architectural radiation underneath the glazing, but it doesn't seem to work very well.

Figure 3.19 Our sometimes-cold chairman and the glazing assembly that is the primary cause of this discomfort.

Now, to address this problem, let's remember that the extent to which one experiences thermal comfort is determined by how well you can maintain a thermal balance between yourself and your surrounding environment (without relying on some corrective thermoregulatory device like shivering!) To maintain that thermal balance you need to sustain appropriate values for the six principal environmental and personal parameters: the air temperature; the net radiant exchange rate between you and your surroundings; the relative humidity of the air in your space; the rate of movement of air around you; your activity rate; and the insulative value of your clothing. Noting that the air temperature is just at the lower boundary of the thermal comfort zone, why an occupant of this space might feel cold could perhaps be explained by the following observations:

(a) As the fourth side of the space — the north elevation — is composed of single-pane glazing and uninsulated concrete, on days when the external air temperature is low, the interior surfaces of this fourth side will have appreciably lower temperatures than the room air and the various internal objects. Thus, there will be a significant net positive radiant exchange from the chairman to this north elevation (i.e., causing the occupant to lose heat).

(b) On days when the external air is cold, these north elevation surfaces will be at appreciably lower temperatures than the room air. Thus, there will be convective exchange from the room air to these envelope surfaces, where the glass and concrete then conduct the heat out of the building. The path of the convective air layer at the inside surface of this north elevation will be downward as the air in this layer grows colder, less buoyant, and then "falls" past these surfaces. At the floor the cold air will "puddle," will flow out from the wall, and will form a draft, cooling the occupant's lower body.

(c) Generally, the occupant's activities are sedentary and, therefore, involve low metabolic rates (i.e., with relatively little internal heat generation).

SIDEBAR 3.6 "Fixing" the chairman's office

There are a series of remedial actions that could be taken to improve the performance of the room and to make the occupant more often thermally comfortable. Concerning the occupant, wearing a sweater over one's shirtsleeves or adopting other warmer clothing ensembles will reduce heat loss rates. Similarly, engaging in activities that require higher internal heat production, when possible and in keeping with the chairman's role, will aid in establishing a thermal balance. But perhaps the range of solutions that will most greatly contribute to the thermal comfort of future occupants of this room would include modifications to the north elevation. Some of these alterations could be: replacing the single-pane assembly with a double-pane construction or reducing the area of the glazing or providing floor-to-ceiling drapes; placing insulating materials over the uninsulated concrete; and fixing and

using the architectural radiation. Additionally, operating the room with a higher air temperature could offset the other failings of the space and its pattern of use. Other solutions such as using the space for other purposes are also possible. Lastly, as the room is finished in fairly austere furnishings and colors, it has been suggested that enlivening the room with bright and cheery-colored surfaces and well-padded and "warm" furniture will improve the ambience of this room; however, there are insufficient data from the professional literature to support this suggestion without some reservation. But, ultimately, the corrective strategies that can and should be adopted must also involve considerations of costs, tradition (i.e., the space has been used as the chairman's office since the opening of the building), image, and other nontechnical factors.

(d) Also, people tend to regard building interiors as "shirtsleeve" environments (i.e., occupants engage in work after removing their suit jacket). Thus, the insulation values of their clothing ensembles are frequently inadequate. Taking off a suit jacket and putting on a woolen sweater would seem the proper way to adopt an informal — and warm — manner.

3.6.2   WHAT CLOTHES ARE APPROPRIATE FOR SKIING?

We have heard reports of people, who ski in the Sierras and Rockies, sometimes wearing as little as T-shirts and shorts or even swimsuits. The use of this apparently unusual ski apparel has been observed on sunny days with air temperatures at about 8–12 °C (the high 40's and low 50's in °F). Seemingly, these people are thermally comfortable and do not wear these ensembles strictly as fashion statements. So, let's explore how they might attain thermal comfort.

As we stated in the previous example, the essential requirement for establishing thermal comfort is the maintenance of a thermal balance between the person and his or her environment (without relying on corrective thermoregulatory devices). Further, the ability of an individual to maintain this balance is dependent on the six primary environmental and personal parameters we have discussed previously.

For this example, the conditions that will contribute to the disruption of the thermal balance (i.e., the removal of heat from the body) are the ambient air temperature is well below the normal comfort zone; the skiers are wearing clothing of low insulative values (approximately 0.3 CLO); and the air movement rates around them as they ski down the slopes will be significantly greater than those prescribed for normal thermal comfort conditions. All three of these factors will accelerate the rate of heat loss from the body to the environment. Conversely, there are some characteristics of the environment or the situation that add heat to the skiers or otherwise work to offset the heat loss mechanisms. Among these are that the skiers are likely quite active, producing heat internally at a rate several times that of the ordinary sedentary person, and the skiers will experience substantial radiant heat gains not only from the solar radiation coming from the sky, but also from the reflection of solar radiation off of the white, crystalline surface (which is highly reflective). Thus, thermal comfort would probably be maintained for the skiers because the increased activity rates and the intense solar radiation gains will offset the heat loss mechanisms and a balance will be sustained. However, once the skiers cease their activities or if the sky becomes cloudy, the thermal balance experienced by the skiers will no longer exist, and the skiers will very probably begin to feel cold.

Section 3.7 | SOME THOUGHTS ABOUT HOW ONE'S STATE-OF-MIND AND OTHER FACTORS CAN AFFECT THERMAL COMFORT

So far in this chapter we have described how the physical principles of heat transfer and the physiology of the human body can determine one's ability to be thermally comfortable. In this last section we will report on some observations suggesting that psychological factors may (or can) override the strictly physical or physiological ingredients that determine how an individual experiences the surrounding environment. A variety of studies exist in the professional and scientific literature documenting how one's feelings of thermal comfort can be affected by conditions that depend on one's state-of-mind. Unfortunately, no systematic exposition has been written about how various psychological factors (e.g., responses to the colors of building surfaces; the presence of bothersome noise; excessive brightness and glare in the view field; influences of motivation and cognition; and so forth) will influence the response of the human body to the thermal environment. Thus, the treatment in this section will necessarily be anecdotal.

3.7.1   THE ROLE (AND LIMITATIONS) OF SENSATION IN DESCRIBING THERMAL COMFORT

For the designer and the builder an important task in creating a building is to provide desirable thermal conditions within the building. Therefore, being able to establish thermally comfortable conditions requires that you can identify what these conditions are. In virtually all of the systematic research on thermal comfort, the basic study procedure has involved test subjects rating how they felt when they were exposed to certain thermal conditions. The subjects were usually asked to describe the test conditions using a range of responses from "cold" to "hot." The researchers then took these responses and correlated them with specific numerical values that characterized the environmental and personal parameters set for the given test. As such, the subjects were reporting on their thermal sensations. These sensations were matched subsequently to the physical conditions of the test and the physiological performances of the subjects' bodies. Thus, thermal sensation was used as a first-approximation estimate of whether a subject was thermally comfortable.

A potential discrepancy between sensation and comfort arises from the fact that *sensation* concerns one's awareness of the environment, whereas *comfort* is a state of pleasantness or well-being. The dilemma inherent in this dichotomy has been considered by Auliciems, who suggests that four scales could be used to characterize the most desirable thermal conditions: neutral sensation, least discomfort, thermal preference, and optimum thermal conditions for performing some activity. Further, this researcher emphatically has contended that these four scales are not strictly interchangeable and are hardly identical in meaning. Rather, Auliciems stipulates that the four descriptions are indeed quite different ways to express how subjects perceive the thermal environment and do not correlate directly to the physiological state of thermal comfort.[13]

3.7.2   DIFFERENTIATING BETWEEN THERMAL PREFERENCE AND THERMAL COMFORT

The distinction between thermal *comfort* and thermal *preference* is one that a number of researchers have investigated. As a starting point, Fanger has maintained that the interrelationship between the environmental and personal parameters, which characterize thermally comfortable conditions, is essentially the same for everyone, without regard to ethnicity, sex, age, body size, or other major demographic variable.[14] But several studies have shown that the thermal conditions preferred by various peoples are different. For instance, Webb has shown that native Malaysian people preferred thermal conditions approximately 2 °C (4 °F) warmer than European subjects.[15] Macfarlane reports that a group of Australian test subjects examined repeatedly throughout the year preferred a higher air temperature in summer than in winter. Moreover, he notes that among these subjects—for the winter period testing—the men preferred a higher air temperature than did the women, even though the men wore clothing with a higher insulation value.[16] These studies raise two questions: do these variations in preferred temperatures demonstrate that differences in the comfort zone may exist; or do these studies simply indicate that some groups may be better able than others to withstand conditions outside of the comfort zone? These two papers—by Webb and Macfarlane—indicate differences in temperature preference among peoples having alternative ethnic backgrounds, sex, and seasonality. Other conditions for which questions about thermal preferences can be addressed include: to what extent are people sensitive to day-to-day weather shifts (e.g., where one day has an average external temperature about 30 °C [86 °F] and the next has an average of about 20 °C [68 °F]) or are preferences (and/or comfort) affected by appreciable differences between indoor and outdoor temperatures? Preference is seemingly more subjective in its assessment, in contrast to thermal comfort reporting. Thermal comfort is supposedly based on physical conditions and physiological mechanisms, whereas preference is at least partially based on one's feelings (and, thus, psychology). Recognizing that the fundamental test for thermal comfort consists of asking test subjects whether they are comfortable for some set of thermal conditions, there are clearly opportunities for one's psychological state to become involved in the assessment of the thermal environment.

3.7.3   WHAT HAPPENS TO ONE'S THERMAL COMFORT WHEN YOU ALTER NONTHERMAL ASPECTS OF THE ENVIRONMENT?

We have heard a number of psychologists argue that by creating environments with especially pleasing or displeasing attributes, one can affect people's assessment of their degree of thermal comfort. However, when we have surveyed the professional and scientific literature for specific examples to support this argument, we have found that, at best, the results are mixed. For instance, Rohles reports that, for subjects seated alternatively in cloth and vinyl-covered furniture, the subjects experienced a greater degree of thermal comfort at lowered temperatures when seated in the cloth-covered chairs. For subjects seated either on the cloth or vinyl-covered chairs, comparisons of measurements of the subjects' skin temperatures showed that these temperatures were not altered by the covering of the chairs.[17] In a previous study Rohles et al. observed similar results when the decor of the test facility was alternatively "plush" or "stark": in the more plush setting the subjects experienced greater degrees of thermal comfort. But the skin temperatures of the subjects and their reported thermal sensations in these alternative settings showed no differences when the thermal conditions were similar.[18] In both these studies the authors found that different lighting schemes had little effect on thermal comfort assessments. In the second of these studies the authors also observed that—for test periods longer than one hour—subjects did not report differences in thermal comfort assessment whether the room decor was predominantly blue or orange! The question of whether color will affect one's assessment of thermal comfort concerns the "hue-heat hypothesis" (i.e., that "warmer" colors will make people feel warmer than will "cooler" colors). In a separate study by Bennett and Rey those authors found that, in fact, warmer colors did not affect the degree of thermal comfort that subjects had.[19] Similar results—that thermal comfort assessments were not affected by alternative predominant room colors or the presence of noise—have also been reported by Fanger et al.[20]

One area of thermal comfort research that provides generally positive support for psychologists' contention that thermal comfort can be affected by one's state-of-mind concerns how cognitive and motivational factors can influence subjects' assessments. Howell and Stamler have examined whether comfort test subjects were influenced by a variety of cognitive variables: for instance, "perceived temperature tolerance," "perceived performance," "perceived adjustment," "perceived cold-naturedness," and "perceived comfort." The authors found good correlations between the variables and how the subjects assessed the thermal environment.[21] Carlton-Foss and Rohles have performed an equally interesting study on how motivational influences and personal history may affect thermal comfort assessments. These authors have found that "cultural conventions and personality may be significant factors in explaining individual differences in thermal acceptability and comfort."[22] A third, related study conducted by Selvamurthy et al. has found that men practiced in yogic exercises were better able to withstand cold environmental conditions than a control group of other men who, instead of performing the yogic exercises, engaged in common physical training exercises.[23] Explanations of this "improvement in cold tolerance" for the yogic practitioners include suggestions that they enjoy better nervous system control, increased muscular efficiency, and altered biochemical performance.[24] The mechanisms enabling these physiological improvements amongst yogic practitioners have not been defined, although the improvements appear to result from mental disciplines involving meditative states and personal thought control. Thus, in these three studies are foundations to support the notion that assessments of thermal comfort can require additional (or alternative) explanations beyond simply relying on descriptions of the physical conditions of the environment and the physiological operations of the human body.

3.7.4   CONSEQUENCES OF LONG-TERM EXPOSURES TO DIFFERENT THERMAL ENVIRONMENTS

So far, in this section, we have discussed how one's perceptions of the thermal environment can be affected by factors other than the strictly physical and physiological determinants. One additional factor that can possibly modify an individual's response to the thermal environment is a process of acclimatization that may result after someone, who is a native of one location with a characteristic climate, moves to another location with a substantially different climate. After an extended period of time — usually, over several years — the individual may observe an increased tolerance to the adopted climate. With these diminished reactions to the vagaries of the new climate, one becomes acclimated to it. How this acclimatization occurs has not been systematically established, although

SIDEBAR 3.7 What influence might "mission orientation" have on a person's feelings of thermal comfort?

Another set of questions about how perceptions of thermal comfort may be affected by factors other than physical and physiological ones arises from anecdotal reports that people are able to exist or perform well in thermal conditions that are decidedly not within the comfort zone. Examples of this phenomenon can be found among attendees of late autumn football games and sportsmen who fish or hunt in conditions that are, at best, described as cold. Another group of individuals who seemingly are able to override considerations of their thermal conditions are jet plane pilots and the astronauts and cosmonauts. Many of these people, when asked to describe the thermal conditions that they experienced during their particular activities, will be oblivious to such concerns. Rather, they will be so "mission-oriented" that they will not recognize discomfort. To a marked extent, many of these people probably would feel uncomfortable, if they thought about it. But, for reasons of motivation, they have unconsciously blocked such feelings from their awareness. Here, then, are other instances where one's state-of-mind can subvert strictly physical and physiological interpretations of one's involvement with the thermal environment.

the topic has been studied. A fundamental component of the process, however, is *habituation,* that is, collectively, the diminished reactions that one experiences as one becomes accustomed to the adopted environment. Habituation is manifested as the individual reacts progressively better to these new conditions (i.e., is made less uncomfortable by the stimuli of the new environment). A second significant component of this acclimatizing process is learning, in which an individual gradually discovers how he or she can exist, feeling less distress from the adopted environment. A now-classic example of individuals undergoing acclimatization was the European of the 17th through the early 20th centuries who traveled from Europe bound for the western and southern hemispheres. Many of these individuals left experiences of one climate and migrated to regions with distinctly different climates. These people ultimately became acclimatized to their new locales (and the attendant thermal environments).[25, 26] The length of time required for acclimatization to occur usually requires a period lasting from several years to a decade or more.

We should also note the existence of many population groups that live in otherwise uncomfortable thermal environments with comparatively few aids to make their living more pleasant. Wulsin has identified a number of these groups and has described the climates in which they live, the resources they draw upon for providing shelter, and their life styles.[27]

Lastly, we can cite the alternative example of a people following an ages-long tradition of living in a sometimes-difficult climate with comparatively limited thermal environmental controls: the Japanese historically have sought to heat themselves rather than heating their buildings. The devices used are directed at the "inner self" and outer body, whereas the traditional building form and composition tend to offer relatively little protection to cold winter weather.[28]

The essential point for those individuals who have emigrated to regions with different thermal environments or for the peoples who are natives of rigorous climates and have limited control devices to modify their environments is that these people are able to become accustomed to their climatic settings. But, in terms of the central theme of this chapter (i.e., thermal comfort), to what extent they experience thermal comfort must remain an issue for further research. It seems probable that their preferences for thermal environments may be different than the typical subject employed in the thermal comfort studies that have been conducted in the United States, England, and Europe. From the research reports that we have cited above, it also appears likely that their definition of thermally comfortable conditions would be similar to the average of the many test subjects. Necessarily, then, the abilities of these individuals and peoples to exist in these challenging conditions suggest that they are able to employ some state-of-mind capacities to limit dissatisfaction with their inability to attain thermal comfort.

There seems to be little question that one's state-of-mind can affect one's state-of-being. Studies that document this observation are beginning to appear in the scientific literature. Let us say then that the state of being thermally comfortable is determined by physical and physiological conditions. The human body senses these conditions, and the body responds to them. But how one evaluates the thermal environment will, to a marked extent, be dependent on one's psychological state.

Section 3.8 | SELECTED REFERENCES FOR HUMAN THERMOREGULATION AND COMFORT

In this chapter we have discussed the thermal regulation of the human body; what thermal comfort is; what conditions are needed for maintaining thermal comfort; and the notion that the state-of-mind of an individual can influence one's assessment of the thermal environment. Below we list a series of books and review papers that can serve as source material for further study of these subjects.

First, for discussion of the physiology of heat regulation, we suggest:

Davis, B.O., N. Holtz, and J.C. Davis, *Conceptual Human Physiology,* (Columbus, Ohio: Charles E. Merrill Publishing Company, 1985); see Chapter 22.

Guyton, A.C., *Basic Human Physiology* (2nd edition), (Philadelphia: W.B. Saunders Company, 1973); see Chapter 47.

Second, for descriptions of research on human thermal comfort, summary statements defining thermal comfort, and extensive bibliographies about thermal comfort, we suggest:

Clark, R.P., and O.G. Edholm, *Man and His Thermal Environment,* (London: Edward Arnold Publishers Ltd., 1985).

Fanger, P.O., *Thermal Comfort: Analysis and Applications in Environmental Engineering,* (New York: McGraw-Hill Book Company, 1972).

Brager, G.S., and R.J. de Dear, "Thermal adaptation in the built environment: a literature review," *Energy and Buildings,* 27, 1998, pages 83–96.

———. "Thermal comfort," *2001 ASHRAE Handbook of Fundamentals,* (Atlanta: American Society of Heating, Refrigerating, and Air-Conditioning Engineers, Inc., 2001), Chapter 8 (pages 8.1–8.29).

For information about thermal comfort envelopes, zones, and indices, as well as definitions of the environmental and personal parameters that affect the thermal comfort state, see

Givoni, B., *Man, Climate, and Architecture* (2nd edition), (London: Applied Science Publishers, Ltd., 1976); note Chapter 5 ("The thermal indices"), pages 75–102.

Markus, T.A., *Buildings, Climate, and Energy,* (London: Pitman Publishers, 1980).

Olgyay, V., *Design with Climate,* (Princeton, New Jersey: Princeton University Press, 1963); see pages 14–23.

———. "Thermal comfort," *2001 ASHRAE Handbook of Fundamentals,* (Atlanta: American Society of Heating, Refrigerating, and Air-Conditioning Engineers, Inc., 2001); see Chapter 8 (note, specifically, pages 8.16–8.22).

As we noted in Section 3.7, there has yet to be written an extended survey treatment concerning how psychological factors can affect the attainment and maintenance of thermal comfort. We have cited a series of papers as footnotes to the main text. Two books that discuss aspects of this topic are:

Glaser, E.M., *The Physiological Basis of Habituation,* (London: Oxford University Press, 1966).

Harrison, G.A., editor, *Human Adaptation,* (Oxford, England: Oxford University Press, 1993).

ENDNOTES and SELECTED ADDITIONAL COMMENTS

1. Givoni, B., *Man, Climate, and Architecture* (2nd edition), (London: Applied Science Publishers Ltd., 1976), page 54.
2. Dagostino, F.R., *Mechanical and Electrical Systems in Construction and Architecture,* (Reston, Virginia: Reston Publishing Company, Inc., 1978), page 150.
3. Fanger, P.O., *Thermal Comfort,* (New York: McGraw-Hill Book Company, 1972), page 13.
4. Fanger, P.O., Ibid., page 13.
5. Yaglou, C.P., "Indices of comfort," in Newburgh, L.H. (ed.), *Physiology of Heat Regulation and The Science of Clothing,* (New York: Hafner Publishing Company, Inc., 1968), page 268.
6. Clark, R.P., and O.G. Edholm, *Man and His Thermal Environment,* (London: Edward Arnold Publishers Ltd., 1985), pages 196–199.
7. Brager, G.S., and R.J. de Dear, "Thermal adaptation in the built environment: a literature review," *Energy and Buildings,* 27, 1998, pages 83–96.
8. ———. *2001 ASHRAE Handbook of Fundamentals* (Atlanta: American Society of Heating, Refrigerating, and Air-Conditioning Engineers, Inc., 2001), page 8.19.
9. Olgyay, V., *Design with Climate,* (Princeton, New Jersey: Princeton University Press, 1963), pages 17–23.
10. Arens, E.A., R. R. Gonzalez, L.G. Berglund, P.E. McNall, and L. Zeren, "A new bioclimatic chart for passive solar design," *Proceedings of the 5th National Passive Solar Conference* (edited by J. Hayes and R. Snyder), (Newark, Delaware: American Solar Energy Society, 1980), pages 1202–1206.
11. Fanger, P.O., *Thermal Comfort,* (New York: McGraw-Hill Book Company, 1972).
12. Emery, A.F., D.R. Heerwagen, C.J. Kippenhan, and G.B. Varey, "Developing Office Building Design and Operation Strategies Using UWENSOL and the COMFORT Routine," *ASHRAE Transactions,* 76(1), 1980.
13. Auliciems, A., "Towards a psycho-physiological model of thermal perception," *International Journal of Biometeorology,* 25(2), 1981, pages 109–122.
14. Fanger, P.O., *Thermal Comfort,* (New York: McGraw-Hill Book Company, 1972), Chapter 3 (pages 68–106).
15. Webb, C.G., "An analysis of some observations of thermal comfort in an equatorial climate," *British Journal of Industrial Medicine,* 16, 1959, pages 297–310.
16. Macfarlane, W.V., "Thermal comfort studies since 1958," *Architectural Science Review,* 21, December 1974, pages 86–92.
17. Rohles, F.H., Jr., "New directions in comfort research," *ASHRAE Transactions,* 89 (Part II), 1983, pages 634–646.
18. Rohles, F.H., Jr., C.A. Bennett, and G.A. Milliken, "The effects of lighting, color, and room decor on thermal comfort," *ASHRAE Transactions,* 87 (Part II), 1981, pages 511–527.
19. Bennett, C.A., and P. Rey, "What's so hot about red?" *Human Factors,* 14(2), 1972, pages 149–154.
20. Fanger, P.O., N.O. Breum, and E. Jerking, "Can colour and noise influence man's thermal comfort?" *Ergonomics,* 20(1), 1977, pages 11–18.

21. Howell, W.C., and C.S. Stamler, "The contribution of psychological variables to the prediction of thermal comfort judgments in real world settings," *ASHRAE Transactions,* 87 (Part II), 1981, pages 609–621.

22. Carlton-Foss, J.A., and F.H. Rohles, Jr., "Personality factors in thermal acceptability and comfort," *ASHRAE Transactions,* 88 (Part II), 1982, pages 776–790; see page 783 for the quoted material.

23. Selvamurthy, W., U.S. Ray, K.S. Hegde, and R.P. Sharma, "Physiological responses to cold (10 °C) in men after six months' practice of yoga exercises," *International Journal of Biometeorology,* 32(3), 1988, pages 188–193.

24. Ibid., pages 188 and 192.

25. Glaser, E.M., *The Physiological Basis of Habituation,* (London: Oxford University Press, 1966).

26. For a survey of research on acclimatization, see Chapter 7 ("Man is a tropical animal") in Clark, R.P., and O.G. Edholm, *Man and His Thermal Environment,* (London: Edward Arnold Publishers Ltd., 1985), pages 134–154.

27. Wulsin, F.R., "Adaptations to climate among non-European peoples," in Newburgh, L.H. (ed.), *Physiology of Heat Regulation and The Science of Clothing,* (New York: Hafner Publishing Company, 1963), pages 3–69.

28. Stinchecum, A.M., "Enduring cold the Japanese way," *Natural History,* 90(10), October 1981, pages 50–55.

CHAPTER FOUR

Weather and Climate (As Determinants of Building Form)

4

IN CHAPTER I WE STATED that an essential requirement for buildings is that they must provide internal environments that are comfortable for their occupants. We also stated that the "amount" of building that is necessary for maintaining occupant comfort is directly dependent on the character of the external environment (i.e., how severe or mild that environment is dictates the extent of support that a building must provide). In this chapter, to depict the range of natural environments that exist across the surface of the Earth, we will identify the various climates that characterize these environments. This discussion will portray the principal attributes of both weather and climate and will consider the behaviors that each presents. We will also describe a classification scheme that has been developed by climatologists to link regions experiencing similar climatic patterns. Then, by modifying this classification scheme, we will introduce a simpler view of four fundamental climatic types, each of which displays properties that dictate how *responsive* buildings should be created. Finally, we will present an analytic procedure that can be used by designers and builders to identify what building devices and forms are appropriate for insuring the thermal comfort of future occupants.

In Chapter 5, we will offer catalogues of basic design guidelines for buildings that are to be constructed in regions displaying each of the four fundamental climatic types.

Section 4.1 | WHAT ARE WEATHER AND CLIMATE?

4.1.1 DISTINGUISHING BETWEEN WEATHER AND CLIMATE

Weather and climate are basic properties of the atmosphere that encircles the Earth. Understanding how weather and climate occur is not requisite knowledge for designing buildings. But, as the climate of some locale is largely a regular quality of that locale, designers and builders should be able to create buildings which respond well to the characteristics of the climate, which ensure adequate thermal comfort for the occupants, and which operate efficiently.

Weather is *a collection of atmospheric phenomena that occur over some place for a short period of time* (i.e., for as short an interval as a few hours to as long a duration as perhaps a week or more). The phenomena include such actions as the movement of air (relative to the ground), the presence of water vapor in clouds or as precipitation, the magnitude of the pressure of the atmosphere over the ground, and the transfer of thermal energy to or away from the ground. These actions result, fundamentally, from the passage of solar energy to the Earth and the subsequent distribution of that energy around the Earth, *by the air in the atmosphere and the water in the oceans.* The movement of this thermal energy around the Earth occurs in recognizable patterns. Additionally, the energy movement determines the nature of the atmospheric processes that are present over any locale at any moment in time. These atmospheric processes include the exchange of short-wave (solar) and longwave (terrestial) radiation between the sky and the surface of the Earth, the existence of atmospheric pressure systems, and the motions of air in wind systems and of water in ocean currents. All of these atmospheric features contribute to the formation of the weather that occurs above (and across) the surface of the Earth.

The weather that is experienced at some locale is commonly described using such parameters as the air temperature, the moisture content of the air (identified as the relative humidity), the presence of wind (noting both its velocity and direction), the atmospheric pressure, the existence of cloud cover (characterized in terms of its type, the height, or ceiling, of its bottom-most layer, and the degree of completeness of the cover over the whole sky vault), the presence or absence of precipitation (and its type, when present), and the visibility (or visual clarity of the air near the ground). When weather conditions are reported by government agencies or news organizations, other parameters that are often noted include: the intensity of solar radiation received by horizontal or vertical surfaces, the behavior of ocean currents, tidal variations at sites along a shore, and/or the presence of particulate matter or various gaseous pollutants in the atmosphere over some locale (e.g., the existence of airborne dust from sandstorm actions or industry-caused smog suspended in the air over a city).

Alternatively, climate is *a statistical composite of weather conditions for some place viewed over a long period of time* (e.g., usually, a duration of at least 20 or 30 years). Thus, the essential distinction between weather and climate focuses on the element of time. Whereas weather is a short-term summary of the phenomena present in the atmosphere around you, climate describes the atmospheric conditions that have existed over a much longer time. Note, however, that what we identify as a climate is *not* simply an average of all the weather events that occurred during those years. Although averages of air temperatures, wind speeds, precipitation rates, and solar radiation intensities are essential features of a climate, attention should also be paid to such features as *(1) the frequency of specific occurrences* (e.g., how often precipitation was observed); *(2) the range of values* (e.g., how much precipitation happened during each June across the 20- or 30-year sample) and *the extreme values* (e.g., what were the greatest and least amounts of precipitation during the 20 or 30 Junes that were recorded for this study period); and *(3) the variability of values or occurrences* (e.g., how did the precipitation rate in June differ from the rates at other times of the year, *or* were there groups of years when the precipitation rates were substantially different from the average). All three attributes can be significant factors in distinguishing the climate of one region from another (and, thus, for determining how one should design buildings for that locale).

As an example of the properties that characterize weather and climate for a particular locale, let us consider the day-by-day records of weather conditions in Seattle for the years of 1988–1990 (Figure 4.1). First of all, the Seattle climate can generally be described as mild or temperate. It displays neither the overheated qualities of many regions located closer to the Equator, nor the underheatedness of lands found further north. The average annual air temperature is 10.8 °C (51.4 °F), and the average daily maximum and minimum air temperatures are 14.9 and 6.1 °C (58.9 and 43.0 °F), respectively. The average annual precipitation rate is 980 mm (38.6 in), with nearly half of that total usually occurring during the period from November through January (about 457 mm [18.0 in]). Note, also, that the summer months are quite dry (i.e., the average total precipitation for June, July, and August is only about 86 mm [3.4 in]). The ambient sky conditions match these periods of high and low precipitation rates: the skies over Seattle are largely overcast for much of the latter half of the fall and all of the winter, whereas the summer skies are most often clear or only partly cloudy.

SIDEBAR 4.1 The relevance of frequency and variability of occurrences for characterizing climates

As a means of demonstrating how the *frequency* and *variability* of atmospheric occurrences can elucidate how a climate appears, let us offer an anecdote that recognizes such differences between three regional climates.

We are commonly asked by friends who live on the eastern coast of the United States about how we can stand all the rain in Seattle! We respond that, after all, it's not so bad; it keeps everything green. But, in fact, we receive an annual precipitation total of about 980 mm (38.6 in) in Seattle, whereas the average totals for New York City (Manhattan) and Boston are 1120 and 1112 mm (44.1 and 43.8 in), respectively. Of course, in Seattle we experience about 160 rain-days per year, whereas the totals for New York and Boston are each about 120: note that a rain-day is defined as any day—a 24-hour period—in which at least 0.25 mm (0.01 in) of rain is measured. But during the summers in Seattle, the total average rainfall for the months

of July, August, and September are 86 mm (3.4 in) compared to the average New York and Boston rainfalls, for the same periods, of 292 and 249 mm (11.5 and 9.8 in), respectively. Indeed, the average monthly precipitation amounts in New York and Boston are comparatively uniformly spread out throughout the year. Instead, what has given Seattle the reputation for being a rainy place is not the average annual amount of precipitation, but rather the fact that in Seattle it seems to rain every day from the middle of autumn to the middle of spring. So, for this anecdote, the relevant issues about climate are not averages, but rather the frequency and variability of occurrence.

The climatic data we report here have been derived from the book *Climates of the States* (3rd edition), (Detroit: Gale Research Company, 1985); see page 521 of Volume 1 and pages 785 and 1199 of Volume 2.

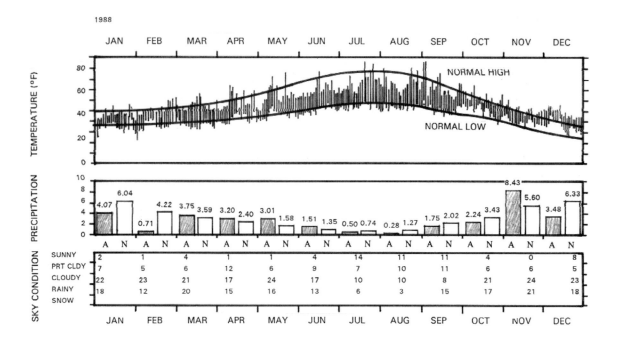

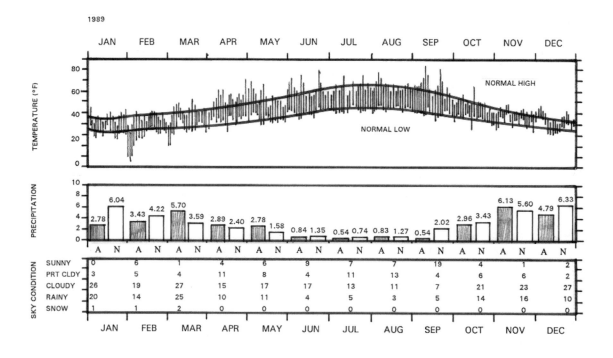

Figure 4.1 (pages 70 and 71) Seattle weather records for the years 1988–1990. Note that the data used to create these illustrations were originally assembled by staff of *The Seattle Times*. Permission to reproduce these data has been purchased from *The Seattle Times* (Copyright 1988–1990 Seattle Times Company. Used with permission).

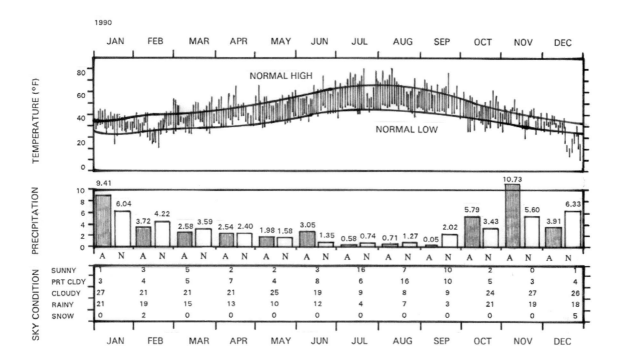

The weather records shown in these three annual summaries for Seattle indicate, nonetheless, many occasions when the actual daily temperature ranges differed from the range of averaged high and low temperatures. For instance, the highest daily temperature — averaged over the 30-year period employed for this record — usually occurs in late July and early August. But, during 1989, there were two prolonged periods in that September when the maximum daily temperatures were substantially higher than the average maximum daily temperatures both throughout September and for the year as a whole. Alternatively, there was a short interval in February 1989 when air temperatures were much less than the normal air temperatures for those dates (i.e., the lowest air temperature reached −14 °C (7 °F) on the fourth of February, whereas the normal lowest temperature for that date has been about 2 °C (35 °F).

One significance of these *extreme* conditions for building design and construction is that if buildings are created to provide occupant thermal comfort only for *averaged* climatic conditions, then during periods displaying extreme weather conditions the buildings may not be able to respond adequately, and occupants will be uncomfortable. Consequently, supplemental environmental control capabilities should be provided in buildings to accommodate occupants when atmospheric conditions stray from average trends to extreme events.

One other example of how short-term weather conditions can deviate significantly from more normal patterns occurred in November 1990. During the typical November in Seattle, the precipitation rate for the month is about 142 mm (5.6 in). But during November 1990 the measured rainfall totaled 272 mm (10.7 in). Further, on the single day of November 9th of that year, 74 mm (2.9 in) of rain fell. Such deviations from normal atmospheric processes further demonstrate how, for at least brief periods, weather conditions can drastically diverge from the usual climatic history for a locale.

We will offer one further distinction about the difference between *weather* and *climate*. Suppose you look out your window and see that it is raining. Thus, you say that the weather is rainy. But if today is Thursday, the seventeenth of October and you ask what is the probability that it will rain two weeks from today, then you would need to examine the climate record for your locale to establish an educated answer. For this latter case you would be relying on the history of atmospheric processes that have occurred over your locale to decide on the likelihood that rain may be encountered in late October. But, for the former instance, the rain you are seeing on this particular seventeenth of October is the result of some short-term atmospheric process. Therefore, the rain is a major component of the weather you endure today, whereas the presence of rain on the seventeenth of October may or may not be seen as a common condition when you look back at the climatic record for your locale.

4.1.2   THE VARIABILITY OF CLIMATES

The weather occurring at many locales across the surface of the Earth varies substantially, whether we speak in terms of day-to-day or seasonal changes. As evidence of such variation we need only to consider how the weather appears in any mid-latitude region. Day-to-day changes can range from sunny, warm conditions on one summer day to cooler, rainy weather on the following day. Alternatively, the variations in *average* temperature between January and July in many North American locales can be as great as 30–40 °C (54–72 °F).

The climate of a locale, conversely, shows much less variation, if we consider successive 20- or 30-year averages. But some variation can nevertheless be seen when *long-term* climatic averages are examined. For instance, Lamb has formulated average temperatures

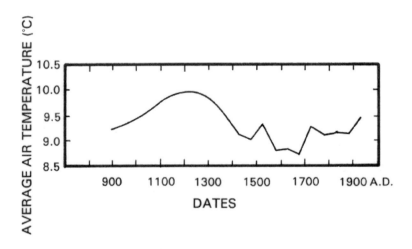

Figure 4.2 The variation of the average air temperatures for 50-year periods over central England is displayed for the years 900 to 1900 A.D. This drawing has previously been published in the paper by Lamb, H.H., "The early medieval warm epoch and its sequel," *Palaegeography, Palaeoclimatology, Palaeoecology,* 1, 1965, pages 13–37. Permission to reproduce this drawing has been granted by the publisher, Elsevier Science Publishers B.V.

in 50-year increments for central England for the period from 900 through 1900 AD (see Figure 4.2). Across this millennium the average temperature ranged from a low of about 8.7 °C (47.7 °F) to a high of 10.2 °C (50.4 °F).[1] Other evidence of even longer-term climatic variations is available to us if we think about the cyclic migration of glaciers that have covered (and receded from) much of the Northern Hemisphere during past ice ages; the presence of oil under the tundra of the North Slope of Alaska; and the former existence of prehistoric, apparently heat-loving beasts like the dinosaurs in such northerly locales as the states of Montana and Wyoming.

Section 4.2 | SHOULD YOU CREATE BUILDINGS TO RECOGNIZE THE PROPERTIES OF WEATHER OR CLIMATE?

A most direct answer to this question is that a building should be created so that it provides an adequate response to the climate experienced at the building site. Thus, to ensure that a building offers satisfactory thermal performance, the design of the building must be predicated on the nature of this climate. Note, however, that information used to characterize the climate should not consist strictly of averages of atmospheric conditions at the site. Instead, a climate record — to be complete — must also include data about the presence and extent of variations for such conditions. The natures of these variations are revealed in the *frequencies* with which weather events occur, the *range* of conditions experienced during these events, and the *variability* (e.g., are conditions similar on a year-to-year basis or by how much do they vary over the year). So the record of a climate must indicate not only what the average atmospheric conditions are, but also what variations have been observed. To create a thermally effective building, the designer and/or builder must employ a summary of the climate for a building site that also includes information about weather extremes, their magnitudes, and how variable conditions have been.

Having buildings that satisfy precisely the averaged conditions would suggest that the building would be underdesigned at least half of the time. Clearly, if you created a building that would be comfortable specifically when the average atmospheric conditions were present, then future occupants might be uncomfortable whenever nonaverage conditions occurred (i.e., depending on the extent of the variations away from the average condition). But by accounting for all the variations present in a climate (i.e., so that occupants could be comfortable inside regardless of what weather was happening outside), then the building could seemingly be overdesigned for a significant time each year (and would likely operate inefficiently except at the extreme weather conditions). Thus, what would seem necessary is to design, first, for the average condition and then to provide some reserve capability so that when variations away from the average were experienced, the building operator could employ these reserves and remain comfortable. The choice of what conditions to design for ultimately concerns how much reserve to include in the conditioning capability for any building. The greater the reserve, the more likely the building will be comfortable inspite of more greatly varying external conditions. A smaller reserve will narrow the ability of the building to have comfortable conditions. However, the smaller reserve will generally enable the building to be operated at greater efficiency for the nonextreme conditions. But, regardless of how this argument about providing reserves is settled, some resources should be held as a cache so that the internal environment of the building can at least provide shelter from the climate.

As a practical example of how this question of what conditions to design for enters into providing adequate environmental control, we would cite a practice that has been followed in North America by engineers and subcontractors designing residential heating systems. The heating capacity of these systems is frequently established by taking the air temperature design condition for the winter and providing enough heating capacity to operate the residence at a comfortable indoor air temperature. In the days before the 1973 oil embargo common practice was to cite an exterior air design temperature that was thought to be a relatively extreme value for the locale (e.g., for Seattle, −9 °C (15 °F)). Thus, if designers were allowed to make certain that residences could be heated internally to at least 21 °C (70 °F), the heating systems would have to be sized to provide enough heating capacity to manage this 30 °C (55 °F) temperature difference. But, following the introduction of governmental regulations to make residential heating systems more energy-efficient, the external design temperature for Seattle has been raised to −3 °C (26 °F) and the permissible system heating capacity has been decreased so that a 23 °C (42 °F) temperature difference now becomes the allowable range. Thereby, an appropriately designed heating system will only be capable of maintaining an internal air temperature of 20 °C (68 °F), when the outside air temperature matches the air temperature design condition. Limiting the capacity of the system is intended to make the system more efficient. But a liability for this gain in efficiency is experienced when the external air temperature falls below −3 °C (26 °F). In that situation the ability to maintain thermally comfortable conditions within the residence is compromised (unless the occupant is willing to put on a sweater or can employ some alternative, nonregulated heat source like a wood-burning stove).

Section 4.3 | CLIMATE CLASSIFICATION (AS A BASIS FOR BUILDING DESIGN)

If you pause to think about the climate that exists over the area where you live, you can likely identify the approximate magnitudes of its principal attributes. For instance, the climate you experience could be depicted in terms of the following attributes: the average air temperatures for various days and months and for the year; daily, monthly, and yearly air temperature ranges; monthly and annual precipitation rates; whether these monthly rates show uniform distribution across the year or precipitation is concentrated or absent in one (or more) season(s); the daily, monthly, and annual patterns of relative humidity; prevalent wind directions and velocities throughout the year; and the degree(s) of sky clearness and/or cloud cover on a daily, monthly, or annual basis. Necessarily, year-to-year weather conditions will differ at least slightly from the overall climatic averages. But, generally, these differences will be small. Alternatively, you probably recognize that distant locales — perhaps closer to either the equator or one of the poles — undergo climates that are dissimilar from the one you experience. For these disparate climates the magnitudes for the climatic attributes identified above can be substantially different from those to which you are accustomed.

For instance, if you live in the middle Atlantic or lower Midwestern regions of the United States, you will experience a different climate from those found in Los Angeles, Rio de Janeiro, Bombay, or Shanghai. But the climates in New York and St. Louis are remarkably similar to those present in Seoul and Bucharest. Each of these four cities experiences a warm summer lasting about three to four months, a cool winter of about three months duration, and intermediate periods showing a gradual transition between the summer and the winter. Air temperature extremes, averages, and ranges are all reasonably similar. The precipitation rates are fairly evenly distributed throughout the year in these cities, although the summers tend to be wetter than the winters. Although the climate of Los Angeles is different from that of New York, other cities such as Beirut, Perth, and Santiago all experience climates quite similar to it. Further, the climate of Shanghai is, in many respects, like those of Atlanta and Sydney.

The climatic similarities that exist amongst these various groups of cities (and the regions in which the cities are located) suggest that *some basic set of climates may prevail across the surface of the Earth.* During the last century numbers of meteorologists and climatologists have considered the existence of these climatic likenesses and have defined various classifying strategies based on these similarities. These climate classification systems have initially been created to aid in the investigation of atmospheric conditions across regions experiencing similar climates. But any of these systems can also be used as a foundation for identifying the capabilities that buildings located in these regions should have.

4.3.1   THE DEVELOPMENT OF CLIMATIC CLASSIFICATION SYSTEMS

The role of classification systems, generally, is *to facilitate the organization of information.* Classification thus commences as someone searches for commonalities amongst the elements of various alternative situations or items (i.e., identifying *like* properties as bases for relating these situations or items). The process will typically involve a series of steps: (1) establishing the properties or criteria by which commonalities can be identified (from amongst the elements of alternative situations or items); (2) gathering sufficient information about each situation or item to enable ready testing against a list of properties or criteria; (3) performing such tests; (4) searching for patterns once commonalities have been identified; and (5) resolving discrepancies where they exist in alternative situations or items (which otherwise have recognizable commonalities) and then selectively fine-tuning the establishment of the lists of criteria or properties (to highlight the more important criteria or properties). Ultimately, someone conducting a classification process seeks to ensure that it is comprehensive, objective, rigorous, and still relatively easy to employ.[2]

The climate of a region or locality is characterized by several atmospheric parameters: air temperature, the rate and form of precipitation, the rate of evaporation (of liquid water), humidity, cloudiness (including the amount and type of clouds), solar and longwave radiation rates, wind speed and direction, and air pressure. These attributes are the fundamental properties of a climate. If we wish to describe a climate explicitly, then the greater the detail we can offer about all these parameters the better the description will be. But some parameters have greater influence on the nature of a climate than do others. Thus, it is feasible to offer a good approximation of any climate by citing only a few of these parameters. However, what parameters are fundamental depends upon the viewpoint of the person considering the climate. For instance, if the individual is involved in farming or gardening, then air temperature, precipitation, evaporation rate, and incident solar radiation might be the most important (because these attributes have the greatest influences on plant growth). Alternatively, as we are primarily concerned with the efficient operation of buildings and the maintenance of occupant thermal comfort in these buildings, the most important parameters of any environment in which we may locate a building will likely be the air temperature, radiant exchange rates between occupants and their environments, relative humidity, and air velocity. After all, these are the four primary environmental parameters that directly affect people's thermal comfort.

Numerous climate classification systems have been devised during the past century.[3] From our perspective, there appear to be three principal types: those based strictly on climatological data, those founded on the existence of environmental conditions suitable for natural plant growth, and those which evaluate environmental conditions in terms of the ready maintenance of human comfortability.

In the early decades of the twentieth century Köppen developed what has become the most widely used climate classification system.[4] This system is fundamentally based on monthly air temperature averages and seasonal and annual precipitation rates, which have been observed at monitoring stations across the Earth. Additionally, Köppen also considered vegetation forms, using them as confirming evidence when specific climatic data for various locales were only available as anecdotes or approximations. His system identified five major climatic groups. Four groups were founded principally on air temperature ranges, and the fifth was based on the annual rate of precipitation. Subsequent to this major effort by Köppen, a number of climatologists have offered modifications to this system, seeking to create general or specific improvements (yet still retaining the basic form and substance of Köppen's system).

4.3.2   DESCRIPTION OF THE TREWARTHA CLIMATE CLASSIFICATION SYSTEM[5]

One of the several alternative classification systems derived from the Köppen model has been contributed by Trewartha. The Trewartha system is based principally on the attributes of air temperature, humidity, and the potential evaporation rate (i.e., an amount of ground surface and plant-emitted water that would evaporate, if that amount were indeed present). In the subsequent discussion in the remainder of this chapter and in Chapter 5 we are going to employ this Trewartha classification system as the foundation for providing further descriptions of climates. Our selection of the Trewartha system has been made because this system has been established principally on air temperatures and moisture presence throughout the world. These two attributes have great influence on how well buildings can provide for human shelter and thermal comfort. So a good match should exist between the climate characterization implicit in the Trewartha system and the design and construction of buildings for the various climates described by the Trewartha system.

Maps showing the Trewartha distribution of climates throughout the Eastern and Western Hemispheres are displayed in Figures 4.3 and 4.4. The maps indicate six basic climatic groups: five (identified as *Groups A* and *C–F*) are based primarily on characteristic air temperature ranges, and the sixth (identified as *Group B*) is determined by precipitation and potential evaporation rates. Most of these basic groups have subcategories, which are used to distinguish secondary characteristics of the climates. Table 4.1 identifies the essential features of these groups and subcategories.

Figure 4.3 The Western Hemisphere climate classification map based on the Köppen system (as modified by Trewartha and Horn). This map has previously been published in the book by Trewartha, G.T., and L.H. Horn, *An Introduction to Climate,* 5th edition, (New York: McGraw-Hill Book Company, 1980). Permission to reproduce this map has been sought from The McGraw-Hill Companies.

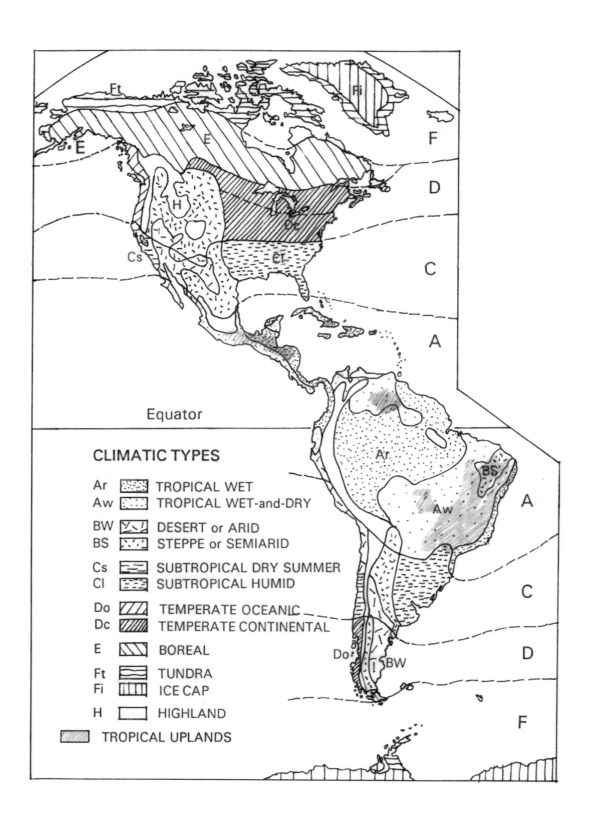

CLIMATIC TYPES

Ar		TROPICAL WET
Aw		TROPICAL WET-and-DRY
BW		DESERT or ARID
BS		STEPPE or SEMIARID
Cs		SUBTROPICAL DRY SUMMER
Cl		SUBTROPICAL HUMID
Do		TEMPERATE OCEANIC
Dc		TEMPERATE CONTINENTAL
E		BOREAL
Ft		TUNDRA
Fi		ICE CAP
H		HIGHLAND
		TROPICAL UPLANDS

Equator

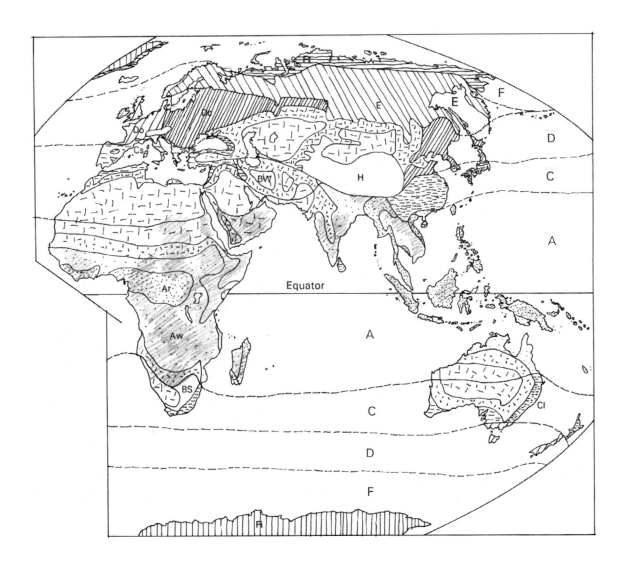

Figure 4.4 The Eastern Hemisphere climate classification map based on the Köppen system (as modified by Trewartha and Horn). This map has previously been published in the book by Trewartha, G.T., and L.H. Horn, *An Introduction to Climate,* 5th edition, (New York: McGraw-Hill Book Company, 1980). Permission to reproduce this map has been sought from The McGraw-Hill Companies.

TABLE 4.1
THE TREWARTHA & HORN CATALOGUE OF CLIMATE GROUPS AND SUBCATEGORIES

GROUP A: TROPICAL CLIMATES

Basic features include: no killing frost and the coldest month has a monthly average air temperature (hereafter, **MAAT**) greater than 18 °C (65 °F)

With subcategories:

Ar: *Tropical wet* (with at least 10 months wet)

Aw: *Tropical wet-and-dry* (including a dry season of duration longer than 2 months, occurring during the winter)

As: Similar to Aw, except that the dry season occurs during the summer (a rare climate)

GROUP C: SUBTROPICAL CLIMATES

Basic features include: 8 to 12 months with **MAAT** greater than 10 °C (50 °F) and the coldest month having a **MAAT** less than 18 °C (65 °F)

With subcategories:

Cs: *Subtropical dry summer* (with at least three times as much precipitation in the winter half year compared with the summer half; the driest summer month has less than 30 mm (1.2"); and the annual total is less than 890 mm (35")

Cw: *Subtropical dry winter* (with at least ten times as much precipitation during the summer half year than during the winter

Cf: *Subtropical humid* (no dry season; the difference between the driest and wettest months is less than those required for the Cs and Cw conditions; the driest summer month has more than 30 mm (1.2")

GROUP D: TEMPERATE CLIMATES

Basic features include: 4 to 7 months with **MAAT** greater than 10 °C (50 °F)

With subcategories:

Do: *Temperate maritime* (with coldest month having a MAAT greater than 0 °C (32 °F)

Dc: *Temperate continental* (with coldest month having a MAAT less than 0 °C (32 °F)

Dca: *Temperate continental warm summer* (as with Dc, except that warmest month has a MAAT greater than 22 °C (72 °F)

Dcb: *Temperate continental cool summer* (as with Dc, except that warmest month has a MAAT less than 22 °C (72 °F)

GROUP E: BOREAL CLIMATES

Basic feature is that 1–3 months have a **MAAT** greater than 10 °C (50 °F)

GROUP F: POLAR CLIMATES

Basic feature is that no month has a **MAAT** greater than 10 °C (50 °F)

With subcategories:

Ft: *Tundra* (warmest month has a MAAT between 0–10 °C (32–50 °F)

Fi: *Ice cap* (all months have MAAT less than 0 °C (32 °F)

(continued on next page)

TABLE 4.1 (continued)

THE TREWARTHA & HORN CATALOGUE OF CLIMATE GROUPS AND SUBCATEGORIES

GROUP B: DRY CLIMATES

Basic feature is that potential evaporation exceeds precipitation annually

With subcategories:

BS: *Steppe* or *Semiarid*[i] (note that steppe or semiarid climates commonly experience 10"–20" (254 mm–508 mm) of precipitation per year)

BW: *Desert* or *Arid*[ii] (note that desert or arid climates experience less than 10" (254 mm) of precipitation per year)

With the further qualifiers:

(added to the BS or BW classifications)

h: *hot* (basic feature is that 8 months or more will have a MAAT greater than 10 °C (50 °F))

k: *cold* (basic feature is that fewer than 8 months will have a MAAT greater than 10 °C (50 °F)

s: *summer dry*

w: *winter dry*

n: *frequent fog*

GROUP H: HIGHLAND CLIMATES

Generally, the term *highland* refers to locales above about 1830 m (6000′). This climatic type is less precisely defined than are the other six groups, partially because of the lack of data for a number of sites in highland locales sufficient to create a general model and the great range of climates observed in highland regions.[iii]

Source: This table has previously been published in the book by Trewartha, G.T., and L.H. Horn, *An Introduction to Climate* (5th edition), (New York: McGraw-Hill Book Company, 1980.) Permission to reproduce this table has been sought from The McGraw-Hill Companies.

Notes:

i. The boundary between the "humid" and "steppe" climates (for regions in which the yearly precipitation is not concentrated during a season) is defined by Trewartha and Horn as when the condition $R = 0.44T - 8.5$ is satisfied (where R is the rainfall in inches and T is the average annual air temperature in °F.) See Trewartha, G.T., and L.H. Horn, *An Introduction to Climate* (5th edition), (New York: McGraw-Hill Book Company, 1980), page 228.

ii. Similar to the separation between "humid" and "steppe," the distinction between "steppe" and "desert" climates is that the rainfall (R′) will be half of R (or, $R' = 0.22T - 4.25$.)

iii. For further information about the characteristics of highland climates, see Trewartha, G.T., and L.H. Horn, *An Introduction to Climate* (5th edition), (New York: McGraw-Hill Book Company, 1980), pages 332–345.

4.3.3   A BRIEF EXPLANATION OF THE BASIC PREMISES OF THE TREWARTHA CLIMATIC CLASSIFICATION SYSTEM

The fundamental organization of the Trewartha system is based on the air temperatures present across the surface of the Earth. First, Table 4.2 displays a list of mean annual air temperatures for the different latitudes. Second, maps of the average sea-level air temperatures for January and July appear as Figures 4.5 and 4.6. From Table 4.2 and the maps, it can be observed that the average temperatures for any locale are generally established according to the distance of the site from the equator. So as one progresses further north or south away from the equator, air temperatures decrease. The principal reason for this behavior is that, on average, equatorial and subtropical regions receive more solar radiation annually than more poleward latitudes do. The regions further from the equator receive less solar radiation and are commonly less warm. Therefore, if you examine the climatic groups shown in Figures 4.3 and 4.4, you can see that those groups determined basically by temperature occur in bands that are parallel to the equator. For instance, the *Group A* climates occur between the tropic of Cancer and the tropic of Capricorn. Similarly, the *Cs* climate is present in a band between 30° and 40° north and south of the equator.

The other major feature of the Trewartha climatic classification system is the presence of substantial areas that experience dry climates. These dry regions are usually found in two locations: either on the west sides of continents in the latitude bands from 20° to 30° north or south of the equator or in the midst of large continental land masses as far as 50° from the equator.

Thus, the Trewartha map is based on a two-layered model of climatic behavior. First, climates are laid out according to average air temperatures that decrease as one moves poleward from the equator. Second, a virtual overlay specifically incorporating the dry areas of the Earth has been placed on top of this temperature-banded pattern. Thus, this

TABLE 4.2
MEAN ANNUAL AIR TEMPERATURES FOR DIFFERENT LATITUDES, IN °C (°F)

LATITUDE	NORTHERN HEMISPHERE	SOUTHERN HEMISPHERE
0°	26 (79)	26 (79)
10°	27 (80)	25 (77)
20°	25 (77)	23 (73)
30°	20 (68)	18 (65)
40°	14 (57)	12 (54)
50°	6 (42)	6 (42)
60°	−1 (30)	0 (32)
70°	−10 (14)	−11 (12)
80°	−17 (2)	−20 (−4)

Source: This table has been previously published in the book by Landsberg, H.E., *Physical Climatology*, (State College, Pennsylvania: School of Mineral Industries, The Pennsylvania State College, 1942). Permission to reproduce this table has been granted by the Department of Energy and Geo-Environmental Engineering, Pennsylvania State University.

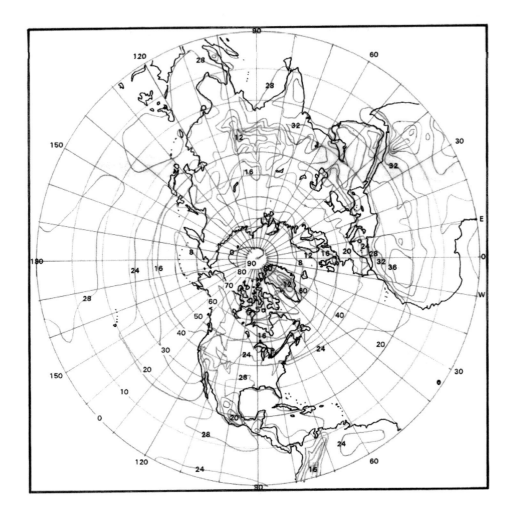

Figure 4.5 The mean ambient air temperatures near the surface of the Earth are shown for the month of January. These temperature contours (or isotherms) essentially coincide with—lay parallel to—lines of latitude across the Earth, except where the contours pass over (and are diverted by) continental landmasses. This map has been previously published in a book compiled by Crutcher, H.L., and J.M. Meserve, *Selected Level Heights, Temperatures and Dew Points for the Northern Hemisphere* (as prepared by the Environmental Science Services Administration [of the Environmental Data Service] for the U.S. Navy, January 1970).

two-tiered model integrates the essential importance of temperature and moisture in defining the various climatic groups.

A number of additional qualifications affect this basic model and help to resolve apparent discrepancies between the basic model and what we can observe in the climatic group maps. Perhaps the most significant of these qualifications is that there are a number of regions either along the coasts of the continents or within the midsts of the larger continents where average air temperatures differ from the basic latitude-wide average temperatures. For the *coastal* regions, one finds that these areas generally experience warmer winters and

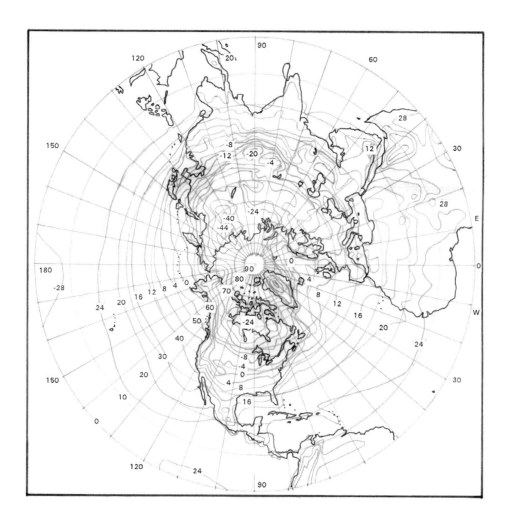

Figure 4.6 Similar to Figure 4.5, the mean ambient air temperatures for the month of July are shown in this map. This map has been previously published in a book compiled by Crutcher, H.L., and J.M. Meserve, *Selected Level Heights, Temperatures and Dew Points for the Northern Hemisphere* (as prepared by the Environmental Science Services Administration [of the Environmental Data Service] for the U.S. Navy, January 1970).

cooler summers than do other land-based locales along the same latitude. Alternatively, regions *in the midst of the continents* undergo greater heating in the summer and greater cooling in the winter. In both instances — for the coastal and mid-continental regions — these variances from the latitudinal average temperatures are known as *isoanomalies.*[6] Examples of these variances can be seen for the Pacific Northwest region of North America where the air temperatures are anywhere from 4–12 °C (7–22 °F) warmer in January and 4–8 °C (7–14 °F) cooler than their respective latitudinal averages, *or* for the central region of Asia which is anywhere from 4–8 °C (7–14 °F) warmer in July and as much as 22 °C (40 °F) cooler in January.

Another significant feature within this two-tiered climatic classification model concerns how precipitation occurs across the Earth. Answers to questions about how much precipitation falls and when does such precipitation happen are central for characterizing the climate of any locale. Thus, the description of a climate must include information that indicates, for precipitation, what the annual rate is; whether the precipitation is uniform across the year or, instead, is concentrated seasonally (i.e., into wet and dry periods); whether the precipitation occurs in occasional, heavy showers or frequent, sustained periods of light rain; and how regular the annual total rainfall is on a year-to-year basis across any period of many years. To demonstrate the relevance of these issues we can cite the following examples. First, rainfall in tropical rainforest areas commonly exceeds 2500 mm (about 100 in) of rainfall annually, whereas precipitation in temperate continental regions usually totals about 875 to 1250 mm (35 to 50 in) per year. Second, the presence of separate wet and dry seasons is a common phenomenon in many regions of the world (e.g., Los Angeles receives 89 percent of its annual precipitation during a period from November through March). Third, examples of rain-day totals for three cities—each characteristic of their respective climate types—are as follows: Pensacola, Florida has, on average, 1575 mm (62 in) of rain/year with 119 rain-days (where a rain-day is any day during which at least 0.25 mm (0.01 in) of precipitation occurs); Boston averages 1090 mm (43 in)/year with 128 rain-days; and Seattle has 965 mm (38 in)/year with 160 rain-days.[7] And, fourth, the "dustbowl" conditions that were present in the Plains area of the United States in the 1930s are thought to be a reoccurring phenomenon that will repeat every 30 to 50 years. Indeed, during the dustbowl years, that region experienced several years of uncommon dryness, resulting in great economic hardship particularly for the inhabitants of the area.[8]

4.3.4 A COMPRESSION OF THE TREWARTHA SYSTEM FOR BUILDING DESIGN AND CONSTRUCTION

In the Trewartha climatic classification system, six primary climatic groups and approximately 20 subcategories are used to delineate the range of climates observed across the Earth. Generally, the distinctions between these groups and subcategories are substantive for climatologists and geographers. But, for designers and builders, a compression of the many climatic groups and subcategories (into a fewer number of types) can be accommodated without losing the significance or accuracy of the overall model). The key issue in performing this compression is to identify the *predominant* feature for each of the various groups and subcategories and to use this feature as the basis for performing the compression. Thus, we suggest that all the various climatic groups and subcategories can be compressed into four distinct (building) climate types:

(1) *Warm, humid:* From the Trewartha classification system, all of the *tropical humid* (Group A) climates and the *subtropical humid (Cf)* climate would thus be included within this designation. The subtropical humid (Cf) climate is incorporated with the tropical humid (Group A) climates because its predominant feature is the sustained period of warm, humid weather. When one designs and builds for this (building) climate type (i.e., warm, humid), the primary responsibility for maintaining thermal comfort is to provide means for offsetting the commonly excessive heat and humidity.

(2) *Hot, dry:* The Trewartha subcategories fitting within this (building) climate type are *desert* (or *arid*) *hot (BWh), steppe* (or *semi-arid*) *hot (BSh)*, and *subtropical dry summer (Cs).* Each of these subcategories experiences a lengthy period of weather that is both dry and over-heated. Thus, the fundamental design and construction problems are to create an

internal building environment that keeps inside what moisture is available *and* to control the large temperature gradients that are present between the exterior and interior of the building. This second requirement generally involves reducing the rates of heat transfer through building envelopes.

(3) *Cold:* This designation includes all of the following Trewartha groups and subcategories: *temperate continental cool summer (Dcb), boreal (E), polar tundra (Ft), polar ice cap (Fi), desert* (or *arid*) *cold (BWk), steppe* (or *semi-arid*) *cold (BSk)* and, potentially, *highland (H).* The dominant feature for each of these climates is that they have *sustained periods of cold weather.* That some of the subcategories also depict climates that are dry is a secondary concern. The essential need for buildings in regions with these climates is to minimize heat loss through the building envelope.

(4) *Temperate:* The two Trewartha subcategories that fit within this (building) climate type are *temperate continental warm summer (Dca)* and *temperate oceanic (Do).* The remarkable feature about this designation is that, generally, the overall climate is neither too warm nor too cold. Rather, though there are short periods of overheated or underheated weather, the climate is moderate. Fundamentally, buildings for this climatic type should have means that enables variable responses to the changing nature of this climate (e.g., minimizing heat loss during the comparatively mild winters and opening the building envelope to permit cooling by natural forces during the occasional periods of summer overheatedness).

In Chapter 5 we will consider specific properties of these four climate types. We will also suggest formal organizations and operating strategies that should be applied when designing and constructing buildings in regions experiencing these climates. Thus, by adopting such planning and operating guidelines, we should be able to ensure that thermal comfort and efficient usage can be provided for the occupants of these buildings.

Section 4.4 | DERIVING BUILDING DESIGN GUIDELINES FOR A SPECIFIC CLIMATE

A fundamental notion of this text is that the design and construction of a building should recognize the nature of the climate in which the building is to be located. Thus, both the building form and the manner in which the building is operated should acknowledge the various attributes of the climate (e.g., air temperature, solar radiation, relative humidity, and so forth) and the needs of the building occupant for maintaining thermal comfort. Necessarily, the nature of any climate involves a number of properties, each of which can vary widely during any year and certainly over the useful life of the building. To prepare a thorough analysis of a climate can be a time-consuming task. In fact, such analysis may lead the designer or builder away from the basic purpose of the analysis: to identify the aspects of the climate, which must be accommodated if the building is to provide comfort and work efficiently and is not to rely substantially on active control systems. Therefore, what the designer or builder then requires is an easy-to-use, quick, and relatively comprehensive device for examining climatic data so that useful guidelines can be determined for designing and constructing a building.

In this section we will describe two devices that can be used for examining the climate of a locale (in recognition of occupant thermal comfort needs) and generating a catalog of simple, useful guidelines for establishing site layout and building spacing, the internal organization of a building, and the composition of the building envelope. These guidelines are intended for use during the preliminary schematic phase of building design and therefore are cast as approximations. Finding more specific information for doing

---

SIDEBAR 4.3 Differentiating between *skin-load-dependent* and *internal-load-dominant* thermal behaviors for buildings

---

The one qualification about the use of either of these devices is that both are better suited for establishing design guidelines for skin-load-dependent buildings (in contrast to internal-load-dominant buildings). The *skin-load-dependent* building is one in which the rates of heat gain and loss that occur through the building envelope fundamentally determine the thermal performance of the building. Thus, whether an envelope experiences a heat gain or loss, this behavior at the envelope (or building skin) will determine if the building interior needs to be cooled or heated for occupant thermal comfort to be maintained. Alternatively, the *internal-load-dominant* building is one in which the

production of heat by internal sources within the building (e.g., from people, electric lights, office equipment, appliances, manufacturing and production machines, and so forth) is substantially greater than the rate of loss or gain experienced at the building envelope. For the internal-load-dominant building the primary need for conditioning the building interior will involve the cooling of occupied spaces. Thus, how the natural environment surrounding an internal-load-dominant building varies climatically can be of secondary concern when one considers how the building can best be operated.

"fine-tuning" during design development and the later phases of the building design process will subsequently require the user to apply more rigorous, analytic calculational procedures and/or simulation techniques.

Lastly, as we introduce these two devices, let us emphasize that, because these devices relate occupant thermal comfort needs and the climate of a locale, it is only necessary to employ either of these devices once for a locale. In other words, after once using either of these devices for a given set of climatic information, you will not need to employ the other device also. Rather, by referring to the results from the original application of either device, you can use those results for all subsequent buildings constructed for that locale.

4.4.1   USING THE MAHONEY TABLES (FOR EXAMINING WARM AND HOT CLIMATES)[9]

The Mahoney Tables offer a recipe for examining the properties of climates that are either predominantly warm and humid or hot and dry. These tables require consideration of the magnitudes and ranges of the air temperature, relative humidity, wind direction, and precipitation experienced at a locale. The examination of these climatic features proceeds by comparing observed climatic properties to conditions that are thermally comfortable. By using these tables a designer can thus identify design guidelines that will promote the creation of buildings that respond well to such climates.

The principal steps in applying the Mahoney Tables consist of securing appropriate climatic data for the intended building locale; filling the data into the tables; and taking off the suggested results from these tables to use in schematic designing. The Mahoney Tables consist of six tables: the first four tables (Tables 4.3–4.6) are employed for comparing aspects of the climate of some locale with occupant thermal comfort needs, and the last two tables are applied for deriving design recommendations (Tables 4.7–4.8). We will include a set of the six Mahoney Tables here in the text.

4.4.1.1 **Establishing the requisite climatic data**   The use of the Mahoney Tables
requires that climatic information be secured for air temperatures, relative humidity, rainfall, and wind direction (for any locale that is to be examined). Specific data that are
needed include the monthly mean maximum and minimum air temperatures (where the
monthly mean maximum air temperature is established by taking the maximum air temperature for each day of a month, summing these daily temperatures for all the days of the
month, and dividing by the number of days in the month); the monthly mean maximum
and minimum relative humidities (where the maximum value normally occurs in the
morning and the minimum value happens in the afternoon); the monthly precipitation
totals; and the prevailing (and secondary) wind directions.

Primary published sources for obtaining such monthly data are for cities in the United States, particularly, *Climates of the States*[10]*;* and for cities throughout the world, either
World Survey of Climatology[11]*,* or *Selected Climatic Data*[12]*.* Additionally, other sources of
monthly climatic data include documents prepared by the U.S. Air Force, U.S. Navy, several United Nations organizations (e.g., World Meteorological Organization), and various
national governments.

4.4.1.2 **Filling in the Mahoney Tables**[13]   The use of Table 1 (Table 4.3) requires cataloging the *monthly mean maximum* and *monthly mean minimum air temperatures* for the
locale and filling these values into the table (in Rows 1.1 and 1.2). The *monthly mean*

TABLE 4.3
AIR TEMPERATURES (MAHONEY TABLE #1)

ROW	JAN	FEB	MAR	APR	MAY	JUN	JUL	AUG	SEP	OCT	NOV	DEC
1.1 Monthly Mean Maximum												
1.2 Monthly Mean Minimum												
1.3 Monthly Mean Range												

Maximum Monthly Mean Maximum =

Minimum Monthly Mean Minimum =

AMT = (Max Mon Mean Max + Min Mon Mean Min)/2 =

AMR = (Max Mon Mean Max − Min Mon Mean Min) =

Tables 4.3–4.12 have previously been published in the book by Königsberger, O., C. Mahoney, and M. Evans, *Climate and House
Design: Design of Low-Cost Housing* (Volume 1), (New York: Department of Economic and Social Affairs, United Nations Center for
Housing, Building, and Planning, 1971). Permission to reproduce these tables has been granted by the Office of External Publications,
Department of Public Information, United Nations, New York.

TABLE 4.4
HUMIDITY, PRECIPITATION, & WIND (TABLE #2)

ROW		JAN	FEB	MAR	APR	MAY	JUN	JUL	AUG	SEP	OCT	NOV	DEC
2.1	Ave Monthly Rel Humidity												
2.2	Humidity Group												
2.3	Monthly Precipitation												
2.4	Prevailing Wind Direction												
2.5	Secondary Wind Direction												

ANNUAL PRECIPITATION = [   ]

range (Row 1.3) is found by subtracting the monthly mean minimum air temperature from the monthly mean maximum air temperature. Use of Table 1 also requires listing the highest monthly mean maximum temperature and the lowest monthly mean minimum temperature. Finally, the user needs to calculate the *annual mean temperature* (AMT) and the *annual mean range* (AMR): the *AMT* is found by averaging the highest monthly mean maximum air temperature and the lowest monthly mean minimum air temperature; and the *AMR* is found by subtracting the lowest monthly mean minimum air temperature from the highest monthly mean maximum air temperature. Note that all temperature data used in these Mahoney Tables must be entered using the Celsius scale.

The initial step in using Table 2 (Table 4.4) consists of filling in the table with data about the *monthly average relative humidity* values (in Row 2.1). To complete Row 2.2, the user needs to compare the monthly average relative humidity values with those in Table 4.9. Then, fill in the corresponding *Humidity Group* number (from Table 4.9) in the appropriate location for each month. *Monthly precipitation* data should be listed in Row 2.3 (and expressed in terms of millimeters (mm) of precipitation). In Row 2.4, the *prevailing wind direction* for each month should be inserted. If *secondary wind direction* data are available, then these data should be entered in Row 2.5.

The purpose of Table 3 (Table 4.5) is to compare the climatic data catalogued in Tables 1 and 2 with acceptable occupant thermal comfort conditions. *Humidity Group* data for Row 3.1 are taken directly from Row 2.2 of Table 2 (Table 4.4). The *monthly mean maximum air temperature* values for Row 3.2 can be filled in using the values from Row 1.1 of Table 1. Similarly, the *monthly mean minimum air temperature* values for Row 3.5 can be found in Row 1.2 of Table 1.

TABLE 4.5
COMPARISON OF COMFORT CONDITIONS & CLIMATE (TABLE #3)

ROW		JAN	FEB	MAR	APR	MAY	JUN	JUL	AUG	SEP	OCT	NOV	DEC
3.1	Humidity Group												
3.2	Mon Mean Max Temp												
3.3	Day Comfort Temp Max												
3.4	Day Comfort Temp Min												
3.5	Mon Mean Min Temp												
3.6	Night Comfort Temp Max												
3.7	Night Comfort Temp Min												
3.8	Thermal Stress Day												
3.9	Thermal Stress Night												

The *permissible daytime thermal comfort temperature ranges* (for entry in Rows 3.3 and 3.4) and *permissible nighttime thermal comfort temperature ranges* (for entry in Rows 3.6 and 3.7) are listed in Table 4.10. The "range" values that should be written into Rows 3.3–3.4 and 3.6–3.7 are established by referring back to the annual mean temperature (AMT) found in Table 1. Depending whether the AMT for your climate is greater than 20 °C, somewhere at or between 15 to 20 °C, or less than 15 °C, you would use the pair of columns according to the *AMT* value. Then, while comparing the monthly Humidity Group (shown already in Row 3.1) with the AMT, you can determine the *suggested maximum and minimum air temperatures* for the day and night times for each month. These suggested maximum and minimum air temperatures — when found from Table 4.10 — can then be entered in Rows 3.3–3.4 (for the daytime) and 3.6–3.7 (for the nighttime).

Once Rows 3.3–3.4 are filled, the next step is to compare the monthly mean maximum temperature (MMMaxT) of Row 3.2 with the daytime comfort temperature range in Rows 3.3–3.4, on a month-by-month basis. If the MMMaxT (for instance, for January) is above the daytime comfort temperature range, then enter an *H* in Row 3.8 (for *daytime thermal stress*). If the MMMaxT is within the daytime comfort temperature range, do not enter anything in Row 3.8. If the MMMaxT is below the daytime comfort temperature

TABLE 4.6
INDICATORS (TABLE #4)

ROW	JAN	FEB	MAR	APR	MAY	JUN	JUL	AUG	SEP	OCT	NOV	DEC	TOTAL
FOR HUMID CONDITIONS													
H.1 Air Movement Essential													
H.2 Air Movement Desirable													
H.3 Rain Protection Needed													
FOR ARID CONDITIONS													
A.1 Thermal Storage Needed													
A.2 Outdoor Sleeping Useful													
A.3 Cold-Season Problems													

range, then enter a *C* in Row 3.8. Thus, for the month of January, you would be establishing whether a person would be thermally stressed (i.e., "hot" or "cold") or not ("neutral") during the daytime. In a similar manner, you should then compare the monthly mean minimum temperature (MMMinT) with the nighttime comfort temperature range. Depending whether the MMMinT is above, within, or below the nighttime comfort temperature range, then you would enter an *H*, nothing, or a *C* in the January box for Row 3.9. After you have completed the January thermal stress boxes, you should complete Rows 3.8–3.9 for the other months of the year.

Table 4 (Table 4.6) is the final one of the four tables used for comparing climatic data with occupant thermal comfort needs. Its function is to relate the thermal stress identified in Table 3 with certain fundamental building operation *indicators* (a term chosen by Carl Mahoney and meant to point out what can be thought of as fundamental operation strategies for buildings exposed to "humid" and "arid" climates).[14] To fill in Table 4, one needs to compare the natures of the thermal stress, the *Humidity Group,* and the mean monthly temperature range (as found in Row 1.3 of Table 1), on a month-by-month basis throughout the year. So for any month in which any of the following criteria is satisfied (see Table 4.11 for a listing of those criteria), enter a checkmark in the appropriate Rows (i.e., rows H.1–H.3 and A.1–A.3 in Table 4.6).

After filling in the appropriate boxes (i.e., for the 12 months and the six rows), add up the number of checkmarks in each row and enter that number in last column *(Total)*. This step thus completes the *prerecommendation* tables.

From Tables 5 and 6 (Tables 4.7 and 4.8, respectively), the user is able to identify series of design guidelines and rules-of-thumb suitable for application in schematic design. Table 5 provides guidelines generally for the building as a whole, whereas Table 6 offers directives for specific components of the building. The use of both tables follows the same procedure: basically, you enter the results from Table 4 into Tables 5 and 6, identify conditions in Tables 5 and 6 which match the results from Table 4, and then read off the recommendations where matches occur. In the following paragraph, we will describe the *matching process* more carefully and demonstrate the use of Tables 5 and 6 with some limited examples.

First, the use of Table 5 begins with the transfer of the *Total* results from Rows H1–H3 and A1–A3 of Table 4 into Row 5.1 of Table 5. Then, for each column of Table 5 (H1–H3 and A1–A3), you should compare the number in Row 5.1 with the numbers shown in Rows 5.2–5.21 for that column. Where the number in Row 5.1 matches the number (or one number within a sequence of numbers) in any one of the 20 rows beneath, then you should circle the matching entries in Rows 5.2–5.21.[15] After you have completed matching each of the Row 5.1 boxes with the succeeding boxes in Rows 5.2–5.21 (i.e., by moving down each column), then you are ready to look for *satisfactions* on a row-by-row basis (i.e., by moving horizontally). The bases for these satisfactions are listed in Table 4.12.

Once these satisfactions have been found, then the rows in which the satisfactions exist should be identified and the recommendations at the right side of Table 5 should be noted (for those rows). These recommendations are the *design guidelines* that should be employed during schematic designing.

The use of Table 6 is conducted in the same manner as the use of Table 5. Again, transfer the *Total* results of the Rows H1–H3 and A1–A3 of Table 4 into Row 6.1 of Table 6. Circle the numbers in Rows 6.2–6.21 for each column where the number in Row 6.1 corresponds with the number or range of numbers in the 20 boxes below the 6.1 box. Then, identify the satisfactions (on a row-by-row basis) and note the design guidelines listed in the column, Recommendations.

4.4.1.3 A worked example using the Mahoney Tables for analyzing the climate of Miami, Florida   As an example of how the Mahoney Tables can be utilized, we will provide completed tables for Miami, Florida. First, we obtain suitable climatic data for Miami (see Table 4.13). From these data we are able to fill in Tables 1 and 2 (see Tables 4.14 and 4.15).[16] We complete Table 3 (Table 4.16) using the data from Tables 1 and 2 and the comfort range temperatures set out in Table 4.10. From Table 4.16 (Table 3) we see that for the months from May through October, the daytime climate has monthly mean maximum (air) temperatures (in Row 3.2) that are above the daytime comfort maximum temperature (in Row 3.3); thus, people exposed to these air temperature and humidity conditions would experience daytime thermal stress (i.e., overheatedness). Alternatively, during nighttimes in the months of December through February, the monthly mean minimum (air) temperatures would be below the nighttime comfort minimum temperature, and people would feel a cold thermal stress (or under-heatedness).[17]

TABLE 4.7
SCHEMATIC DESIGN RECOMMENDATIONS (MAHONEY TABLE #5)

| Row | HUMID | | | ARID | | | | RECOMMENDATIONS |
	H1	H2	H3	A1	A2	A3		
5.1								
LAYOUT								
5.2				0–10				Buildings oriented on east-west axis to reduce sun exposure
5.3				11–12	5–12			
5.4				11–12	0–4			Compact courtyard planning
SPACING								
5.5	11–12							Open spacing for breeze passage
5.6	2–10							Same, but watch hot/cold wind
5.7	0–1							Use compact planning
AIR MOVEMENT								
5.8	3–12							Rooms single-banked, provide openings for wind passage
5.9	1–2			0–5				
5.10	1–2			6–12				Double-banked rooms w/temporary means for wind passage
5.11	0	2–12						
5.12	0	0–1						No wind passage required
OPENINGS								
5.13				0–1		0		Big openings, 40–80% of N & S walls
5.14				11–12		0–1		Very small openings, 10–20% of walls
5.15		All other conditions						Medium-sized openings, 20–40%
WALLS								
5.16				0–2				Low mass; no insulation required
5.17				3–12				High mass or well-insulated
ROOFS								
5.18				0–5				Low mass and well-insulated
5.19				6–12				High mass or well-insulated
OUTDOOR SLEEPING								
5.20					2–12			Provide outdoor sleeping space
RAIN PROTECTION								
5.21			3–12					Protect from heavy rainfall

TABLE 4.8
DESIGN DEVELOPMENT RECOMMENDATIONS (MAHONEY TABLE #6)

Row	HUMID			ARID				RECOMMENDATIONS
	H1	H2	H3	A1	A2	A3		
6.1								

SIZE OF OPENINGS

Row	H1	H2	H3	A1	A2	A3		RECOMMENDATIONS
6.2				0–1		0		Big, 40–80% of N & S walls
6.3				0–1		1–12		Medium-sized, 25–40% of
6.4				2–5				vertical envelope area
6.5				6–10				Composite, 20–35% of wall area
6.6				11–12		0–3		Small, 15–25% of wall area
6.7				11–12		4–12		Medium-sized, 25–40% of wall area

POSITION OF OPENINGS

Row	H1	H2	H3	A1	A2	A3		RECOMMENDATIONS
6.8	3–12							Openings in N & S walls at body
6.9	1–2			0–5				height on windward elevation
6.10	1–2			6–12				As above, but including openings
6.11	0	2–12						in internal walls

PROTECTION FOR OPENINGS

Row	H1	H2	H3	A1	A2	A3		RECOMMENDATIONS
6.12						0–2		Exclude direct sunlight
6.13			2–12					Provide protection from rain

WALLS AND FLOORS

Row	H1	H2	H3	A1	A2	A3		RECOMMENDATIONS
6.14				0–2				Low mass (low heat capacity)
6.15				3–12				High mass or well-insulated

ROOFS

Row	H1	H2	H3	A1	A2	A3		RECOMMENDATIONS
6.16	10–12			0–2				Low mass; reflective; cavity assembly
6.17	10–12			3–12				Low mass & well-insulated
6.18	0–9			0–5				
6.19	0–9			6–12				High mass or well-insulated

EXTERNAL SURFACE TREATMENTS

Row	H1	H2	H3	A1	A2	A3		RECOMMENDATIONS
6.20					1–12			Provide outdoor sleeping space
6.21			1–12					Have good rainwater drainage

TABLE 4.9
DETERMINING RELATIVE HUMIDITY GROUPS

AVERAGE RELATIVE HUMIDITY	HUMIDITY GROUP
0–29%	1
30–50%	2
51–70%	3
71–100%	4

TABLE 4.10
PERMISSIBLE DAY & NIGHTTIME THERMAL COMFORT TEMPERATURE RANGES

HUMIDITY GROUP DAY	AMT > 20 °C		AMT BETWEEN 15 to 20 °C		AMT < 15 °C	
	NIGHT	DAY	NIGHT	DAY	NIGHT	DAY
1	26 to 34	17 to 25	23 to 32	14 to 23	21 to 30	12 to 21
2	25 to 31	17 to 24	22 to 30	14 to 22	20 to 27	12 to 20
3	23 to 29	17 to 24	21 to 28	14 to 21	19 to 26	12 to 19
4	22 to 27	17 to 21	20 to 25	14 to 20	18 to 24	12 to 18

In Table 4 (Table 4.17) we compare the monthly combinations of the thermal stress conditions, Humidity Group, and monthly mean temperature range with the conditions identified in Table 4.11. From these comparisons we can see that for the six months from May through October, *air movement is essential for maintaining thermal comfort;* and for the three months from November through January, *air movement is recommended.* Rain protection is warranted for June and September (although this factor is not strictly a need for establishing occupant thermal comfort). Also, we can see that no arid climate conditions or cold-season problems exist for Miami.

For Table 5 (Table 4.18) the numbers that should be inserted in Row 5.1 are, respectively, 6, 3, 2, 0, 0, and 0 (as these are the numbers listed in the *Totals* column of Table 4.17). Comparing each of the six boxes in Row 5.1 with each of the six columns underneath the 5.1 boxes produces the encircled matches shown in Table 4.18. Now, going row-by-row down Table 4.18, Row 5.2 has a satisfaction condition fulfilled (i.e., the one number in Row 5.2 is circled).[18] But Row 5.4 does not (because there are two boxes in Row 5.4 with *printed* numbers in them, and only the numbers in one of these boxes is encircled). Similar to the Row 5.2 situation, Rows 5.6, 5.8, 5.13, 5.16, and 5.18 also have satisfaction conditions fulfilled. Rows 5.9, 5.11, and 5.14 are each similar to the Row 5.4

TABLE 4.11

CRITERIA FOR ASSESSING THE EXTENT OF THE THERMAL STRESS
(for use with the Mahoney Tables, Tables 4.5–4.10)

For any month which meets any of the following criteria sets,

place a checkmark in the corresponding box (i.e., month vs. row)

FOR ROW H1

- If the "daytime thermal stress" = H and the humidity group = 4

or

- If the "daytime thermal stress" = H and the humidity group = 2 or 3 and the mean monthly temperature range < 10 °C (18 °F)

FOR ROW H2

- If the "daytime thermal stress" is within the comfort range and the humidity group = 4

FOR ROW H3

- If the "monthly rainfall" > or = 200 mm (8 inches)

FOR ROW A1

- If the "humidity group" = 1, 2, or 3 and the mean monthly temperature range > 10 °C (18 °F)

FOR ROW A2

- If the "nighttime thermal stress" = H and the "humidity group" = 1 or 2

or

- If the "daytime thermal stress" = H and the "humidity group" = 1 or 2 and the monthly mean temperature range > 10 °C (18 °F)

FOR ROW A3

- If the "daytime thermal stress" = C

TABLE 4.12

CONDITIONS FOR WHICH SATISFACTIONS EXIST FOR MAHONEY TABLES 5 & 6

SATISFACTIONS are identified when either of the TWO following conditions is met:

    (a) If there is only one box in any row that has a printed number in it and that number is (circled;)

  or

    (b) If there are two boxes in a row that have printed numbers in them and both of those numbers are (circled.)

Note: However, a Satisfaction is not present if there are two boxes in a row that have printed numbers in them and only one of those numbers is (circled.)

TABLE 4.13
MIAMI, FLORIDA CLIMATIC DATA

ROW	JAN	FEB	MAR	APR	MAY	JUN	JUL	AUG	SEP	OCT	NOV	DEC	ANNUAL
Mon. Mean Max. Temp	23.9	24.3	26.3	28.0	29.5	30.6	31.5	31.8	31.0	29.0	26.6	24.6	
Mon. Mean Max. Temp	15.1	15.4	17.8	20.1	22.2	23.7	24.6	24.7	24.3	22.0	18.8	16.0	
Monthly Temp. Range	8.8	8.9	8.4	7.9	7.3	6.9	6.9	7.1	6.7	7.0	7.8	8.6	
Ave. Monthly Rel.Humidity	72	70	70	67	71	76	74	77	78	76	73	71	
Ave. Monthly Precipitation	53	52	48	78	166	232	152	178	205	181	69	47	1462
Prevailing Wind Direction	NNW	ESE	SE	ESE	ESE	SE	SE	SE	ESE	ENE	N	N	
Ave. Monthly Wind Speed	4.2	4.5	4.6	4.7	4.2	3.7	3.5	3.4	3.7	4.2	4.2	4.0	

The data employed to create this table have previously been published in the document, *Climates of the States,* Volume 1 (Detroit, Michigan: Gale Research Company, 1980), page 158. Permission to reproduce these data has been purchased from the Gale Group, Farmington Hills, Michigan).

TABLE 4.14
FOR MIAMI, FLORIDA
Application of TABLE 4.3: AIR TEMPERATURES (MAHONEY TABLE #1)

ROW		JAN	FEB	MAR	APR	MAY	JUN	JUL	AUG	SEP	OCT	NOV	DEC
1.1	Monthly Mean Maximum	23.9	24.3	26.3	28.0	29.5	30.6	31.5	31.8	31.0	29.0	26.6	24.6
1.2	Monthly Mean Minimum	15.1	15.4	17.8	20.1	22.2	23.7	24.6	24.7	24.3	22.0	28.8	16.0
1.3	Monthly Mean Range	8.8	8.9	8.5	7.9	7.3	6.9	6.9	7.1	6.7	7.0	7.8	8.6

Maximum Monthly Mean Maximum =	31.8
Minimum Monthly Mean Minimum =	15.1
AMT = (Max Mon Mean Max + Min Mon Mean Min)/2 =	23.5
AMR = (Max Mon Mean Max − Min Mon Mean Min) =	16.7

TABLE 4.15
FOR MIAMI, FLORIDA
Application of TABLE 4.4: HUMIDITY, PRECIPITATION, & WIND (MAHONEY TABLE #2)

ROW		JAN	FEB	MAR	APR	MAY	JUN	JUL	AUG	SEP	OCT	NOV	DEC
2.1	Ave Monthly Rel Humidity	72	70	70	67	71	76	74	77	78	76	73	71
2.2	Humidity Group	4	3	3	3	4	4	4	4	4	4	4	4
2.3	Monthly Precipitation	53	52	48	78	166	232	152	178	205	181	69	47
2.4	Prevailing Wind Direction	NNW	ESE	SE	ESE	ESE	SE	SE	SE	ESE	ENE	N	N
2.5	Secondary Wind Direction												

ANNUAL PRECIPITATION = 1462

TABLE 4.16
FOR MIAMI, FLORIDA
Application of TABLE 4.5: COMPARISON OF COMFORT CONDITIONS & CLIMATE (MAHONEY TABLE #3)

ROW		JAN	FEB	MAR	APR	MAY	JUN	JUL	AUG	SEP	OCT	NOV	DEC
3.1	Humidity Group	4	3	3	3	4	4	4	4	4	4	4	4
3.2	Mon Mean Max Temp	23.9	24.3	26.3	28.0	29.5	30.6	31.5	31.8	31.0	29.0	26.6	24.6
3.3	Day Comfort Temp Max	27	29	29	29	27	27	27	27	27	27	27	27
3.4	Day Comfort Temp Min	22	23	23	23	22	22	22	22	22	22	22	22
3.5	Mon Mean Min Temp	15.1	15.4	17.8	20.1	22.2	23.7	24.6	24.7	24.3	22.0	18.8	16.0
3.6	Night Comfort Temp Max	21	23	23	23	21	21	21	21	21	21	21	21
3.7	Night Comfort Temp Min	17	17	17	17	17	17	17	17	17	17	17	17
3.8	Thermal Stress Day					H	H	H	H	H	H		
3.9	Thermal Stress Night	C	C		H	H	H	H	H	H	H		C

TABLE 4.17
FOR MIAMI, FLORIDA
APPLICATION OF TABLE 4.6: INDICATORS (MAHONEY TABLE #4)

ROW		JAN	FEB	MAR	APR	MAY	JUN	JUL	AUG	SEP	OCT	NOV	DEC	TOTAL
FOR HUMID CONDITIONS														
H.1	Air Movement Essential					X	X	X	X	X	X			6
H.2	Air Movement Desirable	X										X	X	3
H.3	Rain Protection Needed						X			X				2
FOR ARID CONDITIONS														
A.1	Thermal Storage Needed													0
A.2	Outdoor Sleeping Useful													0
A.3	Cold-Season Problems													0

situation and do not have satisfaction conditions fulfilled. Finally, Row 5.13 is the lone example in Table 4.18 (Table 5 for Miami), for which there are two boxes in a row with numbers in each and both numbers (or groups of numbers) are encircled. From Table 4.18, then, guidelines are offered for laying out the floor plan of the building; establishing building spacing; accounting for air movement; sizing the openings (or windows and doors) for the vertical envelope; choosing the basic compositions of the walls and roof; and accommodating heavy rainfalls.

In Table 4.19, a completed Table 6 for Miami is shown. The rows for which a *satisfaction* is present are 6.2, 6.8, 6.12, 6.14, 6.18, and 6.21. The recommendations suggested here include guidelines for the size and position of the openings in the vertical envelope; the need to provide rain protection and shading for these openings; wall, floor, and roof compositions; and carrying rainwater away from the building.

Thus, by completing this Mahoney Table analysis for Miami, designers and builders can determine fundamental guidelines about how a building should be organized to respond to the climate for that locale. These guidelines specifically focus upon passive

TABLE 4.18
FOR MIAMI, FLORIDA
Application of TABLE 4.7: SCHEMATIC DESIGN RECOMMENDATIONS (MAHONEY TABLE #5)

Row	HUMID			ARID				RECOMMENDATIONS
	H1	H2	H3	A1	A2	A3		
5.1	6	3	2	0	0	0		

LAYOUT

Row	H1	H2	H3	A1	A2	A3		RECOMMENDATIONS
5.2				(0–10)			x	Buildings oriented on east-west
5.3				11–12	5–12			axis to reduce sun exposure
5.4				11–12	0–4			Compact courtyard planning

SPACING

Row	H1	H2	H3	A1	A2	A3		RECOMMENDATIONS
5.5	11–12							Open spacing for breeze passage
5.6	(2–10)						x	Same, but watch hot/cold wind
5.7	0–1							Use compact planning

AIR MOVEMENT

Row	H1	H2	H3	A1	A2	A3		RECOMMENDATIONS
5.8	(3–12)						x	Rooms single-banked, provide
5.9	1–2			0–5				openings for wind passage
5.10	1–2			6–12				Double-banked rooms w/temporary
5.11	0	2–12						means for wind passage
5.12	0	0–1						No wind passage required

OPENINGS

Row	H1	H2	H3	A1	A2	A3		RECOMMENDATIONS
5.13				(0–1)		(0)	x	Big openings, 40–80% of N & S walls
5.14				11–12		0–1		Very small openings, 10–20% of walls
5.15		All other conditions						Medium-sized openings, 20–40%

WALLS

Row	H1	H2	H3	A1	A2	A3		RECOMMENDATIONS
5.16				(0–2)			x	Low mass; no insulation required
5.17				3–12				High mass or well-insulated

ROOFS

Row	H1	H2	H3	A1	A2	A3		RECOMMENDATIONS
5.18				(0–5)			x	Low mass and well-insulated
5.19				6–12				High mass or well-insulated

OUTDOOR SLEEPING

Row	H1	H2	H3	A1	A2	A3		RECOMMENDATIONS
5.20					2–12			Provide outdoor sleeping space

RAIN PROTECTION

Row	H1	H2	H3	A1	A2	A3		RECOMMENDATIONS
5.21			3–12					Protect from heavy rainfall

TABLE 4.19
FOR MIAMI, FLORIDA
APPLICATION OF TABLE 4.8: DESIGN DEVELOPMENT RECOMMENDATIONS (MAHONEY TABLE #6)

	HUMID			ARID			
Row	H1	H2	H3	A1	A2	A3	RECOMMENDATIONS
6.1	6	3	2	0	0	0	

SIZE OF OPENINGS

Row	H1	H2	H3	A1	A2	A3		RECOMMENDATIONS
6.2				(0–1)		(0)	x	Big, 40–80% of N & S walls
6.3				0–1	1–12			Medium-sized, 25–40% of
6.4				2–5				vertical envelope area
6.5				6–10				Composite, 20–35% of wall area
6.6				11–12	0–3			Small, 15–25% of wall area
6.7				11–12	4–12			Medium-sized, 25–40% of wall area

POSITION OF OPENINGS

Row	H1	H2	H3	A1	A2	A3		RECOMMENDATIONS
6.8	(3–12)						x	Openings in N & S walls at body
6.9	1–2			0–5				height on windward elevation
6.10	1–2			6–12				As above, but including openings
6.11	0	2–12						in internal walls

PROTECTION FOR OPENINGS

Row	H1	H2	H3	A1	A2	A3		RECOMMENDATIONS
6.12						(0–2)	x	Exclude direct sunlight
6.13			2–12					Provide protection from rain

WALLS AND FLOORS

Row	H1	H2	H3	A1	A2	A3		RECOMMENDATIONS
6.14				(0–2)			x	Low mass (low heat capacity)
6.15				3–12				High mass or well-insulated

ROOFS

Row	H1	H2	H3	A1	A2	A3		RECOMMENDATIONS
6.16	10–12			0–2				Low mass; reflective; cavity assembly
6.17	10–12			3–12				Low mass & well-insulated
6.18	(0–9)			(0–5)			x	
6.19	0–9			6–12				High mass or well-insulated

EXTERNAL SURFACE TREATMENTS

Row	H1	H2	H3	A1	A2	A3		RECOMMENDATIONS
6.20					1–12			Provide outdoor sleeping space
6.21			(1–12)				x	Have good rainwater drainage

components of the building. However, by encouraging the careful selection of these passive features, the more efficient operation of the building is likely. Thus, the provision of occupant thermal comfort should be enhanced, and the subsequent reliance on active control systems should be reduced.

4.4.2 USING THE MODIFIED MAHONEY TABLES (FOR EXAMINING TEMPERATE AND COOL/COLD CLIMATES)[19]

Application of the Modified Mahoney Tables follows a procedure similar to the one employed for the Mahoney Tables. You begin by gathering climatic data about the intended building locale. Then, you record the data in the tables, perform some manipulations, and read off the guidelines for schematic designing. Modified Mahoney Table samples are shown in Tables 4.20–4.24. Note that these were constructed using *Imperial* units; a version using SI units is not available. The tables consist of five tables, the first three to be used for analyzing and summarizing the climatic data and the last two employed for generating design guidelines. For the last two tables, the next-to-the-last (Table 4.23) provides guidelines for planning the site and the overall building, whereas the last (Table 4.24) offers information for selecting envelope components.

4.4.2.1 Establishing the requisite climatic data The climatic data needed for the Modified Mahoney Tables include the *monthly* and *annual average air temperatures,* the *average monthly wind velocity* and the *prevailing wind direction,* and the *monthly "percentage of possible sun."* The best sources for collecting the needed data are those three documents that are cited in Section 4.4.1.1, although numbers of other sources exist and can be used.

4.4.2.2 Filling in the Modified Mahoney Tables The use of Table 4.20 (Table 1M) begins with the recording of the monthly average air temperature (in °F) in Row 1M.1. For each month subtract the monthly average air temperature from 60 °F and place the

---

TABLE 4.20
EVALUATION OF AIR TEMPERATURES (modified MAHONEY TABLE #1M)

ROW	JAN	FEB	MAR	APR	MAY	JUN	JUL	AUG	SEP	OCT	NOV	DEC	SUM
1M.1 Mon Ave Air Movement													
1M.2 (60°F − Mon Ave Air Temp)													
1M.3 (60°F− Mon Ave Air Temp)/5													T =

TABLE 4.21
EVALUATION OF WIND PRESSURES (modified MAHONEY TABLE #2M)

ROW	JAN	FEB	MAR	APR	MAY	JUN	JUL	AUG	SEP	OCT	NOV	DEC	SUM
2M.1 Ave Mon Velocity (mph)													
2M.2 Prevailing Wind Direction													
2M.3 Mon Ave Air Temp													
2M.4 Ave Annual Air Temp													
2M.5 (Ave Mon Velocity) /10*													W =

Note: * indicates including those months for which the mon ave air temp is less than 60°F.

difference in Row 1M.2. Where a monthly average air temperature is greater than 60 °F, enter a zero (0) for that month. Then, for Row 1M.3, divide the difference found in Row 1M.2 by 5. Round off the dividend to the nearest whole number and enter that number in the appropriate box for that month. Sum these *integer dividends* across Row 1M.3 to accumulate an annual total and enter that total value in the column headed by "SUM." This total is thus set equal to the parameter T.

For Table 4.21 (Table 2M), record the monthly average wind velocity (in mph) and the prevailing wind direction in Rows 2M.1 and 2M.2, respectively. From Row 1M.1, fill in the monthly average air temperatures in Row 2M.3. Note which months have monthly average air temperatures less than 60 °F: you may wish to circle those months. Also, include the average annual air temperature in Row 2M.4 in the column headed "SUM." Noting the monthly average wind velocities from Row 2M.1, divide the velocities for the circled months by 10. Record the dividend, including the first number to the right of the decimal (i.e., the *tenths* digit), in the box for the month in Row 2M.5. For the months when the monthly average air temperature was equal to or exceeded 60 °F, enter a zero (0) in the appropriate box for each of those months in Row 2M.5. Then, sum the values in the 12 boxes in Row 2M.5 and record the sum in the column marked "SUM." This sum is set equal to the parameter W.

The use of Table 4.22 (Table 3M) commences with the recording of the monthly average air temperatures that were initially used in Row 1M.1. Next, for the latitude of your specific locale, establish the monthly clear-day solar heat gain factors from Table 4.25

TABLE 4.22
EVALUATION OF SOLAR HEATING POTENTIAL (modified MAHONEY TABLE #3M)

ROW	JAN	FEB	MAR	APR	MAY	JUN	JUL	AUG	SEP	OCT	NOV	DEC	SUM
3M.1 Mon Ave Air Temp													
3M.2 Clear-day Sol Ht Gain Fac**													Lat =
3M.3 Percent of Possible Sun													
3M.4 Product of (3M.3 x 3M.4)													
3M.5 (Delta T) permissible***													
3M.6 (Delta T) actual ****													
3M.7 Months when (Delta T)per is less than (Delta T)act													R =
3M.8 Months when Mon Ave Air Temp is greater than 60°F													S =

Note: ** See Table 4.25 for solar heat gain factors

*** indicates (i) for single-pane glazing, $(Delta\ T)_{per} = (3M.3 \times 3.M.4)/44.1$
(ii) for double-pane glazing, $(Delta\ T)_{per} = (3M.3 \times 3.M.4)/25.8$
(iii) for triple-pane glazing, $(Delta\ T)_{per} = (3M.3 \times 3.M.4)/20.1$

and **** indicates $(Delta\ T)_{actual} = (60\ °F - Mon\ Ave\ Air\ Temperature)$.

TABLE 4.23
GUIDELINES FOR PRELIMINARY SCHEMATIC DESIGN (modified MAHONEY TABLE #4M)

ROW						
4M.1	Ave Ann'l T =	T =	W =	R =	S =	
						WIND PROTECTION
4M.2	Greater than or equal to 50 °F		0–7			Optional windbreaks* & vestibules
4M.3			8–10			Recommended usages of windbreaks & vestibules
4M.4			11–12			
4M.5	Less than 50 °F	0–7				Optional windbreaks* & vestibules
4M.6		8–10				Recommended usages of windbreaks & vestibules
4M.7		11–12				
						BUILDING SPACING
4M.8		< 29				May use detached spacing (especially if natural ventilation is required)
4M.9		30–39				Suggested attached or rowhouse configuration (along east & west elevations)
4M.10		> 40				Required usage of attached or rowhouse configuration (along east & west elevations)
						PLAN LAYOUT
4M.11				0-1		Single-banked floor plan needed
4M.12				2–3		Double-banked floor plan suggested with primary living spaces (LR/DR/Study) on south elevation; use rectangular floor plan with E-W axis to N-S ratio of 1.5 to 2
4M.13				> 4		Compact shape (cubical) & double-banked

* If in rural or suburban areas, use coniferous trees or fences upwind from buildings; if in urban areas, use attached or rowhouse configurations with narrow streets oriented normal to the windward direction (of greatest intensity).

TABLE 4.24
GUIDELINES FOR DEVELOPING THE SCHEMATIC DESIGN (modified MAHONEY TABLE #5M)

ROW						
5M.1	Ave Ann'l T =	T =	W =	R =	S =	
						FENESTRATION ASSEMBLIES
5M.2		0–9				Area determined by ventilation needs; use double-pained assemblies
5M.3		10–19				Area may be 20–30% of vertical envelope; use double-pained assemblies
5M.4		20–29				Area may be 10–20% of vertical envelope; use double-pained assemblies
5M.5		30–39				Two alternatives are reasonable: (1) Area=10–20% w/triple-paned assemblies (2) Area < 10% w/double-paned assemblies
5M.6		Greater than or equal to 40				Area less than or equal to 10% of vertical envelope w/triple-pained assemblies and night insulation (R-5 minimum)
						SHADING NEEDS (FENESTRATION)**
5M.7					Greater than or equal to 7	Appropriate devices are required
5M.8					2–6	Appropriate devices are recommended
5M.9					0–1	Appropriate devices are optional
						OPAQUE ENVELOPE INSULATION NEEDS (for floors, walls & roofs, in order)
5M.10		0–19				R-11***, R-11, R-19
5M.11		20–29				R-11***, R-11, R-30
5M.12		30–39				R-19, R-19, R-38
5M.13		Greater than or equal to 40				R-30, R-40, R-60

Continued on next page

TABLE 4.24 (continued)
GUIDELINES FOR DEVELOPING THE SCHEMATIC DESIGN (modified MAHONEY TABLE #5M)

ROW						
5M.14	Ave Ann'l T =	T =	W =	R =	S =	
						SOLAR HEATING POTENTIAL
5M.15				0–1		May be used on a room-by-room basis with equator-facing windows therein
5M.16				2–3		Solar heating is suggested w/east-west orientation for major axis; place most window area on equatorward elevation; area may exceed amount recommended under "Fenestration assemblies" above; night insulation suggested (R-5 minimum)
5M.17				Greater than or equal to 4		Solar heating is of marginal value; night insulation (R-5 minimum) required on all windows

** If fixed devices are used, then employ overhangs for equatorward-facing windows and fins for east and west-facing windows; variable devices (including blinds or drapes) can be placed on equatorward, east, and west facing windows.
*** If a slab-on-grade is used instead of wood-framed flooring, employ two inches of a foam board (rated R-10) or use the equivalent.

and record these values in Row 3M.2. From the climatic data set find the monthly percentage of possible sun present at your locale and enter these monthly percentages in Row 3M.3.[20] To find the monthly available solar radiation (MASR), multiply the monthly entries from Rows 3M.2 and 3M.3 together on a month-by-month basis and enter the monthly products in Row 3M.4. Anticipating the number of panes of glazing that you would employ in your fenestration assemblies (e.g., one, two, or three panes), use the equations given here to determine your (delta T)$_{permissible}$ on a monthly basis and enter these values in Row 3M.5, recording the values to the nearest whole number:

For single-pane glazing, $(\text{delta T})_p = \text{MASR}/44.1$
For double-pane glazing, $(\text{delta T})_p = \text{MASR}/25.8$
For triple-pane glazing, $(\text{delta T})_p = \text{MASR}/20.1$

The (delta T)$_{actual}$ is found by subtracting the monthly average air temperature from 60 °F (i.e., as previously found and recorded in Row 1M.2). Again, as for Row 1M.2, when any monthly average air temperature exceeds 60 °F, then enter a zero ("0") in the box for that month. The (delta T)$_{actual}$ is entered in Row 3M.6. Compare the values in Rows 3M.5 and 3M.6 on a monthly basis (i.e., (delta T)$_{permissible}$ versus (delta T)$_{actual}$)

TABLE 4.25
MONTHLY CLEAR-DAY SOLAR HEAT GAIN FACTORS
(for use in TABLE 4.22 [Table #3M] of the modified Mahoney Tables)

LATITUDE	JAN	FEB	MAR	APR	MAY	JUN	JUL	AUG	SEP	OCT	NOV	DEC
24	1670	1390	910	500	380	370	370	480	910	1340	1650	1740
26	1690	1440	980	540	400	380	400	530	970	1380	1660	1730
28	1710	1490	1050	580	430	400	430	580	1030	1420	1670	1720
30	1710	1530	1110	640	460	420	460	640	1090	1460	1680	1710
32	1710	1560	1170	700	500	450	500	700	1150	1500	1670	1690
34	1700	1580	1230	780	540	480	540	760	1200	1530	1660	1670
36	1680	1600	1280	850	590	520	580	820	1250	1560	1650	1640
38	1650	1620	1330	930	640	560	640	870	1300	1580	1630	1600
40	1610	1630	1380	1010	700	610	690	930	1340	1590	1600	1550
42	1570	1640	1420	1080	760	670	750	990	1380	1590	1560	1490
44	1510	1640	1470	1140	820	730	810	1050	1420	1580	1510	1420
46	1450	1630	1500	1200	890	790	870	1110	1450	1570	1460	1340
48	1380	1620	1530	1250	950	860	930	1160	1470	1540	1370	1240
50	1300	1590	1550	1300	1020	920	1000	1210	1490	1510	1280	1120
52	1200	1560	1570	1340	1080	980	1060	1260	1510	1480	1190	990
54	1080	1520	1580	1380	1130	1050	1120	1310	1520	1440	1080	840
56	960	1470	1590	1410	1190	1110	1190	1360	1540	1400	950	680
58	830	1380	1590	1440	1250	1170	1240	1390	1540	1370	830	570
60	680	1310	1580	1470	1310	1230	1290	1420	1510	1260	670	400
62	520	1230	1570	1500	1370	1290	1340	1450	1490	1160	460	180
64	280	1120	1560	1530	1420	1360	1390	1480	1460	1050	280	20

and record, in Row 3M.7, a "1" for each month in which the (delta T)*permissible* is less than the (delta T)*actual*. For any month when the (delta T)*actual* is more than the (delta T)*permissible*, enter a "0" in the appropriate box in Row 3M.7. Then, add the "ones" and "zeros" and set that value equal to the parameter R in the last column of Row 3M.7. Finally, for Row 3M.8, enter a "1" for any month for which the monthly average air temperature is greater than 60 °F (and enter a "0" for each of the other months). Add up the values in Row 3M.8 and set that sum equal to the parameter S in the last column of Row 3M.8.

Noting the values for the parameters T, W, and R and the annual average air temperature recorded in Row 2M.4, enter those values in Row 4M.1 of Table 4.23 (Table 4M). In the top portion of Table 4.23 select the annual average air temperature (that corresponds to your climatic data) and match the parameter W (found in Row 2M.5) with the alternatives in either Rows 4M.2–4M.4 or 4M.5–4M.7. Then, follow the row with the matched condition across to the recommendations column and read off the appropriate guideline. For Rows 4M.8–4M.10 (for the parameter T) and Rows 4M.11–4M.13 (for the parameter

R), match the parametric values (established in Rows 1M.3 and 3M.7, respectively) with the quantities listed in Table 4.23 (Table 4M) and read the guidelines.

For Table 4.24 (Table 5M) perform similar matchings between the parameters—T, S, and R—and the quantities shown in the columns of Table 4.24. Then, read off the related guidelines.

An example of how these Modified Mahoney Tables can be applied is presented in Tables 4.27–4.31, employing climatic data for Minneapolis, Minnesota (offered in Table 4.26).

TABLE 4.26
MINNEAPOLIS, MINNESOTA CLIMATIC DATA

ROW	JAN	FEB	MAR	APR	MAY	JUN	JUL	AUG	SEP	OCT	NOV	DEC	ANNUAL
Monthly Mean Maximum Temp	21	26	37	56	68	77	82	81	71	61	40	27	
Monthly Mean Minimum Temp	3	7	20	35	46	57	61	60	49	39	24	11	
Monthly Average Temp	11	18	29	46	58	68	73	71	61	50	33	19	45
Monthly Temp Range	18	19	17	21	22	20	21	21	22	22	17	16	
Ave. Mon. Rel. Humidity (in %)	71	69	70	64	63	66	67	69	72	70	75	75	
Ave. Monthly Precipitation	0.073	0.084	1.68	2.04	3.37	3.94	3.69	3.05	2.75	1.78	1.2	0.089	25.94
Prevailing Wind Direction	NW	NW	NW	NW	SE	SE	S	SE	S	SE	NW	NW	
Ave. Monthly Wind Speed	10.4	10.5	11.3	12.2	11.2	10.4	9.3	9.1	9.9	10.4	10.9	10.1	
Percentage of Possible Sun	51	57	54	55	58	63	70	67	61	57	39	40	

The data employed to create this table have previously been published in the document, *Climates of the States*, Volume 1 (Detroit, Michigan: Gale Research Company, 1980), page 403. Permission to reproduce these data has been purchased from the Gale Group, Farmington Hills, Michigan).

Note that the temperature data are expressed in degrees Fahrenheit, the precipitation in inches, and the wind speed in mph.

TABLE 4.27
FOR MINNEAPOLIS, MINNESOTA
Application of TABLE 4.20: EVALUATION OF AIR TEMPERATURES
(modified Mahoney Table #1M)

ROW	JAN	FEB	MAR	APR	MAY	JUN	JUL	AUG	SEP	OCT	NOV	DEC	SUM
1M.1 Mon Ave Air Temp	11	18	29	46	58	68	73	71	61	50	33	19	
1M.2 (60°F − Mon Ave Air Temp)	49	42	31	14	2					10	27	41	
1M.3 (60°F − Mon Ave Air Temp)/5	10	8	6	3	1					2	5	8	T = 43

TABLE 4.28
FOR MINNEAPOLIS, MINNESOTA
Application of TABLE 4.21: EVALUATION OF WIND PRESSURES
(modified MAHONEY TABLE #2M)

ROW	JAN	FEB	MAR	APR	MAY	JUN	JUL	AUG	SEP	OCT	NOV	DEC	SUM
2M.1 Ave Mon Velocity (mph)	10.4	10.5	11.3	12.2	11.2	10.4	9.3	9.1	9.9	10.4	10.9	10.1	
2M.2 Prevailing Wind Direction	NW	NW	NW	NW	SE	SE	S	SE	S	SE	NW	NW	
2M.3 Mon Ave Air Temp	11	18	29	46	58	68	73	71	61	50	33	19	
2M.4 Ave Annual Air Temp					45	45							
2M.5 (Ave Mon Velocity Temp) /10 *	1.0	1.0	1.1	1.2	1.1					1.0	1.1	1.0	W = 8.5

Note: * indicates including those months for which the mon ave air temp is less than 60 °F.

TABLE 4.29
FOR MINNEAPOLIS, MINNESOTA
Application for TABLE 4.22: EVALUATION OF SOLAR HEATING POTENTIAL
(modified Mahoney Table #3M)

ROW	JAN	FEB	MAR	APR	MAY	JUN	JUL	AUG	SEP	OCT	NOV	DEC	SUM
3M.1 Mon Ave Air Temp	11	18	29	46	58	68	73	71	61	50	33	19	LAT = 45N
3M.2 Clear-day Sol Ht Gain Fac**	1480	1635	1485	1170	855	760	840	1080	1435	1575	1480	1380	
3M.3 Percent of Possible Sun	51%	57%	54%	55%	58%	63%	70%	67%	61%	57%	39%	40%	
3M.4 Product of (3M.3 x 3M.4)	755	932	802	644	496	479	588	724	875	898	577	552	Suppose triple-pane glazing
3M.5 (Delta T) permissible***	38	46	40	32	25	24	29	36	44	45	29	27	
3M.6 (Delta T) actual****	49	42	31	14	2					10	27	41	
3M.7 Months when (Delta T)per is less than (Delta T)act	X											X	R = 2
3M.8 Months when Mon Ave Air Temp is greater than 60°F						X	X	X	X				S = 4

Note: ** See Table 4.25 for solar heat gain factors

*** indicates (i) for single-pane glazing, (Delta T) $_{per}$ = (3M.3 × 3.M.4)/44.1
(ii) for double-pane glazing, (Delta T) $_{per}$ = (3M.3 × 3M.4)/25.8
(iii) for triple-pane glazing, (Delta T) $_{per}$ = (3M.3 × 3M.4)/20.1

and **** indicates (Delta T) $_{actual}$ = (60 °F − Mon Ave Air Temperature).

TABLE 4.30
FOR MINNEAPOLIS, MINNESOTA
Application of TABLE 4.23: GUIDELINES FOR PRELIMINARY SCHEMATIC DESIGN
(modified MAHONEY TABLE #4M)

ROW						
4M.1	Ave Ann'l T = **45**	T = **43**	W = **8.5**	R = **2**	S = **4**	
						WIND PROTECTION
4M.2	Greater than or equal to 50 °F		0–7			Optional windbreaks* & vestibules
4M.3			8–10			**Recommended usages of windbreaks & vestibules**
4M.4			11–12			
4M.5	(LESS THAN 50 °F)	0–7				Optional windbreaks* & vestibules
4M.6			(8–10)		→	**Recommended usages of windbreaks & vestibules**
4M.7		11–12				
						BUILDING SPACING
4M.8		< 29				May use detached spacing (especially if natural ventilation is required)
4M.9		30–39				Suggested attached or rowhouse configuration (along east & west elevations)
4M.10		(> 40)			→	**Required usage of attached or rowhouse configuration (along east & west elevations)**
						PLAN LAYOUT
4M.11				0–1		Single-banked floor plan needed
4M.12				(2–3)	→	**Double-banked floor plan suggested with primary living spaces (LR/DR/Study) on south elevation; use rectangular floor plan with E-W axis to N-S ratio of 1.5 to 2**
4M.13				> 4		Compact shape (cubical) & double-banked

* If in rural or suburban areas, use coniferous trees or fences upwind from buildings; if in urban areas, use attached or rowhouse configurations with narrow streets oriented normal to the windward direction (of greatest intensity.)

TABLE 4.31
Application for TABLE 4.24: GUIDELINES FOR DEVELOPING THE SCHEMATIC DESIGN
(modified MAHONEY TABLE #5M)

ROW						
5M.1	Ave Ann'l T = 45	T = 43	W = 8.5	R = 2	S = 4	
						FENESTRATION ASSEMBLIES
5M.2		0–9				Area determined by ventilation needs; use double-paned assemblies
5M.3		10–19				Area may be 20–30% of vertical envelope; use double-paned assemblies
5M.4		20–29				Area may be 10–20% of vertical envelope; use double-paned assemblies
5M.5		30–39				Two alternatives are reasonable: (1) Area = 10–20% w/triple-paned assemblies (2) Area < 10% w/double-paned assemblies
5M.6		(Greater than or equal to 40)			→	**Area less than or equal to 10% of vertical envelope w/triple-paned assemblies and night insulation (R-5 minimum)**
						SHADING NEEDS (FENESTRATION) **
5M.7					Greater than or equal to 7	Appropriate devices are required
5M.8				→	(2–6)	**Appropriate devices are recommended**
5M.9					0–1	Appropriate devices are optional
						OPAQUE ENVELOPE INSULATION NEEDS (FOR FLOORS, WALLS & ROOFS, IN ORDER)
5M.10		0–19				R-11***, R-11, R-19
5M.11		20–29				R-11***, R-11, R-30
5M.12		30–39				R-19, R-19, R-38
5M.13		(Greater than or equal to 40)			→	**R-30, R-40, R-60**

** If fixed devices are used, then employ overhangs for equatorward-facing windows and fins for east and west-facing windows; variable devices (including blinds or drapes) can be placed on equatorward, east, and west facing windows.

*** If a slab-on-grade is used instead of wood-framed flooring, employ two inches of a foam board (rated R-10) or use the equivalent.

TABLE 4.31 (continued)
Application for TABLE 4.24: GUIDELINES FOR DEVELOPING THE SCHEMATIC DESIGN
(modified MAHONEY TABLE #5M)

ROW						
5M.14	Ave Ann'l T =	T =	W =	R =	S =	
				SOLAR HEATING POTENTIAL		
5M.15				0–1		May be used on a room-by-room basis with equator-facing windows therein
5M.16				(2–3)	→	Solar heating is suggested w/east-west orientation for major axis; place most window area on equatorward elevation; area may exceed amount recommended under "Fenestration assemblies" above; night insulation suggested (R-5 minimum)
5M.17				Greater than or equal to 4		Solar heating is of marginal value; night insulation (R-5 minimum) required on all windows

4.4.3 SOME THOUGHTS ABOUT DETERMINING WHICH OF THESE TWO CLIMATIC ANALYZERS TO USE

For climates that are clearly *warm and humid* or *hot and dry,* the Mahoney Tables will provide the greater utility. From these tables, the user can obtain design guidelines that relate the nature of the climate with issues of occupant thermal comfort and building siting, layout, and envelope composition. Similarly, for climates that are largely *cold,* the Modified Mahoney Tables will best provide the necessary design guidelines. However, for climates that are generally *temperate* (i.e., neither particularly warm nor cold) *or* that demonstrate a wide variation of conditions between winter and summer, deciding which of these two climate analyzers to use can be difficult. As we have written previously, when designing or building in a temperate region, the primary feature of that climate is its variability. To accommodate such variability, you will need to provide a building form and a means of building operation that often must respond equally well to both the warmth and coldness experienced during the year. Thus, when analyzing such climates, it may be prudent to employ both sets of tables. Using both will identify what devices are most appropriate for the different climatic segments across the year (i.e., the two different table sets will show what types of environmental control are needed for the winter and for the summer).

Finally, with the goal of reducing the time you might spend in analyzing a climate, we will offer two suggestions that may increase your efficiency. First, we suggest that, for climates in the temperate regions (or that display periods of pronounced warmth *and* coldness), you first begin your climatic analysis with the Mahoney Tables, completing the

TABLE 4.32
ANNUAL HEATING DEGREE-DAY (HDD) TOTALS FOR NORTH AMERICAN CITIES

CITY	T&H CLIMATE DESIGNATION	ANNUAL HEATING DEGREE-DAY TOTALS (65 °F BASE) ASHRAE
Boston, Massachusetts	Dca	5634
Chicago, Illinois	Dca	6639
Cincinnati, Ohio	Dca	4410
Columbia, Missouri	Dca	5046
Dodge City, Kansas	Dca	4986
Richmond, Virginia	Dca	3865
Washington, DC	Dca	4224
Medford, Oregon	Do	5008
Seattle, Washington	Do	4424
Albuquerque, New Mexico	BSk	4348
Atlanta, Georgia	Cf	2961
Austin, Texas	Cf	1711
Denver, Colorado	BSk	5524
Miami, Florida	Aw	214
Mobile, Alabama	Cf	1560
Santa Maria, California	Cs	2967
Spokane, Washington	BSk	6655
Phoenix, Arizona	BWh	1765
Halifax, Nova Scotia	Dcb	7361
Edmonton, Alberta	E	10268
Ottawa, Ontario	Dcb	8735
Winnipeg, Manitoba	Dcb	10679
Vancouver, British Columbia	Do	5515

The data employed to create this table have previously been published in *1980 ASHRAE Handbook: HVAC Systems*, (Atlanta: American Society of Heating, Refrigerating, and Air-Conditioning Engineers, Inc., 1980), pages 43.2–43.7, and have been reproduced with the permission of the Society (© American Society of Heating, Refrigerating, and Air-Conditioning Engineers, Inc., www.ashrae.org).

SIDEBAR 4.4 Finding heating degree-day totals for various cities

The annual heating degree-days are determined accordingly: first, for each day of the year find the average daily external air temperature; second, if the average daily temperature is less than 65 °F, then subtract it from 65 °F, thereby arriving at the number of heating degree-days for that day; and third, then sum up the heating degree-days per day over the 365-day year. For example, if the average daily temperature for January 1st and 2nd are 34 °F and 28 °F, respectively, then one would experience 31 and 37 (or a total of 68) degree-days for these first two days of the year. A formula for computing heating degree-days can be written as follows (for the base of 65 °F):

$$\text{Heating degree-days/year} = \sum_{n=1}^{365} (65\ °F - \text{Average Air Temperature for day n})$$

Note that, for days when the average daily air temperature is greater than 65 °F, then there are no (or zero) heating degree-days for that day.

Two primary references listing heating degree-day totals are the two-volume document *Climates of the States* (2nd edition), (Detroit: Gale Research Company, 1980) and the *1980 ASHRAE Handbook: Systems,* (Atlanta: American Society of Heating, Refrigerating, and Air-Conditioning Engineers, Inc., 1980), pages 43.2–43.7.

analysis through Table 4 (Table 4.6). If the *Indicator* totals for Table 4 show the greater need for attention to "cold-season problems" instead of for providing for air movement or thermal storage, then the dominant feature of the climate is its coldness. In this instance we counsel that you cease using the Mahoney Tables and proceed with the application of the Modified Mahoney Tables. Alternatively, if the Mahoney Table analysis through Table 4 shows greater attention is required for problems of a warm or hot climate, then we suggest that you proceed through to Tables 5 and 6 of the Mahoney Tables (Tables 4.7 and 4.8).

The second general suggestion for facilitating analyses of temperate or variable climates is that, where possible, you ascertain the *annual heating degree-day total* for the location of the proposed building (see Table 4.32). If that total is less than about 3000 heating degree-days/year (using a base of 65 °F), the dominant conditioning need for the building will likely be cooling. Thus, the more useful table set for analysis of such climates should be the Mahoney Tables.

Section 4.5 | A BRIEF SUMMARY FOR CHAPTER 4

In this chapter we have discussed topics concerning weather, climate, climate classification, and, lastly, a means for analyzing climates, which can be used to generate information for schematic designing. Our premise in presenting this discussion is that a building should be designed and constructed so that its future occupants can be thermally comfortable and can operate the building efficiently. As we stated in the introduction to this chapter, we believe that developing comfort and efficient operation is dependent upon the securing of a good match between the comfort requirements of occupants, the nature of the climate to which a building is exposed, *and* the capacity of the building to respond to any discrepancies between comfortable conditions and the natural environment (in which a building is to be located). The means that designers and builders have for insuring occupant comfort and the efficient operation depend upon four groups of issues including how a building should be sited, how it should be organized horizontally and vertically (i.e., in terms of floor plans, elevations, and sections), what the composition of its envelope should be, and what finishes and furnishings should be employed within the building. How these issues are resolved during design and construction will affect markedly whether occupants will be comfortable and to what extent efficient operation can be realized. In Chapter 5 we will provide an extensive cataloging of ways in which buildings can provide for occupant comfort and efficient operation, when these buildings are placed in locales experiencing any one of the four major climate types (which we have described in Section 4.3.4).

ENDNOTES and SELECTED ADDITIONAL COMMENTS

1. Lamb, H.H., "The early medieval warm epoch and its sequel," *Palaeogeography, Palaeoclimatology, Palaeoecology,* I, 1965, pages 13–37. Lamb has also presented further discussion about these formulations in his book, Lamb, H.H., *Weather, Climate, & Human Affairs,* (London: Routledge, 1988); note pages 49–55, especially.

2. Basic goals and approaches, which may be considered during classification processes, have been discussed in the following articles: Johnston, R.J., "Choice in classification: the subjectivity of objective methods," *Annals of the Association of American Geographers,* 58(3), September 1968, pages 575–589; and Warburton, F.E., "The purposes of classifications," *Systematic Zoology,* 16(3), September 1967, pages 241–245.

3. One extensive listing of alternative classification systems is available in the book by Oliver, J.E., *Climate and Man's Environment,* (New York: J. Wiley & Sons, Inc., 1973); see pages 170–191. A second catalogue of classification systems can be found in the book by Barry, R.G., and R.J. Chorley, *Atmosphere, Weather, & Climate* (5th edition), (London: Methuen & Co. Ltd., 1987); see Appendix 1, "Climatic classification," pages 411–427.

4. The first complete presentation of this classification system was published in a book by Köppen, W., *Grundriss der Klimakunde,* (Berlin: DeGruyter, 1931). For a description about how Köppen developed his classification system, see the paper by Wilcock, A.A., "Köppen after fifty years," *Annals of the Association of American Geographers,* 58(1), March 1968, pages 12–28. Additionally, Professor Wilcock has provided an extensive bibliography that identifies other articles that have been written about the Köppen system and later efforts by more contemporary scientists to modify Dr. Köppen's system.

5. An extensive treatment of this classification system and systematic discussions of the various climatic groups appear in the book by Trewartha, G.T., and L.H. Horn, *An Introduction to Climate* (5th edition), (New York: McGraw-Hill Book Company, 1980). See chapters 7–12.

6. See Trewartha, G.T., and L.H. Horn, *An Introduction to Climate* (5th edition), (New York: McGraw-Hill Book Company, 1980), pages 197–199.

7. The City of Pensacola resides on the northwestern coast of Florida and experiences a *subtropical-humid (Cf)* climate; Boston undergoes a *temperate continental warm summer (Dca)* climate; and Seattle has a *temperate oceanic (Do)* climate.

8. For further discussion about precipitation variability, see the document by Legates, D.R., "A climatology of global precipitation," *Publications in Climatology,* XL(1), 1987.

9. These tables have been taken from the United Nations document, *Climate and House Design: Design of Low-Cost Housing* (Volume 1), (New York: Department of Economic and Social Affairs, United Nations Center for Housing, Building, and Planning, 1971). O. Königsberger, C. Mahoney, and M. Evans prepared this document.

10. ———. *Climates of the States* (2nd edition), (Detroit: Gale Research Company, 1980).

11. Landsberg, H.E. (ed)., *World Survey of Climatology,* (New York: Elsevier Publishing Company, Ltd). The initial set consisted of 14 volumes, the first of which was published in 1969 and the fourteenth in 1981. Recently, Volumes 1–3 have been issued under the title, *General Climatology,* edited by O.M. Essenwanger (Amsterdam, The Netherlands: Elsevier Scientific Publishing Company, Ltd., 2001).

12. Mueller, M.J., *Selected Climatic Data for a Global Set of Standard Stations for Vegetation Science,* (The Hague: Dr W. Junk Publishers, 1982).

13. We believe that the information generated by the careful completion of the Mahoney Tables can be a very useful contribution to the schematic designing of buildings. However, we recognize that the process is somewhat cumbersome. So, we suggest that it should be performed with patience. We advocate carefully reading of the directions in this section, studying the *worked* example in the following section, and then taking some time to think about the how the process relates climatic data *and* information about the conditions under which people experience thermal stress or thermal comfort. Only after these three steps have been thought through, should one attempt to analyze some climate to develop design guidelines. Lastly, let us emphasize that once you have performed an analysis for a specific climate, there should be no need to replicate this analysis for that climate (i.e., when you design another building in a locale having the same climate).

14. Page 91 of *Climate and House Design: Design of Low-Cost Housing* (Volume 1), (New York: Department of Economic and Social Affairs, United Nations Center for Housing, Building, and Planning, 1971). O. Königsberger, C. Mahoney, and M. Evans wrote this document.

15. Note that, when no number shows in any box, this "emptiness" should not be interpreted as a "zero." Rather, the "emptiness" should be read as an indication that there is no meaningful relationship between the number in the Row 5.1 box and that particular row.

16. Note, for Table 2, that the maximum relative humidity for the hours listed occurs at 0700 hours and the minimum relative humidity at 1300 hours.

17. The overheatedness during the nighttime hours for the months of May through October has little significance in this use of the tables for the Miami climate. Instead, if you were analyzing a locale with a hot, dry climate (perhaps Phoenix, Arizona or Baghdad), nighttime overheatedness would have particular significance. The occurrence of such overheatedness would necessitate providing outdoor sleeping spaces for the building occupants.

18. Again, note that the *satisfaction* conditions are described in Table 4.14.

19. These tables were developed by D. Heerwagen and have not been published previously.

20. For some weather stations outside of North America the "possible sun" presence may be described in terms of either *oktas* or *tenths*. Both terms relate to the degree of cloudiness present in the day sky. Oktas are an alternative way for describing cloudiness in terms of eighths. So, a seven-okta sky means that the sky was seven-eighths cloudy. To find the *percentage of possible sun* from such a value, convert the okta reading to a cloud cover reading in tenths and use the following correlation:

% possible sun = 117.58 – 106.6 × cloud cover (as a decimal fraction)

As an example, for this seven-okta sky, the cloud cover in tenths would be expressed as 8.75 tenths (or, as a decimal fraction, as 0.875). Thus, the *percentage of possible sun* would be found by entering this decimal fraction in the correlation equation and solving it:

% possible sun = 117.58 – 106.6 × 0.875 = 24.3%

Alternatively, a cloud cover condition expressed in tenths requires no conversion. For example, a sky described as having a cloud cover of 6 tenths is 6/10 cloudy or 60% cloudy. The decimal fraction value (i.e., 0.60) can be used directly in the correlation above to find the "percentage of possible sun." You might note that, even for a 10 tenths cloud cover, some solar radiation will penetrate through the cloud cover (although this radiation will be largely diffused).

CHAPTER FIVE

Guidelines and Other Approximations for Creating Buildings with Good Thermal Performances

5

IN CHAPTERS 2, 3, AND 4 we have asserted that if a building is designed and constructed to accommodate the local climate (i.e., by utilizing appropriate building components and operation strategies), then the achievement of occupant thermal comfort and efficient operation in the building will be greatly supported. We have described thermally comfortable conditions and the attributes of the four principal climates of the Earth. In this chapter we will characterize further these principal climates and offer more specific information about such environmental parameters as common air temperature ranges, wind and precipitation presences, and vegetative forms. We will also note other potential building design and construction problems that are traceable to the natures of these climates and that require attention when one creates buildings in regions experiencing these climates. Then, for the four principal climates, we will identify basic building forms and operation strategies whose adoption should provide comfortable and efficient occupant settings. Additionally, we will show examples of existing buildings that have been constructed applying these forms and strategies.

Let us make one essential admonition: our intent throughout this text is to present information about *passive* environmental controls that can manage the internal environments of buildings (and spaces immediately external to buildings). Thus, in this chapter, we will focus our discussion on the employment of such passive controls. In many instances for these four principal climates, the careful selection and implementation of passive controls can provide occupant comfort and efficient building operation, without relying on *active* control systems. But, necessarily, we are neither suggesting the avoidance of using active systems nor are we proposing that occupant comfort and efficient operation can be unilaterally achieved, depending strictly on the careful use of passive controls. Rather, our fundamental premises are that by applying passive controls well to the task of environmental control, one can achieve better comfort and efficiency (without operating active systems unnecessarily); for any climate, there are many occasions for which comfortable and efficient building operations can only be achieved with the judicious application of active control systems; and the successful long-term operation of most buildings (i.e., for comfort and efficiency) will require a well-balanced integration of passive environmental controls and active control systems.

Section 5.1 | DESIGNING AND BUILDING FOR THE WARM-HUMID CLIMATE

The *warm-humid* climate is a composite of three related climatic types: *tropical wet (Ar)*[1]; *tropical wet-and-dry (Aw);* and *subtropical humid (Cf).* The *Ar* and *Aw* climatic types generally occur on either side of the equator and extend outward from the equator to about 20° north or south. Alternatively, the subtropical humid climate is found in the latitude bands of 25 to 40° north or south. The fundamental characteristics of these climatic types are that they offer warm air temperatures, high humidities and extensive rainfall, a substantial cloud cover, slight air movement, and frequent periods of fog and heavy dew. Generally, the major challenge to maintaining thermally comfortable conditions is the overheated, quite humid natural environment. In regions where the subtropical humid climate exists, a relatively brief winter often occurs, and this winter period will also require some attention by designers and builders.

5.1.1   LOCATIONS AND CHARACTERISTICS OF THESE CLIMATIC TYPES

5.1.1.1   Features of the *tropical wet* climate   The *tropical wet (Ar)* climatic type is present at the equator and extends poleward to regions characterized by either reduced air temperatures or reduced rainfall. Generally, all of the regions experiencing a tropical wet climate are coastal or extend inward from a coast. The *tropical-wet* climate commonly occurs only at lower elevations, where the typical terrain is comparatively flat.

SIDEBAR 5.1 Preparation of the several climate description graphs in Chapter 5

The three horizontal lines for each rectangle within each climate graph represent *for a month*—from top to bottom, respectively—the average daily maximum air (dry-bulb) temperature, the average daily air (dry-bulb) temperature, and the average daily minimum air (dry-bulb) temperature; and each circle indicates the amount of monthly precipitation. The data used to create each graph have been taken from the book by Müller, M.J., *Selected Climatic Data for A Global Set of Standard Stations for Vegetation Science,* (Amsterdam, The Netherlands: Dr. W. Junk Publishers, 1982). Permission to employ these data has been granted by Kluwer Academic Publishers, Dordrecht, The Netherlands, and by Professor Müller.

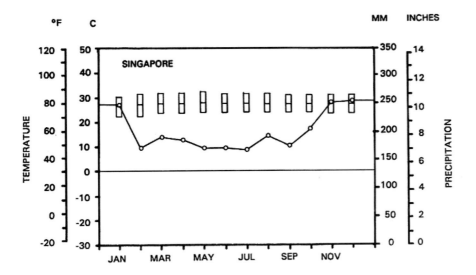

Figure 5.1 The climate of *Singapore*. The three horizontal lines for each rectangle within this graph represent *for a month*—from top to bottom, respectively—the average daily maximum air (dry-bulb) temperature, the average daily air (dry-bulb) temperature, and the average daily minimum air (dry-bulb) temperature; and each circle indicates the amount of monthly precipitation.

SIDEBAR 5.2 Positioning the sun in the sky

The sun will be at the zenith of the sky hemisphere (the point in the sky with which a line drawn perpendicular to a horizontal surface will intersect) at noon on June 21st for locations along the tropic of Cancer (23° 27' N) and at noon on December 21st for locations along the tropic of Capricorn (23° 27' S). So, for instance, all locations on the Earth south of the tropic of Cancer at noon on June 21st will see the sun from the north.

SIDEBAR 5.3 Land-sea breezes

During evenings in many coastal regions, when the land is warmer than the water, a sea breeze will move from the water toward the land: the convective transfer from the warmed earth to the atmosphere above causes the air just above the land to become more buoyant and rise, encouraging the more dense air over the water to move inland. Alternatively, during mornings, when the land has cooled down over night and is cooler than the adjoining water surface, a breeze from the land will move seaward. As explanation, the air over the water experiences a greater rate of convective heat transfer and rises, enabling the more dense air above the land to move out across the water surface.

Figure 5.2 The rain forest near Lago de Yojoa, Honduras, featuring numerous broadleaf evergreen plants.

The characteristic tropical-wet climate has constantly warm weather with abundant rainfall. Temperature patterns present for this climatic type include average annual air temperatures of about 25 to 27 °C (77 to 80 °F) with an annual temperature range—the difference between the highest monthly mean air temperature and the lowest monthly mean air temperature—of about 3 °C (5 °F). Common daily temperature maxima are 29 to 34 °C (85 to 93 °F), with daily minima of 20 to 24 °C (68 to 75 °F). The diurnal temperature range is between 6 to 14 °C (10 to 25 °F) (see Figure 5.1). Thus, the *annual* temperature range is small compared to the *daily* range, providing the basis for a saying that is much quoted by climatologists and inhabitants of these regions, "Night is the *winter* of the tropics." The second major feature of this climatic type is the copious rainfall. The annual amounts of precipitation vary from about 1750 mm (70 in) to more than 2500 mm (100 in). The rain tends to fall in heavy showers, rather than the extended day-long rainy periods experienced in areas further from the equator. In fact, much of the precipitation occurs in thunderstorms having short, but intense rainfalls. There may be as many as 250 rain-days per year in the regions closest to the coasts: a rain-day is any day in which the precipitation total is equal to or greater than 0.25 mm (0.01 in). Additionally, the time that rainfall occurs during a day generally is determined by the proximity of a locale to the ocean. If the locale is along the coast or on an island, the rainfall will most likely occur at night. If the locale is within the continent, the rainfall will most often happen during the afternoon.

Other important properties of this climatic type include the character of available solar radiation, the presence of cloud cover, and the behavior of winds. In the equatorial latitudes, solar radiation can be strongly incident on both the north and south sides of buildings. Also, the position of the sun tends to remain high in the sky throughout much of the day. But the cloud cover in these areas is commonly quite substantial, reducing the magnitude of the incident solar radiation. The most intense solar radiation occurs during the driest times of the year, when the sky is clearest. Necessarily, the periods when air temperatures are highest coincide with the times when incident solar radiation is greatest. Winds in these equatorial regions generally are light and variable (i.e., the rate of movement is slow and varies widely over any period of time). Areas substantially inland from an ocean usually have quite still air, whereas coastal regions experience more air movement (which is caused by land-water surface temperature differentials).

The other significant feature of this climatic type is the wide range of biological forms that exist here. The prevalent native biome is the *rain forest* (see Figure 5.2), which displays a huge variety of plants, insects, and animals. Ecologists say that there are more species of life forms in a few acres of a tropical rain forest than in the entirety of Europe.[2] The dominant vegetation is broad-leaved evergreens. The rain forest is composed of three principal components: occasional, very tall trees that stand well above the general canopy layer (reaching heights as great as 50 m (150 ft); the general canopy layer that exists at a height of about 25–30 m (80–100 ft) and is composed primarily of broadleaved evergreens; and an underlayer that is not dense unless there is a break in the canopy to let in enough solar radiation to enable more plant growth. Climbing vines wind among the trees making the forest denser.

The rain forest represents a major resource for the world-at-large not only as a treasure-trove of life forms, but also for its generation of oxygen for animal life everywhere on this planet. Unfortunately, significant areas of the equatorial rain forest are currently being destroyed to enable increased agricultural development (to support greatly expanding populations). Because much of the nutrients present in the rain forest are trapped in the vegetation, when it is removed, the remaining nutrient quantities are small. Consequently, newly converted areas have proved comparatively poor for agriculture (unless major

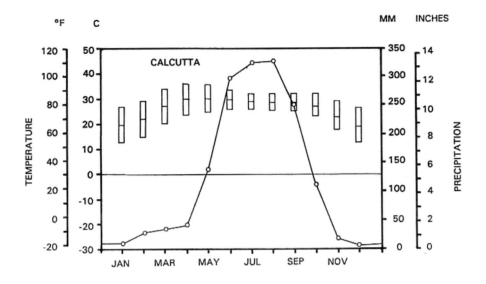

Figure 5.3 The climate of *Calcutta*.

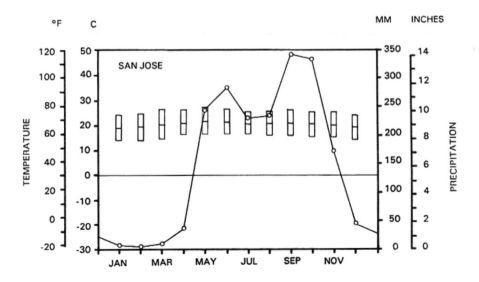

Figure 5.4 The climate of *San Jose, Costa Rica*.

nutrient sources are added). Appreciable areas of these once richly forested lands are becoming barren wastes, approximating deserts. There is even some evidence that the regional climates in these newly wasted areas are beginning to change in response to the destruction of rain forest vegetation.

5.1.1.2   Features of the *tropical wet-and-dry* climate   The *tropical wet-and-dry* climate is present in regions adjacent to those containing the *tropical wet* climate. The tropical wet-and-dry climate is found in bands running from about 5–10° from the equator to 15–20° north or south. Whereas the *tropical wet* climate tends to be found along coastal regions or on islands, the tropical-wet-and-dry climate tends to be present within the continents. Also, the tropical wet-and-dry climate can be found in more elevated regions, occurring in uplands at altitudes of 600 m (2000 ft) or higher.

The principal differences between the tropical wet and the tropical wet-and-dry climates are that the wet-and-dry climate shows greater variation in monthly average temperatures and month-to-month precipitation amounts. For this climatic type a distinct dry season occurs during which hardly more than trace amounts of rain falls each month for periods of between three to six months. Alternatively, rainfall during the wet season (generally, of six to eight months duration) will average 100–300 mm (4–12 in) per month. The annual total for this climatic type usually range from about 1000–1500 mm (40–60 in). The cloud cover patterns follow the rainfall with abundant cloud cover during the wet season and clear skies during the dry. Monthly patterns of air temperature are inextricably linked to this cloud cover and the accompanying rainfall. The average monthly temperatures vary across the year from 3 to 8 °C (5 to 15 °F), with the warmest months occurring toward the end of the dry season. The diurnal temperature variations differ substantially between the dry and wet seasons (6.7 to 8.3 °C [12 to 15 °F] for the wet season and 14 to 16.7 °C [25 to 30 °F] for the dry. So, for the dry season, monthly mean maximum temperatures can be as high as 40 °C (105 °F) with corresponding monthly mean minimum temperatures as low as 13 to 16 °C (55 to 60 °F). The relative humidity will be high during the rainy season (between 65 and 85 percent) and much lower during the dry season (25 to 35 percent). Finally, the dry season commonly occurs during the winter and the wet season during the summer (see Figures 5.3 and 5.4).

Figure 5.5 The savanna viewed from the air during the *dry* season (near Amboseli, Kenya).

The principal biome for the tropical wet-and-dry climate is the *savanna,* which consists of grasslands with occasional groups of trees or individual trees (see Figures 5.5 and 5.6). The numbers of species on the savanna are much smaller than are present in the rain forest. In fact, Odum reports that frequently single species of grass or trees will dominate large areas.[3] The savanna, however, is home to many animals. Among the grazing animals are the elephant, zebra, giraffe, gnu, and various species of antelope. The predatory animals include the lion, tiger, cheetah, and hyena.

Figure 5.6 The savanna viewed from the air during the wet season (Kenya).

5.1.1.3   Features of the *subtropical humid* climate   Similar to the *tropical wet-and-dry* climatic type, the *subtropical humid* climate displays a seasonality. For the *tropical wet-and-dry* climate, this seasonality is displayed in the substantial variation in the monthly amounts of rainfall. In regions of the subtropical humid climate, the principal variation is the shift in temperature levels. Generally, there is a warm period lasting six to eight months. But a brief winter will also exist and have air temperatures that are considerably cooler than those experienced during the sustained warm period. This climatic type exhibits high humidities year-round, thus demonstrating a principal connection to the tropical wet and tropical wet-and-dry climates. Rainfall is fairly evenly spread throughout the year, although the summers tend to have relatively more and the winters relatively less.

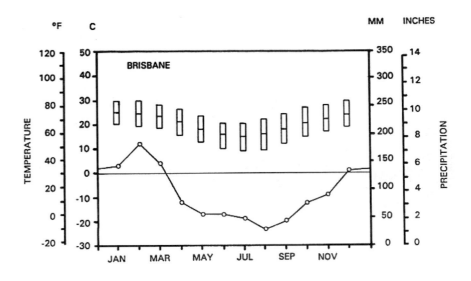

Figure 5.7 The climate of *Brisbane, Queensland, Australia.*

Regions having a subtropical humid climate generally are found on the southeastern sides of continents in the latitude range of 25° to 35° north or south. These areas are coastal, although this climate can stretch inland as much as 1000 to 1250 km (about 600 to 800 miles) from the coast. Generally, west of regions with this subtropical humid climate is the *semiarid* or *steppe (BS)* climatic type. As such, the subtropical humid climate separates the semiarid climate from large bodies of water. There are, however, two exceptions to the observation that a semiarid climate will exist westward of a subtropical humid climate. These exceptions occur where a subtropical humid climate is present on an island (e.g., Japan and the northern island of New Zealand). In these instances no semiarid climate will be adjacent. The principal distinction between the subtropical humid and semiarid climates is that the latter experiences about half as much rainfall annually as the former. Commonly, regions of *temperate* climates *(Dc and Do)* will exist poleward of the subtropical humid climate. These temperate climates are cooler and drier than the subtropical humid type.

The principal characteristic of the subtropical humid climate is that it displays a summer of warmth and high humidities similar to the tropical wet climate. The mean annual air temperatures vary between approximately 16 to 22 °C (from about 60 °F to the low 70's), with annual temperature ranges spanning from about 11 to 22 °C (20 to 40 °F). The monthly mean maximum air temperature is usually about 32 °C (90 °F), but for some locales within the subtropical humid climate the monthly mean maximum air temperature may be as low as about 25 °C (or the high 70's in °F). The monthly mean minimum air temperature will be anywhere from just about freezing to 6–8 °C (the middle to high 40's) (see Figure 5.7). The relative humidity in the subtropical humid regions is uniformly high throughout the year. The range of annual mean relative humidities for this climate is from the high 60's to about 80 percent. Many cities in these regions show monthly mean relative humidity values varying from about 65 percent to about 85 percent, thus demonstrating the high humidities present for this climatic type. Precipitation rates can total as much as 2000 mm/year (80 in/year) for some locales, but commonly the more typical amount is about 1000 to 1250 mm/year (40 to 50 in/year). Summers tend to be wetter than winters. The typical rainfall, particularly during the warmer portion of the year, is intense but of limited duration. Two remarkable weather phenomena that are present in southeastern North America and, also, along coastal China and southern Japan are the hurricane and the typhoon, respectively. These very intense storms provide rainfall rates and wind speeds that are grossly atypical. Further, because of the severity of these storms, building design and construction in affected regions must provide special treatments to safeguard life and property.

The mature biome native to subtropical humid regions is the *temperate deciduous forest*.[4] This form consists of both hard and softwood trees, shrubs, and groundcovers. The temperate forests of the southeastern United States and eastern Asia, where existent, have the greatest numbers of species of plants and animals outside of the tropical forests.[5] However, many areas throughout the world that display this subtropical humid climate are heavily populated. Consequently, forested lands in these areas have been greatly exploited, and present biomes seldom represent mature states. Further, in addition to mankind's exploitation of the deciduous forest for its useful products, the vegetation is subject to destruction by fire, resulting from both natural and human initiation.

5.1.2   CHALLENGES AND PROBLEMS FOR HUMAN OCCUPANCY IN THESE CLIMATIC TYPES

In Chapter 3 we identified four environmental and four personal parameters that affect the maintenance of occupant thermal comfort. The environmental parameters were the temperature of the air around the occupant; the *net* radiant exchange rate between the occupant and the surroundings; the relative humidity; and the rate of air movement around the occupant. The two important personal parameters were the activity rate of the occupant and the insulation value of the occupant's clothing ensemble. As we stated in Chapter 1, two fundamental roles for buildings are that they should provide for occupant comfort and should operate efficiently. In the following section (5.1.3) we will identify a variety of environmental control devices that can establish thermal comfort and efficient operation in

---

SIDEBAR 5.4 The use of heating degree-days to characterize climates

One indication of the characteristic temperatures of climates is the number of *heating degree-days* required. A definition of what are heating degree-days is provided in Sidebar 4.4 of Chapter 4. Using the base temperature of 65 °F, the American Society of Heating, Refrigerating, and Air-Conditioning Engineers, Inc., has calculated heating degree-day totals for cities in the United States and Canada. For cities that are located within the *subtropical humid climate* region defined by Trewartha and Horn, the range of heating degree-days is about 500 to 4000 per year (e.g., Brownsville, Texas has an annual total of 600, whereas Nashville, Tennessee experiences 3578). That both cities are located in the subtropical humid climate region is evidence that, despite the warmth and humidity of this area, regard must be maintained for winter conditions. For a catalog of heating degree-day totals for various North American cities, see Table 4.32.

buildings exposed to a *warm-humid* climate. However, prior to cataloging these devices, we will summarize a series of attributes of this principal climate group (and some related aspects of the natural environments affected by this warm-humid climate group) that could hinder the designer and builder from attaining occupant comfort in and efficient operation of future buildings.

The primary nature of the warm-humid climate is that it has air temperatures and relative humidities that are beyond the thermal comfort zone for much, if not all, of the year. The tropical wet and tropical wet-and-dry climates are warm throughout the year, and the subtropical humid climate is warm for at least a significant majority of the year. The tropical wet and the subtropical humid climates have high relative humidities year-round, whereas the tropical wet-and-dry climate has high humidities for all but its three to four-month dry season.

The warm-humid climate poses several other potential difficulties that may constrain comfortable building occupancy. These problems require resolution during building design and construction. For example, in the warm-humid climate, the sun is a major heat source when skies are clear. Solar heat gain can be substantial within buildings, particularly if direct-beam solar radiation is permitted to enter. Further, objects that are exposed to the sun and that exhibit high absorptivity for solar radiation will gain heat readily and re-radiate this gained heat to the surroundings (including people).

Winds in the tropical and subtropical regions, where the warm-humid climate group exists, tend to occur most often as gentle breezes, particularly when air temperatures and relative humidities approach their maxima. Rainfall is frequently intense and can be wind-driven, if the rains occur as part of coastal squalls (which display greater wind speeds than the more typical gentle breezes). Provisions will be needed to carry rainwater away from buildings. In these warm, moist climates insect presence is rampant and can cause discomfort and illness to people unless preventive measures are taken. Building materials (and occupants' personal effects) must be able to withstand biological attack (e.g., mold, fungi, mildew, and rot). Iron-based alloys must be adequately treated, or they will rust. Wood must be conditioned against termites. Additionally, jointure involving wood assemblies (e.g., furniture) must be allowed to expand (and contract) according to changes in relative humidity levels.

SIDEBAR 5.5 Direct-beam solar radiation

Direct-beam solar radiation is that component of solar radiation that is unscattered by the atmosphere (i.e., in contrast to the diffuse component of solar radiation, which is indeed scattered by the gases and particulate matter present in the atmosphere). The direct-beam and diffuse components comprise total (global) solar radiation. On clear-sky days (or even days with partly cloudy skies), the direct-beam component of solar radiation will be substantially more intense than the diffuse component. For such days special care may have to be taken by designers and builders to provide means for shading the interiors of buildings. Otherwise, the interiors of these buildings may be substantially overheated by the transmission of the direct-beam component, particularly through fenestration assemblies. Transmission of direct-beam solar radiation can also have discomforting visual effects for building occupants. For information about the effects of the direct-beam component on daylight presence in buildings (and some means for reducing these effects), see Section 9.2.1 of this text.

Finally, the warmth and humidity present in the warm-humid climate dictate building forms whose adoption can require personal and lifestyle adjustments. For instance, a common building response to the overheated, humid climate is to encourage the movement of air around the building occupant. To achieve good air flow the building envelope must be open. This openness, however, can work against occupant privacy, both visually and acoustically. Further, the largely open envelope makes it more difficult to secure the building interior from entrance by intruders. A third problem arises from the very bright skies present in these regions: the contrast between normal illumination levels within a building and external levels can cause significant discomfort for the occupant whose view field may include both interior and external images (i.e., particularly where the building envelope needs to be relatively open).

Thus, devices chosen specifically to respond to climatic conditions may lead to other difficulties for living and working. Inevitably, the resolution of these conflicts may require that trade-offs be analyzed in terms of their associated benefits and liabilities.

5.1.3   SELECTING BUILDING FORMS AND OPERATING STRATEGIES TO RESPOND TO THE WARM-HUMID CLIMATE

5.1.3.1   Fundamental operation strategies   Given the warmth, high humidity, and other related features of the warm-humid climate, four *passive* operation strategies require overriding attention: providing natural ventilation of the building interior; fostering shading of the interior from solar radiation; employing a lightweight building envelope (to permit the prompt transfer of heat during the overheated times); and waterproofing the building. The first three strategies focus on aiding the establishment of occupant thermal comfort. The fourth concerns maintaining the integrity of building materials and construction assemblies used in the building.

As the warm-humid climate presents challenges of overheatedness and high humidity, the primary means for creating thermal comfort—using natural (or passive) forces—is through evaporative cooling and, to a secondary extent, convective cooling of the occupants. Both of these cooling mechanisms can best be accomplished by relying on natural ventilation to move air around the occupants. Shading devices are also important because they inhibit the admission of direct beam solar radiation and its attendant heating of already-warm interiors. The use of lightweight building materials will minimize the

---

SIDEBAR 5.6 Providing winter protection for residents of the subtropical humid climate regions

An additional problem exists for designers and builders who create buildings in the subtropical humid climate region. The subtropical humid climate requires that most buildings make accommodations for the cold temperatures present during the short winter. Thus, whereas the predominant feature of this climatic type is excessive warmth and humidity, buildings must have provisions for dealing with periods of insufficient warmth. The principal responses for buildings exposed to the subtropical humid climate will be to have *convertible envelopes*—ones that can be open during the overheated portion of the year and closed during the short winter—and *internal heat sources*.

storage of heat gained from both exterior and interior sources over the course of the day. So, if heat gain and storage during the day can be controlled, then the nighttime can be relatively cooler (both to offer a respite from the heat of the day and, especially, to facilitate sleeping). Ensuring waterproofing means keeping the rain out of the building, carrying rainwater away from the building perimeter (and foundation), and choosing materials (or treating them) so that they are less readily affected by the high humidity and the associated degradation by bacterial and fungal rots (which commonly have accelerated growth rates in warm, moist environments).

5.1.3.2 Specific design and construction guidelines for warm-humid climates

FOR SITE DEVELOPMENT

(WH1) *Place buildings to establish a ready air flow through the buildings.* The principal means for enhancing occupant thermal comfort is through evaporative and convective cooling, both of which requires moving air past the occupants. For site design one must ensure that adjacent buildings have adequate space between them and that any nearby vegetation does not hinder airflow around the buildings.[6] Among the planning methods that can provide sufficient spacing is staggering buildings when multiple units are contemplated; not placing taller buildings upwind of smaller buildings (unless there is adequate separation); and where vegetation exists upwind from buildings (and is to be retained), raising the floors of the working and living areas off the ground.

SIDEBAR 5.7 Using building materials to store thermal energy (heat)

In Chapter 2 we discussed how heat is transferred through building materials and assemblies when temperature differences (or gradients) exist across materials and assemblies. An alternative behavior for common materials and assemblies is that they can store heat (i.e., to retain some of the thermal energy as the energy passes through them). This behavior is generally referred to as *heat storage.* Indeed, stored heat will tend to leave its place of storage after the temperature gradient has lessened. So, heat stored by envelope materials during a warm day could be released during the cooler night, thus continuing to overheat the occupants.

The primary material properties that determine the capability to store heat are the mass of the material and its specific heat. *Specific heat* is defined as the ratio of the amount of heat required to raise some mass (weight) of a material one temperature degree compared to the amount of heat required to raise the same mass (weight) of water one temperature degree.

Materials placed in a building that has greater masses or higher specific heats or both are better heat retainers (or, can store heat better). But, as most common building materials have specific heats of similar magnitudes, the primary determinant of the storage capacity of a building component is usually the amount of mass present in the component. Thus, materials and assemblies that are comparatively lightweight will be less able to store heat because they have less mass.

As examples we can cite using a wood-frame assembly versus a concrete block construction. The wood-frame assembly, by virtue of its much lower mass, will store heat less well than the concrete block and, therefore, will offer better thermal performance for the *warm-humid* climate. How well each assembly will withstand other rigors of the warm-humid climate (e.g., termites, rot, and so forth) is another significant question. Such competing bases (for choosing building materials) will often necessitate resolving trade-offs.

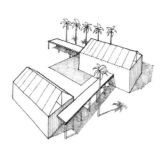

Figure 5.8 Covered walkways are provided between buildings to shade pedestrian movement.

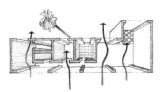

Figure 5.9 A single-banked floor plan offers the least resistance to air movement through the building.

(WH2) *Use ground cover that has low reflectance (but be careful of placing dark, high-mass materials near building envelope openings).* One should reduce the possibility of reflecting direct beam solar radiation into the building (off of reflective surface materials). Such reflections would increase the heat load contributed to the building interior. In addition, the placement of dark, massive surfaces under or near openings in building envelopes can lead to additional heat being admitted. The dark surfaces will absorb solar radiation, and then heated air will convect off of these surfaces and may flow into the building. Thus, black-topped surfaces (e.g., for parking lots) either should be placed underneath buildings at their ground floors (so that these surfaces are shaded by the buildings) or should be located so that the surfaces are downwind of the buildings or away from them altogether.

(WH3) *Provide covered walkways between buildings to offer both sun and rain protection* (see Figure 5.8). Because of the intense solar radiation on clear days and the high rates of precipitation during rainstorms, the comfort of occupants will be enhanced if covered walkways are included in site development.

(WH4) *Use vegetation for shading, both for activity spaces outdoors and for openings in building envelopes.* As an alternative to employing built forms for shading outdoor spaces and building openings, vegetation can accomplish the same function. But one must be careful when using vegetation in this manner so that it does not impede air movement into or out of buildings or across outdoor activity spaces.

(WH5) *Provide channels, catch basins, and related storm drainage devices to handle the copious amounts of rain that fall during storms.* Adequate planning for community or private storm drainage is essential when building in locales with heavy rainfall rates common to regions with the warm-humid climate. The requirements for these drainage systems will be determined by the amount of ground areas covered by buildings and paving for outdoors activities, walkways, and vehicular access and parking.

FOR BUILDING LAYOUTS

(WH6) *Orient the major axis of the building along the east-west compass axis line.* For the latitudes in which the warm-humid climate occurs, the sun moves across the sky vault along paths that place it quite high in the sky for much of each day throughout the year. Consequently, along the upper parts of these paths, direct beam radiation reaches the ground at angles approaching or at perpendicularity. Thus, it is relatively easy to shade the south and north elevations of buildings. But for early morning and late afternoon hours, direct beam radiation will be incident on the east and west walls at much lower angles, making adequate shading of any openings in these elevations more difficult. By placing the major axis of a building along the east-west compass axis line, using greater amounts of envelope openings on the north and south elevations, reducing openings on the east and west elevations, and using appropriate shading devices for the openings on the south and north elevations, solar heat gains for the building interior will be reduced.

(WH7) *Organize the floor plan of the building so that it is* single-banked *(i.e., one room wide)* (see Figure 5.9). A principal operating strategy for buildings located in *warm-humid* regions uses natural ventilation to enhance evaporative and convective cooling of occupants. Thus, a building should impose as little resistance as possible to airflow through it. To achieve low resistance the building should be *open-planned* (i.e., with few, if any, intermediate partitions). Buildings with single-room widths or widths composed of a single room and an adjoining circulation space (with little fixed wall separation between the room and the circulation space) are essential for insuring low airflow resistance.

SIDEBAR 5.8 Siting and organizing buildings for natural ventilation

---

A major trade-off situation may arise if the prevailing wind direction is not from the north or south or some reasonably close variant (i.e., some direction within about 45° of north or south). If the prevailing wind comes from, say, the west or east, then devices for shading east or west-facing envelope openings and for enhancing wind flow from the east or west through the building may operate in conflict.

Chandra has reported that when prevailing wind directions are up to about 45° from a line drawn normal to a vertical building surface, wind pressures on this windward side will enhance air flow into the building. However, when the prevailing wind direction is at an incident angle greater than 45°, wind pressures on this principal elevation will decrease to about zero at 60°. At incident angles greater than 60°, the wind pressure on the principal elevation will be negative, meaning that the wind will act in suction on this principal side. An instructive booklet that offers much useful information about how to organize buildings to foster natural ventilation has been written by Chandra, S., P.W. Fairey III, and M.W. Houston, *Cooling With Ventilation* [prepared at the Florida Solar Energy Center, Cape Canaveral, Florida], (Golden, Colorado: Solar Energy Research Institute, December 1986).

Regarding the sizing of envelope openings to foster natural ventilation, if openings on the windward and leeward elevations cannot be equally sized, then it is better to have the windward size be smaller and the leeward size be larger than vice versa. If the windward opening were larger, nonuniform air flow would result, leaving some floor areas with little moving air and others with gusting and turbulence. For further information about sizing openings, see either the book by Olgyay, V., *Design With Climate*, (Princeton, New Jersey: Princeton University Press, 1963), 102–112, or the paper by Chandra, S., "A design procedure to size windows for naturally ventilated rooms," *Proceedings of the Eighth National Passive Solar Conference* (J. Hayes and D.A. Andrejko, editors), (Boulder, Colorado: American Solar Energy Society, Inc., 1983), 105–110.

For further information about the use of wing-walls, see the paper by Chandra, S., P. Fairey, M. Houston, and A. Kerestecioglu, "Wingwalls to improve natural ventilation: full-scale results and design strategies," *Proceedings of the Eighth National Passive Solar Conference* (J. Hayes and D.A. Andrejko, editors), (Boulder, Colorado: American Solar Energy Society, 1983), 855–860.

Finally, two papers that describe the principles of stack ventilation and present specific design information have been written by Wilson, A.G., and G.T. Tamura: "Stack effect in buildings," *Canadian Building Digest #104,* and "Stack effect and building design," *Canadian Building Digest #107,* (Ottawa: Division of Building Research, National Research Council of Canada, August and November, 1968, respectively). Additionally, two examples of houses constructed to employ stack ventilation as a primary cooling mechanism have been described in the following articles: Alvarez, M., "Florida cracker house," *Fine Homebuilding,* No. 3, June/July 1981, 56–59; and Gerner, J., "The deja-vu house," *Solar Age,* 10(10), October 1985, 24–27. The form and operation of this second house, designed by Robert Ford, have been derived from earlier American South housing styles. Professor Ford has described the historical linkage between his house design and its predecessors in a booklet, *Mississippi Houses: Yesterday Toward Tomorrow* (2nd edition), (Mississippi State, Mississippi: Mississippi State University, 1987). Among the housing forms discussed in this booklet are the "dogtrot," the "beauvoir," and the Neshoba County Fair cabins.

(WH8) Create a building form that lifts the primary living and working areas off of the ground (see Figures 5.10 and 5.11). Air movement is better as one gets above grade level because the ground form and objects close to the ground (e.g., low vegetation, single-story buildings, fences, and the ground itself) offer resistance to airflow. By raising the building on columns and providing a first floor that is at least a few meters (or more) above grade, better natural ventilation will be likely.

(WH9) For residential buildings, place activities according to the occupants' need for thermal comfort. Two specific suggestions are appropriate here: first, locate the kitchen to the leeward side of the main living or working area; doing so will reduce the penetration of heat into other parts of the house from cooking and other food preparation procedures; and, second, locate the bedrooms so that they are exposed to minimal solar heat gain and enhanced air flow. To accomplish the latter, it is sometimes desirable to locate the bedrooms on a level above the primary living and working spaces and to shield the bedroom areas with extended roofs that provide adequate shading.

FOR ENVELOPE COMPOSITION: VERTICAL OR HORIZONTAL (SEE PAGE 127)

(WH10) Employ the following building envelope forms:

(a) *Create a largely open building envelope (i.e., one that will readily allow the passage of external air to flow through the building).* The open area should be between 40 to 80 percent of the vertical envelope for the tropical wet and tropical wet-and-dry climates and between 30 to 50 percent for the subtropical humid climate. However, for the subtropical humid climate, a means of closing off the open area is necessary for reducing heat loss during the winter. For all three of these climates large open areas should be deployed on the elevations facing into and away from the prevailing winds and at wall heights suitable for encouraging air flow across the occupants (whether sitting or standing).

(b) *Use wingwalls and related vertical protrusions adjacent to envelope openings to enhance airflow through the openings into the buildings* (see Figure 5.12). These

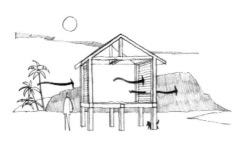
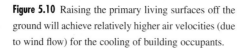

Figure 5.10 Raising the primary living surfaces off the ground will achieve relatively higher air velocities (due to wind flow) for the cooling of building occupants.

Figure 5.11 A Cambodian native hut.

devices are especially desirable in the subtropical humid climate where the envelope openings are incorporated into otherwise fixed, opaque parts of the envelope.

(c) *Use shading devices to minimize the admission of direct beam solar radiation through the envelope openings into the building interior* (see Figures 5.13 and 5.14). These devices can include either blinds or louvers that are placed over the openings and are operable (thus readily permitting air flow through the openings) or overhangs or awnings that extend outward from the vertical plane of the envelope.[7]

(WH11) *Employ the following building envelope materials:*

(a) *Use envelope assemblies with low thermal capacities (i.e., to minimize heat storage).* Massive assemblies with large thermal capacities are not suitable for buildings located in warm-humid regions as they collect and retain the heat of the day long after the peak heat has passed.

(b) *Employ light-colored finishes for the exterior surfaces of the vertical envelope.* Light-colored surfaces commonly absorb little solar (shortwave) radiation and mostly reflect incident solar radiation. Thus, heat transfer rates through light-colored building envelopes, resulting from absorbed solar radiation, will be kept low.

(c) *For the tropical-wet and tropical-wet-and-dry climates, provide jalousies or other adjustable means for covering envelope openings* (see Figures 5.15 and 5.16). Such adjustable window devices can be used *selectively* to keep out wind-driven rain or unwanted external noise and to offer privacy and security. These jalousies can also direct air flow upwards or downwards into the building.

(d) *For the subtropical humid climate, use window assemblies that are operable,* to encourage natural ventilation during warm weather and reduce heat loss during cold weather. To provide adequate resistance to heat loss during cold weather, employ double-pane glazing assemblies.

(e) *Equip all envelope openings in buildings for these climates with insect screening.*

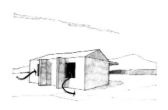

Figure 5.12 Including wingwalls alongside windows will aid the penetration of wind into the building (especially, when the direction of the incident wind is at some angle to the window other than perpendicular.)

Figure 5.13 Louvered slats (e.g., Venetian blinds) are particularly useful for shading vertical openings. Here, jalousies are supplied to cover vertical envelope openings, keeping out solar radiation and rain, but still permitting the ready flow of air through the building.

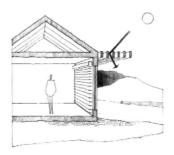

Figure 5.14 One alternative to the use of a vertical shading assembly is the horizontal overhang: this shading type should be particularly effective in regions where the sun is quite high in the sky throughout the year (e.g., between the two tropics of Cancer and Capricorn.) Using a partially open overhang will furnish good shading for the window underneath the overhang, as well as permitting warm air to rise convectively and pass through the open spaces.

FOR ENVELOPE COMPOSITION: HORIZONTAL

Figure 5.15 A multiple-story building in Calcutta with louvered, shuttered window coverings.

Figure 5.16 A very well-developed sloped roof appears on this 19th century meeting house built at Hanalei on the north shore of the island of Kauai. Note how the vertical envelope on the porch (or principal entrance) side of the building is set well back from the roofline.

(WH12) *Employ the following roof forms:*

(a) *Slope the roof substantially to permit adequate run-off for heavy rains* (see Figure 5.16). Also provide a suitable drainage scheme for roof run-off by using gutters and downspouts or ground troughs to channel water.

(b) *Provide extensive overhangs beyond the planes of the vertical envelope, both for offering rain protection and for shading the building interior* (see Figure 5.16).

(c) *Use double-skin or cavity roof structures to reduce solar heat penetration into the building interior* (see Figure 5.17). A cavity roof is a double-layered assembly, with a thermal break between the layers. The top layer, exposed to solar radiation, warms up and conducts the heat to its underside. Then, air passing beneath this topmost layer and above the lower roof layer captures the heat and carries it off, thus preventing it from entering the occupied space below the lower roof layer.

(d) *Employ stack ventilation for promoting air movement through building spaces in which wind-driven airflow is inadequate* (see Figures 5.18 and 5.19). Stack ventilation operates by the natural convection of warmed air. As air inside a building is warmed by internal sources (or external sources whose heat has entered the building), the air will rise. If there are suitable openings at the top of the space, the warmed air will leave, inducing air from outside the building to move into the building through openings below (e.g., usually through vertical envelope openings). Roof forms that can readily permit stack ventilation air to leave the building interior include *monitors* and *cupolas*.

(WH13) *Employ the following roof materials:*

(a) Consistent with the use of low thermal capacity vertical envelopes, *use roof assemblies that also possess low thermal capacities.* The primary framing materials for such roofs are either wood or steel, each treated against degradation by moisture and insects or corrosion, respectively.

Figure 5.17 Heat (from absorbed solar radiation) conducts through the upper layer of the roof, warming up the air space between the upper and lower layers of this double-skin, cavity roof. The warmth induces a convective movement of the air between these layers, drawing the heated air out and pulling outside air into this cavity.

Figure 5.18 Stack ventilation can be employed to bring outside air into the building: thus, air movement can aid the evaporative cooling of occupants, as well as the removal of heat gained through the envelope or produced by internal sources (e.g., people, lights, cooking apparatus, electrical appliances, and so forth.)

(b) *For the subtropical humid climate, use ventilated attics with insulation included in the ceiling above the uppermost-occupied space.* The use of insulation is strongly suggested—if indeed it is not required by local regulations—to minimize heat loss through the roof of the building during cold weather. Further, if solar radiation is absorbed by the external roof surface and the absorbed thermal energy conducts into the attic space, insulation in the ceiling assembly above the uppermost-occupied space will resist the downward transfer of heat into the living areas. The use of the insulated ceiling can thus serve as an alternative to the double-layered or cavity roof suggested in Guideline WH12.

(WH14) *For floor assemblies ensure that whatever materials are used will be adequately treated against the vagaries of these climatic types.* If wood is used in or near the ground, make certain it is treated against moisture, organic degradation, and insects. Alternatively, if steel is used, treat it for corrosion and rust resistance. For on-the-ground flooring, use concrete poured as a slab-on-grade.

FOR DEVELOPMENT OF THE BUILDING INTERIOR

(WH15) *Plan the building interior without using* full-height partitions. The building interior should be organized using *open-planning* concepts so that air movement through the building is not obstructed. Where intermediate partitions are required for privacy or security, they should be constructed of operable assemblies. These assemblies can be opened to allow air movement to pass through when the needs for privacy or security are lessened.

(WH16) *Provide high ceilings in occupied spaces.* These high ceilings will allow warmed air to rise toward the upper part of the spaces and will generally improve air movement throughout rooms. Openings in the upper walls should also be provided to enable warmed air to exit the space (see Figure 5.19).

(WH17) *Use furniture constructed to withstand the warmth and high humidity common to the warm-humid climate.*
   (a) *Wood furniture must be detailed to allow for substantial expansion and contraction,* in response to changes in humidity levels in the surrounding air.
   (b) *Furniture for occupants to sit on or lie in should be constructed of webbed or woven straps* (i.e., instead of using continuous fabrics) to permit air to flow readily through the supporting surfaces.
   (c) *Sleeping spaces, in rooms where envelope openings are not covered with insect screens, should be provided with mosquito netting* (see Figure 5.20).

Figure 5.19 Upper wall openings in spaces with high ceilings enhance the stack ventilation of a building interior. Note that the rotating fan can aid the upward movement of the warm air. This building is an airline reservation office in Zihautanejo, Mexico.

Figure 5.20 Using mosquito netting will minimize the discomfort that sleepers can experience from flying insects.

5.1.4   FURTHER REFERENCES FOR DESIGNING AND CONSTRUCTING BUILDINGS FOR WARM-HUMID CLIMATES

An outstanding text that offers informed discussion and many interesting examples has been written by Maxwell Fry and Jane Drew, *Tropical Architecture in the Dry and Humid Zones* (2nd ed.), published by R.A. Krieger Publishing Company of Malabar, Florida, in 1982. Other good and useful discussions of strategies for building for these climates can be found in:

Evans, M., *Housing, Climate, and Comfort,* (London: The Architectural Press, Ltd., 1980).

Fullerton, R.L., *Building Construction in Warm Climates* (Volume 3), (London: Oxford University Press, 1977).

Königsberger, O.H., C. Mahoney, and M. Evans, *Climate and House Design* (Volume 1 of *Design of Low-Cost Housing and Community Facilities*), (New York: United Nations, Department of Economic and Social Affairs, 1971).

Königsberger, O.H., T.G. Ingersoll, A. Mayhew, and S.Z. Szokolay, *Manual of Tropical Housing and Building,* (London: Longman Group Ltd., 1974).

Konya, A., *Design Primer for Hot Climates,* (London: The Architectural Press Ltd., 1980).

Watson, D., and K. Labs, *Climatic Design,* (New York: McGraw-Hill Book Company, 1983).

Section 5.2 | DESIGNING AND BUILDING FOR THE HOT-DRY CLIMATE

The hot-dry climate represents a composite of three of the Trewartha and Horn[8] climatic types. The predominant feature of all three types is that they are *dry*. In addition, they have *hot weather for significant periods of the year*. The first two of the three types are the *arid* or *desert* type with hot summers (identified in the Trewartha and Horn nomenclature as *BWh*) and the *semiarid* or *steppe* type with hot summers (represented as *BSh*). The third type is the *subtropical dry-summer* category (represented as *Cs*). Regions experiencing this third climatic type have near desert-like dryness during the summer. During the comparatively mild winters of the subtropical dry-summer climate regions, there is somewhat more rainfall than is experienced for the semiarid climate.

The basic characteristics of these three climatic types include dryness (both in rainfall and relative humidity), hot summers with cool winters, clear skies, and hot winds. Rainfall is meager in comparison to most other climates. Significant variations are observed from year-to-year concerning *when* the rainfall happens and *how much* rainfall occurs. Rainstorms, when they take place, tend to be brief and intense. The amount of solar radiation reaching the ground in these regions is generally the highest worldwide. Winds are commonly brisk during daytime hours and result from convective movement of the atmosphere over hot ground surfaces. Because ground cover in these hot-dry regions is often sparse, windborne dust causes frequent discomfort for residents of these regions.

Dryness presents the principal challenge for occupants of these regions. Odum has written that there are two types of mammals: those that use water to regulate body temperature and those that do not.[9] The human being, among the former group, is poorly adapted to living in dry climates without environmental supports of various kinds. The primary reason for this poor adaptation is that the principal means of heat exchange between the human body and a hot environment is evaporative cooling (which is largely based on sweating). Because sweating involves the loss of body water, appreciable sweating in response to hot air temperatures can lead to dehydration, heat stroke, and, ultimately, death, unless the water can be replenished. Thus, human beings living and working in *hot-dry* climates need to regulate water loss and, when water loss is substantial, to match the loss with a corresponding water intake. So, in areas exposed to the warm-humid climate, human beings may find that they are uncomfortable. But they do not lack for any of the basic requirements for sustaining life. Conversely, in hot-dry lands, the shortage of water creates potentially life-threatening conditions.

Traditional settlement practices, particularly in the hot-dry regions of the Third World, have been founded on seeking out available ground water and then using it wisely. A common life pattern in these regions is *nomadism,* where people move from place to place in search of water, food, and grazing lands. Alternatively, agriculture in this climate is a high-risk venture because of the uncertainty surrounding the water supply. Populations wishing to sustain long-term settlements require a diversified economic base as a hedge against the vagaries of water supply and the often-tenuous production of food. Thus, any permanent settlement requires the careful use of natural resources and finely adjusted controls on the size of the settlement.

5.2.1 LOCATIONS AND CHARACTERISTICS OF THESE CLIMATIC TYPES

5.2.1.1 Features of the hot-arid and hot-semiarid climates The common climatological definition for the existence of these two dry climate is that the annual precipitation rate—water gain—is less than the sum of the potential rate of evaporation of ground water and the water lost by the transpiration of plants (i.e., the two forms of water loss in the natural environment). Instead, when the precipitation rate matches or exceeds the summed evaporation and transpiration rates, a humid climate exists. Trewartha and Horn point out that, in regions experiencing these two dry-climate types, there will be no constantly replenished ground water supplies. They further state that permanent, moving bodies of water (i.e., rivers) cannot begin in dry climate regions, but can flow through these regions.[10]

An alternative definition of the boundary between *dry* and *humid* climates was offered by Köppen and has since been simplified by Patton. Both scientists employed the amount of rainfall as the boundary condition and related this rainfall amount at some locale to the average annual temperature and the percentage of rainfall occurring during the winter at that place.[11] Thus, as the average annual temperature increases (i.e., basically as one moves closer to the equator), the amount of rainfall needed to sustain a humid climate likewise increases.

The amount of annual rainfall present in the *hot-semiarid* region commonly varies between 250 to 500 mm (10 to 20 in), although the amount can be as much as 750 mm (30 in) per year. A large majority, if not virtually all, of the rainfall will occur in a short moist season. This season is normally spread over a three or four-month period and may occur during either the hot or cool time of the year. The occurrence of the moist season is regular for a specific region or locale (i.e., it will occur at the same time and for about the same length of time each year). Alternatively, the *hot-arid* regions generally experience less than 250 mm (10 in) of rainfall annually. The months sustaining the greatest rainfall are frequently in late summer, although in some regions the monthly rainfall totals are similar across summer and winter months. However, despite when the rainfall occurs in both the hot-semiarid and hot-arid climates, the sky is generally clear, particularly during the summers. Rainfall, when it does happen, is characteristically brief and intense.

Air temperatures for both the hot-semiarid and hot-arid climates vary widely through the day. During summers, temperatures exceeding 38 °C (about 100 °F) are common with nighttime low temperatures being 14 to 17 °C (25 to 30 °F) *less*. The mean monthly maximum air temperatures usually are about 35 °C (95 °F) and the mean monthly minimum air temperatures are about 22–24 °C (72–76 °F). Winter temperatures range from mean

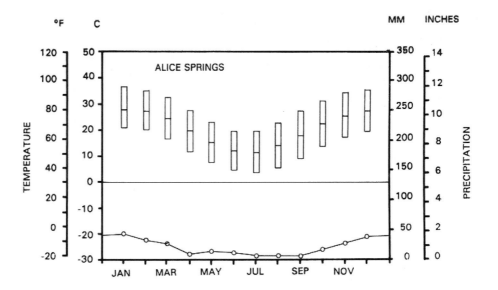

Figure 5.21 The climate of *Alice Springs, Northern Territory, Australia.*

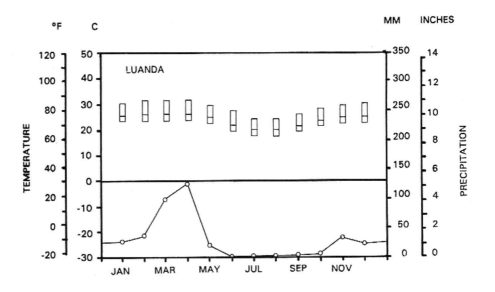

Figure 5.22 The climate of *Luanda, Angola.*

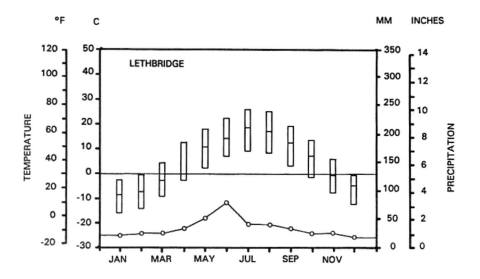

Figure 5.23 The climate of *Lethbridge, Alberta.*

monthly maxima of about 15 to 21 °C (60 to 70 °F) to mean monthly minima near or just above freezing (see Figures 5.21 and 5.22).

In the *mid-latitude* dry regions (cold-semiarid and cold-arid) the summertime mean monthly maxima are about 27 to 32 °C (80 to 90 °F) with large diurnal temperature swings over night. Winter mean monthly maximum and minimum temperatures differ widely depending on the distance a specific locale is poleward from the equator. For instance, the average daily high and low temperatures for January in Albuquerque, New Mexico, are 8 and −4 °C (46 and 24 °F), respectively, whereas these average temperatures for Williston, North Dakota, are −8 and −20 °C (17 and −4 °F). Both of these locales are represented by the same climate designation (as cold-semiarid climates). That both locales are considered to experience similar climates is an indication that the essential factor in describing these climates is the *dryness* (and not the differing temperature extremes) (see Figure 5.23).

The hot-semiarid and hot-arid climates are commonly bounded by the 20° to 30° latitude lines, north and south of the equator. The semiarid (steppe) climate presently covers about 14 percent of the surface of the Earth, whereas the arid (desert) climate accounts for another 12 percent. Trewartha and Horn characterize the existence of these dry regions noting three related factors:

(1)   The regions are generally within the interiors of large continental land areas, and often mountain ranges separate these areas from the oceans; both conditions make these dry lands distant from primary moisture sources;

(2)   The regions frequently experience high pressure systems, which reduce the ability of more stormy weather systems to pass over; and

(3)   The major wind systems do not reach into these dry areas (i.e., the lands are too far poleward to be affected by the equatorial trade winds, too far equator-ward to

be affected by the mid-latitude westerlies, and too far inland to be influenced by onshore and oceanic wind systems).[12]

Figure 5.24 This hillside was photographed in Tucson, Arizona in the early spring of a year (i.e., after the normally wettest months of the year, which usually occur in the winter.)

These three factors explain the fundamental causes of these dry regions. However, the combination of regional climate changes and the effects of human occupation on marginal lands (especially, the mismanagement of lands due to poor agricultural techniques and the destruction of native vegetation) is causing an increase in the formation of dry land across the Earth — essentially, as *desertification* — at a rate of 14 million acres per year![13] The recent famines occurring in East Central Africa are too-graphic examples of how fragile land can be transformed from being able to support its occupants to becoming a desert-like region capable of supporting little. There, poor crop management and the overgrazing of the land (the result of a human population ravaged by civil war) have dramatically altered an environment.

A profile of vegetation present in the semiarid and arid regions can offer revealing information about the character of these climates (see Figure 5.24). Examining the native vegetation (to see how it survives) can also suggest means by which occupants can respond to the dry climates. Fundamentally, there is a relationship between the amounts of rainfall and indigenous plant forms. The development of forests usually occurs where annual rainfall exceeds 750 mm (30 in). When yearly rainfall ranges between 250 to 750 mm (10 to 30 in), grasslands occur, although — if the rainfall is seasonally distributed — grass growth may also be equally seasonal. Below 250 mm (10 in) of rainfall annually a number of desert plant forms can successfully adapt to the dryness. These plant forms follow one of three basic growth strategies: they can exist as *annuals* that grow when moisture is available and "hibernate" during dry seasons; they can be *succulents* that take in and store water when it is present in the environment and then slowly consume the stored water during long dry seasons; or they can endure as *desert shrubs* that grow during moist periods and then shed parts of the plants during the droughts.[14]

Figure 5.25 This fountain and the lush, grassy lawns exist — in the September of a year — on the University of New Mexico campus in Albuquerque, New Mexico. Clearly, the addition of enough water and suitable nutrients to the soil and strong solar radiation from the cloudless sky enable healthy plant growth.

A key strategy for both plant and animal life in the dryness of the semiarid and arid lands is that an equilibrium must exist between the available resources and the population size (or, alternatively, the sizes of the individuals). If the population grows to a point where it exceeds the available resources, individuals within the population will die out until a balance is reestablished between resources and needs. However, when resources (i.e., particularly, water) are made available in sufficient quantities to permit vegetative growth, plant life can indeed abound (see Figure 5.25). Generally, if the soil texture and its nutrient presence are suitable for plant growth (or the basic soil can be improved accordingly), then the addition of water will enable dry lands to become greatly productive. A significant reason for this growth is that solar radiation is present over these dry lands in amounts greater than anywhere else on Earth. Thus, land along the Nile has sustained human occupation for more than five thousand years and areas around Lubbock, Texas and the Imperial Valley in California enable growth of significant quantities of cotton and produce, respectively. In all three instances, where adequate water exists, so, too, can successful agriculture. Generally, the only limitation on the continued growth of cash-producing crops — beyond the continued supply of water — is the sometime build-up of inorganic salts in the dry soils, which must be washed out of the soil periodically for plant growth to be continued.

5.2.1.2 Features of the subtropical dry-summer climate The *subtropical dry-summer* climate is present over a relatively small portion of the surface of the Earth. This type is primarily a coastal climate and is located around the Mediterranean Sea and along

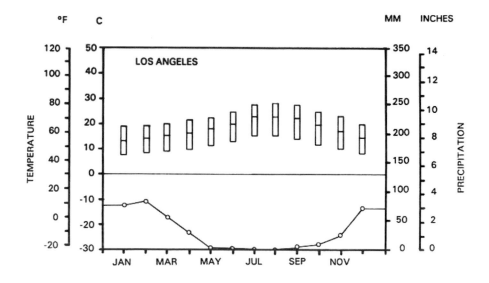

Figure 5.26 The climate of *Los Angeles, California.*

the west coasts of the United States, Chile, South Africa, and Australia. A number of major cities experience this climate, including Los Angeles, Algiers, Barcelona, Rome, Istanbul, Beirut, and Perth, Australia. This climate is located primarily between the latitudes between 32° to 36° N or S (see Figure 5.26).

The climate consists basically of dry, warm-to-hot summers and cool, wet winters. The warmest months have mean monthly maximum air temperatures of about 27 to 32 °C

SIDEBAR 5.9 Plant and animal life in semiarid and arid regions

For further information about plant and animal life in arid and semiarid regions, see the following books: Cloudsley-Thompson, J.L., *Man and the Biology of Arid Zones,* (London: Edward Arnold, Ltd., 1977) and MacMahon, J.A., *Deserts* (An Audubon Society Nature Guide), (New York: Alfred A. Knopf, 1985). Additionally, sections of chapters in two books provide good introductory descriptions of plant and animal life in these regions: Furley, P.A., and W.W. Newey, *Geography of the Biosphere,* (London: Butterworth & Co., Ltd., 1983), see pages 309–320; and Tivy, J., *Biogeography: A Study of Plants in the*

Ecosphere (2nd edition), (London: Longman Group Limited, 1982), see Chapter 14 and pages 363–374, especially. One further source of information about desert vegetation can be found in the journal called *Desert Plants* (published by The University of Arizona for the Boyce Thompson Southwestern Arboretum, Superior, Arizona). A special issue of this Journal, "Biotic Communities of the American Southwest—United States and Mexico" (edited by D.E. Brown), appeared as Volume 4, Numbers 1–4, 1982. This issue offers a comprehensive listing of plant and animal life native to that region.

(80 to 90 °F), whereas the coolest months have mean monthly minimum air temperatures of 4 to 10 °C (40 to 50 °F). The annual average air temperature in this climatic zone commonly falls between 15 to 21 °C (60 to 70 °F). The presence of freezing weather or snow is rare, happening perhaps once in a decade. The rainfall for the regions with this climate can range from approximately 380 to 900 mm (15 to 35 in) per year. But the most significant feature of this subtropical dry-summer climate is its six-month-long dry season. This dry season occurs between May through October in the Northern Hemisphere and November through April in the Southern Hemisphere. During the dry season rainfall is limited to less than one tenth to one-third of the annual total. Thus, areas around Los Angeles experience a total of less than 25 mm (1 in) of rain during the dry period. Similarly, cities like Haifa and Santiago report six-month totals of about 40 mm (1.5 in). Thus, a fundamental concern for human occupancy in these regions is the ability to withstand the desert-like dryness of these periods.

Finally, inspite of this sustained dryness, these areas are frequently regarded as prime locations for human residency and for such special activities as resort development. If sufficient water can be provided by irrigation, these regions can also serve as garden spots, affording highly successful agricultural ventures. With virtually year-round growing seasons (because this climate is generally frost-free) and abundant solar radiation, plants grow vigorously, as long as needed water is present.

5.2.1.3   Features of the cool coastal arid climate   One other climate for which dryness is the essential feature is the *cool coastal arid* (desert) climate. The cool coastal arid climate is present in only five somewhat limited land areas of the Earth: the Peruvian-Chilean coast of South America, the Mexican Baja, and three coastal regions of Africa. The areas encompassing the west coast of South America and Namibia in Southwest Africa are the driest places on Earth, receiving no precipitation at all for periods lasting as long as several years. The average annual rainfall in cool coastal arid climate regions is commonly about 25 to 50 mm (1 to 2 in). Water is present in the atmosphere, however, in the form of *fog,* which is a basic feature of this climatic type. Lima, Peru, for instance, receives about 0.5 inches of rainfall per year, but experiences fog at least 300 days per year.

People reside in these regions, but special accommodations must be made to deal with the extreme dryness. Plant growth occurs drawing upon evolutionary adaptations. Some plants harvest moisture from the fog, and others grow only when rainfall occurs (even if this means waiting for years between growth periods!).

5.2.2   CHALLENGES AND PROBLEMS FOR HUMAN OCCUPANCY IN HOT-DRY CLIMATES

To summarize the characteristics of the hot-dry climate group, let us emphasize the following aspects. First, the climate is fundamentally one in which the central challenge is acquiring enough water to enable human activity. The climate basically offers little rainfall and low humidities throughout the year. However, one must note that when rainfall does occur, it generally does so in concentrated storms. For those infrequent occurrences, rain protection is a requirement because of the potential for flooding due to rapid run-off.

A second feature of this climate is that quite hot air temperatures are present during summers, and cool air temperatures exist during comparatively brief winters. A complicating factor concerning the air temperatures is that large diurnal temperature swings are widespread because of the dry, clear skies that predominate in these regions. The very clear skies, day and night, enable very intense solar radiation during the day and substantial longwave radiational cooling at night. This radiational cooling occurs because of the large apparent temperature differences between natural and built surfaces that have been heated throughout the day by the strong solar radiation and the clear, cold night sky vault. Regarding this sky vault as a heat *sink,* its "effective temperature" is generally estimated to be about –45 °C (–50 °F). Thus, the sky vault functions as if it were a surface to which heat from the warmed built and natural surfaces near the ground can radiate. The result of this radiational cooling is that large diurnal air temperature variations commonly exist for the hot-dry climate group.

The third principal aspect of this climate is the intense solar radiation that results from the low humidities and concomitant clear skies. In addition to serving as a major heat source, the bright sunlight also imposes a significant *glare* source for human occupancy (a topic to be discussed further in Chapters 7 and 9). The fourth important feature of this climate is the frequent presence of a brisk wind. This wind — in addition to bearing heated air — will also pick up and carry the loose, easily blown soil. Thus, dusty air movement further accentuates the already-too-dry air.

To derive a catalogue of building construction and operation strategies suitable for this climate, we can compare these four features against the environmental and personal parameters — identified in Chapter 3 — that determine how well occupant thermal comfort can be maintained. From such a comparison it is evident that the natural environment for the hot-dry climate greatly inhibits the achievement of thermal comfort. Generally, the natural environment will be too hot. It will impose an excessive *net* radiant exchange (to a person from the sun or from surfaces made hot by absorbed solar radiation or by convective exchange with the air). In addition, the ambient air is almost always too dry. Further, moving air will not only be hot and dry, but also laden with dust. Acceptable clothing for this climate then should be lightweight and light-colored (to reflect, particularly, incident solar radiation) and should serve to retard body moisture loss. Prevention of dehydration due to excessive sweating is especially important for persons living in a hot-dry climate. Indeed, a standard clothing strategy in many hot-dry Third World countries is to wear clothing ensembles consisting of multiple layers. Thus, sweat absorbed by the innermost layer of clothing is inhibited from being lost by the outer layers. Lastly, activity rates should be kept as low as possible.

5.2.3   SELECTING BUILDING FORMS AND OPERATING STRATEGIES THAT RESPOND TO THE HOT-DRY CLIMATE

5.2.3.1   Fundamental operation strategies   If a building is to be life-sustaining and ensure occupant thermal comfort, then the building must inhibit moisture loss from its internal spaces and keep out heat. The following passive strategies will provide the needed control. First, minimize the use of water for space conditioning (primarily by reducing the volume of the space requiring conditioning). Second, use a heavily massed or well-insulated building envelope to prevent — or, at least, to retard — the day heat from entering the building. Third, provide shading devices to block out solar radiation from entering through limited-area envelope openings (i.e., those that are present to enable the admission of daylight and some fresh air). And, fourth, cool the building interior using evaporative techniques (where sufficient water is available) and air movement (when the heat and dust can be removed from the external air).

5.2.3.2   Specific design and construction guidelines for hot-dry climates

FOR SITE DEVELOPMENT

Figure 5.27 This drawing presents the typical form of cityscapes found in the lands spanning from the western coast of North Africa to Iran. The cityscape is densely-packed with low-rise residential buildings which have plain, nearly fully opaque envelopes facing narrow streets. The narrowness of the streets provide protection from the sun and hot winds that ravage people who traverse more open land. The buildings commonly open up inwardly to private courtyards.

(HD1) *Employ narrow, shaded streets to protect paths of circulation* (see Figures 5.27–5.29). For the hot-dry climate minimizing incident solar radiation is essential. People and places should be shaded, particularly from direct beam solar radiation, so that overheating by excessive radiant exchange can be reduced. Closely spaced buildings with moderate heights will afford public accessways into which little direct solar radiation can penetrate. Alternatively, one can use coverings that span from one side of an accessway to the other. These coverings can be horizontal or domed, can be permanent or temporary forms, and can be made of a range of materials from cloth to woven mats to masonry. Note, however, that a dichotomy can exist concerning the appropriate width of accessways. For instance, if the primary function of the pathway is for people to pass among buildings, then providing shaded or covered walkways is essential. If the accessway is for vehicular traffic, then its width must necessarily be greater and coverings will be less needed (as the vehicle can offer shelter from the sun).

(HD2) *Use ground covers that offer low reflectance and that will prevent the dusty, sandy soils from becoming airborne.* Ground covers should possess low reflectances to minimize reflection of incident solar radiation that can produce glary view fields and can increase the heat gain into buildings through envelope openings. Alternatively, surfaces with high absorptances (e.g., asphalt) should not be placed directly under

---

SIDEBAR 5.10 Literature describing cityscapes in hot-dry regions

Many interesting reports about cityscape and building forms of the Islamic world have been published recently. Even a selective, though representative, list of these reports is well beyond the intent of this text. Thus, here we will note a few sources to serve as starting points for readers who wish to relate the guidelines presented in this text with the urban and individual building forms of the Islamic world. A most interesting, thoughtful study of building and urban forms (displayed in the cities of North Africa and the Middle East) is presented in the book by Hakim, B.S., *Arabic-Islamic Cities: Building and Planning Principles* (2nd edition), (London: Kegan Paul International, 1988). An article describing a townscape formed of medium-rise buildings, that is otherwise placed in an organization resembling the traditional village, has been written by Breton, J-F., and C. Darles, "Shibam and the Wadi Hadramaut," *MIMAR*, No. 18, October–December 1985, pages 8–20. The village of Shibam is located in South Yemen. Thirdly, an article that portrays life in a traditional Saudi town and how the living practices and building forms have been altered by renovation efforts has been written by Parssinen, J., and K. Talib, "A traditional community and modernization: Saudi Camp, Dhahran," *Journal of Architectural Education*, 35(3), Spring 1982, pages 14–17. For a report that describes the urban form, selected community buildings, and residences of a relatively typical Pakistani settlement, see Hassan, I., "The indigenous architecture of Chitral, Pakistan," *MIMAR*, No. 17, July–September 1985, pages 68–76. Alternatively, we recommend a summary paper that catalogues a variety of building forms in North Africa and the Middle East: see Sayigh, A.A.M., "The Arab world," in the *Proceedings of the International Passive and Hybrid Cooling Conference* (edited by Bowen, A., E. Clark, and K. Labs), (Newark, Delaware: American Solar Energy Society, 1981), pages 934–961.

openings because the surfaces will absorb heat from the sun and will give off heat by convective exchange to the air and by longwave radiation to surrounding objects. Further, the ground-covering materials should prevent the dusty, sandy soils from becoming wind-blown. Perhaps the ground cover that will best satisfy both of these requirements is grass. Various grass species will grow well in hot-dry climates (when adequate water is present), will display relatively low reflectances (and low tendencies to initiate convection), and will hold loose soil in place (see Figure 5.25).

(HD3) *Use plantings selectively for creating shading (or for simply providing refreshing differentiations from dry, dusty city and townscapes).* The contrast between the occasional item of vegetation and the fundamentally dry environment can offer appreciable (psychological) relief to the inhabitants. As such, these occasional plantings can serve as "oases." Trees and appropriate shrubs can also offer shading to adjacent buildings and for people to sit under. Maintaining such plantings in this climate depends on having an adequate water supply.

(HD4) *Provide channels, catch basins, and related storm drainage facilities to handle the occasional rains that occur.* Although precipitation does not happen frequently in the hot-dry regions, it tends to be intense. Because the amount may be substantial, the rain duration brief, and the soil relatively poor at absorbing the water, torrential runoff can happen. Thus, paths for such runoff must be planned and constructed.

FOR BUILDING LAYOUT

(HD5) *Establish the orientation of the major axis of the building along the east-west compass line.* For most of the year, if direct-beam solar radiation is permitted to enter buildings through envelope openings, substantial overheating of the building interior may result. Thus, all openings must be shaded. Because the sun is higher in the sky vault during the middle of the day, simple overhangs are generally sufficient for shading openings on the south elevation (or north elevation in the Southern Hemisphere). During the early mornings and late afternoons, when the sun is lower in the sky and more nearly perpendicular to the east and west elevations, respectively, the successful shading of openings requires using more elaborate devices. For these early morning and late afternoon times, shading of envelope openings will necessitate applying coverings that can either diffuse or reflect the solar radiation. Two examples of such devices are cloth blinds and heat-reflective glazing assemblies.

(HD6) *Develop the building floor plan so that it is double-banked (i.e., two rooms wide)* (see Figure 5.30). For the hot-dry climate, wind flow through the building during the day is seldom desirable (unless the air has been appropriately conditioned to comfortable temperature and humidity levels). So there is little reason to encourage air flow across the building interior. The particular worth of double-banking is that the outer "bank" (or room) can be used to prevent the heat of the day from penetrating the inner "bank" that serves as the primary living area. Double-banked floor plans are common throughout the Middle East, where the outer rooms are used as entry halls or for storage and nonessential activities, and the inner rooms are used for daytime living.

(HD7) *Turn the focus of the building inward away from the street and toward a courtyard, if one can be provided* (see Figures 5.30 and 5.31). This strategy is

Figure 5.28 A narrow street path as it appears in the "old city" district of Algiers.

Figure 5.29 In some urban settings across the North African–Middle Eastern lands streetscapes are covered by vaulted arches, wooden beams covered with woven materials, or, simply, vegetation (where adequate water exists to enable growth.) This scene is an approximation of any one of a series of masonry-covered bazaars present in a number of Iranian cities. Such coverings protect the residents from the hot sun and the accompanying high air temperatures of the summer (and the cold, nearly-as-dry winter.)

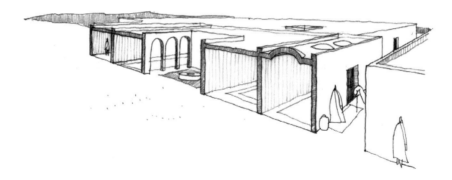

Figure 5.30 A double-banked building layout with the inner rooms located around and opening onto a courtyard. A fountain has been located at the center of this courtyard which is enclosed by a large home in Algiers.

Figure 5.31 This pool and the accompanying trees, shrubbery, and grass occur in the courtyard of the Madrasseh of the Mother of the Shah in the Iranian city of Isfahan. For additional drawings, photographs, and text about the city of Isfahan, see the May 1976 issue of *Architectural Review,* 159(5).

directly linked to the strategy of the double-banked floor plan (with the building wound around a central courtyard and the inner rooms having operable envelopes that face out upon the courtyard). As a family's economic means permit, the courtyard can be the site for a garden and/or a fountain with both devices serving to condition physically — as well as spiritually — the central space. Vegetation and running or standing water can also affect the thermal environment of the courtyard. The water will cool it evaporatively, just as the plants will provide shading from the sun (while also serving as sources for evaporative cooling due to the transpiration of water from their foliage). For buildings that are double-banked and inward turning, the central space can offer privacy from the street and a site for social or business-related activities.

(HD8) *For residential buildings, place activity spaces according to the occupants' needs for thermal comfort.* A predominant feature of the hot-dry climate is its over heatedness, especially during the daytime. Thus, to avoid the penetration of external heat, a fundamental operation strategy is to close off the building from the outside. Additionally, to reduce the contribution of further heat to the amount that passes through the building envelope, the generation of heat from internal sources should be minimized. But, if internal heat production is inevitable (e.g., for food preparation), then the next best solution is to isolate these heat sources away from living areas. Secondly, accommodations must be made to permit comfortable sleeping. If the building has become overheated during the course of the hot day and is uncomfortably warm at night, the occupants can set up sleeping facilities on the rooftop (or in bedrooms located at the top story of the building, which could be opened up to the night sky). Rooftop sleeping is widely practiced throughout the hot-dry regions of Africa, the Middle East, and South Asia. Screens (or parapet walls) will usually shield these areas to provide privacy (see Figure 5.32). But otherwise the sleeping areas will be open to the night sky. The night sky in these regions is clear (cloudless) and serves as a major radiant heat sink for absorbing stored-up daytime heat. Further, because of the large diurnal air temperature swing, nighttime air temperatures will generally be quite comfortable for sleeping (and bed covers will regularly be needed).

FOR ENVELOPE COMPOSITION: BOTH HORIZONTAL AND VERTICAL

(HD9) *Employ the following building envelope forms:*

(a) *Openings in the vertical envelope should be modestly-sized, equaling perhaps between 20 to 40 percent of the vertical surface area.* The need for openings in the vertical envelope should be based more on providing contact with the outside and admitting daylight, than on permitting ventilation of the building interior. Thus, the locations of envelope openings should be established more for view, than for allowing air to flow across occupants.

(b) *Coverings should be provided for these openings* (see Figures 5.33 and 5.34). First, shading of the openings is essential to minimize the penetration of incident solar radiation (and, especially, the direct beam component) into the building. Second, fenestration assemblies—whether composed of multiple-paned glazing materials or of glazing materials with draperies or supplemental insulating covers—can reduce the transmission of airborne heat through the openings. However, note that heat is transmitted in much greater quantities through even the best fenestration assemblies than through well-insulated or massive *opaque* envelope assemblies.

(c) *If the admission of daylighting into the building interior is needed, then use clerestories (for low-rise buildings) and atria (for high-rise buildings).* First, using daylight for building illumination is a significant way to reduce heat production within a building (i.e., by reducing the need for supplemental electric lighting and its concomitant heat generation). Second, as an alternative to relying solely on openings in the vertical envelope for daylighting the building interior, roof openings can markedly enhance this daylighting. But do not use skylights or other unshaded roof openings.

Figure 5.32 The rooftop is used throughout numbers of countries in the Middle East as a sleeping area. The external heat of the day slowly warms up the interiors of residential buildings over the course of the day. But once the sun sets, the outside air cools rapidly. When it is time for the occupants to retire for the night, the temperature of the outside air is suitable for sleeping (whereas the building interior is still quite warm.) So, many people in these regions sleep on rooftop platforms. To attain visual privacy, these platforms are hidden from view using screens like the ones that appear at the edges of the roof for this Iraqi house.

SIDEBAR 5.11 The courtyard house as cultural artifact and thermal regulator

---

The courtyard house is widely found throughout North and Central Africa, the Middle East, and South Asia, where the Islamic religion strictly influences the various cultures (note that this housing form also is employed in the American Southwest and Latin and South America). In the countries where Islam is the principal religion, the inward-turning residences relate directly to the search for privacy for the family and to religious tenets like *purdah* (i.e., the seclusion of women from public observation). An article that discusses various social benefits of the courtyard housing form has been written by Aksoylu, Y., "Courtyard house form: response to the traditional and modern needs of man," *The Journal of Architecture and Planning Research,* 4(3), 1987, pages 228–240. We also recommend two articles that summarize recent building projects using the courtyard form: Santelli, S., "Self-built urban housing, Rabat and Tunis," *MIMAR,* 17, July–September 1985, pages 41–48; and "Shushtar New Town, Iran," *MIMAR,* 17, July–September 1985, pages 49–53.

For a description of the thermal performance of courtyards in the city of Colima, Mexico, see the article by Reynolds, J.S., J.-F. Blassel, and G. Papers, "The courtyard: passive cooling performance and shading variables," *Proceedings of the Eighth National Passive Solar Conference* (edited by Hayes, J., and D.A. Andrejko), (Boulder, Colorado: American Solar Energy Society, Inc., 1983), pages 843–848. Another discussion about the use of the courtyard for providing thermal benefits has been written by Dunham, D., "The courtyard house as a temperature regulator," *The New Scientist,* 8, September 8, 1960, pages 663–666. Regarding this last paper, also see the qualifying statement offered by J. Harvey in a letter to the editor of *The New Scientist,* published in the October 6, 1960 issue, page 944.

Figure 5.33 Alternative window coverings have been used for this Saudi Arabian house. Note the horizontal poles that protrude outward from the upper left-hand side of the envelope (i.e., where a covering structure once was present).

Figure 5.34 A sun screen that fills in an opening in an Indian building which was formerly a palace.

Figure 5.35 A traditional building form used in the American Southwest and Mexico is shown here. The massive opaque envelopes are composed of *adobe* (i.e., a clay-containing earthen material), which retards heat transfer through it. Wooden poles are used horizontally to support a roof assembly that consists of smaller wooden pieces spanning in a direction perpendicular to the poles, a matting (approximating a decking) above the wooden pieces, and then adobe placed on top of the matting.

Figure 5.36 In the southeastern Italian area called Apulia, these stone houses have been constructed by the residents for many generations. This housing form is known as Trulli. A well-illustrated, informative book that documents this housing form and the Apulian region has been written by Allen, E.B., *Stone Shelters,* (Cambridge, Massachusetts: The MIT Press, 1970).

(HD10) *Employ the following building envelope materials and assemblies:*

(a) *Opaque envelopes should be constructed either of massive assemblies or of well-insulated assemblies.* Because of the characteristic overheatedness of the hot-dry climate, it is essential to reduce passage of external heat through the building envelope into the building interior. Two fundamental alternatives exist for restricting external heat from entering the interior: massive materials can be used to store the external heat of the day, thus slowing its passage through the envelope (see Figures 5.35 and 5.36); or insulating materials can resist the flow of heat. Which strategy to employ depends on at least two factors: whether either envelope technology is readily available in a region (e.g., are insulating materials produced and sold and is the use of insulation consistent with established building practices in the region) and how can heat transfer rates best be controlled during the underheated winter period. Examples of suitable massive materials include concrete and other masonry materials, mud-earth bricks or adobe, and rammed earth. Another alternative for employing a massive envelope to retard heat transfer into a building is to employ earth-sheltering or berming techniques (i.e., thus, using the ground as a barrier between the building interior and the external air).

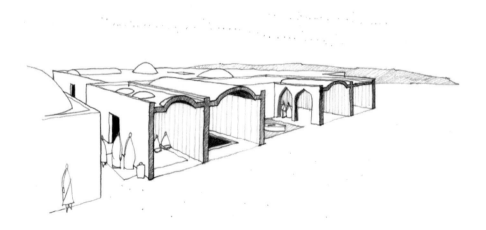

Figure 5.37 Vaulted, domed, or flat roof forms are common in these *hot-dry* regions (i.e., where fending off precipitation is a less frequent concern).

(b) *Flat, vaulted, or domed roofs may be used for this climate because of the small amounts of rainfall* (see Figure 5.37). If massive materials are used as the principal building material, then vaults or domes may be required to span the (horizontal) distances between vertical walls. Additionally, flat roofs can be used as open-air sleeping platforms (see Figure 5.32).

(c) *External building surfaces should be light-colored to reduce the absorption of incident solar radiation.* If solar radiation can be reflected away by the building surface, then the external surface temperature will be lessened and the temperature gradient between the external surface and the air in the building will also be less, reducing the "driving force" for heat transfer to occur through the building envelope.

FOR OPERATING THE BUILDING: CONVECTIVE COOLING

(HD11) *Use cool night air to remove the heat of the day from the building interior* (see Figure 5.38). First, buildings in the hot-dry climate will acquire heat throughout the day both from heat transferred through the envelope and from internal sources. Second, large diurnal exterior air temperature swings occur between day and night, with the nighttime air being appreciably cooler than the daytime air. If the nighttime *external* air temperature is below the end-of-the-day air temperatures *within the building,* then bringing in external air can cool the building.

Three distinct means can be used to propel the air through the building. First, *cross-ventilation* can be established by having operable openings in adjacent or opposite walls and allowing wind pressure to move the air. Thus, cool air from the exterior can be drawn in and warm internal air dumped to the exterior. Second, *stack ventilation* can be induced by enabling warmer air near the ceiling to exit the building through envelope openings close to the ceiling, while letting in cooler air drawn through openings near the floor (on the same, adjacent, or opposite wall). Or, third, *motor-driven fans* can be used to pull in cool air and to move it around the building through ducting.

Figure 5.38 By opening up buildings to the cool night air, one can cool the interior of a building. The interior of the massive envelope can effectively store this *coolth* over night so that, as the next day's heat begins its assault on the building occupants, they have a cooled interior environment.

(HD12) *Provide storage mass in the building that can be cooled with nighttime exterior air; then, during the following day, cool interior air by moving it past the cooled mass.* Cool night air admitted to the building interior can replace air warmed by the activities of the day. This cool air can "soak up" heat from the warmed interior building mass. Thus, the admission of the night air will cool both air and surface temperatures in the building. The next day the building interior will feel cool when

SIDEBAR 5.12 Stack ventilation

Stack ventilation (i.e., warm air rising and leaving the building while cooler air enters at a lower place in the building) is a result of the free convection of the air. The warmer air is less dense and more buoyant, whereas the cooler air is heavier. Here, the building surfaces serve to warm up the air, releasing the heat they have acquired over the course of the day. Stack ventilation is frequently present in medium and high-rise buildings, in which warmed air rises up through several stories becoming progressively warmer. At the top of a multiple-story zone the air will frequently be substantially warmer than at the bottom. Generally, high-rise buildings (in any climate) must be designed to minimize this stack effect happening unintentionally between floors. The stack ventilation process is also known as *thermosiphoning* or as an *adiabatic chimney effect.*

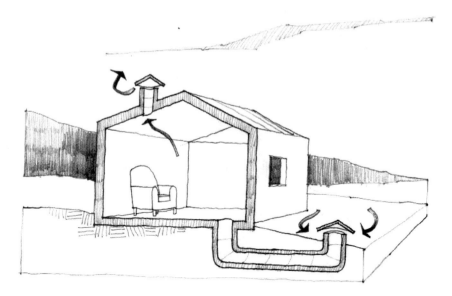

Figure 5.39 The temperature of the Earth a meter or more (about three or more feet) below the grade level will commonly be substantially less than the outside air temperatures reached during the hottest parts of the day. Earth-tube cooling thus functions by drawing outside air into a duct located under the ground, passing this air along the duct for some distance, where the inside surfaces are at the below-grade temperature, and then introducing this lowered-temperature air into the building interior. This airflow can be encouraged with the operation of one or more fans placed strategically in the ducting and the building.

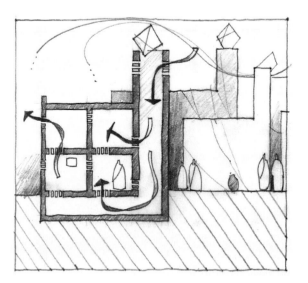

Figure 5.40 A traditional *wind scoop* structure found in South Asia and the Persian Gulf region. Wind pressure forces air down the chimney-like volume. As the air descends, it is cooled by its contact with the below-grade surfaces. The cooled air is then induced to rise upward through the dwelling as the warmed air above exits from the upper volumes of the dwelling.

outside the building the natural environment will be hot. Mass can be deployed use-fully in at least two means within a building: simply spread uniformly throughout the building in the walls, floors, ceilings, and furnishings; or placed in a concentrated form at one location in the building. A specific example of this latter mode is to use a rock bin through which air can be moved. As cool night air passes through the bin, heat stored in the rocks will be transferred to the air, thus cooling the rocks. Then, the next day, ventilation air—warmed from passing through spaces occupied by peo-ple—can be blown through the bin transferring heat to these now-cooler rocks.

(HD13) *Use external air for ventilation during the day if the air is cooled first (before being introduced into the space).* We will identify four alternative methods here for cooling external air. A fifth will be described in Guideline HD16 below. The first method employs the widely used *active heat exchanger.* For this device, external air is blown across the heat exchanger, transferring heat from the incoming external air to the exchanger sink (e.g., some refrigerated material). The second cooling alterna-tive uses the ground as the heat sink by passing the external air through an underground duct for some distance before introducing it into the building. This underground ducting is known as a *cool tube* (see Figure 5.39).

The third alternative applies a device that has long been incorporated in traditional buildings throughout the Persian Gulf states and South Asia. This device, called a *wind scoop,* has a chimney that runs vertically from above the rooftop to a below-ground space (see Figure 5.40). An *operable* baffle is placed at the very top of the chimney. When the baffle is opened, the wind scoop will "catch" the wind and direct it down the chimney. The wind pressure—in conjunction with stack ventilation effects inside the building—can impel the air down to the underground space. Once the air reaches this space, the air is cooled as it comes in contact with the cool underground surfaces in the space. Then, by stack ventilation, this cool air rises up through the building, con-ditioning the spaces and taking the heat away from the occupied zones.

The fourth means of cooling external air before admitting it to the occupied zones is to draw the air through a rock bin that has been precooled (i.e., using the procedure suggested in Guideline HD12 above). The use of a rock bin may be less efficient than some of these other alternatives because it may have limited mass (and, therefore, limited storage capacity).

All four methods rely on stack ventilation as the means for inducing air movement. Note that for all four methods a motor-driven fan can enhance air movement.

SIDEBAR 5.13 Using cool-tubes to provide well-tempered air to a building interior

The premise for passing the external air through underground ducting is that the earth that surrounds the ducting maintains a temperature that is approxi-mately equal to the *average annual air temperature* for the locale. Earth at this reduced temperature (rel-ative to the hot exterior air) can be found a depth that is usually a few to several feet below grade level. The actual ground temperature profile (i.e., temperature versus depth) for any location also depends upon a number of secondary factors including how closely packed the earth is and what its density is, the amount of organic materials present, the wetness of the earth, and so forth. See the article by Francis, E., "Cooling with earth tubes," *Solar Age,* 9(1), January 1984, pages 30–33.

FOR OPERATING THE BUILDING: RADIATIVE COOLING

(HD14) *Open the closed building at night to permit trapped heat from the day to be radiated away.* Two significant nighttime heat sinks are available in the hot-dry climate: the many objects outside of the building whose surface temperatures are similar (in magnitude) to the external air temperature and the night sky. We have written previously about the often-large diurnal air temperature swings that exist for the hot-dry climate. The temperatures of *nonmassive* objects will rise and fall at rates corresponding to changes in the external air temperature. Even the surface temperatures of massive objects will decrease as the night air temperature falls. Thus, all of these objects can serve as sinks to receive heat radiated (by longwave radiation) from warmer building surfaces. Alternatively, the characteristically clear night sky of the hot-dry climate operates as a virtually infinite heat sink for absorbing heat radiated from warmer surfaces below. As the clear night sky has an effective temperature of about −45 °C (−50 °F), the heat transfer rate between building surfaces and the sky vault can be substantial.[15]

(HD15) *Employ a roof pond as a heat-radiating device for night cooling* (see Figure 5.41). The primary built application of this guideline is a house designed and constructed by Harold Hay in Atascadero, California.[16] The building, known as the *Skytherm House,* has a flat roof composed of steel decking on which are laid bags of water. Removable insulating and shading panels cover the bags. The operation of this composite roof proceeds, *for the hot part of year,* in the following manner. During the day the panels cover the water bags protecting them from incident solar radiation and the daytime heat. Heat from the house rises up to the steel deck ceiling and conducts through the steel and into the water, with the water serving as a heat sink throughout the day. Then, at night, the panels are rolled away exposing the water bags so that the stored heat can radiate to the sky. By morning, after the water has cooled, the reflecting and insulating panels are moved back to cover the water bags (thus, shading them from the daytime heat). Then, the water can serve as a heat sink for the following day.

SIDEBAR 5.14 Literature sources describing wind scoops

For more definitive discussions on the *wind scoop,* see the following articles: Bahadori, M.N., "Passive cooling systems in Iranian architecture," *Scientific American,* 238(2), 1978, pages 144–154; Bahadori, M.N., "An improved design of wind towers for natural ventilation and passive cooling," *Solar Energy,* 35(2), 1985, pages 119–129; Karakatsanis, C., M.N. Bahadori, and B.J. Vickery, "Evaluation of pressure coefficients and estimation of air flow rates in buildings employing wind towers," *Solar Energy,* 37(5), 1986, pages 363–374; and Chand, I., and P.K. Bhargava, "Studies on design and performance of a non-conventional system of natural ventilation in buildings," *Solar & Wind Technology,* 7(2/3), 1990, pages 203–212. Also, see the description of the use of the *malqaf* and *badgir,* which are regional adaptations of the wind scoop device, offered in the book by Fathy, H., *Natural Energy and Vernacular Architecture: Principles and Examples with Reference to Hot Arid Climates,* (Chicago: The University of Chicago Press, 1986), pages 56–61 (with illustrations shown on pages 114–136).

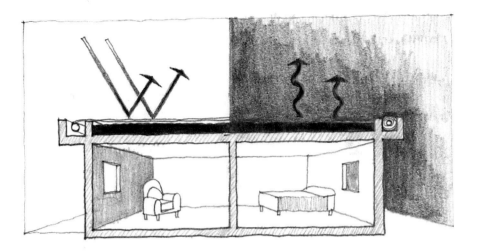

Figure 5.41 The rejection of daytime heat using the rooftop reflecting panels and the passage of stored heat (acquired from the building interior during the daytime) to the night sky show how the *Skytherm* principle is employed during *hot-dry* weather.

Also, note that by reversing the operation of the panels (i.e., by opening them during the day to expose them to the incident solar radiation and closing them at night), it is possible to provide a radiant heating source for the cool weather of the winter.

FOR OPERATING THE BUILDING: EVAPORATIVE COOLING

(HD16) *Use evaporative cooling devices in the building to cool the interior.* Evaporation is an *endothermic* event (i.e., it requires energy to make it happen). Thus, by introducing water droplets into the building air that then evaporate, the air is cooled (and made more humid). Two examples of devices that can cool building interiors *evaporatively* are the swamp cooler and direct (and indirect) evaporative coolers. The *swamp cooler* is essentially a wire-mesh bucket filled with wood chips (see Figure 5.42). Water drips onto the wood chips, wetting them and providing a large surface area off of which evaporation can occur. Blowing air — using a motor-driven fan — across the surfaces of the wetted wood chips air will increase the rate of evaporation. The result of this simple, effective device is cooled, more humid air (that may even have a pleasant odor if the chips are aromatic.

The *direct (and indirect) evaporative coolers* are fan-driven air movers into whose air streams water droplets are injected.[17] The water droplets either drip from a trough or are "tossed" into the air by a paddle wheel or blade. As the hot air rushes past the water droplets, the water evaporates, cooling and humidifying the air. Various modifications to this simple device have been developed and are available commercially throughout the world. Note that both this type of evaporative cooling device and the swamp cooler are effectively passive-hybrid systems that utilize electrical power only to drive the fan (and, if present, the paddle wheel).

A number of variations exist for performing the evaporative cooling of air entering a building. In Guideline HD7 we described the placement of a fountain in the courtyards

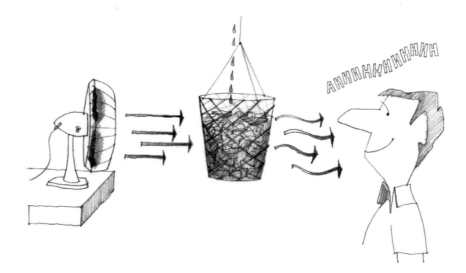

Figure 5.42 The swamp cooler can use air driven by the wind or by a fan. In either instance, the evaporative cooling of the air should enhance occupant thermal comfort.

Figure 5.43 A water spray used for roof surface cooling: the sprayed water evaporates from its contact with the hot roof surface, fostering the cooling of the roof surface (and reducing the temperature difference between the roof surface and the inside air). Thus, the amount of heat transferred through the roof to the space below would be lessened.

of buildings. Whether the water in the fountain is static or forced into the air with a pump, evaporative cooling of the surrounding air will result. Alternatively, for Guideline HD13 we stated that a fifth means for cooling external air is available. Using various evaporative cooling strategies in association with the four devices described for Guideline HD13 will indeed promote even better passive (or passive-hybrid) cooling of the building interior. For instance, in numbers of locations in the Third World, *wind scoops* are used in conjunction with water jars (or other means of holding water) placed in the chimney, and the air passing down the chimney is cooled evaporatively. Thus, the air flowing down the chimney will be cooled both by evaporation and by convective exchange with the chimney and underground surfaces.

(HD17) *Spray water onto roofs to cool them* (see Figure 5.43). This technique — another passive-hybrid operating strategy — uses water to wet the roof surface, causing the evaporative cooling of that surface. One reference states that the surface temperature of a roof may be reduced by up to 50 °F (about 28 °C) by applying a fine spray of water in a dry climate.[18] Necessarily, this technique requires the ready availability of water. Thus, this technique will be unsuitable for locales with limited water supplies.

FOR OPERATING THE BUILDING: PASSIVE SOLAR HEATING

(HD18) *Provide passive solar heating capabilities for cool weather periods during winters.* Virtually all of the regions that experience the hot-dry climate undergo a number of months when the external air is cool to cold (i.e., *underheated*). Depending on a number of factors (e.g., the temperature of the external air; the type of use for which the building is intended; the nature of the building envelope; and so forth), buildings located in these regions may need some heating capability. Because a fundamental characteristic of the hot-dry climate — even in winter — is that the sky is rarely cloudy, passive solar heating of a building should be an attractive means for thermal conditioning. In Section 5.4 we will discuss the principles of passive solar heating and offer a series of guidelines for incorporating passive solar heating features with other components of the buildings.

5.2.4   FURTHER REFERENCES FOR DESIGNING AND CONSTRUCTING BUILDINGS FOR HOT-DRY CLIMATES

Maxwell Fry and Jane Drew have written the outstanding book about creating buildings for the hot-dry climate, *Tropical Architecture in the Dry and Humid Zones* (2nd edition), (Malabar, Florida: R.E. Krieger Publishing Company, 1982). Other books presenting useful information for building for the *hot-dry* climate include:

Fathy, H., *Architecture for the Poor: An Experiment in Rural Egypt,* (Chicago: University of Chicago Press, 1973).

Fathy, H., *Natural Energy and Vernacular Architecture,* (Chicago: The University of Chicago Press [for the United Nations University], 1986).

Givoni, B., *Man, Climate, and Architecture* (2nd edition), (London: Applied Science Publishers Ltd., 1976).

Königsberger, O.H., C. Mahoney, and M. Evans, *Climate and House Design* (Volume 1 of *Design of Low-Cost Housing and Community Facilities*), (New York: United Nations, Department of Economic and Social Affairs, 1971).

Konya, A., *Design Primer for Hot Climates,* (London: The Architectural Press, Ltd., 1980).

Saini, B.S., *Building in Hot Dry Climates,* (Chichester, England: John Wiley & Sons Ltd., 1980).

Three other books that present information that can be helpful for designing and constructing buildings for the hot-dry climate are:

Brown, G.Z., and M. DeKay, *Sun, Wind, and Light: Architectural Design Strategies,* 2nd edition, (New York: John Wiley & Sons, Inc., 2000).

Olgyay, V., *Design With Climate,* (Princeton, New Jersey: Princeton University Press, 1963).

Watson, D., and K. Labs, *Climatic Design,* (New York: McGraw-Hill Book Company, 1983).

Lastly, we also recommend the very fine journal *MIMAR: Architecture in Development* (published by Concept Media Pte Ltd., Singapore). *MIMAR* focuses on the built environment of the Islamic world. Thus, much interesting information about creating buildings in *warm-humid* regions is also present in the journal.

Section 5.3 | DESIGNING AND BUILDING FOR COLD CLIMATES

Predominantly cold climates occur only in the Northern Hemisphere and are located, to a marked extent, within the continents (away from the coastal regions). The cold climate is essentially a composite of four climatic types: the *temperate continental with cool summer (Dcb),* the *boreal (E),* the *polar (F),* and, to a somewhat limited extent, the *highland (H).*[19] Except for the highland climate, these types are normally found north of the 45° latitude line. The fundamental characteristic of this climate is its absence of sufficient heat. Although the temperate continental with cool summer climate has a short summer with occasional hot days, the primary concern for designers and builders in the composite cold climate is to keep heat in the building, using well-insulated and tight envelopes. Generally, human life in this environment cannot be sustained year-round without the existence of some form of built shelter. Further, in addition to the provision of a well-insulated and tight envelope, there is an essential need for passive and active heat sources (to be used within many buildings) for a major part of the year.

5.3.1   LOCATIONS AND CHARACTERISTICS OF THESE CLIMATIC TYPES

5.3.1.1   Features of the temperate continental with cool summer climate   *The temperate continental with cool summer* climate is present in three regions of the Northern Hemisphere: the northern tier of the United States, running from Massachusetts to North Dakota, and southeastern Canada, including the maritime provinces; the European portion of Russia, the Ukraine, Byelorussia, the Baltic States and the Eastern European countries

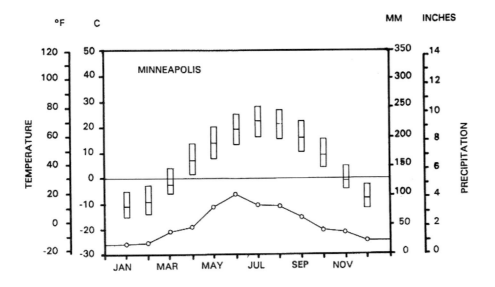

Figure 5.44 The climate of *Minneapolis, Minnesota.*

from Poland south to Rumania, and the island of Hokkaido and northern Manchuria. Thus, this climatic type generally occurs either on the northeastern coasts of continents or within continental land masses.

The fundamental temperature range shows a variation of average monthly air temperatures from 22 °C (72 °F) (or less) for the warmest summer month to below 0 °C (32 °F) for the coldest winter month. Further, average annual air temperatures for four cities representative of the temperate continental with cool summer climatic type are, for Boston, 9.4 °C (49 °F); for Berlin, 8.8 °C (48 °F); for Moscow, 3.3 °C (38 °F); and for Winnipeg, 2.8 °C (37 °F) (see Figure 5.44). Generally, regions experiencing this climate have protracted winters of between six to eight months with shorter, comparatively cool summers. Precipitation varies between 500 to 1000 mm (20–40 in), with wetter areas being closer to the coasts of continents and drier regions well inland. The majority of this precipitation usually occurs during the summers. Winters are drier, and much of that precipitation falls as snow. One qualification should be noted about the averaged annual precipitation amounts for locales within the continents: there is appreciable variation on a year-to-year basis for these annual amounts. As a result, sustained droughts over a multiple-year period occasionally happen.

In some parts of these regions the snow cover may remain for several months. Alternatively, in other areas, intermittent periods of a few comparatively warm days will cause the snow cover to disappear. Blizzards—a combination of heavy snowfall over a short period and greater than usual wind speeds—happen occasionally throughout these areas and pose special hazards for public safety. Generally, though, overall wind speeds tend to be greater for coastal regions and lower for areas within the continents. Wind conditions, particularly during the winter, are highly variable with some days showing quite rapid ambient air movement and well-established gusting, and other days showing calm air and little movement. Thus, monthly averaged wind speed records do not necessarily display conditions for which any special attention should be paid when designing or constructing

Figure 5.45 A tall grass prairie meadow near Madison, Wisconsin.

buildings (although, for some locales in the cold climate, the designer and builder will need to be aware of wind conditions).

The predominant vegetation forms for this climatic type are the *deciduous forest,* in the areas with annual precipitation rates exceeding 750 mm (30 in), and *grasslands,* in locales with precipitation amounts of less than 750 mm (30 in) (see Figure 5.45). In the forested areas herb and shrub layers will also be well developed. Deciduous trees are the primary form for the mature forest biome (or ecological community), although both deciduous and coniferous trees will commonly exist in the developing biome. Animal life in the forests varies from larger mammals like deer, moose, and bear to smaller mammals like squirrels and foxes. On the grasslands the characteristic animals are either running or burrowing types. However, animals introduced for farming have replaced many of these once-native running animals. Still, burrowing animals like the gopher and ground squirrel remain, even in farming areas.[20]

SIDEBAR 5.14 Literature sources describing wind scoops

For more definitive discussions on the *wind scoop,* see the following articles: Bahadori, M.N., "Passive cooling systems in Iranian architecture," *Scientific American,* 238(2), 1978, pages 144–154; Bahadori, M.N., "An improved design of wind towers for natural ventilation and passive cooling," *Solar Energy,* 35(2), 1985, pages 119–129; Karakatsanis, C., M.N. Bahadori, and B.J. Vickery, "Evaluation of pressure coefficients and estimation of air flow rates in buildings employing wind towers," *Solar Energy,* 37(5), 1986, pages 363–374; and Chand, I., and P.K. Bhargava, "Studies on design and performance of a non-conventional system of natural ventilation in buildings," *Solar & Wind Technology,* 7(2/3), 1990, pages 203–212. Also, see the description of the use of the *malqaf* and *badgir,* which are regional adaptations of the wind scoop device, offered in the book by Fathy, H., *Natural Energy and Vernacular Architecture: Principles and Examples with Reference to Hot Arid Climates,* (Chicago: The University of Chicago Press, 1986), pages 56–61 (with illustrations shown on pages 114–136).

SIDEBAR 5.15 Heating degree-day totals for various cities experiencing the Boreal climate

One further indication of the severity of the Boreal climate can be found in the *heating degree-day* index. As we defined this index in Sidebar 4.4, the suitable formula for determining heating degree-days (for the base of 65 °F) is:

$$\text{Heating degree-days/year} = \sum_{n=1}^{365} (65 - \text{Ave. Air Temperature for day n})$$

Degree-day totals for a range of American cities are: Los Angeles, 1349; San Francisco, 3001; Seattle, 4424; New York, 4871; Boston, 5634; Chicago, 5882; Minneapolis, 8382. For some North American cities which experience a boreal climate degree-day totals are: Anchorage, 10864; Fairbanks, 14279; The Pas, Manitoba, 12281; Churchill, Manitoba, 16728; and Dawson, Yukon Territory, 15067. (Source: *1980 ASHRAE Handbook: Systems,* (Atlanta: American Society of Heating, Refrigerating, and Air-Conditioning Engineers, Inc., 1980), pages 43.2–43.7).

With the exception of Hokkaido most of the land areas exhibiting the temperate continental with cool summer climate have extensive human development, either in farming or in well-populated suburban and urban communities. Some of these areas are among the most productive and heavily populated lands on the Earth. Additionally, these areas have hosted a significant portion, historically, of the development of Western civilization.

5.3.1.2   Features of the boreal climate   The *boreal* climatic type is largely present in two broad bands of land between 50° and 60° north latitude: one spans westward from the Atlantic Ocean to the Bering Sea in the Western Hemisphere and the other covers much of Sweden and Finland and a broad swatch of Russia and its neighboring republics across to the shores of the Bering Sea. The primary factors in determining the character of this climatic type are that these regions are far from the equator (and receive markedly lesser quantities of solar radiation than areas closer to the equator) *and* are generally distant from the moderating influences of oceans.

The Trewartha and Horn definition of regions experiencing a boreal climate is that they must have between one and three month(s) with average monthly air temperatures equal to or greater than 10 °C (50 °F).[21] Generally, the warmest average monthly air temperature for locales exhibiting this climate is about 18 °C (65 °F) and the coldest average monthly temperature is about −18 to −15 °C (0 to 5 °F). Average annual air temperatures for four cities having boreal climates are, for Anchorage, Alaska, 1.6 °C (35 °F); for Goose Bay, Newfoundland, 0 °C (32 °F); for Murmansk, Russia, 0 °C (32 °F); and for Trondheim, Norway, 5 °C (41 °F). For Anchorage, the maximum mean monthly air temperature (in July) is 18 °C (65 °F), and the minimum mean monthly air temperature (in January) is −15 °C (5 °F). For Fairbanks, Alaska—a location perhaps less affected by its proximity to the ocean—the maximum mean monthly air temperature (in July) is 22 °C (72 °F), and the minimum mean monthly air temperature (in January) is −19 °C (−2 °F). For areas with a *boreal* climate there are commonly only about 50 to 70 days per year that are frost-free.[22]

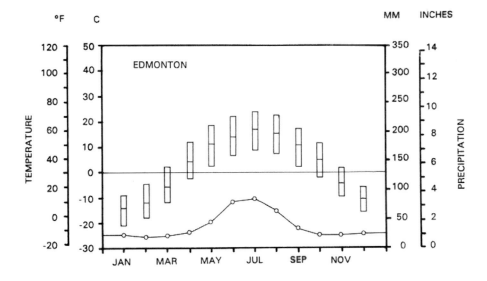

Figure 5.46 The climate of *Edmonton, Alberta.*

Figure 5.47 An aspen forest in Alberta (at the approximate boundary between the *boreal* and *temperate continental with cool summer* climatic types).

Figure 5.48 The coniferous forest at the Gulf of the St. Lawrence River in Quebec, Canada: this forest is commonly present in the *boreal* climate region.

Figure 5.49 A stave bog and stream in northern Sweden, above the Arctic Circle and north of the timberline.

The amounts of solar radiation received in the *boreal* regions show some interesting characteristics of the climate. First, the amount of solar radiation received at 60° north latitude in July is equal to the amount of solar radiation found at the equator at the same time. A primary reason for this is that at 60° north latitude, the length of time that the sun is above the horizon is approximately 18 hours per day in July. But during the winter the daytime length is brief, and the intensity of solar radiation is weak (i.e., because of the thickness of the atmosphere through which the solar radiation must penetrate). A further reason for the ineffectiveness of the solar radiation for heating the boreal regions is that with snow on the ground for long periods of the year, much of the solar radiation is reflected away.

Annual precipitation for the boreal regions usually is less than 500 mm (20 in) per year, with many areas reporting as little as 250 to 375 mm (10 to 15 in). This amount is similar to rainfall found for most locales experiencing a semiarid (steppe) climate, thus indicating that the boreal climate is dry as well as cold! (See Figure 5.46).

The majority of the precipitation in these regions happens in the summers. During the long winter period precipitation will occur virtually only as snow, and a snow cover will be present continuously for at least five to seven months. Consistent with the comparative dryness of the winter, the winter cloud cover averages about three-tenths, whereas the summer cloud cover is about seven-tenths.[23] The clear winter sky enables the weak solar radiation to reach the snow-covered ground, but also permits any reflected solar radiation to pass upward through the atmosphere. Further, clear skies will readily allow longwave radiation to pass from the ground and built surfaces near the ground to the night sky. Thus, the clear sky accentuates the negative heat balance between the energy received from the sun and the energy given off from the ground (i.e., more heat is lost to the sky than is gained from the sun).

The principal vegetative form in the boreal regions is the northern coniferous forest.[24] This forest stretches ubiquitously across the land areas of both the North American and Eurasian continents and shows little of the diversity of species found in more temperate climates equatorward. Spruce, fir, and pine trees are the major plant form in this forest (see Figures 5.47 and 5.48). Because the density of tree life is less here than in more temperate forests, extensive shrub growth can be observed amongst the trees. Lakes and bogs are also quite common in the boreal forests, although for much of the year these remain frozen (see Figure 5.49). *Permafrost* is a widely present ground condition in the northern areas of the boreal climatic region. Where permafrost exists, only the top few feet or so of the ground will thaw during the summer. Otherwise, the ground will be permanently frozen to great depths. The principal forms of animal life include larger mammals like the moose, wolf, bear, and lynx and smaller animals like squirrels, hares, and a variety of birds. Well-established predator-prey organizations exist and form the basis for the survival of numbers of these species.[25]

For the human being, life in the boreal regions is difficult. The growing season is short, and agriculture is a high-risk venture (particularly because of occasional mid-summer frosts). Commonly, human activity in these areas occurs primarily for the exploitation of natural resources, whether for hunting and fishing or for the seeking out and processing of rich mineral deposits. To a marked extent, occupancy in at least the more northerly areas of the boreal region is dependent upon supplies transported into the region from more temperate locations.

5.3.1.3 Features of the polar climate   The *polar* climate manifests itself in two forms: the *polar tundra* and *polar ice cap* types. The tundra climate is found only in the northern hemisphere, beginning as far south as about 60° north latitude in northeastern Canada,

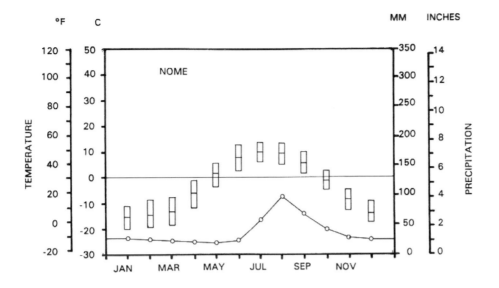

Figure 5.50 The climate of *Nome, Alaska.*

western Alaska, and eastern Siberia, and continuing northward to the northerly extremes of the continents. The polar ice cap climate is present on land masses within the island of Greenland and throughout Antarctica. The boundary between the tundra climate and the boreal climate occurs wherever at least a single month of the year has an average monthly air temperature equal to or greater than 10 °C (50 °F).

An example of a community located in the *tundra* region is Point Barrow, Alaska. There, the average annual air temperature is −12 °C (10 °F), with the highest monthly mean maximum and lowest monthly mean minimum air temperatures of 7.8 and −31.7 °C (46 and −25 °F), respectively. Annual precipitation commonly amounts to less than 250 mm (10 in), and snow cover is present for all but a few weeks (see Figure 5.50). For areas north of the Arctic Circle (66°4′ N), during at least some of the winter, no solar radiation

SIDEBAR 5.16 Permafrost conditions

Permafrost may be present in any of three zones: sporadic, discontinuous, or continuous. The distinction between these three zones is based on how extensive the permafrost exists geographically (e.g., sporadic implies that permafrost is present here and there; discontinuous suggests that permafrost occupies a significant fraction of the land area; and continuous means that all of the land in a region is permafrost). Which form will be present is dependent predominantly on how far north the land is. Sporadic permafrost can be observed as far south as 50° north latitude, whereas the discontinuous permafrost boundary begins at about 60° north. The construction of buildings in permafrost regions requires the use of special foundation assemblies (i.e., one must be careful not to cause the melting of otherwise permanently frozen ground; to do so will severely reduce the bearing capacity of the ground).

will reach ground surfaces at sea level. However, during the summer the sun will remain above the horizon for all 24 hours of the day. Even when the sun is above the horizon, the solar radiation is generally weak except in the most southerly areas of this climate (e.g., in northern Quebec and Newfoundland).

Continuous permafrost is present for most of the tundra region. During the brief summer when the uppermost depth of the ground loses its snow cover and thaws, the native vegetation consists of grasses, lichen, mosses, and low shrubs. Numerous small ponds and bogs also are present at that time. But no forestation is evident in the tundra climate. A number of warm-blooded mammals live in this climate, including the caribou (or reindeer), hares, musk ox, and foxes. Migratory birds also fly in during the summers. Lastly, prodigious quantities of mosquitoes and black flies can be found throughout the wet ground areas of the tundra.[26]

SIDEBAR 5.17 Climatic differences with increased elevation

To exemplify how climate changes with increased elevation, we might consider what vegetative forms are encountered as one climbs Mount Kilimanjaro, located at 3° south latitude in Tanzania. The base of the mountain lies on a lowland plateau at an altitude ranging from 800 to 1300 m (2500 to 4000 ft), where the primary biome is the equatorial savanna with its trees and grassland. Human habitation occurs at the upper range of this plateau (1300 m), where coffee plantations are present and animal herding is observed. Banana trees are also found at this elevation and, also, slightly higher. The native vegetation immediately above the plateau—on the lower sides of the mountain—is the rain forest, consisting of dense broadleaf coniferous trees and brush, including palms and ferns. Human habitation does not extend above about 2200 m (7000 ft) on this mountain, but the rain forest persists to about 2500 m (8200 ft), at which elevation tree presence is less dense. From about 2500 to 3000 m (8200 to 10,000 ft) heather—like that found on the Scottish moors—exists, except on Mount Kilimanjaro this plant grows to heights of two to three m (about six to ten ft). In some locations the heather reaches twelve m (forty ft) or taller. The tree line—the elevation above which few, if any, trees grow—is at about 3000 m. Waist-high grasses also persist from 2500 to 3500 m (8200 to 11,500 ft). Above this band of grasses and heath trees, an alpine region is present up to about 4250 m (14,000 ft). In this regime low heather and moss predominate. This alpine region is also quite dry and shows little surface water. Finally, above 4250 m two conditions exist: first, dry, sandy soil with little vegetation for at least a short distance up the mountain, and, second, at about 4250 m and continuing to the summit at 5890 m (19,390 ft), ice and snow fields, along with a series of well-developed glaciers. The lowest elevations at which these glaciers appear range from about 4400 to 5300 m (14,500 to 17,400 ft), depending on which side one looks. The freezing point (in the overlying air) is usually found at an average elevation of about 4600 m (15,000 ft). The average air temperature at the summit is about −8 °C (18 °F). Thus, at a location only about 300 km (180 mi) from the equator, snow and ice are constantly present at the top of Mount Kilimanjaro. Alternatively, a rain forest and tropical vegetation grow just a short, horizontal distance away from the snow and ice.

For further information about the plant and animal life forms present on and near Mount Kilimanjaro, see the books by Dundas, C., *Kilimanjaro and Its People,* (London: Frank Cass & Company Limited, 1968); note pages 11–32, particularly; and Ricciuti, E.R., *Wildlife of the Mountains,* (New York: Harry N. Abrams, Inc., 1979; note pages 28–29 and 105–117. Also, vegetation presences in the highland Andes and for a middle-latitude mountain are catalogued in Trewartha, G.T., and L.H. Horn, *An Introduction to Climate* (5th edition), (New York: McGraw-Hill Book Company, 1980); see pages 335–337.

Regions exhibiting the polar ice cap climate are the most inhospitable thermally. The designation polar ice cap indicates that a permanent ice cover exists at any site within this climatic type. Two principal areas that experience the polar ice cap climate are the interior of the island of Greenland and the whole of Antarctica. Few, if any, continuously inhabited communities exist in the interior of Greenland, so meteorological data are sketchy at best. Alternatively, a number of continuously peopled stations operate in Antarctica, primarily for research purposes. Average annual air temperatures at *coastal* Antarctic stations vary between about −4 to −18 °C (25 to 0 °F), depending on the latitude of the facility. The average annual air temperatures *within the continent* are as low as about −50 °C (−60 °F) (although most of the reporting stations are at elevations between 2600 to 3000 m [8500 and 10,000 ft]).

5.3.1.4 Features of the highland climate The final climatic type displaying characteristics of the generalized cold climate is the highland type. The designation *highland* characterizes those locales whose climates depend as much on their specific *elevations* as their locations across the surface of the Earth. The fundamental notion of this designation is that if the region were not at *some elevation well above sea level,* then its climate would likely be significantly different. Generally, the principal climatic difference between *high* and *low-elevation* locales, which are otherwise in reasonably close proximity, is that the air temperatures at the higher location will be less.

One example of this phenomenon is Mount Kilimanjaro, which is located about 3° south of the equator. The areas just to the east and west of the mountain experience a tropical-wet-and-dry climate, whereas the land at the base of the mountain, which rests on a plateau at an elevation of about 1000 m (3300 ft), exhibits tropical rain forest vegetation. As one climbs further up the mountain, one encounters locales displaying, in sequence, temperate, boreal, and ice cap climates.

Lands (and communities) located at elevations substantially above sea level will experience markedly different climates than areas in the same latitudes that are nearer sea level. So designers and builders must account for the effects of elevation, particularly when the increased altitude manifests itself through coldness.

5.3.2 CHALLENGES AND PROBLEMS FOR HUMAN OCCUPANCY IN THESE CLIMATIC TYPES

In Chapter 3 we defined the thermal comfort envelope as occurring when the air temperature is between 20 to about 27 °C (68 to 80 °F) with reasonably balanced radiant exchange rates, relatively still air, and moderate relative humidity (when a person is sedentary and wearing a clothing ensemble rated at 1 CLO). For these cold climates the predominant feature is the sustained periods of coldness (or, even, extreme coldness). Related climatic conditions that accentuate this coldness are the comparative dryness (both in terms of precipitation and the humidity in the ambient air), the reduced solar radiation during the winter (because of the shortened periods that the sun is above the horizon and the low angles of the sun above the horizon), and winds that produce the blowing and drifting of snow. Further problems for these poleward regions exist: daytime commonly is a period of little daylight (due to shortened days and low sun angles), the landscape is relatively barren of life, and the snow cover creates a dreary uniformity to the landscape.

Other problems presented by these cold climates include the short growing season and the precariousness of agriculture in general, the inhibitions against moving about in cold, snow-covered areas, the difficulty in constructing buildings in cold weather, and the permafrost presence in the more northerly regions (with its attendant problems for setting foundations for buildings). Thus, between the challenges offered by the climate directly and the constraints placed on life activities indirectly, it is evident that existing in such climates often requires tangible concessions to the natural environments.

Several strategies can be identified for easing the burdens of living and working in cold climates. First, settlements should be organized to create microclimates as favorable as possible. Accommodations—that should be made for both spaces within buildings and for immediately external places—include providing ready solar access, insuring wind control (to reduce wind chill effects and the blowing and drifting of snow), and admitting daylight to as many locations as possible. Reliance on private transportation systems should be reduced, and covered (and possibly enclosed) walkways should be created between buildings. But densely packed residential development, particularly, should be avoided (although commercial development can be closely arranged and still successful). Scandinavian experiences with communities in the northern regions of these countries have shown that high-density residential communities suffer from too little variety between units and areas, family groupings that grow too large, and noise problems (that result from having groups of people confined in often too-small enclosures).

The natural environment around residential groupings, especially, and urban and suburban communities, generally, should be developed for recreational purposes. Further, these recreational facilities need to be placed as close as possible to the residential development and will work best if vehicular transportation is not required for moving between these areas. Vegetation should be planted wherever possible throughout communities, and variation in vegetative forms should be provided, choosing plants that can withstand the indigenous climate.

Buildings will have to be constructed that minimize heat and moisture loss to the external environment. Humidification of internal building spaces is a likely requirement. Glazing should be provided in building envelopes, both to provide view relief and also to admit solar radiation and daylight. Buildings must be placed so that they do not disrupt permafrost conditions. And, recognizing the length and rigor of the winter, construction techniques must be employed that accommodate the limitations imposed by the climate, for example, the use of prefabrication at the site (in a temporarily erected production facility) or the fabrication of components in a factory at some distance from the building site with the units then transported to the site for final assembly.

5.3.3 BASIC FORMS OF HEAT LOSS EXPERIENCED IN BUILDINGS

There are two fundamental modes by which heat loss occurs across the envelope: *transmission* and *infiltration*. These happen by largely natural means (although the rates with which these two modes lose heat can be controlled by devices and strategies that we will discuss in the next sections). A third mode of heat loss may be present, depending on whether external air is intentionally introduced into buildings as a source of ventilation for occupants.

5.3.3.1   Heat transmission: what is it and how can we control it?   Heat transmission occurs as a result of a temperature difference (or gradient) existing from one side of a building envelope to the other. For example, if it is warmer in the building than outside, heat loss happens across the envelope (by transmission). Alternatively, if it is warmer outside (say, on a warm summer day), then heat gain by transmission occurs through the envelope, with the thermal energy moving into the building. Thus, if a temperature difference exists from one side of the envelope to the other, heat transmission occurs (as a consequence of the Second Law of Thermodynamics).

Three parameters determine the rate of heat transmission occurring across a building envelope (i.e., how much energy is transferred per unit time): the amount of *resistance* present in the envelope (that retards energy flow through the envelope); the *surface area* of the envelope that separates the room interior from the outside; and the magnitude of the *temperature difference* between the inside and outside air. Of these three parameters a designer or builder can directly control the first two. The third parameter—the magnitude of the temperature difference—is a property both of the climate of the region in which a building is constructed and the needs of its occupants. The inside air temperature depends on the thermal comfort conditions maintained within the building. The external air temperature, of course, is determined by the weather for some moment (or by the climate, if employing a longer time perspective).

Thus, if the designer or builder wishes to minimize the rate of transmission loss that can happen across a building envelope in a cold climate, s/he can employ a lot of resistance in the building envelope and/or keep the surface area of the envelope, that separates the building interior from the exterior, to a practicable minimum.

5.3.3.2 Heat exchange by infiltration: what is it and how can we control it?   Transmission heat exchange across a building envelope happens when *temperature* differences exist between the interior air and the air outside of the building. Alternatively, infiltration heat exchange occurs as a result of *pressure* differences between the exterior and interior air. Such pressure differences occur when wind blows against the building envelope. In addition,

SIDEBAR 5.18 Resistance of building materials to heat transmission

The amount of resistance that an envelope has is described in terms of units of "R": thus, an envelope with an R of 22 will be more resistant to heat transfer than an envelope with an R of 14. In much of the United States and Canada the amount of resistance that an envelope should have is now dictated by "energy codes" that have been promulgated by local, county, state, or provincial governments. Typically, an energy code will stipulate what amount of R should be present in roofs, walls, and floors, or—alternatively—what materials are appropriate for composing these envelopes. Generally, the most effective material for resisting heat transmission is insulation, a generic identifier for a range of products. The most common insulation products are batts made of glass or mineral fibers and foam boards consisting of either expanded polystyrene or polyurethane. Other insulation materials are available and can be used, depending on localized practices and preferences.

Quantities of resistance, such as R-22 or R-14, are based on the Imperial unit system and have the specific units of hours-square feet-°F/Btu. An R-11 designation matches the resistance provided by a 3.5 in. glass fiber batt, whereas the R-19 rating requires a 5.5 in. batt. The conversion factor between this unit set and the comparable SI unit set of m²-K/Watt is 1.0 hr-sqft-°F/Btu = 0.18 m²–K/W. Therefore, the two batt thicknesses identified above—R-11 and R-19—would have ratings of 1.94 and 3.35 m²/K/W for thicknesses of 3.5 and 5.5 in. (89 and 140 mm), respectively.

For additional information about the resistances of various materials and procedures for calculating the "overall coefficient of heat transmission" (the U-factor) for a building envelope, see Chapter 25 ("Thermal and water vapor transmission data") of the *2001 ASHRAE Handbook of Fundamentals,* (Atlanta, Georgia: American Society of Heating, Refrigerating, and Air-Conditioning Engineers, Inc., 2001).

infiltration can occur as a result of the *stack effect,* in which warm air rises throughout a building and exits at some relatively high location. As warm air leaves the building creating a reduced pressure zone, external air at some lower place will be drawn in.

Thus, the fundamental mechanism for infiltration heat loss is that cold air enters the building, replacing warm building air that exits the building. This cold air then has to be heated in some manner to raise its temperature to whatever level is desired for the interior air (i.e., for the sake of maintaining occupant thermal comfort). Whether the cold exterior air is forced into the building by the pressure difference created by the wind and/or exerted by the stack effect, air will flow through the envelope wherever openings, cracks, and/or other discontinuities are present in the envelope separating this air pressure gradient.

Infiltrating air moves through the building envelope along any of several *continuous air paths* in the envelope. Typical locations include at doors or windows that are open temporarily, while someone enters or leaves a building, or more permanently, when someone opens a window; along cracks around closed windows or doors where the movable pieces do not fit tightly within their frames; or even at cracks between rough framing members in a wood-framed envelope (e.g., where the wood plates meet foundation walls or a prefabricated window assembly is placed in the rough-framed opening).

There are two primary controls for reducing air infiltration (and its attendant heat loss). First, you can reduce the pressure differences that occur across the envelope and, second, you can create as airtight a building as possible. If you can block the wind or cause it to go around or over the building, then the pressure differences between the windward air and the air in the building will be significantly reduced. Alternatively, when infiltration may occur due to the stack effect, then reducing the resulting pressure differences (between the building interior and exterior) can best be accomplished by minimizing pathways for warmed air to rise throughout the building (i.e., by closing off any pathways that exist between floors).

Once adequate means for the reduction of pressure differences are in place, attention can be directed at creating a comparatively airtight building envelope. Often, establishing tight envelopes will require a cooperative approach by the several people (or groups) responsible for the production and use of the building. Initially, the designer must provide a building design (with its component details) that will enable the builder to construct the building well. Secondly, the builder must then exercise due care to ensure that the construction is well performed. Thirdly, the occupant must use the building wisely by not introducing situations that could disrupt the careful design and construction of the building (e.g., permitting excessive moisture to accumulate and cause condensation damage to window frames); *and* provide periodic maintenance, repair, and replacement for the various devices used in the envelope to ensure adequate tightness. Combating air infiltration and its attendant heat loss require on-going attention throughout the design, construction, and operation of a building.

5.3.3.3   Heat loss by ventilation: how does it happen and what controls are reasonable?

Whereas heat losses by transmission and air infiltration happen naturally, ventilation heat loss commonly occurs as a result of direct intervention by the building operator. For a building to be healthful for occupant use, some fresh air must be introduced throughout the building in an on-going, systematic manner. One source of this fresh air can be air that has been previously used within the building and then has been scrupulously cleansed of airborne dirt, pollutants (e.g., tobacco smoke), and odors (e.g., from cooking or people). Alternatively, fresh air generally can more easily be obtained by bringing outside air into a building. The primary limitation to the use of this external air, however, is that, if the

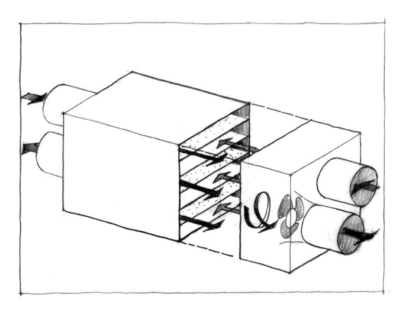

Figure 5.51 A schematic diagram of an air-to-air heat exchanger (AAHX). Note that each air stream will usually be fan driven and that the streams cross—over-to-under and vice versa—within the exchanger box. A residential AAHX commonly has dimensions of about 1.0–1.5 meters (36–60 in) long by 0.5–0.7 m (18–24 in) high by 0.3–0.4 m (12–15 in) wide.

temperature of the external air is very low (as it might be for many locations in the cold climate regions), then substantial heating will be required (and the operation of the building may thus not be very energy-efficient). But, often, the combination of taking in and heating the cold external air is more cost-effective (though less energy-efficient) than performing the scrupulous cleansing required for the re-use of internal air.

Ventilation of the building interior proceeds generally by exchanging equal quantities of fresh, but cold, outside air with used, warm inside air. In this arrangement the heat present in the used inside air is essentially "dumped" to the exterior of the building. Recently, however, an alternative means for thermally conditioning the cold air (using heat other than that derived from a furnace or some other *active* device) has become available, and is likely to be cost-effective in some of the colder regions. To capture most of the "dumped" heat when the used air is vented to the building exterior, a basically passive-hybrid device called an *air-to-air heat exchanger* has been developed (see Figure 5.51). In operation, the exchanger draws warm, used air from the building and moves it past the cold, fresh air in *parallel, but separated, streams*. The exchanger thus enables the entering cold air to gather heat from the departing warm air. Energy to drive the fans used for moving the air streams is all that is required for accomplishing this useful heat exchange. Manufacturers of these exchangers claim efficiency rates (i.e., for heat recovery) as great as 85 percent.[27]

Air passage through most ventilation systems occurs because of the creation of a positive pressure differential by fan operation. Thus, ventilation air flows through such a system at a pressure that is slightly greater than the ambient atmospheric pressure.

Individual spaces in a building will be slightly "pressurized" and, depending on the magnitude of any pressure differential resulting from external air movement (by the wind), may be able to resist all or at least some of the wind force that causes air infiltration. Therefore, this pressurizing of the building can minimize infiltration heat loss. Necessarily, in using a ventilation system, outside air would still enter the building. But it would do so at a centralized location, where it could then be thermally conditioned with an air-to-air heat exchanger or by mixing in some warm, used air.

5.3.4   SELECTING BUILDING FORMS AND OPERATING STRATEGIES THAT RESPOND TO COLD CLIMATES

5.3.4.1   Fundamental operation strategies   We have previously identified a series of needs for site planning and building form; compliance with these needs should provide comfortable and efficient structures in cold climates. Of these requirements the most important is the ability of the building envelope to keep the heat inside a building from escaping out of the building envelope (i.e., to minimize the transfer of heat through this envelope).

5.3.4.2   Specific design and construction guidelines

FOR SITE DEVELOPMENT

(C1) *Provide windbreaks upwind of buildings to reduce pressure differences across building envelopes and, thus, the rates of air infiltration.* As the magnitude of wind pressure is proportional to the square of the wind velocity, anything that can be done to reduce the velocity of wind incident on a building will lessen the rate of infiltration. Windbreaks should be placed between the building and the direction from which the prevailing (or most frequent) winds come. These windbreaks should be located perpendicular to this prevailing direction. The windbreaks can consist of relatively closed (i.e., non-porous) barriers such as fences, vegetation, out buildings, or ground forms. If vegetation is employed, then coniferous varieties are most appropriate for blocking the wind, especially during winter.

(C2) *Provide barriers to prevent the blowing and drifting of snow across the landscape.* Snow covers the ground continuously for a significant portion of the year in most cold climate regions. Snow will become airborne in winds with more than light velocities. To prevent wind-blown snow from being a hazard to those living in these regions, fences, vegetation, or ground forms should be employed to impede it.

(C3) *Employ covered or enclosed walkways in settled areas (especially between buildings).* Alternatives for protecting pedestrians can include the use of narrow streets between medium-rise buildings (to provide wind-shadowed walkways), pathways lined with vegetation or ground forms like berms, and roof covers over walkways that can be deployed temporarily during the winter season to ward off wind and falling snow.

(C4) *Organize building units (e.g., houses, office spaces, stores, and so forth) so that they are attached rather than detached).* Several benefits can be achieved by following this guideline. First, the attached buildings will function as continuous windbreaks for

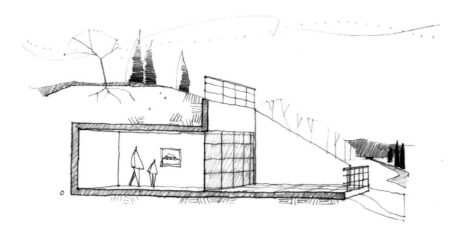

Figure 5.52 A prototypical below-grade building space. Setting the space underground should markedly reduce infiltration heat loss (i.e., the surface area of the building exposed to the wind will be much less than for a comparable above-grade building).

buildings that are downwind of them (thus, reducing the potential for air infiltration in the downwind buildings). Second, creating such windbreaks establishes partially enclosed and protected walkways for circulation between buildings. Third, by attaching buildings, you decrease the surface area of each building that is exposed to the exterior air and thus subject to transmission heat loss.

(C5) *Where the composition of the ground at the building site is suitable, place the building (or a significant portion of it) below grade level* (see Figure 5.52). Usually at a depth of one to one-and-one-half meters (about three to five feet) below the existing grade level, the temperature of the soil, *if dry,* will be relatively constant throughout the entire year. At this depth, the soil temperature will be approximately equal to the average annual temperature of the air for the locale. So, by placing a building below grade, the temperature difference between the inside air and the soil on the external side of the envelope will be significantly less for much of the heating season (i.e., than the temperature difference across a building envelope that separates inside air and outside air). By reducing this temperature difference, one can decrease transmission heat loss. Further, by using earth-sheltering techniques, one also reduces the surface area exposed to the wind. Thus, infiltration heat loss is also reduced.[28]

FOR BUILDING LAYOUTS

(C6) *In areas with frequent high-velocity winds, construct buildings with streamlined shapes to reduce wind loading (and infiltration heat loss)* (see Figure 5.53). Instead of having bluff surfaces facing into the prevailing direction of a winter wind, building surfaces—particularly, roofs—should be canted to ease the wind flow up and over the building. One further means of assisting wind flow over a building (without the wind significantly loading the building envelope) is to construct the building partially below grade (i.e., with the windward elevation built into the earth and with the

Figure 5.53 A traditional saltbox house located in Rehoboth, Massachusetts. The steeply sloped roof on the elevation opposite to the main entrance presents a streamlined shape which will assist the passage of wind up and over the building.

Figure 5.54 High berms placed on three of the four sides of the pool protect it from off-the-ocean winds. The clubhouse protects the fourth side. This swim club is located at the Sea Ranch, some one hundred miles (160 km) north of San Francisco, California.

roofline sloping gradually up from near the grade line). Another related strategy is to create a gently sloping berm on the side of the windward elevation, thus making the transition between ground form and building surface as smooth as possible for the oncoming wind (see Figure 5.54).

(C7) *In locales experiencing substantial snow amounts, use steeply pitched roofs to minimize the accumulation of snow loads on the roofs.* Accumulated snow can create a large deadweight on structures and may lead to roof leakage (from ice dams at the edges of roofs).[29] To minimize the build-up of snow, roofs should be steeply inclined so the snow slides off before there is significant accumulation. Of course, means must be provided to ensure that any snow that does slide off roofs does not fall on pedestrians, causing injuries to them.

(C8) *Align the major axis of the building along the east-west compass line where there are suitable quantities of incident solar radiation and solar heating would benefit the operation of the building* (see Figure 5.55). By placing the major axis along this compass line, the major elevations will be south and north, respectively. The south elevation is the best one for locating glazing to admit solar radiation for the passive solar heating of building interiors (as will be discussed in Section 5.4). A rule-of-thumb for determining whether the passive solar heating of a building is an appropriate

---

SIDEBAR 5.19 Qualifications about the benefits of using compact building shapes

One widely held belief is that a compact shape (e.g., such as a cubical building form) is the most energy-efficient. To what degree this belief is true depends on a number of factors, including the insulation levels attainable in the various parts of the envelope, the possibility that passive solar heating may be employed, and the types of activities that are performed in the building (and, thus, the air temperatures requisite for maintaining occupant thermal comfort). Regarding practicable insulation levels, we can note that, for wood-frame envelopes, wall cavities into which insulation may be placed tend to be *less deep* than flat ceilings (below ventilated attics) or sloped roofs (over cathedral-ceiling spaces). Thus, *more insulation can be placed in the roof than can be built into vertical walls.* So, it may make more sense to have greater roof surface areas and smaller wall surface areas. But in a cubically shaped building constructed with a wooden structural system, the surface areas of the walls greatly exceed the roof area. Therefore, at least on the basis of this first qualifier, the general notion that compact shapes are more efficient is not necessarily true.

Whether insulating materials can be more easily placed in walls or roofs of concrete, masonry, or steel-framed buildings is, of course, greatly dependent on a range of factors, including the types of vertical and horizontal envelope assemblies, the activities for which a building is used, the acceptable thicknesses for the various envelope assemblies, and so forth. To a marked extent, what shapes will provide the best performances thermally and how heat losses can best be limited are questions that may require substantial analysis for any given building project.

The effect of the second qualifier on this notion—employing passive solar heating strategies for building operation—is highly variable. The benefits gained from developing solar heating capabilities (and not using a compact building shape) may outweigh the liabilities imposed by creating a less compact building form. How the third qualifier can influence building performance—that the activities present in a building often dictate that certain building forms be adopted—will be addressed in Guideline C11.

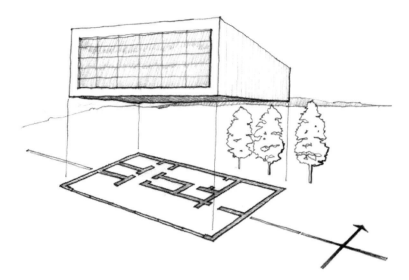

Figure 5.55 To enhance the solar heating of a building, orient the building so that its major axis lies as nearly parallel to the equator as possible. Limit the amount of glazing on elevations that are not used for solar energy collection (but at least provide some glazing for regularly-occupied room so that occupants can see out and gain some daylight for illumination.) Two qualifiers should be noted about this guideline. First, for skin-load-dependent buildings, glazing usually causes the greatest heat loss through the envelope. Thus, for elevations where the opportunity for solar energy collection may be minimal, keeping glazing areas small for these elevations can significantly help to minimize heat loss. Further, small glazing areas should also enable the maintenance of better thermal comfort conditions for occupants who sit or stand near the windows. Second, for internal-load-dominant buildings, deciding upon acceptable heat loss and gain rates through windows and the appropriate sizes and locations of windows in the building envelope can be more complex. For such buildings, the admission of solar radiation can create additional needs for cooling the building interior (i.e., to provide thermally comfortable conditions for the occupants). And, although the presence of glazing may offset some of the heat produced internally within the building — by fostering heat loss through the glazing — such heat loss will occur only at the perimeter of the building and will offer little respite for the overheated interior. Note also that even if a building operates in an internal-load-dominant mode and loses heat at the perimeter, occupants who exist near these windows will probably be thermally uncomfortable due to the cold glazing surfaces (unless active control systems are included in the building to increase the surface temperatures of the glazing.)

operation strategy suggests that for climates with heating degree-day totals greater than 8000 to 9000 per year (based on the 65 °F reference temperature), the benefits will be of marginal economic gain. However, in this northerly cold climate, seeing the sun and feeling its radiation can have important psychological benefits. Thus, the intangible gains from having positive contact with the natural environment might outweigh strictly economic concerns for many inhabitants of these regions.

(C9) *Make efforts to minimize the surface areas of the building exposed to the external air.* Transmission heat loss is especially dependent on the amount of area of the envelope that separates the building interior from the exterior. Infiltration heat loss is not directly dependent on surface area, but a smaller surface will provide less area over

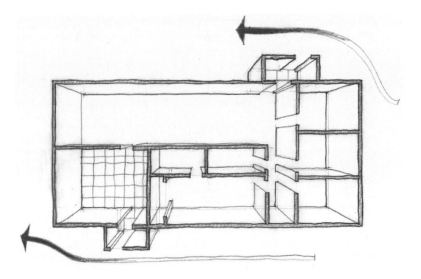

Figure 5.56 Building entrances should have vestibules—or revolving doors, if entry rates are high—to minimize infiltration heat loss when people enter or leave.

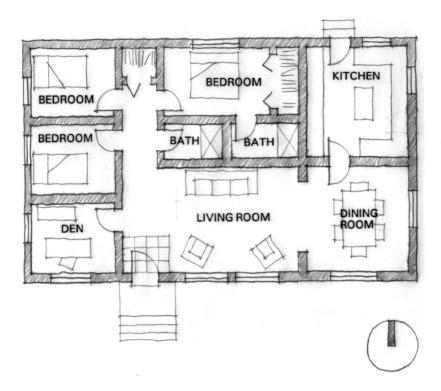

Figure 5.57 Locating spaces in accordance with activity rates and the possibility of gaining passive solar heating.

which the pressure of the wind can act. Also, buildings with smaller surface areas tend to have smaller volumes: the presence of smaller internal volumes suggests that less air will have to be warmed, if infiltration does occur through the building envelope.

(C10) *Place primary doors and windows on the leeward side of the building, and, for doors, provide vestibules or airlocks* (see Figure 5.56). The primary sites at which air infiltration occurs are doors and windows and at the places where these components join the overall framing system of the building envelope. Thus, placing these infiltration-prone sites on the leeward side of the building where they will not be subjected to incident wind pressure should reduce infiltration heat loss.

Using vestibules and airlocks provides a double-door arrangement. Since one door is kept closed as the other one is opened during the entry and exiting of occupants, smaller volumes of building air will leak out of the building (and smaller volumes of infiltrating air will have to be warmed up). These vestibules and airlocks should optimally be placed on the prevailing leeward elevation of the building, simply to reduce wind pressure effects.

(C11) *For residential buildings, organize the floor plan to have sedentary activities on the side facing the equator and more active functions and storage spaces on the side facing away from the equator* (see Figure 5.57). Sedentary activities commonly require higher air temperatures for occupants to feel thermally comfortable, whereas people pursuing active functions will find lower air temperatures suitable. It is generally acceptable to maintain bedrooms (and storage areas) at even lower air temperatures (e.g., when in bed, one has adequate covering to maintain the feeling of warmth). Bathrooms and dressing spaces should be placed within the building interior (thus removed from exterior walls). In bathrooms and dressing areas occupants frequently are in a state of undress and will require comparatively higher air temperatures to maintain thermal comfort.

The primary reason for placing sedentary activities on the south side of the building is that this elevation may receive incident solar radiation to warm the equator-facing spaces. Additionally, in many Northern Hemisphere locations, the coldest winds (and, commonly, the prevailing ones) come from northerly directions. Thus, the north-facing spaces are most likely to experience cold air infiltrating through the building envelope.

(C12) *In some building (or environmental) situations, to ensure that thermally comfortable conditions are most efficiently established, create a small enclosed space—often within an existing building—and provide greater-than-usual insulation amounts and extra heating capabilities* (see Figure 5.58). Sometimes, rather than constructing an entire building with suitable amounts of insulation and heating capabilities, it may be more efficient to set up a limited portion of the building with substantially better environmental controls. This approach can be particularly useful when a building is being renovated. Alternatively, for building applications like warehouses, factories, sports arenas, and other large-volume spaces, specific areas requiring greater levels of thermal comfort can be provided, without forcing the whole building to meet such a heightened standard. Thus, an office area in a warehouse or factory or a locker room in a sports arena can be constructed to offer better thermal conditioning than for other volumes in such buildings.

Figure 5.58 A cardinal rule for achieving energy-efficiency in building operation is to create small spaces, make certain that they are well-insulated, well-built, and well-operated. Then, if you provide a good active or passive heating system, the occupant(s) should be thermally comfortable. This enclosure is used as a refuge against the cold for the outside porter at a New York City hotel.

Figure 5.59 In cold climates, particularly, use well-insulated building envelopes.

FOR ENVELOPE COMPOSITION

(C13) *Ensure that the opaque envelope is well-insulated* (see Figure 5.59). The roofs, floors (above unheated crawl spaces), and walls of any heated building constructed in these cold climates should have appropriately thick layers of insulation, which will provide resistance to transmission heat loss through the envelope. What kind of insulation and how much insulation are questions whose answers will likely differ according to the specific region in which buildings are placed. Minimum amounts of insulation for walls, roofs, and floors are, perhaps, R-19, R-30, and R-19, respectively (note Sidebar 5.18 for information about these resistance amounts). If basements are present instead of floors-above-unheated-crawl-spaces, then the basement walls should be insulated by either attaching insulation to the exterior of the wall or including it within the interior of the wall assembly. If the floor of the building is a slab-on-grade, then insulation may be placed either at the perimeter of or underneath the slab. The specific quantities of insulation for basement and slab-on-grade applications should be at least consistent with building codes for the locale in which buildings are sited.

(C14) *Limit the area of glazing in the building envelope.* The resistance of glazing assemblies to transmission heat loss tends to be about one-fifth to one-tenth (or even less) of the resistances present in insulated opaque envelopes. Thus, transmission heat loss through glazing assemblies will occur at rates five or ten times *greater* than through insulated opaque envelopes.

The area of glazing appropriate for use in a building should be established from regional or local building (or energy) codes consistent with Guideline C13. Some glazing may be required as a means of egress, and glazing is justifiable for permitting the viewing of exterior sights. Further, glazing provides for the admission of daylight. An acceptable minimum area of glazing from these cold climates could be about 10 percent of the surface area of the vertical envelope, although greater or lesser amounts may indeed be required or permitted by applicable building regulations.

(C15) *If passive solar heating of the building interior is considered practicable for your locale* and *heating is needed for the operation of your building, then place the majority of the glazing area on the south elevation of the building* (see Figure 5.55). By doing so, you may provide significant energy savings by utilizing solar radiation as a heat source. Glazing areas on the east and west elevations are commonly less efficient sources of solar heat gain. But before you eliminate glazing on the east, west, and/or north elevations, you should recognize that, as we noted in Guidelines C13 and C14, some glazing should be provided for daylighting the interior and for view purposes.

Note, however, that buildings whose thermal performance can be characterized as *internal-load-dominant* (i.e., when internal heat sources produce more heat than is lost through the envelope) may not benefit from admitting solar radiation through the envelope. For these buildings either glazing may need to be shaded to reduce solar gain or glazing should be placed on building elevations that would receive lesser amounts of solar radiation.

Figure 5.60 An insulating roller blind used in a passive solar house in North Carolina.

(C16) *Ensure that all fenestration used in buildings located in cold climates is composed of insulating glazing assemblies.* To reduce transmission heat loss through glazing, one should employ either multiple-paned assemblies (e.g., double-pane, triple-pane, or quadruple-pane) or double-pane glazing with one of the special treatments like "hard-coating." If passive solar heating is desired, then the glazing assembly should be composed of clear glass (and not have any heat-reflecting or heat-absorbing properties).

(C17) *Provide thermal shutters or night insulation for glazing, particularly where large areas of glazing are used (e.g., for passive solar heating)* (See Figure 5.60). These movable, insulating devices, when placed over glazing, will reduce transmission heat loss that would otherwise occur through the uncovered glazing. The thermal shutters or night insulation should be employed either past sunset or on cloudy days when the solar heat gain rate is low.

SIDEBAR 5.20 Energy conservation codes as requirements for building design

In the United States numbers of governmental jurisdictions have promulgated energy conservation codes that specify the amount of resistance that walls, floors, and roofs are required to have. For the specific requirements that you should observe, you should determine whether the locale hosting a building site is bounded by such a code and then find out what the tenets of that code are. We can note, generally, that many energy conservation codes have been based on a series of standards developed by the American Society of Heating, Refrigerating, and Air-Conditioning Engineers, Inc. One example standard is ANSI/ASHRAE/IESNA Standard 90.1-1999, *Energy Standard for Buildings Except Low-Rise Residential Buildings,* (Atlanta: American Society of Heating, Refrigerating, and Air-Conditioning Engineers, Inc., 1999).

(C18) *In buildings that do not have air-handling systems for ventilating occupied spaces, allow some glazing to be operable to permit the natural ventilation of the building interior (especially for periods of warm weather).* Many locales that experience cold climates have a number of days during the summer when the weather is warm (and even hot). For those days, the windows should be operable to let outside air in to cool the interior.

However, for *internal-load-dominant* buildings (i.e., in which internal heat production rates exceed the heat loss rate at the envelope), reliance on operable windows as a primary means of the cooling the interior can foster occupant discomfort. Operable windows offer little direct control of how the outside air enters the building and where this air goes after it enters. Natural ventilation is a worthy means of cooling comparatively simple buildings (wherein the admission and movement of outside air can be more readily controlled). But, when one operates a complex building (e.g., a school or an office building), air handling should be provided by a well-developed HVAC system.

(C19) *Provide any operable openings with insect screening.* Insects that are present in the comparatively brief summer season for this climate are voracious and can cause much discomfort for unprotected human inhabitants. Thus, means must be provided to keep such insects from entering buildings through any openings in the building envelope.

(C20) *Attend to details such as including vapor retarders in walls and placing weatherstripping and caulking with care.* Although these topics more commonly concern the preparation of construction documents (for buildings), they are still worthy of mention here. Vapor retarders in walls and, if handled correctly, in roofs are essential to control moisture migration through the envelope. In cold climates grievous damage to envelopes can occur if sufficient moisture migrates into an envelope and then condenses and freezes. Alternatively, the application of caulking and weatherstripping to joints and places where operable parts of the envelope come together is most important for tightening the building envelope (against infiltration heat loss).

SIDEBAR 5.21 Tightening building envelopes

Vapor barriers are also useful for limiting the rate of air infiltration through opaque envelope assemblies. Generally, when the vapor barrier is intended as a means to limit infiltration, its edges will be lapped and taped to ensure, as nearly as possible, the creation of a *continuous* barrier. One qualification about such continuous vapor barriers concerns the fact that air infiltration can serve as a path for bringing fresh air into a building. In buildings where continuous vapor barriers are used, the infiltration rates can be reduced to 0.1 air changes per hour or less (i.e., well below healthful levels of fresh air supply). So, for such buildings, other means of fresh air introduction is virtually mandatory. Either an active air handling system or the passive-hybrid *air-to-air heat exchanger* should be included to ensure adequate admission of fresh air. Alternatively, occupants in buildings with limited fresh air may resort to opening windows: the introduction of fresh air by this means — in a cold climate — is *not* energy-efficient.

5.3.5 FURTHER REFERENCES FOR DESIGNING AND CONSTRUCTING BUILDINGS FOR COLD CLIMATES

For insights about the climate, the rigors that it imposes upon the inhabitants of the cold regions, and the cold lands themselves, we recommend the following book:

Lopez, B.H., *Arctic Dreams: Imagination and Desire in a Northern Landscape,* (New York: Charles Scribner's Sons, 1986).

For information about buildings designed and constructed to withstand the severity of the cold climate, we suggest these books:

Latta, J.K., *Walls, Windows, and Roofs for the Canadian Climate* [NRCC 13487], (Ottawa: Division of Building Research, National Research Council of Canada, October 1973).

Matus, V., *Design for Northern Climates,* (New York: Van Nostrand Reinhold Company, Inc., 1988).

Shurcliff, W.A., *Superinsulated Houses and Double-Envelope Houses,* (Andover, Massachusetts: Brick House Publishing Company, 1981).

Whiteson, L., *Modern Canadian Architecture,* (Edmonton, Alberta: Hurtig, 1983).

A comprehensive survey of Ralph Erskine, an architect who has devoted his entire practice to creating buildings for habitation in cold climate regions, is presented in the following special issue of the journal, *Architectural Design:*

Egelius, M., "Ralph Erskine" [AD Profile 9], in *Architectural Design,* 47 (11–12), 1977, pages 751–852.

Additionally, much useful information about designing and constructing buildings for cold climate regions appears in the on-going document series, *Canadian Building Digests,* produced by the Division of Building Research, National Research Council of Canada, Ottawa, Canada.

Section 5.4 | DESIGNING AND BUILDING FOR THE TEMPERATE CLIMATE

The fourth major climate represents a combination of two climatic types identified by Trewartha and Horn: the *temperate continental warm-summer (Dca)* and the *temperate maritime (Do)*.[30] Though these two climatic types together occupy a relatively small total land area across the Earth, the regions exhibiting these climates are some of the most populous. Further, these regions are host to some of the highest levels of cultural and economic development. The temperate continental warm-summer climate type exists only in the middle latitudes of the Northern Hemisphere, whereas the temperate maritime climate can be found in the middle latitudes of both hemispheres. The fundamental characteristic of these climates is that during significant parts of the year, they possess *both* the warm weather of the more tropical (and subtropical) climates and the cool to cold weather of the more poleward climates. As such, the designer and builder will need to respond to both conditions in creating buildings that perform well passively. Thus, the fundamental challenge is to develop building forms and operations that permit a *variability of response* to the range of climatic conditions experienced throughout the year.

5.4.1 LOCATIONS AND CHARACTERISTICS OF THE TEMPERATE CLIMATE

5.4.1.1   Features of the temperate continental warm-summer climate   The *temperate continental warm-summer* climate can be found in the United States starting from the middle Atlantic states and running westward through the central Midwestern states; the eastern European nations surrounding the Danube basin; portions of coastal northeastern China and most of Korea; and approximately the northern half of the island of Honshu. In terms of latitude, these regions are all within the range of 35° to 45° north.

Because the temperate continental warm-summer climate exists between regions we have previously identified as warm-humid and cold, it should seem reasonable that the

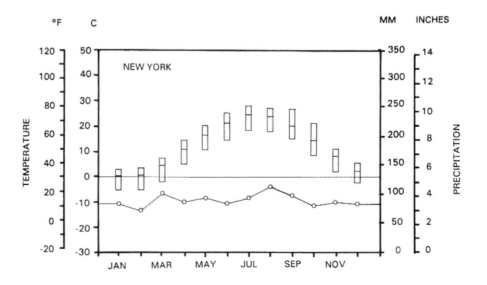

Figure 5.61 The climate of *New York, New York.*

temperate continental warm-summer climate will display the predominant features of each. Indeed, the typical characteristics of the temperate continental warm-summer climate show a sustained period of four to six months of warm weather and a briefer, but continuous, winter season of about three to four months.

The average annual air temperatures range between 10 to 14.5 °C (50–58 °F), with the highest monthly mean maximum air temperatures of about 27 to 29 °C (80–85 °F) and the lowest monthly mean minimum air temperatures between −7 to −1 °C (20–30 °F). These regions experience occasional days with air temperatures at or slightly above 38 °C (100 °F) and at or just below −18 °C (0 °F) annually. Yearly rainfall totals commonly range between 250 to 500 mm (20–40 in), although in coastal areas close to the boundary with the warm-humid climate the rainfall total may be as great as 1250 mm (50 in) per year (see Figure 5.61). The summer will be comparatively wetter than the winter with perhaps twice as much rainfall during this warm season. Additionally, in relatively southern cities experiencing a temperate continental warm-summer climate such as Richmond, Virginia, and Seoul, South Korea, the rainfall in the wettest month can be as much as five times greater than that in the driest month. Precipitation during the winter may occur as snow. Snow covers will last for brief periods in the coastal and more southerly regions of this climate. In more continental locations, particularly in the northerly areas, the snow covers will frequently remain for some weeks at a time. Average monthly relative humidities range between 65 to 75 percent throughout the year, and the summer season can have a substantial number of days with warm air temperatures and high humidities (i.e., much like the neighboring subtropical humid climate).

Wind velocities tend to be light during the summers. But average velocities are greater during the winter with substantial gusting (i.e., localized increases in velocity two or three times greater than ambient wind conditions) occurring during winter storms. Consistent with the comparatively drier winter seasons, solar radiation intensities during the winter are generally sufficient to warrant the use of passive solar heating for building operation.

The primary native vegetative community for these temperate continental warm-summer climate regions is the *broadleaf deciduous forest* (see Figure 5.62). These forests, where still present, usually consist of three distinct layers—arranged horizontally by descending height—of trees, low to middle-height shrubs, and low herbs. Common trees include the oak, beech, maple, chestnut, and cherry. These hardwood trees (and the accompanying shrubs and herbs) shed their leaves with the approach of winter. Leaf-shedding is a response to the cold weather, when growth is curtailed. Note that this behavior is *not* motivated by drought, which is an operational strategy employed by some plants in the semiarid (steppe) and arid (desert) regions. Few of these native-forested areas remain

Figure 5.62 The Esopus Creek in the Catskill Mountains region of New York State. Note the well-developed broadleaf deciduous forest on both sides of the Creek. Numerous species of wildlife abound in the Catskills and the Esopus, and other nearby lakes and streams are renowned habitats for a wide variety of waterfowl and fish.

SIDEBAR 5.22 Temperature isoanomolies

A *temperature isoanomaly* exists for a region (or locale) when the average air temperature is either significantly warmer or cooler than the average air temperature for *all locations across the specific latitude at which the region is located.* As an example, Seattle at approximately 48° north latitude is nearly 8.5 °C (15 °F) warmer in January than the average of January air temperatures for locations at 48° north latitude around the world. For other examples of (and maps showing) isoanomaly conditions for both January and July, see Trewatha, G.T., and L.H. Horn, *An Introduction to Climate* (5th edition), (New York: McGraw-Hill Book Company, 1980), pages 193–199.

Figure 5.63 Low grasslands in eastern Kansas. Once greatly populated by the American bison and other naturally migrating herd animals, these lands are now used primarily for cattle ranching and grain farming.

throughout much of these regions because of the long-established practice of clearing the land for settlement and agriculture. The replacement vegetative forms, where forests have been removed and the land is subsequently allowed to return to its once-native state, are usually low to middle-height grasses (see Figure 5.63). The native soils in these regions are commonly rich in organic materials and can be excellent for agricultural development.

Native animal life consists primarily of grazing and browsing varieties. The grazers exploit the grasslands that exist between the forested areas, and the browsers (i.e., those who feed on the leaves of trees and middle-height shrubs) do well in forested areas. Typical examples of native animal life are deer, bear, various squirrels, foxes, and bobcats. In addition to these native animals, several domesticated animals are present as components of agriculture (e.g., the dairy cow, sheep, hogs, goats, and so forth).

5.4.1.2   Features of the temperate maritime climate   The character of the *temperate maritime* climate is determined strictly by its proximity to the oceans. The principal land areas displaying this climate type are western Europe including the British Isles and southern coastal Norway; the Pacific Northwestern coast of North America (from about 40° to 55° north latitude); southern coastal Chile (from 38° to 55° south latitude); and the southern island of New Zealand, Tasmania, and the southern tip of the Australian state of Victoria. All these areas, except the South Island of New Zealand, are present on the west coasts of continents, and the climates are strongly dependent on the presence of well-established ocean currents. For example, the climate of western Europe is greatly affected by the Gulf Stream, whereas the Pacific Northwestern area of North America receives much of its weather from the North Pacific current. Both of these ocean currents cause the *isoanomalies* of temperature exhibited for these two regions (as discussed in Section 4.3.3).

The essential nature of the temperate maritime climate is that it displays little evidence of extreme temperature and precipitation. The average air temperature is approximately 11 to 13 °C (52 to 55 °F), with the highest monthly mean maximum air temperatures between 21 to 24 °C (70 to 75 °F) and the lowest monthly mean minimum air temperatures about 0 to 4 °C (32 to 40 °F). The air temperatures in these regions rarely exceed 32 °C (90 °F) on the hottest days of the summer, and the coldest days of the winter usually have air temperatures just below freezing (i.e., somewhat less than 0 °C [32 °F]) (see Figures 5.64 and 5.65).

Annual rainfall amounts range between 625 to 1000 mm (25–40 in), although some areas of Chile and Norway receive significantly larger totals. For instance, Bergen, Norway receives about 1960 mm (77 in) annually and Valdivia, Chile records approximately 2490 mm (98 in) per year.[31] The rainfall may be uniformly distributed throughout the year or there may be appreciably greater amounts in some one season (e.g., for regions with seasonal concentrations, there seems to be nearly equal tendencies for the greatest amount to occur in the winter or the summer). These different rainfall patterns appear to be caused by features secondary to the effects of the ocean currents. One characteristic property of the precipitation distribution for all the temperate maritime climate regions, however, is that the number of *rain-days* per year is usually appreciably larger than is observed in land areas adjoining these regions. Thus, whereas the *total* precipitation in the temperate maritime climate regions may be comparatively modest, *how often* precipitation occurs is generally substantially greater than in nearby areas. Snow falls occasionally during the winters in the temperate maritime climate regions, but the amount produced in any one snowstorm is comparatively light (perhaps 5 to 15 cm [2–6 in], typically). Snow cover usually remains on the ground for less than a week.

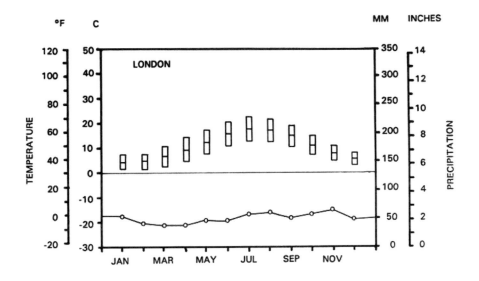

Figure 5.64 The climate of *London, England.*

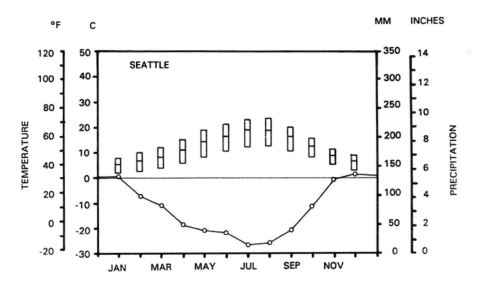

Figure 5.65 The climate of *Seattle, Washington.*

Figure 5.66 A redwood forest in northern California exhibiting old-growth timber.

Throughout the temperate maritime climate regions the average annual relative humidity is approximately 75 percent, a further indication of the large amount of moisture present in the atmosphere. Because of the frequent rainfall and the high humidity levels, the predominant sky condition is overcast. The solar radiation that penetrates the cloud layer tends to be largely diffuse, offering, at best, marginal promise for passive solar heating of buildings. But in temperate maritime climate areas where distinct wet and dry seasons are present, the sky during the dry season will often be mostly clear. Winds throughout these regions tend to have low velocities (i.e., generally less than 4.4 m/sec [10 mph] on average). But occasional winter storms coming off of the oceans will bring higher ambient wind velocities (9 to 18 m/sec [20 to 40 mph] with localized gusts of appreciably greater speeds.)

The native vegetation of these temperate maritime regions varies according to the latitude of any specific region. In the Pacific Northwest region of North America the overall vegetative form is the *temperate evergreen forest* (see Figure 5.66). In its most southerly reaches in northern California the primary tree is the sequoia. Further north through coastal Oregon, Washington, and British Columbia, the forests include fir, pine, and hemlock trees with bushes of laurel, rhododendron, and holly. Then, in the coastal areas of northern British Columbia and southern Alaska, the primary tree becomes the sitka spruce. The forestation that covered much of southern England and northwestern Europe in medieval times has been gone for at least three to four hundred years. The native vegetation, when it still existed, was primarily the *broadleaf deciduous forest,* similar in most respects to that found in temperate continental warm-summer climate regions. Currently, where land has been left uncultivated or undeveloped, grasses and small shrubs grow. In southern England laurel, rhododendron, and holly are also quite common. Alternatively, in Scotland, native vegetation forms are dwarf shrubs, heather, and mosses. Chile and Southeastern Australia, Tasmania, and the South Island of New Zealand have been or are largely forested, albeit with somewhat different forms of forestation than are present in the North American and European temperate maritime climate regions.

5.4.2 CHALLENGES AND PROBLEMS FOR HUMAN OCCUPANCY IN THESE CLIMATIC TYPES

For the major climates discussed in sections 5.1 to 5.3, the primary challenge to comfortable and efficient human occupancy is *unimodal:* a single problem exists whose parameters are so specific and rigorous that attention must be focused on them, if one is to create a successful building. For instance, in the *hot-dry* climate, air temperatures consistently exceed comfortable conditions and atmospheric moisture — whether as rain or as relative humidity — is less than that needed to sustain human activity. These parameters, combined with the intense solar radiation and brisk, hot wind, establish needs for buildings that must be dealt with to ensure the survival and well-being of the inhabitants of the hot-dry climate regions. Dealing with these parameters is of paramount importance. That a cool season is also present for the hot-dry climate introduces a problem of lesser significance. Some means to keep heat in the building (and to provide supplemental heating for the sake of space conditioning) is required, but the cool season is brief and not especially rigorous in comparison to the magnitude of the problems posed by the overheated, dry season. Therefore, the problem of building design and construction in the hot-dry climate can be described as essentially unimodal.

Similarly, we might say that the other two major climates — the *warm-humid* and the *cold* — also require essentially unimodal building responses. For the first, the overheatedness and attendant high humidity are not life-threatening, but instead are causes of thermal discomfort. Buildings, thus, require the use of devices to create more comfortable conditions. For the areas of the warm-humid climate in which a brief cool winter season is experienced (e.g., the southeastern United States), relatively minor adjustments to one's buildings will permit the maintenance of thermal comfort and efficient building operation. For the cold climate, the underheatedness of the climate is of such rigorous proportions that buildings must be developed to minimize heat transfer from the building interior to its exterior. Although some warm weather is present in the more southerly areas of cold climate regions, those periods of overheatedness are brief and do not foster significant thermal discomfort. Each of these two major climates thus dictates that buildings be designed and constructed to afford shelter, comfort, and efficient operation for a principal thermal season. If one has satisfied the needs for the major challenge, then responding to the secondary thermal season will present fewer problems.

Now, for the *temperate* climate regions, the basic challenge is *bimodal*. Two problem phases exist in this climate: namely, a generally warm, humid summer and a cool to cold winter. Both of these phases impose thermal stress on the individual, although rarely to the extent of the stress in the other major climates. Instead, the fundamental challenge is to respond to two different climatic conditions of near-equal severity. The temperate climate is somewhat overheated for periods of the summer and underheated for periods of the winter. Maintaining thermal comfort in the summer will depend on being able to reject the excessive heat gains posed by elevated air temperatures, high humidity, and solar radiation. Alternatively, for the winter, establishing thermal comfort will depend both on how well heat loss to one's surroundings can be limited and on whether some beneficial heat gain can be found from a natural source like the sun. Thus, in many respects, a building designed and constructed for this climate must be convertible: it must include capacities that can be altered to meet these two contrasting seasons. Though the temperate climate does not impose the severity of weather seen in the other major climates, the task of creating buildings that offer a sufficiently flexible climatic responsiveness can be more difficult than building for the other three major climates.

5.4.3   AN OVERVIEW OF OPERATING STRATEGIES FOR THE TEMPERATE CLIMATE

To describe what operating strategies are appropriate for these climates we will initially divide the discussion so that we may separately consider the overheated and underheated seasons of the year. Then, for each of these two seasons, we will differentiate between the *temperate continental warm-summer* climate type and the *temperate maritime* climate type.

5.4.3.1   Operating strategies for the *overheated* season   The aspects of the overheated season of the temperate climate that need attending by designers and builders include: air temperatures above the comfort zone; accompanying high relative humidities; strong solar radiation; little wind movement; and brief, intense thunderstorms. Generally, the strength of these conditions will be greater (and, thus, more challenging to establishing occupant comfort) in the temperate continental warm-summer climate regions than in the temperate maritime climate regions. In fact, in locales with the temperate maritime climate, summer conditions commonly will be quite pleasant, including air temperature and relative humidity combinations that are within the thermal comfort zone. For the temperate maritime climate regions, then, the only accommodation needed may be blocking the strong solar radiation that often is present on warm days. Thunderstorms tend also to occur less often in the temperate maritime climates and, consequently, require little attention.

Three operating strategies should be accounted for in the design of the building envelope. First, to keep solar radiation off of inhabitants, shading devices should be provided for openings in the envelope. Coverings for walkways may also be included. Second, to offset too-warm air temperatures and excessive relative humidities, means for naturally ventilating the building interior should be employed. Third, to handle the often-drenching summer rainstorms, rain protection for buildings and drainage systems for built-up areas are necessary.

5.4.3.2 Operating strategies for the *underheated* season   The duration of the underheated season for the temperate climate typically is somewhat briefer than that of the overheated season. But the magnitude of the thermal stress experienced during the underheated season is usually greater than that found in the overheated season. The primary attributes of the *cold season* are air temperatures that are well below the comfort zone, air that is less moist than air present in warmer times, gusting winds (sometimes of comparatively high velocities), some rain and snow; and occasional-to-frequent periods of bright solar radiation. The temperate maritime climate commonly imposes less severe winter conditions than does the temperate continental warm-summer climate. For instance, regions having the temperate maritime climate experience—during this underheated season—comparatively higher air temperatures, lower wind velocities, more rain and less snow, and more heavily overcast skies with weak solar radiation.

Two primary operating strategies for the temperate climate during this underheated season are essential: buildings must be well-designed, constructed, and maintained to minimize the transfer of heat from the inside to the exterior (by transmission and infiltration); and where sufficient solar radiation is present to justify its use as a principal heating source, then passive solar heating strategies should be employed. However, a basic qualification about relying on passive solar heating techniques in the temperate climate is that, first, you should provide a well-insulated, tight envelope; and, second, after this first step is assured, you can proceed with the inclusion of solar heating. In other words, *this qualification advocates first using whatever resources (e.g., economic) are available to reduce potential heat loss, before employing solar heating.* If you follow this prescription, both the building and the solar heating capability will likely be more efficient.

5.4.3.3 A short explanation about how *passive* solar heating assemblies function
The operations of both *active* and *passive* solar heating systems include five functions: the admission of solar radiation; the collection of solar (thermal) energy; the storage of thermal energy; the distribution of stored energy through the areas to be conditioned with the energy; and the control of the operation of the solar system. The primary differences between active and passive systems include the following features. Usually, the active system is developed separately from the basic building envelope and interior, whereas the passive system will be composed of parts of the envelope and interior. Secondly, whatever moves in the active system (e.g., gases or liquids for the collection, storage, and distribution of thermal energy) will do so because some active energy source—for example, electricity—is applied. Alternatively, in passive systems, movement of these gases or liquids occurs naturally (i.e., without relying on active energy sources). Lastly, the controls for an active system commonly promote automatic operation, whereas in the passive system the building occupant will control it by working the system parts manually. In addition, many variations derive from the simpler, more common organizations of these systems. In such variations, the distinctions separating the systems can become fuzzy.

The number of parts involved in a solar heating system can vary, and some parts can perform more than one function. In most passive systems operations proceed in the following manner. First, solar radiation passes through an aperture (i.e., a transparent or translucent material that separates the system interior from the exterior air). Second, most of the solar radiation is absorbed by a collector surface. In some passive systems the collector surface and the storage medium will be one and the same. In others, collection and storage of thermal energy will be performed by different components, and the collected energy will be transferred by the three means of sensible heat exchange (specifically, conduction, convection, and radiation). Third, if we consider the type of passive system where the collector surface and the storage medium are physically joined (e.g., flat black paint applied to a concrete wall), the energy absorbed by the collector surface will be conducted into the storage medium and will gradually heat up this medium. Fourth, as the storage medium is warmed and a temperature difference develops between the surface of the medium and the air surrounding it, heat transfer will occur between the surface of the medium and the air by natural convection. Similarly, as temperature differences develop between the surface of the medium and nearby objects, then these objects will gain heat by longwave radiant transfer from the medium (i.e., the *net* radiant transfer will proceed from the medium to the objects). And, fifth, in passive systems, *control* of this heating procedure usually occurs manually. A variety of controls can be exercised, including deploying a shading device (when the building becomes too hot from admitted solar radiation), putting up some night insulation over a glazed aperture (to reduce heat loss from the warm interior to the cold exterior), or opening vents (small passages through which naturally convected, warmed air can move to heat an adjoining space).

5.4.3.4   The basic types of passive solar systems   There are three principal types of passive solar systems: *direct gain, indirect gain,* and *isolated gain.* The primary difference between these types involves the physical relationship between the building occupant and the aperture and collector for the system. In the direct gain passive system, the aperture, collector, storage medium, and occupant all share the same space (see Figure 5.67). In the indirect gain system the collector and storage medium separate the occupant from the aperture (see Figures 5.68 and 5.69). In the isolated gain system, the aperture and collector (and, possibly, the storage) are located in some remote space away from the occupant (see Figure 5.70).

The two principal forms of the *direct gain* passive system are the *sunspace* and the *greenhouse.* In these two systems the collector and storage devices are the walls and floor of the building. Further, for greenhouses, the earth or water in which the plants grow may also collect and store solar radiation. For direct gain systems solar radiation enters the space through the aperture and is absorbed by various surfaces in the space. These surfaces (and their underlying materials) warm up, serving as heat sources for promoting natural convection and longwave radiant exchange throughout the space. Because these surfaces are present within the spaces occupied by the building inhabitants, the heating process is said to be direct.

For the *indirect* gain passive system the primary forms are the *masonry wall* (frequently called a *Trombe wall*) and the *water wall.*[32] In these systems the collector surface and storage medium are encompassed within a masonry or water wall that is placed between the aperture and the living space. The water wall is usually composed of a series of translucent or opaque plastic cylinders that contain water. These cylinders are placed in a row separating the aperture (window) from the living space. They generally have

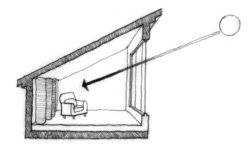

Figure 5.67 A prototypical *direct gain* passive solar system, showing the aperture for admitting the solar radiation and the water cylinders which serve as the collectors and storage medium for the solar energy.

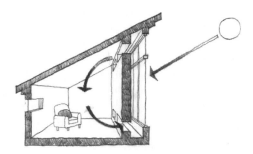

Figure 5.68 An *indirect gain* passive solar system, based on a Trombe wall with its operable vents at the bottom and top of the wall (which enables a convective air loop connecting the air channel between the wall and glazing and the occupied volume).

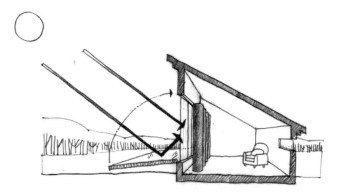

Figure 5.69 A water-wall indirect gain solar system. Note the use of a convertible reflector surface which will redirect solar radiation reaching the reflecting surface toward the water wall. This reflecting surface is part of an insulating shutter that can be pulled up, at night, to cover the glazing reducing the rate of heat loss through the fenestration. This combination of a reflecting surface-shutter and a water wall (as collector and storage) was introduced by Steve Baer of the Zomeworks, Albuquerque, New Mexico.

diameters of about 0.33–0.50 m (12–18 in) and heights equal to the distance from the floor to the top of the aperture.

If we consider a masonry wall as the storage medium, the operation of this indirect gain system commences with solar radiation passing through the aperture and onto the surface of the wall. As the surface of the wall becomes warmer, the thermal energy gained is transferred by conduction into the wall. Some of this heat will be stored in the mass of the wall, and the remainder will slowly flow through it. Over the passage of time (usually a few to several hours), some of the transferred heat will reach the other side, warming it. Then, the warmth on the side of the wall facing the living space will transfer heat by natural convection and longwave radiation to the internal space and objects within the space. The fact that the wall separates the sun from the occupied space is the reason why this system is called an indirect gain system (i.e., because there is no general "line-of-sight" between the sun and the occupant).

One modification that is frequently used with the masonry wall system is the inclusion of operable vents at the top and bottom of the wall (see Figure 5.68). When the outer surface of the wall is warmed by the incident solar radiation, the channel air will also become warm. If the vents at the top and the bottom of the wall are then opened, the heated air from the channel will pass through the top vents into the occupied space and cooler air near the floor of the occupied space will pass out through the bottom vents into the channel. Thereby, air circulation between the channel and the occupied space occurs.

Note that a *roof pond* (see Figure 5.41) can also be used as an indirect gain system. When the water bags are exposed — the covering panels are removed — to solar radiation, the water will be heated. After the sun has set, the insulating panels can cover the heated water bags. The heat stored in the water bags will conduct through the supporting ceiling creating a warm ceiling surface. This warmed ceiling surface can then function as a radiant source that provides heat for the occupants.

The primary differences between the *isolated gain* system and the other two passive systems are that the collector and storage components for the isolated gain system are located away from the occupied space (i.e., are isolated from the living area) and generally separated from each other. The collector may be placed either external and separate from the building or attached to the building. Alternatively, the storage device will usually be a part of the building, but not immediately adjacent to the occupied space. In an isolated gain system, an aperture covers the collector surface, and an air channel exists between the aperture and surface. Solar energy heats the collector surface, and the channel air grows warm (see Figure 5.70). The warmed air rises and passes out of the collector, either to the occupied space or into a storage medium like a rock bin. If the air enters a rock bin, then the heat from the air will warm the rocks and they will store the thermal energy. Cooler air exiting the rock bin or the occupied space will pass back into the air channel at its bottom and be warmed once again. Thus, a convective loop transfers heat from the collector to storage or the occupied space. In operation a daytime loop exists between the collector and the storage bin, warming up the rocks. Then, at night, air movement past the aperture is closed off, and air circulation between the rock bin and the occupied space is opened. Thus, the heat stored in the rocks passes into the occupied space by natural convection. Throughout the isolated gain system air can move either through vents between adjacent spaces or via ducts. If ducts are employed, then air movement can be aided by employing electric fans. Lastly, a principal reason for employing an isolated gain system is that its presence will have comparatively little impact on the physical form of the building served by the system. Because the collector can be placed outside the

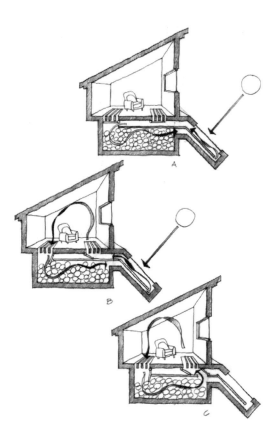

Figure 5.70   The inclusion of a rock bin as a storage facility for an isolated gain passive solar system. In View (A), the collected solar energy is passed to the circulating air, and the heat entrained in the air is transferred to the rocks. In View (B), the collected solar energy is transferred to the circulating air that enters the occupied volume of the building to warm it. In View (C), the stored heat from the rock bin is used to warm the occupied area.

SIDEBAR 5.23 Generating "rules-of-thumb" for passive solar designing

These rules-of-thumb, consistent with most short-cuts employed in the passive solar building industry, have been generated by computer simulation to predict the likely thermal performances of passive buildings. Simulation of a building proceeds by describing its thermal performance with a series of equations that portray heat transfer throughout the building. Then, the computer solves these equations iteratively, thus modeling how the building would behave if it were built and subjected to stimuli like external weather and occupant activities.

Rules-of-thumb are widely used in the passive solar building industry and have been found to offer accuracies (of performance prediction) consistent with the level of approximation commonly sought in the early phases of building design. More precise methods for assessing the likely performance of solar buildings are available and are appropriate for the later stages of building design. Volume 3 of the *Passive Solar Design Handbook* presents some of these evaluative techniques.

building—whether attached to or separated from it—and any storage can be remotely located from occupied spaces, the spaces will not have to accommodate the storage devices of the direct gain system nor will the solar system have to be bounded by a masonry wall or a waterwall. The isolated gain system will necessitate little compromise between the requirements and the organization or appearance of the occupied spaces. Thus, the isolated gain system offers perhaps the greatest freedom in laying out a building interior.

5.4.3.5 Three "rules-of-thumb" for rough-sizing the basic elements of a passive solar system   Scientists at the Los Alamos National Laboratory have produced the most comprehensive set of information for designing and constructing passive solar buildings. Much of their work is recorded in the three-volume document, *Passive Solar Design Handbook.*[33] In the *Handbook* the authors describe, generally and specifically, how to create passive solar systems. They then offer various methods for analyzing the likely thermal performance of the systems (and the buildings associated with these systems). We will introduce three "rules-of-thumb" offered in Volume 2 of the *Handbook,* which may be considered as the essential guidelines to begin the designing of passive solar buildings.

> **First Rule:** "A solar collection area of (column A1 of Table 5.1) to (column A2) of the floor area can be expected to reduce the *annual heating load* of a building in the identified city by (Column H1) to (Column H2), or, if night insulation valued at R-9 is used, by (Column H3) to (Column H4)."[34]

This rule has been prepared for approximately 240 cities in the United States and Canada. For a sample application, please look at Table 5.1. There, find the city in which the solar-heated building is located. Then, note the quantities in columns A1 and A2. These quantities suggest the area for the aperture of the solar system *as percentages of the floor area to be heated by the solar system* (i.e., multiply the floor area by these percentages to find the requisite aperture area). The values in columns H1 and H2 will tell you what percentage of the anticipated *annual heating load* can be met by using a passive solar system to condition your building in this location. The quantities in column H3 and H4 indicate what percentage of annual heating load can be provided by the solar system, *if the system includes night insulation (or thermal shutters) rated at R-9*. A specific notion of this rule-of-thumb is that if you create an aperture larger than the maximum size suggested by this rule, then the future occupants will probably experience overheating of the solar-conditioned space, and a *decreased* percentage of the annual heating load, supplied by solar heat gain, may result.

For an example, if we use the table to establish a recommendation for Washington, D.C., the rule tells us that a solar collection area of 12 to 23 percent of the floor area can be expected to reduce the annual heating load of a building in Washington, D.C., by 18 to 28 percent, or, if night insulation valued at R-9 is used, by 37 to 61 percent. The quantity by which the annual heating load is reduced (by including the solar heating capability) is known as the *Solar Savings Fraction* (or SSF). The significance of the Solar Savings Fraction is that it tells you by how much you can reduce your heating load annually by capturing solar energy within your building. You should note that that quantity of the heating load not supplied by solar energy has to be provided by some other source (e.g., an oil-burning furnace or a wood-burning stove). Note also that the reason why the fraction of the annual heating load provided by solar heat gain may be *decreased* (if the aperture is oversized) is that *overheated* occupants may manipulate components of their building

TABLE 5.1
RECOMMENDED SOLAR COLLECTION AREAS FOR NORTH AMERICAN CITIES
(note that these cities are the same as those listed in Table 4.32)

CITY	T&H ClimDes	A1	A2	H1	H2	H3	H4
Boston, MA	Dca	15	29	17	25	40	64
Chicago, IL	Dca	17	35	17	23	43	67
Cincinnati, OH	Dca	12	24	15	23	35	57
Columbia, MO	Dca	13	26	20	30	41	66
Dodge City, KS	Dca	12	23	27	42	46	73
Richmond, VA	Dca	11	22	21	34	37	61
Washington, DC	Dca	12	23	18	28	37	61
Medford, OR	Do	12	24	21	32	38	60
Seattle, WA	Do	11	22	21	30	39	59
Albuquerque, NM	BSk	11	22	29	47	46	73
Atlanta, GA	Cf	08	17	22	36	34	58
Austin, TX	Cf	06	13	27	46	37	63
Denver, CO	BSk	12	23	27	43	47	74
Miami, FL	Aw	01	02	27	48	31	54
Mobile, AL	Cf	06	12	26	44	34	60
Santa Maria, CA	Cs	05	11	31	53	42	69
Spokane, WA	BSk	20	39	20	24	48	68
Phoenix, AZ	BWh	06	12	35	57	45	73
Dartmouth, NS	Dcb	14	28	17	24	45	70
Edmonton, ALA	E	25	50	NR		54	72
Ottawa, ONT	Dcb	25	50	NR		59	80
Winnipeg, MAN	Dcb	25	50	NR		54	74

EXPLANATIONS FOR THE ABBREVIATIONS:

T&H ClimDes = Climate classifications taken from the book by Tre-wartha, G.T., and L.H. Horn, *An Introduction to Climate* (5th edition), (New York: McGraw-Hill Book Company, 1980), see pages 228ff.
A = Minimum south-facing glazing area (reported as a percentage of the floor area served by this glazing area)
A2 = Maximum south-facing glazing area
H1 = Minimum percentage of an annual heating load (that a passive solar system would provide if the south-facing glazing area is equal to some value between A1 and A2)
H2 = Maximum percentage of an annual heating load (achieve by matching the same condition listed for R1)

H3 = Minimum percentage of an annual heating load (that a passive solar system would provide if the south-facing glazing area is equal to some value between A1 *and* A2 and night insulation with a resistance rated at R-9 is employed)
H4 = Maximum percentage of an annual heating load (that a passive solar system would provide if the south-facing glazing area is equal to some value between A1 *and* A2 and night insulation with a resistance rated at R-9 is employed)
NR = Attempts to operate a passive solar system without night insulation for the solar aperture are *not recommended*

Source: Balcomb, J.D., D. Barley, R. MacFarland, J. Perry, Jr., W. Wray, and S. Noll, *Passive Solar Design Handbook* (Volume 2: *Passive Solar Design Analysis*), (Springfield, Virginia: National Technical Information Service, U.S. Department of Commerce, 1980).

space in an effort to reestablish their thermal comfort. For instance, as their spaces grow too warm, they might open a window or close the blinds behind the solar aperture. Either of these steps would reduce the effectiveness of the passive solar system, leading to a *decrease* in the Solar Savings Fraction.

> **Second Rule:** "A thermal storage mass of (60 times the annual heating load reduction percentage) in pounds of water or (300 times the annual heating load reduction percentage) in pounds of masonry is recommended for each square foot of south-facing glazing."[35]

For this rule you take whatever *percentage of the annual heating load reduction* that you have decided to aim for after using the First Rule and *multiply that percentage by either 60 or 300* (depending on what kind of storage mass you intend to use). The resulting product is the *number of pounds of mass that must be provided* per square foot of south-facing glazing area. The Los Alamos scientists note that three specifications must be observed for this mass (i.e., to ensure that the mass is adequate for storing the solar energy): the mass must be located in the space to be conditioned with solar radiation; the mass must have a direct "line-of-sight" with the sun, and *the surface area of the mass should be at least three times the area of the south-facing glazing;* and there should be no insulation between the air in the space (separating the aperture and the mass) and the mass. Moreover, as a fourth specification, the solar energy-absorbing mass should have dark-colored, matte finishes. Generally, if you cannot comply with the Second Rule and these qualifications (i.e., you have an inadequate amount of mass for storing the solar energy), then your space will probably overheat on clear, sunny days.

Now we can apply this Second Rule, continuing with the example begun previously for a passive-solar-heated building in Washington, D.C. If you have chosen to aim for an annual heating load reduction (or Solar Savings Fraction) of 25 percent—from your use of the First Rule—then you would need a south-facing glazing area of about 20 percent of floor area (presuming that you are not going to use any night insulation). And if the floor area for the space you want to condition with solar energy is 400 square feet, then you will need a glazing area of 80 square feet. The amount of mass (of masonry) needed

---

SIDEBAR 5.24 Consequences of deviating from optimal sitings

A former student of ours explored the consequences of facing a Trombe wall (for a house he wished to build) toward the *southwest* (45° west of true south), rather than toward the south. This house was to be constructed in Yokohama, Japan. The Yokohama climate—though in a subtropical humid climate zone—is actually quite similar to that experienced in Washington, D.C. because of local factors including a well-developed smog layer. His studies of this indirect gain system showed that the southwest-facing Trombe wall system would gain about 35 percent less solar energy than a similar Trombe wall system that faced true south. For further information about the bases and results of the study, see the paper by Waki, T., A.F. Emery, D.R. Heerwagen, and C.J. Kippenhan, "A parametric study of a passive solar-heated house with special attention on evaluating occupant thermal comfort," *Proceedings of the Sixth National Passive Solar Conference* (edited by J. Hayes and W. Kolar), (Newark, Delaware: American Solar Energy Society, 1981), pages 450–454.

will be 0.20 times 300 (or 60) pounds of masonry *per square foot of glazing area.* The total amount of mass should then be 60 pounds/square foot of glazing times 80 square feet or 4800 pounds of mass. This mass should also have a surface area of at least three times the glazing area and, therefore, should be spread out over 3 times 80 (or 240) square feet.

Third Rule: "The orientation of the solar glazing should lie between 20° east and 32° west of *true* south." [36]

The Los Alamos scientists found that to obtain the optimal performance from a passive solar heating system, the solar glazing (or aperture) should generally face true south. However, locating the glazing so that it was oriented within the range cited in this Third Rule would provide performances no less than 90 percent of the optimal behavior. Some exceptions to orientations of true south, however, were noted in the Los Alamos studies: these were explained by local climatological conditions. For example, one exception was for Santa Maria, California, where fog is frequently present during mornings throughout the times of the year when passive solar heating would be advantageous. For Santa Maria, then, the Los Alamos scientists' computations suggested that the optimal orientation for the solar glazing would be 30° west of true south. [37] Otherwise, for solar glazing oriented outside of the range cited in this Third Rule, the fraction of the annual heating load saved by the passive solar heating system would be lessened.

5.4.4   SELECTING BUILDING FORMS AND OPERATING STRATEGIES THAT RESPOND TO THE TEMPERATE CLIMATE

The fundamental character of the temperate climate is that it is variable across the year. Therefore, for a building to be successful in satisfying the different challenges posed by the climate, it will have to vary its response or be *convertible.* Where the building cannot provide a variable response — for example, the cost to offer such convertibility would be prohibitive — then the more favorable strategy likely would be to develop a building that responds better to one season or the other. The choice of which season to design or build for should be dictated either by specific needs of the future occupants (when these needs are known) or, when the needs are unknown, according to the preferences of the designer or builder. Trying to respond to the variability of a climate when you cannot build in such a variable response is one of the primary trade-offs (or conflicts) for creating comfortable, efficient buildings.

In the following list we will specifically include guidelines that present variable responses. The designer or builder *who wishes to focus a response to one season or the other* should instead review the guidelines suggested for the warm-humid climate and the cold climate and focus upon their applications to create an energy-efficient building.

FOR SITE DEVELOPMENT

(T1) *Examine the building site for insights about its microclimate.* First, the temperate climate has a variable character across the seasons of the year. Second, the periods of quite hot and very cold weather occur relatively infrequently. Third, the ranges of these extreme conditions — how overheated or underheated these periods are and how long they last — are relatively less pronounced than the extreme conditions are for the other three major climates. Consequently, the temperate climate is more uniform comparatively than these other major climates.

Given this relative uniformity, a small variation in the climate around a building may have a comparatively large effect on the thermal performance of the building. What could cause such variations would be some localized condition. For example, if the site were on the side of a valley or on the valley floor, the microclimate in either situation could be expected to be different from a site on a relatively flat plain. Alternatively, if the site were surrounded by well-developed vegetation or if the site were near a sizable body of water, the microclimate in either instance would likely be different than would be found at a site with neither significant vegetation nor a large water area near it. Among the qualities of the site that can affect its microclimate are the nature of the terrain (e.g., whether it is in an area of general flatness, sloped lands, or rolling hills), the vegetation present on or near the site, the patterns of adjacent buildings and settlement, proximity to a large body of water, different soil types, and so forth. Estimating how the character of the site will determine the microclimate is at best an imprecise exercise: there has been too little systematic measurement work done to enable specific quantification of the effects of these qualities. Perhaps the best advice that we can offer is to encourage designers and builders to recognize that all of these qualities will affect the microclimate of a site (making it somewhat different from the regional macroclimate) and to suggest that the designer and builder be sensitive to the properties of sites and develop, over time, a personal database of experiences.

(T2) *Consider the airflow paths over and through the site.* For the temperate climate, reducing infiltration heat loss from the building during the winter and enhancing

---

SIDEBAR 5.25 Issues concerning the use of vegetation for solar shading

One qualification about using deciduous vegetation as a seasonally-selective shading device concerns the relative openness of the trunk and branching structure. If there is substantial trunk and branch development, then—even with the leaves gone—the vegetation could be quite closed to the penetration of direct-beam solar radiation. For further information, see the papers by Montgomery, D.A., S.L. Keown, and G.M. Heisler, "Solar blocking by common trees," *Proceedings of the Seventh National Passive Solar Conference* (edited by J. Hayes and C.B. Winn), (Boulder, Colorado: American Solar Energy Society, Inc., 1982), pages 473–478; and McPherson, E.G., R. Brown, and R.A. Rowntree, "Simulating the shadow patterns for building energy analysis," *Proceedings of the Tenth National Passive Solar Conference* (edited by A.T. Wilson and W. Glennie), (Boulder, Colorado: American Solar Energy Society, Inc., 1985), pages 378–382.

A very nice discussion relating the times when buildings may be overheated with the shading potential of native vegetation has been provided in the book by V. Olgyay, *Design With Climate,* (Princeton, N.J.: Princeton University Press, 1963), pages 74–77.

One other point to consider when thinking of vegetation either as a useful shading device or as a block to the penetration of direct-beam solar radiation is that vegetation is necessarily a living, *growing* entity. Note that a plant, when delivered from the nursery to the building site, may not be of sufficient height or form (unless you are willing to pay an additional sum to secure a suitable plant) and therefore will not furnish the shading you had planned on. Alternatively, the designer or builder, who thinks at the time of construction that existing vegetation will not interfere with a passive solar heating scheme, may have to provide selective cutting and pruning services some years later.

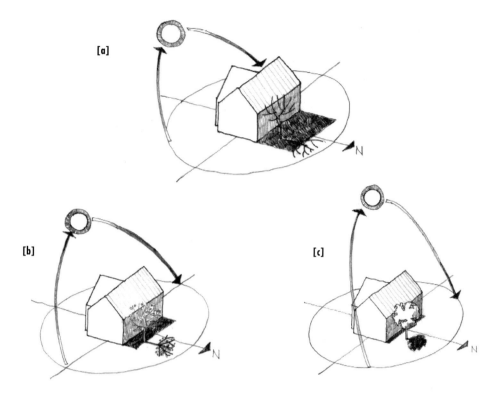

Figure 5.71 Solar paths across the sky vault: (a) at the winter solstice; (b) at the spring/autumn equinox; and (c) at the summer solstice.

natural ventilation through the building during the summer may be primary operational goals. The designer and builder will need to ascertain the prevailing directions for winter and summer winds. Then, decisions can more readily be made about where and how to place windbreaks and how to open up channels through which summer winds can flow.

(T3) *Determine whether direct-beam solar radiation can reach the proposed building at the various times of the year* (see Figure 5.71 a–c). Knowing whether direct-beam solar radiation will be incident on glazing surfaces will enable you to determine if the building can be passively solar heated and/or if shading devices will be needed to reduce solar heat gain loads within the building (see Figure 5.72 a–c). Note that deciduous vegetation (e.g., trees, shrubs, and vines) can shade the building during the summer. Alternatively, upon losing its foliage at the end of the growing season, the vegetation will pass direct-beam solar radiation to building surfaces during the winter. When selecting vegetation to use for shading, try to match the time of the year when the building interior is most likely to be overheated (and needs shading) with the period when a plant has substantial foliation.

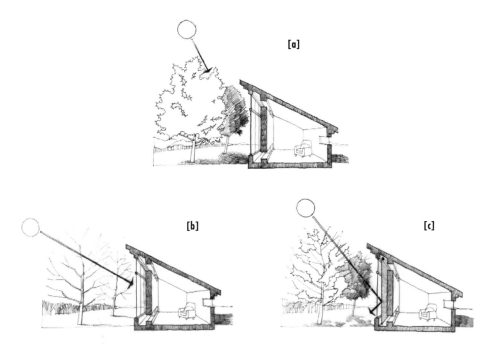

Figure 5.72 The effects of vegetation on the performance of a passive solar system: (a) the fully-leafed vegetation functioning as shading during the warm summer; (b) the leafless vegetation permitting the ready admission of solar radiation during the winter; (c) during the spring, the shading offered by the partially-leafed vegetation can be augmented by using a roller shade that is pulled down to reflect away entering solar radiation.

FOR BUILDING LAYOUT

(T4) *Use a basic building form that is more rectangular than square.* Employing this form will enable you to achieve better solar heating for winter operation and natural ventilation for summer operation. Also, consistent with the discussion offered for Guideline C9 in Section 5.3, the cubical building is not necessarily the most energy-efficient. In most respects the rectangular building form offers the greatest flexibility for responding to the alternative climatic challenges of opposing seasons.

(T5) *Orient the major axis of the building along the east-west compass line.* By placing the building axis in this fashion you will have the major elevations, in terms of surface area, on the south and north sides of the building. Placing glazing on the south elevation will enable you to promote the passive solar heating of the building interior. Also, south-facing glazing can be shaded more effectively than glazing on east or west elevations (especially, when external shading devices are to be employed).

Figure 5.73 Promoting air movement through a building for summer cooling.

(T6) *Develop a building organization that permits air movement across the building* (see Figure 5.73). Air movement from natural ventilation will enable an occupant to be cooled during humid, overheated summers. Thus, paths across the building are needed for airflow. These paths can be achieved by using single-banking of floor plans or by having operable partitions that separate multiple-banked spaces. Another alternative is to use roof monitors or clerestories, with operable glazing, to permit air to enter at the perimeter of a space and to rise by natural convection (i.e., by stack ventilation) and exit through the opened glazing in the roof.

(T7) *For residences, place spaces in which less vigorous activities occur along the elevation that faces the equator and such spaces as kitchens, bedrooms, and storage on the elevation that faces the pole. Also, place bathrooms and dressing areas within the building interior (away from exterior walls)* (see Figure 5.57). During winters, spaces in which less active tasks are performed can benefit from passive solar heating. Maintaining thermal comfort in other spaces will be easier because, respectively, people are more active in kitchens, they have additional bed coverings in the bedrooms, and they use storage areas only occasionally. For the warmer season occupants will go to spaces where less active tasks occur to overcome the summer heat. If the glazing in these equator-facing spaces is operable and shaded, then natural ventilation of the space — across the floor plan or between windows in adjacent elevations — will promote cooling.

FOR ENVELOPE COMPOSITION

(T8) *Insulate the opaque envelope.* The walls, floors above unheated volumes, and any ceilings below unheated air should all contain insulation. The amount of insulation that should be employed often cannot be precisely established. In the United States and Canada, many municipalities, states, and provinces have energy conservation codes that stipulate the amounts of insulation required for building envelopes. Designers and builders should comply with those regulations (and may wish to provide additional insulation, when such inclusions would be consistent with building and occupant needs).

(T9) *Naturally ventilate insulation placed in ceilings or in roofs.* Moisture present in warmed air that has risen to the top of occupied spaces will commonly diffuse through the exposed ceiling material and the insulation above this material. To provide a path of removal for this moisture, the air above the insulation should be continuously changed by natural ventilation.

(T10) *Slope roofs to permit the run-off of precipitation and to minimize the build-up of occasional snow.* The amounts of rainfall experienced in the temperate climate regions are not as great as those found in the warm-humid climate regions. Alternatively, whereas the amounts of snowfall found in temperate climate regions may be as great as those experienced in cold climate regions, the likelihood that the snow will accumulate on roofs over time is less. Nonetheless, sloped roofs will perform better and require less maintenance than flat roofs. Also, storm drainage facilities should be provided to carry water from roofs and away from foundations of buildings.

(T11) *Provide a glazing area of about 15 to 25 percent of the vertical envelope for residential buildings and perhaps as much as 35 percent of the vertical envelope for commercial buildings.* Specific glazing area maxima may be set by energy conservation codes; the designer and builder should examine such regulations for permissible maximum standards. For passive solar heated buildings, some regulatory agencies allow glazing areas greater than those permitted for non-solar-heated buildings. But note that use of additional glazing (for increasing opportunities for the passive solar heating of a building) may require employment of thermal shutters or night insulation; such window-covering insulation reduces the rate of transmission heat loss through the glazing assemblies during nighttimes.

(T12) *Use glazing composed of insulating assemblies (i.e., double-pane or storm sash).* Using insulated glazing assemblies will reduce the amount of transmission heat loss that a building will experience.

(T13) *Employ glazing in the vertical envelope that is operable and has insect screening.* Opening the glazing will permit natural ventilation during periods of warm weather. The glazing should be distributed in opposite or adjacent walls to enable good cross-flow. One alternative to creating cross ventilation is to use stack ventilation (as in Guideline T6) by deploying roof monitors and clerestories. Because insects are plentiful, particularly in the temperate continental warm-summer climate zone, screening over any opened window is required.

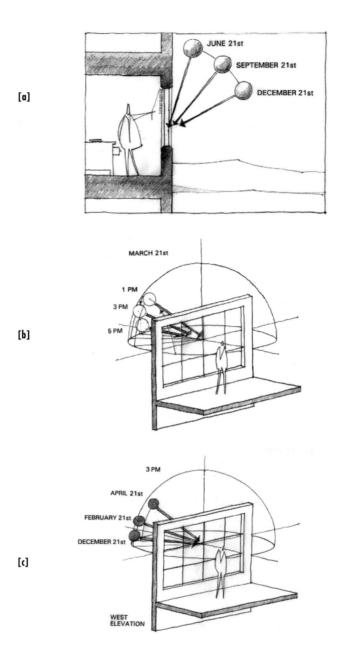

Figure 5.74 Note the solar positions across the sky vault for various times of the day and year: (a) for the south-facing window of a building located in the middle latitudes of the Northern Hemisphere, the sun appears low during the winter and high during the summer; (b) for a west-facing window of a building placed in the middle latitudes of the Northern Hemisphere, on March 21st, the sun moves further west and becomes progressively lower in the sky as the day passes; and (c) similarly, for a west-facing window at 3 pm on various days of the year, the sun will appear at different points of the sky vault. For the creation of shading devices, for these three conditions — (a)–(c) — different approaches will have to be considered. Operable devices may offer attractive possibilities, but will require the cooperation of building occupants to provide the selective admission and/or blocking of solar radiation.

(T14) *Shade glazing areas during times when incident solar radiation would cause overheating of the building interior* (see Figures 5.74 a–c and 5.75). Shading devices should either be operable or should be designed for the selective admission of solar radiation. If using operable devices (e.g., awnings or drapes), then incident solar radiation can be selectively admitted to suit an occupant's comfort needs (see Figure 5.76). Alternatively, shading devices may be designed that will block the admission of direct-beam radiation from the summer sun and that will permit the admission of direct-beam radiation from the winter sun; the sun passes high overhead in the summer, while during the winter the path of the sun is lower as it passes across the sky vault.

FOR BUILDING OPERATION

(T15) *Selectively employ vestibules and air-to-air heat exchangers to reduce infiltration heat loss (depending on the relative severity of the local climate).* Use of these two devices is strongly advocated for the cold climate, but for the *temperate* climate neither device should specifically be mandated. Whether the designer or builder wishes to include either device in a building should be determined by such issues as personal experience, occupant wishes, or cost factors.

(T16) *Carefully install and maintain vapor barriers in walls and the weatherstripping and caulking of building joints to reduce infiltration heat loss.* These topics are generally attended to during later stages of the design process. However, it seems appropriate to mention them here also to emphasize their importance.

5.4.5 FURTHER REFERENCES FOR DESIGNING AND CONSTRUCTING BUILDINGS FOR TEMPERATE CLIMATES

In Sections 5.1.4 and 5.3.5 we have identified publications that provide further information about the warm-humid and cold climates, respectively. Since the temperate climate contains elements of both of these other major climates, the publications cited for each of these two climates should be useful for gathering information about how to create buildings for at least *one of the two* extreme climatic periods found in the *temperate* climate. Alternatively, perhaps those books that present their information in a basically climate-independent manner would be the most appropriate for looking for additional information for designing and building in temperate climate regions (i.e., because it is an amalgam of the other two climates). Among such publications, we would specifically recommend the books by Brown, G.Z., and M. DeKay, *Sun, Wind, and Light: Architectural Design Strategies,* 2nd edition, (New York: John Wiley & Sons, Inc., 2000); and Watson, D., and K. Labs, *Climatic Design* (New York: McGraw-Hill Book Company, 1983).

Additionally, for those readers who live in areas of North America where energy conservation codes have been adopted, we suggest that you consult your regional code for design and construction guidelines. Also, for a number of these energy conservation codes informative booklets explain their use and interpretation. To determine whether such booklets exist for your state (or province), we suggest you communicate with the appropriate office responsible for regulating energy use in buildings.

Figure 5.75 The use of fixed overhangs as a means to shade equator-facing glazing. These overhangs will shade glazing during the summer months and periods during the later spring and early autumn: if the overhangs are well-developed, they should admit solar energy during the winter to provide some passive solar heating of the building interior.

Figure 5.76 Operable awnings are especially useful for the selective blocking or admission of solar radiation.

Figure 5.77 Some buildings along a thoroughfare in Port-Au-Prince, Trinidad. Note the juxtaposition of the vernacular buildings with their traditional means for climate control and the modern high-rise building with its reliance on a higher-technology envelope and the active conditioning system (whose presence is manifested by the apparatus displayed on the roof of the building).

Section 5.5 | A GENERAL PROVISO CONCERNING A LIMIT FOR THE APPLICATION OF THE GUIDELINES PRESENTED IN SECTIONS 5.1 THROUGH 5.4

In Chapter 3 we introduced the four environmental parameters—air temperature, radiant exchange rates, humidity, and air movement—that directly affect the establishment of thermally comfortable environments for human beings. We also identified what values these environmental parameters should have if thermally comfortable conditions are to exist. This listing of acceptable parametric values indicated that a human being will be thermally comfortable only within comparatively narrow ranges for each of these parameters.

In Sections 5.1 through 5.4 of this chapter we have described the characteristics of the four principal climates worldwide, for which buildings are designed and constructed. Each of these climates presents environmental conditions that are substantially outside of the ranges of parametric values that need to be maintained to ensure thermal comfort. As responses to these climatic conditions, we have suggested guidelines for the design, construction, and operation of buildings. These guidelines, if followed, should generally produce more energy-efficient places for people to live and work.

The guidelines have emphasized the inclusion and utilization of passive means of environmental control to achieve the energy-efficient operation of buildings constructed for these climates. However, by focusing strictly on passive (and the occasional passive-hybrid) means, *we do not intend to suggest that by relying* only *on these various passive means you can produce thermally comfortable buildings.* Further, for numerous aspects of these climates, the use of active control systems will considerably enhance the ability of a building occupant to establish thermally comfortable conditions. For other aspects of these climates, the operation of active control systems is essential if a building is to provide shelter and comfort for its occupants. Instead, *our purpose through this chapter has been to identify design and construction guidelines based on passive elements of buildings, whose use will reduce an absolute reliance on active control systems* (see Figure 5.77). We advocate the careful use of passive devices so that the capacities of active systems can be reduced to practicable minimum levels and the frequency and extent of operation of these active systems can also be curtailed. Finally, only by designing, constructing, and operating well-integrated passive and active systems can building occupants have *both* thermally comfortable and energy-efficient buildings.

ENDNOTES and SELECTED ADDITIONAL COMMENTS

1. The symbol *Ar* is consistent with the climate classification system introduced in Chapter 4 (derived from the book by Trewartha, G.T., and L.H. Horn, *An Introduction to Climate* (5th edition), (New York: McGraw-Hill Book Company, 1980), see pages 214–229, especially.) This symbol set will be employed throughout the remainder of this chapter.

2. Odum, E.P., *Fundamentals of Ecology* (3rd edition), (Philadelphia: W.B. Saunders Company, 1970), pages 400–401.

3. Ibid., pages 391–392.

4. Odum, E.P., *Basic Ecology,* (Philadelphia: Saunders College Publishing, 1983), page 525.

5. Ibid., page 529.

6. The amount of space between buildings that is required to re-establish relatively smooth-moving air flow, can seldom be determined precisely (primarily, because of the large number of parameters that control wind behavior). However, in the professional literature, various rules-of-thumb are cited for estimating what distance should be provided between buildings: for instance, see the book by Watson, D., and K. Labs, *Climatic Design,* (New York: McGraw-Hill Book Company, 1983), page 86.

7. The use of awnings is particularly appropriate in the more-poleward subtropical humid areas that experience comparatively cooler winters. In such areas the passive solar heating of the building interior may be justifiable, and the retractable nature of awnings may better enable the admission of direct beam solar radiation.

8. Trewartha, G.T., and L.H. Horn, *An Introduction to Climate,* pages 228–229.

9. Odum, E.P., *Fundamentals of Ecology,* page 396.

10. Trewartha, G.T., and L.H. Horn, *An Introduction to Climate,* page 346.

11. The basic relationship set forward by Patton is

    $$R = T/2 - Pw/4$$

    where R is the amount of annual rainfall (in inches), T is the average annual temperature (in °F), and Pw is percentage of annual rainfall that occurs during the winter season. For more information, see the article by Patton, C.P., "A note on the classification of dry climates in the Köppen system," *California Geographer,* 3, 1962, pages 105–112.

12. Trewartha, G.T., and L.H. Horn, *An Introduction to Climate,* pages 350–351.

13. Ibid., page 348.

14. Odum, E.P., *Fundamentals of Ecology,* page 393.

15. Clark, G., "Passive/hybrid comfort cooling by thermal radiation," *Proceedings of the International Passive and Hybrid Cooling Conference* (edited by Bowen, A., E. Clark, and K. Labs), (Newark, Delaware: American Solar Energy Society, 1981), pages 682–714.

16. Hay, H., "Atascadero Residence," *Passive Solar Heating and Cooling Conference and Workshop Proceedings,* (Springfield, Virginia: National Technical Information Service, 1976), pages 101–107.

17. Yellott, J.F., "Evaporative cooling," *Proceedings of the International Passive and Hybrid Cooling Conference* (edited by Bowen, A., E. Clark, and K. Labs), (Newark, Delaware: American Solar Energy Society, 1981), pages 764–772.

18. Reaves, F.M., and J.S. Reaves, "Evaporative cooling of the roof," *Proceedings of the International Passive and Hybrid Cooling Conference* (edited by Bowen, A., E. Clark, and K. Labs), (Newark: Delaware: American Solar Energy Society, 1981), pages 240–243.

19. Trewartha, G.T., and L.H. Horn, *An Introduction to Climate,* pages 228–229.

20. For more specific information about animal and plant life in regions with the *temperate continental with cool summer* climate type, see *(a)* Furley, P.A., and W.W. Newey, *Geography of the Biosphere,* (London: Butterworth & Co. Ltd., 1983), pages 250–260; and *(b)* Walter, H., *Vegetation of the Earth* (3rd edition), (New York: Springer-Verlag, 1985), Chapter VI, pages 188–223.

21. Trewartha, G.T., and L.H. Horn, *An Introduction to Climate,* pages 228–229.

22. Ibid., page 319.

23. *Cloud cover* is an index used by meteorologists in North America to describe the cloudiness of the sky and is recorded in terms of tenths. Ten-tenths is a fully overcast sky whereas zero-tenths would suggest a completely clear sky. Cloud cover readings are commonly taken on an hourly basis and are established by a knowledgeable person making a visual observation of the sky.

24. For more information about the vegetation in the boreal forest region, see *(a)* Turk, J., and A. Turk, *Environmental Science* (3rd edition), (Philadelphia: Saunders College Publishing, 1984), pages 124–125; and *(b)* Furley, P.A., and W.W. Newey, *Geography of the Biosphere,* pages 241–250.

25. Furley, P.A., and W.W. Newey, *Geography of the Biosphere,* pages 245–246.

26. Odum, E.P., *Fundamentals of Ecology,* pages 380–383; Tivy, J., *Biogeography: A Study of Plants in the Ecosphere* (2nd edition), (London: Longman Group Ltd, 1982), pages 353–363; and Furley, P.A., and W.W. Newey, *Geography of the Biosphere,* pages 225–240.

27. One manufacturer of air-to-air heat exchangers suitable for either residential or commercial building applications is the Des Champs Laboratories, Inc., East Hanover, New Jersey 07936, USA. A second manufacturer is Conservation Energy Systems, Inc., Saskatoon, Saskatchewan S7K 7G9, Canada. Less proprietary information about air-to-air heat exchangers, generally, can be found in the book by Shurcliff, W.A., *Air-to-Air Heat Exchangers for Houses,* Andover, Massachusetts: Brick House Publishing Company, 1982).

28. Numerous books, conference proceedings, and journal articles have been composed recently about earth-sheltered building opportunities. One book that provides a useful summary of the various issues, applications, and technologies involved in earth-sheltering has been written by Boyer, L.L., and W.T. Grondzik, *Earth Shelter Technology,* (College Station, Texas: Texas A&M University Press, 1987.) The book also presents an extensive bibliography about this topic.

29. An ice dam develops on sloped roofs when snow builds up at the eave of the roof and the underlayer of this snow melts (due perhaps to heat that is transferred up through the roof). Simultaneous with the underlayer melting, water close to the eave line freezes creating a dam. This dam holds back the remaining water (from the melted snow), which can then seep under the roof cover, leading to water leakage into occupied spaces underneath the roof. For further information about ice dams and their formation, see Latta, J.K., *Walls, Windows, and Roofs for the Canadian Climate,* (Ottawa: Division of Building Research, National Research Council of Canada, 1973), pages 63–64.

30. Trewartha, G.T., and L.H. Horn, *An Introduction to Climate,* pages 284–315.

31. Müller, M.J., *Selected Climatic Data for A Global Set of Standard Stations for Vegetation Science,* (The Hague: Dr. W. Junk Publishers, 1982).

32. The *water wall* is usually composed of a series of translucent or opaque plastic cylinders that contain water. These cylinders are placed in a row separating the aperture (window) from the living space. They generally have diameters of about 0.33–0.50 m (12–18 in) and heights equal to the distance from the floor to the top of the aperture.

33. Volumes 1 and 2 have been available from the National Technical Information Service, U.S. Department of Commerce, Springfield, Virginia 22161. Volume 3 is available from the American Solar Energy Society, Inc., Boulder, Colorado 80302.

34. Balcomb, J.D., D. Barley, R. MacFarland, J. Perry, Jr., W. Wray, and S. Noll, *Passive Solar Design Handbook* (Volume 2: *Passive Solar Design Analysis*), (Springfield, Virginia: National Technical Information Service, U.S. Department of Commerce, 1980), pages 20–23.

35. Ibid., pages 25–28.

36. Ibid., pages 28–29.

37. Ibid., page 29.

CHAPTER SIX

The "Physics" of Light

THIS CHAPTER AND Chapters 7 and 8 will describe light, human vision, and the use of daylight for illuminating buildings. Chapter 9 will then offer a series of guidelines for admitting daylight into buildings and controlling the daylight once it has entered the buildings. Electric lighting fixtures and lamps will not be discussed directly in these four chapters. Also, the design and selection practices associated with creating electric lighting for buildings will only be considered in the most limited of manners.[1]

As a preface for these four chapters, we will state what we believe are the responsibilities of designers and builders for creating a well-illuminated building. First, designers and builders should have some sense of how human beings see. An understanding also is necessary of what means can be employed to enhance the visual performance of people (i.e., to ensure that they can see well enough to conduct normal work, living, and play activities). Further, what environmental conditions afford visual comfort—for work, living, or play—should also be known. Second, designers and builders should know where lighting is needed in a building and how much lighting will be required at the various locations throughout the building. Third, the designer and builder should understand the properties of building materials, both regarding how these materials can affect the presence of light in the building and how they can influence the vision of occupants carrying out common visual tasks. Fourth, the designer and builder should be aware of the capabilities of various lighting sources, including where and how these sources should be located, how much light will be emitted by the sources, and what directional controls are required. And, fifth, the designer and builder must be able to integrate the knowledge pertaining to the first four responsibilities during the design and construction of buildings.

These four chapters will thus offer information about what light is and how it behaves, the operation of the human vision system, and the properties of daylight and means for using it to illuminate buildings. Finally, information will be presented about the arrangement and sizing of windows and the selection of materials and other accessories for building fenestration.

Section 6.1 | SOURCES OF LIGHT

Fundamentally, light is one form of *electromagnetic radiation,* which is a basic means of energy transfer between objects throughout our universe. Electromagnetic radiation occurs in a variety of types, including cosmic, X-ray, and thermal radiation, as well as radio waves and sub-audio radiation. Light is remarkable only because we can see with it! After all, what we describe as light comprises just a small fraction of the entire electromagnetic radiation spectrum. Further, light exists naturally as a relatively weak form of radiation, when compared to such higher-energy forms like cosmic and X-ray radiation. However, as we can sense light and use it to learn about our environment and ourselves, light is unquestionably the most important form of electromagnetic radiation for us.

Light is one of the three principal forms of *thermal* radiation, the other two being ultraviolet radiation and infrared radiation. Differentiation between the three basic forms of thermal radiation is usually specified in terms of the wavelength range over which each exists. Ultraviolet radiation happens in the range of 0.005 to 0.38 micron (5–380 nanometers [nm]), light occurs over the range of 0.38 to 0.78 micron (380–780 nm), and infrared radiation is present in the range of 0.78 to more than 50 microns (780–50,000 nm).

6.1.1   LUMINOUS SOURCES

Prevost's Law states that all bodies with temperatures above absolute zero (i.e., that are warmer than −273 °C [−460 °F]) emit electromagnetic radiation. Thus, virtually all objects on Earth are continuously giving off electromagnetic radiation. These objects also will emit radiation *simultaneously* over a range of wavelengths (i.e., they do not send out single-wavelength radiation, but radiate at multiple wavelengths at the same instant). Some of the radiation that is emitted by these objects may be visible, whereas the remainder will not be visible. For instance, if you switch on a heating element of an electric cooking range to "high heat," the element will gradually began to emit a deep red light. This red light is one form of visible radiation. At the same time as the heating element emits red light, the element also emits infrared radiation. To verify that infrared radiation is present, you could turn the selector from high heat to a lower setting and wait until the deep red light is no longer visible. Then, if you hold a finger over the element, you will feel the infrared radiation warming your finger. The infrared radiation is present when the element is at a lower temperature as well as when the element appeared red: your visual system just does not see the infrared radiation.

The conditions that separate visible radiation from the remainder of the electromagnetic radiation spectrum are whether the radiation produced by any object has wavelengths in the portion of the spectrum that can be seen by our visual system and whether the radiation in the visible wavelengths has sufficient intensity so that we can discern it. For example, when you go out at night and look about you and everything seems dark, the reason you are unable to see anything is not that there is no radiation passing between you and the objects about you. Rather, the radiation that travels between you and these objects is not visible because it occurs primarily at wavelengths that you are unable to sense with your eyes, and any secondary wavelengths that would otherwise be visible do not have sufficient intensity to be detected. These conditions, thus, set the limiting requirements for generally being able to see electromagnetic radiation: the radiation must be in wavelengths that the human visual system can sense, and the radiation must have sufficient intensity to be registered by the light receptors in your eyes.

Light—visible electromagnetic radiation—is emitted from two primary groups of materials: those that exist in a solid state and those that are present in a gaseous state.[2] For solid sources there are two principal mechanisms by which light is produced: *incandescence* and *luminescence*. Light produced by *incandescence* is commonly referred to as

SIDEBAR 6.1
The effect of gradually heating a lamp filament

When you flip a wall switch and an electric lamp is turned "on," the electric current flows virtually instantaneously through the filament in the lamp, and the lamp commences immediately to produce light. However, if you could slow down this flow of electrical energy to the lamp and its filament, you would see that the filament turns (and emits) progressively a series of colors before it ultimately gives off the common white light. One way to demonstrate the effects of gradually heating a tungsten filament is to place a rheostat in the electric circuit that includes the light bulb (see Figure 6.1). The rheostat is a device in which the amount of electric current resistance presented by the rheostat can be varied. If you switch on the circuit with the rheostat at its maximum resistance setting, little current will pass to the filament (and the filament will not emit any visible radiation). Then, by slowly decreasing the resistive setting of the rheostat, more and more current will pass to the filament. The filament will begin to glow red and then will progressively change color, ultimately producing white light.

When the filament appears to be white (at its operating temperature), the wavelength range with the

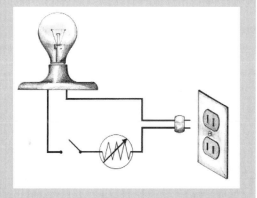

Figure 6.1 This simple electrical circuit, which includes a rheostat for regulating the amount of current flowing to the electric lamp, will enable the operator to dim or brighten progressively the light emitted by the lamp.

greatest intensity is still within the infrared radiation range. But radiation from the wavelength ranges of each of the other colors (from red to violet) all will have sufficient intensity to appear to be integrated and are thus perceived by the human eye as white light.

"hot" light because incandescent light results when a solid is heated to a temperature high enough that it glows (i.e., emits visible radiation). For example, in Chapter 2, we described radiation emitted from a light bulb. In that description we stated that an electric current passing through a tungsten filament within the light bulb will heat the filament. As the filament starts to warm up, it will initially not give off any visible radiation. But, after some moments, reddish light will begin to be visible. Then, as the filament grows progressively hotter, the color of the filament will sequentially change from red to orange to yellow and finally to white. Each of these colors has a characteristic wavelength range: for instance, red light has a range from approximately 0.63 to 0.70 micron (630–700 nm). When the filament gives off red light, other radiation is also being emitted, including infrared radiation, radiation of each of the other colors, and even some ultraviolet radiation. But the human eye sees the red light because the red light has sufficient intensity to be visible (and it has a characteristic wavelength range that our visual system can perceive). Actually, the most intense radiation being emitted by the filament when it is perceived as red is infrared radiation. Whereas the filament is also emitting radiation in other wavelengths in the visible spectrum (i.e., at the other colors), the human eye does not sense the other wavelengths because the "red" wavelength range is intense enough to obscure the others.

The moments while the red light is dominant occur when the filament is within a particular temperature range. For the radiation that we see as red light, the filament will be at a temperature of about 820 °C (1500 °F). As the filament turns from red to orange to yellow, the temperature of the filament will increase correspondingly. When the filament emits white light, the filament will have reached its normal operating temperature of about 3000 °C (5500 °F). Thus, this light is produced by the incandescence of the filament. Note, also, that another example of an incandescent source is the electric cook-top heating element which, when turned on to high heat, appears "red hot."

The other means by which light is emitted from solid materials is by *luminescence*. Here, objects give off visible electromagnetic radiation without heating up (as was true for incandescent objects). Consequently, light from luminescent sources is called "cold." Light will be emitted from these solid objects after they have been excited by a variety of electrical, mechanical, or chemical processes. The firefly is an example of a creature that displays bioluminescence.[3] Numbers of crustaceans, fish, and other undersea organisms also exhibit this light-generating capability. Generally, bioluminescence results from chemical reactions that occur within the body or at the body surface of these creatures. The length of time that a luminescent organism or creature will emit light can vary from seconds to hours.

The other major group of light sources includes those that exist in a gaseous state. This group also has two primary mechanisms for the production of light: first, as *flames* and, second, by *electric discharge*. Candles and the sun are two examples of sources that produce light with flames. A candle generates light as its fuel burns (generally, paraffin wax or animal fat). The heat of combustion raises the temperature of the gases produced by the burning of the fuel to *incandescence,* and light results. Alternatively, the sun creates its heat by the *fusion* of hydrogen into helium near the core of the sun. Then, this heat migrates out to the outer layer of the sun (or *photosphere*), where the thermal energy moves out into space as electromagnetic radiation. Some of this solar radiation ultimately reaches the surface of the Earth (and buildings constructed upon it) in the three forms of ultraviolet, visible, and infrared radiation (see Figure 6.2).

Light produced by the discharge of electricity through gases (enclosed in glass vessels) encompasses an important group of light sources. Common examples of these electric

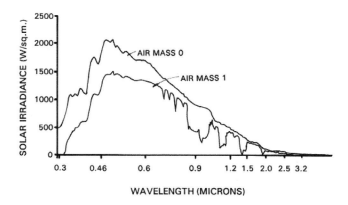

Figure 6.2 This graph shows the amounts of solar radiation that reach the outer edge of the atmosphere of the Earth (usually identified as *extraterrestial solar radiation*) and arrive at the surface of the Earth (often called the *global solar radiation*). These two curves display — across this wavelength range — how much of the extraterrestial solar radiation is excluded from reaching the surface of the Earth due to its atmosphere. The several sharp decreases in the global solar radiation intensity in the wavelength range from about 0.65 to 1.90 microns are largely the result of the absorption of the solar energy by various atmospheric gases. These curves have been constructed using data published on pages 38–39 of a paper by Thekaekara, M.P., "Data on incident solar energy," from the document edited by Thekaekara, M.P., *The Energy Crisis and Energy from the Sun* (Supplement to the Proceedings of the 20th Annual Meeting of the Institute of Environmental Sciences, Washington, D.C., April 1974), pages 21–49. Permission to present this graph using data from the noted publication has been granted by the Institute of Environmental Science and Technology (www.iest.org) who owns the copyright for the publication.

sources include neon, mercury or sodium vapor, and fluorescent lamps. The dominant feature of the electric (or high-intensity) discharge lamp is that, as an electric current is passed through the gas that is enclosed in the lamp, the gas becomes ionized and electromagnetic radiation is emitted. In the neon, mercury vapor, and sodium vapor lamps, the current passes between two electrodes, ionizing the gas. The ionizing gas glows, emitting light. The observer's eyes perceive light from each of these lamps as having a characteristic color (e.g., bluish-green for mercury, orange for sodium, and red for neon). The color in each instance thus demonstrates the principal wavelength amongst the visible spectrum, which each lamp produces.

For the fluorescent lamp (see Figure 6.3), the glass tube has a tungsten electrode at each end and is filled with a mixture of argon and mercury vapor. A current is generated between the electrodes and through the gas mixture, ionizing the gases. The ionization produces some small quantity of visible radiation and a significantly larger amount of ultraviolet radiation. The internal surface of the tube is coated with a layer of phosphors. The ultraviolet radiation is absorbed by the phosphors, and the phosphors *fluoresce* and emit visible radiation. The process of *fluorescence* thus involves the absorption of the ultraviolet radiation by the phosphor and the production of visible radiation (that is created in a substantially greater quantity than was generated by the ionizing of the enclosed gas). Note that, in contrast to the output of the incandescent lamp, there is little heat present on the surface of the tube (except at the ends of the tube in the vicinity of the electrodes).

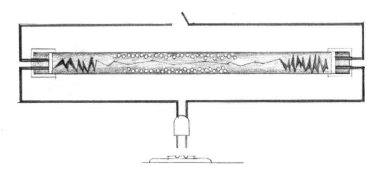

Figure 6.3 A typical fluorescent lamp is depicted in this drawing. Note the electrical discharge that passes through the gas mixture and the presence of the phosphors on the inside surface of the glass tube. These phosphors are the materials that fluoresce, providing light (with its the characteristic color).

There are two additional, important sources of light: daylight (from the sky vault) and laser light. We will discuss the characteristics of daylight throughout Chapter 8. Alternatively, lasers comprise a special group of light sources. The term *laser* is the acronym for *Light Amplification by Stimulated Emission of Radiation*. The laser is a very concentrated beam of light. Among its most significant properties are that it is virtually monochromatic (i.e., consists of a quite narrow spectral band); it can have energy intensities high enough to melt some metals; and it will show little divergence over extremely long distances separating a target from a source. Lasers are used primarily in scientific work (e.g., for patient care in the health sciences, physics research, and microelectronics assembly). Lasers are also employed in a variety of the visual arts. In the building industry their primary application currently occurs during the construction of buildings, when careful alignments and/or measurements are required.[4]

SIDEBAR 6.2 Phosphors and the colors of fluorescing lamps

Phosphors are various inorganic crystalline compounds to which small percentages of metals have intentionally been added. When these phosphors are irradiated with ultraviolet radiation they emit light. The predominant color of the fluorescing lamp (e.g., whether it is "warm-white" or "cool-white") is determined by the choice of the phosphor coating. For additional discussions of the principles of the fluorescent lamp and its alternative color characteristics, see *IES Lighting Handbook,* 8th edition, (New York: Illuminating Engineering Society, 2000); and/or Murdoch, J.B., *Illuminating Engineering,* (New York: Macmillan Publishing Company, 1985), pages 211–232.

The efficiency of a light source is described in terms of its *luminous efficacy*, which is the ratio of the amount of light produced by the source versus the amount of power required to sustain the production of light. The fluorescent tube has a higher luminous efficacy than the incandescent bulb. A primary reason for this higher luminous efficacy is that the incandescent bulb emits radiation as its filament is heated to and maintained at an quite elevated temperature, whereas the fluorescent tube operates at a substantially lower temperature. In the case of the incandescent bulb the largest share of the energy consumed to produce radiation goes to the generation of infrared radiation (i.e., consistent with the presence of the elevated temperature, which is needed to create incandescence). Conversely, the fluorescent tube produces comparatively less infrared radiation, and thus less energy is spent for producing the invisible infrared radiation. Lastly, note that sodium and mercury vapor lamps have higher luminous efficacies than fluorescent lamps. Metal halide lamps—another form of high-intensity discharge light source—also display higher luminous efficacies than do fluorescent tubes. Further information about the performance of these lamp sources, including power versus wavelength graphs, can be found in the *IES Lighting Handbook,* 8th edition, (New York: Illuminating Engineering Society, 2000).

6.1.2 HOW DO YOU SEE A LIGHT BEAM?

If you think about daylight entering a window, light from the headlights of a car, or even candlelight, you will readily acknowledge that their light illuminates the spaces near these sources. But, *unless you are looking directly at the source* or *you have some intermediate device, which will enable you to "capture" light,* you cannot actually see the light that emanates from these sources. Certainly by looking out a window at the daylighted sky or by looking at a car headlight or at a candle, you can tell that light is being emitted by these sources. Additionally, you can use some light-sensing instrument or material to demonstrate the presence of light. For instance, we can tell that light is present if we employ photographic film or the light-sensitive cell of a light meter. We can look for shadows, as solid objects interrupt the passage of light. Or, if the air (or a transparent liquid) through which light passes is dusty or dirty, then we can see the light reflected off of the particles suspended in the fluid. On a day when the sun shines directly through your window and there is air movement in your room, you can likely see the motes of dust moving throughout the sunlight.

Thus, the principal way that we see light is not by looking at the source. Rather, we see light as it is reflected off of *nonluminous* surfaces. But these natural and man-made objects do emit electromagnetic radiation. However, the emitted radiation is virtually entirely in the "long" infrared wavelengths. Any radiation emitted by these "cool" sources (which is in the visible wavelength band) is of such marginal intensity that our eyes cannot sense it. So, we see building surfaces, a companion's face, or the words on this page all by the reflection of light passing from the sky or from electric lamps (or from both). The light that reflects off of these surfaces passes to your eyes, which sense the reflected energy. For instance, your eyes can discern the words on this page because of the difference in reflection between the black type and the white page on which the type lies. The white page readily reflects incident light, whereas the black letters absorb it. Thus, we could say that we do not directly sense the blackness of these letters. Instead, we see the light reflected from all around the letters, and our visual system — our eyes and brain — determines what the letters are by identifying the patterns of these light-reflecting cavities.

Most of the information that we gather with our visual system does not come directly from luminous sources, but arrives from all of the nonluminous surfaces that surround us. We rely on these nonluminous, reflecting surfaces to indicate the character of the environment in which we live. Normally, in our buildings and in the natural (and human-modified) environments outside of buildings, there are only a few light sources. The sun and the concomitant daylight are essential natural sources of light. Electric lamps and open flames from candles and fires are among the most important artificial light sources. But there are huge numbers of surfaces that reflect light to us from these few sources. Just a few of these surfaces are the moon, mirrors, our food, our bodies and the clothes we wear, the surfaces of buildings and of furnishings within buildings, and all the various kinds of vegetation that exist in nature surrounding us and our buildings.

Section 6.2 | SELECTED PROPERTIES OF LIGHT

Light provides us with a fundamental resource for sensing and understanding our world. Thus, we must understand the behaviors of light if we wish to control both it and the environment. The quality and quantity of light available in any environment enable us to examine that environment and to use the environment for satisfying our various needs and wishes. But, as we talk of using light to scrutinize an environment, we must necessarily recognize that the environment will alter the character of the light that enters the environment. Thus, to develop strategies for using light in our natural and built environments, we need to understand what light is and how light will behave as it interacts with the component materials and surfaces of our environments.

6.2.1   LIGHT AS A MEANS OF MOVING ENERGY

Light is one form of electromagnetic radiation, and all forms of electromagnetic radiation exist as conveyors of energy from one location to another. The fundamental significance of light for human beings is that we are able to sense this small portion of the electromagnetic spectrum with our eyes (and interpret it with our brains). Thus, we can see the light energy flowing from luminous sources and nonluminous surfaces alike. Light serves us by carrying information about these sources and the surfaces (which reflect or absorb light). The sources illuminate the surfaces and enable us to gain data about the characteristics of these surfaces: where they are; how close they are to us; what color they are; whether they are rough or smooth; whether they are safe to touch; and so forth.

Now, let's ask *what are the essential properties of light that enable it to carry such information to us.* To begin with, light is a form of thermal radiation, and thermal radiation is emitted from objects whose electronic structures are in states of oscillation. This radiation is basically energy that propagates outward from a source. The propagation of energy is accompanied by *electrical and magnetic fields* that essentially surround the energy flow.

The presence of these electrical and magnetic fields is the basis for why this radiation is referred to *electromagnetic*. These fields vary cyclically (i.e., with time) and exist in planes at right angles to each other and at right angles to the direction of the energy propagating from the radiation source (see Figure 6.5). Thus, radiation emanating from some

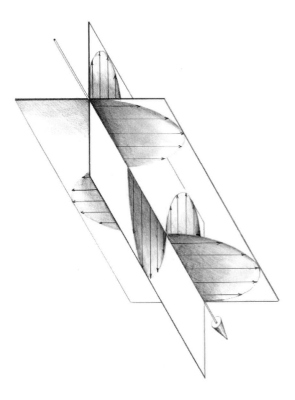

Figure 6.5 The electrical and magnetic fields vary sinusoidally in directions that are each perpendicular to the direction of the energy travel (and to each other.) Thus, this energy movement occurs by means of *transverse* waves.

SIDEBAR 6.4 Electrical and magnetic fields

A field can be thought of as a region, zone, or volume that contains a central point that exerts an electrical, magnetic, gravitational, or other force on the region, zone, or volume. For example, if you have a horseshoe magnet, then a magnetic field is spread outward from the two poles (ends) of the magnet (see Figure 6.4). These fields are represented graphically as having lines of force. Thus, a field line may be defined as "an imaginary line drawn in such a way that its direction at any point (i.e., the direction of its tangent) is the same as the direction of the field at that point." (from Sears, F.W., M.W. Zemansky, and H.D. Young, *University Physics,* 6th edition, (Reading, Massachusetts: Addison-Wesley Publishing Company, 1984), page 479.

Figure 6.4 A common horseshoe magnet with its corresponding magnetic field lines appears here. Note that the field lines emanate outward from the opposite poles (at the two ends of the magnet).

oscillating source flows as energy and creates electrical and magnetic fields that *disturb* — electrically and magnetically — *the space through which the radiation passes.* How much the space is disturbed by the radiation as it passes some point in the space is established (at that point) by the intensities of these cyclically varying electrical and magnetic fields. This behavior — energy being propagated in a direction that is perpendicular to the electrical and magnetic fields that accompany the energy — is described as exhibiting the form of a *transverse wave.*

Light, whether passing through the vacuum of outer space or through some Earth-bound medium like air or a transmitting liquid, displays the same properties as all the other forms of electromagnetic radiation. These basic properties include that the radiation forms are periodic in both time and space (i.e., occurring with a regular frequency having a characteristic number of cycles per second [or Hertz {Hz}]); that they transport energy from a source to a receiver; that their velocities in a vacuum are the same; and that the wave surfaces they create are three-dimensional. Further, all radiation is said to be composed of a basic unit called a *photon.* The *photon* can be thought of essentially as a *bit of energy,* the magnitude of which is *discrete* and which is proportional to the frequency of the radiation. As such, radiation is made up of bundles of photons, where these bundles consist of whole-number multiples of photons. The view of radiation being composed of photons suggests that it will exhibit behaviors as particles do. Thus, by means of these particle-like photons, radiation will transport energy, move through a vacuum at the constant velocity, carry momentum, and exert a pressure on the receiver. But, almost contrarily, the photon has no mass. Finally, the primary difference between the various forms of radiation is the frequency (and, thus, the wavelength) of the several radiation forms.

So far, we have described the radiation emanating from a source as having the form of a *transverse wave.* We can also state that radiation propagates from a source in all three dimensions. So, if we have a *point source* of *light* with nothing obstructing the emission of the light (i.e., nothing external to the source blocks the propagation of the radiation in any direction), then the geometry of the *wavefront* will be truly spherical. However, if we mask the point source with a shade that has a pinhole in the shade, then a light beam will propagate from the side of the shade away from the source. This light beam will be conical in shape, and the cross-section of the beam at any distance from the pinhole (and parallel to the shade) is circular (see Figure 6.6(a)). The formation of this beam indeed provides us with a basis for representing light that comes from a partially masked or bounded source (i.e., the type of source that we commonly find in buildings, where lamp fixtures or window frames partially bound the propagation of light from, respectively, electric sources or the sun and sky vault). To show graphically the path of a light beam, we can employ the axis of the light cone, noting that the axis will pass through the centers of the pinhole and the point source. Thus, a single line overlaying this axis defines a *light ray* that represents

---

SIDEBAR 6.5 Transverse versus longitudinal waves

The alternative waveform observed in nature is the *longitudinal* wave. For this second wave form, the direction of wave propagation and the direction of the disturbance of the space coincide. A primary example of the longitudinal wave is the *sound* wave, where the sound energy emanates out from a source and compresses the molecules that surround the source. Thus, the direction of the molecular compression (i.e., the disturbance of the medium through the wave passes) is the same as the direction of the wave.

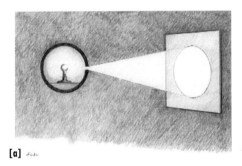 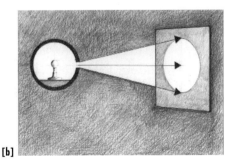

[a] **[b]**

Figure 6.6 A light source is bounded by a light-tight enclosure that has a very small pinhole in one side. The escaping light passes as a conical light beam to a screen, where a circular area is illuminated. Note that (in the right image) *rays* are used to delineate the paths that light beams take when passing from a source to nonluminous surfaces (where the incident beams undergo various behaviors including reflection, absorption, and other phenomena.) As we note in the written text (Section 6.2.2), these rays are commonly drawn at the center of the beam. Sometimes, rays will also be drawn at the edges of the cone to signify the spread of the light beam. In all these instances—whether we consider a central or boundary ray—these rays are essentially approximations that are useful for studying how light will behave as it passes from a source to some receiving surface.

the center of the light beam. Alternatively, light rays can be drawn at the edges of the beam to indicate the degree of divergence of the cone of light (Figure 6.6(b)). Note that any ray will be perpendicular to the wavefront. We emphasize, though, that *light* (or any other form of electromagnetic radiation) *does not actually propagate by rays.* Instead, drawing these rays can aid us in describing and exploring how light behaves.

6.2.2 THE INTERACTION OF LIGHT WITH SURFACES AND MEDIA

A principal reason why we should consider how light behaves when it passes through different media and reaches various surfaces is because, by understanding such behaviors, we will be better able to comprehend the world around us. We have said that the two fundamental services that light provides us with are, first, to enable us to learn about the sources of the light and, second, to examine visually all the various surfaces that surround us. When light is incident on surfaces or passes into media, basic properties of light determine how this radiant energy interacts with the surfaces and the media. Thus, to understand the information our eyes (and brains) receive from these surfaces and media, we need to examine the several physical properties of light.

6.2.2.1 The transmission of light Light transmission is not a surface phenomenon; rather, it involves the passage of light through some medium. Solar radiation passing through the atmosphere is one example of light transmission. Alternatively, light which has reflected from this printed page and which reaches your eyes through a pair of glasses that you may be wearing is another example of the transmission of radiant energy. A third instance of the transmission of radiation is the transfer of light through the lens at the front of each of your eyeballs (i.e., light from the external world passes through each lens and falls onto the light-sensitive cells of the retina).

How readily light (or any other radiation form) will propagate through a medium is described in terms of the *transmittance* (or transmissivity) of the medium for the wavelength range that the radiation exhibits. Transmittance is defined as the ratio of the amount of radiant energy that passes through the medium compared to the amount of radiant energy that is incident on—reaches—the surface of the medium. The transmittance of some medium will generally be different for alternative wavelengths of radiation. Thus, many media display *selective* behaviors toward various forms of electromagnetic radiation. For example, light—visible radiation (incorporating wavelengths from 0.38 to 0.78 microns [380–780 nm])—will pass readily through common clear window glass (see Figure 6.7). However, this glass is virtually opaque to most infrared radiation (that having wavelengths longer than about 2 microns [2000 nm]). The same glass will also be quite opaque to ultraviolet radiation (that has wavelengths shorter than about 0.3 microns [300 nm]). Thus,

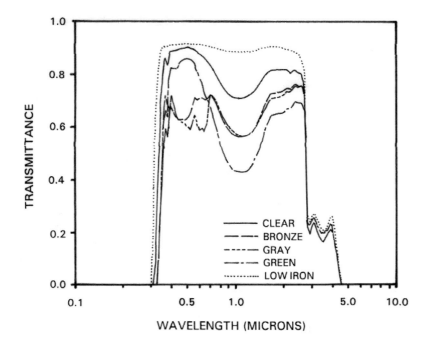

Figure 6.7 The wavelength-dependent transmissivities for five different glasses used in buildings are shown here. Note that solar radiation reaching the surface of the Earth has a wavelength range from about 0.3 to 2.2 microns (300 to 2200 nm) (see Figure 6.2) and visible light has a wavelength range from 0.38 to 0.78 micron (380 to 780 nm). The low-iron glass is often specified for buildings that are to be passively-heated with solar radiation: this glass has a uniformly greater transmissivity than does clear glass. Alternatively, the bronze, grey, and green glasses are used in buildings to reduce the rates with which solar radiation can enter a building. Thus, these glasses serve as shading devices (e.g., particularly for *internal-load-dominated* buildings, where the rate of internal heat production resulting from people and electric lights and equipment exceeds the rate of envelope heat loss, and air cooling is required for much of the time when these buildings are occupied). For additional discussion about internal-load-dominance, see Section A.2.2. This graph has previously been published in the paper by Rubin, M., "Optical properties of soda lime silica glasses," *Solar Energy Materials,* 12, 1985, pages 275–288. Permission to reproduce this graph has been granted by Elsevier Science Publishers B.V. (copyrighted by Elsevier Science Publishers B.V., 1985).

common clear window glass will still transmit some ultraviolet radiation (that having wavelengths from about 0.30 to 0.38 microns [300–380 nm]) and some infrared radiation (that having wavelengths from about 0.78 to about 2.0 microns [780–2000 nm]). A result of this capacity to transmit some solar radiation, whose wavelengths are beyond the range of visible radiation, is that daylight and solar radiation transmittance numbers, which are reported for various glasses, will commonly be different (i.e., the solar radiation transmittances will be greater).

Three general types of envelope media are used in buildings: transparent, translucent, and opaque. The first two are light-transmitting, although translucent materials limit the resolution (for an observer) of objects present on the side of the material opposite to the observer. Opaque materials are those media whose daylight transmittances are essentially zero. Ordinary single-paned clear window glass — which is thought of as being entirely transparent — often has a daylight transmittance approaching 0.90 (which is nearly the highest value for common envelope materials; note, however, that *low-iron glass* transmittance values are greater than ordinary clear glass for the entire wavelength range of visible radiation [see Figure 6.7]).[5] Alternatively, there are numbers of other glasses (and various polymeric substances) whose daylight transmittances are substantially less than 0.90. In fact, some of these transmission-restricting glasses (and plastics) may have daylight transmittances as low as 0.20 to 0.40. These glasses (and plastics) are often applied in situations where occupants would like to be able to see out of buildings, but the solar radiation transmission must be restricted as greatly as possible (i.e., to reduce the potential overheating of the building interior resulting from solar radiation heat gain). Such glasses are usually identified as *heat-absorbing* or *heat-reflecting*. Their compositions include either tinting agents present within the glass itself or reflecting films bonded to a surface of the glass.

One other example of selectively transmissive glazing is the various colored glasses used in the stained-glass windows of many churches. In these stained-glass windows, the colored glass will selectively filter the *white* light (of sunlight or daylight) so that colored light — matching the color of the glass itself — will be admitted into the building.

6.2.2.2 The absorption of light   The process of absorption involves the collection of radiant energy that is incident on the surface of any medium. Thereby, the material accumulates some of the radiant energy that reaches the surface of the material. Absorption is dependent principally on the nature of the surface of the material. Further, the ability of a material to absorb radiant energy is also determined by other material properties including the mass and the heat capacity of the material. The amount of incident radiation that will be absorbed by a surface is described in terms of the *absorptance* (or *absorptivity*) of the surface (which is defined as the ratio of energy gathered in by the surface versus the energy incident on the surface).

Similar to how the transmittances of various media are characterized, the absorptances of most material surfaces will vary across the radiation spectrum: a material may absorb relatively shortwave radiation better than it may absorb longer wavelength radiation (or vice versa). For most *transparent* and *translucent* media, absorptances in the visible radiation wavelength band are small, ranging from about 0.05 to 0.20. But some special materials — like heat-absorbing glasses — are used in buildings because these glasses have considerably higher absorptances (and reduced transmittances).

One example where the absorption of light is essential to all of us is for the promotion of *photosynthesis*. The process of photosynthesis involves the combining of water and carbon dioxide in the cells of plants to form oxygen and carbohydrates, this last product being the basis for plant growth. For green plants, the chemical reaction occurs in the presence of

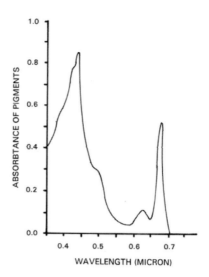

Figure 6.8 The absorption of the chlorophyll-bearing plant cells is comparatively greater in the wavelength ranges from about 0.35 to 0.47 micron and from 0.65 to 0.68 micron. Light in this lower wavelength range appears to human beings as the colors violet and blue, whereas light in the higher wavelength range is perceived as red. Alternatively, across the light spectrum where the absorptivity is lowest occurs in the wavelength range of about 0.50 to 0.63 micron. In this middle segment of the light spectrum, the characteristic colors for these wavelengths are green, yellow, and orange, successively. This graph has previously been published in the paper by Gantt, E., "Phycobilisomes: light-harvesting pigment complexes," *BioScience,* 25(12), December 1975, pages 781–788. Permission to reproduce this figure has been granted by Professor Gantt and the American Institute of Biological Sciences (copyrighted by the American Institute of Biological Sciences, 1975).

the pigment *chlorophyll.* What energizes this reaction is the absorption of radiant energy by molecules of the pigment (see Figure 6.8). Thus, from the absorption of light incident on the surfaces of plants comes the energy needed to produce tissue development in the plants.

6.2.2.3   The reflection of light   This property is strictly a surface phenomenon. The reflecting capability of a surface is described in terms of its *reflectance* (or *reflectivity*) that is characterized as the ratio of radiant energy that is rejected (not gathered in or transmitted) by a surface versus the radiant energy incident on the surface. Determining the nature of a reflection that will occur at a surface depends on a variety of features of that surface. Whether the surface is rough or smooth, shiny or matte-finished, and black, white, or some other color, all of these qualities will affect how light will reflect off of a surface. If the surface is quite smooth, then the reflection will be *specular;* whereas, if the surface is rough, then the reflection will be *diffuse* (see Figure 6.9). A specular reflection is what you find when you direct a light beam — perhaps with a flashlight — at a mirror. The beam will remain collected and not spread out after it has reflected off of the mirror surface. If you shine the flashlight beam at a diffuse surface (e.g., the plasterboard of a wall or a ceiling; a linoleum-covered floor that has not been waxed lately; and so forth), you will be able to see the spot where the beam strikes the surface. However, there will not be any apparent reflection from the surface. Instead, the incident beam is reflected diffusely: the reflected

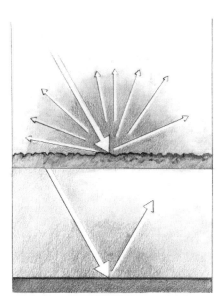

Figure 6.9 In the top image a light beam is reflected diffusely as the beam falls upon a rough surface. In the bottom image a similar light beam reflects specularly as the beam strikes a smooth, mirror-like surface.

radiation will be spread out and distributed relatively evenly in all directions as the light moves away from the reflecting surface. How you can determine whether the surface will appear smooth or rough to the incident radiation is by comparing the magnitude of the wavelength of the incident radiation and the average depth of the surface irregularities. If the depth of these irregularities is much larger than the wavelength of the radiation, then the surface will diffuse the radiation. Such is the case for light incident on most building surfaces, where the light is diffused off of these surfaces. Alternatively, if the depth of the irregularities is smaller than the wavelength of the radiation reaching the surface, then the reflections will be specular (e.g., as with a mirror or, possibly, a highly polished surface like marble or well-waxed linoleum).

One other significant behavior of a light beam incident on smooth surfaces producing specular reflections is that the angle of reflection off of a surface is equal to the angle of incidence onto the surface. The angles of the incident wave and reflected wave are both determined relative to a line drawn perpendicular to the surface at the point where the incident wave falls on the surface. Further, the pathlines (or rays) of the incident and reflecting waves and the line perpendicular to the surface at the point of incidence will define a plane. The reflected wave also will travel at the *same velocity* and with the *same wavelength* as the incident wave.[6] A verification of this fact is that when you are wearing a blue sweater and you look at yourself with a mirror, your sweater appears blue!

Similar to the descriptions for the transmittance and absorptance of surfaces and materials, how reflective a surface is depends on the wavelength of the incident radiation. For instance, in Table 2.1, we have identified the absorptances and reflectances for characteristic shortwave and longwave radiation incident on a number of opaque building materials.

The roughness of a surface and how it affects radiation is a quite relative experience. For instance, you can scarcely see your image if you peer at a wall whose surface consists of white paint covering gypsum wallboard. The roughness of the paint-covered wall is great compared to the very small wavelengths of light, and your image is greatly diffused. But, alternatively, if the wall is struck by microwaves from your oven—with wavelengths of up to a few centimeters (or just less than an inch)—then the surface roughness of the wall will be small in comparison, and any beamed microwaves will reflect off of the wall specularly.

One other requirement for producing a specular reflection is that the surface reflecting the incident wave must have a dimension that is greater in the transverse (or cross-wise) direction than the wavelength of the incident wave. Otherwise, the incident radiation will be scattered in all directions, being totally diffused.

From that table one can see that some materials display similar reflective behaviors at these two wavelengths (i.e., 0.6 micron [600 nm] for the shortwave radiation and 9.3 microns [9300 nm] for the longwave radiation). Other materials show strong differences. A further condition where the reflectances of surfaces can be considerably different occurs when colored light strikes a colored surface (e.g., red light incident on a red surface or green light directed at a red surface; these last examples will be discussed in Section 6.3).

Section 6.3 | SOME THOUGHTS ABOUT COLOR FROM A PSYCHOPHYSICAL POINT OF VIEW

The range of colors that the many objects in the built environment possess is one of several attributes that make possible our ability to sense and understand this environment. Seeing color enables us to identify such features as the composition, location, order, and texture of both the environment and the individual elements existing within it. Whitfield and Wiltshire have suggested that the presence of color serves three basic roles for the occupant.[7] First, color provides *ergonomic* information: with color, we are better able to see the overall environment and its many components and to distinguish between these components. For instance, because of the different colors of such devices, we see (and understand the implications of) yellow lines on roadway surfaces, traffic signals and stop signs, light switches on building walls, exit markers in buildings, and changes in floor surfaces (particularly, on step surfaces in stairways). The second role for color is that the use of color affords *structural* information about the environment. The coloring of objects in the environment enhances our perception of *the organization in spaces.* Because of structural data, we are better able to grasp the content of a space and recognize whatever patterns may exist in the space. Thus, color permits us to see the furnishings in a room and to ascertain their functions. Thirdly, color offers an *aesthetic* appeal to our visual sense. The use of color stimulates feelings of pleasure and satisfaction with the natural and built environments. Color can motivate delight and satisfaction with these environments, and these responses fulfill emotional needs that all of us experience.

If these roles describe the function of color, particularly, in the built environment, then—to understand its structure and essence—we should ask, What is color? and How can we distinguish alternative colors?

6.3.1   WHY IS A RED ROSE "RED"?

Color is a property of both our visual system and the material or light source that we see as having color. Indeed, we can describe color as being a *subjective* property of both. When light — visible radiation — of a narrow wavelength range reaches our eyes, we perceive that light as being colored. For instance, if we see light having a wavelength range of, say, 0.45 to 0.49 micron (450–490 nm), we will recognize this light as being blue. Physically, the light does not possess color. Rather, our visual system, which includes our brain, interprets the light of this wavelength range as exhibiting color. The color, then, is a product of how our visual system reacts to the receipt of light in this narrow-wavelength range.

When we look at a car or a tomato or a wool sweater, our eyes receive light reflected from the surfaces of these objects. If we perceive each of these objects to be *red*, we do so because the light reflected by these surfaces has a predominant wavelength range of about 0.63 to 0.70 micron (630–700 nm) (see Figure 6.10). If these objects are illuminated with

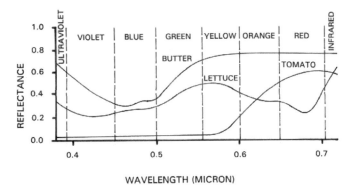

WAVELENGTH (MICRON)

Figure 6.10 This graph shows the reflectivities for three common edible materials: butter, lettuce, and a toma-to. The color of an object is basically determined by what portion of the light spectrum is most reflected by the surface of the object. Butter, when viewed under daylight, appears yellow because the butter readily absorbs vio-let and blue light and some of green light radiation. Light that has wavelengths equal to or longer than about 0.550 micron (550 nm) is mostly reflected by the butter, thus causing human beings to perceive it as yellow. Day-light, when used to illuminate lettuce, will be most greatly reflected in the green-yellow wavelength range. Thus, lettuce is perceived as being green. A tomato fully absorbs the shorter-wavelength light and most strongly reflects red light, producing its characteristic red color. Lastly, let us emphasize one further issue about these reflective behaviors and the colors perceived by human viewers: to predict what color will be perceived when viewing some object, it is essential to know the spectral characteristics of the lighting source. For example, if you viewed a tomato under a lamp that only produced red light — radiation in the 0.63–0.70 micron (630–700 nm) wavelength range — the tomato would of course appear red. But looking at butter under the same red lamp would result in the butter appearing red, rather than yellow. Alternatively, a tomato viewed under a blue lamp would appear black, because very little of the incident blue radiation would be reflected by the surface of the tomato. One final issue about this behavior might then be to consider what color would be perceived if a lettuce head is viewed under red light: we will leave this issue as a question for the reader to resolve. This graph has previously been printed in a paper by Gordon, G., "The design department" in the Volume 1(5), May, 1987 issue of *Architectural Lighting*. The copyright for this graph was owned by the General Electric Company. The General Electric Company has granted permission for the reproduction of this graph.

daylight—perhaps, from an overcast sky—then the other wavelength components of day-light (from 0.38 to about 0.63 micron [380–630 nm]) are not reflected as readily by the surfaces of these objects. Instead, the light having wavelengths outside of this 0.63 to 0.70 micron (630–700 nm) range *is largely absorbed* by the surfaces of these objects. The surfaces of these objects thus display *selective reflection* (and selective absorption).

SIDEBAR 6.7 Color-blindness

One necessary qualification about the ability of human beings to perceive color is that a small percentage of human beings have difficulty in discerning some colors or all colors. This partial or total color-blindness is present predominantly in males. In the various industrialized countries where tests have been conducted, about eight to ten percent of males experience some limitation toward their color vision.

Amongst females studied in similar tests, less than one percent displayed similar limitations. A brief discussion about the types of color-blindness and the percentages of people having such difficulties is presented in the book by Hunt, R.W.G., *Measuring Colour,* (Chichester, England: Ellis Horwood Limited, 1987), pages 28–30.

SIDEBAR 6.8 Color mixing and subtraction

Most surfaces will not be highly reflective to light of one wavelength range and minimally reflective to light outside this range. Instead, surfaces will commonly be somewhat more reflective to one wavelength range and relatively less reflective to other ranges. The color of the surface will thus result from the comparative strengths of the reflecting wavelengths (i.e., color will be determined by whatever wavelength range is strongest). Alternatively, the color that the surface appears may be due to a mixture of wavelength ranges (e.g., note that for butter—as displayed in Figure 6.10—the only wavelength range where the surface of butter is a weak reflector is in the 0.41 to 0.50 micron range [410–500 nm]). The color by which a surface appears can thus result from the mixing of wavelength ranges. Such a process is known as *color mixing* or, more specifically, *additive color mixing.*

The filtering out of colors essentially involves the process of color *subtraction.* Thus, the skylight filter used on cameras provides for the selective transmission of incoming light. This filter screens out, particularly, the short wavelength radiation in the ultraviolet and violet light range, thus helping to deemphasize bluish tints

that occur when photographic images include substantial portions of the sky (e.g., when taking pictures of relatively far-distant landscape scenes). Some new skylight filters will also absorb slightly greater quantities of blue-green light, helping to accentuate the orange-red tones that are important when photographing human subjects (to make the human skin colors seem more natural).

An alternative example of color subtraction occurs when you shine green light on a red glass filter and no light passes through the filter (i.e., all the incident radiant energy will be absorbed by the filter). To clarify how color subtraction operates, consider white light—the mixture of the basic or primary colors—as it passes through a colored filter. Some of the primary colors, that combine to produce white light, will be removed (or subtracted) from the light beam, leaving one (or more) primary color(s). For further explanations of the additive and subtractive color processing, see the books by Williamson, S.J., and H.Z. Cummins, *Light and Color in Nature and Art,* (New York: J. Wiley & Sons, Inc., 1983), pages 17–30; and Overheim, R.D., and D.L. Wagner, *Light and Color,* (New York: J. Wiley & Sons, Inc., 1982), pages 41–45.

So, let's now address the question, Why is a red rose red? The answer is that the petals of the rose absorb most of the radiant energy for the wavelengths of light other than those wavelengths of light that we perceive as red. So, the rose appears red because, when full-spectrum daylight falls on the petals of the rose, the light that is predominantly reflected is in the range of 0.63 to 0.70 micron (630–700 nm). Alternatively, look again at Figure 6.8 (which shows the relative absorptivity of chlorophyll, the active agent in the process of photosynthesis). In this graph we see that the green plant material absorbs virtually all of the radiant energy in the light spectrum, *except for those wavelengths we view as green.* Thus, the plant material appears green because the only wavelengths of light that are reflected by the material are perceived by our visual system as green (i.e., light with the characteristic wavelengths between 0.49 to 0.56 micron [490–560 nm] is viewed as green).

Another instance of coloration occurs when light passes through a colored filter. If daylight is transmitted through a blue filter, then the light passing out of the filter will be limited to the wavelength range of about 0.45 to 0.49 micron (450–490 nm) (i.e., that portion of the light spectrum we perceive as blue). The remainder of the light spectrum will not be transmitted through this blue filter. Similarly, if we consider Figure 6.11 where a prism disperses white light and the color components then are filtered by a red glass, the light passing to (and out of) the second prism will be red. The red filter will transmit no other light wavelengths (except for those of red light).

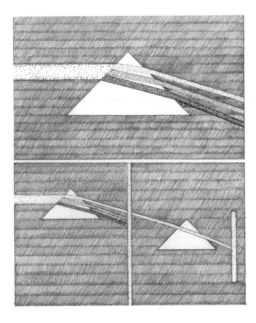

Figure 6.11 In the top image, white light passes through a prism and is dispersed into the various colors of the visible spectrum. The principal colors that will appear—from the top to the bottom of the intercepting screen—are, in order: red, orange, yellow, green, blue, and violet. For the bottom image, the dispersed light components (produced by passing white light through the first prism) then fall upon a red glass filter. Only the red light will pass through this filter and continue on to the second prism (i.e., light of each of the other colors will be absorbed by this red filter.) So, only the red light can pass into the second prism and come out the other side of this prism (as red light).

A third issue in assessing the color that a surface will display concerns the character of the source whose light falls on the surface. Daylight is a full-spectrum source, meaning that the radiant energy present in daylight is well spread out across the visible spectrum.[8] Alternatively, many electric lamp sources produce amounts of radiant energy, which are significantly greater for a few relatively narrow wavelength ranges than are present across the whole visible spectrum. For example, fluorescent tubes are commonly sold as *warm-white* and *cool-white*. The *warm-white* lamps have stronger radiant emissions in the orange-red portion of the spectrum, whereas the *cool-white* bulbs have stronger radiation in the blue-green portion. Surfaces that are more orange or red when viewed under these warm-white lamps will appear more vibrant and lively. Alternatively, these same surfaces, when looked at under the light from a cool-white bulb, will seem more subdued and less distinct. Lastly, if we direct a beam of green light at a red surface, the surface will appear black to our eyes. This result occurs because the red surface will absorb virtually all of the incident green light.

Using light sources whose rates of radiant emission correspond well with the reflectivity patterns of the surfaces that are to be viewed under the light can enhance the nature of these surfaces. One example of matching electric lighting sources with reflecting surfaces occurs in health clubs and spas. In these facilities, warm-white fluorescent lamps are commonly deployed. Thus, serious (and not-so-serious) athletes can be encouraged by their healthy skin tones (which these people will exhibit as they "pump iron" and perform aerobic exercises). One other example of how these accentuated-emissions lamps can affect the color appearance of objects can be observed in clothing stores. We suggest that, the next time you try on a sweater or a pair of slacks, you note the character of the lighting in the store. If the store is illuminated with fluorescent fixtures, you might want to examine what the colors of the fabric will look like under daylight!

6.3.2   CLASSIFYING COLORS[9]

A basic problem in working and living with color is determining what color some object is. You can say that your sweater is red, a tomato is red, and a rose is red. But are they all the same red? Likely, the answer must be, no: the red of the tomato has some orange present; your sweater may perhaps appear to be more maroon than strictly red; and the rose is a darker shade of red than the tomato. Such differences among similar colors can be even more exacerbated, if the light source illuminating these three objects has a spectral bias (e.g., a *warm* fluorescent lamp is used rather than a *cool* fluorescent lamp, thereby emphasizing the *red-orange* portion of the visible spectrum). Further, if you ask several people what colors they each perceive when they look at these objects, you will probably find that their answers differ.

What these examples display are the principal variables in the assessment of colors: the nature (or appearance) of the reflecting surface, the character of the illuminating source, and the variation between people's visual systems (and their mental stores of color experiences). When working with color, we often need to describe the color that some object exhibits (at least, to us) or to match two or more colors (e.g., to establish to what extent they are similar or to determine to what degree they complement each other).

This chapter is presented chiefly to characterize light in strictly physical terms. But, in this section where we are describing color, we must digress to a *psychophysical* treatment (i.e., because color is a product of our visual system, any description of color must recognize how the mind directs the perception of color). So, whereas *physics* is the study of the events and processes that occur throughout the world around us (focusing particularly on the interactions between matter and energy), *psychophysics* involves the examination of how the operation of the mind affects how physical events are perceived. The central topic in psychophysics generally concerns how we sense physical events and the nature of sensory (and other) responses to external stimuli. A variety of devices and descriptions have been developed across the past few centuries to define and/or to coordinate the colors of objects. In the following two subsections we will identify a very few of these color descriptions and systems and will suggest other literature where additional explanations can be found.

6.3.2.1 Colorimetry   Colorimetry is the science of color classification. As such, colorimetry involves the search for rational bases for describing and measuring the colors of objects (and light). Though early studies in this science were conducted by such eminent scientists as Isaac Newton, Thomas Young, and James Clerk Maxwell, most currently employed methods for describing, measuring, and matching colors are those which have been developed in the last 70 years. Recent scientific work has sought to relate colorimetric methods with the processes by which the human visual system perceives color. As the understanding of how the visual system interprets color has developed further, so also have methods evolved for describing color.

Before offering a description of the perhaps most widely applied colorimetric procedure, let us explain briefly how the human visual system senses color. In recent years information about the anatomy and physiology of human color vision has been integrated with observations about how well the color vision components perform. This merger of the two knowledge chains has produced a better, more comprehensive view of how we perceive color.

The principal component in the visual system for color sensation is the retina, which is the innermost layer of the eyeball. The retina is composed of a large number of cells that capture light from external objects and sources, as the light enters the eyeball through its pupil. These light-sensitive cells are present in two forms, and one of these forms is able to discriminate among light of different colors. Thus, the color-discriminating cell form responds to specific wavelengths of light that we see as color.

Three types of this cell form are found in the retina and are designated as R, G, and B cells. Each of these three cell types displays a different spectral sensitivity (i.e., how well the cell type will respond to light of specific wavelengths). These three types have been designated R, G, and B because the greatest sensitivities for these cell types occur, respectively, in the red, green, and blue portions of the color spectrum (see Figure 6.12). Color vision thus is based on these R, G, and B cell types: operating in an almost limitless number of combinations, these three cell types enable us to see all the colors we experience across the light spectrum.

The principal description of colorimetry results from work performed under the auspices of the Commission Internationale de l'Eclairage (abbreviated as the *CIE*), an international organization of leading scientists concerned with light and human vision.[10] In 1931 — before the more recent anatomical and physiological studies *which identified the presence of the R, G, and B retinal cells* (as described above) — the CIE published two sets of curves: each set portrayed the capacities of human beings to distinguish colored objects. These curves were based on experiments conducted in the 1920s with large numbers of people. The experiments tested the capabilities of people to see color (i.e., the studies were *psychophysical* in nature). One result of those studies was the definition of what was called a *standard colorimetric observer* (essentially, a *normative* estimation of how people see color).

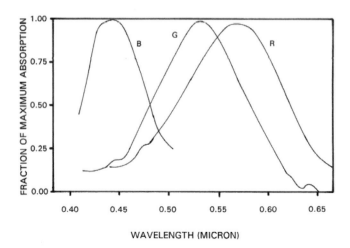

Figure 6.12 The retina contains three types of color-sensitive cells. One type absorbs most strongly light having a wavelength of about 0.430 micron (430 nm). This retinal cell type is thus designated as the B-type because it is most sensitive to blue light. The second type is most sensitive to light having a wavelength of about 0.530 micron (530 nm) and is designated as the G-type cell. The third type is most sensitive to a wavelength of about 0.580 micron (580 nm). This cell type is regarded as an R-type. The color vision present in most human beings results from the combined actions of these three retinal cell types. Some human beings, however, have defects in the operation of one cell type (or more): these people experience color blindness. Permission to reproduce this figure has been purchased from its graphic artist, Alan D. Iselin.

For this standard colorimetric observer, it was found that a combination of three *essentially hypothetical* color vision components, when integrated variously, could describe people's abilities to see color. Each of these three components could be represented by a curve that displayed the relative strength of detection for the component versus the light wavelengths over which the component was effective. Coincidentally, the first set of these three curves used the labels R, G, and B, for the three components (see Figure 6.13). The second set, which was based on a simple mathematical transformation of the values present for these RGB curves, used the designation x, y, and z (see Figure 6.14). Both sets of curves were called *color-matching functions.*

So, color-matching proceeded first by taking some amount of each of these x, y, and z components. Then, these components were mixed, and the character of the illumination used for this color-matching was noted. From a correlation of the mixture and the illumination character, it was possible to arrive at a unique description of any color. The three amounts which, when mixed together to produce a specific color, were then identified as *tristimulus values.*[11] In 1964 a third set of color-matching function curves were introduced—identified by the letters u, v, and w. These curves were based on enhancements—made upon the xyz set—which more closely tied the color-matching functions to a newer, better model for the perception of color. This uvw set of matching functions serves as the basis for the CIE 1964 Uniform Color Space.[12]

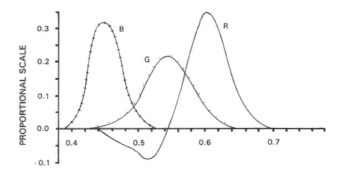

WAVELENGTH (MICRON)

Figure 6.13 The psychophysical experiments leading to the definition of the *standard colorimetric observer* by the CIE produced a model of human color vision based on three components in the eye. The performance of each one of these three components was demonstrated by one of the three curves shown in this graph. Thus, the curve with a maximum rating at about 0.440 micron (440 nm) suggests the presence of a strong capacity for viewing blue light. The curve having a maximal rating at 0.540 micron (540 nm) supports the capability for viewing green light. Lastly, the third curve with its maximum rating at about 0.600 micron (600 nm) indicates a strong ability to perceive red light. Thus, the *standard colorimetric observer* has been shown to have color vision based on capacities that most strongly perceive blue, green, and red light, respectively, and that integrate these separate capacities to enable perception of the full visible spectrum. These curves have been constructed from data — the r, g, b (spectral tristimulus) values — published by the Commission Internationale de l'Eclairage (CIE) in Table 2.5, pages 66–67 of their document, "Colorimetry" (CIE 15.2-1986). Permission to employ these data has been granted by the Commission Internationale de l'Eclairage. Note that the full publication can be purchased from the CIE Central Bureau, Kegelgasse 27, A-1030 Vienna, Austria.

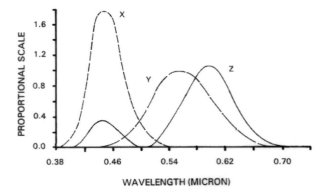

WAVELENGTH (MICRON)

Figure 6.14 This second set of curves is produced using data — the x, y, z (spectral tristimulus) values — published by the CIE in Table 2.1, pages 56–58 of their document, "Colorimetry" (CIE 15.2-1986). These data are the results of numerical transpositions performed by CIE scientists. Consistent with the curves shown in Figure 6.13, the curves here describe the performances of the three human color vision components as predicted from psychophysical experiments. Permission to employ these data has been granted by the Commission Internationale de l'Eclairage. Note that the full publication can be purchased from the CIE Central Bureau, Kegelgasse 27, A-1030 Vienna, Austria.

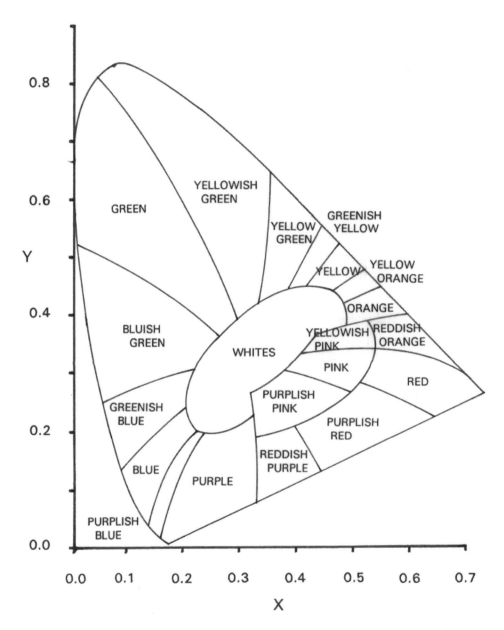

Figure 6.15 This chromaticity diagram enables a user systematically to establish what colors will result when two or more colors are mixed. First, the outer boundary line — the curvilinear portion — comprises all the monochromatic colors from violet (at one end of the visible spectrum) to red (at the other end of the visible spectrum). The enclosed area inside this boundary line (identified as the "locus," within the main text) contains all the color mixtures that either are created by mixing two (or more) monochromatic colors or by mixing two (or more) mixed colors. The identifications of the various color areas within the locus are approximate (i.e., a "green" at the point [0.1, 0.7] will be different from the "green" at the point [0.2, 0.45].) This figure has been published in an article by Sarver, C., and D. Ranada, "True colors," *High Fidelity,* 37(3), March 1987, pages 48–52. Permission to reproduce this figure has been extended by the editor of the journal, *Sound & Vision.*

These color-matching functions and tristimulus values are used primarily to describe the color-sensing capabilities of the human visual system. Instead, when someone wishes to determine — predict — how a mixture of colors will appear after the colors are combined, the device that is employed is a *chromaticity diagram.* This diagram is derived by computing x- and y-axis coordinate values for the wavelengths from 0.38 to 0.78 microns and then plotting a graph of (x, y) coordinates versus wavelengths. The x- and y-axis coordinate values are established from the following formulas:

$$x = X/(X + Y + Z) \text{ and } y = Y/(X + Y + Z) \text{ [also, } z = Z/(X + Y + Z)]$$

where the X, Y, and Z values are the tristimulus values for specific wavelengths. When the (x, y) coordinates have thus been calculated and are plotted against the specific wavelengths (for which each (x, y) coordinate has been established), the resulting graph will have a horseshoe-shaped locus that is left-leaning (see Figure 6.15). Along this locus (i.e., for the set of (x, y) coordinates falling on this locus), all its points represent *monochromatic* colors. Any such point depicts a *pure* color (i.e., one that exists along the spectral range from violet to red). By connecting any two points along this locus with a straight line, we can demonstrate the range of color mixtures that can be produced with these two pure colors. The relative distance from one or the other of the locus coordinates (representing the pure colors) denotes what color the mixture will have.

Further, all points within the area bounded by the locus embody various color mixtures (of the pure colors depicted by points along the locus). Such mixed colors can in turn be mixed. To identify what color will be produced when two mixed colors are combined, a straight line is drawn between the two coordinates that respectively delineate the two mixed colors. Indeed, this straight line forms a continuum of all the color mixtures that can be produced by combining the two mixed colors in various ratios.[13]

6.3.2.2   Color systems   The identification of a color is often required in various building industry applications (e.g., simply, as a response to the question, What color is this?) Whereas colorimetric techniques can be employed to derive a suitable answer, another approach can be to apply one of the many color systems. These systems are basically samples of color, organized according to some recipe or scheme. The major functions of color systems are to demonstrate the range and number of colors (or, at least, the range and number of colors in some principal set) and to portray relationships amongst all the various colors in a system.

Color systems have been in use since the early 17th century, and numerous distinguished scientists and artists have proposed different systems across the past four centuries.[14] There are a variety of color systems in use today, each with its supporters and opponents. No one system is universally accepted or adopted, although several are quite well regarded.

Perhaps the most widely recognized system today is the one developed by Albert Munsell in 1915. Munsell first described this system in a book entitled, *The Atlas of the Munsell Color System.* The colors in the *Atlas* were arranged in a manner generally consistent with most other color systems. The colors in the Munsell system are differentiated according to three essential properties: *hue, value,* and *chroma.* The word *hue* portrays the basic color present in a sample. According to the Munsell system there are five principal hues: red, yellow, green, blue, and purple. Alternatively, there are also five intermediate hues: yellow-red, green-yellow, blue-green, purple-blue, and red-purple. These 10 hues (or colors) can be described in terms of their dominant wavelengths (or wavelength ranges). *Value* in the Munsell system describes the lightness of a color sample. The range

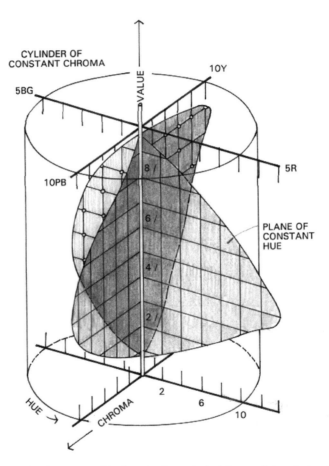

Figure 6.16 The Munsell color system solid relates the three principal characteristics of color: *hue, value,* and *chroma*. For the Munsell system these characteristics are shown using a cylinder. *Value* varies along the axis of the cylinder, with white at the bottom of the axis (value = 0) and black at the top (value = 10). *Hue* varies around the circumference of the cylinder from red (hue = 5R) at one point on the circumference and blue-green (hue = 5BG) at another point on the circumference that is diametrically opposite to this red. Note that the hue scale has 10 segments (1 to 10). *Chroma* varies along any radius from the spectral color at the circumference (chroma = 10) into the chroma-lacking—essentially, some shade of gray—condition along the *value* axis (chroma = 0). This figure has previously been published on page 262 in the book by Judd, D.B., and G. Wysecki, *Color in Business, Science, and Industry* (3rd edition), (New York: J. Wiley & Sons, Inc., 1975.) Permission to reproduce this drawing has been granted by John Wiley & Sons, Inc. (copyrighted by John Wiley & Sons, Inc., 1975).

of value progresses from white, at one extreme, to black, at the other extreme. Value thereby depicts whether a sample is light or dark. *Chroma* represents the strength that a color sample shows. Two words that are often substituted for chroma are *intensity* and *saturation*. All three words — *chroma, intensity, and saturation* — refer to how pure a color appears. A color viewed directly from the spectrum will be very pure (or "highly saturated," displaying deep or great intensity). Instead, a relatively unsaturated color will contain comparatively little of the main hue. Thus, pink has a weaker chroma in comparison with the spectral red color.

Similar to many of the color systems, the color samples in the Munsell system are shown arrayed in a three-dimensional solid that displays the relationships amongst the many colors (see Figure 6.16). The Munsell color solid is organized around a *value* axis where the two poles are, respectively, white and black. In between these poles are a variety of grays, ranging from grayish-white to grayish-black. Around this axis the many colors are deployed in a form approximating a cylinder. The 10 principal and intermediate *hues* are spaced out regularly around the circumference of this cylinder. The *chromas* for the various hues vary radially outward from the axis. So, the hue red is located at the circumference of this solid, maximally distant from the value axis. This red is spectrally pure. Alternatively, the chroma of the samples, lying along the radius from the *value* axis to the out-lying spectral red, will progress from a grayish-red near the axis to various middle shades looking like brick red to the spectral red placed at the extremity of the radius. The grayish-red color sample next to the axis has a weak chroma. Each color sample lying progressively further away from the axis has a stronger chroma (than the sample just inside of it). Moving upward along the outer edge of the color solid from the spectral red toward the white pole, the colors will have lessening values. Passing along the circumference of the solid from the spectral red, in one direction the next color encountered is the intermediate hue, yellow-red (or orange). Traveling in the other direction around the circumference the next *hue* is the intermediate, red-purple. Thus, by using this color solid and the three color properties (dimensions) of hue, value, and chroma, the Munsell system provides a means for displaying the range of colors and the relationships between them.[15]

As we have stated, the Munsell color system is simply one of many such systems that are in use (or disuse) today. Numerous papers frequently appear in the professional literature identifying alternative systems (and the professional groups advocating the applications of these systems), and recent color texts have also described numerous color systems. Generally, at least several attributes distinguish these various color systems from one another. For example, the spacings between color samples in some systems are determined by subdividing the total apparent *color difference* for a color property like value or chroma (i.e., taking the amount of the difference from one extreme to the other and dividing the difference by some integral number). Other systems employ results of *perceptual tests* of human subjects to establish appropriate spacings. The organizations of some systems are based of the establishment of *color harmonies* (i.e., colors which when used adjacently seem to be aesthetically pleasing). Other systems have been derived based on the character of the light source and the light level under which the color samples will be viewed (and, thus, on how these factors will affect how the various colors appear). And still other systems have been developed to accommodate the sizes of the color samples; the area (and the appearance of the area) surrounding the sample can also influence how colors will be judged. Such attributes as these can thus contribute to different viewer responses or preferences when alternative color systems are considered.

SIDEBAR 6.10 **Additional literature about color systems and their structures and differences**

For examples of alternative color systems, see any of the following papers: Nickerson, D., "OSA [Optical Society of America] uniform color scale samples: a unique set," *Color Research and Application,* 6(1), Spring 1981, pages 7–33; also, note the earlier paper by MacAdam, D.L., "Uniform color scales," *Journal of the Optical Society of America,* 64(12), December 1974, pages 1691–1702; Hard, A., and L. Sivik, "NCS—Natural Color System: a Swedish standard for color notation," *Color Research and Application,* 6(3), Fall 1981, pages 129–138; and Nemcsics, A., "Color space of the Coloroid Color System," *Color Research and Application,* 12(3), June 1987, pages 135–146. Note that the differences between these three systems and others that have been created in the recent past are both general and specific.

An extensive catalogue of color systems (presented with a well-developed bibliography) appears in the book by Hunt, R.W.G., *Measuring Colour,* (Chichester, England: Ellis Horwood Limited, 1987); note,

particularly, Chapter 4 ("Colour order systems"), pages 74–104.

For further information about how human perception can influence color vision, see the paper by Hunt, R.W.G., "Perceptual factors affecting colour order systems," *Color Research and Application,* 10(1), Spring 1985, pages 12–19.

Additional information about how alternative systems may be compared is presented in the following two papers: Wright, W.D., "The basic concepts and attributes of colour order systems," *Color Research and Application,* 9(4), Winter 1984, pages 229–233; and Robertson, A.R., "Colour order systems: an introductory review," *Color Research and Application,* 9(4), Winter 1984, pages 234–240.

And, finally, a brief paper that describes how color systems can be applied to building design and construction has been written by Spillman, W., "Color order systems and architectural color design," *Color Research and Application,* 10(1), Spring 1985, pages 5–11.

Section 6.4 | MEASURING LIGHT FROM SOURCES AND NONLUMINOUS SURFACES

Often when we think about light that is present in a space or that falls on a work surface, we must address the question of whether enough light exists to permit us to conduct some task. We thus need means for characterizing the quantity of light emanating from a source and/or a nonluminous surface and the amount of light reaching a surface. In the following section (6.4.1), we will introduce four cardinal means for describing light. These four characterizations will concern the rate of light emitted from a source, the spread of light over a surface, the physical brightness of a source (or a nonluminous surface), and the reflectance of a nonluminous surface. Then, in Section 6.4.2, we will describe some basic light measurement (photometry) techniques.

6.4.1 PARAMETERS FOR QUANTIFYING LIGHT

6.4.1.1 Rate of light emission   Light is one form of electromagnetic radiation, and all radiation forms are vehicles for moving energy from one location to another. The significance of light for human beings is that we are able to see it (or surfaces illuminated by it). Thus, light furnishes us with visible information about luminous sources and nonluminous surfaces, which are present around us.

We characterize the amount of light propagated by a source in terms of its flow rate. This rate of light flow is referred to as the *luminous flux,* which is the quantity of light energy emitted by the source for some length of time. Luminous flux from a source — whether a candle, a lamp, or the sky — is described by the unit *lumen* (we will provide a definition for this unit in the next subsection). Alternatively, the generalized quantity, *energy per unit time,* is also a description of the *power* that a source of any radiation manifests, and power is described in terms of the unit *watt.* Although a watt and a lumen are not numerically equivalent (or mathematically precise), they both represent the same parameter, *energy (of radiation flux) per unit time.* For instance, the amount of solar radiation reaching some receiver is described in terms of watts, which is a unit of power. As light is one component of solar radiation and light is expressed in lumens, the linkage between lumens — as an expression of light energy per unit time — and watts — as an expression of solar (radiant) energy per unit time — is evident.

6.4.1.2 Spread of light over a surface

This parameter — also called *illuminance* — considers how much light reaches a surface (from all sources and nonluminous surfaces surrounding the receiving surface). The basic quantity here relates the amount of light falling on the surface versus the area of the surface. As described above the amount of light flow is described in terms of luminous flux. So, the parameter (for characterizing the spread of light over a surface) becomes *luminous flux/surface area* and is expressed as either lumens/square foot (lm/ft^2) or lumens/square meter (lm/m^2). The former expression, lumens/square foot, is alternatively identified as *footcandles.* The latter expression, lumens/square meter, is more often cited as *lux* (see Figure 6.17). Also, recognizing that one meter is equivalent to 3.28 feet, the conversion factor between footcandles and lux is that one footcandle is equivalent to 10.76 lux.

To provide a definition for lumens and to set an example for illuminance, let us consider the light emanating from an ordinary wax candle. If we imagine a sphere being constructed with the candle placed at the center of the sphere and the surface of the sphere set one foot away from the candle (so that the radius of the sphere is one foot), then the *luminous flux/unit surface area* received at any point on the surface of the sphere (or the illuminance) is one lumen/square foot. Further, because the surface area of the sphere is 4π ft^2, the candle is emitting 4π lumens of light.

A catalog of recommended or probable illuminance values for various situations is presented in Table 6.1.

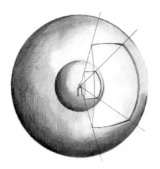

Figure 6.17 Here, we locate a candle inside two concentric spheres, one with a radius of one foot and the other with a radius of one meter. The sphere with the one-foot radius will have an illuminance of one lumen/square foot (or one footcandle.) Alternatively, if we remove the inner sphere and let the light from the candle fall on the surface of the sphere with the one-meter radius, then that surface will have an illuminance of one lumen/square meter (or one lux.) Further, because the distance of 1 m is equivalent to 3.28 ft, then the area of 10.76 ft^2 equals 1 m^2. Consequently, an illuminance of one footcandle will be equivalent to the illuminance of 10.76 lux.

TABLE 6.1
ILLUMINANCE AMOUNTS IN VARIOUS BUILDING AND OTHER CONDITIONS

expressed in lux (with foot-candle magnitudes in parentheses)

Moonlight (maximum) 0.43 (0.04)	**Classroom** (recommended) 200–1000 (19–93)
Starlight (maximum) 0.002 (0.00019)	**Drafting studio** (recommended) 500–2000 (46–186)
Total from sun & clear sky (maximum) 105,000 (9,760)	**Corridors** (recommended) 50–150 (4.7–14)
Direct-beam sunlight (maximum) 90,000 (8,360)	**Basketball, for organized competition** (recommended) . . . 300–500 (28–46)
Clear, diffuse sky (maximum) 14,000 (1,300)	**Tennis** (indoor) 500–1000 (46–93)
Overcast sky (maximum) 45,000 (4,180)	**Handball/squash** (indoor) 200–500 (19–46)
Reading room (recommended) 200–500 (19–46)	

6.4.1.3 Physical brightness of a source or surface   The *physical brightness* of a source or a surface characterizes the amount of light that leaves the source or surface *and proceeds in a specific direction.* Its application is based on the fact that many light sources and surfaces do *not* have light leaving uniformly in all directions. Rather, there is a preferential distribution of light outward from these sources and surfaces (i.e., more light passes in some directions than in others).

To characterize a directional distribution of light, let us begin with a point source of light (i.e., light emanates from a source that is quite small). The directionality of the source is manifested by a cone, pointed outward, with its vertex located at the point source. The amount of light cast outward through this cone is some quantity of luminous flux. The dimension over which the flux is spread—the "angular width" of the cone—can be described in terms of the *solid angle* of this spread. This solid angle is an angle in three dimensions (see Figure 6.18). To determine the solid angle for some cone, think of a sphere of radius r that the cone intercepts. The solid angle then is equal to the *portion* (designated as A) of the surface area of the sphere, *intercepted by the cone,* divided by the square of the radius (or, the solid angle is equivalent to A/r²). The unit for a solid angle is *steradian.* As the total surface area of a sphere with radius r is $4\pi r^2$, the number of steradians for the sphere is 4π. For an analogy, think in terms of how a length of a portion of the circumference of a circle is described in terms of *radians.* The entire length of the circumference is $2\pi r$, where r is the radius of the circle, and this entire length is described as being 2π radians.

So, to quantify the light that spreads outward *in some direction* from a point source, we would characterize it as the *luminous flux/solid angle* (of the spread). This quantity is identified as the *luminous intensity* of a source in some direction. Note that, although we used a point source as the basis for this explanation, luminous intensity can be used to describe either point or larger sources (for which we wish to consider the spread of light in some direction). Similarly, luminous intensity also describes the amount of light that can emanate from a nonluminous surface (whether the surface is very small or somewhat larger). The term *luminous intensity* (or lumens/steradian) bears the unit *candela.* In the previous example of the candle, we have said that it emits a luminous flux of 4π lumens over the surface of the sphere. As the solid angle for the entire sphere is 4π, then the luminous intensity (or luminous flux/solid angle) for this candle is *one candela.*[16]

The luminous intensity describes the light leaving a directional source. If we wish to determine the amount of light *reaching a surface from this source,* then we would divide the luminous intensity by the area of the surface on which this light is incident. Here, the surface area is that which is bounded by the solid angle as it intercepts the surface. This quantity *luminous intensity/surface area* (or luminous flux per solid angle per surface area) is known as the *luminance* and has the unit of either candela/square foot or candela/square meter. The unit *foot-Lambert* has been employed as an alternative expression for *candela/square foot.* But, recently, with the decline in use of the Imperial units system, application of the term *foot-Lambert* is becoming archaic. Instead, the unit *candela/square meter* (or cd/m²) has widely replaced the application of the foot-Lambert term. However, where foot-Lamberts appear in the professional literature, the conversion factor between foot-Lamberts and cd/m² is 1 foot-Lambert is equivalent to 3.46 cd/m².[17]

One consequence of luminous flux being spread outward *radially* within a solid angle is the *Inverse-Square Law.* This Law states that the illuminance (or luminous flux/surface area) is proportional to the luminous intensity of the source and inversely proportional to the square of the distance separating the receiving surface from the source. As a means for visualizing this Law, think of the sphere of radius r that is intercepted by the solid angle.

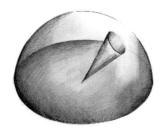

Figure 6.18 Planar and solid angles are shown in this figure. The chord of the circle subtends the planar angle in the two-dimensional view. The segment of the hemisphere subtends the solid angle in the three-dimensional view. Alternatively, we could write that the three-dimensional view shows the areal portion of the hemisphere bounded by the solid angle.

The total surface area of the sphere is defined as $4\pi r^2$. Thus, as the radius r of the sphere increases (or, as the surface becomes more distant from the source), the surface area increases as the square of this radius. The flux passing from the source through the boundaries of the cone is constant. So, the flux/solid angle (or luminous intensity) is constant, whereas the surface area on which the flux is incident increases as the square of the distance (see Figure 6.19).[18]

For a catalog of luminance values for a variety of sources and common nonluminous surfaces, see Table 6.2.

6.4.1.4   Reflectance of nonluminous surfaces

The light leaving a *nonluminous* surface will be some fraction of the amount of light that has been incident on the surface (and has come from some source or other surface). This exiting light is thus reflected by this nonluminous surface. To establish what *the reflectance of the surface* is, we divide the amount of light leaving the surface by the amount of light incident on the surface. The amount of light that is incident on the surface is its *illuminance*. And the amount of light that leaves the surface is the *luminance* of the surface. So, to determine the reflectance of a surface we

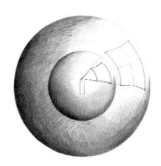

Figure 6.19 Suppose we create two spheres, the first with a radius of one meter and the second with a radius of two meters. Then, we place two identical wax candles, one in the one-meter-radius sphere and the other in the two-meter-radius sphere. If each candle has a luminous flux of one lumen, then the illuminance on the inner surface of the one-meter radius sphere will be one lumen/(π) square meters and the illuminance on the inner surface of the two-meter-radius sphere will be one lumen/($4 \times \pi$) square meters. So, as the radius from the first to second spheres increases two-fold, the illuminance on the inner surface of the second sphere is one-fourth of the illuminance on the inner surface of the first sphere. Thus, the inverse-square law is fulfilled.

TABLE 6.2
LUMINANCE VALUES FOR VARIOUS NATURAL AND ARTIFICIAL OBJECTS

SOURCE	LUMINANCE (cd/m²)
The star, Sirius	15,000,000,000
The sun	1,700,000,000
Snow in sunlight	30,000
The moon	3,000–5,000
Overcast sky	2,000–5,000
Clear blue sky	600–4,000
Xenon lamp	650,000,000
Mercury vapor lamp	1,500,000–31,000,000
Sodium vapor lamp	6,000,000
Tungsten filament lamp (inside surface frosted)	
500W	330,000
100W (standard coiled-coil filament)	170,000
60 W (standard coiled-coil filament)	55,000
Fluorescent lamp, 30 W, T-8	10,000
Fluorescent lamp, 40 W, T-11	4,000
Flame of a candle	5,000–6,000

Source: Stimson, A., *Photometry and Radiometry for Engineers*, (New York: J. Wiley and Sons, Inc., 1974), pages 80–81. Permission to reproduce this table has been granted by John Wiley & Sons, Inc. (copyrighted by John Wiley & Sons, Inc., 1974).

divide the luminance by the illuminance. The one qualification to this approach is that the surface must be *equally diffuse in all directions:* there should be no specularity to the surface (i.e., there should be no preferential reflection in some one, or more, directions). For most building materials this qualification is readily satisfied, and the reflectance established by this approach is an accurate portrayal of a surface.

6.4.2   MEASURING LIGHT

The operation of virtually all photometric sensors employed today is based on the *photoelectric effect.* In this effect photons of light fall on the surface of a receiver and pass energy to the electrons of the surface atoms. If the receiver is connected to other materials so that a completed electric circuit exists, the excited electrons will travel around the circuit as an electric current. Generally, the number of photons falling on the surface per unit time will determine the rate of the electron flow—and, thus, the magnitude of the current—through the circuit (i.e., this rate of falling photons is a direct indication of the *luminous flux* reaching the surface of the receiver). This current can be readily measured to determine the amount of light reaching the metal surface. The sensors—the surfaces of photon receivers—used in most photometric detectors often are sensitive to a wavelength range (of electromagnetic radiation) wider than simply the visible radiation band: thus, these receiver targets will also sense some ultraviolet and/or infrared radiation. As a result, filters are incorporated into these photometers to limit the wavelength range that the sensors can detect (i.e., so that they will measure radiation only in the visible wavelength band or about 0.38 to 0.78 micron [380 to 780 nm]). Thereby, the sensors respond to the same wavelength range as the human eye.

A variety of photometers are commercially available. At the University of Washington the two photometric sensors that we use most often are the Sekonic Studio DeLuxe Light Meter (Model L-398) and the LiteMate/SpotMate Photometer System. The Sekonic meter (see Figure 6.20) is a hand-held instrument of comparatively modest cost. This meter offers enough accuracy to be useful for field applications that also require portability and quick-and-easy measurements. The meter is supplied with a series of accessories that permit specialized readings, including illuminance, luminance, and surface reflectance. This Sekonic meter is also *cosine-corrected.* The LiteMate/SpotMate Photometer is a handheld, portable light-measuring instrument suitable for professional-quality work. This photometer is supplied in two parts (see Figure 6.21): the LiteMate component that is operated like a standard *illuminance*-sensing device; and the

---

SIDEBAR 6.11 Cosine-correction of light rays by photometers

Cosine-correction accounts for light rays that are incident on sensors from nonperpendicular angles of incidence. Meters with this correction produce measurements that include compensation for these nonperpendicular rays. The protocol for including this compensation by a photometer involves establishing the product of *the luminous flux found for a meter held perpendicular to these otherwise nonnormal rays* and *the cosine of the angle of incidence* for these nonperpendicular rays. Then, this product is added to the quantity of the luminous flux for the rays arriving at the surface of the sensor from a perpendicular direction.

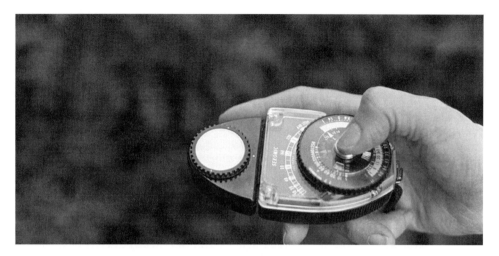

Figure 6.20 A Sekonic light meter is shown in this photograph.

[a]

[b]

Figure 6.21 The Litemate/Spotmate is displayed here in its two principal formats: the Litemate senses illuminance incident on horizontal or vertical surfaces; and the Spotmate measures luminance from luminous sources and nonluminous surfaces.

Figure 6.22 A two-part Spectral Pritchard photometer is exhibited in this photograph. The hand-held sensing component appears on the right: an eyepiece is on the back of this unit, and the lens that is to be pointed at the source or surface for evaluation is on the front. The meter on the front of the left component indicates the magnitude of the parameter that is being sensed. This unit is most often used in refined applications that require precise measurements. Its somewhat considerable cost likely makes it too expensive for common architectural practices. Instead, it is a device that would most probably be confined to specialized consulting organizations, testing laboratories, and research facilities.

Figure 6.23 This photograph displays a Li-Cor datalogger and some Li-Cor Photometric Sensors.

SpotMate which, when attached to the LiteMate, enables measurement of *luminance* for both sources and nonluminous surfaces. The LiteMate/SpotMate Photometer System includes two special probes: a fiber optic probe and a microreader probe. The fiber optic probe can be used to measure illuminance in models. Alternatively, both probes are suitable for measuring the luminances of back-lighted surfaces or the luminances of more distant sources.

In addition to these two portable photometers — the Sekonic and the LiteMate/Spot-Mate — we also employ three other photometric systems. First, we have a Spectra Pritchard Photometer (Model 1980A), which also is manufactured by Photo Research Corporation, Chatsworth, California. This photometer is a laboratory-quality device that can be applied either portably in the field or with a test stand in a laboratory (see Figure 6.22). It will measure illuminance, luminance, and luminous intensity. Further, this device can also be used to determine the relative chromaticity and chromaticity coordinates of surfaces as well as the color temperature for special luminous sources. Second, we have previously used a Megatron Architectural Model Light Meter — manufactured by Megatron Limited — in laboratory work. We employed this device, in conjunction with an artificial sky chamber, for the measurement of lighting levels in building models. We found the Megatron Meter to be particularly well-suited for modeling work, and it was much used in our daylighting classwork. Recently, however, we have altered our laboratory procedures to incorporate, first, data acquisition systems produced alternatively by either Campbell Scientific Company or Li-Cor, Inc. and, second, a series of Li-Cor Photometric Sensors (Model LI-210SZ). We presently use a Campbell Scientific data acquisition (Model CR21) or a Li-Cor datalogger (Model Li-1000-8) (see Figure 6.23). Either of these data acquisition devices can be utilized in both laboratory and field applications. Each is intended for use in fixed locations, rather than as portable devices (i.e., their applications usually involve taking a series of readings over some period of time). Their costs are reasonable, and they offer a level of accuracy that is well-regarded in the professional and scientific community. Our applications for the Li-Cor sensors include measurements of illuminance and luminance within buildings, in building model studies, and of the sky vault.[19]

ENDNOTES and SELECTED ADDITIONAL COMMENTS

1. For information and guidance about electric lighting systems, we suggest reading any of the books noted below (i.e., after reading the four chapters in this text). See, for example, the following texts: Hopkinson, R.G., and J.D. Kay, *The Lighting of Buildings.* (London: Faber and Faber Limited, 1972); Lam, W.M.C., *Perception and Lighting As Formgivers for Architecture,* (New York: McGraw-Hill Book Company, 1977); Egan, M.D., *Concepts in Architectural Lighting,* (New York: McGraw-Hill Book Company, 1983); Stein, B., and J.S. Reynolds, *Mechanical and Electrical Equipment for Buildings* (9th edition), (New York: J. Wiley & Sons, Inc., 2000); Murdoch, J.B., *Illumination Engineering,* (New York: Macmillan Publishing Company, 1985); and Sorcar, P.C., *Architectural Lighting for Commercial Interiors,* (New York: J. Wiley & Sons, Inc., 1987).

2. Elenbaas, W., *Light Sources,* (London: The MacMillan Press, Ltd., 1972).

3. Sobel, M.I., *Light,* (Chicago: The University of Chicago Press, 1987), pages 154–160.

4. Waldman, G., *Introduction to Light: The Physics of Light, Vision, and Color,* (Englewood Cliffs, New Jersey: Prentice-Hall, Inc., 1983), Chapter 6.

5. Note that the *low-iron glass* identified in Figure 6.7 has transmittance values greater than ordinary clear glass for the entire wavelength range of visible radiation.

6. For the reflected wave and the incident wave to have the same velocity and wavelength, the condition that must be maintained is that *the incident and reflected waves must be traveling in the same medium.* If, somehow at the point of incidence with the reflecting surface, the reflected beam passed into some other medium than the one in which the incident wave had been passing, then the reflected wave would display a changed velocity and wavelength.

7. Whitfield, T.W.A., and T.J. Wiltshire, "The aesthetic function of colour in buildings: a critique," *Lighting Research & Technology,* 12(3), March 1980, pages 129–134.

8. Henderson, S.T., *Daylight and Its Spectrum* (2nd edition), (New York: J. Wiley & Sons, Inc., 1977).

9. *Standard Definitions of Terms Relating to Appearance of Materials,* ASTM E284-87, (Philadelphia: American Society of Testing and Materials, 1987).

10. The CIE is also known by its anglicized name, the International Commission on Illumination. The CIE operates as a standards-writing body, producing recommendations on virtually the entire range of topics that address the availability and control of illumination to support human activities. This organization is based in Vienna and functions principally through a variety of conferences, professional meetings, and published standards.

11. This technique is described in the CIE publication, *Colorimetry: Official Recommendations of the International Commission on Illumination,* No. 15 (E-1.3.1). 1971, (Paris: Bureau Central de la CIE, May 1970). Note that a second version of this standard has been re-issued by the CIE in 1986 and is identified as No. 15.2). An additional source of information about this technique can be found in the ASTM Standard, *Standard Method for Computing the Color of Objects by Using the CIE System,* (E308-85), (Philadelphia: American Society for Testing and Materials, 1985). Further, a paper by F.W. Billmeyer, Jr. and H.S. Fairman identifies some of the development work that was undertaken for the preparation of the revised CIE document No. 15.2. The title of this paper and the journal in which it was published are "CIE method for calculating tristimulus values," *Color Research and Application,* 12(1), February 1987, pages 27–36. Note that, in the bibliography for the Billmeyer and Fairman paper, there are citations for several other studies that were pursued as part of the revision process (for reworking the 1971 CIE document).

12. *Colorimetry: Official Recommendations of the International Commission on Illumination,* No. 15 (E-1.3.1) 1971, (Paris: Bureau Central de la CIE, 1970).

13. For further information see the following books by Hunt, R.W.G., *Measuring Color,* (Chichester, England: Ellis Horwood Limited, 1987); MacAdam, D.L., *Color Measurement: Themes and Variations* (2nd edition), (Berlin: Springer-Verlag, 1985); Overheim, R.D., and D.L. Wagner, *Light and Color,* (New York: J. Wiley & Sons, Inc., 1982); and/or Williamson, S.J., and H.Z. Cummins, *Light and Color in Nature and Art,* (New York: J. Wiley & Sons, Inc., 1983). Additionally, a journal, *Color Research and Application,* is devoted specifically to issues concerning the science, technology, and application of color.

14. Hesselgren, S., "Why colour order systems," *Color Research and Applications,* 9(4), Winter 1984, pages 220–228.

15. Munsell, A.H., *A Color Notation,* 14th edition, (Baltimore, Maryland: Munsell Color Company, Inc. (a division of Kollmorgen Corporation), 1981).

16. A definition for the candela and the lumen have been developed and adopted by the Bureau International des Poids et Mesures, Sevres, France. The definition for the candela is "The candela is the luminous intensity, in a given direction, of a source that emits monochromatic radiation of frequency 540×1012 Hertz and whose radiant intensity in that direction is 1/683 Watt per steradian." This statement occurs in the article by Giacomo, P., "News from the BIPM," *Metrologia,* 16, 1980, pages 55–61. An argument for this definition of the candela (and a definition for the lumen) appears in an earlier paper by Blevin, W.R., and B. Steiner, "Redefinition of the Candela and the Lumen," *Metrologia,* 11, 1975, pages 97–104.

17. For further information and more extended derivations of the concepts of the solid angle and luminance, see Keitz, H.A.E., *Light Calculations and Measurements* (2nd edition), (London: Macmillan and Co., Ltd., 1971), pages 18–38; Murdoch, J.B., *Illumination Engineering—From Edison's Lamp to the Laser,* (New York: Macmillan Publishing Company, 1985), pages 28–33; and/or Stimson, A., *Photometry and Radiometry for Engineers,* (New York: J. Wiley & Sons, Inc., 1974), pages 6–10.

18. See Kietz, H.A.E., *Light Calculations and Measurements* (2nd edition), (London: Macmillan and Co., Ltd., 1971), pages 78–80; and/or Meyer-Arendt, J., *Introduction to Classical and Modern Optics* (2nd edition), (Englewood Cliffs, New Jersey: Prentice-Hall, Inc., 1984), pages 385–390.

19. The Sekonic Studio DeLuxe Light Meter (Model L-398) is manufactured by Hakodate Sekonic Co., Ltd., Norima-ku, Tokyo, Japan. The Web address for Hakodate Sekonic is http://www.h-sekonic.co.jp/sekonic-e/sekonicE.htm. The Li-Cor Photometric Sensors and Datalogger are manufactured by Li-Cor, Inc., Box 4425, Lincoln, Nebraska. The main Li-Cor Web address is http://www.licor.com/. The mailing address for Photo Research—the manufacturer for both the LiteMate/SpotMate Photometric System and the Spectra Pritchard Photometer—is 9330 De Soto Avenue, P.O. Box 2192, Chatsworth, California 91313. The Web address for Photo Research is http://www.photoresearch.com/newpage1/index2.htm. A mailing address for Campbell Scientific, Inc. is Box 551, Logan, Utah 84321. The Web address for Campbell Scientific, Inc., is http://www.campbellsci.com/. The mailing address for Megatron Limited is 165 Marlborough Road, London N19 4NE, England.

CHAPTER SEVEN

What Do We See?

THE HUMAN VISUAL SYSTEM is a truly marvelous creation, both for the capabilities with which it provides us and for its complexity. Our visual system enables us to sense light that permeates the environment that surrounds us. This system also permits us to gather information from the light, thereby determining the natures of objects and their surfaces. The visual system includes our eyes and brain, as well as some intermediate components that connect the eyes to the brain. Both the eyes and the brain are composed of vast quantities of individualized components. Indeed, our eyes and brain are likely the most complex organs in our bodies. Together, they comprise an essential means for sensing and, ultimately, for utilizing the environment around us.

In this chapter we will briefly describe the mechanisms of *seeing*. We will catalog the major components of the human visual system, discuss the process of interpreting light received from sources and nonluminous surfaces, and identify what attributes of the surrounding environment are required to make possible — even, to aid — our sensing of these sources and nonluminous objects. Lastly in this chapter, we will identify environmental conditions whose presence are necessary for maintaining visual comfort in our working and living environment.

Section 7.1 | VISION AS A SENSORY EXPERIENCE

7.1.1   IDENTIFYING COMPONENTS OF THE SENSORY PROCESS

Before discussing how the visual system operates, let's first think about what is involved, generally, in our several abilities to sense any environment that surround us. Fundamentally, our five senses — touch, taste, smell, hearing, and sight — provide us with capabilities to observe the environment around us and to gain useful (and extraneous) information from it. Thus, these senses enable us to characterize this environment (e.g., by seeing a dangerous animal moving toward you; smelling aromatic food being cooked; feeling a caress by a loved one; and so forth). Each of these sensory experiences has attributes that are common to the others. These attributes include means for *sensing* the world around you, *communicating* "messages" received by the sensing elements (to other parts of the human body), and *integrating* the messages (generally, analyzing individual messages and relating them to one another). The process of integration involves taking information gained from more than one sensory system, analyzing the messages from the different systems, and developing insights about the whole experience. For instance, if you are confronted by a large dog running towards you and the dog is barking loudly, you may be greatly intimidated by the approaching animal. Necessarily, you probably know that large dogs can bite! But, if you look at the dog and recognize that it is your pet and that the dog is inviting you to play with it, then you will not experience a sense of danger, but rather one of delight. So, the process of integration involves not only joining messages from different sensory systems together, but also drawing upon and including information that has been stored from prior experiences.

The sensory process begins, generally, with a *receptor* being stimulated by something external to one's body. In response to the acquisition of this *stimulus,* the receptor generates some form of an electrical *signal*. This signal then is passed along some *nervous system network* (a collection of components that tie the receptor to the *brain*). The nervous system network not only serves as a means of communication between the receptor and brain, but may also modify the form of the *signal,* thereby contributing to the interpretation of the stimulus. However, our brain conducts much of this interpretation (i.e., as it analyzes the content of the message presented by the stimulus).

What the brain thus obtains from the nervous system network is a message that has been broken down into simpler units. The process of analysis by our brain includes examination of the units, searching for the properties of these units and for relationships between the units. Then, comparisons involving the units with previously acquired experiences are undertaken. From such a multistep analysis the brain gathers enough information to synthesize a *representation* that embodies characteristics of the initial stimulus. How the brain performs this analysis and synthesis is largely unknown to today's scientists. In any case, once a representation of the stimulus is achieved, then the brain can go about deciding whether and how to respond (see Figure 7.1). Necessarily, any response that the brain initiates (using bodily parts) will frequently affect the original stimulus and cause new inputs to reach the receptors. New messages (from the receptors to the brain) may thus be created; such later messages can offer additional information to the brain and help it to understand better the characteristics of the stimulus.

The activity of the receptors during the sensation of a stimulus is *information gathering.* The several steps commencing with the generation of a signal by the receptor to the

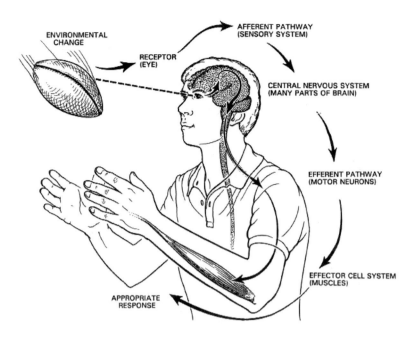

Figure 7.1 Here, a change in the environment—the arrival of the ball—leads to a response: the person sees the ball moving through the air, prepares to catch it, and does.

---

analysis of the information by the brain involve *information processing*. These steps of gathering and processing information about the surrounding environment provide the means for a person to examine the environment. Further, they enable the person to determine how to interact with the environment. Fundamentally, the reason why an individual observes an environment is to determine the guidelines or procedures needed to exist and prosper within that environment.

There are two types of sensory systems in the human body: the *somesthetic* and *special* senses.[1] The *somesthetic* senses include the sensation of touch (including sensing heat and "coolth", pressure, and pain). The *special* senses are those of vision, hearing, smell, and taste (and the maintenance of equilibrium). Both types of sensing mechanisms have three principal component groups: *specialized receptors* (which sense some form of energy that is a property of the surrounding environment and which convert that energy into an electrical message); a *pathway* that transports the electrical message to the brain; and *some particular region of the brain* where the message is processed. For instance, three essential components of the visual system are the *eyes,* which capture light and convert the energy embodied in this electromagnetic radiation into an electric message; the *visual pathways,* which transport the message to the brain; and the *primary visual cortex* of the brain, where the electrical message undergoes significant interpretation. The principal differences between the somesthetic and special sensing systems are also three-fold: there are many somesthetic sensing receptors, whereas the special receptors are comparatively few in number (e.g., we have two eyes and two ears); the somesthetic sensory receptors tend to be located generally over the entire surface of the body, whereas the receptors for the special senses are concentrated in one's head (i.e., close to the brain); and the special sensory receptors are greatly more complicated. As evidence of a somesthetic sensory system, you know that your sense of being touched is active over all of your body. But the "touch" sensor is not sufficiently complex to enable you to discern much from the experience, other than whether the object with which you are in contact is hot or cold, rough or smooth, or sharp or blunt. The receptor that senses when something comes in contact with your body essentially only registers an increase in pressure applied to the body. This receptor can discern where pressure is applied on the body, but comparatively little else. For instance, you may remember how, when you were a child, you were ticklish over many locations of your body. When someone tickled you, you could sense the application of pressure at some place on your body. But you could discern little else about the stimulus.

Alternatively, we have only two eyes. But each eye is able to distinguish great detail about the environment from which the eye gathers light (and, thus, information). As we shall describe in the Section 7.2, the eye is a very complex structure.

7.1.2   WHY DO WE SENSE LIGHT?

What is remarkable about light is not the light itself. After all, it exists only as one narrow band in the electromagnetic radiation spectrum. Instead, what is extraordinary about light is that human beings—and other animal and plant organisms—can sense it. We have eyes that are sensitive to this particular form of electromagnetic radiation and a neurological system that processes the energy embodied in the light. Our ability to discern and interpret this radiation has developed through the evolution of countless lower creatures over perhaps billions of years (so, we are genetically tied to light). Ultimately, our ability to sense this narrow band of radiation *defines* the radiation as *visible* (and makes this radiation band highly significant to us!).

A fundamental question that we then might consider is, Why are we able to sense light? First answers to this question certainly lie in the nature of light itself. As we have noted in Chapter 6, light is a form of energy that can be transmitted across both short and long distances. This convenient ability of light to pass from a source or a nonluminous object to the sensing mechanisms, which creatures have, makes light a very effective way of gathering information about the environment. Another likely factor leading to both plant and animal life being able to sense light is that light is a principal form of thermal radiation. Because thermal radiation is emitted from hot objects (the primary source being the sun), there is a substantial quantity of thermal radiation in the natural environment in which plant and animal life has evolved. Further, the ready interaction of thermal radiation with surfaces of nonluminous objects (e.g., by reflection or absorption) provides creatures with yet better information-gathering abilities. Lastly, a major answer to this fundamental question must also be that—for any life form to be able to maintain itself—the life form must be able to sense and adapt to its environment. The ability of creatures to sense light necessarily provides them with information about the surrounding environment. This information then can be integrated with stored memories, which together can be used to determine how to respond to whatever stimulus light emanates from.

To a great extent, human beings, specifically, and animal and plant life, generally, have become what they are because of the ready presence of light in the many environments of the Earth. Certainly, the evolution of sensing capabilities in these life forms has occurred in partnership with light. Although it may seem like an exercise in science fiction, one could speculate about what life forms might have resulted—and whether they would have evolved to higher states at all—if early organisms had been able to sense *preferentially* some other portion of the electromagnetic radiation spectrum. Other radiation types like the very-short-wavelength X-rays and the quite long-wavelength radio waves have only existed in very limited presences on Earth until very recently, when human beings learned how to produce them artificially. So, any historical development (or evolution) based on these or other less-present radiation types would have had to be very sensitive indeed to detect their presences. Further, such sensory systems would have had to be able to screen out the relatively much greater quantities of thermal radiation.

Section 7.2 | THE COMPOSITION AND OPERATION OF THE VISUAL SYSTEM

The essential parts of the human visual system are the eye, which senses light and converts the light energy into a series of electrical impulses; the visual pathway, which conveys these impulses to the brain; and the brain, which conducts the major interpretation of the impulses. The principal functions of the eyes are the receipt of light from the surrounding environment, the focusing of the light onto cells that are stimulated by the light, and the transformation of these light-induced stimulations into messages that are transmitted along the visual pathway to the brain.

Essentially, when we look at the world around us, much of what we see is light that is reflected from nonluminous surfaces. This light is received and processed by our visual system. Somehow, the visual system enables us to form understandings about the natures of these surfaces and then to identify objects bounded by the surfaces. Unfortunately, knowledge of the human visual system (by the present-day scientific community) is incomplete. Consequently, we cannot describe explicitly how the system operates or how we perceive objects in the world around us. Nor do we know if, after determining all of the areas of the brain that participate in vision and the activities in which these areas are engaged, we will someday be able to explain the integration that leads to the recognition of objects. In fact, an explanation of how all the components of the visual system work physiologically may not address important synergistic capacities that may occur in our brain and about which we are not yet knowledgeable. So, in Section 7.2 we will present an overview of important features determining about how human vision occurs. We include Section 7.2, specifically, to provide a foundation for information presented in Sections 7.3 and 7.4, which begin the cataloguing of guidelines for creating well-lighted building spaces.

Figure 7.2 A frontal view of the human eye is shown here.

7.2.1 THE STRUCTURE AND FUNCTION OF THE OUTER EYE

The eye is basically an oblong globe about two-and-one-half centimeters (one inch) in diameter (see Figure 7.2). It is composed of three layers of tissue, two chambers containing liquids, and a light-admitting-and-focusing lens system at its front. The human eye is placed frontally in the head: this location differs from many other mammalian species for which the eye occurs in a lateral position (e.g., the dog). The human eye rests within an orbit—a bony cavity within the skull—and is cushioned on all sides but the front with fatty tissue. The eyelid is composed primarily of muscle tissue and provides a protective cover over the eye. The front surface of the eye is continuously washed with tears, which

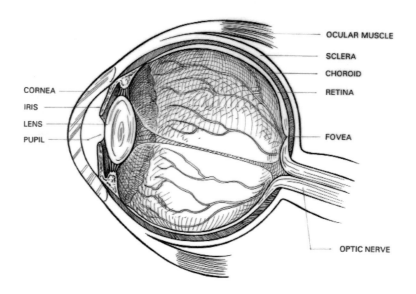

Figure 7.3 The principal components of the human eyeball are displayed in this cross-sectional view. Light enters the eyeball through the cornea, the aqueous humor, and the pupil, passes through the lens and the vitreous humor, and falls upon the surface of the retina, where the light is received and the processing of the light commences.

are secreted from tear glands and are released toward the top front of the eyeball. The tears are a salt-water solution that has antiseptic properties. Lastly, six extra-ocular muscles that are attached to the skull cavity walls control the placement and movement of the eyeball.

The basic components of the eye are shown in Figure 7.3. The surface of the eyeball is composed of three layers of tissue: the *sclera* (the outermost), the *choroid* (the middle layer), and the *retina* (the innermost). The retina is the light-sensitive layer and is an essential component of the visual system. However, before we describe the structure of the retina (which we will do in the next section), let us indicate how light reaches the retina. The outer tissue layer — the sclera — is semirigid and maintains the overall shape of the eyeball. The front part of the sclera is called the *cornea*. The cornea differs from the rest of the sclera: the cornea has virtually no blood vessels running through it and is, thus, comparatively transparent. As such, it functions as a window to the exterior world, letting light pass through it. But the cornea also prevents elements of the outer world (e.g., air, water, and so forth) from entering into the eyeball. The cornea serves as a *refractive* element that affects the formation of an image on (or near) the retina. Immediately inward of the cornea is a chamber that is filled with a clear, watery liquid. This liquid is bounded by the cornea on the front and by the crystalline lens in the rear. The middle tissue layer — the choroid — is generally brownish in color over much of its spherical surface except in the front of the eyeball. The principal parts of the choroid layer are the *iris* and a series of muscles that control the form of the crystalline lens (as the eye focuses on near or distant objects). The iris is the most forward portion of this layer and surrounds the *pupil* that is the opening through which light penetrates into the inner eye. The iris regulates the amount of light that enters the eye, increasing or decreasing the diameter of the pupil.

Behind the pupil (or, really, the opening in the iris) is the *lens,* an elastic, crystalline structure that is transparent and is composed of protein fibers. The shape of this lens is basically biconvex and has a variable thickness (i.e., the lens shape varies from a small diameter with larger thickness along its optical axis to a larger diameter with relative thinness at the optical axis). By changing the thickness of the lens, the *refractive power* of the eye is altered (see Figure 7.4).

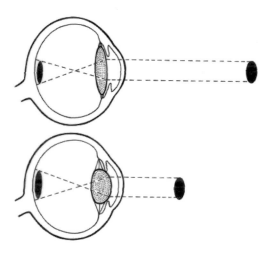

Figure 7.4 In the upper image the lens of the eye is relatively thinner to enable accurate sensing of objects that are further from the eye. Alternatively, in the lower image the lens becomes thicker to provide better resolution for objects that are close to the eye.

SIDEBAR 7.1 How the eye enables seeing near or distant objects

Throughout the process of lens shape variation, the primary need for the lens is *to focus the entering light on the retina surface.* For an object that is located quite close to the eye, more refraction (i.e., a greater bending of the light rays) is needed to see the object and the lens becomes quite thick. Alternatively, for a more distant object, the lens grows thinner so that less refraction occurs as the light passes through the lens.

The *ciliary muscles* (that are part of the front portion of the choroid layer) control the changing of the shape of the lens. This capacity to focus on objects

occurring at different locations is one that is affected by increasing age. As an individual grows older, the lens becomes less pliant and more resistant to changing shape (particularly, to becoming thick). Thus, the process of viewing close objects grows more difficult, and eyeglasses (corrective lenses) are generally required for seeing these close objects.

This process of varying the shape of the lens according to the distance of the object from the eye is identified as *visual accommodation.*

Inward from the lens is a second liquid chamber that contains an inert, transparent, and gelatinous liquid. The primary function of this chamber is simply to fill the volume between the lens and the tissue layers, thus maintaining the basic oblong shape of the eyeball.

7.2.2   THE ROLE OF THE RETINA IN HUMAN VISION

The retina is the innermost principal layer of the eye and effectively encloses the interior liquid chamber. Studies of human embryo development have shown that the retina develops out of the same tissue from which the brain forms. Thus, the retina is essentially an extension of the central nervous system. The primary functions of the retina are to sense light admitted through the front of the eyeball and to convert the light energy into electrical signals that then pass on to the brain. The retina has a highly complex structure and is itself composed of a series of principal sublayers (see Figure 7.5): the photoreceptor cells (located in the cell layer that is most removed from the interior liquid chamber and is adjacent to the choroid layer) and several intermediate cell layers (present between the photoreceptor cells and the interior liquid chamber).

The photoreceptor cells are the basic light-sensing components of the eyeball. There are two types of photoreceptor cells: *rods* and *cones*. Each of these two cell types have been named to reflect their basic shapes (i.e., the portions of these cells that are photosensitive). Rods function primarily at low light levels, whereas cones operate at higher light levels. Across the surface of the retina there are approximately 120 million rods and six million cones, *spread nonuniformly*. The cones are more highly clustered in the center of the retina in a region called the *macula*. There are relatively few rods in this center: most are clustered outward from the center (in the periphery). Light is preferentially focused on the macula by the crystalline lens, and indeed the macular area of the retina is where light reception is best. Further, more conal cells exist in the macula than elsewhere on the retina, and there are relatively fewer rodal cells. But, away from the macula the concentration of the rods increases greatly per unit area, whereas the cones, though present, are significantly fewer (both in numbers and in terms of areal density).

The operation of the photoreceptor cells commences with photons of light falling on to the light-sensitive surfaces of the rod and cone (photoreceptor) cells. The energy present in the photons is absorbed by the light-sensitive surfaces, leading to the initiation of chemical changes within the photoreceptor cells. In each cell the chemical reactions cause the cell to become electrically charged, resulting in the passage of electrical impulses out from the photoreceptor cell. These impulses pass on from the photoreceptor cells to various intermediate retinal cells (and then to the visual pathway and the brain).

The light that activates photoreceptor cells arrives at these cells as the conveyor of information about the world external to the human body. When we talk of "light," we are — to a great extent — speaking generally about the composition of the light and the character of the messages it bears. In fact, light reaches our eyes from an immense number of objects. These objects possess different forms, brightnesses, locations, colors, and other features that distinguish them one from another. The light from each of these objects falls on the photoreceptor cells — the approximately 120 million rodal cells and six million conal cells of each eye — and causes individual photoreceptor cells across the surface of the retina to respond. Where light from any object falls on the surface of the retina — whether in the macula toward the center of the retina or away from the center toward the periphery of the retina — depends on where the object is in the field of view and how the lens of the eye refracts the light rays incident on the surface of the lens. *We are best able*

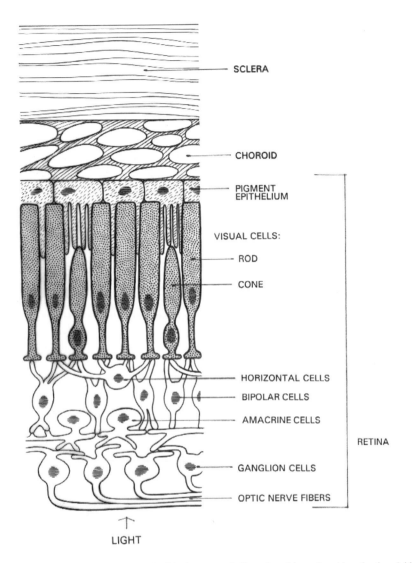

SCLERA

CHOROID

PIGMENT
EPITHELIUM

VISUAL CELLS:

ROD

CONE

HORIZONTAL CELLS

BIPOLAR CELLS

AMACRINE CELLS

RETINA

GANGLION CELLS

OPTIC NERVE FIBERS

LIGHT

Figure 7.5   The three principal layers at the back of the human eyeball are the schlera, choroid, and retina. Additionally, the retina is composed of a series of sublayers as shown here. Light reaching the retina from the environment outside of the eyeball encounters a series of cell layers before this light is sensed by the photoreceptor cells—the rods and cones.

to see when the light from an object we are looking at is received by the photoreceptors that are located at the center of the macula. Thus, we will consciously employ strategies that will focus the light, from something we want to see clearly, on to this area of the retina (e.g., turning our heads, trying to get more light to illuminate the object, using an external lens, spending more time looking at an object, and so forth). Simultaneously, our visual system will employ unconscious mechanisms that can also aid in enhancing vision (e.g., opening the pupil to let more light enter the eye).

The electrical impulses that leave the conal cells located across the macula contain much more detailed information about the light received at these conal cells than impulses flowing from more peripheral areas of the retina (because out in these more peripheral areas, the rods predominate in numbers).

So, the representations of light — from the peripheral rodal photoreceptors — are substantially *more generalized* than those established from the central conal cells. Light reaching the central conal cells will thus provide the most vivid information about an object or a surface, whereas the light reaching the periphery of the retina will offer a less incisive view of the external environment.

The messages the rodal and conal photoreceptor cells send "upward" toward the brain describe the amounts of light that are sensed (by these photoreceptor cells). After these messages leave the photoreceptor cells, other, intermediate retinal cells take the information about the intensity of the light, as initially sensed by the photoreceptor cells, and the intermediate cells produce altered messages that relate *differences in light intensities*. Indeed, these altered messages reveal the existence of *contrasting areas of light* (i.e., *showing relationships between areas of lightness and of darkness*). Thus, these messages concern the existence of light *contrast* amongst adjoining, very small external areas (very many of which compose the view field). So, the intermediate cells formulate messages that indicate less about the absolute level of light previously sensed by the photoreceptors and more about where (and, also, about how) surfaces of lightness and darkness exist external to the eye. Lastly, the overall retinal structure does not discriminate between environmental features, when the environment is *uniformly* lighted. Instead, differences in illumination levels — the establishment of *contrast* between adjoining surface areas — are essential for good detection of the nature of the view field.

The role of contrast as an essential property for differentiating environmental features is evident, for instance, if we think about viewing objects under either overcast or sunny skies. With an overcast sky the illumination appears to have a nearly uniform distribution. Instead, with a clear sky with direct-beam solar radiation incident on surfaces in the view field, the illumination will be *unevenly* distributed. An object viewed with an overcast sky will appear undifferentiated, bland, and even amorphous. The same object when sunlight falls on it, can be much more sharply defined as the sunlight highlights the edges, contours, and textures which the surface of the object possesses.

The features of the environment that are most readily recognized by the retinal structure are, thus, separations between adjacent light and dark areas of the view field. Such separations would include edges, lines, bars, and even corners of surfaces. All of these geometric forms — particularly, when seen on the printed page — will bear sufficient contrast, so that these forms can be easily detected.

7.2.2.1   Light sensitivity: scotopic versus photopic vision   The operation of the retina can be regarded as a competition between having sensitivity to light and resolving detailed information. The benefits of this competition thus allow a viewer to identify objects and their characteristics, as these objects appear in a person's view field. In other words, the retina senses light across a great range of light levels from quite dim to very bright. The retina is also able to sense the existence of substantially different light levels — dimness and brightness — in closely proximate areas (of the view field). The retina can achieve both capacities because it has the two distinct types of photoreceptor cells. Each cell type offers special capabilities which, when working in combination with the capabilities of the other type, create a highly flexible and proficient visual system (see Table 7.1).

TABLE 7.1

LIGHT-SENSING CAPABILITIES OF THE HUMAN VISUAL SYSTEM

LUMINANCE (candela/square meter)	LUMINANCE OF WHITE PAPER WHEN VIEWED UNDER...*	OPERATION OF THE HUMAN RETINAL CELLS & OTHER PROPERTIES OF THE VISUAL SYSTEM
1,000,000,000		Damage to the retina is possible.
1,000,000		
10,000		
	Sunlight	Photopic vision (approximate upper limit of useful conal vision)
		Best acuity (from 100 to 10,000 cd/m²)
100	Ordinary room lighting	Good color vision
		Very good visual acuity
		Saturation of rodal cells begins
		(all of these behaviors at about 100 cd/m²)
1		
	Moonlight	Mesopic vision (both rods and cones function;
		in range of about 0.001 to 10 cd/m²)
0.01		
	Starlight	Threshold of conal cell operation
0.0001		No color vision; poor visual acuity
		Scotopic vision (rodal cell operation) (from about 10^{-7} to 10^{-3} cd/m²)
0.000001		
		Absolute threshold of human vision

* In other words, when a piece of white paper is viewed under each of the following light sources, the measured luminance of the white paper would have the matching value (e.g., white paper when viewed under sunlight would exhibit luminances of about 100,000 cd/m²).

This table has been reproduced from the paper by D.C Hood and M.A. Finkelstein, "Sensitivity to Light," that was published in the book edited by Boff, K.R., L. Kaufman, and J.P. Thomas, *Handbook of Perception and Human Performance*, Volume 1: Sensory Processes and Perception, (New York: John Wiley & Sons, Inc., 1986), page 5-3. Permission to reproduce this table has been granted both by Professor Hood and John Wiley & Sons, Inc.

Scotopic vision is effective at very low light levels (i.e., at luminances between 10^{-6} and 10^{-3} cd/m²).[2] A primary scotopic vision situation occurs at night when the only light sources are the moon, the stars, and/or light from distant buildings or street lamps. At these light levels only rods are able to sense light. The quality of vision produced by this *rod-only* sight is quite poor, and the opportunities for discriminating detail and for discerning the color of objects in the view field are virtually nonexistent. The rods, which are located mainly away from the center of the retina, provide only reduced capabilities for separating out the *small differences in light and darkness,* which are needed for seeing detail. When these low light levels exist, the center of the macula (where the conal photoreceptor cells greatly predominate) is virtually blind. Generally, scotopic vision is considered to be *quantity-vision,* a condition for which the principal need is simply to see (i.e., to detect the presence of any small quantities of light). Finally, scotopic vision can usually provide the greatest amount of information when light from an object that you wish to see falls in the retinal area about 10° to 20° out from the macula. Thus, you can frequently see best at night, not by looking directly at an object, but rather by skewing the primary direction of your view field slightly away from the object. By looking slightly askance you reduce reliance on the fovea—the central area of the retina that has the greatest concentration of conal cells—and increase reliance on the rodal cells that function better at lower light levels.

Photopic vision exists at considerably higher light levels (i.e., at luminances above 3 cd/m²). For these light levels only cones operate (i.e., the rods are inoperable). Because the distribution of cones is comparatively high across the *macula* (and is greatest near the center of the macula) and the electrical impulse signals passing from these cones upward to the brain provide better information about the light falling on these conal photoreceptors, photopic vision provides the ability to discern finely detailed structures. Indeed, such *detail-seeing* vision is made possible by the capacity *to distinguish readily between adjacent areas of lightness and darkness.* Thus, photopic vision is regarded as a *quality-vision* condition (i.e., enabling the performance of tasks that require dealing with complex and closely differentiated surfaces). Such photopic vision also facilitates our recognition of edges and permits us to discern that adjacent objects and/or surfaces are separate. Photopic vision is generally operable in the natural environment during periods of daylight (excepting at the times of dawn or dusk) and within buildings that are well-illuminated (by daylight or electric lighting).

Mesopic vision is present at light levels that are intermediate between scotopic and photopic vision conditions (usually, for luminances between 10^{-3} and 3 cd/m²). Generally, under these light levels, both rods and cones will operate and will contribute to the visual experience. Some ability to discern color and surface detail will be present. But this ability will be limited.

So, the retina works in a duplex fashion. It has one set of photoreceptor cells—the rods—that make possible vision at light levels of low intensity. Alternatively, the other photoreceptor cells—the cones—permit detailed work at greater light levels. That the rods and cones are spread differentially across the surface of the retina also dictates the character of vision possible with each. In the *macula* and, more specifically, at its center,

---

SIDEBAR 7.2 Some suggestions about how the rods and cones came to be

If you wonder about how this duplicity of photoreceptor cells evolved, let us offer one plausible explanation. Clearly, the rods—being better at sensing low levels of light—would have provided a mechanism for our ancestors of long ago to remain safe at night from menacing animals. Also, the fact that the rods are in greater density and number away from the fovea—at the periphery of the retina—suggests a second survival mechanism. These peripheral rodal cells, whereas not especially useful in determining the detailed nature of objects, would still have been successful in detecting the presence of moving objects (e.g., menacing animals). Thus, simply being able to establish that something near you was moving

would have offered an initial warning. Then, the viewer could have turned to face the moving object, thereby gathering light from the object which could fall closer to the macula (i.e., the retinal location for detailed vision).

Alternatively, the ability to discern finely detailed objects would seem to complement the development of other capabilities linked to the primates (e.g., the prehensile thumb and walking on two legs). Thus, the ability to gather detailed information from the surrounding environment would have furnished more data for examining the environment and making decisions about its properties.

conal cells can sense highly differentiated messages about the presence of adjacent light and dark regions from the cone-dominated vision. Thus, surfaces with fine detail can be recognized and understood. Alternatively, away from the macula, the rodal cells predominate and there are few cones in the periphery. In these noncentral areas, discrimination of detail is comparatively poor. Instead, these surrounding areas are better for providing general vision during periods of lower luminances and *peripheral* vision (i.e., seeing objects located at the periphery of our primary view field, during conditions of either low or higher luminances).

7.2.2.2 Spectral sensitivity in the retina   We are able to sense electromagnetic radiation—to see light—in the wavelength band from about 0.38 to 0.78 micron (380 to 780 nm). But our eyes are not uniformly sensitive across this band. In fact, both the rods and the cones display varying sensitivities throughout the range of wavelengths of light. All the rods in the human retina show the same spectral sensitivity characteristics. The rods have a maximum sensitivity at about 0.505 micron (505 nm) (i.e., the wavelength for bluish-green light, although for the luminances at which the rods function, no color is discernible). The sensitivities of the rods at wavelengths on either side of this wavelength decline substantially (see Figure 7.6).[3]

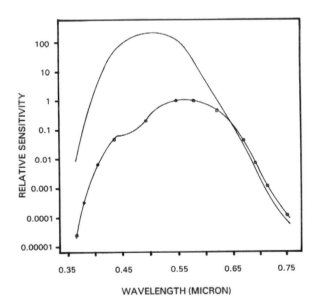

Figure 7.6   This graph displays the spectral sensitivities of the rodal cells—the upper curve—and the cones (located in the fovea)—the lower curve (with the dots). Note that the rods are substantially more sensitive to low levels of light. Thus, these rodal cells are able to respond to amounts of illumination that are much less intense than are required to activate conal cells (whether these conal cells are located at the fovea or the periphery of the retina). The conal cell behavior shown here is a composite description for the three types of conal cells (i.e., the R, G, and B cones, whose behaviors are differentiated in Figure 7.7). This graph has been reproduced from a paper by Wald, G., "Human vision and the spectrum," *Science,* 101(2635), June 29, 1945, pages 653–658. Permission to reproduce this graph has been granted by the publisher of this journal, the American Association for the Advancement of Science.

The cones also display sensitivities that correspond to the wavelength of incident light. For *generalized* photopic vision—essentially, an aggregated or averaged performance for all conal cells—the wavelength at which maximum sensitivity is achieved is 0.555 micron (555 nm) (i.e., a wavelength for which light appears greenish-yellow). At shorter or longer wavelengths the generalized photopic vision is less sensitive. A principal difference in performance, however, between the rods and the cones is that, whereas the rods all display the same pattern of spectral sensitivity, there are three different types of cones. A fundamental distinction between these three conal types is manifested by the fact that each of the three has its maximal light sensitivity at a particular wavelength. The three cones are commonly referred to as the *blue* cones with a maximal sensitivity at 0.440 micron (440 nm) (for blue-green light); the *green* cones with a maximal sensitivity at 0.550 micron (550 nm) (for yellow-green light); and the *red* cones with a maximal sensitivity at 0.570 micron (570 nm) (for orange-yellow light). Each of these three cone types has its characteristic behavior. Variations in the respective sensitivities for each conal type are shown in Figure 7.7. Note that each conal type, though it responds maximally to some single wavelength, actually is sensitive to a wide range of wavelengths. For instance, the red cones will be excited by light in wavelengths all the way from blue-green through red, whereas the blue cones will respond to light that spans the spectrum from violet to orange-red. Thus, there is considerable overlap between the sensitivities of these three conal types. When light of a particular color reaches these cones, all of the cones that have sensitivity to that wavelength will generate electrical impulses of intensities matching their relative abilities to absorb it.

The ability to discriminate between one color and another is founded on sensing the composition of the mixed signals sent by the three conal types. For example, if light with

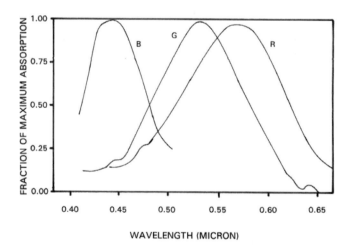

WAVELENGTH (MICRON)

Figure 7.7 The spectral sensitivities of the three types of human cones are displayed by this graph. The three types of human cones—B, G, and R—are most sensitive to blue-green, green-yellow, and yellow-orange, respectively. This graph has been reproduced from a paper by Rushton, W.A.H., "Visual pigments and color blindness," *Scientific American,* 232(3), March 1975, pages 64–75. Note that this graph was also employed as Figure 6.12; we suggest reading and comparing the discussion in Section 6.3.2.1 (on the relevance of Figure 6.12) with the information presented in Section 7.2.2.2. Permission to reproduce this drawing has been purchased from the graphic artist, Alan D. Iselin.

a wavelength of about 0.500 micron (500 nm) reaches the cones, all three types will sense the light (i.e., the blue cones have an absorptivity of about 0.35 at 0.500 micron [500 nm]; the green cones, an absorptivity of about 0.70; and the red cones, an absorptivity of 0.35). Thus, the message passed on from the cones upward to the brain would show a ratio of response of 0.35:0.70:0.35 for the three cones. This ratio would then be interpreted as *green* light.

7.2.3 DERIVING IDEAS ABOUT CREATING BUILT ENVIRONMENTS FROM THIS DESCRIPTION OF THE VISUAL SYSTEM

As a summary of this discussion about the structure and operation of the eye (and the photoreceptor cells of the retina) for the human being, we can state that, first, a series of processes enable us to gather *visible* information from the environment and to interpret this information. These processes include acquiring the light from external stimuli in the surrounding environment, changing the light energy to electrical signals, routing these signals from the eye to the brain, and having the brain conduct the necessary analysis (and synthesis) of the information.

For us as designers and builders, our responsibilities for fostering good conditions for vision include insuring *appropriate qualities* and *quantities* of light in the built environment. The acquisition of light, transmitted from external objects to our eyes, is the first step in seeing and understanding what surrounds us. Creating a visually satisfactory environment requires that enough light passes from an object to our eyes so that the photoreceptor cells in the retina will be excited by the light and that sufficient contrast is present between such objects and their surrounds and backgrounds. Being able to sense numerous objects across a view field depends on having enough variability in the view field so that these objects can be distinguished. Uniformity in surface appearances will degrade a person's ability to discern the properties of objects or to differentiate between objects. Further, diffused light provides little basis for the visual system to separate detailed information. Instead, illumination must highlight the edges, contours, textures, and other surface features that distinguish objects. Lastly, selecting the overall magnitude of light in the view field is less important (i.e., as long as there is enough light for one or the other of the retinal photoreceptors—the rods and the cones—to be operational).

In Sections 7.4 and 7.5 we will continue this catalogue of environmental properties, which are necessary for us to see well.

Section 7.3 | VISUAL PERCEPTION AS A FUNDAMENTAL STEP IN SEEING

In this section we will offer some discussion about how our brains integrate the many bits of information that our eyes detect. An explicit description of how this integration occurs is not possible because there still appears to be much that is unknown about how the human visual system operates. Yet, there are numerous textbooks and a substantial number of professional and academic journals, all of which discuss theory, research, and practice about this subject. Because of both the breadth and depth of the field we can hardly provide a short, comprehensive view of its contents. Instead, we will present a brief explanation of the apparent steps involved in the visual perception of external objects.

7.3.1   SOME THOUGHTS ABOUT HOW VISUAL PERCEPTION OCCURS

The operation of the visual system is, ultimately, one part of the continuum of the human experience. The visual system provides us with information about the world around us, enabling us to understand the environment external to our bodies. Other sensory systems (e.g., hearing, smell, touching, and so forth) also supply information, thus providing more data for our interpretation of the environment. However, how well we gain insights about this environment will also depend on many additional parameters including the levels of our physical and mental abilities, the complexity of the surrounding environment, and the technical (or artificial) aids we have for enhancing our abilities to sense the environment. Furthermore, the character of the knowledge we establish (in our search for insights about the surrounding environment) will likely change from moment to moment. Thus, this development of understanding about the world around us is really a very active and continuing process.

In Section 7.2 we have briefly described how light stimulates the photoreceptors of the retina. Now, let us consider how the products of that stimulation can guide our interactions with the surrounding environment.

The fundamental operation of the visual system proceeds on a *stimulus-response* relationship. The receipt of light from some external object initiates action by the system. The system then decomposes the object (or, more specifically, the light from the object), generating a sort of code. This code then passes on to a central processor, where the code is interpreted, first alone and then in comparison with information stored from previous experiences. The central processor evaluates the results of these analyses and formulates a *model* that will include as much of the information that the processor is able to gather about the external object (and about similar, past experiences with comparable objects). Essentially, this model functions as a *hypothesis,* which the processor can test for how well it seems to describe the external object. When the processor is satisfied that the model is reasonable (or when the processor decides that no further time is available), the processor makes a decision to accept the model or to construct a new one. If the processor elects to proceed with this model (or an alternative one), then the processor identifies some action that the body can take concerning the external object and causes the body to undertake that action. When this action is commenced, the processor will likely receive new signals—stimuli—from the object and its environment, which can lead to further data

processing. Acquiring this additional information may subsequently produce a better definition of what the nature of the external object is and what action concerning it would be
most appropriate. As an example, think about how you might perceive a moving animal.
First, your eyes see patterns of light reflected off of the animal's body. These patterns can
provide information about the size, color, form, and rate of movement of the animal. The
light information is processed into electrical signals that pass from the eyes to the brain.
The brain constructs a perceptual model and compares this information with previous
experiences. Then, the brain synthesizes conclusions from these comparisons. So, if your
brain recognizes that the animal is large, appears mean, and is running toward you, the
brain will identify possible actions (e.g., running away, climbing a tree, drawing a weapon
and preparing to use it, and so forth) and will initiate some action.[4]

This description identifies a reasonably simple composition for a *stimulus-response*
relationship. This process not only includes the components and operation of the visual
system, but also specifies the larger context (i.e., some human experience) in which the act
of seeing is integral. Thus, what we are describing here is the *purpose* for — or the function of — the visual system and the information with which it provides us: the acquisition
of light from an external object and the interpretation of information borne by the light are
one major part in our striving *to perceive* the world in which we exist. Other principal
components in this process are relating what is viewed by the visual system to prior experiences, conducting comparisons among the alternative bits of information (about this one
event and prior experiences), and establishing tentative conclusions about that which is
being viewed presently. Thus, the integration of this sensory process — vision — with
these mental processes leads to *visual perception.* An additional step in the overall experience is the testing of the accuracy of the conclusions and, if these conclusions are found
to be reasonable, their addition to the individual's personal set of experiences. This last
step leads to *cognition* (i.e., the development of knowledge or learning about some thing).

Visual perception, then, encompasses both the collection of visible information about
some external object (which is obtained with the visual system) and the mental processing of that information. The goal of this processing is to identify the patterns of light
received by the eyes. So, perception involves the sensing of the external object and the

---

SIDEBAR 7.4 A small bibliography concerning visual perception

Numerous books have been written on the subject of
perception. Among the large numbers of such books,
we will recommend the following books as excellent
sources for further information: Sekuler, R., and R.
Blake, *Perception,* (New York: Alfred A. Knopf, Inc.,
1985); see pages 1–23, particularly; Bruce, V., and P.
Green, *Visual Perception: Physiology, Psychology, and
Ecology,* (London: Lawrence Erlbaum Associates,
Ltd., 1985; Gibson, J.J., *The Ecological Approach to
Visual Perception,* (Hillsdale, New Jersey: Lawrence
Erlbaum Associates, Inc., 1986); Kaufman, L., *Sight
and Mind: An Introduction to Visual Perception,* (New
York: Oxford University Press, 1974); Marr, D.,
Vision, (New York: W.H. Freeman and Company,
1982); Rock, I., *Perception,* (New York: Scientific
American Books, Inc., 1984); and Beck, J., editor,
Organization and Representation in Perception,
(London: Lawrence Erlbaum Associates, Inc., 1982).
This last text is a collection of essays written by sever-
al distinguished psychologists specializing in visual
perception. The scientific points of view expressed in
these essays range widely, offering an interesting,
cross-sectional glimpse of the field.

association of what is sensed with mental products of past experiences (i.e., memories). Two distinctions are present here. First, we can distinguish between the visual system, which includes the eye and the parts of the brain directly involved in vision, and the mind, which encompasses all the entire mental processes of the brain (i.e., the operation of the various sensory systems, as well as other conscious and unconscious activities). Second, we can also distinguish between the products of the visual system, which provides *sensations* about the external world, and the products of the mind, which enables us to form *percepts* (or understandings) about the external world. Ultimately, then, perception is an essential step in the process by which our sensory systems gather information about the external world and our mind incorporates that information into our set of life experiences. Therefore, *seeing* requires more from the human being than simply having an operant visual system. For perception to occur successfully, both the visual system and the mind must perform in concert. Objects in the external world also must have properties, which enable these objects to be perceived.

7.3.2   ATTRIBUTES OF THE VISUAL PERCEPTION PROCESS

Perception involves the *input* of some information to a body *unit* capable of sensing the stimulus, the subsequent *manipulation* of the information by the sensory *system* and our mind, and the production of some *output* (or percept). Using this simple model for perception,

$$\text{input} \rightarrow \text{manipulation} \rightarrow \text{output}$$

let us identify attributes for each of these three steps.

The input for *visual* perception consists, first, of information taken from the external world. This information is obtained from the stimulus that activates the sensory system (i.e., light falling on the retinal photoreceptor cells of the visual system). Thus, several parameters can affect the quality of the available information (and how easily these data can be manipulated by your mind subsequently). For instance, the *information* provided by the stimulus may be *incomplete:* the stimulus can present a blurred image or the receptor system may not be able to view the stimulus well because the object is too far away). However, if the information is indeed incomplete but still is comparatively *familiar* (it emanates from a much-used object), then understanding may still occur readily. Another source of information for visual perception comes from one's memory. Stored images can be used as comparison bases for developing understandings about the nature of the stimulus. For stored images to be useful, the information obtained from the stimulus must be sufficiently *well defined* and appear *similar to stored images,* so that meaningful comparisons can be executed. The later recognition of information can also be aided if the information is presented in a *context* and/or the information exhibits a *directionality* (i.e., the information exists in some form or order that makes it more easily interpretable by the perceiver). Context can greatly aid the observer. For instance, even if one word in a sentence is blurred, the presence of other words that appear clearly enables the viewer to determine the blurred word from the meaning of the sentence. Just so, the presence of an informative context can enable the accurate perception of an object—a word in a sentence or the face of an old classmate at a reunion party—even when the object is not entirely familiar. Similarly, when visual materials are presented with a specific directionality or well-established pattern, then the perception of elements in such a pattern will be more easily accomplished. For instance, a traffic light controlling vehicular passage across an intersection changes from green to yellow to red. Some color-blind people would have trouble identifying these colors, if the three colors appear in other random settings. But, because these people can readily learn the color progression that the traffic signal employs, their color-blindness would not limit their abilities to interpret the meaning of the traffic signal. Also, *information derived from some other sensory system* can aid your visual perception. Say, for example, you go on a hike in the woods and, while walking, you see a small, black animal moving through some underbrush ahead of you. Although your vision of the animal may be partially obscured by the vegetation, the presence of an overwhelming stench can quickly help you to determine that the creature is most likely a skunk and not some cat or small dog! Lastly, the perceptual process *does not end with the cessation of the stimulation.* In fact, perception may continue for significant periods of time following the end of the receipt of light from a stimulus. For example, you glimpse something suddenly while looking around and, when you look back to confirm what you think you saw, the object is no longer present, so you have to recreate an image from "memory." Or you look at an object, form an image of the object, and then you later wonder if your original impression of the object were indeed accurate. Anyway, all of these parameters can affect the input of information and thus may influence your perception of some activity or object. Further, these parameters can also determine by what means and how well the input data will be manipulated (as you struggle to perceive external objects and features).

The manipulation procedure for this input information has several important features. First, it has a *temporal* dimension (i.e., it is a process that involves *time*). Perception does not occur simultaneously with the arrival of light at the retinal photoreceptors. Instead, some time will elapse between the acquisition of the light and the realization of what is being viewed; one estimate is that seeing and perceiving a common object require about

SIDEBAR 7.5 How perceptions can be aided in the conduct of everyday activities

Let us offer two examples of conditions that can adversely affect the manipulation of the input information. First, you are driving your car and feeling anxious about whether you are going to arrive at your destination with sufficient time to call a business associate; thus, when you see a large pothole in the road surface ahead, you are unable to react quickly enough to avoid driving over this pothole. And, second, as you try and read a set of directions, a colleague is speaking to you about operating the device whose directions you are reading (thus confusing your reading comprehension). Each of these two experiences involves having streams of data input, which arrive simultaneously, thus causing an overload of sensory information. A third example, which shows how input information can be manipulated successfully, consists of having you stand waiting for your playmate to throw the ball to you: you know that the ball will arrive at a fast rate, so you block out other thoughts and concentrate your mind (and body) on getting ready to catch the ball (e.g., placing your hands in an outstretched position and forcing your eyes to peer only at the ball, which presently rests in one of your playmate's hands [note, again, 7.1]).

Your *visual* ability to perceive some condition can thereby be modified by a host of various factors. Some of these factors you may be able to control only if all your faculties are focused on the perceptual process; alternatively, other factors may impose constraints on your ability to perceive some object, thus limiting your ability to be successful in recognizing the object or its environment.

0.3 seconds. Second, perception *does not happen automatically.* That is, we have many actions—conscious as well as unconscious—that aid perception. Such unconscious acts as moving one's head to see an external object better or squinting to limit the amount of light getting to the retina can improve the performance of the visual system. Additionally, perception can be affected by a host of other factors (e.g., one's emotional state; some input from another person; the application of some thought process initiated by prior training; and so forth). The involvement of any of these factors can modify (and possibly enhance or complicate) the perceptual process.

Third, perception is a highly *selective* process in which *all or only some* of the information from the stimulus will likely be treated and compared with just some of the vast store of memories that a human being maintains. The fact that the information from any visual experience will be manipulated against only snippets of one's memory seems unavoidable and most efficient. To summon up your entire memory store to compare with information obtained from viewing a single object would be hopelessly inefficient and time-consuming. Thus, your mind has to have some means of choosing what are the most relevant bits of memory to call upon, as you try to perceive some object. How this process of stored memory recall and comparison occurs—to what extent it is random or structured—is unknown and currently only a subject for conjecture. A fourth attribute of this manipulation phase of perception is that much of the process seems to be *sequential.* The acquisition of a signal from the stimulus and its handling by the visual system clearly appear orderly up to the processing that happens beyond the first vision areas in the human brain. The treatment that occurs during further manipulation is thought to be sequential, rather than random, if for no other reason than it would seem to be more efficient and timely. The fifth attribute of the manipulation phase is the existence of a *rate sensitivity* for the process. Thus, how long an individual has to acquire information and manipulate it (or its components) will greatly affect the accuracy of the process. The results of a brief glimpse of some object and a hurried judgment about its composition both can usually be improved upon when increased amounts of time are made available.

The output (or product) of the perceptual process will be greatly dependent upon the successful implementation of the first two steps of this process. For instance, if information gained about some object is incomplete because of poor environmental conditions or if the object is unfamiliar and insufficient time is available for a more careful scrutiny, then the understanding derived about the object could be relatively limited. Alternatively, suppose that the information gained from some object indeed is incomplete. Even, though data about the nature of the object are limited, the information so gained may be just the right fraction. Recognition can still take place if similar experiences occurred previously (i.e., so that the portion of information, which is obtained from the external object, appears familiar). Thus, whether the outputs of the perceptual process for these two examples are useful or not will be determined by the sensory and mental activities that precede the generation of the output.

The principal attribute of the output is *integration.* The output involves bringing together information gained from observing an external object, recalling results of past experiences, comparing the present and past sets of information, and deciding on the nature of the external object. The other attribute of this step is that *learning may result* as a new element is added to one's set of stored experiences. Of course, if the information gathered in the input phase was sufficiently unfamiliar or there was insufficient time for adequate manipulation of the information or any of the several attributes were not suitably taken care of, then the output would likely be misleading and would provide disinformation. So, inevitably, before one can be confident about the quality of a perception that has been formed, some testing may be warranted. This testing may require additional thought or the collection of further information (e.g., if an electric element on a stove appears "red hot," holding your hand close to the element can confirm that it is indeed hot).[5]

Section 7.4 | BEING ABLE TO SEE WELL: DESCRIBING ENVIRONMENTAL ATTRIBUTES THAT AFFECT VISION

In the previous two sections we have described how the visual system operates and have offered a brief commentary about how we perceive external objects. How well the visual system functions establishes, to a great extent, how well one sees. But various attributes of the surrounding environment also can significantly influence a person's ability to see. In this section we will identify what those attributes are. We will also describe how changes in these attributes can alter our quality of vision.

7.4.1   HOW CAN WE ASSESS WHAT ENVIRONMENTAL ATTRIBUTES AFFECT VISION?

In Section 7.2 we have described how light from external objects—either sources or reflecting surfaces—is received by the retinal photoreceptors and how the received light causes the initiation of electrical signals that pass to the human brain. So, when we look at the pages of a book or a traffic sign or a movie screen, we receive light that is reflected from any of these surfaces. The analysis of this acquired light proceeds due to the fundamental *antagonism* that our visual system has toward light and dark areas in the visual field. The visual system, at a primary level, thus differentiates between the amounts of light reflected from adjacent areas in this field. Identification of such elemental shapes as bars, edges, corners, and so forth is made possible by the ability of our visual system to discriminate among these areas with various degrees of light and darkness. Therefore, the visual system operates by discerning *contrasting* areas in the visual field (and finding boundaries between areas). To ensure that such contrasts can be observed accurately, adequate light must reach surfaces in the view field. Lastly, uniformity in the appearance of surfaces will minimize the ability of our visual system to distinguish what properties these surfaces display.

When vision scientists consider which (and to what extent) environmental attributes can affect how well we see, these scientists have traditionally employed two types of measures. The first measure assesses the *visual acuity* that human subjects display, whereas the second examines the *visual performance* that human subjects can manifest. Both measures are undertaken to determine what *attributes* are important to having good vision and to establish what particular combinations of *attribute conditions* will provide good vision.

Studies of *visual acuity* examine how readily an observer can detect or recognize finely detailed spatial information. These tests present objects possessing a variety of features that are both small and having high contrast (e.g., between the detailed object and the background on which the object rests or between the detail on the object and the overall surface of the object). Subjects are then asked to discriminate amongst these features and select those consistent with instructions offered by the examiners. From these acuity tests indices, descriptions of the sharpness or clarity of the subject's vision may be formulated (e.g., individuals taking the Snellen letter test, which is widely used by ophthalmologists and opticians, are scored in terms of a ratio like 20/20 or 20/100). In addition to tests

SIDEBAR 7.6 Techniques for measuring subjects' visual acuity

Three types of visual acuity tests are widely applied: those involving the *detection* of detail; those requiring the *recognition* of detail; and those based on the *resolution* of detail. *Detection* tests usually are organized so that the viewer is expected to identify the smallest detail among a group of objects. For instance, a row of dots of decreasing size may be presented to a viewer and the person will be requested to point out the smallest dot detectable. In *recognition* tests the viewer is requested to identify an odd or different character from amongst several characters of similar appearance. Two recognition tests that are often employed are the Snellen and Landolt C measures. The Snellen test involves the use of individual letters on a chart arranged with the largest letters at the top and progressively smaller letters arrayed in parallel rows beneath (see Figure 7.8). Ophthalmologists and opticians commonly apply such an arrangement to examine the performance of patients' visual systems (e.g., for the selection of eyeglass lenses). The Landolt C test has parallel rows of C's, printed in groups of six or eight, printed on a page (see Figure 7.9). These C's are circular in form and have the single gap (in the circular ring) located at different locations (e.g., some with the gap horizontal and on the right side of the ring; some with the gap vertical and at the top or bottom of the ring; and some with the gap horizontal and on the left side of the ring). The viewer of these rows of Landolt C's is then asked to identify all of the C's whose gap has a particular orientation. The *resolution* tests require a viewer to point out the degree of separation between objects. The viewer may be shown sets of gratings where each set of gratings is a series of black, parallel lines (on a white background) (see Figure 7.10). Across the range of grating sets the spacings between lines in each set become smaller (until the grating sets appear to be single black rectangles). The viewer observing these sets of gratings will be asked to point out the grating set for which the white spaces between the parallel lines of the grating are still discernible. A fourth visual acuity test is also occasionally employed. In this fourth alternative the procedure involves a *vernier* measure, in which two parallel lines, one above and the other below, are slightly separated (or offset). The amount of separation (or offset) between these two parallel lines is the fundamental variable that the viewer is asked to identify. In addition to using offset lines as a study vehicle, vernier testing also may employ offset dots or lines tilted one-to-another. In all of these vernier tests the basic measurement involves the identification of the smallest detectable offset between two or more elements.

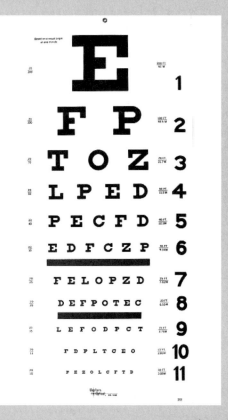

Figure 7.8 A typical Snellen eye testing chart is shown in this illustration. As stated in Section 7.4.1, 20/20 vision is regarded as an optimal performance (but it is not necessarily a normative level). This illustration is a photograph of a Snellen eye testing chart (that was printed by the Western Optical Corporation, formerly of Seattle). Permission to reproduce this image has been granted by the Western Ophthalmics Corporation — Western Optical Ophthalmic Instruments, Lynnwood, Washington.

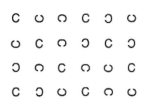

Figure 7.9 A small array of Landolt C symbols is shown in this illustration. Commonly, visual performance tests employ sheets having perhaps 30 to 50 such rows of these symbols, organized in random orientations. Test subjects are given these sheets and are asked to mark C's having a specific orientation, while the examiners measure the time required to complete the task.

Figure 7.10 Here, a typical group of alternatively spaced gratings are displayed. On the right the spacings between the grating lines are wide, whereas on the left the spacings are almost so narrow that the viewer can scarcely distinguish the presence of such openings.

SIDEBAR 7.7 What are common levels of visual acuity?

The numbers in the ratio 20/20 (or 20/100) have the following significances: the numerator represents a distance (here, in feet) that a test subject is from the test chart; the denominator is the relative size of a feature (object or letter) that the subject can readily discern at that distance. Thus, vision rated at 20/20 is comparatively better than that rated at 20/100 because the latter condition requires that the feature be approximately five times larger than is necessary for clear vision by someone with the former condition (i.e., 20/20).

The ratio 20/20 is generally understood by many to be an optimal level. In fact, a large segment of the population of the world displays better vision (e.g., 20/15). The quality of one's vision has been found to degrade with advancing age. Generally, one's vision will be most acute at about the age of twenty-five years and will slowly degrade until the age of sixty years, when the *rate of degradation* will increase.

SIDEBAR 7.8 Measuring a person's visual performance

There are three groups of tests that are commonly employed for measuring visual performance: threshold recognition, the conducting of simplified, representative tasks, and the carrying-out of simulated tasks.

For the first group—the detection of some threshold condition—one common test uses a stimulus such as a lamp having variable intensity. The threshold recognition test can be conducted in either of two ways. First, the intensity of the lamp is adjusted from "not visible" to "visible" and, when the test subject is able to detect the light, the intensity of the lamp is noted by the examiner; for the subject, that intensity will be known as the *absolute threshold*. Such threshold intensities are determined for a number of subjects, and graphs are drawn plotting threshold intensities versus the numbers of subjects reporting for various intensities. Alternatively, two lamps can be used in a test wherein one lamp has a fixed intensity and the other lamp has a variable intensity. This test proceeds by having the subject vary the intensity of the second lamp until the individual believes that its intensity matches the intensity of the first lamp. The examiner then notes the intensity of the variable lamp, compares it with the intensity of the first (the fixed one), and records whether indeed the intensities matched or, if one were higher, which one was. Data are recorded about how often matching did occur and how often the intensity of one lamp exceeded the other. These results can then be plotted (e.g., how often one is stronger than the other versus the number of tests conducted). This procedure is known as a test for a *difference threshold*.

The second group of visual performance tests employs a collection of easily recognized images and asks subjects to detect differences amongst them (or, otherwise, to discriminate between these images). The lengths of time required by the subjects to perform these detection tasks and/or the degrees of accuracy that the subjects display are recorded and plotted, thus showing levels of performance. The images can be either strings of letters and/or numbers (i.e., alphanumeric character strings) or simple pictures. Examples of such letter-based tasks include the Snellen letters (found in many vision-examination charts and the Landolt "C" test (see Sidebar 7.6 for further information about these two tests). A third kind of letter-based test uses groups of letters arranged in columns and requires the test subject to look through the columns for some specific letter or collection of letters.

A third group of visual performance test procedures is the *simulated task*. In this procedure a subject is asked to perform some simplified task that is supposed to approximate an activity which one might encounter in a normal situation. Two examples are suggested by Boyce: trying to move a needle indicator on a meter scale through a certain pre-planned pattern of movements; the measurements taken for this task were the errors in execution produced by the subjects and the amount of time it took the subjects to complete the test; and running a number of objects by on a conveyor moving at a fixed speed and asking the subject to perform actions including the general identification of objects and the selection of particular ones; the primary measurement was then the errors of omission and commission. A primary concern of some researchers with these types of tests is whether the results found provide an accurate indication of visual performance. These critics contend that such simulated tasks are too job-specific, and the results obtained for a specific test will frequently not match other simulated tasks that rely on different work conditions. The supporters of simulation tasks maintain, however, that these simulated tasks enable experimenters to examine parameters that other commonly accepted tests do not address.

For further discussion about these simulation techniques and their potential problems, see Boyce, P.R., "Age, illuminance, visual performance, and preference," *Lighting Research and Technology,* 5(3), 1973, pages 125–145. Additional information about the first two groups of visual performance tests can be found in the book by Boyce, P.R., *Human Factors in Lighting,* (London: Applied Science Publishers Ltd., 1981). Chapter 3 of that book—see pages 79–110—describes the procedures followed in these tests, the advantages and disadvantages associated with the tests, and some typical test applications.

All three groups of these visual performance tests can be employed to study how some one (or more) of the environmental attributes can affect the visual performance of test subjects. For example, as the amount of light that reaches a task surface—the illuminance on that task—is varied by an examiner, a test subject will likely find that he or she is better or less well able to perform the task. The examiner can then vary this illuminance systematically over some range and observe how well the subject can complete the task. The length of time required to complete the task and the degree of accuracy that the subject displays are both indicators of the effect that the illuminance variation had on the test. Thus, the examiner can determine whether an optimum illuminance condition exists or over what range of illuminance adequate performance is present. From such tests (i.e., for illuminance and the other attributes), the examiner can establish what conditions would be appropriate to ensure good visual performance.

examining how an environmental attribute can affect acuity, these measures are often employed to evaluate the adequacy of one's vision (to determine the need for and/or preparation of vision aids like eyeglasses) or to ascertain whether a person has any of several vision health problems such as cataracts. This ability to distinguish among small things depends on one's visual system, the nature of the objects that one is trying to see, and the environment in which the person and objects are. Further, as visual acuity is frequently a *measured* description of some situation involving vision, visual acuity can also depend on the criteria used for deciding whether a successful detection of some image has occurred (i.e., the degree of acuity can depend on the test used to determine whether some detail can be identified accurately).

The concept of *visual performance* has two meanings. First, the more general meaning for this term concerns the ability of a person to proceed with a task that requires vision. Second, *visual performance* refers to the result (or product) of a testing process that has been undertaken to establish the quality of the visual conditions available for the carrying-out of some task. This second meaning thus is central to assessments that are used to examine the environmental attributes that affect vision (i.e., in our working and living spaces). These tests are conducted either to study how well people can perform tasks under specific visual conditions or to investigate how each of these attributes can affect the quality of performance. When an environment (and its combination of attribute conditions) are evaluated, any one (or more) of five questions may then be considered as the study focus: how accurately can a task be performed; how quickly can the task be completed; will a person experience visual fatigue while carrying out the task; to what extent is the person comfortable while doing the task; and how easy or difficult has the task completion been? So, for example, such evaluations may concern how readable some text is or how precisely you can distinguish between small parts on an electronic circuit board or how easily you can see a tennis ball moving toward you. Ultimately, all of these tests of visual performance embrace the degree of *productivity,* which a person exhibits while performing a task.[6]

7.4.2   HOW THE WORLD AROUND US AFFECTS VISUAL ACUITY AND PERFORMANCE [7]

For the surrounding environment to be supportive, one fundamental requirement is that this environment must enable us to have clear, sharp vision. Possessing clear, sharp vision will thus allow us to obtain accurate information and to carry out this information gathering (and identifying) as promptly as possible. The ability to gather visual information from some scene or about some object, accurately and in a timely fashion, depends on five primary environmental attributes and several secondary parameters (i.e., where *primary* and *secondary* are determined by the relative degree of influence that each attribute or parameter is likely to have on the ability of a person to conduct a visual task). The five *primary* attributes are the *size* of the object that is being viewed; the amount of *contrast* existing between the object and the visual area immediately surrounding the object; the *luminance* incident on the object; the *luminance distribution* across the task object, the area immediately surrounding the object, and the area adjoining the immediate surround;[8] and the *amount of time* that the subject has to see the task (see Figure 7.11).

7.4.2.1   The primary attributes affecting acuity and performance

A. Size. The dimension of an object most responsible for determining whether good vision can be obtained is the size of the smallest *detail* within the object that must be seen for the visual task to be successfully completed. Detail concerns such attributes as texture, pattern, color, or even some aspects of form. For example, if you read a book, then you will likely need to differentiate between individual letters within words. But, if you select some paper currency to pay for some item, then you will likely need to read only the number that identifies the denomination of that paper bill. Alternatively, while reading the book you will undoubtedly find that seeing the larger, main text is easier than reading

Figure 7.11 The marketing of pearls requires that they be carefully assessed and then graded according to a number of attributes. Among the attributes used as a basis for sorting the pearls are, at least, size, color, luster, and uniformity. To be able to distinguish the properties of these pearls, a sorter must have very good visual acuity, as well as workstation and environmental conditions that facilitate this difficult visual task.

the smaller footnotes. So, the larger some detail is, the more readily it can be seen accurately (see Figure 7.12). However, if the detail is small, then we can often improve its visibility by increasing *either* the amount of contrast between the detail and its surrounding area *or* the magnitude of the light directed at the detail, or by increasing *both* the contrast and the light magnitude.

B. Contrast. Contrast is the difference in physical brightness between an object and its immediate surround. More precisely, contrast is defined as the ratio between the *algebraic difference* between the luminance of the surround and the luminance of the object *divided by the luminance of the surround* (i.e., contrast can be defined via an equation, $C = (L_s - L_o)/L_s$, where L_o is the luminance of the object and L_s is the luminance of the surround; note also that the terms *luminance* and *physical brightness* are interchangeable). How much contrast exists between an object and its surrounding area is dependent on how incident light reflects off of the surfaces of the object and the surround. For instance, black type will reflect little light, whereas a white page will reflect nearly all of the incident light. Alphanumeric characters—letters and numbers—printed on the white page of a book can exhibit high contrast, if the letters have been written with a black ink and the characters are accurately and clearly printed. But neither gray characters printed on white paper nor black letters on gray paper will display the same degree of contrast as black characters on a white

The quick, brown fox jumped over the lazy, yellow dog and ran into the forest.

The quick, brown fox jumped over the lazy, yellow dog and ran into the forest.

The quick, brown fox jumped over the lazy, yellow dog and ran into the forest.

The quick, brown fox jumped over the lazy, yellow dog and ran into the forest.

The quick, brown fox jumped over the lazy, yellow dog and ran into the forest.

The quick, brown fox jumped over the lazy, yellow dog and ran into the forest.

Figure 7.12 Two examples demonstrate how the size of an object can affect the degree of difficulty involved in the viewing process. For the top image, as the size of the dots increases, the visibility likewise increases. Alternatively, for the bottom image, a reader's ability to discern the words printed in these six different sizes will no doubt increase as the print size increases.

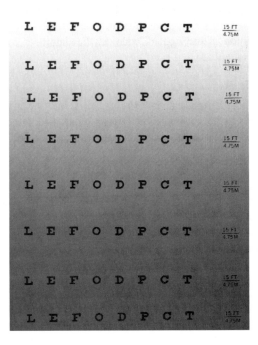

Figure 7.13 This illustration demonstrates how contrast between printed words and the surface on which the words are printed can influence visual acuity and performance. Here, ordinary black type has been printed on a page whose surface color varies gradually from white through darkening shades of gray to black. As the contrast between the black letters and the background surface lessens, a reader's ability to discern what is printed will decrease.

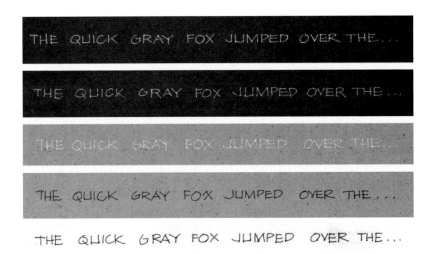

Figure 7.14 A series of words and backgrounds are printed and cast in black, gray, and white. We invite the reader to consider these alternatives to determine which combinations offer the most favorable viewing conditions.

paper (see Figures 7.13–7.15). Thus, the essential issue regarding the role of contrast in enabling good visual acuity and performance concerns the ability of an observer to see relevant visual information when this information is set upon some background.

Further, let us suggest two other examples of environmental situations where the degree of contrast between an object and its surround affects how much success a viewer will have (i.e., for identifying the object). First, think about the problems of seeing objects when the weather is foggy. Whether you are trying to drive a car or land an airplane or see a ship passing across a body of water, boundaries, edges, and surfaces which are obscured by the fog will display little contrast: recognition of the surfaces and other surrounding

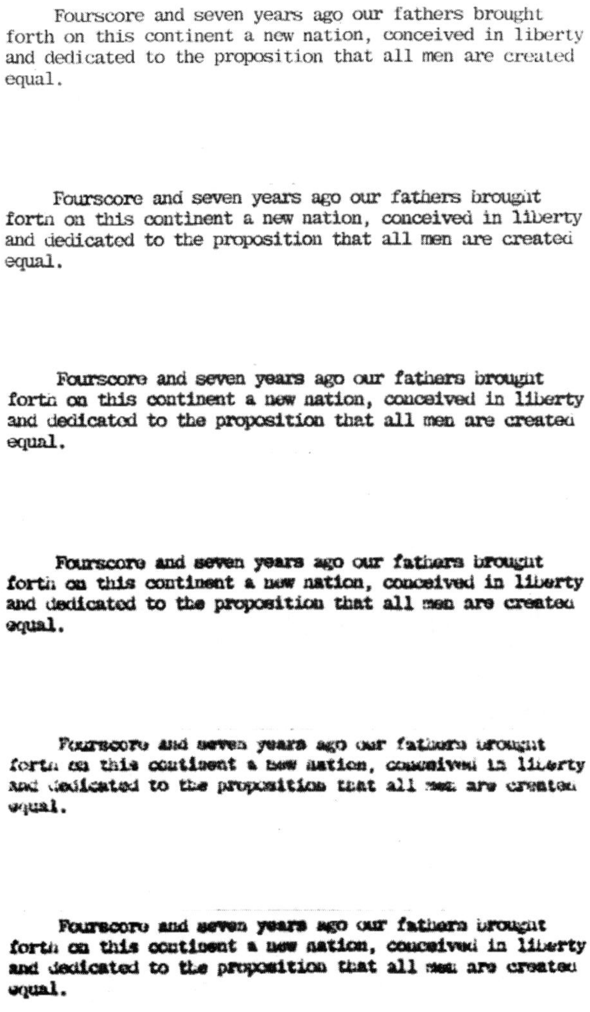

> Fourscore and seven years ago our fathers brought forth on this continent a new nation, conceived in liberty and dedicated to the proposition that all men are created equal.

> Fourscore and seven years ago our fathers brought forth on this continent a new nation, conceived in liberty and dedicated to the proposition that all men are created equal.

> Fourscore and seven years ago our fathers brought forth on this continent a new nation, conceived in liberty and dedicated to the proposition that all men are created equal.

> Fourscore and seven years ago our fathers brought forth on this continent a new nation, conceived in liberty and dedicated to the proposition that all men are created equal.

> Fourscore and seven years ago our fathers brought forth on this continent a new nation, conceived in liberty and dedicated to the proposition that all men are created equal.

> Fourscore and seven years ago our fathers brought forth on this continent a new nation, conceived in liberty and dedicated to the proposition that all men are created equal.

Figure 7.15 This illustration presents a typewritten printing and five successive carbon-copy generations of this printing (i.e., the first carbon-copy under the original, the second carbon-copy under the original, and so forth). Note how the distinctiveness of the letters degrades progressively as the copy generations increase in number so that the fifth-order copy is nearly illegible.

objects can be greatly inhibited. Second, a skier schussing down a snow-covered hill will look ahead for variations in the surface that need to be planned for (before the skier reaches them). A hillock or mogul will be difficult to see because the brightness of the snow — particularly when incident sunlight is bright — will be great and little brightness variation may be noticeable between the general surface contours and the surface details around the mogul. For this latter example the skier's visual performance can be negatively affected not only by the lack of contrast between the mogul and the general surface, but also by the very brief amount of time that the skier may have for recognizing the presence of the mogul.

Vision scientists examining the degree of contrast present in a viewing opportunity will commonly question whether adequate contrast exists so that relevant information is at least minimally detectable. Further, these individuals may consider how surface detail can be made more visible, when the degree of contrast is low. A principal means for improving visibility for low-contrast material is to direct greater amounts of light toward the surface that bears the relevant information.

C. Luminance. Visual performance depends not only on the luminances of the object and its surround (i.e., indicating how well they reflect incident light), but also on the magnitudes of light that reaches these surfaces. The light falling on the task surface can be described, alternatively, in terms of either *luminance* or *illuminance.* In the first case, the luminance of the incident light addresses that component of light that reaches the task surface after emanating from a specific source (or, alternatively, from some specific nonluminous surface). As such light has both magnitude and directionality it is described in terms of its luminance. For the second case, the light generally reaching the task surface is described in terms of its illuminance: this light has no preferential direction.

What lighting level is available for conducting a visual task will influence how readily the task can be carried out. For instance, in Table 7.2, several office tasks have been compared in terms of their relative visual task difficulties. The principal attributes affecting the tasks identified in this list include the size of the task objects (e.g., alphanumeric characters), the amount of contrast between the task objects and their surround, and how well these objects are formed (i.e., whether the characters are each partially or fully printed). Each of these three parameters is a basic determinant of task visibility.

Commonly, providing enough light to ensure that vision by the retinal conal photoreceptors can occur will foster good visual acuity and performance. However, once lighting conditions necessary for *conal* vision exist, then increasing lighting levels cannot greatly improve the visibility of the task surface. But, if the contrast or size of the task object is inadequate for vision under normal levels of lighting, task visibility can sometimes be improved, at least fractionally, by increasing the amount of light incident on the task. Information about how much light is recommended for the conducting of various tasks will be addressed in Section 8.4.

D. Luminance distribution. The range of luminances spread across the task surface and its surrounding surfaces can markedly affect how well visual acuity and performance are realized. One significant fact about the luminance amount reaching a task surface is that the human eye can process light of alternative strengths ranging over approximately 13 orders of magnitude (i.e., this range spans from the magnitude of light gained from a star-illuminated sky to a snow-covered field that is illuminated by direct-beam sunlight). But abrupt changes in luminance levels can produce discomfort and accompanying decreases in visual acuity and performance. Thus, changes in luminance — across both space and time — must be gradual, allowing the eye to adjust to such variations. Generally, lighting directed at the task surface should be two to three times stronger than the

Figure 7.16 Consider the range of luminances that are present in this visual task setting. A worker sitting at the computer monitor will experience different luminances from the monitor screen, from the surrounding monitor surfaces around the screen, from paper surfaces adjacent to the monitor, from the window glass, from the window frame, and from the various opaque surfaces near the window frame.

lighting directed at the immediately surrounding surfaces. The outlying background—surfaces beyond the immediate surround—should then have incident luminances that are about equal to the luminance falling on the immediate surround (see Figure 7.16).

The principal issue about the luminance distribution across task and nearby surrounding surfaces concerns how well the viewer's eyes are *adapted* to this range of luminances. *Adaptation* is the process by which the eye (and, more specifically, the retina) becomes accustomed to a different light intensity. As an example, when you enter a comparatively darker room after having been in a well-lighted space, your eyes will take anywhere from a few minutes to a half hour to adapt to the change in light intensity (i.e., to be able to see well in this darker environment). So, if one's eyes are well adjusted to the luminance distribution within a space and you suddenly attempt to view an object that is

---

TABLE 7.2
RELATIVE VISUAL TASK DIFFICULTY FOR COMMON OFFICE TASKS

VISUAL DIFFICULTY TASK DESCRIPTION	RATING (1 = easiest; 15 = most difficult)
Large black object on white background	1
Book or magazine, printed matter, 8-point type & larger	2
Typed original	2
Ink writing (script)	3
Newspaper text	4
Shorthand notes, ink	4
Handwriting (script) in No. 2 pencil	5
Shorthand notes, No. 3 pencil	6
Washed-out copy from copying machines	7
Bookkeeping	8
Drafting	8
Telephone directory	12
Typed carbon, fifth copy	15

Source: Lighting and Thermal Operations: Energy Conservation Principles Applied to Office Lighting, (prepared by Ross & Baruzzini, Inc., Consulting Engineers, St. Louis, Missouri, under contract to the [U.S.] Federal Energy Administration, April 1975), Conservation Paper Number 18, Federal Energy Administration, Washington, D.C. 20461. This table appears on page V-6 of this document.

Note: On page V-7 of the source document the following set of instructions is included for using the task-difficulty values identified in this table:

Table 2 may be used as a guide in evaluating the degrees of visual difficulty for office work. It is based on the concept that visual difficulty for this kind of work is not only a function of the intrinsic characteristics of the task and the lighting system, but also of the length of time the task must be performed.

To use this table, multiply the difficulty rating, as shown in the table, for each task performed at a given work place by a single worker times the number of decimal hours per day it is performed, for example, 3 hours 15 minutes = 3.25 decimal hours. Add the products for each task. If the sum is greater than 40, provide 75 footcandles on the work station. If the sum is greater than 60, provide 100 footcandles on the work station. Multiply the difficulty factors by 1.5 if the operator is over 50 years of age, or if he/she has uncorrectable eyesight problems.

Figure 7.17 Windows on two vertical elevations of a room or a vertical side and a roof offer better opportunities to achieve the balancing of daylight illumination (than when daylight is admitted from a single vertical side or roof).

SIDEBAR 7.9 Having your sensory systems adapt to new environmental conditions

To understand the visual adaptation process, think of the different natures of the two sets of photoreceptor cells in the human retinas. The rods function at low light levels, whereas the cones operate at comparatively higher light levels. Thus, when you pass from a well-lighted space to a darkened space, your eyes pass from conal vision to rodal vision (i.e., thus, becoming dark-adapted). For example, if some night you were in a brightly lighted rural farmhouse—away from the lights of other human habitation—and you walk out into a field away from the house, the transfer from conal to rodal vision might take as long as thirty minutes for your eyes to become fully-adapted (to be able to see the full range of stars present in the night sky). Alternatively, when you pass into a well-lighted area after having been in a darkened space (e.g., leaving a theater after seeing a movie or a darkened classroom following a slide show and going out into daylighted spaces), the transfer from rodal vision to conal vision usually requires a few minutes. This difference in adaptation times is directly related to the photochemistry of the two types of photoreceptor cells.

This adaptation behavior exists in all of the sensory systems that are present in the human body. For instance, if you have ever tried to buy perfume, you know that, after smelling three or four samples, your nose becomes fatigued and you will be unable to distinguish among any additional perfumes. To recommence your perfume sampling, you will have to let your nose "rest" for a few minutes before it can again be receptive to new fragrances.

substantially brighter than the ambient conditions, then you will likely experience diffi-culty in seeing the object (for at least some period of time until your eyes can adapt to this brighter object).

One instance where the luminance distribution across a space should be carefully considered is when a designer or builder lays out window locations and selects surfaces that will surround the windows (for one example, see Figure 7.17). Commonly, window surfaces during daytime hours will appear brighter than adjoining interior surfaces. To lessen the range in luminance distribution when these windows may be quite bright, the surrounding surfaces should be covered with some light color and may indeed need to gain illumination from the windows (e.g., by splaying the surrounding surfaces toward the window surface).

E. Time for seeing. Lastly, if one has a greater amount of time to see an object, then the acuity and performance associated with that visual opportunity will commonly be bet-ter. Vision, like hearing, is an integrative process during which bits of information are observed and synthesized. Such integration necessarily evolves across time, rather than arising instantaneously. In various studies of reaction times using simple psychophysical tests, successful recognition or detection of target images have been readily achieved in fractions of a second. Of course, the nature of the target — how well-structured, complex, or familiar — can affect such times. But these tests have also shown that having adequate contrast between the task object and its surround is a particularly important attribute. The amount of illuminance incident on the task object also strongly affects what reaction times are measured: increasing illuminance will provide reduced times for comparable levels of acuity or performance (i.e., up to specific illuminance amounts — depending on the nature of the test — at which little or no further improvements can be observed).[9]

7.4.2.2 Secondary attributes that affect acuity and performance In addition to the five *primary* environmental attributes that principally control our ability to see well, there are a number of secondary environmental factors that also can affect our vision. To a marked extent, these secondary factors largely influence aspects of the five primary attrib-utes. In the following paragraphs we will identify these secondary factors and relate them to the primary attributes.

A. Concerning the size of the object. How an object is laid out or displayed can affect visual acuity and performance. For instance, the *configuration of detailed informa-tion* can facilitate or impair vision. If the detailed information is presented in a regular, well-spaced format, it may more easily be sensed. However, if the spacing of the detailed information is uneven or there is a mixing of large and small detail, then such information will likely be more difficult to view. As an example, this book is composed of a main text, which is presented in a relatively large type, and a series of endnote indicators, which are printed in a reduced-size type. By rendering the endnote indicators in a reduced-scale, our intent is to lessen their visibility. The *distance of the task surface from the observer* affects how readily vision can be conducted. Being close — without being too close — to the task will aid in seeing the object and its details, whereas viewing a task surface at some greater distance can inhibit how readily the visual system can discern what the object and its com-ponents are. The *size of the visual field* regards how large the whole image is. One issue here concerns whether a viewer must take in the whole object before recognition occurs. A second point bears on how much of the detail, spread across a large object, must be viewed to enable recognition.

B. Concerning the contrast between the object and the surroundings. *The pres-ence of "noise" in the visual field* can decrease the effectiveness of one's vision (see

Figure 7.18 This photograph presents a scene of Saturday shopping at the Pike Place Market in Seattle. The photograph is included here to demonstrate how "noise" can intrude into the visual field. Amongst the veritable sea of faces is one for which a viewer may be searching. Initially, for the search to be successful, the viewer must likely possess a good mental image of the subject (of the search). Then, the viewer must be able to exclude all of the information that is not relevant or useful.

Figure 7.18). Almost invariably a visual field will contain extraneous information (i.e., information which is not useful for the recognition of an object). When irrelevant (and possibly conflicting) details exist in the view field, successful recognition of the salient object will require that the field be regarded selectively and that this "noise" be ignored.[10]

C. Concerning the illuminance incident on the object. *Specularity of detailed information and its surroundings* can render vision more difficult. If the surface of an object or, alternatively, its immediate background reflects incident light specularly (i.e., without diffuse reflection), then such a surface may appear excessively bright, causing discomfort or distraction (see Figure 7.19). To minimize the possibility that discomfort or distraction may occur, both the primary task surface and its surroundings should have matte (or nonspecular) reflective surfaces. *The presence of shadows falling on the task surface* can negatively affect seeing by reducing the amounts of light that reach across a task surface and/or by creating uneven patterns of light on the task surface (see Figure 7.20). Shadows can also create distraction and some discomfort, where this discomfort results from the need of the viewer's eyes to adapt anew to different conditions. *The spectral power distribution of the light incident on the task surface* can also cause distractions for the viewer. If light reaching a surface is preferentially biased toward (i.e., has more of) a particular portion of the spectrum, this bias will accentuate the appearance of specific colors in the task surface and its background. Attention may then be drawn to those colors, causing useful emphasis or potential distractions. Using light with a biased spectral distribution (i.e., to emphasize some aspect of an object) must be done with care to avoid decreasing visibility for other parts of the object.

Figure 7.19 Note the difference in luminances — and thus the contrast — between the dark screen covering the fence behind the tennis court and the very bright wall of the building that looms over the screen. The brightness of the building wall is caused partly by the inclusion of specular-reflecting stones in the surface finish of the wall.

Figure 7.20 One example of how shadows may fall across a task surface and affect a person's visual performance is displayed here. The person in the near court will experience an approaching tennis ball — one hit to this person — passing from an area of brightness to area of dimness. Thus, for the receiver to hit the approaching tennis ball accurately, either the receiver must be able to adapt rapidly to the change in apparent brightness or the receiver must sense the moving ball while it is still on the well-lighted side and then project (estimate) the location when the ball arrives near the receiver. In either instance the process of seeing the approaching ball, preparing to attempt its return, and striking the ball must be executed in a very brief time period.

Figure 7.21 How time for seeing can influence the accuracy of a person's vision is portrayed in this photograph. The two dogs are twin sisters and look somewhat alike, although with adequate time the differences that separate their appearances can be comparatively easily distinguished. But acquiring the time to detect such differences is often difficult because, as with any puppies, they are seldom at rest for long enough periods of time (which may partially explain the fuzziness of the details in this photograph).

D. Concerning the time available for seeing an object. Whether *an object is stationary or moving* can greatly affect visual acuity and performance. A viewer can look at a stationary object for as long as this person is willing to commit time to the viewing of that object. Conversely, if an object moves across the view field, then the viewer may have significantly less time to see the object (see Figure 7.21). *The recognizability of the object* can also be time-dependent. If the object is reasonably familiar to the viewer, then the person will likely require less time to identify the object. Alternatively, if the object is unfamiliar, then either more time must be allowed for the viewer to look at the object or some cues or aids must be established to improve acuity and performance (e.g., using enhancements such as italicizing specific words or employing colors to emphasize some detail(s) of an object).

7.4.3 PERSONAL FACTORS THAT CAN INFLUENCE TASK VISION

In addition to these several primary and secondary *environmental* attributes, a number of *personal* factors can also influence the visual acuity and performance that one achieves. Some of these factors can directly determine how well a person's visual system operates, whereas others can alter how the mind processes whatever information the visual system supplies. Here, then, is a list of such factors.

A. The sensitivity of a person's visual system to *light* (and, particularly, the *intensity* and the *wavelength* of the light).[11] We have written in Section 7.2.2.1 that the two sets of retinal photoreceptor cells operate best at alternative illuminance levels (i.e., the rods function at low illuminance levels, whereas the cones require substantially higher illuminance levels). The cones, particularly those located in the fovea of the retina, provide substantially better vision of small, detailed information. So, incident illuminance levels should be scaled to ensure that adequate light exists for conal vision.

Further, we have noted in Section 7.2.2.2 that the conal cells, when active, are selectively sensitive across the visible radiation spectrum. There are three types of conal cells (e.g., ones most sensitive to red, green, or blue light). If there is sufficient light, the presence of colors in the visual task surface can affect how readily the task can be carried out (by the viewer's ability to see the colors). Also, if sufficient light exists and the light displays a bias in its spectral power distribution—the light is colored—then this color may affect how well visual acuity and performance are achieved for the task.

B. The sensitivity of a person's visual system to the size of the object (or of the detailed information in or on the object). The spacing of the retinal cones, particularly those concentrated at the retina center, determines the minimum size of objects that the eye can see (under adequate light). Blurring will be experienced if the image contains details finer than the conal spacing at this center. A secondary issue here concerns where, on the retina, light falls after being reflected from an object (or from some detail on the surface of the object). If reflected light from the detail reaches the retinal periphery, then that vision will be mostly rodal and will not be very good at discerning the detail (because of the averaging nature with which rodal cells generally process incident light).

C. The sensitivity of a person's visual system to the contrast present in the visual field. Contrast is basically a comparison between adjacent areas in the view field (or on the surface of a task object) where one area displays a greater physical brightness—luminance—than the other area. A lighter-appearing area reflects more incident light; the

---

SIDEBAR 7.10 Age-dependent changes in the eyes of elderly human beings

The process of focusing on near and/or far objects is known as *accommodation* (see Figure 7.4). It involves the lens of the eye changing shape to enable focusing of light from differently placed objects onto the retinal photoreceptors. The lenses in eyes of older people are less able to undergo shape changes (i.e., the lenses become less elastic), making accommodation for near objects less successful.

The retinal photoreceptor cells—the rods and cones—are essentially at the "bottom" of the layering of the retina (i.e., a variety of other cells all lie "upward" from the photoreceptors [see Figure 7.5]). Light entering the eyeball and passing to the retina must pass around these "upper" cells before incident light reaches the photoreceptors. Thus, some

absorption and reflection of the entering light occurs, reducing the amount of light that falls upon the photoreceptor cells. And, with advancing age, the percentage of light reflected and absorbed before the light reaches the photoreceptor cells increases, leaving less light energy to be incident on these photoreceptors. A second cause of reduced light reaching the photoreceptor cells among the aged is that the lens (at the front of the eyeball) slowly *yellows* with increasing age, thus further decreasing the amount of light that gets to the photoreceptors. Thirdly, some elderly people are also affected by cataracts, which is a clouding of the eyeball lens and which also reduces the amount of light passing into the eyeball.

darker-appearing area reflects less. Having adjoining areas that manifest such different reflective behaviors results in contrast. The precision with which retinal photoreceptors can discriminate between potentially small differences in luminance establishes how well the eye can separate detailed information.

D. The sensitivity of a person's visual system to the time available for seeing an object. When retinal photoreceptors receive incident light, these cells respond by undergoing photochemical changes (which lead to the emission of electrical impulses). The change to a "light-excited" state and the subsequent return to the pre-excitation condition by these photoreceptor cells take time. So, if one can only look briefly at some object, then the quality of seeing will be dependent on how long the cycling of the photoreceptor cells requires (i.e., if the photochemical cycling period for a photoreceptor cell has a duration that is longer than the length of time available for some object to be glimpsed, then that cell can only gather information about the object once).

E. The ability of a person's eyes to adapt to changing conditions. Adaptation is the process by which the photoreceptor cells gradually become accustomed to the amount of light present in a space. This process is dependent upon the rate with which such an adjustment can occur. As a person moves from place to place or the lighting conditions vary in a space or across a task surface, then the adaptation process will determine how well the person can see in these situations.

F. The presence of glare in the visual field. Glare is a condition in which the eye is exposed to luminance from some source, which is substantially greater than the general luminance to which the eye is well adapted. Having a glare source within the field of view can make the seeing of an object more difficult or even impossible. To a great extent, the tolerances people display to withstanding glare are widely variable (e.g., for a condition that one person finds to be intolerably glare-ridden another person may just be aware of the glare source).[12]

G. The age of the person viewing an object. As people age, the performances of their visual systems tend to degrade. Such degradation is particularly evident in the functioning of the eyes. Three specific failings occur: each eye becomes less able to focus on objects in the *near* foreground; light entering each eye is more greatly absorbed and/or scattered before the light reaches the retinal photoreceptors; and the diameter of the pupil of each eye decreases with increasing age for specific adaptive conditions. All of these failings work in concert, causing deterioration in how readily older people can see detailed information.

H. Physiological conditions. A person's state of health can affect the person's ability to see. Having a cold or an allergy attack or a more serious malady (e.g., diabetes) can cause a person's visual system to work less well (for a short or long period).

I. Motivational, emotional, and cognitive factors. These last personal factors cover a range of mind states, in which how a person feels "psychologically" can markedly affect how well that person sees. Alternatively, if the person pays special attention or exerts an extra effort to the visual task (i.e., if someone wants to see something quite intently), then adverse environmental conditions can be overcome. Conversely, if a person feels alienated perhaps about a work assignment or people with which the person is interacting, then quite adequate physical conditions may not promote good vision.

7.4.4   SOME GUIDELINES FOR TREATING THE ENVIRONMENTAL AND PERSONAL FACTORS THAT AFFECT SEEING

Each of the *environmental* and *personal* attributes that we have identified in Sections 7.4.2 and 7.4.3 can influence how well a person sees. However, some of these attributes have greater significance for promoting good vision than others: thus, those attributes deserve more attention during the creation of building spaces. In this section—and later in Chapter 9—we will identify guidelines for developing effective visual conditions. The guidelines presented here will specifically relate to the five primary environmental attributes which we have identified in Section 7.4.2.1: *the size of the object (or the detail on the surface of the object); the amount of contrast between the detail and the surface on which the detail is located; the illuminance falling on the task surface; the luminance distribution around the task;* and *the amount of time available for viewing the task.* Further, these guidelines suggest conditions for the task surface and its surrounding environment, which should be met if vision is to be comparatively easy and which should provide opportunities for vision that are well beyond the minimal requirements usually needed just to maintain vision at the threshold of detection. Therefore, these task and environmental conditions are those that might commonly be expected to exist in a typical office or schoolroom setting.

A. For the size of the object (or the detail on the surface of the object). *Visual acuity and performance will be better when our eyes are relatively close to the object (or the detail).* But getting too close to the task surface can inhibit acuity and performance. *The size of detailed information and its contrast needed for good vision are not independent.* Usually, as the size of the detail increases, the need for contrast can decrease without loss of acuity and performance. However, there are no widely accepted, simple relationships that suggest what are optimal conditions between the size of an object (or its detailed information) and the amount of necessary contrast.[13] *The size of the immediate surround (around the task surface) should be as large as possible.* Generally, visual acuity and performance improve as the size of the surround increases. But increases in surround sizes beyond some limits will produce no further benefit for acuity and performance.

B. For the contrast between the detailed information and its immediate surface. *Visual acuity and performance will both improve as the amount of contrast increases.* Increases in contrast can be established by increasing the *difference* between the luminance displayed by the detail and the luminance of the surface surrounding the detail. Thus, insuring that printed alphanumeric characters are well-inked and fully-formed[14] will promote high contrast between detailed information and its background (i.e., contrarily, text copies produced from multiple-layered carbon copies, some photocopy machines, or computer printers whose ribbons are worn out will often appear "washed-out" (i.e., the characters are not wholly formed and show discontinuities in their formation). Interestingly, white detail on a black background has been found to provide better visual performances than black detail on white surfaces, particularly for low illuminance levels. Further, black detail on white surfaces provides better performances than red detail on green surfaces. Tests of red detail on green surfaces have shown better results than green detail on red surfaces (except at quite low illuminance levels).[15] *High contrast reduces the need for high illuminance on the task surface (for equal degrees of visual acuity).*[16] *Attempting to see detail that has lower contrast can often cause the viewer to experience visual fatigue (and discomfort).*

C. For the illuminance on a task surface. *Visual acuity and performance will improve continuously up to some limit as the illuminance on the task surface increases.* What this limit will be is subject to a number of conditions including the degree of contrast present between detailed information and its background surface, the size of the detail (or object), the nature of the task, the amount of time for viewing the task, and so forth.[17] *If the illuminance on a task surface is suitable for good vision, then the size of the object (or detail) will have less significance for providing good visual acuity and performance. Also, as the size of detailed information (or of a task object) increases, the illuminance on the object can be lessened and visual acuity and performance will be unaffected.* But the illuminance can only be decreased to some lower limit before a viewer encounters a threshold condition, below which the detailed information (or the task object) will no longer be recognizable. Necessarily, what the limit may be will vary depending on what values the several other critical attributes that the task and the environment display (e.g., the degree of contrast between detail and its background, the luminance distribution across the task surface and the view field, and so forth). We have noted previously that elderly people generally see less well than young people. However, *increasing the illuminance on task surfaces (or the illuminance directed at detailed information) that elderly people encounter will not necessarily improve their visual acuity or performance.*

D. For the luminance distribution around the task surface. *The luminance of the task surface should be slightly greater than the luminance of the immediate surrounding surfaces* (e.g., one approximation that is often suggested by lighting designers is that the luminance of the task surface should be about two to three times greater than the luminance of the immediate surrounding area). *An optimal condition will generally be present when the luminance of the outlying background is equal to the luminance of the immediate surround.* However, it has been found that when the luminance of the outlying background is less or greater than the surround luminance, visual *acuity* will be reduced.[18] The essence of these two guidelines then is that a nonuniform distribution should be maintained across the entire view field, with the luminance from the surface of the object (or its detailed information) being somewhat greater than the luminances from both the immediate surround and the outlying background. *The nature of the luminance distribution across the outlying background will have comparatively little effect on visual performance.* But, ultimately, the consequences of not satisfying these recommendations about luminance distribution are that viewers quite likely will experience visual discomfort.[19]

E. For the time available for seeing an object (or detailed information on the surface of the object). Generally, *if visual conditions are of a marginal quality and the viewer has more time to see some object (or detailed information on its surface), then the visual performance for the person will be better.* But, *if the illuminance on the task is sufficient to permit reasonable seeing, then the amount of time required to see some object (or detail) will not be reduced by increasing the illuminance.* In other words, once the ability to see some task is established, increasing the illuminance will not further improve visual performance.[20]

Section 7.5 | VISUAL COMFORT: ENVIRONMENTAL FACTORS AND HUMAN RESPONSES

The environment that surrounds us — whether inside or outside of a building — is composed of assorted light sources and many nonluminous surfaces (which nevertheless reflect light). In any environment there is likely to be a great range in the brightnesses of these sources and objects. Some will appear bright, and others will seem quite dull. When a person spends time in such an environment, the person's visual system will *adapt* to some specific level of brightness. This level may match the brightness manifested by a task surface or, perhaps, a brightness approximately equal to an average of brightnesses of various objects across the field of view.

Although our eyes will commonly *adapt* to some specific, ambient brightness level in a space, our eyes are also naturally *attracted* to brighter-than-average objects and will move to view them (a physiological property called *phototropism*). When our eyes, which are adapted to some brightness level, encounter a significantly greater brightness level, then our eyes (and our visual system as a whole) are challenged to *re-adapt,* thereby compensating for the presence of a different brightness level. Whether our eyes will indeed adapt to this "new" brightness level may depend on such issues as the size of the object from which the brightness emanates, how comparatively brighter the object is, where the object is in the view field, and so forth. In any event, our eyes (and/or the visual system) may possibly have to undergo a substantial change in their condition during this re-adaptive process.

If the re-adaptive process does indeed require a significant change, the person may experience feelings of physiological irritation or, even, pain. This re-adaptation may also constrain the person from looking at an object in the view field. Having sensations like physiological irritation or pain will inevitably lead to a state of discomfort (and may cause a person to become dissatisfied with the environment).

Of the various circumstances in which a bright object exists in the field of view and causes visual distress, the most common situation occurs when *glare* is present. Other circumstances for which a bright object can cause distress or discomfort include when *veiling reflections* interfere with a person performing some visual task; when light from a source or a reflecting, nonluminous object *flickers* (i.e., the stimulus occurs intermittently); or when *excessively bright color* is present in the view field. The characteristics of glare and these other conditions will be described below.

The presence of objects whose brightness levels are different from ambient conditions and which exist in a person's view field can also have *positive* features. Two examples where dissimilar brightness levels may foster compelling visual effects are placing a bright light or object at some point to accentuate its particular location in a space (i.e., relying on *phototropic behavior* to draw the attention of people to that point); and using a bright object (or, instead, a dark part of a space) to create alternative moods within the space (e.g., having a darkened church interior with a well-lighted altar). In the first example, when an object of greater-than-average brightness is used in an otherwise well-lighted area, this brighter object is said to create *sparkle.* Sparkle can highlight the presence of an object in the view field, accentuating its existence and encouraging observers to concentrate their

SIDEBAR 7.11 Defining *visual comfort*

A definition for *visual comfort* has been suggested by Hopkinson as "the absence of a sensation of physiological pain, irritation, or distraction (that could be felt as a result of some visual condition." Note that this definition includes no concern for whether, in experiencing a field of view, we find a view that we like or that is aesthetically satisfying. Rather, this definition considers only the gathering of light and the physiological steps in its processing. The source for this definition (and for further discussion about it) is an essay written by Hopkinson, R.G., "The brightness of the environment and its influence on visual comfort and efficiency," in his book, *Architectural Physics: Lighting,* (London: Her Majesty's Stationery Office, 1963); see page 252.

vision at the object. One specimen of sparkle can occur when moving water is illuminated by bright sunlight. If water flows outward from a fountain and cascades over roughened surfaces, strong lighting directed at (or from behind) the moving water will often exhibit many points of sparkle.[21] For the second example, the darkened interior of a chapel can instill contemplative moods amongst parishioners. Then, if the altar and its immediate surround are comparatively brighter (particularly during the time of the service), the attention of the parishioners will focus there (see Figure 7.22). This juxtaposition of light and dark areas can thus work towards invoking a feeling of awe or mysticism from the parishioners toward the service and the clergy.

For the designer and builder, light can be a powerful device both for creating ambience and for emphasizing the presence of particular objects in a building space. But care must be exercised when placing light sources or reflecting, nonluminous surfaces so that visual problems do not result. The designer and builder should consider where differing brightness levels might exist within a building. Particular forethought should be given to circumstances where sources and/or objects are placed which could be substantially brighter (or duller) than the average condition. Lastly, the designer and builder should also recognize how these brightness levels may affect the visual acuity and performance of occupants in any building.

Figure 7.22 One example of how a church altar may be lighted to direct attention there is ably demonstrated in the chapel at the Massachusetts Institute of Technology, Cambridge, Massachusetts. A diffusing skylight and complementary electric lighting (included within the skylight assembly) illuminate this altar area. The remainder of the chapel is usually operated at a much lower illumination level (thus emphasizing the lighted area immediately surrounding the altar).

7.5.1 THE PRESENCE OF GLARE IN THE VIEW FIELD AND MEANS FOR ITS CONTROL

Glare is excessive or unwanted brightness that is present in the visual field of an observer. Why the brightness of a source or an object may be excessive—resulting in the sensation of glare—is because too great a difference in brightness exists between the source or task surface and the immediate surrounding and background for the source or surface. Three common glare sources are a window that admits the bright light of an overcast sky into a relatively dark space (see Figure 7.23), bright lamps located in an otherwise dull room (see Figure 7.24), and a shiny surface that reflects light brightly toward an observer (when the other surfaces surrounding the shiny one have matte finishes and appear dim). For each of these examples, glare is the response to a stimulus whose brightness differs markedly from the brightness(es) of the surroundings.

    Glare is also a subjective experience: to what extent a bright source or surface may seem glary often differs from person to person. So, a condition that one person finds to be glare-ridden, another person may scarcely notice. When people have been tested for their responses to a potentially glary condition, the range of responses has varied from bare awareness of the source to outright discomfort and, even, pain. The extent of the glare experience is fundamentally dependent upon how each person's visual system operates. But what specifically occurs within the individual's visual system as the person reacts to the glare source is not well understood. Instead, what the limited research on people's responses to glare shows is that tolerance levels differ substantially. Also, when specific experimental subjects are tested repeatedly in potentially glary conditions, the responses each person offers are quite uniform across time (i.e., the responses do not vary from day to day or season to season).

Figure 7.23 The glary conditions in this room exist not only because of the windows present an overly-bright, large surface area, but also because the surfaces surrounding the windows are dark. To reduce the experiences of glare, either the brightness of the windows must be reduced (e.g., using drapes or tinted glazing) or the surfaces surrounding the windows should be made less dark (e.g., by illuminating these surfaces and/or finishing the surfaces with lighter colors).

Figure 7.24 Having a single bright light source in an otherwise dark space can create both a localized area of excessive brightness and a more general, larger area of gloominess. Both conditions can produce unpleasant visual sensations.

Figure 7.25 One example of how a bright background can obscure the features of a relatively darker foreground object is displayed in this photograph. This mostly glazed building entrance presents a visual "antagonism" for a viewer's eyes. When one's eyes are quickly exposed to a large, bright view field (after having experienced a view field of lesser brightness), they will attempt to adapt to the change in brightness. But, if the view field also contains a darker surface—that indeed is what the viewer most needs (or wishes) to see—then the adaptation process will be beset with conflict.

Two types of glare are commonly observed: *disability glare* and *discomfort glare*. *Disability glare* can be experienced when there is either a small bright source in a generally dull field of view or a dim surface present in otherwise bright surroundings. One example of the former condition can occur when you are walking down a relatively dark corridor that has a window at its end and someone walks toward you. If you look at the person's face (and it overlays the bright plane of the window), you will be unable to distinguish the features of the face (see Figure 7.25). Alternatively, for the second example, suppose you are walking by a shallow brook on a sunny day and you look down into the water. The reflected sunlight will make the surface appear very bright, whereas any object beneath the water will be comparatively dim. Thus, you will likely have difficulty in determining the natures of any underwater object. In either instance the *disability glare*-ridden condition creates a *loss of visibility,* interfering with the viewer's ability to determine the characteristics of an object. Visual acuity thus is negated entirely; the eyes will be unable to distinguish the presence of any contrast in or about the object. If the object is part of some task requiring seeing, then an observer may commit numerous errors while performing the task or may require significantly longer periods of time to complete the task. Basically, the presence of *disability glare* can greatly increase the difficulty a viewer experiences while gathering information about the task. *Disability glare*, however, will not usually cause the observer any discomfort.[22]

Discomfort glare results when there is an area whose luminance differs substantially from the ambient luminance conditions. As the eyes of an observer traverse back and forth across areas with markedly different luminances, essentially a competition for suitable adaptation—within the visual system—will occur. But these differing luminances will prevent the establishment of a satisfactory adaptation. Thus, as the observer attempts to resolve the luminance differences, eye strain (or visual fatigue) will result. Additionally, an observer may have to *squint* to offset the effects of these differing luminances. A common example of how discomfort glare is experienced in buildings is when one occupies a comparatively dark room that has a window with a view of some portion of the sky. At times when the sky is brightly overcast or sunlight enters the space directly and this bright window area is in the occupant's field of view, the occupant can experience substantial discomfort glare. Having conditions present that cause discomfort glare will not reduce

SIDEBAR 7.12 Explaining glare physiologically

The sensing of glare seems to result from an "overloading" of any one (or more) of the several parts of the human visual system. For instance, excessive brightness can essentially cause retinal photoreceptor cells—generally or in some region of the retina—to overload, thus not being able to respond with enough specificity to incoming light. These deluged cells will not be able to provide useful "messages" about the received light, and the rest of the visual system will be helpless to analyze whatever messages pass upward from the retinal cells.

The sensing of glare also can ensue from a dysfunctioning of some part of the visual system. A discussion of some of the optical disorders that can lead to experiences of glare appears in the chapter by Prager, T.C., "Essential factors in testing for glare," in the book edited by Nadler, M.P., D. Miller, and D.J. Nadler, *Glare and Contrast Sensitivity for Clinicians,* (New York: Springer-Verlag, Inc., 1990), pages 33–44. This chapter by Dr. Prager also lists a number of references that identify how various maladies can promote the sensation of glare.

visual acuity. But these conditions will produce a situation where an occupant's visual performance will suffer. If the occupant is forced to experience the conditions for some time, the individual's vision will progressively degrade as the fatigue and discomfort increase.

Environmental conditions that are most responsible for the sensation of glare (and, especially, *discomfort glare*) include having some object (or objects) within the view field whose brightness is excessive and having the contrast between the object and its surroundings and background appear too great. Essentially, both factors must be present for one to sense glare. Having great contrast between an object and its surroundings will not alone cause glare; actually, high contrast can foster visual acuity and performance, *if the illuminance on the object is reasonable*. Alternatively, a task object that appears excessively bright will not alone cause glare. An entire field of view—including the task surface—may seem very bright (e.g., when a building space is illuminated with light from an arc lamp or a desert landscape is lighted by direct-beam solar radiation). For these examples, if the luminance distribution across the view field is relatively uniform, glare will not be the specific sensation. Rather, our eyes cannot adapt upward sufficiently to withstand the brightness. Thus, our ability to tolerate such brightness is limited. For these conditions people will experience great discomfort, but the discomfort is not strictly glare-related.

There are several environmental parameters that can affect the sensing of glare (i.e., can contribute to a condition in which glare is present). Further, the likelihood that occupants will experience glare is dependent on the extent (magnitude) of any one (or more) of these parameters. First, glare is more likely to be sensed when a large variability in surface luminances exists throughout the environment. Second, whether or not glare is observed will often depend on the sizes of the surfaces (displaying the range of luminances). Third, the positions of the surfaces within the view field also can establish the extent that glare is present (i.e., are bright surfaces central in the primary view field or do they lie off to one side and only are seen by one's peripheral vision?) Fourth, how large the distance is between the surface and the object can affect the sensing of glare. Indeed, distance is, to some degree, a qualifier for the first and second parameters because if one is some distance from a potential glare surface, the effect of the surface brightness may be lessened because the surface will occupy a smaller areal percentage of one's view field. And, fifth, what are the luminance conditions for the surfaces surrounding—forming the background for—the potential glare surface? Thus, how might these surrounding surfaces influence the adaptation process of the observer's visual system?

SIDEBAR 7.13 References for gathering further information about glare

One author who has written widely about the presence and nature of glare in buildings is R.G. Hopkinson. Dr. Hopkinson has authored (or co-authored) a number of texts and scholarly papers about glare. An excellent *first* reference would be the selection, "Glare and visual comfort," from Dr. Hopkinson's book, *Architectural Physics: Lighting*, (London: Her Majesty's Stationery Office, 1963), pages 201–290. Additional information about discomfort glare can be found in a paper by

C.A. Bennett, "Discomfort glare: concentrated sources—parametric study of angularly small sources," *Journal of the Illuminating Engineering Society*, 7(1), October 1977, pages 2–15. This latter paper describes research that examined how small, bright sources could promote discomfort glare and what effects some related environmental parameters might have on the glare sensation.

For instance, suppose you are sitting in a room with glazing along one side. As we stated in the previous paragraph, the probability that you will experience glary conditions in this room will be determined by a series of factors. First, the brightness of the sky can be an important stimulus (e.g., is the sky brightly or darkly overcast or is the sky clear with sunlight entering the window?). Second, is the window a small area or a large area? A small area may occupy less of the overall view field. But the brightness that a small window may display could create a greater level of contrast across the room and, thus, across the view field (i.e., the window surface may appear very bright, whereas many surfaces in the room could be quite dim). To marked extent, the position of the window can determine what effect a significant contrast gradient can have when an occupant looks at the view field. If the window lies at the periphery of view, its direct ability to cause glare will be reduced. Instead, for a window that will only be seen peripherally, a designer or builder might then be more concerned with how the window influences — contributes light to — the brightnesses of other internal surfaces within the room. But if the window lies at the center of view, then whether the window causes glare can depend on the percentage of the view field the window occupies and the magnitude of the contrast difference that exists

---

SIDEBAR 7.14 Assessing (or predicting) the likelihood that glare will be experienced by occupants of proposed building designs

Relationships between the environmental parameters identified in these paragraphs have been used to derive formulas for a *glare constant* and a *glare index*. Indeed, the *glare constant* and *glare index* are intended for use during the building design process to predict whether glare may be present in a space if it were constructed as proposed. The *glare constant* is calculated for each potential glare source within the space. Then, the various *glare constants* are summed, and the sum can be further manipulated mathematically to produce the *glare index* for the space. The resulting number for the *glare index* can then be compared to values suggested for the application(s) for which the space is to be used (i.e., to establish the likelihood that luminous conditions may cause glare). Additional information about this prediction method appears in Chapter 9 ("Glare and visual discomfort") of the book by Hopkinson, R.G., *Architectural Physics: Lighting,* (London: Her Majesty's Stationery Office, 1963), pages 96–108.

Otherwise, measurements of glare are not possible in the same manner that you can measure the intensity of a lamp or the heat from a fire. Glare is a subjective experience, and people respond to it differently. However, you can measure the *physical brightness* of a potential glare source (i.e., in terms of its luminance). You can also measure the luminances for the area immediately surrounding the potential glare source and for the background area. By noting how a space is or will be laid out, you can ascertain geometrical information about the potential glare experience (e.g., where viewers may sit or stand; in what directions they will be looking when they view the source; will the source lie in the center or periphery of their view; how large does the source appear to be; and so forth). From these data you can deduce the likelihood that glare may be present (i.e., by using calculations suggested in Chapter 9 of the Hopkinson book).

Alternatively, indirect methods can be used for testing whether glare is present in a space or what effect glare may have on the occupants of a space. To determine if disability glare exists in a space, traditional visual acuity tests are employed (e.g., such as those described in Section 7.4.1). To examine the effects of discomfort glare, the methods employed generally include various subjective tests wherein subjects are presented with an environment in which a glare source exists and then are asked to describe their reactions or feelings about their experiencing of the space (or some set of tasks they are asked to perform in the space).

between the window and its surrounding surfaces. For the fourth parameter—the distance between the observer and the window—the extent to which glare may be experienced will be lessened as one moves away from the window (as long as other parameters like the brightness, the real size, and the position of the window in the view field remain the same). And, fifth, the adaptive state of the observer's visual system can be greatly affected by the characteristics of the surfaces surrounding the window. If these surfaces are relatively bright themselves, then the contrast gradient between the window and these surfaces will be less. The visual system, looking at the window-wall combination, could be well adapted. Alternatively, if the surrounding wall is dark and the visual system is basically adapted to the wall luminance, then glare will likely be experienced whenever the window appears bright.

While studying these five environmental parameters, researchers have made a series of observations about how changes in these parameters can affect one's sensing of glare. For example, one major suggestion is that the luminance of any light source (or nonluminous, reflective surface) should not be significantly greater than the luminances of the immediately surrounding surfaces (or those luminances of the areas that form the background for the surround).[23] Further, it has been found that, as the luminances of the source and the surround differ ever more greatly (i.e., the larger the degree of contrast existing between the source and the surround becomes), the likelihood increases that discomfort will be experienced by the observer. Regarding the sizes of a luminous source (or a nonluminous reflecting surface) and its surround, decreasing the size of the source (or surface)—if it causes glare—will have little effect on the extent of the discomfort experienced. Increasing the size of the area surrounding a glare source also does little to improve the sensation of discomfort. In other words, discomfort glare cannot be lessened by increasing the size of the surrounding area. Instead, *to improve a glary situation, you must reduce the difference in luminances between the source and the surround.* One other research finding concerns the position of the glare source in the field of view: generally, *having the source be directly in (or near) the center of the view field will cause more discomfort than if the source is located to the side of the view field.*[24]

Glare is most often experienced in buildings when excessively bright light sources are present in comparatively dim spaces. Common examples where these too-bright sources can cause glare include when daylight (or sunlight) is transmitted through windows and when electric bulbs or tubes are not adequately shaded from the direct view of occupants. Additionally, glare can also result when nonluminous interior finishes reflect light from excessively bright sources into the view field of an occupant. Of these various glare problems, creating windows in building envelopes requires the greatest amount of attention to ensure glare mitigation. Daylight or sunlight passing through windows produces surfaces whose luminances are often substantially greater than the luminances of the surfaces immediately surrounding the windows. Thus, a fundamental issue in window design is how to reduce the luminance differences between windows, surrounding surfaces, and the ambient conditions of the interior space. One principal solution to this problem is to treat the window surface so that its luminance is not excessive. Using transmitting materials other than clear glass (e.g., tinted or heat-reflecting glasses) is one widely applied solution. Alternatively, external or internal physical devices (e.g., awnings, permanent overhangs or fins, drapes, blinds, and so forth) can restrict the transmission of daylight and/or sunlight. Other solutions for glare mitigation include employing light-colored internal opaque surface finishes near the window and locating the windows so that they are lower in the window-wall surface and do not present so much of the sky (i.e., the sills (and tops) of these windows are closer to the floor). We will describe, in Chapter 8, the roles of windows in building envelopes. Then, in Chapter 9, we will discuss how windows should be located to admit daylight, and we will further identify strategies for controlling the rate of daylight (and/or sunlight) admission. *But, for now, let us emphasize that the creation of windows for the building envelope involves some of the most complex decisions that designers and builders must make!*

7.5.2   VEILING REFLECTIONS, FLICKER, AND VISUAL FATIGUE

In addition to the visual discomfort or disability caused by the presence of glare sources (and surfaces) within the view field, there are a number of other situations involving lighting that can also cause visual system dysfunction. Here, we will address two specific conditions and a third somewhat general one: veiling reflections, flicker, and visual fatigue.[25]

Veiling reflections occur when light enters an observer's field of view by reflection off of a task surface and when the luminance of this light is substantially brighter than the generalized light illuminating the task surface (i.e., where the generalized light results from all the other sources and nonluminous surfaces in the environment [see Figure 7.26]). A source of veiling reflections produces localized lighting that intrudes on the general lighting condition for a task surface. The veiling reflection thus establishes a nonuniform

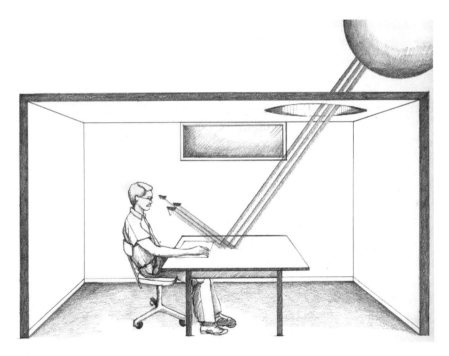

Figure 7.26 The person seated at this desk will experience veiling reflections off of any reading or writing surfaces placed directly in front of him or her (i.e., whenever bright light enters through the skylight and falls on this workstation surface. Indeed, the presence of veiling reflections will be especially discomforting when direct-beam sunlight passes through the skylight and reflects off the task surface upward at this person. Note also that electric illumination that has any sort of directional nature can also create veiling reflections when light from the electric source reflects off task materials toward the viewer.

distribution across the task surface. The veiling reflection and a common glare source are similar in nature (e.g., both result from excessively bright light entering the view field). The principal difference between veiling reflections and common glare sources, however, is that the veiling reflection specifically results from light reflected off of a *task surface* (i.e., whereas glare sources (and surfaces) simply occur in the generalized view field of an occupant).[26]

Veiling reflections are often experienced in tasks involving reading. For instance, suppose a person sits at a table reading a book and employing a light source that specifically illuminates the book surface. If the light source is located in front of and above the reader and is brightest in a particular direction (i.e., the source does not simply emit an evenly diffused light), then light from this source can reflect off of the book surface and pass to the reader's eyes. If the reflected light from this light source strongly exceeds the light resulting from other sources and nonluminous surfaces, then a veiling reflection will exist and cause visual discomfort (or disability). The effect of this veiling reflection is that it reduces the contrast between the print on the page and the page itself (i.e., by increasing the amount of light reflected off of the printface). With a decrease in contrast between the print and the page surface, the reader's visual performance will suffer and/or the reader will require more time for reading. Additionally, the reader may report that the task with its veiling reflections is visually uncomfortable.

The possibility that veiling reflections will be encountered during reading tasks can be minimized if the designer or builder exercises caution when locating and orienting where the reader and the task surface will be placed and in selecting and arranging the principal light sources. For instance, if daylight entering through a window is the primary light source, then the window should not directly face the reader. Rather, *place the reader so that the person sits alongside the window and has the daylight falling perpendicular to the direction of viewing the book surface* (see Figures 7.27 and 7.28). Two other guidelines suggested for improving the visual comfort of readers are *do not use glossy paper as the page material; instead, use a matte-finished paper to minimize the possibility that too-bright light may be reflected into the reader's view field* and *avoid having people read pencil-writing* (i.e., particularly, with hard graphite pencils). Pencil-writing often provides insufficient contrast between the written words and the page surface; alternatively, if enough graphite is transferred to the page, the graphite can itself become moderately reflective.[27]

Flicker is a visual problem created most commonly by electric lighting and, particularly, with fluorescent lamps. Flicker is the sensation that one experiences when a light source cycles on and off rapidly (i.e., cycling many times per second as lamps can when powered by alternating-current electricity). This cycling of the light source produces an intermittent stimulation of the retinal photoreceptor cells and creates discomfort due to visual fatigue.[28] Environmental parameters that most readily affect a viewer's sensitivity to and awareness of flicker include the luminance of the flickering source, the amount of contrast between the source and its surround, the frequency (or rate) of flickering of the source, and the color of the light emitted by the flickering source (if, indeed, the color is not white). Generally, flicker will be more readily discerned when the source appears within a reasonably large view field whose ambient luminance is of a moderate intensity. A flickering source occurring within a smaller, more concentrated view field of higher luminance will be less noticeable. So, then, a flickering source will be more evident when increased contrast exists between the source and its surround. The effect of color on the sensing of flickering sources seems to be that shorter-wavelength colors (e.g., violet and blue) are more discernible and, thus, more bothersome than the longer-wavelength colors (e.g., orange and red). Some commentary has been published about the relationship between the "warmth" of the colors and their respective tendencies to be readily discerned

Figure 7.27 This office setting presents a condition where gazing at the computer monitor will often subject the user to visual discomfort. The cause of the discomfort will probably be the substantial luminance difference between the monitor screen, the window glass, and the opaque surfaces that surround the window and the monitor, respectively. An immediate improvement could be achieved by pulling the shade down to cover the window. But such action would eliminate any daylight and would certainly require reliance on electric illumination.

Figure 7.28 By pulling the shade over a window that is directly in front of the worker's desk, the potentially excessive brightness of the window can be negated (from disrupting the worker's view field). Alternatively, by admitting light from the window along the side of the desk, the worker is much more likely to experience a comfortable visual condition.

and/or discomforting. But these comments appear anecdotal, and we have not been able to find any systematic research that supports these anecdotal reports. In any case, the best solution necessarily to reducing discomfort due to flicker is to remove any flickering light source from a primary view field. Further, it would be prudent to not use sources that may be conducive to flickering or to make possible the easy replacement of any sources that may be prone to flicker.[29]

Lastly, visual discomfort can also result from the accumulation of visual fatigue. Often, such fatigue occurs as the product of trying to perform visual tasks in settings where there is insufficient support for good vision. Such conditions can include not having adequate illuminance on a task surface or enough contrast between the detailed item and its background (e.g., the printed word and the page on which it resides). Alternatively, the visual task may be a comparatively difficult one involving very small, detailed information (even when adequate illuminance and contrast are present). Or the information may be of an appropriate size, the lighting conditions satisfactory, and enough contrast may be present, but the viewer has too little time to observe the material and experiences fatigue and discomfort as a result. Thus, visual fatigue and discomfort can happen in environments that are in most respects supportive, but which have some one condition that places a strain on the visual system. Such strain, when experienced for a lengthy period of time, creates fatigue and discomfort and inevitably leads to lessened visual acuity and performance.[30]

Section 7.6 | A BRIEF SUMMARY FOR CHAPTER 7

This chapter has been organized to describe aspects of the human visual system, to provide some insight into current thinking about how an object in the external world is seen and understood to be (i.e., is perceived), to suggest some of the ways in which the external world affects seeing, and to begin the presentation of guidelines that can be used to create well-lighted spaces (additional guidelines will be offered in Chapters 8 and 9). The visual system acts as an information gatherer and processor. By doing so this system tells us more about the external world around us than any of the other senses.

What the visual system reveals is determined by its physical structure and physiological operation. But the act of discerning the composition of the external world appears to involve a greater enterprise than that which can be described in terms of physiological operations. Instead, the perception of some object requires activity that scarcely can be limited to a progressive building-up of partial images. Perception occurs essentially every time we see something (or, how else would we know that we saw it?).

Finally, in Sections 7.4 and 7.5, we have begun to describe how our environment should be created if we want to foster good conditions for seeing. We have discussed means for insuring visual acuity and performance, relating how a task object (or surface) should appear with regard to its surrounding and background environments. We have identified a series of environmental conditions that cause visual discomfort and/or disability. Lastly, we have suggested some guidelines for minimizing visual dysfunction that might otherwise result from environmental characteristics. In Chapter 9 we will expand this catalog of design and building guidelines.

ENDNOTES and SELECTED ADDITIONAL COMMENTS

1. These two terms are employed in the text by Davis, B.O., N. Holtz, and J.C. Davis, *Conceptual Human Physiology,* (Columbus, Ohio: Charles E. Merrill Publishing Company, 1985); see pages 181–187. A more extended discussion of these concepts is presented by Bloch, G., *Body and Self,* (Los Altos, California: William Kaufmann, Inc., 1985), pages 77–105.

2. In addition to the information shown in Table 7.1, see also the book by Boyce, P.R., *Human Factors in Lighting,* (London: Applied Science Publishers, 1981), pages 44–45.

3. The classic reference describing rodal (and conal) sensitivities to alternative wavelengths is Wald, G., "Human vision and the spectrum," *Science,* 101, 1945, pages 653–658. Also, for instance, see Sekuler, R., and R. Blake, *Perception,* (New York: Alfred A. Knopf, Inc., 1985), pages 88–98.

4. Hubel, D.H., "The visual cortex of the brain," *Scientific American,* 209(5), November 1963, pages 54–63.

5. Some of the discussion about the attributes of the perceptual process has been derived from ideas presented in the chapter, "Information processing of visual stimulation," from the book by Haber, R.N., and M. Hershenson, *The Psychology of Visual Perception,* (New York: Holt, Rinehart and Winston, Inc., 1973); see pages 157–175.

6. See the following two articles: Boyce, P.R., "Current knowledge of visual performance," *Lighting Research and Technology,* 5(4), 1973, pages 204–212; and Rea, M.S., and M.J. Ouellette, "Visual performance using reaction times," *Lighting Research and Technology,* 20(4), 1988, pages 139–153.

7. A number of documents address this topic and the subject that will be discussed in Section 7.4.3. Two that we recommend are by Crouch, C.L., "Lighting for Seeing," in Volume 1 ("General Principles") of *Patty's Industrial Hygiene and Toxicology,* revised edition (edited by Clayton, G.D., and F.E. Clayton), (New York: J. Wiley & Sons, Inc., 1973); and Boyce, P.R., *Human Factors in Lighting* (London: Applied Science Publishers Ltd, 1981), see Chapters 2–3, particularly.

8. Note that when the immediate surround and the area beyond the immediate surround are considered together, the combined area is described generally as the *background.*

9. Concerning the detection of detailed information and the effect of detail size on vision, see the following two papers: Guth, S.K., and J.F. McNelis, "Visual performance: a comparison in terms of detection of presence and discrimination of detail," *Illuminating Engineering,* January 1968, pages 32–35; and Blackwell, H.R., "A comprehensive quantitative method for prediction of visual performance potential as a function of reference luminance," *Journal of the Illuminating Engineering Society,* October 1982, pages 40–63.

   For additional information about contrast and its influence on visual acuity and performance, see any of the following papers (or book): Cannon, M.W., Jr., "Contrast sensation: a linear function of stimulus contrast," *Vision Research,* 19, 1979, pages 1045–1052; Rea, M.S., "Visual performance with realistic methods of changing contrast," *Journal of the Illuminating Engineering Society,* 10(3), April 1981, pages 164–177; Rinalducci, E.J., L.F. Cosgrove, and J. Walker, "Optimum sensitivity to contrast vs. luminance," *Journal of the Illuminating Engineering Society,* 14(2), April 1985, pages 568–580; Bradley, A., and I. Ohzawa, "A comparison of contrast detection and discrimination," *Vision Research,* 26(6), 1986, pages 991–997; and Wolfe, J.M., "An introduction to contrast sensitivity testing," in the book edited by Nadler, M.P., D. Miller, and D.J. Nadler, *Glare and Contrast Sensitivity for Clinicians,* (New York: Springer-Verlag, Inc., 1990), pages 5–23.

   For additional discussion about some experiments concerning tasks with various levels of difficulty, see the paper by Yonemura, G.T., and R.L. Tibbott, "Equal apparent conspicuity contours with five-bar grating stimuli," *Journal of the Illuminating Engineering Society,* 10(3), April 1981, pages 155–163.

Regarding how the time available for viewing can affect visual acuity and performance, see any of the following papers by Harwerth, R.S., and D.M. Levi, "Reaction time as a measure of suprathreshold grating detection," *Vision Research,* 18, 1978, pages 1579–1586; Thompson, P., "Perceived rate of movement depends on contrast," *Vision Research,* 22, 1982, pages 377–380; Rea, M.S., P.R. Boyce, and M.J. Ouellette, "On time to see," *Lighting Research and Technology,* 19(4), 1987, pages 101–103; and Rea, M.S., and M.J. Ouellette, "Visual performance using reaction times," *Lighting Research and Technology,* 20(4), 1988, pages 139–153. Additionally, a review chapter on these topics has been written by A.B. Watson, "Temporal sensitivity," in the book edited by Boff, K.R., L. Kaufman, and J.P. Thomas, *Handbook of Perception and Human Performance (Volume I: Sensory Processes and Perception),* (New York: J. Wiley & Sons, Inc., 1986), pages 6–1 through 6–43.

10. Cohn, T.E., and D.J. Lasley, "Visual sensitivity," *Annual Review of Psychology,* 37, 1986, pages 495–521; note pages 501–506, particularly.

11. Hood, D.C., and M.A. Finkelstein, "Sensitivity to light," in the book edited by Boff, K.R., L. Kaufman, and J.P. Thomas, *Handbook of Perception and Human Performance (Volume 1: Sensory Processes and Perception),* (New York: J. Wiley & Sons, Inc., 1986), pages 5–1 through 5–66.

12. Heerwagen, J.H., A.F. Emery, D.R. Heerwagen, D. MacGowan, and G.B. Varey, "Human variability: the comfort 'annoyance factor'," *Proceedings of the 10th National Passive Solar Conference* (edited by A.T. Wilson and W. Glennie), (Boulder, Colorado: American Solar Energy Society, 1985), pages 632–637.

13. Four recent papers have addressed the creation of such models and the problems involved in their development: Clear, R., and S. Berman, "A new look at models of visual performance," *Journal of the Illuminating Engineering Society,* 12(3), July 1983, pages 242–250; Rinalducci, E.J., L.F. Cosgrove, and J. Walker, "Optimum sensitivity to contrast vs. luminance," *Journal of the Illuminating Engineering Society,* 14(2), April 1985, pages 568–580; Rea, M.S., "Toward a model of visual performance: foundations and data," *Journal of the Illuminating Engineering Society,* 15(2), Summer 1986, pages 41–57; and Rea, M.S., and M.J. Ouellette, "Visual performance using reaction times," *Lighting Research and Technology,* 20(4), 1988, pages 139–153. The last three papers suggest models that relate visual performance to variations concerning detail size, contrast, and luminance present for visual tasks.

14. Text copies produced from multiple-layered carbon copies, some photocopy machines, or computer printers whose ribbons are worn out will often appear "washed-out" (i.e., the characters are not wholly formed and show discontinuities in their formation).

15. Foxell, C.A.P., and W.R. Stevens, "Measurements of visual acuity," *British Journal of Ophthalmology,* 39, 1955, pages 513–533.

16. Stone, P.T., A.M. Clarke, and A.I. Slater, "The effect of task contrast on visual performance and visual fatigue at a constant illuminance," *Lighting Research & Technology,* 12(3), 1980, pages 144–159.

17. Blackwell, H.R., "A comprehensive quantitative method for prediction of visual performance potential as a function of reference luminance," *Journal of the Illuminating Engineering Society,* 11(4), October 1982, pages 40–63.

18. Foxell, C.A.P., and W.R. Stevens, "Measurements of visual acuity, *British Journal of Ophthalmology,* 39, 1955, pages 513–533.

19. Collins, B., *Evaluation of subjective response to lighting distributions: a literature review,* NISTIR 5119, (Gaithersburg, Maryland: Building and Fire Research Laboratory, National Institute of Standards and Technology, February 1993).

20. A few literature sources present guidelines similar to these (i.e., suitable for providing good seeing conditions). We have previously cited the material composed by Crouch, C.L., "Lighting for seeing," in *Volume 1: General Principles of Patty's Industrial Hygiene and Toxicology,* revised edition (as edited by Clayton, G.D., and F.E. Clayton), (New York: J. Wiley & Sons, Inc., 1973); and Chapters 2–3 of the book by Boyce, P.R., *Human Factors in Lighting,* (London: Applied Science Publishers, 1981).

Two other books that discuss how good seeing can be maintained are Hopkinson, R.G., *Architectural Physics: Lighting,* (London: Her Majesty's Stationery Office, 1963), see Chapters 1–2; and Hopkinson, R.G., and J.B. Collins, *The Ergonomics of Lighting,* (London: Macdonald & Co., 1970), see Chapter 3, especially.

21. For photographic examples of fountains and waterfalls where sparkle can be observed, see Section 13.3.2.3.

22. Fisher, A.J., and A.W. Christie, "A note on disability glare," *Vision Research,* 5, 1965, pages 565–571.

23. Note that this suggestion is entirely consistent with one of recommendations set forth in Section 7.4.4.

24. Chauvel, P., J.B. Collins, R. Dogniaux, and J. Longmore, "Glare from windows: current views of the problem," *Lighting Research & Technology,* 14(1), 1982, pages 31–46.

25. A fourth cause of visual discomfort or disability involves the presence of excessive amounts of color in the view field.

26. Boyce, P.R., *Human Factors in Lighting,* (London: Applied Science Publishers Ltd, 1981); see pages 314–317.

27. For further information about planning and designing visually comfortable settings for reading and writing, see the following three sources: DeBoer, J.B., "Performance and comfort in the presence of veiling reflections," *Lighting Research & Technology,* 9(4), 1977, pages 169–176; Chapter 7 ("Avoiding discomfort") in the book by Boyce, P.R., *Human Factors in Lighting,* (London: Applied Science Publishers Ltd, 1981), pages 284–342; and/or "Office lighting for good visual task conditions," *Building Research Establishment Digest* #256, December 1981 (as prepared by the Building Research Station, Garston, Watford, WD2 7JR, England).

28. Wilkins, A.J., I. Nimmo-Smith, A.I. Slater, and L. Bedocs, "Fluorescent lighting, headaches, and eyestrain," *Lighting Research and Technology*, 21(1), 1989, pages 11–18.

29. For further information about *flicker* see the material by Hopkinson, R.G., "Flicker discomfort due to intermittent light stimulation," in his book, *Architectural Physics: Lighting,* (London: Her Majesty's Stationery Office, 1963), pages 269–290. Also, note the chapter by Brown, J.L., "Flicker and intermittent stimulation," in the book edited by Graham, C.H., *Vision and Visual Perception*, (New York: J. Wiley & Sons, Inc., 1965), pages 251–320.

30. See the following source for further information about visual fatigue: Boyce, P.R., *Human Factors in Lighting,* (London: Applied Science Publishers Ltd, 1981), pages 216–221.

Using the Sky as a Light Source

8

TWO PRINCIPAL THEMES will be addressed in this chapter. First, daylight offers a pervasive source for illuminating the activities of human beings. Thus, means for admitting daylight into buildings should be accommodated during their design and construction. Second, the window, which is the essential component through which daylight enters buildings, should be designed with care. In this chapter we will use the term *window* generically (i.e., to include any opening in the building envelope, whose range of purposes at least includes the admission of daylight). Consequently, the term *window* will also account for clerestory and skylight forms.

When we create windows to admit daylighting into a building, we must recognize that the sky has a dual character. The hemispherical sky vault—whether overcast, partly cloudy, or clear—commonly presents a relatively uniform source of daylighting illumination. Alternatively, the sun—when not obscured by clouds—is a localized, directional, and intense source of illumination. Because these two sources—the sky vault and the sun—function in concert, the light gained from them can be highly variable, both in its composition and intensity.

Lastly, although windows present a series of benefits for the building occupant, but they can also pose liabilities. Generally, however, the benefits outweigh the liabilities. For instance, if you ask, Why should one be interested in admitting daylight into a building, then we can answer that it enables us to see within the building. Further, daylight — used to illuminate building interiors *passively* — will reduce the amount of electrical energy that will have to be purchased (i.e., to complement daylighting illumination). Daylight can also be applied as a design element that will enliven and add dash and verve to the building form and the activities that occur in the building. However, there are situations wherein the liabilities will be more significant. For these situations, buildings may need to be windowless. Therefore, in this chapter, we will also consider the benefits and liabilities associated with window presence.

Section 8.1 | WHY DO WE HAVE WINDOWS IN BUILDINGS?

8.1.1 BENEFITS AND COSTS OF WINDOW PRESENCE

Window design is fundamentally a problem of *optimization:* each time you locate a window in a building envelope you have to balance a series of benefits and liabilities, which will be associated with that window during the occupancy of the building.[1] Perhaps the primary benefit of a window is that it admits daylight, providing illumination for working, reading, and living. In addition, some scientists have recently pointed out that daylight also fosters the maintenance of one's health, thus making the presence of daylight necessary for the well-being of the building occupant. Windows also admit sunshine that not only brings strong intense light, but also potentially useful heat. Other significant benefits

---

SIDEBAR 8.1 Health benefits resulting from exposure to daylight

Among the health benefits attributed to daylight are influences on daily biological rhythms (e.g., maintenance of the core body temperature); enhancement of one's abilities to form Vitamin D3 and to absorb calcium; treatment of a variety of skin diseases; inhibition of the formation of melatonin which induces sleep and modifies secretion of a number of hormones from the endocrine glands; and the alteration of the development of reproductive organs and the timing of the reproductive cycle. These health benefits have been discussed in the article by Wurtman, R.J., "The effects of light on the human body," *Scientific American,* 233(1), 1975, pages 69–77. Three other papers have discussed how light can be used therapeutically. First, confirmation of the initial report and an expansion of its subject have been offered by Hughes, P.C., and R.M. Neer, "Lighting for the elderly: a psychobiological approach to lighting," *Human* *Factors,* 23(1), 1981, pages 65–85. Second, an examination of how light presence (and wavelength composition of the light) can induce chemical changes in human beings has been described by Hollwich, F., and B. Dieckhues, "The effect of natural and artificial light via the eye on the hormonal and metabolic balance of animal and man," *Ophthalmologica,* 180, 1980, pages 188–197. Third, an article, addressing how colored light can influence physical well-being, has been written by Kaiser, P.K., "Phototherapy using chromatic, white, and ultraviolet light," *Color Research and Application,* 9(4), Winter 1984, pages 195–205. And, fourth, bright lights have been applied as a therapeutic device for people suffering from seasonal affective disorder (SAD), a condition in which afflicted individuals experience greater levels and frequencies of depression during the short, relatively darker days of winter.

that windows offer the building occupant include a target to look at (and through) to permit eye muscle relaxation; contact with the exterior and the provision of views of the exterior[2]; the passage of air through the envelope (as ventilation and exhaust); the offering of a means of escape from within the building (as in the event of a fire or some other calamity); and the enhancement of the aesthetic experience that buildings can create (i.e., daylight thus can be employed to draw attention to and accentuate the building form).

The liabilities of window presence generally involve conditions where *too much* of something potentially good passes into a building. For instance, we have stated that sunshine can be a positive commodity. But sunshine also can have negative effects if too much of it enters the building and causes the building interior to overheat. Additionally, windows can be responsible for excessive heat loss from buildings. Strong daylight (and sunshine) can produce glary conditions in buildings. Sunshine can also cause the deterioration of organic materials and the fading of dyed, painted, or inked markings on paper and fabrics. Exterior noise from outside of the building will often pass through window assemblies with less attenuation—noise reduction—than through nearly all opaque envelope assemblies (unless the window assemblies are fabricated with special noise-transmission-reducing treatments). Windows permit people from outside to look into a building, thus disturbing an occupant's privacy (see Figure 8.1). Even worse, windows can

---

SIDEBAR 8.2 Identifying differences between sunlight and sunshine

Sunlight is to be distinguished from *solar radiation,* where the former term is limited to just the visible portion of the radiation that arrives at the surface of the Earth from the sun and the latter is the total radiation emitted by the sun that reaches the Earth (including ultraviolet, visible, and infrared radiation forms). This total solar radiation is called *sunshine* by E. Ne'eman in his paper, "Visual aspects of sunlight in buildings," *Lighting Research & Technology,* 6(3), 1974, pages 159–164. The terms *sunlight* (and *sunshine*) are commonly used to describe, respectively, light (and radiation) from the sun, when one is referring to the condition where there is a definite *directionality* for the light (and radiation)—as when the sky is clear or lightly hazy—and the *solar disk* of the sun is distinguishable.

SIDEBAR 8.3 Why looking at distant objects rests one's eyes

The focusing of light as it passes through the eyeball lens and falls on to the retina requires the action of the ciliary muscles. These six muscles around the human eyeball regulate the shape of the lens. The lens changes shape to enable the eyeball to focus on objects that are, alternatively, near or far from the viewing person (see Section 7.2.1 and Sidebar 7.1). When a person reads or performs other work involving small, detailed objects, these muscles need to be maintained in a constant configuration. As with any muscle group that remains in a constant position, the muscles tire and require resting. Looking away from a near target and allowing one's vision to focus on some distant object outside of a building can achieve this resting. Such distant targets have been identified by E.C. Keighley as "visual rest centers" in his paper, "Visual requirements and reduced fenestration in office buildings—a study of window shape," *Building Science,* 8, 1973, pages 311–320.

[a]

[b]

Figure 8.1 The fenestration assemblies for an office building on the University of Washington campus are composed of a heat-reflective glazing. One elevation of this building is located next to a bus stop. Inevitably, while people wait for the arrival of their buses, individuals will use the almost mirror-like glazing to adjust clothing, check their cosmetics, and even consider facial and body movements (e.g., note the behavior exhibited in (a)). However, although the glazing is largely reflective, some light is transmitted through, more particularly when viewed from the inside of the building. In this second photograph (b), you can indeed verify that people inside of the building can see the outside of the building (i.e., note the presence of the dancing child in the center of the glazing panel). Thus, for the office workers inside the building whose desks are placed at the building perimeter, the behaviors of people outside of the building are often distracting and sometimes unnerving.

serve as the means of entry for thieves and other ne'er-do-wells. Lastly, window assemblies generally cost more to construct than do the opaque envelope assemblies that are used in place of windows.

Regarding these benefits and liabilities for window use, we might offer two qualifications. First, the form, composition, placement, and use of any window can be *controlled*. For instance, drapes can be employed inside a building to reduce the penetration of heat from sunlight, to shut out excessively bright daylight, or to protect one's privacy (see Figure 8.2). So, whether windows present benefits or costs for occupants can be determined greatly by the provision (and use) of appropriate controls. Second, the *proximity* of occupants to windows will markedly influence the degree to which windows positively or negatively affect the people. How the issues of *control* and *proximity* are treated during the design and construction of the building will determine the success with which the future occupant can use the windows. So, a designer or builder should not simply provide windows in a building envelope because they represent the common practice. Instead, the selection and placement of windows should be thoughtfully carried out, and the designer or builder should be able to state rationally why windows appear where and how they do in a building.

8.1.2   THE ROLE OF VIEW IN WINDOW PLANNING

A major benefit of windows is that they enable the occupant to see what exists outside of the building. Fundamentally, this benefit involves two components: the occupant can maintain contact with the outside world; and the occupant can learn about the conditions and content of the outside world. *Establishing contact* means that the occupant can sustain a psychological sense of the outside world and that there is a continuum between the building interior and external spaces. Thus, whether you are in your home looking out at your backyard or

[a]   [b]

Figure 8.2 (a & b) A pair of interior shutters are available for controlling view and the penetration of exterior light for a window in the Hill House in Glasgow, Scotland. Note that the presence of the small openings in the shutters still allows a small amount of daylight to enter when the shutters are closed (i.e., so that some daylight will be admitted when the occupant might otherwise be seeking privacy).

SIDEBAR 8.4 Problems with sitting near windows

A window can cause thermal discomfort for a building occupant who sits near it. If the interior surface of the window is cold, then discomfort can result from the radiant exchange between the occupant and the window and the convective drafts that may flow from the window to the occupant. Alternatively, when direct-beam solar radiation enters through the window and "falls" on the occupant, the person may become overheated. Various window controls can be utilized to reduce the extent of thermal discomfort otherwise created by uncontrolled windows: catalogues of suitable thermal and daylighting controls appear in Chapters 5 and 9, respectively. A discussion of heat transfer mechanisms near a window appears in Section 2.2 of this text. Additionally, the discomfort caused by trying to work near a cold-surfaced window has been discussed in Section 3.6.1.

From 14th Floor

From 24th Floor

From 34th Floor

From 44th Floor

From 54th Floor

Figure 8.3 This series of photographs was taken in a high-rise office building in Seattle (while the building was under construction). In the basic view shown in this series an occupant looks northward from the business district toward the Seattle Center—the home of the 1962 World's Fair—and, beyond, to some of the residential areas of Seattle. The five views in this series were taken, respectively, from the 14th, 24th, 34th, 44th, and 54th floors in the building. For all of these photographs the camera was set at a distance of 12 ft (3.66 m) from the window surface and was held horizontally at a height of 62 in (1.57 m) above the floor.

What these photographs demonstrate is how the view that a building occupant can enjoy changes as one ascends in a building. In the lower views there is more information about the city near the building, whereas in the upper views the scenes display information about the more distant landscape. Thus, the occupants of the lower floors would be better able to maintain contact with the nearby area they inhabit. Alternatively, the occupants of the upper floors would be furnished with a greater sense of the locale beyond the immediate city in which the building is located. As long as no other tall buildings are constructed north of this building, all five views will present information about the sky and the weather present around and north of the building.

on the thirty-fourth floor of an urban high-rise looking out at the cityscape, you can partake of the exterior while remaining inside (see Figure 8.3). A quotation cited by Ruys (and attributed to Lawrence Perkins) captures the essence of this benefit:

> I have seen the importance of the window diminishing as a lighting device, and have gained an increased awareness of its importance as a psychological device… In my office, for example, I don't depend on my windows for light, but I do depend on them for sanity — and a sense of general relationship to the world outdoors. The feeling that we're part of a larger environment than the cubic one we happen to be in is made possible by windows. This is their primary function.[3]

Alternatively, *learning* about the exterior of the building means that you can seek information about the external world and use it positively, either to reinforce what you know and feel or to refresh your mental state. In both instances, what you see when you look out of the window is important to your well-being. Thus, the *view* that a window offers is an important factor in window planning. Indeed, having attractive and pleasant views from windows has been linked to the promotion of physical and mental health by a number of researchers (especially, for those people confined to the building interior, such as hospital patients and prison inmates). In a recent review paper J.H. Heerwagen reports that:

> A recent study by Ulrich found that hospital patients whose rooms looked out on a small grove of deciduous trees had a significantly more positive post-surgical recovery process than a matched control group in the same hospital whose view consisted of a brick wall. Patients in rooms with the tree view stayed in the hospital for a shorter time, took fewer narcotic analgesics, and had fewer post-surgical complications. Two studies of health care in prison settings have produced similar results. Moore found that inmates whose view consisted of adjacent farmlands had lower rates of sick call than did inmates whose windows looked out upon the prison yard…West found that inmates whose windows were facing a meadow or mountains had significantly lower rates of stress-related sick call than inmates whose views consisted mainly of the prison courtyard and buildings.[4]

What then should a view provide the occupant of a building? Or, what content should a view have? These questions have been discussed in the professional literature by a number of authors. The consensus suggests that a view, to be most pleasing and useful, should furnish elements of six parameters: the information presented in a view should be organized in *horizontal layers;* the view should display *complexity;* the view should show *diversity;* the view should have *variability;* the view should support the occupant's *privacy;* and the view should contain *elements of nature.*[5]

Ideally, when you look out a window, the view should be composed of three zones (or layers): first, a lower layer should present what is happening close to the building; a middle layer should include everything from the edge of the building-proximate zone to physical objects, vegetation, and other features at or near the horizon; and an upper layer should show the sky (see Figure 8.4). The lower and middle layers should contain information about artifacts created by human beings (e.g., other buildings or street scenes) and items of nature. Alternatively, the sky should indicate the weather conditions and the time of day. Having *complexity* within the view ensures that it will not be boring. But the degree of complexity must be controlled and moderate: too much complexity will render the view confusing or incomprehensible. Ludlow has written that "people assess views essentially as a coherent whole and not as a series of parts."[6] To be most successful, then, the view should include information that identifies what is present and how it is structured. *Diversity* suggests that the view should be made up of a number of components and not just a

Figure 8.4 This photograph shows the view from the author's former fourth-floor office at the University of Washington. Because of the presence of the roof deck just outside of the office, there is little view of the area immediately surrounding the building (i.e., the recommended *lower layer*). However, the other two principal layers are well represented. The *middle layer* shows a series of university buildings and a public thoroughfare south of this building, the Portage Bay waterway, and a residential area on the other side of the water. Then, an unimpeded view of the sky constitutes the *upper layer.* Further, the view out of this window displays a *complex,* interesting cityscape. The presence of a range of building forms, transportation alternatives, and landscape scales all contribute to a wealth of *diversity* (which is captivating and hardly confusing). Likewise, these features also contribute *variability* and dynamism to the view. *Elements of nature* are certainly present, both in terms of the vegetation and the waterway. Finally, the view is largely a *private* one (except when college functions occur on the roof deck and others cluster along the railing to partake of the view).

Figure 8.5 This photograph shows the west elevation of Larsen Hall, one of the buildings of the Harvard University Graduate School of Education in Cambridge, Massachusetts. Each of the four elevations of this building has quite limited quantities of fenestration, and many perimeter spaces within the building are basically windowless.

few items (or even just a lot of one thing). The view should not be too predictable or too regular. It should also include components, some of which are near the building and others that are further away. Elements within the view should be *variable,* so that these elements (or their appearances) change over a period of time. For instance, having deciduous trees in the view can display a seasonal variation: the tree branches form buds in early spring; leaves come forth from these buds later in the spring and provide greenery and shade throughout the summer; the leaves change color in early autumn; and the trees drop their leaves in late autumn. Variability can also include objects that move (e.g., boats sailing or people walking by, trees swaying in the wind, and so on). Sustaining *privacy* in one's view generally requires that a person can watch what goes on outside of the building, without being seen by people external to the building. Further, an occupant will be able to look over the exterior without feeling isolated from it. The occupant should sense that he or she can participate in or take advantage of external activities or presences (e.g., walking amongst some vegetation). Lastly, the view should have *natural elements* present within it. These pieces of nature can be vegetation, a scene containing water (a lake or a stream), some portion of the sky, animals and birds, and so forth. Numbers of recent papers about window use state that the existence of natural elements is a fundamental need in occupants' views.[7] Scenes of nature emphasize the ready connection between the building occupant and the outside world. Views of nature offer respites from work-related anxiety and stress. Additionally, these natural scenes have been found to demonstrate restorative powers that improve the health and well-being of occupants.

You may note that these six properties of view content overlap. For example, a view including a grove of deciduous trees will have a natural component; show seasonal change (variability); and display motion as the wind moves the leaves and branches (thus offering information about the weather). These trees, if present with ground cover, low bushes, and animal and bird life, would also include substantial diversity and complexity. One could even argue that such a grove of trees affords some degree of privacy, depending on the vantage point of the occupant and where people external to the building may be. Thus, such overlap can reinforce and enhance the positive qualities of a view and make it more interesting and appealing to the occupant who has the good fortune to see it regularly.

8.1.3   IS THERE A SUBSTANTIVE BASIS FOR OR AGAINST WINDOWLESS SPACES?

Windowless buildings (or buildings with numbers of spaces without windows) have been popular with facilities planners, designers, and administrators at various times during the past several decades (see Figures 8.5 and 8.6). Whether one might call the development of windowless buildings a "fad" is unclear. But strong enthusiasms have arisen periodically for creating windowless buildings. Generally, the primary benefits that windowless buildings appear to offer occupants are a reduction in vandalism, particularly that caused by people outside of buildings; a reduction in the distraction levels experienced by people inside of windowless buildings; and the ability to create a more uniform internal environment (i.e., in terms of heat, light, and sound). A fourth justification for windowless spaces is that, in large buildings, it is often difficult to provide all of the occupants with access to the building perimeter (and, thus, those located in the interior of the building will necessarily be without windows).

Research about windowless spaces has been conducted to determine what effects windowlessness may have on the feelings and activities of the occupants. For instance, studies in primary and secondary schools in California and Michigan have evaluated the reactions of teachers and students to windowless spaces.[8] Generally, these studies showed little statistical difference in occupant preference, performance, or health (the last as evidenced by rates of absenteeism), when comparisons were made between occupants of windowed or windowless spaces. Teachers liked the windowless spaces better because they found that students were more attentive. Also, the teachers believed that the windowless spaces were more conducive to the needs of teaching (e.g., there was more blackboard surface, better lighting control, and so forth). The reactions of the students tended toward ambivalence, although some noted that they disliked not having the presence of sunlight within their rooms and not being able to grow plants. Further, some reported feeling claustrophobic. But, overall, the major conclusion that could be drawn across these studies seemed that little difference was evident between how occupants felt and performed in the windowed and windowless spaces.

Some research has also been conducted on how workers in windowless spaces feel about these spaces. A study by Ruys surveyed 139 female office workers at the University of Washington. All occupied private, one-person offices without windows, and they all performed work with a "routine" focus (e.g., secretarial, accounting, record-keeping, etc.). Ninety percent (90%) of these workers reported that they wanted a window in their space. Fifty percent (50%) said that they believed that the lack of windows adversely affected their work performance. Further, when asked what they missed most about not having windows, the most frequently cited items were daylight and not having any information about the weather. In response to questions about how they most often felt in their windowless offices, these workers mentioned feelings of isolation, claustrophobia, anxiety, and depression. Ultimately, the conclusion drawn from this research was that these workers did not like the windowless spaces and had not adapted to being in such spaces.[9]

Wyon and Nilsson have performed a study on windowless spaces for a large sample of professional and clerical workers throughout Sweden. This sample was divided into a number of discrete groups whose feelings and attitudes could then be compared one to another: those in windowed spaces versus those without windows; those from five different job classifications, each of which had members that worked in windowed or windowless spaces; those from northern Sweden versus those from southern Sweden; and a series of blind (sightless) workers, some of whom occupied windowed spaces and some of whom had windowless spaces. Much of the research employed surveys and the solicitation of spontaneous comments by the workers about their work environments. Among the several findings three are most interesting: people with windowed spaces felt more strongly about having windows than people in windowless spaces felt about *not* having windows; people with what were identified as "boring" jobs wanted windows more than did people with "interesting" jobs; and the blind workers were the most positive group in support of having windows within their work space. These blind workers gained sensory information (e.g., sound, air movement from ventilation) from the windows and used this information as cues about their environment.[10]

A third study brings together the seemingly disparate issues of windowlessness and view content. J. Heerwagen and Orians have investigated what *adaptations* office workers at the University of Washington made to their workplaces.[11] Some of these workers occupied windowed spaces, whereas others occupied windowless spaces. Serving as a principal study instrument, a detailed content analysis was performed of visual decorations used by individuals in these two groups. The authors found that the workers in the windowless spaces used more than twice as many visual devices to decorate their offices; the visual materials employed by the windowless workers most frequently presented a sense of a view (rather than simply some decorative item); and these "surrogate

Figure 8.6 An exterior view of the chapel at the Massachusetts Institute of Technology is presented in this photograph. The main space for worship has no vertical fenestration, although there is a diffusing skylight in the roof of the building and a low-wall horizontal ring of glazing along the interior perimeter of this space (i.e., so that a bit of daylight might reflect off the water in the external, surrounding moat, pass through the glazing ring, and illuminate the interior walls of the space). An interior view of this chapel appears as Figure 7.22 in Chapter 7; in that view nearly all of the illumination displayed results from three flood lamps incorporated into the diffusing skylight assembly.

views" were predominantly scenes of nature, rather than of suburban or cityscape settings. To highlight these points, the authors have written:

> The results of this study underscore people's apparent strong need for contact with nature in some form. The number of landscapes and nature-dominated visual materials in the windowless office spaces in this study clearly indicates that people want to see the natural world, even if the contact is a surrogate one provided by posters and paintings. It is instructive here to note some of the ways in which office staff…have gone to great lengths to create naturescapes indoors. In one windowless employees' lounge, staff members hung a wall-length mural of a marsh. To enhance its effectiveness as a picture window, they hung curtains that, of course, are never drawn. Another office has a wall-length mural of a Hawaiian sunset, and a third has a large poster of a country scene that has a window frame and curtains in the picture.[12]

Considering these several studies together, no basis appears to exist for making a definitive case *for* or *against* windowless buildings. Windowless spaces offer certain benefits to building occupants and administrators, but these spaces also pose liabilities. To a marked extent, whether or not to employ a windowless design strategy for some space — where a choice is possible — should depend on the circumstances involved in the building situation. But, *if windowless spaces are to be created, then the occupants of those spaces should be allowed special consideration in how they modify — or otherwise adapt to — their spaces.*

Section 8.2 | THE AVAILABILITY OF DAYLIGHT

Using daylight to illuminate the building interior requires that the building envelope contain windows to admit the light. These windows must be adequately sized and placed to ensure that enough light will enter the building. To establish what indeed are the appropriate sizes and locations for windows, you will need information about how much daylight is available from the sky. You will also require data about the extent of variation in the amount of daylight across time (i.e., for a day or throughout a year). Additionally, you will need information about how uniform the sky is at any given time (e.g., whether the same amount of illumination can be obtained from all parts of the sky at any time or whether the amount of illumination is variable). Further, some knowledge about what causes these variations may also be useful, both for planning window placement and sizing and for anticipating how well a building can be daylighted.

In fact, there are perhaps five topics for which data are needed if one is to carefully locate and size windows for the admission of daylight. First, some data are required about *average* conditions and the likely *maximum* and *minimum* values of daylight availability. The maximum and minimum values should be established for the times of the day (throughout the year) when the building is occupied. Thus, if the building you are planning is a school and it is not used during the summer, then there is little need to consider what the maximum amount of daylight will be in late June or early July (presuming that we are discussing school use in the Northern Hemisphere). If, for example, we were designing windows for a school in New Zealand, then the designer would less likely consider sky conditions in December or January (i.e., that time of the year when New Zealand schools are in summer recess). Alternatively, the minimum amount of daylight will probably be zero for early mornings and late afternoons during the winter in upper *Northern Hemisphere* latitude areas. Second, as the amount of daylight can significantly differ for *clear* and *cloudy* sky conditions, you should seek information that presents average and extreme daylight amounts for these conditions. Third, the extent to which the *amount of daylight varies across the day* (or, at least, during the time the building will be occupied) is also relevant. Fourth, presuming that windows will likely be placed on more than one elevation of the building, you will need to consider *how uniformly the daylight is present across the sky*. And, fifth, information will be needed about *how often these various conditions occur*. For instance, what is the frequency (or the number of hours) that a clear or cloudy sky will be present? Or, is an average condition the average for a month or for the entire year? And, if the value is an average, in fact how many hours per day (or month or year) does the sky have that amount of daylight?

When you plan windows, you will need to select some sky condition against which to prepare your design. So, you should have some rational basis for selecting a sky condition. This sky condition will, in turn, serve as the basis for locating and sizing the window. The window location and size will then determine how much light can be admitted into the building. But, though the location and size of any window — once installed — is invariant, an occupant can still enjoy a great amount of flexibility in establishing how much light enters the space at any time. By including, with a basic window, one (or more) variable control(s) (e.g., blinds, drapes, shading devices, light shelves, and so forth), flexibility can be ensured.

8.2.1   LIGHT FROM THE SKY (AND THE SUN)

The daylight that we gain from the hemispherical sky vault over us is solar radiation. Thermal energy from the sun radiates, as this *beamed* radiation, across space to the upper layers of the atmosphere of the Earth. Much of this beamed radiation does not reach surfaces on the Earth. Instead, a substantial fraction is reflected and scattered by components in the atmosphere. Also, some of the beamed radiation is absorbed by these atmospheric components. In the process of being scattered and absorbed this radiation is *diffused* throughout the atmosphere and reaches the surfaces on which it falls as *diffuse* radiation. However, some fraction of the original beamed radiation will still pass unhindered through the atmosphere and reach these surfaces as *direct-beam* radiation (see Figure 8.7).

The solar radiation that passes through the atmosphere is composed of ultraviolet, visible, and infrared radiation. Of these three forms, only visible radiation can be seen by the human eye. So when we speak of the *visible* portions of diffuse and direct-beam solar radiation, we call them, respectively, *diffuse illuminance* and *direct-beam illuminance*. These two components, when summed, form the *total illuminance*.

The amount of illuminance at a building site is chiefly dependent on three parameters: the *climate* of the region and the *microclimate* of the specific site; the *sky condition* above the site; and the *altitude of the sun* in the sky. The temperature of the air above a site and the amount of water vapor in the air — as manifestations of the climate and, to a lesser extent, of the microclimate — principally determine whether clouds exist over the site (and, if they are indeed present, what forms the clouds will have). The presence or absence of clouds is a fundamental feature of the sky condition. Other elements that contribute to the sky condition are dust particles and industrial and vehicular-produced pollutants. The clouds and these other elements affect the ability of the beamed radiation to pass undisturbed through the atmosphere. So, when the air is dry and there is little dust or few pollutants in the air, the sky will be clear, the amount of diffuse illuminance will be low, and we will see the sun (as a well-defined solar *disk*). At such times the amount of

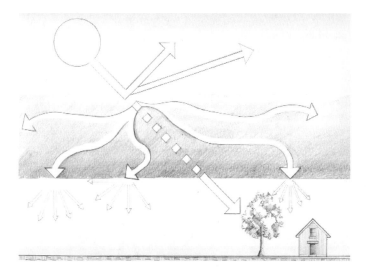

Figure 8.7 The transmission of solar radiation through the atmosphere of the Earth results in the presence of diffused sunlight (which emanates from the sky vault generally) and direct-beam sunlight. How intense either component will be, at a building location, depends on the characters of the regional climate, the sky condition above the building, and the altitude of the sun at some moment in time.

SIDEBAR 8.5 Locating the sun in the sky

The location of the sun as it passes across the sky vault is described in terms of the *solar altitude angle* and the *solar azimuth*. The solar altitude angle is formed at the intersection of two lines, one the path of the direct-beam (from the sun) to the ground plane and the other a line defined by two points, first, where the direct-beam intersects the ground plane and, second, where a line from the apparent position of the sun will be perpendicular to the ground plane. The solar azimuth angle is bounded by the north-south compass line and a line determined by two points, first, where the line from the apparent position of the sun will be perpendicular to the ground plane and, second, the location of the compass. Note that the solar azimuth angle may be referenced to either the North or South compass direction depending upon what organization provides the azimuthal data (i.e., some organizations prefer defining the azimuthal reference based on the North compass direction, whereas others use the South). (See Figure 8.8.)

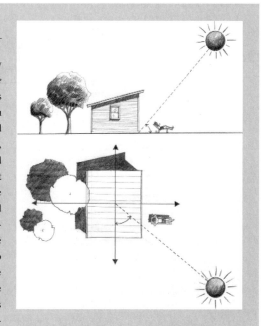

Figure 8.8 This drawing demonstrates the solar altitude (in the top drawing) and solar azimuth angle between the sun and a place on the Earth (in the bottom drawing).

direct-beam illuminance will be high, and the sunlight entering a building directly will be very bright.[13] Alternatively, on overcast days (when you rarely see the solar disk), the direct-beam illuminance will be relatively weak, and the majority of the illuminance received at the surface of the Earth will be *diffuse illuminance* (i.e., most of the daylight will appear to come from the sky vault).

8.2.2   RATES OF SKY ILLUMINANCE

Sky illuminance has been measured at various stations located at high or low latitudes on both sides of the equator. The principal determinants of illuminance amounts are whether the sky is clear or cloudy (fully or partly cloud-covered) and what the solar altitude angle is. Typical relationships between illuminance and the solar altitude angle are shown in Figures 8.9 and 8.10, for *clear* and *overcast* (fully cloud-covered) *skies* in San Francisco, respectively. Both graphs display an essentially linear relationship between the illuminance values and the solar altitude angle (for each of the two sky conditions). In another recent study, similar measurements have been taken in the Washington, D.C. area. This second study produced relationships between illuminance amounts and solar altitude angles similar to those established in the San Francisco study.[14]

A number of researchers have developed *frequency distributions* that describe how often the skies over their measurement stations display particular amounts of illuminance. For instance, in Figure 8.11, distribution curves for *global* (or *total*) and *diffuse* illuminance values have been generated for the San Francisco sky. Further, in Figure 8.12, from data measured in Nottingham, England, distribution curves are plotted for the amounts of illuminance and the solar altitude angles. These frequency distributions are determined fundamentally by the climates present at the measurement sites, as the amount and type of cloud cover are both properties of any climate. Recent studies of daylight illuminance values in England and Australia have further verified the principle that sky illuminances over a site can be readily determined, if climatic data (concerning the amount and type of cloud cover) and solar altitude angles are well-known.[15]

Lastly, a literature survey collating measured values of illuminance has found reasonable agreement among recorded *minimum* amounts for *diffuse* illuminance.[16] Most of these reported values were derived to meet the criterion that about 90 percent of the working hours throughout the year would have diffuse illuminance amounts greater than these minima. Thus, such amounts may initially be employed as *design conditions,* when one wishes to size a window to accommodate the minimum presence of daylight. The catalogued values vary between about three and ten kilolux (or, about 280 to 930 footcandles).

What the numerical values cited in Figures 8.9–8.12 display is that, first, well-developed relationships exist and correlate sky illuminances, solar altitude angles, and sky conditions. Second, the frequency distributions for measured illuminances further qualify daylight availability. Third, daylight availability is linked directly to the amount and type of cloud cover, which in turn relate to the properties of the climate at a site. Thus, by having information about climatic parameters and knowing the solar altitude angles at a site, *one can predict daylight availability for that site over long periods of time.*

One additional approach exists for estimating illuminance values. This approach has been developed because, though the measurement of illuminance has occurred at a number of scattered research stations around the Earth, there are still many locations where no illuminance measurements have been or are being conducted. So, whereas illuminance has been measured at comparatively few sites, *irradiance* (or solar radiation) has instead been measured at many more. Using an index called the *luminous efficacy* of daylight and irradiance data gathered for a site, very good estimations can be generated for what the rates of illuminance will be for the site. The *luminous efficacy* is defined as the ratio of the illuminance (established for a short time period) to the irradiance (for the same time period). Essentially, this term *luminous efficacy* indicates the amount of daylight available for a unit amount of solar energy. Usually, reports of illuminance and irradiance are published for one-hour-long periods. The units employed in this ratio are, for illuminance, lumens per square foot and, for irradiance, watts per square foot. Thus, the *luminous efficacy* ratio has the unit set of *lumens per watt*.

Researchers have determined the luminous efficacy at various measurement stations around the Earth. Their results show that the luminous efficacy displays consistent values for particular sky conditions and for whether direct-beam, diffuse, or global (total) radiation is being considered. Additionally, the luminous efficacy values (achieved for these sky conditions and radiation types) are generally *independent of the specific locations at which*

SIDEBAR 8.6 Relating sky illuminance and solar altitude angles

The graphs in Figures 8.10 and 8.11 are based on measurements conducted in San Francisco by scientists working at the Lawrence Berkeley Laboratory. These (and additional, related) graphs appear in a paper by Navvab, M., M. Karayel, E. Ne'eman, and S. Selkowitz, "Daylight Availability Data for San Francisco," *Energy and Buildings*, 6(2–4), 1984, pages 273–281.

Equations have been derived based on the data shown in these graphs. These equations can thus be used to predict illuminance values for any solar altitude angle and either clear or overcast skies. The two equations are:

FOR CLEAR SKIES,
Illuminance on a horizontal surface =
$0.927 + 117.2 \times (\sin SAA)^{1.325}$ (in kilolux)

**AND FOR OVERCAST
(FULLY CLOUD-COVERED) SKIES,**
Illuminance on a horizontal surface =
$0.357 + 0.578 \times SAA$ (in kilolux)

where, for both equations, SAA represents the solar altitude angle. Note that most measurements of illuminance are conducted with sensors facing upward to record horizontal illuminance.

From the data used to generate Figure 8.12, two equations have also been developed for predicting the *average* total horizontal illuminance at any solar altitude angle. These two equations are:

**FOR LOW SOLAR ALTITUDE ANGLES
(-5° TO 2.5°)**
Average horizontal illuminance =
$10.5 \times (SAA + 5)^{2.5}$ (in lux)

**FOR ALL BUT THE LOW SOLAR
ALTITUDE ANGLES (2.5° TO 60°)**
Average horizontal illuminance =
$73700 \times (\sin SAA)1.22$ (in lux)

where the SAA represents the solar altitude angle. For further information about these equations, see page 72 of the paper written by Tregenza, P.R., "Measured and calculated frequency distributions of daylight illuminance," *Lighting Research & Technology*, 18(2), 1986, pages 71–74.

Note that one kilolux approximately equals 92.9 footcandles (or 1 footcandle equals 10.76 lux). See Section 6.4.1.2 for more information about the conversion of these illuminance units.

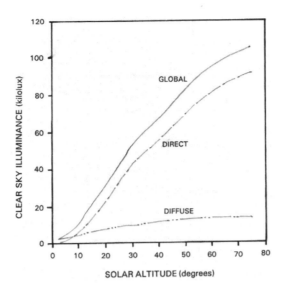

Figure 8.9 This graph displays the total (global) and component (direct-beam and diffuse sky) amounts of illuminance for a *clear sky* plotted versus the altitude of the sun (or solar disk). Note that these illuminance amounts have been measured for a horizontal surface. This graph has previously been published in a paper by Navvab, M., M. Karayel, E. Ne'eman, and S. Selkowitz, "Daylight availability data for San Francisco," *Energy and Buildings,* 6(2–4), 1984, pages 273–281. Permission to reproduce this figure has been granted by the publisher of the journal, Elsevier Science.

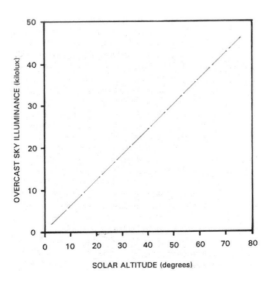

Figure 8.10 This graph shows the amount of illuminance for an *overcast sky* plotted versus the altitude of the sun. These illuminance amounts have been measured on a horizontal surface. This graph has previously been published in a paper by Navvab, M., M. Karayel, E. Ne'eman, and S. Selkowitz, "Daylight availability data for San Francisco," *Energy and Buildings,* 6(2–4), 1984, pages 273–281. Permission to reproduce this figure has been granted by the publisher of the journal, Elsevier Science.

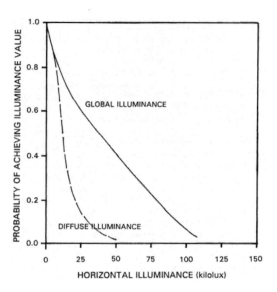

Figure 8.11 The likelihood (or probability) of observing alternative amounts of illuminance from global (total) and diffuse-sky component measurements, for a horizontal surface, is shown in this figure. This graph has previously been published in a paper by Navvab, M., M. Karayel, E. Ne'eman, and S. Selkowitz, "Daylight availability data for San Francisco," *Energy and Buildings,* 6(2–4), 1984, pages 273–281. Permission to reproduce this graph has been granted by the publisher of the journal, Elsevier Science.

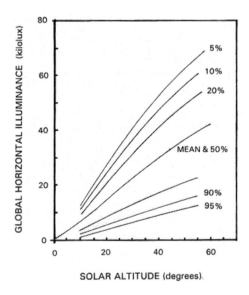

Figure 8.12 This graph relates the amount of illuminance (measured on a horizontal surface) for the global (total) sky to the altitude of the sun. Similar to information shown in Figure 8.11, this graph incorporates probability as a variable, thus indicating how frequently particular illuminance values should be anticipated. This graph has previously been published in a paper by Tregenza, P.R., "Measured and calculated frequency distributions of daylight illuminance," *Lighting Research and Technology,* 18(2), 1986, pages 71–74. Permission to reproduce this graph has been granted by The Lighting Division of the Chartered Institution of Building Services Engineers and Arnold Publishers, Ltd.

the luminous efficacy is sought (i.e., these values do not differ from station-to-station). The luminous efficacy also tends to be independent of the solar altitude angle (except at times close to sunrise and sunset when the solar altitude angles are low).

Therefore, for a clear sky condition, the luminous efficacy of global radiation has been found to be about 108 +/− 7 lumens/watt. Similarly, for an overcast sky, the luminous efficacy of global radiation appears to be slightly higher (at, perhaps, 115 +/− 5 lumens/watt).[17] Using efficacy values such as these and representative solar radiation data (irradiance) for a building location, a window planner can then estimate illuminance values.

8.2.3   HOW UNIFORM IS THE DAYLIGHTING SKY?

A simple answer to this question is that the sky is generally not uniform. It may contain clouds. These clouds may cover some or all of the sky. The clouds may be wispy or may constitute a thick cloud bank. Alternatively, the solar disk may or may not be visible. The portion of the sky near the horizon may appear brighter or duller, depending on whether the sky is cloudy or clear. The presence of smoke, dust, pollutants, and other transient, airborne materials may also contribute to the nonuniformity of the sky. That such nonuniformity exists is significant because *any window of a building will look out on only a portion of the sky.* So, if that sky portion is markedly lighter or duller than the average sky condition, then one should account for this disparity during the design of the building. Such accounting may involve sizing windows to suit the different sky conditions for the various elevations and/or including provisions that enable building occupants to modify the performance of windows.

A description showing how uniform (or nonuniform) the sky vault is over a building site can be accomplished by charting the *luminance distribution* across the sky vault. To describe the sky vault, we begin by regarding it as being composed of a series of point sources (or small areas) from which light emanates (i.e., toward building surfaces and the ground). Then, by measuring the physical brightness—*luminance*—of each of these many points of light, we can show how the amounts of light radiating from the sky vary across the hemispherical vault. So, by recording these luminance values for the sky vault, we develop a *luminance distribution* for the sky at any time (see Figure 8.13).

Because the sky character can be highly changeable, the luminance distribution of the sky will also be subject to change. In fact, the luminance distribution across the sky can undergo appreciable variation in comparatively small periods of time (e.g., certainly on an hour-by-hour basis and commonly for much shorter periods).[18] However, most building occupants are seldom aware of changing sky conditions (i.e., unless the change is severe and occurs over a brief interval, such as preceding a thunderstorm on a warm, humid summer day when the sky may progress from partly cloudy to fully cloud-covered with dark, foreboding clouds). Thus, because creating windows to comply with alternative sky conditions can often pose special difficulties, building designers generally establish window schemes for specific sky conditions. As an aid to designers, the *Commission Internationale De L'Eclairage* has published *standards* describing the likely patterns of luminance distribution for a *typical clear sky* and a *typical overcast sky.* Both of these distributions are essentially *idealized models* of how sky conditions will be when sky vaults are *clear* or *overcast.* But, even though these models exist only as *likenesses* of real skies, the models present workable approximations that can be used while designing window assemblies.

The *clear sky model* displays three luminance regions. First, a small area around and including the sun—called the "circumsolar" region—has great brightness. Second, a very large area covers much of the rest of the sky. The area is distinguished by having brightness

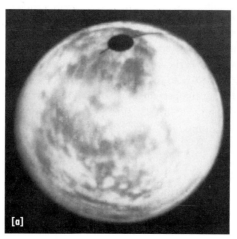
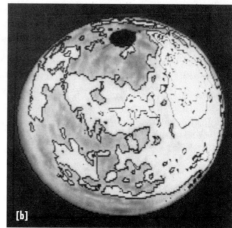

Figure 8.13 Photograph (a) shows a hemispherical sky vault for a partly cloudy sky. The lighter regions of this sky vault are the cloud-covered areas, whereas the darker areas are locations where the blue sky appears. The black spot at the top of this sky vault photograph is a shading device which obscures the solar disk or the place where the solar disk would be seen if the sky were not partly cloudy or cloudy (i.e., the solar disk is excluded from view because its great brightness would hinder getting a meaningful exposure for the remainder of the sky vault). Photograph (b) is a contour mapping of the sky vault shown in (a), thus demonstrating the luminance range across this sky vault at the moment at which photograph (a) was taken. These contours have the units of thousands of foot-lamberts (where 1 foot-lambert is equivalent to 3.426 cd/m²).

These two photographs have been provided by Theodore W. Cannon of the U.S. National Renewable Energy Laboratory (formerly, the U.S. Solar Energy Research Institute), Golden, Colorado. Photograph (b) has previously been published in a paper by Robbins, C.L., K.C. Hunter, and T. Cannon, "Mapping sky and surface luminance distribution using a flux mapper," *Energy and Buildings*, 6(2–4), 1984, pages 247–252. Permission to reproduce photograph (a) has been granted by Mr. Cannon. Permission to reproduce the photograph (b) has been granted by Mr. Cannon and the publisher of the journal, Elsevier Science.

SIDEBAR 8.7 Characterizing the luminance of any sky vault area

We have previously defined—in Section 6.4.1.3—luminance as the *luminous intensity* leaving a source *divided by the area of the surface* on which the light falls. As a basis for repeating that definition, first, think of the sky as being composed of a multitude of small areas, each essentially approximating a "point source." Thus, the light (or luminous intensity) from a small area of the sky vault can be described as the amount of light leaving the area (or source) divided by the solid angle of the spread of that light. Note that the amount of light leaving the area (or source) is also identified as the *luminous flux* of the area (or source). So, the luminous intensity of the sky source (or its *luminous flux*

divided by the solid angle across which the light is spread) is expressed in the units of *lumens per steradian* (or *candela*). The amount of light reaching a surface from this point source is then the *luminous intensity divided by the area of the receiving surface* (i.e., where the bounds of the receiving surface are established by the solid angle intersecting this receiving surface). The units here are *candela per square meter* (cd/m²). This quantity, *luminous intensity per unit surface area*, is characterized as the *luminance* of the sky source (or the small area of the sky vault from which the light emanates).

levels that gradually diminish as one looks away from the sun. This large area also includes a small relatively dark zone (that is located on a great circle [defined by the sun and the zenith point] and is about 80°–90° from the sun). And, third, there is a region that generally lies just above the horizon all around the sky vault. This third region has a brightness about midway between the sun and the dark spot. A sample luminance distribution map of this clear sky model is shown in Figure 8.14.[19]

The *overcast sky model* is somewhat simpler and is based on work initially performed by Moon and Spencer.[20] In this second model the luminance at any point in the sky is determined by the equation

Luminance at sky point p = (Luminance at zenith) × [(1 + $2\sin$ AA)/3],

where the angle AA is the altitude angle between the point p and the horizon. This simple equation is a convenient means for determining the luminance at any location in the overcast sky, as long as the *zenith luminance* is known. If the zenith luminance is not known but the global illuminance (on a horizontal sensing surface) can be established (from one of the Figures 8.9–8.12), then an equation such as the one shown in Sidebar 8.10 can be employed.

Using the equation shown for determining the luminance at point p, one can see that, for the *overcast sky,* the sky will be least bright at the horizon. The physical brightness of the overcast sky will increase as the altitude angle (between the horizon and point p) increases. Thus, the overcast sky will be most bright at the zenith (i.e., the luminance of the overcast sky will be the greatest at the zenith).

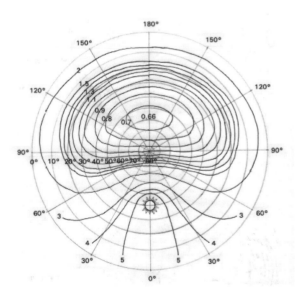

Figure 8.14 The CIE-standardized luminance distribution for the clear sky model, with the sun located at an altitude of 40°, is presented in this illustration. The three regions described in the written text can be readily seen here. Note also the ratio of the brightness levels for these three regions.

This drawing is a reproduction of an illustration in the document produced by the Commission Internationale de L'Eclairage, *Standardization of Luminance Distribution on Clear Skies* (CIE Publication No. 22 (TC-4.2) 1973), page 28. Permission to reproduce this drawing has been granted by the CIE.

SIDEBAR 8.8 What is the Commission Internationale De L'Eclairage (CIE)?

The CIE is a major international forum organized to foster the study of the presence and use of light in a variety of human endeavors and to write standards about illumination in nature, in buildings, and in other settings of human endeavor (e.g., for mines, roadways, tunnels, stadiums, and so forth). The CIE is comprised of member nations, who each appoint an individual representative to participate in the CIE. In conjunction with formal meetings of these spokespeople, the CIE maintains a large number of technical committees whose responsibilities include the study of illumination and the writing of the technical standards noted.

These committees are usually composed of lighting researchers, consultants, designers, and selected governmental officials. The CIE has its principal headquarters in Paris and holds international conferences every three or four years, at which technical papers are presented and various recommendations by the technical committees are discussed and voted upon for adoption (i.e., to augment existing standards and/or to create new ones). One article that describes the function of the CIE and how its various technical committees operate has been published in *Lighting Research & Technology*, 16(2), 1984, pages 85–97.

SIDEBAR 8.9 Approximate brightnesses for areas of the CIE clear or overcast skies

For the clear sky, a rule-of-thumb sometimes used to relate the luminances of the dark spot, the luminous region around the horizon, and the sun suggests a brightness ratio of 1:3:9, respectively, when the solar altitude angle is at least 40°. A corollary of this rule-of-thumb offers a brightness ratio of about 1:4:20 (or greater [for the brightness of the solar disk]) when the solar altitude angle is 30° or less.

A simple rule-of-thumb, which is used to describe the *overcast* sky, suggests that the zenith luminance will be three times more physically bright than the luminance at the horizon. Noting the equation

for establishing the luminance at point p (as presented in the text), the trigonometric term (2sin AA) must vary between 0 and 2 as the altitude angle varies between 0° and 90°. So, when point p is at the horizon (AA = 0°), then the luminance at the horizon will be one-third of the zenith luminance. Further, any point in the overcast sky between the horizon and the zenith will have a luminance that is some fraction of the zenith luminance (where the fraction is determined by the term (1 + 2sin AA)/3. Thus, the rule-of-thumb complies with this equation.

SIDEBAR 8.10 Relating global illuminance and zenith luminance for an overcast sky

A correlation between global illuminance and zenith luminance (for the overcast sky) is:

$$\text{Zenith luminance} = \text{global illuminance} \times \text{zenith luminance factor}$$

where the global illuminance excludes direct sunlight and the zenith luminance factor for the *overcast* sky is established as 1.286 in the following paper:

"Recommended practice for the calculation of daylight availability" (prepared by the Illuminating Engineering Society (IES) Calculation Procedures Committee), *Journal of the Illuminating Engineering Society*, July 1984, pages 381–392. Note that this equation may also be used for predicting the zenith luminance for clear or partly cloudy skies and that tables which catalog zenith luminance factors for clear or partly cloudy skies are presented in this *JIES* paper.

Both of these CIE sky vault models are, of course, simplifications of real-life conditions and should be treated only as approximations. Currently, more precise models are being derived by a number of researchers throughout the world. Such work includes both the further measurement of sky vault parameters (which affect luminance distributions for the skies) and the development of better relationships between these parameters (i.e., which can then be used for simulation and prediction).[21]

Section 8.3 | USING THE DAYLIGHT FACTOR TO DESCRIBE THE PRESENCE OF DAYLIGHT IN BUILDINGS

The term *Daylight Factor* describes how much daylight falls on a surface in a building space (as the light passes through one (or more) opening(s) in the building envelope). The Daylight Factor functions as a metric either for measuring or predicting daylight presence in a building. It can be quickly employed to size windows during schematic designing, evaluate design suggestions at the end of schematic designing, or fine-tune building proposals during design development. As such, the Daylight Factor can serve both as an estimating device — to determine how much daylight might enter a space — and as a testing device — to establish whether a window opening is adequately sized and placed.

The Daylight Factor is defined as *the ratio of the illuminance measured at some point within a building to the external illuminance, where this external illuminance is measured for* an unobstructed view of an overcast sky (see Figure 8.15). The specification that the sky be overcast requires that the sky cannot contain the solar disk and the attendant, identifiable

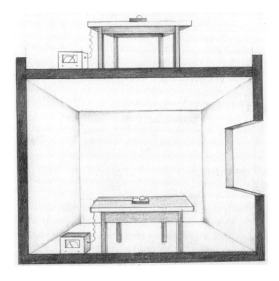

Figure 8.15 This drawing demonstrates how Daylight Factors would be established for this daylighted space. First, the sky is checked to make sure that the sky vault is overcast (i.e., without a recognizable solar disk visible). Second, the internal illuminance is measured in the space at some representative location on a workplane. Third, at the same time, the external illuminance is determined, with the observer verifying that this external illuminance is obtained for an unobstructed view of the sky vault. Then, the internal illuminance is divided by the external illuminance, producing the Daylight Factor value for the location at which the internal measurement was performed.

direct-beam sunlight. For this qualifier, when photometers measure the internal and external illuminances, neither should have direct-beam sunlight incident on its sensor surface. Further, the Daylight Factor method is founded on the notion that the overcast sky will approximate, in composition, the CIE Standard Overcast Sky.

The Daylight Factor (as a ratio of internal to external illuminance) is expressed as a percentage. Commonly, the Daylight Factor is identified for a horizontal surface in the building space (e.g., a desk top). Alternatively, though less frequently, the Daylight Factor may be determined for a location on a vertical wall surface such as for a display case or a blackboard. When you specify the Daylight Factor for a horizontal surface—unless otherwise stated—the surface is thought to be *76 cm (30 in) above the floor.* If, on the other hand, you need to specify a Daylight Factor for a work surface that is some other height (e.g., the table top of a drill press or a laboratory work bench), then you would identify the height of that particular surface. In any event, whatever horizontal surface is chosen for the Daylight Factor estimation, this location is described as the *workplane height.*

The Daylight Factor is fundamentally an indication of how much daylight from the sky vault can penetrate into a space (through an opening in the building envelope). The amount of daylight that can enter *through a window* depends on at least the following parameters: the location of the daylighted space in a building (on which elevation and how high above the ground plane the space is), the size and shape of the window, the window material(s), the presence of any shading devices in the window assembly, and, lastly, even whether layers of dirt build up on the window surfaces. Further, the amount of daylight *reaching a workplane* will depend not only on these parameters, but also on a variety of factors which characterize the internal space to be daylighted: the geometry of the space, the surface reflectances of internal surfaces in the space, the presence of any occluding objects or planes within the space, and so forth. In addition to these building, window, and space properties, the quantity of daylight entering the space can be greatly affected by the presence of any obstructions external to the window that can inhibit the sky vault daylight from even getting to the window (e.g., such obstructions may include other buildings, vegetation, fences, and so forth). So, to proceed with the designing of windows for daylighting a space, information about these properties must be established.

8.3.1   HOW DAYLIGHT FACTORS ARE USED

The principal application for the Daylight Factor method is as a guideline for creating windows for buildings. To use this technique, a designer begins by looking in a table to ascertain the amount of illumination required for a particular building application (e.g., an office or a classroom). The designer establishes the amount specified in terms of a Daylight Factor. Then, the individual can proceed to rough out a schematic window design, using any one of a series of physical design aids (that can be applied for matching the recommended Daylight Factor with the physical form and composition of the window(s)). The central premise for the use of the Daylight Factor as a metric is that the sky vault is the illumination source. Thus, the success of window design will depend on how well you can open a building up to the sky and permit the light energy from the sky vault to enter the building and reach a work surface (see Figure 8.16). The utility of daylighting a space will also depend on the nature of the sky vault—whether the sky is clear, overcast, or some condition in between—and how much light energy is available from the sky vault.

The daylight reaching any point on a work surface arrives from as many as three different source components. The first of these components is the daylight that passes from

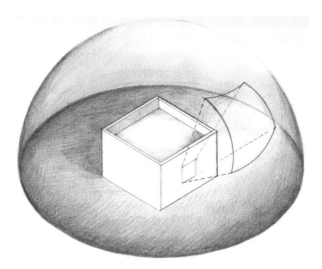

Figure 8.16 The essence of designing for daylight is to enable diffuse illumination from the sky vault to enter through windows and reach workplanes within building spaces. Thus, the source of this diffuse illumination, *for any window,* is some portion of the hemispherical sky vault that overlays the building. To ascertain how much daylight may enter through a window, the designer must determine how much of the sky vault the window "sees" and where that portion of the sky vault is. For the rectangular window shown here for this simple building, the portion of the sky vault seen by the window is the spherical rectangle outlined on the sky hemisphere. So, this spherical rectangle is the daylighting source for the window (and the space inside it).

the sky vault through the envelope opening and falls upon the work surface. This daylight amount is identified as the *Sky Component* (SC) (see Figure 8.17). The Sky Component is defined as the ratio of the amount of illuminance received at the reference location on the work surface directly from the sky vault versus the external illuminance (i.e., *for the overcast sky*). Note that the Sky Component is identified as a percentage.

In addition to this Sky Component, daylight may also be received at a point on the work surface by the reflection of light into the daylighted space from external objects (especially, where these objects may obstruct sight of some portion of the sky vault when looking from the window). The amount of daylight that enters through the window as a result of reflections off of external objects is called the *Externally-Reflected Component* (ERC). The ERC is defined as the ratio of illuminance at the reference point on the work surface due to these external reflections versus the illuminance of an unobstructed and overcast external sky. Consistent with the Sky Component, the Externally-Reflected Component is displayed as a percentage.

The third contribution to the amount of daylight found at a point on the work surface is the *Internally-Reflected Component* (IRC), which accounts for the daylight that enters through the opening, falls initially on other surfaces within the building space, and then is reflected from these other surfaces, one or more times, until the light reaches the reference location. Not all of the light incident on the other surfaces in the space will reflect to the location on the work station: commonly, only a small fraction of the daylight entering through the envelope opening will do so. The IRC is defined as the ratio of illuminance reaching the reference location due to the internal reflections of entering daylight versus

the external illuminance for the unobstructed, overcast sky. And the IRC is also presented as a percentage.

Thus, the amount of daylight reaching a reference location on a work surface—
resulting from daylight passing through an envelope opening—will be the sum of these
three components. Indeed, we can write a generalized equation to show that the Daylight
Factor at some point on a work surface is the sum of the components,

$$DF = SC + ERC + IRC$$

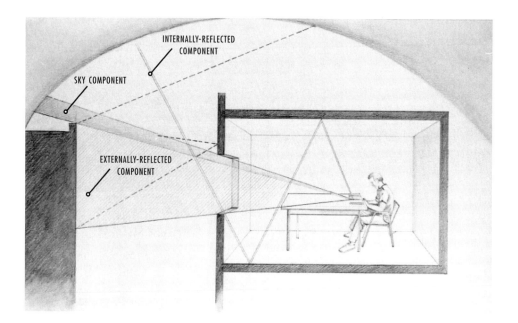

Figure 8.17 The three components that comprise the Daylight Factor methodology (the Sky, Externally-Reflected, and Internally-Reflected Components) are displayed in this drawing. Each of these components is a means
by which illumination from the sky vault can reach a workplane in a building space.

SIDEBAR 8.11 Using a recommended illuminance quantity as a starting point for designing envelope openings

Alternatively, the designer may find the amount of
recommended illuminance (specified in terms of lux
or footcandles) that should be incident on the workplane (i.e., measured at the workplane surface). In
this instance, then to use the daylight factor method,
the designer will need to select a *representative* sky
illuminance value. This chosen illuminance value will
thus constitute the *design condition* for the sky vault.

This illuminance amount can be chosen from one of
the approaches identified in Section 8.2 or from a
published table that has been prepared for a specific
locale. Once the representative illuminance value for
the sky vault has been selected, then dividing the recommended illuminance value for the workplane
surface by the sky vault illuminance will furnish a
Daylight Factor suitable for further design work.

8.3.2.   ESTIMATING DAYLIGHT ADMISSION USING THE DF PROTRACTORS

One means of determining the Daylight Factor for an envelope opening involves use of the *BRS Daylight Factor Protractors* (see Figure 8.18). Both the Sky Component and the Externally-Reflected Componet can be established using the protractors. The Internally-Reflected Component may then be found by utilizing a graph and some relatively simple calculations.[22]

To apply these protractors for estimating daylight presence, one begins with a plan and a sectional view of the opening and its adjoining building space, drawn to some convenient scale (see Figure 8.19). These drawings should also show any potential external obstructions, indicating how the Sky Component would be limited and permitting determination

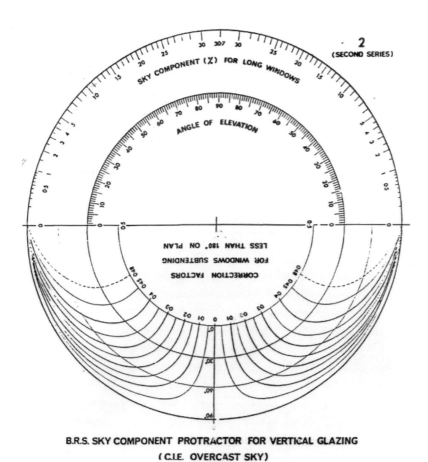

Figure 8.18 One of the several Daylight Protractors is shown in this figure. In addition to this protractor, which is used for vertical glazing with an CIE-standard overcast sky, other protractors in the BRS Daylight Protractors set accommodate horizontal and 30°- and 60°-tilted glazed openings for either the CIE-standard overcast sky or the "uniform" sky condition. Further, two additional BRS Protractors are available for unglazed openings for either of these two sky conditions. The several Protractors are described in the document by Longmore, J., *BRS Daylight Protractors,* (London: Her Majesty's Stationery Office, 1968).

of the Externally-Reflected Component. Following the use of these protractors for estimating the SC (and ERC), the Internally-Reflected Component can be found by applying the materials identified in Endnote 21.

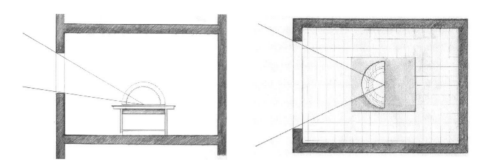

Figure 8.19 Use of the BRS Protractor exhibited in Figure 8.18 occurs in two steps. First, the upper-half of the protractor is placed over a building section that includes the daylighting window. The Daylight Factor percentage (for the Sky Component) can then be read from the semicircular protractor scale. Then, if the window has a limited width (i.e., any width such that the window subtends less than 180°, when viewed from the reference location on the plan drawing), a correction factor to account for this limited width is found from the lower-half of the protractor and is used to modify the Daylight Factor percentage (for the Sky Component) established for the window height.

SIDEBAR 8.12 Literature citations for the Daylight Factor method

Both of these design aids — the BRS Daylight Factor Tables and the BRS Daylight Factor Protractors — have long been in use. The key developments in these aids have primarily been made by scientists and practitioners at the Building Research Station (now, the Building Research Establishment) of the United Kingdom. The earliest use of tables for estimating daylight presence in buildings was formalized by the Waldrams in the early 1920s. Subsequently, these tables were modified and developed further until the "BRS Simplified Daylight Tables" were introduced in 1958. In a parallel effort, the BRS Daylight Factor Protractors were introduced in 1946. A reference for the Waldrams' work is: Waldram, P.J., and J.M. Waldram, "Window design and the measurement and predetermination of daylight illumination," *Illumination Engineer* (London), 16, 1923, pages 90ff. An extended description of the BRS Simplified Daylight Factor Tables is present in the book by Hopkinson, R.G., *Architectural Physics: Lighting,* (London: Her Majesty's Stationery Office, 1963), pages 54–70. The initial work on the BRS Daylight Protractors is described by Dufton, A.C., "Protractors for the computation of daylight factors," *Building Research Technical Paper,* No. 28, (London: His Majesty's Stationery Office, 1946).

For further historical information about the development of the Daylight Factor and other daylighting technologies, see the paper by Collins, J.B., "The development of daylighting — a British view," *Lighting Research & Technology,* 16(4), 1984, pages 155–170.

SIDEBAR 8.13 The utility of the Daylight Factor as a design tool

In this explanation we have proceeded from the premise that a designer had some idea about what an envelope opening should be like and wished to determine how much daylight could enter the building space. Once the designer estimated the Daylight Factor achievable with the opening, the estimate could be compared with some specific value suggested for the building application (e.g., as identified, perhaps, in an industry standard such as the one shown later in this chapter as Table 8.4). If the estimate matched the specified value, then the designer could continue on with further design work knowing that the windows would admit a satisfactory quantity of daylight. But, if the Daylight Factor estimate did not closely (or loosely) match the specific value stipulated for the building function, the designer could modify the size of the opening, its shape, or the materials intended for use.

After performing this modification, s/he could re-estimate the Daylight Factor. In this fashion, estimating the Daylight Factor would guide one through initial schematic design work (or in evaluating a design proposal).

Alternatively, the designer could begin with a statement of the amount of daylight needed in some building space (e.g., relying on a Daylight Factor amount stated by some industry standard such as the one presented here as Table 8.4). Then, s/he could use this requirement as a guide for sizing and shaping the opening and choosing the appropriate materials. In this latter approach the designer would be working in an alternative direction from the one described in the preceding paragraph. But either direction should provide a successful window design.

SIDEBAR 8.14 The availability of two additional DF Protractor sets

This discussion of this Daylight Factor methodology, generally, and the Daylight Factor Protractors, particularly, has emphasized reliance on the CIE Standard Overcast Sky as the sky condition fundamental to this methodology. Actually, two other sets of protractors have been developed, permitting development of Daylight Factors for other sky conditions. In the period preceding the adoption of the CIE Standard Overcast Sky model, the basic sky condition used for Daylight Factor analysis was a "uniform sky." This uniform sky was essentially a fully overcast sky that was described as showing no luminance variation from horizon to zenith (i.e., in contrast to the specific luminance variance present in the CIE Standard Overcast Sky). Because this uniform sky often poorly matched actual overcast sky conditions, the uniform

sky description is rarely applied for Daylight Factor estimation. Daylight Factor Protractors for determining Daylight Factors for this uniform sky condition are discussed in the booklet by Longmore, J., *BRS Daylight Protractors,* (London: Her Majesty's Stationery Office, 1967). Another set of Daylight Factor protractors has been developed for use with clear skies. These clear sky protractors can be employed in manners similar to those used for modeling overcast skies. For further information about these clear sky protractors, see the paper by Bryan, H.J., and D.B. Carlberg, "Development of protractors for calculating the effects of daylight from clear skies," *Journal of the Illuminating Engineering Society,* 14(2), April 1985, pages 649–662.

Once the magnitudes of the three components have been determined (or the magnitudes of the two components, if there are no external obstructions), the magnitudes are summed to reveal the Daylight Factor for the *unfilled* envelope opening. Then, to acknowledge the insertion of a window assembly into the unfilled opening, some modification of this component sum will be necessary. These modifications account for the type of window materials which are present in the window assembly, the presence of dirt or other atmospheric residue which will likely accumulate on the external window surface during building occupancy, and the presence of window-framing members (e.g., mullions and other area-occupying elements that reduce the opening area through which daylight may enter into the space). All three of these modifiers are expressed as decimal fractions that are to be multiplied together with the sum of the DF Components. Thus, each modifier reduces the amount of daylight illumination that reaches the work surface.

8.3.3   REPRESENTATIONS OF DAYLIGHT FACTORS ON BUILDING DRAWINGS

The Daylight Factor can be employed in building design not only as a means *to predict* or *to evaluate* the daylight presence within a proposed building, but also *to describe* how much daylight illumination will reach into the building. Thus, the Daylight Factor functions as a device for communicating to other designers, building developers, governmental officials, or even future occupants how daylight will appear in a building space. The goal of furnishing such descriptions of daylight presence often is to indicate the pattern of daylighting in a building space.

There are two basic *representational* devices that are widely employed: the *isolux contour* and the *Daylight Factor profile*. The isolux contour diagram shows a series of contour lines—analogous to a topographical map—that indicate *equivalent Daylight Factor levels* (see Figure 8.20). Each contour line then is a *locus* of points (or locations within the building space), along which the same Daylight Factor is found (e.g., 1 percent, 2 percent, 5 percent, and so forth). The Daylight Factor profile is commonly derived from an isolux contour diagram. The DF profile will be shown in a sectional view of the space that is being investigated or described. The profile is established by creating a vertical plane drawn perpendicular to the window surface and projecting into the building space. This DF profile is usually drawn for a plane constructed at the mid-point of the window width. Where the plane intersects each isolux contour line, a point on the vertical plane is generated (i.e., the magnitude of the Daylight Factor corresponds to the height of the point on the plane; the higher the Daylight Factor, the higher the point appears on this vertical plane). When the various points of intersection are identified, a line connecting these points can then be drawn. Thus, a graph is constructed of the magnitudes of the Daylight Factor contours versus the distance of any contour point from the window (see Figure 8.21). The resulting line on this graph demonstrates how the amounts of the Daylight Factor will vary from the front to the back of the building space. This line—the Daylight Factor profile—also shows how effectively daylight will penetrate into the space. The utility of these DF profiles is dual: by drawing a line parallel to the abscissa (the x-axis) *representing the minimum acceptable Daylight Factor requirement* for the activity for which the space is to be employed, the designer can see what parts of the space will have adequate daylighting; and the shape of the DF profile can display the *rate of change* of illumination levels across the space. Where this change rate is large, occupants may often experience excessive brightness and even visual discomfort due to the presence of glare (see Figure 8.22).

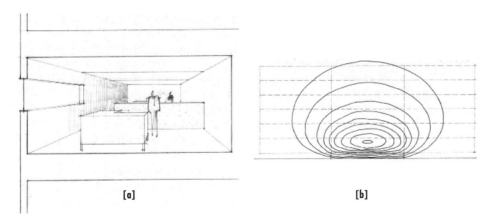

[a]   [b]

Figure 8.20 In (a), a view of a typical open-plan office is shown with a single-sided window that delivers daylight into the office space. In (b), the Daylight Factor contours (for the Sky Component) are displayed for the window. Each point along a contour will have the same Daylight Factor value as any other point on the contour (thus, each contour is an *isolux* contour). In this representation, the heavy, solid line at the base of the image is the inner (perimeter) edge of the exterior wall. Each of the dotted rectangles matches the size of the window. Additionally, the distance that the workplane (on which daylight is measured) stands above the floor is equal to the distance from the heavy, solid line at the base of this image and the first dotted line running parallel to the heavy, solid line. The furthest solid contour has a value of 1 percent, and each succeeding contour moving inward toward the exterior wall increases by an increment of 1 percent. Thus, the Daylight Factor values (for the Sky Component) *along* the small elliptically shaped line in the "center" of the contour rings are 8 percent.

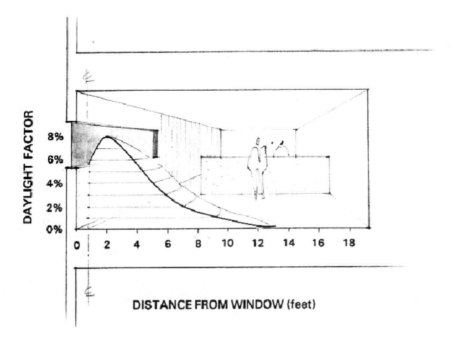

Figure 8.21 The Daylight Factor profile for the window shown in Figure 8.20(a) and for the Daylight Factor contours displayed in Figure 8.20(b) is presented.

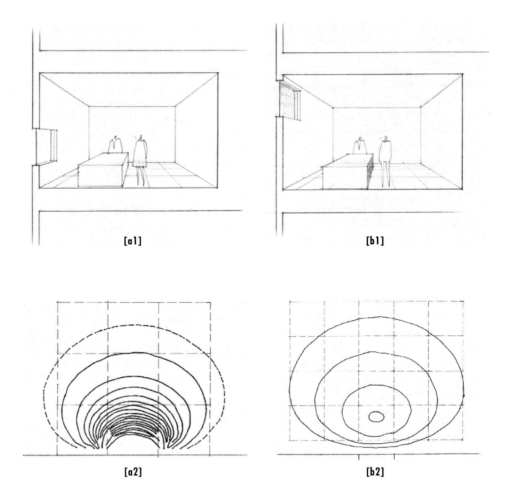

[a1]　　　　　　　　　　　[b1]

[a2]　　　　　　　　　　　[b2]

Figure 8.22 In (a1), a single-sided window is shown for an office space. This window, seen in elevation, is basically square. The DF contour pattern (for the Sky Component) for this window is presented in (a2). Alternatively, in (b1), a similarly square, equal-sized, single-sided window for another office space is shown. And, in (b2), the DF contour pattern (for the Sky Component) for this second window is presented. The difference in formats for these two windows is their relative locations in the window wall: the (a) window occurs with its sill at approximately the height of the workplace, whereas the (b) window is a clerestory with its sill above the heads of the office workers. The resultant DF contour patterns (for the respective Sky Components) for these two alternative-height windows show that, for (a), the pattern displays a large brightness gradient across the workplane area near the window and that, for (b), a much more gentle brightness gradient occurs across a workplane (at 76 cm or 30 in). For occupants working in (a) with the low window in their view fields, excessive brightness and glare will frequently be problems. Instead, workers using daylight from the clerestory in (b) will experience a much more uniform light distribution and will likely find little glare around the workplane.

This example has been derived from the *Graphic Daylighting Design Method Workbook* (developed by M.S. Millet and J.R. Bedrick of the Department of Architecture at the University of Washington).

SIDEBAR 8.15 Difficulties arising from too dim or too bright lighting

Having inadequate daylighting across a space can create a dimness or murkiness in areas some distance from windows, which occupants may find bothersome. Lighting designers and consultants describe this ill-lighted condition as *gloom*. The presence of gloom in work and other building spaces often causes occupant dissatisfaction with the spaces. Anecdotal reports about gloomy spaces have indicated that workers' attitudes are more negative and the performances of these workers suffer. However, descriptions of what constitutes gloom are often manifestly subjective. Further, statements about what lighting conditions are acceptable or not frequently vary widely across any randomly chosen population. So, the definition of gloom and the conditions that cause gloom have been only loosely studied. Some recent studies have been initiated to provide more precise information about the properties of gloom (or, indeed, the properties of spaces that are gloomy). Reports about these studies appear in papers by Rothwell, S.E., and F.W. Campbell, "The physiological basis for

the sensation of gloom: quantitative and qualitative aspects," *Ophthalmic and Physiological Optics*, 7(2), 1987, pages 161–163; and Shepherd, A.J., W.G. Julian, and A.T. Purcell, "Gloom as a psychophysical phenomenon," *Lighting Research and Technology*, 21(3), 1989, pages 89–97.

Solutions for overcoming these problems—having too little daylight or having too steep a DF gradient—are similar. Some solutions include altering the proposed window (e.g., its size or material), adding other windows, and/or furnishing electric illumination. Changing the window shape can modify the isolux contours and the DF profile, perhaps furnishing more light or reducing the DF gradient. Adding other windows or electric illumination could increase the illuminance, thus improving the brightness levels. Such solutions should all seek to create a more-balanced distribution of illumination across the space. Further discussions about potential solutions will be presented in Chapter 9.

8.3.4   DESIGNING WITH ALTERNATIVE DAYLIGHT FACTOR DESIGN AIDS

Estimation of Daylight Factor magnitudes and the resulting demonstration of daylight distribution patterns for a building space can enable a designer to predict whether adequate illumination is present. Developing isolux contour lines and DF profiles—to examine daylight distribution patterns—for a building space can be performed in any of four ways. First, for a given building design—when planar and sectional views have been drawn and information is known about the nature of any window assembly (e.g., what the shape, location, and materials of the window are)—a designer can iteratively estimate the Daylight Factor magnitude at each of several locations within the proposed space using a Daylight Factor Protractor. Then, using these DF values for the locations, the designer can lay out these DF values on the building plan and connect locations of equal DF levels (thus, identifying isolux contours). Subsequently, the designer can derive a DF profile for the contour pattern (i.e., by taking a sectional cut at whatever location along the window width seems appropriate).

A second means for generating isolux contours for a given window and building space situation employs an extensive catalog of Sky Component contour *templates* that have been derived for various (vertical) window and (horizontal) skylight geometries. This catalogue of templates is known as the *Graphic Daylighting Design Method Workbook.*[23] This *Workbook* can be found at the address http://www.caup.washington.edu/gddm.

The utility of the *Workbook* is dual. First, it offers an accelerated means for establishing Sky Component isolux contours and, thus, a much more rapid means of deriving Daylight Factor contours for a window or a skylight. Second, the template catalog enables the quick determination of which window shapes and locations will supply appropriate daylight distribution patterns. Thus, a designer can compare alternative templates — representing different window shapes and locations — to establish which window shape and location will furnish a sought-after daylight distribution pattern.

To use this *Workbook,* a designer first identifies a *shape parameter* and a *location parameter* for a given opening. Then, using these two parameters, s/he looks through the series of contour templates, seeking the one that is uniquely identified by the combination of the two parameters. When the appropriate template is found, the Sky Component contour pattern for the opening is thereby established. For instance, for a vertical window, the *shape parameter* is the ratio of the dimension of the opening in the vertical direction versus the dimension of the opening in the horizontal direction (expressed as a decimal fraction). The *location parameter* is the ratio of the vertical distance between the sill of the

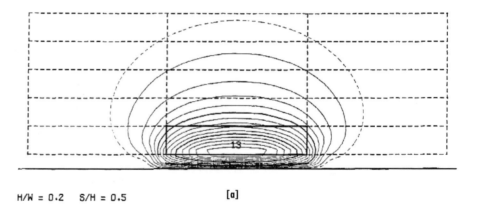

H/W = 0.2   S/H = 0.5   [a]

Figure 8.23 These two images are templates from the *Graphic Daylighting Design Method Workbook.* Template (a) is for a skylight that has equal-sided width and length and a height above the workplane that is 1.8 times the width of the skylight. Template (b) is for a (vertical) window with a height-to-width ratio of 1:5 and a sill height above the standardized workplane that is equal to 0.5 times the window height.

For this example we have set the window height as 4' (1.22 m) and the window length as 20' (6.09 m). The skylight is 4' (1.22 m) by 4' (1.22 m) and is 7'-2 1/2" (2.19 m) above the workplane.

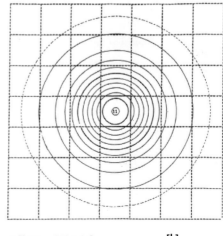

L/W = 1   S/W = 1.8   [b]

opening and the work surface (for which the daylight factor contours are sought) versus the dimension of the opening in the vertical direction. The location parameter is also, expressed as a decimal fraction. For a skylight, the shape parameter is the ratio of the "long" dimension versus the "short" dimension, and the location parameter is the ratio of the height of the skylight above the work surface versus the "short" dimension. In either instance (whether for window or skylight), when the designer or consultant finds the isolux contour pattern identified by the combination of the two parametric values, the template thus establishes the Sky Component (see Figure 8.23). The addition of the Internally-Reflected Component to the Sky Component magnitudes must be made by hand (although this is a comparatively easy step). To determine Daylight Factor values, the magnitudes of the Sky Component and the Internally-Reflected Component are added. Then, the resulting sum is modified by multiplying it by the correction factors to account for the transmittance of the window material, the fraction of the window consisting of framing, and how clean is the window surface.

Note, however, that identifying the Sky Component isolux contour pattern fundamentally establishes the form of the ultimate Daylight Factor contour pattern for the window or skylight. Adding the Internally-Reflected Component and multiplying the sum (of the SC and IRC) by the materials, framing, and maintenance factors result in changes in the magnitude for each contour line, but the overall pattern will remain unchanged even after performing these addition and multiplication procedures.

If a designer is simply looking for a good approximation of what the DF contours will be within the space, then s/he may ignore the IRC value altogether (i.e., the magnitude of the IRC often tends to be small relative to the magnitude of the Sky Component). One additional thought about the *Graphic Daylighting Design Method* is that it is especially suitable for examining the daylight presence when there are two (or more) openings in the building envelope that encloses a space. In the situation where multiple openings are present, then the designer can establish the isolux contour pattern for each opening. By superimposing—overlaying—the patterns on top of one another and adding the DF values accordingly, a designer can develop a total representation (see Figure 8.24).

SIDEBAR 8.16 Accounting for the Externally-Reflected Component when using the Graphic Daylighting Design Method contours

The *Graphic Daylighting Design Method* as it was developed does not directly accommodate the Externally-Reflected Component. If a precise description of Daylight Factor contours on some work surface is needed, the use of these templates can be limited to situations for which no external objects cause obstructed views of the sky. Alternatively, if the DF contours are being sought to provide an approximate indication of daylight presence within a building, then either the ERC could be ignored or an estimate could be made using something like the BRS Daylight Protractors to determine the ERC. To a marked extent, when selecting which of these latter two approaches to take concerning the ERC, it might be better to perform a few sample calculations of the ERC and consider their magnitudes in comparison to the SC. If, indeed, the ERC is substantially smaller than the SC, then neglecting the ERC is a quite reasonable judgment. If the ERC is more like 25 percent (or more) of the SC, then making some adjustment to the SC defined by these templates would be warranted.

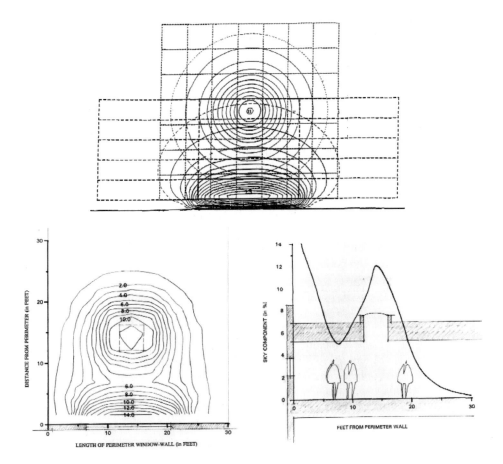

Figure 8.24 The top image is a composite overlay of the two templates shown in Figure 8.23. For this overlay the scales of the two templates have been resolved to a common scale. In the lower left image a summary contour map has been derived showing the Sky Component composite for these two envelope openings. Then, in the lower right image a composite Sky Component profile is presented for the openings. To derive a Daylight Factor Profile from the SC profile it would be necessary to add in the value for the Internally-Reflected Component and then multiply the resulting sum by the correction factors for the window assemblies.

The third method for generating isolux contours and DF profiles is to use any one of a number of computer programs that have been written specifically to create such representations. The particular utility of these programs is that the amount of time required for determining the daylight presence in a building space can be reduced substantially in comparison to the time required for similar determinations by other means. Some of these programs are comparatively easy to use, whereas others are intended primarily as research packages. Generally, the simpler ones offer relatively approximate solutions and are usable only for building situations in which there are at most one or two openings in the envelope. Alternatively, the more elaborate programs may be able to evaluate daylighting in building spaces, where as many as 10 or more discrete openings, complicated space geometries, and alternative window materials are proposed for the envelope.

SIDEBAR 8.17 Identifying some computer programs for the modeling of daylight presence in buildings

Three daylight simulation programs that are well-regarded by the professional community and that are commercially available are *Lumen Micro,* which has been developed by Lighting Technologies, Inc., of Denver, Colorado (see http://www.lighting-technologies.com/); *Lightscape,* which has been composed by Autodesk, of San Rafael, California (see http://www.lightscape.com/); and *Radiance* and *Desktop Radiance,* which have been developed by the Lawrence Berkeley National Laboratory, of Berkeley, California (see http://radsite.lbl.gov/radiance).

The fourth means for predicting daylight presence in buildings employs physical, reduced-scale models. During schematic designing or later design phases, models of proposed buildings and their envelope openings can be constructed. Common scales that are used for schematic designing range from 1:100 to 1:10. Once a scaled model has been constructed, the nature of the illumination entering through envelope openings can be studied under either clear or overcast sky conditions (i.e., using either direct-beam or diffuse illuminance). The particular utilities of reduced-scale models are that both qualitative and quantitative studies of daylight admission can readily be performed. Modification of these models, once they are constructed, is often comparatively easy so that alternative window designs can be evaluated.[24]

The choice of which of these four methods of representation to use (or whether to use any representation at all) will depend on what you want to know and what you need to show. A technique like the BRS Daylighting Protractors can be used very quickly and is best for addressing simple window situations. These protractors will furnish approximate results with relatively little effort and should not get in the way of the flow of schematic designing. Alternatively, the *Graphic Daylighting Design Method* requires more time and attention as a technique for representing (or evaluating) daylighting presence in a proposed design. But a cardinal strength of the *GDDM Workbook* is that it serves as a *catalogue* of isolux contours. This catalogue can be applied as a reference document to see what daylighting capabilities any likely window-and-space situation will offer. The computer programs should probably be reserved for use in *evaluating* schematic design alternatives, particularly where multiple openings are present, or for *fine-tuning* envelope opening designs during the design development phase. Lastly, the construction and testing of building models offer means for visualizing how daylight will illuminate modeled spaces across a day and throughout the year.

Section 8.4 | HOW MUCH LIGHT DO YOU NEED?

In the previous sections of this chapter we have treated windows and the sky as resources that illuminate human tasks: the sky serves as the natural light source; windows admit the light into the building. In addition, we have described the character of the sky and a device for predicting or evaluating the performance of windows. The next question that we will consider, then, is how much light do we need to perform the various tasks that we encounter during our work and life activities? In turn, we will identify a series of industry standards that recommend or prescribe the quantities of light needed for task performance. Further, we will explain the bases for these standards.

8.4.1   WHAT ARE THE BASES FOR LIGHTING STANDARDS?

The principal intention in setting lighting standards is to ensure that people will have sufficient illumination to perform their various life tasks. These tasks can occur within buildings or out-of-doors. The standards offer guidelines for designers, builders, and managers, indicating what amounts of lighting are recommended. These standards also suggest, generally in less detail, how light should be provided (e.g., what are the "quality" issues associated with providing illumination and what devices might best supply the recommended illumination). The term *quality* concerns such topics as insuring visual comfort (e.g., minimizing glare), controlling color presence and distribution, and generally providing suitably aesthetic treatments. Because of the intangible natures of these and related issues, it is frequently difficult to offer — within standards — quantitative or well-bounded descriptions about such issues. In some instances, standards may suggest that a designer or manager should consider such issues. But, commonly, the standards will not offer explicit definitions about such issues (or how to approach them). The physical means for supplying the illumination levels are, of course, left to building designers, builders, and managers to select, assemble, and operate. But, throughout, the fundamental basis for the various lighting standards is the intention of insuring that occupants will have enough light to perform visual tasks.

In Section 7.4.2.1 we identified the five major environmental parameters that determine our abilities to perform visual tasks (i.e., that enable us to see well). These parameters affect how readily we can gather visual information from the world around us and process that information so that we understand it. These five parameters include the *size* of the object to be seen; the amount of *contrast* between the object and the area around it; the *light* falling on the object; the *luminance distribution* across the object and the background area surrounding the object; and the amount of *time* that an individual has to see the object. The effects of these five parameters on insuring good visual conditions are interrelated (e.g., if the object is large, we need less time to see it; if the contrast between the object and its background is appropriately high, the object can be made smaller; and so forth). So, when we ask how much light we need to provide for the performance of some task utilizing vision, we should recognize that the natures of these other four parameters would markedly affect how much light is needed.

SIDEBAR 8.18 Standards versus codes

An essential point concerning standards is they are simply recommendations offered, mostly, by specific professional organizations and, occasionally, by a national governmental body. The difference between a standard and a code (or regulation) is that the standard commonly has no force of legislative fiat behind it, whereas a code will generally have some law that mandates that designers, builders, and building managers must comply with the tenets of the code. Thus, three of the lighting level standards that we will identify in Section 8.4 are simply recommendations that have been offered by professional organizations. The fourth is part of the British building code.

Relationships between the amount of light incident on the task surface and the other four task (and environmental) parameters have been studied for more than 100 years. The methods of testing lighting conditions have involved either examinations of the physiology of human vision or evaluation of the abilities of subjects to perform tasks comparable to common work (or life) situations. Because the human visual system is complex and its operation is not entirely understood, these tests generally employ procedures that only reveal limited insights, about the system and its operation. So, the chief problem for scientists who have examined the human visual system and its performance has been how to integrate the many different studies and their results. A related problem has concerned how to distill—from these studies—guidelines about what lighting levels should be provided to enable the performances of various tasks.

A committee of the Commission Internationale De L'Eclairage (CIE) has prepared a report discussing the relationships between lighting levels, the other four parameters, and their combined effects on visual performance.[25] The report offers perhaps the most comprehensive summary of research results about the human visual system and how these five task (and environmental) parameters should be interpreted for generating lighting levels. Insights about these parameters and how they influence visual performance (and visual acuity) have been offered in Section 7.4.2. In the next section—8.4.2—we will briefly describe how lighting standards have been derived in relation to these parameters.

The principal concern in defining lighting levels is to foster confidence that these levels will enable good visual performances. Further, insuring good visual performances means that an occupant working or living under these levels can complete visual activities with a minimum of visually induced errors and as little visual discomfort as possible.[26] One other concern that must be confronted when specifying lighting levels is to ensure that these levels will not be excessive: too much light or too nonuniform distributions can produce conditions like excessive brightness and glare. Indeed, one possible consequence of having too much light incident on a task surface is that there will be a need to increase light on the

---

SIDEBAR 8.19 A qualification to defining lighting needs based simply on luminance assessments

The characterization of lighting conditions based solely on luminance appears not to recognize the influence that the spectral properties of light can have on the utility of the light. Recent studies indicate that the brightness of light—as sensed and reported on by test subjects—does not always match measured luminance amounts. Such differences between brightness and luminance amounts are attributed to the spectral properties of the test lighting, which is revealed by the sensing of brightness and is left unaccounted for by simple luminance measurements. Thus, at some future time, lighting standards will likely have to integrate statements about both the spectral properties and the luminance of light supplied for task performance. A series of articles describe the research on this topic: Burns, S.A., V.C. Smith, J. Pokorny, A.E. Elsner, "Brightness of equal-luminance lights," *Journal of the Optical Society of America,* 72(9), September 1982, pages 1225–1231; Altman, D.H., M.E. Breton, and J. Barbour, "New results on the brightness matching of heterochromatic stimuli," *Journal of the Illuminating Engineering Society,* 12(4), July 1983, pages 268–274; Howett, G.L., "The coming redefinition of photometry," *Journal of the Illuminating Engineering Society,* 15(2), Summer 1986, pages 5–18; and Berman, S.M., D.L. Jewett, G. Fein, G. Saika, and F. Ashford, "Photopic luminance does not always predict perceived room brightness," *Lighting Research and Technology,* 22(1), 1990, pages 37–41.

background surfaces. Thus, additional energy will have to be expended to create a suitable luminance distribution across the visual field. Alternatively, too bright conditions can cause visual discomfort if the eye cannot adapt upward to the brightness or if the eye cannot adapt quickly enough (i.e., when the time for viewing is comparatively brief).

One further consideration in defining lighting levels for human activities is to establish what amounts are *acceptable* and what amounts are *preferable.* The definition of what is acceptable should no doubt be determined by considering visual performance requirements. But the lowest acceptable lighting levels for an application will also depend upon the value ranges for the other four environmental parameters. So, for instance, lighting levels for a workstation should be specified by recognizing the range of contrast that will likely be present between the task surface and its background. Similarly, the decision about the lighting level at a workstation should also be based on the range of object sizes that will probably be experienced. But, still, an acceptable lighting level for the performance of some task may not be the amount of lighting that people would prefer.

Virtually all of the research that has served as the basis for defining lighting levels has examined the question of what lighting conditions are needed — thus, are acceptable — for performing some sort of test. A small number of studies, however, have explored what lighting conditions people *would prefer to have* for living and work activities. Amongst this latter category, most research has addressed color preferences under artificial illumination. But a few studies have permitted subjects to define what lighting conditions they preferred.

One study by Tregenza et al. placed subjects, one at a time, in a windowless room. These subjects — female secretarial workers at the University of Nottingham — were asked to perform a series of typing, reading, and sorting tasks. While doing these tasks, each subject was asked to adjust the lighting conditions within the room so that these conditions were most suitable for the performance of these tasks. Six electric lamps directed light at the four walls, ceiling, and work surface; each could be independently controlled. The results of this test appear mixed. There was wide variation in the amount of illumination that was preferred. Generally, the amount of illumination preferred became greater as the age of the subject increased and as the visual difficulty of the task increased. To some extent, the preferred amount of lighting varied directly with the lighting levels at the start of each test (i.e., the higher the starting level, the higher the overall preferred level was). But the amount of increase (from the starting levels) seemed to be similar across the study group. Perhaps the two most interesting results were that the subjects — considered collectively — appeared to be satisfied with a broad range of conditions and, when these subjects

---

SIDEBAR 8.20 Seasonal Affective Disorder

Seasonal Affective Disorder is a condition that appears to link feelings of depression with seasonality. Specifically, during the winter months when the days are both shorter and the skies are more frequently overcast (and darker), numbers of individuals report feelings of increased depression. Individuals affected by SAD report that their depressive states occur more often and are more intense than those they experience during other times of the year. Presently, one form of therapy that is being tested for these individuals is placing them for a sustained period of time daily — usually, up to an hour — in front of a bank of lamps with very high brightness. Further information about SAD can be found in the book edited by Rosenthal, N.E., and M.C. Blehar, *Seasonal Affective Disorders and Phototherapy,* (New York: Guilford Press, 1989).

were tested repeatedly over a period of some two weeks, the responses of the subjects were consistent. The authors of this study closed their report with the proviso that, despite the results listed here, there was no clear identification of any illuminance magnitude that seemed best or most preferable.[27]

J. Heerwagen has conducted a second study that offers some insight about preferred lighting conditions. While testing a comparatively heterogeneous group of 20 subjects in Seattle about a condition known as Seasonal Affective Disorder (SAD), information was also sought about lighting level preferences for performing office tasks. One principal result of this study is the finding that one group of subjects — that identified themselves as suffering from SAD — consistently preferred lighting levels on the work surface one-and-one-half to three times brighter than the other subjects (who indicated no especial SAD affliction). Further, when tested for the preferred brightness of a *simulated* window (i.e., a screen that showed a scene similar to what a window might and whose brightness could be controlled by adjusting an electric lamp combination placed behind it), this first group demonstrated brightness preferences that were generally two to three times greater than the second group did.[28]

A third study described by Van Ooyen et al. has examined preferred luminances and luminance distributions for work settings. In this experiment the researchers employed three two-person offices, each of which had wall reflectances different from the other two. The lighting in the rooms — achieved either by daylighting or with electric fixtures — was organized to provide a constant illuminance measured on the task surface (750 lux) and variable luminances directed at the work surface immediately surrounding (and supporting) the task surface and the walls of each room. The luminances of light directed at the work surface and at the walls varied across the ranges of 20–200 cd/m² and 12–92 cd/m², respectively. The subjects were asked to perform one of four common office tasks — reading a

SIDEBAR 8.21 Two additional office space lighting studies

Two other studies that provide interesting information about office lighting needs have been written by Henderson, R.L., J.F. McNelis, and H.G. Williams, "A survey of important visual tasks in offices," *Lighting Design & Application*, 5(1), January 1975, pages 18–25; and McKennan, G.T., and C.M. Parry, "An investigation of task lighting for offices," *Lighting Research & Technology*, 16(4), 1984, pages 171–186. The paper by Henderson et al. presents a summary of the visual tasks usually performed in offices. The natures of these tasks are then characterized, including both examples and viewing conditions (which will improve seeing). The second paper — by McKennan and Parry — describes a study in which an office environment was simulated and subjects performed a series of common office tasks. The authors examined the subjects' preferences for task and/or uniform lighting conditions and found that task lighting was preferred. But these researchers noted that if the fixtures providing uniform lighting conditions were carefully placed, the resulting lighting was also favorably regarded by the subjects. A further, interesting outcome of this study was that well-developed lighting conditions — involving suitable task and surrounding surface lighting distributions, but operating at lower-than-usual levels — could provide occupant satisfactions equal to those found for other distributions that used higher lighting levels. Thus, by employing distributions with these reduced lighting levels, future occupants would likely be satisfied with the lighting and could operate the lighting systems with lowered rates of energy consumption (i.e., relative to other conventional lighting solutions).

glossy-paged magazine; writing something out on matte paper; working at a workstation monitor; or conducting an interview with another subject—and then to complete a brief questionnaire that asked the subjects to describe what degree of visual comfort and satisfaction they experienced as they performed the task. The researchers reported a series of conclusions, four of which we will mention here. First, the subjects preferred to have the work surface luminance and the wall luminance vary inversely (i.e., as the work surface luminance was increased, the subjects sought lowered wall luminances, and vice versa). Second, the particular combinations of work surface and wall luminances, which were preferred for each task, depended on the task: generally, the subjects preferred lower luminances on both the work surface and the wall surfaces when working with a workstation monitor and higher luminances on the work and wall surfaces for completing the other office tasks. Third, the preferences espoused by the subjects were strongly determined by the magnitudes of the wall luminance; the work surface luminances were deemed to be less significant. And, fourth, the ratio of preferred luminances on the task surface, the surrounding work surface, and the walls was 10:4:3. For the three tasks (other than the workstation monitor), the preferred luminances ranged from 30–60 cd/m² for the walls and 45–105 cd/m² for the work surface; for the workstation monitor, the preferred luminances ranged from 20–45 cd/m² for the walls and 40–65 cd/m² for the work surface. Whether these values are generally applicable to offices will seemingly require further verification. However, the most significant result derived from this report of *preferred* luminance values would appear to be that there are considerable differences, across a group of individuals, about what lighting conditions are indeed preferred.[29]

These three studies suggest that although people can generally perform useful work at lower lighting levels, at least some individuals will actually prefer substantially higher levels, if they can be attained. For the designer, then, the primary responsibility is to ensure that some minimally acceptable level can be maintained. Then, the designer should seek to offer sufficient flexibility so that higher lighting levels can be provided, if individuals wish (or need) them. Further, care must be taken to ensure that these higher levels will not cause excessive brightness.

8.4.2   WHAT ARE THE PRIMARY LIGHTING STANDARDS?

The amount of illumination considered necessary for performing some task has undergone substantial redefinition in the century since lighting standards were first written. A general trend of the first 70 years of this period was a continuing increase in minimally acceptable levels (for examples, see Figures 8.25 and 8.26). Figure 8.25 presents *reported* lighting levels (for the years from 1910 to about 1930) and then *recommended* lighting levels (for the years from 1930 until about 1975) for offices and schools in Great Britain. This graph displays a steady rise in levels continuously from 1910 until the late 1960s.[30] From Figure 8.26 one can see that a similar pattern of lighting level increases has occurred in the United States for much of the same period.[31] Explanations for this regular increase occurring up to about 1970 are two-fold: first, results from scientific research—conducted up to the late 1960s—on the physiology of vision and the measurement of visual performance encouraged the continuing increases in minimum lighting levels; and, second, during this period electric lighting became the primary means for providing adequate illumination. Further, through a series of technical innovations, the luminous efficacy of lamps also steadily increased, (i.e., providing ever more light from a given amount of electricity).

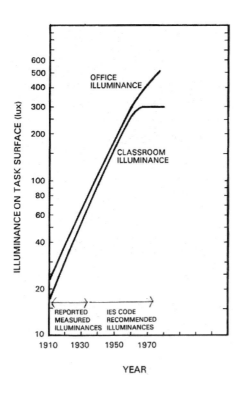

Figure 8.25 This graph shows the change in recommended task illuminances for British offices and classrooms for the period from 1910 until the 1970s.

This graph has previously been published in a paper by Collins, J.B., "The illuminating engineer in a changing world," *Lighting Research & Technology,* 9(1), 1977, pages 1–10. Permission to reproduce this graph has been granted by Arnold Publishers, Ltd.

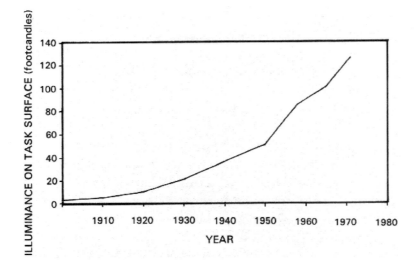

Figure 8.26 This graph displays recommended illuminances on (undesignated) task surfaces in the United States from 1910 until 1970. The source of the information from which this figure has been plotted is a paper by Cooper, B.C., "A statistical look at the future of lighting," *Lighting Design and Application,* 1(1), July 1971, pages 14–23. Permission to publish this graph has been granted by the Illuminating Engineering Society of North America (IESNA).

TABLE 8.1
RECOMMENDED LIGHTING LEVELS (attributed to the CIE)

VISUAL TASK	ILLUMINANCE, IN LUX (foot candles)	WORK SITUATIONS
Simple	300 to 750 (27.9 to 69.7)	Rough industrial work
Normal	500 to 1000 (46.5 to 92.9)	Offices, machine shops, carpentry
Fine	1000 to 2000 (92.9 to 185.9)	Drawing offices, tailoring, quality inspection

---

This table was introduced by J.B. de Boer, who was president of the CIE, in an address—the Trotter-Paterson Memorial Lecture, presented at a meeting of the CIBS Lighting Division at the RIBA in London on 10 March 1982—that was subsequently published in the journal, *Lighting Research & Technology,* Volume 14, No. 4, 1982, pages 207–221. Permission to reproduce this graph has been granted by the Chartered Institution of Building Services Engineers.

TABLE 8.2
RECOMMENDED MAXIMUM LIGHTING LEVELS
(AS SPECIFIED BY THE U.S. FEDERAL ENERGY ADMINISTRATION, 1975)

TASK or AREA	LIGHTING LEVELS (in foot candles)	HOW MEASURED
Hallways or corridors	10 +/– 5	Measured average (allowable minimum = 1 fc)
Work and circulation areas	30 +/– 5	Measured average surrounding work stations
Normal office work, such as reading & writing (on task only), store shelves, and general display areas	50 +/– 10	Measured at work station
Prolonged office work that is somewhat difficult visually (on task only)	75 +/– 10	Measured at work station
Prolonged office work that is visually difficult and critical in nature (on task only)	100 +/– 20	Measured at work station
Industrial tasks	See ANSI Standard A11.1-1973	As maximum

Source: *Lighting and Thermal Operations: Energy Conservation Principles Applied to Office Lighting,* (prepared by Ross & Baruzzini, Inc., St. Louis, Missouri), (Washington,D.C.: Federal Energy Administration, April 1975), page V-6.

Recent developments have shown some reductions in this pattern of increasing lighting level minimums. Two reasons seem most significant for these changes from past history. First, following the oil embargoes of the early and middle 1970s, electricity costs increased substantially, leading to a rapid rise in the cost of space lighting. Such price increases encouraged rethinking about what industry standards might say about acceptable lighting levels. Second, at about the same time as the oil embargoes, some of the research that had served as bases for the recommended increases in lighting levels was being questioned. The questioning concerned whether the older studies were accurate and thus served as reasonable bases for the setting of lighting level guidelines. One issue that was raised was whether the *experimental* tasks used to derive prescribed lighting levels were really comparable to the *actual* tasks encountered in work, school, and home settings. Another subject of concern addressed the validity of using *simulated* environments as locations for testing. A third series of questions considered how well the results of the studies were integrated with tests about the other four major (and some of the less major) environmental parameters that affect visual acuity and performance (i.e., as we presented in Section 7.4).

Presently, acceptable lighting levels tend to be somewhat lower than those defined in the period up to 1970. New research about suitable lighting levels is being conducted, and the results from these studies will likely influence the writings of future standards and codes. Additionally, issues of economics and resource availability also contribute to the settings of new standards (e.g., needs to match *fixed* electrical generation capacities with *expanding* electricity demands are inducing positive conservation efforts in many locations throughout the industrialized world).

We will identify four lighting level standards that are (or have been) used for building designing in various locations throughout the world. To some extent, these standards are not directly comparable, primarily because they consider somewhat different lighting conditions and are expressed with alternative unit systems. Thus, you should exercise some care in selecting from among these four standards. Nevertheless, the four standards are "recommended lighting levels" from the Commission Internationale De L'Eclairage; "recommended maximum lighting levels" originally espoused by the (U.S). Federal Energy Administration (a precursor to the U.S. Department of Energy); "currently recommended illuminance categories and illuminance values for lighting design" from the Illuminating Engineering Society (of North America); and "recommended values of general or minimum daylight factor in buildings" from the Illuminating Engineering Society (London). Other standards exist; for instance, many national lighting codes are observed throughout the world. We have selected these four to indicate the diversity of their contents and to show a range of different means for presenting these standards.

First, "recommended lighting levels" specified by the CIE are shown in Table 8.1. These levels are founded on the character of the detail that will be experienced — or the size of objects that must be discriminated — in the performance of some visual task.

Second, "recommended maximum lighting levels" is a standard that was published by the (U.S). Federal Energy Administration (see Table 8.2). For this standard the organization identified six groups of tasks considering the severity or difficulty of the visual task as the basis for the groupings. Then, for each such grouping, a *maximum* lighting level was recommended. In spite of the fact that the Federal Energy Administration no longer exists, this standard still has relevance as a historical reference.

Third, "currently recommended illuminance categories and illuminance values for lighting design" is a standard that has been published in the *Illuminating Engineering Society (of North America) Handbook.*[32] This standard identifies nine *categories of activity* and lists ranges of illuminances recommended for these activities (see Table 8.3). These illuminance ranges depend on the difficulty of the visual task involved in performing the specific activity type. Application of this standard occurs by identifying the specific task in which occupants of a space will likely be engaged and determining what *category of activity* matches the specific task (i.e., a process that involves searching the extensive catalogue of tasks and finding what activity category corresponds to the task).[33]

Fourth, "recommended values of general or minimum daylight factor in buildings" presented by the Illuminating Engineering Society (London) are not stated in terms of illuminance values (as are the other three standards cited here). Rather, this standard specifies lighting levels for various building applications in terms of *Daylight Factors* (see Table 8.4).

TABLE 8.3
DETERMINATION OF ILLUMINANCE CATEGORIES

Orientation and simple visual tasks. Visual performance is largely unimportant. These tasks are found in public spaces where reading and visual inspection are only occasionally performed. Higher levels are recommended for tasks where visual performance is occasionally important.

A	Public spaces	30 lx (3 fc)
B	Simple orientation for short visits	50lx (5 fc)
C	Working spaces where simple visual tasks are performed	100 lx (10 fc)

Common visual tasks. Visual performance is important. These tasks are found in commercial, industrial and residential applications. Recommended illuminance levels differ because of the characteristics of the visual task being illuminated. Higher levels are recommended for visual tasks with critical elements of low contrast or small size.

D	Performance of visual tasks of high contrast and large size	300 lx (30 fc)
E	Performance of visual tasks of high contrast and small size, or visual tasks of low contrast and large size	500 lx (50 fc)
F	Performance of visual tasks of low contrast and small size	1000 lx (100 fc)

Special visual tasks. Visual performance is of critical importance. These tasks are very specialized, including those with very small or very low contrast critical elements. Recommended illuminance levels should be achieved with supplementary task lighting. Higher recommended levels are often achieved by moving the light source closer to the task.

G	Performance of visual tasks near the threshold	3000 to 10,000 lx (300 to 1000 fc)

---

* Expected accuracy in illuminance calculations are given in Chapter 9, Lighting Calculations [of the *2000 IESNA Lighting Handbook*]. To account for both uncertainty in photometric measurements and uncertainty in space reflections, measured illuminances should be with ± 10% of the recommended value. It should be noted, however, that the final illuminance may deviate from these recommended values due to other lighting design criteria.

Reprinted from page 10-13 of the *IESNA Lighting Handbook,* 2000, courtesy of the Illuminating Engineering Society of North America.

TABLE 8.4
RECOMMENDED VALUES OF GENERAL OR MINIMUM DAYLIGHT FACTOR IN BUILDINGS
(AS SPECIFIED BY THE [U.K.] BUILDING RESEARCH ESTABLISHMENT)

BUILDING TYPE	RECOMMENDED DAYLIGHT FACTOR (IN %)	QUALIFICATIONS AND/OR RECOMMENDATIONS
DWELLINGS		
Kitchen	2	Over at least 50% of floor area (minimum of 50 sqft or 4.5 m2)
Living room	1	Over at least 50% of floor area (minimum of 75 sqft or 7.0 m2)
Bedroom	0.5	Over at least 75% of floor area (minimum of 60 sqft or 5.5 m2)
SCHOOLS	2*	Over all teaching areas and kitchens
HOSPITALS	1	Over all ward areas
OFFICES		
General	1	Side-lighted, at a penetration of 12 ft or 3.5m
	2	Top-lighted, over whole area
Drawing offices	6	On drawing boards
	2	Over remainder of working area
Typing and composing	4	Over whole working area
LABORATORIES	3 to 6	Depending on dominance of side or top lighting
FACTORIES	5	General recommendation
ART GALLERIES	6	Maximum on walls or screens where no special problems of fading
CHURCHES	1	General, over whole area
	1.5 to 2	In sanctuary area
PUBLIC BUILDINGS	1	Depending upon function, the recommendation may exceed 1%, but a minimum value of 1% is generally desirable for amenity in most public buildings

* Statutory requirement, The Standard for School Premises Regulation, 1959.

This table is reprinted from the document by Longmore, J., *BRS Protractors,* (London: Her Majesty's Stationery Office, 1968), page 21.

Section 8.5 | DESIGNING FOR DAYLIGHTING

8.5.1 ALTERNATIVE APPROACHES FOR USING THESE STANDARDS FOR DESIGNING WINDOWS

These first three standards presume that a designer will mix daylight and electric light sources to provide the recommended levels of illumination. If, however, a designer wishes to determine whether daylighting alone can be used for illuminating a space, then it is possible to evaluate a proposed window (and building space) design for daylight presence. The procedure that the designer employs begins with the identification of the recommended illuminance level for the space. Then, the designer identifies a likely sky illuminance value (e.g., from information present in Section 8.2). Dividing the recommended internal illuminance by the external (sky) illuminance leaves, effectively, a daylight factor magnitude. This magnitude then becomes the target for the designer to achieve in composing the window(s) for the space. If the designer uses this daylight factor magnitude as a starting point in creating a building solution, then the designer might employ the isolux contour patterns shown in the *Graphic Daylighting Design Method Workbook* to establish a window form and location. Alternatively, the designer can use one of the rules-of-thumb that are identified in Section 9.5.2 for sizing the window(s).

But, if the designer wishes to evaluate the daylight presence that will likely be present for a *proposed* building space, then this person can employ the Daylight Factor tables or protractors or one of a number of computer programs. Either of these design tools will enable the designer to generate a Daylight Factor profile. Then, the designer can compare the DF profile for the proposed design against the recommended lighting level (as expressed as a Daylight Factor magnitude). Where values along the profile exceed the recommended level, then sufficient daylight will be present in that portion of the proposed space. Further, if the Daylight Factor magnitudes found for a proposed space are substantially greater than the recommended daylight factors for the projected tasks, then some means of controlling the admission of daylight should be incorporated in the design. For instance, either the size and/or shape of the window should be modified or some variable control device should be introduced (e.g., blinds or drapes on the inside of the window or some form of shading device on the outside). Where the recommended lighting level is greater than the values along the DF profile, daylight would be insufficient as the sole means for providing illumination, and electric lighting would be needed as a supplement.

When a designer can begin this procedure with a Daylight Factor magnitude already suggested for some particular application — as the fourth of these standards specifies — the process of design or evaluation will be that much simpler. For creating a design, the person can either use the rules-of-thumb suggested in Section 9.5.2 or employ the many patterns presented in the *Graphic Daylighting Design Method Workbook*. Or, if the designer wishes to evaluate a proposed design against this fourth standard, the individual can use the Daylight Factor tables or protractors or some computer program to determine the Daylight Factor profile. Then, the designer can compare the found values against the standard.

8.5.2   A WORKED EXAMPLE SHOWING A PROCEDURE FOR DESIGNING FOR DAYLIGHT ADMISSION

The principal steps involved in this worked example include starting with a likely room form, prospective window-wall area(s), and a probable choice of a glazing assembly; determining how much light is needed on the task object on the work surface; establishing what sky illuminance is likely to be available; calculating the magnitude of the Daylight Factor that is needed (by comparing the required illuminance on the task object versus the sky illuminance); accounting for the correction factors (i.e., for the transmissivity of the glazing assembly, the surface dirt, and the framing elements); solving for the magnitude of the Internally-Reflected Component and then the Sky Component; examining alternative window templates from *the Graphic Daylighting Design Method Workbook,* looking for window shapes and locations which supply isolux contours similar to or matching the required Sky Component; and, finally, verifying that the selected window(s) provide adequate daylight admission, good view opportunities, and visual comfort maintenance.

In this worked example we will describe a procedure for creating a window solution for a small office space in a suburb of Seattle, one of a series of such offices arranged modularly (see Figures 8.27 and 8.28). The office will have a floor area of 800 square feet (74.4 m²), share walls on the east and west elevations with adjoining office spaces, have a main entrance into a single-loaded corridor on the south elevation, and have single-sided daylight admission on the north elevation. A proposed floor plan presents dimensions of 25 feet wide (along the north and south elevations) and 32 feet long (along the east and west elevations) (7.62 m × 9.76 m). The proposed roofline involves a two-way shed roof with an intermediate vertical plane for incorporating a clerestory window.

The design goal is to provide a daylighting illumination level of 20 footcandles (about 200 lux) across the floor area of the office on a horizontal work surface 30" (76 cm) above the floor. Daylighting will be furnished from an overcast sky. Note that an illumination level of 20 footcandles (about 200 lux) is recommended as a lower limit for many visual tasks undertaken in traditional offices (see Table 8.3). The designer anticipates that occupants will use small task-specific desk lamps to supplement the daylight illumination.

To estimate the likely available sky illuminance we recommend use of the Tregenza frequency distribution graph shown as Figure 8.12. This graph displays the probabilities of attaining magnitudes of sky illuminance for alternative solar altitude angles. For this worked example we are basing our design condition on the situation where the solar altitude angle is 20°. A solar altitude angle of 20° is achieved in Seattle (situated at 48° North Latitude at 10 AM and 2 PM during the months of February and October. We will also seek a daylighting solution for the 90th percentile frequency distribution. The 20° solar altitude angle and 90th percentile frequency combination essentially means that, for only 10 percent of the time, when the solar altitude angle is equal to or greater than 20°, the sky illuminance will be less than the magnitude shown on this graph.

For this 20° altitude angle and 90th percentile combination, the sky illuminance is 560 footcandles (6000 lux). Then, the required Daylight Factor magnitude × 100% is (20/560) × 100%, or 3.6%. Alternatively stated, the Daylight Factor magnitude required to achieve 20 footcandles on a horizontal surface when the solar altitude angle is 20° and the 90th percentile frequency is sought is 3.6 percent.

If the designer elects to use a clear double-pane glazing assembly with a daylight transmissivity of about 0.8, assumes that in a suburban area the dirt layer on the exterior surface of the glass will impose about a 10 percent reduction in daylight transmission, and

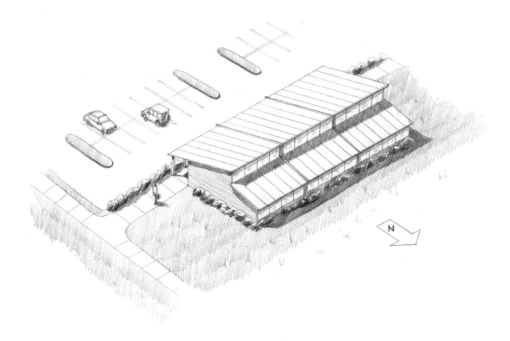

Figure 8.27 A bird's-eye view of several of these modular offices.

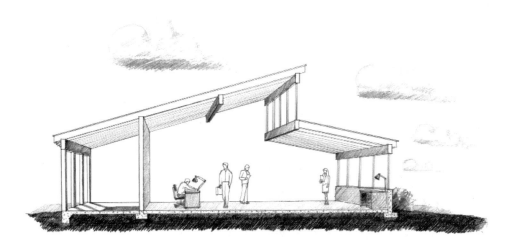

Figure 8.28 A three-dimensional sketch of one of the proposed modular offices.

expects that about 10 percent of the window area will be composed of framing materials, then the overall magnitude of daylight transmitted through the window will be 0.8 × 0.9 × 0.9 (or 0.65) of the daylight that actually reaches the exterior surface of the window. So, if the Daylight Factor magnitude at the task surface is to be 3.6 percent, the Daylight Factor *at the external surface of the glazing assembly* will need to be 3.6%/0.65 or 5.5%.

The next step involves estimating what the Sky Component and Internally-Reflected Components are (we are assuming that there will be no exterior obstructions impeding the admission of daylight into the office space). Determination of the Internally-Reflected Component depends on the areas and reflectances of the various interior surfaces. Once the surface areas and reflectances have been established, then the graph in Figure 8.29 can be used to find the Internally-Reflected Component.

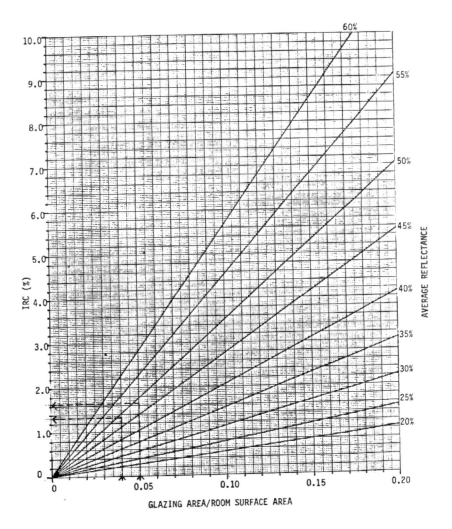

Figure 8.29 This graph affords means for determining the Internally-Reflected Component for side-lighted rooms. This graph has been reproduced from the document by Millet, M.S., and J.R. Bedrick, *Graphic Daylighting Design Manual Workbook,* (Seattle: Department of Architecture, University of Washington, 1980). See http://www.caup.washington.edu/gddm).

To gain a first approximation of the window area for the north wall elevations, we use the rule-of-thumb equation identified in Section 9.5.2,

$$DF_{minimum} = 0.1 \times (\text{glazing area / floor area})$$

If the $DF_{minimum}$ on the horizontal workplane is to be 3.6 percent and the floor area is 800 square feet (74.4 m²), then the recommended glazing area on the north elevation should be 288 square feet (26.8 m²). From this glazing area approximation, we propose to install two window areas, each with a rectangular shape of 4'-8" high by 24' long (1.42 m × 7.32 m). One window area would be placed with the sill at about workplane height; the other area would be set with the sill at a clerestory height (Figure 8.30).

We have proposed that the office space would have a two-direction shed roofline, east and west elevations as shared walls with adjoining offices, the south wall facing onto a single-loaded interior corridor, and the north wall used principally for daylight admission. The resulting surface areas for this scheme then are a floor area of 800 square feet (74.4 m²), a ceiling area of 830 square feet (77.2 m²), an opaque wall area (total) of 1170 square feet (108.7 m²), and a north-wall glazing area of 230 square feet (21.4 m²). We will presume conventional surface reflectances of 0.80, 0.50, 0.20, and 0.10 for ceiling, walls, floor, and glazing, respectively. A calculation of the average area-weighted surface reflectance for the office space then produces a value of 0.47. The ratio of north wall glazing area (230 square feet or 21.4 m²) to the overall interior surface area of the office space (3,040 square feet or 282.5 m²) yields a decimal fraction of 0.076. When these values — 0.47 for the average surface reflectance and 0.076 for the area ratio — are entered into Figure 8.29, the Internally-Reflected Component is found to be 2.3 percent. Note that this amount is the contribution present at the exterior surface of the glazing assembly.

Figure 8.30 North elevation view of initially proposed fenestration.

So, if the Internally-Reflected Component is estimated to be 2.3 percent and the Daylight Factor magnitude required at the exterior surface of the glazing assembly needs to be 5.5 percent, then the Sky Component at the exterior surface of the glazing should be 3.2 percent. The goal then for placing windows in the north elevation for the office space involves finding window forms and locations which provide Sky Component contours largely of 3 percent or greater. As we have already established that the desired window shapes will be rectangular with a dimensional ratio of 4'-8" high by 24' long (1.42 m × 7.32 m), the design issue thus becomes determining at what sill heights the windows should be placed.

For information about Sky Component contours we employ the window templates from the *Graphic Daylighting Design Method Workbook*. The *shape parameter* for this proposed rectangular window (h/w) is 0.19 (or, approximately, 0.2): see Figure 8.31 for the definition of the shape parameter. If we then propose to use a window with a sill at

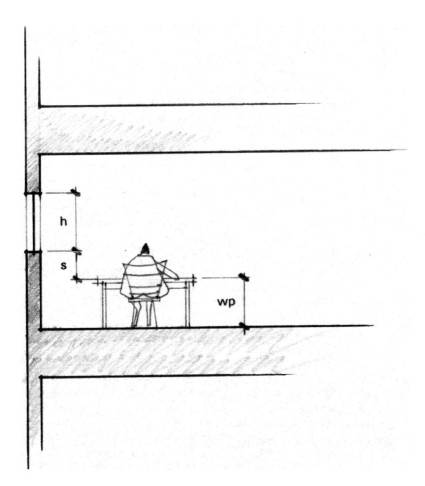

Figure 8.31 The definitions for the shape and location parameters used in the *Graphic Daylighting Design Method Workbook* (hereafter, *GDDM Workbook):*

   h/w = height/width for the envelope opening

   s/h = distance of the sill above the workplane/height of the window

where the opening height is distance from the opening sill to the opening header.

2'-6" from the floor and a clerestory window with a sill height at 11'-0" above the floor, the *location parameters* (s/h) are 0 and 1.8, respectively. The matching templates for the combinations of a shape parameter of 0.2 and location parameters of 0.0 and 1.8 are Window #33 and Window #38, respectively (see Figures 8.32 and 8.33).

To evaluate the composite daylight distribution, the two templates can be placed over one another, accounting for the different horizontal sill locations (see Figures 8.34 and 8.35), to see how the templates are rotated from their vertical modes onto the projected horizontal workplane surface. The resulting overlaid contours are shown in Figure 8.36. For judging the amount and quality of the *composite* daylight distribution a Daylight Factor Profile is constructed at the centerline of the widths of these windows. This profile is displayed as Figure 8.37, with the Sky Component values shown as blackened squares and the Daylight Factor magnitudes (*on the task surface*) identified as open squares.

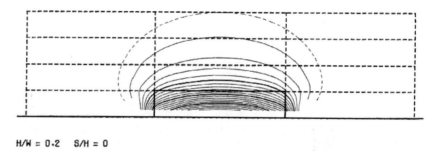

H/W = 0.2   S/H = 0

Figure 8.32 The template for the lower windows from the *GDDM Workbook* (Window #33).

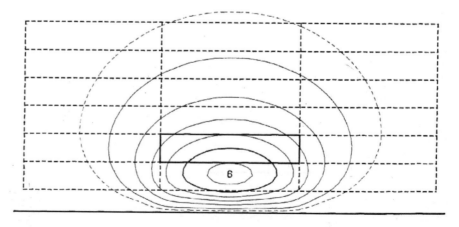

H/W = 0.2   S/H = 1.8

Figure 8.33 The template for the clerestory windows from the *GDDM Workbook* (Window #38).

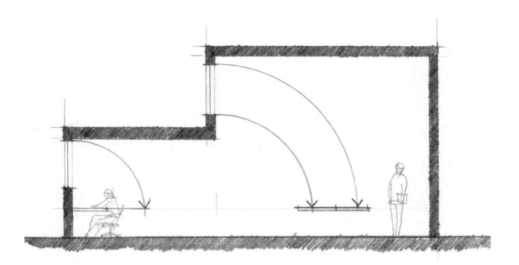

Figure 8.34 The generic rotation process for *GDDM Workbook* templates from vertical mode onto a projected horizontal workplane surface (as seen in an elevation view).

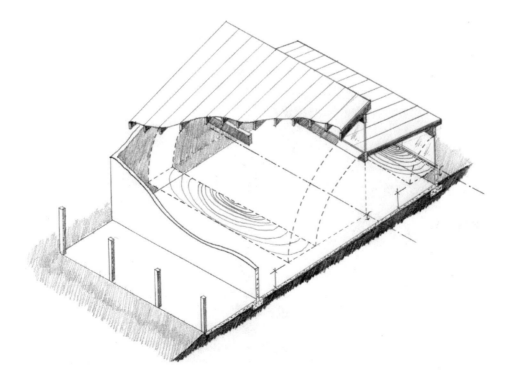

Figure 8.35 The rotation of the two templates for the proposed initial solution (as seen in a section view).

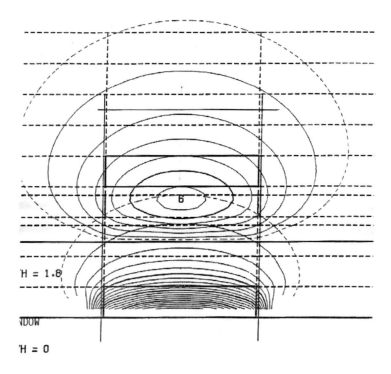

'H = 1.8

'DOW

'H = 0

Figure 8.36 The overlaid contour patterns for (vertical opening) Templates #33 and #38: note the placement of these contour patterns in relation to the rectangular floor plan. The utility of these overlaid patterns is that they demonstrate how the daylighting will be distributed across the space.

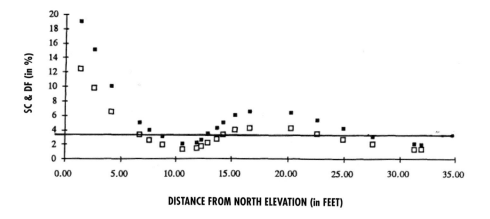

Figure 8.37 The Sky Component and Daylight Factor profiles for the composite contour pattern shown in Figure 8.36.

Figure 8.38 The north elevation view for the revised window assemblies.

Looking at the Daylight Factor magnitudes we can see, first, that some points along the projected horizontal workplane will have magnitudes less than the required 3.6 percent. Second, the variation in these Daylight Factor magnitudes — thus, in brightness — ranges from a high of 12 percent to a low of about 1.5 percent at a distance of about 12 feet [3.7 m] in from the lower part of the north elevation and another low of equal magnitude toward the south elevation. The brightness ratio for someone sitting perhaps halfway between the north and south elevations and facing this north elevation would be 8:1. In Section 7.4.4 (D) we have written that desirable brightness ratios — or luminances on task surfaces and surrounds — should most often be 3:1 or less. Thus, the brightness ratio resulting from this combination of window locations would present excessive brightness and discomfort glare. It is also possible that occupants seated in the darker areas or facing these darker areas may experience some sense of visual dimness and gloom. Therefore, the daylight distribution offered by this initial window location proposal is inadequate and needs further development.

Consequently, a modification in the location of the lower window is warranted because it is the source of the excessive brightness. For the modification we advocate raising the sill of the lower window to a height of 4'-10" (1.47 m) above the floor plane (see Figure 8.38). The Sky Component template matching this new window location — the shape parameter, S/H, would be 0.5 — is Window #35 (see Figure 8.39). When this new template (Window #35) is overlaid on the clerestory template (Window #38), a different Sky Component and Daylight Factor profiles are drawn (see Figure 8.42), the minimum Daylight Factor magnitudes are about 4 percent, and these occur on the horizontal workplane essentially at the south elevation (i.e., at the opposite side of the office space from the north window-wall). Further, a comparison of the maximum Daylight Factor value with the minimum value presents a ratio of about 11:4 (or less than the recommended maximum allowable ratio of 3:1).

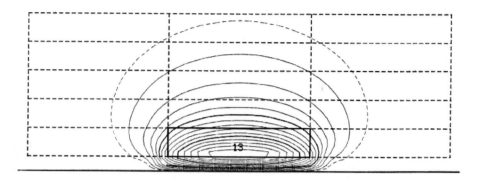

H/W = 0.2   S/H = 0.5

Figure 8.39 The template for the revised design for the lower windows from the *GDDM Workbook* (Window #35).

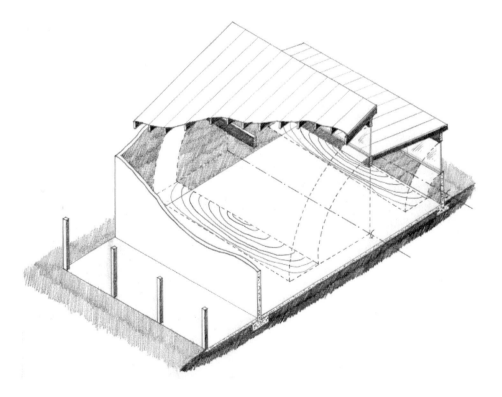

Figure 8.40 The rotation of the two templates for the revised solution (as seen in a section view).

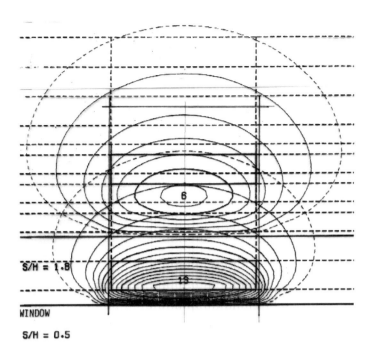

Figure 8.41 Overlaying the contour patterns for window templates #35 and #38.

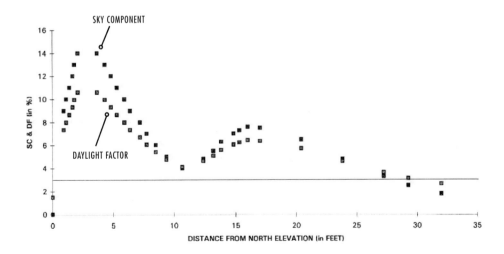

Figure 8.42 The Sky Component and Daylight Factor Profiles for the contour pattern shown in Figure 8.41.

Figure 8.43 Some glazing areas have been included on the left and right sides to better enable viewing of the exterior landscape by seated occupants. To reduce the likelihood that glary conditions might be present with these views we advocate using tinted glass for these areas.

Thus, this new combination of a clerestory window and a window with a sill slightly elevated above the workplane height produces sufficient daylight. Further, the Daylight Factor profile shows evidence that visual comfort will be maintained. The one additional concern with this new combination of windows is whether adequate view opportunities will be afforded. In Section 8.1.2 we have written the views from windows should present three layers of information: a lower layer showing areas close to the building, a middle layer showing information from the edge of this building-proximate area to the horizon, and a sky layer. With a sill height of 4'-10" (1.47 m) above the floor plane, occupants seated at conventional workstations would only see the sky layer. To furnish views of the lower and middle layers of the view field it will be necessary to incorporate some additional glazing areas below the sill height of the main window (see Figure 8.43). Since such lower areas could admit excessively bright daylight and since they are not included to foster additional daylight admission, some glazing material other than ordinary clear glass should most likely be used. To allow occupants to see out (without letting more daylight in), a tinted glass might be installed, or instead an ordinary clear glass assembly might be used *in combination with a venetian blind.*

Section 8.6 | A BRIEF SUMMARY FOR CHAPTER 8

We have written this chapter to demonstrate, first, that windows should be designed with forethought and care and, second, that daylight furnishes an important resource for illuminating a building. Necessarily, the amount of daylight present in the sky varies according to a number of parameters, including the climate, generally, and the weather, specifically; the composition of the sky; the time of day and year; and so forth. We have identified a number of records that can be used to predict how much light is present in the sky for any combination of these parameters.

Though our discussion in this chapter has focused on windows as a means for admitting daylight into a building, we want to emphasize that windows offer a number of other very important benefits to the occupants of buildings. When you design and select windows in the future, please consider these other benefits as bases for making decisions about the character of your building envelopes.

In this chapter we have also described a principal design tool for indicating daylight presence in buildings, namely the Daylight Factor. We have also suggested means for using this design tool. Additionally, we have identified a series of standards that can be used as targets, when seeking to ensure the adequate presence of daylight for building operation. In addition, we have offered an example (in Section 8.5.2) of how windows used to admit daylight can be systematically sized and set in the building envelope.

Lastly, we will suggest six books that can be used for further study on at least some of the topics treated in this chapter.

The two most useful books on daylighting, generally, as well as on detailed topics discussed in this chapter, are:

Hopkinson, R.G., P. Petherbridge, and J. Longmore, *Daylighting,* (London: William Heinemann Ltd., 1966).

Hopkinson, R.G., *Architectural Physics: Lighting,* (London: Her Majesty's Stationery Office, 1963).

Two additional books that discuss daylighting use in buildings include:

Moore, E.F., *Concepts and Practice of Architectural Daylighting,* (New York: Van Nostrand Reinhold Co., Inc., 1991).

Robbins, C.L., *Daylighting: Design and Analysis,* (New York: Van Nostrand Reinhold Co., Inc., 1986).

A text that discusses a number of the measurement and descriptive issues associated with daylight availability (and its admission into buildings) is:

Murdoch, J.B., *Illumination Engineering: From Edison's Lamp to the Laser,* (New York: Macmillan Publishing Company, 1985).

Finally, an information source that presents an almost encyclopedic treatment of issues about daylighting in buildings (and for many other related, important lighting topics) is:

Rae, M., editor, IES *Lighting Handbook* (8th edition), (New York: Illuminating Engineering Society of North America, 2000).

ENDNOTES and SELECTED ADDITIONAL COMMENTS

1. Markus, T.A., "The function of windows: A re-appraisal," *Building Science,* 2, 1967, pages 97–121.

2. Stewart, D.M., "Attitudes of school children to daylight and fenestration," *Building and Environment,* 16(4), 1981, pages 267–277.

3. Ruys, T., "Windowless offices," unpublished Master of Architecture thesis, University of Washington, Seattle, Washington, 1970.

4. This quotation appears on pages 430–431 of a paper by Heerwagen, J.H., "The Role of Nature in the View from the Window," *1986 International Daylighting Conference: Proceedings II,* (Bales, E.J., and R. McCluney, editors), (Atlanta: American Society of Heating, Refrigerating, and Air-Conditioning Engineers, Inc., 1989), pages 430–437. Citations for the other references include: Ulrich, R., "View through a window may influence recovery from surgery," *Science,* 224, 1984, pages 420–421; Moore, E.O., "A prison environment: its affects on healthcare utilization," unpublished Doctor of Philosophy dissertation, University of Michigan, Ann Arbor, Michigan, 1982; and West, M., "Landscape views and stress response in the prison environment," unpublished Master of Landscape Architecture thesis, University of Washington, Seattle, Washington, 1986.

5. For instance, see Markus, T., "The function of windows: a reappraisal," *Building Science,* 2, 1967, pages 97–121; Ludlow, A.M., "The function of windows in buildings," *Lighting Research & Technology,* 8(2), 1976, pages 57–68; and/or Collins, B.L., "Review of the psychological reaction to windows," *Lighting Research & Technology,* 8(2), 1976, pages 80–88.

6. Ludlow, A.M., op. cit., page 59.

7. For instance, see Kaplan, R., "Nature at the doorstep: residential satisfaction and the nearby environment," *Journal of Architecture and Planning Research,* 2, 1985, pages 115–127; Ulrich, R., "Aesthetic and affective response to the natural environment," in Altman, I., and J.F. Wohlwill (editors), *Behavior and the Natural Environment,* (New York: Plenum Press, Inc., 1983), pages 85–125; and/or Ulrich, R., "Human response to vegetation and landscapes," *Landscape and Urban Planning,* 13, 1986, pages 29–44.

8. One paper that described research conducted in a California school has been written by Demos, G.D., S. Davis, and F.F. Zuwaylif, "Controlled physical environments," *Building Research,* 4, 1967, pages 60–62. The study of windowless schools in Michigan is described in a report edited by Larson, C.T., *The Effect of Windowless Classrooms on Elementary School Children,* (Ann Arbor, Michigan: Architectural Research Laboratory, Department of Architecture, University of Michigan, 1970). Both of these studies are cited in a literature review prepared by Collins, B.L., *Windows and People: A Literature Survey,* (U.S. National Bureau of Standards Building Science Series No. 70), (Washington, D.C.: U.S. Government Printing Office, 1975). A revised version of this third document has been published as Collins, B.L., "Review of the psychological reaction to windows," *Lighting Research & Technology,* 8(2), 1976, pages 80–88.

9. Ruys, T., "Windowless offices," unpublished Master of Architecture thesis, University of Washington, Seattle, Washington, 1970.

10. Wyon, D., and B. Nilsson, "The experience of windowless environments in factories, offices, shops, and colleges in Sweden," *Proceedings of the 1980 Symposium on Daylighting,* (Paris: Commission Internationale de L'Eclairage, 1980), pages 216–225.

11. Heerwagen, J.H., and G.H. Orians, "Adaptations to windowlessness: a study of the use of visual decor in windowed and windowless offices," *Environment and Behavior,* 18(5), September 1986, pages 623–639.

12. Ibid., page 636.

13. In a note in Section 8.1 we distinguished between *sunshine* and *sunlight:* sunshine is the combination of ultraviolet, visible, and infrared radiation, which emanate from the sun and proceed to the Earth (as solar radiation), whereas sunlight is only that portion of sunshine, which is visible as light.

14. Gillette, G., W. Pierpoint, and S. Treado, "A general illuminance model for daylight availability," *Journal of the Illuminating Engineering Society,* 13, July 1984, pages 330–340.

15. See Ruck, N.C., "Representation of skylight availability in Australia in different climatic zones using regression procedures," *Lighting Research & Technology,* 17(2), 1985, pages 72–78; and Seckler, S.M., and P.J. Littlefair, "Daylight availability and lighting use: geographical variations," *Lighting Research & Technology,* 19(2), 1987, pages 25–34. Note that this latter paper also presents information relating daylight availability to the numbers of hours of electrical lighting operation in daylighted buildings. The paper suggests that such information can also be used to predict the extent of electrical lighting use in these buildings. Three earlier papers also discuss the relationship between variations in daylighting presence and local climates: Kittler, R., "Skylight availability under typical nebulosity conditions," *Lighting Research & Technology,* 13(4), 1981, pages 199–202; Seckler, S.M., "Regional variations of daylight availability—a review of measured data and estimating methods," *Lighting Research & Technology,* 15(3), 1983, pages 151–156; and Kittler, R., and N. Ruck, "Definitions of typical and average exterior daylight conditions in different climatic zones," *Energy and Buildings,* 6(2–4), 1984, pages 253–259.

16. Ruck, N.C., and S. Selkowitz, "A Review of Measured Skylight Availability Data" (extended abstract*), Proceedings of the 1986 International Daylighting Conference, Volume 1,* (Zdepski, M.S., and R. McCluney, editors), (McLean, Virginia: 1986 International Daylighting Organizing Committee, 1986), pages 67–71.

17. An extensive review of the literature concerning the luminous efficacy of daylight has been prepared by P.J. Littlefair and has been published as, "The luminous efficacy of daylight: a review," *Lighting Research & Technology,* 17(4), 1985, pages 162–182. This paper also identifies values of luminous efficacy, which have been found by other researchers. Four additional papers which have described the derivation and use of this luminous efficacy term include Gillette, G.L., and S.J. Treado, "Correlations of solar irradiance and daylight illuminance for building energy analysis," *ASHRAE Transactions,* 91(1), 1985, pages 180–192; Perez, R., K. Webster, R. Seals, R. Stewart, and J. Barron, "Variations of the luminous efficacy of global and diffuse radiation and zenith luminance with weather conditions—description of a potential method to generate key daylight availability data from existing solar radiation data bases," *Solar Energy,* 38(1), 1987, pages 33–44; Littlefair, P.J., "Measurements of the luminous efficacy of daylight," *Lighting Research & Technology,* 20(4), 1988, pages 177–188; and Perez, R., P. Ineichen, R. Seals, J. Michalsky, and R. Stewart, "Modeling daylight availability and irradiance components from direct and global irradiance," *Solar Energy,* 44(5), 1990, pages 271–289.

18. McCluney, R., and H.J. Bornemann, "The Time Rate of Changing Daylight", *1986 International Daylighting Conference: Proceedings II,* (Bales, E.J., and R. McCluney, editors), (Atlanta: American Society of Heating, Refrigerating, and Air-Conditioning Engineers, Inc., 1989), pages 24–30.

19. ———, *Standardization of Luminance Distribution on Clear Skies* (CIE Publication No. 22), (Paris: Commission Internationale De L'Eclairage, 1973).

20. Moon, P., and D. Spencer, "Illumination from a nonuniform sky," *Illuminating Engineering,* 37(12), December 1942, page 707ff.

21. For instance, see Littlefair, P.J., "The luminance distribution of an average sky," *Lighting Research & Technology,* 13(4), 1981, pages 192-198; Karayel, M., M. Navvab, E. Ne'eman, and S. Selkowitz, "Zenith luminance and sky luminance distributions for daylighting calculations," *Energy and Buildings,*

6, 1984, pages 283–291; Kittler, R., "Luminance models of homogeneous skies for design and energy performance predictions," *1986 International Daylighting Conference: Proceedings II,* (Bales, E.J., and R. McCluney, editors), (Atlanta: American Society of Heating, Refrigerating, and Air-Conditioning Engineers, Inc., 1989), pages 31–37; and Nakamura, H., M. Oki, Y. Hayashi, and T. Iwata, "The mean sky composed taking account of the relative sunshine duration," *1986 International Daylighting Conference: Proceedings II,* (Bales, E.J., and R. McCluney, editors), (Atlanta: American Society of Heating, Refrigerating, and Air-Conditioning Engineers, Inc., 1989), pages 38–50.

22. Tabular information about determining the Internally-Reflected Component can be found in each of the following three documents: Hopkinson, R.G., *Architectural Physics: Lighting,* (London: Her Majesty's Stationery Office, 1963), pages 63–68; Hopkinson, R.G., P. Petherbridge, and J. Longmore, *Daylighting,* (London: William Heinemann Ltd., 1966), pages 249–256; and Hopkinson, R.G., J. Longmore, and A.M. Graham, *Simplified Daylight Tables* [National Building Studies Special Report No. 26], (London: Her Majesty's Stationery Office, 1958), pages 16–20.

23. This method was developed by M.S. Millet and J.R. Bedrick at the Department of Architecture, University of Washington, Seattle, Washington. Its release date was March 1980.

24. A very informative videotaped description of model making and study techniques has been produced and is distributed by the Lighting Design Lab (400 East Pine Street, #100, Seattle, WA 98122-2360; or http://www.lightingdesignlab.com). Alternatively, see the paper by Bryan, H., "The use of physical scale models for daylighting analysis," in the *Proceedings of the Sixth National Passive Solar Conference,* 1981, pages 865–869.

25. ———. *An Analytical Model for Describing the Influence of Lighting Parameters upon Visual Performance.* This document was prepared by the CIE Technical Committee 3.1 and is identified as CIE Publications No. 19.21 and 19.22, 1981.

26. Yonemura, G.T., "Criteria for recommending lighting levels," *Lighting Research & Technology,* 13(3), 1981, pages 113–129.

27. Tregenza, P.R., S.M. Romaya, S.P. Dawe, L.J. Heap, and B. Tuck, "Consistency and variation in preferences for office lighting," *Lighting Research and Technology,* 6(4), 1974, pages 205–211.

28. Heerwagen, J.H., "Affective functioning, 'light hunger' and room brightness preferences," *Environment and Behavior,* 22(5), September 1990, pages 608–635.

29. See Van Ooyen, M.H.F., J.A.C. van de Weijgert, and S.H.A. Begemann, "Preferred luminances in offices," *Journal of the Illuminating Engineering Society,* Summer 1987, pages 152–156.

30. Collins, J.B., "The illuminating engineer in a changing world," *Lighting Research & Technology,* 9(1), 1977, pages 1–10.

31. Cooper, B.C., "A statistical look at the future of lighting," *Lighting Design and Application,* 1(1), July 1971, pages 14–23.

32. ———. The *IESNA Lighting Handbook: Reference & Application, 9th edition* (Rea, M.S., editor), (New York: Illuminating Engineering Society of North America, 2000).

The illuminance values expressed in this standard have been established in a report prepared by a committee of members of the Illuminating Engineering Society (of North America). The report is entitled, "Selection of illuminance values for interior lighting design" and is identified as the "RQQ Report No. 6." For further information about this report, see the document, "IES Transaction: Selection of illuminance values for interior lighting design (RQQ report no. 6)," *Journal of the Illuminating Engineering Society,* April 1980, pages 188–190.

CHAPTER NINE

Guidelines for Creating Buildings with Good Daylighting

IN THIS CHAPTER WE WILL PRESENT a series of guidelines for creating buildings that are illuminated with daylight. Our goals in offering these guidelines are to describe building forms and conditions which can provide well-lighted settings for working and living, to ensure that occupants will experience visual comfort when relying on daylighting illumination, and to suggest means for operating buildings efficiently (by employing daylighting as a principal source of illumination). Major issues concerning the use of daylight for illuminating buildings include: recognizing the properties of the sky (as the light source); gaining information that describes the illumination needs of the occupants; and then establishing a catalogue of methods for getting the light into the building and controlling the light once it has been admitted. In Chapters 6 through 8 we have reported on the nature and properties of light; the operation of the human visual system; environmental and other parameters for insuring good vision and visual comfort; the role of windows in buildings; daylight and sunlight availability; procedures for predicting and/or analyzing daylight presence in buildings; and industry standards for illuminating buildings.

In keeping with an overall focus of this text, we will concentrate our attention in this chapter on the use of daylight as a *passive* means for controlling the internal building environment. We will also discuss such daylighting design topics as the identification of building forms that foster daylight usage; the placement and sizing of windows in building envelopes;

and the selection of fenestration materials. Lastly, we will offer only brief comments about the use of electric illumination. However, we acknowledge that electric illumination supplies a fundamental means for lighting buildings. So, in your subsequent study and work, you should explore how daylighting and electric illumination can be integrated.

Section 9.1 | SITE DEVELOPMENT GUIDELINES FOR DAYLIGHT

9.1.1 ACCESSIBILITY TO THE SKY VAULT

Provide uninterrupted lines-of-sight between the building interior and the sky vault. When daylight is used as a major illumination source for a building interior, unobstructed views of the sky vault must be accessible from within the future building. Daylight is gained both from *direct-beam sunlight* and the *diffused* light from the sky vault. For direct-beam sunlight to pass into a building, there must be an unobstructed line-of-sight between the solar disk, the window through which the sunlight will enter, and the surface that will be illuminated by the sunlight. Ground forms, vegetation, fences, or buildings can interfere with this line-of-sight, thus shading the window (and the building interior). So, when you begin the creation of a building, examine the environment around a building to determine if these exterior forms may prevent the admission of sunlight.

Alternatively, the hemispherical sky vault is the source of the *diffused* daylight. To gain this diffuse illuminance from the sky vault, a line-of-sight should exist between the sky vault and the fenestration in the building envelope (although daylight from the sky vault can still enter the building by being reflected off of buildings, vegetation, and other objects external to the fenestration). However, any ground form, vegetation, fencing, or other building that interferes with this line-of-sight can substantially reduce or even negate the availability of the diffused daylight.

SIDEBAR 9.1 Issues of solar and daylight access

When a designer or builder considers how to introduce daylight into a building, some thought should be given to anticipating whether, at some future time, buildings or other forms may be created on adjacent land. In areas that are undergoing real estate development, occupants of first-constructed buildings can often face the possibility that later buildings will obstruct the passage of solar radiation and daylight into the earlier-built buildings. Necessarily, then, there is a modicum of risk associated with relying on daylight as an illumination source. This issue of maintaining a "right-of-way" between the windows of a building and the sky vault is generically categorized as having *daylight* (or *solar*) *access*. To ensure good daylight (or solar) access for the occupants of current buildings, the heights and shapes of future buildings will need to be regulated (by standard or ordinance).

9.1.2 USE OF VEGETATION FOR CONTROLLING THE ADMISSION OF DAYLIGHT

Employ vegetation, particularly the deciduous varieties, as means for reducing excessive daylight brightness. In Section 8.2.3 we have written about daylight variability. The principal point of that discussion is that the intensity of daylight reaching a window varies widely depending on the time of day and year, the portion of the sky a window faces, whether the daylight consists of direct-beam sunlight or diffused radiation from the sky vault, and so forth. The two factors that most greatly determine how bright the sky will appear from a window are whether or not direct-beam sunlight is incident on the window and what the solar altitude angle is. Direct-beam sunlight is substantially brighter than daylight that emanates from either an overcast or clear sky. Further, the intensity of daylight increases markedly as the solar altitude angle increases. A third factor that can also strongly affect the daylight brightness is the climate of the region. For instance, the numbers of overcast and clear days will differ for winter and summer seasons. Wintertime generally produces many periods of overcast sky conditions (with largely diffused daylight), whereas the summertime sky will usually consist of more clear-sky conditions *with the frequent presence of direct-beam sunlight.* Concomitantly, the solar altitude angles are much lower throughout the winter.

Windows are commonly sized and located in building envelopes to accommodate sky conditions when the sky brightness is substantially less than its maximum value. For instance, windows may be selected to provide daylighting from the wintertime overcast sky. So, during the summer with its greater frequency of clear sky conditions and the attendant direct-beam sunlight, these windows—sized and located for wintertime daylight—will likely require some provision to moderate very bright sky conditions. One means that can be used to inhibit the entrance of excessively bright daylight, when it occurs during the summertime, is to employ deciduous vegetation external to windows (see Figure 9.1). The foliage of deciduous vegetation should then match this need for seasonal shading. Further, if the particular species of vegetation are chosen carefully, it is often possible to obtain plants whose foliation period occurs simultaneously with the time when such shading is needed most.[1]

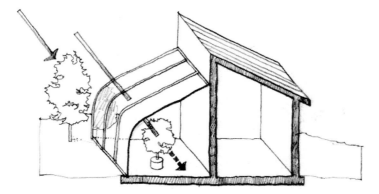

Figure 9.1 Using vegetation to block direct-beam sunlight (and its often-excessive brightness).

9.1.3   REFLECTANCES OF SURFACES EXTERNAL TO A BUILDING

Exercise care in selecting external surfaces. The choices of external surfaces near a building can either enhance or detract from the character of the illumination within a building. Surfaces that have higher reflectances—commonly, those that are light-colored—can reflect light into a building. Similarly, glossy surfaces—those that provide specular reflections—also can reflect light into a building. Bodies of water—liquid or frozen—and snowfields are two naturally occurring examples of surfaces that will often display high reflectances. Alternatively, building materials like aluminum, stainless steel, and concrete with a high sand content also can be highly reflective (see Figures 9.2 and 9.3).

Having highly reflective surfaces near a building can create visual difficulties for the building occupant. When an occupant's view field includes such surfaces, their reflections may appear excessively bright. For instance, an occupant whose view out a window includes a highly reflective surface (e.g., the side of an adjacent building) may frequently receive direct-beam sunlight reflected from that surface (see Figure 9.4). The brightness

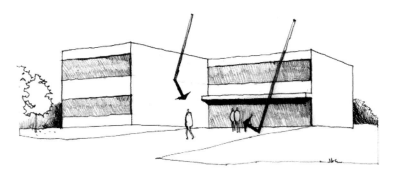

Figure 9.2 High-reflectance building and ground-surface materials can cause visual discomfort for people, whether they are inside looking out or are outside and simply walking by.

Figure 9.3 This sidewalk surface in Portland, Oregon, contains many highly reflective sand particles. The sand, when illuminated with direct-beam sunlight, produces a sparkly effect that is visually discomforting for pedestrians.

of reflected sunlight will be substantially greater than the sky vault or, possibly, the internal surfaces surrounding the window. Thus, the occupant can often experience *glare* when a view field contains highly reflective surfaces.

So, unless you specifically wish to have reflected daylight (or direct-beam sunlight) enter your building, external surfaces should have low reflectances (i.e., dark colors and matte finishes). However, if you want to reflect light into the building, you will need to employ materials and surfaces with high reflectances, light colors and, possibly, that offer specular reflections. If high reflectance surfaces and materials are used, then they must be placed so that their reflections do not coincide with the view fields of building occupants and people passing.

Section 9.2 | CHOOSING BUILDING FORMS TO ENHANCE THE DAYLIGHTING OF BUILDING INTERIORS

The guidelines presented in this section are intended for use in organizing the gross form of buildings (i.e., particularly for developing overall floor plans). Subsequently, in Section 9.6, we will offer guidelines about specific building components whose use can encourage the daylighting of building interiors.

9.2.1 ORGANIZING BUILDINGS WITH NARROW WIDTHS FOR DAYLIGHT PENETRATION

Design buildings with narrow depths to facilitate the admission of daylight (see Figure 9.5). Many building spaces will only have vertical windows on a single side of the space. For such single-side-lighted spaces, a standard rule-of-thumb—used for predicting daylight presence—suggests that *the depth* (the dimension from a window surface into the space) *that daylight will penetrate usefully is equal to approximately two-and-a-half times the height of the window.* So, if the height of a window is limited by how high the ceiling is—commonly, about eight to nine feet (2.4 to 2.7 m) in many residential, commercial, and institutional buildings—then the approximate maximum distance from the building envelope that daylight may provide useful illumination is about twenty feet (6.1 m). This

Figure 9.4 This building is fenestrated with a heat-reflective glazing assembly. Such assemblies often have almost mirror-like appearances. Further, in addition to reflecting much of the incident solar radiation (and its heat gain potential), the glazing will also reflect much of the daylight. On days with clear or partly cloudy skies when direct-beam sunlight is present, these surfaces can appear very bright and cause appreciable visual discomfort, when they intrude into people's view fields. This photograph has been furnished by the Libbey-Owens-Ford Company. Permission to reproduce the image has been granted by the Pilkington North America Company.

SIDEBAR 9.2 Examples of disability and discomfort glares

Depending on the nature of the reflecting surface and where it is within the view field, glare can be categorized as either *disability* or *discomfort glare* (see Section 7.5.1 for information about the natures of these glare experiences). A large brightly reflective surface like a walkway made of light-colored sandy concrete would cause discomfort glare if, for instance, you sat near it and tried to watch people pass by. And,

on a bright, cloudless winter day, ground covered with fresh snow would also produce discomfort glare. You might experience disability glare if direct-beam sunlight reflected off of a water puddle on a asphalt-covered surface (e.g., like on a roof or a roadway). Or you might experience disability glare trying to see out of a dirt-covered window when direct-beam sunlight falls on the window surface.

Figure 9.5 A narrow-width building which permits daylight to enter from at least two elevations (to achieve more balanced daylight distributions; see Section 9.3.2 for further information about balancing daylight admission by locating windows on two (or more) enclosing planes of a building space).

Figure 9.6 "Borrowing" daylight from a perimeter space to illuminate an intermediate space will generally be acceptable as long as the activities in the intermediate space do not require significant amounts of light.

dimension thus establishes a practical maximum depth for a building space, *in which daylight is to serve as a major source of illumination.*

Necessarily, two such building spaces, each with windows located on a single-side of the room, can be placed back-to-back with a double-loaded corridor running between them. To provide daylight for the corridor in this scheme, some glazing could be used in the internal walls opposite the perimeter window-walls. This glazing will permit light from the perimeter spaces to pass into the corridor. Thus, the corridor can be said to *borrow light* from the perimeter spaces (see Figure 9.6). If visual separation must be maintained between a perimeter space and the corridor — likely, as a means of insuring visual privacy — then glazing could be placed in the upper wall that separates the perimeter space and the corridor. In this manner the glazing would function as a transom window. Though the amount of daylight reaching the corridor from transom windows on either side of it may be relatively low, such comparative dimness can be suitable: recommended illumination levels for corridors are usually quite low, as the activities performed there usually present little visual difficulty.

Two other design strategies that can be employed to get daylight into interior spaces are, first, to place skylights in the roofs above the spaces and, second, to increase the ceiling height of the spaces (above that of the perimeter rooms on either side) and include clerestories in the uppermost vertical walls. The use of upper wall transoms for passing light from perimeter to interior spaces is a technique that can be applied when a building has multiple floors. But skylights or clerestories employed to admit daylight into interior spaces will only be effective for single-story buildings or for the top floors of multiple-story buildings (i.e., unless additional means are incorporated with the skylights or clerestories to get the daylight deeper into the building).

9.2.2   THE USE OF ATRIA FOR BRINGING DAYLIGHT INTO BUILDING INTERIORS

Employ atria as a means for increasing the penetration of daylight into buildings. An atrium is essentially a covered light well or cavity that *vertically* opens up the interior of a building (see Figures 9.7 and 9.8). The atrium volume usually includes a central courtyard space that is placed on the bottom floor of the atrium. The floors above the courtyard level often have balcony areas or open corridors which overlook the courtyard. The heights of atrium volumes can range from a few stories to perhaps 20 floors (or more).

Many atria are roofed with skylights or have clerestory windows included in the uppermost vertical walls. These skylights and/or clerestories will enable daylight to penetrate

---

SIDEBAR 9.3 Allowable heights for atria

The height that an atrium may have is often governed by the applicable building codes. Generally, permissible heights are determined by fire-resistive practices required for buildings in a municipality. For further information about how building codes issues affect the creation and use of atria, see Leslie, R.P., "Core daylighting: building code issues," *1986 International Daylighting Conference: Proceedings II*, (Bales, E.J., and R. McCluney, editors), (Atlanta: American Society of Heating, Refrigerating, and Air-Conditioning Engineers, Inc., 1989), pages 314–324.

Figure 9.7 An internal courtyard (or atrium) enables daylight entering through clerestories and skylights at the roof to penetrate throughout this building. Classroom doors, which open off of the walkways on the various floors, have glazed panels to let the daylight from this courtyard enter into the classrooms.

Figure 9.8 Here, a comparatively "narrow thickness" and an open-to-the-air courtyard facilitate the daylighting of much of the floor area of this office building.

deeply into buildings. Spaces on the floors surrounding an atrium can then be illuminated with the daylight that passes down the atrium. Alternatively, spaces at the *perimeter* of a building (with an atrium at its center) can be daylighted conventionally, through windows in the building envelope. Thus, the span of any floor that is illuminated by daylight can be at least four spaces wide: on each side of an atrium, the interior space adjoining the atrium will receive daylight from the atrium, and the spaces at the building perimeter will gain daylight from windows in the building envelope. If an interior corridor is used between the interior and perimeter spaces and upper window transoms line the corridor, then the corridor can gain daylight from fenestration in both the perimeter and atrium elevations (utilizing the *borrowed light* scheme). One additional option is to layout the space in an *open-planned* fashion, without intermediate walls to break up the space.

How deep an atrium can be—and still provide useful daylighting for areas that lie adjacent to the atrium—is variable. The character and quantity of the daylight as it reaches the lower floors of a building containing an atrium will greatly depend on the means used to admit daylight into the atrium volume, the geometry of the atrium space, and the choice of materials used throughout the atrium. Further, the success of an atrium as a device for admitting daylight into the interior of a building will also depend on the types of activities that are to be conducted there: the amounts of illumination that an atrium can furnish and that are needed for particular activities should be matched carefully to ensure good fits.

One further development of the atrium concept as a means for admitting daylight into building interiors employs the use of *light pipes* (or *light tunnels*). These devices are essentially vertical pathways that channel daylight from the roof of a building to lower floors much below the roof. The effectiveness of light pipes can be substantially increased if direct-beam sunlight is the principal daylight component passed through them. To enhance the utility of the direct-beam component, a collection system may be implemented using mirrors to capture and redirect and lenses to focus and pass the beamed sunlight down the light pipe. At the lower end of the pipe, the beamed sunlight can then be diffused to provide a softer, more general illumination level.

9.2.3   APPROPRIATE ORIENTATIONS FOR ADMITTING DAYLIGHT

For obtaining daylight without appreciable solar gain, locate windows on building elevations away from the principal solar collection side. As an example, for buildings sited in the Northern Hemisphere at latitudes north of the tropic of Cancer, northward-facing windows will receive only minimal amounts of the direct-beam component of solar radiation. So, these windows can have full views of the sky vault without experiencing appreciable solar heat gain. Additionally, occupants looking out of these windows will experience little of the excessive brightness (and potential glare) commonly associated with direct-beam sunlight.

Recognize that windows facing east and west can also introduce visual comfort problems. In the morning for east-facing windows and the afternoon for west-facing windows, when the sun shines most directly, it also tends to be lower in the sky. Thus, the paths of the direct-beam component of the solar radiation will generally coincide with the primary view fields of building occupants who look out of these windows. The presence of direct-beam sunlight in the view field can create significant visual *discomfort* because of the excessive brightness of this sunlight. Occupants with east and west-facing windows will frequently experience glare within their view fields (and possibly, veiling reflections on their work surfaces), when their workstations face these windows. To mitigate these conditions

SIDEBAR 9.4 Literature about the use and development of atria

See the book by Saxon that presents a catalogue of buildings having atria as a principal design feature: Saxon, R., *Atrium Buildings: Design and Development* (2nd edition), (London: Architectural Press, Ltd., 1986). Several research papers have described model and full-scale studies of atria. For instance, see Navvab, M., and S. Selkowitz, "Daylighting data for atrium design," *Proceedings of the Ninth National Passive Solar Conference*, (Hayes, J., and A. Wilson, editors), (Boulder, Colorado: American Solar Energy Society, Inc., 1984), pages 495–500; Bednars, M.J., "An analysis of daylighting design factors in atria," *Proceedings of the Tenth National Passive Solar Conference*, (Wilson, A.T., and W. Glennie, editors), (Boulder, Colorado: American Solar Energy Society,

Inc., 1985), pages 111–114; Kim, K., and L.L. Boyer, "Development of daylight prediction methods for atrium design," *1986 International Daylighting Conference: Proceedings II*, (Bales, E.J., and R. McCluney, editors), (Atlanta: American Society of Heating, Refrigerating, and Air-Conditioning Engineers, Inc., 1989), pages 345–359; Treado, S.J., and G.L. Gillette, "The daylighting and energy performance of building atria," *1986 International Daylighting Conference: Proceedings II*, (Bales, E.J., and R. McCluney, editors), (Atlanta: American Society of Heating, Refrigerating, and Air-Conditioning Engineers, Inc., 1989), pages 360–371; and Navvab, M., "Outdoors indoors," *Lighting Design & Applications*, 20(5), May 1990, pages 6, 24–31.

SIDEBAR 9.5 Literature describing the use of light pipes and tunnels

For data about the various components involved in executing a functioning light pipe for a Toronto office building (e.g., sun-tracking reflectors, focusing mirrors, the light piping, and automatic controls), see Whitehead, L.A., J.E. Scott, B. Lee, and B. York, "A demonstration of large scale core daylighting by means of a light pipe," *1986 International Daylighting Conference: Proceedings II*, (Bales, E.J., and R. McCluney, editors), (Atlanta: American Society of Heating, Refrigerating, and Air-Conditioning Engineers, Inc., 1989), pages 297–301. Alternatively, a review paper by Littlefair explains a light pipe that has been used for illuminating some below-grade floors of an engineering building at the University of Minnesota. In this paper descriptions are provided for the several parts of this device, as well as possible alternatives for these parts. To examine this review paper, see Littlefair, P.J., "Innovative daylighting: review of systems and evaluation methods," *Lighting Research and Technology*, 22(1), 1990, pages 1–17. Two other papers present the engineering principles which govern the performance of light pipes: Whitehead, L.A., R.A. Nodwell, and F.L. Curzon, "New

efficient light guide for interior illumination," *Applied Optics*, 21(15), 1 August 1982, pages 2755–2757; and Fraas, L.M., W.R. Pyle, and P.R. Ryason, "Concentrated and piped sunlight for indoor illumination," *Applied Optics*, 22(4), 15 February 1983, pages 578–582. Both of these latter papers also discuss the possible application of fiber optics as means for channeling sunlight through buildings (i.e., as alternatives to hollow-shaft light pipes). Lastly, a fifth paper introduces a sun-tracking and projecting device whose development includes a capability to adjust the configuration of the reflecting surface. This adjustment permits a more favorable acquisition and channeling of sunlight into and through a building interior. For information about this device, see the paper by Howard, T.C., W. Place, B. Andersson, and P. Coulter, "Variable-area, light-reflecting assemblies (VAL-RAs)," *1986 International Daylighting Conference: Proceedings II*, (Bales, E.J., and R. McCluney, editors), (Atlanta: American Society of Heating, Refrigerating, and Air-Conditioning Engineers, Inc., 1989), pages 390–409.

of excessive brightness, glare, and veiling reflections, shading treatments will have to be included for these windows (see Figures 9.9 and 9.10).

One other problem with east and west-facing windows occurs when external surfaces near the windows—particularly, horizontal ones—consist of highly reflective materials. These surfaces will readily reflect low-angled direct-beam sunlight so that it enters the view field of occupants who look out of these windows. Reflected sunlight in the view field obscures the character of the ground surface from someone who is looking at it (i.e., an instance of *disability glare*). One special example is when a building is located next to a body of water. Reflections off of the water (or ice, when the water is frozen) can produce appreciable glare. Snow-covered fields can also create similar visual difficulties.

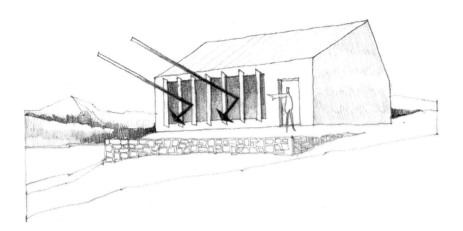

Figure 9.9 Shading devices for east and west-facing windows are usually more effective when these devices can be deployed vertically (i.e., so they offer the possibility of covering the whole height of the window). For example, here, vertical fins can block direct-beam sunlight even when the sun is low in the sky. Alternatively, diffused daylight will readily pass around these fins.

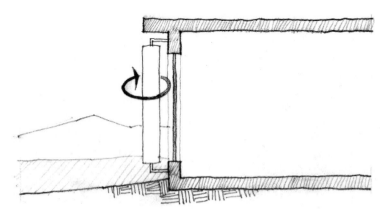

Figure 9.10 If the vertical shading devices described in Figure 9.9 can be rotated, their ability to block the direct-beam sunlight can be further enhanced. By rotating these vertical blinds to a closed (or nearly closed) position, it will be possible to close off the window (behind the blinds).

Suitable window treatments are needed to block direct-beam sunlight when glazing is located on the principal solar collection elevation. For instance, in the northern hemisphere above the tropic of Cancer, principal solar energy collection occurs on the south elevation. With the application of suitable shading devices, diffused daylight can be admitted through south-facing windows, whereas direct-beam sunlight will be blocked from entry (see Figures 9.11 and 9.12).

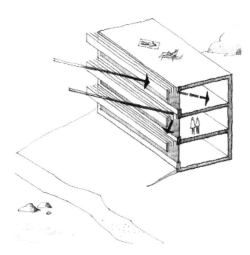

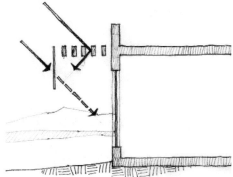

Figure 9.12 Looking at the basic device shown in Figure 9.11 in a sectional view reveals its components. The louvered overhang blocks the direct-beam sunlight from reaching the upper portion of the window, whereas the vertical panel reduces the intensity of the sunlight as it falls upon the lower portion of the window. Note that one reason for using a louvered (partially open) overhang is to permit warmed air near the external window surface to rise convectively away from the building (thus, reducing heat gain potentials; see Section 5.1.3.2 and Figure 5.15).

Figure 9.11 Shading devices on elevations which serve as the principal solar radiation collection surfaces — the south elevation at locations north of the tropic of Cancer and the north elevation at locations south of the tropic of Capricorn — can be beneficially installed as horizontal overhangs. Alternatively, vertical panels of translucent or tinted, transparent materials may also be usefully employed.

SIDEBAR 9.6 The influence of latitude on window elevation decisions

Choosing a window orientation that will escape significant solar heat gain, but which will still admit daylight, depends greatly on the latitude of the site at which you will construct a building. The north orientation is appropriate for locations in the Northern Hemisphere above a latitude of 23° 27'. Between the 23° 27' north and 23° 27' south latitudes, windows on elevations oriented to the four cardinal compass directions will receive significant solar heat gain during at least some part of the year. Beginning at 23° 27' south and proceeding southward toward the south pole, the window orientation that will be least likely to receive significant solar heat gain is the southern one. The cause of this variation is the tilt of the rotational axis of the earth (23° 27') relative to a line normal (perpendicular) to the revolution plane of the earth around the sun. Thus, the path that sun appears to take through the sky varies across the year for any location on Earth and across the latitudes for any given moment of the year.

Section 9.3 | SUGGESTIONS FOR LOCATING WINDOWS FOR THE DAYLIGHTING OF BUILDING INTERIORS

9.3.1   HIGHER WINDOWS FOSTER BETTER DAYLIGHTING THAN DO LOWER WINDOWS

A cardinal guideline for locating windows has been offered by Evans, *"Bring daylight in high and let it down softly."*[2] Specific window types that satisfy this guideline include: vertical windows that extend toward the ceiling of a space, clerestories, and skylights (whether the glazing or other light-admitting materials are placed horizontally or are tilted). These window types can be applied individually or used in various combinations (e.g., when many tilted skylights are present in a *sawtooth* roof assembly). Also, these higher windows can be used to provide general lighting or to illuminate quite specific work surfaces or living areas (see Figures 9.13–9.15).

9.3.1.1   Using windows in vertical walls and as clerestories   A window placed *higher*—rather than lower—*in a wall* will provide a more uniform distribution of daylight throughout a space. A *Daylight Factor profile* drawn at the mid-width of this higher-placed window will display a less steep light distribution gradient than is found for the same-sized window set lower in the window-wall (see Figure 9.16). If this window can be placed sufficiently high, the actual location of the maximum Daylight Factor magnitude will occur at some distance from the window-wall (i.e., in contrast to the lower window for which the maximum Daylight Factor magnitude will be very near the internal window surface). A benefit of a less steep DF profile is that the ratio of maximum brightness versus minimum brightness for this higher window will be lessened—again, in comparison to the brightness ratios exhibited by lower windows. Further, this decrease in the brightness ratio will reduce the likelihood that occupants may experience glary conditions when looking towards the window.

Employing higher windows provides an additional benefit in that the window surface (and its concomitant brightness) will be less likely to intrude on an occupant's view field. Placing the window higher in the window-wall can also reduce the possibility that an occupant will experience the glary conditions associated with too-bright surfaces. However, an attendant liability of the higher window is that it decreases opportunities for the occupant conveniently to find views (i.e., the occupant may have to stand to see out of a higher window or, if the window is a clerestory, the occupant may not be able to see anything but the sky vault). Here, then, a fundamental trade-off arises concerning the placement of windows in a building envelope: whether to use high windows to facilitate daylight admission or to employ lower windows to improve the view. One possible compromise for this situation is to include some windows that will provide greater daylight entry and others that enhance one's view of the external world (for instance, see Figure 9.17).

The second part of Evans' guideline stipulates that daylight—entering through these higher windows—should be *"let…down softly."* This qualification means that daylighted spaces should not be excessively bright. Instead, the entering daylight should be well controlled to avoid wide variations in brightness levels: light distribution should be more, rather than less, uniform. Daylight passing into a building from an overcast sky will likely not appear overly bright unless the space to which the daylight is admitted is comparatively dark. Where the space may indeed be dark, either additional means for bringing daylight

Figure 9.13 This reading room is illuminated by two strips of glazing. The principal skylight glazing (on the left side of this photograph) faces north, whereas a secondary glazing (along the right side of the photograph) faces south but is fully shaded by a medium-rise portion of the building, immediately adjacent to the reading room. Daylight accounts for the majority of the ambient light in this room and is supplemented primarily by table lamps that illuminate the readers' books.

Figure 9.14 In the Mount Angel Abbey Library, Saint Benedict, Oregon, daylight enters this central space through a ring of skylights arrayed across the roof of the building. For further information about this library, see the article, "Aalto's second American building: an abbey library for a hillside in Oregon," *Architectural Record,* May 1971, pages 111–116.

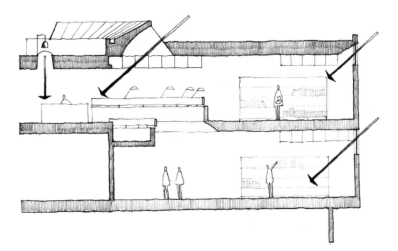

Figure 9.15 A sectional view of the library space shown in Figure 9.14 indicates some of the various means by which daylight is admitted. The main skylight illuminates the central space and, through the opening in the upper floor, some of the lower floor. Additionally, a series of localized, domed skylights admit daylight to the librarians' central workstation. Vertical glazing at the perimeter also contributes daylighting in the stack areas (see Figure 9.36). This drawing is a reproduction of an image presented in the article, "Aalto's second American building: an abbey library for a hillside in Oregon," *Architectural Record,* May 1971, pages 111–116. Permission to reproduce this image has been sought from The McGraw Hill Companies, Inc.

into the space should be considered or the daylight must be further softened. If daylight enters as *direct-beam sunlight,* then this sunlight must be diffused. Such diffusion will provide a more even illumination distribution across a sizeable area of a space.

Techniques for diffusing direct-beam sunlight include the use of fenestration materials that are basically *translucent* or surfaces that will reflect the sunlight in a diffusing manner. A wide range of suitable fenestration materials exists, and several alternative materials and assemblies will be discussed in Section 9.7. For surfaces employed to reflect bright daylight or sunlight, the essential requirement is that they do *not* foster specular reflection. Probably the most appropriate reflecting surfaces will be those that are reasonably smooth and have been painted — or are otherwise finished with some coating

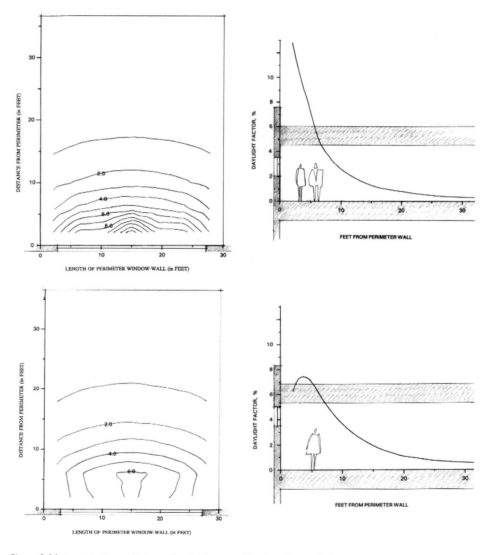

Figure 9.16 Daylight Factor (DF) profiles for lower- and higher-placed windows are shown. Note that daylight entering from the higher-placed window is both less intense near the window-wall and more uniform as it spreads across the width of the space.

Figure 9.17 The vertical windows here enable the occupants to view the cityscape outside of this building. Alternatively, the horizontal window offers daylight admission. An extensive horizontal overhang exists on the exterior of the building just outside of these windows and shades them.

SIDEBAR 9.7 Why "higher" windows may be preferable

An explanation for why higher windows (in comparison to lower windows) create less steep DF profiles is that for most points on the workplane lying along a line perpendicular to the window, those points will "see" a higher segment of the sky vault (than the points would with a lower window). The significance of "seeing" the higher sky vault is that, for the *overcast sky condition* (see Section 8.2.3), the luminance of the sky increases as one looks progressively upward from the horizon to the zenith of the sky vault. This benefit, however, is modified by the geometrical relationship between the angle defined by the point on the workplane and the window and the portion of the sky vault subtended by this angle (projected outward from the window). A point on the workplane close to a lower window will actually "see" a substantially greater portion of the sky vault than would the same point "looking" through a higher window. This greater area results in the comparatively larger Daylight Factor magnitudes for the workplane points close to the lower window (and produces the steep gradient observed for the DF profile drawn for the lower window).

SIDEBAR 9.8 The potential presence of gloom

In some buildings (e.g., high-rise office buildings) spaces usually will have fenestration restricted to one elevation. Additionally, these spaces are often open-planned with no floor-to-ceiling partitions from the perimeter to the walls of the central service core (i.e., distances in the range of 33–50 feet [10–15m]). One potential problem that can arise with such single-sided windows is that at some distance from the fenestration the illumination level from daylight will be relatively low making the interior of the space appear gloomy. For further discussion about the problems and sensing of gloom, see Sidebar 8.15 (in Chapter 8).

Figure 9.18 For this airport concourse, the principal illumination comes from two clerestories in the roof envelope. Electrical illumination sources are built into this roof structure and serve as complements to the daylighting.

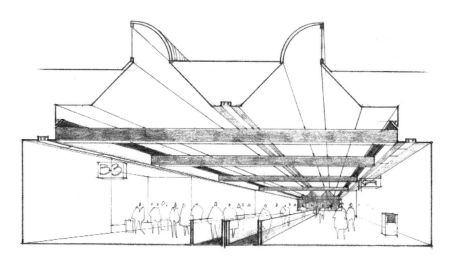

Figure 9.19 This drawing presents a sectional view of the roof structure shown in the Figure 9.18. The clerestory windows are parts of roof monitors. The internal surfaces of these monitors diffuse any direct-beam sunlight that may enter through the clerestories.

material—in a light color. The finished surfaces should thus have a matte appearance. Most common building materials like gypsum wallboard, plaster, plywood, or concrete, after being coated with a light-colored paint or some other paint-like finishing material, can serve satisfactorily as a diffuse-reflecting surface. The principal surfaces to avoid using—when the diffusion of bright lighting is needed—are any of the shiny metals or other smooth materials that have been polished (to remove all but the finest surface irregularities) and subsequently coated with a finish that leaves a glossy appearance.

Placement of shiny metal and other smooth surfaces so that they may reflect and diffuse direct-beam sunlight should be determined in accordance with the geometry describing the path of the sunlight to the admitting window. A single reflection of direct-beam sunlight on a matte surface can be sufficient to diffuse the sunlight. But multiple reflections of the sunlight can further ensure its proper diffusion and provide greater uniformity for the entering light. From the standpoint of visual comfort, any window admitting direct-beam sunlight will be very bright; thus, any such window should be hidden from the view field of the occupant. Alternatively, reflecting surfaces that will readily diffuse the direct-beam sunlight can be present in the view field, as long as these surfaces do not have brightnesses that are substantially greater than those of other surfaces appearing in the view field. The configurations in which these reflecting surfaces can be arranged are limitless and therefore should be chosen not only to promote the diffusion and distribution of the daylight, but also to enhance the form of the building (see Figures 9.18 and 9.19).

Daylight emanating from the general sky vault is solar radiation that has been diffused by the gases and entrained particulate matter in the atmosphere of the Earth. The brightness of the daylight that comes from the general sky vault is much less than the great brightness of direct-beam sunlight. So, ordinarily, the principal steps in handling the diffused daylight is to admit it into the building and channel it to the location(s) where illumination is needed. How this light may be channeled to a workplane will depend greatly on the placements of the windows and the workplane. Further, what means is most appropriate for channeling the daylight will also depend on the amount of light needed for performing the task that occurs at the workplane. If comparatively more brightness is required for task performance, then the diffused light from the sky should directly fall on the workplane. But, if the task needs a relatively lesser amount of light, then the daylight can be conveyed to the workplane by reflecting it off of one or more surfaces. Also, keep in mind that, as the surfaces of most building materials are not perfect reflectors and do scatter light, the intensity of reflected light grows less with each succeeding reflection.

You should note that, even though daylight from the general sky vault is much less bright than direct-beam sunlight, the diffused daylight could still be quite bright. If the brightness from the sky vault is seen through a window that is surrounded by relatively dark surfaces, then the encompassing view field will probably appear glary.

9.3.1.2 Windows used as skylights   Much of the discussion about vertical windows in Section 9.3.1.1 can be applied to the placement of fenestration in roofs. Nonetheless, one principal qualification on using skylights is that, for a space to be illuminated with skylights, the space must be on (or at least near) the top story of the building. A second major qualification concerns whether the admission of daylight will have to be controlled as it passes through the skylight. This second qualification specifically involves whether the daylight is diffuse daylight from the general sky vault or direct-beam sunlight.

First, let us consider the practice of admitting diffused daylight into a building using skylights. Skylights present a very good means for getting daylight into a space at some distance from a perimeter window-wall. The daylight provided by a vertical window—as

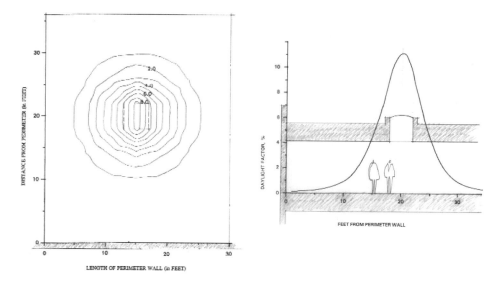

Figure 9.20 The DF contour and DF profile produced by this skylight under an overcast sky.

demonstrated by a *Daylight Factor profile* (see Figure 9.16) — generally tends to be quite bright near the window-wall and to grow progressively dimmer as one moves away from the envelope. Alternatively, the characteristic isolux contour pattern for a skylight indicates that illumination will be brightest directly under the skylight (see Figure 9.20). As one moves out from under the skylight, the amount of illumination will decrease. Thus, a skylight — placed over a workplane area some distance away from the window-wall — can serve as a very useful means of evening out the daylight distribution in a space that has daylight entering at the window-wall.

The daylight pattern created by a skylight depends primarily on the shape of the skylight and its location (i.e., where the skylight is in the roof and how far the roof is from the workplane or floor). Alternative daylight patterns can range from those that display quite gentle drop-offs in daylight presence across a space to others that show a very sharply changing profile (see Figure 9.21). Where a Daylight Factor profile has a steep form, then there will be a substantial variation in brightness from directly under the skylight to some short horizontal distance away. If an occupant's view field includes the region where this sharp variation occurs, then the occupant's eyes may potentially have difficulty adapting across the range of brightnesses. Further, the occupant may also find the viewing of objects on the workplane glare-ridden.

The other significant problem with the use of skylights is how to treat direct-beam sunlight that can enter through a skylight. First, direct-beam sunlight will be very bright. Additionally, because this sunlight would be entering a space in its midst (rather than near the perimeter window-walls), the brightness of the sunlight would likely appear all the more intense. So, the low brightness levels found in an interior space surrounding the skylight will be sharply different from the very bright sunlight falling in a concentrated pattern underneath the skylight (see Figure 9.22). To use this beamed sunlight effectively and to maintain the occupants' visual comfort, the sunlight must be diffused (see

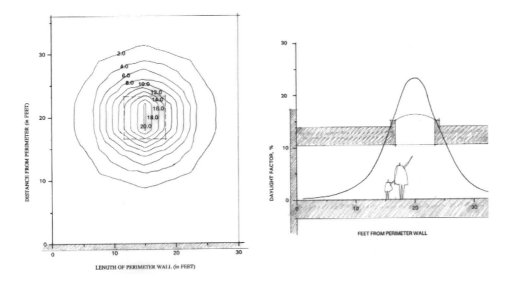

Figure 9.21 The DF contour and DF profile for a skylight that is somewhat larger than the one shown in Figure 9.20, also under an overcast sky.

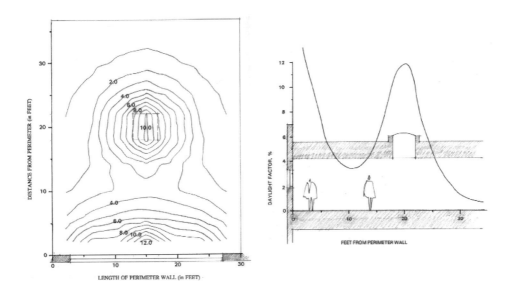

Figure 9.22 Section through a building space with a combination of a single-sided window-wall and one (or more) interior skylights and the resulting DF profile.

Figure 9.23 At an United Airlines concourse at O'Hare International Airport in Chicago, the roof is largely glazed with glazing panels that diffuse much of incident direct-beam sunlight.

SIDEBAR 9.9 Veiling reflections resulting from skylight presence

An additional problem that may result from using skylights to illuminate work surfaces is the presence of veiling reflections across these surfaces. Veiling reflections can be avoided by arranging work surfaces so that the skylight illumination does not reach the worker from in front of the person. Rather, illumination should fall upon the work surface from the left or right sides of the work surface. See Section 7.5.2 for more information about veiling reflections and means for controlling them.

Figure 9.23). Generally, such diffusion can be achieved with reflecting surfaces and/or with special glasses (acting as lenses or filters).

Besides brightness, a second formidable problem created by the admission of direct-beam sunlight is the substantial amount of heat gain that will accompany the sunlight. In many instances, it will be much easier to diffuse the sunlight and reduce its brightness than to keep this excessive heat out of the space. Often, the best means for excluding solar heat gain from a skylight will also significantly reduce the amount of daylighting that can be admitted. One potential solution that will greatly reduce solar heat gain while admitting useful daylight is to *employ tilted skylights* and *face them away from the primary directions from which solar radiation falls* on the building (see Figure 9.24). A second, ingenious solution to this problem is shown in Figures 9.25–9.27. We will discuss additional solutions to this problem in Section 9.7.

Figure 9.24 A skylighted entrance has been included in the Justice Center in Portland, Oregon. This half-cylindrical skylight has an east-west main axis. The skylight is shaded by the high-rise building component on the east and vegetation on the west. To reduce solar gain, a variety of glasses have been used in the skylight (and the other window assemblies adjacent to this skylight). For further information about this building and its materials and assemblies, see the articles by Crosbie, M.J., "An essay in integral decoration," *Architecture*, 73(2), February 1984, pages 70–73; and Brenner, D., "Balancing the scales of justice," *Architectural Record*, 172(7), June 1984, pages 126–135.

SIDEBAR 9.10 Preferable orientations for tilted skylights

The best orientation for tilted skylights in locations north of the tropic of Cancer is north (or, possibly, northeast and northwest). South of the tropic of Capricorn tilted skylights should be oriented toward the south (or southeast and southwest). In the equatorial region between the two tropics, external shading devices (such as those described in Section 9.7) must be applied to tilted skylights (regardless of tilt orientation) to exclude solar heat gain.

9.25

9.26

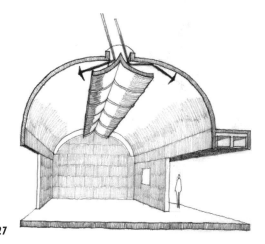

9.27

Figures 9.25–9.27 These three illustrations present the basic daylighting scheme for the Kimbell Art Museum in Fort Worth, Texas. A fundamental problem in the building of art museums and galleries is how to admit daylight so that it approximates the quantity and quality of light under which the displayed artifacts were created. In Fort Worth, the climate offers sustained periods of clear skies with very bright direct-beam sunlight. Alternatively, numbers of the artifacts present in the Kimbell collection were created under the largely diffused daylighting conditions common to Northern Europe. Thus, a challenge for the architect was how to bring bright Texas daylight into the museum in a manner so that the light would match the much softer Northern European illumination. The solution involves the use of semicylindrical lenses placed at the apex of each concrete half-cylindrical vault; a strip-opening in each vault (below a lens) so that daylight can pass into the building; two quarter-cylindrical, mirrored panels which reflect the admitted daylight upward on to the ceilings of the concrete vault; and a reflective coating placed on the ceiling to reflect the daylight downward toward the artifacts (and people). Thus, the very bright daylight is admitted and diffused multiply so that the interior light is soft and well-distributed. In addition to this multiple-reflection solution, some daylight is also admitted through small openings at the vertical ends of the half-cylindrical roof vaults. Substantial literature exists about the Kimbell Art Museum: for example, see the article written by Speck, L., "Evaluation: the Kimbell Museum," *AIA Journal*, 71, August 1982, pages 35–43.

9.3.2 USING WINDOWS ON MULTIPLE SPACE-ENCLOSING PLANES TO BALANCE ILLUMINATION

To create a more uniform distribution of illumination throughout a building space, *employ windows on more than one of the envelope planes that enclose the space.* A common problem with building spaces that have windows on a single enclosing plane — whether a vertical wall or a roof — is that the illumination distribution resulting from daylight entrance is nonuniform. Thus, there will be a region, usually near the window(s), where the illumination is much brighter than in the remainder of the space. Occupants located elsewhere and looking towards this window will frequently experience glare. Alternatively, for occupants who may be near the window-wall and face the interior of the space, the space will seem *gloomy.* This sense of gloom is mainly caused by the significant variation in illumination levels across the space.

A principal solution for these glare and gloom presences is to admit daylight through openings located on more than one enclosing plane of the space. For instance, placing a window on a second vertical side of the space — whether on an adjacent or opposite wall — will appreciably improve the illumination distribution across the space (see Figure 9.28).

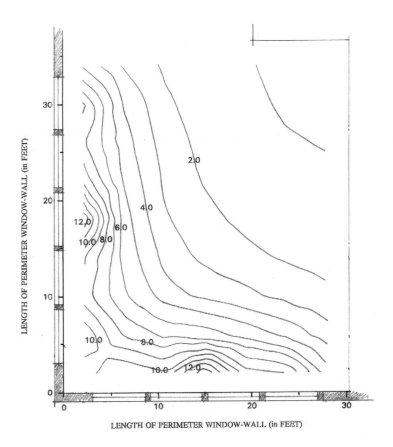

Figure 9.28 An open-planned (landscaped) office area with windows on two window-walls and the DF contour pattern for that office.

A second means of improving the daylight distribution within a room is to use a clerestory or skylight as a complement to fenestration located along a single side of a room. Either a clerestory or skylight—especially when suitable reflecting (diffusing) surfaces are present—can bring daylight into areas of a building space, where otherwise a space with a single window-wall would be gloomy. The clerestory or skylight, if used to create a more uniform illumination distribution within the space, would also reduce the likelihood that glare would be experienced in view fields that included the primary window. The likelihood of glare being experienced is lessened because the overall illumination level across the room would be higher and, thus, an occupant's eyes would *adapt* to this higher overall level. Concomitantly, a lower brightness ratio would exist between the surface of the primary window and the other space surfaces because these other surfaces would gain illumination from the secondary source.

9.3.3 USING LOW WINDOW SILLS TO REDUCE GLARE PRESENCE FROM WINDOWS

A fundamental problem for window design is that windows that admit daylight often have much brighter surfaces than the internal room surfaces that surround the windows. Consequently, the contrast (or brightness) ratios that exist between the windows and the surrounding surfaces can be quite large. A common result of having these large contrast ratios in occupant view fields is that the occupant may experience glare. One solution for mitigating this glare is to *locate windows so that they have low sills and look out upon immediately external surfaces that have low reflectances* (see Figure 9.29).[3] A lowered sill height enables a greater amount of daylight to enter a space, thereby increasing the ambient daylight throughout the space and the relative brightness of internal surfaces surrounding the window. By increasing both the ambient illumination level and the brightnesses of surfaces near the window, the range of brightnesses will be lessened

Figure 9.29 A house in Ojai, California: note the use of glazing on the adjoining sides of this dwelling.

between the window surface, the surfaces surrounding the window, and other surfaces that may appear in the view field when an occupant looks toward the window. Thus, the likelihood that the occupant will experience glare, when looking at or through the window, can be reduced. Two qualifications should nonetheless be noted for these lowered sills: if the sills are lowered below the height of the work surfaces, then the benefit of the extra window area (for workplane illumination) may be negligible; and any surfaces external to windows with low sills should have low reflectances so that glare is not caused by bright light reflecting off of these surfaces.

SIDEBAR 9.11 Human vision and glare

The human eye is drawn to bright objects: this property of the visual system is known as *phototropism*. When a person observes a bright object in an otherwise dimly lighted view field, very often the viewer will experience glare. Having a bright window in the view field—particularly when the surfaces inside a building and surrounding the window are dark—can cause glare. There are five parameters of the window-viewing experience that jointly affect the extent that glare may be encountered: the brightness (luminance) of the sky (or portion of the sky) seen through the window; the apparent size of the sky portion observed (i.e., how large the sky is relative to the rest of the view field or the fraction of the view field the sky constitutes); the position of the sky in the view field (i.e., where the sky appears in the overall view field: in the midst or at the periphery of the view field); the distance of the window (and its bright surface) from the observer (for an occupant seated close to a window, the window will represent a greater fraction of the view field than if the occupant were located further from the window); and the adaptation conditions within the building space (i.e., the brightness levels for the surfaces surrounding the window and the other surfaces that appear in the view field). These five parameters define the luminous conditions associated with having a window in a building occupant's view field.

Various researchers have studied these parameters seeking observations about how they affect visual comfort and what conditions should be satisfied to promote visual comfort. Their studies show the following results. First, the more nearly equal the luminances of the window surface (and the portion of the sky seen from the window) and its surrounding surfaces are, the lower the probability that glare will be experienced. Alternatively, the greater the contrast between the window surface (and the sky portion seen from the window) and the surrounding interior building surfaces, the greater the likelihood that the viewer will experience visual discomfort. Second, decreasing the apparent size of the source—the portion of the sky seen from the window—does little to increase visual comfort; similarly, increasing the size of the surfaces surrounding the window (i.e., by decreasing the size of the window surface) also provides little benefit for visual comfort. And, third, when the source—the portion of the sky seen through the window—is directly in the middle of the view field, the visual discomfort is more likely to be greater than when the source is located at the periphery of the view field.

We have discussed glare and its effects on visual comfort in Section 7.5. For additional discussions, see the paper by Chauvel et al., which presents an excellent description of the research about glare and offers more detailed information about means for its control in buildings: Chauvel, P., J.B. Collins, R. Dogniaux, and J. Longmore, "Glare from windows: current views of the problem," *Lighting Research & Technology*, 14(1), 1982, pages 31–46. A second source that explains the general causes of glare and suggests means for reducing it in buildings is a chapter by Hopkinson, R.G., and P. Petherbridge, "Discomfort glare and the lighting of buildings," published in the book by Hopkinson, R.G., *Architectural Physics: Lighting*, (London: Her Majesty's Stationery Office, 1963), pages 201–224.

Section 9.4 | WHAT SHAPE SHOULD A WINDOW HAVE?

In Section 8.1 we stated that the two principal reasons why we have windows in buildings are that windows provide occupants with views of the exterior (i.e., contact with what is outside of the building) and admit daylight for illuminating the activities that occur within the building. These essential roles for windows should then be the bases for defining what *shapes* windows should have.

A first guideline for establishing the shape of a window is *use wide, horizontal windows for admitting daylight and tall, vertical windows for enabling the view of the exterior.* One qualification that is central to the choice of whether a window should be long in *either* its horizontal *or* vertical dimension — *and not long in both* — is that the area of fenestration in buildings presently tends to be limited by various governmental regulations. In other words, because fenestration permits greater heat gain and/or loss through it than through virtually all opaque envelope assemblies, regulatory agencies have increasingly set limits on how much fenestration can be present in a building envelope. Thus, a designer or builder can seldom specify windows in a building, which are *long* both in the horizontal and vertical dimensions.

Using a wide, horizontal window in the window-wall of a building space will provide a relatively uniform illumination distribution *across the width* of the space. How deeply into the space daylight from this window can penetrate effectively will be determined by the height of this horizontal strip above the floor. The higher the strip is in the window-wall, the deeper daylight will flow usefully into the space. But a trade-off for having a higher window is that the *seated* occupant will be unable to see anything through the window except for the sky vault. Thus, the higher horizontal strip, although enhancing daylight presence within the room, will reduce view capabilities for the occupants. Alternatively, a lower horizontal strip, which will permit a better range of view for seated occupants, will provide relatively poorer daylight admission. The higher horizontal window (compared with the lower horizontal window) will also see more of the upper sky. When the sky is overcast (and the daylight largely diffused), this upper sky commonly tends to have greater physical brightnes, luminance, than the lower sky. However, for times when the sky is clear, the higher window should be provided with means for blocking or diffusing the direct-beam sunlight that might enter the room (with its substantial brightness and accompanying solar heat gain).

Windows that are tall will enable the occupant, whether seated or standing, to enjoy a greater view range. With such a window shape, the occupant can more readily partake of the three horizontal layers that comprise the ideal view: the area close to the building;

SIDEBAR 9.12 Energy-efficiency and window assembly selection

It is, of course, possible to create fenestration assemblies that have quite low rates of heat loss and heat gain. But, generally, the most energy-efficient assemblies are also the most expensive. The additional costs that must be paid to employ more energy-efficient assemblies can only be justified when a client will accept such extra costs or when other special considerations dictate or justify these expenses (e.g., when the external climate is especially rigorous, or occupants are likely to be particularly sensitive to thermal comfort maintenance, (such as in health care facilities or nursing homes).

everything from the area just beyond the building to the horizon; and the sky. The vertical window is best suited for displaying these three layers, both from various locations in a room and for seated and standing occupants. This window also will generally provide a greater variation in brightness from the bottom to the top of its expanse than one experiences for a wide, horizontal window. The daylight distribution illumination — resulting from the tall and narrow window — will present a high magnitude along a vertical plane perpendicular to the window and significantly lower magnitudes in areas on either side of the plane perpendicular to this vertical window (see Figure 9.30). So, the tall, narrow window can effectively bring usable daylight further into the room than can the long, horizontal window. But this area of useful daylight will be quite narrow, and the distribution of light across the width of the room will be highly nonuniform.

A third issue that can perhaps impel decisions about window shapes concerns how they can affect an occupant's visual comfort. The principal study of how visual comfort can be influenced by window shape has been conducted by Hopkinson. In that research he examined a range of shapes of *equal-sized* windows to determine whether these shapes might cause discomfort for building occupants.[4] His special interest focused on to what degree glare would be experienced. The study examined six particular shapes whose dimensions varied, in terms of *a ratio of length to height,* from 1:10 to 40:1. Hopkinson's research protocol employed a model room (constructed at a scale of about 2" = 1'-0") for which the illumination could be widely altered. He asked a number of subjects to look into the model room through an opening in an "interior" wall. What the subjects saw was one of the *equal-sized, different-shaped* windows placed opposite the "interior" wall opening. For each window shape, the conditions of source and surround brightness were varied, and the subjects were asked to assess how they found the lighting conditions (e.g., did they experience glare?). The results that he reported from this experiment were that observers found, *for the same conditions of environmental brightness,* a wide, horizontal window caused no more glare than did a square window; a tall, narrow window provided the most glare; and the window causing the least glare had a length-to-height ratio of 10:1.

The finding that a tall, narrow window (looking out to the daylighted sky) would be the most glary is not surprising because the *variation in brightness* from the bottom to the top of such a window *would generally be substantial.* This variation would be present whether the sky was clear or overcast (i.e., the clear sky would be brighter near the horizon, whereas the overcast sky would commonly be brighter as one's view ascended toward the zenith). Thus, *when tall, narrow windows are used in buildings — to enhance view opportunities — devices should be included to mitigate glare presence.* These devices could obscure the upper — or lower — part of the sky, thereby reducing the vertical fraction of the sky vault observed (e.g., shading could be provided with an overhang or an awning). Alternatively, the brightness of the tall, narrow window might be filtered, using a device that decreases the transmittance of the overall fenestration assembly (such as is found with tinted or heat-reflective glasses).

Knowing that a wide, horizontal window will offer a more uniform daylight distribution within a space and that a tall, narrow window will provide better view capabilities, we could ask whether a square window might afford a successful compromise between these two extreme shapes. But the square or nearly square shape simply presents some of the useful *and* limiting qualities of both extremes and has no special basis for recommending its use. So, a square shape should be chosen by a designer or builder for reasons other than those of acquiring better views or better daylight distributions. For instance, the square window might be chosen because it best suits some activity pattern or a furnishing style that is to be present in a space.

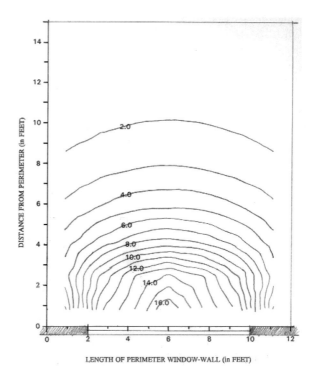

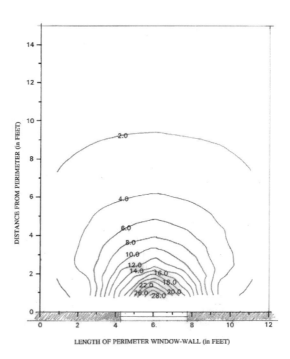

Figure 9.30 The daylight distributions for *equal-sized* windows with dimensions that are, on the left, long in the horizontal dimension and short in the vertical dimension and, on the right, short in the horizontal dimension and long in the vertical dimension.

Finally, picking an appropriate shape for a skylight requires somewhat different considerations than for a window (see Figure 9.31). One must determine whether the skylight will be used as a primary source of light or to complement windows in a vertical window-wall; whether the skylight will be a large single unit or a number of smaller, multiple units (e.g., in the form of a sawtooth arrangement); and whether the skylight will be tilted or flat. In addition, one must determine at what locations within the space to place the skylights present, to what extent might the brightness of the skylights intrude into an occupant's view field, and so forth. Most likely a skylight cannot be counted upon to provide a view experience. But a central reason for incorporating one or more skylights in a roof is to bring daylight in from the overhead sky. Thus, the shape (and height above the work surface) of the skylight should be established by satisfying the daylight distribution a designer or builder wants to offer the occupants of the space. A square or nearly square skylight will provide daylight in a relatively concentrated area underneath the skylight. Alternatively, a long, narrow rectangular skylight — of the same surface area as the square skylight — can offer a greater area of potentially useful daylight. So, for any skylight, the choice of its shape should be based primarily on how the space beneath the skylight will need to be illuminated. Also, note that skylights with the same shape but located at heights progressively further above the workplane will spread daylight further outward and will generally promote wider, more uniform distributions. But the maximum Daylight Factor amounts achieved with these higher skylights decrease as the distances between the workplane and the skylight increase (see Figure 9.32).

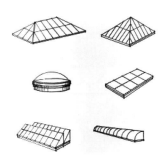

Figure 9.31 A number of alternative rooftop daylight-admitting devices.

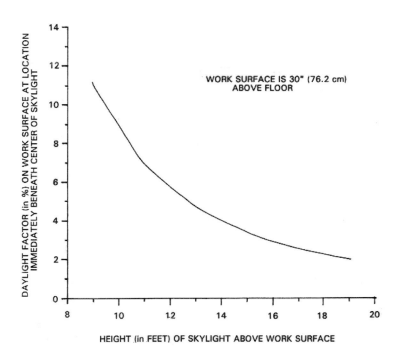

HEIGHT (in FEET) OF SKYLIGHT ABOVE WORK SURFACE

Figure 9.32 Considering a prototypical horizontal skylight, the variation in the vertical distance from the surface of the skylight to the workplane surface has been plotted versus the Daylight Factor (in %) for a location on the workplane directly underneath the center of the skylight.

SIDEBAR 9.13 Further information about Hopkinson's study of window shapes

First, the six window shapes that Hopkinson employed for his study were (as ratios of length-to-height): 1:10; 1:2.5; 1:1; 2.5:1; 10:1; and 40:1. Second, to control carefully the precise levels of physical brightness used in the model facility Hopkinson chose to employ electric lighting (i.e., rather to rely on daylight) as the illumination source. Thereby, he was assured that specific lighting levels were reproducible whenever he needed to apply them. Third, the observers that Hopkinson employed in this experiment (and a number of his other studies of glare conditions) had been specially selected to participate because of their abilities to provide similar observations across a time span (i.e., their responses to specific lighting conditions would be the same). Hopkinson described his use of these "human meters" in a brief section, "The human being as a meter," of his book, *Architectural Physics: Lighting*, (London: Her Majesty's Stationery Office, 1963), pages 8–9.

Section 9.5 | HOW LARGE DO WINDOWS NEED TO BE?

Ever since the on-set of the oil supply embargoes, which were imposed on the industrialized nations in the 1970s, designers and builders in these countries have exercised greater care when sizing windows. In fact, for the period between the oil embargoes and the present, window areas have generally been reduced substantially (i.e., in relation to the amounts of glazing that were used in building envelopes before the 1970s). The principal argument that has been cited by regulatory agencies as the justification for these mandated decreases in window area is that both heat gain and heat loss through the building envelope can be reduced if glazing areas are decreased (i.e., as rates of heat loss and heat gain are reduced, the amounts of energy required for heating and cooling buildings can be decreased, thus reducing fuel consumption). Therefore, many regulatory agencies have specified allowable glazing areas based on thermal performance issues. Indeed, these agencies have tended to disregard topics such as the admission of daylight or insuring occupant contact with the external environment when decisions about the amount of glazing have been formulated.

9.5.1   DEFINING WINDOW SIZE BASED ON STUDIES OF OCCUPANT SATISFACTION WITH REDUCED WINDOW AREAS

Research that has focused on the definition of window sizes *based on occupant needs or wishes* is comparatively sparse. However, the few studies that have been completed offer interesting results. The first of four studies we will cite was performed by Ne'eman and Hopkinson.[5] These authors used a reduced-scale model room (constructed at $1'' = 1'\text{-}0''$) that they had test subjects look into. Across the room from where the subjects viewed, there was a window that looked out on to a London townscape and sky. The size of this opposite window could be varied. The model room was illuminated using electric lamps, and the illumination within the model room remained constant for all the tests. The parameters of the test facility which could be varied included: the dimension of the window height above a sill fixed at three feet (in scale); the number of segments for the opposite window; the total opening area of the window; the content of the outside view; and the character of the weather and the sky brightness. The conditions for these parameters during any test period were either established by the researchers or were those that were available at that time (e.g., for the outside view, the weather, and the sky brightness). The subjects, after being introduced to the test conditions, were then asked to adjust the size of the opposite window to create "the minimum acceptable window opening."

What Ne'eman and Hopkinson concluded from this study was that the amount of daylight that entered through the window, the position of the sun, and the sky brightness were *not* the principal issues that caused the subjects to establish a "minimum acceptable window opening." Rather, the subjects concentrated primarily on the *view* that could be provided by a window of this minimum size (i.e., they most wanted to maintain contact with the external environment). A second conclusion of the researchers was that no simple dimensional relationship was evident in terms of the width and the height for the minimum window opening. The preferred minimum width was found to be directly proportional to the distance that an occupant was from the window. The researchers derived a "window ratio" to describe the minimum acceptable width: the window width (employed in the test) divided by the distance that the occupant was from the window. For the studies that the researchers conducted, they determined that the window ratio that provided the preferred width was approximately 0.50. As an alternative method for expressing the width for the minimally acceptable window, these researchers suggested considering the *viewing angle* that an occupant would have with the window (i.e., the angle formed using the occupant as the origin and the opposite sides of the window (in the horizontal plane) as the boundaries of the view angle). Ne'eman and Hopkinson observed that the subjects preferred view angles of between 30° and 60°. When the window was long enough to create view angles greater than 60°, the subjects expressed no greater satisfaction. On the subject of a preferred height for the windows, the researchers uncovered no definitive result (i.e., what they observed they regarded as contradictory and requiring further study). Thirdly, the researchers found that whether there were one large window or several small ones had no influence on observer satisfaction, as long as the view angle provided was between 30° and 60°. In fact, the several smaller windows were looked upon, effectively, as being additive. Fourthly, Ne'eman and Hopkinson noticed that 50 percent of the subjects were satisfied if the window length was at least 25 percent of the window

---

SIDEBAR 9.14 Other qualifications concerning the Ne'eman and Hopkinson study

Necessarily, the view angles would be strongly dependent on the locations of the occupants in a building space. For people close to an opening, to sustain the view angle criterion of 30° to 60°, the window could be less long than for someone further removed from the window. Presumably, if one were sizing a window to furnish a minimum acceptable view angle for anywhere in the room, the position furthest from the window would have to be chosen as the location from which this view angle was cast.

After developing the reduced-scale model and the associated testing methodology, Ne'eman and Hopkinson carried out similar test procedures in a full-scale building space as a check on the validity of their approach. These full-scale tests provided results similar to those found in the early stages of the work with the reduced-scale model, thus supporting the use of the model as a testing device.

wall and 85 percent of the subjects were satisfied if the window length was 35 percent of the window wall.[6] Finally, a "minimum acceptable window opening" was found to be one-sixteenth — 1/16th —of the room floor area.

A second study about the sizing of windows has been conducted by Keighley.[7] The basic methodology of Keighley's research was similar to that employed by Ne'eman and Hopkinson. Test subjects were asked to look into a reduced-scale model of an office that was illuminated with electric lamps. Various window configurations were placed on the elevation (of this reduced-scale room) opposite from the one the subject looked through. Any one of three specific views was projected onto the window surfaces. Each subject was then asked to rate the satisfaction that he or she felt with the window configuration-view combination. The four primary variables examined by Keighley were the effect of mullion width (for glazing assemblies composed of multiple panels); the number of window panels; the height of the window above the sill; and the area of the window. Two sets of tests were run to investigate the effects of these four variables: where the area of the window was fixed at 20 percent of the window-wall and where the area of the window was anywhere between 11 and 65 percent of the window-wall.

The results that Keighley found in this study included, first, that neither the mullion presence nor the number of window panels that made up the overall window area had much effect on how the subjects rated the schemes. Instead, the principal findings were that the most satisfactory windows were those that had their primary — longer — dimension along the horizontal, rather than the vertical edge; that had sufficient length across the window-wall so that they provided an uninterrupted view angle of 12° to 16° (*when measured from the center of the room*); and that this length should be between 60 to 75 percent of the wall length. Additionally, the optimum window area was established to be about 30 percent of the window-wall. Thus, this suggested window area closely matched the 35 percent amount found by Ne'eman and Hopkinson.

A third study about window size preferences has been reported by Tabet and Sharples.[8] These authors have also employed a research protocol similar to those used by Ne'eman and Hopkinson and by Keighley. The results from this latest research both confirm the earlier studies and offer further insight into occupant preferences about window

---

SIDEBAR 9.15 Qualifications of the Keighley study

Note that the ratings for both of these parameters—the presence of mullions and the number of window panels—were largely influenced by the character of the view. For views with small detail, if the mullion presence (or the opaque space between window panels) blocked the seeing of the small detail, then the subjects were less favorably disposed toward the window configuration. But, for a view with large items—whose identities could be deduced by seeing only portions of the items—then less dissatisfaction was expressed by the subjects about mullion presence or using multiple window panels.

The stipulation of a viewing angle by Keighley of 12° to 16° (from the center of the room) provides a "window ratio" of approximately 0.25, which is one-half of the window-ratio value established by Ne'eman and Hopkinson. Without further information (i.e., the research data collected in the two studies), resolution of this apparent dichotomy is not possible. Thus, until other studies are performed that can offer additional insight, both values should perhaps be regarded as disputable, and other guidelines for setting minimum window widths should instead be employed.

sizing. For instance, regarding the minimum and optimum sizes for windows, Tabet and Sharples found area ratios that match those previously found by Ne'eman and Hopkinson and by Keighley. But Tabet and Sharples also found that view content can be a significant determinant for both size and shape. Generally, if the view was interesting, then the subjects selected window sizes and shapes that enabled the subjects to see the views wholly. But, if the view was relatively "featureless and repetitive,"[9] then smaller windows were acceptable. One further result of this latest study concerns the heights for window headers and sills. For window headers, the optimum height was approximately 1.5 to 2.0 times the eye level of a seated occupant. Seemingly, the feature that most subjects sought after when they arranged the window header height was the skyline (i.e., the horizon or visual edge between the cityscape and the sky). Alternatively, the preferred sill height depended on whether the view the subjects were shown was either that which would be seen from a ground-floor office or one that an occupant would experience from a mid-height floor of a high-rise office building. For the ground-floor office, the preferred sill height ranged from 0.65 to 0.80 m (about 25 to 31 1/2 inches), whereas the preferred sill height for the higher floors was about 0.40 to 0.60 m (about 16 to 24 inches). The lowered sill for the upper floors enables the occupants to see more of the cityscape close to the simulated building. The higher sill for the ground floor does not prevent views of the areas close to the simulated building, and this greater sill height would provide more visual privacy from passersby.[10]

One other issue that a designer or builder should consider when selecting a suitable window area is how the size of a window can affect the maintenance of visual comfort. This question has been examined by Chauvel et al.[11] This team of authors has suggested that as long as the window area was at least 1.2 percent of the floor area of the space served by the window(s), any glare that was present would not be caused by the window size or the room size.[12] Instead, the glare would result primarily from the luminance of the window (or, really, the sky luminance) and, secondarily, from the reflectances of the room surfaces adjoining the fenestration assembly. So, for most building situations, windows sized to be about 30–35 percent of the window-wall will be substantially larger than windows sized to match the 1.2 percent of floor area suggested here. Thus, whether glare is experienced as a building occupant looks towards a window should not be the overriding factor in establishing the size of some window(s). Indeed, the size of the window is not the primary cause of the glare. Rather, glare would result from the brightness of the sky and the apparently great difference between the brightness of the window and the brightnesses of the internal surfaces in the view field surrounding the window.

To summarize — as design guidelines — the findings of these four research studies, we can state that *window(s) in a window-wall should be laid out with the horizontal dimension — the width — being greater than the height; the window width should be at least 60 to 75 percent of the total width of window-wall; the window(s) area should be about 30 to 35 percent of the total area of the window-wall and should also be equal to or greater than one-sixteenth of the floor area of the space that is served by the window-wall; and the sill and header heights should be chosen to accommodate the likely views that occupants can experience.* The first three studies have emphasized that *the essential benefit of windows* — which the test subjects demonstrated as they evaluated the various window schemes — was *contact with the outside* (i.e., the provision of a view of the world external to the building). Thus, where permitted by building codes and other local construction industry practices, windows must be sized and shaped to accommodate the viewing of the exterior. Lastly, using windows as means for admitting daylight to the building interior was seemingly deemed to be of lesser importance by the subjects of these various tests (although it should be noted that the use of electric lamps as the illumination source in these studies would have diminished the importance of seeking daylight admission).

These guidelines apply to windows located in the vertical planes of a building envelope. Their applications for the sizing of skylights appear problematic. A primary limitation to using these guidelines for sizing skylights is that the guidelines were derived from tests of subjects, in which they indicated that maintaining contact with the exterior—seeing views—was the principal reason for having windows. Providing daylighting for illuminating the building interior was only a secondary goal. Skylights, on the other hand, would seem useful primarily for providing daylight and will likely offer few opportunities for views of anything but the sky (although sky views can at least offer information about the weather and time of day). Thus, the basis for developing the vertical window guidelines—people's wishes to have views—would not be relevant for setting guidelines for sizing skylights. Instead, what sizes skylights should have will be discussed in Section 9.5.2.

9.5.2   ESTABLISHING MINIMUM WINDOW AREAS FOR ADMITTING DAYLIGHT: SOME RULES-OF-THUMB [13]

Here we will present some rules-of-thumb which can be used as an alternative means for sizing windows. These approximations differ fundamentally from the guidelines offered in Section 9.5.1, the basis of which were the sizing (and shaping) of windows to enable occupants to view the external world. The foundation for these rules-of-thumb is the sizing of windows to admit daylight to the building interior. Two sets of these guidelines will be provided: those for vertical windows and those for roof fenestration.

9.5.2.1   Rules-of-thumb for sizing windows in the vertical envelope   Two rules-of-thumb are suggested for *vertical windows:*

$$DF_{average} = 0.2 \times (\text{glazing area / floor area})$$

$$DF_{minimum} = 0.1 \times (\text{glazing area / floor area})$$

The distinction between *average* and *minimum* concerns how much daylight should enter the space. The *average* Daylight Factor should be used when you wish to illuminate a space with daylight so that the *illumination level on the workplane averaged across the space* is the one established by this Daylight Factor rule. Alternatively, if you wish to ensure that *at least some minimum daylight illumination level is present across a workplane* (i.e., located at any point throughout a space), then you should employ the rule-of-thumb for the *minimum* Daylight Factor.

For example, suppose you are designing a classroom that is to have a floor area of 500 square feet. The suggested Daylight Factor for schools is 2 percent (from Table 8.4). If you want to have enough vertical glazing to provide a DF of 2 percent *averaged across the 500 square feet* (i.e., so that some areas on the workplane would have more and other areas would have less), then you would only need 50 square feet of glazing. But, if you wanted to ensure that the *minimum DF* that you would find *anywhere* on the workplane in the room was 2 percent, then you would need 100 square feet of vertical window.[14]

The rule-of-thumb for *sizing clerestories* is similar to that for providing an *average* DF illumination level with vertical windows:

$$DF_{average} = 0.2 \times (glazing\ area\ /\ floor\ area)$$

So, if a clerestory (or a series of clerestories) is sized according to this rule-of-thumb, then the *average* illumination level across the workplane in the daylighted room will match the daylight factor you have chosen as your design target.

9.5.2.2 Rules-of-thumb for sizing roof openings The roof openings we will address are the skylight and the sawtooth monitor. Essentially, these building elements are two variations on a single theme: both serve to admit daylight into the interior of a building (i.e., at some distance inward from the envelope for the building). For the sake of these rules-of-thumb, the essential difference between the skylight and the sawtooth monitor relates to the positioning of the fenestration. For the skylight, the fenestration is deployed horizontally, whereas, for the sawtooth monitor, the fenestration is tilted (sloped). The fenestration material that is used in the skylight and the sawtooth monitor can either be flat or curved.

The horizontal skylight, unless specially treated, will permit both diffused daylight and direct-beam sunlight to pass into the building space beneath the fenestration. As the admission of direct-beam radiation—both the sunlight and the accompanying nonvisible thermal radiation—can cause discomfort for building occupants (e.g., in terms of excessive brightness and substantial heat gain loads), horizontal skylights should be accompanied by means to reject or at least diffuse the direct-beam sunlight. Note also that simply diffusing the direct-beam sunlight will only partially reduce the heat gain that accompanies the entrance of the sunlight. Methods for controlling the passage of direct-beam sunlight through fenestration are discussed in Section 9.7.

The sawtooth monitor can also admit direct-beam sunlight into a building space, if the surface of the sawtooth monitor faces the sun. To avoid the admission of direct-beam sunlight through a sawtooth monitor, you should either orient the monitor away from the sun or provide shading devices that would block (or diffuse) the direct-beam sunlight. In the Northern Hemisphere north of the tropic of Cancer, for instance, sawtooth monitors should face toward the north. Alternatively, south of the tropic of Capricorn, sawtooth monitors should face southward. In the higher latitudes both north and south of the respective tropics, shading devices may be needed during the summer months because early morning and late afternoon direct-beam radiation can fall on sawtooth monitor surfaces facing away from the equator. For the area between the two tropics, any sawtooth monitors will require the use

---

SIDEBAR 9.16 Using these rules-of-thumb for multiple window forms

One strategy that can be employed, if some combination of vertical windows and roof fenestration is desired, is to set the individual Daylight Factors for each opening type to "smaller values" than the total Daylight Factor amount sought for the space. As illumination provided by daylight (and by electric sources) is to a great extent additive, then you could set these smaller values for the opening types so that they added to equal the total Daylight Factor amount sought.

For an example, if you were designing the 500 square foot classroom described in Section 9.5.2.1 and you wished to have an averaged Daylight Factor of 2 percent, you might decide that a Daylight Factor of 1 percent could be provided for vertical windows along one elevation and that sawtooth monitors could be used to provide the other 1 percent. Using their respective rules-of-thumb to size the two fenestration forms would give you reasonable size estimates for them.

of shading devices, as direct-beam radiation will fall on surfaces sloped in any of the four cardinal compass directions for at least significant periods of time throughout the year.

The rules-of-thumb for these two fenestration forms are, for the horizontal skylight,

$$DF_{average} = 0.50 \times (glazing\ area\ /\ floor\ area)$$

and, for the sawtooth monitor,

$$DF_{average} = 0.33 \times (glazing\ area\ /\ floor\ area)$$

Two qualifications should be noted about using these rules-of-thumb. First, both formulas are suitable for generating *averaged* daylighting presence across the workplane in a space. One concern about the use of the rule-of-thumb for skylights is that openings, sized with the rule to provide a desired average DF amount, *may often exhibit large light level gradients* at the workplane height. These large gradients can frequently cause problems by introducing excessive brightness and glare. Further, these skylights may also produce veiling reflections. Generally, though, to ensure that a more uniform distribution of illumination is achieved across a workplane, the best layout strategy is to apportion the area of the opening as uniformly as possible over the envelope surface in which the opening(s) is (are) to be present (i.e., essentially, to divide the suggested skylight area into a series of skylights, each with a fraction of the overall suggested area). The second qualification about both formulas is that their application presumes that either the skylight or the monitor would provide the only daylight that enters the building space. Thus, if you wish to size a skylight to supplement a vertical window, then these rules-of-thumb are somewhat less useful (although an approximating approach described in Sidebar 9.16 can be beneficially employed).

Necessarily, these rules-of-thumb should be used only as quick approximations for the *preliminary schematic* phase for building design. More careful sizing approaches—utilizing the Daylight Factor protractor method, the *Graphic Daylighting Design Method Workbook* method, or computer programs—should be applied during the subsequent *design development* of the proposed building and its fenestration openings.

Section 9.6 | ALTERNATIVE WINDOW TREATMENTS FOR PASSING DAYLIGHT DEEPER INTO BUILDINGS

In Section 9.2 we have stated that the depth of a building into which daylight can penetrate *usefully* is limited. How deeply daylight will enter into a building space—when an ordinary window is used—depends on several parameters including the area and shape of the window, the height of the window above the floor (or the workplane), the choice of window materials, and so forth. But, generally, daylight entering a building through an opening in the vertical envelope will have an intensity that is higher near the window and that decreases as one moves further away from the window. At some distance into the building from the window, the intensity of the daylight becomes sufficiently weak enough so that intended activities cannot be performed while relying on this daylight illumination.

In Sections 9.2 and 9.3 we have identified some design strategies that would enable daylight to penetrate farther into building interiors. Those devices involve *the overall form of a building* (e.g., the layout of narrow buildings or the use of atria and/or light tunnels). We will now describe three additional strategies that specifically concern *the composition*

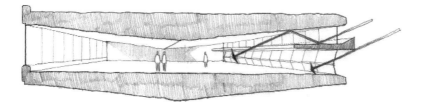

Figure 9.33 This building cross-section shows a light-shelf assembly which has been effectively used as both a means to foster the passage of daylight deeper across a building space and a shading device for reducing the brightness and heat gain of direct-beam radiation (and sunlight). This cross-section is an approximation of the actual form of the Lockheed Office Building #157 in Sunnyvale, California. This drawing is a reproduction of an image presented in the paper by Benton, C.C., B. Erwine, M. Warren, and S. Selkowitz, "Field measurements of light shelf performance in a major office installation," *Proceedings of the 11th National Passive Solar Conference,* pages 291–295. Permission to reproduce this image has been granted by the American Solar Energy Society and C.C. Benton.

or organization of fenestration assemblies: light shelves, clerestories (and roof openings), and "borrowed" light. Each of these three devices can be used singly, or any two or all three can be applied in concert.

9.6.1   USING LIGHT SHELVES TO BRING LIGHT INTO BUILDINGS

Employ light shelves for admitting daylight deep into spaces. A light shelf is essentially a horizontal plane that protrudes out from the vertical plane of a fenestration assembly and into the building interior (see Figures 9.33 and 9.34). This shelf is usually located toward the upper part of the window-wall and is rarely set at heights less than about six-and-one-half or seven feet (2.0 to 2.1 m) above the floor. The function of the light shelf is to reflect daylight—both the diffuse component from the sky vault and direct-beam sunlight—on to the ceiling of the space. Then, this daylight is expected to reflect off of the ceiling and enter into the building interior (at depths greater than would be common with simple vertical windows). The pattern of reflection between the shelf and the ceiling may involve multiple reflections: this pattern will be dictated by the geometry between the ceiling and the shelf and, particularly, the angle with which the direct-beam sunlight reaches the shelf. To enhance reflection of daylight inward, the top surface of the light shelf can be finished to promote specular reflections. Then, if the ceiling surface is comparatively rough (e.g., composed of wallboard, plaster, or acoustic tile), it will diffuse any specular reflections that emanate from the light shelf.

The placement of the light shelf above the eye level of a standing (and, thus, a sitting) occupant is important: first, at that height the light shelf will not obscure the view that the occupant sees when looking out of the lower portion of the window and, second, there will be virtually no opportunity for the *top* of the light shelf to enter into the view field of an occupant. As very bright light may reflect off of the top surface of the light shelf—and likely cause glare if that bright light were to enter the view field—occupants should not be able to see this top surface.

The light shelf can serve effectively as a means to introduce direct-beam sunlight into a space. Direct-beam sunlight will reflect off of the light shelf onto the ceiling. The

Figure 9.34 The light shelf shown here occurs in the Emerald Public Utility District Office Building in Eugene, Oregon.

Figure 9.35 A typical clerestory is shown in this drawing.

Figure 9.36 This clerestory application occurs in the Mount Angel Abbey Library, Benedictine, Oregon. These windows are located along the perimeter adjacent to the library stacks (see the building section of this library shown in Figure 9.15).

reflection diffuses the light, making it more tolerable as it enters the view field. Enabling *diffused* direct-beam sunlight to enter as light reflected off of a light shelf should still be done with some care because the diffused sunlight will be very bright compared to the generally diffused daylight (from the sky vault) that enters through the lower window. To ensure that there would not be a large brightness ratio between *the light coming in above the light shelf* and *the light entering below the light shelf,* the light shelf should have sufficient depth (into the room from the vertical envelope) to allow for the development of a multiple-reflection pattern between the top of the light shelf and the bottom of the ceiling. One other benefit that the light shelf may provide is that it can serve as a means of shading the window below it from direct-beam solar radiation (thus keeping excessively bright light and the potential solar heat gain from entering the space).[15]

9.6.2   USING CLERESTORIES AND ROOF-TOP OPENINGS TO ADMIT DAYLIGHT INTO THE BUILDING INTERIOR

The primary function for the clerestory, skylight, and sawtooth monitor is to promote the admission of daylight, possibly deep into the building interior. All three forms are located above the occupant's eye level. As such, their capacities for offering views of the external world are limited to scenes of the sky or of any very tall vegetation, landforms, or buildings.

A clerestory is essentially a window form that may be located either in the vertical plane of any principal elevation of a building or as vertical fenestration somewhere on the roof surface of a building (see Figures 9.35 – 9.37). When placed in one of the vertical envelope faces of a building, the ability of the clerestory to admit light more deeply into the building space is better than a vertical window which occurs at an occupant's eye level (again, note Figure 9.16). But, when a clerestory is incorporated into the roof plane of a

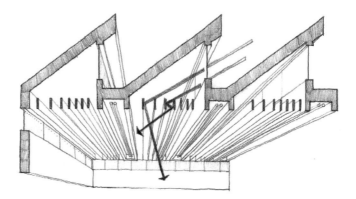

Figure 9.37 As we have noted, a basic difficulty in bringing bright daylight in through a mid-roof clerestory (or skylight) is how to soften the intensity of the light so that it does not cause visual discomfort for the occupants. One very nice solution to this need for brightness softening has been achieved at the Mount Airy Public Library in North Carolina. As bright daylight or even direct-beam sunlight passes amongst a multiple-slatting assembly, the light is diffused and its intensity is reduced. The resulting daylighted interior has sufficient intensity for the reading activities that occur throughout the floor area under these clerestories. For further information about this library, see the document by Reece, N., *Savings from the Sun: Passive Solar Design for Institutional Buildings*, (Report Number DE90000348), (Boulder, Colorado: American Solar Energy Society, June 1990).

building, then daylight will be admitted into the space beneath the clerestory. For example, if you are designing or constructing a building with a large floor area—perhaps a one-story school or a shopping center—then clerestories can be placed away from the perimeter of the building thereby readily admitting daylight into the interior.

Horizontal skylights and sawtooth monitors can similarly be used to bring daylight into spaces with large floor areas. These roof features can be located near the perimeter of the building or can be placed in the midst of a roof plane. However, one qualification about the use of these skylights or monitors toward the center of a roof plane is that the daylight entering with either of these devices can often appear very bright (in contrast to the more dim illumination provided by electric lighting fixtures). Therefore, when using skylights or monitors, arrangement should be made to soften the brightness of the penetrating daylight, especially if direct-beam sunlight might enter through the rooftop fenestration.

9.6.3 BORROWING LIGHT FROM A PERIMETER SPACE TO USE IN BUILDING INTERIORS

The use of opaque interior walls in buildings is dictated for a variety of reasons. Such walls can provide acoustic separation, a sense of security and privacy, place definition, and so forth. Whether in residences or multistory commercial buildings, floor-by-floor areas of these buildings are commonly divided into discrete, smaller areas. However, from the standpoint of trying to illuminate a building with daylight, the primary problem—which the presence of interior walls creates—is how to get daylight into internal areas separated from the building perimeter.

One solution that is satisfactory for single-story buildings is to use clerestories and roof top openings in the manner described in the Section 9.6.2. Alternatively, for multiple-storied buildings, you can employ atria and light tunnels (as considered in Section 9.2.2). But, if the daylight can only be admitted at the perimeter of the building—for example, the building has too many stories to use light tunnels or atria; roof-top openings are inappropriate for reasons of style and form; and so forth—then to get daylight into more internal spaces, the daylight must be able to penetrate through the separating, interior walls. Such penetration can only be accomplished if at least some of the interior walls are composed of translucent or transparent materials.

The use of transparent materials (e.g., glass and clear plastics) in an internal wall will permit daylight to pass through the wall. But some primary limitations exist for the presence of these materials in internal walls: they can offer poor acoustic separation; they do not provide visual privacy (unless they are used in conjunction with drapes or other coverings, which would limit the daylight penetration through the resulting assembly); they are comparatively more costly than conventional opaque assemblies; and they present occasional safety problems. To overcome these difficulties one solution is to use *composite* interior walls (i.e., partitions that are constructed, by area, of two or more different compositions). Thus, to accommodate daylight transmission through a space-dividing partition, you can create a wall having its lower two meters (about 80 inches) composed of an opaque assembly and then install a glazed assembly running from the top of the opaque assembly to the finished ceiling. The lower assembly will provide privacy, better acoustic separation, and be less costly and safer. The upper glazed assembly will allow daylight to penetrate from a perimeter space into an internal space (see Figure 9.38).

This design strategy of bringing daylight into the interior of a building through a glazed portion of a space divider is described as *borrowing light*. Generally, the amount

Figure 9.38 An example of borrowed light occurs in this office building. Daylight is admitted through the tilted skylights and illuminates the secretarial space directly underneath the skylight. The daylight passes through the vertical glazing into an office area beyond the composite wall on the left. Additionally, a small fraction of the daylight entering the secretarial space in the central portion of this photograph also passes through the large-windowed walls on the right into adjacent private offices.

of light that can be borrowed is not great and will be insufficient for tasks requiring any handling of detail-containing items. But having some daylight pass through a composite partition will enable interior spaces to be employed for activities such as circulation and socializing. Additionally, the entrance of even low levels of daylight can foster the sense that the exterior is nearby, even for occupants of internal spaces.

9.6.4   USING THESE THREE DEVICES IN PAIRS OR ALLTOGETHER

All three of these devices are basically secondary means for bringing light into a building. Clerestories and roof top openings are infrequently employed as the principal (or only) entries for illuminating a space. Light shelves and the borrowed light strategy both function best as supplements for windows that are located in the vertical envelope.

However, the three strategies can be used beneficially in various combinations to improve the performance of windows in the vertical envelope. Similarly, any one of these three strategies can be applied to enhance how the other two will function. For example, light shelves used in vertical fenestration assemblies will increase the amount of daylight that can pass into internal spaces through partly glazed partitions (that are used for borrowing light). Clerestories located at the perimeter of the building will aid in getting light to the glazing of such composite partitions. Alternatively, a light shelf — or, simply a reflecting panel — can be placed external to a clerestory to reflect daylight

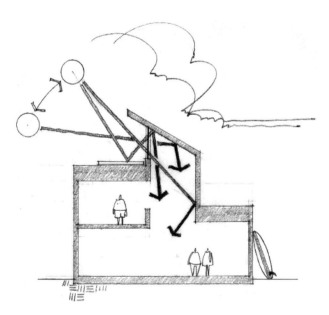

Figure 9.39 A clerestory monitor is displayed here with a reflecting panel located just outside the vertical glazing. To employ this reflecting panel effectively, maintaining visual comfort, the entering light should be diffused before it passes down to where occupants are located. To accomplish this diffusion (or "softening"), direct-beam sunlight (or bright daylight from the overcast sky vault) can be reflected off of the ceiling of the clerestory assembly or scattered by an internal reflecting device like the one shown in Figure 9.37 or an intermediate window material (see Section 9.7 for examples).

(and, especially, direct-beam sunlight) in through the clerestory fenestration [see Figure 9.39]). Frequently, providing daylight successfully for occupant use will require applying these (and other) strategies and devices in combination.

Section 9.7 | ALTERNATIVE FENESTRATION ASSEMBLIES AND MATERIALS

In Chapter 2 we have described how electromagnetic radiation—of which light is one form—behaves in three fashions when it reaches the surface of a solid material: The radiation can be transmitted through the material, reflected by the surface of the material, and absorbed at the surface of the material. In this section we will identify and describe a variety of fenestration materials and assemblies that can be used to control how readily light—and, more generally, solar radiation—will enter a building.

Fundamentally, light is one form of solar radiation. What distinguishes it from the other forms is that light is *visible*. This visible radiation—seen by animal forms as daylight—has two basic components: the direct-beam sunlight, which is the light that reaches the observer or the building surface directly from the sun, and the diffused light that comes from the sky vault and is scattered by the gases and other materials present in the atmosphere of the Earth.

In Section 8.1 we have identified a series of benefits and liabilities associated with having windows in buildings. Among the liabilities that we cited, two in particular can be dealt with by selecting appropriate fenestration assemblies. The first liability is that buildings may overheat substantially from the admission of solar radiation through windows. The second liability is that entering daylight can be excessively bright (causing visual discomfort for occupants).

How to control solar heat gain through windows is a topic involving trade-offs. Solar heat gain in buildings results largely from the passage of solar radiation through windows. Necessarily, daylight is one form of solar radiation. So, many devices that can be employed to reduce the rate with which solar heat gain enters a building will also reduce the admission of daylight. Often, therefore, the trade-off concerns how to get daylight to pass into the building without promoting the entrance of the accompanying solar heat gain.

The excessive brightness of daylight is also basically a problem of dealing with solar radiation. Daylight has two components: direct-beam sunlight and light from the diffusing sky. On a day when the sky is clear, direct-beam sunlight will have a brightness which is many times greater than the brightness of its blue-sky background. Alternatively, on a day with an overcast sky, the upper sky can be as much as three times as bright as the lower sky

---

SIDEBAR 9.17 Significance of the term *assembly*

The term *assembly* is used to indicate that the fenestration incorporates both the materials through which light—or, more generally, solar radiation—enters a building space and the devices that may be present inside and/or outside of these materials (e.g., drapes or overhangs and fins). The major purpose for assembling the light-passing materials and the inside and/or outside devices is to control the manner in which light—or solar radiation—enters the building interior.

(near the horizon). Further, on days that are partly cloudy, there can be significant variation in sky brightness over the course of the day (i.e., as clouds move across the sky and the solar disk is visible or not). Thus, choosing window materials also requires resolving problems concerning the magnitude of and variation in brightness.

9.7.1   WHAT ARE THE PRINCIPAL MATERIALS FOR WINDOWS?

The primary material used in windows is glass. The complicating factor about building with glass, however, is to select which kind of glass. Glass varies widely in composition, in the manner in which it is manufactured, in the types of assemblies in which it is available (or can be placed into), and, lastly and most importantly, in the range of properties that it and its assemblies can display (see Figure 9.40). The primary properties with which we are concerned here are those that dictate the rates of heat gain and loss through the glazing assembly and the ability of daylight to pass through the assembly. Other topics, such as the strength of glass, its resistance to breakage, safety features for occupants, cost, noise transmission characteristics, and so forth, are important parallel issues for designers and builders. But these topics do not directly affect the visual and thermal performances of glass.

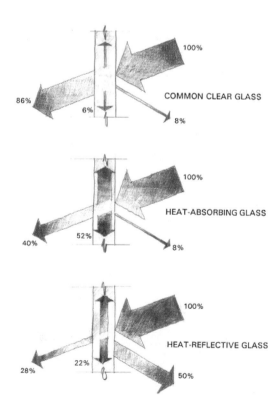

Figure 9.40 Three common glazing materials are identified here, along with their respective daylight transmittances, absorptances, and reflectances.

The other primary light-transmitting materials used in window assemblies are several polymeric compounds (known most generally as "plastics"). These compounds include polymethyl methacrylate (PMMA), polycarbonate (PC), polyvinyl chloride (PVC), and a few epoxies.[16] A number of these materials have properties that make them useful substitutes for glass: for instance, polycarbonate has a very high resistance to fracture and polyvinyl chloride can be easily formed into shapes that would be difficult and very costly to achieve with glass. Generally, many offer good transparency, whereas others are at least translucent. But, conversely, many of the polymeric materials have liabilities associated with their use: they often are easily scratched; they generally display much higher thermal expansion characteristics (than glass); numbers of these materials will become yellowed and/or will craze[17] with long-term use; and so forth. Thus, the selection of a polymeric material as a substitute for glass must be made with some care.

9.7.2 CHOOSING WINDOW MATERIALS FOR LUMINOUS PERFORMANCE

Controlling the brightness of the daylight that will enter a building depends ultimately on how much daylight reaches the window and how much of that daylight then is transmitted through the window assembly. We will treat the issues affecting the rate of light passage first. Then, we will discuss devices and techniques that can be used to control the amount of light that reaches the external window surface.

9.7.2.1 Controlling radiation transmission through glazing *Use low-iron glass to promote solar radiation transmission.* There are some applications for which one may wish to have as high a rate of radiation passage as possible (e.g., for the passive and active solar heating of buildings or for plant growth indoors). For these applications glass with a *low-iron content* will provide the highest transmittance of any common commercial product.[18]

Select glazing materials and assemblies displaying lowered-transmittances to reduce the admission of solar radiation. The passage of solar radiation into many buildings can cause occupant discomfort, both visually and thermally. To reduce the heat gain and/or excessive brightness resulting from solar radiation transmission, window materials should be employed that have reduced transmittance rates. At least five alternatives exist and are widely used to satisfy this need. First, tinted or colored glasses can be used. Examples include common gray glass that is often used in office buildings or the various tinted (or "stained") glasses found in the windows of religious buildings. Second, metallic or polymeric films can be affixed to a surface of a window glass. The films that are applied generally present a mirror-like appearance to the exterior of a building. From this appearance (and the fact that they will reflect much of the incident solar radiation, as well as incident daylight), the glasses that have such films attached are identified as *heat-reflective* (see Figure 9.4). A third approach to reducing the transmittance of a glass is developed by creating textures on the surface of the glass; this texturing is generally accomplished by rolling glass sheets while they are still hot during the initial production of the glass. The texturing will cause the glass to lose its *transparency*. But the textured surface will at least remain reasonably *translucent*. Fourth, glazing assemblies may be used that are composed of multiple panes of glass (i.e., arranged in series). Each pane by itself may permit a significant fraction of radiation to pass through the glass. For a multiple-pane assembly, however, the overall transmittance is approximately equal to the multiplication product of the transmittances for each of the two or more panes that comprise the assembly. Thus, multiple-pane assemblies will display overall transmittances that are less than the transmittance of any single pane of glass present in a multiple-pane assembly. The basic multiple-pane assembly consists of two clear glass panes. Alternatives to this basic unit include having more than two panes in an assembly (i.e., triple-pane or quadruple-pane assemblies); using tinted glass in the assembly or placing a metallic film on one surface in the multiple-pane assembly (generally, the film is placed on one surface within the "dead air" space that exists between the panes); employing glass blocks — whether composed of clear, textured, or heat-reflecting glass — to create a fenestrated area (see Figure 9.41); or using a double-pane assembly that has a venetian blind incorporated between the two panes of glass. Fifth, to reduce the transmittance of radiation through fenestration, the glass — whether used as a single pane or in multiple-pane assemblies — can be set in walls so that the glass is *tilted* out of its normally vertical orientation (see Figure 9.42). Thus, the glass will be tilted toward the ground, forming an acute angle of, perhaps, 80° or so.

All of these five alternative glazing types can be employed to reduce the passage of solar radiation through the fenestration. Using these glazing types will thereby reduce the solar heat gain that accompanies the solar radiation admission (and that can contribute to the overheating of buildings). The application of these reduced-transmittance glazing types will also decrease the amount of daylight that can enter into a building. Thus, when considering the possible use of any of these reduced-transmittance glazing types, the designer or builder must confront the trade-off between the benefit of decreasing solar heat gain and the liability of diminishing the amount of daylight that will be admitted through the glazing.

Figure 9.41 The building shown in this photograph is the Carpenter Center for Visual Studies located at Harvard University, Cambridge, Massachusetts. Note the use of glass blocks in the right foreground.

Figure 9.42 The window here is sloped downward relative to the vertical, producing a reduction in the transmittance of solar radiation (and thus creating a shading effect). This building is the national headquarters for the (U.S.) National Association of Home Builders and is located in Washington, D.C..

SIDEBAR 9.18 Further thoughts about some special glasses

Tinted glasses have various chemicals mixed with the basic glass compounds to produce specific colors. The chemicals—usually various metallic salts—are added while the glass exists in a molten state during its manufacture. The range of colors achievable by this tinting process is great and includes many of the primary (and the secondary) colors found across the rainbow.

Heat-reflective glasses present substantially increased reflectances and reduced transmittances compared to ordinary window glass. For instance, ordinary clear sheet window glass will have a transmittance of about 85 to 88 percent and a reflectance of about 8 to 10 percent. Transmittances of a typical single-sheet heat-reflecting window glass—a pane of glass to which a metallic or polymeric film has been affixed—will more commonly be anywhere from about 20 to 50 percent with reflectances of about 40 to 70 percent.

One further alternative has been employed in the Beinecke Rare Books Library at Yale University, in New Haven, Connecticut. There, instead of using a tinted glass as the primary fenestration material, large sheets of marble serve as the principal light-admitting elements of the vertical envelope. These marble sheets are sufficiently thin enough to enable light to pass through the material (see Figures 9.43 and 9.44).

Figure 9.43 This building is the Beinecke Rare Books Library at Yale University in New Haven, Connecticut. Daylight enters through the marble sheets that fill the openings between the concrete framing elements for the second through the sixth levels.

Figure 9.44 The radiation passing through the marble is greatly diffused, offering a very soft, delicate character. Further, because of the striations and veining present in the marble, the daylight appears to have an aura and complexity, which sets it apart from illumination that passes through the conventional window. We believe that the admitted light must closely approximate the quality (and quantity) of illumination that would have been present at the medieval and Renaissance centers of learning, art, and religion where many of the works now stored in this present-day library were created.

9.7.2.2 Using devices external to the window to control the admission of radiation into buildings *To reduce the amount of solar radiation — or the degree of excessive brightness — incident on the window surface, use external shading devices.* One principal alternative to the use of reduced-transmittance glazing is the inclusion of *shading devices* placed external to the window-wall of a building (see Figure 9.45). These external shading devices block direct-beam sunlight from reaching the window surface, thus minimizing the amount of solar radiation that reaches the window. To be effective, the external shading devices must be deployed so that they stand in the direct path between the solar disk and the window surface. Given that the solar disk moves across a range of altitude and azimuthal angles over the course of a year, the geometry of any external shading device must be carefully established to ensure that the device will provide shading of direct-beam sunlight, when needed.[19]

Match the color and degree of openness of any external shading device to other needs for the window assembly. A number of types and forms of external shading devices exist. The more common types are horizontal overhangs and vertical fins that are placed above and alongside, respectively, windows in vertical window-walls. These overhangs and fins can also be used in concert to create *egg crate* assemblies that are attached to external vertical building surfaces. Other types of external shading devices include screens and blinds that are hung vertically from horizontal supports that project out from window-walls. The vertical screens can consist of a solid, but transparent, material (e.g., such as a sheet of tinted glass or plastic). These screens can also be built of latticework or composed of louvers, similar to a venetian blind. Whether the screens are solid or open (i.e., holes or gaps between the components of the screen) is a decision for the designer or builder to make. A primary reason for having holes or gaps is to permit air to pass through, so that the *natural ventilation* of the building can occur without significant inhibition. Alternatively,

Figure 9.45 The horizontal overhangs and vertical fins shown here offer an example of a well-developed external shading device. By choosing the appropriate geometries for overhangs and fins (i.e., carefully matching the horizontal and vertical projections with angles between the position of the sun and planar surfaces on the Earth), these shading devices can provide very effective heat gain and glare controls.

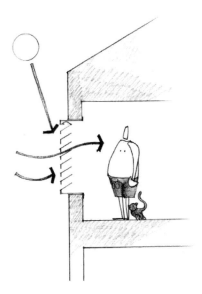

Figure 9.46 The shading devices on this building façade operate as operable blinds, enabling the building occupants to adjust the orientation of the blinds to exclude direct-beam sunlight or to admit daylight. The building is the Ministry of Education, Rio de Janeiro, Brazil.

Figure 9.47 The roles for this shading device are dual: to exclude direct-beam sunlight, while permitting the natural ventilation of the building interior. The design requirement in creating this device involves orienting the blinds to block the sunlight and yet spacing them adequately to enable airflow.

openness achieved with holes or gaps between *opaque* components of a screen will enable daylight from the diffusing sky vault to reach the window. If screens are to include gaps between the solid opaque components, then the degree of openness should be determined principally by the geometry between the sun (as it moves across the sky) and the building window-wall (see Figures 9.46 and 9.47).

Similarly, the color of any external shading device should be established according to whether you wish solar radiation (and light) to be reflected through a window (e.g., using the top sides of the blinds to reflect the radiation onto the ceiling of the room, much as a *light shelf* does). The *degree of openness* of screens and blinds along with the *color and geometry* of blind assemblies will affect the transmittance that an external screen displays. Whereas a screen or blind is generally deployed to reduce the amount of solar radiation reaching external window surfaces, it should be remembered that two essential reasons for having windows are to provide occupants with the view of the exterior and to admit daylight for task performance.

Choose the type and form of any external shading device according to the elevation in which the window occurs. The selection of an external shading device should include matching the type and form of the device with the specific building elevation on which the shading device will be employed. The factor that dictates which type and form would perform best for a given elevation is the geometry of the path that the sun follows across the sky vault. For example, consider building locations in the more northerly latitudes. There, overhangs are commonly very effective external shading devices for south-facing elevations, particularly when the sun is high in the sky during the middle of the day. But, for these northern latitudes, buildings with windows on east and west elevations will require screens or blinds in front of the windows for shading because the sun is lower in the sky during early mornings and late afternoons. Windows on north-facing elevations will generally need minimal shading. For locations between the tropic of Cancer and the tropic of Capricorn, overhangs can effectively be used to shade both south and north-facing windows because the sun will be high in the sky vault during the middle of days throughout the year and will approach buildings on one elevation or the other depending upon the season. However, in early morning and late afternoon hours in lands between the two tropics, the sun is lower in the sky and is incident on the east and west elevations, respectively. During these daytimes vertical screens and blinds are the most effective external devices for shading windows. For buildings constructed in the southern latitudes below the tropic

---

SIDEBAR 9.19 Potential liabilities using external blinds

The use of *operable* blinds or louvers permits building occupants to set these external devices according to their visual or thermal needs. For instance, if the occupants wish to exclude solar radiation entirely, they may close the blinds altogether. If they wish some light penetration, then they can open the blinds.

The choice of color for external blinds should be made with some forethought: if a light color or a glossy finish is employed to enhance the reflectance of the blind (so it works like a light shelf), then the reflecting surfaces can serve as *glare* sources for the building occupant. To ensure that these surfaces do not function as glare sources, the surfaces must be designed so that they do not coincide with the view field of any occupant. One other potential problem created by seeking to reflect direct-beam sunlight (and solar radiation) into the building is that this reflected radiation can become a significant heat source (that may have to be overcome if occupant thermal comfort is jeopardized).

SIDEBAR 9.20 Further effects of solar geometries on designing external shading devices

One qualification about the utility of overhangs concerns the altitude that the sun reaches on a day-by-day schedule across the year. At noon on the summer solstice the sun will be at its highest point in the sky, whereas at noon on the winter solstice the sun will be at its lowest. Thus, an overhang created to shade a window at noon on the summer solstice will scarcely be useful for shading the same window at noon on the winter solstice. Consequently, if the prevention of direct-beam solar radiation from entering a window is important throughout the year, then a shading geometry or device — other than a simple, fixed overhang — will need to be employed.

In the region between the equator and the tropic of Cancer (at 23° 27' N), for the days from the September equinox to the March equinox, the sun will primarily face the south elevation during the midday; and, from the March equinox to the September equinox, the sun will primarily face the north elevation during the midday. Alternatively, in the region between the equator and the tropic of Capricorn (at 23° 27' S), for the days from the March equinox to the September equinox, the sun will primarily face the north elevation during the midday; and, from the September equinox to the March equinox, the sun will primarily face the south elevation during the midday. Note the summer period in the region immediately north of the equator is the winter period for the region immediately south of the equator: the converse of this is also true.

of Capricorn, overhangs will offer good performances for windows on north-facing elevations. But vertical screens and blinds are most useful for east- and west-facing elevations. Lastly, providing external shading devices on south-facing elevations generally requires little attention in these more-southerly latitudes.

External shading devices serve, principally, to block the incidence of direct-beam sunlight on the external surface of windows. As such, these shading devices will also reduce the incidence of solar radiation on the windows and the attendant solar heat gain load. One other benefit that external shading devices will commonly afford is the blocking of the view of the upper sky. For overcast skies, the upper region—near the zenith—is appreciably brighter than the lower areas near the horizon. Thus, if a building occupant has a substantial view of the upper sky, occupants may find areas of excessive brightness within their view fields (and glary conditions may result), unless viewing of the upper sky region is curtailed.

9.7.2.3 Employing internal shading devices to control the admission of solar radiation

The third means for controlling how much light (and solar radiation) can enter through a window is the application of various devices like drapes, venetian blinds, and roller blinds, which are used to cover the internal surface of windows. All of these internal devices provide control by reducing the radiation transmittance through the overall fenestration assembly. The degree of transmission reduction depends on the character of each specific device. For drapes the principal attributes that determine transmittance are the color and weave of the drapery material. A light-colored material would reflect a substantial portion of the solar radiation (and light) that would be incident on the material. Alternatively, a dark material would absorb a much larger fraction of the incident radiation. The nature of the weave will influence how readily radiation can pass through the material. If a weave is relatively open (i.e., has fewer, thinner fibers per unit area), then the transmittance of the cloth will be quite high. Other factors that can also affect the transmittance of the material include how thick it is and whether it forms a single layer across a window or, instead, is gathered and bunched into a virtual multiple layering. For instance, if the material is a thin, loosely woven cloth that is neither gathered nor bunched, then the radiation transmittance will be high (i.e., perhaps 80 or 90 percent). But if the drape is a medium or heavyweight velour that may be bunched even when pulled out across the window, then its transmittance will be much lower. Indeed, if the drape is composed of some flexible polymeric sheeting, the drape may be virtually opaque to incident radiation.[20]

The abilities of venetian and roller blinds to control the transmittances of solar radiation (and light) are determined by much the same parameters that affect the transmittances of drapes: the colors, spacing between the elements of the blinds, and the extent with which the elements overlap. One other important parameter that will determine the performance of these blinds is whether the material of the blind slats is opaque or translucent. Generally, a blind composed of light-colored, opaque slats that are well overlapped will provide greater blockage of direct-beam sunlight (or the excessive brightness from an overcast sky) than will a dark-colored or translucent or loosely lapped slatted blind.

9.7.2.4 The benefit of using operable radiation controls

To promote the selective admission of daylight, the blockage of direct-beam sunlight, and the curtailment of excessive brightness, use operable internal and external shading devices. The penetration of direct-beam sunlight through windows can occur when a *line-of-sight* path exists between the sun and the windows. Further, the extent to which the extreme brightness of direct-beam sunlight can enter the view field of a building occupant will be similarly determined

Figure 9.48 Awnings, whether fixed in place or operable, offer promising opportunities for controlling admission of direct-beam sunlight through fenestration assemblies or for permitting daylight entrance when the sky vault is overcast.

by a line-of-sight relationship between the sun and the view field. Thus, the effectiveness of any external or internal shading device will be substantially determined by how well the device can impede these lines-of-sight. Because line-of-sight conditions between the sun and building windows are dependent upon how the sun moves across the sky vault, the patterns of these lines-of-sight are greatly changeable across a day and throughout the year. So, if external and internal shading devices can be selected to meet these changing conditions (i.e., by having the ability to be manipulated), the devices would offer flexibility for blocking direct-beam sunlight (see Figure 9.48). Additionally, these changeable devices could allow the admission of daylight from the diffusing sky vault (for those times when direct-beam sunlight is not incident on a specific elevation) or could simply constrain the entrance of excessively bright light from the sky vault. This flexible response would enable the building occupant to establish how much daylight might be admitted into an individual's space and, to some extent, what the character of that daylight might be.

Lastly, two further strategies that will enable building occupants to control the selective admission or blockage of light (and/or solar radiation) include: using a *retractable device* (e.g., a screen or awning that can be easily removed or pulled back when not needed) (see Figure 9.48); and (2) employing *translucent* materials in these devices to reduce the extreme brightness of the light, thus softening it and making it useful.

9.7.3   SELECTING WINDOW-FRAMING ELEMENTS FOR LUMINOUS PERFORMANCE[21]

This discussion of window materials has so far considered glazing (or other light-admitting substances). The manner in which window-framing components — sills, mullions, reveals, and other related hardware and surfaces — are incorporated into an overall fenestration assembly can also affect an occupant's visual comfort and ability to see external objects.

Use window-framing elements that are light-colored and have matte finishes. Opaque window-framing components — whether placed intermediately between window areas (e.g., as mullions) or used as borders that surround the windows (e.g., as sills, headers, or reveals) — should be light-colored and have a matte finish. Virtually anytime daylight enters a window, the sky vault from which the daylight emanates will be a generally bright light source. So, when an occupant looks out of the window and sees this bright sky, the window-framing materials should have surface properties that minimize the contrast between these surfaces and the sky vault. However, if these window-framing materials are dark or highly reflective, the occupant may experience discomfort glare.

One other reason for using light-colored, matte-surfaced window-framing materials is that they can serve as transition areas between the bright window surface and the often relatively darker opaque wall areas that surround the window assemblies. Using such transition areas can help the occupant's eyes to adjust to any significant contrast that exists between bright windows and the less-bright internal surfaces of a building.

Make these window-framing elements as small as possible and provide tapered cross-sections for these elements (see Figure 9.49). To reduce the effect of substantial contrast ratios between bright window surfaces and relatively darker window-framing elements, these elements should be made as small as possible. Reducing the area and thickness of the framing elements will help the occupant's eyes to slide over them when the individual looks at the window surfaces. Additionally, to foster better contrast ratios between the window surfaces and the framing elements, these elements should be tapered so that some of the daylight from the sky vault might fall on the edges of these framing members.

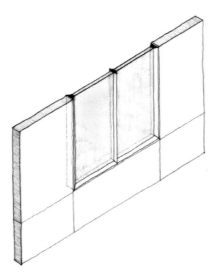

Figure 9.49 Window frames and mullions should be tapered and finished in some light color to ease the transition of the eye across the alternative surfaces of glass and framing materials.

Section 9.8 | INTERNAL BUILDING SURFACE SHAPES AND FINISHES

After accommodations have been made to get daylight into a building in a controlled fashion, the next responsibility of the designer and builder is to ensure that the daylight is well treated within the building. We have written in Section 9.3 about how entering daylight should be reflected off of diffusing surfaces so that the daylight is "let down softly" into the building space employed by the occupant. As a corollary for this principal guideline, some attention should also be given to the character of the surfaces that surround windows, *particularly where these windows and surfaces are readily present in an occupant's view field.*

9.8.1   SHAPING BUILDING SURFACES SURROUNDING WINDOWS

Splay or round opaque surfaces adjacent to windows (see Figure 9.50). Generally, wall surfaces near vertical windows and ceiling surfaces beneath horizontal and sloped skylights should all be tapered away from the internal window surfaces. This tapering can be accomplished by splaying or rounding inward the internal wall or ceiling surfaces adjacent to the window or skylight. Where possible, such splaying and rounding should be provided at all the edges that surround the fenestration. The principal reason for shaping these surfaces accordingly is to allow the daylight that enters through the window to wash over the surfaces and makes them appear bright. By brightening these surfaces adjacent to windows, the contrast ratios between the window surfaces and the adjacent surfaces will be kept suitably low (i.e., contrast ratios of about 3:1 should be sought between window luminance and the luminances of adjoining surfaces). With lowered contrast ratios, the likelihood of glare from bright windows will be reduced and the visual comfort of occupants can be enhanced.

Figure 9.50 The walls adjacent to a window assembly should be splayed away from the window surface. Thus, light entering through the window will lighten the wall surfaces, reducing the contrast between the window surface and the surrounding wall surfaces. Creating a gradual transition in both the relative brightnesses between surfaces and the shapes of these surfaces will make seeing window assemblies and their surrounding surfaces more comfortable visually. This window assembly is found at the Mount Angel Abbey Library.

9.8.2   FINISHING BUILDING SURFACES NEAR WINDOWS

Employ light-colored surfaces with matte finishes near windows when these surfaces may be present in the occupant's view field. The purpose of this guideline is similar to the one stated in Section 9.8.1: to ensure the maintenance of the visual comfort of building occupants, the contrast ratio between bright window surfaces and the adjoining opaque wall and ceiling surfaces should be kept as low as possible. By using light-colored surfaces next to windows the contrast ratio between the window and its near surfaces will likely be acceptable. Further, matte-finishing these surrounding surfaces will enhance the nondirectional spread of light entering through the window.

9.8.3   RECOMMENDED REFLECTANCES FOR INTERIOR SURFACES

Use surface finishes for the ceiling, walls, and floor, which have average reflectances (for light) of 80 percent, 50 percent, and 20 percent, respectively (see Figure 9.51). This guideline relates the need to spread light inward from window-walls (at the perimeter of building spaces) and the concern for having reasonable contrast ratios in the primary view fields. The ceiling and upper walls should generally serve as the principal surfaces for reflecting exterior light into rooms. For the seated or standing occupant the principal view field will commonly encompass the walls and furnishings at a middle-height (i.e., from about 0.5 to 2.0 m [two to six or seven feet] from the floor). The occupants will not ordinarily see much

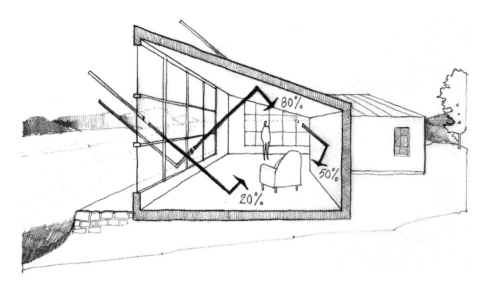

Figure 9.51 Recommended reflectances for floors, walls, and ceilings are shown here.

of ceilings. Thus, the ceiling surface can have higher reflectances to promote the transporting of daylight inward without introducing too-bright surfaces and unfavorable contrast ratios into the principal view field. Using reduced reflectances for the wall areas close to the floor and for the floor itself will minimize opportunities for too-bright surfaces to appear in the view field. There will be fewer occasions for disability glare to intrude into one's view field as an occupant moves or looks about. Given that the very bright direct-beam sunlight (and daylight from the overcast upper sky) are most likely to fall on floor and lower wall surfaces, then making sure that such bright light will not be reflected upward into the occupant's view field is important. These lower room surfaces should also have matte finishes so that no specular reflections can occur.

Section 9.9 | THREE CONCLUDING GUIDELINES FOR DESIGNING AND BUILDING FOR DAYLIGHT

9.9.1   MATCH DAYLIGHTING NEEDS AND SPECIFIC WORK AND LIFE ACTIVITIES

Provide enough daylight so that building occupants can perform necessary tasks. Insuring that enough daylight illumination can be present in building spaces requires a three-step methodology. First, we suggest that designers and builders carefully anticipate, for each building space they create, the range of tasks that will likely be conducted in that space. The designers and builders should next establish how much illumination is needed (e.g., in terms of suggested daylight factors). Then, these people should determine the appropriate location, shape, and size for each window that can be used to admit the requisite daylight.

9.9.2   TAKE CARE WITH BRIGHT LIGHT SOURCES AND SURFACES

Avoid having bright light enter into the occupant's view field. The essential issue that this guideline addresses is that, whereas the human eye displays phototropism, the human eye loses its capacity to see well when light in the view field is too bright. Light sources or transmitting or reflecting surfaces that have luminances that are excessive will cause discomfort for the viewer. The presence of an over-bright source or surface in the view field will usually result in high contrast ratios between the source or the surface and the surrounding or background objects, making vision difficult for the viewer. Thus, a fundamental requirement for designers and builders is to anticipate the possibilities that such bright sources or surfaces could exist in a building. Where the presence of bright light is expected, then accommodations must be provided to ensure that the future occupant's vision will not be impaired. In the previous sections of this chapter we have discussed a variety of means for exercising such control with daylight (e.g., sizing and locating windows adequately, employing shading devices to keep out direct-beam sunlight, and so forth). These various strategies must be integrated into the building form so that visual comfort and good visual performance are maintained.

9.9.3   TEACH BUILDING OCCUPANTS TO USE DAYLIGHTING WISELY

Educate building occupants about how to employ daylight illumination for building operation. This final proviso extends well beyond the scope of this text. But using daylight to illuminate a building involves the application of a profoundly passive means of environmental control. As with virtually all passive environmental controls, some manual effort must be expended by the occupants of buildings to take advantage of the best features and performances of these passive controls. For instance, closing blinds and drapes is fundamental to shutting out direct-beam sunlight, whereas opening the blinds or drapes is essential for admitting light from the overcast sky. Alternatively, when electric illumination is provided for balancing and supplementing daylight, this electric illumination should not be used generally and continuously just because it is there. For spaces with provisions for both daylight and electric light, daylight can commonly offer sufficient illumination for most activities and tasks, at least during the daytime hours. This daylight can often provide more interest and definition within the space, due to its variability and its ability to highlight features of the building interior. Therefore, electric illumination should not be provided by the designer and builder simply because it is expected. Similarly, the occupant should not rely on electric illumination because it is easy to use (e.g., by flipping a switch). The occupant should employ electric illumination selectively and with forethought so that the electric illumination complements daylighting, instead of replacing the daylight. To encourage the occupant to use daylight as a complement for electric illumination, the occupants of a building should be educated about how best to use these alternative sources of light. Additionally, suitable automatic (and manual) control devices for electric lighting systems should also be incorporated into the building design, and occupants should be instructed about the use of these control devices.[22]

Section 9.10 | THINKING ABOUT DESIGNING FOR ELECTRIC LIGHTING

The goal for this text is to present information about environmental controls and systems that can be incorporated during the schematic designing of buildings. In Chapter 7, discussions about the visual process have been presented, including the parameters that affect visual acuity, performance, and comfort. In Chapter 8 and earlier in this chapter, the light properties that daylight can display have been described. Then, means for admitting daylight into buildings have been identified and guidelines for distributing the daylighting have been offered. The focus throughout these chapters has been to demonstrate how the daylighting of building spaces and the selection of building forms to enable daylighting are inextricably linked. Thus, making provisions to admit daylight and using the daylight to enable occupancy of building spaces should be considered during the earliest designing of any building.

Whether similar attention should be paid to designing electric illumination during schematic designing is arguable. Creating successful electric illumination requires that attention be paid not only to fixture (and luminaire) selection and location, but also to the establishment of appropriate visual qualities gained from the relationships between the lighting devices and the building forms and surfaces. Determining building forms, of course, occurs during schematic designing. But defining the specific textures and colors of surfaces, the nature of furnishings, the system controls, and perhaps even how to achieve the balancing of daylight and electric illumination throughout the spaces seems better left to later design phases. Much of the design challenges involving the electric lighting of building spaces rests upon detailed information that will be better grasped in these later phases.

9.10.1 BASIC CAPABILITIES TO BE FURNISHED BY LIGHTING SYSTEMS

There are, however, some design considerations and practices that, if applied during schematic designing, can enable the more successful, subsequent integration of electric illumination systems with the overall building. As a basis for identifying these considerations and practices, we will first describe a series of fundamental properties that lighting systems — composed of daylighting and/or electric illumination — should offer to building occupants. These four capabilities are the creation of ambience, the accenting of localized spaces and objects, the support of task performance, and the exhibiting of decorative features.

The function of ambient lighting is to provide a luminous surround or general lighting quality that pervades a space. The purpose of furnishing this general lighting quality is that it establishes a foundation on which the other lighting capabilities can be built. Whether an entire space should be supplied with a suitable luminous ambience or whether one or more principal surfaces should be suffused with a generalized light quality is the choice of the designer.

Using lighting for the accenting of an environment can serve multiple objectives. First, lighting can highlight specific features in a space. Second, lighting can dramatize how a space or an attribute of the space is perceived. The lighting can be employed to draw an occupant's attention to a spatial feature, such as some artifact like a painting or a piece of furniture. Or some bit of a room can be emphasized: an alcove can be made to seem more private with softened lighting or a dining table can have attention drawn to it with concentrated lighting.

To support task performance, adequate and comfortable light must be furnished on the surfaces that the occupant will use to accomplish the task. Note that task surface areas will usually comprise only a small to intermediate fraction of an overall space. Lighting to enable task performance should then bring enough light from the appropriate directions to the task surface. The surface should be shadow-free, and the spread of light across the surface should be uniform. Areas for food preparation, craft production, machine assembly, drafting, and/or reading are but a few examples of situations where the furnishing of adequate and comfortable lighting is essential.

Creating decorative lighting is perhaps a subset of the mission for establishing lighting for accenting an artifact or a portion of a building space. Lighting to accent objects or areas is undertaken to call attention to these objects or areas. Alternatively, the goal for decorative lighting is to create lighting that is itself the artifact. Thus, rather than using light to highlight some component of a building or a sculpture, the lighting is presented to please the occupants and to lend an artistic quality to their visual experiences.

Achieving each of these four qualities requires the careful selection of fixtures and luminaires and the application of supportive building forms. Defining the properties of alternative fixtures and luminaires and providing directives for choosing amongst such alternatives are assignments that are better conducted during the design development phase. But some design guidelines can be offered for employment during schematic designing.

9.10.2 SIMPLE GUIDELINES FOR ANTICIPATING LATER PLACEMENT OF ELECTRIC LIGHTING SYSTEMS

Ambient lighting primarily serves as a background condition, particularly when surfaces can be "washed" with a soft, general illumination level. Minimized variation in the lighting level across a large surface or across a room is a common goal for the use of ambient lighting. To attain such uniform lighting levels indirect sources are best applied. These sources can supply light upward or downward, but they should illuminate room surfaces—walls or a ceiling—rather than surfaces used in work or for common living functions. Sources for producing ambient lighting are often hidden or recessed, placed behind opaque assemblies such as valences or shades that reflect the light away from occupants.

Sources of accent lighting will often have directional properties that enable the sources to be aimed at some feature in a space. These sources will commonly have compact shapes. Further, the sources will require finer, more specific controls, both for establishing the necessary directionality and for issuing an appropriate intensity. Accenting sources can be placed remotely in a room and directed in a concentrated fashion at some object or room feature, or can be located more closely to a target for the light.

Task sources will usually be placed near the specific surface area that is to be illuminated. To be effective the task illumination must be accurately aimed so that the lighting arrives at the task surface without causing shadows, glare, or discomfort. Also, if task surfaces are numerous in a space or their locations are likely to change over time, then it is useful to be able to alter the placement of the task sources. Changing the placement of task sources can be attained either by using portable sources or by employing sources that are mounted on fixed wall or ceiling surfaces, but that are directional and can be readily aimed to localized surface areas.

9.10.3 USING BUILDING FORMS THAT CAN ACCOMMODATE ELECTRIC LIGHTING FIXTURES

Two significant issues concerning the planning for electric lighting should be considered during schematic designing. First, in any final design solution for a building, it is incumbent on the designer to present the successful integration of daylight and electric illumination. And, second, the designer should anticipate the sorts of electric lighting devices that might be subsequently added to the building solution—during design development, for instance—and where those devices might best be located.

Integrating daylight and electric illumination involves recognizing the differences between each resource. Daylighting consists of a mixture of diffuse-sky and direct-beam illumination. The quantity and quality of daylighting vary across the day and across the year. And daylighting can be directional or not. Electric illumination devices can be chosen so that they display variability in quantity or directionality. But more often electric lighting devices will be static, aimed in a single direction (or having no particular directionality), and will furnish a uniform amount of illumination. Typical electric lighting devices are much more controllable and predictable than is daylighting. Lastly, electric illumination is available on demand—by switching a fixture or system "on" or "off"—whereas daylight is present only during the daytime.

In this chapter we have provided guidelines for designing building envelopes to admit daylight. We can suggest here—as an addendum—that the admission of daylight from the diffuse sky might serve as the primary source of ambient illumination in building spaces throughout a day. In addition, the admission of sunlight can be used as an accenting illumination. But using sunlight in this fashion will require particular care by the designer because sunlight can be very bright, glary, and if it arrives from an inappropriate direction, discomforting. Perhaps, more safely, a designer might employ daylight from the diffuse sky and rely on electric lighting systems as sources for accent and task performance.

During schematic designing a designer should begin to think generally about what sorts of electric lighting systems and devices might likely be incorporated in the final design product. Establishing the specific systems and devices, however, is probably not necessary in schematic designing. But the designer should recognize that various systems and devices will impose specific requirements on building forms.

For instance, when formulating illumination strategies, the designer will need to consider whether certain surfaces or areas in rooms will need particular attention. Should such surfaces or areas be illuminated generally, or should accenting or decorative lighting be furnished? Where might occupants conduct specific tasks, and how much light will be required at these task surfaces? Also, can decisions about window size, shape, and placement produce needs for electric illumination to balance daylight admission? These are but a few of the questions that a designer might consider during schematic designing when making decisions about daylight admission, sunlight control, window form, and so forth, and then contemplating the electric lighting systems and devices to include later in the building design process.

One other important decision area that is commonly arrived at during schematic designing concerns setting ceiling heights for occupied rooms. As many electric lighting systems and devices are hung from ceilings or attached to upper parts of walls, ceiling placement will potentially influence how well any system or device provides useful illumination. Other issues involved in setting ceiling heights include establishing an acceptable floor-to-floor dimension, determining the space needed for structural and HVAC systems hardware, finding an acceptable relationship between the length and width of a room and the ceiling height, and perhaps considering how the ceiling height might affect room acoustics.

In Section 9.3.1 we have advocated bringing daylight in from high wall positions and letting it fall softly on to room surfaces. Generally, to achieve more uniform and comfortable daylight distributions, daylight should enter from windows in upper walls or from roof monitors, thus requiring that ceilings be adequately high. If a ceiling is placed high above the floor, then recessed electric lighting fixtures — mounted as incandescent cans or in-the-ceiling fluorescent troffers — may furnish good ambient lighting, but probably not be useful for accent or task lighting. Alternatively, if task lighting is sought, then a pendant fixture could be hung from a ceiling to above a work surface or one (or more) desktop fixture(s) could be mounted on or near the work surface. On the other hand, if a low ceiling height is needed — perhaps because of a limited floor-to-floor dimension — then fixtures that are surface-mounted on the ceiling or recessed into the ceiling would likely be effective in furnishing both ambient and task illumination. But for a low ceiling height, pendant or hung fixtures would be less useful for supplying ambient illumination and would only be effective for task illumination if they were located directly over work surfaces.

So, in summary, we assert that decisions about admitting daylight should be considered and made during schematic designing. Alternatively, for electric illumination, a designer should begin thinking during schematic designing about what sort of lighting capabilities — for ambience, accenting, task performance, and decoration — should be present in a space. The designer should also consider how decisions about room forms, the incorporation of other active systems, and probable furniture locations — arrived at during schematic designing — might influence later opportunities for designing electric illumination systems and devices.

Section 9.11 | ADDITIONAL READINGS

9.11.1 ADDITIONAL READINGS ABOUT DESIGNING FOR PROVIDING DAYLIGHT

This chapter has set forth guidelines about introducing and controlling daylight in buildings. These guidelines are intended for use in the preliminary schematic phase of building design. As such, they function as a number of directives that designers and builders can employ when they begin to create the form and specify the operating strategies for a building. Following the completion of this preliminary form generation and the approximate definition of how the building is to be operated, the designers and builders will need to develop aspects of the building solution more carefully. At that time the following books may serve as sources of much useful information.

For the further development of a daylighted building, see:

Hopkinson, R.G., P. Petherbridge, and J. Longmore, *Daylighting,* (London: William Heinemann Ltd., 1966);

Lam, W.M.C., *Sunlighting As a Formgiver for Architecture,* (New York: Van Nostrand Reinhold Company, 1986);

Moore, E.F., *Concepts and Practices of Architectural Daylighting,* (New York: Van Nostrand Reinhold Company, 1991); and

Robbins, C.L., *Daylighting: Design and Analysis,* (New York: Van Nostrand Reinhold Company, 1986).

9.11.2 A BRIEF BIBLIOGRAPHY ABOUT ELECTRIC ILLUMINATION DESIGNING

A major literature source about daylighting, electric lighting systems, and their integration is the following book,

Rae, M., editor, *IES Lighting Handbook* (8th edition), (New York: Illuminating Engineering Society of North America, 2000).

For additional information about electric lighting equipment, designing with electric lighting equipment, predicting the likely behaviors of this equipment in building interiors, and the citing of good applications of this equipment, see

Egan, M.D., and V.W. Olgyay, *Architectural Lighting,* (New York: McGraw-Hill Book Company, 2002);

Johnson, G.M., *The Art of Illumination: Residential Lighting Design,* (New York: McGraw-Hill Book Company, 1999);

Lam, W.M.C., *Perception and Lighting As Formgivers for Architecture,* (New York: McGraw-Hill Book Company, 1977);

Murdoch, J.B., *Illumination Engineering: From Edison's Lamp to the Laser,* (New York: Macmillan Publishing Company, 1985);

Smith, F.K., and F.J. Bertolone, *Bringing Interiors to Light,* (New York: Whitney Library of Design, 1986).

Stein, B., and J.R. Reynolds, *Mechanical and Electrical Equipment for Buildings* (9th edition), (New York: J. Wiley & Sons, Inc., 2000);

Tregenza, P., and D. Loe, *The Design of Lighting,* (London: E. & F.N. Spon, 1998).

ENDNOTES and SELECTED ADDITIONAL COMMENTS

1. Olgyay, V., *Design with Climate,* (Princeton, New Jersey: Princeton University Press, 1963), pages 74–77.

2. Evans, B.H., *Daylight in Architecture* (New York: McGraw-Hill Book Company, 1981), page 54.

3. Chauvel, P., J.B. Collins, R. Dogniaux, and J. Longmore, "Glare from windows: current views of the problem," *Lighting Research & Technology,* 14(1), 1982, pages 31–46.

4. Hopkinson, R.G., *Architectural Physics: Lighting,* (London: Her Majesty's Stationery Office, 1963), page 209.

5. Ne'eman, E., and R.G. Hopkinson, "Critical minimum acceptable window size: a study of window design and provision of view," *Lighting Research and Technology,* 2(1), 1970, pages 17–27.

6. These percentage figures have been deduced and presented by B. Collins in the paper, "Review of the psychological reaction to windows," *Lighting Research & Technology,* 8(2), 1976, pages 80–88; see page 82 for the discussion about this specific topic.

7. Keighley, E.C., "Visual requirements and reduced fenestration in offices — a study of multiple apertures and window area," *Building Science,* 8, 1973, pages 321–331.

8. Tabet, K.A., and S. Sharples, "Climatic and cultural preferences in window design," presented at the Second European Conference on Architecture: Science and Technology at the Service of Architecture (organized by the Commission of the European Communities, UNESCO), Paris, December 1989.

9. Ibid, page 3.

10. Another study has reached similar conclusions about window size preferences and the importance of view content. See the paper by Butler, D.L., and B.L. Steuerwald, "Effects of view and room size on window size preferences made in models," *Environment and Behavior,* 23(3), May 1991, pages 334–358.

11. Chauvel, P., J.B. Collins, R. Dogniaux, and J. Longmore, "Glare from windows: current views of the problem," *Lighting Research & Technology,* 14(1), 1982, pages 31–46.

12. Ibid., page 38.

13. Millet, M.S., and J.R. Bedrick, *Graphic Daylighting Design Method Workbook,* (Seattle, Washington: Department of Architecture, University of Washington, 1980), pages 5–6. Rules-of-thumb similar to those offered here have also been identified in a section, "Single-stage daylight factor calculation based on flux-transfer methods," in the book by Hopkinson, R.G., P. Petherbridge, and J. Longmore, *Daylighting,* (London: William Heinemann Ltd., 1966), pages 279–282.

14. You might note that, in Table 8.4, the minimum Daylight Factor in British schools is actually to be 1 percent; thus, illumination equivalent to at least 1 percent of the sky illuminance should reach all horizontal workplane surfaces (at the typical height) within classrooms.

15. Benton, C., B. Erwine, M. Warren, and S. Selkowitz, "Field measurements of light shelf performance in a major office installation," *Proceedings of the Eleventh National Passive Solar Conference,* (Boulder, Colorado: American Solar Energy Society, Inc., 1986), pages 290–295; Benton, C., M. Warren, S. Selkowitz, and J. Jewell, "Lighting system performance in an innovative daylighted structure: an instrumented study," *1986 International Daylighting Conference: Proceedings II,* (Bales, E.J., and R. McCluney, editors), (Atlanta: American Society of Heating, Refrigerating, and Air-Conditioning Engineers, Inc.), pages 286–294; and Littlefair, P.J., "Innovative daylighting: review of systems and evaluation methods," *Lighting Research and Technology,* 22(1), 1990, pages 1–17; note pages 10–12, particularly.

16. Dietz, A.G.H., *Plastics for Architects and Builders,* (Cambridge, Massachusetts: The MIT Press, 1969).

17. *Crazing* is the development of many hairline-like cracks within a polymeric material. These cracks form over time and are particularly noticeable in transparent polymeric materials. The development of such cracks seems to result from the materials being stressed, particularly by bending (i.e., alternatively loading the materials in tension and compression).

18.   Rubin, M., "Optical properties of soda lime silica glasses," *Solar Energy Materials,* 12, 1985, pages 275–288.

19.   Olgyay, V., and A. Olgyay, *Solar Control and Shading Devices,* (Princeton, New Jersey: Princeton University Press, 1957).

20.   ———, "Fenestration" (Chapter 30) of the *2001 ASHRAE Handbook of Fundamentals,* (Atlanta: American Society of Heating, Refrigerating, and Air-Conditioning Engineers, Inc., 2001): note the discussion, "Solar-optical properties," pages 30.18–30.36.

21.   Chauvel, P., J.B. Collins, R. Dogniaux, and J. Longmore, "Glare from windows: current views of the problem," *Lighting Research & Technology,* 14(1), 1982, pages 31–46.

22.   ———, "Lighting controls and daylight use," *Building Research Establishment Digest #272,* April 1983 (as prepared by the Building Research Station, Garston, Watford, WD2 7JR, England).

The "Fundamentals" of Sound

10

IN CHAPTERS 10 THROUGH 13 we will discuss how sound can be controlled in buildings and in external spaces adjacent to buildings. As part of this discussion, we will begin by describing properties of sound. We will consider how sound — like light — enables us to learn about the physical world around us and to gather information from other occupants of our world. Sound is a basic means for communication, whether we send information forth or we receive information. We will stipulate that a principal responsibility for designers and builders is to enhance communication in the natural and built environments. In these chapters we will also address the presence of noise in our modern world and discuss how it affects us. Necessarily, a second major responsibility for designers and builders is to establish means for minimizing the presence of noise (or *unwanted sound*) in the built and natural environments. Lastly, we will identify design guidelines and operation strategies whose applications can promote the attainment of good acoustics in the built and natural environments.

There are many types of sound which we experience during our everyday lives: the bark of a dog, the sighing of the wind, the distant *whoosh* of urban traffic, the rock-and-roll from a "boom-box," and the gurgle of a baby are but a few examples. Two principal communication forms to which designers and builders must pay particular attention are *speech* and *music*. Most of our discussion in these four chapters will focus on establishing good

---

SIDEBAR 10.1 Defining speech and music simply

As definitions for *speech* and *music*, we can state that speech is *a series of sounds that are formed into words and that are used to transmit knowledge* and music is *a collection of sounds that are strung together for the* *aesthetic stimulation of the auditor (or the pleasure of the performer)*. These definitions may be regarded as providing first approximations of what speech and music encompass.

SIDEBAR 10.2 Transduction of the mechanical energy of sound waves

---

The transmission of sound from a source to our ears involves mechanical energy that is embedded within the sound. In our ears the mechanical energy is transformed into electrical energy, a process identified as *transduction*. The electrical energy then travels along auditory nerve fibers to portions of our brain, where perception and interpretation of the sound happens. The capabilities that this process provides will be developed in Chapter 11.

---

hearing for speech. But many of the principles that will promote speech communication can be applied usefully to enhance listening to musical performances.

There are five steps involved in our hearing: the production of sound by a source; the transmission of the sound from the source to us; the collection of the sound by our ears; the transduction of the sound within our inner ears; and the interpretation of the sound by our brain. In this chapter we will discuss the production and transmission of sound, as well as a number of other physical properties and characteristics that sound displays. Then, in Chapter 11, we will describe the capabilities of our hearing and speech systems. In Chapter 12 we will characterize the types and range of noise that fill our environments. Further, we will consider the many difficulties that noise can cause us. Finally, in Chapter 13 we will present design and building guidelines for enhancing communication with sound, separating noise out from our built and natural environments, and, generally, trying to make our acoustical experiences more useful and pleasant.

Section 10.1 | WHAT IS SOUND?

Let us begin our description of what sound is with a paradoxical question sometimes raised by whimsical folks and philosophers: If a tree falls in the forest and no one is there to hear it fall, is any sound produced? To answer this question we must first establish a definition for *sound*. Second, we shall follow this definition with portrayals of a number of common sources and the media in which sound propagates. Then, we can return to this question and offer an unequivocal answer for it.

10.1.1 SOUND EMANATES FROM A VIBRATING BODY

If we look in a dictionary for a definition of *sound*, we will see that there are indeed several ways for defining sound.[1] Two definitions that seem most appropriate to our discussion suggest that sound is either a sensation that we experience with our ears (and the rest of our auditory system) or a mechanical energy form that is transmitted through some medium. Let us put aside the first definition — we will return to it for later development — and explore the attributes present within the second. Sound emanates from a source that has acquired enough energy to emit sound. As the sound travels through the medium, the energy that the sound has alters the medium. So, the fundamental physical components of sound — according to this definition — are a *source* and a *medium* through which *mechanical energy* passes.

To establish a basis for characterizing sound sources, first, let's consider a tuning fork. The fork, when struck with a mallet or when hit against some hard object, will emit a sound. If we touch the *prongs* (or tines) of the fork as sound emanates from it, we can feel that they *vibrate*. The presence of vibration is a fundamental property of anything that emits sound: a body — or at least some part of it — must vibrate to produce the sound. This vibration commences with the imposition of mechanical energy on the fork when it is hit by something or, alternatively, is struck against something. If we could look closely

---

SIDEBAR 10.3 Affecting the vibration pattern of a tuning fork

The tuning fork has several physical properties that affect this simple vibration behavior. First, the fork possesses some *mass*. The mass is acted upon by a force (i.e., the action that initiates the vibrations in the fork). The force causes the prongs of the fork to deflect *elastically*: the prongs bend, but they will return to their initial shape. Second, the fork behaves like a spring, and the degree of *springiness* of the fork determines how readily the fork will vibrate. A limp material can be made to deflect easily, whereas a more rigid material requires a greater force to make it vibrate. Third, the fork displays *inertia* as it is struck: the prongs will continue to vibrate after the force that initiated the vibrations has ceased. But, because of friction within the fork, the prongs will eventually stop vibrating. And, fourth, the *shape* and even the *size* of the fork affect the vibration pattern. A bigger fork, having more mass, would require more force to set the fork into vibration than would a smaller fork, if both are composed of the same material. Similarly, the cross-section of the prongs of the fork can also influence the nature of vibration. For example, a prong with a solid, circular cross-section would vibrate more readily than a prong whose cross-section was organized in an I (or H) shape, as long as both had equal cross-sectional areas. A further discussion of how these properties influence the vibration patterns of sources can be found in Chapters 1–3 of the book by Hall, D.E., *Musical Acoustics*, (Belmont, California: Wadsworth Publishing Company, 1980), pages 1–59. Chapter 3 of that book provides a particularly interesting basic description of how these properties determine the performance of various types of musical instruments. An alternative description of the vibration behavior of the tuning fork and the physical properties of the fork that affect the pattern of vibration can be found in Chapter 2 of the book by Backus, J., *The Acoustical Foundations of Music* (2nd edition), (New York: W.W. Norton & Company, 1977), pages 22–31.

enough, we would find that the vibration pattern of *either* prong has a very regular, repeating form. The prong deflects out from its rest position to some maximum place, swings back past the rest position and continues (toward the other prong) to a maximum deflection point inward and opposite the maximum outward deflection point, and then swings outward toward the rest position.

We can introduce some vocabulary to describe this vibration pattern. The rest position is called the point of *equilibrium*. The movement of the prong from this equilibrium position to the maximum outward deflection point, back to the maximum inward deflection point, and on again to the equilibrium position is known as a *cycle*. The number of cycles that a prong vibrates through in a second is the *frequency* of vibration. The length of *time* that it takes for the prong to move through one cycle (or, in other words, the *time per cycle*) is the *period* of the vibration. The points of maximum deflection outward and inward for a tuning fork are of equal distance from the equilibrium point. Also, the distance from either of these points of maximum deflection is known as the *amplitude* of the vibration. Lastly, we can describe the vibration pattern of the tuning fork graphically by relating the amount of *displacement*—the deflection of the prong from its equilibrium point—versus the amount of time for this displacement to occur (from some beginning moment when the prong was at the equilibrium point). Such a graph will show a *sinusoidal* variation (Figure 10.1).

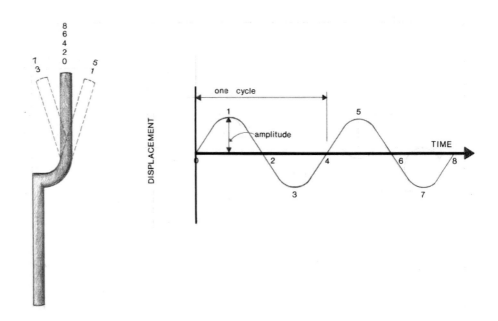

Figure 10.1   The vibration pattern of the tuning fork can be described by comparing the amount of displacement of a prong of the fork—shown on the y-axis—against the moment in time—shown on the x-axis—when the prong is located at that point of displacement.

10.1.2 THE WAVE NATURE OF SOUND

If we strike a tuning fork—giving it energy to vibrate—the prongs of the fork will move outward and then back to their equilibrium positions (thus, completing half of a vibration cycle). Each prong, as it deflects outward, encounters air molecules and pushes these molecules together. A *localized, compressed* volume of molecules develops in the vicinity of each prong. The molecular volume displays a *denser packing* than the ambient air that surrounds the volume. Consequently, this volume exhibits a pressure that is higher than (and a density that is increased above) the ambient air that generally surrounds this volume. Indeed, the compression squeezes the molecules together, taking them from what may be thought of as their "equilibrium" positions (i.e., where they would likely be if the tuning fork were not vibrating) and pushing them into an intermediate, compressed formation.

All of this compressive action results from molecules being forced together by the outward movement of the deflecting prong. So, when the prong subsequently retreats inward (toward its equilibrium and, subsequently, its maximum inward positions), the force that pushed the molecules together is removed. The compressed molecules "relax," proceed back toward their "equilibrium" positions, and move even further apart creating a localized volume that is less densely packed than is present in the ambient air. At the same time that the prong is moving inward, the pressurizing force, however, continues outward and acts on the molecules that were just beyond those that were initially pushed together by the prong when it first deflected outward. These just-more-distant molecules, acted upon by the pressurizing force, become more densely packed (Figure 10.2).

After the prong has deflected to its maximum location inward, the prong will once again deflect outward. As the prong moves outward, it will create a new localized volume of more densely packed molecules (by pushing the air molecules from their equilibrium positions into a pressurized volume). Meanwhile, the initially pressurizing force continues to move outward, and a second higher-than-ambient pressure region forms further out from the prong. As the prong reaches its maximum outward displacement (on this second vibration cycle) and retreats inward, the pressurizing force that caused the formation of the new localized volume will also continue to move outward. As the prong moves inward to complete its second vibration cycle, the molecules "relax," proceed back toward their equilibrium positions, and then move further apart creating another lower-than-ambient pressure region.

Thus, this pattern of creating increased and decreased pressure zones continues as the tuning fork prong vibrates iteratively. The air molecules acted upon by these pressure zones only move progressively from equilibrium positions to more densely packed positions to equilibrium positions to less densely packed positions to equilibrium positions. *However, these molecules do not move ever outward from the tuning fork prong.* Instead, *each greater-than-ambient pressure region* (formed at each instance when the prong

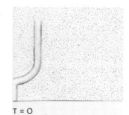
T = 0

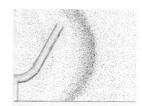
T = 1

T = 2

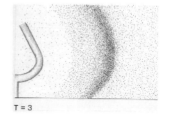
T = 3

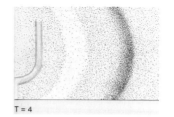
T = 4

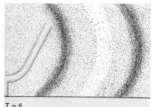
T = 5

Figure 10.2 For a vibrating prong of the tuning fork, formations of more tightly packed and less tightly packed volumes of molecules (or zones of "compression" and "rarefaction," respectively) are shown in this drawing. The outwardly moving prong compresses the molecules close to it, imparting momentum to the molecules. This momentum then passes to molecules progressively outward from the originally compressed volume of molecules thus carrying the sound wave away from the prong.

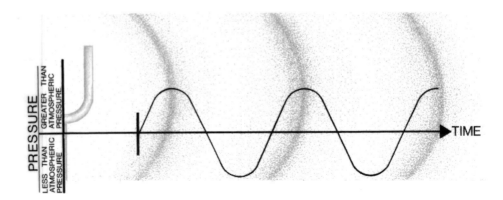

Figure 10.3 The variation in the amount of pressure change of the air molecules, resulting from the vibrating fork prong, is plotted versus the moment in time when each specific amount of pressure change occurs.

SIDEBAR 10.4 Waves as disturbances of transmitting media

A wave is fundamentally a disturbance in some medium, which results from some action carried out upon the medium. For example, switching on a light bulb sends light waves throughout the room containing the light bulb, or turning on an infrared heat lamp sends out heat as electromagnetic radiation, or depressing a key on the piano produces sound waves that emanate from the instrument. A primary characteristic of a wave is that, after the disturbance has passed some point away from the wave source, the medium at that point will return to its quiescent state (unless the wave source continues to send out additional waves). So, for instance, if we turn off the light bulb, the light waves will cease to be present and the room becomes dark.

In addition, the pressure wave (which moves away from the tuning fork) is *longitudinal*. In longitudinal waves the elements of the medium (e.g., the air molecules), which convey the wave, move back and forth along the same axis or line as the wave propagates.

Contrary to this longitudinal wave behavior, electromagnetic radiation travels in *transverse* waves. The electric and magnetic fields that are essential components of electromagnetic radiation vary in direction *perpendicular to the axis* along which the radiation wave flows. Setting up waves in a water tank is a commonly used modeling technique for showing wave behavior. But the water waves that result from disturbing the water (e.g., tossing a pebble into the water) are also transverse waves, as the wave motion in the water consists of the localized volumes of the water moving upward and downward as the wave spreads outward from where the disturbance was initiated. For a further discussion of longitudinal and transverse wave behaviors, see "Mechanical Waves," in Sears, F.W., M.W. Zemansky, and H.D. Young, *University Physics* (6th edition), (Reading, Massachusetts: Addison-Wesley Publishing Company, 1984), pages 403–419. Alternatively, for a treatment of the properties and behaviors of sound waves, see "Waves," in Rossing, T.D., *The Science of Sound*, (Reading, Massachusetts: Addison-Wesley Publishing Company, 1983), pages 31–47.

deflects outward) *continues to move away* from the tuning fork. This pressurizing force essentially is a *disturbance* that moves through the ambient air that surrounds the tuning fork. *The movement of this disturbance*—caused by the vibrations of the tuning fork— *thus occurs as a wave.* So, the variation of the pressure at any location away from the tuning fork also exhibits a wave-like pattern between greater-than-ambient pressures to less-than-ambient pressures.

For the tuning fork we can draw a graph relating the *pressure variation versus time* (Figure 10.3). The organization of this graph will be similar to the *prong displacement versus time* curve (Figure 10.1) that we presented earlier. The maximum and minimum amplitudes in Figure 10.3 have equivalent magnitudes though with opposite signs. The pattern of variation is also regular and periodic and shows a smooth pressure change from greater-than-ambient to ambient to less-than-ambient to ambient and so forth. The frequency of the pressure changes—or the number of pressure cycles that occur in a given unit of time—is constant (and also is equal to the frequency of the prong vibration (or deflection) rate shown in Figure 10.1). As a result, this pressure variation versus time curve in Figure 10.3 is definitely *sinusoidal*.

10.1.3 MEDIA IN WHICH SOUND WAVES PROPAGATE

A commonly used physics classroom demonstration employs an alarm clock, a glass bell jar, and a vacuum pump. First, the instructor turns on the alarm clock and lets it ring strong and clear (i.e., the alarm in the clock consists of a small clapper striking a bell). Then, the *ringing* alarm clock is placed inside of the bell jar, the vacuum pump is connected to the bell jar and is switched on, and the air within the bell jar is gradually evacuated. After a period of having the air drawn from the bell jar, the ringing of the alarm clock can no longer be heard. The cessation of the alarm clock noise, however, does not occur because the alarm clock clapper has stopped hitting the bell. Rather, the air within the bell jar has been nearly totally removed, and thus there is nothing to transport the energy from the vibrating alarm clock bell to the ears of those observing this demonstration. The principal intent of this display is to indicate that a *medium* is needed to propagate the sound. Here, the medium is air (which, of course, is a mixture of gases). Additionally, sound can also be transported through liquids and solids.

The two essential properties of air that enable it to propagate sound are that it has *mass* and is *compressible*. The air is composed of molecules, and the molecules can be squeezed together (or drawn apart) into localized volumes that are more densely packed (or less densely packed) than the ambient air that surrounds the sound source. Similarly, the basic properties of liquids and solids which allow them to transport sound waves are that they also have *mass* and, whereas liquids and solids are generally *incompressible*, they are *elastic*. The mass thus provides a medium in which sound waves can be propagated. The elasticity—even if the material is only slightly elastic—allows vibrations to be set up within the material.

So, if we return now to the question of whether a tree falling in the woods will cause the production of sound, we must conclude that, yes, sound—which is ultimately a physical phenomenon—is produced. As the tree strikes the ground, pressure waves will emanate from the impact point. If the waves are strong enough and someone is close enough to sense these waves, then the sound of the tree striking the ground will also be heard. Otherwise, the sound waves will propagate outward and will dissipate, unheard.

Section 10.2 | SELECTED BEHAVIORS OF SOUND WAVES

In this section we will describe a series of behaviors that sound waves display as they propagate outward from a source. This catalogue of behaviors will provide the basis for subsequent descriptions of our hearing capabilities and how the built environment can be used to improve our hearing. Understanding these behaviors is fundamental to designing and building for good acoustic performance. Note that some behaviors can occur in both open and closed spaces. Others will be observed only in enclosed spaces. In the following discussions, closed spaces are those that are bounded by surfaces like walls which limit the movement of the sound wave. Alternatively, open spaces are essentially free of these surfaces (e.g., a grassy meadow).

10.2.1 THE TRANSMISSION OF SOUND WAVES

So, let's begin by considering a sound wave that is propagating outward from its source (e.g., a tuning fork). The sound wave travels through air that surrounds the tuning fork, the air serving as the medium for the transmission of the wave. The sound wave travels away from the source because the source has imparted mechanical energy to the wave. This energy is passed progressively across the air molecules that comprise the surrounding medium, causing localized volumes of molecules to grow alternatively more dense and then less dense as the wave travels outward. As the source continues to vibrate, giving off mechanical energy, sound waves will continue to propagate away from this source, moving through the medium. Only when the source ceases to vibrate do the sound waves stop forming at the source. Then, no further mechanical energy will flow outward from what had been the source.

Necessarily, our discussion about the propagation of sound waves so far has concentrated on the movement of the mechanical energy through air. But sound waves can also be transmitted along a telephone wire and across a drumhead. As long as the medium has mass and is elastic — or, in the case of a gas (or a mixture of gases like air), has mass and is compressible — the transmission of sound waves can occur readily.

10.2.2 THE REFLECTION OF SOUND WAVES

When a sound wave that is propagating through one medium encounters a medium of a different type, the sound wave will be at least partially reflected by the second medium. For example, a sound wave moving in air reaches the wall of a room and reflects off of the wall. Reflection involves the sound wave undergoing a change in direction at the boundary between the two media and then passing back through the first medium following this new direction (Figure 10.4). Additionally, the incident sound wave will also experience two other behaviors: some fraction of the mechanical energy carried by the wave will be *absorbed* by the second medium, and another fraction of the mechanical energy will be *transmitted* into the second medium. Further, some of the mechanical energy that is transmitted into the second medium may even pass through and emerge at an opposite boundary of the second medium (if the thickness of the second medium is not very large and does not impose great resistance to such passage).

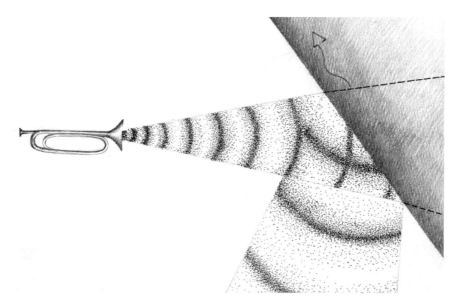

Figure 10.4 A hard surface intercepts sound waves from a bugle and reflects most of the energy back to the surrounding air. Some of the mechanical energy of the sound wave will pass into the material of which the surface is composed. A bit of the energy of the sound wave that passes into the material will be transmitted on through the material. And the material will absorb the remainder of the energy of the sound wave that has not been reflected nor absorbed.

10.2.2.1   How the mechanical impedances of adjoining media affect the reflection of sound waves   Any medium that transmits sound displays *mechanical impedance*. This mechanical impedance is characterized as a ratio of the force that needs to be exerted to drive a sound wave through a medium versus the velocity at which the sound wave moves in the medium. As such, the mechanical impedance is a measure of how much resistance the medium exerts on this transporting of mechanical energy (by a sound wave) through that medium. For instance, little force needs to be imposed on air to cause sound waves to be transmitted through it. Thus, air has low mechanical impedance. Alternatively, to move sound waves through water requires substantially greater force, and, although the speed of sound in water is slightly more than four times greater than in air, the mechanical impedance of water is very much larger than that of air.[2] The properties of a material that most determine its mechanical impedance are likely to be its density and elasticity (or, in the case of a gas, how compressible the gas is). Therefore, a material like a soft, springy rubber — that has a moderate to low density (among solids) and is very springy — has a low mechanical impedance. Alternatively, concrete with its high density and virtually inelastic character has a large mechanical impedance value.

The magnitudes of the mechanical impedance that materials display strongly affect the reflection of sound waves. When a sound wave traveling in one medium reaches the boundary separating the first medium from the second, the ability of the sound wave to move from the first medium into the second depends on how closely matched the mechanical impedances of the two media are. If the media have nearly similar mechanical impedances, then the sound wave will pass readily from the first medium to the second medium. But if the first medium has a very much smaller mechanical impedance than the second medium, nearly all of the mechanical energy that the sound wave had while moving in the first medium will be reflected by the second medium. Such is the case when a sound wave in air encounters the surface of water: very little of the airborne sound wave will enter the water (i.e., because the mechanical impedance of water is much greater than that of air). So, for example, if you are swimming underwater, then you cannot hear someone who is standing above the water and yelling at you: virtually all of the mechanical energy in the yell is reflected off the water surface and remains in the air above (Figure 10.5).

To ensure that a sound wave will readily pass across a boundary that separates two materials and that the sound wave will be well-transmitted in the second medium, the two materials must be chosen so that an "impedance match" exists between the two materials (i.e., so that they have similar impedances).

10.2.2.2   Predicting the direction that a reflecting sound wave will follow   As a first approximation for describing the direction that a sound wave will follow as it leaves a reflecting surface, we can state that the reflection will occur specularly (i.e., the angle of reflection will be equal to the angle of incidence). To facilitate envisioning the path that incident and reflecting sound waves will travel, we can introduce a modeling technique that is useful when designing for acoustical performance. First, we should recognize that a sound wave incident on a reflecting surface arrives at that surface after emanating from a vibrating source. So, we can—by means of drawing—connect the source and the reflecting surface with a straight line (or arrow). We call this line a *ray* and say that it portrays the path that the sound wave has traveled before reaching the reflecting surface.

Representing the intersection of this ray and the reflecting surface with a two-dimensional (sectional) view, we thereby establish the *angle of incidence*. Using this view and the angle of incidence, we can then construct the *angle of reflection*—at the point where the ray intersects the surface—by using the equal angles law. This procedure of employing a ray to indicate the path of a sound wave and examining the likely paths that sound waves traverse is known as *ray diagramming* (Figure 10.6). This method of predicting where reflecting waves will travel can be used even when the reflecting surfaces are curvilinear.

For a curved surface, you establish where the sound wave (ray) will be incident on the surface. Then, using a two-dimensional (sectional) view, you draw a line tangent to the curved line at the point of incidence. This tangent line and the incident ray determine the angle of incidence. An angle of reflection (equal to the incidence angle) can then be generated at *the point of incidence on the tangent line* (Figures 10.7 and 10.8).

10.2.3   THE ABSORPTION OF SOUND WAVES

A sound wave passes through some medium because a vibrating sound source has imparted mechanical energy to the medium. When the sound wave bearing this mechanical energy reaches a boundary separating the medium from an adjoining medium, three types of behavior will be present: a sound wave possessing some of the energy from the incident wave will reflect off the boundary; some of the energy will drive the sound wave across the boundary and enable the wave to pass into the second medium; and a fraction of the energy from the incident sound wave will enter the second medium and will be dissipated as heat (i.e., converted from mechanical to thermal energy). This third behavior—the conversion of mechanical to thermal energy and the gathering-in of the thermal energy by the second medium—is called *absorption*. How much energy is devoted to each one of these

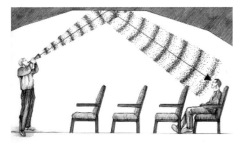

Figure 10.5 When a sound wave, present in one medium, reaches the boundary separating the first medium from a second medium, the sound wave (and the mechanical energy of the wave) will mostly be reflected at this boundary if the mechanical impedances of the two media are different. Thus, a mother calling to her swimming child will not be heard by the child (because of the large difference in the mechanical impedances of air and water).

Figure 10.6 A ray diagram is a simple, yet quickly useful approximation for showing the behavior of sound waves. By drawing a ray to represent the sound waves emanating from a horn, we can easily determine whether these waves will reach a listener after reflecting off of the ceiling surface (i.e., knowing that the pattern of reflection of the wave will follow the Law of Reflection).

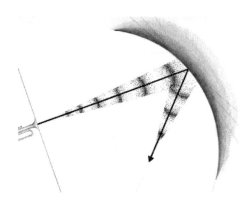

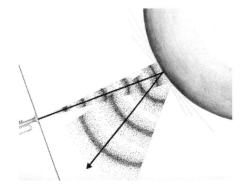

Figure 10.7 Sound waves reflecting off of a concave surface will be focused or concentrated toward some place, where its location is determined by the nature of the curvature. In built spaces created with concave curvilinear surfaces, listeners will observe some locations in the spaces where sound seems unusually strong ("hot spots") and other locations where the sound is very weak ("voids"). Designers and builders including concave-shaped surfaces in buildings should be aware that anomalous sound conditions will likely be present unless special treatments are provided for these surfaces.

Figure 10.8 A convex reflecting surface will cause incident sound waves to diffuse as they strike the surface. The diffusing of the sound waves spreads the mechanical energy of the waves outward, creating a more uniform energy distribution away from the surface. For more information about sound wave diffusion, see Section 10.2.4.

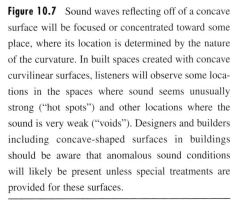

behaviors depends not only on the nature of the second medium, but also on the character of the sound wave.

To understand what happens during absorption, think in terms of a sound wave emanating outward from a tuning fork. The sound wave is essentially a disturbance in the air: this disturbance is manifested as a pressure variation where the air molecules become more densely packed as the wave passes and then relax after the wave has moved on. When the air molecules close to the surface (of what will be the reflecting medium) clump together and come in contact with that reflecting surface, they experience friction. Some of the mechanical energy present in the sound wave thus is converted to heat (thermal energy), reducing the amount of mechanical energy remaining in the reflected sound wave (Figure 10.9).

Absorption can also occur when sound waves impinge on panel structures (e.g., plywood suspended from wood-framing or gypsum wallboard attached to wall studs). Some of the mechanical energy of the sound wave will be transferred to the panel. The transferred energy will cause the panel to flex and bow (Figure 10.10) in a manner similar to how a drumhead vibrates when struck by a drumstick. This transference of mechanical energy from the incident sound wave to the panel produces a reflecting wave with less energy than the incident wave had. The vibration energy imparted to the panel eventually is lost to the surrounding air as heat (i.e., friction is experienced within the panel, slightly warming the panel).

The ability of a material to absorb mechanical energy from a sound wave depends on the surface of the material, its composition, and how the material is mounted (e.g., whether it is suspended — or hung — in free space or secured to some more rigid structure). Generally, materials having the following properties will readily absorb mechanical energy from a sound wave: surfaces that are roughened, textured, or fissured; materials that have low densities or are porous; or materials that are soft or that have parts (e.g., fibers) that can be made to vibrate (thus, taking mechanical energy from the incident sound wave). Examples of materials that are commonly used in buildings for promoting absorption include cloths, fiber batts and blankets, acoustic tiles, wood panels (when hung away from structural framing), gypsum wallboard, and so forth.

The ability of a material or a construction to absorb mechanical energy is described in terms of its *absorption coefficient*, which is defined as the ratio of the amount of energy absorbed by the material (when a sound wave reaches it) versus the amount of energy present in the incident sound wave. Absorption coefficients of common building materials and constructions will range from 0 to 1. The ability of a material or construction to absorb mechanical energy — and, thus, its absorption coefficient — commonly will vary with the frequency of the incident sound wave. Some materials and constructions will be better absorbers of higher-frequency sounds, whereas other materials and constructions will offer better absorption for lower-frequency sounds.

10.2.4 THE DIFFUSION OF SOUND WAVES

Sound wave diffusion is a special category of the reflection process. In the generalized reflection process, a sound wave that is incident on a large, smooth surface will be matched by a reflecting sound wave. The form of this reflecting wave, though it is diverging, is still comparatively well defined and bounded (Figure 10.4). The direction of the reflecting sound wave will be determined both by the shape of the reflecting surface and where the incident wave impinges on this surface (i.e., in the manner described in Section

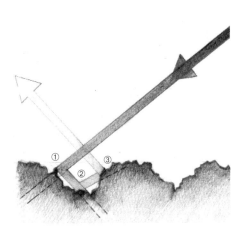

Figure 10.9 Sound waves (represented by the ray) strike a textured surface. With each reflection of the ray some of the entrained mechanical energy is exchanged to the surface material. After each reflection, the ray is comparatively weaker than it was before the reflection. Thus, after the three reflections shown here, the ray that passes off the surface back into the ambient air is decidedly less powerful than the incident ray. For instance, if after each reflection the ray retains 80 percent of its incident energy and the ray undergoes three such reflections, then the ray that returns to the ambient air has only 51 percent of the energy possessed by the ray that first struck the absorbing material.

Figure 10.10 A panel structure, which has a comparatively smooth surface, absorbs mechanical energy by being set into vibration (i.e., by flexing and bowing), when struck by sound waves. Low frequency sounds (with longer wavelengths) will be more greatly absorbed by these panel structures than will higher frequency sounds (with shorter wavelengths). Note that the relatively less powerful reflecting wave is not shown in this drawing.

SIDEBAR 10.5 Bending materials and heat production

Evidence that warming of the panel will occur, when the panel is caused to flex and bow, can be found by thinking about what happens when you bend a thin piece of metal back and forth. As you bend it repeatedly, the metal—particularly, at the area of bending—grows warm. When you cease bending the metal, either because it has failed or you have grown tired of the exertion, the heat developed in the strip will gradually dissipate to the surrounding air. Certainly, a panel induced to vibrate by the mechanical energy of a sound wave may not acquire as much thermal energy as the strip of metal. But some mechanical energy from a sound wave is nonetheless transferred to the panel, converted to thermal energy, and ultimately exchanged with the surrounding air.

10.2.2.2 above). However, when a surface contains many small irregularities, an incident sound wave reflecting off of the surface will be *scattered* across a wide angle of dispersion. This dispersion—or diffusion—produces a reflection pattern in which the mechanical energy of the incident sound wave is spread out virtually uniformly over this wide angle without an apparently preferred direction (Figure 10.11). The amount of energy in any specific direction will be much less than would be present in the case where the same incident wave reflected off of a large, smooth surface.

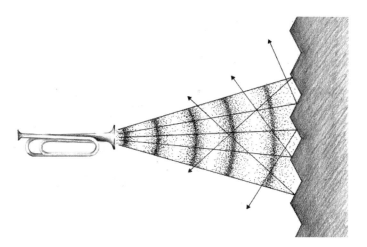

Figure 10.11 A sound wave intercepted by a rough surface undergoes diffusion, and the entrained energy in the sound wave is spread out widely from the surface.

SIDEBAR 10.6 Differentiating between sound wave diffusion and sound wave absorption

Note that the diffusing and absorbing processes are indeed different. Absorption happens when the mechanical energy of a sound wave impinging on a surface is converted to thermal energy. The amount of energy in the reflecting wave may be substantially less than was present in the incident wave. But the reflecting wave still is comparatively well defined and bounded. However, when an incident wave is diffused by a reflecting surface, comparatively little of the mechanical energy of the wave converts to thermal energy. In fact, the large majority of the mechanical energy embedded within the incident wave will remain in the first medium. Instead of having the well-defined and bounded shape of the incident wave, the diffusing energy of the "reflecting" wave will be greatly spread out over a wide angle. Thus, in absorption, much of the energy from the incident wave will be lost to the second medium, although the form of the reflecting wave will still continue to resemble the incident wave. Alternatively, for diffusion, little of the energy from the incident wave will be transferred to the second medium and most will remain in the first medium. But the diffused waveform will be widely spread out: thus, an even—though less concentrated—distribution of energy is produced over a large volume.

To achieve the diffusion of an incident sound wave, the necessary criterion is that *the wavelength of the wave must be less than the size(s) of the surface irregularities*. The wavelength is the distance that exists between corresponding points in two adjacent localized volumes of air molecules (within a wave): for instance, the wavelength is often cited as the distance between the location where one volume is most densely packed to the location where the next volume is most densely packed. This distance can also be regarded as the amount of space for a wave to undergo one complete cycle in its pressure variation. The wavelength is described in terms of a unit of length (e.g., inches or meters).

The wavelength of a sound wave is not an independent parameter of the wave. In fact, *the product of the frequency of the sound wave* (the number of cycles of pressure variation per unit time) *multiplied by the wavelength* (the distance the wave moves in completing one cycle of its pressure variation) *equals the velocity of sound* (for the medium in which the sound wave is traveling). The speed of sound is expressed as distance per unit time (for example, for air at sea level, 344 m/s or 1130 ft/s). A relatively high-frequency sound wave thus has a short wavelength, and a comparatively low-frequency sound has a longer wavelength (i.e., the frequency and wavelength of a sound vary inversely with respect to each other).

So, to promote the diffusion of incident sound waves, the size of the surface irregularities must be greater than the wavelength of the sound wave that is to be diffused. Alternatively, if the wavelength of an incident sound wave is substantially larger than the surface texturing, the sound wave will simply reflect off of the surface with no diffusion occurring.

The benefit of achieving diffusion of incident sound waves is that the mechanical energy embodied in the waves is spread relatively uniformly throughout a built space. Developing a uniform spread of a sound energy from a source is often an important factor in establishing good hearing conditions (particularly, in musical performance spaces). We will discuss the development of good diffusion capabilities further in Section 13.6.5.

10.2.5 THE DIFFRACTION OF SOUND WAVES

Sound waves moving through a medium (e.g., air) can encounter individual obstacles that are small enough not to enclose the wave. When a wave runs into such an obstacle, the wave may pass around the obstacle and continue beyond it. This behavior is one of two situations in which *diffraction* of sound waves occurs. Diffraction can also happen when a sound wave reaches a narrow opening in what would otherwise be an enclosing surface. The sound wave will pass through the opening and propagate onward past the enclosure. In both of these situations diffraction results from the wave brushing against the edge of a surface. The part of the wave closest to this edge is impeded, while the remainder of the wave, away from the edge, readily passes on. The net effect is that the direction of the wave is bent outward from the edge and spreads out. The extent that diffraction will occur depends on the wavelength of the sound wave and either the size of the opening or the form of the edge. In the case of a *sound wave passing through an opening*, diffraction will be most pronounced when the wavelength of the sound is substantially bigger than the opening. If the wavelength is smaller than the dimension of the opening, some limited diffraction will be present at the edges of the opening. The portion of the sound wave closest to the edge will be bent and will spread outward. But the major fraction of such a small wave will pass by unimpeded. Alternatively, for *a sound wave coming in contact with the edge of some obstacle of limited size*, diffraction results primarily when the sound wavelength

Figure 10.12 Sound waves, leaving our mouths as we speak, undergo diffraction with the spread of the sound waves becoming appreciably greater than might otherwise seem likely given the size of our mouths.

Figure 10.13 If you speak through a megaphone, much as a cheerleader does at a sporting event, your voice will appear much more powerful than if you speak without the megaphone. The megaphone does not add energy to your voice: rather, it concentrates the energy by minimizing its diffractive spread outward (i.e., thus, the megaphone combats the diffraction of sound waves as they leave your mouth).

is substantially larger than the obstacle. When small-wavelength sounds run into a larger obstacle, these sound waves will most likely be reflected by the obstacle (i.e., instead of being diffracted and then passing around the obstacle).

One common example of diffraction happens with the emission of long-wavelength—low-frequency—sounds from a loudspeaker. For instance, a 200 Hz sound has a wavelength of 1.7 m (about five feet). The diameter of the typical bass-response speaker, however, is usually about one-third to one-half of a meter. Because of diffraction, the low-frequency sound waves leaving the speaker front will bend and spread outward, filling the space in which the speaker rests. A second example of diffraction occurs when you speak. Speech contains sounds that span a wide frequency range,[3] but the more powerful components of speech occur from about 250–500 Hz for men and at about 500 Hz for women. The wavelengths for 250 and 500 Hz sounds are, respectively, about 1.4 and 0.7 meters (or 4.5 and 2.3 ft). The size of one's mouth is clearly much smaller. So, the lower-frequency sound waves that emanate from your mouth will undergo appreciable diffraction (Figures 10.12 and 10.13).

A third example—one involving the built environment—involves the passing of sound waves over a mid-height partition (perhaps, 1.5 meters or five feet high) in an *open-planned* space where the ceiling may be suitably higher. In this situation sounds initiated on one side of the partition will often be easily heard on the other side of the partition, even though there is no "line-of-sight" between a source and an office worker. With a high

Figure 10.14   The diffraction of sound waves by a mid-height partition is shown in this drawing. The extent of this diffractive behavior will be further described in Section 13.3.2.1.

ceiling the reflection of sound waves off of the ceiling will probably *not* be the principal mechanism for communication. Instead, sound waves passing over the partition will most likely be diffracted by the edge of the partition and will spread downward to auditors who are on the other side of this partition (Figure 10.14).

Section 10.3 | THE EXISTENCE OF SOUND FIELDS

How sound waves behave in an environment is determined both by the nature of the source from which the sound waves emanate and the physical properties of the environment. For instance, the size (or volume) of the environment and the presence and natures of surface materials within the environment are essential determinants of behavior. For the source, parameters such as how the source is induced to vibrate, whether the energy supply causing vibration of the source is continuous or intermittent, and by what means the source is deployed in the environment will all affect the behavior of the sound waves. Generally, the presence of sound waves in an environment—whether from one or several sources—results in the formation of sound *fields*. The several kinds of fields that we will describe below display a variety of properties that result from the character of the environment in which the sound waves exist. These properties determine how and what we hear from sound sources in an environment.

The first, and perhaps the most basic, pair of sound fields are the *open* and *closed* fields. An open field—also described as a *free* field—exists when one or more sound sources are present in an environment for which there are either no enclosing planes or the enclosing planes are so distant from the source that they have little effect on the sound waves that emanate from the source. Thus, in the typical open field there will be no vertical (wall) or horizontal (ceiling) surfaces to reflect sound waves. Instead, sound waves

SIDEBAR 10.7 Sound production in large, covered sports stadiums

If you have many people present at a sporting event in one of these domed stadiums, it is possible to create sound strengths that are sustained by the reflections of sound off of the many surfaces in such stadiums. There have recently been numbers of anecdotal reports, published in the popular press, about the noise strength that has been created by enthusiastic spectators at various events. In fact, sustained noise levels as high as 125 decibels were reported during the 1991 World Series games at the Metrodome in Minneapolis, Minnesota. For such activities and with the many sound sources present, the open-field conditions are lost.

leaving a source will continue moving out until the mechanical energy from them is exhausted. The loss of propagating strength results from air absorbing the energy of the sound waves as they flow through the air. This weakening of the outward-moving sound wave is known as *attenuation*.[4] Any sound that propagates in an open field travels from the source to the receiver by a direct — or *line-of-sight* — path: the only wave reflections that may be present will be those that bounce off ground plane surfaces (and these reflections will contribute comparatively little to the strength of the sound message that reaches a receiver). Two examples of open field conditions can be found in flat-topography meadows and in large field houses or roof-enclosed sports stadiums. The undeveloped flat terrain found in the North American prairie lands (especially where the ground covering is low or is cut close to the ground) is an excellent example of where open-field conditions may be experienced (for example, Figure 5.63). Alternatively, domed sports stadiums that exist in several North American cities (e.g., the Astrodome in Houston, Texas) also generally provide open-field conditions: the distances that exist between walls, the heights of the roofs, and the large volumes within these enclosures are great enough to cause single sounds created in these buildings to die out before reflection can occur.

When sound waves from a single or multiple sources are bounded by vertical and horizontal planes — such as by the walls, floor, and ceilings in buildings — a *closed field* exists. When these enclosing planes are present, sound waves will be reflected off of the planes. These reflecting waves will *reinforce* the message carried by direct ("line-of-sight") sound waves, thereby contributing substantially to the strength of any message received by an auditor. The character of a closed field is greatly dependent (as are the messages produced within this field) on the locations of the various enclosure surfaces and the natures of the materials that constitute these surfaces. Additionally, surfaces other than these enclosing planes will also reflect sound waves present in the space. Depending on where these other surfaces are and how extensive they are, these additional surfaces can have profound effects on sound wave behavior in an enclosed space.

An important subcategory of the closed field is the *reverberant field*. This latter field condition is created within an enclosed environment and is a short-term, *transient* phenomenon. Its development occurs when a sound source within an enclosure ceases to emit sound waves. Sound waves that had previously left the source — before it ceased vibrating — continue to move through the space and to reflect off of enclosing (and other) surfaces. Consequently, a *subtle prolongation* of the sound can be observed. The strength of this prolonged sound will decrease with time, as the reflecting sound waves lose their propagating energy (after further reflections and the concomitant absorption of this mechanical energy). The length of time it takes for the prolonged sound to decay a specified amount is known as the *reverberation time* of the enclosure. This reverberation time usually ranges from about one-half of a second for small rooms (e.g., seminar classrooms and offices) to three or four seconds for very large built spaces like cathedrals. The primary properties of a space that determine the extent of reverberation (and the length of the reverberation time) are the volume within the enclosure through which sound waves can move and the amount of surface materials that will absorb the mechanical energy from the reflecting waves.

When a reverberant field exists in a space, the sound energy will be uniformly distributed throughout the space (except in the volume very near the source, where the localized sound energy density will exceed the uniform spread of energy). This uniform distribution develops through the mixing and dispersion of direct and reflected sounds: sound in the reverberant field will appear to be well blended. Sound will also appear to be well diffused, and the reverberant field is sometimes identified as a *diffuse field*. The principal requirements for providing good diffuse field conditions in enclosed spaces are that there will be numerous opportunities for sound reflection to occur and much of the reflecting surface area will be able to diffuse sound waves (i.e., by having *irregularities of varying sizes* on the reflecting surfaces and *intermixing* surfaces which are either good reflectors or good absorbers of sound waves). The creation of the diffuse field condition is particularly important in enclosures in which music is performed and listened to.

The last two field conditions that are significant for building operation are the *near field* and the *far field*. Both of these are most often subcategories of the closed field. The near field condition exists only in a localized volume that immediately surrounds a sound source (Figure 10.15). In the near field the sound present in this localized volume results from waves coming directly from the sound source *without the reinforcement of reflected waves*. In the near field (compared to elsewhere in an enclosed space), the strength of the sound will be greatest because the mechanical energy carried by the waves has not had any opportunity to be absorbed (or attenuated). Also, in the near field, the density of the sound energy will be constant. Just beyond the near field, a far field exists where the density of sound energy decreases slightly with increasing distance away from the source. The approximate dividing line between the near and far fields is suggested by Durrant and Lovrinic to be at a distance of a few wavelengths from the source[5] (therefore, the location of the dividing line will depend on the frequency of the source with high-frequency sounds having a very compact near field and low-frequency sounds having a much larger near field).[6] Also, in many enclosures, the presence of the reverberant field will take over the volumes of the near and far fields, once the sound source has ceased vibrating (again, the reverberant field is the volume in which a uniform sound energy density builds up resulting from the multiple reflections of sound waves).

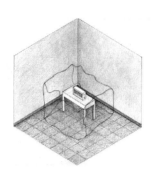

Figure 10.15 The near field around this table radio will be an irregularly shaped volume that will vary in shape and size as sounds of various wavelengths emanate from the radio speaker. The intensity of sound within this near field will be greater than the sound intensity found elsewhere in the room (i.e., in the far field).

Section 10.4 | FOUR BASIC PROPERTIES OF SOUND

In Section 10.1 we described how a vibrating source produces sound waves. In Sections 10.2 and 10.3 we considered how sound waves behave in various environments. In this section we will discuss four primary properties of sound waves: *frequency, intensity, waveform,* and *time*. We will also show—in Section 10.5—how these properties can be used to characterize specific sources and to distinguish among alternative sources.

10.4.1   THE FREQUENCY OF A SOUND WAVE

In Section 10.1 we described how a tuning fork vibrates when struck: the prongs of the fork bend outward and inward from their equilibrium—or rest—positions. As the prongs deflect, they create waves that pulse outward from the tuning fork. Each wave moves through the air that surrounds the tuning fork and causes the creation of alternating localized volumes of air, which are either more densely packed or less densely packed than the ambient air. Each wave moves progressively through the surrounding air, and at any point along the path of the wave the degree of packing varies continuously from some greatest density to some least density. The number of times that this density variation for the wave completes a cycle—say, from greatest density to least density to greatest density—is described as the *frequency* of the source. An alternate way of determining what the frequency of a sound source is—for a source that *continuously* emits waves—would be to pick some point along the path that the sound waves are traveling and to count how often the localized volume reaches its greatest (or least) density per second. Using either approach, the most common way of characterizing the frequency of a sound source is to establish the number of cycles completed or the number of instances that the maximum (or minimum) density occurs *for a second of time*. Thus, for example, the frequency of a sound source will bear the units of *cycles per second*. And this unit ratio is most commonly expressed in terms of *Hertz* (or, in its abbreviated form, as Hz).

For the tuning fork, this density (or pressure) variation can be represented graphically with a sine curve. This sine curve shows that the density variation is continuous and indicates the maximum and minimum levels of the density variation.

10.4.2   THE INTENSITY OF A SOUND WAVE

Sound waves propagate outward from the tuning fork because mechanical energy passes from this source to the surrounding medium. The energy from the vibrating tuning fork thus propels the waves as they travel through air. The *amount of energy* that the tuning fork gives up to the surrounding air *for some time duration* is defined as the *power* of the wave. This power is commonly described with the unit *watts*.

The sound waves that emanate from the vibrating tuning fork are approximately spherical in shape. The power driving a wave will thus be spread out over this spherical wave. At any point along the path that the outward-moving wave follows, the area of the wave sphere will be proportional to the square of the distance of this point from the source (Figure 10.16). Dividing the *power* of the wave by the *surface area* of the spherical wave at any point away from the source defines the *intensity* of the wave. So, intensity has the units of watts per square meter (or, sometimes, watts per square centimeter is used).

One other way of defining the intensity of a sound wave is to relate the pressure that the wave exerts on the air molecules as the wave passes through the air, the density of the air through which the sound wave travels, and the speed of the sound wave as it moves through the air. We have previously written about how a sound wave forms alternating regions with greater and lesser densities of air molecules. The physical property *density* is directly proportional to the *pressure* that a propagating sound wave exerts. Thus, when we talk of a region of higher or lower density, we can easily substitute *pressure* into the discussion. In other words, as the wave passes through air, the wave creates localized regions in which the air molecules are under greater or lesser pressure. *Note that in all instances of this pressure variation, when we say that the air molecules are under greater or lesser*

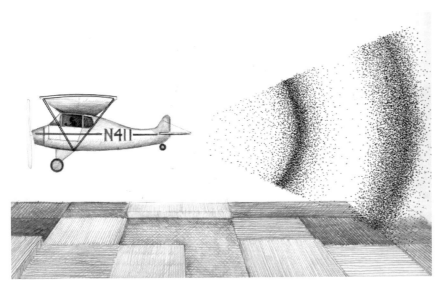

Figure 10.16   This airplane (or, rather, its single engine) is a point sound source that sends out spherical sound waves. As each sound wave emanates outward from the airplane, the surface area of the sphere expands. The amount of expansion is proportional to the square of the radius of the sphere. As the surface area of the spherical wave increases (as the wave moves away from the source), the intensity of the sound wave decreases. This result is essentially a consequence of the Inverse Square Law.

SIDEBAR 10.8 Describing sound wave movement mathematically

Written as an equation, power is equal to energy divided by time (or, algebraically, $P=E/t$, where P is the power of the source, E is the mechanical energy given off by the source to the surrounding air in wave formation, and t is the time period during which the energy is measured.

The formula for finding the area of the wave sphere is $A=4\pi r^2$, where r is the distance (or radius) from the source to the wavefront. The intensity of the sound wave at any point out from the source along the path that the wave travels is equal to the power of the source divided by the surface area for the wave sphere

at this point. Written in algebraic form, $I=P/A$, where I is the intensity, P is the power of the source, and A is the wave surface area (or $4\pi r^2$, where r is the radius of the wave sphere).

With the intensity of the sound wave defined as the power of the source divided by the product of $4\pi r^2$, the square of the radius of the spherical wave, then this intensity relationship follows the *Inverse Square Law* (i.e., that some effect at a distance r from its source will vary in an inverse proportion to the square of the distance).

pressure, we are speaking of amounts that are in comparison to the atmospheric pressure of the ambient air. Establishing greater pressure means then that the molecules in a localized region will be under a pressure that is greater by some *increment* than the ambient atmospheric pressure. Similarly, where the wave causes a region of lesser pressure, then the molecules in that localized region will exist under a pressure that is incrementally less than the ambient pressure.

The specific relationship—between the intensity of the wave and the (incremental) pressure of the wave, the density of the air, and the speed of sound in air—states that the intensity is equal to the square of this pressure divided by the product of the density multiplied by the speed of sound.[7]

10.4.3 SIMPLE AND COMPLEX SOUND WAVE FORMS

We have described the tuning fork as vibrating at a *single* frequency. The behavior of the vibrating fork can be further described—whether we consider the displacement of the prongs of the fork, the incremental pressure exerted on the localized air molecules, or the power of the wave—in terms of a sinusoidal curve. All three of these parameters vary with time, and the patterns of these variations are characterized by a smooth waveform. This vibration behavior of the tuning fork is identified as *simple*.

Most sound sources, however, vibrate not only at some lowest frequency, but also *additionally* with a number of other, higher frequencies. These sources are regarded as *complex*. For a complex source, higher-frequency vibrations that occur simultaneously with the lowest-frequency vibration combine with this lowest frequency to produce a complex wave that represents the presence of these multiple, overlaying frequencies.

Let's suppose that we have a guitar. An acoustic guitar—as differentiated from the electric guitar—has either six single strings or six pairs of strings, all of which are commonly made of steel or nylon. The strings are mounted between a cross (or tail) piece that is attached to the top plate of the guitar body and to six or twelve pegs at the end of the fingerboard. Just down the fingerboard from the pegs is a ridge piece over which each of the strings is pulled. The strings are maintained under tension, which is established by fastening the strings to the cross piece and winding them around the pegs. The guitar is generally played by plucking the strings with the fingers of one hand or with a plastic pick (held by a forefinger and thumb). Simultaneous with this plucking, the fingers of the player's other hand will commonly move up and down the fingerboard holding various strings against the fingerboard to change the sounds that are produced by the plucked strings.

When we pluck a guitar string, it appears to vibrate between the two restraints—the cross piece and the ridge (at the end of the fingerboard)—with a motion where the *middle part of the string* curves out on one side of its rest position, passes back across this rest position, curves outward on the other side of the rest position, and then passes across the rest position, moving outward again as it did initially. This movement *for the mid-part of the string* from its rest position to fully deflected on one side to fully deflected on the other side and back to the rest position is one cycle of vibration for the string. The number of cycles that the string completes in a second is called the *fundamental* frequency for the string.

The reason why this frequency is regarded as the *fundamental* is that the string also experiences other vibration patterns *at the same time* that this fundamental vibration happens. What distinguishes each additional vibration pattern from the fundamental is that, instead of a single deflection occurring between the two restraints (as it does for the fundamental), multiple such deflection patterns happen along the string. To illustrate this notion, let us begin with the fact that at the restraints the string does not deflect at all (i.e., it is fixed at both locations). For the fundamental vibration these two points are called the *nodes*. Now, for the first additional vibration pattern, a third node occurs along the string, specifically *at the middle of the string* (Figure 10.17). At this middle node the string will undergo no deflection (identical to the end nodes) and will appear to be at rest. Alternatively, the string on either side of this middle node will deflect, although in a direction opposite to what is happening on the other side of this middle node. Thus, deflections occur for each half of the string (i.e., for the string length from one end node to the middle node and the middle node to the other end node). Each of the two deflection patterns has the same form as the fundamental, but these deflection patterns occur along only one half of the length of the string.

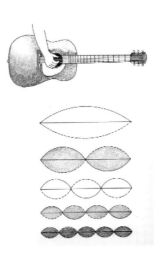

Figure 10.17 The vibrational patterns of a guitar string, displaying the fundamental note and several overtones.

For the fundamental vibration the length of the string is essentially one-half of the wavelength for waves leaving the string. For the first additional vibration—the one with the node at the middle of the string—*one-half of the wavelength for the waves leaving the string will be one-half of the length of the string*. Thus, as the product of the frequency of a sound wave and its wavelength are equal to the speed of sound (which is a constant value), the frequency of this first additional vibration pattern will be *twice* what the frequency of the fundamental vibration is. This first additional vibration pattern is traditionally called the *first overtone*.

The *second* additional vibration pattern has four nodes, one at each end of the string and one each at the *third* points of the string (Figure 10.17). The vibration pattern for this second condition then will have two places *intermediate along the string length* where no deflection will occur (i.e., at both of these intermediate nodes the string will remain at the rest position). Deflection will occur on either side of these intermediate nodes, although the deflection will be in opposite directions. The vibration patterns along each of these three segments of the string will have forms similar to the fundamental vibration. But for this pattern, one-third of the string length will be equal to one-half of the wavelength of the waves created by this pattern. Consistent with the discussion in the previous paragraph, the frequency for these waves will be three times what the fundamental frequency is. This second additional vibration pattern is called the *second overtone*.

Overtones in addition to these first two (e.g., a third, fourth, fifth, and so on) can often be found. Each succeeding overtone will have a frequency that is a whole number multiple of the fundamental. So, the fourth overtone will have a frequency that is five times the fundamental (e.g., if the fundamental frequency is 147 Hz, then the fourth overtone would have a frequency of 735 Hz). The principal limitations on the existence of overtones for a vibrating string are where the string was plucked (i.e., if the string were plucked at a location where an overtone has a node, then that overtone will not exist),[8] and that there is sufficient energy imparted to the string to cause it to vibrate in many modes, rather than in only a few modes. Necessarily, the number of tones including the fundamental frequency of the string plus the existing overtones is equal to the number of *modes of vibration*. The fundamental frequency and the overtones, whether few or many, together are called the *harmonic series* for the string.[9] In most instances, each higher overtone for a vibrating string will display a smaller intensity than will be present for lower overtones, with the greatest intensity usually present for the fundamental frequency.

The vibration pattern of the guitar string will thus include the fundamental frequency and a number of overtones. To determine what the waveform—a summary graphic representation of the intensity versus time variation for this harmonic series—will look like, we can layout each intensity-versus-time curve for the component frequencies and add up

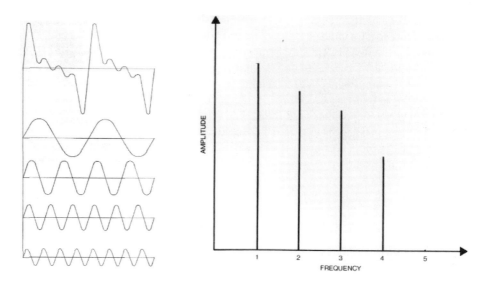

Figure 10.18   A complex waveform and its amplitude spectrum are shown in these two photographs.

the intensity values instant by instant. The intensity-versus-time curve for *each individual frequency* will be a sine wave (which is a *simple wave*). The resultant summation of these simple (sine) waves is called a *complex wave* (or waveform) and will generally not have the smoothness that is present with any sine wave curve (Figure 10.18). Note, however, that the waveforms for the fundamental frequency and the complex wave will both have the *same period* (i.e., the period being the time required for the variation in intensity for the two waveforms to undergo a complete cycle).

10.4.4   THE ROLE OF TIME IN THE BEHAVIOR OF SOUND

Time is an essential parameter for describing sound. When an object vibrates, sound waves emanate from the object. The nature of the waves depends strongly on time (e.g., the number of pressure cycles that pass some location per unit time; the length of time sound takes to travel from a source to a receiver; the existence of temporal differences between two sources when they are both present in a space; and so forth). One vivid example of how sound and time are linked is our perception of lightning and thunder. Lightning in a rainstorm occurs with a sudden flash of light. Though the lightning strike may occur several kilometers away from an observer, the individual sees the light at virtually the same instant that the lightning happens. This instantaneous experience results from the extraordinarily rapid velocity of light passage (i.e., 300,000 km/s [186,000 miles/s]). We have noted that velocity of sound is only 344 m/s (or 1130 ft/s), a far slower speed than light. So, if the strike occurs some distance away from the person, the sound of the thunder may take several seconds to reach the observer (e.g., the thunder from a strike that is 3.25 km [two miles] distant will take nearly ten seconds to reach the individual).

A second condition where time is an essential parameter for describing sound is evident when two (or more) sound sources are present in a space. If these sources both vibrate periodically (have regular rates of vibration), their amplitudes and frequencies are identical, and they have commenced vibrating at the same moment, we say that the sound waves are *in phase*. Often, such sources may begin vibrating at different moments and, consequently, the waves will be *out of phase*. Alternatively, the amplitudes and frequencies of the sources may only be similar, but not identical. Or the amplitudes and frequencies of the sources may differ, one from the other, by whole-number factors (for example, the second source vibrates at a rate twice that of the first). In these instances, the sources are also out of phase. When sources are out of phase, the extent of this condition is described in terms of a *phase difference* (which defines the time separation that exists between the vibrations of the sources). The relevance of phase relationships between two (or more) sources present in a space concerns the fact that the sounds may contribute additively to create a sound that is stronger and more dominant than the individual sounds. Or, instead, the sounds may work destructively and reduce an individual's ability either to distinguish between the two sources or to detect either.

Time is also an important parameter determining a human being's ability to hear sounds. Generally, there is a minimum amount of mechanical energy that must be acquired from a source before our auditory system can detect sound. The acquisition of a minimum energy amount will necessarily depend on the power of the source and the length of time available for listening to the source. We will further discuss the role of acquisition time in the human auditory process in Section 11.1.

Section 10.5 | QUANTIFYING THE NATURES OF COMMON SOUNDS

10.5.1 SOUND LEVELS AND THE DECIBEL SCALE

The auditory system of the human being is fully as wondrous as the visual system. One example of the spectacular capability with which the auditory system furnishes us is the great dynamic range of sounds across which we are able to hear. At one extreme, we can discern the rustle of tree leaves, the sighing of the wind, and the chirp of a cricket. Alternatively, we can withstand the very intense sounds that come from an amplified rock band or from jet engines as an airplane powered by them takes off. For the former examples, the sound waves that emanate from these sources have very weak intensities. For the latter sources, their sound waves have enormous intensities.

10.5.1.1 Defining the intensity level of a sound The intensity of a sound wave is defined as the power of a source divided by the surface area of the resulting spherical wave, as the wave moves outward from the source. Accordingly, the intensity of the sound wave is characterized in units of watts/square meter (or, W/m²). The human ear can detect sounds whose intensities are as small as 10^{-12} W/m². This intensity is identified as the *threshold of audibility*. In contrast, the average ear can *briefly* tolerate sounds that have intensities as great as 10^0 W/m². The dynamic range of hearing therefore occurs across 12 orders of magnitude: the most intense sounds we can stand (at what is described as the *threshold of pain*) are 10^{12} times as intense as the smallest intensities we can discern. Alternatively stated, these most intense sounds are one trillion times as powerful (or

. . . . .

SIDEBAR 10.9 Deriving decibels from Bels

The basic unit for characterizing the relationship between the intensity of some sound to a *reference* sound—the intensity of sound at the threshold of audibility—is the Bel, a term chosen to honor Alexander Graham Bell (who is widely credited with inventing the telephone). The use of the Bel proceeds from the relationship

$$IL = \log_{10}(I_{\text{some sound}} / I_{\text{threshold of audibility}})$$

where the intensity level is described in terms of Bels. Thus, sound from a normal conversation might have an intensity level of between 5 and 5.5 Bels, and the intensity level of a whispered conversation might be about 2 Bels. The difficulty that initially arose with this unit system was that the human auditory system was (and is) substantially more sensitive than the power factors suggested by a 1 Bel increase or decrease (i.e., the auditory system can discern changes in intensity level as small as 0.05 Bels (or 0.5 decibels; see Section 11.1.4 for further information about our abilities to differentiate between various sounds). Consequently, tenths of a Bel were commonly reported, and the Bel-based system became awkward. To ease this difficulty, a unit system based on the decibel was subsequently adopted and is now the standard unit.

This minimum—or *reference*—value for the sound intensity at the threshold of audibility is stipulated in the ANSI document, *Acoustical Terminology* (S1.1-1994 [R1999]), (New York: American National Standards Institute, Inc., 1994).

the least! So, the ability of the human ear to recognize sound sources across this huge dynamic range is remarkable.

In Chapter 11 we will briefly describe the capabilities of the human auditory system and how it operates over this range. Here, however, we will introduce a *relational* means for describing the intensity of any sound source. This means allows us to represent the intensity of the source without having to rely on the very great numbers cited above (this *relational* device is widely used because of its convenience). The device is based on a *comparison* of the intensity of some sound source versus the intensity of a sound at the *threshold of audibility* (i.e., the lowest intensity at which we can discern sound). The resulting ratio—$I_{\text{some sound}} / I_{\text{threshold of audibility}}$, where the letter I is an algebraic symbol for intensity—is then manipulated by finding the logarithm of this ratio, using the base of 10. Once the logarithm of the ratio is determined, that logarithmic value is multiplied by the factor of 10. The quantity that is produced from these manipulations is known as the *intensity level* of the sound and is expressed with the unit of *decibels* (shown commonly in the abbreviated form *dB*). Expressed as a formula, these manipulations can be written as

$$IL = 10 \times \log_{10}(I_{\text{some sound}} / I_{\text{threshold of audibility}})$$

where IL is the intensity level (in decibels) for the sound and $I_{\text{threshold of audibility}}$ has the value of 10^{-12} W/m². Most often in the professional literature, when the intensity at the threshold of audibility is written algebraically, the symbol used is I_0.

An important distinction between the intensity of a sound and the intensity level of that sound is that the intensity is an *absolute* (or strictly physical) description of the power of the sound and the intensity level is a *comparative* representation of the sound. Indeed, the *intensity level* is a representation that relates the intensity of a sound to the intensity of the *threshold* sound, for human beings (i.e., 10^{-12} W/m²). As the threshold of audibility is founded on what sound a human being can detect, the intensity level is fundamentally a *human-centered* characterization of sound intensity. Note also that the magnitude of the intensity this threshold sound is a *nominal* value.

Examples of the intensity level are shown in Table 10.1. For instance, first, the intensity of voices spoken in normal conversation is usually about 1,000,000 times more intense than a sound at the threshold of audibility, so the intensity level of these voices would be 60 dB; second, a parent speaking softly to a baby may have an intensity that is

TABLE 10.1
COMMONLY OBSERVED SOUND INTENSITY LEVELS FOR EVERYDAY SITUATIONS

EVENT	TIMES MORE POWERFUL THAN AUDIBILITY THRESHOLD	INTENSITY (W/sq.m.)	SOUND INTENSITY LEVEL, in dB
Gunshot (in the near field)	100,000,000,000,000	100	140
Rock concert (in an enclosed theater)	316,000,000,000	0.316	115
Gasoline-powered leaf blower (at 2 m [7 ft])	15,800,000,000	0.0158	102
Gasoline-powered lawn mower (at 5 m [16 ft])	6,310,000,000	0.00631	98
City bus with faulty muffler (from about 5 m [16 ft])	1,000,000,000	0.001	90
Interior of a DC-10 jet plane during take-off	631,000,000	0.000631	88
Interior of a well-built car running at 100 km/hr (62.5 mph)	10,000,000	0.00001	70
University lecturer (without amplification in medium-sized classroom)	3,162,000	0.00000316	65
Car traffic on a suburban commercial street	1,585,000	0.00000158	62
Normal conversation	316,200	0.000000316	55
Noise in a typical office	31,620 to 100,000	0.0000000316 to 0.0000001000	45 to 50
Quiet urban residential neighborhood	10,000	0.00000001	40
Bedroom at night in a typical suburban single-family detached residence	3,160	0.00000000316	35
Bedroom at night in a rural single-family detached residence	316	0.000000000316	25

about 3,160 times greater than the threshold, thus producing sound with an IL of 35 dB; and, third, an electronically amplified rock band may have intensities as large as 100 billion times greater than a threshold sound, and its intensity level would then be 110 dB.

10.5.1.2 Describing sound in terms of sound pressure levels

As an alternative to the intensity level, the expression *sound pressure level* is also widely employed to characterize the magnitude of the power of a sound wave. The sound pressure level (abbreviated as *SPL*) compares the incremental pressure (above ambient atmospheric pressure) for a sound wave versus a threshold pressure, where the magnitude of this threshold pressure is 2×10^{-5} Newton/meter^2.[10] The specific relationship between the sound pressure level and these pressure increments appears in either of the following forms:

$$SPL_{\text{some sound}} = 10 \log_{10} [(P_{\text{some sound}})^2 / (P_{\text{threshold}})^2] \text{ or}$$
$$SPL_{\text{some sound}} = 20 \log_{10} (P_{\text{some sound}} / P_{\text{threshold}})$$

where the SPL is expressed in decibels and $P_{\text{threshold}}$ has the value of 2×10^{-5} N/m^2.[11] Further, please note that preference is most often written in the professional and scientific literature as P_0.

The SPL nomenclature is widely used by engineers and physicists to characterize sound presence. Also, note that a sound presence reported in terms of either its intensity level (IL) or its sound pressure level (SPL) will show a numerical value very similar to the other.

SIDEBAR 10.10 Working with logarithms

Because many designers and builders have not confronted the use of logarithms perhaps since their secondary school or college freshman days, we will offer here some suggestions about working with logarithms. The logarithm is an arithmetic operator, just as an exponent is an operator (e.g., writing a^2 to indicate that the quantity a should be multiplied by itself or, $a \times a$). In fact, finding the logarithm of a number is basically identifying the exponent for some numerical base, which, when the base is raised by that exponent, will equal that number. Stated algebraically, we can say:

$$\log_N x = y \text{ or } N^y = x$$

where N is the numerical base, x is the number, and y can be viewed as either the exponent in the second

equation form or, in fact, the logarithmic value of the number x using the base N. Thus, the logarithm of 2 to the numerical base 10 is 0.3010; the logarithm of 14 to the base 10 is 1.1461; and the logarithm of 0.23 to the base 10 is −0.6383. A second set of formulas for working with logarithms includes:

$$\log_N xy = \log_N x + \log_N y$$
$$\log_N x/y = \log_N x - \log_N y$$

so that, for example, the logarithm to the base 10 of the number 635 can be written as

$$\log_{10} 635 = \log_{10} 6.35 + \log_{10} 100 =$$
$$0.8028 + 2.0000 = 2.8028$$

SIDEBAR 10.10 (continued)

Working with logarithms and converting between the intensities and intensity levels for various sounds can be made easier if one employs virtually any handheld calculator. Most calculators available today (and in the recent past) have keys for logarithmic and other mathematical operations involving exponents: our advice to the reader is that if you anticipate needing to perform calculations about sound intensity levels, then you will benefit from using a calculator that can perform these various operations.

One final series of instructions concerns the problem of establishing what will be the total magnitude of sound presence when more than one source exists in a space. In such instances the basic operational guideline is that you should combine the intensities of the two or more sources: do not add their intensity levels! For example, if we have two trumpets in a room and each emits sound with an intensity level of 63 dB, to determine what the combined intensity level is we must (a) find the intensity for each of the two sources, (b) add these intensity values, and then (c) convert the intensity sum back to an intensity level by comparing the sum to the reference intensity (i.e., 10^{-12} Watt/meter^2):

    (a) If $IL_{trumpet} = 63$ dB, then $I_{trumpet} = 1.9952 \times 10^{-6}$ W/m^2;

    (b) so 2 trumpets will have a combined intensity of 3.9905×10^{-6} W/m^2;

    (c) and the $IL_{(2\ trumpets)} = 66$ dB.

When seeking to determine the total intensity level when multiple sources are present in a space, an alternative to converting and manipulating intensity and intensity level values is to use a graph such as the one shown in Figure 10.19. This graph will enable you to establish an overall intensity level for several sources (e.g., for three sources, first, find the subtotal IL for two sources; then, find the overall total by relating the subtotal IL and the third source IL). In this manner you can "add" up a few or many sources to find a total IL.

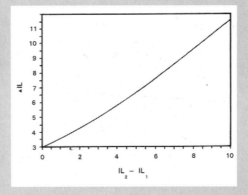

Figure 10.19 This graph may be used to "add" decibel values. The basic instructions for using this graph (for addition) are:

1. Determine the difference between the intensity levels of the two sounds (i.e., for IL_1 and IL_2).
2. Noting the quantity $(IL_2 - IL_1)$ along the x-axis and using the curve, find the ΔIL on the y-axis.
3. Add ΔIL to IL_1 to find IL_{total}.

To perform decibel "subtraction" using this graph, follow this procedure:

1. Establish $(IL_{total} - IL_1)$, which equals ΔIL.
2. Noting ΔIL along the y-axis and using the curve, find $(IL_2 - IL_1)$ on the x-axis.
3. Add the quantity $(IL_2 - IL_1)$ to IL_1 to find IL_2.

Note that this graph and these procedures may also be used for adding and subtracting sound pressure levels (SPL's). Simply substitute the term SPL wherever IL appears for the axis labels of the graph and in these procedures.

10.5.2 WHOLE AND ONE-THIRD OCTAVE BANDS

People with good hearing can hear sounds across a spectral range that encompasses frequencies from 20 to about 20,000 Hz (see Section 11.1.1 for further information about human hearing capabilities). Many common sounds that occur in our everyday work and living environments have energy spread out throughout this spectral range. For instance, if you pluck a guitar string, you can hear the presence of a fundamental tone and a series of overtones. The amount of energy that emanates from the guitar, when the string is plucked, can then be determined from the sound pressure levels (or intensity levels) produced for each of these tones.

To describe the spectral composition and range—the frequencies present—in a sound or a group of sounds, the term *octave* is employed. An octave is the interval—between any two sounds where the ratio of the frequency of one sound to the frequency of the other is either two or one-half.[12] For instance, there is a single octave between sounds with frequencies of 250 and 500 Hz; and there are four octaves between frequencies of 250 and 4000 Hz.

Two sets of frequencies have specifically been standardized for use in various acoustical measurements and writings.[13] In the first set, the frequencies are separated by whole-octave intervals: for instance, those frequencies present across the audible spectral range for a person with good hearing are 31.5, 63, 125, 250, 500, 1000, 2000, 4000, 8000, and 16,000 Hz. Necessarily, this whole-octave frequency set can be extended further downward and upward beyond this audible range (e.g., below 63 Hz to 31.5, 16, and so forth; and above 16,000 Hz to 32,000 Hz, and so forth). A second set of standardized frequencies include values where the frequencies are separated by one-third octave intervals: again, for the range listed above (with the whole-octave numbers shown in boldtype), 20, **31.5**, 40, 50, **63**, 80, 100, **125**, 160, 200, **250**, 315, 400, **500**, 630, 800, **1000**, 1250, 1600, **2000**, 2500, 3150, **4000**, 5000, 6300, **8000**, 10,000, 12,500, **16,000**, and 20,000 Hz. Similar to the whole-octave set, the one-third octave set also extends downwards and upwards outside of this audible range.

Lastly, the word *band* is used to encompass a range of all the frequencies from some one frequency to some other frequency (e.g., a frequency band from 224 to 280 Hz would include all the frequencies in this interval and would have a *one-third octave* band center frequency of 250 Hz). Alternatively, an *octave band center* at 250 Hz would encompass all the frequencies between 177 and 354 Hz.

Section 10.6 | SOME BASIC METHODS FOR MEASURING SOUND PRESENCES

10.6.1 SOME QUALIFICATIONS ABOUT SOUND MEASUREMENT STRATEGIES

There are several reasons why you might wish to measure the sound (or noise) around you. For example, any of the following situations will require sound (or noise) measurements (i.e., to establish what design and construction solutions are warranted). First, you may want to fine-tune the operation of a musical performance space, making the sound produced there seem fuller and richer. Or you could need to optimize the performance of a home or business high-fidelity music system (i.e., so that your favorite music is more appealing). Second, a parcel of land on which you wish to develop a series of houses lies along a busy thoroughfare. Being prudent, you elect to determine when noise levels from vehicular traffic are at their worst and what amount of noise along this highway will carry onto your site. For this situation a principal concern will be to exclude the traffic noise from entering the buildings you intend to build. Alternatively, you might be asked to renovate an existing office building. Present occupants have complained that the ventilation system seems excessively noisy. So, you would like to establish the character of the noise, and then create some means for repairing, improving the operation of, or simply replacing whatever is producing the noise. Third, while serving as a manager of a manufacturing factory, you may be concerned that the hearing capacities of some of your workers are being damaged by the presence of noisy machines. You wish to identify which machines are especially noisy, what are the noise properties of these machines, and whether various solutions you propose and implement will indeed improve the acoustical environment of this workplace.

All of these examples represent situations in which sound (or noise) must be measured, either on a one-time basis or over an extended period of time. Some of these conditions involve finding out about the properties of a sound (or noise) *field*. Others concern the characterization of a sound (or noise) *source*. Both the fine-tuning of the performance space and the optimization of the high-fidelity system will include measurements about *reverberant fields* (i.e., to find answers for questions such as how long are the reverberation times of the rooms, what effect will the placement of additional absorption materials have on the times, and so forth). Alternatively, the traffic noise may occur in an essentially *open field*. Measurements of this traffic noise might include determining whether buildings located at some distance from the thoroughfare will experience less noise. Or the developer might propose construction of a noise barrier between the highway and the building property and may wish to test this proposal by erecting a temporary barrier and examining if subsequent noise levels reaching the property are indeed reduced. The noise produced by the ventilation system and the factory machines are sounds that are produced at specific sources. To treat and reduce these noises, it will be necessary to ascertain how the noises are produced and to measure what the characteristics of the noises are (e.g., thereby to explore whether some part within the source is specifically at fault and, by modifying or replacing the part, the source will be less noisy). For instance, the noise produced by the ventilation may result from vibrations of the vanes of the ceiling diffusers, which flutter as the fan-forced ventilation air rushes past these vanes. A solution may be to replace the diffuser with one that has more rigid vanes (i.e., vanes that can be less readily driven to vibrate).

Generally, measurements of sound fields will involve testing of the sound levels—either pressure or intensity levels—present in these fields. These measurements may involve determining the total energy, thus assessing the energy across the whole frequency spectrum to which an instrument is sensitive. Or the tests may analyze sound levels at specific octave or one-third octave band centers, thereby revealing whether energy distribution is concentrated at specific frequencies or is spread generally over some spectral range. Alternatively, testing of various sound (or noise, where noise is simply *unwanted* sound) sources usually is undertaken to elicit information about the intensity (and power) that a source displays. The intensity (and power) measurements for a source can be conducted within the near field of the source (although these measurements may also be taken in other field conditions).

Another characteristic of a sound field or source that must be accounted for when measurements are conducted is whether the production of sound is *steady* or *variable*. If the sound occurs continuously with a uniform intensity, measurement can usually be more easily obtained. However, the sound may vary, either in terms of time or intensity. The production of such variable sounds may happen intermittently or impulsively, with or without regularity. The sound may also display a rising and falling intensity, a pattern that repeats with some periodicity or does not. Further, the variation of the sound with time and intensity can essentially be random and have no discernible or identifiable character. Determining whether production of a sound is steady or unsteady and, if the sound varies, whether some pattern of variation exists, are basic questions for any measurement procedure.

Lastly, there are usually a series of pragmatic issues that will inevitably influence how measurements can or should be undertaken. The basic question for any measurement program will be, What information do you wish to gain from the testing? Developing an answer for this question will, first, require considering the project with which you are involved (e.g., what are the natures of the sound or noise sources; what kinds of sound fields are likely to be present; what is the physical environment like; what expectations will future occupants have for the built spaces which you are engaged in creating; and so forth). Second, you will have to assess what level of accuracy is needed from the measurement series. And, third, you must establish how much time and money can be devoted to these measurements and the subsequent analysis of their results.

Generally, for the various sensing devices that are used for measuring the presences of heat, light, or sound (and noise) in the natural or built environment, sound-measuring equipment will be the most costly. Thus, selecting what measurement strategy you wish to employ will be strongly determined by your ability to purchase or rent suitable equipment. A second pragmatic worry concerns where the sound (or noise) source is located, whether the source is a single object or many objects (e.g., a noisy factory or many vehicles traveling along a highway), and for what period you need to conduct measurements (e.g., for a few hours, days, or for selected periods over a longer time frame). Some sound-measuring equipment is portable and can be used in the field, whereas other testing devices are really suitable only for laboratory-based applications. Additionally, some physical conditions encountered during field-testing can adversely influence results of sound-measuring activities (e.g., wind and rain).

SIDEBAR 10.11 Measuring the power of a sound or noise source

In Section 10.4 we defined the intensity of a source as the sound power of the source divided by the surface area of the sound wave sphere that radiates outward from the source. So, to determine the power of a source, it is necessary only to find an averaged intensity for the source *over some implied spherical surface* (outward from the source) and multiply the averaged intensity by the surface area of this implied sphere. Alternatively, if the source does not radiate outward in a strictly spherical pattern, then it will be more appropriate to establish a more representative shape for the radiative pattern and to find the surface area for that pattern. See Rasmussen, G., "Intensity—Its measurement and uses," *Sound and Vibration*, 23(3), March 1989, pages 12–21; and Baade, P.K., "Standards and test codes for measuring the noise emission of stationary sources," *Noise Control Engineering*, 29(1), July–August 1987, pages 18–25.

In many instances where a designer or builder may need information about the presence of sound (or noise) in an environment, the best approach to achieving good information at a still-reasonable cost will be to hire a qualified acoustical consultant who can perform the appropriate measurements and offer informed judgments about the collected data.

10.6.2 COMMON SOUND (AND NOISE) MEASUREMENT DEVICES

Presently, there are perhaps four primary types of *airborne* sound-measuring devices (used for studies of common natural and built environments): the sound level meter, the octave (or one-third octave) band analyzer, the real-time analyzer, and the sound intensity analyzer. In addition to these primary types, there are a number of other instruments that are used for more specialized applications.

The **sound level meter** (Figure 10.20) measures the pressure of sound waves existing in a sound field—open or closed—and provides a reading of the sound pressure level in the field (in decibels).[14] The principal elements of the generic sound level meter are a microphone, an amplifier, a frequency-weighting system, a time-controlling device, and an output indicator. The microphone senses the pressure increment created by the sound field and establishes an electrical current whose magnitude is increased by the amplifier. The sound detected by the microphone usually consists of a number of frequency components, spread over a potentially wide spectral range (i.e., thus, the sound is described as *broadband*). At each of these frequencies, the broadband sound displays different pressure amounts. So, a weighting mechanism modifies the pressure amounts for the various frequency components and performs a summing process that provides a single-valued response (in decibels). This response then passes to the output device, where the measured sound pressure level is shown with an analog or digital view meter. The other principal element of the sound level meter is a time-controller. This controller determines the time length during which the meter will gather energy from incident sound waves before the meter displays an output. A *fast* setting provides a much shorter-duration response: the time length is usually about 125 milliseconds. For a *slow* setting, the time length over which the energy is sensed and averaged is, typically, 1000 milliseconds.

The weighting process involves the use of an electronic filter to selectively pass sound energies for the various frequencies that the sound meter can sense. These energies, after filtering, proceed to an accumulator (or summing device). The selective filtration of broadband sounds enables the sound meter to condition its response (i.e., to weight the importance of specific frequencies). Most sound level meters will have at least two (and as many as five) such weighting filters (or schemes). The most commonly employed weighting schemes are the A and C filters (Figure 10.21), with the other filters designated as B, D, and E.[15] The A-filter excludes much of low-frequency sound energy and admits, with little qualification, middle and upper-frequency sound energy: this pattern closely resembles how our auditory system works (i.e., we generally hear low-frequency sounds less well than we hear middle and upper-frequency sounds). Thus, *there is an excellent correlation between sound levels found with A-filtered sound meters and our subjective responses to the sounds*. Alternatively, the C-filter provides a relatively unmodified passage of energies from across the entire audible frequency range (i.e., the C-filter screens out little of the sound energy). As such, the C-filter most accurately portrays the total physical sound energy that is present in a sound field. Lastly, note that when any weighting filter is used for measuring the sound level in a field, the measured value will be presented in any literature based on the measurement as dB(x), where x indicates the

Figure 10.20 A very inexpensive and simple sound level meter is shown in this photograph. This meter provides A- and C-scale weightings, slow and fast response rates, and a sensitivity range from 50 to 126 dB (A or C). The meter is a Realistic Model No. 33-2050 (which is manufactured for Radio Shack).

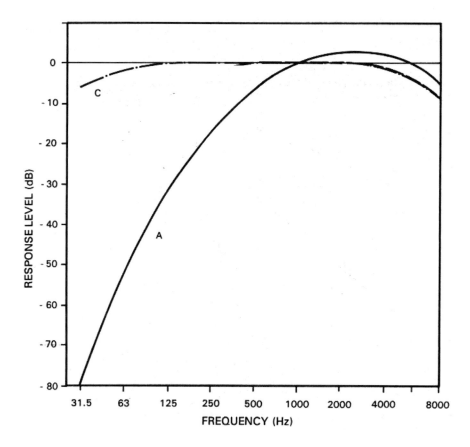

Figure 10.21   These curves describe, respectively, the weighting values for the A- and C-weighting scales found on many sound level meters. Each curve indicates, for the range of frequencies shown, how sound levels at these frequencies are weighted—having numerical coefficients attached—prior to the summation of the sound energy. For instance, the A-weighting scale greatly de-emphasizes low-frequency sounds. So, for a sound having energy evenly distributed across a wide band of the spectrum (including low frequencies), an A-weighted reading will show the sound with a lower pressure level than would be revealed with an unweighted measurement. The wide use of the A-weighting scale follows from the fact that this scale closely approximates how the human auditory system functions (i.e., our hearing is less sensitive to lower frequency sounds and best able to discern middle-spectral-range sounds). Reprinted from ANSI S1.42-2001, American National Standard *Design Response of Weighting Networks for Acoustical Measurements,* © 2001, with the permission of the Acoustical Society of America, 35 Pinelawn Road, Suite 114E, Melville, NY 11747, USA. Copies of the Standard may be purchased from the Standards Store at http://asa.aip.org.

specific filter that has been applied. So, if a sound meter with A- and C-filters is used to measure a sound field with each of these filters, the values would be reported in terms of dB(A) and dB(C), respectively.

An **octave (or one-third octave) band analyzer** is essentially a sound level meter that has a filter set allowing measurement of sound levels at specific octave (or one-third octave) frequency centers (Figure 10.22). The filters in these frequency analyzers enable the meters to be set to specific frequencies (identified in Section 10.5.2), which comprise the several octave (or one-third octave) centers across the audible sound spectrum. Thus, instead of measuring the *summed* energy in a sound field—produced by a *broadband* source—using a weighting filter (e.g., the A-weighting scale), you can determine individual sound levels at each of the various frequencies. Some applications where sound levels at these frequencies may need to be found include examining the characteristics of environmental noise, determining the performance of absorption materials in a built space, or measuring the degree of noise isolation provided by a building envelope. In each instance, sound pressure levels can be plotted against octave (or one-third octave) center frequencies to establish the nature of some type of sound (or noise) field.

Decisions about using a frequency analyzer to study a sound (or noise) should be made following some thoughtful anticipation of the nature of the source and its resultant field. Necessarily, the act of measuring sound levels at several frequencies will require a period of time (e.g., a few minutes or longer). If the source emits sound for only a short duration, then there may not be adequate time to conduct all of the various measurements needed to describe the characteristics of a sound field. In such instances, an alternative approach to measuring a short-lived sound directly can involve the use of a tape recorder. After recording the sound (or noise), it can be played back iteratively to permit careful measurements of sound levels for the several test frequencies.

A **real-time analyzer** is ultimately a yet more sophisticated sound meter than the octave (or one-third octave) band analyzer (Figure 10.23). Using a real-time analyzer enables an observer to measure *simultaneously* sound levels at each of the octave (or one-third octave) band centers across the sound spectrum. Thus, within a sound field a person may sample the spectral characteristics of the field continuously, noting how sound levels may vary with frequency and time. The sound levels measured at frequencies from 31.5 Hz (or lower) to 20,000 Hz either are shown on a digital display screen on the front of the analyzer or can be written out with an attached printer. Generally, real-time analyzers also have the capability to store and "replay" measured results so that these results can be compared against each other. Most frequency band analyzers and real-time analyzers also will have one or more weighting scales and a range of response rates—for instance, slow and fast—present as alternative measurement settings.

The fourth of these measurement strategies involves determining the sound intensity of a sound (or noise) source. Whereas the establishment of the sound level in a field is based on measuring the sound pressure, finding the intensity of a source requires sensing both the amount of sound energy flowing from the source and the direction of energy flow from the source to the sensor. The sound intensity measurement is performed using a probe with two microphones that face each other and that are held apart by a rigid divider. The probe is attached to a display device (e.g., a frequency band analyzer or a real-time analyzer, for which the probe replaces the pressure-sensing microphone of the analyzer). Then, the probe is moved systematically around a sound (or noise) source to establish the intensity of the source. A primary benefit of sound intensity measurements is that they enable an observer to investigate the performance of one or more sources, rather than simply examining the field in which the sources are present. Thus, it is possible to study how a source behaves when the sound from the source exists as part of a sound field (i.e., the sound field forms a background which the source sound lies within). This measurement technique also enables the analysis of individual sources when they are mixed and when separation of their components is needed to elicit their characteristics. Lastly, the use of sound intensity measurements is particularly useful for identifying, testing, and treating noise sources (i.e., those devices which interfere with occupant performance in and/or enjoyment of the built environment and which, consequently, need modification or removal).

Figure 10.22 A professional/scientific-grade frequency band analyzer appears here. This analyzer has a series of amplitude ranges, performs A- and C-scale weightings, and enables octave-band and one-third octave band measurements. Output signals from measurements of sound can be sent to a personal computer and then on to a printer to establish "hard-copy" records. Additionally, a variety of measurements taken for periods of time—integrating pressure readings over time—can be made; these time-integrated measurement schemes are described in Section 12.2.4. The manufacturer of this frequency band analyzer is Larson-Davis Laboratories, Pleasant Grove, Utah; the model number of the analyzer is 800B.

Figure 10.23 This real-time spectrum analyzer provides sound level values at third-octave band centers at three rates (slow, medium, and fast). The analyzer performs A- and C-scale weightings. And the analyzer has memory locations for storing up to six different SPL versus third-octave band center curves; these memories enable comparison of alternative measurements. The measured values can also be written out using a portable printer. The manufacturer of this analyzer is Audio Control Industrial, Mountlake Terrace, Washington; its model number is SA-3050A. Its cost is comparatively modest in contrast to the often very expensive professional or scientific-grade real-time analyzers.

ENDNOTES and SELECTED ADDITIONAL COMMENTS

1. *Webster's Seventh New Collegiate Dictionary,* (Springfield, Massachusetts: G. & C. Merriam Company, 1967), page 834.

2. The speed of sound in air is 344 meters/second, whereas the speed of sound in water is 1478 m/sec, a ratio of 1:4.30. But the ratio of the mechanical impedances of air versus water is 1:4165, thus indicating the substantially greater force that must be applied to move sound waves through water.

3. The frequency ranges and power (expressed in terms of sound pressure levels) present in speech for men and women are identified in Section 11.2. A further discussion of speech sounds and their characteristics is provided in the chapter, "Speech perception," in Gelfand, S.A., *Hearing: An Introduction to Psychological and Physiological Acoustics,* (New York: Marcel Dekker, Inc., 1981), pages 323–354.

4. Kurze, U., and L.L. Beranek, "Sound propagation outdoors," in Beranek, L.L., (editor), *Noise and Vibration Control,* (New York: McGraw-Hill Book Company, 1971), pages 184–193.

5. Durrant, J.D., and J.H. Lovrinic, *Bases of Hearing Science* (2nd edition), (Baltimore, Maryland: Williams & Wilkins, 1984), page 45. Also, in that book the authors provide additional information about the various sound fields that are described in this section.

6. Beranek, L.L., "The measurement of power levels and directivity patterns of noise sources," in Beranek, L.L., (editor), *Noise and Vibration Control,* (New York: McGraw-Hill Book Company, 1971), pages 138–163 (see pages 139–142, especially); and Lord, H.W., W.S. Gatley, and H.A. Evensen, *Noise Control for Engineers,* (Malabar, Florida: Robert E. Krieger Publishing Co., Inc., 1987), pages 71–74.

7. Algebraically, $I = p^2/(d \times c)$, where I is the intensity (in Watts/square meter), p is the *incremental* pressure (in newtons/square meter), d is the density (in kilograms/cubic meter), and c is the speed of sound (in meters/second). For further discussion of this relationship and a derivation of it, see Sears, F.W., M.W. Zemansky, and H.D. Young, *University Physics* (6th edition), (Reading, Massachusetts: Addison-Wesley Publishing Company, 1984), pages 434–437. For more information about the frequency and intensity of sound waves, see Franken, P.A., "The Behavior of Sound Waves," in Beranek, L.L., *Noise and Vibration Control,* (New York: McGraw-Hill Book Company, 1971), pages 2–17 (Chapter 1).

8. The overtone will not exist because the string will be in motion at what would have been one of the nodes for that overtone. For a specific overtone to exist, the string must be at rest at each of the locations along the string where a node would occur. Thus, if the string is plucked at its middle, only the fundamental tone, second overtone, fourth overtone, and so forth can be present. See Rigden, J.S., *Physics and The Sound of Music* (2nd edition), (New York: John Wiley & Sons, Inc., 1985), pages 117–147.

9. Another way in which the fundamental frequency and the various overtones are identified is that the fundamental frequency is called the *first harmonic,* the first overtone is the *second harmonic,* the second overtone is the *third harmonic,* and so forth. Thus, this combination of the fundamental tone and a series of overtones is called a *harmonic series.*

10. Just as with the reference *intensity* value (I_0), this reference pressure value (p_0) is defined in the ANSI document, *Preferred Reference Quantities for Acoustical Levels* (S1.8-1969), (New York: American National Standards Institute, Inc., 1969), page 8.

11. The foundation for this comparison is the relationship stating that the intensity *(I)* of a sound wave is equal to the pressure increment raised to the second power divided by the product of the density of the medium *(d)* multiplied by the velocity *(c)* of the sound wave in that medium. The algebraic form of this relationship is shown in Endnote 7 above.

12. This explanation is derived from the ANSI document, *Acoustical Terminology* (ANSI S1.1-1994 [R1999]), (New York: American National Standards Institute, 1999). An alternative definition for *octave* is also presented in this ANSI Standard and concerns its usage for differentiating the *pitch* interval between two tones: there, an octave exists when one tone has a pitch that is twice (or one-half) the pitch of the other. We will further discuss *pitch* in Section 11.1.

13. This standard is described in the ANSI document, *Preferred Frequencies, Frequency Levels, and Band Numbers for Acoustical Measurements* (ANSI S1.6-1984 [R1997]), (New York: American National Standards Institute, 1997).

14. ———, *Specification for Sound Level Meters* (ANSI S1.4-1983 [R2001]), (New York: American National Standards Institute, 2001).

15. ———, *Design Response of Weighting Networks for Acoustical Measurements* (ANSI1.42-1986 [R1998]), (New York: American National Standards Institute, 1998).

Hearing and Speech

11

IN THIS CHAPTER we will describe selected properties of human hearing and speech. To fully understand how human hearing functions, three fundamental questions need to be addressed: what is acoustic information; how do perceptions arise from our acquisition of the information; and how do these perceptions lead to our understanding of the information?

First, acoustic information is that which we gain from the sounds around us. These sounds may come from natural sources (e.g., raindrops hitting the roof overhead or the sighing of the wind), human or animal sources (e.g., a child speaking to you or a cat "meowing" for its supper), or, even, artificial sources — something created by people — like the squeal of a car's brakes. The basic quality of all of these sources and their sounds is that they enable us to learn about and understand what is happening around us. Thus, each source provides us with *useful data* about the world and the things within it.

Second, the development of perceptions from this acoustic information requires an ability to analyze the newly acquired sound (i.e., to process it and find what is useful in it). This analysis generally includes breaking the new sound into its elements and relating the sound (and its elements) to sounds that have accumulated in our memories. The remembered sounds inform this analysis. Thus, we compare new data with old experiences. During the formation of perceptions we effectively create hypotheses about what these data represent. Then we test these hypotheses to make sure we do indeed understand these new sounds and the messages they carry. Through this process of hypothesizing and testing (all of it internalized within our brains), we become aware of what the sound sources are, and we perhaps even add the new information to our memory.

Thirdly, reacting to newly gained information provides a further opportunity to test any such hypothesis. Such reaction can validate the perception or show its limits (and weaknesses). By matching the reaction (and the results that the reaction produces) with the acquired sound, an individual can then fine-tune whatever understanding has been gained from hearing the sound.

Thus, sound provides a basic means to gather information both from the environment and from the occupants of the environment. Sound also provides an individual with a principal capacity to communicate with other human beings. Fundamental to our capability to communicate with sound are speech and language, the former as a mechanism for creating sounds and the latter as a means for organizing and rationalizing the sounds. Speech and the other sounds that we hear enhance our life experience and enable us to participate in the activities around us.

In Chapter 10 we have defined sound *physically* and have identified its major physical properties. In this chapter, we will indicate how sound is collected by our auditory system and is processed selectively to ascertain what is useful information.

Section 11.1 | PROPERTIES OF THE HUMAN AUDITORY SYSTEM: SENSITIVITY AND PERFORMANCE

At the beginning of Chapter 10 we identified five basic steps in our hearing of sounds: the production of sound by a source; the transmission of the sound from the source to us; the collection of the mechanical energy by our outer ears (and its passage to the inner ear); the transduction of the mechanical energy within the inner ear, where electrical energy "messages" about the properties and composition of external sounds are produced; and the interpretation of these electrical energy messages (and, thus, the external sounds) by our central auditory system. In this section we will present information about the sensitivity of our auditory system. Our intent here is to offer at least an *indirect* view of how the various messages may be interpreted and what the component products of these interpretations are. Basically, our auditory system receives "information" borne by sound waves. This information is decomposed by the auditory system, and the contents of the information are revealed. The processing of a communication involves both the initial perception of the sound waves and then the various cognitive activities employed in thinking about the information existent amongst the sounds.

In Section 10.4 we stated that the four basic properties of sound are its frequency, intensity, waveform, and temporal content. These four properties are, strictly, the *physical* (or *objective*) manifestations of sound. As such, these properties describe the form and substance of sound. These properties can be measured, quantified, and even modeled using numerical relationships.

When the human auditory system is stimulated by sounds created external to our bodies, the information that the system receives is defined in terms of the four basic physical properties of sound. But, in the process of sensing and interpreting the physical properties of a sound, the information distilled by the auditory system becomes *subjective* and is personalized. The personalization of the physical properties of a sound is dependent on how sensation, perception, and cognition occur. We will not write directly about the perceptual and cognitive routines that render these physical properties into subjective assessments. But in this section we will introduce products of these assessments, describing how the properties of a sound appear after they have been sensed and interpreted by our auditory system.

11.1.1 THRESHOLDS OF HEARING

The human auditory system is capable of sensing sounds that occur across a very large range of frequencies and intensities. For those with the most acute hearing, the audible frequency range extends from about 20 to 20,000 Hz. To put this range into perspective, the lowest note on a piano sounds at 27 Hz and the highest at about 4100 Hz. The highest note that can be readily produced with a common musical instrument is one of about 4500 Hz, which can be created with a piccolo. The frequencies present in human speech extend from as low as 50 Hz to as high as 8000 Hz, although the range for conversational speech is about 200 to 3500 Hz.

The ability of a person with good hearing to sense a sound is also dependent on the intensity of that sound. There is indeed a minimum intensity for any sound frequency, below which the sound cannot be discerned. This minimum is identified as the *threshold of hearing* (or, alternatively, as the *threshold of audibility*). A typical definition for this threshold is shown in Figure 11.1 (i.e., the lower curve on this graph describes the threshold of hearing). This figure indicates that sounds with comparatively low or high frequencies — particularly, up to about 500 Hz and also above about 8000 Hz — require substantially greater pressure levels to be readily detected. Sounds with frequencies in the mid-range, from approximately 500 to 8000 Hz, are more easily heard. The frequency at which human hearing is commonly most acute is 3500 Hz, although hearing is nearly as good from about 1000 to 6000 Hz.

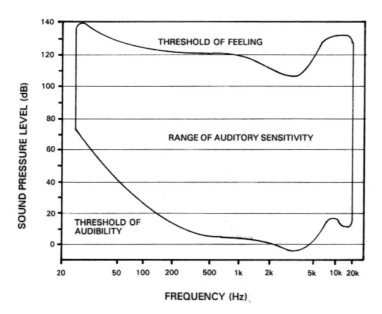

Figure 11.1 For the human being, the pressure level range of auditory sensation occurs between the *threshold of audibility* and the *threshold of feeling,* respectively. The high-frequency limit depends on a number of factors, including the age of the person (see Figure 11.2.)

In addition to the frequency and intensity of a sound, the threshold of audibility is also determined by the duration of the sound. The intensity that a sound must have to be discernible is dependent upon the length of time that a continuous source lasts or the repetition rate that an intermittent source manifests. To be detected, short-duration sounds must be more intense than longer sounds. But as the duration of a sound source increases, the threshold of audibility will decrease (i.e., the minimum pressure level required at a specific frequency for sound to be detected will lessen). For sounds that last longer than about 0.2 seconds, the threshold will *not* be affected by duration. One further qualification concerning the effect of time on hearing thresholds is that *for short-duration sounds* (those lasting less than about 0.2 seconds), *the threshold level increases as the frequency of a sound decreases.* Or, stated alternatively, short-duration sounds with low frequencies will require greater intensities to be heard than will similarly short sounds exhibiting higher frequencies.[1]

Research about the hearing capabilities of the general population indicates that these capabilities are greatly age-dependent and subject to deterioration from environmental noise. Recent studies show that our hearing at birth is less acute but gradually improves until we are between six and ten years old.[2] Then, our hearing capability begins a slow decline that continues until our death.[3] How this change in acuity is manifested is that from birth until the ages of six to ten years the *threshold* slowly *descends* (across the frequency range) to a lowest level. Then, after the age of ten years is passed, this threshold gradually rises with advancing age (see Figure 11.2). A second effect of this age-determined hearing degradation is that the upper frequency limit at which sounds can be detected decreases. For instance, a typical 40-year-old person has a upper limit of 13,000 Hz; a 60-year-old person, 9000 Hz; and an 80-year-old person, 5000 Hz.[4]

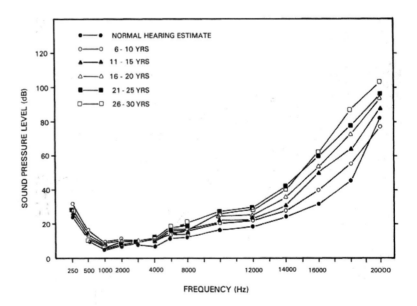

Figure 11.2 Our hearing capability deteriorates with advancing age, particularly for higher-frequency sounds. Evidence of this gradual hearing loss is demonstrated in this graph. This graph has previsouly been published in a paper by Schechter, M.A., S.A. Fausti, B.Z. Rappaport, and R.H. Frey, "Age categorization of high-frequency auditory threshold data," *Journal of the Acoustical Society of America,* 79(3), March 1986, 767–771. Permission to reprint this image has been granted by Dr. Schechter and the Acoustical Society of America.

Noise present in the workplace or experienced as part of the activities of everyday life can also cause significant losses in hearing acuity. To what extent such noise will cause hearing loss depends both upon the intensity of the noise and the length of exposure. Generally, when an individual experiences intense noise, the individual's hearing threshold will increase (i.e., the minimum pressure levels required for the individual to detect sound rise substantially above the standardized *threshold of audibility*). This increase in the minimum threshold (of audibility) is called a "shift of the threshold." Depending upon how intense the noise causing the threshold shift and how long the noise endured, this shift may be *temporary* (lasting a few hours to a few weeks) or *permanent* (such that the individual subjected to the intense noise has experienced a permanent hearing capability loss). As an example of conditions causing a permanent threshold shift, think of a factory worker who operates a noisy machine for several or many years; this individual is likely to sustain significant hearing loss that will increase with the continued operation of the machine (unless the worker begins wearing hearing protection devices). We will further discuss the effects of noise on hearing in Section 12.2.

11.1.2   LOUDNESS AND THE EQUAL-LOUDNESS-LEVEL CURVES

Sound is a physical (or objective) product of a vibrating source. The basic characteristics of a sound are its intensity and frequency, its duration, and the nature of its waveform (simple or complex). All of these characteristics are measurable and can be described in terms of common physical units (or dimensions). Alternatively, a sound sensed by a listener creates a subjective experience for that person. Though the sound remains a physical entity, the perception of that sound (and the impression that the sound invokes for that person) will not be strictly tangible. So, whereas the physical manifestation of a vibrating object is a sound, we identify the product of our sensing this sound as a *tone*. Thus, a tone is the *personalized* account of the sound, which is rendered by our auditory system. Any tone has a number of distinguishing properties, which we will describe throughout the remainder of this section. For instance, if a sound has a strictly sinusoidal waveform, then the perceived tone will be pure (or simple). Instead, if the sound has a complex waveform (i.e., having a mixing of frequencies), the resulting tone will also be complex.

The *intensity* of a sound is perceived by our auditory system in terms of the *loudness* of the corresponding tone. Therefore, loudness is the subjective response to the amount of energy that a sound wave has (as it impinges on our ears). Loudness characterizes how great the auditory sensation appears. A number of physical parameters will affect what we perceive the loudness of a tone to be: the intensity of the sound wave that initiated the sensation; the frequency content (whether the sound is simple or complex and how low or high the component is or the components are); the duration of the sound; and whether there are sounds which exist in the background. But, fundamentally, loudness is a personalized account of the intensity of a sound. How each of us describes the loudness of a tone depends greatly upon the attributes of our individual auditory systems: how well we hear. Other subjective considerations that influence the apparent loudness include: the relationship of the listener to the source (i.e., is the listener involved causing the sound *or* is the sound extraneous to what the listener is doing) and the degree to which the listener can control the source. Such considerations suggest that loudness can be affected by psychological factors (e.g., is a sound intrusive and/or annoying or, alternatively, is the listener a patient and easy-going person?) So, personal factors can influence an individual's perception of loudness. But when the loudness of some sound is considered *normatively* (i.e., by many people), the effects of individual biases can be discounted and the generalized loudness of the sound will seem independent of these factors.

To demonstrate this normative experience, suppose we start with two sounds and compare them to establish which one appears louder. What we will basically discover is that if the frequencies of the two sounds are the same, then the more intense sound will seem louder; and if the intensities of the two sounds are the same, the sound with the lower frequency will often seem less loud than the sound with the higher frequency. In one of the early studies of loudness, Fletcher and Munson sought to find some way to define a loudness relationship between alternative sounds.[5] Because loudness is a *subjective* assessment of sound, there could not be a direct measurement. So, instead, these researchers began with the basic question of what sounds of differing intensities and frequencies seemed *equally loud.* For their experimental methodology they asked test subjects to compare sounds displaying various combinations of intensity and frequency and to pick out those combinations that appeared to have equal loudness. So, for instance, starting with a 1000 Hz sound produced at a sound pressure level of 40 dB, the researchers found that combinations such as a 100 Hz sound at 52 dB and a 4000 Hz sound at 33 dB were identified by the subjects as being equally loud. Fletcher and Munson continued these tests for the frequency range of 20 Hz to 15,000 Hz and for the intensity range from the threshold of audibility up to about 120 dB. The fundamental result of their work — including some modifications and extensions provided by later scientists — is the set of *equal-loudness-level contours* shown in Figure 11.3.[6]

This figure indicates that along any contour, any *combination of frequency and intensity* falling on that contour will appear to have a loudness that matches any other frequency

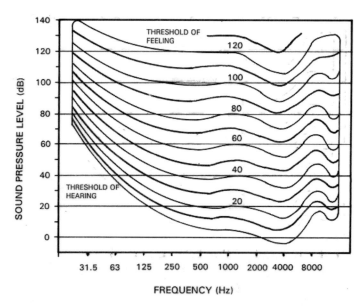

Figure 11.3 This graph presents the equal-loudness-level contours. This graph has previously been published in a book by Doelle, L.L., *Environmental Acoustics,* (New York: McGraw-Hill Book Company, 1972), page 18. Permission to reproduce this image has been granted by The McGraw-Hill Companies, Inc.

and intensity combination that also falls on that contour. Each one of these contours is identified in terms of its *loudness level* (rather than in terms of a sound pressure level). A quantitative means for characterizing these loudness levels is provided by the unit *phon,* with the specific phon value for a contour set to match the sound pressure level of the 1000 Hz sound for the contour. Thus, for the contour including the point having the coordinates of (40 dB, 1000 Hz), this contour is recognized as the 40-phon curve. Similarly, for a curve passing through the (50 dB, 1000 Hz) point, the curve is designated as the 50-phon contour.

These contours distinguish sounds that create *sensations of equal loudness.* But they do not provide a direct comparison of the loudnesses between sounds falling on different contours. To remedy this need, another scale has been developed. This second index uses the unit of *sones* and characterizes the loudness of one tone relative to the loudness of another. A sound with a loudness level of 40 phons (or a sound pressure level of 40 dB at 1000 Hz) is rated as exhibiting a 1-sone loudness. A second sound that appears to be twice as loud as this 40-phon sound will be rated at 2 sones; one set of frequency and intensity level properties that match this rating is a sound with a sound pressure level of 50 dB at 1000 Hz. A sound that seems to be four times as loud as the 1-sone sound will be described as displaying a loudness of 4 sones; one example would be a sound with a sound pressure level of 60 dB (at 1000 Hz). Alternatively, a sound that appears to be one-half as loud as a 1-sone sound will be rated at 0.5 sone; a sample frequency and intensity level combination matching this sone rating would be a sound with a sound pressure level of 30 dB at 1000 Hz. Thus, the distinctions between loudness and loudness level and sones and phons are that the loudness level—expressed in *phons*—essentially follows the sound pressure level for a 1000 Hz sound, and the loudness—in *sones*—increases by a factor of two for every incremental loudness level increase of 10 phons. Or, for every adjustment of 10 phons up or down, the loudness will be doubled or halved, respectively.

So far, our treatment of loudness and loudness level has focused on a sound with a single frequency (namely, 1000 Hz). Now, let's consider the loudness characteristics of broad-banded sounds (i.e., those for which a range of frequencies are present). If we start our observation with relatively narrow-band sound and gradually increase the width of the frequency range (holding the intensity constant), we will initially find that the sound for this broadening range will not appear any louder than the sounds with narrower ranges. But upon reaching a frequency range (or bandwidth) called the *critical band,* the sounds which have frequency ranges greater than this critical band will indeed appear louder than the narrower-banded sounds (even though the intensities of the sounds have not changed). Thus, *the loudness of a sound will increase as the bandwidth of the sound grows larger* (after the bandwidth exceeds the *critical band*). This critical bandwidth varies between 125 and 200 Hz for sounds with frequency band centers up to 2000 Hz. For frequency ranges with band centers above 2000 Hz, the critical bandwidth becomes about 10 percent of the numerical value of the band center.[7]

White noise is a collection of sounds for which the amplitudes vary randomly with time and there are no discernible or dominant frequencies. Essentially, the frequencies present in white noise occur across the audible range with an equal probability of occurrence for any specific frequency value. What white noise appears like then is the sound that an FM radio makes when tuned to a dial location in between recognizable stations.

The loudness of white noise can appear up to two times as great (i.e., achieving a doubling of the loudness [described in sones]) relative to the loudness for the 1000 Hz reference sound, even though both the white noise and the reference sound have the same intensity. The explanation for this difference in our subjective response is that our auditory system is driven by its acquisition of sound energy. The white noise occurring over a broad frequency range will possess a greater energy aggregate than is present with a narrow-band or single-frequency sound. Thus, the more energetic white noise will seem louder to our auditory system. How much louder a broad-band sound may seem in comparison to a narrow-band sound—with each sound having the same intensity—depends on the component frequencies present in both the broad- and narrow-band sounds. Presently, there appears to be no comprehensive relationship to predict likely loudness differences between sounds with various alternative bandwidth differences (or spectral compositions).[8]

Another important issue concerning our perception of loudness arises when the sound occurs in conjunction with background sound (or noise). If a source emits a sound at, say, 70 or 80 dB for some single frequency and there is background sound at 80 or 90 dB (which has a more broadly banded frequency range), then the single-frequency sound may appear indistinct or it may be undetectable, even though a 70 to 80 dB sound would otherwise be perceived as loud. Thus, our ability to hear a sound can depend greatly on the context in which that sound occurs. For this example the more intense sound will partially or wholly *mask* the less intense sound. In this masking the louder background sound effectively imposes a new threshold of hearing, thus shifting the minimum level that a foreground sound must have to be distinguished. For a less loud foreground sound to be perceived, the intensity of this sound must generally surpass this new threshold. The presence of a masking sound thus inhibits (or may instead deny) the ability of the auditory system to distinguish components of other sounds. The masking sound can be a single tone, a narrow-banded sound, or a wide-banded sound. One qualification that determines to what extent a louder, narrow- or broad-banded sound may mask the single-frequency sound is the intensity that the background sound has at the frequency matching that of the single-frequency sound. If the intensity of the background sound is less at that frequency than the single-frequency sound, then the masking will only be partial. The foreground sound then can be detected, but will not appear as distinct as it would if the background sound were not present. If the frequency-specific intensities of the two sounds are similar (or the intensity of the background sound is greater), then the masking will be partially or wholly complete (i.e., and the foreground sound will be nearly or fully undetectable).[9]

SIDEBAR 11.1 Relating sound intensities, intensity levels, loudnesses, and loudness levels

---

An equation for calculating loudness of a 1000 Hz sound when its intensity is known has been suggested by Stevens. This equation is

$$L = kI^{0.3}$$

where L is the loudness in *sones*, I is the intensity expressed in *watts per square centimeter*, and k is 0.06. Stevens has also provided an alternative relation,

$$\log L = 0.03 N - 1.2$$

where L is the loudness in sones and N is the intensity level of the sound in decibels. Both of these equations appear in the paper by Stevens, S.S., "The measurement of loudness," *Journal of the Acoustical Society of America*, 27(5), 1955, 815–827.

For further development of *phon* and *sone* scales and loudness and loudness level, see pages 560–564 of Beranek, L.L., *Noise and Vibration Control*, (New York: McGraw-Hill Book Company, 1971); or pages 39–42 of Lord, H.W., W.S Gatley, and H.A. Evensen, *Noise Control for Engineers*, (Malabar, Florida: Robert E. Krieger Publishing Co., Inc., 1987).

We suggest two guidelines for insuring a sound will have adequate loudness when there is likely to be background noise: *a worthwhile sound present in a noise-ridden environment will need to be more intense if the sound is to appear as loud as it would in a quiet environment;* and *the sound pressure level increment by which the worthwhile sound should exceed the hearing threshold imposed by the environmental noise may need to be as much as 30 dB higher* (i.e., the worthwhile sound would need to be 30 dB greater than the environmental noise for the former sound to be discernible). Two qualifications for these guidelines are that when the loudness of the background noise is quite high already,

---

SIDEBAR 11.2 Further thoughts about the masking of sounds

Another qualification about a background sound masking a foreground sound is that the two sounds do not have to occur simultaneously. Instead, background sounds happening just before or after the foreground sound can also achieve a masking condition. For such conditions, the masking is referred to as either *forward masking* (when the masker precedes the foreground sound) or *backward masking* (when the masker follows the foreground sound).

The concept of the critical band has been introduced to show how the loudness of a sound appears greater if the sound has a sufficiently wide frequency range. The notion of the critical band may also be used to describe masking behavior. Scharf has written that "the critical band is the bandwidth at which subjective responses rather sharply change." The interaction of the critical band with masking behavior arises from the observation that the threshold of a pure tone will not vary unless the frequency bandwidth of the masking sound is less than some critical bandwidth. But when the masking bandwidth is less than the critical bandwidth, the threshold of the pure tone declines, allowing a more ready perception of the pure tone. This behavior appears consistent with the fact that a sound having frequency bandwidths less than the critical bandwidth will appear less loud. Thus, when the frequency bandwidth of a masking sound is greater than the critical band, the masker will appear louder and will effectively raise the threshold for a pure tone present with the masking sound.

In the paragraph above, the quoted statement attributed to Scharf is taken from a chapter by B. Scharf, "Critical bands," which appears in the book edited by J.V. Tobias, *Foundations of Modern Auditory Theory, Volume 1*, (New York: Academic Press, 1970). The quoted statement occurs on page 159. Other information sources about the role of the critical band in masking include Fletcher, H., "Auditory patterns," *Reviews of Modern Physics*, 12, 1940, pages 47–65; Hamilton, P.M., "Noise masked thresholds as a function of tonal duration and masking noise band widths," *Journal of the Acoustical Society of America*, 29(4), April 1957, pages 506–511; and pages 93–94 of the book by Moore, B.C.J., *An Introduction to the Psychology of Hearing* (2nd edition), (London: Academic Press Inc., Ltd., 1982).

Masking of sounds has been widely studied, and a large body of literature exists about the phenomenon. For further information about masking, we suggest such comparatively early papers by Tanner, W.P., Jr., "What is masking," *Journal of the Acoustical Society of America*, 30(10), October 1958, pages 919–921 and Small, A.M., Jr., "Pure-tone masking," *Journal of the Acoustical Society of America*, 31(12), December 1959, pages 1619–1625; a recent paper (as an example of contemporary studies) by Relkin, E.M., and C.W. Turner, "A re-examination of forward masking in the auditory nerve," *Journal of the Acoustical Society of America*, 84(2), August 1988, pages 584–591; and a review paper by Patterson, R.D., and D.M. Green, "Auditory masking," which appears as Chapter 9 of the book edited by Carterette, E.C., and M.P. Friedman, *Handbook of Perception, Volume IV: Hearing*, (New York: Academic Press, 1978), pages 337–361. A more recent review about masking appears in the book by Kryter, K.D., *The Effects of Noise on Man* (2nd edition), (Orlando, Florida: Academic Press, Inc., 1985), pages 39–56.

then the sound pressure level increment may need to be even greater than the 30 dB suggested here; and the frequency content of the background noise can also affect how much more intense a worthwhile sound (of narrow bandwidth) will need to be.

The procedure that is employed to determine the loudness of a sound of unknown intensity requires a test subject to listen to, first, the unknown sound and, second, a reference sound having a frequency of 1000 Hz and an intensity of 40 dB. Then, the subject is asked to tell by what multiple the unknown sound is louder (or softer) than the reference sound. The reference sound is rated as having a loudness of 1 sone. So, by using the multiplier suggested by the subject, the researcher can establish the loudness of the unknown sound in sones. From this loudness (in sones), one can convert to loudness level (in phons) using the relationship that for every doubling or halving of the loudness of the 40 dB, 1000 Hz sound, the loudness level will change 10 phons.[10] An alternative procedure that can be applied to ascertaining the loudness of a sound when its spectral composition is known — perhaps after the sound has been measured with a frequency band analyzer — is suggested by Stevens. This procedure calculates the loudness in the following manner. The intensity for each of a series of specific frequencies is multiplied by a factor (depending on the frequency), and the several products are summed. The resulting sum is the loudness of the sound. To find the loudness level (in phons) a one-line equation can then be employed.

11.1.3 PERCEIVING PITCH

Just as intensity is a basic physical property of a sound wave, so, too, is the frequency. The intensity of a sound, however, is interpreted by our auditory system in terms of loudness and leads us to a *subjective* assessment of the physical stimulus. Similarly, the auditory system responds to the frequency of a sound wave in terms of *pitch,* where pitch is also a subjective assessment of the physical stimulus.

A sound in the physical environment is internalized by our auditory system as a *tone.* When we hear a sound that has a low frequency, we say that the resulting tone will be low-pitched. Or, when the sound frequency is high, then its tone will be high-pitched. We also can speak in terms of *simple* and *complex* tones. The simple tone has a single pitch (resulting from a source that vibrates at a single rate), whereas the complex tone has more than one pitch and is composed of a *fundamental* tone and a series of *overtones.* For example, a sound heard as the fundamental tone may have a frequency of 200 Hz: its several overtones have frequencies of 400 Hz, 600 Hz, 800 Hz, 1000 Hz, and so forth. This fundamental tone and its overtones are also known as *harmonics.* The fundamental tone (here, at 200 Hz) is the first harmonic; the first overtone (at 400 Hz) is the second harmonic; the second overtone (at 600 Hz) is the third harmonic; and so forth.

Because pitch is a subjective attribute of a physical stimulus, pitch cannot be measured. Although we can certainly measure the frequency of some sound, we can only rely on our auditory system to ascertain whether some sound appears to be low or high-pitched. The most common strategy for identifying the pitch of some tone is to compare this tone with the tone from a known reference source, thus establishing whether the unknown tone is higher, equal, or lower-pitched than the reference. In such comparisons the person conducting the test will often employ an electronic frequency generator (which will produce a pure tone for a known frequency). An important qualifier for the performance of this test is that when a complex tone of unknown pitch is compared to a known simple tone, the different tonal qualities of the complex tone may confound the comparison and create spurious results (i.e., the presence of a number of harmonics, in the complex tone, may mislead the auditor).[11]

Although a good general correlation exists between the frequency of a sound and the pitch that is perceived for that sound (i.e., a low frequency sound is heard as a low-pitched tone and a high frequency sound is heard as a high-pitched tone), there are still some peculiarities between what is perceived by the auditory system and the nature of the physical stimulus. For instance, suppose we consider a pure tone resulting from a source producing a 1000 Hz sound. If we double the vibration rate of this source, we will have a 2000 Hz sound. But if we listen to the two tones from these sounds and compare their pitches, we will discover that the pitch of the 2000 Hz sound does not appear to be twice as high as the pitch of the 1000 Hz sound. In fact, to find a sound that seems to have a pitch that is twice as high as the pitch of the 1000 Hz sound, we will need to employ a source that vibrates at about 3000 Hz. Further, to find a sound that appears to have a pitch that is three times as high as the pitch of the 1000 Hz sound, we will then need to employ a source vibrating at approximately 9000 Hz. So, clearly our auditory system does not interpret (and compare) the frequencies of a sound in a strictly linear fashion.

A second peculiarity about pitch concerns how its perception is altered by changes in the intensity of a stimulus. For instance, when the intensity of sound creating a low-pitched *pure* tone is increased, the tone seems to become even lower-pitched. Alternatively, when the intensity of a sound heard initially as a high-pitched *pure* tone is then increased, the tone appears to be become more highly pitched. The transition point (or frequency) at which the direction of this pitch shift changes seems to occur around 3500 Hz (e.g., for sounds with rates of simple vibration below 3500 Hz, increasing the intensity of the sound will result in lowered pitch).[12] But when the intensities of sounds displaying *complex* tones are changed, the perceptions of pitch appear to depend on the spectral character of these sounds. According to research conducted by Terhardt, a tone with discernible harmonics below 1000 Hz—when its intensity is increased—will appear to become lower-pitched. Similarly, when the intensity of a complex tone—which has discernible harmonics above 1000 Hz—is increased, the pitch will seem to be raised. For a complex tone with perceptible harmonics both below and above 1000 Hz, an increase in intensity will produce no apparent change in the pitch of the tone.[13] Lastly, the perception of the pitch of a complex tone seems to depend as much on the composition of the tone (i.e., what the harmonics are) and how the components appear (i.e., what the relative intensities of these harmonics are), as it does on the composite tone itself. Thus, assessing how pitch is modified by other sound factors like intensity can be highly subjective.[14]

In these paragraphs we have essentially described *pitch* from a physical standpoint. Alternatively, we could have written extensively about the role of pitch as it is linked to musical scales. Pitch perception is extremely important to any musician and to those who enjoy listening to music. Numbers of textbooks discuss the interrelationship between music and the physics of sound and the role of pitch and its perception in music.[15]

11.1.4 DISCRIMINATING AMONG CHANGES IN THE FREQUENCY AND INTENSITY OF SOUNDS

Our ability to discriminate between sounds is fundamental to our ability to communicate. One of the primary differences between human beings and the other primates is our superior ability to distinguish between sounds. This capacity enables us to create and employ highly developed spoken languages and thereby to express our thoughts and feelings. We are also able to differentiate between various musical sounds and their relationships, so that we may perceive and enjoy music. The extent to which we can sense differences in spoken and musical sounds is fundamental to our understanding of other people, crea-tures, and the physical environment around us. With this concern in mind, let's consider our capacity to distinguish between sounds.

In the middle of the 19th century the psychophysicist Fechner proposed a theory describing the ability of human beings to discriminate between changing conditions for a physical stimulus. This theory stated that a ratio of the amount of change in a stimulus (which must be accomplished so that there is a *just noticeable difference* in that stimulus) versus the magnitude of the stimulus before it changed is constant.[16] A basic notion of Fech-ner's model is that a relationship between changes in a stimulus and the response by the sensing system is, to a marked extent, linear. Thus, one can infer from this principle that the sensing and perceiving human system and the physical stimulus, which causes the acti-vation of the system, must therefore be linked (i.e., that the development of the system has occurred in a manner to accommodate the stimulus). A key element of the theory concerns the basic ability of the sensing system to discern a small change (i.e., the just noticeable difference) in the stimulus. Being able to detect the just noticeable difference means that the sensing system can recognize the stimulus and at least one of its properties. How the sensing system identifies and interprets the character of the stimulus thus becomes central to understanding the stimulus and how its changes are manifested.

Determining what the magnitude of the just noticeable difference is for any particular stimulus and how well the sensing system operates (so that it can recognize the just notice-able difference) have become fundamental topics of study in psychophysics: establishing the just noticeable difference demonstrates how sensitive the system (or some component in the system) is to a stimulus. Assessing the discriminating capability of a sensing sys-tem (i.e., by examining the just noticeable difference for a stimulus) also can provide insight about what amount and type of environmental support will be necessary to enable the satisfactory performance of tasks associated with the stimulus (e.g., how intense a sound should be to ensure good hearing, and whether increasing the intensity will aid in the performance of a task related to the sound).

The capacity to perform frequency discrimination is one of the significant abilities of the human auditory system. The extent of this capability—meaning how finely a person can separate out the sound of one frequency from another—depends on a series of sound parameters including: where the frequency occurs across the audible spectrum (i.e., whether the frequencies are low or high); to what extent the sound intensity is above the threshold of audibility (this difference between the intensity of a sound and the intensity at the threshold is known as the *sensation level*); what is the duration of the sound; and how much time exists between succeeding sounds. Of these four parameters, the two fac-tors that appear to have the greatest influence in establishing what the just noticeable difference is between adjacent sounds are the location of the sounds in the audible spec-trum and the difference in intensities between some sound and the hearing threshold (i.e., the magnitude of the sensation level). Research on human hearing has shown that the sizes of just noticeable differences in the frequency range differ between lower and higher fre-quencies. For example, for lower frequency sounds, just noticeable differences are as large as 5 percent of the base frequency at very low intensities to about 1 percent at intensities up to about 40 dB; and for mid-range and higher frequencies, just noticeable differences are 1 to 2 percent of the base frequency at low intensities to about 0.2 to 0.4 percent of the base frequency at intensities of 40 to 80 dB.[17]

The primary significances of these results are two-fold. First, the size of the just noticeable difference shown in these results varies across the spectrum with the just notice-able differences being substantially smaller for the higher frequency sounds than for the lower frequency sounds (i.e., we are better able to discriminate between adjacent frequency values when the sounds occur at the middle and upper ends of the audible sound spectrum). Second, and more important, to ensure good discrimination between sounds of adjacent frequencies, there must be suitably large intensities for these sounds (i.e., their tones must appear sufficiently loud).

Similar research about the ability of human beings to discriminate between comparable sound intensities shows somewhat different results. Jesteadt et al.[18] have found that intensity discrimination was not frequency-dependent (i.e., the frequency for adjacent intensities had little effect on test subjects' abilities to discern just noticeable differences in intensity values). Instead, the only parameter that had an influence on the just noticeable differences was the base intensity at which the tests were conducted. At lower intensities the change in the intensity required for discrimination between sounds was larger on an absolute basis. At higher intensities the change in sound intensities needed for a just noticeable difference was less. The specific values of a change in sound intensity reported in terms of decibels were 1.5 dB at low intensities (about 5 dB above threshold), 1.0 dB at middle intensities (about 40 dB above threshold), and 0.5 dB at high intensities (about 80 dB above threshold).[19]

These values for frequency and intensity discrimination suggest that the relationship proposed by Fechner only loosely describes how the human auditory system reacts to physical stimuli. Further, the lack of close agreement between the subjective assessment and the physical stimulus demonstrates that behavioral models based on linear relationships are too simple. Indeed, the auditory system and how it interprets sound exhibit substantial complexity. A further confirmation of the intricacy of this system and its workings is shown by the number of individual sounds that the system is thought to recognize. For instance, the number of just noticeable differences on the frequency scale across the auditory spectrum, which an adult human being can recognize, has been estimated to range from more than 1500 to as many as 11,000.[20] Given the work on frequency discrimination cited above, neither of these two extreme numbers seem accurate, and probably the true number of frequency just noticeable differences is somewhere in between. The research on intensity discrimination—also identified above—suggests that, from the threshold of audibility upward, there are perhaps as many as one hundred or more intensity just noticeable differences (i.e., across the intensity range from the threshold of audibility to the threshold of feeling). Thus, recognizing that frequency and intensity are the two most basic properties that differentiate individual sounds, it seems reasonable to accept the probable accuracy of Stevens and Davis's projection that the human auditory system can distinguish as many as 340,000 specific sounds![21]

11.1.5 SOME ADDITIONAL TONAL QUALITIES OF SOUND

Loudness and pitch are the most significant tonal qualities that a sound can have: these are the essential bases for our assessment of different sounds. But some other qualities provide further definition. Perhaps the most important additional quality is *timbre*. Timbre is the tonal quality that results from the mixing of a fundamental tone with one or more overtones. The composition of the tonal mix—encompassing such physical properties as the number of overtones distinguishable (and which ones they are), the intensities of the fundamental tone and overtones, and how they relate to one another temporally—determine the timbre that a complex tone will have. For instance, one can take a violin and play the same note on two strings (say, producing tones with fundamentals at 440 Hz). With the loudness and pitch of these tones from the alternative strings being equal, the tones will still appear different. This difference is indeed the result of timbre.[22] Thus, timbre is an extremely meaningful tonal quality for musical performance, providing essential definition, character, and color to the sounds. Musical tones with well-developed timbre will seem, to knowledgeable listeners, to be "full," "rich," "well-rounded," and "brilliant," whereas tones devoid of timbre will appear to be "thin," "brittle," and even "opaque."

Of the principal sound properties, intensity has the greatest influence on the development of timbre. When sounds occur with higher intensities, more overtones will be discernible. Thus, the resulting tones will appear fuller and have more developed timbre.

Three other tonal qualities may be noted for the benefits they offer to the definition of individual tones. First, of these is *duration*. As we stated in Section 11.1.1, sounds must exist for an adequate duration if they are to be perceived. The minimum exposure time the auditory system needs to sense and perceive a physical stimulus depends on the acquisition of sufficient sound energy. The principal determinant of how long a sound must endure to be heard is the intensity of the sound: as the intensity increases, then the minimum amount of time can decrease. A secondary influence appears to be that if the frequency of a simple sound (or the fundamental of a complex sound) is high, then perception of the sound may occur in less time.

The last two tonal qualities are ones suggested by Stevens and have been called *volume* and *density*.[23] Volume is a quality that is not strictly related to the intensity of a sound. Instead, the volume that a tone is said to display is determined by its capability to occupy a space. For instance, the low-pitched tones of a bass viol or a bassoon will spread out and fill a room, whereas the high-pitched tones of a piccolo or a clavichord seem directed and precise and maintain a localized and tightly bounded domain. The former tones are full and can be described as possessing substantial volume; alternatively, the latter tones will have little volume. The term *density*, when used, can almost be taken as the converse of *volume*. Density refers to the extent that a tone will be "compact" or "loose" (i.e., to what extent the sound energy is contained as it leaves its source). Commonly, sounds emitted from higher-pitched instruments will seem piercing and compact, and sounds from lower-pitched instruments will appear diffused and loose. Comparing the volume and density of tones, one can say that as the frequency of a sound increases, the volume of the resulting tone will appear to decrease and its density will increase. Alternatively, as the intensity of a sound increases, the volume and density of its tone will both seem to increase. The significance of these last two terms is that they provide more expressive descriptions for the subjective assessment that the human auditory system provides. In many cases, defining a tone in terms of its loudness, pitch, and timbre will be sufficient for conveying its feeling to the listener. But, occasionally, using terms like *volume* and *density* can evoke a greater regard for the sentiment and emotion that a tone (or a series of tones) can embody.[24]

Section 11.2 | SPEECH AS A FUNDAMENTAL FORM OF COMMUNICATION

Communication between people exists so that we may state ideas and concepts and share emotions and feelings; all of these qualities are essential to the performance (and enjoyment) of living and working activities. There are five generic, widely used forms of communication: speech, the printed word, drawings, music, and dance. All five types employ various accepted conventions—practices and techniques—for displaying thoughts and feelings. Speech and the printed word require language. Drawings are enhanced if done with perspective, color, and the contrasting of light and dark areas. Music relies on melodies, harmonies, and rhythms. Dance (and other interpretative or representational movement) utilizes ritualized or structured actions to convey meaning. All five of these communication forms are powerful means of expression, but none is useful for all occasions and circumstances. A blind person cannot see a drawing or a dancer or read pages printed with ink on paper (i.e., like this text). However, a blind person can read when the printed word is displayed in the Braille system. Alternatively, a deaf person cannot hear speech or music, although the individual may read lips or understand a signed language or feel the vibrations produced by various musical instruments. There are many cultural differences among peoples that limit the general application of any one form of communication (e.g., whereas most people can speak, the number of languages—and dialects—used throughout the world is large). Thus, all of these basic forms of communication have conditions that limit their global acceptance.

Of these five, though, speech is the most powerful and ubiquitous, if we exclude the problem of understanding different languages. In most respects—among people with a common language—speech is the easiest and least restrictive communication form to use. The variety of ideas that can be expressed with speech are equal to the printed word and greater than what can be shown with drawings, music, or dance. Speech is the most natural communication form (i.e., speech can be produced without artifice). Alternatively, the printed word, drawings, and music all require the use of instruments or tools. Dance, which sometimes employs natural body rhythms, more often applies highly stylized conventions. Of course, song can also be produced naturally, but for this discussion we will regard song as a more grand form of speech.

In this section, we will explore the properties of speech, including how it is produced and how it can be characterized. Throughout this discussion we will focus on conditions of direct communication (i.e., people talking to people without intermediate aids). But much of the discussion will also apply to situations where aids such as telephones and various audio-visual devices are employed (e.g., amplification, generally, or the use of electronic media like radios or televisions).

11.2.1 SPEECH PRODUCTION

Speech happens as one action of respiration. As we breathe out, we expel respiratory gases from our lungs. These gases pass up the trachea into the larynx and the pharynx and then out of our mouth or nose (see Figure 11.4). Speech can be produced when the expelled gases move across the vocal cords (see Figure 11.5). The vocal cords are controlled by a series of muscles, which when activated will cause the vocal cords to vibrate (i.e., following "instructions" received from our brain). The exiting gases convey the vibratory energy, which takes on the form of sound waves. As these sound waves progress upward and out of our mouth and nose, the vocal tract—consisting of the pharynx and either the mouth or the nose—modifies the sound waves, adding resonance to the exiting sounds. Thus, speech production involves a sound source—the vibrating vocal cords—and a resonance-inducing system (which enhances sounds having specific frequencies).[25]

The principal anatomy of the speech system includes the lungs, trachea, larynx, pharynx, mouth, and nose. The trachea is basically a tube of about 100 to 120 mm (4 inches) in length that connects the lungs and the larynx. The larynx serves two purposes. First, the larynx keeps food—that descends from the back of the mouth cavity through the esophagus into the stomach—from entering into the lungs. Second, speech is initiated at

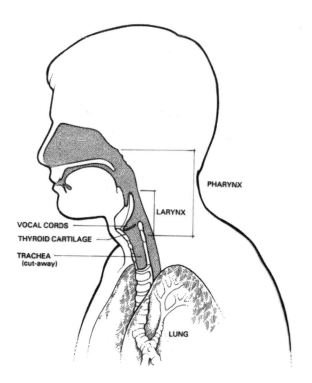

Figure 11.4 The anatomy of the speech tract.

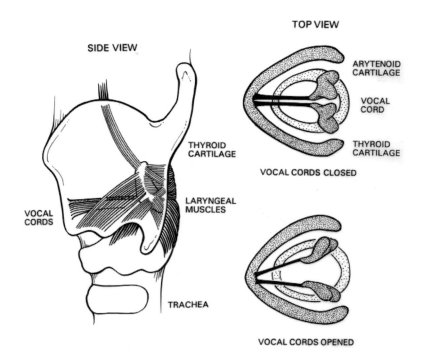

Figure 11.5 Vocal cords (in plan and elevation views), both open and closed.

the vocal cords. In the upper length of the larynx are two sets of vocal cords (or membranous folds) that open and close across the larynx. Generally, these folds remain open during breathing. However, the muscles that control these folds can alternatively open and close the folds, as well as induce vibrations within the folds (or cords). The exiting gases, after passing by these cords enter the pharynx, which is a volume leading from the larynx to the mouth and the nasal cavities. As the expelled gases leave through the mouth, several components in this cavity — the teeth, gums, tongue, palate, and lips — all can affect the passage of the gases, altering the character of the sound waves which proceed into the external environment. Sounds borne by gases leaving through the nasal passages are also modified as the gases traverse along these alternative passageways.

The manners in which all of the various components of the speech system act upon the sounds so that they appear as speech are complex. But this complexity is essential in providing us with the capabilities to create the range of spoken (and sung) sounds that we can produce.

SIDEBAR 11.3 The resonance of sound waves

Any passageway, container, or vessel through which a sound wave may propagate has one (or more) natural frequency (frequencies) of vibration. At a natural vibrational frequency the vessel will vibrate with a greater strength than would be present if some other rate of vibration were induced in the vessel. A natural vibrational frequency is a property of the vessel and is determined by such other physical properties as its mass, degree of elasticity, configuration, and size.

Sound waves passing through any vessel will cause the vessel to vibrate (i.e., the sound waves induce vibrations in the vessel). When the frequency of the sound wave does not match a natural vibrational frequency of the vessel, the vessel will vibrate nonetheless. But, for the condition when the frequency of the sound wave is identical to the natural vibrational frequency of the vessel, the force of the vibrations in the vessel will be at a *maximum* value. At this matching of the sound wave and vessel vibration frequencies, *resonance* is said to exist. With resonance, the force of the sound wave leaving the vessel will be appreciably greater than the original force of the entering sound wave.

In a *resonant* condition, the initial force of the sound wave activates the vessel, causing the vessel to vibrate at its natural frequency). Then, the vibration of the vessel contributes energy to the sound wave,

increasing the energy that the sound wave will display when it leaves the vessel. The consequence of resonance is essentially that it amplifies the sound wave, making the wave more powerful.

Three common situations where resonance is demonstrated involve blowing down the throat of a sodapop bottle; using a resonating box with a tuning fork to increase the sound power shown by the tuning fork; and singing in the shower (when the shower is located in a *small* bathroom). If you take a narrow-necked bottle and blow into the bottle, you can feel the bottle vibrate. Further, if you vary your blowing, you can find a condition where the sound will seem fuller and more powerful. In this condition resonance exists. Alternatively, in demonstrations carried out in physics classes, tuning forks — which produce relatively low amounts of sound energy when struck — are stuck into hollow wooden boxes. When the instructor strikes the tuning fork set into a resonating box, the sound created has much greater power and will be more easily heard by observing students. Thirdly, if your shower is located in a small bathroom that is lined with hard, smooth surfaces, you can sing while showering and make your voice appear much fuller and richer than it might otherwise be (without the aid of resonance).[26]

SIDEBAR 11.4 The components of language

Robbins states that the three essential features of language are *phonetics, grammar,* and *semantics. Phonetics* concerns how speech occurs—its physiology—and how it sounds. *Grammar* describes how words are linked together to form sentences: thus, rules are set forth to develop contexts that can be anticipated (by readers or listeners) and which help to convey appropriate meanings. *Semantics* involves the establishment of meaning for individual words and words linked together in phrases (e.g., as the words appear in various idioms). For further information, see the article by Robbins, R.H., "Language," in the *Encyclopedia Brittanica*, 10 (Macropedia), (Chicago: Encyclopedia Brittanica, Inc., 1980), pages 642–662.

11.2.2 BASIC COMPONENTS OF SPEECH

Speech is a progression of sounds that occur over a range of frequencies and intensities (see Figure 11.6). In any sequence of sounds there are generally considerable variations in frequency and intensity from one sound to the next. A significant feature of speech is that these changes in frequency and intensity occur rapidly, essentially taking place from moment to moment. Thus, speech consists of large numbers of sounds, each different from the next in terms of basic characteristics but all linked together in a context and having apparent relationships. *In normal conversation,* a syllable lasts about one-eighth of a second; on average, approximately four syllables will be spoken per second; and common speech using the English language will occur at the rate of about 200 syllables per minute.[27] The frequency range over which speech occurs spans from about 100 to 8000 (or higher) Hz, and the change in sound pressure levels, during normal conversation, varies by as much as 30 decibels.[28] So, speech is a complex assemblage of sounds that happen very quickly and display great variety in such basic characteristics as frequency and intensity. Given this complexity, our ability to recognize speech is all the more remarkable.

Speech is founded upon language, which is basically an organization of sounds. Language is composed of a series of units—identified as *words*—and is structured with a set of rules—known as *grammar* or *syntax.* These units (or words) represent objects, describing how we feel about them and how we relate to them, explaining how these objects pertain to one another, and telling what activities occur between us and the objects. Alternatively, the rules by which words are joined in combinations exist by tradition or convention and are loosely or closely followed by the users of a language.

The basic element of the spoken word is the *phoneme.* A dictionary definition of *phoneme* states that it is "a member of the set of the smallest units of speech that serve to distinguish one utterance from another in a language or dialect."[29] As examples, what differentiates the spoken words *pear, bear, fair, mare,* and *share* are the respective phonemes *p, b, f, m,* and *sh.* The number of phonemes that are recognized as existing in any language varies to some extent by interpretation (i.e., by who is doing the cataloging). For *generic American* English there are between 10 to 20 phonemes based on vowel sounds and another approximately 25 phonemes based on consonant sounds. These phonemes by themselves do not possess meanings: they are simply specific elemental sounds. Instead, the phonemes are combined to form syllables, which are combined to form words. The

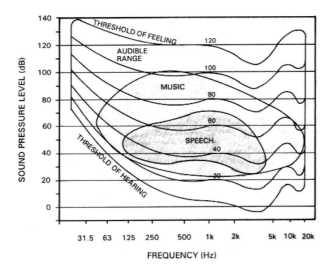

Figure 11.6 The approximate ranges of frequency and sound pressure levels for speech (and music) as portrayed against the hearing capacity of a young adult (see Figure 11.1.) This drawing has been published previously in a brochure, "Human-Environment Measures," composed by Bruel & Kjaer S.V. Permission to reprint this drawing has been granted by Bruel & Kjaer S.V.

words then are joined in sentences, which express ideas. Most English words have between two to five phonemes (although there can be as few as one and as many as ten or more in any word). The number of syllables in the English language is estimated to be in range of 1000 to 2000, and the English language contains as many as several hundred thousand words.

The significance of these various phonemes — and the many syllables that are developed with them — is that they provide the basis for discriminating between spoken words. As all of the words in any language are composites of phonemes and syllables, *the quality of spoken communication depends on our ability to distinguish among these elemental sounds.* To distill the meaning in spoken communication, we must first identify the disparate sounds presented in speech. For instance, if we take two nonsense sentences, "the bear ate the pear" and "the fair gates are paired," we can behold — by speaking these sentences aloud — that comparatively little separates how these sentences sound. But their "meanings" are quite different. If these dissimilar meanings are to be noted by the listener, then it is essential that the individual be able to differentiate between the various sounds present in the sentences. As we shall develop below, any interfering noise that can inhibit one's ability to differentiate among various sounds will markedly affect the quality of speech communication.

11.2.3 SOME ACOUSTICAL QUALITIES OF SPEECH

11.2.3.1 Characteristics of elemental sounds in speech   The human voice is a tremendously flexible and varied instrument: a fundamental characteristic is that it is ever changing. An individual can raise or lower his or her voice, speak with alternative frequencies (i.e., to

SIDEBAR 11.5 Formant frequencies in human speech

For instance, for the phoneme *ee* (which is pronounced as a "long e" as in the word *heat*), the first formant frequency — averaged for adult males — is 270 Hz; the second formant frequency is 2290 Hz; and the third formant frequency is 3010 Hz. For the average female adult, the averaged first, second, and third formants are, respectively, 300, 2790, and 3310 Hz. Generally, the pressure levels for the second and third formant frequencies will be less than the pressure level of the first formant. For the phoneme *ee*, the pressure levels for the second and third formants are commonly 20 and 24 dB less than the first formant.

make sounds appear to be lower- or higher-pitched), talk more slowly or quickly, and even use combinations of these capacities together. Basic properties of voice are thus *temporal* and *spectral*. Temporal qualities of speech are manifested in the rapidity with which an elemental sound — a phoneme — is expressed. A phoneme must achieve enough intensity to be perceived, exist for sufficient time to be recognized, then must fade away so that it does not impede perception and recognition of succeeding sounds. So time is an essential parameter, affecting the formation, duration, and decay of successive phonemes.

Equally important for the creation of these speech components are the voice capabilities that enable expression of all the various speech sounds with their alternative combinations of frequency and pressure level. Speech is a combination of vowel and consonant sounds (i.e., the phonemes appear as vowels and consonants). These vowel and consonant sounds (and their characteristic frequencies and pressure levels) are directly determined by the physiology of the body parts involved in producing speech. Speech is initiated as the vibrational energies of the vocal cords are transferred to respired gases exiting the lungs. The patterns of the vibrations are established by the physical properties of the larynx and the vocal cords (or folds). These properties include the mass and length of the larynx and the tension present in the larynx and its associated muscles (e.g., greater mass will usually produce lower-frequency sounds; more tension will create higher-frequency sounds; and so forth). So, the sound waves resulting from these vibrations will feature presences of fundamental frequencies and of series of overtones (i.e., each vowel or consonant will be characterized by a specific fundamental frequency and a number of overtones).

The configuration and behavior of the vocal tract also strongly influence the appearance of each elemental sound. The vocal tract includes, as its main parts, the pharynx, mouth, and nasal cavity. This tract resembles a tube or pipe and is gas-filled. As a consequence, the air passing through this tract experiences resonance, which strengthens sounds of particular frequencies. The addition of resonance to some of the sound waves created at the vocal cords thus fills out and enhances selected basic sounds. As the length and shape of the vocal tract can be varied by the individual — for instance, by opening and closing of the mouth, locating the tongue in different positions, raising and lowering one's head to alter the length of the tract, and so forth — the frequencies at which resonance will occur are subject to wide adjustment (note Sidebar 11.3).

The frequencies at which these resonances happen are identified as *formant* frequencies. For any specific configuration of the vocal tract — established as its length and shape vary — a number of frequencies exist for which resonance is present. As a result, there are multiple formant frequencies in many elemental sounds. These alternative formant frequencies are catalogued numerically beginning with the lowest frequency: the frequency range for the first formant for the various English phonemes is between about 250 to 800 Hz; the second formant occurs in the range between 800 to 2000 Hz; and the third formant is present in the range between 2200 to 3500 Hz. Generally, about three formant frequencies must be audible if a phoneme is to be recognizable.

These formant frequencies exist principally for vowel sounds that benefit from the resonances achieved along the vocal tract. The vowel sounds are spoken with greater pressure levels. The greater pressure levels result from the general openness present in both the vocal cords and the vocal tract, while these vowel sounds are enunciated. Alternatively, *consonant sounds are spoken with lesser pressure levels,* primarily because the vocal cords are partially or nearly closed at the initiations of these sounds and there will generally be some attendant constriction in the vocal tract (as the respired gases exit the tract). The relative powers with which these various basic vowel and consonant sounds are commonly spoken have been identified by Fletcher and are shown in Table 11.1. The accompanying graph (Figure 11.7) relates the power of each of these basic sounds in speech with the apparent frequencies at which the sounds are heard.

TABLE 11.1
RELATIVE PHONETIC POWERS OF FUNDAMENTAL SPEECH
SOUNDS AS PRODUCED BY AN AVERAGE SPEAKER[1]

SOUND	SAMPLE WORD	RELATIVE POWER	SOUND	SAMPLE WORD	RELATIVE POWER
o	talk	680x	ch	chat	42x
a	to	600x	n	no	36x
o	ton	510x	j	jot	23x
a	tap	490x	zh	azure	20x
o	tone	470x	z	zip	16x
u	took	460x	s	sit	16x
a	tape	370x	t	tap	15x
e	ten	350x	g	get	15x
u	tool	310x	k	kit	13x
i	tip	260x	v	vat	12x
e	team	220x	th	that	11x
r	err	210x	b	bat	7x
l	let	100x	d	dot	7x
sh	shot	80x	p	pat	6x
ng	ring	73x	f	for	5x
m	me	52x	th	thin	1x

1. Thus, the phonetic sound o (as used in the word talk) is spoken with 680 times the power employed to express the phonetic sound th (as used in the word thin). Similarly, for instance, the sound a (as used in the word top) is spoken with six times as much power as the sound l (as used in the word let). This table is reprinted from the book by Fletcher, H., *Speech and Hearing in Communication,* (New York: D. Van Nostrand Company, Inc., 1953), pages 85–86.

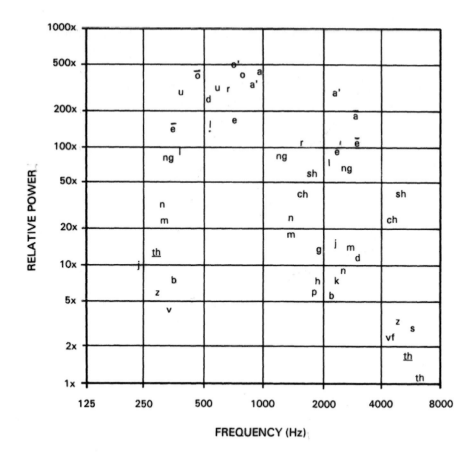

Figure 11.7 A plotting of the relative power for the elemental speech sounds — phonemes — versus apparent frequencies for these sounds. This graph is reprinted from the book by Fletcher, H., *Speech and Hearing in Communication,* (New York: D. Van Nostrand Company, Inc., 1953).

Other conditions also determine how intense these elemental sounds may appear. For instance, the speech context in which the sounds occur and whether a sound is stressed (or otherwise emphasized) in its enunciation during speech will both influence the intensity that a specific sound may have. Two additional factors will also affect how elemental sounds are perceived: consonant phonemes commonly have shorter durations, and the expression of these consonant phonemes in speech passes quickly from one sound to the next (i.e., causing the sounds to appear to run together). The characteristic frequencies of the vowel sounds are generally lower than those of the consonant sounds. Consequently, the benefit attained by having lower-frequency formants for vowel phonemes is that these sounds tend to be masked less by environmental noises. And the vowel sounds have lower probabilities that they will be overridden by noises that can interfere with speech perception.

In this description of the differences between elemental vowel and consonant sounds our discussion has focused on American English (i.e., English language sounds spoken by

SIDEBAR 11.6 Great American English and other dialects

It is perhaps overly simple to refer to an "American English as spoken by an average American" because the English language, more than any other modern language, is a composite of many other languages; and there are many dialects and regional pronunciations present throughout the United States. However, there are well-based suggestions that "Great American English," which encompasses the speech of many people in the midwestern and western United States, is perhaps speech that has the least accenting or other

regional tonality among the various American dialects. Thus, this "Great American English" may be regarded as an "average" expression of American English. For more information about the various forms of American English, see the book by Hendrickson, R., *American Talk: The Words and Ways of American Dialects,* (New York: Viking Penguin Inc., 1986). On page 17 of that book, Mr. Hendrickson indicates that there are three principal American dialects: New England, Southern, and General American.

an average American). However, our intent here is to describe, generally, the composition of a spoken language. As we have identified the principal sounds in the language, we have thus established the characteristics of speech based on this language.

Finally, concerning the extent to which characteristics of basic American English sounds can be generalized to other spoken languages, we can cite a study conducted by von Tarnoczy.[30] Von Tarnoczy found that among six European languages (English, German, Hungarian, Italian, Russian, and Swedish), the characteristic frequency ranges and pressure levels used to express speech were similar to the other languages and displayed only small variations. These variations tended to be exhibited primarily in the frequency band of 800 to 2500 Hz. Overall, the energy levels of sounds created in the six languages were quite similar.

11.2.3.2 Sound pressure levels across the sound spectrum for speech So far, we have treated the properties of speech in terms of its fundamental elements (i.e., the vowel and consonant sounds which comprise American English). Let's now consider the range of pressure levels and frequencies across which speech most often occurs. For evidence, we will cite a study that measured speech levels for about one hundred American talkers, who spoke at five different vocal efforts (*casual, normal, raised, loud,* and *shouting*). The results of these measurements are shown in Figures 11.8–11.10. Pressure levels for speech—by men, women, and children, respectively—are found to be (in dB(A)): for normal conversation, 57–58, 55, and 57–58; for speaking to a small group with a raised voice (as in a lecture format), 64–65, 62–63, and 64–65; and for talking in a low tone of voice, 52–53, 50, and 52–53. Whispering can be conducted at pressure levels as low as 20 to 25 dB(A). When sound pressure levels are measured across the octave bands over which speech occurs, then the spectral distributions show substantial pressure level variations. For instance, for male speech conducted at normal conversational levels, the greatest pressure level (54 dB) occurs at 500 Hz with minima at the low frequency end of the distribution (44 dB at 160 Hz) and at the high frequency end (30 dB at 10,000 Hz). Similar spectral distributions are also exhibited for raised or casual voice levels.[31]

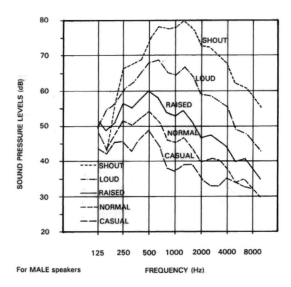

Figure 11.8 Mean spectral information (sound pressure levels versus frequency) for male speakers at five vocal efforts. As examples, the *lowered* speech level for males is approximately 52–53 dB(A); the normal conversational speech level is 57–58 dB(A); and the raised speech level (perhaps as one might lecture to students in a class) is 64–65 dB(A). This graph is reproduced from the document by Pearson, K.S., R.L. Bennett, and S. Fidell, *Speech levels in various noise environments* [PB-270053], (Washington, D.C.: National Technical Information Service, U.S. Department of Commerce, May 1977).

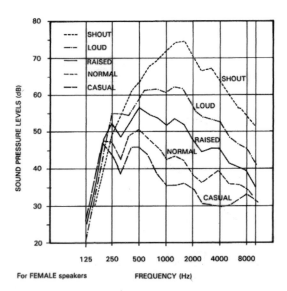

Figure 11.9 Mean spectral information (sound pressure levels versus frequency) for female speakers at five vocal efforts. As examples, the *lowered* speech level for adult females is approximately 50 dB(A); the normal conversational speech level is 55 dB(A); and the raised speech level (perhaps as one might lecture to students in a class) is 62–63 dB(A). This graph is reproduced from the document by Pearson, K.S., R.L. Bennett, and S. Fidell, *Speech levels in various noise environments* [PB-270053], (Washington, D.C.: National Technical Information Service, U.S. Department of Commerce, May 1977).

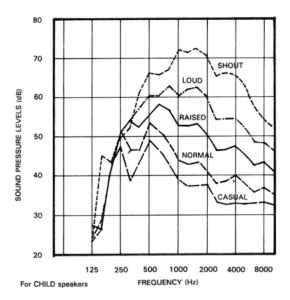

Figure 11.10 Mean spectral information (sound pressure levels versus frequency) for children speakers (aged less than 13 years) at five vocal efforts. This graph is reproduced from the document by Pearson, K.S., R.L. Bennett, and S. Fidell, *Speech levels in various noise environments* [PB-270053], (Washington, D.C.: National Technical Information Service, U.S. Department of Commerce, May 1977).

The relative pressure levels (produced around your head) as you speak are shown in Figure 11.11. Note that pressure levels are substantially higher close to the speaker and decrease with increasing distance. Also, *recognize that the pressure levels behind the speaker are considerably lower than in front of the speaker* (i.e., as one might expect with a directional source). One significance of this fact — that the pressure levels behind a speaker's head will be substantially less than those levels measured in front of the speaker — is that speech intelligibility will be reduced for listeners who are not facing the speaker.

Additionally, to enhance speech communication, one must be concerned about the characteristic frequencies of any noise. If noise frequencies overlay the frequencies of elemental sounds, then the noise frequencies may mask the audibility of these phonemes, rendering them inaudible. As speech is based on combinations of vowel and consonant phonemes and the consonant phonemes are more "fragile," more attention needs to be given to supporting the audibility of these consonant sounds, if speech perception is to be ensured.

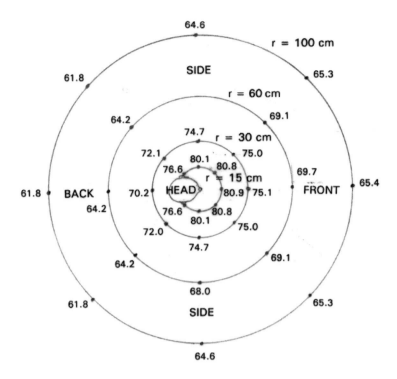

Figure 11.11 Sound pressure levels for various distances and angles relative to a speaker's mouth. This graph is reprinted from the book by Fletcher, H., *Speech and Hearing in Communication,* (New York: D. Van Nostrand Company, Inc., 1953).

11.2.4 SPEECH INTELLIGIBILITY

11.2.4.1 Basic requirements for maintaining speech intelligibility   The intelligibility — or comprehension — of speech concerns how well spoken words are perceived and understood. Speech is composed of many elemental sounds that are linked together in a virtual continuum. Thus, speech flows along much as a mountain stream, having its eddies and swirls and variations in volume rates. In speech there are constantly shifting patterns of sound: the frequencies and pressure levels of the many sounds change across a conversation. Additionally, the presences of *stress* — the intentional marking of individual sounds to emphasize meanings and contents in speech — and *intonation* — the repeated, gradual raising and lowering of pitch during speech — both affect how speech appears to and is understood by the listener. These two latter devices are commonly employed to amplify specific words or phrases, to differentiate statements and questions, and to indicate lulls and continuities between thoughts in speech.

The hearing and understanding of speech depend on several factors involving the characteristics of the spoken words, the environment in which speech is conducted, and the personal capabilities and styles of the speaker and the listener. An initial, fundamental requirement for good speech intelligibility is that *the listener should have good hearing*

SIDEBAR 11.7 The cocktail party effect

One example of the *reverberant* field is the stereotypical cocktail party. In that setting a number of people will be talking. There will be noises from the mixing of drinks, food preparation, and other such related activities. Indeed, music may also be played. All of these contribute to the creation of a constant din which will make the holding of easy conversation virtually impossible. Success in treating such continuous noise will be limited. Providing a great amount of absorbing surface materials will have some benefits. Making certain that people can arrange themselves in small groups which are separated by very short distances will also enhance speech intelligibility in these circumstances. But, finally, the mostly likely means for a person to increase his or her chances of being heard and understood is to raise one's own speech level (thus, further exacerbating these noisy conditions). Additionally, using this increase in the pressure level of one's speech to override the background noise level can lead to a straining (or tiring) of speech faculty. A likely concomitant effect will be the reduction in the length of conversations.

---

capacity.[32] If a listener's hearing is impaired, then either remedial action must be taken to upgrade the acuity of the person or some form of amplification of the speech — most likely with electronic means — will be needed. But presuming that the auditor hears well, then a first need for insuring good speech intelligibility is that the speaker talks *clearly* with *adequate loudness.* Speech intelligibility depends particularly on the maintenance of suitable *pressure level ratios of the useful sounds versus the background noise.* Speech should thus have pressure levels that are intense enough to exceed those of any unwanted sounds (i.e., *noise*). But, more than simply having adequate sound pressure levels for speech, establishing intelligibility requires the provision of *sufficiently large sound-to-noise ratios, particularly at frequencies involving consonant sounds.* Regarding the development of intelligibility, Cavanaugh et al. have written that virtually all of the sound energy present for speech is roughly in the frequency range between 200 to 6000 Hz. Most of this sound energy is concentrated in the frequency band from about 200 to 800 Hz, whereas the more essential determinants for good intelligibility — many of the consonant phonemes — appear at frequencies greater than 800 Hz. And the contribution that any frequency bandwidth between 200 to 6000 Hz offers toward speech intelligibility is dependent on the extent that the pressure level for that bandwidth is above the pressure level of ambient noise for the bandwidth, the width of the bandwidth itself, and the "importance" of the bandwidth in determining intelligibility (where the most important frequencies for creating intelligibility occur in the range between about 1250 to 3150 Hz). Referring back to Figure 11.7, note that few of the *consonant* phonemes have characteristic frequencies less than about 1500 Hz, and those consonant phonemes that do have characteristic frequencies less than 800 Hz are relatively weak in comparison to the much stronger vowel phonemes. Thus, if hearing elemental consonant sounds is essential to establishing good speech intelligibility and most consonant sounds are comparatively weak, then some means of enhancing these consonant sounds will have to be provided. Also, related to this requirement that there be adequately high speech signal-to-noise ratios, it is quite possible that, without such high signal-to-noise ratios, ambient noise or even some speech components will mask other elemental sounds which are necessary for insuring good intelligibility.[33]

A second requirement for establishing good intelligibility is that speech be able to occur across a wide frequency range. Thus, no noise source should be present that might mask some frequency bands. Or a speech source should not be limited to a narrow frequency, such as with a radio whose amplifier or speaker is defective. Intelligibility is enhanced when all the various elemental sounds—phonemes—can be easily heard. Third, good intelligibility depends on the provision of a *context* for the words. As phonemes comprise syllables and syllables form words, the understanding of single words is enhanced when they are offered in a continuum. Thereby, the listener can take in an overall thought or concept (expressed in speech) and employ the thought or concept to determine possibly indistinct elemental sounds (or words). A fourth property of *conversation* that can contribute to good intelligibility concerns the *nature of the behaviors in which the speaker and listener are engaged.* For example, hand-gesturing and body movement by a speaker can demonstrate the strength of a person's feeling and impart emphasis to specific words, phrases, or sentences. Such body actions can reinforce attention to what is said. Alternatively, these actions may express an emotion or mood that is inadequately conveyed with speech alone. And, fifth, the *acoustical properties of the space* in which speech occurs will affect intelligibility. Providing short distances between speakers and listeners or between conversants is important. Alternatively, the surfaces of these spaces should be more absorptive (or diffusing) than reflective, thereby reducing the development of reverberant fields.

11.2.4.2   The Articulation Index and the Speech Interference Level   The extent that speech intelligibility exists for some situation or within a space can be described numerically using a scale known as the *Articulation Index* (or, simply, as the AI). This index was first suggested by Collard, later developed extensively by French and Steinberg, and then codified into a useful evaluation (and prediction) method by Kryter. The Articulation Index is founded on a series of subjective measurements of speech intelligibility. Test subjects are read lists of carefully selected words containing the various basic elemental sounds and are asked to write out what they hear (and understand). The percentages of correctly interpreted words are subsequently correlated with a calculation-derived scale (see Figure 11.12). The fundamental parameters affecting this index are voice level and background noise (i.e., how readily can elemental sounds be heard and comprehended and to what extent will ambient noise inhibit the understanding of speech).

The Articulation Index is expressed as decimal fractions between 0.0 and 1.0. Pirn has matched AI values for a room with occupant assessments of whether acoustic privacy or good communication conditions exist in the room (see Table 11.2).[34] Generally, low AI values (from 0.0 to 0.2) indicate that environmental conditions will provide poor communication qualities and good speech privacy. Alternatively, high AI values for a room (from 0.5 to 1.0) suggest that the room will offer good to excellent communication conditions and marginal to no speech privacy.

The Articulation Index can be employed as an evaluative or predictive tool. For example, to determine the AI for a space where speech between occupants is a principal activity and background noise is reported as an inhibiting factor, measurements of the sound pressure levels of the speech and the noise are performed. These sound pressure levels for the speech and the noise can then be entered into an empirically derived equation, and the AI value for the space can be calculated. Alternatively, how intelligible speech will appear in a space can be estimated, if environmental noise levels are known (or can be predicted) and likely speech levels can be established from data such as those shown in Figures 11.8–11.10. Ultimately, computing the AI for a given situation will show that with higher

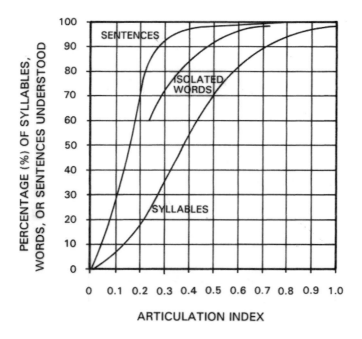

Figure 11.12 Correlations between the percentages of syllables, words, and sentences understood versus the Articulation Index. Note that the intelligibility of sentences is higher than it is for isolated words (and for individual syllables) principally because the sentences provide context to better enable understanding of individual words within the sentences. Thus, hearing a series of words promotes the understanding of any individual word within the series. This graph is reprinted from the paper by French, N.R., and J.C. Steinberg, "Factors governing the intelligibility of speech sounds," *Journal of the Acoustical Society of America,* 19(1), January 1947, pages 90–119. Permission to reprint this graph has been granted by the Acoustical Society of America.

TABLE 11.2
RELATIONSHIPS BETWEEN THE ARTICULATION INDEX VALUES, PERCENTAGES OF CORRECTLY UNDERSTOOD SYLLABLES & WORDS, AND SUBJECTIVE FEELINGS ABOUT COMMUNICATION & PRIVACY CONDITIONS[1]

PERCENTAGE OF CORRECTLY UNDERSTOOD SYLLABLES	PERCENTAGE OF CORRECTLY UNDERSTOOD ISOLATED WORDS	ARTICULATION INDEX VALUES	SUBJECTIVE IMPRESSION
3	—	0.00 – 0.05	confidential privacy
3 to 18	—	0.05 – 0.20	normal privacy
18 to 45	— to 78	0.20 – 0.35	marginal privacy
45 to 70	78 to 9	0.35 – 0.50	fair communication
70 to 85	92 to 97	0.50 – 0.65	good communication
85 to 98	97 to —	0.65 – 1.00	excellent communication

1. This table is synthesized from information provided in the papers by French, N.R., and J.C. Steinberg, "Factors governing the intelligibility of speech sounds," *Journal of the Acoustical Society of America,* 19(1), January 1947, 90–119; and Pirn, R., "Acoustical variables in open planning," *Journal of the Acoustical Society of America,* 49(5), 1971, 1339–1345.

noise levels, there will be lower AI values and poorer speech intelligibility (i.e., unless speech pressure levels can be raised sufficiently to override the noise presence).

An alternative, streamlined version of the Articulation Index has been derived and is called the *Speech Interference Level* (or SIL). The SIL, expressed in decibels (dB), is an average of the sound pressure levels of ambient noise at the four frequency bands centered at 500, 1000, 2000, and 4000 Hz that will permit "just reliable communication" among speakers and listeners who are face-to-face. Note that these just reliable communication conditions will provide an Articulation Index score of approximately 0.30. The most significant variables affecting the SIL—the average acceptable noise level—are the distance separating a speaker and a listener and the voice level used by the speaker. The application of the SIL is based on the expectation that—whatever noise is present—this noise will have a broadband character (i.e., the energy of the noise will be spread somewhat evenly across the spectral range of speech). Acceptable average noise levels for the four frequency bands—used for determining the SIL—can be related to the distance between the speaker and the listener (see Figure 11.13). As an example, if a speaker and

---

SIDEBAR 11.8 Assessing the Articulation Index for an environment

A history describing the early development of the Articulation Index appears in a paper by Bowman, N.T., "The Articulation Index and its application to room acoustics design," *Journal of Sound and Vibration,* 32(1), 1974, pages 109–129. Citations for J. Collard's reports appear in Professor Bowman's paper. A seminal paper on the AI has been written by French, N.R., and J.C. Steinberg, "Factors governing the intelligibility of speech sounds," *Journal of the Acoustical Society of America,* 19(1), January 1947, pages 90–119. The mathematical formalization of the Articulation Index proceeds from the paper by Kryter, K.D., "Methods for the calculation and use of the Articulation Index," *Journal of the Acoustical Society of America,* 34(11), November 1962, pages 1689–1697.

The technique for determining the AI for an environment is defined in the ANSI Standard S3.5-1997, *Methods for the Calculation of the Articulation Index,* (New York: American National Standards Institute, Inc., 1997). This procedure requires that ambient noise pressure levels in an environment be measured on a frequency bandwidth-by-bandwidth basis (i.e., using either one-third octave bands or octave bands). Speech pressure levels in each of the same bandwidths are also measured. The ambient noise pressure levels are subtracted from the speech pressure levels, and the

pressure level difference at each bandwidth is then multiplied by a weighting factor. The products of the pressure level difference times the weighting factor, for all of the bandwidths, are summed. The total is the Articulation Index for the environment and situation. The particular frequency bandwidths used in the AI calculation, the weighting factors, and calculational form sheets for the AI calculation can be found in the ANSI Standard noted above. Also, note that, recognizing the importance of elemental consonant sounds in fostering intelligibility, the weighting factors are higher in the frequency range between 1250 to 3150 Hz (specifically, the frequency range in which many of the elemental consonant sounds (phonemes) have their characteristic frequencies).

Lists of the test words mentioned in the main text above can be found in the ANSI Standard 3.2-1960 (R1971), *Monosyllabic Word Intelligibility,* (New York: American National Standards Institute, Inc., 1971). Each list is composed of 50 *phonetically balanced* words (i.e., words that contain all of the elemental speech sounds whose frequency of presence in each list matches the "frequency of occurrence in normal speech." [this quoted phrase is taken from page 7 of the Standard.]) These lists are commonly referred to in the professional and scientific literature as *PB-lists.*

listener are about 6 feet (2 m) apart and the speaker is talking at a normal conversational voice level, then the average noise level (or SIL) for these four frequency bands must be equal to or less than about 52 dB. However, if an observed average noise level for these four bands is greater than 52 dB (and a just reliable communication condition is to be sustained), then the distance separating the speaker and listener must be lessened, the sound pressure level of the speaker must be increased, or some way must be found to lessen the average noise level. Alternatively, if an AI rating higher than 0.3 is required (i.e., communication conditions better than just reliable communication are needed), then at least one of these three problem resolutions must be accomplished. But if one or more of these three actions cannot be successfully undertaken, then the speech intelligibility will be reduced for the given situation (i.e., understanding speech communication in the environment will be more difficult). Also, note that the A-weighted noise level equivalent to this SIL value of 52 dB is 60 dB(A) (i.e., a noise having a SIL value of 52 dB — a noise pressure level average for these four frequency bands — when measured using the A-weighting scale would register 60 dB(A)).

Lastly, a third scale for estimating speech intelligibility has recently been introduced and is gaining acceptance in the professional building acoustics community. This scale, known as the *Speech Transmission Index* (or STI), extends the Articulation Index and is particularly useful for fine-tuning existing rooms used for listening to single speakers (e.g., lecture rooms and classrooms) and for fine arts performance spaces (e.g., theaters and playhouses).

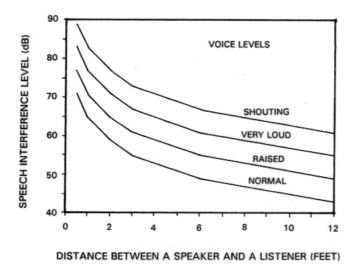

Figure 11.13 Speech interference levels (SIL) acceptable for alternative voice levels and distances separating speakers and listeners. The significance of each of these voice level curves is that the SIL for any voice level will decrease as the distance between a speaker and a listener increases. Thus, as the background noise level increases — as the SIL increases — for any voice level, a speaker and a listener must be closer together for good speech intelligibility to occur. This graph has been reprinted from ANSI S3.14-1977 (R1997), *American National Standard for Rating Noise with Respect to Speech Interference,* © 1997, with the permission of the Acoustical Society of America, 35 Pinelawn Road, Suite 114E, Melville, NY 11747, USA. Copies of the Standard may be purchased from the Standards Store at http://asa.aip.org.

SIDEBAR 11.9 Further information about the Speech Interference Level

The original concept for the Speech Interference Level was suggested in a paper by Beranek, L.L., "Noise control in office and factory spaces," *Transactions of the Industrial Hygiene Foundation of America (Bulletin)*, 18, 1950, pages 26–33. The paper identified a Speech Interference Level (SIL), which used octave bandwidths spanning from 600 to 1200, 1200 to 2400, and 2400 to 4800 Hz. At the time (1950) that Dr. Beranek wrote the paper describing the SIL, those bandwidths were standard. Since that time, the definition of which octave bandwidths are regarded as standard has changed. Now, the octave band centers at 500, 1000, 2000, and 4000 Hz are among those accepted as standard for the sound spectrum. For more information about octave bands and the frequency centers, see Section 10.5.2. Subsequent to the development of the original SIL, a Preferred Speech Interference Level (PSIL) was suggested, based on noise levels measured at the octave centers of 500, 1000, and 2000 Hz. For information about the PSIL, see Beranek, L.L., "Criteria for noise and vibration in

communities, buildings, and vehicles," (Chapter 18) of the book edited by Beranek, L.L., *Noise and Vibration Control,* (New York: McGraw-Hill Book Company, 1971), pages 558–560.

The present version of the Speech Interference Level has been established by a Standard written by the Acoustical Society of America, *Rating Noise with Respect to Speech Interference,* ANSI S3.14-1977 [R1997], (New York: American National Standards Institute, 1997). The two phrases shown in quotation marks in the text are taken from page 3 of the Standard. Note that the SIL, using the four octave band centers as the basis for determining its value, is abbreviated as *SIL (0.5, 1, 2, 4).*

For a more extended discussion (and comparison) of the Articulation Index and the Preferred Speech Interference Level and their applications, see the book by Kryter, K.D., *The Effects of Noise on Man* (2nd edition), (Orlando, Florida: Academic Press, 1985). Note Chapter 4, generally, and pages 89–101, especially.

SIDEBAR 11.10 Seeking additional information about the Speech Transmission Index (STI)

Many papers describing the use of the Speech Transmission Index (STI) have been published. Two papers that introduced the STI scale are by Steeneken, H.J.M., and T. Houtgast, "A physical method for measuring speech-transmission quality," *Journal of the Acoustical Society of America,* 67(1), January 1980, pages 318–326; and Houtgast, T., H.J.M. Steeneken, and R. Plomp, "Predicting speech intelligibility in rooms from the modulation transfer function; part I: general room acoustics," *Acustica,* 46, 1980, pages 60–72. Three papers that compare the STI scale with other means for assessing speech intelligibility include: Lazarus, H., "Prediction of verbal communication in noise — a review: part I," *Applied Acoustics,* 19, 1986, pages 436–464; Bradley, J.S., "Predictors of

speech intelligibility in rooms," *Journal of the Acoustical Society of America,* 80(3), September 1986, pages 837–845; and Schmidt-Nielsen, A., "Comments on the use of physical measures to assess speech intelligibility," *Journal of the Acoustical Society of America,* 81(6), June 1987, pages 1985–1987. Additionally, a formalization of the STI scale has led to the development of the Rapid Speech Transmission Index (RASTI). For information about the RASTI, see either Orfield, S.J., "The RASTI method of testing relative intelligibility," *Sound and Vibration,* December 1987, pages 20–22; or Horrall, T.R., and T. Jacobsen, "RASTI measurements: demonstration of different applications," *Bruel & Kjaer Application Notes,* (Naerum, Denmark: Bruel & Kjaer, 1986).

In summary, speech is composed of a number of elemental sounds arranged essentially into a continuum of syllables, words, and sentences. Speech often proceeds at a comparatively rapid rate, approaching 200 words per minute. The comprehension of speech by listeners depends greatly on the clarity of the sounds and whether masking noise is present. Noise can severely affect the intelligibility of spoken words. Thus, noise must be controlled in environments where speech communication is a major activity.

ENDNOTES and SELECTED ADDITIONAL COMMENTS

1. Watson, C.S., and R.W. Gengel, "Signal duration and signal frequency in relation to auditory sensitivity," *Journal of the Acoustical Society of America,* 46(4), Part 2, 1969, pages 989–997.

2. Schneider, B.A., S.E. Trehub, B.A. Morrongiello, and L.A. Thorpe, "Auditory sensitivity in preschool children," *Journal of the Acoustical Society of America,* 79(2), 1986, pages 447–452.

3. Schechter, M.A., S.A. Fausti, B.Z. Rappaport, and R.H. Frey, "Age categorization of high-frequency auditory threshold data," *Journal of the Acoustical Society of America,* 79(3), 1986, pages 767–771.

4. Hinchcliffe, R., "The anatomical locus of presbycusis," *Journal of Speech and Hearing Disorders,* 27, 1962, pages 301–310.

5. Fletcher, H., and W.A. Munson, "Loudness, its definition, measurement, and calculation," *Journal of the Acoustical Society of America,* 5(4), 1933, pages 82–108.

6. The researchers usually credited for the construction of the equal-loudness contours in the form that is widely employed today are D.W. Robinson and R.S. Dadson. The paper by these authors that includes the contours is "A re-determination of the equal-loudness relations for pure tones," *British Journal of Applied Physics,* 7(5), May 1956, pages 166–181.

7. Scharf, B., "Critical bands," in Tobias, J.V. (editor), *Foundations of Modern Auditory Theory, 1,* 1970, pages 157–200. An alternative treatment of how the critical band affects the perception of loudness has been presented in a paper by Zwicker, E., G. Flottorp, and S.S. Stevens, "Critical band width in loudness summation," *Journal of the Acoustical Society of America,* 29(5), May 1959, pages 548–557.

8. A paper by R. Hellman and E. Zwicker suggests that the use of a "loudness meter" may produce better descriptions about differences in loudness for sound sources with alternative spectral compositions. See Hellman, R., and E. Zwicker, "Why can a decrease in dB(A) produce an increase in loudness?" *Journal of the Acoustical Society of America,* 82(5), November 1987, pages 1700–1705.

9. Scharf, B., "Loudness," (Chapter 6), pages 187–242 of Carterette, E.C., and M.P. Friedman (editors), *Handbook of Perception, Volume IV: Hearing,* (New York: Academic Press, 1978). See pages 212–215, especially.

10. As an example, suppose that the subject reports that an unknown sound seemed 10 times as loud as the reference sound (i.e., that the sound has a *loudness* of 10 sones). Then, using the second equation identified in an earlier endnote (where N is the intensity level and L is the loudness)

$$\log L = 0.03\,N - 1.2$$

we can calculate what intensity level a 1000 Hz sound would need to have to appear 10x as loud. From this equation we can determine that the *intensity level* would be 73.3 dB (for the 1000 Hz sound) and that its corresponding loudness level would be 73.3 phons.

11. Wightman, F.L., and D.M. Green, "The perception of pitch," *American Scientist,* 62, March–April 1974, pages 208–215.

12. Geldard, F.A., *The Human Senses* (2nd edition), (New York: John Wiley & Sons, 1972), page 197.

13. Terhardt, E., "Influence of intensity on the pitch of complex tones," *Acustica*, 33, 1975, pages 344–348.

14. For further information about the perception of complex tones and their components, see the paper by Peters, R.W., B.C.J. Moore, and B.R. Glasberg, "Pitch of components of complex tones," *Journal of the Acoustical Society of America*, 73(3), 1983, pages 924–929.

15. Backus, J., *The Acoustical Foundations of Music* (2nd edition), (New York: W.W. Norton & Company, 1977), Chapters 7 and 8 (pages 107–160); Hall, D.E., *Musical Acoustics: An Introduction*, (Belmont, California: Wadsworth Publishing Company, 1980), pages 114–140; Rigden, J.S., *Physics and the Sound of Music* (2nd edition), (New York: John Wiley & Sons, Inc., 1985), pages 48–55 and 234–253; Rossing, T.D., *The Science of Sound* (2nd edition), (Reading, Massachusetts: Addison-Wesley Publishing Company, 1990), Chapters 6–8 (pages 85–168).

16. Sekuler, R., and R. Blake, *Perception*, (New York: Alfred A. Knopf, 1985), pages 449–452.

17. Wier, C.C., W. Jesteadt, and D.M. Green, "Frequency discrimination as a function of frequency and sensation level," *Journal of the Acoustical Society of America*, 61(1), 1977, pages 178–184.

18. Jesteadt, W., C.C. Wier, and D.M. Green, "Intensity discrimination as a function of frequency and sensation level," *Journal of the Acoustical Society of America*, 61(1), 1977, pages 169–177.

19. A more recent paper has explored another approach to defining *just noticeable differences* for intensity. This paper suggests that intensity discrimination should instead be considered in terms of *loudness*, rather than strictly in terms of the ratio of the change of intensity versus the original intensity (as would be the case if Weber's Law were accurate for this application). For a further explanation, see Zwislocki, J.J., and H.N. Jordan, "On the relations of intensity jnd's [just noticeable differences] to loudness and neural noise," *Journal of the Acoustical Society of America*, 79(3), 1986, pages 772–780.

20. The smaller number was proposed by Shower, E.G., and R. Biddulph, "Differential pitch sensitivity of the ear," *Journal of the Acoustical Society of America*, 3, 1931, pages 275–287. The larger number is credited to E. Luft by F.A. Geldard in his book, *The Human Senses* (2nd edition), (New York: John Wiley & Sons, Inc., 1972), pages 194–195.

21. Stevens, S.S., and H. Davis, *Hearing*, (New York: John Wiley & Sons, Inc., 1938), page 153.

22. Olson, H.F., *Music, Physics, and Engineering* (2nd edition), (New York: Dover Publications, 1967), pages 254–256.

23. Stevens, S.S., "The attributes of tones," *The Proceedings of the National Academy of Science*, 20, 1934, pages 457–459.

24. Geldard, F.A., *The Human Senses* (2nd edition), (New York: John Wiley & Sons, Inc., 1972), pages 201–206.

25. See Chapters 6 and 7 ("The speech mechanism as sound generator" and "The vocal tract," respectively) of the book by Fry, D.B., *The Physics of Speech*, (Cambridge, England: Cambridge University Press, 1979), pages 61–81.

26. One very informative discussion of the principles of resonances appears in the book by Fry, D.B., *The Physics of Speech*, (Cambridge, England: Cambridge University Press, 1979), pages 49–60. The vocal tract in the human being, which might be thought of as a column that extends from the vocal cords to the lips (see Figure 11.4 in this text), displays multiple resonances. The most powerful one occurs at about 500 Hz, and secondary and tertiary resonances are present at approximately 1500 and 2500 Hz.

27. French, N.R., and J.C. Steinberg, "Factors governing the intelligibility of speech sounds," *Journal of the Acoustical Society of America*, 19(1), January 1947, pages 90–119.

28. Dunn, H.K., and D.W. Farnsworth, "Exploration of pressure fields around the human head during speech," *Journal of the Acoustical Society of America*, 10(1), January 1939, pages 184–199.

29. *Webster's Seventh New Collegiate Dictionary*, (Springfield, Massachusetts: G. & C. Merriam Company, Publishers, 1967), page 635.

30. Von Tarnoczy, T., "Das durchschnittliche Energie-Spektrum der Sprache (für sechs Sprachen) [The mean energy-spectrum of speech (for six languages)]," *Acustica,* 24(2), 1971, pages 57–74.

31. Pearson, K.S., R.L. Bennett, and S. Fidell, *Speech levels in various noise environments* [PB-270053], (Washington, D.C.: National Technical Information Service, U.S. Department of Commerce, May 1977).

32. Kamm, C.A., D.D. Dirks, and T.S. Bell, "Speech recognition and the Articulation Index for normal and hearing-impaired listeners," *Journal of the Acoustical Society of America,* 77(1), January 1985, pages 281–288. Also, see Duquesnoy, A.J., "The intelligibility of sentences in quiet and in noise among aged listeners," *Journal of the Acoustical Society of America,* 74(4), October 1983, pages 1136–1144; and Gelfand, S.A., N. Piper, and S. Silman, "Consonant recognition in quiet and noise with aging among normal hearing listeners," *Journal of the Acoustical Society of America,* 80(6), December 1986, pages 1589–1598. Also, a review paper cataloging studies on issues of hearing loss, aging, and speech recognition has been prepared by the Working Group on Speech Understanding and Aging for the Committee on Hearing, Bioacoustics, and Biomechanics, National Research Council and published as, "Speech understanding and aging," *Journal of the Acoustical Society of America,* 83(3), March 1988, pages 859–895.

33. Cavanaugh, W.J., W.R. Farrell, P.W. Hirtle, and B.G. Watters, "Speech privacy in buildings," *Journal of the Acoustical Society of America,* 34(4), April 1962, pages 475–492.

34. See Table II (on page 1341) of the paper by Pirn, R., "Acoustical variables in open planning," *Journal of the Acoustical Society of America,* 49(5), 1971, pages 1339–1345.

Noise in the Built and Natural Environments

12

AT THE BEGINNING OF CHAPTER 10 we stated that sound offers two fundamental benefits for human beings: first, it provides us with a means for gathering information from the surrounding environment, and, second, it enables us to exchange information with other occupants of the world. In both instances, whether we are receiving or creating sound, its essential role is to promote communication. Thus, as long as a basic purpose of any built environment is to enhance activities that human beings carry out, then buildings (and areas immediately external to these buildings) must foster communication.

A prime constraint to achieving good communication with sound is the presence of noise. To define noise simply, we can say that it is *unwanted sound.* Thus, noise is any sound that interferes with our ability to gather useful information from the world around us, that impairs our pursuit of some activity (e.g., sleeping or talking with a friend or performing some work function), or that merely annoys us. Besides posing problems of impairment, interference, and annoyance, noise can also cause hearing loss. And some observers believe that noise can induce stress-related health problems for those exposed to it (e.g., producing such nonauditory difficulties as hypertension and/or gastrointestinal maladies).

Many sources of noise exist in our urban, suburban, and rural environments. Among the sources that generally create the greatest consternation amongst people exposed to these sources are vehicular traffic, airplanes engaged in landings and takeoffs, and industrial plant operations. Other comparatively less significant, transient sources can include garbage trucks, "boom box" radios, barking dogs, and lawnmowers. Even groups of people can produce significant noise problems for occupants who seek quieter living or working settings. Ultimately, noise is a *pollutant* much like noxious combustion gases and road dirt spewed by motor vehicles or the smoke, odors, and liquid-borne wastes created by industrial operations. A dictionary characterization of the word *pollutant* suggests that it is something that causes "the loss of purity and cleanliness through contamination."[1] Noise sources in our external environments certainly do taint and befoul our living and working spaces, making them unfit for many activities that we seek to perform there.

In this chapter we will describe noise presence in the built environment, the extent to which noise interferes with communication, and how noise affects human beings. We will also explain how noise can be controlled, either by relying on regulatory agencies or by employing physical devices. Necessarily, the alternative mechanisms for intervening against noise encompass what we can identify as the *PEST* issues (i.e., *p*olitical, *e*conomic, *s*ocial, and *t*echnical solutions that can combat the environmental problems created by noise sources and presence). For instance, how to regulate noise (or what degree of regulation should be imposed against a noise producer) is a contentious topic that is argued by both those who cause noise and those who must put up with it. For these adversarial groups, noise control is decidedly a political issue. Alternatively, actions taken to control noise must inevitably address economic concerns: manufacturers could make virtually noiseless motorcycles or builders could construct essentially noise-tight building envelopes. But the basic economic question related to each of these products is could the consumer sustain the additional costs that would enable the fabrication of such creations? In the social realm, many noises exist because the industrial plant or the airplane that generates noise also provides some useful service to the community (or, at least, some group in the community). To reduce the extent of these noises may require that the sources substantially curtail the services that they offer the community. Thus, questions about control of such sources will necessarily entail consideration of the effects the attendant cutbacks in services might have on the community (or groups therein). Lastly, numerous technical means exist for controlling noise, and useful innovations are regularly being created. One common problem for noise control specialists is staying abreast of all the various alternatives now available for curtailing noise. Another related problem is establishing how to integrate technical controls into present-day products. A third difficulty is figuring out how to relate technical solutions to existing political, economic, and social concerns. Ultimately, establishing noise control practices often requires trade-off analyses and the optimizing of resources. For instance, a somewhat high noise level for a factory may be permitted because it is socially and politically expedient — the factory provides jobs for a community — and the required noise control would cost too much.

One other important, general observation about noise control concerns the overall structure of any noise problem. There are three basic components of any such problem: a source, a transmitting pathway, and a receiver. Development of noise controls can focus on any of these three components, or it can combine strategies that include two or even all three components. The initiation of a noise control program will inevitably require the identification of the characteristics of the noise source (e.g., how the noise is produced; is it continuous or intermittent; how intense is it; what are its spectral features; and so forth). Second, information about how the noise is borne to the receiver should be sought (e.g., can this pathway be interrupted; what control alternatives exist; what are the costs associated with these restraints; etc.). Third, questions will have to be answered about what environmental conditions need to be provided for people engaged in some activity. For instance, how quiet should their ambient environment be; how likely is it that increased noise will affect people's activities; can they initiate localized controls which will limit noise levels and enable their activities to occur unaffected; and so forth. Noise control is a necessary and important environmental requirement throughout the world today. The means for achieving it are numerous. Indeed, the general problem for the designer and/or builder confronting a noisy environment is to select an appropriate solution and then be able to execute it for the betterment of the occupants of the environment.

Section 12.1 | PHYSICAL (AND PSYCHOSOCIAL) CHARACTERISTICS OF NOISE

To better understand how noise can interfere with speech and what other effects noise can have on occupants of built environments, let us now identify a variety of noise *sources* and describe the properties of the noises which these sources emit. We will also introduce a series of noise rating schemes that can be employed to describe how much noise is present in an environment. Then, in Section 12.2 we will discuss how these noises can affect us — the *receivers* of the noise — as we live and work in noisy environments.

12.1.1 COMMON (AND UNCOMMON) NOISE SOURCES

We can perhaps divide all the various noise sources into four classifications: *mechanical, electrical, animal,* and *natural* (see Figure 12.1). Necessarily, these classes are very general and sources identified within these classes will overlap somewhat. But the inherent value in establishing such classes may be that by recognizing what the origins of noises are, we can then examine each source, searching for means to control the noise that the source emits. However, before we begin categorizing noise sources, we must acknowledge one important qualification: what is noise to one person may be a pleasing sound to someone else. The perception of noise involves subjective, as well as objective, assessments. As an example, what one's daughter listens to on her radio may be music to her, but just as likely her parents may regard it simply as noise!

Mechanical sources are basically those that involve motors and machinery. Vehicles — whether ground, air, or water-based — are one common group. Powered devices used around the home are another: air-conditioners, vacuum cleaners, food processors, clothes dryers, lawnmowers, and so forth. Office equipment represents a third group, including computers (with their fans), tape drives, copiers, printers, and typewriters. Then, there is a great range of machines used in industrial and manufacturing processes. All of these mechanical sources involve the presence of moving parts that can rub against each other, strike each other, or simply vibrate.

If we consider any one of these groups, we can identify a variety of conditions that will determine how much or little noise any source type will emit. For instance, if we examine ground-based motor vehicles, a number of parameters — concerning mechanically powered transportation — are evident as determinants of noise levels. These determinants include the volume of traffic overall (how many vehicles pass by some site per hour); the percentages of cars, trucks, motorcycles, and buses present in the overall volume (each type has its own noise signatures); whether, at an observation site, the traffic is stop-and-go or is free-flowing; if the traffic is comparatively free-flowing, what the ambient (or average) velocity of the vehicles is; the presence of a road gradient (so that vehicles must brake

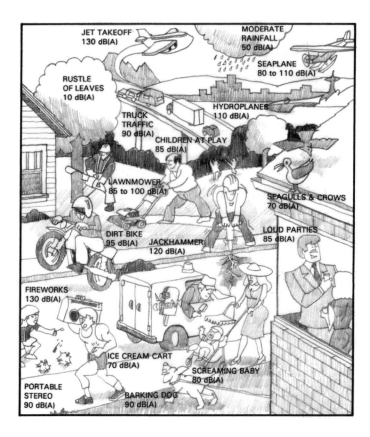

Figure 12.1 A variety of urban sounds and their pressure levels. A variety of urban noises and their pressure levels. This illustration was originally drawn by Steve McKinstry, *Seattle Times* staff, and published in the *Seattle Times* on July 1, 1984. © 1984 Seattle Times Company. Reprinted with their permission.

going downhill or increase engine speeds going uphill); whether noise barriers (vegetation or fences) between the roadway and the roadside are present to alter the noise appearance; the placement of a roadway below the common grade level or perhaps lowering and covering the roadway; and so forth. Each of these attributes can have a demonstrable effect on noises emitted by the traffic flow.

Electrical noises — as distinct from electrically powered motors that drive machinery — are primarily those emitted by such electrical devices as radios and other high-fidelity recording-and-playing equipment, power transformers (used for regulating municipal electrical supplies), and ballasts for fluorescent lamps. None of these electrical devices has the ubiquitous moving parts that are common to machinery and motors (i.e., other than switches to begin and curtail operation). But all of these devices still have parts that vibrate with sufficient energy and at frequencies that render them audible (and disturbing) to people near to them. Probably the most obvious noisemaker among this class is the portable radio: deserving particular attention, as a noise source, is the "boom box" that has become an often-heard presence in North American and European urban areas. Alternatively, the hum that ballasts produce can be especially bothersome when they operate in quiet interiors such as are found in libraries and museums.

Animal sources include people, domesticated animals, and the various creatures that live amongst or near people (if not directly as parts of people's extended families). Examples of noises produced by these sources are barking dogs, the cawing of crows or other more sonorous birdcalls, and people talking in conversation. Birdcalls may generally appear melodic and pleasing. But if they occur during the early morning hours and cause a human being to awaken, then that person may regard the birdsong as noise. Similarly, declaring that some conversation is noisy depends ultimately on one's point of view. Normal conversation is inherently not noisy: it occurs at moderate loudness levels; people do not screech or whine; and, depending on the content of the exchange, the talking can be interesting, pleasant, and even soothing to the listener. But when a conversation happens between two people within the hearing of a disinterested third person, then the conversation can indeed be regarded as noise for the third person. Such an observation is, of course, greatly subjective and is entirely contingent on when and where the talking occurs and what it disrupts.

Finally, the fourth class of noise sources encompasses *natural* sounds. The sound from a waterfall displays the power of running water and will generally be regarded by its beholders as awesome. But the roar of the cascading water makes conversation difficult and unintelligible. A gentle breeze on a warm summer day creates pleasant sounds as the wind rustles the leaves of nearby trees. But the shriek of a hurricane or the wail of a blizzard will be unpleasant, perhaps less for the sounds accompanying the storms and more for the discomfort and danger that the weather can create.[2] For these natural events, what are pleasing sound and unfortunate noise depends on one's situation and perspective. For this class of sources, as with the other three classes, treating the sources may often require thinking not only of what causes the sounds (that are considered to be noisy), but also why people regard them as noisy. Analyzing and understanding the subjective responses of people to noise can thus be critical to developing *adequate and reasonable* solutions. Another related issue that affects people's responses is the degree of control that the auditors can exercise when they experience the noise (i.e., the ability to control the noise source often makes the noise seem less bothersome).

12.1.2 PROPERTIES OF NOISE SOURCES

To establish the magnitude of any noise problem and to search for a solution, we need to catalog the properties of the noise and its source(s). Generally, most noise will demonstrate variable behaviors. Overcoming the noise and its effects on people will require finding the dominant qualities of the noise and dealing with them. We can identify three property classes that noises display. First, we can ask, what are the strictly physical features of a noise and its source? Second, what is the nature of the interaction between a noise and the surrounding sonic environment (how does the environment affect the noise)? And, third, how do we perceive and feel about the noise (i.e., to what extent can we accept the noise and its source)?

12.1.2.1   Physical properties of noise   The physical attributes of a noise — like those of any sound — involve frequency, intensity, temporal, and spatial characteristics. In terms of *frequency content,* noise can show many different forms. A noise can occur as a mixture of sounds spread over a wide spectral range without one overwhelming tonal presence (e.g., the static that exists between stations on a FM-band radio). Alternatively, a noise can have an essentially monotonic structure either with no other tonal presence or with a very weak wide-spectral-band background. Or the noise can be composed of multiple layers.

For instance, some narrow frequency band sounds may be superimposed over a less powerful, but still discernible, background consisting of a wide spectral range (e.g., the squeal of the brakes of a stopping car overlaying the general noise of the car itself).

A second important physical feature of a noise (and its source) concerns the *duration* of the noise. Does the noise happen *impulsively, intermittently,* or *continuously? Impulsive* noises commonly are isolated occurrences that happen randomly (across time). Such sudden noises arise often without forewarning and display intensities that are substantially greater than any sound levels underlying them (e.g., the backfire from a car). *Intermittence* implies that a noise repeats itself and has some sort of an identifiable repetition rate (which, for the sake of noise control, will require determination). One example of an intermittent noise is the "whooshing" of cars that pass by someone standing along the side of a highway. This phenomenon is especially noticeable when the cars are traveling at high velocities. A second example of a *repeating* noise that occurs *impulsively* is the sound that emanates from a typewriter when the keys or typing element strike(s) the paper held next to the roller. Each strike produces an impulsive noise whose pressure level is substantially greater than the usual ambient office noise level and that has a duration of a fraction of a second. A *continuous* duration suggests that the noise takes place over a sustained length of time (but it does not mean that the noise intensity is necessarily constant). Examples of continuous noise sources include air-conditioning systems in buildings and the general noise experienced when riding in a car at highway speeds.

A third physical property of noise involves the *sound pressure level of the noise and the extent to which this level fluctuates across time.* Some noise sources will create a comparatively uniform noise level (e.g., the noise inside a car), whereas other sources will emit noise at greatly variable levels. One typical urban noise problem that displays fluctuating noise levels occurs when buses move along urban streets, stopping and starting every few blocks to pick up and discharge passengers. The varying level of noise emitted by such buses can be strongly exacerbated if the street is inclined, requiring the bus driver to race the engine each time the bus pulls out from the street curb.

A fourth property of noise (and its source) concerns *how the noise appears spatially* (i.e., what is the character of the sound field that emanates from the source?) The two most common field types are those encountered with *point* and *line* sources. For the point source (e.g., an airplane or a factory, when each is heard from a distance), sound waves travel outward spherically. When these waves pass outward without interruption or reflection (as in an otherwise open field), the sound pressure level measured away from a point source will decrease by an increment of six decibels for each doubling of the distance from the source (see Figure 12.2). Alternatively, for a line source (e.g., a busy highway or a train with many cars), the noise waves will move out from the source with a cylindrical shape. For such line sources, when the noise waves can travel outward without interruption or reflection, the sound pressure level will decrease by an increment of three decibels for each doubling of the distance from the source (see Figure 12.3).

12.1.2.2 Perceptual properties of noise (or how physical properties can have subjective components)

Any noise is, first of all, a sound, with all the physical properties that exist for any sound. But what makes a sound appear noisy is the subjective reaction that a listener has toward it. Indeed, the "unwantedness" of a sound renders the sound noisy. The willingness of people to accept or reject the presence of noise (or its source) does not constitute a physical property of the noise. But physical attributes of a noise will generally affect whether we can accommodate the noise presence or not. When confronting the presence of noise (and determining how to resolve its existence), we will

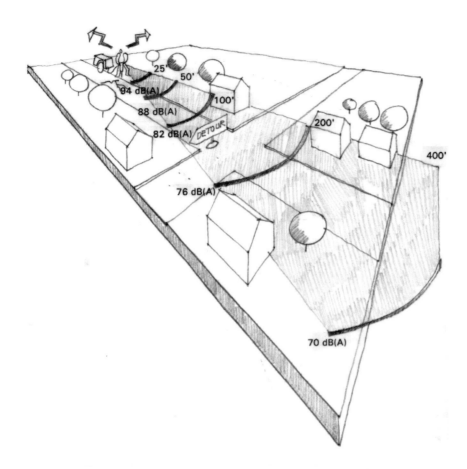

Figure 12.2 When a *point source* sounds in an open field its sound pressure level will decrease with increasing distance. The magnitude of the sound pressure level (SPL) decrease will be six decibels for each doubling of the distance away from the point source.

often need to show why the noise is unwanted and how it interferes with human activities (i.e., by identifying what physical aspects of the noise provoke our reactions to it).

One physical property of noise that invites a subjective response is *the time when the noise occurs*. Whether a noise happens during the day or at night or during the summertime or wintertime can markedly affect how the noise appears to a person. For instance, nighttime noise can disrupt sleep. Alternatively, daytime noise outside of a building may not readily enter the building during the winter. But during the summertime, when building occupants open windows to furnish natural ventilation, external noise can often interfere with activities inside the building.

A second quality of a noise that can affect the perception of noisiness is *whether an individual expects the noise to be present*. If a person lives near an airport and knows that the greatest number of aircraft departures happens between 7:00 and 8:00 AM, then that individual can try to accommodate such noise occurrence peaks (e.g., trying not to sleep during that hour). Thus, where noise happens according to some recognizable schedule,

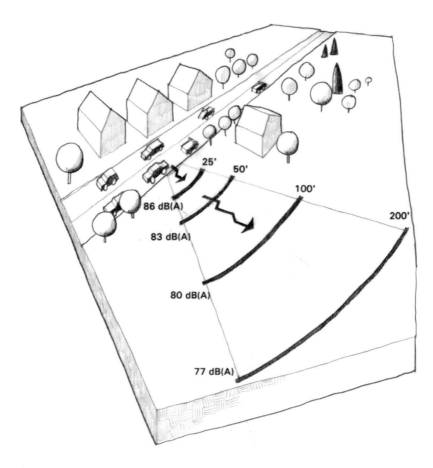

25'
50'
100'
200'

86 dB(A)

83 dB(A)

80 dB(A)

77 dB(A)

Figure 12.3 When a *line source* sounds in an open field its sound pressure level will decrease by three decibels for each doubling of the distance away from the line source.

establishing what that schedule is may enable the development of some strategy to minimize the adversity posed by the noise.

A third attribute of a noise source that can influence how one may regard the source is *the utility of the source.* For example, if noise is a by-product of a commercial or industrial process that exists for the good of the community, then people living and/or working near the noise-making facility will likely be more tolerant of the noise and will also be apt to regard it less harshly. So if the noise source is a manufacturing plant that provides local workers with jobs and that contributes taxes to the local economy (thereby supporting community services like schools, health care, and recreational facilities), then the benefits afforded by such a plant can outweigh a liability like excessive noise.

A fourth attribute of many noisy situations (and of the sources that produce the noise) concerns *the amount of control that affected people may exercise to limit the noise.* If an environment is noisy and people can do little to reduce the noise presence, often these people will fault the noise and strive to change it. But when a noise source is permitted to exist by common agreement (i.e., perhaps because it offers some significant benefit to those people), then the noise can seem much less egregious than it would to a visitor to the locale. Whereas the noise level can seem objectionable to an uninvolved person, the noise may appear less offensive to the inhabitants because these people have accepted it by mutual consent. One situation where higher noise levels are readily accepted by building occupants is in open-plan offices: background noise masks other potentially distracting noise, creating acoustic privacy for the occupants.

A fifth sound property that can influence the extent to which people will regard a sound as noisy is the *nature of the interference* that the noise imposes. If a noise disrupts normal conversation, then people may find the noise quite disagreeable. For instance, a noisy workplace can inhibit communication by speech, causing the workplace to be discomforting and even unsafe (e.g., in a noisy factory, a worker may not be able to advise another of some condition that might be injurious).

A sixth factor—that less directly describes any noise itself—may influence how greatly a person may regard a sound as noisy; this factor concerns *the natures of the personality, health, and emotional state of the listener.* For instance, how patient, obsessive, or committed a person may feel towards getting a task done—when working in a generally noise-ridden environment—can greatly influence how noisy the environment appears to the individual. An occupant who is already beset with hypertension or other symptoms of stress may be more likely to react strongly to noisiness. Alternatively, a person who is particularly desirous of completing some project may be better able to ignore the noise (or, indeed, may be wholly unaware of it).

For all of these attributes of noise that focus on people's reactions to and acceptance of the noise, the common component is the subjective response of the listener. The extent to which a sound appears noisy is thus based on the personal, *affective* reactions that an individual has when confronted with the sound.

The final property class of noise addresses the issue of *the content* of the noise. Some initial questions about noise content might ask whether *the noise has informational matter embodied within it, has recognizable repetitive components, or is strictly random in its organization.* For instance, music played over electric systems as background sound in offices, shopping malls, and recreational facilities often has discernible content and structure. When queried about such background sound, many people will report being able to

---

SIDEBAR 12.1 White and pink noise

White noise is broadband sound whose pressure level and spectral content—frequency components—vary without any apparent pattern. The variation does not have to be strictly random, but it may often be. The static produced by a FM-radio, when the station selector is tuned to a point between stations, is essentially white noise. Alternatively, *pink* noise is, to some extent, a subset of white noise. Pink noise is also broadband sound. But it has the property that—for specific frequency components present in the continuum of the noise—the pressure level of these components decrease as the frequency increases. Thus, for the higher-octave frequency components present in pink noise, these octaves will have lower pressure levels than will lower-octave frequency components. Pink noise generally appears less harsh and strident than white noise.

recognize specific musical phrases within the sound. For them, this background music can affect their work performance (i.e., their ability to concentrate on their work may be lessened), and sounds that might otherwise be pleasing become noise. Alternatively, the use of white or pink noise in these building types satisfies needs to have background noise and to ensure that this noise has no identifiable content or structure. Another content issue for noise is *whether the listener can identify the noise and the source from which the noise is emitted.* Being able to recognize a noise and its source may be essential when the noise occurs in a potentially injurious or dangerous setting (e.g., on an assembly line when a production step fails to operate properly or in the home when a smoke alarm emits its shrill sound). In both instances, being able to identify the noise and its source are imperative, if one is to continue safely.

So, thinking of noise as simply sound that is too loud may often lead to mistaking the significance of a noise and/or may cause adoption of improper corrective measures. When a designer or builder is asked to treat some noise in an existing environment, a careful analysis of the noise is an essential step for confronting the noise. Alternatively, if a designer or builder is planning to create a new building and anticipates that noise may be present in an environment in which the new building is to be created, then similarly the potential noise (and its sources) should be carefully considered.

12.1.2.3   Transmission mechanisms of noise through buildings   The general concern about noise transmission in buildings is that noise produced in one space will be perceivable in another space, leading to the disruption of activities that are occurring in the second space. There are two basic ways that noise can be transmitted through building envelopes: first, by *airborne routes* and, second, by the *impact loading* of rigid structural members.

Airborne noise transmission exists when airborne sound (noise) waves are produced by a source in one space and pass into an adjoining space or when noise is produced outside of a building and is audible inside the building. One means by which airborne noise transmission occurs is when there is a *continuous air path* between the space in which the noise source is present and the space in which noise (from this source) is observed. An example where a continuous air path can be found is when two adjacent rooms both open onto a common hallway. Airborne noise can pass from one room into the hallway and then enter the second room from the hallway. Alternatively, airborne noise transmission will likely still be observable when the hallway doors for these rooms are closed, but gaps are present between the bottoms of the doors and the floor. Thus, even with closed doors, a continuous air path will exist from the interior of the noise source room to the interior of the receiving room. Other examples of continuous air paths that lead to noise transmission between spaces include the following: through *cracks or discontinuities* present between structural framing and door or window frames; through holes cut in horizontal or vertical planes to enable pipes or ducts to pass from one space to another; or through ducts that serve two or more spaces (i.e., noise from one room will pass into the duct, travel along the duct, and come out in another room).

A second mechanism by which airborne noise is transmitted from one space to another is the *diaphragmatic action* of flexible wall, floor, and ceiling assemblies. Generally, these building assemblies have internal structural members—like studs or joists—and are surfaced with panel compositions like gypsum wallboard, plaster-on-lath, or plywood. Airborne waves produced by a sound source in one room will strike a flexible wall, floor, or ceiling surface of the room, causing the surface panel to bow inward and outward (e.g., similar to a drumhead which oscillates when struck). The bowing of the surface panel creates pressure

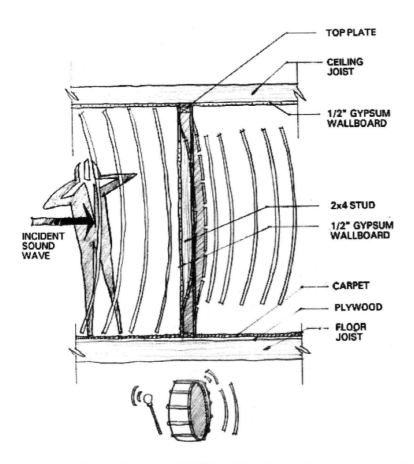

Figure 12.4 The diaphragmatic action of an envelope assembly is displayed here.

waves—sound waves—in the enclosed air space within the assembly (i.e., between the structural members and the surface panel). The pressure waves pass across this enclosed air space, striking the surface panel on the other side of the assembly and causing that panel to oscillate inward and outward. This second oscillating panel thus initiates pressure waves at the surface of the second room. These pressure waves then pass into the air of this second room, where occupants can perceive them as noise (see Figure 12.4). The internal structural members—studs or joists—will also conduct the noise energy from one surface panel to the other surface panel. Note that *there is no transfer of air between the two adjoining rooms.* Instead, there is a transfer of noise energy from one room to the second room through the common wall, floor, or ceiling assembly that separates the rooms.

The other major form of noise transmission occurring in buildings results from the impact loading of rigid structural components. Impact noise transmission happens when, at some location in a building, a structural component is induced to vibrate (e.g., by trying to drill into a concrete column, by dropping a heavy object onto a concrete floor, or by people running and jumping down a set of stairs). The vibration from this impact loading can cause sound waves to pass into the air of an immediately adjacent room, thus to be perceived as noise. Or the vibrational energy created by the impact loading can traverse some distance in the rigid structure and initiate sound waves at some remote location(s) throughout the building. The sound waves that enter into the air of some distant room will be heard there as noise. So, for instance, in a multistory, rigid-frame building, someone drilling into the frame on one floor might be the source of noise for occupants two or three or more stories away. Such passage of vibrational energy from impact loading can move horizontally, as well as vertically, throughout a building. This impact-induced noise transmission is often referred to as being *structure-borne* (i.e., in contrast to airborne noise transmission).

Comparing these two noise transmission mechanisms—airborne and structure-borne—the typical sources that create airborne transmission usually display comparatively lower power than the impact-loading sources. But the airborne sources will often persist for relatively longer time periods than the impact-loading sources (unless the impact source is indeed something like the concrete drill suggested above). So, in summary, noise from impact-loading sources will commonly appear more intense and impulsive; noise from airborne sources generally will demonstrate comparatively lower pressure levels and will more likely be continuous.

12.1.2.4 Noise rating schemes Noise is disruptive and adversely affects intended or required behaviors. It can also be annoying, causing those who hear it to experience dissatisfaction and even anger with their environment. The physical properties of noise—as described in Section 12.1.2.1—show that it can have great variability in its temporal character, magnitude, spectral content, and even when its peaks happen. Whether we consider community noise or noise within a building, being able to describe the character of noise is an important capability (e.g., for evaluating the extent of noise; for determining what actions must be taken to reduce noise; or perhaps even for predicting community or occupant reaction to noise). Any description of noise presence in an external or internal environment should thus correlate with how people respond to—feel about—noise.

In this section we will describe a series of noise rating schemes that are employed to characterize noise that exists in *community* settings. These noise ratings have two purposes: to describe the noise physically, and to relate the noise to some aspect of human perception or experience (i.e., how a typical person would likely feel about some noise condition). Indeed, the physical description should provide information about the amount of energy produced by a source or measured at some location, the length of time that the source endures or that noise can be measured, or the times of the day and/or night when noise occurs. Regarding people's perception of noise, Schultz has written that various schemes can predict how people will react to noise events. The three categories of rating schemes he identifies include those that indicate *interference with speech intelligibility;* those that characterize noise in terms of *how loud it appears;* and those that suggest *how likely people will be annoyed* by the noise presence. These three categories can thus serve as the three dimensions for people experiencing community noise.[3] The interference of noise with speech intelligibility can best be shown by finding the Articulation Index or Speech Interference Level for some situation and comparing the value with AI or SIL numbers suggested for speech or privacy conditions (see Table 11.2 or Figure 11.13). The loudness of noise is most easily described using the dB(A) or dB(C) scales (see Section 10.6).

However, determining whether some noise will annoy people or the degree of annoyance people will feel toward noise can be shown from measures like the *Perceived Noise Level* (PNL) or any of a series of time-based procedures like the *Day-Night Average Noise Level* (LDN) or the *Noise Exposure Forecast* (NEF). Further information about measures like the PNL, LDN, and NEF will be presented in the following paragraphs.

The A-weighted scale is widely used to describe *single-event* noise (i.e., as if taking a "snapshot" of a noisy experience). But when noise occurs over some period of time and significant variations exist in the characteristics of the noise, then other means for describing the noise experience are needed. Three groups of devices are used for reporting on community noise experienced at some location: those that describe the *total noise energy measured;* those that indicate the *amount of time* during which noise of some magnitude is found; and those that report on the *number of noise events* — how many discrete times — for which some noise level is exceeded. Each of these three groups of noise descriptors is commonly reported for 24-hour periods (although shorter or longer time periods may also be cited). Note, also, that most of these *total noise energy* rating devices use the A-weighting scale as the measurement basis.

For describing the total noise energy measured at a site, the basic reporting device is called the *Equivalent Sound (Noise) Level* (and is abbreviated as either L$_{eq}$ or LEQ). Establishing the Equivalent Sound (Noise) Level involves two steps. First, all the noise energy received by a measurement sensor at some location is summed. Then, this sum is divided by the time over which the measurements have been conducted. The noise energy is sensed

---

SIDEBAR 12.2 Working with A-weighted sound pressure levels

In Section 10.6 we have written about measuring sound (and noise). There, we discussed the use of weighting scales—especially, the A- and C-weighting measures—for describing sounds that have energy spread over wide spectral ranges (i.e., such as that over which human hearing occurs). Of these scales the most commonly employed is the *A-scale*.

The wide acceptance and use of the A-weighted scale is based on two facts. First, establishing weighted scale values occurs by taking energy spread over the spectral range and summing this energy to derive a representative single number (that can function as a useful, quick description). Second, the scale approximates the human hearing response by deemphasizing the lower frequency sounds (which are less well-heard by the human auditory system) and by permitting the middle and higher frequency sounds to contribute without penalty to the overall rating scale. The A-scale, because of its apparently good approximation to how human hearing occurs, provides a good correlation with both one's sensing of the loudness of a noise and the degree of interference that noise can cause for speech communication.

In fact, the Speech Interference Level (SIL)—see Section 11.2.4.2—can be predicted approximately

when the A-weighted measurement of noise has been established. The following relationship can be used for this purpose:

$$SIL = L_A - 7$$

where L$_A$ = the A-weighted sound level in decibels. Note that the degree of approximation between the SIL and the A-weighted sound level will depend on the spectral composition of the noise. Similarly, values for the Articulation Index (AI)—also see Section 11.2.4.2—are closely related to A-weighted measurements. But how well the A-weighted scale correlates to people's annoyance with noise depends on factors beyond simple loudness. These factors will be identified in the Section 12.2.1.

The A-weighting scale does however have some limitations. First, when a sound (or noise) consists principally of low frequency components, then the A-weighting will underestimate the actual energy presence. And, second, when the sound (or noise) includes higher-intensity narrow-spectrum tones or monotones overlaying a lower-intensity wide spectrum, the A-weighting will be biased by these superimposed tones and will likely display inaccurate readings.

on an instant-by-instant basis and is recorded using an A-weighted scale. As such, the LEQ describes the *average noise level* for the time period during which the measurements are performed.[4]

One alternative means for reporting on the total noise energy measured is performed using the *Sound Exposure Level* (SEL). The SEL is found by summing all of the noise energy measured for some period of time and then determining a noise amount *occurring for one second,* which would be equal to the total energy found for the measurement time period. This SEL scheme is also known as the *Single Event Noise Exposure Level* (SENEL).[5] One application for the SEL scheme is the description of the amount of noise energy created by an airplane during its take-off or its approach and landing. Commonly-observed SEL's for commercial jet airplanes from take-offs range between 90 to 110 dB(A), when measured at distances of about 4500 meters (15,000 feet) from the roll start and about 500 meters (1600 feet) from the flight path (as an airplane ascends near the measurement site).[6]

Two modifications of the LEQ are more commonly used to report on community noise, particularly when the noise events occur in the evening or night (i.e., the times of the 24-hour day when noise can be the most disrupting or annoying). The first of these alternatives is known as the *Day-Night Average Noise Level* (and is normally written as L_{dn} or LDN). The basis for the LDN descriptor is that a "penalty" is built into this reporting device for noise events measured between the hours of 2200 to 0700 (10 PM to 7 AM). For noise events recorded during these hours, an incremental penalty of 10 dB(A) is added. Typical values for the LDN are shown in Table 12.1.

A second alternative for reporting on community noise observed over time is identified as the Community Noise Equivalent Level (and is designated as either CNEL or L_{cen}). The CNEL is a derivative of the LDN and is used to impose an additional penalty on noise that occurs during the daily hours of 1900 to 2200 (7 PM to 10 PM). The noise level increment that is added to noise measured between these hours is 5 dB(A).[7]

TABLE 12.1
TYPICAL DAY-NIGHT AVERAGE NOISE LEVEL (LDN) VALUES
FOR A VARIETY OF COMMUNITY NOISE EXPERIENCES

SETTING (OUTDOOR LOCATION)	LDN VALUE (IN DB(A))
Ambient wilderness	35
Rural wilderness area	39
Agricultural crop land	44
Wooded residential area	49
Urban row housing on major avenue	68
Urban high density apartment	78
Downtown with some construction activity	79
Site 0.75 mile away from touchdown point at a major airport	86
Apartment next to freeway	87

Source: Protective Noise Levels – Condensed Version of EPA Levels Document [PB82-138827], prepared by the U.S. Environmental Protection Agency, (Washington, D.C.: National Technical Information Service, U.S. Department of Commerce, November 1978), page 8.

The second group of rating schemes used for reporting on noise presence are those which portray the amount of time that noise of some level is experienced. Two alternative schemes are employed: TA, which is *the total time in minutes for which a specific noise level, measured with the A-weighting scale, is exceeded during some reporting period* (e.g., a 24-hour day); and L_x, which is *the percentage of time for which some noise level is exceeded during a reporting period* (when also measured with the A-weighting scale).[8] The TA scheme is usually written as *TA N,* where *N* is a noise level specified for study (e.g., *TA 70* indicates the total time in minutes that the ambient noise level at the measuring location exceeds 70 dB(A)).

The second rating scheme, L_X, is often identified as the *statistical sound (noise) level.* Establishing the statistical sound (noise) level requires three steps. First, minute-by-minute noise level values are measured using the A-weighted scale. Second, these minute-by-minute values are sorted by magnitude (from the highest to the lowest). Third, these ranked values are grouped into *decile* "bins." When the values that comprise the highest 10 percent of the minute-by-minute measurements are established, then the level value that separates this highest decile from the next lower is designated as the $L10$ noise level. Similarly, the $L50$ and $L90$ values are commonly measured for noise presences and reported along with the $L10$ value (i.e., for the highest 50 percent and 90 percent magnitudes, respectively).

Finally, a number of rating schemes are employed to report on the number of times that some particular noise level is exceeded. The two most commonly used schemes of this type are the *Composite Noise Rating* (CNR) and the *Noise Exposure Forecast* (NEF). Both of these schemes are employed primarily for describing noise presence around airports. These two schemes show reasonably good correlations with community reactions to noisy conditions, particularly as indicated by the extent to which people will be annoyed by aircraft noise. The numerical value for each scheme is found by mathematically deriving the *noisiness*[9] expressed in terms of the *apparent* loudness levels of the several aircraft that may operate at an airport with the number of fly-overs for each aircraft type.

Note that the Composite Noise Rating (CNR) and the Noise Exposure Forecast (NEF) and the two schemes involving time-related penalties—LDN and CNEL—are useful in estimating the *likely degree of annoyance* that will be experienced by communities exposed to noise. Thus, the utility of these two rating schemes—CNR and NEF—is that their applications foster land use planning (i.e., by helping to identify what activities will be compatible with the noise levels that are present at various locations around an airport).

In summary, all of these various rating procedure can offer insight about community reactions to noise presence. No one procedure is uniquely the optimal choice for the wide range of noise sources that exist around us (e.g., noise from ground vehicles, aircraft, industry, the community generally, and so forth). Lastly, a variety of studies have compared the utility of selected schemes and developed algebraic relationships between the numerical values established by the schemes.[10]

Section 12.2 | HOW DOES NOISE AFFECT US?

Noise is one of the basic ingredients of urban and suburban life in the 21st century, whether we speak of the industrialized nations or the developing countries. However, this statement does not mean that noise has been a recent invention. Instead, noise in urban areas has been present at least as long ago as the early days of the Roman Empire. Some authors of that time wrote about the noise created by metal-covered chariot wheels clanking along over the cobblestone streets of Rome in the 1st century, AD. Also, the hubbub found in the bazaars and trading areas of the urban centers around the Mediterranean Sea was said to be contentious and cacophonous.

Because noise is so pervasive and produced by so many sources, anyone concerned with the creation of the built environment must confront the question of the effects noise will have on people who work and live in its presence. The professional literature of the last 25 years has provided extensive treatment of this question. Here, we will provide a brief synopsis of that discussion.

The most often cited effects of noise upon people include the following results. First, noise interferes with the ability to communicate with speech. Second, people exposed to noise will experience auditory fatigue (and a temporary hearing threshold shift). Third, when noise has a great enough intensity and one's exposure to it is prolonged, the noise experience can cause the permanent loss of hearing. Fourth, nighttime noise will result in the loss of sleep. Fifth, noise — whether present during the day or night — can contribute to stress-related illnesses and can increase the tendencies toward the development of various maladies. Sixth, noise in the workplace can cause reductions in the performance of skilled tasks (both in terms of production quality and work rates). And, seventh, community noise is often noted as a major source of annoyance for residents exposed to the noise.

Formal complaints brought by residents are further evidence that noise creates difficulties and unpleasantness for those exposed to it. Additionally, legal action is increasingly being initiated against the purveyors of noise, and declines in property values are being reported for once-quiet locales that are newly subjected to noise. Finally, noise is frequently identified as a prime negative factor when "quality-of-life" surveys are conducted.[11]

12.2.1 DISTINGUISHING BETWEEN *LOUDNESS, NOISINESS,* AND *ANNOYANCE*

These three terms are widely used to describe noise, and they are often taken to be interchangeable. But in the professional literature, these words are employed to express different conditions. What sets apart the three terms are the steps involved in perceiving a sound and deciding that it is noise. *Loudness* is what one *perceives* the intensity or pressure of a sound to be (see Section 11.1.2). Loudness describes the magnitude of the sound stimulus as we hear it. Thus, what we declare to be the loudness of a sound is our *subjective estimate* of the amount of energy that the sound displays. This estimate will likely differ somewhat from person to person. The *noisiness* of a sound is the quality that makes a sound seem "noisy." Essentially, noisiness refers to the physical properties — identified in Section 12.1.2.1 — that characterize noise (e.g., spectral content, duration, fluctuating pressure levels, and so forth). For instance, when a sound has a too-strong component in the low-frequency range or occurs with an intermittence that makes it seem abrupt and discordant, then the sound will appear to be noisy. *Annoyance* is the feeling that a person may have when exposed to nuisance noise (i.e., noise that is bothersome or disrupting). How annoying a noise may appear commonly is directly related to *how much* the noise is unwanted. The extent that a noise interferes with the performance of some activity (e.g., conversation or sleeping) will determine how much annoyance a person experiences in that situation.[12]

As the pressure level of a sound (or noise) is increased, so will the loudness of the sound increase. For example, when you turn up the output volume of a radio, then its loudness will be greater. If a sound appears noisy — has characteristics that make it seem noisy to the listener — and its pressure level is increased, then the sound will have greater loudness and will also have greater noisiness. But a sound can appear loud (or louder) and still not be noisy. What separates the loudness and the noisiness of a sound is founded within our acquisition of the sound. As a model of this acquisition, we can identify the following basic steps:

| sound production | → | receipt by auditory system | → | perception and cognition | → | commencement of activity in response |

Determining the loudness of a sound employs the first two steps in this model, whereas assessing the noisiness of the sound requires at least the first three steps and may include the fourth.[13] Thus, the mechanism that a person uses to establish whether a sound is noisy or not involves a comparative process by which the individual not only hears the sound but also analyzes it sufficiently — mostly by unconscious means — to reach an assessment about its noisiness.

The properties of a noise that will make it annoying to the listener are those that we identified in Section 12.1.2.2 as largely being of a personal nature. When noises *intrude upon and disrupt* activities, we most often regard these noises as annoying. Noises that *occur unexpectedly* — that startle us — are also annoying. For example, a dog's bark and the sound of a book falling off of a table are both impulsive noises whose suddenness can be unnerving. Annoyance is a frequent result when *our mood or emotional state does not enable us to respond with grace* to a noise. If we are anxious about work we are doing (i.e., we are concerned about completing it or about its quality), then noisy sounds will more likely be annoying. When noises *are emitted from sources that we cannot control* — for example, noise produced by public transportation vehicles — we will often find them to be annoying. Lastly, an important determinant of whether a noise will be annoying is *the content (and, possibly, the meaning)* of the noise. If our child cries out, we will likely be tolerant of the intrusive sound. But if someone else's child cries out, then we might be more likely to regard such an utterance as noise and feel that it is annoying.[14]

Some purely physical properties of a noise can influence the degree to which we find the noise annoying. High-magnitude sound pressure levels will cause greater feelings of annoyance than will sounds with lower sound pressure levels. Additionally, if the sound pressure level grows as a listener hears the sound, the listener's annoyance often will increase. It is generally true that high-frequency sounds will be more annoying than low-frequency sounds, if both have the same loudness. Further, if the noise overlays (or is background to) useful sound, then the noise can be especially annoying (e.g., suppose you are listening to your favorite radio program and your dog starts barking, thus masking an important program segment).

The development of people's annoyance with community, industrial, or vehicular noise is a topic that has been addressed in a number of studies conducted during the past 25 years. One example of such work is a study performed by Schomer for a municipal airport in Illinois.[15] This airport was located at the eastern perimeter of the built-up area of a town. With the exception of a small commercial strip located near the airport, most of the land use in the town was residential with single-family houses placed on half-acre lots. The residential zone lay primarily to the west and north of the airport. The airport had two runways, one of which was used by medium-sized commercial and military jet and prop-jet airplanes and the other of which was used almost entirely by small private propeller-driven airplanes. Helicopters also used the airport with a limited frequency.

Noise level measurements were taken southwest of the airport where a new residential development was being projected. Measurements were also made along routes used by aircraft during take-offs and landings. These measurements showed Day-Night Average Noise Levels (LDN) ranging from 55 to 66 dB. Current residents of the area southwest of the airport were surveyed to determine their attitudes about the noise created by the use of the aircraft (and by other nonrelated sources). The primary result of the survey showed a good correlation between the LDN values and the number of people who were highly annoyed by the aircraft noise: *as the LDN increased, so did the number of highly annoyed people.* Additionally, computer-based predictions of what noise levels would likely be found for the study area provided good comparisons with the measured noise levels. Schomer wrote that this result had also been reported in earlier studies. Thus, the LDN rating scheme (and the LDN noise zone maps that can often be generated for airports using computer simulation programs) served as good indicators for assessing — predicting — likely future community reactions and making land-use planning decisions.

Schultz has conducted a second study of community annoyance that is widely cited in the literature.[16] In this research Schultz compared the results of 11 previous surveys that had been undertaken to evaluate community attitudes toward transportation noise. These 11 surveys had been done in five European countries and in the United States. Throughout, these surveys focused on noise created by aircraft, street traffic, and railroad vehicles.

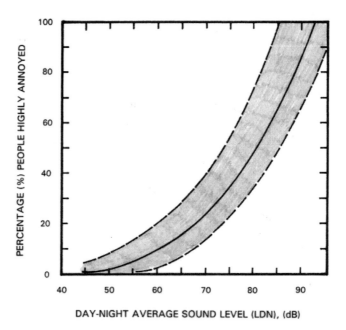

Figure 12.5 This graph shows the results of Schultz's analysis of 11 studies about the reaction of people exposed to noise (from both North America and Europe). The curves display the correlation between the *Day-Night Average Noise Level* (LDN) and the percentage of people who were highly annoyed by the noise. The solid line indicates the average (mean) correlation between the LDN and the percentage of highly annoyed people. The dashed lines present values that are one standard deviation away from the average correlation. This graph appeared in a paper by Schultz, T.J., "Synthesis of social surveys on noise annoyance," *Journal of the Acoustical Society of America,* 64(2), August 1978, pages 377–405. Permission to reprint this graph has been granted by the Acoustical Society of America.

The comparison and analysis of the results of these surveys were undertaken especially to establish the extent with which people were annoyed by noise. From this synthesis of the 11 surveys, Schultz found that a direct relationship between the percentage of people who were highly annoyed by the transportation noises and the Day-Night Average Noise Levels (LDN). This relationship is shown in the graph of Figure 12.5 and demonstrates that *as the LDN increases, so also will the percentage of people who will be "highly annoyed" by the noise.*

In a subsequent paper Kryter further analyzed results from the various studies Schultz employed in his paper cited above. Then, Kryter developed a series of correlations, one of which is produced here as Figure 12.6. This second graph (Figure 12.6) shows relationships between LDN (for two vehicular types), the percentage of the population annoyed when exposed to an LDN amount, and four categories of annoyance. These two graphs (Figures 12.5 and 12.6) display somewhat different numerical relationships between the LDN numbers and the percentages of annoyance. But, more importantly, the two graphs do exhibit similar trends in the relationships, suggesting that both graphs present good information about people's responses to community noise.[17]

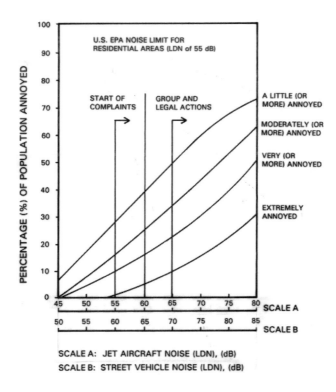

Figure 12.6 This graph displays results of analyses performed by Kryter relating the percentage of people who were annoyed by two types of traffic noise versus the *Day-Night Average Noise Level* (LDN) (as an indicator of the noise levels experienced by these people). This graph appeared in the paper by Kryter, K.D., "Community annoyance from aircraft and ground vehicle noise," *Journal of the Acoustical Society of America,* 72(4), October 1982, pages 1222–1242. Permission to reprint this graph has been granted by Dr. Kryter and the Acoustical Society of America.

Lastly, two recent studies have explored whether cultural differences between peoples will influence the degree of annoyance felt by people who are exposed to noise. In the first study researchers contrasted attitudes of residents of apartment buildings in Germany and Japan who experienced community noise—particularly, noise caused by neighbors.[18] This study found that the German occupants felt greater annoyance with noise created by their neighbors than did the Japanese. The Germans were described as being "more sensitive" to noise and more likely to initiate corrective actions. In the second study the scientists examined behavioral patterns, "ways of thinking" about noise, and the feelings of annoyance accompanying exposure to noise, for residents of apartment buildings in the United States, England, and Japan.[19] The results of this latter study indicated that the English and American residents had more liberal attitudes about the existence of community noise and were generally more tolerant of noise caused by neighbors. Alternatively, the Japanese occupants indicated greater apprehension about causing noise themselves and were more likely to bear the costs involved in creating dwellings with lower rates of noise transmission. The authors of this second study concluded that their studies showed differing concepts of and attitudes about community noise for the nationalities examined. These second authors also suggested that developing international standards for noise control (as means to reduce occupant annoyance with noise) would probably not be successful.

Independently of these two latter studies, Job has examined a series of previous reports concerning people's reactions primarily to traffic and aircraft noise sources.[20] In this review the author cited studies involving European, North American, Japanese, and Australian nationalities. Generally, Job found similar reactions to noise exposures for the several nationalities, although there was evidence that differences did exist in noise sensitivities and in attitudes about noise when comparing the various nationalities. Job's results that indicate differences in national sensitivities and attitudes converge with the two studies cited in the preceding paragraph.

12.2.2 THE EFFECTS OF NOISE ON SPEECH INTELLIGIBILITY

Whether we consider the home, the workplace, or some outdoor location in a town or cityscape, the presence of noise can interfere with the hearing of spoken words. For any speech communication when noise is present, there are three major parameters that determine how well speech can be understood: the ratio of the pressure level of the speech signal versus the pressure level of the background noise for the range of frequencies over which speech occurs; whether the spoken words have a variety of spectral components (phonemes) occurring across the frequency bandwidth of speech; and what the distance is between the speaker and the listener. Three other important parameters include the degree of complexity of the speech; whether a verbal context exists so that individual words can be deduced from some continuum of speech; and whether the speaker and listener face each other. Of these six parameters, the most crucial is the maintenance of *adequately high speech-to-noise level ratios* for the spectral components.

Pearsons et al. have found that when this ratio was 10 dB or greater, high sentence intelligibility would usually be present (i.e., that nearly 100 percent of all spoken sentences would be understood by listeners).[21] Alternatively, a general rule-of-thumb offered by Kryter suggests that noise levels above 45 dB(A) can cause speech interference when the noise is steady; and peak noise levels above 55 dB(A) can interfere with speech when the noise has variable levels.[22]

Webster has shown more explicitly how the first three parameters cataloged above interact to control speech intelligibility (see Figure 12.7).[23] Generally, the graph shows that if intelligibility is to be maintained while the ambient noise level increases, either the distance between a speaker and listener must be lessened or the speaker must raise his/her voice level. The numerical information listed beneath the labels for the abscissa identify what values the Articulation Index will have—when speaker and listener are three feet (0.9 m) apart—for the various ambient noise levels and the four voice levels.

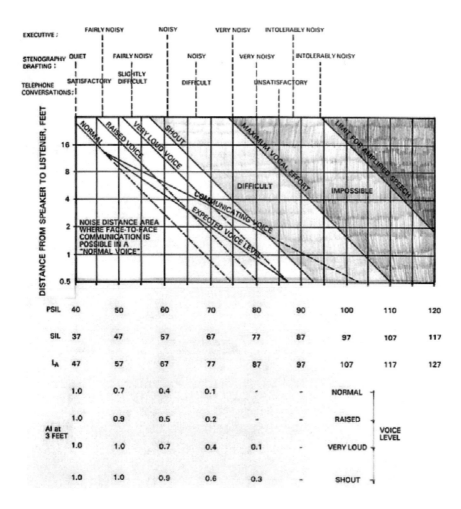

Figure 12.7 This graph by Webster shows a series of subjective evaluations of noise and relates a number of indices that are used to characterize noise levels. This graph appeared in a paper by Webster, J.C., "Effects of noise on speech intelligibility," in Ward, W.D., and J.E. Fricke (editors), *Noise as a Public Health Hazard*, (Washington, D.C.: The American Speech and Hearing Association, 1969), pages 49–73; the graph appears on page 69. Permission to reprint this graph has been granted by Dr. Webster and the American Speech-Language-Hearing Association (© American Speech-Hearing-Language Association).

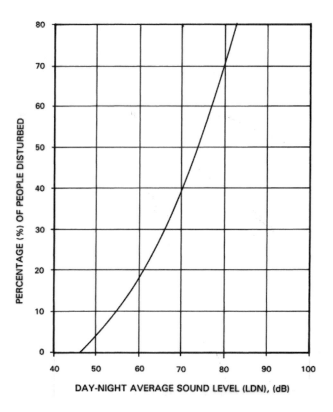

Figure 12.8 This graph was prepared by Schultz to show how noise interferes with *speech.* The graph relates the *Day-Night Average Noise Level* (LDN) versus the percentage of people disturbed while attempting to understand speech that is embedded in background noise. This graph appeared in a paper by Schultz, T.J., "Synthesis of social surveys on noise annoyance," *Journal of the Acoustical Society of America,* 64(2), August 1978, pages 377–405; the graph was printed on page 388. Permission to reprint this graph has been granted by the Acoustical Society of America.

Schultz has also developed a graph demonstrating how noise will interfere with or will disturb conversations.[24] This graph (shown as Figure 12.8) relates noise levels — expressed in terms of Day-Night Average Noise Levels or LDN — and the percentage of people who will be disturbed by the noise levels. This graph is a synthesis of results from several European and American studies, all of which were conducted to examine the effects of transportation noise (as described in Section 12.2.1).

The other physical property of noise that can have a significant effect on speech intelligibility is the spectral composition of the noise. The principal issue about the spectral composition concerns the extent that noise can *mask* spoken sounds. In Section 11.2.3.2 (and Figures 11.8–11.10) we have described the spectral content of speech (at various voice levels): speech occurs over a wide spectral range with greater pressure levels exhibited in the lower middle frequencies for any particular voice level and lesser pressure levels at the low and high ends of this spectrum. Miller found that low-frequency noise does not mask speech until the pressure level of the low-frequency noise has been increased greatly. He also noted that mid-to-high-frequency noise will mask speech even at low pressure levels, but increases in these pressure levels for the mid-to-high-frequency noises did not appreciably heighten the masking effect. Indeed, noises that include higher-frequency components will more readily mask lower-frequency sounds, even when these higher-frequency components may have comparatively lesser pressure levels (than the lower-frequency sounds). A third observation that Miller made was that low-frequency noise was less annoying to those trying to converse than was higher-frequency noise and that intermittent, variable noise was more annoying than continuous noise.[25] Later work by Pickett and Kryter supported Miller's findings. Writing about how the spectral characteristics of noise affect speech intelligibility, these authors stated that low-frequency noise had comparatively little effect on the understanding of speech when speech intelligibility was high; when intelligibility had already been lessened, then the presence of low-frequency noise reduced intelligibility further; high-frequency noise curtailed high levels of intelligibility (i.e., when conditions would otherwise have provided good hearing); and when intelligibility was already less good, then high-frequency noise had a smaller influence on understanding speech.[26]

Several corrective actions can be taken to reduce the effect of noise on the understanding of speech. First, *increase the sound pressure level of the spoken words* (either by having the speaker raise his/her voice level, by using a passive device such as cupping one's hands together or employing a megaphone, or by using electronic amplification. Second, *decrease the distance between the speaker and the listener.* Third, *reduce the sound pressure level of the noise* (by imposing controls on its source, by isolating the source, or by separating the speaker and listener from the noise). Fourth, wherever possible, *simplify the message content.* Fifth, *reinforce the spoken message using alternative means of communication* (e.g., using written words or complementary body motions). And, sixth, *enhance the consonant phonemes, specifically, by electronic means* (i.e., amplify the middle-to-upper-frequency phonemes that are the most greatly overridden by even low to moderate noise levels and that are essential for the promotion of speech intelligibility).

12.2.3 THE EFFECTS OF NOISE ON HUMAN HEARING AND HEALTH

The issue of how the hearing and health of human beings are affected by noise has been widely discussed in the popular and technical literature at least since the late 1940s. For instance, Kryter in his book *The Effects of Noise on Man* (2nd edition) cites 244 references—through 1983—for the chapter that considers how noise affects health.[27] The reason so much attention has been paid to this issue is that noise presence contributes to— and may directly cause—such personal failings as hearing loss, stress-related maladies, and sleep loss (and its attendant reduction in work efficiency and performance).

Unfortunately, the extent to which prolonged noise exposure directly causes physiological or psychological stress and related maladies is not still well established from the research that has been conducted to-date on this subject. Kryter has suggested that there can reasonably be two fundamental hypotheses about the relationship of noise and nonauditory system damage for human beings: the extensive presence of noise can indeed create damage to the human physiology; or the presence of noise does not create damage, but simply exacerbates existing problems.[28] As an example, Cohen and Weinstein have noted in a review paper that industrial workers exposed to job-related noise have been found to experience increased anxiety and feelings of psychological stress.[29] However, these authors also note that at the same time these workers experienced the job-related noise, they had also been subjected to increased task demands and increased risks associated with fulfilling these tasks (i.e., thus leaving open the root causes of the anxiety and stress).

Indeed, Cohen and Weinstein present a number of other instances where researchers have found apparent linkages between prolonged noise exposures and various health and mental health problems. But for nearly all of the studies these two authors cite, Cohen and Weinstein have written that either methodological failings exist in the cited works or that other explanations could be reasonably suggested to account for the various researchers' results. Additionally, the two authors note, in the latter instance, that these other explanations had not been treated in the cited studies.[30] Among the various studies which Cohen and Weinstein examined in their review paper, a number of studies considered physiological and psychological maladies that were thought to be noise-induced. Among the range of maladies identified were the following ailments: increased incidence of nausea, rapid mood shifts, headaches, and anxiety in industrial workers; higher admission rates to mental health facilities for individuals living in areas affected by aircraft noise levels; various cardiovascular problems, including increased blood pressure, reduced circulation rates, higher cholesterol levels, and cardiac morbidity; increased presence of gastrointestinal problems; and so forth! Again, Cohen and Weinstein did not state that these various maladies were not noise-induced. Rather, they have written that insufficient evidence existed to support the hypotheses and claims made by the several researchers. Clearly, as these maladies can be of serious consequence to individuals who experience them, the potential linkage between prolonged noise exposure and the acquisition of these maladies must be studied further and the hypotheses and claims substantiated or not. Until such additional work has been performed and more *reliable* answers established, the two fundamental hypotheses suggested by Kryter above will remain unresolved.

Two topics relating noise exposure and health problems, for which significant research has been conducted and well-established views do exist, are *hearing loss is caused by exposure to prolonged, excessive noise,* and *people's sleep is disrupted by community noise.* We will discuss these two topics in the paragraphs below.

12.2.3.1   Hearing loss from noise exposure   Exposure to excessive noise can produce either *temporary* or *permanent* hearing loss, which will commonly be manifested by a raised threshold (of audibility). Thus, the lowest sound pressure levels for which sound can be heard will be increased above the population-wide *threshold of audibility.* So, for a sound to be heard by someone with reduced acuity, the sound will have to be more powerful than a sound at the nominal audibility threshold. In addition, for persons with hearing loss, what is actually heard can often appear distorted.

Whether the loss of hearing acuity due to noise exposure is *temporary or permanent* depends on the sound pressure levels of noise, the spectral content of noise, the duration of exposure, how many times one is exposed to noise, and other factors including whether hearing protection devices are employed and what the capabilities of these devices are. The period of temporary hearing loss can be greatly variable, extending from a few hours or days to several weeks. The extent of hearing loss — temporary or permanent — can be an increase in an individual's audibility threshold of a few decibels or as much as thirty to forty decibels.

Four types of hearing loss conditions are found throughout the industrialized nations. The first of these conditions is *presbycusis,* which is the gradual deterioration in hearing acuity that occurs with *advancing age.* This loss in acuity is marked by the increase in the minimum threshold of audibility, a loss in frequency-selectivity, generally, and a loss in ability to sense higher-frequency sounds, particularly (see Section 11.1.1).[31] The second general condition is *sociocusis,* which is hearing loss resulting from exposure to *everyday living activities* (i.e., disregarding workplace noise exposures). Examples of noise leading to sociocusis are common urban street noise created by public transportation vehicles, building and road construction, noise from industrial plants, and heavily amplified music (such as one experiences at rock concerts and night clubs). The third hearing loss condition is *nosocusis,* which results from injuries to the auditory system and illnesses that can adversely affect the auditory system. Nosocusis can be produced by blows to the head—as may be suffered in boxing matches—or from various respiratory maladies such as those associated with allergic reactions to environmental substances. The fourth condition leading to hearing loss is that which is caused by *exposure to severe noise in the immediate workplace.* People in close proximity to jackhammers, various industrial plant machinery, aircraft engines, and other powerful noisemakers will often experience significant hearing loss during and after the time they are exposed to these sources (unless the workers wear protective hearing devices).[32]

Kryter has performed a major study of hearing loss caused by presbycusis, sociocusis, and nosocusis.[33] In the study he examined a number of surveys about hearing acuity that had previously been conducted in several countries. Among the findings of his examination were that the *threshold of audibility* was not dependent on either race or sex and that there was little difference in hearing acuity for these two major parameters across the populations studied. When the hearing acuity of *young people from a preindustrial society* (from the Sudan) was compared with *young people from industrialized Western societies,* little difference in acuities was indicated; but *when people of advanced age (55 years of age and older) for the two different societal groups were compared,* those from the preindustrialized society (the Sudanese) were shown to have substantially reduced hearing loss (i.e., their acuity was superior). *Women in industrialized societies* tend to show less evidence of sociocusis and nosocusis than do *men from the same societies.* And *factory workers* demonstrated substantially poorer hearing acuities—or greater hearing losses—than *other members of the industrialized societies.*

The consequences of these hearing loss conditions for designers and builders are three-fold. First, tendencies toward presbycusis and nosocusis cannot be mitigated in any significant way by environmental controls. Instead, only the effects of sociocusis can be reduced by careful noise control (and, thus, aspects of the environment should be planned to lower the everyday noise that causes sociocusis). Second, presbycusis is a fundamental condition of advancing age, and the built environment should be planned and constructed to augment hearing acuity, particularly where older users will be present (e.g., by reducing background noise levels, especially, and by promoting speech intelligibility conditions, generally). And, third, noise control in noisy industrial environments is essential (e.g., using built objects such as noise barriers and enclosures or personal devices such as earplugs and earmuffs).

12.2.3.2   The effects of noise on sleep   Environmental noise can have an adverse effect on both the duration of sleep and the ability to reach and sustain deep sleep (i.e., that experienced in the stage characterized by *rapid-eye-movement* (or REM) sleep).

Kryter has written that if sleep is to be undisturbed, *allowable noise levels* are—*for steady sources*—35 dB(A) and—*for the peak levels of varying sources*—45 dB(A).[34] Alternatively, Schultz in his major study examining the several surveys concerning the effects of transportation noise on people produced a graph—see Figure 12.9—relating Day-Night Average Noise Levels (LDN) versus the percentage of people whose sleep was disturbed by the attendant noise levels.[35]

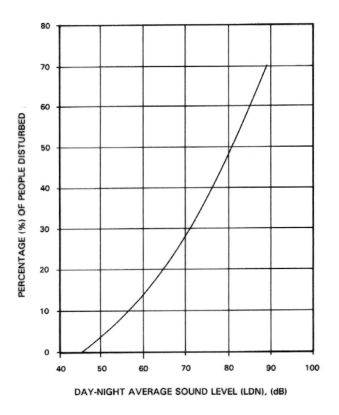

PERCENTAGE (%) OF PEOPLE DISTURBED

DAY-NIGHT AVERAGE SOUND LEVEL (LDN), (dB)

Figure 12.9 This graph is a companion to the one shown in Figure 12.8. Here, Schultz demonstrates how noise can interfere with *sleep*. Similar to Figure 12.8, the graph shows the relationship between the *Day-Night Average Noise Level* (LDN) and the percentage of people who reported being disturbed while attempting to sleep. This graph appeared in a paper by Schultz, T.J., "Synthesis of social surveys on noise annoyance," *Journal of the Acoustical Society of America,* 64(2), August 1978, pages 377–405. Permission to reprint this graph has been granted by the Acoustical Society of America.

The loss of sleep and the prevention of reaching and maintaining deep sleep—both which will result from excessive noise—was examined by an international research team working in several European countries. Wilkinson and Campbell[36] examined a series of adults living in single-family houses in two English cities who were exposed to comparatively high nighttime traffic noise. The average Equivalent Noise Level (LEQ) in the subjects' bedrooms for the normal sleep periods *at the beginning of the test period* was 46.6 dB(A) (with a range between 42 to 52). After this average noise level was established as a control condition, the windows in the subjects' bedrooms were changed from single-pane assemblies to double-pane assemblies. After these modifications the *new* average equivalent noise level in the bedrooms was 40.8 dB(A) (with a range between 36 to 47). Thus, the addition of the second pane of glass provided an average noise reduction of 5.8 dB(A). For the time periods with the two alternative glazing assemblies in place, the subjects were examined using various physiological, subjective, and work performance tests to assess how the change in the window assemblies affected their sleep (and, consequently, how well-rested the subjects were from their sleep).

The results of these tests showed that there was an apparent increase in the amount of deep sleep experienced by the subjects (i.e., following the change to double-pane assemblies); the subjects performed better on reaction-time tests (where such tests are considered to be good indicators of how alert people were during the testing period; thus, *better* performances demonstrated that good sleep patterns had been achieved on the nights preceding these reaction-time tests); and the subjects also stated that they slept better and that they experienced fewer awakenings.

A subsequent paper employed German adults as test subjects.[37] These people were residents of single-family urban housing units. The research design had the subjects sleep according to their normal practices for a "control" period during which the Equivalent Noise Levels (LEQ) in the bedrooms were measured. The Equivalent Noise Levels were found to range from 35.4 to 48.2 dB(A). Then, for a test period half of the subjects were asked to wear earplugs and the other half were requested to sleep with the windows of their bedrooms opened (i.e., this latter group had normally slept with their windows closed). For this second half group the average LEQ increase resulting from the window openings was 6.5 dB(A). Following this test period, a second "control" period was carried out during which the subjects were asked to return to their previously normal sleep practices. Consistent with the first study the subjects were tested using physiological, subjective, and work performance procedures.

Selected results from this study included that sleep onset was delayed for the entire group of subjects. Also, the length of time required to pass from light sleep into deep sleep was increased for the entire test group. The sleep quality was reported as being worse for the group who slept with their windows opened. And the reaction time was longer for the entire test group (when work performance test times were compared for the "nights before" and the "mornings after"). These researchers then stated that the quality of sleep is determined more by factors of personality and personal differences (e.g., age and sex) than by tangential factors like noise. But, when the scientists compared their results with those of the other researchers for this European consortium, the overall conclusions of the total project were that the noise presences caused a decrease in deep sleep, more wakefulness, increases in reaction time (on performance tests conducted during the mornings which followed nights with noise exposure), and a decrease in sleep quality. Another overall conclusion was that a strong correlation existed between the Equivalent Noise Levels (LEQ's) and the heart rate of the test subjects and the degree of variability in their heart rates (i.e., higher LEQ's produced greater heart rate variability). A final observation was that *no habituation occurred* for the test subjects: *thus, people still reacted to noise even after prolonged exposure to it over periods of several years.*

12.2.4 THE EFFECTS OF NOISE ON WORK PERFORMANCE

The popular conception that noise presence in the workplace will significantly impede the successful conduct of work tasks appears not to be supported by the technical literature addressing this topic. Indeed, the literature about this topic is as extensive as the writings about the effects of noise on nonauditory human systems and health. But, similar to the studies that seek to relate noise presence and health effects, research on how noise presence can influence work performance has also produced ambiguous results and contradictory reports. Several review papers about this subject have all noted the comparative scarcity of clear-cut findings and have explained this dearth in terms of a variety of factors inherent to this type of research.[38] Among the factors cited — to explain the lack of definitive evidence — are the often-complex work settings, the involved personal relationships present in the workplace, work tasks that are based on multiple steps and complicated procedures, the fact that such research usually requires long and painstaking study, and the likelihood that examination of workers and their work settings can induce the Hawthorne Effect to distort the findings. Alternatively, *laboratory* studies of how noise presence can affect work performance have been conducted using research tests that are perhaps overly simplistic (i.e., missing the environmental and task complexities inherent in industrial settings). These laboratory studies have likewise shown inconsistent and generally conflicting results.

Some *field* tests, however, have overcome such experimental design problems and have shown correlations between particular behaviors and noise presence.[39] So, drawing upon the field test results and the suggestions made by the observers, we will briefly note the highlights presented by these sources.

The first influence that noise presence appears to have on work performance is that *noise competes for the attention of the worker.* Thus, noise can cause the loss of concentration on work tasks, contributing to distraction and a concomitant reduction in work efficiency. A related problem occurs wherein noise will over-stimulate a worker. The noise presence, taken in conjunction with normal work tasks, essentially overloads the capacity of the worker to deal with both the noise and the task. Constant, unchanging noise — that exists over months or years in the workplace — can also create a monotonous condition in which a worker will become habituated to the noise. Whether this condition will lead to a sustained reduction in work performance is unclear, but such an effect seems plausible. A

SIDEBAR 12.3 The Hawthorne Effect

The Hawthorne Effect is a change in behavior, usually marked by the improved performance of workers, which results from the apparent display of increased concern by some set of researchers (or perhaps by management) towards these workers. The observation of this effect was first noted in a study conducted in the late 1930s at the Hawthorne Works (of the Western Electric Company) in Chicago. One principal component of that study concerned the improving of the work environment and determining what effect such an improvement might have on worker productivity. In that specific component two groups were identified who worked in similar facilities. In one facility the illumination conditions were markedly improved to facilitate seeing the finely detailed objects employed in the assembly process and inspection of the assembled results. The other facility was left as it had been originally (i.e., to serve as a "control" device for the experiment). Tests of worker performance and satisfaction subsequently showed that both groups — the one in the newly improved setting and the other in the "control" space — performed better and that, in fact, their levels of performance were virtually equal. Later explanations for this behavior were that by having researchers show increased interest toward the workers and their tasks (whether by renovating the workspace and testing its occupants or simply by testing the "control" group), both groups of workers were motivated to perform better. The original document that describes this research was written by Roethlisberger, F.J., and W.J. Dickson and was entitled, *Management and the Worker* (Cambridge, Massachusetts: Harvard University Press, 1939). A critical review of the research has been presented by Parsons, H.M., in the article, "What happened at Hawthorne?" *Science*, 183, 1974, pages 922–932.

complicating factor about such noise is that different results can be expected depending upon whether the noise is continuous or intermittent. Loeb noted that as intermittent noise is more noticeable than continuous noise (i.e., one can be expected to habituate to the continuing source), intermittent noise will create a greater distraction.[40] The explanation for the greater level of distraction is that the intermittent noise will more likely interfere with discrimination among fine-grained images or complicated ideas and will impede the decision-making processes which workers employ. Further, if the noise contains recognizable components (e.g., conversation between other people or music from a radio), then the degree of distraction will be even greater. Lastly, one other consequence of noise competing for the worker's attention is the increased incidence of accidents in noisy workplaces (in contrast to quieter ones). Cohen has documented this result in well-conducted research.[41] In his studies he found that workers involved in particular, complex tasks experienced higher rates of accidents for a noisy workplace compared to a quieter one. Additionally, he showed that the accident rate declined when a policy was instituted requiring the use of ear protection devices.

A second effect of noise presence in the workplace is that *noise has been shown to cause reductions in the accuracy of task performance.* A study undertaken by Broadbent and Little examined worker performance in a film-manufacturing factory.[42] The workers carried out their normal tasks in adjoining rooms, one of which had a lower noise level achieved by applying various noise control techniques. From an analysis of performance these researchers found that fewer errors and shutdowns due to operator-caused defects occurred in the quieter room. But the rates of production were virtually the same in both rooms.

A third, and perhaps most important, effect of noise presence is that *it will inhibit the hearing of the workers.* Essentially, noise will *mask* useful sounds. One result of such masking is that workers will be unable to distinguish between useful sounds that characterize the work procedure. For instance, many machines emit a particular sound when they are running correctly. Being able to discern whether that sound is present or not could indicate whether the machine needs to be "tuned." So not being able to hear that sound, due to masking noise, could lead to less efficient operation. Additionally, noise can greatly constrain aural communication. Thus, communicating with speech can be difficult in many noisy situations and will be impossible in some. Communication between workers then may have to be based on various nonverbal forms. The use of such forms can slow down communication, reducing worker efficiency (when communication between workers is necessary for job performance). Further, employing such nonverbal signals will probably limit what can be expressed. Masking noise can also curtail one's ability to sense sound-based warning signals (e.g., fire and smoke alarms, assembly-line breakdown indicators, and so forth).

Other consequences of noise presence in the workplace suggested in the professional literature include the increasing of worker fatigue[43]; the slowing of motor reflexes; and the growing annoyance with noise and its sources, subsequent displays of anger, and the collapse of interpersonal relationships.

Finally, there appear to be at least two positive consequences of having noise in the work environment. First, noise can sometimes counteract an otherwise boring, repetitive task. Loeb has written about such noises as being "facilitative," rather than "detrimental."[44] However, what the characteristics of such noises are (i.e., how they should appear so as to foster worker interest without distracting or disrupting the completion of the work) has not been well defined. Second, moderate noise can provide *acoustic privacy,* separating workers by aural means when visual barriers are not present or are inadequate.

Section 12.3 | DEFINING ACCEPTABLE NOISE LEVELS

Some noise will be present in virtually any building or in areas immediately exterior to a building, as long as human beings live and/or work in its vicinity. The fundamental questions then — given that some noise is inescapable — are how much noise should one anticipate finding in any locale and how much should one have to tolerate? In this section we will identify levels of noise that are considered to be reasonable maxima for operating buildings and for the external spaces that surround these buildings. The identification of permissible (or acceptable) noise levels commonly is established from answers to the question, What sound pressure levels can a noise source produce before the noise interferes with an activity? Thus, defining acceptable noise levels will depend on what aural qualities a space should have (i.e., so that the space can still enable the performance of some programmed set of activities).

The permissible noise levels we will describe here are industry standards that generally have wide acceptance within the American building industry. In many cases these standards are simply recommendations and do not exist as codes. In other instances the noise level maxima have been established by legislation. Defining what noise levels are acceptable (and desirable) must inevitably be subject to the PEST issues that we identified at the beginning of this chapter. For most projects, complying with noise control requirements, as specified by a code, can be sufficient. However, a building project team may confront some situations for which the provision of yet-better noise control practices may be desirable and perhaps should be undertaken. As a general rule, technical means will nearly always exist which, if elected, can enable yet better noise control. But when the designer, builder, property owner, and/or the occupant group confronts the need to provide noise control, each must weigh the political, economic, and social costs that will have to be defrayed for developing it. Determining what noise control capability should be selected for a specific project may thus entail analyzing the trade-offs between the benefits that can be gained against the costs that will have to be met.

Various noise level numbers — that we will identify in this section — are cited in current noise control standards and codes. The specific reasons justifying the selection of these numbers are not always readily apparent. As we view these standards and codes, we believe that three principal justifications can support the numbers identified therein. First, for setting guidelines for community noise, the fundamental concern must be the mitigation of annoyance that community residents would experience with severe noise problems. Guidelines established to control community noise must be based on how loud, noisy, and/or annoying a noise source can appear and how likely people will find some noise particularly bothersome or disturbing. A second principal justification for the various standards and codes is that most activities involving human beings are best pursued within some sound pressure level range. Whether this range is dictated by the need to minimize noise interference of speech or the fact that noise may intrude on people's work tasks, in such human enterprises noise must be maintained at levels below those at which disruption would result. A third major reason for the setting of noise control guidelines is the need to provide hearing protection for people subjected to high noise levels (e.g., on a factory floor, a construction site, or in a transportation facility). Thus, noise control should be set up expressly to minimize the hearing loss of workers and others exposed to these excessive noise levels.

12.3.1 SINGLE-NUMBER ACCEPTABLE NOISE LEVEL STATEMENTS

There are two generic forms in which these standards and codes are expressed: as single-number recommendations and as sets of performance curves. Most of the single-number guidelines are founded on A-weighted noise level measurements. Some of these guidelines are presented simply as rules-of-thumb, whereas others are offered as prescriptive statements. For an example of such rules-of-thumb, in Section 12.2 we noted that Kryter has suggested that *to minimize speech interference in a space,* the noise level *in the space* should be equal to or less than 45 dB(A) when the source was steady and should have peak values no greater than 55 dB(A) when the source was variable; and to minimize sleep disruption in a space, the noise level in the space should be equal to or less than 35 dB(A) for a steady source and should have peak values no greater than 45 dB(A) when the source was variable.[45] Alternatively, for an indication of how a performance curve may be used, we could refer to Schultz's graph (Figure 12.5) as a basis for establishing acceptable community noise levels. This graph displays a relationship between the Day-Night Average Noise Level (LDN) and the percentage of the population that will be "highly annoyed" when exposed to a specific noise level. Using this graph would thus provide us with a solid foundation for setting a noise level guideline that is closely tied to popular feelings about community noise.

The American National Standards Institute has established recommendations for maximum Day-Night Average Noise Levels (LDN's) for *land use compatibility.*[46] These recommendations indicate the *yearly* LDN's allowed for specific land uses—activities that future building occupants are likely to pursue—"at a site for *buildings as commonly constructed.*"[47] The basis of these recommendations is the expectation that buildings constructed with common materials and practices will reduce by some amount noise transmission through the building envelope. Thus, considering what noise levels are permissible within a space used for a specific activity, it is possible to establish what the maximum external noise level can be *if the external noise is not to interfere with the internal activities.*

Another example of using the LDN rating scheme as a single-number index of noise presence is its application for fostering noise control near airports. The Aviation Safety and Noise Abatement Act of 1979 (for the United States) mandated that airport operators were required to establish—either by measurements or with the use of computer simulation programs developed and approved for this application—noise level contours for land surrounding airports. Thus, by matching measured or predicted noise levels against permissible community noise levels, land use compatibility could be determined. Where the measured or predicted noise levels exceeded permissible levels, then the airport operators were required to purchase buildings (at a fair market value) or to oversee the improvement of building envelopes (i.e., to ensure that adequate noise insulation techniques had been added to the building, thus reducing the likelihood that the occupants would be greatly annoyed by the aircraft noise).[48]

One other principal application of a single-number noise level rating to specify the maximum *permissible* noise levels that can be present in work settings. The purpose of this rating is to ensure that workers, when exposed to noisy conditions, will have adequate hearing protection. For instance, in the United States the Occupational Safety and Health Administration (OSHA), an organization within the U.S. Department of Labor, sets controls for occupational noise exposure.[49] The OSHA regulation of noise exposure for

SIDEBAR 12.4 Problems resulting from relying on single-number noise level guidelines

The use of these single-number noise level recommendations is fraught with limitations. A single-number index is generally employed because of its ease of application. But such a single-number index is often an average value calculated for many events. Or, less commonly, the index may be equal to some selected value that is representative of the many events, without specifically being an average or a maximum or a minimum. In any of these instances, the single-number index does not show the variability of the values describing the many events (e.g., none of the statistical properties characterizing the pattern of variation is usually shown; thus, the range, the deviation from a mean, and the frequency distribution will not be revealed).

These qualifications are inherent in the use of any single-number index to represent variable behavior. In addition to these generic qualifications, using a single-number index to define acceptable noise levels offers some further limitations. First, a single-number index like the annual average day-night noise level (LDN) relies on matching a physical measure with people's perceptions of the noise. Such a match is not always well founded. For instance, one's perceptions concern how loud, noisy, or annoying a source may appear. Depending on the spectral characteristics of the noise or whether the noise is continuous, intermittent, or impulsive can greatly affect how an individual perceives the noise. However, relying on a single-number index essentially provides an averaged view of the noise, removing the idiosyncrasies of the noise that may make it particularly noisy or annoying.

A second reason why relying on an index like the annual LDN may be ill founded is that the condition of the building envelope, the building's use, or the character of the noise source may change seasonally. For instance, from winter to summer, the performance of a building envelope can be modified by the opening and closing of windows (for natural ventilation and cooling). Alternatively, for buildings located near a highway, the daily LDN may change appreciably from winter to summer as traffic flow rates vary.

A third reason why a single-number index like a daily LDN value may provide poor definitions of noise presence is that the source (or sources) contributing to the derivation of the LDN value may be highly variable. As an example, noise measurements on American airports are conducted to establish daily LDN values. Basic to the LDN rating scheme is the 10 dB(A) increment that is added to all noise readings that occur between the hours 0000 to 0700 and 2200 to 2400. So, at many airports the operators seek to minimize the numbers of landings and take-offs between these hours and to bunch flight activities into the hours just after 0700 (and, to a lesser extent, between 1700 to about 2100). Such behavior circumvents the basic tenet of the LDN scheme (i.e., that seeks to impose penalties on nighttime noise sources). But the resulting flight schedules with their take-off frequencies as rapid as one every 60 to 90 seconds can create great annoyance for nearby residents and workers.

Finally, the use of single-number indices occurs because, in most cases, they are easy to derive and they are comparatively easy to apply. However, the designer and builder should be aware that the indices indeed have limitations and often provide only an approximate picture of noise presence. Thus, the designer and builder should be willing (or may need) to make accommodations beyond what a strict interpretation of the single-number index would suggest.

TABLE 12.2

MAXIMUM PERMISSIBLE NOISE LEVELS FOR SPECIFIC PERIODS OF EXPOSURE

(according to the Occupational Safety and Health Administration, U.S. Department of Labor)

DURATION PER DAY (in Hours)	SOUND LEVEL (in dB(A)) 'slow response'
8	90
6	92
4	95
3	97
2	100
1.5	102
1	105
0.5	110
0.25 or less	115

Source: Volume 29 of the U.S. Code of Federal Regulations (7-1-87 edition), Occupational Safety and Health Standards, Subpart G: Occupational Health and Environmental Control; Section 1910.95, Table G-16.

Note that when two or more exposure periods at different noise levels occur per day, then a weighted summation of the total condition is required to be less than the level limit for the corresponding total period length.

workers is structured along two tracks. First, the *maximum permissible noise exposure*— specified in terms of noise level versus duration of exposure — is catalogued in Table 12.2. The regulation mandates that whenever workers are exposed to noise for conditions that exceed this combination of noise level and duration, "engineering controls shall be utilized"[50] to reduce noise exposures. Second, a *hearing conservation program* must be implemented by the employer for his/her employees "whenever employee noise exposures equal or exceed an 8-hour time-weighted average sound level (TWA) of 85 dB measured on the A scale."[51] The tenets of the hearing conservation program further stipulate that workers exposed to time-weighted average sound levels (TWA's) equal to or greater than 85 dB(A) must be provided with hearing protectors that furnish adequate noise attenuation and must be administered regular audiometric tests to ensure that personal hearing capacities are being maintained.[52]

12.3.2 THE NOISE CRITERION CURVES

The other widely used device for defining acceptable noise levels is the *Balanced Noise Criterion (NCB) Curves* (see Figure 12.10). These curves were originally developed by Beranek and were called the *Noise Criteria* (NC) rating method.[53] Later, Schultz modified the Noise Criteria rating method.[54] And, more recently, Beranek further revised the Noise Criteria method, creating the Balanced Noise Criterion method.[55] In this latest revision Beranek has introduced the Balanced Noise Criteria (NCB) curves, which serve as an enhancement of the Noise Criterion (NC) rating method.

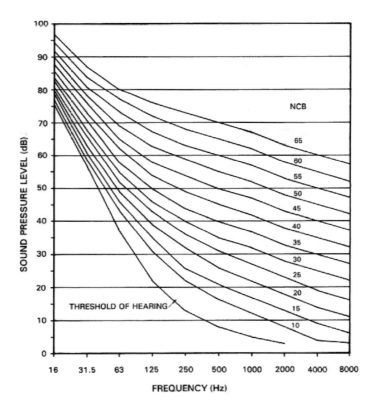

Figure 12.10 This graph identifies the Balanced Noise Criteria (NCB) curve set developed by L.L. Beranek. These curves accompany the information presented in Table 12.3. This graph has been reproduced from a paper by Beranek, L.L., "Building noise-criterion (NCB) curves," *Journal of the Acoustical Society of America,* 86(2), August 1989, pages 650–664. Permission to reproduce this graph has been granted by Dr. Beranek and the Acoustical Society of America.

The purpose of the Balanced Noise Criterion family of curves is to indicate what *background noise level* may be maintained in a building interior without the noise interfering with the performance of activities intended for the interior. For various building applications (e.g., retail sales, office work, church service, and so forth), specific Balanced Noise Criteria ratings have been established dictating what background noise levels can be tolerated (i.e., levels which will not disrupt an application). By keeping background noise levels below the appropriate NCB rating, the building operator can ensure that the background noise will appear suitably quiet and that speech communication typical for the activity for which a space is intended will not be compromised. The conditions for using this family of curves as a *design goal* for a building space are that the usual noise sources will be present external to the building; the space will be unoccupied; and a heating, ventilating, and air-conditioning system appropriate to the space will be operating. The Balanced Noise Criteria ratings recommended for specific activities appear in Table 12.3: these NCB ratings correspond to the similar-numbered NCB curves in Figure 12.10.

Application of these curves proceeds by comparing anticipated noise levels across the frequency spectrum — those that will probably be present in a space — with allowable noise levels (as delineated by a specific NCB curve). If the anticipated noise levels are less than what the NCB curve stipulates for the particular activity, then background noise will be sufficiently quiet and will not interfere with the intended activity. However, if at some frequency the anticipated noise level exceeds that of the recommended noise criterion curve, then some accommodation should be made to minimize the interference resulting from the higher-than-acceptable noise level. Two approaches to reaching accommodation with this potential noise intrusion are to reduce the background noise or to decide if the interference created by the offending background noise will pose serious consequences to the performance of the intended activity. Strategies and devices that can be employed to reduce background noise levels will be discussed in Chapter 13.

Let's consider an example of how to use this family of curves. Suppose you are designing and building a public library along a busy thoroughfare. Standing in an existing building near the site of your project, you measure background noise levels (across the frequency spectrum) for an internal space bordering this street. If the construction of the existing building and the one you are creating will be similar, you can proceed with comparisons of the noise levels measured in the existing building with those recommended for the new library. The suggested noise criterion range for libraries — see Table 12.3 — is NCB-30 to NCB-40. When you compare the NCB-40 curve with the background noise levels measured in the existing building, you find that the recorded noise levels exceed the recommended noise levels at two frequencies. Your options when confronted with these data are several. You can elect to disregard the probability that background noise levels

---

SIDEBAR 12.5 Deriving the original Noise Criterion (NC) curves

The Noise Criterion (NC) curves were derived from studies that Beranek and his colleagues conducted on office workers whose speech communication was disrupted by the presence of noise. The character of the noises — noting sound pressure levels at particular frequencies — was first established in terms of *speech interference levels* (SIL's). When workers' ratings of noisy conditions were compared with various combinations of sound pressure levels and frequencies (especially noting the *three* specific frequency bandwidths for which the SIL was *first* determined), a family of curves resulted similar to those shown in Figure 11.13. These curves were then identified in terms of a Noise Criterion number that matched the speech interference level (i.e., the average of the sound pressure levels measured at the three frequencies used for determining the speech interference level). The present Balanced Noise Criterion (NCB) curves have been developed using similar techniques.

One additional product of these curves is the fact that the loudness level for any combination of sound pressure level (SPL) and frequency that lies along one of the noise criterion curves will be 22 phons greater than the SIL in dB(A). Alternatively, one can state that the sum of (the NC curve rating + 22) will equal the loudness level for any noise source whose noise level (SPL) and frequency lies on the NC curve. As a consequence of the relationship between the SIL and the loudness level, these NC curves and the Equal-Loudness Level curves (Figure 11.3) presented in Section 11.1.2 have similar shapes. For further information about the derivation of the NC curves and the linkage between the NC curves, SIL's, and loudness levels, see the paper by Beranek, L.L., "Revised criteria for noise in buildings," *Noise Control,* 3(1), 1957, pages 19-27.

TABLE 12.3
RECOMMENDED RANGES OF NCB CURVES FOR VARIOUS OCCUPIED ACTIVITY AREAS

TYPE OF SPACE (and accoustical requirements)	NCB CURVE (see Fig.12.11)	APPROXIMATE SPL, dB(A)
Broadcast and recording studios (distant microphone pickup used)	10	18
Concert halls, opera houses, and recital halls (for listening to faint music)	10 to 15	18 to 23
Large auditoriums, large drama theaters, and large churches (for very good listening conditions)	Not to exceed 20	28
Broadcast, television, and recording studios (close microphone pickup used only)	Not to exceed 25	33
Small auditoriums, small theaters, small churches, music rehearsal rooms, large meeting and conference rooms (for very good listening), or executive offices and conference rooms for 50 people (with no amplification)	Not to exceed 30	38
Bedrooms, sleeping quarters, hospitals, residences, apartments, hotels, motels, etc. (for sleeping, resting, relaxing)	25 to 40	38 to 48
Private or semiprivate offices, small conference rooms, classrooms, libraries, etc. (for good listening conditions)	30 to 40	38 to 48
Living rooms and drawing rooms in dwellings (for conversing or listening to radios and televisions)	30 to 40	38 to 48
Large offices, reception areas, retail shops and stores, cafeterias, restaurants, etc. (for moderately good listening conditions)	35 to 45	43 to 53
Lobbies, laboratory work spaces, drafting and engineering rooms, general secretarial areas (for fair listening conditions)	40 to 50	48 to 58
Light maintenance shops, industrial plant control rooms, office and computer equipment rooms, kitchens and laundries (for moderately good listening conditions)	45 to 55	53 to 63
Shops, garages, etc. (for just acceptable speech and telephone communication). Levels above NC- or NCB-60 are not recommended for any office or communication station.	50 to 60	58 to 68
For work spaces where speech or telephone communication is not required, but where there must be no risk of hearing damage	55 to 70	63 to 78

This table has been reproduced from a paper by Beranek, L.L., "Application of NCB noise criterion curves," *Noise Control Engineering Journal,* 33(2), September–October 1989, pages 45–56. Permission to reprint this table has been granted by Dr. Beranek and the Institute for Noise Control Engineering.

will be too high; some background noise may thus be offensive, but perhaps it will not be too bad. You can construct your library with greater noise separation capabilities (e.g., providing a more transmission-resistant envelope). Or you might explore whether the external noise levels can be reduced by some means (e.g., having the velocities of the external vehicles decreased by getting the speed limit reduced or constructing some sort of an external barrier that will separate the street and its vehicles from the new library). Your choice will probably depend on the so-called PEST issues that we introduced in the beginning of this chapter. One of your responsibilities, as designer and/or builder, will thus be to advise your clients and the future user group about the various means for dealing with this problem and what the likely consequences of any noise control method(s) will be.

Section 12.4 | A BRIEF SUMMARY FOR CHAPTER 12

Noise causes several difficulties for people, the most serious being that it impairs communication based on sound. The most important *physical* properties of noise are its spectral composition, duration, sound pressure level, and the extent to which the pressure levels fluctuate across some time period. Because noise is fundamentally a subjective experience — noise is *unwanted* sound and the determination of unwantedness is based on one's sensations and feelings — noise also has *psychosocial* (or personal) properties. These psychosocial properties are greatly determined by how accepting individuals are toward noise. The characteristics that influence how noisy a sound appears include when the sound (noise) occurs, whether the sound is expected (or can be anticipated), how important the source of the noise may be to the individual or the community in which the person lives or works, how disruptive the sound is to the person hearing it, and the state of mind of the

---

SIDEBAR 12.6 The Room Criteria (RC) sound rating system

The Room Criteria sound rating method was initially developed by Blazier and has since been modified, again by Blazier, to its present form as the RC Mark II Room Criteria Method. Both the original and the newer modified rating methods are intended as mechanisms for describing noise levels generated by HVAC systems. Similar to the NC and NCB rating methods, the RC and RC Mark II rating methods are based on a series of curves. These curves indicate permissible noise levels for systems operation. One variant from the NC and NCB rating methods is the inclusion of notations that are used to identify situations where low-frequency rumble, mid-frequency roar, and high-frequency hiss noises, individually or in combination, are present during system operation.

Principal citations for descriptions of the Room Criteria and the RC Mark II methods include Blazier, W.E., Jr., "Revised noise criteria for application in the acoustical design and rating of HVAC systems," *Noise Control Engineering*, 16(2), 1981, pages 64–73; Blazier, W.E., Jr., "Revised noise criteria for design and rating of HVAC systems," *ASHRAE Transactions*, 87(1); and Blazier, W.E., Jr., "RC Mark II: A refined procedure for rating the noise from heating, ventilating, and air-conditioning (HVAC) systems in buildings," *Noise Control Engineering Journal*, 45(6), November–December 1997. Additionally, summaries of the RC and RC Mark II methods, along with brief descriptions of the NC and NCB rating methods, appear in the chapter, "Sound and Vibration" of the *2001 ASHRAE Handbook of Fundamentals*, (Atlanta: American Society of Heating, Refrigerating, and Air-Conditioning Engineers, Inc., 2001), pages 7.1–7.18.

auditor at the moment of experiencing the noise. A third set of properties of noise that can influence how people will feel about the noise concerns whether the noise has an informational content (that perhaps will impair concentration) and whether the noise has identifiable (or recognizable) components that may compete for people's attention.

In addition to the possible disruption of speech, noise can also have other deleterious effects on people. People's feelings of annoyance toward noise are well-established through research. Workers and other individuals exposed to high levels of noise will commonly experience hearing capability loss, both temporarily and permanently (depending on a series of exposure parameters). The extent to which noise can cause physical and mental health failings of an individual who is exposed to it is still subject to question. But there are at least some well-qualified studies that suggest that, in limited circumstances, health can be adversely affected by noise presence. Similarly, there are some well-documented instances wherein noise exposure has reduced work performance, creating decreases in productivity.

Defining acceptable noise levels in buildings depends greatly on how one defines the basis for acceptability. The principal issue generally concerns the determination of what noise levels will interfere with any activity. We have identified *single-number* noise level guidelines for minimizing speech and sleep interference, establishing land use compatibility, and limiting noise presence in the workplace. The use of the *Balanced Noise Criterion* (NCB) curves has also been described, including matching particular NCB curves with activities (i.e., as bases for setting acceptable noise levels for these activities).

ENDNOTES and SELECTED ADDITIONAL COMMENTS

1. *Webster's Seventh New Collegiate Dictionary,* (Springfield, Massachusetts: G. & C. Merriam Company, Publishers, 1967). Page 180.
2. Miller, L.N., "Sound levels of rain and of wind in the trees," *Noise Control Engineering,* 11(3), November–December 1978, pages 101–109.
3. Schultz, T.J., *Community Noise Ratings,* (London: Applied Science Publishers Ltd., 1972), pages 6–9.
4. Goldstein, J., "Descriptors of auditory magnitude and methods of rating community noise," in Peppin, R.J., and C.V. Rodman (editors), *Community Noise,* ASTM STP 692, (Philadelphia: American Society for Testing and Materials, 1979), pages 38–72 (see pages 56–58, particularly); and Kryter, K.D., *The Effects of Noise on Man* (2nd edition), (Orlando, Florida: Academic Press, Inc., 1985); see pages 20–21.
5. Goldstein, J., op. cit., page 61.
6. Bishop, D.E., A.P. Hays, H.H. Reddingius, and H. Seidmam, *Calculation of Day-Night Levels (LDN) Resulting From Civil Aircraft Operations* (Report No. EPA–550/9-77-450, prepared by Bolt, Beranek & Newman, Inc., for the U.S. Environmental Protection Agency), (Washington, D.C.: National Technical Information Service, U.S. Department of Commerce, 1976).
7. ———, *Protective Noise Levels: Condensed Version of the EPA Levels Document,* prepared by the U.S. Environmental Protection Agency, (PB82-138827), (Washington, D.C.: National Technical Information Service, U.S. Department of Commerce, 1978).
8. Winer, D.E., "Aircraft noise exposure: the problem of definition," *Sound and Vibration,* 13(2), February 1979, pages 22–27.
9. Kryter, K.D., *The Effects of Noise on Man* (2nd edition), (Orlando, Florida: Academic Press, Inc., 1985), pages 14–19.
10. Simpson, M.E., and D.E. Bishop, "Correlations between different community noise measures," *Noise Control Engineering,* 1(2), Autumn 1973, pages 74–78; Shepherd, W.T., "Time of day corrections to aircraft noise assessment metrics," *Sound and Vibration,* 16(2), February 1982, pages 10–12; and

Flynn, D.R., and S.L. Yaniv, "Relations among different frequency rating procedures for traffic noise," *Journal of the Acoustical Society of America,* 77(4), April 1985, pages 1436–1446.

11. Kryter, K.D., *The Effects of Noise on Man* (2nd edition), (Orlando, Florida: Academic Press, 1985); Miller, J.D., "Effects of noise on man," *Journal of the Acoustical Society of America,* 56(3), September 1974, pages 729–764; and Mackenzie, S.T., *Noise and Office Work: Employee and Employer Concerns* (Key issues series, No. 19), (Ithaca, New York: New York State School of Industrial and Labor Relations, Cornell University, 1975).

12. Berglund, B., U. Berglund, and T. Lindvall, "Scaling loudness, noisiness, and annoyance to aircraft noise," *Journal of the Acoustical Society of America,* 57(4), April 1975, pages 930–934; and Berglund, B., U. Berglund, and T. Lindvall, "Scaling loudness, noisiness, and annoyance of community noises," *Journal of the Acoustical Society of America,* 60(5), November 1976, pages 1119–1125.

13. Scharf, B., "Loudness and noisiness — same or different?" in Snowden, J.C. (ed)., *Proceedings of the 1974 International Conference on Noise Control Engineering* (Inter-Noise 74), (Poughkeepsie, New York: Institute of Noise Control Engineering, 1974), pages 559–564.

14. Broadbent, D.E., "Noise in relation to annoyance, performance, and mental health," *Journal of the Acoustical Society of America,* 68(1), July 1980, pages 15–17.

15. Schomer, P.D., "A survey of community attitudes towards noise near a general aviation airport," *Journal of the Acoustical Society of America,* 74(6), December 1983, pages 1773–1781.

16. Schultz, T.J., "Synthesis of social surveys on noise annoyance," *Journal of the Acoustical Society of America,* 64(2), August 1978, pages 377–405.

17. Kryter, K.D., "Community annoyance from aircraft and ground vehicle noise," *Journal of the Acoustical Society of America,* 72(4), October 1982, pages 1222–1242; Schultz, T.J., "Comments on K.D. Kryter's paper, 'Community annoyance from aircraft and ground vehicle noise'," *Journal of the Acoustical Society of America,* 72(4), October 1982, pages 1243–1252; and Kryter, K.D., "Rebuttal by Karl D. Kryter to comments by T.J. Schultz," *Journal of the Acoustical Society of America,* 72(4), October 1982, pages 1253–1257.

18. Kuwano, S., S. Namba, and A. Schick, "Cross-cultural survey on noise problems in apartment houses," *Proceedings of the 1985 International Conference on Noise Control Engineering* (Inter-Noise 85), (Zwicker, E., and H. Steinhardt, editors), (Dortmund, West Germany: Federal Institute for Occupational Safety, 1985), pages 937–940.

19. Florentine, M., S. Namba, and S. Kuwano, "Concepts of loudness, noisiness, noise, and annoyance in the U.S.A., Japan, and England," *Proceedings of the 1986 International Conference on Noise Control Engineering* (Inter-Noise 86), (Lotz, R., editor), (New York: Noise Control Foundation, 1986), pages 831–834.

20. Job, R.F.S., "Community response to noise: a review of factors influencing the relationship between noise exposure and reaction," *Journal of the Acoustical Society of America,* 83(3), March 1988, pages 991–1001.

21. Pearsons, K.B., R.L. Bennett, and S. Fidell, *Speech Levels in Various Noise Environments* (a report prepared for the U.S. Environmental Protection Agency by Bolt, Beranek, and Newman, Inc), [NTIS Report No. PB-270 053], (Washington, D.C.: National Technical Information Service, U.S. Department of Commerce, 1977), pages 3–4.

22. Kryter, K.D., *The Effects of Noise on Man* (2nd edition), (Orlando, Florida: Academic Press, Inc., 1985), page 138.

23. Webster, J.C., "Effects of noise on speech intelligibility," in Ward, W.D., and J.E. Fricke (editors), *Noise as a Public Health Hazard,* (Washington, D.C.: The American Speech and Hearing Association, 1969), pages 49–73; the graph appears on page 69.

24. Schultz, T.J., "Synthesis of social surveys on noise annoyance," *Journal of the Acoustical Society of America,* 64(2), August 1978, pages 377–405. This graph appears on page 388.

25. Miller, G.A., "The masking of speech," *Psychological Bulletin,* 44(3), March 1947, pages 105–129.

26. Pickett, J.M., and K.D. Kryter, *Prediction of Speech Intelligibility in Noise,* U.S. Air Force Cambridge Research Center Technical Report 55-4 (1955), as reported on page 57 of the paper by Webster, J.C., "Effects of noise on speech intelligibility," in Ward, W.D., and J.E. Fricke (editors), *Noise as a Public Health Hazard,* (Washington, D.C.: The American Speech and Hearing Association, 1969), pages 49–73.

27. See Chapter 10 ("Non-auditory system response to noise and effects on health") in Kryter, K.D., *The Effects of Noise on Man* (2nd edition), (Orlando, Florida: Academic Press, 1985), pages 389–524.

28. Ibid., page 390.

29. Cohen, S., and N. Weinstein, "Nonauditory effects of noise on behavior and health," *Journal of Social Issues,* 37(1), 1981, 36–70. See page 54.

30. Ibid., pages 56–57.

31. Robinson, D.W., and G.J. Sutton, "Age effect in hearing—a comparative analysis of published threshold data," *Audiology,* 18, 1979, pages 320–334.

32. Szanto, C., and M. Ionescu, "Influence of age and sex on hearing threshold levels in workers exposed to different intensity levels of occupational noise," *Audiology, 22,* 1983, pages 339–356; Lane, C.L., R.A. Dobie, D.R. Crawford, and M.S. Morgan, "Standard threshold shift criteria: an investigation of the most reliable indicator of noise-induced hearing loss," *Journal of Occupational Medicine,* 27(1), January 1985, pages 34–42; and Thiery, L., and C. Meyer-Bisch, "Hearing loss due to partly impulsive industrial noise exposure at levels between 87 and 90 dB(A)," *Journal of the Acoustical Society of America,* 84(2), August 1988, pages 651–659.

33. Kryter, K.D., "Presbycusis, sociocusis and nosocusis," *Journal of the Acoustical Society of America,* 73(6), June 1983, pages 1897–1917.

34. Kryter, K.D., *The Effects of Noise on Man* (2nd edition), (Orlando, Florida: Academic Press, Inc., 1985), page 138.

35. Schultz, T.J., "Synthesis of social surveys on noise annoyance," *Journal of the Acoustical Society of America,* 64(2), August 1978, pages 377–405; see page 388.

36. Wilkinson, R.T., and K.B. Campbell, "Effects of traffic noise on quality of sleep: assessment by EEG, subjective report, or performance the next day," *Journal of the Acoustical Society of America,* 75(2), February 1984, pages 468–475.

37. Griefahn, B., and E. Gros, "Noise and sleep at home, a field study on primary and after-effects," *Journal of Sound and Vibration,* 105(3), 1986, pages 373–383.

38. Jones, D.M., "Noise," in Hockey, G.R.J. (editor), *Stress and Fatigue in Human Performance,* (Chichester, England: J. Wiley & Sons Ltd., 1983), pages 61–95; Chapter 9, "Mental and psychomotor task performance in noise," in Kryter, K.D., *The Effects of Noise on Man* (2nd edition), (Orlando, Florida: Academic Press, Inc., 1985), pages 343–387; and Chapter 9, "Noise and task efficiency," in Loeb, M., *Noise and Human Efficiency,* (Chichester, England: J. Wiley & Sons Ltd., 1986), pages 171–216.

39. A paper that discusses (a) the limitations of laboratory studies used as means for examining "real-world" behavior and (b) the settings in which this behavior occurs has been written by Cohen, S., G.W. Evans, D.S. Krantz, and D. Stokols, "Physiological, motivational, and cognitive effects of air craft noise on children," *American Psychologist,* 35(3), March 1980, pages 231–243.

40. Loeb, M., *Noise and Human Efficiency,* (Chichester, England: J. Wiley & Sons Ltd., 1986), page 209.

41. Cohen, A., "Industrial noise and medical, absence, and accident record data on exposed workers," in Ward, W.D. (ed.), *Proceedings of the International Congress on Noise as a Public Health Problem,* (Washington, D.C.: U.S. Environmental Protection Agency, 1974), pages 441–453; and Cohen, A., "The influence of a company hearing conservation program on extra-auditory problems in workers," *Journal of Safety Research,* 8, 1976, pages 146–162.

42. Broadbent, D.E., and E.A.J. Little, "Effect of noise reduction in a work situation," *Occupational Psychology,* 34, 1960, pages 133–140.

43. Loeb, M., *Noise and Human Efficiency,* (Chichester, England: J. Wiley & Sons Ltd., 1986), pages 203–205.

44. Ibid., page 220.

45. Kryter, K.D., *The Effects of Noise on Man* (2nd edition), (Orlando, Florida: Academic Press, Inc., 1985), page 138.

46. ———, *Sound level descriptors for determination of compatible land use* [ANSI S3.23-1980], (New York: American National Standards Institute, 1980).

47. Ibid., page 4.

48. Firle, T.E., "Ldn dictates local options: why?" *Proceedings of the 1986 International Conference in Noise Control Engineering,* (Inter-Noise 86), Lotz, R. (editor), (New York: Noise Control Foundation, 1986), pages 973–978.

49. ———, "Occupational noise exposure," *Code of Federal Regulations, Volume 29,* Chapter XVII, Section 1910.95 (Washington, D.C.: U.S. Government Printing Office, July 1987), pages 179–194.

50. Ibid., page 179.

51. Ibid., page 179.

52. Cluff, G.L., "Noise dose from impulse and continuous noise," *Sound and Vibration,* 16(3), March 1982, pages 18–25; and Staiano, M.A., "OSHA noise exposure due to intermittent noise sources," *Sound and Vibration,* 20(5), May 1986, pages 18–21.

53. Beranek, L.L., "Revised criteria for noise in buildings," *Noise Control,* 3(1), 1957, pages 19–27.

54. Schultz, T.J., "Noise-criterion curves for use with the USASI preferred frequencies," *Journal of the Acoustical Society of America,* 43(3), 1968, pages 637–638.

55. Beranek, L.L., "Balanced noise-criterion (NCB) curves," *Journal of the Acoustical Society of America,* 86(2), August 1989, pages 650–664; and Beranek, L.L., "Application of NCB noise criterion curves," *Noise Control Engineering Journal,* 33(2), September–October 1989, pages 45–56.

CHAPTER THIRTEEN

Guidelines for Controlling Sound and Noise in the Built Environment

13

THE FUNDAMENTAL ISSUE in acoustic designing and construction is how to promote communication. Whether we consider speech, music, other sounds made by living creatures, or sounds produced by inanimate objects, all provide us with information about what happens around us. To acquire this information, we must first be able to hear these sounds. Then, we must be able to understand the "messages" borne within them. Hearing and understanding sounds thus require that we can identify their sources, differentiate their characteristics, and interpret their messages. So, if our auditory systems function at least reasonably well, then the acquisition and interpretation of sounds will depend on how good hearing conditions are in the surrounding environment.

A secondary, but still important, need for acoustic designing and construction involves the control of noise. When we are sleeping, working, or simply sitting and thinking, noise can intrude and possibly interfere with the function or task. Further, noise can annoy the occupants of a space or otherwise detract from experiencing the space (and the activities for which the space is used). Identifying and implementing strategies to reduce noise — or at least its effects — therefore become critical tasks during design and construction.

Thus, in this chapter we will introduce a series of guidelines for creating spaces that perform well acoustically. We will also explain the bases for these guidelines, providing linkages between them and the concepts that we have introduced in the preceding three chapters.

Section 13.1 | THE FOUR BASIC REQUIREMENTS FOR GOOD HEARING [1]

The reason for considering the presence of sound in a building or in an external area is to ensure that the space will enable occupants to perceive and understand sound (i.e., as well as they are capable). Thus, listeners should readily and accurately be able to hear sounds emanating from other occupants and any inanimate sound-producing devices that are present within a space. To create a building or an external area in which conditions for good hearing exist, four requirements of the environment must be met. These requirements include:

(a) There must be *a quiet background.* Noise levels must be low enough so that they will not interfere with the hearing of useful sounds. Establishing a permissible level for background noise requires thinking about a number of factors. First, what is the nature of the activity in which an occupant is engaged? Second, how distant is the occupant from the sound source? Third, what length of time does the occupant have to hear the sound? And, fourth, what is the spectral character of the sound? Sound(s) that an occupant will wish to hear should be substantially more powerful than any noise that is present (i.e., the signal-to-noise pressure level ratio should be sufficiently high). Whether potentially intrusive noise enters from outside or is produced by a source within the space will dictate which mechanisms might be furnished to control the noise. But, regardless of the location(s) of the source(s), any noises entering the space or present within the space must be dealt with to prevent these noises from interfering with useful sounds.

(b) The *sound source(s)* in the occupied space *must be adequately loud.* Thus, any source of useful sound must generate sufficient energy so that a listener can easily hear sounds emanating from the source. Of course, the source should not be too loud, making it offensive to the listener. To ensure that a source will be perceived as having adequate loudness, the source must produce enough energy, the transmission path between the source and the receiver must be unconstrained and as short as possible, and the listener should have a satisfactory hearing capacity. If one of these three needs is likely to be unsatisfied, then one or both of the other two needs may require enhancement. For instance, suppose a listener has impaired hearing (i.e., has a higher-than-normal hearing threshold). Then, people speaking to this listener will likely need to raise their voice levels, increasing the amount of sound energy leaving their mouths. Alternatively, the listener may wish to move closer to a speaker, thereby shortening the transmission path. Such a move may take the listener into the near field surrounding the speaker. Within this near field the sound pressure level of the speaker's voice will be highest. Further, within the near field, the sound arriving from the speaker will be less affected by the reverberant conditions created by the spatial enclosure.

(c) There must be *good distribution of the sound transmitted out from the source and into the space.* Basically, to ensure that sound is well distributed in a space, sound energy should reach into all occupied areas of the space. As many sources project sound energy directionally each source should be placed to ensure that the direct sound will reach the listener via an uninterrupted line-of-sight. Additionally, to reinforce this direct sound, reflecting surfaces should guide some of the sound energy toward the listener. In some applications the best distribution of sound in the space will be one for which the sound energy is uniformly spread throughout the space. For other applications the preferred distribution could include one area (or more) of the space in which the spread of the sound appears to be concentrated, whereas the remainder of the space seems quieter or perhaps even devoid of sound. The optimum sound energy distribution for any given space will depend on the activities for which the space is used.

(d) There should be *an appropriate separation of successive sounds, and yet a proper blending of these sounds.* A fundamental attribute of sound is that it is temporal: sound exists across time. Further, sound will often change over time. Both speech and music occur as assemblages of discrete, though related, sounds. Each component of speech or music has properties that distinguish it from other sounds. But these components also will have accustomed linkages to other sounds (established either by tradition or by habituation). So, to hear speech or music and to understand (or relate to) either, a listener must be able to discern the message components separately and also to recognize how these components are associated with one another. The specific physical features of a space should enhance the appropriate separation and blending of these components. These features necessarily are those that determine the temporal properties of sounds. For example, a space in which communication by speech or music occurs should have a volume appropriate for the activity performed there. There should be adequate opportunity for the reflection of sound (to reinforce direct sound). Noise from outside of the space should be prevented from interfering with specific sound components present in the space. Time gaps between successive sounds should not be too lengthy, and so forth.

Section 13.2 | TO IMPEDE OR PROPAGATE SOUND WAVES?

Creating spaces to promote communication — whether the spaces will be in or external to buildings — requires that the designer and builder think carefully about the acoustical conditions needed in the space. To achieve good communication conditions, a sound source must appear adequately loud; the transmission path between the source and a listener should be short and direct and enable reinforcement by useful reflections; and the listener should be able to hear well. Additionally, any background noise should be weak enough so that its presence does not interfere with the hearing of relevant sounds. Thus, when you set out to create environmental conditions that will provide good communication, a fundamental question is whether a sound emanating from some source is unwanted (i.e., the sound is noise) or whether the sound is useful. If the sound is indeed noise, its propagation must be stopped from reaching the receiver. If the sound is useful, its passage from the source to the receiver must be enhanced.

Generally, the distinction between unwanted and useful sounds can be easily established. Then, means of aiding sound propagation or impeding noise transmission can be developed in a straightforward manner. But occasionally the distinction can be highly subjective. Sounds that one person wishes to hear, another person may regard as disrupting and irritating. For these more difficult circumstances, the application of controls for the sound source, for the path between the source and a receiver, and for the receiver can be flexible. When sounds may be perceived as noisy, controls should ensure that the amount of the noise reaching the receiver is minimized. Such controls can include shutting down the source, blocking the transmission path, or isolating the receiver. Instead, if the sound generated by a source presents worthwhile information to the receiver, the designer and the builder should seek to enhance the production of sound energy and its transfer from the source to the receiver. Such actions may include strengthening the source, shortening the transmission path, and/or placing the listener in a position to most favorably hear the sound.

Determining how to impede noise passage and/or to enhance sound propagation will commonly require the resolution of three fundamental issues. The first issue concerns the creation of enclosures and surfaces within the enclosures. The walls, floor, and ceiling of a room can limit the entrance of noise produced by a source external to the room. Alternatively, these planes can guide and reinforce the flow of sound energy out from a useful source throughout the room. Additional surfaces within a space (i.e., other than the primary space-enclosing planes) are often created specifically to foster noise control or sound propagation. Furthermore, fully bounded enclosures within a space can even be used to minimize how much noise will pass into the rest of the space. The second issue concerns establishing the *shapes* the various enclosure (and other) surfaces within the space should have and the appropriate locations for these surfaces. The third issue concerns what *materials* should be used in the enclosure assemblies and placed on the various surfaces throughout the space.

13.2.1 A GENERAL VOCABULARY OF NOISE CONTROL STRATEGIES

When a building (or external) space is to be created and a noise source is expected to be present, a number of procedures can be employed to limit the loudness of the noise. These nine procedures may be applied singly or in combination.

First, considering the noise source (see Figure 13.1) as the starting point of the problem, the easiest solution is simply to eliminate the source or move it elsewhere. This step can be performed if the source is a nonessential device whose absence would not affect whatever activity occurs in that space. For example, if the noise of an electric typewriter might intrude upon work activities in an office, then removing the typewriter and setting it up in another space could offer a quick solution.

However, if the source cannot be eliminated or moved, then the second noise control step could be to improve its operation. If the noise source involves continuously moving parts that emit squeaks, rattles, whines, or knocks, then lubricating moving parts, replacing defective elements, or tightening loose components may overcome its noisiness (see Figure 13.2). With a typewriter, the principal noise created results from a typing element striking the paper held on the platen. To reduce this noise a moveable plastic cover can be fitted over the cavity in which the platen and typing element reside, keeping the noise from reaching the surrounding environment (see Figure 13.3).

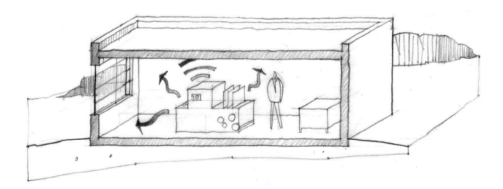

Figure 13.1 A noisy machine can disturb all occupants exposed to its noise.

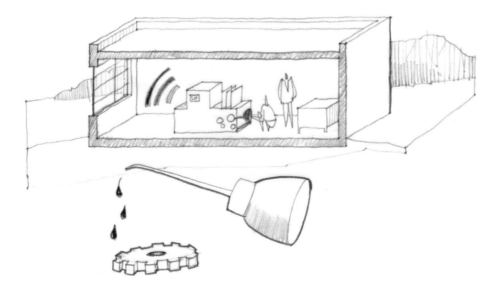

Figure 13.2 Fixing the noisy machine (shown in Figure 13.1) is often the best strategy for dealing with the noise. Such treatments can include periodic maintenance or prompt repair.

Figure 13.3 A moveable plastic cover on an electric typewriter can be lowered over the element-and-platen cavity to reduce noise produced when the typing element repeatedly strikes the paper and platen.

The third approach to noise reduction is to isolate a noise source by enclosing it (see Figure 13.4). Using an enclosure to surround the source will reduce the amount of airborne noise energy that can pass from the source to some nearby person. For example, if a typewriter and its operator can be placed in a small fully enclosed office complete with an operable door, then the noise that travels from the machine to other office workers can be substantially reduced. To increase the amount of noise reduction that the enclosure will provide, a fourth step that can be taken is to apply absorbing materials to the inside surfaces of the enclosure (see Figure 13.5). These materials will absorb some of the energy from the noise source, decreasing the amount of noise that could pass beyond the enclosure.

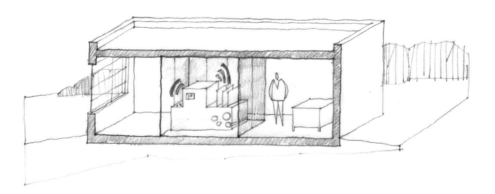

Figure 13.4 An enclosure around a noisy machine can greatly reduce the amount of noise that passes out of the enclosure into adjacent spaces occupied by workers.

Figure 13.5 Placing absorptive materials on the inside surfaces of an enclosure surrounding a noisy source can lower the sound pressure level exhibited in the immediate space. Reducing the internal sound pressure level will, in turn, reduce the sound pressure level outside of the immediate space. An even better means for lowering the external sound pressure level would be to select an enclosure assembly that has a reduced sound transmittance.

Generally, the creation of an enclosure to separate a receiver from a noise source is the best means for accomplishing noise reduction (i.e., other than removing or shutting down the source). However, the *amount* of noise separation displayed by an enclosure is determined by the *composition(s)* of the planes of the enclosure. For instance, an office space enclosure made of single-pane glass is a far less effective separator than an enclosure constructed of gypsum wallboard supported by steel studding. Furthermore, an

---

SIDEBAR 13.1 Factors affecting how much noise separation an enclosure can provide

How much noise separation an enclosure envelope will exhibit is dependent on three physical properties: mass, rigidity (or stiffness), and damping resistance. Each of these properties affects the ability of an envelope—or layers within the envelope—to vibrate. When sound waves arrive at a building envelope, much of the energy of the incident waves will be reflected by the surface of the envelope. However, some of the mechanical energy is transmitted into the envelope. The transmitted energy becomes kinetic energy that is manifested in the vibrations that the envelope undergoes and potential energy that the envelope acquires as it deflects.

First, the amount of *mass* that an envelope has determines how much kinetic energy is required for vibration to occur: kinetic energy varies directly with mass. As the mass of an envelope increases, the resistance to the commencement and continuance of vibration also increases. So, a more massive envelope will provide greater separation than will a less massive envelope. An envelope composed of a thicker layer of some material (e.g., concrete) will offer more separation than will a thinner layer of the same material. And a layer of a more dense material will have a greater separation than a layer of a less dense material, if both layers have the same thickness.

Second, the rigidity of an envelope establishes the amount of potential energy that the envelope can acquire through deflection (as the envelope experiences strain). The more strain that a material layer (in the envelope) can sustain, the greater the quantity of potential energy that the layer can acquire and the less kinetic energy the layer (and envelope) will manifest. Thus, the ability of a material layer to undergo extensive strain contributes to increased noise separation being shown by the layer. And, so, a limp material layer (and envelope)—one which can endure much deformation—will provide a greater noise separation than will a stiffer layer (and envelope).

The third physical property of a material layer (in an envelope) that influences its noise separation is damping, a process that involves the conversion of mechanical energy into thermal energy. This energy conversion occurs due to frictional forces within the layer. As mechanical energy is required to initiate and continue vibratory motion, the conversion of the mechanical energy to thermal energy will reduce the amount of energy available for vibration. Thus, damping imposes resistance to vibration and the transmission of sound waves through a layer. Generally, materials that are soft, pliant, and/or flexible will exhibit good damping. Specific materials (or classes of materials) which display such qualities include various nonrigid plastics and polymeric foams, rubber, silicones, cork, and sand (when used as a bulk filler). Numbers of these materials are described in the technical literature as being *viscoelastic* (i.e., they readily behave elastically, but exhibit some resistance to deformation). The primary applications of materials possessing good damping are as intermediate layers within multiple-layered constructions (e.g., in sheets of glass, where a damping layer of some polymeric material is sandwiched between two layers of glass). Other applications involve using good damping materials where panels need to be supported by more rigid structural elements (i.e., the damping materials will cushion the panels against the structural elements). For example, when glazing panes are set into metal frames, a damping material may be placed between the glass and the metal.

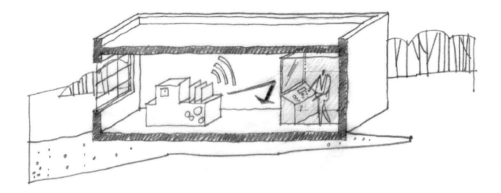

Figure 13.6 A relatively noise-free enclosure within a noisy space — into which an occupant can enter to escape from the ambient noise level — can offer a welcome relief for the occupant.

enclosure of this wallboard assembly will, in turn, be a relatively inferior separator compared with an enclosure composed of concrete masonry units. The choice of enclosure assembly depends on a series of factors, including the massiveness of the enclosure, its stiffness (or rigidity), and its damping resistance.

A fifth noise control option involves the provision of an enclosure in which occupants of a noisy space can enter to escape the noise (see Figure 13.6). Thus, instead of building an enclosure to surround a single noisy source, here we suggest creating an enclosure that will essentially comprise a relatively "noise-free" zone. This latter approach is warranted when several noise sources exist in a space and constructing separate noise enclosures for each of these sources would be too costly. Rather, supplying a single noise-free shelter for occupants would likely be a much less expensive alternative.

A sixth control procedure is the provision of absorbing materials in the space that the receiver occupies. When a noise source is enclosed and the enclosure separates the source from the receiver, placing absorbing materials in the receiver's space will reduce the

SIDEBAR 13.2 Do not design schools with open-plan classrooms

The open-planning of classrooms was a design strategy that was enthusiastically employed in the 1960s and 1970s. The theory that supported open-planning suggested that openness would promote learning through the sharing of resources and the positive interactions between adjacent class groups.

Subsequent examinations of open-plan classrooms built during that period have revealed that the resulting acoustics were inferior. Noise levels were invariably too great. Speech-signal-to-noise-level ratios were too small. Students had difficulties in understanding teachers' speech, generally. And students with any sort of hearing impairment were profoundly isolated. The overall product of open-planned classrooms was that learning suffered significantly.

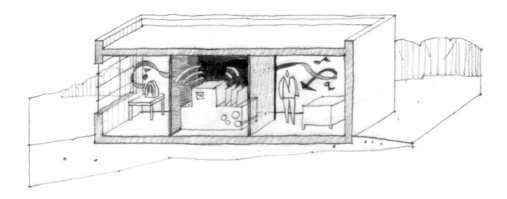

Figure 13.7 Using masking noise to overlay some other less intense, but otherwise objectionable, noise is another strategy for treating the unpleasant, ambient noise.

amount of the noise energy reaching the receiver. Similarly, when the source is unenclosed and there is ready passage of airborne noise from the source to the receiver, installing absorbing materials in the space can reduce the amount of noise energy reaching the receiver. However, enclosing the source and then placing the absorption in the space containing the receiver will nearly always provide substantially better separation than if the source is left unenclosed and absorption is placed on surfaces of the space which the source and receiver share. Again, as we stated above, enclosing the source *or* the receiver — thus, separating one from the other — provides the best means of reducing the amount of noise that an occupant will experience (i.e., when one (or more) noise source(s) must be present).

A seventh noise control strategy applies masking sound (or noise) to override the noise from the source (see Figure 13.7). The intent is not to lessen the amount of noise energy emanating from the source, rather to make the source noise indistinguishable. Examples of this procedure are often used in open-plan (or landscaped) offices or shopping centers. There, to reduce the intrusion that other people's conversations can pose for an uninvolved person, background noise is introduced into the space to mask, or make unintelligible, these "third-party" conversations. Furnishing the masking noise thus establishes speech privacy for those people engaged in conversation and minimizes annoyance that an uninvolved receiver might otherwise experience. This technique is most suitably employed in spaces where a high background noise is permissible and will not conflict with activities that commonly occur in these spaces.

An eighth strategy for noise control involves the wearing of ear coverings or ear plugs by the receiver (see Figure 13.8). In environments with high ambient noise levels, often it will be easier to treat the occupant(s) rather than the noise source(s) or the environment. Such is often true in industrial plants where noise is a by-product of manufacturing or other processes. In these settings, because noise will emanate from many sources that cannot all be individually or multiply enclosed, neither the sources nor the transmission paths can be controlled. Here, workers are encouraged to wear hearing protectors (e.g., earmuffs or earplugs). One limitation presented by the use of these devices is that speech communication between workers will be constrained and other means of communication will

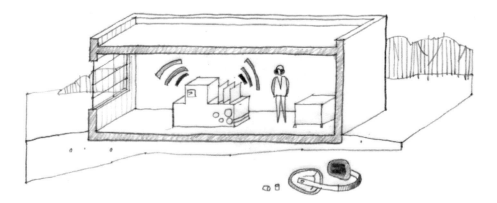

Figure 13.8 Wearing ear plugs or ear coverings is the most appropriate noise reduction method when excessively loud noise sources cannot be enclosed and occupants must share space with them.

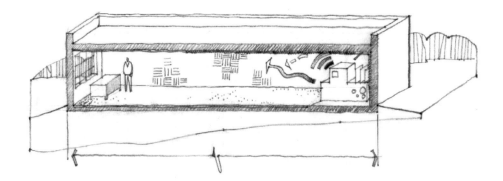

Figure 13.9 Increasing the distance between a noise source and a listener can reduce the adverse effects of the noise on the listener, *as long as both the source and the listener are in a basically open field.*

have to be used (e.g., hand signals or written messages). In such excessively noisy spaces, the primary reason for using these protection devices is to foster hearing conservation among the workers.

The ninth and last strategy for providing noise control is to substantially increase the distance between the source and a receiver (see Figure 13.9). This technique is generally useful only in an open (or free) field, where enclosing surfaces will not reflect sound waves (because the surfaces are widely separated). With open field conditions the intensity of the sound wave decreases according to the Inverse Square Law. So, by lengthening the transmission path, the noise level experienced at some distance from the source will be less than is found at a position closer to the source.

All of these nine noise control devices and strategies can be used singly or in various combinations. Generally, when a designer or builder confronts a noise control problem, developing a solution will require working with several of these control devices in combination. For instance, if we again consider how to treat the noise problem created by having a typewriter in an office space, a variety of noise control solutions are available. We could place a plastic cover over the typewriter cavity containing the platen and typing element. We could apply absorbing materials on the walls and ceiling surrounding the workstation. We could even furnish earplugs to the typewriter operator and any work associates who may also be present in the space containing this workstation. Alternatively, we could create a separate, enclosed space for the typewriter and its operator. By selecting this latter approach, we would then have to establish how much noise separation should be provided by the enclosure (i.e., what the compositions of the walls, floor, and ceiling should be). As a further response, we could also elect to place absorption in the space outside of the typewriter enclosure. So, any two or more of these solutions could be employed, in combination, to solve this noise control problem.

The provision of noise control features in building and external spaces is an essential responsibility during design and construction. However, treating likely noise problems will demand the resolution of conflicting alternatives. Regarding such trade-offs, we previously introduced the notion of the PEST issues at the beginning of Chapter 12 and noted how these issues influence the selection of methods of noise intervention. For such circumstances, choosing the most favorable solution will almost always involve difficult decisions.

13.2.2 GENERAL STRATEGIES FOR ENHANCING COMMUNICATION BY SOUND

Just as there are a number of approaches that will foster noise control in buildings and external spaces, there are also several strategies that will promote sound propagation. Like the various noise control practices, these seven sound-enhancement strategies should generally be employed in combination.

First, ensure that there is a suitably quiet ambient noise level (i.e., that the background noise level is sufficiently low). The specific level that is acceptable in a space depends upon the nature of the activities that occur there. In Section 12.3.2 we identified the acceptable background noise levels for various activities (in terms of the Balanced Noise Criterion curves). Alternative noise control devices that can be applied have been described in Section 13.2.1.

Second, encourage the flow of *direct sound* from the source to the receiver (see Figure 13.10). The path across which sound waves will travel between the source and the receiver must be unobstructed and direct. While planning a space the designer should make certain that uninterrupted lines-of-sight will exist between all of the locations where a source and a receiver will likely be. To confirm that these unobstructed lines-of-sight are present, the designer should employ the *ray-diagramming* technique (described in Section 10.2.2.2).

Third, keep the distance between the source and the receiver as short as possible. Maintaining short path lengths for sound wave passage will ensure that the sound waves will undergo little attenuation. Thus, there will be little loss of sound intensity. Short transmission path lengths will generally offer fewer opportunities for obstructions to interfere with transmission. But the lengths of sound transmission paths are also subject to other considerations. One example where trade-offs arise occurs in the creation of large multipurpose performance spaces. For these facilities, contrasting needs will usually exist between providing strong, direct sound waves (by maintaining short path lengths) and establishing sufficiently great volumes (to foster sound wave reflection and the build-up of reverberant fields).

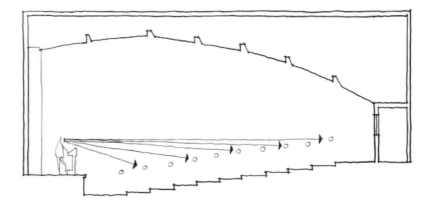

Figure 13.10 When good sound propagation is important, a direct *line-of-sight* sound path should readily exist between any source and the receiver(s).

Figure 13.11 In this large classroom improved lines-of-sight between a speaker and the listeners are achieved by stepping the chair rows. From any chair in the classroom a listener should readily be able to see — and establish a clear line-of-sight — with the lecturer.

SIDEBAR 13.3 Designing for line-of-sight between source and receiver

For situations where speech is the principal communication form, lines-of-sight should be sought between a speaker's mouth and the heads (or, more precisely, the ears) of the listeners. Thus, sound waves should be able to pass from the speaker to each listener without anything interfering with the wave transit (e.g., someone else's head). For example, in a classroom, each listener should be able to see the speaker: after all, the listener's eyes and ears are at the same height. One practice that can improve the likelihood that an unobstructed line-of-sight will exist between a listener and a speaker is to place the more-distant listeners' chairs

on a gentle incline (see Figure 13.11). This incline should become gradually steeper as the distance between the speaker and listener increases. By providing such an incline, listeners in more distant seats will be better able to look—maintain uninterrupted lines-of-sight—over people sitting in less distant chairs. One other practice that is also useful for developing good sight lines in larger spaces is furnishing the speaker with a raised platform on which to stand (e.g., a stage). The height of such a platform above the audience floor will depend on the size of the room and the number of people in the audience (see Figure 13.12).

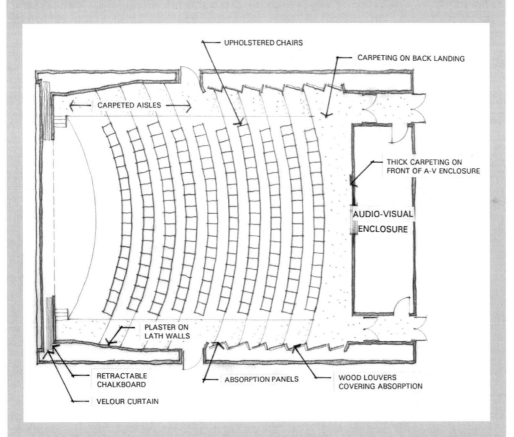

Figure 13.12 Here is a seating plan for a conventional lecture room. An essential issue in designing this space is to ensure that all areas of the audience should have good sight lines toward the stage (i.e., the location of potential sound sources).

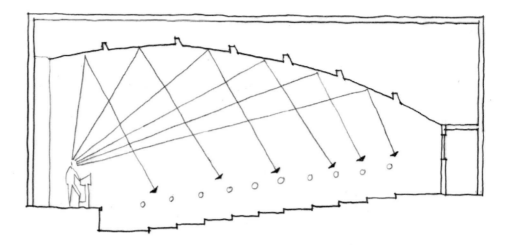

Figure 13.13 Placing reflecting panels near, above, and in front of a speaker can greatly improve the beneficial reflection of sound waves toward a listener.

Fourth, employ reflected sound to reinforce the direct sound. Thus, surfaces should be provided near the sound source to reflect some of the energy of the direct sound waves toward the receiver. It is critically important that reflected sound waves arrive at the receiver from nearly the same direction as the direct sound wave. In virtually no circumstance should the direct wave arrive at the front of the receiver and a reflected wave, which is strong enough to be perceived easily, reach the receiver from the back. The value of providing reflected sound waves to augment direct sound is that these reflected waves essentially amplify the direct sound, offering additional energy to the message transmitted from the source (see Figure 13.13).

By making sure that the direct and reflected sound waves arrive from the same (or an approximately similar) direction, there will also be less confusion about the location of the sound source. If the sound waves come from appreciably different directions, the capability

---

SIDEBAR 13.4 Sound wave attenuation

The attenuation of sound waves—a gradual loss of mechanical energy as the waves travel through air—occurs because the air absorbs the sound wave energy. In small spaces (e.g., classrooms for 30 to 50 people, conference rooms, and so forth), attenuation is not a significant effect. But in larger lecture halls and auditoriums, the loss of sound intensity due to attenuation can be substantial. For these larger spaces using space planning techniques like inclining the seat rows to shorten the distance between source and listener can reduce the extent of attenuation (see Figures 13.11 and 13.12). The amount of attenuation is also frequency-related: attenuation is greater for middle-to-high-frequency sounds (i.e., from about 1000 Hz upward).

to *localize* on the sound will be greatly reduced. One additional corollary to this strategy is that the path of the reflected waves should be kept as short as possible (to minimize the difference in time between when the direct wave and the reflected wave reach the receiver). Examining likely reflection paths is easily done using the ray-diagramming technique, when estimating the likely behaviors of sound waves in proposed spaces.

Fifth, place absorbing materials on appropriate surfaces throughout a space. Generally, two questions must be considered when allocating sound absorption materials: how much absorption is needed; and where should the absorption be located? Resolving this first issue depends on what kind of communication activities will occur in the space and whether the space should appear more "lively" or more "dead." In more lively spaces, sound waves will experience prolonged travel (i.e., the length of time that a sound wave will travel before it ceases to be audible will be relatively longer). For these lively spaces, surfaces should be finished to promote the reflection of sound waves (with a concomitant reduction in the use of absorbing surfaces). Alternatively, in comparatively dead spaces, surfaces will be more absorbent and will display a lessened ability to reflect sound (resulting in shorter passage lengths for the sound waves). As a general rule, spaces in which speech is the principal form of communication should appear slightly deader than spaces in which music is the primary communication. Where absorption is best placed should be determined by considering which surfaces should be used to reflect sound waves and which surfaces should diminish the energy of the incident sound waves, minimizing their abilities to spread further. Establishing solutions for this two-part problem is one of the more difficult and uncertain tasks in acoustical designing.

One general guideline, however, concerning the use of absorption materials is that the space planner should minimize the presence of unwanted reflections. To accomplish this objective the planner must anticipate the paths that sound waves will follow as they move outward from one (or more) source(s). Then, considering where building surfaces in the space will probably be located, the planner must decide whether these surfaces should be primarily reflective or absorbent. To make such a decision the planner should ascertain the extent to which reflecting waves will enhance good hearing conditions in the space. Specifically, the planner needs to think about the directions from which the reflecting waves will come (versus the directions of the direct waves) and how lively or dead the space should be. If the direction of a potential reflected wave is substantially different from the probable directions along which direct waves will arrive at a listener, then absorption should be placed on the surface from which the reflecting wave had "bounced." Further, the use of reflected waves to reinforce direct waves should be limited to first reflections (i.e., those for which the original wave "bounces off" of only one surface before proceeding toward the receiver). Second-order and other higher-order reflections happen when a sound wave reflects consecutively off more than one surface on the way to the receiver. These multiple-order reflections should be discouraged because the time delay between the arrival of the direct sound and the arrivals of the multiple-order reflections can be large (see Figures 13.14 and 13.15). Such time delays between direct and higher-order reflected sounds will generally be too long. The result of long-delayed sounds (from a multiple-order reflection) arriving at a receiver well after the direct wave is that the receiver will likely experience confusion. The person will be hearing, at the same time, both earlier-produced sounds that have taken circuitous reflection paths to the listener and other later sounds that are transmitted along direct routes.

Note that the time delay between the arrival of sound traveling directly from the source to the listener and sound that has reflected off one (or more) surfaces(s) can be found by determining the difference in the distances that the reflected and direct sounds travel in reaching the listener. Then, dividing this difference of travel lengths (distances) by the speed of sound will indicate the time delay between the arrivals of the two sounds. Generally, time delays—between the arrivals of direct and reflected sounds—greater than about 0.035 seconds should be avoided.

Sixth, the volume of the space should be chosen to fit the activities that will occur in the space. The volume should be neither excessively large nor small. What volume is

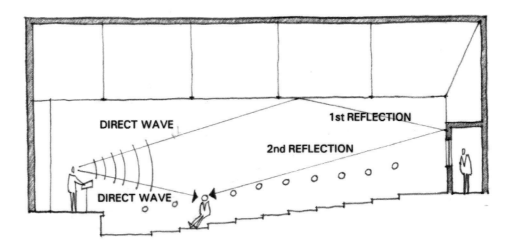

Figure 13.14 The pathway for the second-order reflection demonstrates how a long-delayed reflection can arrive at a listener from an unfortunate direction (i.e., competing with the arrival of the direct sound).

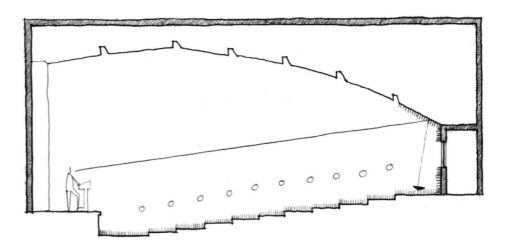

Figure 13.15 Absorption should be placed on surfaces that can cause the formation of long-delayed reflections. Generally, placing absorbing materials on ceiling and wall areas toward the back of rooms used for speaking will minimize potentially bothersome long-delayed reflections.

appropriate for a given activity will depend on the character(s) of the sound source(s), the number of people who will want to hear the source(s), and whether the primary communication form is speech, music, or both. The major concern in achieving a suitable volume for communication is to ensure that the source(s) will be adequately loud. Generally, spaces where speech is the principal means of communication should be smaller than comparable spaces in which music is predominantly executed (because the average person's voice possesses less power than can be produced by musical instruments, especially when these instruments are used in combination).

Lastly, carefully choose the shape of the enclosure in which sound communication is important (i.e., whether the enclosure shape is looked at in plan or sectional views). Generally, reflecting surfaces will function best if they are planar. Curvilinear shapes — whether rounded or elliptical — must be introduced with care. Convex surfaces provide very good means for diffusing sound energy, thereby contributing to the build-up of a uniform spread of sound energy throughout a space. But concave surfaces should be avoided in both plan and section. Concave-shaped surfaces cause the formations of areas with concentrated sound energy — resulting from the focusing of sound waves into these areas — and areas with little or no sound energy. Further, cubical spaces and square plan shapes are also not desirable.

Necessarily, the guidelines presented here in this section are general. They are intended as starting points for thinking about how a space should be organized, particularly when communication by sound is an important feature of the space. These general guidelines can be used for creating very rough (or approximate) space designs. But, probably, the designer and builder should examine the more specific guidelines that are presented in the remainder of this chapter.[2]

Section 13.3 | SPECIFIC SITE-PLANNING GUIDELINES

For site planning the principal issue for creating spaces that will have good acoustical performance — whether external to or within buildings — is controlling the level of noise that reaches the site. As a simple, but effective, rule, if you can keep the site of a building (or an external-use space) quiet, it will be substantially easier to keep the interior of the building quiet. In this section we will describe some planning and operating strategies and some physical devices that can be employed to reduce the effects of environmental noise on people. The discussion will focus on noise control approaches that will reduce how much noise reaches external use spaces and the envelopes of buildings located near noise sources.

In Section 12.1.1 we identified a variety of noise sources. Some of these sources are usually found in the external environment, whereas the others are present within buildings. Major noise producers occur outside of buildings. Examples include aircraft — either those taking off, landing, or simply flying over a site — or ground transportation — cars, buses, trucks, motorcycles, and trains. Construction activities and industrial plant operations often generate substantial noise. And even town and cityscape inhabitants and participants can be noisy (e.g., crowds of people, delivery of goods, lawnmowers, barking dogs, fire alarms and vehicles, and so forth).

A source such as traffic moving along a major expressway will provide constant noise, day and night. The noise level in an urban business district will be sustained (and high) for the majority of each business day. Alternatively, this same area will often be relatively quiet during the evenings and on weekends. Noise created by aircraft taking off and landing at airports is intermittent depending on when the flights start and conclude.

Noise from airplanes flying over a neighborhood will similarly be episodic and not constant. Industrial plants can operate during specific hours or continuously day and night. Construction activities can create substantial noise levels when a building or a roadway is under construction. However, after the project has been completed, the site may once again appear as quiet as it was before the initiation of the construction work.

Further, the noise source(s) will probably exhibit variable intensity levels. Consequently, designers and builders should consider what noise sources may exist around a building site and should determine what characteristics these sources will display. Once such information is gathered, then the building planners can investigate means for overcoming the potential disruption (by these external noises) of activities expected to occur inside the future building.

13.3.1   Site planning and operating strategies for noise control   In Section 13.2.1 we have catalogued a number of noise control strategies: some of them are especially relevant for consideration during site planning. For instance, when noise sources are present near a site (see Figure 13.16), getting a noise source removed or having operation of the source made less noisy are two prominent control solutions. Finding means to have the sources eliminated, or even curtailed, may require political action involving regulatory agencies or

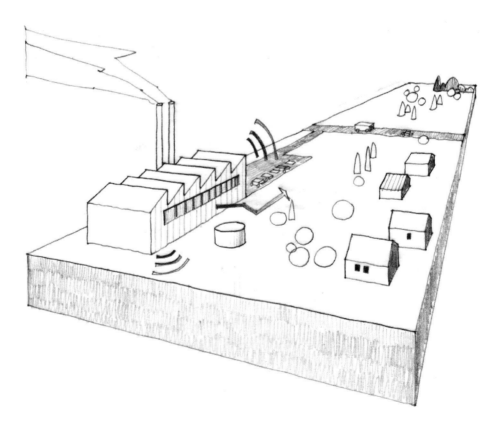

Figure 13.16 Industrial plants can generate high noise levels that spread across a surrounding community.

negotiation between the developers of a new building and the operator of the noise source. But these control efforts, if successful, can make subsequent building design and construction easier and will likely ensure better performance within buildings (or in spaces external to buildings). A third strategy — increasing the distance between a noise source and a new building (or external-use space) — can provide effective noise control, if adequate ground space is available and nearly free-field conditions exist (see Figure 13.17).

Two additional strategies can also be applied for noise control. First, where noisy events occur and cannot be restricted by any one of the three strategies mentioned in the previous paragraph, then you might seek to alter the schedule of the events producing the noise. For instance, you might attempt to have the regularity with which noise is generated decreased or to have the times when the noise is produced shifted to some other time of the day or week. One example of this strategy has been widely employed at airports to reduce night-time noise levels (i.e., to reduce sleep interference from noise created by aircraft). Second, it is incumbent on the designer and builder to consider land use compatibility when seeking

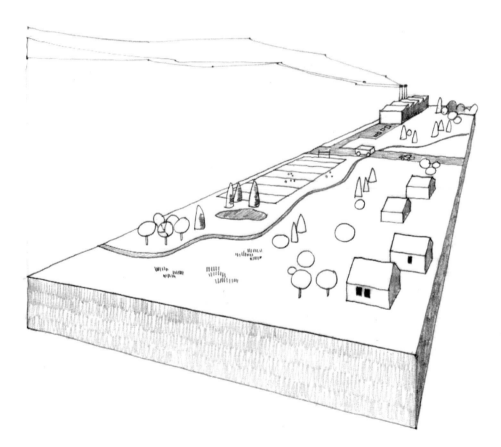

Figure 13.17 One solution to the presence of a noisy industrial plant is to develop a zone around the plant in which only buildings whose activities can withstand similar noise levels will be located. For building applications requiring sites with lower ambient noise levels, placing such buildings at considerable distances from the noisy plant can reduce the noise levels that will reach these buildings. Note that the noise from the plant will behave as a point source.

land on which to place a building (or an external-use space). Thus, an individual should try not to construct a building (or external-use space), if the building (or space) will require quiet conditions and adjacent land has noisy activities present (and these activities cannot be controlled by any of the previously mentioned site-planning strategies). For instance, locating a church or a movie theater near an urban highway can pose significant problems: the interior of either facility needs to have a relatively silent background noise level, and the external noise level created by the highway can be quite high. Further, the opening of doors or windows during a church service—to permit latecomers to enter or to facilitate natural ventilation on warm days—will provide direct paths for external noise to enter into and intrude upon the service. So, constructing the church or the theater on a quieter site away from traffic noise can simplify establishing a quiet interior for either building use.

13.3.2 MANIPULATING PHYSICAL FORMS (AND FUNCTIONS)

13.3.2.1   Using barriers to reduce site noise   One means of reducing the amount of noise that a listener will hear from a nearby noise source is to increase the distance between the source and the listener. But in many urban and suburban situations, it is not possible to employ this strategy because land availability is limited and, commonly, a site

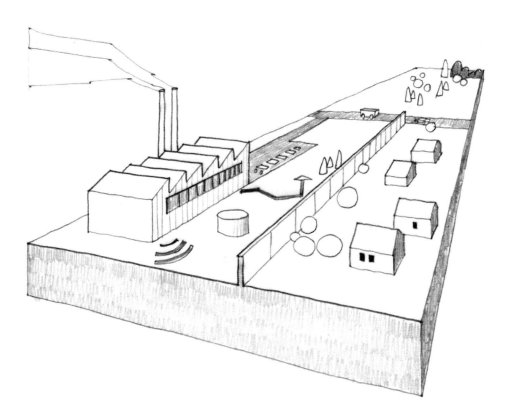

Figure 13.18 A barrier can be used to reduce the amount of noise created by a noisy industrial plant that will be incident on the surrounding community.

that a client furnishes a designer or builder is the only one that can be used. In such instances an alternative means for separating the receiver from an adjacent source is to create a physical barrier between them (see Figure 13.18). Various noise barriers that can be employed include masonry walls, wooden fences, or earth berms. Occasionally, buildings or hillocks—if they already exist on a site—can be employed to separate newly placed receivers from noise sources. Generally, the best performing built-up barriers will be those that are constructed of dense, rigid materials.

The most prevalent reason for using noise barriers is to reduce traffic noise that can impinge on adjacent building and external-use spaces (see Figure 13.19). A secondary, though still important, application of barriers occurs at urban airports where walls are placed at the ends of runways as "blast fences." These blast fences divert the noise and hot gases emitted by jet engines as aircraft prepare for take-offs.

The primary function of a noise barrier is to obstruct the line-of-sight between sources and a receiver. Essentially, the sound waves emanating from the sources are

Figure 13.19 A large, tall precast concrete barrier is used along a major thoroughfare in Seattle to reduce the noise that would otherwise impinge on the adjacent residential community.

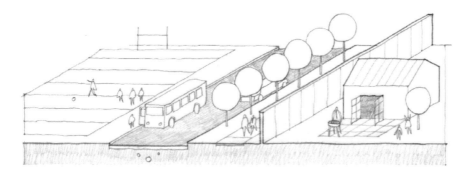

Figure 13.20 A house placed in the sound shadow of a barrier can experience reduced sound pressure levels from noise than would otherwise be present if the barrier did not exist.

deflected up and over the vertical barrier, creating a *sound shadow* behind the barrier (see Figure 13.20). The principal parameter determining the extent of the sound shadow created behind a barrier is the height of the barrier relative to the locations of the source and the receiver (see Figure 13.21). Commonly, the higher a barrier is, the greater distance the sound shadow will extend away from the barrier. With a well-designed barrier the noise levels in such a sound shadow can be 20 or more decibels less than those levels found on the barrier side adjacent to the noise source. Thus, by locating a building or external-use space within the sound shadow, a relatively more silent background noise level results (see Figures 13.21 and 13.22).

The value of these barriers can, however, be limited by any of three factors. First, a common behavior of sound waves is that they will be diffracted by the edges of a barrier as they pass over it. This diffraction will cause the waves to bend downward toward receivers who are present behind the barrier, decreasing the effectiveness of the noise shadow. To what extent the effectiveness of a barrier will be reduced by diffraction is related to the wavelength of the noise wave: as the wavelength lengthens — as the frequency of the noise gets lower — then the noise reduction capability of the barrier is further reduced. So, the typical noise barrier will be less effective in creating sound shadows for low-frequency sources than for higher-frequency sources.[3] A second qualification about noise barriers is that they will be substantially more effective if they run continuously for some distance past the area that they are shielding. For instance, if a barrier terminates at the property line for the land area that is to be protected by the barrier, the noise will pass horizontally around the barrier, thus *flanking* it and markedly reducing its utility. The third qualification about the performance of barriers, generally, is that they must be airtight. If air can pass through them, then so, too, can noise. Thus, a picket fence such as one might employ in front of a residence will provide less separation than a continuous, solid fence. For a slatted fence, some of the energy from a noise source is indeed reflected back by the fence staves. But much of the incident energy will pass between the slats. A further limitation on the noise separation provided by such fences is that the presence of gates will also reduce how much noise reduction the fence will supply.

In addition to the height of a barrier, the other major determinant of its noise-reducing capability is its shape. For barriers of equal height, a comparatively thin upright wall will provide better noise reduction than a triangular-shaped wedge which, in turn, will perform better than a three-sided wedge (i.e., for this last shape, the top (or middle) side of the wedge will have a finite width). Hutchins et al. have compared these shapes and a

---

SIDEBAR 13.5 How flanking can occur

The mechanism of this flanking action depends upon where a noise source is located relative to the barrier. If the source and the receiver are on opposite sides of the barrier, some noise will pass around the barrier by the diffraction of sound waves moving horizontally. For this instance, flanking results from the diffraction of sound waves around the edges of the barrier. However, if the source is located beyond the end of the barrier and there is a line-of-sight between the source and the receiver, then the noise energy will pass readily toward the receiver. So, for sources that move horizontally along and past a barrier (e.g., motor vehicles in urban traffic), the effectiveness of the barrier will greatly depend upon how far beyond a receiver the barrier extends in the horizontal direction.

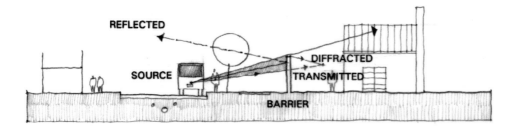

Figure 13.21 The behaviors of noise waves incident on a barrier are displayed here. Depending on the composition of the barrier, more or less noise energy will be reflected by, transmitted through, and/or diffracted over it. The extent that diffracted energy will pass over and down from the top of the barrier is shown in the next illustration, Figure 13.22.

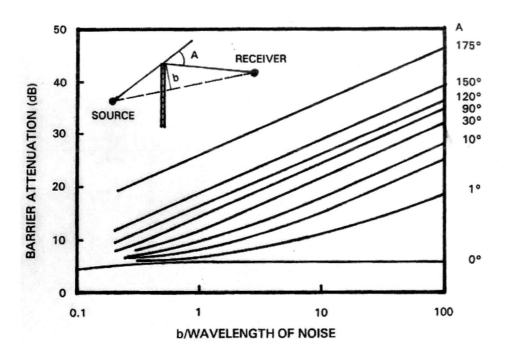

Figure 13.22 This chart predicts the noise-separating performance of a reasonably heavy, rigid barrier. Note that how readily diffraction of incident sound waves occurs is dependent on the wavelength (and, thus, the frequency) of the sound wave and the physical positions of the source and the receiver, relative to the barrier. This illustration has been previously published in a paper by Kurze, U.L., "Noise reduction by barriers," *Journal of the Acoustical Society of America,* 55(3), March 1974, ppg 504–518. Permission to reprint this illustration has been granted by Dr. Kurze and the Acoustical Society of America.

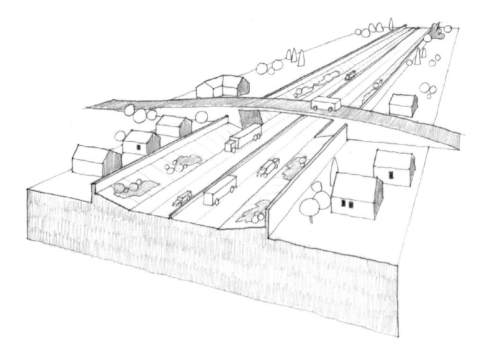

Figure 13.23 A combination barrier is shown here consisting of a grass-covered berm sloping away from the roadway and a thin, vertical concrete wall. Such a combination barrier may be used on one or both sides of a highway, depending on where noise control is required.

number of others, both for situations where a barrier occurs along one side of a roadway (between the noise source and the receiver) and where barriers of like composition are present on both sides of the road. From these tests, the researchers concluded that the most promising barrier form was one which had—on both sides of the roadway—a gently inclined, grass-covered berm sloped from near the road surface up to an upright, thin-walled barrier (see Figure 13.23). When they employed this parallel barrier set-up, they found noise reductions as high as 25 decibels for noise frequencies around 1000 Hz. However, at other frequencies the noise reduction levels were less: for instance, the noise reductions were about 15 decibels at 200 and 500 Hz and 10 to 15 decibels at other frequencies across the spectrum from 100 to about 800 Hz.[4]

13.3.2.2   Depressing urban noise sources below grade levels   A strategy that has been used in numbers of North American and European cities for reduction of noise from urban thoroughfares is to sink the roadways below the surrounding grade levels (see Figure 13.25). For instance, in one study researchers found that by depressing a roadway about 3.66 m (12 ft) below the ambient ground level, a noise reduction of seven to ten decibels was observed across a wide area of the upper ground plane.[5] A further means of reducing noise from these depressed roadways is to cover the roadway as it passes through the urban center (i.e., essentially tunneling the roadway below grade; see Figure 13.26). One example of this latter technique has been created in Seattle where a major interstate roadway

SIDEBAR 13.6 Vegetation as a noise-separating barrier

The performance of vegetation, when used as a noise barrier, is determined by properties other than those that affect how well masonry, wood, or earthen barriers establish noise separation. Barriers constructed of masonry, wood, or earth are generally dense, rigid, and massive. These barriers function by resisting the transmission of noise energy through the barrier. Alternatively, vegetative barriers usually consist of stands of trees (see Figure 13.24). These tree groups do not have the same massiveness or rigidity. Instead, such tree stands reduce noise penetration by scattering (diffusing) and absorbing the energy present in the sound waves. The ability of a tree stand to scatter noise energy is dependent on the number of trees per unit of ground area and the size of the trees — the trunk diameters — and, to a lesser extent, the presence of horizontal branching. Absorption of noise energy is determined primarily by the amount of foliage on the trees and secondarily by the size of the leaves. The other principal factors that establish the noise separation of a tree stand are the depth of the tree stand (i.e., the distance across the stand between the noise source and a receiver) and the frequency of the noise. In fact, tree stands have been found to provide little noise separation for noise frequencies lower than about 500 Hz and considerably better noise reduction for noise frequencies at or above 1000 Hz. Further, the type of tree — whether deciduous or coniferous — also is an important variable. For instance, one study of tree stands reports noise separation capabilities of about 0.1 decibel per meter of depth for densely placed pine trees

and high frequency noise and suggests that the separation rate of 0.05 db/meter would be more representative of typical mixed-species forests. Another study has found a noise separation of eight decibels for a specific red pine forest and virtually no separation provided by a forest of similar dimensions, which was largely composed of *leafless* deciduous trees (e.g., mostly maple, some oak, and a small percentage of hemlock).

One additional benefit — beyond the actual noise reduction capability — that vegetative barriers apparently can offer is an emotional boost for listeners experiencing noise and viewing the vegetation. We have found no empirical evidence to substantiate how much a tree stand — versus, for instance, a concrete wall — can make noise seem more tolerable. But it appears from anecdotal information that vegetative barriers, when used for noise reduction, can indeed provide more effective noise separation than strictly objective measurements would suggest.

For further information about these issues, see the papers by Bullen, R., and F. Fricke, "Sound propagation through vegetation," *Journal of Sound and Vibration,* 80(1), 1982, pages 11–23; Fricke, F., "Sound attenuation in forests," *Journal of Sound and Vibration,* 92(1), 1984, pages 149–158; and Heisler, G.M., O.H. McDaniel, K.K. Hoddon, J.J. Portelli, and S.B. Gleason, "Highway noise abatement in two forests," *Proceedings of the 1987 International Conference on Noise Control Engineering* (Noise-Con 87), (Tichy, J., and S. Hayek, editors), (New York: Noise Control Foundation, 1987), pages 465–470.

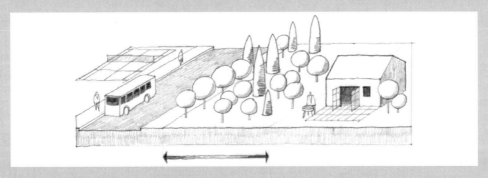

Figure 13.24 A vegetative barrier affords some noise separation, although less than would be provided by a rigid, massive barrier.

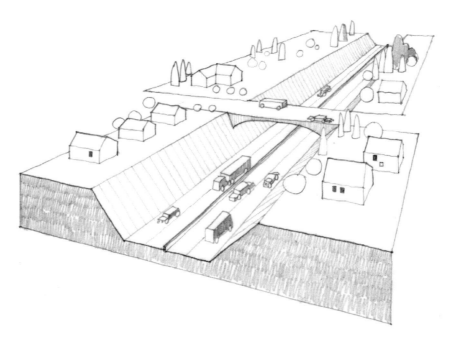

Figure 13.25 Depressing a thoroughfare below the ambient grade plane used for the surrounding buildings and external spaces can reduce the noise levels impinging on these buildings and external spaces.

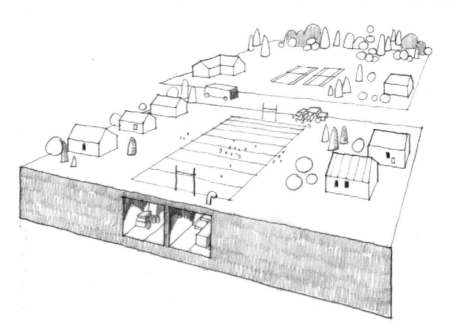

Figure 13.26 Covering below-grade thoroughfares is a very good way to reduce the amount of noise that can reach nearby buildings and external spaces. For further information about methods of reducing noise from busy interurban roadways and results of studies to determine the amount of noise separation achieved with these results, see the paper by Maekawa, Z., "Shielding highway noise," *Noise Control Engineering,* 9(1), July–August 1977, pages 38–44.

runs through the midst of the cityscape. The roadway has been depressed below grade level and covered. A park consisting of alternating areas of vegetation and concrete furnishings has then been constructed on top of the roadway covering (see Figures 13.27 and 13.28). Noise measurements conducted near and along the side of the roadway, in areas near this Seattle park, and in the park itself show noise reduction levels greater than 20 decibels (i.e., noise levels in the park are 20 dB(A) less than those observed along and near the roadway).

Figure 13.27 An aerial view of Freeway Park, an urban park created over a major interstate highway that passes through the business district of Seattle.

Figure 13.28 A space within Freeway Park: the mixture of vegetation, flowing water, and concrete join together to form a quiet, restful place for people to enjoy a bit of nature while in the midst of a busy city center.

Figure 13.29 This urban oasis—Paley Park—has been created amid the frenetic hubbub in mid-town Manhattan (New York City). For those sitting within this park area, the noise of the busy New York City street that fronts Paley Park is completely masked out. Instead, the combination of the sonorous rushing water and the vegetation create a wonderful, refreshing experience for people who can pause a few minutes to sit down and enjoy the ambience of this setting.

Figure 13.30 An urban fountain immediately adjacent to a busy city street in the business district of Seattle offers a pleasant and soothing location for local workers to enjoy lunch or to be away from their offices.

13.3.2.3 Using more pleasant maskers to override off-site noises   One other device that can be used to overcome the effects of intrusive off-site noise is the application of masking sounds to overlay the ambient noise.[6] This technique is based on the presumption that the on-site sounds will be found by auditors to be more pleasant than off-site noises. For this technique to be successful, the masking sound must be generated with sufficient power to enable this intentional sound to override off-site noise. For instance, one sound masker that is occasionally used to overlay off-site noise is running water, whether in a fountain or a waterfall. Further, because the moving water will provide pleasant visual sensations, the sound of the water may also seem all the more agreeable (see Figures 13.29 and 13.30).

Successfully applying on-site maskers to override off-site noise will depend on the pressure levels and spectral composition of the off-site noise. If it appears particularly loud or has some narrow-tone component that is very conspicuous, developing a pleasant masking noise may not be possible (i.e., because any masker that could overlay the off-site noise would also be objectionable). But, by careful design of a watercourse and the regulation of the flow rate, it is often possible to adjust (or tune) the water movement so that the moving water can selectively mask off-site noise. Such tuning and regulation can also create — if produced (and integrated) with attractive visual features — an especially appealing local environment. The use of moving water, notably in courtyard settings, can develop feelings of an oasis (away from the hurly-burly of the cityscape).[7]

Section 13.4 | APPROACHES FOR LAYING OUT BUILDINGS

Once whatever environmental noise control that can be readily accomplished is achieved, then the next step is to explore what techniques can be employed to minimize noise transmission into the proposed building and to enhance sound communication within the building. In this and the following two sections we will describe design and construction strategies and devices for attaining these two goals. In this section we will identify guidelines for laying out buildings to achieve good noise control. In the next section (13.5) we will present information for creating building envelopes to ensure good noise separation. In Section 13.6 we will suggest a variety of interior devices and means whose use can enhance sound communication in building spaces.

13.4.1 PLANNING DEVICES TO USE WHEN THE BUILDING SITE IS NOISY

The first guideline suggests that you do not place a space in which activities occur that require a quiet background next to a place where noisy activities are present. For instance, constructing a library reading room immediately adjacent to a busy thoroughfare will inevitably lead to traffic noises interfering with the reading and concentration that library-goers seek to accomplish. Alternatively, attempting to answer a telephone — trying to hear what the calling person is saying — will be difficult in an office that has an operating photocopy machine. Or having an operating outdoor fan unit (condenser) of a residential heat pump just outside of and underneath a bedroom window will likely disturb the sleep of most people who occupy the bedroom. The fundamental problem for each of these situations is that the noise level in the quiet space needs to be low and the adjacent space has excessive noise.

Often it is technically feasible to create an envelope (or enclosure) that can provide adequate noise separation. But the production of a virtually noise-proof envelope (or enclosure) will require that comparatively difficult and expensive noise control procedures be applied. In many instances, however, clients, designers, and/or builders will elect not to employ suitable noise control features, and the subsequent occupants will suffer. So, instead of having to rely on the development of extraordinary noise controls, it is greatly preferable to avoid placing noisy activities and spaces requiring a quiet background close to each other.

When a space requiring a quiet background must be placed near a space (or an environment) in which noisy events are common, one good solution is to create an intermediate buffer zone between the noise source and the receiver. One common example is the placement of a lobby or foyer in the front of the entrances to movie theaters or concert halls (see Figure 13.31). Thus, the intermediate space works as a sound trap for street noise. When a fully developed lobby cannot be included in (or is not appropriate) for some building, then a designer or builder may employ a vestibule to serve as the sound trap (see Figure 13.32). Having doors at the ends of a vestibule that operate in opposition (i.e., one remains closed when the other is opened) will enhance the ability of the vestibule to work as a noise separator. One additional method for keeping street noise from entering through doorways is to use revolving doors instead of the conventional swinging doors (see Figures 13.33 and 13.34). The use of an opposing-door operation is intended for the times when the passage rate through the vestibule will be relatively low. Normally, these types of door control can be overridden when there is need for rapid admission to or evacuation from the inner space.

Overall, each of these strategies is intended to place the space requiring comparatively quieter conditions in the midst of the building and to reduce the opportunities by which street noise can enter into this quiet space. In fact, a common practice that is employed when performing arts centers are constructed in areas with potentially bothersome site noise is the encircling of the performance space with a series of other spaces. Thus, dressing rooms, practice rooms, offices, lobbies, and so forth surround the quiet-needing space

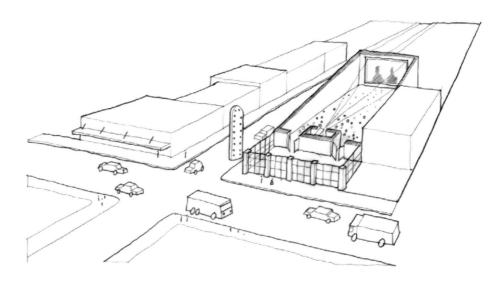

Figure 13.31 A lobby can be used as an intermediate sound "lock" to resist the flow of site noise into the midst of a quiet building space.

Figure 13.32 A vestibule can serve as a "sound trap" when the presence of a lobby is not warranted (e.g., by reason of inadequate space availability or financial resources).

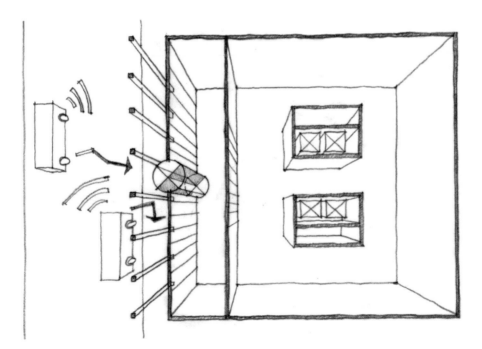

Figure 13.33 A revolving door, used as an entrance to a building, can reduce noise transmission into the lobby of the building.

Figure 13.34 For a high-rise office building in Boston, Massachusetts, a revolving-door entry has been included to reduce noise transmission (and to help maintain air pressure within the building).

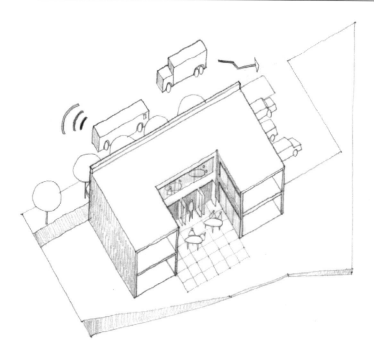

Figure 13.35 An urban courtyard can offer a peaceful alternative to the busy streetscape. This technique of surrounding an enclosed garden area with a series of adjacent buildings is one that is used in numerous restaurants which have both indoor and out-of-doors seating areas (i.e., the outdoor area is used for food service when weather permits).

Figure 13.36 Street noise that may intrude into the courtyard can be masked by the more pleasant sounds of the moving water of this fountain.

with a ring of buffer zones. Activities conducted in these perimeter spaces can occur even if the activities are exposed to high noise levels (i.e., resulting from the transmission of external noise into these perimeter spaces). When performances occur within the central space, the various activities that ordinarily transpire in the perimeter spaces are shut down, minimizing the possibilities that noises from these spaces might disrupt a performance.

This principle can also be applied when a quiet exterior space is sought and the street-side noise levels are high. Then, the creation of a courtyard bounded by a surrounding building is warranted (see Figures 13.35 and 13.36). With the courtyard surrounded by adjoining multiple-story buildings, this exterior space should enjoy noise levels many decibels less than those existing at the fronts of the buildings.[8]

A third practice for reducing sound transmission into buildings that are located adjacent to noisy spaces is to place the building entry on an elevation of the building that faces away from the noise events (see Figure 13.37). By establishing the entry on a side of the building away from the noisy front elevation, the intensity of the sound waves incident on this secondary side of the building will often be substantially less than those sound waves that impinge on the front elevation. One additional strategy that will complement this practice is to minimize the presence of any reflection paths by which noise from the street can get to the secondary-side entrance. Accomplishing this latter strategy may include the use of a privacy wall or cul-de-sac that faces away from the street elevation (see Figure 13.38) or a vestibule at the entryway.

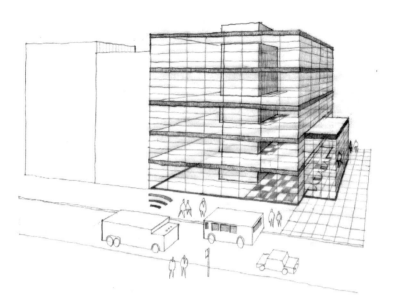

Figure 13.37 Locating a building entrance on an off-street side of a building, rather than on the front (where the front side faces a busy street) will reduce the amount of noise which will likely pass through the entry.

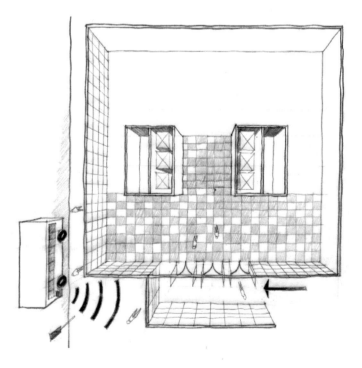

Figure 13.38 Surrounding a building entry with an enclosure that does not open directly onto a busy street—thus forming a cul-de-sac for the entrance—can reduce the opportunity for street noise to penetrate into the building.

Section 13.5 | CRITERIA FOR THE SELECTION OF BUILDING ENVELOPE COMPOSITIONS

To establish good acoustical conditions within a building, the fundamental role for the building envelope involves minimizing the amount of external noise that can enter the building. In Section 12.1 we have identified various common environmental noise sources and have described the characteristics of the noises that they generate. Three major factors determine how well a relatively quiet background can be maintained inside a building when there is substantial external noise. The first factor involves the sound pressure levels and spectral patterns of the external noises (e.g., how loud or noisy do the external sources appear, and do the sources produce high or low frequency sounds?). The second factor concerns the compositions and surface areas of the elements of the building envelope (i.e., how much fenestration will be present; how readily does the fenestration assemblies transmit noise; and so forth?). The third factor concerns how well the envelope is assembled (e.g., what are the natures of the details for sealing the envelope components, and with what degree of care is the construction of these joints conducted?).

Other issues can also affect how well a quiet background can be maintained in a building space. These other issues include the noise levels generated in the immediate space and in any adjacent spaces, the compositions and surface areas of the partitions that separate the immediate space from others, and the presence of absorbing materials in the immediate space. But, necessarily, the latter three issues describe how the interior of a building is developed, rather than suggesting what the character of the building envelope should be.

13.5.1 DESCRIBING THE ADMISSION AND CONTROL OF EXTERNAL NOISE

Noise can enter a building either from sources that emit airborne sound waves or from impacting sources that set the building (or selected components of the building) into vibration. These two noise types have previously been identified and described in Section 12.1.3. We will offer further discussion here on methods that can be employed to reduce airborne sound transmission. Note that establishing treatments for impact noise separation will more often be performed during the design development phase of the building design process (i.e., after many of the early building planning and envelope composition issues have been resolved during schematic designing).[9]

Sound transmission into a building by airborne sound waves occurs by either of two mechanisms: through continuous air paths that exist in the building envelope or by diaphragmatic action of the envelope. For the first of these mechanisms, any crack, opening, or other discontinuity, which enables air to pass from one side of the building envelope to the other, will allow external sound waves to enter the building. Uncaulked joints between framing components of a building envelope or open windows and doors are two common paths by which noise passes through an envelope. Normally, by systematically closing off such paths, sound transmission through the affected envelopes can be significantly reduced.

Noise admission by diaphragmatic action occurs when sound waves incident on the envelope induce it to flex repeatedly (i.e., much as a drumhead flexes when struck). The inward-flexing motion will cause pressure waves to be initiated on the internal side of the envelope. These interior pressure waves thus effectively perpetuate the noise presence that exists external to the building, albeit at lower relative pressure levels. Also, note that sound transmission by this diaphragmatic action occurs without any external air actually passing through the envelope to the interior. Instead, sound transmission happens by some of the mechanical energy of the external sound wave being transferred across the envelope. The fraction of the mechanical energy that does reach the interior surface of the envelope creates pressure waves in the interior room air. If these entering pressure waves have sufficient intensity, then occupants of the interior space will perceive the entering sounds. Generally, the solution to inhibiting sound transmission by diaphragmatic action is to develop mechanisms that will permit as little of the mechanical energy of the incident sound waves to be transferred through the envelope. To accomplish this task, envelopes should either resist the initiation of flexural vibrations or absorb the mechanical energy before it passes across the envelope.

13.5.2 NOISE-SEPARATING BEHAVIORS FOR ENVELOPE COMPOSITIONS

An important question that must be confronted during the design of a building is, what should be the composition of its envelope? Necessarily, a variety of factors—many of which involve issues other than noise separation—will need to be considered. However, for many buildings, the ability to keep external noise from disrupting activities within the building will be a cardinal requirement. Here, we will further describe some properties and other features that are major determinants of how well an envelope can resist the penetration of external noise.

13.5.2.1 Opaque walls as noise separators A first question about the composition of opaque walls concerns whether any wall should be made up of single or multiple layers. Single-layered walls will often be less complicated and less costly to build. But obtaining all the desired properties from a single-layered wall is usually not possible. Instead, when one employs a single-layered wall, choosing its composition will require facing difficult trade-offs. As an example, two of the most important material properties determining the transmission loss of an envelope are mass and stiffness. Generally, to maximize the noise separation that an envelope can provide, the envelope must be massive and limp. But finding a single material that demonstrates these two properties and satisfies other envelope requirements (e.g., weatherproof, resistance to heat transfer, and so forth) is unlikely. As a result, envelopes are most commonly composed of several layers, with each layer fulfilling some specific requirement. Thus, by selecting a multiple-layered envelope, the envelope, in aggregate, will more nearly display all the required properties.

As we have written previously in Sidebar 13.1, the primary properties that establish how well an envelope can reduce sound transmission are the mass, rigidity, and damping of the envelope. Now, let's consider how these properties affect opaque wall performance. First, as a general rule, doubling the mass of a wall will increase its noise separation rating by an increment of approximately 6 decibels. Second, no single such rule exists for describing the benefits gained by altering the rigidity (stiffness) or the damping of a wall. Because walls that are massive tend to use materials that also are comparatively stiff, there are few means for simultaneously increasing the mass and lessening the apparent stiffness of a wall. Third, including dead air spaces in walls can increase their noise separation capacities by as much as 10 decibels. Fourth, filling a dead air space with a sound-absorbing material like batt insulation will usually offer a three to four decibel improvement (i.e., versus similar walls built without this sound-absorbing material). What increase in noise separation would be obtained when a wall assembly includes both a dead air space and sound-absorbing material—in series—has not been reported in the professional literature. But it appears likely that such a combination might create an improvement approximately equal to the sum of the individual gains produced when either a dead air space or sound-absorbing material is independently added to wall assemblies.[10]

13.5.2.2 Floors and roofs Noise separation for floor and roof assemblies that are exposed to the external environment must include treatment not only to reduce transmission by airborne noise sources, but also to minimize transmission induced by impact loading. Lessening airborne sound transmission through floors and roofs can generally be ensured, if these assemblies have properties comparable to those wall compositions that offer good noise separation. For instance, using assemblies with considerable mass provides better separation than will be found for lighter-weight assemblies (e.g., concrete slabs will commonly show superior noise separation performance versus wood-framed floors). Second, employing suspended ceilings underneath structural roof (or flooring) constructions can also increase the noise separation of the envelope. Third, placing insulation batts in the air space between a suspended ceiling and the structural roof construction will also increase the noise separation for the assembly. The magnitude of improvements in the noise separations afforded by floor or roof assemblies—gained by using these envelope modifications—will generally be similar to those found for opaque walls.

Controlling impact sound transmission through floors is an important subject that is commonly better dealt with after the preliminary schematic design phase has been completed. Even so, a number of strategies can be employed to increase separation of impact-caused noises. First, placing a soft material—such as carpeting (and perhaps an underlying pad of rubber or woven hemp fiber)—on top of the structural flooring will usefully reduce impact-noise loading. Second, a more ambitious approach uses a built-up or floated flooring that rests over the structural flooring (see Figure 13.39). For a floated floor, furring strips or pads are laid at regular intervals on top of the structural flooring and

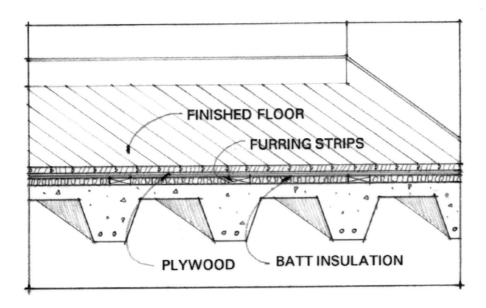

Figure 13.39 A floated floor assembly is shown in this sectional view.

then covered with wood-decking (e.g., plywood and a finished flooring material like a hardwood or, instead, carpeting). Batt insulation is commonly laid between the strips or pads, to serve as a noise-absorber. With this floated flooring the magnitude of the impact-loading on the structural flooring will be significantly reduced.[11] A third strategy applies a suspended ceiling hung below the structural flooring. When the top of a floor assembly is impact-loaded — causing the structural floor to vibrate — energy passes through the flooring producing airborne noise (i.e., by the diaphragmatic action of the flooring). If the structural flooring has a suspended ceiling hung underneath the flooring, then the intensity of the airborne noise entering into the space below will be substantially less than would be present if the suspended ceiling were not present. Fourth, as a modification to the third strategy, laying a sound-absorbing material like batt insulation on top of the suspended ceiling will further reduce the intensity of impact-induced sound waves that enter the occupied space below.

13.5.2.3   Window assemblies   The noise-separation capabilities of glazing assemblies are most sensitive to the same properties that affect opaque envelopes: specifically, the amounts of mass, stiffness, and damping present within these glazing assemblies. Increasing the mass of a glazing pane — by increasing its thickness — will produce yet better noise-separation capabilities. Thus, a 0.5 in (13 mm) glazing pane will provide five more decibels of noise separation than will a 0.125 in (3 mm) glazing pane.[12] These noise-separating capabilities can be further improved by *laminating a thin film* of a clear polymeric material between two "half-thicknesses" of a single-pane assembly (e.g., bonding a film layer between two pieces of glass). Since film layers often used in these laminated panes have thicknesses of approximately 0.030 in (0.76 mm), the overall thickness of a laminated pane is nearly the same as a monolithic pane. But the presence of the film layers improves the noise separation of the laminated panes by an increment of about 3 dB above the comparable monolithic panes. This improvement results from the laminated pane having greater flexibility and displaying better damping. Thus, a laminated pane is better able to transform the mechanical energy of incident sound waves into thermal energy.

Multiple-pane glazing assemblies also generally provide a distinct noise-separation improvement over comparable single-pane glasses. Often, double-pane glazing assemblies are more massive (by virtue of having two panes of glass present in the assembly rather than the one). Further, considering the effect of the intermediate air space between the panes, Quirt has reported that, for each doubling of the air space thickness, the noise separation increases by an increment of three decibels. Further, by doubling the thickness of each pane in a double-pane assembly, the noise separation of the assembly with the twice-thick panes will have an noise separation capacity approximately six decibels greater than the double pane assembly with the once-thick panes.

Additional tests on multiple-pane glazing assemblies indicate that triple-pane assemblies and double-pane assemblies — each having the same total air space thickness — show very similar noise separation capacities. Also, nonparallel-pane assemblies and parallel-pane assemblies perform equally well, when the average air space dimension for the former is the same as the air space thickness for the latter. And placing a sound-absorptive material, like batt insulation, between the panes at the perimeter of the air space will improve the noise separation properties of a multiple-pane assembly, in the middle- to high-frequency range. However, using a sound-absorptive material at the air space perimeter offers no benefit at lower noise frequencies (because the materials employed offer little absorption at these lower frequencies).[13]

SIDEBAR 13.7 Describing sound transmission through envelopes (and partitions)

The ability of an envelope to transmit mechanical energy from incident sound waves is described in terms of the *transmission coefficient* of the envelope (or partition). This transmission coefficient is defined as the ratio of amount of mechanical energy transmitted through the envelope to the amount of mechanical energy incident on the envelope. The transmission coefficient is thus a fraction (with values ranging from zero to one). Commonly observed values for the coefficient range from approximately 0.01 to 0.000001. Note that this coefficient can describe either a single material in an envelope or an entire envelope assembly composed of several materials. Also, for most envelope materials and assemblies, the transmission coefficient varies with frequency.

Describing sound transmission with transmission loss

The direct use of the transmission coefficient is limited both by the range of magnitudes demonstrated by this term and the apparent lack of an immediate relationship to sound pressure levels (as expressed in decibels). To combat these difficulties, an alternative term *transmission loss* is more commonly applied to describe the transmissive character of an envelope. The transmission loss indicates how much the sound pressure level of a noise *will be* reduced as the noise penetrates an envelope (or partition) (see Figure 13.40). Thus, the transmission loss expresses how well an envelope will remove mechanical energy from a sound wave that is incident on the envelope.

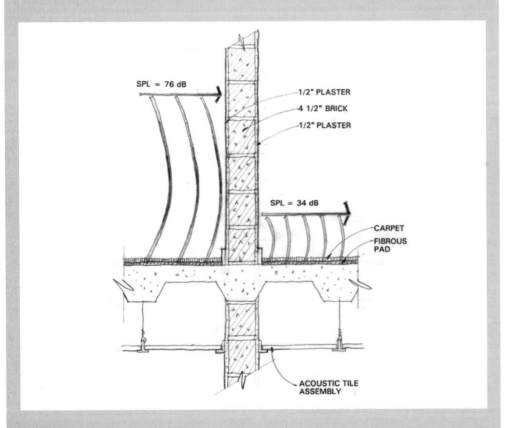

Figure 13.40 The transmission loss exhibited by a masonry wall is displayed in this illustration. The transmission of noise by this wall would essentially occur by the *diaphragmatic* action of the wall (i.e., the wall would bend inward and outward, much as a drumhead does when struck).

Sidebar 13.7, continued

The transmission loss of an envelope is found using the equation

Transmission Loss (TL) =
$10 \log_{10} (1/\text{transmission coefficient})$

Similar to the sound pressure level (SPL), transmission loss bears the same unit, decibels. The noise-separation behavior represented by the transmission loss is the converse of that manifested by the transmission coefficient. As the transmission coefficient (i.e., the amount of energy passing through an envelope versus the amount incident on the exterior of the envelope) grows smaller, the transmission loss that the envelope displays becomes larger.

For virtually all envelopes—whether composed of a single layer or an assembly of several layers—the transmission loss for the envelope will vary across the sound spectrum. Commonly, the range in noise-reducing performance for many envelope assemblies will be as great as three orders of magnitude across the spectrum (i.e., the TL at one frequency may be as much as 30 (or more) decibels greater than at another frequency). In Figures 13.41 and 13.42, we show examples of how transmission losses for two envelope assemblies vary across the spectrum. For each of these assemblies the transmission loss values tend to be smaller at the lower frequencies; increase toward the middle-frequency range, dip in the 2000–3000 Hz range, and then increase again for the higher frequencies: this overall shape is characteristic of many envelope assemblies.

Note that the magnitude of the transmission loss at each frequency is dependent on three physical properties: mass, rigidity (or stiffness), and damping. See Sidebar 13.1 for a further explanation of how these three properties can affect sound transmission through a building envelope (or partition).

**Describing envelopes in terms
of Sound Transmission Class**
As we have noted, the transmission loss of an envelope varies across the sound spectrum. Typically, to show how the transmission loss of the envelope varies, a large amount of numerical data is required. To simplify the description of the noise-separating ability of an envelope, an alternative index—the *Sound Transmission Class*—has been developed. This index is a single-number rating that enables direct comparison of the airborne-noise-separating capacities for many common envelope compositions. The Sound Transmission Class (STC) summarizes the various transmission loss values that an envelope displays for the one-third octave frequency centers between 125 and 4000 Hz. The choice of this frequency range for the Sound Transmission Class emphasizes the importance that this range has for the maintenance of good speech intelligibility conditions. The purpose of using the STC rating system is to enable selection of an envelope (or a partition inside a building) that will keep noise from entering into a space and disrupting communication.

Each STC index is defined in terms of a standardized-curve shape, identifying transmission loss (TL) values extending over this frequency range. A typical STC curve is shown in Figure 13.43. The standardized shape comprises a straight-line TL rise of 15 decibels from 125 to 400 Hz, a straight-line TL rise of 5 decibels between 400 to 1250 Hz, and a straight-line with no TL rise from 1250 to 4000 Hz. The TL value at 500 Hz for each STC curve is used as its distinguishing number. Because the STC curves have a common, standardized shape, establishing the difference in behaviors between any two STC-rated envelopes is straight-forward. For instance, the difference between two envelopes, one rated at STC-42 and the other at STC-45, is that the latter envelope will exhibit, on average, transmission losses three decibels greater than the former for each third-octave frequency point across the spectral range from 125 to 4000 Hz.

Lastly, the STC ratings are intended for establishing what envelope assemblies are needed to create silent backgrounds in buildings. To emphasize this intention we note that the following statement appears, in the *ASTM Standard* E413–87 (1999), defining the STC: "the rating [STC] is designed to correlate with subjective impressions of the sound insulation provided against the sounds of speech, radio, television, music, and similar sources of noise in offices and dwellings."

Sidebar 13.7, continued

Note that the test procedure for establishing the transmission losses of an envelope (at the one-third octave frequency points) has been defined by the American Society for Testing and Materials. This protocol is described in the ASTM Standard E90-02: *Standard Test Method for Laboratory Measurement of Airborne Sound Transmission Loss of Building Partitions and Elements*, (Philadelphia: American Society for Testing and Materials, 2002). The quotation in the previous paragraph of this sidebar has been published in *Classification for Rating Sound Insulation*, (ASTM E413-87 [1999]), (Philadelphia: American Society for Testing and Materials, 1999).

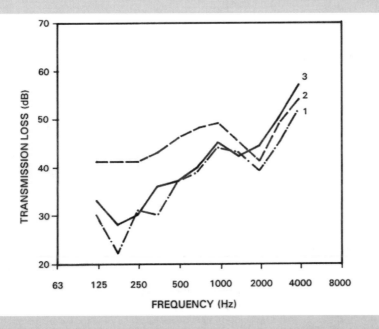

Figure 13.41 The frequency-dependent transmission losses for three stud wall assemblies appear in this graph: (1) Assembly #1 consists of a 2×4 wood-framed stud wall with the studs spaced 16" on center and attached to 2×4 floor and ceiling plates; the studs are covered on each of the two vertical sides with a single layer of 5/8" gypsum wallboard which is nailed to the studs; the wallboard joints are taped and finished; the surface weight of Assembly #1 is 7.2 lbs/ft^2 and its STC is 36 dB; (2) Assembly #2 is a wood-framed, staggered stud wall; the vertical studs are 2×3's attached to 2×4 floor and ceiling plates; the vertical studs are spaced 8" on center with alternating studs supporting gypsum wallboard; on each side of this assembly are two layers of wallboard, with each layer nailed to the supporting studs; all exposed wallboard joints are taped and finished; the surface weight of Assembly #2 is 13.4 lbs/ft^2 and its STC is 44 dB; and (3) Assembly #3 is a 2×4 wood-framed wall, similar in all respects to Assembly #1 except that *two* layers of 5/8" gypsum wallboard are nailed to each side of the vertical studs; all exposed wallboard joints are taped and finished; the surface weight of Assembly #3 is 12.9 lbs/ft^2 and its STC is 41 dB. All data used in creating this graph have been taken from the document, *A Guide to Airborne, Impact, and Structureborne Noise Control in Multifamily Dwellings* (prepared for the U.S. Federal Housing Administration by the U.S. National Bureau of Standards), (Washington, D.C.: U.S. Government Printing Office, 1974); see pages W-29, W-32, and W-35.

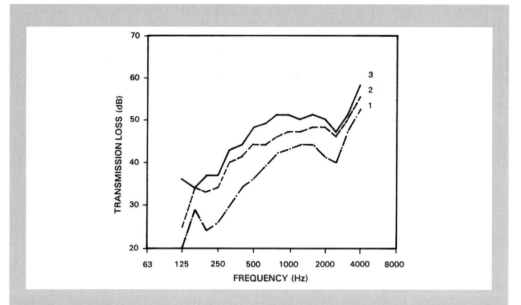

Figure 13.42 The frequency-dependent transmission losses for three double-pane assemblies are shown in this graph. Assembly #1 consists of two 1/4" (6.3 mm) panes, separated by a 1/2" (12.7 mm) air space; its STC is 39 dB. Assembly #2 has one pane of 1/4" (6.3 mm) thickness and the other pane of 3/16" (4.8 mm) thickness, with a separation between the two panes of 2" (51 mm). The STC for Assembly #2 is 46. Assembly #3 consists of the same two panes used in Assembly #2, but for Assembly #3 these panes are separated by 4" (102 mm). The resulting STC for Assembly #3 is 48 dB.

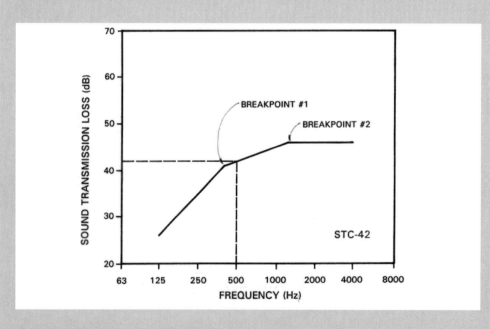

Figure 13.43 The standardized shape for the Sound Transmission Class curve is presented in this graph.

Section 13.6 | DEVELOPING BUILDING INTERIORS FOR GOOD ACOUSTICAL PERFORMANCE

Good acoustical performances can occur in buildings when two guidelines are satisfied. First, good communication should be achievable between speakers and listeners. Second, acoustical privacy should also be present for those seeking to communicate independently of (away from) nearby activities (i.e., occupants should be able to communicate without fear of being overheard). Also, acoustic privacy should be available so that occupants can pursue a task without being intruded upon by other nearby conversations (e.g., a person seeking a quiet setting to read a book). Acoustic privacy is necessary, too, to enable an occupant to engage in a task without intruding sonically on another person in an adjoining workstation (e.g., a person wanting to listen to a radio without disturbing another worker).

13.6.1 SEPARATING INTERIOR SPACES FOR SOUND AND NOISE CONTROL

Acoustic privacy can best be established by minimizing sound transmission between spaces and by reducing noise levels produced within a space. Basically, the two design and construction tasks that must be undertaken to create good acoustic privacy are the development of adequate space separations and the selection, location, and placement of materials for interior building surfaces.

Three means of noise separation are directly applicable for use in building interiors. First, the distance between adjacent activity spaces should be maximized. Second, physical barriers (walls or partitions) must be provided to impede sound transmission between spaces. Third, masking noise with high enough pressure levels can be employed so that this intentional noise will overlay any noise entering from adjacent areas.

For masking noise to be an effective isolator, the activities present where the masking is used must be unaffected by comparatively high background levels. Otherwise, the presence of masking noise can interfere with the performance of these activities (and the useful sounds that may accompany them). Alternatively, in many building settings, the ability to establish adequate distances between adjacent spaces is often limited for reasons of cost and the need to have a greater number of workers occupy some floor area. So, of these three strategies the most comprehensive and generally useful solution for creating quiet interiors—both to enhance communication and ensure acoustic privacy—is the reliance on wall and partition systems.

13.6.1.1 Acoustical characteristics of partition systems   Choosing a suitable wall or partition system should focus on a series of factors. These factors should generally include how much noise isolation is needed; how much the system components cost; how the system appears; its fire-rating; whether it is operable or fixed-in-place; how the system is structured; how it can be installed; and so forth. As with many decisions involved in selecting building components, selecting a wall or partition system involves trade-off analyses encompassing these factors. In the following discussion we will identify what we believe are the more important properties of common wall and partition systems. However, we will not comment directly on how decision-making about such systems might be carried out.

The most important acoustical requirement of a partition system is that the wall should reduce sound transmission from one space to another. Further, any noise that does pass through a wall should not be intelligible—recognizable—to occupants in the receiving room. Therefore, the basic design issue is to select a partition system that will provide

SIDEBAR 13.8 Alternative partition systems

There are perhaps four major types of vertical enclosure systems: permanent, demountable, operable, and portable.

The major components of *permanent* walls at least include framing elements (studs) that are usually attached directly to the structural system of the building and finished surfaces that cover the studding (see Figure 13.44). Fibrous batts or blankets are often placed between the studding. The permanent wall is usually assembled by skilled craftspeople employing basic wall components (e.g., studding and wallboard). This assembly most often occurs during the original construction of the building. But, if occupants' needs change (sometime after the initial occupancy of a building), even such permanent walls can be removed, and newly permanent walls can be constructed at other locations in a building.

Demountable (or relocatable) walls usually have cross-sections similar to permanent walls. But the demountable walls will commonly be manufactured, off-site, as a series of panels. These panels will essentially function as modular units. The panels then can be placed where a wall is needed, interlocking to form a

continuous wall. Assembly involves installing a series of ceiling and floor tracks that are secured to the structural system. Then, each panel is inserted into the tracks, joined to the tracks, and attached to each other (see Figure 13.45). The initial erection and any subsequent relocation of these demountable walls will generally have to be done by skilled craftspeople. Alternatively, some American manufacturers produce demountable wall systems in which floor and ceiling tracks, frames, and surface finishing materials are shipped to the building site as many individual components. There, the tracks are mounted in the required positions, the frames are inserted into the tracks (and braces are added), and the finishing panel surfaces are attached to the frames. Because of the nature of the connections used in this assembly process, the completed wall can be disassembled at a later time and rebuilt in some other location.

Operable walls differ from permanent and demountable walls by virtue of the fact that they will be moved regularly and easily to accommodate differing activities. For instance, in a gymnasium or a school

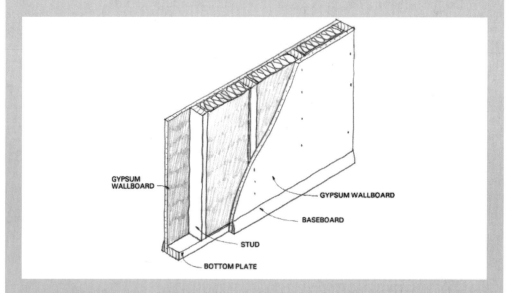

Figure 13.44 This wood-framed wall assembly is conventionally employed as a permanent partition. The assembly consists of top and bottom horizontal plates, vertical studs, fiberglass batt insulation, and gypsum wallboards on both surfaces.

Figure 13.45 A series of offices have been created using a demountable, glazed partition assembly.

Figure 13.46 This operable wall assembly is used to divide two adjacent classroom spaces.

cafeteria, an operable wall (or walls) can be used to divide a large open area into smaller, enclosed sub-areas. The operation (or moving) of these walls can be accomplished manually or, in numbers of applications, using motor systems and controls. The operable walls will ride in ceiling-mounted tracks and will effectively be hung from these tracks (see Figure 13.46). Some operable wall systems are composed of modular panels, which are installed as individual or continuously hinged units. Generally, these operable panels will have cross-sections consisting of steel skins and an underlying steel frame. The skin of these panels may be covered with cloth or a polymeric film. Alternatively, other operable panels are available as accordion-bellows-like curtains that are comparatively lightweight: these panels are hung from tracks attached to the structural system and can be quite easily drawn out of or compressed into storage receptacles. Initial installation of any of these operable partition systems will require skilled labor. But subsequent operation can often be accomplished by anyone, without special training.

The fourth type of partition is the *portable* unit. Portable partitions consist of panels that can be installed in an office or commercial setting without having to be attached to any permanent system (e.g., structural, ceiling, or flooring). Thus, the erection of these portable panels can be done quickly and without interfering with business activities. Similarly, with little fuss the portable panels can also be taken down and arranged in new configurations. The portable panels commonly are composed of steel skin attached to a steel frame. The skin will most often then be covered with cloth, a polymeric material, or some utility surface like a tackboard or a chalkboard. The essential premise of the portable partition is that it offers temporary or longer-term space enclosure with relatively little expense for initial installation or later rearrangement and it provides visual and acoustic separation (see Figures 13.47 and 13.48). Further, the portable partition is ideal for office and commercial situations where work relationships change frequently and space layouts must be reordered to accommodate such changes.

Door and window frames (and the accompanying doors and glazing) can readily be integrated with

SIDEBAR 13.8, continued

all of these four partition systems, allowing personal and visual access through the barriers created with these systems. Additionally, wiring for computer devices, telephones, and other electronic services can also be easily included within these partition systems without greatly affecting their appearance or utility.

Note that these partition systems are variously produced in three sets of height dimensions: *low or high railings* (usually, 1.2–1.4 m or 1.8–2.0 m [48–54 inches or 72–78 inches], respectively); *cornice height* (usually, 2.4–3.0 m [or 90–120 inches]), which establishes contact between the partition and the bottom surface of a finished ceiling; and *structural member height*, where the vertical partitions extend to the underside of the structural system and thus form tight connections both at the floor and roof.

Figure 13.47 Portable walls have been used in this office to separate several workstations.

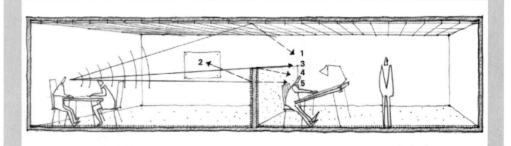

Figure 13.48 Sounds from the conversation occurring between the two workers in the left half of this drawing behave in the following manners: (1) direct waves reflect off of the ceiling; (2) direct waves reflect off of the intermediate-height, portable barrier back toward the conversants; (3) direct waves pass over the portable barrier; (4) some of the sound energy embodied in the direct waves noted as (3) will undergo diffraction and bend downward toward the worker sitting in the sound shadow of the barrier; and (5) some of the sound wave energy incident on the left side of the barrier will be transmitted through the barrier toward the desk worker.

adequate noise separation. Determining what amount of noise separation is needed involves contrasting the likely ambient noise level that will be present on the source side and the acceptable background noise level on the receiving side. Other issues that can merit consideration include whether the noise level on the source side is continuous or intermittent and how important to the performance of the activities occurring on the receiving side is the maintenance of a suitably low background noise level.

The acoustical performances of the various partition systems range greatly according to the composition of the partition, its height, the inclusion of window and door assemblies, and how each partition unit is secured to the floor, ceiling, and adjacent units. *Permanent* interior walls will generally perform as well as any exterior envelope assembly with the behavior of the interior wall determined by virtually the same properties that affect building envelopes. Glazed assemblies are available with substantial noise separation capacities, if needs warrant and the associated expenses can be sustained. For *demountable, operable,* and *portable* partition systems, noise separation capacities can be quite good, though these three systems usually perform less well than the permanent systems.

One qualification about noise separation ratings for wall systems should be noted. Most ratings have been established in laboratory tests, wherein sound transmission through the wall can be assured to be the major pathway for noise to pass from a space to the adjacent space. However, for walls assembled in normal buildings, other significant transmission routes may often be present. For this alternative instance, transmission occurs by *flanking.* Flanking results when continuous air passageways exist between a source space and a receiving room (see Figure 13.49).

SIDEBAR 13.9 Flanking situations in buildings and some solutions

Potential flanking paths in buildings are multitudinous: under wall systems attached to structural floors; over a wall whose top ends at a finished ceiling (where the ceiling may serve as a plenum for active environmental control systems); under or around a door where the door fits loosely in its frame; through open doors or windows (particularly when these openings exist along a single- or double-loaded corridor of offices or classrooms); or through a ventilation system that serves a series of adjacent spaces with a single duct run (see Figure 13.49). Flanking occurs in these situations because there are gaps, discontinuities, or open pathways in these space-enclosing assemblies. Thus, airborne noise may pass through.

Solutions to the problem of flanking are several and commonly require close attention to the proper choice of enclosure system components, the development of good detailing practices, and well-crafted and closely inspected construction efforts. Specific solutions can include seeking to have as few joints as possible between components, to employ caulking or gasketing at these joints, to apply flexible flaps over joints, or even to use pressure-tightening seals at the joints. Vertical walls should run continuously from the floor to the undersides of the structural system members (thus, curtailing sound transmission over wall tops that end at the finished ceiling). Where noise passes between adjacent offices or classrooms because of open doors or windows, conditions should be enhanced in the individual spaces so that the doors and windows can be kept closed without adversely affecting environmental conditions within the spaces. For instance, if windows or doors are opened to seek better ventilation, then a mechanical ventilation system — local or centralized — can be introduced. And where noise may pass between spaces along a duct run, then multiple duct runs can be included in the building design (so that each run might serve alternating offices, rather than every one). Further, such duct runs can be lined with noise-absorbing materials.

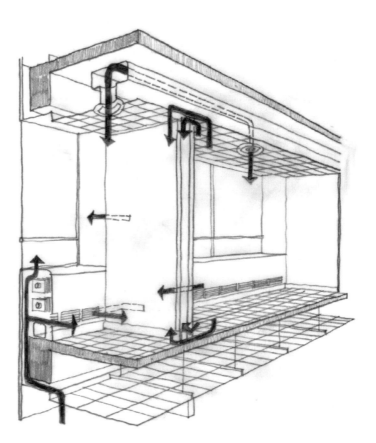

Figure 13.49 Several alternative flanking paths around a wall system are shown in this illustration, which is a modification of a drawing published previously in the article, "Architectural Engineering (Special Report #4), Noise control in architecture: more engineering than art," *Architectural Record,* October 1967, page 198. Permission to reproduce this drawing has been sought from the publisher of *Architectural Record,* The McGraw-Hill Companies, Inc.

13.6.2 DESIGNING BUILDING SPACES FOR GOOD COMMUNICATION

The first part of this section has dealt with means for creating a quiet building interior. In this second part we will present space planning guidelines that can be employed to enhance communication within building interiors. The initial set of guidelines will focus on developing proper shapes for rooms and the enclosing surfaces of a room. Then, we will discuss the use and placement of absorbing materials and of diffusing surfaces.

13.6.2.1 Recommended room shapes Spaces that are used for communication by speech or music should be laid out with rectangular floor plans. Rectangular floor plans should never be square, but rather there should be a long dimension and a short dimension. Generally, the aspect ratio—expressed in terms of width-to-length—should be greater than 1:1.2 and less than 1:3. Indeed, a number of room shape ratios are thought to produce very good communication conditions. These shape ratios are presented in terms of height-to-width-to-length and appear as (a) 1.0:1.14:1.39; (b) 1.0:1.26:1.59; and (c) 1.0:1.6:2.4.

The source(s)—whether a speaker or one (or several) musical instrument(s) or singer(s)—should be placed near one end of the centerline axis that spans the long dimension of the rectangle. The receivers should be located along the centerline axis and facing the source(s). When several or many receivers are present, then they should be spaced incrementally and proportionally away from the centerline. The best-quality sound usually exists along the centerline axis.

Other dimensional guidelines can also be suggested. For instance, the maximum distance between a source and a receiver should usually be 18.3 m (60 feet), unless electronic amplification can be provided to strengthen the intensity of the source. To ensure that there are good lines-of-sight between a source and the receivers, the source should be elevated above the floor level for the front-most receivers (i.e., the source should be placed on a raised stage). Also, to better enable the receivers to see—maintain good lines-of-sight with—the source(s), the receivers who are more distant from the source(s) should be elevated relative to the front-most receivers. One other dimensional guideline stipulates that the maximum useful angle of spread for sound emanating from a source is 135°. Thus, no receivers should be located outside of a cone with this angular dimension, when measured from the mouth of a speaker (or singer) or the sounding element of an instrument.

13.6.2.2   Room shapes to be avoided   We can also suggest a series of room and enclosure shapes whose use should not be employed in buildings.[14] Each of these five shapes, if used, will produce acoustical defects that will often require rehabilitative treatment after the building has been occupied. First, avoid the creation of long, narrow rooms. In such rooms the sidewalls would be comparatively close together, and the end walls would be much further apart (e.g., an aspect ratio [width-to-length] of 1:4 or greater). Sound produced at either end of rooms with aspect ratios of this magnitude or greater will inevitably develop flutter echoes, a condition where sound will reflect multiply between the sides of room without undergoing significant intensity loss. The presence of these flutter echoes will greatly impair speech intelligibility.

Second, do not employ high ceilings in corridors. Most corridors in nonresidential buildings will have hard-sided walls, and many may have hard-surfaced floors. In such instances, noises created by people moving through these corridors will reflect readily off

---

SIDEBAR 13.10 Similarities between corridor noise and cocktail parties

The high noise level created in corridors due to the presence of many sources and the increasing of sound pressure levels by individual sources attempting to override the ambient din is analogous to what commonly occurs at cocktail parties. There, the generally high background noise level—generated by many people speaking at once—forces individuals to raise their voices appreciably in order to be heard. As the many individuals all raise their voice levels, the sound pressure levels increase yet more. These high noise levels can be accentuated by excessive reflections from the ceiling and any hard-surfaced walls. To reduce this "cocktail-party" effect, absorbing materials should be used to cover the reflecting surfaces. A number of authors have written about the cocktail party effect; as an example, see the paper by Plomp, R., "Acoustical aspects of cocktail parties," *Acustica*, 38, 1977, pages 186–191.

Figure 13.50 A corridor in an engineering classroom and laboratory building on the University of Washington campus displays characteristic features that can often cause adverse noise conditions: a long, narrow-walled space; parallel surfaces; vertical walls and floor composed of hard, relatively smooth materials; and high ceilings. Additionally, mechanical system ducting running in the near-ceiling space can provide unpleasant background noise levels.

of the hard surfaces, causing the development of conditions similar to a diffuse sound field. These reflections will cause noise levels to be sustained, and you may even find that noise levels do not decrease with increased distance (i.e., as you move away from the apparent sources). Rather, the corridor can resemble a tunnel in which the sound waves propagate to the very end. If high ceilings are also employed, then the noise levels will be that much greater (see Figure 13.50). By lowering these ceilings and placing absorptive materials on the ceiling and floor, and, where possible, on the walls, the build-up of the nearly uniform noise levels can be reduced.[15] One additional consequence of noisy corridors is that people, trying to converse, will raise their voices to overcome the loss of speech intelligibility caused by the high ambient noise levels. The result will be a further increase in the sound pressure levels in these corridors. For people in rooms adjacent to the corridors such noise will often be transmitted through the walls and doorways that separate the corridor from the rooms.

Third, refrain from creating spaces that have nearly cubical dimensions. The major problem with spaces with cubical shapes is that, because there is no preferential dimension, a receiver will often be unable to discern from which direction sound has emanated. Thus, the receiver would be unable to localize on the sound and could be confused about the context in which sound is produced. Because context can play an important part in deciphering sounds, establishing good speech intelligibility could be severely hampered. Rather, spaces that have floor shapes that are more rectangular, perhaps with aspect ratios that are 1:1.5 or 1:2 than 1:1, will offer better localization opportunities for the occupants.

The fourth guideline suggests that you should not produce rooms that have large floor areas and low ceilings. The result of creating such a room is that the room will appear very dead. In rooms with too-low ceilings, sounds generated will often have nonuniform distributions. The loudness of these sounds will usually appear to be adequate only locally. A principal explanation for the failing of these rooms is that little chance will exist for the development of first-reflected sounds to reinforce direct sound. Instead, the overall sound in such rooms will appear to be very thin and to have little fullness. What heights are appropriate for rectangular-shaped rooms should be determined by satisfying volumetric requirements, which are based on the type of communication for which a space will be employed. We will identify a series of these volumetric guidelines in Section 13.6.4.

Lastly, the fifth guideline states that you should avoid using concave shapes to enclose rooms (in which satisfactory sound communication is needed). Whether enclosure surfaces are round, elliptical, or simply generally curved outward (relative to a source), sound waves incident on these surfaces will tend to have their reflected waves *converge* at various points within the space (see Figure 10.7). Such convergence will produce sound energy concentrations at these points called "hot spots." At these hot spots sound levels will appear to be increased substantially in contrast to other locations in the room where the reflected waves do not converge. Additionally, in rooms with these curved surfaces, little or no reflected sound energy will reach other places. The result for occupants located at any of these latter places will be significantly lowered sound pressure levels; these locations are referred to as "voids." At these voids occupants will only be able to hear the direct sound waves from a source and will receive virtually none of the reflected sound. The overall consequence of using concave surfaces as reflectors is that they will create decidedly uneven, nonuniform distribution of sounds throughout any room enclosed by these surfaces.

The use of convex shapes and surfaces, however, can serve as a significant benefit in sound control. Such convex surfaces are often employed to diffuse sound, thus helping to create uniform distribution of sound energy throughout the space.

SIDEBAR 13.11 Practical solutions when concave shapes are unavoidable

In some large rooms such as those used as lecture halls or music performance spaces — where the audience may number several hundred or more — the back wall (opposite the lectern or stage) will often be curved in a concave shape. The placement of absorbing materials on the back wall is, of course, a primary option. These absorbing materials will minimize the ability of the surfaces to produce sound concentrations and voids.

But in some facilities the total amount of absorption materials will need to be limited to achieve adequate liveliness and reverberation. For those facilities an alternative solution may be used. To minimize the effects of the concavity, first, the wall can be composed of a number of rectilinear surfaces (essentially, as segments of the overall curve). Second, these surfaces either should have *diffusing* elements built onto the surfaces (see Figure 10.12) or should have *convex shapes* that will diffuse sound waves incident on the surfaces (see Figure 10.8). For the approach where each segment of the wall has a diffusing shape, one way to form each segment would be to have the segment appear as a rectangular section in a plan view and as a convex curvilinear section in a top-to-bottom view. The result of using these diffusing strategies would be that the diffused sound energy would contribute to the overall sound pressure level in the space and would help to make sound in the space appear fuller and richer.

13.6.3 USING ABSORBING MATERIALS TO CONTROL THE PRESENCE OF SOUND AND NOISE

There are four dominant reasons for applying absorption materials throughout building interiors. First, absorption materials reduce the pressure levels of noise occurring in building interiors. For instance, for each doubling of the amount of absorption present in a space, the reduction of the sound pressure level accompanying this absorption increase will be three decibels. Second, absorption controls the development of a reverberant field within interior spaces. As we have stated in Section 10.3, the reverberant field develops as sound waves from a source within a space reflect off the various surfaces, and the sound energy reaches a comparatively uniform level throughout the space. Producing this reverberant condition depends upon having adequate amounts of reflecting surfaces within the space. If some of these reflecting surfaces are instead covered with absorbing materials, then a lesser quantity of reflection will result, and the reverberant field will have less energy distributed throughout the space. Also, the length of time — the reverberation time — that reflections endure will be shortened. Thus, generally, as the amount of absorption material in a space is doubled, the length of the reverberation time for that space will be halved.

Third, absorbing materials applied to selected surfaces in a space control the directionality that sound waves appear to have. By installing absorption on particular surfaces, it is possible to virtually eliminate reflections coming off of such surfaces (i.e., the energy present in incident sound waves may be absorbed sufficiently so that the reflected sound waves have much lower energy levels and become imperceptible). This selective negating of sound reflections can especially influence our ability to determine the location of sound sources.

And, fourth, absorbing materials can reduce the energy levels of higher-frequency sounds, making a space feel "warmer" to the occupants. Thus, any tendency of sound to appear shrill or strident can be largely minimized by applying suitably absorptive materials. Sound produced in a space with a lot of high-frequency absorption can seem richer, fuller, and generally more responsive and pleasurable.

SIDEBAR 13.12 Limits to applying ever greater amounts of absorption

Each doubling of the amount of absorption produces a three-decibel improvement in the ambient noise level. Thus, when you are confronted with a noisy situation in some space, it would seem to make sense to add much absorption to the space, with the express purpose of reducing the noise level. But, practically, there are often limits concerning how much absorption can be installed in such a space (i.e., many surfaces in a building space will serve other purposes and will not be available for having absorbing materials located on

them). For instance, vertical walls may be glazed, covered with chalkboards, hung with storage systems or cabinets, and so forth. Ceiling surfaces will often be occupied by lighting fixtures. Floors may have carpeting, but the carpeted surface areas exposed directly to the ambient air in the space will likely be limited by the presence of furniture. So, being able to successively double and redouble the surface area of absorption in a space is often limited by issues of practicality.

13.6.3.1 The two major types of sound-absorptive materials and assemblies All building materials, enclosure assemblies, and equipment pieces or appliances will display some ability to absorb mechanical energy from incident sound waves. However, specific types of materials and assemblies will function better than others as absorbers, and these types are the ones on which we will focus discussion. There are two major categories of absorption materials. Additionally, there are a series of other assemblies and devices that can also be used to absorb the energy of sound (or noise) waves. The first major group includes materials that are *porous or fibrous* in composition and structure. The second major group incorporates materials that are employed in the form of *panels and large sheets*. Generally, the ability of any material or assembly to absorb the mechanical energy embodied in sound waves is dependent upon four attributes: its composition, thickness, surface finish, and how it is mounted to other materials or assemblies.

Porous or fibrous materials that serve as good sound absorbers typically have distinctive physical properties. First, the materials will possess a great amount of air entrainment with the air present in numerous small pores (or pockets). These pores are usually open-celled, allowing air molecules to pass readily in and out of the material. Second, the overall board or batt, which contains the air pores and the matrix material, will have a low density and can deform elastically when stressed.

Common examples of these porous or fibrous materials include the following: most fabrics (especially, those that are relatively heavy and that can be draped like wool or velour); carpeting (particularly, compositions with deep pile or shag); mineral and vegetable fiber batts, blankets, and boards (for instance, acoustic tile); boards composed of wood fibers and some impregnating resin; open-celled polymeric foams (like urethane or Styrofoam); and some ceramic foams.

The absorption of the mechanical energy from incident sound waves results from the matrix material being set into vibration by the sound waves. Then, the bits of the vibrating matrix material experience friction by rubbing against each other. Thus, mechanical energy is converted to thermal energy, and this thermal energy is dissipated into the material and the surrounding air.

SIDEBAR 13.13 Other forms of absorbing materials and assemblies

Other types of absorbent materials and assemblies include cavity resonators, perforated panel absorbers, space absorbers, acoustical plaster, and air. Each of these first four devices offers specialized capabilities. For instance, most *cavity resonators* provide excellent sound absorption capabilities in a narrow frequency range. A cavity resonator consists of an enclosed volume of air that is connected to the primary occupied space by a small hole or slot in the volume enclosure (see Figure 13.51). Mechanical energy of incident sound waves is absorbed by inducing the air around and in the volume enclosure to pulse in and out of the enclosure as sound waves move toward the enclosure. Thus, the enclosed air behaves like a spring.

The cavity resonator generally displays very good absorption for *one* narrow frequency range. Most often, the applicable frequency range will be somewhere between 125 to 250 Hz, although frequencies of maximum absorption as high as 300 to 400 are sometimes encountered. Such cavity resonators are especially useful absorbers when there is a dominant noise source within a room that emits sound in a narrow frequency range. One particular form of cavity resonator is a hollow concrete block with two or three narrow linear slots on the block side facing into a room, with these slots running from the bottom to nearly the top of the block. The slots either can have a rectangular cross-section through the block skin or a

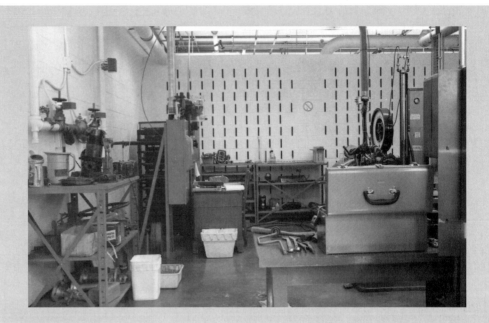

Figure 13.51 Cavity resonator blocks are used in this machine shop to absorb low-frequency noise.

cross-section that flares inward. The performance of these blocks can be significantly enhanced by including a fibrous batt inside the cavity of the block (with the batt faced with a metallic membrane on the inner side of the batt). For the blocks with batt-filled cavities, a high absorption coefficient will be observed at some one frequency, but at other higher frequencies the absorption coefficients will be much improved over blocks that do not include the batting. The significant contributions that these batt-filled, slotted blocks provide are that they offer good absorptive performances in a frequency range which is comparatively higher than usually found for cavity resonators and they also possess structural integrity and can be used as load-bearing members. Conversely, most other materials that present good absorptive characteristics at these higher frequencies are soft, have low densities, and usually can be used only in decorative or finishing applications.

A second specialized absorption type is the *perforated panel absorber*. This device is a compound assembly, using some common fibrous or porous absorption material faced with a slatted or perforated rigid covering (see Figure 13.52). The fibrous or porous material serves as the principal absorption. Alternatively, the covering material protects the soft, low-density under-material (reducing the abrasion of its surface and dirt accumulation on it). Further, this covering offers an attractive finish to the assembly. The covering can consist of regularly spaced wood slats, metal screens that have been fabricated with many small gaps, or ceramic mats also with many little perforations. These perforated panel absorbers behave like an aggregation of many cavity resonators. Generally, these assemblies will display useful absorption for sounds with frequencies up to (and often) beyond 4000 Hz. In comparison to uncovered fibrous or porous absorbers, the perforated panel absorbers normally will show better absorption performance at lower frequencies and somewhat lower coefficients at higher frequencies.

The third specialized type of absorption is the *unit space absorber*. These devices are essentially panels or partial (or whole) cylinders of porous or fibrous materials, which are attached to metal or wooden frames (to ensure maintenance of appropriate shapes). The units are often hung from ceiling or roof structures, thus maximizing the area of exposure to sound waves. Unit space absorbers are most often employed in buildings for noise reduction, particularly in areas that are subjected to high noise levels (e.g., factories, recreational facilities, shopping malls, and so forth). Planar-shaped unit absorbers generally will offer better absorptive performances than cylindrically shaped unit absorbers. Thicker unit absorbers will similarly provide better performance than will thinner absorbers. Further, unit absorbers suspended with their largest surface areas oriented vertically will afford better performances than those hung with the primary surface areas arranged horizontally. Lastly, the increase in sound absorption will ordinarily be greater when fewer — rather than more — unit absorbers are deployed: with fewer unit absorbers, each one will be more open to receiving sound waves and, consequently, there will be less interruption of the surrounding sound fields. Specific performance values for these unit space absorbers are dependent not only on the several properties identified here, but also on other parameters such as size and the particular materials used in unit absorbers (see Figure 13.53).

Acoustical plaster is the fourth of these specialized absorption devices. This material is basically a plaster compound to which a significant component of organic or mineral fibers and/or flocculating agents has been added. The acoustical plaster is generally sprayed wet — in a water-based slurry — on to enclosure surfaces (e.g., wood, lath, masonry, and so forth), and a layer with definite thickness is built up and allowed to dry. The resulting product is lightweight and has a surface texture that is stippled and wavy (i.e., resembling frosting on a layer cake). The acoustical plaster behaves similarly to porous and fibrous absorbers, showing greater absorption for sound waves with middle to higher frequencies and comparatively lower absorption for the lower-frequency sounds. Thicker layers, with thicknesses up to two inches (five cm), will commonly provide better absorptive performances than will relatively thinner layers.

The last of these special absorption types is *air*. In fact, air is not special as a "material." But its ability to absorb sound wave energy makes the presence of air something to consider during acoustical designing. Generally, the amount of absorption demonstrated by a volume of air is regarded as inconsequential unless the volume is quite large, as in a performing arts hall or a sports arena. Air is most effective as an absorber in the upper frequency range (1000 Hz and up). The ability of air to absorb sound wave energy is further evidence that sound waves passing through air in an open sound field undergo attenuation (i.e., a weakening of the sound waves as they pass away from their source).

Figure 13.52 Perforated (slatted) panel absorption is employed at either end of this classroom. The simple assembly consists of fiber batts covered with cedar slats, which are placed regularly across the wall.

Figure 13.53 Unit space absorbers are hung from the ceiling of this office space. Most of the wall surfaces and the ceiling surfaces are quite reflective. The unit space absorbers will help to overcome any excessive reverberation.

The second major type of absorbing materials and assemblies that are widely used in buildings are panels and large sheets (i.e., usually, membranes that separate volumes of air). The absorption of the mechanical energy of sound waves by panels and large sheets occurs when incident sound waves induce vibrations in these assemblies. A panel or sheet will flex and bow at a rate like the frequency of the wave. These panels and sheets thus behave as diaphragms (i.e., like the head of a drum). Some of the mechanical energy of the incident sound waves is transferred to the panels and sheets as the oscillations continue, thereby reducing the amount of energy that will be present in the reflected wave. Vibrations—flexing and bowing—of the panel (or sheet) then disperse as thermal energy (heat) to the surrounding air.

Typical panel and sheet absorbers include plywood, gypsum wallboard, wood paneling, suspended ceiling assemblies, glass, doors, and wood floors (covering furring strips or for raised stages above hollow spaces). The amount of absorption that a panel or sheet provides will depend on the geometry of the diaphragm and its damping character. Better absorption will commonly be obtained if the panel or sheet has fewer connections to supporting members, particularly when the supporting members are more widely spaced. For example, a 4 ft × 8 ft (1.22 m × 2.44 m) plywood sheet supported by framing members running along the two eight-foot edges will generally be more absorptive than an identical sheet that is supported by framing members laid out at sixteen-inch intervals along the eight-foot dimension. Similarly, the absorptive performances of these membrane materials are enhanced if the diaphragm covers an air space—even of a comparatively small thickness (e.g., 1 in [25 mm] or less)—rather than being fixed directly to another solid surface. The presence of an air space will enable the panel or sheet to vibrate resonantly. Alternatively, the absorption capacity of a panel or sheet can be improved by attaching a porous or fibrous material glued to the back of the panel or sheet (e.g., 0.5 in to 1 in (about 12 to 25 mm) of felt or a fiberglass blanket).

SIDEBAR 13.14 Describing the absorbing capabilities of materials and assemblies

---

The ability of materials, generally, to absorb the energy of incident sound waves is highly frequency-dependent (i.e., how much energy will be absorbed by any material varies according to what frequency is—or frequencies are—present in a sound). Some materials display superior capacities for absorbing middle-to-higher frequency sounds, whereas other materials are better at absorbing lower frequency sounds. To indicate how well (or poorly) some material can absorb sound, we can employ a term called the *absorption coefficient*. This coefficient is defined as the ratio of the difference between the energy present in the incident wave and energy remaining in the wave reflecting from the absorbing surface divided by the energy present in the incident wave. Written as an equation, the definition appears as

$$\text{Absorption coefficient} = (E_{\text{incident}} - E_{\text{reflected}})/E_{\text{incident}}$$

This coefficient will have values ranging between 0 and 1. Also, because the absorption capability of any material is frequency-dependent, the numerical value of the absorption coefficient for the material will vary across the sound spectrum.

For instance, many typical samples of acoustic tile will show absorption coefficients as high as 0.90–0.95—the tiles can absorb 90 to 95 percent of

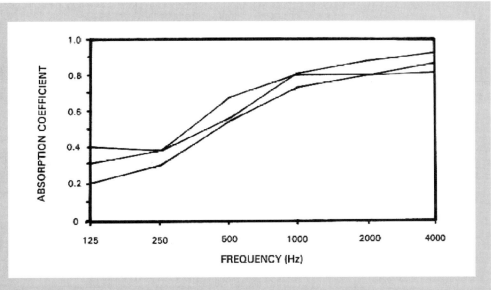

Figure 13.54 The absorption coefficients for three acoustic tile samples are shown here for the portion of the sound spectrum from 125 to 4000 Hz.

the incident sound energy — at about 1000 Hz (see Figure 13.54). At 500 or 2000 Hz, the absorption coefficient for common acoustic tiles will often be about 0.7 to 0.8 (although some tiles will perform better and some will be less good). Similar coefficient values will also be found at 4000 Hz. But, in the lower frequency range (60 to 250 Hz), the absorption coefficients for most tiles will vary from 0.1 to 0.4 depending upon surface texture and the method of mounting. Alternatively, a cloth like heavy velour (which is normally hung in a draped fashion) can show coefficients of about 0.70–0.75 at 1000 Hz, 0.45–0.65 at 500, 2000, and 4000 Hz, and 0.10–0.25 at the lower frequencies. Thus, a distinct performance pattern is displayed for the various porous or fibrous materials (see Figure 13.55). Generally, these materials will absorb incident sound wave energy best in the middle-to-higher frequency range (from about 500 to 4000 Hz) and function less well as absorbers in the lower-frequency range (60 to 300–400 Hz). To understand the basis for these behaviors, we suggest thinking about the relative wavelength sizes for these two frequency ranges. For the higher-frequency range the wavelengths of the

sound waves are quite small, and the waves can readily enter into the air spaces between the matrix materials (that comprise the absorbers). These smaller-wavelength sound waves can more easily interact with the fibers or strands of the matrix material causing them to vibrate and experience friction. Thus, the mechanical energy of the sound waves is readily converted into thermal energy reducing the amount of mechanical energy that a reflecting wave will have (as it leaves the surface of the absorption). So, porous or fibrous materials are characterized by high absorption coefficients for middle-to-high frequency sounds. Alternatively, longer-wavelength — low-frequency — sound waves are less able to pass into the small-pored cavities, and the mechanical energy present in these longer-wavelength waves undergoes lesser degrees of conversion to thermal energy. Consequently, these porous or fibrous materials are relatively poorer absorbers of lower-frequency sounds.

Panel and sheet materials commonly display their best absorption performances in the lower-frequency range (see Figure 13.56). The useful frequency domain for such materials and assemblies is usually from about

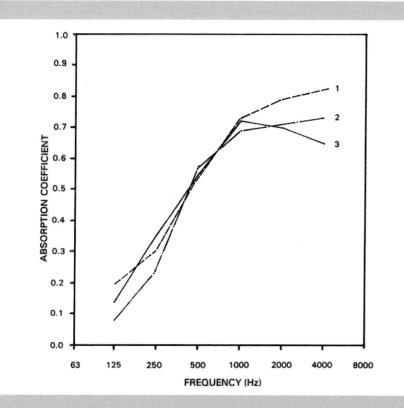

Figure 13.55 The absorption coefficients for three alternative fuzzy (soft-surfaced) materials are displayed here: (1) an acoustic tile, suspended in a lightweight metal frame; (2) heavy wool carpeting laid on top of a foam rubber pad; and (3) velour drapery hung vertically and gathered (to cover a wall surface area less than the area of the drapery when horizontally laid flat).

60 to 400 Hz, although for some products frequencies of 500 Hz or greater can be absorbed to a still beneficial degree. Commonly, the greatest amount of absorption for most of these diaphragmatic absorbers will be evident at frequencies around 100 to 150 Hz. The absorption coefficients for sample materials include for plywood, 0.60 and 0.30 (at 125 and 250 Hz, respectively); for common double-strength window glass, 0.35, 0.25, and 0.18 (at 125, 250, and 500 Hz, respectively); and for 0.5 in (12.7 mm) thick gypsum wallboard nailed to 2×4 studs, with the studs 16 in (0.41 m) on center, 0.29 and 0.10 (at 125 and 250 Hz, respectively).

Absorptive capabilities of materials are basically dependent on four parameters: the nature of the material, its thickness, the method of mounting the material, and whether there is an air space between the material and its supporting structure (and, if an air space exists, what its thickness is). Such material properties as the surface texture, degree of porosity, stiffness, and damping are important determinants of these absorption capabilities. Materials that are more porous offer better absorption in the middle-to-high frequency range. Similarly, well-fissured or stippled surfaces also demonstrate better absorption in these frequency bands. Adequate stiffness and damping in panel absorbers will enable better absorption in the lower frequency range. In terms of material thickness, greater thickness for porous and fibrous materials will commonly increase absorption values. Alternatively,

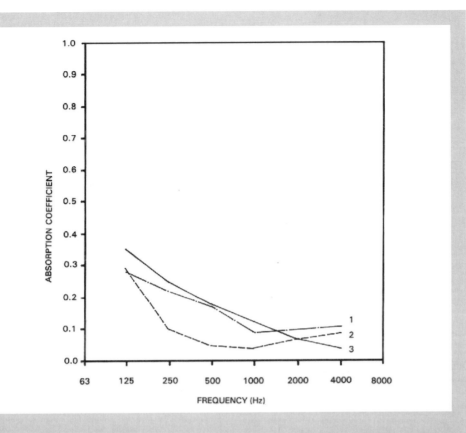

Figure 13.56 The absorption coefficients for three alternative panel assemblies are shown here: (1) 3/8 in (9.5 mm) plywood paneling; (2) 1/2 in (12.7 mm) gypsum wallboard nailed to 2×4 wood studs that are spaced at 16 in (0.41 m) centers; and (3) 1/8 in (3.2 mm) double-strength window glass.

excessive thickness in panel absorbers will reduce their abilities to absorb lower frequency sounds (i.e., because the panels will be too rigid).

Three basic mounting choices exist. First, the absorption material can be attached directly to the surface of the supporting material. Second, furring strips can be used to create comparatively narrow air spaces between the absorption material and the supporting structure. Third, the absorption material can be hung at a greater distance away from the supporting structure (so that a sizeable air space results) (see Figure 13.57). Selecting which method to apply in a given room depends on the location where the absorption is to be placed, what performance is sought for the absorption, and other factors including appearance, fire-rating, and the inherent nature of the material (i.e., whether it is easily abraded, has good tensile and compressive strengths and can be hung horizontally, and so forth).

Generally, porous and fibrous absorbers can be mounted using any of these three methods (i.e., direct attachment, using furring strips, or hanging). However, if these absorbers are suspended horizontally, they must be supported by some sort of a structural frame (e.g., the modular tees and elbows used to hang acoustic tile). Some porous or fibrous materials — when applied vertically — will require protective covering, such as is provided with perforated panels. Employing porous or fibrous materials in horizontally suspended assemblies will enhance the absorption capacity of these materials across the frequency range,

SIDEBAR 13.14, continued

particularly improving their performances at the lower frequency ranges (i.e., in comparison to performances for similar materials cemented directly to rigid supporting surfaces). The placement of perforated panels over vertical porous or fibrous materials will generally reduce the higher-frequency absorptive capabilities of these assemblies, whereas increasing their lower-frequency absorptive capacities. Panel absorbers, to be effective, must have well-developed air spaces between them and any supporting surfaces. And the performance of a panel absorber can often be improved by attaching a fibrous/porous material to the underside of the panel (i.e., the side away from the incident sound waves). The attachment of the fibrous/porous material thus bolsters the damping capacity of the assembly.

Figure 13.57 The three major types of mounting practices for absorption materials are shown in these drawings. The top format (a) portrays the absorption placed on furring strips, set out from the rigid undersurface. The middle format (b) demonstrates the use of perforated (or slatted) panels that cover the absorption. And the bottom format (c) displays absorption supported—usually, hung—well apart from any rigid, structural system. Normally, the distance between the absorption material used in this bottom format and the supporting structural system will be at least 12 in (30 cm) or greater.

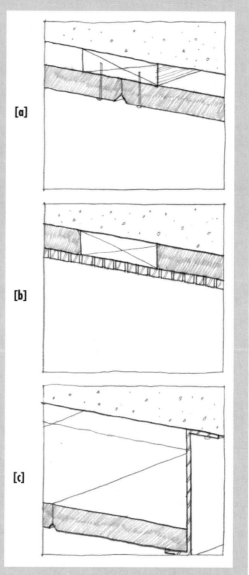

13.6.3.2 Mounting practices for sound-absorbing materials   A number of standard mounting practices for these several absorptive materials are employed in the building industry. To a marked extent, which practice is used for a given material depends upon the character of the material, the nature of the assembly in which the absorption is commonly deployed, and the level of absorption performance sought for the material. For instance, a glass fiber batt—which has little resistance to abrasion, is easily compressed, and offers a not-especially-attractive appearance—is usually employed with some covering to protect the surface of the batt and enhance its appearance (thus, creating a perforated panel assembly). Alternatively, a panel absorber, to be most effective, requires that it be hung or otherwise installed away from any rigid support, with an air space left between the panel and the surface behind the panel.

There are eight standard mounting formats.[16] As such, these mounts encompass the range of installations commonly used in buildings (see Figure 13.57). For two of these mounts the absorptive material is directly attached to some hard, stiff backing. For the third mount the absorption is similarly affixed to a hard, stiff backing, but then is covered with a perforated facing. The fourth mount has the absorption placed out from the stiff backing, resting on regularly spaced furring strips. The fifth and sixth mounts have the absorption suspended from a structural member with a sizeable air space between the absorption and the structure. And the seventh and eighth mounts are employed for utilizing drapes, other cloth materials, and window shades and blinds, which are hung vertically, parallel to wall surfaces.

13.6.3.3 Locating absorption materials in building spaces
When considering where to place absorption materials, the designer and builder must ensure that adequate opportunities are provided for first-reflected sound waves to reinforce direct sound waves and the occupant can readily localize upon a sound source. To accommodate this first goal, it is necessary to encourage the generation of "early" reflections. Such early reflections should emanate from surfaces close to the source. Also, these early reflections should usually arrive at the receiver from directions that are similar to the path that the direct waves travel along (i.e., thus, the early reflections should also arrive at the front or near-front of any receiver who faces a source). The second goal — enabling the receiver to localize easily upon the source — will be most readily satisfied by providing both strong direct and early reflected waves to the listener and discouraging reception of any "later" reflections (by absorbing as much of the energy of these reflected waves as possible). These later reflections generally emanate from surfaces that are more distant from the receiver. Often, such later reflections may come from surfaces that are located well behind the receiver.

SIDEBAR 13.15 Insights about binaural hearing and localization

Many sound sources are directional. Thus, an important property of human hearing is the ability to discern the directionality of a source and to establish from where the sound is emanating. What makes this localizing capability possible is that we hear with two ears (i.e., each ear receives slightly different sound information). From the comparison of sound information "data streams" received at the two ears, the human hearing system is able to determine whether an intensity difference exists between what the two ears sense and whether a time delay is evident between the receipts of sound at the two ears.

A consequence of generating data about intensity differences and time delays is that the location of sound sources within the external environment can be determined. The localization of a sound source requires, first, a sensing of the direction from which the sound is coming and, second, an estimation of the distance that separates the receiver from the source. The intensity of a sound will appear greater to the leading ear (i.e., the one closer to the sound source). This intensity difference (as sensed by the two ears) thus provides information about the direction from which the sound emanates. Additionally, sound waves will arrive at the leading ear before the waves reach the more distance ear. Thereby, a time delay will exist between the two moments of sound arrival. This delay, as well as the sensing of the intensity difference, can be used to estimate the likely distance from the sound source to a person's head (see Figure 13.58).

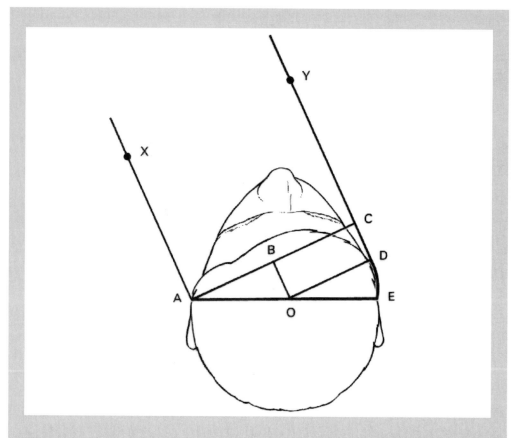

Figure 13.58 Localizing on a sound source depends on the resolution of the difference in time between the sound waves reaching our two ears. A derivation of an approximate time difference between the receipts of the sound wave by our two ears depends on finding the distance (CD + DE) and dividing this summed distance by the speed of sound.

(i) Line ABC is parallel to line OD; thus, angle CAE = angle DOE.

(ii) Length CD = length BO; length BO = (length AO) × sin (angle CAE).

(iii) Length DE approximately equals angle DOE, when the angle is expressed in radians (based on the approximation that the length of arc X is equal to angle X, when angle X is small).

(iv) So, the difference of the distance that the sound waves must travel is equal to [(length AO) × sin(angle DOE)] + [angle (DOE), with the radian length converted to some length unit] and the time delay is equal to this distance sum divided by the speed of sound.

(v) For example, if the circumference of a man's head is 0.56 m (22 inches), the radius (AO) is 0.089 m, and angles CAE and DOE are 30° (or 0.52 radians), then length (CD + DE) = 0.044 + 0.047 = 0.091 m; the speed of sound is 344 m/sec; so, the time delay for this example is 0.26 milliseconds (i.e., the sound waves arrive at the right ear 0.26 milliseconds later than at the left ear).

Our ability to localize on a sound source has been studied by Mills, who found that a minimum audible angle—the smallest angular change of a sound source that can be sensed—is dependent upon the frequency of the sound and the direction from which the sound arrives (e.g., from straight ahead to directly facing an ear). The minimum audible angle can be as small as 1° for mid-range frequencies and sound sources when a person faces frontward). For further details on this localization ability, see the paper by Mills, A.W., "On the minimum audible angle," *Journal of the Acoustical Society of America*, 30(4), April 1958, 237–246.

Thus, these later reflections will arrive at the receiver from directions opposite to those of the direct sound waves and the early reflected sound waves. Sound waves arriving at a receiver simultaneously from opposing directions—from the front and the back—will make localization difficult, at best. Indeed, without some means of identifying the source of a sound (or noise) the receiver can only be confused by the presence of the sound. Thus, it is incumbent on the designer and builder to establish means for minimizing the intensities of any later reflections.

Many noise sources create sound waves that are more nearly omnidirectional. Examples include the screech of moving a chair across a concrete floor, the jarring impact of a book dropped on to a tabletop, the ringing of an alarm clock, the noise of a factory machine, and so forth. Because these noise sources produce sound waves that move spherically outward, one can often have difficulty identifying where the source is. Further, reducing the intensities of such noises by absorbing the direct sound waves will thus require placing absorbing materials in numbers of locations (i.e., rather than in a few areas when you wish to reduce the intensities of reflections from a directional source).

But many useful sound sources in buildings emit sound waves with very specific directions: for example, waves leaving a speaker's mouth, a radio, or many musical instruments all travel along well-defined paths. Generally, the air volume, in which sound from a directional source has its greatest intensity, resembles a diverging cone with the source located at the apex of the cone. Using a ray diagram, you can then determine where sound waves from a directional source will strike an enclosure surface (by drawing a ray from the source along the axis of the cone). If the enclosure surface is reasonably close to the source and flat, then the surface should best function as a reflector. Alternatively, if the enclosure surface is more distant from the source or the surface could cause a reflected wave to reach the receiver coming from a direction opposite to that of the direct and early reflected waves, then the surface should be covered with an absorbing material.

Either the sidewalls of a space or its ceiling can be used to produce early reflections. Generally, selecting whether the wall or ceiling area should be reflective (or absorptive) is best established by considering its relative proximity to sources in the space. If the ceiling is quite high (so that it cannot serve as a good reflector), then the ceiling should be covered with absorptive materials, and the sidewalls should be used to create early reflections. However, if the ceiling is comparatively low or the sidewalls will be used for the display of items (as in a classroom) or the sidewalls will be glazed and have curtains present for light control and establishing privacy, then the ceiling should serve as the primary reflector. When the ceiling functions as a reflector, absorption should be placed along the sidewalls (e.g., by using a heavy cloth drape as a light or privacy curtain). In some situations it may be better to divide the area of a wall or ceiling into two (or more) areas, one (or more) for encouraging reflection and the other(s) for absorption. When dividing the areas of walls or ceiling, the best acoustical performance will probably be produced if the surfaces in the front of the space—near the primary sound source—are reflective and the back surfaces (side and back walls and ceiling) are all absorptive (see Figures 13.59 and 13.60).

It is also possible to use the floor as a reflector, but two points of caution should be considered. First, the floor will commonly be covered with furniture, so little opportunity will exist for good reflection paths to occur between a source and a receiver. And, second, when noise from scuffling feet or moving furniture can disrupt activities carried out in a space, then the floor surface should be covered with carpeting, reducing noise production at the floor.

For many common applications—for example, classrooms, offices, retail stores, and the like—where some attention to good acoustics is warranted, but other factors may

Figure 13.59 In a classroom, the principal absorbing surfaces have been placed at the ceiling. These surfaces are a combination of acoustic tile for absorbing middle and high-frequency sounds and the light-diffusing lens of the fluorescent fixtures, which function as panel absorbers and are better at absorbing lower-frequency sounds.

Figure 13.60 In another classroom, the front area of the ceiling is covered with a reflecting material to create good first-reflection sounds (to reinforce direct sound). The back area of the ceiling is composed of acoustic tile and the upper area of the back wall consists of a perforated panel absorber (e.g., perhaps similar to the perforated assembly shown in Figure 13.52). Both of these rearward areas absorb sound, thereby reducing the energies of any long-delayed reflections.

more particularly determine the form and surface composition of the space, then the best location for placing absorptive materials can be the finished ceiling surface. Several factors lead to this guideline. First, these spaces generally have small-to-medium floor areas with comparatively low floor-to-ceiling dimensions — perhaps, 2.4 to 3.0 m (8 to 10 ft) — and the line-of-sight distance between a speaker and a receiver will be short (no more than 6 to 9 m [20 to 30 ft]). Thus, direct sound waves will largely be the principal form of communication, and "early" reflections for reinforcing the direct sound can emanate off of vertical surfaces. Also, the ceiling area in these small to medium-sized spaces will be large compared to the areas of the vertical walls: so, absorption placement can be limited to one surface. Second, the space immediately above the finished ceiling surface will often be used for containing the several active environmental control systems. So, the finished ceiling is commonly composed of a suspended frame into which acoustic tile is laid (or otherwise fitted). This suspended ceiling — constructed of a porous/fibrous tile and hung as a panel — will provide good absorptive properties across a wide frequency range. Third, most absorptive tiles used in such assemblies are easily abraded, and placing them on an inaccessible surface like a ceiling protects them from degradation by building occupants. Fourth, using needed absorptive materials as a finished ceiling surface allows vertical walls to be employed for decorative materials, for hanging use-surfaces like chalkboards and tackboards in schools and display areas in stores. Alternatively, the vertical walls also will likely contain doors and windows. And, fifth, floors are generally covered by furniture. So, relying on porous or fibrous floor-covering materials to absorb sound waves in the room will often be ineffective (although such floor-covering absorption will still be useful for reducing noise generation from the impact of falling objects or from furniture or shoes scraping the floor).

A final guideline for locating absorptive materials is that absorption should be placed on surfaces that could cause acoustical defects like long-delayed reflections, echoes, or the focusing of sound waves. For example, any surfaces that might allow multiple-order sound wave reflections — second, third, and so forth — to arrive at a receiver should also

---

SIDEBAR 13.16 Suggestions for furnishing absorption materials in rooms

When estimating absorption amounts during preliminary schematic designing, we suggest application of the following two guidelines.

First, when absorption is to be added to a space explicitly to reduce anticipated noise levels, then the amount of absorption in the room must be increased by a factor of at least three times (3x) before any improvement in ambient noise levels will be noticeable to the occupants. Tripling the amount of absorption will decrease the sound pressure level by about five decibels. Similarly, increasing the amount of absorption by a factor of five times (5x) — about the limit that is generally practicable — will create a seven-decibel drop from the original sound pressure level.

The second guideline is a pair of statements that suggest average absorption coefficients for rooms. The first statement recommends the provision of a minimum average absorption coefficient of 0.2 for large spaces, especially where ceilings are quite low and there are relatively few noise sources (or these sources are not severe). Alternatively, for smaller spaces with one (or more) significant and identifiable noise source(s), the maximum average absorption coefficient should be 0.5. The first part of this pair is suggested to keep larger spaces from being too "lively," whereas the

second part is proposed to ensure that smaller spaces do not appear too "dead." If you know the absorption coefficients and surface areas for the principal materials that are likely to be used in a space (or can easily determine these numbers), you can compute rough average absorption coefficients for the space by calculating a surface-area-weighted average.[i]

To render these two statements into predictions about how much surface area of a room can be covered with absorbing materials, we suggest the following approach. A typical good absorbing material will have an absorption coefficient of about 0.8 in the middle to high frequencies. So, for large rooms, about 25 percent (or somewhat more) of the surface area of the room should be covered with a good absorbing material. Alternatively, for small rooms, no more than about 63 percent (or somewhat less) of the surface area of the room should be covered with good absorbing materials. Necessarily, these recommendations are approximate. But they can be taken as starting points during schematic designing.

i. *Sound Control Construction,* (Chicago, Illinois: United States Gypsum Company, 1972), page 31.

be covered with absorbing materials or made to be diffusing. Multiple-order reflections result in long-delayed sounds reaching receivers (creating confusing hearing conditions). When time differentials between the arrival of direct sounds and reflected sounds at a receiver can exceed 0.035 seconds, then special attention must be exercised to treat the surfaces causing these long-delayed reflections. To determine where such long-delayed reflections can occur, look for potential reflected wave pathways that will be more than 12.2 m (40 ft) longer than the direct wave path.

Also, if the distance between a speaker and a surface that could reflect sound waves back to the speaker are separated by more than 12.2 m (40 ft), then this surface should be covered with absorbing materials. When reflected sounds return to a speaker with time delays approaching or longer than about 0.07 seconds, the reflected sounds will be perceived as echoes. Echoes will often confuse a speaker (as well as any receivers in close proximity to a speaker). Alternatively, if a reflecting surface has a concave shape (relative to the location of a source), then the surface should be covered with an absorptive assembly to minimize the likelihood that sound "hot spots" and "voids" will be created in areas where receivers may be present.

13.6.3.4   Determining how much absorption should be provided in rooms   Generally, establishing whether adequate absorption is being provided for a room is best resolved during the latter stages of building design. In those stages of the design process, determining that there is enough absorption for each of the several frequencies can be carried out using appropriate calculations. Settling on necessary amounts of absorption and locating these materials are fundamentally a trial-and-error process. Absorption may thus be thought of as a resource that is to be allocated selectively and with care. Additionally, relevant trade-off analyses that usually must be entertained while locating absorption materials are most readily integrated with other design activities. Nevertheless, it is still possible during preliminary schematic designing to make some approximate decisions about absorption amounts. These decisions, when made early in the design process, can expedite later fine-tuning.

13.6.4   ESTABLISHING VOLUMETRIC STANDARDS FOR SPACES

Figure 13.61 offers guidelines for establishing what are acceptable volumes for rooms according to the type of communications likely to occur there. This graph also relates the room volumes and these communication types to the *reverberation times* suggested for these activities. The intent in presenting this graph is to provide not only a means of selecting volumetric guidelines, but also a basis for deciding upon a room height once the floor area of the room has been determined (by other planning methods and information). For instance, if you need to design a classroom that would seat a certain number of students, you might employ a planning guideline that suggests the floor area required per student. Then, having estimated the total floor area for the room, you could use this graph to establish an appropriate volume. Dividing this room volume by the total floor area would indicate a height that should afford good sound distribution.

13.6.4.1   A definition for the *reverberation times of rooms*   The reverberation time is generally regarded as a major determinant of the quality of sound that a space will display. In Section 10.3 we have previously described the dual notions of a reverberant field and reverberation time. Here, we will expand on that description. A well-developed reverberant

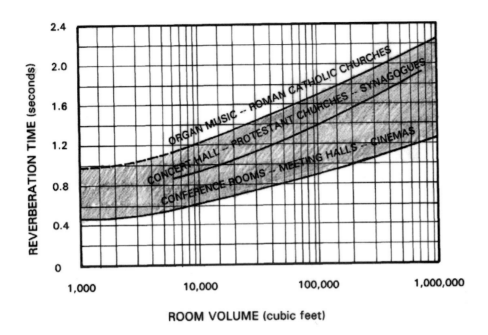

Figure 13.61 This graph suggests reasonable volumes and reverberation times for the several activities identified on the graph. Note that those activities using speech as the principal means of communication should have shorter reverberation times, whereas activities employing music as the major communication form require longer times. This illustration has been published previously in the article by Bolt, R.H., and R.B. Newman, "Architectural acoustics (Article 3, Part Two: Reverberation)," *Architectural Record,* November 1950, page 159. Permission to reproduce this drawing has been sought from the publisher of *Architectural Record,* The McGraw-Hill Companies, Inc.

field will have a uniform distribution of sound energy throughout the volume that the field occupies. This distribution results from one (or more) source(s) producing sounds that reflect off of the numerous surfaces within a space. These reflections thus form a well-diffused—or uniformly distributed—sound field (i.e., the reverberant field).

To measure the reverberation time for a space we employ the following procedure. When the sound emanating from a source in an enclosure appears to have established a uniform distribution, the sound source is shut off. We will then observe that a *subtle prolongation* of the sound will occur past the time of cessation of the source (i.e., the sound will continue to remain audible for some short period after the source has ceased emitting sound energy). This stretching-out of the sound results from the reflections and continued movement of sound waves (which originated from the source before it was extinguished). Accompanying this prolongation will be a gradual decrease in the sound pressure level present throughout the space. The reverberation time of the space is routinely defined as the length of time (in seconds) required for the sound pressure level of the reverberant field in the space to decrease 60 decibels (see Figure 13.62). Note that the reduction of the sound pressure level of a reverberant field may not always occur at a constant rate. Instead, the decrease in the pressure level—from moment-to-moment—may vary depending on

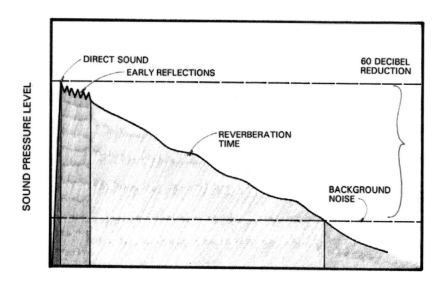

Figure 13.62 In this prototypical reverberation decay period curve a number of components can be seen. First, the pressure level in the space rises quickly as the direct sound wave propagates. Early reflections of the sound wave next occur, sustaining the nearly uniform pressure level. Then, a comparatively long pressure level decay proceeds as the energy from the sound source is depleted. When the remnant of pressure from the sound source falls below the ambient (background) noise level, then the reverberating sound will no longer be recognizable. The time required for the decaying pressure level to decrease by an increment of 60 decibels is the reverberation time for the enclosing space.

the characteristics of the sound source and its enclosing space. This incremental decrease in the pressure level is alternatively called the *decay rate.*

Figure 13.61 indicates that rooms built primarily for speech communication require relatively shorter reverberation times than do rooms where music will be the major communication form. For instance, for speech, the reverberation time should usually be between 0.4 second for a small office up to about 1.0 second for a large lecture hall. Alternatively, the reverberation time lengths for a space will be quite different depending upon the type of music that will be performed. For chamber music, where a small ensemble will generate the music, reverberation times from 1.0 to about 1.3 or 1.4 seconds are appropriate. In chamber music it is often important for the auditor to hear the individual parts that each instrument contributes to the ensemble's product. Thus, being able to separate out the musical components means that the amount of reverberation should only be a little greater than what is optimal for speech (i.e., much as one senses and interprets the individual components in speech). However, for church music — including choral works, chants, and plainsong — a large amount of the music requires that the performers sound as if they were of one voice (or one instrument). Thus, there must be substantial interweaving and blending of the musical components. The lengthening propagation of the musical sound waves and their reflections off of surfaces throughout the space become essential behaviors for spaces in which these musical forms are to be performed. Therefore, the reverberation times in churches may need to be as long as 2.0 to 2.5 (or more) seconds. Lastly, for spaces in which both speech and music will be presented—as in movie theaters and school auditoriums—designers and builders will usually have to seek compromises. For these mixed-use spaces, the amount of reverberation and the reverberation time are usually chosen to be greater than what is optimal for speech and less than what might be suitable for whatever music is heard in the space. The apparent sacrifice in aural quality for these mixed-use spaces is generally acceptable because of the multiple activities and/or communication forms that occur in these spaces. Also, the receivers' attention to the sound produced there may not be quite as fervent as for the lecture room or the concert hall (i.e., because the receivers in a theater or an auditorium will often be involved in visual pursuits as well).

The two room parameters that most directly determine the reverberation time of a space are the volume of the space and the amount of absorption present on the surfaces throughout the space. A simple relationship—originally proposed by Wallace Sabine in the early years of the 20th century—describes how the reverberation time, space volume, and absorption are linked.[17] In this relationship, the reverberation time is proportional to

---

TABLE 13.1
SUGGESTED VOLUME/SEAT RATIOS FOR VARIOUS ACTIVITIES,
IN CUBIC FEET/SEAT (CUBIC METERS/SEAT)

Activity	Doelle [i]	Smith et al. [ii]	Carbonell & Zuccoli [iii]
Conference room	—	—	130 (3.7)
Lecture room	110 (3.1)	100 (2.8)	150 (4.2)
Film theater	125 (3.5)	110 (3.1)	—
Chamber music	—	—	240 (6.8)
Orchestral music	275 (7.8)	250 (7.1)	325 (9.2)
Church	250–350 (7.1–9.9)		—
Protestant	255 (7.2)	—	—
Roman Catholic	300 (8.5)	—	—

i.   Doelle, L.L., *Environmental Acoustics*, (New York: McGraw-Hill Book Company, 1972), page 52.
ii. Smith, B.J., R.J. Peters, and S.Owen, *Acoustics and Noise Control*, (London: Longman Group Limited, 1982), page 34.
iii. We derived these numbers from a series of relationships presented in a paper by Carbonell, J.R., and J.L. Zuccoli, "Volume per seat and variation of the reverberation time with the size of the audience," *Journal of the Acoustical Society of America*, 33(6), June 1961, pages 757–759.

the volume and inversely proportional to the amount of absorption. Thus, for two rooms with equal volumes and unequal absorption amounts, the room with the larger amount of absorption will experience less reflection of sound waves, will have less reverberation, and a shorter reverberation time. So, if you are creating a space in which *speech* will be the principal (or only) form of communication, then you will want to provide more surfaces on which absorption can be placed and more absorption. Alternatively, if the space is to be used primarily for music, then you will want to encourage the reflection of sound and should have less absorption spread out through the space.

A common design practice provides smaller volumes for rooms in which speech will be the major (or sole) communication type and relatively larger volumes for rooms in which music is the major (or sole) communication type. For example, you would want to offer less volume for a lecture room than for a room in which listening to chamber music is the principal use. An indication of the differing volumetric needs for alternative communication types can be seen in Table 13.1 (i.e., in terms of recommended volume-per-seat ratios).

13.6.5 PROVIDING DIFFUSING SURFACES IN BUILDING SPACES

The diffusion of sound occurs when incident sound waves reflect off of irregular surfaces. Then, energy present in the incident waves will pass back into the surrounding space without any dominant directions. This reflected energy spreads out diffusely throughout the space, contributing to the build-up of a uniform energy density and, thus, a diffuse sound field. At the same time as this diffusion happens, sound waves also will likely reflect off of regular surfaces, leading to the development of reverberation. Diffusion enhances the qualities of reverberation by helping to ensure that there is good distribution of the sound energy throughout the space. A space with good diffusing characteristics will seem suitably "lively" (i.e., not too "dead"), without giving the impression of being too lively. Sounds will appear to be equally loud across the space, supporting good hearing conditions. Necessarily, the goal in establishing a sufficient diffusion of sound—equalizing the sound energy across the space—is to ensure that good communication conditions will be present. Diffuse sound conditions are an important attribute for spaces where musical

SIDEBAR 13.17 The acoustic "mean free path" in rooms and its utility

Providing unrestricted passage of sound waves throughout a room will enhance the creation of a *homogeneous* distribution of sound energy within the room. Kosten and a number of other researchers have written about the *mean free path* along which sound waves can travel in rooms with diffuse sound fields. The "free path" is basically the course that sound waves can pass through without encountering blocking (reflecting) surfaces. The equation cited by Kosten for determining the *mean free path* of sound waves in a diffuse field is four times the volume of the room divided by the total area of all the enclosure surfaces in the room. In a truly diffuse sound field—something that is not fully achieved in real spaces—sound waves would be able to travel from one reflecting surface to another over paths equal in length to achieve this mean free path. But, in real spaces with furnishings and other objects used for living and work, such path lengths are not as readily present. For further information, see the paper by Kosten, C.W., "The mean free path in room acoustics," *Acustica,* 10, 1960, pages 245–250.

practice and performance occurs or, more generally, for places of assembly where either presentations of music or speech are made.

Schultz has identified three requirements for assuring that adequate sound diffusion can occur in a space: the space must be appropriately large; the surfaces in the space should specifically accommodate diffusion; and diffusing elements should be included on wall and ceiling surfaces.[18]

Let's now consider each of these guidelines. First, the dimensions of the room should be established while considering what wavelengths of sounds will commonly be present in the space. A suggested relationship between wavelength and the volume of the space is that the volume should be equal to the product of four times the cube of the wavelength of the lowest one-third-octave band center frequency (e.g., perhaps for 63 or 125 Hz sound).[19] As an example, for a sound with the frequency of 125 Hz, the wavelength is 2.75 m (9.04 ft). The minimum volume—to ensure adequate space for the good diffusion of sound—should then be 83.7 m³ (2955 ft³). But, where these proportions cannot be met, less stringent recommendations suggest that the largest and smallest dimensions of the room should differ by a ratio of less than 2:1; and no two dimensions of the room should be the same.[20] Lastly, the smallest dimension for a room should be equal to or greater than the wavelength for the center frequency of the lowest one-third-octave band that is considered to be important for good hearing. Thus, for a 125 Hz sound, the wavelength is 2.75 m (9.0 ft) or for a 63 Hz sound, the wavelength is 5.46 m (17.92 ft).[21] These space-sizing guidelines should be used in combination with those presented in Section 13.6.2.1.

Second, the diffusion of sound within a space can further be enhanced if, in addition to employing the appropriate dimensions, the space planner also includes each of several other features. For example, creating a space with nonparallel surfaces will aid diffusion, especially if the surfaces can be oriented at random angles or—second best—can at least have multiple orientations (within the space). Note that these surfaces do not necessarily have to be the boundary surfaces—walls and ceiling—of the envelope of the room. Instead, these diffusing surfaces may consist of many small or medium-sized attachments connected to the boundary surfaces. Additionally, reducing the amount of furniture and other equipment within the space as much as possible will also improve diffusion. Essentially, furniture and other objects in the space inhibit the movement of sound energy throughout the space. To encourage the development of the diffuse sound field—one in which sound energy is uniformly distributed in a room—sound waves need to pass undisturbed across the interior of the room. These waves then should be reflected randomly by enclosure surfaces that are oriented to diffuse incident waves.

Another strategy for fostering diffusion is to ensure that the diffusing surfaces at the boundaries of the room are adequately sized. As suggested above, these surfaces can be installed as small- or medium-sized attachments to the walls and ceiling of the room. These attachments should have dimensions that are at least as big as one-quarter of a wavelength for the center frequency of the lowest one-third octave band sound for which the room will be designed. So, if a room is to be used strictly as a lecture hall and the most important sound spectral range for speech encompasses sounds with frequencies between 125 to 4000 Hz, then the center frequency of the lowest one-third octave band would be 125 Hz. And for 125 Hz sound the minimum surface dimension should be about 0.7 m (2.3 ft).[22] Diffusing surfaces of lesser dimensions should also be provided to enhance the diffusion of smaller-wavelength (higher-frequency) sounds. Thus, a mixture of diffusing-surface attachments with appropriate dimensions should be present and located on the enclosure surfaces of a room.

Third, a variety of devices and shapes can be used in a room to diffuse sound waves (e.g., see Figure 13.63). Generally, diffuser shapes should either be convex or faceted. These diffuser shapes and devices can be constructed as textured reliefs attached to the walls and ceiling of a room (i.e., thus appearing as a series of protrusions erupting from the boundary surfaces). Diffusers can also be included in a room as hanging panels, moving vanes, or shelving (as in display shelves used in retail stores). As stated above, these diffusing surfaces should best be oriented randomly to encourage a well-scattered spread of the sound energy. But, if a randomized texture cannot be created across the surfaces of the room, then as a first alternative the diffusing surfaces should at least provide multiple orientations for reflecting incident sound waves.

Lastly, one additional solution for minimizing the effects of concave reflecting surfaces is to diffuse the energy of the sound waves incident on these surfaces. Such diffusion can be accomplished by making the surfaces faceted or bowing the surface in a convex shape (i.e., the surface will be basically concave in its primary dimension—side-to-side—but its secondary dimension—top-to-bottom—will be convex).

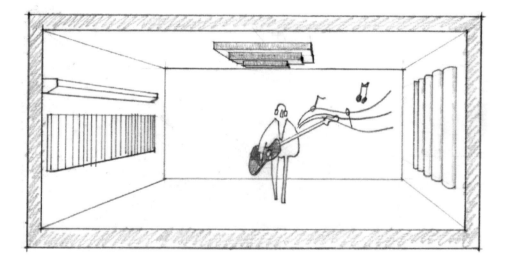

Figure 13.63 Several diffusing surfaces and shapes are shown in this illustration. The devices on the left wall and the ceiling have faceted shapes, and the device on the right wall is a series of half-cylindrical forms placed side-by-side (thus, having convex shapes). The lower paneling on the left wall is intended to approximate the appearance of a reflection phase grating that was initially proposed by M. A. Schroeder. For further information about reflection phase gratings and some of the theory that explains their behavior, see the article by D'Antonio, P., "Fractals and number theory are changing the shape of acoustics," *Sound and Vibration,* 26(10), October 1992, pages 24-30.

13.6.6 PROVIDING SPECIAL FURNISHINGS FOR ROOMS FOR MUSIC AND/OR SPEECH PERFORMANCE

Rooms that are created specifically for the performance of musical compositions or as lecture halls often require special accommodations (i.e., to facilitate and enhance communication between the source and the receiver). As examples, such rooms may need to have out-of-the-ordinary furnishings (e.g., particularly absorbent chairs). The organization of the basic room elements may have to include a stage or raised platform (on which speakers may stand), adjoining service rooms, audio-visual booths, special means for egress, and noise-admission control. Various electronic and other support devices may also be employed to augment, extend, or otherwise embellish the musical performance or lecture.

Many of these accommodations are traditionally dealt with during the later stages of building design (and thus will be excluded from consideration in this text). For further information on these topics we suggest references to the books by Apfel, Cavanaugh et al., Doelle, Egan, Mehta et al., and Parkin et al.[23]

ENDNOTES and SELECTED ADDITIONAL COMMENTS

1. These four requirements were described by Robert B. Newman in his classes on architectural acoustics, which he taught for many years at MIT.

2. For an alternative presentation of these acoustical design fundamentals, see the series of four articles written by Bolt, R.H., and R.B. Newman, "Architectural acoustics," *Architectural Record,* 1950 (April, pages 165–168ff; June, pages 166–169ff; September, pages 148–151ff; and November, pages 158–160ff).

3. Kurze, U.L., "Noise reduction by barriers," *Journal of the Acoustical Society of America,* 55(3), March 1974, pages 504–518; Thomasson, S., "Diffraction by a screen above an impedance boundary," *Journal of the Acoustical Society of America,* 63(6), June 1978, pages 1768–1781; Maekawa, Z., and S. Osaki, "A simple chart for the estimation of the attenuation by a wedge diffraction," *Applied Acoustics,* 18, 1985, pages 355–368; and L'Esperance, A., "The insertion loss of finite length barriers on the ground," *Journal of the Acoustical Society of America,* 86(1), July 1989, pages 179–183.

4. Hutchins, D.A., H.W. Jones, B. Paterson, and L.T. Russell, "Studies of parallel barrier performance by acoustical modeling," *Journal of the Acoustical Society of America,* 77(2), February 1985, pages 536–546. See also the paper by Bowlby, W., L.F. Cohn, and R.A. Harris, "A review of studies of insertion loss degradation for parallel highway noise barriers," *Noise Control Engineering Journal,* 28(2), March–April 1987, pages 40–53.

5. This information is stated in a chapter by Kurze, U., and L.L. Beranek, "Sound propagation outdoors," in the book edited by L.L. Beranek, *Noise and Vibration Control* (New York: McGraw-Hill Book Company, 1971). See page 181 for the specific noise reduction claim. The research study identified by Drs. Kurze and Beranek as the source of this information is a report, *Noise in Urban and Suburban Areas: Results of Field Studies,* prepared by the acoustical consulting firm of Bolt, Beranek, and Newman, Inc., Cambridge, Massachusetts (Report No. 1395, January 1967).

6. See Sections 11.1.2 and 12.3.2 for information about the masking process and the effect that masking noise can have on speech intelligibility.

7. An eloquent description of the use of water (and the wind) to create enchanting aural environments is presented in the chapter, "The soniferous garden," in the book written by Schafer, R.M., *The Tuning of the World: Toward a Theory of Soundscape Design,* (Philadelphia: University of Pennsylvania Press, 1980), pages 246–252.

8. Fricke, F.R., "The protection of buildings against traffic noise," *Noise Control Engineering,* 8(1), January–February 1977, pages 27–32.

9. Information about approaches to impact noise separation can be found in Ver, I.L., and C.I. Holmer, "Interaction of sound waves with solid structures," in Beranek, L.L. (editor), *Noise and Vibration Control,* (New York: McGraw-Hill Book Company, 1971), pages 334–361); and _____, *A Guide to Airborne, Impact, and Structureborne Noise Control in Multifamily Dwellings* (prepared for the U.S. Federal Housing Administration by the U.S. National Bureau of Standards), (Washington, D.C.: U.S. Government Printing Office, 1974).

10. Warnock, A.C.C., "Factors affecting sound transmission loss," *Canadian Building Digest #239,* (Ottawa: Division of Building Research, National Research Council of Canada, July 1985); ———, *A Guide to Airborne, Impact, and Structureborne Noise Control in Multifamily Dwellings* (prepared by the National Bureau of Standards for the Federal Housing Administration), (Washington, D.C.: U.S. Government Printing Office, 1974); and Doelle, L.L., *Environmental Acoustics,* (New York: McGraw-Hill Book Company, 1972), pages 228–237.

11. Fearon, W.W., "Floating floors for impact and airborne noise control," *Sound and Vibration,* October 1986, pages 20–22.

12. Purcell, W.E., "Materials for noise and vibration control," *Sound and Vibration,* July 1982, page 22.

13. Quirt, J.D., "Sound transmission through windows I. Single and double glazing," *Journal of the Acoustical Society of America,* 72(3), September 1982, pages 834–844; Quirt, J.D., "Sound transmission through windows II. Double and triple glazing," *Journal of the Acoustical Society of America,* 74(2), August 1983, pages 534–542; and Quirt, J.D., Sound transmission through windows," *Canadian Building Digest #240,* (Ottawa: Division of Building Research, National Research Council of Canada, July 1985).

14. ———. *Sound Control Construction: Principles and Performance,* (Chicago, Illinois: United States Gypsum Corporation, 1972), pages 38–39.

15. Redmore, T.L., "A method to predict the transmission of sound through corridors," *Applied Acoustics,* 15, 1982, pages 133–146; and "A theoretical analysis and experimental study of the behavior of sound in corridors," *Applied Acoustics,* 15, 1982, pages 161–170.

16. These eight mounting practices are defined by the American Society for Testing and Materials in its Standard E795-00, *Standard Practices for Mounting Test Specimens During Sound Absorption Tests,* (Philadelphia: American Society for Testing and Materials, 2000).

17. Young, R.W., "Sabine reverberation equation and sound power calculations," *Journal of the Acoustical Society of America,* 31(7), July 1959, pages 912–921; Doelle, L.L., *Environmental Acoustics* (New York: McGraw-Hill Book Company, 1972), pages 26–29, 55–58, and 221–224; and Egan, M.D., *Architectural Acoustics* (New York: McGraw-Hill Book Company, 1988), pages 62–66.

18. Schultz, T.J., "Diffusion in reverberation rooms," *Journal of Sound and Vibration,* 16(1), 1971, pages 17–28.

19. ———. *Standard Test Method for Sound Absorption and Sound Absorption Coefficients by the Reverberation Room Method,* ASTM Standard C423-02, (Philadelphia: American Society for Testing and Materials, 2002).

20. ———. *Standard Method for Laboratory Measurement of Airborne Sound Transmission Loss of Building Partitions and Elements,* ASTM Standard E90-02, (Philadelphia: American Society for Testing and Materials, 2002).

21. ———. *Standard Test Method for Sound Absorption and Sound Absorption Coefficients by the Reverberation Room Method,* ASTM Standard C423-02, (Philadelphia: American Society for Testing and Materials, 2002).

22.   ———. *Standard Method for Laboratory Measurement of Airborne Sound Transmission Loss of Building Partitions and Elements,* ASTM Standard E90-02, (Philadelphia: American Society for Testing and Materials, 2002).

23.   Apfel, R.E., *Deaf Architects & Blind Acousticians? A Guide to the Principles of Sound Design,* (New Haven, Connecticut: Apple Enterprises Press, 1998); Cavanaugh, W.J., and J.A. Wilkes (editors), *Architectural Acoustics: Principles and Practice,* (New York: J. Wiley & Sons, Inc., 1999); Doelle, L.L., *Environmental Acoustics,* (New York: McGraw-Hill Book Company, 1972); Egan, M.D., *Architectural Acoustics,* (New York: McGraw-Hill Book Company, 1988; Mehta, M., J. Johnson, and J. Rocafort, *Architectural Acoustics: Principles and Design,* (Upper Saddle River, New Jersey: Prentice-Hall, Inc., 1999); Parkin, P.H., H.R. Humphreys, and J.R. Cowell, *Acoustics, Noise, and Buildings,* (London: Faber and Faber Ltd., 1979).

HVAC Systems for Buildings

Section A.1 | THE BASIC FUNCTIONS OF HVAC SYSTEMS

To paraphrase a definition offered by the American Society of Heating, Refrigerating, and Air-Conditioning Engineers, Inc., a comprehensive heating, ventilating, and air-conditioning (HVAC) system is capable of providing heating and humidification during the winter, cooling and dehumidification during the summer, the supply of fresh air throughout the year, and the capability to furnish each of these services in a controlled manner and when sought by building occupants. Thus, HVAC systems are created in buildings to serve two principal functions: first, these systems provide fresh air for building occupants; and, second, the systems enable the thermal conditioning of the building interior.

Optimally, fresh air is air that is free of particulate matter (alternatively, dust and dirt), allergens, odors, and any of various pollutants (e.g., those produced by industrial sources, motor vehicles, adjacent buildings, and so forth). The fresh air must be supplied in sufficient quantity to ensure that occupants have air of good quality throughout the building. This fresh air may be drawn entirely from the building exterior, or it may be a mixture of outside air and "used" — but still relatively clean — air that has been gathered from within the building.

Thermal conditioning of the building interior involves providing conditions that will ensure that occupants are thermally comfortable. Establishing thermally comfortable conditions in a building requires that the four environmental parameters that determine how occupants experience the thermal nature of their environment are maintained in suitable ranges. Thus, air temperature, radiant exchange rate between occupants and their environment, relative humidity, and velocity of moving air around these occupants must all be adequately controlled (see Section 3.5 for guidelines about what ranges of these parameters foster thermal comfort).

A.1.1   THE PRINCIPAL COMPONENTS OF HVAC SYSTEMS

A fully-developed HVAC system will generally consist of a heating source, a refrigeration (chilling) source, distribution devices for transporting the ventilation air, heat, and coolth to individual spaces in the building, a medium (or media) for doing the transporting, sensors for detecting the natures of the thermal environment and the air quality, and controls for regulating the operations both of the overall system and of individual elements within the system. These components may be collected in a single, stand-alone unit, or they may exist as a series of individual components that are separately placed in various locations throughout a building.

The media most commonly used for ventilating and conditioning building spaces are air, water, and electricity. Moving air not only offers ventilation to individual spaces, but also furnishes an important means of transporting heat and coolth throughout a building. Water passing around a building affords an alternative means for moving heat and coolth. Electricity, whereas not directly capable of carrying heat, coolth, or air around a building, does provide the power to operate localized or centralized system components, which can supply heat, coolth, or air. For example, a commonly applied space-heating device is an electrically powered baseboard radiant strip (similar in function to the finned-tube convector described in Chapter 2; see Figures 2.7 and 2.8).

The distribution devices that enable the passage of air around a building can include fans (for propelling the air), ducts (for enclosing and transporting the air), terminals (used either for modifying the quantity of air flowing along a duct or for altering the thermal properties of the air), outlet devices (for admitting the air into occupied spaces), and intake devices (for gathering up air that has been used in occupied spaces)(see Figure A.1). The distribution of air to individual spaces in a building can be performed using air-handlers that are either arrayed locally, on a floor-by-floor basis, or centrally. In many larger buildings and, even, in some small, yet complicated buildings, more than one air-handling system can be expected to be present.

SIDEBAR A.1 *Coolth as a physical phenomenon*

This term *coolth* was initiated and popularized by the late John Yellott, a distinguished mechanical engineer who practiced in the American Southwest for many years. Its meaning embodies both a cool (or cold) medium and the ability of the medium to absorb heat, thereby rebalancing the thermal environment of the building.

The distribution devices by which water is moved through a building consist of pumps, piping, valves (for regulating flow rates), tanks (for the temporary storage of water), and terminals (for transferring heat or coolth into occupied spaces). Either hot water or chilled water (or both) may commonly be transported around a building, expressly for the thermal conditioning of individual spaces. To enable simultaneous passage of hot water and chilled water, more than one pipe run may connect to a conditioning terminal. Generally, for every pipe run supplying water to a terminal, there will be a paired return pipe run (see Figure A.2).

In many HVAC applications, combinations of air movement and water flow will be employed in the ventilation and thermal conditioning of building spaces. For example, moving air will provide ventilation for a space, and the passage of water will furnish a *supplemental* resource for modifying the thermal properties of the air before it is introduced

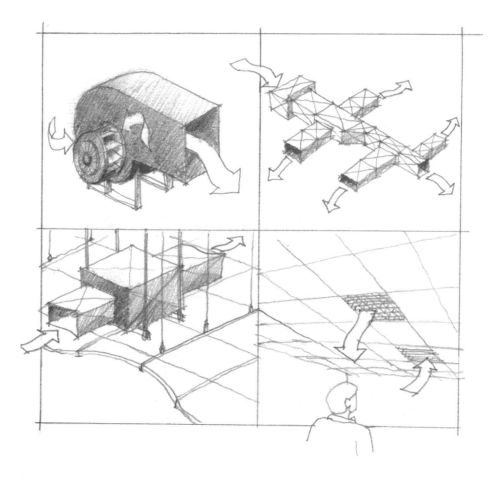

Figure A.1 Four basic components of most central air-handling systems are the fan (for propelling the air), ducting (for conveying air to spaces that are to be conditioned and ventilated), in-the-ceiling terminals (for conditioning the air or regulating the amounts that enter the spaces), and diffusers for admitting air to the spaces and grilles for gathering the air from the space. Other air-handling systems may use other components and in different combinations.

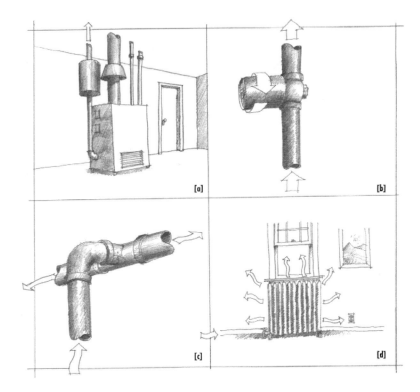

Figure A.2 Four basic components of a hot water (hydronic) heating system (a) are the hot water boiler (for heating the water), (b) a pump (for propelling the water through the system), (c) piping (for transporting the water throughout the building), and (d) a terminal (for exchanging the heat from the water to the occupied space). Other versions of hydronic heating systems may employ alternative components.

into the space. In such an application the hot or chilled water might pass through coils embedded in the air-handling terminal, and the ducted air will flow across the coils. As the air passes around the coils, the temperature (and humidity) of the air can be altered (see Figure A.3). In another instance, a terminal can be mounted at a building perimeter— either as an in-the-wall unit or in the space above a finished ceiling. Air can be drawn into the terminal directly through the wall or by a short duct running between the wall and the ceiling-mounted unit. The air can then be conditioned as it passes across water-carrying coils present in the terminal, where the water is being transported to the terminal from perhaps a central source.

Two other fluids are also used as transport media. One such fluid is steam that is run through well-insulated piping. Generally, for reasons of safety and energy efficiency, its use is often limited to large-scale district heating applications. The other group of fluids is a collection of refrigerants that are used, particularly, in cooling (or chilling) applications. These refrigerants are transported by piping and can be run across either short or intermediate-length distances.

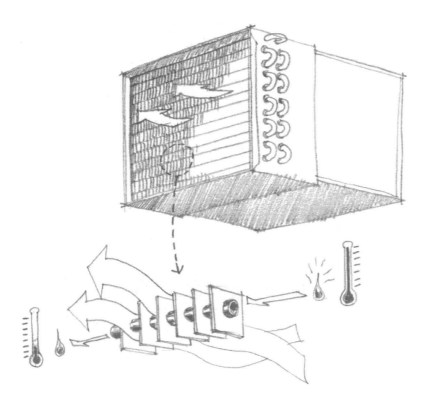

Figure A.3 By passing air across a heating coil, as it moves through ducting, the air can be warmed. Such coils can perform the heating either by having hot water flow through piping embedded in the coil or by having electric resistance heaters present in the coil.

A.1.2   THE TRADITIONAL BUILDING SPACES FOR LOCATING HVAC SYSTEMS

Generally, three types of building spaces are employed to house components of HVAC systems: mechanical (or fan) rooms, service core areas, and horizontal volumes between finished ceilings and the floor (or roof) surface above. Additionally, a fourth type of space — for housing cooling towers or condensers — will commonly be included when buildings have refrigeration machines (chillers) (see Figure A.4).

Mechanical (or fan) rooms will usually contain fans for moving air and/or pumps for moving water. There may be one room or a few rooms in a building if a central air-handling system is used for conditioning the building. As an alternative to a centralized air-handling system air-handlers can be located on each floor of a building. Where such floor-by-floor air-handlers are utilized, they will usually be organized modularly, and each will be housed in a dedicated space (meaning that there will be a fan room on each floor). In between having a single mechanical room for a building and having one fan room per floor of a multiple-floor building, there are a myriad number of permutations. Because single

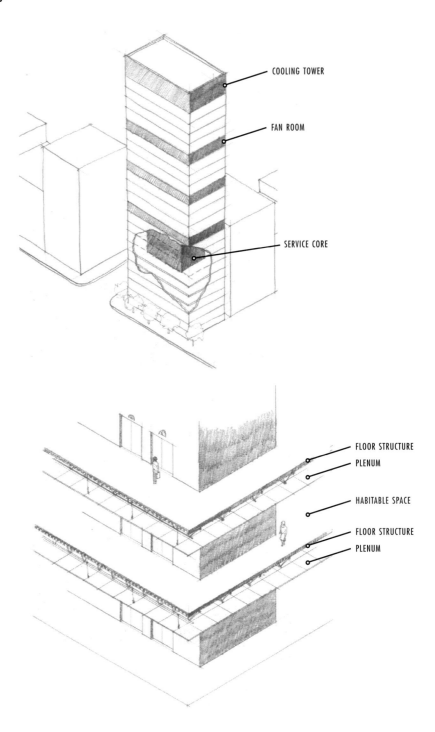

Figure A.4 The four principal HVAC system spaces in a conventional high-rise commercial building are the mechanical (or fan) rooms, the service core (in which vertical shafts are run), the ceiling plenums (in which horizontal ducts are run), and space — usually at the rooftop — for a cooling tower. Note that, whereas the air-handling fans may be spread throughout the building in a series of fan rooms, primary heating and cooling equipment such as boilers, chillers, and pumps will often be concentrated in a single location.

mechanical rooms in large buildings are often quite large spaces, sizing and locating them involve important design decisions.

Service cores exist to organize *vertically* components of the various building services (e.g., toilet rooms, electrical power and communication facilities, vertical transportation, fire safety equipment and evacuation routes, and HVAC systems). In a typical high-rise office building the service core is often located in the center of the building footprint (although it may be placed along a perimeter elevation). As a second alternative the services that are organized vertically throughout a building may be divided, and perhaps half of them will be deployed along one elevation and the remainder placed along the opposite elevation.

The third generic, modular volume will be the space that occurs between the finished ceiling and the finished floor (or roof) above. Into this volume will be placed components of the various systems that provide services for the rooms immediately below and above this volume. These service components will basically be laid out in horizontal layers with each service system occupying its own layer. As such, an apt metaphor is that the organization of these parallel, yet separate layers resembles a bacon, lettuce, and tomato sandwich (so that this finished-ceiling-to finished-floor volume is sometimes referred to as a "ceiling sandwich"). Because of the relative ease, practicality, and efficiency of utilizing this repeating, modular volume for housing the components of these service systems, this layout strategy is employed for most nonresidential buildings.

Section A.2 | DESCRIBING THE HVAC SYSTEM FOR A TYPICAL UNIVERSITY CLASSROOM BUILDING

Gould Hall is a building located on the campus of the University of Washington, Seattle (see Figure A.5).[1] The principal spaces in this building operate as classrooms, offices, meeting rooms, and laboratories (e.g., a wood and metal-working shop and a photography studio and darkroom). The building has a reinforced-concrete structural system; the facade is composed of uninsulated, poured-in-place concrete walls with operable single-paned glazing assemblies (consistent with standard design practices at the time of its construction in 1971). The interior materials are also conventional and are well matched

Figure A.5 An exterior view of Gould Hall

to their use requirements. The building has four floors above grade and two floors below grade. The gross floor area is 62,000 square feet (5760 m²). A central atrium extends from the first floor up to the roof.

A.2.1   DESIGN CONDITIONS

The occupancy characteristics of the building are varied. The building is in use from about 8:00 AM until late in the evening throughout the week (with reduced usage on most weekends). Classroom seating capacities range from a high of 90 occupants to a low of 6 or 8 occupants. Additionally, the rates of use of these classrooms differ across the school day. For instance, a classroom may be used one hour and vacant the next. Also, the degree to which any classroom is fully occupied during a class session can vary appreciably (e.g., the 90-occupant classroom often has back-to-back classes with one class where the room will be fully occupied, whereas for the next class the room will be only one-third full).

The offices tend to be single-person rooms, are generally located along the building perimeter (mostly on the north elevation), and have envelope assemblies that consist of, by area, 70 percent single-pane glazing and 30 percent uninsulated concrete. The university, both at the time when this building was being designed and now, maintains a policy of trying to furnish an air temperature in all offices of 68 °F (20 °C) for the period of the year when heating is required. Further, the university administration generally wishes to maintain a "shirtsleeve environment" (i.e., one in which occupants who spend several hours per day in the building can work in their shirtsleeves or, more specifically, use sweaters or suit coats during the winter and lightweight clothing during the summers).

In addition to these general operating conditions, selected spaces require special accommodations. First, the wood and metal-working shop generates a high level of dust and particulate matter, as well as airborne gases that should not circulate through the rest of the building. Second, in the photography darkroom, various chemicals are used in the processing of film and printing materials. The vapors from such chemicals also should not be permitted to circulate through the rest of the building. And, third, it is undesirable for toilet room odors to pass into other occupied spaces. For these three groups of spaces room air will need to be exhausted to the building exterior, rather than used for recirculation. However, in contrast to these building spaces that require special accommodations, the "used" air from all of the other building spaces can be recirculated.

A.2.2   THERMAL CONDITIONING ISSUES

In many occupied building spaces the presence of occupants, the use of electric lighting, and the operation of various electrically powered equipment (e.g., computers, projectors, and so forth) all contribute to a situation where the rate of heat generation exceeds the rate of heat loss through the building envelope. This condition is described as being *internal-load-dominant* (i.e., the rate of heat production by sources within the building space is greater than the rate with which heat can be lost through the building envelope). For such internal-load-dominant spaces, if the excess heat is not removed from the space, then the air temperature in the room will rise, the room will feel increasingly stuffy, and the thermal comfort of the occupants will be degraded.

In building spaces where the rate of internal heat production is small — occupant densities are low and the amounts of electrical energy used to operate lights and equipment are also low — and heat loss or gain through the building envelope is present and substantial, then the thermal condition of the space can be described as being *envelope-load-dependent* (i.e., the rate of heat transfer through the building envelope determines the thermal behavior of the space). If, in an envelope-load-dependent space, substantial heat loss occurs through the envelope, then the air temperature will fall and occupants will become uncomfortable. Or, if in such a space the heat gain rate through the envelope is large, then the room air temperature will rise and occupants will become uncomfortable.

Each of these two fundamental thermal conditions is commonly present in Gould Hall. The larger classrooms — those with seating capacities of about 25 people or greater — will behave in an internal-load-dominant manner whenever the rooms are filled with people. Further, the number of occupants and the intensity of their usage of electrically powered equipment will determine the magnitude of the internal heat gain. Some spaces may only be marginally internal-load-dominant and have modest overheating, whereas other spaces are likely to be substantially more overheated.

Any space that experiences overheating will need to be cooled (i.e., to have the heat gain extracted or diluted), if thermally comfortable environments are to be maintained. Alternatively, the perimeter office spaces will be envelope-load-dependent. During the conventional heating season — when outside air temperatures are below about 60 °F (15 °C) — then heat will have to be supplied to these offices if they are to remain thermally comfortable.

To summarize the capabilities needed in a heating, ventilating, and air-conditioning system for Gould Hall, first, the system must provide adequate thermal conditioning. The conditioning capabilities must include provisions for cooling overheated spaces, heating spaces along the building perimeter, and varying the amount of cooling according to the intensity of the overheatedness. Additionally, each of the thermal conditioning capabilities must be available simultaneously: some spaces will need to be heated at the same time that others will need to be cooled, and the amounts of cooling to be supplied at any given moment will differ on a room-by-room basis. The amounts of heating required in the various spaces will also vary, although the range of the needs for heating will be less great than for cooling. Second, each of the occupied spaces throughout the building will require the supply of adequate amounts of fresh air.

SIDEBAR A.2 The effects of solar heat gain on internal-loaded and envelope-loaded situations

The heat gain rates in occupied spaces that are internal-load-dominant will often be quite uniform due to the near-constancy of occupant presence and the use of electrically powered devices. But a space that is already internal-load-dominant (because of the presences of people and electrically powered devices) can be rendered even more overheated, if solar heat gain also enters into the space. In some circumstances the rate of solar heat gain can be as great as the rate of heat gain resulting from the internal sources. However, the amount of heat gain from solar radiation will certainly vary across the day and throughout the year (as the path of the sun across the sky vault and the weather change).

The effect of solar heat gain on envelope-load-dependent spaces can be even more profound. On a day with cold external air temperatures and without any solar gain, a perimeter building space will experience heat loss through the envelope. But if solar radiation enters into the perimeter room, it can positively offset heat loss through the building envelope (offering the passive solar heating of the building interior).

A.2.3 THE HVAC SYSTEM FOR GOULD HALL

A.2.3.1 The physical presence of the HVAC system: components, sizes, locations

The overall system can be identified as an *all-air system with supplementary perimeter radiation*. The principal components of this system are a series of air-handlers, a steam-hot water heat exchanger, several pumps, many in-the-ceiling terminals, and an extensive hot water under-windows radiation system. The major building volumes that house these components are a central mechanical room, four shafts for running air and conditioning water vertically through the building, and conventional ceiling plenums (the spaces between the finished ceiling and the finished floor or roof above)(see Figure A.6).

The physical dimensions of the mechanical room are 50 feet (width) by 120 feet (length) by 18 1/2 feet (height; from the finished floor to the bottoms of the ceiling joists) (15.2 m × 36.6 m × 5.6 m). The total cross-sectional area for the four vertical shafts is 336 square feet (31.2 m²). Generally, the vertical dimensions for the finished-floor-to-finished-ceiling and the finished-ceiling-to-finished-floor (or roof) spaces are 10 feet (3.1 m) and 3

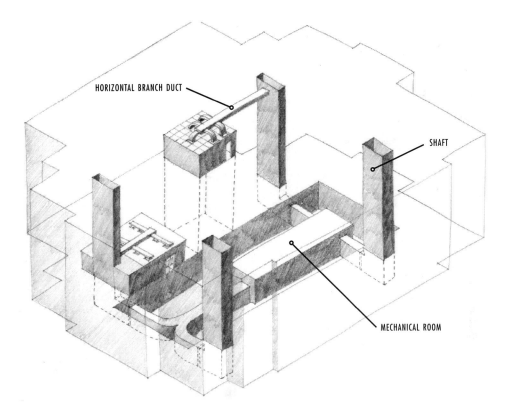

Figure A.6 The major spaces for the Gould Hall HVAC system are presented here. The mechanical room is located in a two-story high space with its flooring set at the sub-basement level. There are four shafts, each located in one of the corners of the building. Off of these shafts numbers of horizontal branch ducts run in ceiling plenums (note that two sets of these horizontal branches are shown in this illustration).

feet (0.9 m), respectively. In addition to these internal building spaces, the external fresh air intakes have a total cross-sectional area of 111 square feet (10.3 m²).

The major HVAC system components located in the mechanical room—when viewed in terms of the quantities of space that they occupy—are the supply air-handler, the return air fan, two exhaust air fans, and a steam-hot water heat exchanger (see Figure A.7). The supply air-handler is a *built-up* assembly consisting of a mixed-air plenum, two sets of filters, a preheat coil, a chilled water coil,[2] a reheat coil, and the supply air fan (see Figure A.8). The return air-handler consists of a return air fan and a return air plenum (that, at one end, connects through a set of dampers to the mixed-air plenum of the supply air-handler)(see Figure A.9). The two exhaust air fans are stand-alone fans and connect to exhaust ducting that run inside the return air plenum to the building exterior. One of the two exhaust air fans removes air from the wood and metal-working shop and from the photography darkroom and studio. The other exhaust air fan withdraws air from the toilet rooms throughout the building.

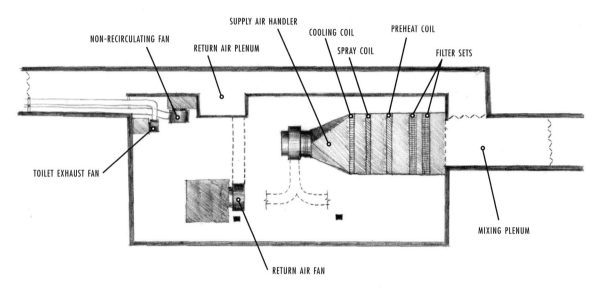

Figure A.7 The four air-handlers (and their associated fans) that are present in the Gould Hall mechanical room are displayed here as well as the air intake plenum and the return air plenum. The four air-handlers are, respectively, the supply air air-handler, the return air air-handler, the toilet exhaust fan, and the non-recirculating air fan. The volume just to the right of the supply air air-handler is the mixing air plenum where the incoming fresh air and (some of) the return air can mix. The five devices shown within the supply air-handler by cross-hatching are, starting from the right (where the air from the mixing plenum enters the air-handler), two sets of filters, a preheat coil, a water spray coil (for adjusting the humidity of the supply air stream), and a cooling coil.

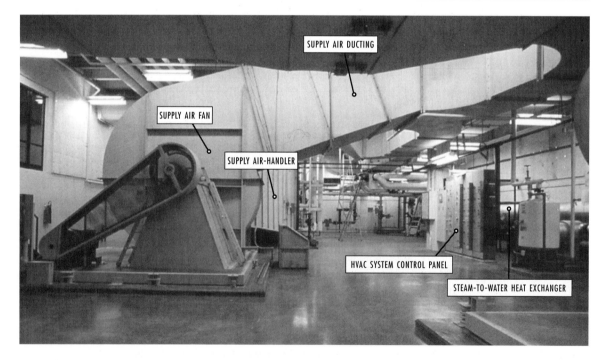

Figure A.8 The supply air fan and the supply air-handler behind the fan are shown as they are surrounded by the control panel, various pipes, the steam-to-water heat exchanger, and supply air ducting.

Figure A.9 The supply air fan and the supply air-handler are in the right foreground. In the center are the return air fan and its housing. In the distance middle right are the two specialized exhaust fans. The system control panel appears on the left.

Figure A.10 The University of Washington Power Plant operates up to five main boilers; the number operating at any given moment depends on the need for heating across the campus. These boilers produce steam that is routed to most of the buildings on the campus through pipes that run in a series of utility tunnels. The newest of the boilers is shown here in this photograph.

Figure A.11 Also present in the power plant are a series of chillers. The one displayed here is an absorption chiller. It has a capacity of 2500 tons (8800 kW). Its product is water chilled to about 37 °F (3 °C) that is transported around the campus through the utility tunnels.

The steam-hot water heat exchanger functions as the principal heat source within the building. Gould Hall is connected to a campuswide utility system and draws its heating resource—steam—from this system. At the center of the campus system is a utility services plant in which steam and chilled water are separately produced (see Figures A.10 and A.11). The steam and chilled water are then distributed across the campus through a series of large pipes running in tunnels that pass under the campus (see Figures A.12 and A.13). Steam from the utility services plant passes into Gould Hall and is piped to the steam-hot water heat exchanger (see Figures A.14 and A.15). The steam enters the cylinder (of the

Figure A.12 This map shows the layout of the utility tunnels that lie beneath the University of Washington campus. To serve this campus of approximately 700 acres (280 ha), nearly eight miles (12.9 km) (linear) of tunnels have been dug and finished at depths of between 10 to 50 feet (3.05 to 15.24 m) below grade. The services that pass through these tunnels include steam, chilled water, compressed air, and cabling for electrical power distribution, computer networks, telephones, and specialized communications (e.g., the clock system for the university). A typical interior of these tunnels is shown in Figure A.13.

exchanger) and flows around coils (present inside the cylinder) through which cool-temperature water passes (see Figure A.16). Once, the steam has transferred some of its heat to the water, the steam (condensate) is piped back through the campus system to the utility services plant (where it is reheated and redistributed). The water exiting the steam-hot water heat

Figure A.13 One of the utility tunnels is shown here. These tunnels are located, on average, two or more stories beneath grade level. On the left in this photograph are a series of large pipes (approximately 24 in [610 mm] in diameter) for transporting the steam and chilled water across the campus. On the right are trays that support electrical cables that run from West Campus substation to many individual buildings (note that this electrical distribution will be discussed in Section D.3.1.

exchanger will have temperatures in the range of 140–160 °F (60–70 °C). This hot water is then piped around the building to perform heating services (see Figure A.17).

Above the mechanical room, which is located in the sub-basement and basement levels of the building, the principal space-occupying HVAC system components are supply air ducting, in-the-ceiling terminals, and supplemental perimeter radiation units. The supply air ducts are located in the four shafts. At the basement level these ducts are approximately 36 in (0.9 m) in diameter, and at the fourth floor level, these ducts have diameters of about 16 in (0.4 m). The horizontal ducts that branch off immediately from these vertical ducts — at all floors — are also about 16 in in diameter (0.4 m). These horizontal branch ducts decrease in size as the tributary floor areas served by them become smaller. The in-the-ceiling terminals to which the horizontal branch ducts run have depths of about 16 in (0.4 m). From these terminals the supply air passes through further, though short, horizontal branches to diffusers, from which the supply air enters the occupied spaces.

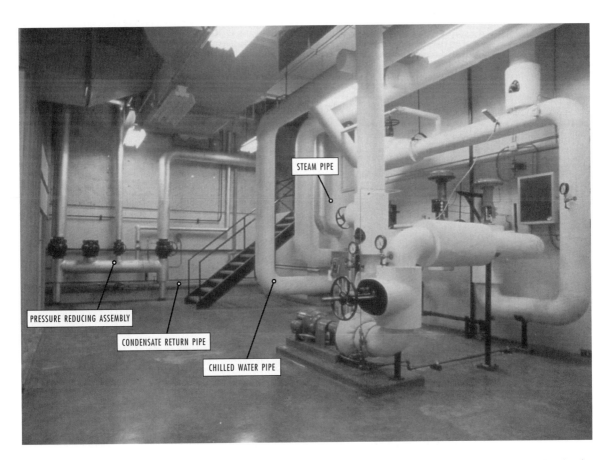

STEAM PIPE

PRESSURE REDUCING ASSEMBLY

CONDENSATE RETURN PIPE

CHILLED WATER PIPE

Figure A.14 At the west end of the mechanical room are the pipe entries for the steam and chilled water supplies that are produced at the university's power plant. The piping assembly in the left background (against the far wall) is a pressure-reducing valve. This pressure-reducing assembly is necessary because the steam arrives at this building at a pressure of about 185 psi. After flowing through the pressure-reducing assembly the steam pressure will be substantially reduced (to about 15 psi) so that it may flow to the steam-to-water heat exchanger and the domestic hot water producer (see Figure A.15) without causing damage to these units or the piping.

STEAM-TO-WATER HEAT EXCHANGER

DOMESTIC HOT WATER GENERATOR

Figure A.15 The small upright cylindrical device in the center foreground is the domestic hot water generator. It operates by exchanging heat from the steam system to potable water. This generator operates on a demand basis: the hot water is produced as it is needed (see Section E.3.2.4 for further information). The larger horizontal cylindrical device behind the domestic hot water generator is a steam-to-water heat exchanger (see Figure A.16). This heat exchanger is the site at which heat from the steam is transferred to water that then can be passed throughout the building to provide space heating.

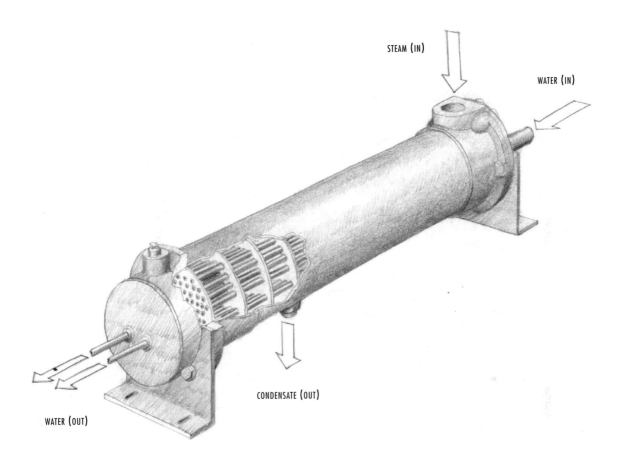

STEAM (IN)

WATER (IN)

WATER (OUT)

CONDENSATE (OUT)

Figure A.16 A prototypical steam-hot water convertor is shown. The steam enters at top back orifice and exits at the bottom. System water enters at the right end, flows through the bundle of tubes, and exits at the left end. The steam passes around the bundle of tubes transferring its heat through the walls of the tubes to the water. In the Gould Hall steam convertor — shown in Figure A.15 — the water leaves at a temperature of about 140 °F (60 °C) and passes into the heating components of the overall HVAC system. The system through which the hot water passes is essentially a closed loop (with minimal water losses during circulation).

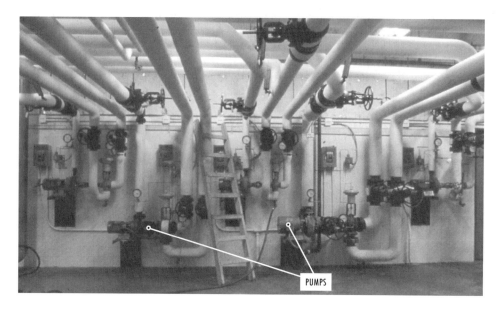

PUMPS

Figure A.17 These several pumps are used for propelling hot water that is used for space heating throughout the building. The hot water comes from the steam-to-water heat exchanger that is along the wall just to the right of the door. Note the pipes that run from these pumps transport the hot water to a variety of systems components, both in the mechanical room and elsewhere in the building.

Figure A.18 A length of architectural radiation is present underneath this window.

All of the glazing assemblies in Gould Hall—principally, because the assemblies are all single-paned—have supplemental radiation lengths placed under them (Figure A.18). Such radiation lengths exist not only under the conventional vertical windows, but also under the vertical clerestory and sloped skylight areas that are parts of the building roof (above the central atrium space). In virtually all instances—whether for window, clerestory, or skylight—the length of each radiation unit matches the width of the glazing assembly that the radiation unit is furnished to condition. Note that these supplemental radiation lengths are basically finned-tube "architectural radiation" (that has been shown in Figures 2.7 and 2.8).

A.2.3.2 The operating protocol for the HVAC system A summary of the operation of the HVAC system is portrayed in Figure A.19. Note that three building volumes are devoted to housing this system: the mechanical room, vertical shafts, and in-the-ceiling plenums.

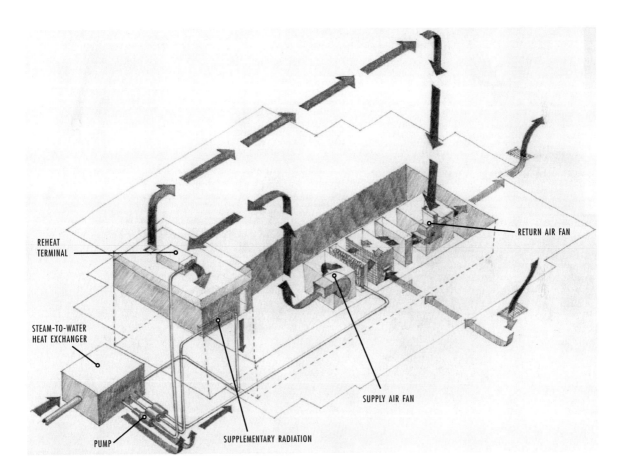

Figure A.19 A summary of the Gould Hall HVAC system is presented here. The circling blackened arrows represent the supply and return airflows from the supply air handler to a classroom on an upper floor to the return air fan. The arrow to the right portrays the return air that is dumped to the building exterior after the air has been used. The arrow at the right front indicates the entrance of fresh air coming in from outside of the building. At the lower left is the steam-to-water heat exchanger. Hot water in pipes flows from this heat exchanger through pumps to the preheat coil in the supply air handler, to reheat terminals, and to supplementary radiation. This drawing has been created as an alternative to the traditional one-line schematic system drawing that often is used to introduce the contents of an HVAC system in a construction documents set.

The fundamental operation for this Gould Hall HVAC system involves the provision of appropriately tempered supply air for each building space. Thus, the air supplied to each room is supposed to be conditioned to present a temperature matching the heat loss or gain circumstances of the room. To attain the requisite temperature for each room, the supply air-handling system has been configured with a series of redundant conditioning capabilities (i.e., there are at least three means of adjusting the temperature of the supply air entering each room).

Beginning in the central supply air-handler, the first means of temperature adjustment occurs in the mixed-air plenum (see Figures A.20 and A.21). There, fresh outside air—having an air temperature identical to the ambient external air temperature—can be mixed with some quantity of the "used" return air (that will have an air temperature matching an approximate average air temperature throughout the building, perhaps at about 68–72 °F

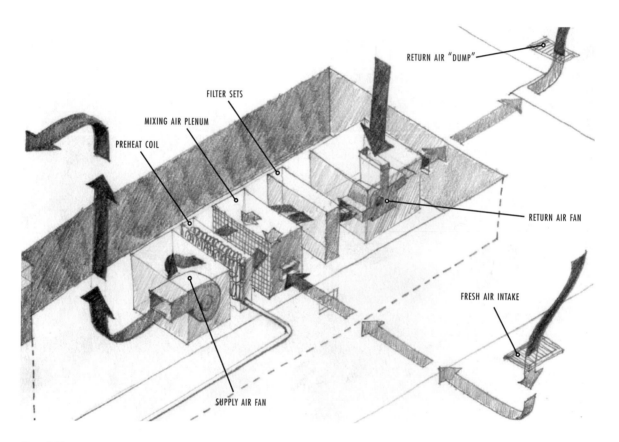

Figure A.20 This drawing presents a portion of Figure A.19, focusing on the supply air-handler (and including the return air fan). The purpose of this illustration is to explain the temperature conditioning process performed in the supply air-handler. Fresh air—represented by the arrow at the lower right—enters the supply air-handler at the ambient external air temperature. The "used" air returns from occupied spaces in the building, at ambient air temperatures present in the building. The fresh air and some fraction of the used air mix in a mixing air plenum, establishing some air temperature that is intermediate between the outside and inside temperatures. Generally, this air temperature will be the air temperature that circulates throughout the building. Further conditioning can be done using hot water that passes through the preheat coil in the air-handler. Yet further conditioning can be performed at the reheat terminals (see Figure A.19).

(20–22 °C). Depending upon the mixing ratio of quantities of fresh air to return air, any temperature in the range between the external ambient temperature and the return (used) air temperature can be attained.[3] The actual mixing of the two air streams is accomplished by regulating the openness of the dampers that separate the return air and fresh air streams (i.e., the more open these dampers are, the greater the quantity of return air that will be mixed with the in-coming outside air). This beneficial mixing of fresh and used air streams — to obtain the needed temperature for the supply air without reliance on active-system heating and/or cooling — is identified as an *economizer cycle*.

A second means of temperature adjustment can be achieved by passing the mixed air stream across a preheat coil. This preheat coil is an assembly within the supply air-handler, to which hot water (from the heat exchanger) is pumped through piping (see Figure A.22). The hot water flows through this preheat coil at a rate sufficient to condition the air, if the mixing process has not already provided adequate temperature adjustment (i.e., the use of the preheat coil as a conditioning capability serves essentially as a back-up to the mixing process). If the mixing process has been successful in achieving the requisite temperature for the air leaving the supply air-handler, then the preheat coil will not be operated.

The air leaving the supply air-handler will have a specific temperature (resulting from the mixing of the air streams and, possibly, the intervention of the preheat coil). According to the operating protocol for this system, this specific air temperature will be set *to furnish the amount of cooling needed in the space with the greatest rate of heat gain* (from people, lighting systems, equipment, and/or solar radiation).

Figure A.21 This photograph displays the supply air-handler described in Figure A.20.

A second qualification about this HVAC system in Gould Hall is that it functions as a *constant volume* system. Thus, the amount of air flowing from the central air-handler and through the system is constant across all the operating hours. Further, the amount of supply air furnished to each building space is established during the system design process, and the system is configured to provide that amount continuously during the operation of the HVAC system. The temperature of the air being supplied to each space, however, is variable according to the thermal conditioning need existent in the space (i.e., as determined by the rate of heat gain or loss occurring in the space). So, whereas the HVAC system is indeed a *constant volume* system, it is also a *variable temperature* system (and is, more generally, categorized as a *constant volume, variable temperature* system). This operating protocol is one of a basic few widely employed HVAC system operating strategies.

Having the supply air temperature set at the supply air-handler to satisfy the thermal needs of the single space with the greatest heat gain rate means that, for all of the other

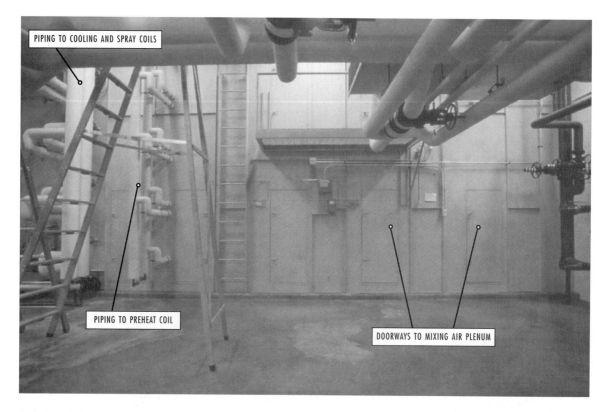

Figure A.22 This photograph presents a side view of the supply air-handler for Gould Hall (as shown in Figure A.21). The air-handler is approximately one-and-one-half stories high. At the floor level of the air-handler are a series of doors that offer access to its various components. The horizontal pipes at the upper edge of this photograph transport hot water to the preheat coil. This preheat coil provides a second means for temperature conditioning of the supply air stream (i.e., the first means being the mixing of the fresh outside air and the "used" return air, which occurs in the mixing plenum that is behind the right-most door). The left-most pipes that enter into the air-handler can supply chilled water to the chilled water coil (although this coil is left nonoperational because of the limited chilled water capacity of the university's central system).

building spaces with lesser heat gain rates, the centrally conditioned supply air temperature will be too cold. To adjust the temperature of the supply air that enters each of these other spaces, these individualized supply air streams must be further conditioned. This *tertiary* level of conditioning is provided by running the supply air stream (before it enters a space) across a *reheat* coil that is a component within the in-the-ceiling terminals (see Figures A.23 and A.24). Hot water is piped from the steam-hot water heat exchanger in the mechanical room to each reheat coil. As the hot water flows through a reheat coil and the supply air passes over the reheat coil, the temperature of the supply air reaching the terminal is increased to match the thermal need for the building space. The amount of heating is determined by a signal sent from a wall-mounted thermostat in the space to the terminal. After this tertiary heating is applied to the supply air stream for the room, the air enters the room (and mixes with the existing room air).

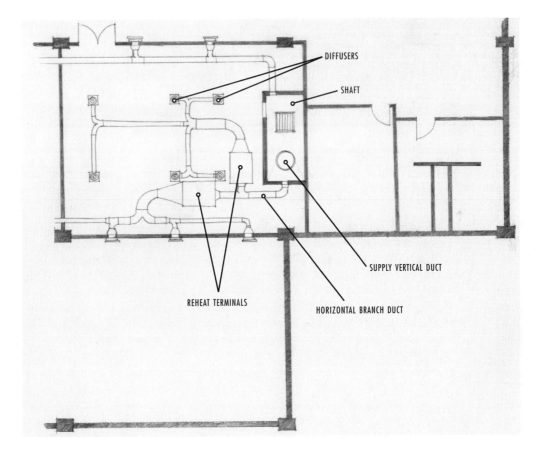

Figure A.23 A reflected ceiling plan shows two reheat terminals. One of these terminals conditions and ventilates the room in which these terminals are placed. The other terminal services the adjoining room. The circle within the enclosed space — one of the four shafts for this building — adjacent to the room is the vertical supply air ducting for approximately one-quarter of the building. The square in this enclosed space represents the hole in the ceiling of the shaft that allows return air to flow downward to the return air fan that is located in the mechanical room.

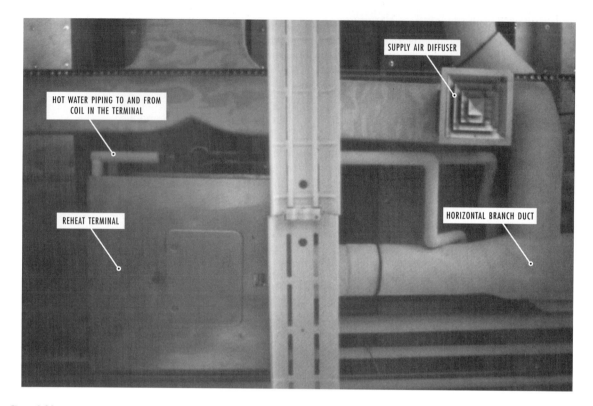

Figure A.24 One of the reheat terminals shown in Figure A.23 is visible here.

To supplement the thermal conditioning and ventilation provided by this air-handling system, lengths of hot-water radiation (also identified as *convectors* or even as *finned-tube convectors*) are placed under all of the glazing assemblies throughout the building. For all of these perimeter-mounted radiation lengths, hot water is piped to them from the heat exchanger in the mechanical room. The function of these radiation lengths is to warm the interior surfaces of the glazing assemblies. Otherwise, cold window surfaces can cause discomfort for the occupants who would experience radiational cooling and drafts (for further discussion about the functioning of these radiation lengths, see Section 3.6.1).

While the supply air-handling system furnishes air to each space, the return air system operates to withdraw used air from each space. The operation of the return air system occurs through the sucking action of the return air fan. In most spaces in Gould Hall the used air is drawn up through ceiling grilles into the enclosed volume between the finished ceiling and the structural flooring (or roof) above. This volume is commonly identified as a *ceiling plenum*. The ceiling plenum for each space will be connected to horizontal ducts that will carry the return air back to the vertical shafts. At these shafts the ducted return air will be discharged into the shaft, and the shaft enclosure itself will serve as the passageway for returning the air to the return air fan in the mechanical room (i.e., no ducting is used for transporting the return air downward in the same manner that a vertical duct in a shaft is provided to carry supply air upward). Once the return air reaches the return air fan, the air will pass through the fan and enter into the return air plenum. In the return air plenum the return air will either pass back to mix with the fresh outside air (in the mixing plenum) or will be dumped to the building exterior at the opposite end of the building.

The two exhaust air fans that are located in the mechanical room (see Figure A.9) operate to evacuate used air that is not fit for recirculation. The first of these exhaust fans services the wood and metal-working shop and the photography studio and darkroom. Air in the shop spaces is laden with particulate matter and with vapors from paint, adhesives, lubricating oils, solvents, and so forth. Similarly, air in the photography spaces becomes contaminated with vapors from chemicals used in the development and production of photographic images, as well as from related oils, paints, solvents, and the like that are applied in other image-rendering processes. The used air from these spaces is drawn out by a *nonrecirculating fan* and ducted through a special duct to the exterior of the building.

The other exhaust fan draws used air from the several toilet rooms located around Gould Hall. Because the air from these rooms will often contain unpleasant odors and may hold excessive water vapor, this toilet room air can also not be recirculated back into the supply air-return air loop. Thus, the toilet exhaust fan operates to draw the used air from the toilet rooms and, through a dedicated duct, to dump the toilet room air to the building exterior.

The shop and photography spaces are furnished with air supplied from the supply air-handler via ducting organized similarly to that used for the remainder of the building. The supply air reaching the shop and the photography spaces demonstrates the same properties as air supplied to the other building spaces.

SIDEBAR A.5 The economizer cycle

Most energy conservation standards and codes require the operation of an *economizer cycle* as the basis for temperature adjustment of incoming fresh air. The basic premise for this requirement for HVAC system operations is that the necessary supply air temperature—for conditioning building spaces—can be established by mixing fresh outside air and "used" return air. This mixing process is energy-conserving because the only active-system energy that will have to be expended to establish the needed supply air temperature is that used to operate the supply and return air-handling fans.

Note that if ambient air is taken in from outside and there were no economizer cycle, then further active-system energy would instead have to be furnished to heat or cool the air stream (i.e., by amounts substantially greater than that required to run fans to create appropriate mixing).

The usual clauses in energy conservation standards and codes pertaining to economizer cycles stipulate that "up to 100 percent outside air" should be drawn in by the economizer cycle operation. Thus, unless the internal heat gain and/or solar heat gain rates are too great, this economizer cycle operation should be fully capable of providing adequately conditioned supply air. Only if the economizer cycle operation is insufficient—the amount of outside air at the ambient air temperature is not large enough—then can active-system cooling be furnished to condition the supply air stream.

The original document that laid out many of the energy-conserving practices cited in most American energy conservation standards and codes was the ASHRAE Standard 90-75, *Energy Conservation in New Building Design,* which was first published by the American Society of Heating, Refrigerating, and Air-Conditioning Engineers, Inc., Atlanta, Georgia, in 1975. Additional discussion of this early standard and more recent versions appears in Section B.3.6.1.

Note, however, that the toilet rooms are *not* directly provided with air supplied through the supply air ducting system. Instead, air entering the toilet rooms does so by passing through door louvers from ventilated hallways adjacent to these rooms. The toilet room air is exhausted through wall grilles that are connected to ducting that carries the air back to the toilet exhaust fan. The air in these toilet rooms is present at a pressure that is slightly less than the air occupying the remainder of the building. The toilet room air is at a negative pressure gradient *relative to* the air pressure elsewhere in the building. Thus, air passage is encouraged from the adjacent hallways into the toilet rooms and not in the opposite direction. Heating for the toilet rooms is furnished via perimeter radiation lengths (placed underneath casement-style windows).

Hot water that is used in the preheat coil of the central air-handler, the many reheat coils located in in-the-ceiling terminals, and all of the lengths of the perimeter radiation pass back to the steam-hot water heat exchanger. This hot water supply and return system operates in a virtually closed loop, requiring only the most minimal amounts of water replenishment.

The Gould Hall HVAC system furnishes fully developed thermal conditioning and ventilating capabilities. Its components and operating protocol are typical of an *all-air system with supplementary perimeter radiation.* The movement of air provides both ventilation and thermal-conditioning capabilities (thus, the "all-air" description). The presence of the three alternative means for the temperature conditioning of the supply air stream presents important redundancy for achieving occupant thermal comfort. The flexibility gained with these alternative means of thermal conditioning ensure that spaces in the building can be used for a variety of activities. The features of the system, its operating range, and its utility all contribute to the system being a first-class service provider.

SIDEBAR A.6 Providing for space cooling for large buildings in warm climates

---

Note that in one instance the Gould Hall system functions differently from many similar buildings located in warmer climates. Because the Seattle climate is temperate and rarely displays hot weather and because the University of Washington central-system refrigeration capacity is limited, no central-system cooling capability is furnished to Gould Hall. Instead, the cooling of building spaces is dependent on the use of the economizer cycle (which operates effectively for as much as 90 percent or more of the year).

In climates that experience longer and more pronounced periods of hot weather, buildings will more likely be reliant on conditioning by refrigeration machinery (e.g., chillers or heat pumps). In such buildings fresh outside air will often need to be cooled substantially before it can be circulated through the building. Also, depending on whether the outside air is humid or dry, the humidity level of the supply air will need to be modified.

Cooling for buildings located in warmer climates can be furnished by central-system cooling sources or by in-the-building refrigeration machinery. Conventionally, the cooling medium from a central system or from localized refrigeration machinery will pass through cooling coils that will be present in supply air-handlers. The supply air stream will flow across these cooling coils, and the supply air will be suitably cooled. Humidity control of the supply air stream will also be performed using any one of a variety of humidifiers.

For further information about nonresidential building cooling equipment, see Chapters 4 ("Central cooling and heating") and 20 ("Humidifiers") of the *2000 ASHRAE HVAC Systems and Equipment Handbook,* (Atlanta: American Society of Heating, Refrigerating, and Air-Conditioning Engineers, Inc., 2000). Building operating strategies that provide suitable space cooling will be described in Section A.3.

Section A.3 | THE FOUR BASIC TYPES OF NONRESIDENTIAL HVAC SYSTEMS

Nearly all nonresidential HVAC systems consist of one of the following four organizational types: all-air, air-water, all-water, and direct refrigerant. The physical features of each of these four types that distinguishes one type from the others include whether air or water is used as the primary means for the thermal-conditioning of building spaces, whether air is transported around a building or is accessed locally from the building exterior, how complex the centralized HVAC equipment will be and what are the spatial requirements for housing the centralized equipment, and what are the spatial requirements and probable locations for locally placed equipment. In addition to distinguishing these four systems types in terms of their physical features, the four types may be differentiated in terms of the natures of the services they provide: how many conditioning zones can be readily treated with systems of each type; what range of occupancy densities can be supported with each type; how much flexibility for supporting alternative activities is present for each system type; and how comprehensive a level of environmental control can be exercised with each system type? Other issues that can affect decision-making when a designer selects which system type to employ for a building can involve what are likely first costs and operating costs, what levels of system reliability are observed with each system type, and what frequencies are expected for the maintenance and the repair of system components?

The following descriptions of these four system types will be organized to provide information, for each type, about the nature of air distribution strategies, the kinds of equipment commonly present, the building locations where the equipment components are most often placed, and the building applications for which the system type is used.

A.3.1 THERMAL-CONDITIONING EQUIPMENT AND PLACEMENT

Three of these four system types—the all-air, air-water, and all-water systems—are commonly organized to utilize hot water and/or chilled water, both of which will be produced at a single location in the building. As an alternative heating source, steam can be produced and circulated, although such circulation is usually limited to passage from a central plant to satellite buildings (e.g., in the manner that Gould Hall is serviced by steam supplied from the University of Washington Power Plant). The actual passage of steam through individual buildings as a conditioning medium—particularly where this steam may pass near or in occupied spaces—has become a seldom-used practice over the past few decades.

A.3.1.1 Producing hot water Hot water for conditioning a building can be produced using steam that has been generated at a central-station or municipal plant and that has been run through a steam-to-water heat exchanger. Alternatively, hot water can be produced directly with an in-the-building boiler (see Figure A.25). Whether a boiler or a heat exchanger is the source, hot water will pass from its source through piping and will be propelled by pumps (see Figure A.26). A boiler or a heat exchanger may be placed in any of several locations: on a below-grade floor, at an on-grade floor, at some floor above the grade level, or even in an immediately adjacent building. This flexibility in placement is made possible by the fact that piping of hot water from its source throughout a building is seldom limited by spatial requirements (i.e., by how much space is needed to run the piping and where piping can be run). Further, as pumps can readily propel hot water around a building, there is rarely a situation where the necessary distance for pumping hot water will be an operation-limiting factor.

One issue that may dictate where a heat exchanger can be located concerns providing a connection between a central or municipal steam supply and the exchanger: if such an out-of-building steam supply is the energy source for the production of hot water, then the heat exchanger should be placed to facilitate the connection between the steam supply service piping and the heat exchanger. Additionally, as a central or municipal steam supply will operate at substantial pressure (to promote its flow and to maintain the heat content of the steam), the pressure will have to be lessened as it enters a building. Therefore, space will be needed for pressure-reducing valve assemblies (that will lessen the pressure on the steam to more manageable levels). Another issue that can dictate where a hot water boiler may be located concerns the energy source that would be used to heat the water. For instance, if fuel oil is used, then a storage tank will be required. Alternatively, if a hydrocarbon gas is used as the boiler fuel, then there will need to be a connection between a municipal gas supply pipe and the boiler or, less likely, between a gas storage tank and the boiler. In either of the examples for which a storage tank is used, then ready access must

Figure A.25 Four modular boilers are arranged to function in a cascading series. The principle for this organization of the boilers is that as one commences service the others will remain inactive. Only when the heating demand of the building approaches or is greater than the capacity of the first boiler will a second boiler begin operation. Thus, each boiler that is in operation—based on demand requirements—will operate closer to its maximum capacity. This operating strategy offers greater efficiency than if one large boiler were used to satisfy relatively low demand levels.

be planned for the delivery and transfer of the fuel to the tank. If the hot water is produced using an electrically powered boiler, then its placement should be quite straightforward and would be guided only by the need to find adequate space to house the boiler.

One last concern when seeking to locate a boiler (and any of the other centralized equipment that will be described below) is that sufficient space should be allowed around any of this equipment for maintenance, repair, and replacement. Usually, installation of these centralized equipment devices will occur during construction. To ensure that the operation of these devices occurs smoothly and efficiently, each device will require regular maintenance and occasional repair. Additionally, boilers and other centralized HVAC equipment will usually have service lifetimes that are shorter than the buildings that house them. Thus, at some moment(s) during the building lifetime, the replacement of parts of a centralized device or even the entire device assembly will likely have to be performed. Space for such work should be planned for, and accessways for removing old parts or assemblies and the bringing in of new parts or assemblies should also be established.

Figure A.26 To propel the hot water generated by the modular boilers shown in Figure A.25, these four pumps are mounted on the wall across from the boilers. The multiple pumps are used to send the heated water to different locations around the building (e.g., to the central air-handler, to reheat terminals, to (under window) baseboard radiation lengths, and so forth).

SIDEBAR A.7 The refrigeration cycle

Heat pumps and vapor-compression chillers—the chillers that rely on electricity rather than on steam absorption—all operate according to a simple, or single-stage, refrigeration cycle. The purpose of the refrigeration cycle is to transfer heat from a lower-temperature medium to a higher-temperature medium and to perform this transfer in an efficient manner. The refrigeration cycle engages four components: an evaporator, a compressor, a condenser, and an expansion device (see Figure A.27). The material moving through each of these components in the cycle is a refrigerant, which is basically a fluid that evaporates at low temperatures (e.g., approximately –60 °F [–50 °C] at atmospheric pressure). The reason machines based on the refrigeration cycle are well-regarded for their efficiencies is that the only "active systems" energy that must be supplied to operate the refrigeration cycle is the electricity used to run the compressor.

The operation of a refrigeration cycle is a continuous process (as long as electricity is supplied to run the compressor). Thus, there is no particular starting point to the cycle (i.e., the cycle can begin at any location along the cycle).

So, if we commence from the left of the expansion device (shown in Figure A.27), the refrigerant (fluid) at this point along the cycle is in a liquid state and is being subjected to a higher pressure. As the refrigerant moves through the expansion device, the pressure on the liquid is greatly reduced. The result of this fluid expansion is a mixture of liquid and vapor.

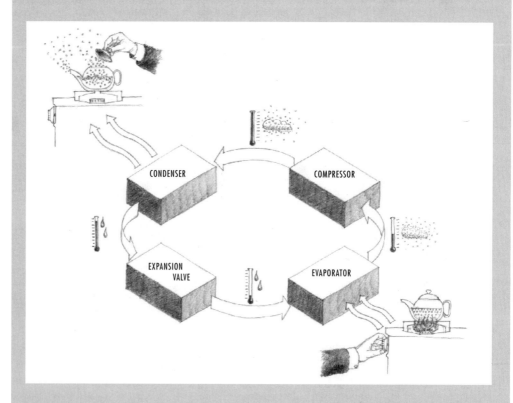

Figure A.27 The refrigeration cycle is presented in this diagram. The four physical components that enable this cycle are an evaporator, a compressor, a condenser, and an expansion valve. How these four devices function during the operation of the cycle is described in Sidebar A.7.

The temperature of the refrigerant mixture—after moving through the expansion device—is also lessened.

In the next step, as this mixture of liquid and vapor passes through the evaporator, environmental heat—heat from the air surrounding the evaporator—is added to the mixture. This addition essentially occurs passively (i.e., no "active systems" energy is furnished here). The addition of heat to the refrigerant in the evaporator causes the liquid fraction (of the refrigerant) to evaporate totally so that the refrigerant exiting the evaporator is entirely a vapor. Further, this vapor is at a relatively low temperature and low pressure.

As the cold, low-pressure vapor passes through the compressor, the action of the compressor increases the temperature and pressure conditions of the vapor. The electricity that is furnished to the compressor enables it to perform work on the vapor, causing the vapor to become hotter and under greatly increased pressure.

In the fourth step, this hot, elevated-pressure vapor passes into the condenser. There, heat from the vapor is exchanged with the environment. This exchange also occurs passively. And, as the heat from the hot, elevated-pressure vapor is given off to the air surrounding the condenser, the vapor changes state to become a liquid. The refrigerant exiting the condenser will continue to flow under high pressure. With this fourth step accomplished, a full loop of the refrigeration cycle will have been completed.

The efficiency and utility of the refrigeration cycle are described by the index, the *Coefficient of Performance* (COP). The Coefficient of Performance for a refrigeration-cycle cooling machine is a ratio of the heat gathered in—removed—by the cycle divided by the electrical energy required to operate the cycle. Common COP's for heat pumps will range from about 3 to 5 (i.e., three to five times as much energy will be extracted as will be required to operate the cycle equipment).

In summertime operations of heat pumps, when indoor air needs to be cooled, the evaporator is the indoor section of the heat pump, and the condenser is the outdoor section. In other words, to cool a building using a heat pump, heat from the building air will provide the energy to promote evaporation of the refrigerant as it passes through the evaporator. Then, this thermal energy—the excess heat from inside the building—is transferred through the compressor to the condenser where this excess heat is "dumped" to the exterior air (that surrounds the condenser).

Lastly, note that the basic operation—the direction of refrigerant flow—of a heat pump is reversed during the heating season when heat from the exterior is collected and passed to the building interior. In the heating mode, the indoor section of a heat pump functions as a condenser, giving heat off to the surrounding inside air. The outdoor section operates as an evaporator, collecting heat from the exterior.

A.3.1.2 Producing chilled water Chilled water is produced with a refrigeration machine (often identified as a "chiller.") There are several alternative processes that are employed in chiller operations. Most are electrically powered, but one—the absorption chiller—uses steam as the energy source. Chillers that operate principally on electricity—not steam—use the electricity mostly to drive compressors.

The other major component in the chilled-water production process is a condenser (which provides means for heat rejection). In the process of chilling water (that will be used for conditioning buildings), heat is generated in the chiller as a by-product. This heat can be passed to a secondary water system that connects the chiller and the condenser and is often identified as "cooling cycle water." Because the cooling cycle water becomes warmer as it passes through the chiller, the heat that the cooling cycle water gains from the chiller operation must be exchanged ("dumped") to the external environment. This heat exchange (or heat rejection) is performed at the condenser (see Figures A.28–A.30).

Three types of compressors are most commonly employed in chillers: reciprocating, helical rotary, and centrifugal. Smaller-capacity chillers—most often, those using reciprocating compressors—can be air-cooled (instead of relying on a cooling cycle water system). Thus, for these air-cooled chillers, air is the medium that carries and exchanges the process heat to the environment (thereby rejecting the heat gained while chilling the water used for conditioning the building). Some of these air-cooled chillers will be stand-alone units (i.e., the air cooling device will be an integral component of the chiller). For other air-cooled chillers, the use of a remote (secondary) condenser will be required.

Larger-capacity chillers—particularly those based on helical rotary or centrifugal compressors or on steam-driven absorption—will use a cooling cycle water system to dump heat that is generated when conditioning chilled water is produced. But instead of using a condenser, a cooling tower will more commonly be used (to transfer the process

Figure A.28 A reciprocating chiller stands in the center of this photograph. To the left are pumps for propelling chilled water around the building and condenser water to the condenser (see Figures A.29 and A.30). In the background (just left of the chiller) is a hot water boiler. For the purpose of estimating the sizes of these devices, use the fluorescent fixture above and to the immediate right of the chiller.

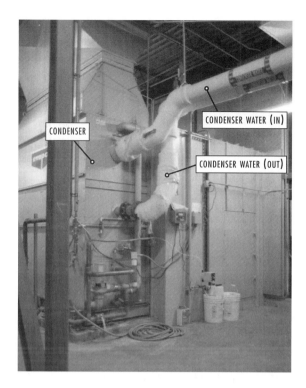

Figure A.29 Here is the condenser that serves the reciprocating chiller that appears in Figure A.28. This condenser is located on the top floor of this building. The condenser water from the chiller enters through the upper pipe and flows downward and exits the condenser through the lower pipe. Air flows across this water stream furnishing the needed cooling. The air stream involves a large louver in the building elevation (see Figure A.30) and a rooftop louver. A fan within this condenser housing drives the air stream.

Figure A.30 The air louver for the condenser shown in Figure A.29 is the circular opening in the upper central portion of the building elevation.

heat to the external environment). Generally, the cooling tower is simply a larger version of the condenser (see Figure A.31).

The chilled water exiting a chiller—for the circulation to air handling devices and the conditioning of building air—can be pumped and piped substantial distances throughout a building. A chiller may even be located in another building that is adjacent or relatively near to the building that is to be conditioned by the chilled water. Thus, the locations where a chiller may be placed are many. If an absorption chiller is to be used, then proximity to a steam source is an important location determinant. Alternatively, for water-cooled chillers, being located near a cooling tower is desirable.

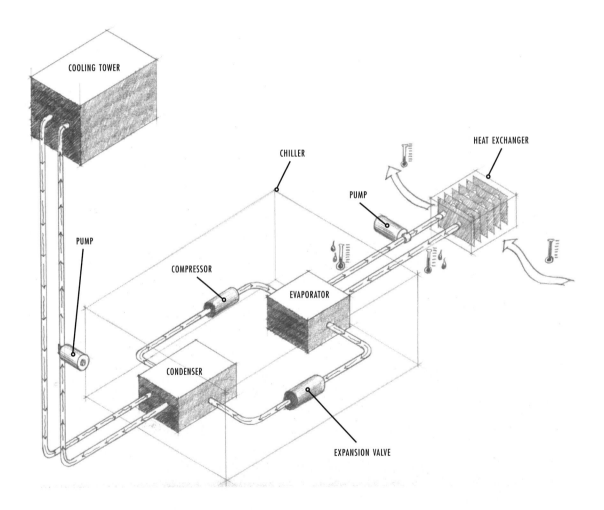

Figure A.31 A basic application of the refrigeration cycle (Figure A.27) is shown here. Electricity-driven chillers will have within their housings the basic four components of this cycle: the compressor, the evaporator, an expansion valve, and the condenser. Warm water from the condenser will be piped and pumped to a cooling tower so that the water can be cooled and passed back to the condenser. The chilled water from the evaporator is piped and pumped to a heat exchanger that would be present in an air-handler. Thus, supply air would pass across this heat exchanger and be cooled so that the air can be distributed through the building to offset any heat gains experienced in the building.

Because most chillers are large, massive, heat-generating (in the immediate space around the chiller), and very noisy, it is generally best to locate chillers away from occupied spaces. Further, pumps will most often be used with chillers—to propel the chilled water throughout a building or simply to central air-handlers. These pumps also will require adequate floor areas in the near vicinity of the chillers (see Figures A.32 and A.33).

A.3.2 ALL-AIR SYSTEM TYPES

For the all-air systems, air is circulated throughout the building, both to provide ventilation for the occupants and as a means of thermal conditioning. Water may be circulated beyond mechanical (fan) rooms, but only to provide for the secondary thermal conditioning of the air (i.e., the primary thermal-conditioning is performed at the air-handler).

A.3.2.1   Air distribution strategies for all-air systems   For nearly every all-air system, air will move from an air-handler through an usually extensive ducting layout to terminals located at the ends of the ducting runs. The air passes into the occupied spaces through diffusers. The entering supply air will then mix with the room air. Simultaneous with the admission of the supply air, some of the room air will flow as return ("used") air back to the location of the supply air-handler (usually with the assistance of a return air-handler). Thus, the passage of air from the supply air-handler into the occupied space and back to a return air-handler (which will likely be connected with the supply air-handler)

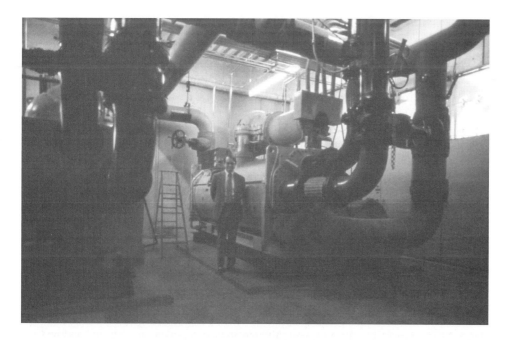

Figure A.32 Two centrifugal chillers—each rated at 700 tons (2460 kW) of refrigeration capacity—are used to provide cooling water for a 20-story office building in Seattle. The floor area served by these two chillers is about 250,000 square feet (23,200 square meters). In addition to the obvious massiveness of the chillers, note also the size of the pipes that are associated with these chillers.

Figure A.33 Across from the two centrifugal chillers shown in Figure A.32 are three pumps that are used for propelling the chilled water to various air-handlers that are located elsewhere in the building. Two pumps run at any one time, with one pump working in conjunction with one chiller and the other pump working with the other chiller. The third chiller provides a back-up capability in the event that one of these other pumps requires servicing.

completes a loop. As fresh outside air is added continuously at the supply air-handler, used air will have to be dumped to the exterior to balance this loop: some of the lost air will exit the building via exfiltration through the building envelope, some will be exhausted by the return air-handling component, and some may be lost by other exhausting pathways (e.g., for toilet rooms and other building locations from which "contaminated" air should not be recirculated).

Two important qualifications can be offered about this generic all-air distribution model. First, the supply ducting can involve a single-duct layout or a dual-duct layout. The single-duct layout offers moving air passing through a building at a single temperature that has been set at the air-handler (although the air temperature can be modified by remote in-the-ceiling terminals). The dual-duct layout employs two ducted air streams running in parallel usually to an in-the-ceiling terminal where the separate air streams are mixed. The function of this parallel ducting is to enable movement of air streams having different temperatures (i.e., most often, one at a suitably cool temperature, the other at a

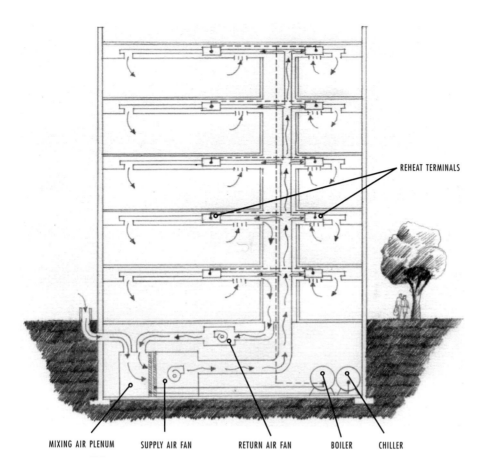

MIXING AIR PLENUM   SUPPLY AIR FAN   RETURN AIR FAN   BOILER   CHILLER

REHEAT TERMINALS

Figure A.34 A basic all-air system with reheat terminals.

suitably warm temperature). The mixing of these two air streams with their different temperatures permits the supply of air into an occupied space at any intermediate temperature between the two extremes. Thus, the role of the in-the-ceiling terminal for this double-duct layout is to mix the air streams to accommodate the requisite thermal-conditioning need for the occupied space. Having this capability to mix the streams accordingly provides broad flexibility for insuring occupant thermal comfort.

The second important qualification about the generic all-air distribution model concerns how the magnitudes of air volume and air temperature are established. In the Gould Hall system described in Section A.2, air distribution operates in a *constant volume, variable temperature* format. Thus, a constant volume of air is supplied to each space — as set by the designer or operating engineer. When the thermal conditioning needs of the space vary from some norm, then the temperature of the air supplied to the space is modified to reinstitute comfortable conditions.

The converse to this model is one in which the supply air passes through the ducting layout at a constant temperature but with a varying volumetric flow rate. For this *constant*

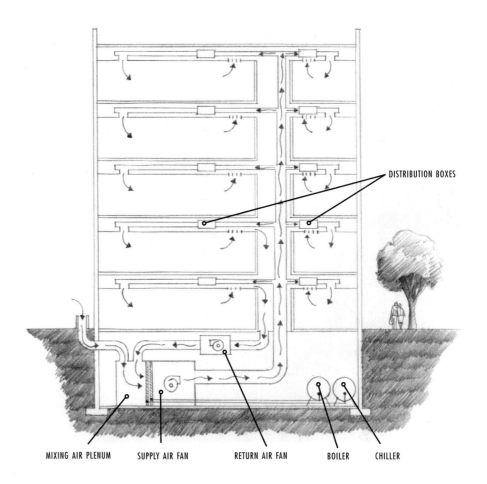

DISTRIBUTION BOXES

MIXING AIR PLENUM   SUPPLY AIR FAN   RETURN AIR FAN   BOILER   CHILLER

Figure A.35 A basic all-air system with a variable air volume (VAV) operating protocol.

temperature, variable volume air distribution format, the temperature of the supply air is established before the air leaves the air-handler and then remains unchanged throughout the rest of its passage into the occupied spaces. The rationale for the application of the constant temperature, variable volume distribution model is that both the thermal-conditioning and ventilation needs of building spaces are dictated by the numbers of occupants present in a space. If only a few people are present, then the heat gain rate may be low and the need for fresh air will similarly be small. So, a lowered-amount of supply air is warranted. Only when the occupancy rate increases would there be a need to furnish more air to the space, providing greater ventilation and thermal-conditioning capabilities (see Figures A.34–A.37).

A.3.2.2   Equipment used in all-air systems   For buildings with large floor areas the use of centralized hot water and chilled water producers — boilers or steam-hot water heat exchangers and chillers, respectively — will be most common. For smaller buildings packaged indoor or rooftop units or commercial split-system climate-changers can readily be

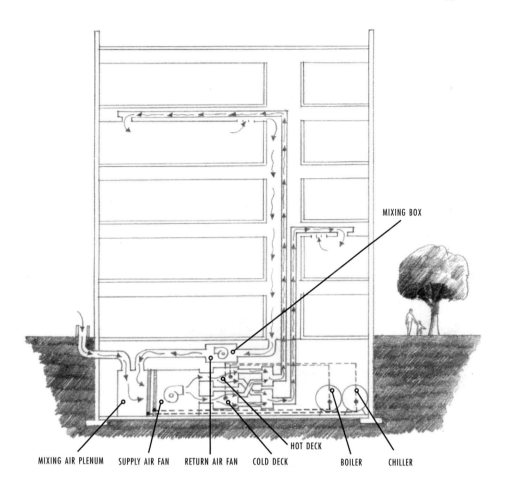

MIXING BOX

MIXING AIR PLENUM   SUPPLY AIR FAN   RETURN AIR FAN   COLD DECK   HOT DECK   BOILER   CHILLER

Figure A.36 A basic all-air system with a multizone operating protocol.

applied. Further, for buildings with larger floor areas it is quite appropriate to use pack-aged climate-changers organized in a modular fashion (i.e., to use more than one such unit so that each unit serves some fraction of the total floor area of the building). Note also that there is no general *floor-area* criterion — some minimum or maximum area — that can effectively determine whether to select a boiler and/or a chiller or a packaged climate changer: the choice between these options is often based simply on design experience.

Air distribution for all-air systems will be accomplished with air-handlers that can be organized centrally or in some modular fashion (see Figure A.38). Thus, there can be as few as a single central air-handler in a building or as many as one air-handler per floor (e.g., as in some high-rise office buildings). And, for some large floor-area buildings such as labora-tories and secondary schools, there may be more than one air-handler per floor. Intermediate organizations are also entirely possible (e.g., one air-handler serving every two or three floors or serving about twenty floors; this latter situation being a common approach for other high-rise office buildings).

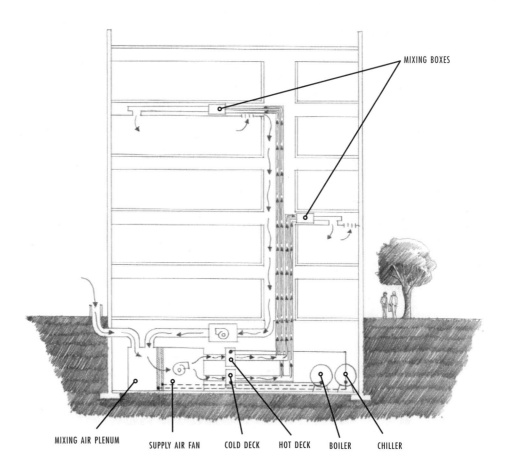

Figure A.37 A basic all-air system with a dual duct hardware scheme.

Selecting the number of air-handlers to employ for the ventilation and thermal-conditioning of a building should be based on issues such as how complex the building is, how many conditioning zones are present, how fine the control of the building environment needs to be, and whether space is available either centrally or modularly to place the air distribution equipment. Each air-handler will need components for mixing fresh and used air streams, filtering the mixed air, performing temperature conditioning, establishing humidity regulation, and then propelling the air through the ducting layout. These supply air-handlers can be built-up or packaged units, with the built-up units more often employed when larger amounts of air circulation are required. The number and location of the return air-handlers should be similar to the number and location of the supply air-handlers.

For each supply air-handler there must be a means of taking in fresh air from the building exterior. The fresh air must then be passed to a mixing plenum in which the fresh air can mix with the returned used air. Similarly, there must be a means for exhausting any returned used air that will not be recirculated. The supply air intake location and

Figure A.38 A floor-by-floor modular air-handler and its ducting are shown. For this building—a 40-story commercial office building—each floor is ventilated and conditioned by an air-handler similar to this one. Fresh air is brought in at the building exterior, ducted to the air-handler, conditioned in the air-handler, and passed out through ducting to occupant spaces. Used air from the various occupied spaces is gathered in ceiling plenums and passed into ducts that terminate at the building exterior where it is expelled.

SIDEBAR A.8 A limiting condition for variable volume systems: indoor air quality

A basic premise for the constant temperature, variable-air-volume operating strategy is that the amount of supply air that enters an occupied space should be determined by the heat gain rate experienced in the space. When the heat gain rate is higher, then a greater volumetric flow rate of supply air should enter the space. Alternatively, when the heat gain rate is less, then smaller amounts of supply air need be furnished. The heat gain rate in a space is often tied to the number of people who occupy the space and their usage of electrically powered equipment.

A problem can arise when there are few occupants in a space (and the heat gain rate is commensurately low). On such occasions less supply air will enter the space. With smaller amounts of supply air, there will be greater tendencies for the room air to stagnate and to become more ridden with localized pollutants. Examples of potential pollutants include dust, allergens, mold, bacteriological substances,

vapors that out-gas from furnishings and surface finishes, and chemicals that are produced by various office equipment. Many of these pollutants will exist in building spaces whether there are only a few occupants present or there are many occupants present.

Clearly, to dilute the concentration of airborne pollutants in a space, greater quantities of supply air should be furnished. Thus, selection of the variable-air-volume operating strategy should be considered carefully to see if future air pollution could cause discomfort and/or disease for future occupants. Alternatively, when variable-air-volume operating strategies are attractive for other reasons, accommodations should likely be provided to ensure that appropriate minimum amounts of supply air would reach such spaces (i.e., enough supply air will be furnished to reduce the potential effects of airborne pollutants).

the return air dumping location should be adequately separated and will be best placed if they occur on opposite vertical elevations of a building.

Ducting will be necessary as means for connecting each air-handler to the in-the-ceiling terminals serviced by the air-handler. In-the-ceiling terminals will be employed whether a single-duct or a dual-duct layout is applied or whether a *constant-volume, variable temperature* or a *variable volume, constant temperature* distribution is used. For the constant volume, variable temperature system the principal function of the terminal will be to provide a final thermal conditioning for the air just prior to it being admitted into an occupied space. For the variable volume, constant temperature distribution format, the terminals regulate the volumetric flow rate of air being admitted into an occupied space. In both instances these terminals operate in response to signals sent by in-the-room thermostats.

A.3.2.3 Locating air distribution equipment for all-air systems

Selecting locations for air-handlers (and the building spaces that house them) depends foremost on how many air-handlers will be employed in the building. If a single air-handler is to service the building, then placing the unit in a basement or on the top floor of the building may be most conventional (presuming, of course, that the building has multiple stories). If more than one air-handler will service the building, then these units may be arrayed modularly (e.g., one per floor, one per some number of floors, or one per some fraction of the total floor area). Alternatively, for a multiple-story building, air-handlers may be located at the top and bottom floors of the building with one air-handler supplying air downward and the other air-handler supplying air upward, each serving perhaps one-half of the total building.

Issues involved in choosing locations for air-handlers across a floor area involve being able to get fresh air to the air-handler (from the exterior), being able to run ducting readily from the air-handler to the terminals (and back to the return air-handler), having sufficient floor area to enable the maintenance and repair of the air-handler, and having adequate noise separation between the air-handler and any adjacent occupied spaces. Preferably, an air-handler should be placed along the perimeter of a building and, more specifically, along the *long-axis* side of the building (in both instances, to facilitate bringing fresh air into the air-handler). One other guideline for placing an air-handler is that it is especially desirable to locate the unit as close to the centroid of the floor area served by the unit, *if* fresh air can still readily be brought into the air-handler *and* vertical ducting can be run upwards or downwards from this centroidal location.

Locating vertical and horizontal ducting that connect the air-handlers to remote terminals must be performed during early space planning (to ensure the most efficient usage of building space and to promote the efficient operation of the air-handling system). If central air-handlers that service two or more floors are used, then shafts for running ducts vertically will be needed. A single shaft can be planned, or two or more shafts can be employed. The choice of whether to use one shaft or two or more shafts will most often depend on the space available for running the vertical shaft(s) and whether simpler horizontal duct runs can be achieved by using more than one shaft.

Locating horizontal *trunk* ducting can generally be easily accommodated in more communal spaces like corridors, when the ducting is to be placed above a finished (dropped) ceiling. Because such horizontal trunk ducts will be larger in cross-sectional areas than will be the *branch* ducting (that the trunk ducting serves), running trunk ducts in more communal spaces generally is preferable. In corridors and other similar communal spaces, greater depths for the volumes between the finished ceiling and the structural grid above can usually be tolerated. Alternatively, placing the horizontal branch ducting in the ceilings above primary occupied spaces can enable having larger floor-to-finished-ceiling dimensions (i.e., because the branch ducting will be smaller than the truck ducting).

In-the-ceiling terminals are usually best placed in the ceiling plenums above the spaces that they condition. One constant volume, variable temperature terminal can usually provide adequate thermal-conditioning for a space having a floor area up to about 1000 square feet (93 m²). However, the amount of floor area that can be served by a single in-the-ceiling terminal will as likely depend on the floor area for each zone (i.e., placement of terminals should match the needs for conditioning zones as readily as possible).

A.3.2.4 Building applications for all-air systems All-air systems offer the capacity to provide thermal conditioning and ventilation for buildings housing multiple activities and having different heating and cooling requirements (i.e., operating different conditioning zones, some of which may require heating while others require cooling, all occurring simultaneously). The all-air systems enable precise thermal conditioning in spaces (e.g., regulation not only of temperature, but also of humidity) and certainly the best air filtration capabilities. Virtually all of the air-handling and thermal-conditioning equipment is located away from occupied spaces: devices such as boilers (or hot water heat exchangers), chillers, and air-handlers are placed in mechanical (or fan) rooms or other spaces remote from occupied spaces. Thus, the noise, heat production, and dirt usually associated with the operation of these central or remote equipment pieces can be prevented from entering into the occupied space. Ducting and terminals are located in building volumes usually adjacent to, but not within, occupied spaces.

The types of buildings in which all-air systems are mostly commonly present include offices (particularly, urban multistory towers), high school and university classrooms, laboratories, hospitals, large recreational facilities, and commons areas in hotels.

A.3.3 AIR-WATER DISTRIBUTION SYSTEMS

Air-water systems are typically composed of the same equipment components as all-air systems. Additionally, in a number of respects, air-water systems also operate in similar means to all-air systems. For both of these system types air is conditioned — both for temperature and humidity — by a central air-handler, is ducted to remote spaces, and is further conditioned (or is distributed without further conditioning) through a terminal, and is introduced into the occupied space (see Figure A.3).

Where air-water and all-air systems differ is in the nature of environmental control achieved with each system type. Air-water systems use ducted supply air as the means for ventilating individual building spaces. But distributed water supply — for either heating or cooling or both — is employed for providing the thermal conditioning of the individual spaces. The centrally distributed air will first be conditioned by the central air-handler. However, in each space a terminal will provide further conditioning for the centrally supplied air. This conditioning will be accomplished with the circulating hot and/or cold water passing through coils in the terminal. The terminal will be located in the room (not in the ceiling plenum as are the all-air terminals).

A.3.3.1 Building applications for air-water systems One principal difference between air-water systems and all-air systems is the magnitude of the volumetric airflow rates transported around buildings by each system type. All-air systems move large quantities of air, thereby providing the means to thermally condition and ventilate spaces

occupied by potentially large numbers of people. Alternatively, air-water systems generally pass air at relatively small volumetric flow rates; thus, these air-water systems are
employed in buildings with relatively low occupant numbers and space densities (i.e.,
where ratios of floor area versus occupant numbers are quite large). With such low airflow
magnitudes, the thermal conditioning of the individual building spaces must then be
accomplished with the circulating water.

Typical building applications in which air-water systems are employed include
libraries (particularly, small-town libraries or urban branch libraries), museums, and various residential types (guest rooms in hotels and motels, patient rooms in hospitals, and for
apartment buildings and college dormitories). In each of these applications the numbers
of occupants in any individual space will generally be small, and the required volumetric
airflow rates needed to ventilate the spaces will also be small. The thermal conditioning
capabilities offered by the in-the-room terminals mean that the occupants can readily dictate how warm or cold a space will be.

Air-water systems are most frequently employed for buildings that have mainly
perimeter spaces (e.g., libraries and museums, both of which have spaces that front on
more than one elevation, and occupant rooms organized along double-loaded corridors for
hotels, hospitals, apartments, and dormitories). Some building applications with internal
spaces can be serviced by air-water systems (e.g., small office buildings). But, for air-
water systems to function well with these internal spaces, the occupant densities must be
low (i.e., the ratio of floor area versus the number of occupants should be large). Often,
buildings with air-water systems will display modest heat gain rates from electric lighting
and equipment. Further, the heat gain rates from solar radiation will be more substantial
than the heat gains from occupancy and electrical devices. Thus, buildings serviced by air-
water systems often display *skin-load-dominant* thermal behaviors.

A.3.3.2 Equipment used for air-water systems   Centrally supplied ventilation air
will come from an air-handler that will be similar in most respects to the air-handlers used
for the all-air systems. Generally, this centrally supplied air stream will function according to a *constant-volume* regime (with the variation in air temperature made at the remote
terminals). Two differences between the air-water and all-air air-handlers, however, will
exist. First, because the magnitude of the volumetric flow rate used for air-water systems
will be substantially less than that for all-air systems, the capacity — and, thus, the size —
of the typical air-water air-handler can be considerably smaller than the all-air air-handler.
Second, also because the volumetric flow rate for air-water systems is relatively small,
there is less incentive to recirculate used air (i.e., because air flow rates are small, the thermal energy lost by dumping the used air will be small). Consequently, up to 100 percent
of the supply air stream may be composed of fresh air. Whether a capability for returning
used air is included in an air-water system is a choice left to the system designer. Without
the inclusion of a return air system, no return air ducting and return air fan are needed.
Thus, a considerable savings in floor area and volume could be realized by employing a
one-way air-water system to ventilate and thermally condition a suitable building.

The air-handler for an air-water system can be located centrally, if one air-handler
will be used. Instead, if building conditions dictate, there can be more than one air-handler installed, and these air-handlers can be arrayed in modular fashion or according to
other useful strategies. For example, a common practice in laying out air-handlers for a
multiple-story hotel is to employ one air-handler per floor and to run a trunk duct in the
corridor ceiling with branch ducts running to each guest room (see Figure A.39).

The typical air-water air-handler will consist of a set of air filters, a preheat coil, a humidification coil, a cooling coil, and a supply air fan. The preheat coil and the cooling coil will be serviced by centrally furnished hot water—from a boiler or steam/hot water heat exchanger—and chilled water, respectively. If the building is composed of multiple stories and a single air-handler is to be employed, then a vertical shaft will be needed for running supply air ducting vertically. Horizontal ducting will then pass from the vertical supply duct and carry supply air to each building space. Alternatively, if the building has a single story (or if each floor is conditioned by a dedicated air-handler), then only horizontal ducting will be required to carry supply air to each space. The supply ducting running to each space will connect to an in-the-space terminal at which further thermal conditioning will occur before the air is admitted to the space.

In conjunction with the passage of supply air from the air-handler to each occupied space, water will be distributed from a central location to each space. Either a single water stream can be circulated—either hot or cold—or both hot and cold water streams can be circulated, depending on occupant needs and budgetary capabilities. The sources of the hot and chilled water streams will be the same as those used for all-air systems (i.e., a boiler or steam/hot water heat exchanger and a chiller, respectively). These hot and/or chilled water sources may be placed in a central mechanical room or in some other building space located remotely from the mechanical room. To move the hot and/or chilled water through the building a series of pumps will be required. These pumps should be located near to the sources of the hot and chilled water. Piping for transporting the water streams through the building can be laid out adjacent to the supply air ducting or in separate pipe runs. Generally, these central supply pipes will be no more than 4–6 in (10–15 cm) in diameter including the thermal insulation wrapping.

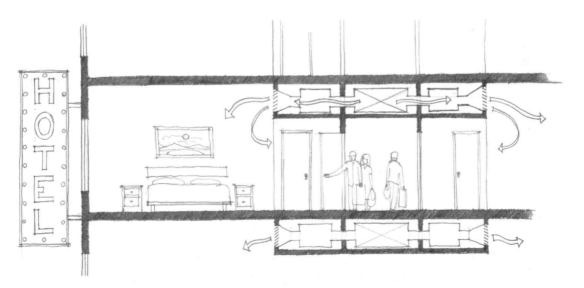

Figure A.39 A typical application of air-water systems that utilize induction terminals occurs in multifamily housing, dormitories, and hotels. A main duct is set in the ceiling plenum of a corridor. Then, off of this horizontal main duct branch, ducts run to induction terminals above the door entries for each living unit. The induction terminals enable a final conditioning of the air streams before the streams enter their respective occupied zones.

The piping runs from the sources to the in-the-space terminals can be grouped either as sets of two or four pipes. Two-pipe sets are used with one pipe transporting water to the terminals and the other pipe returning the water to the source. With a two-pipe set either hot or cold water will be transported depending on the need for the thermal conditioning of a space (or group of spaces). A particular limitation for two-pipe systems occurs during swing seasons when both heating and cooling of spaces are needed at different times of the day or when heating is needed in some building locations while cooling is required in others. The principal alternative to two-pipe systems is the use of four-pipe systems. In four-pipe systems — one pipe each for hot water supply, cold water supply, hot water return, and cold water return — greater flexibility in operation is available. For two-pipe systems the water flow passes through a single coil in the in-the-space terminal. Instead, for four-pipe systems, two separate coils are present in each terminal. Thus, as hot water and cold water can both be transported to a terminal, the choice of whether to heat or cool a space is readily obtainable, and the changeover from one regime to the other requires minimal effort.

Two types of in-the-space terminals are employed for air-water systems: induction units and fan-coil units. The induction terminal (see Figures A.40 and A.41) operates by using the pressure of the supply airflow to draw air from the space into the terminal, thereby inducing the mixing of the fresh and space air. Then, this mixed air passes over a thermal-conditioning coil (or two coils, if the overall system has four-pipe water distribution). After the mixed air has been conditioned, it exits the terminal, flowing into the space. Space air entering the terminal will pass through a cloth screen thereby trapping large dust particles and other common detritus. A thermostat present in the terminal will

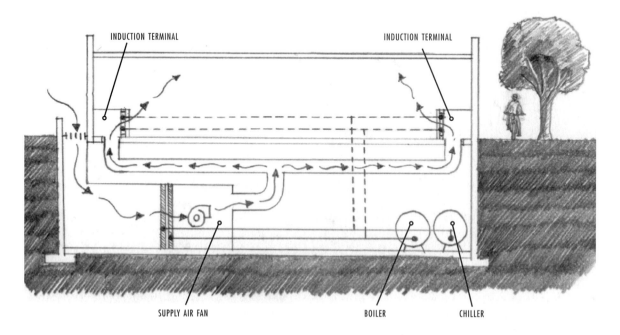

Figure A.40 An air-water system utilizing induction terminals.

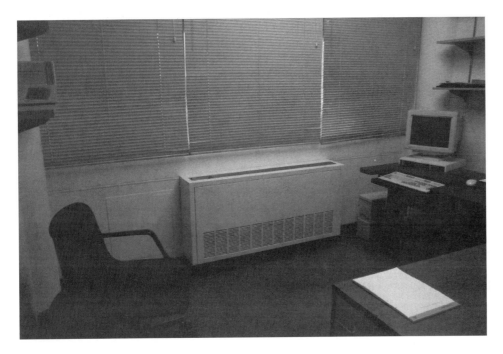

Figure A.41 An induction terminal is installed against the wall and under the windows.

sense the surrounding air and control the operation of the conditioning coil (or coils). Aside from the control devices — to sense the space temperature and to regulate the water flow — no other moving parts are present in this induction terminal.

The fan-coil terminal (see Figures A.42 and A.43) is composed of a fan for drawing air into the terminal and for blowing the air out of the terminal and one (or two) thermal conditioning coil(s). Similar to induction units, most fan-coil units provide minimal air filtration for the airflow prior to the air reaching the conditioning coil(s). While in the terminal the air will pass across the thermal-conditioning coil (or two coils, if a four-pipe water distribution system exists), thus being heated or cooled. The fan-coil terminal offers a wider range of operational possibilities than the induction terminal. First, the fan-coil terminal can function as a stand-alone unit separate from the air supply distribution. For example, the supply air will enter the space, passing through a conventional duct to a diffuser (and mixing with the existing space air). The fan-coil unit will be located on an opposite wall. The operating fan will pull the mixing air into the terminal causing the air to flow over the conditioning coil and then to leave the terminal. Thus, the fan-coil terminal provides space conditioning. A second operational strategy for fan-coil terminals involves distributing the supply air from a duct into the terminal and having the supply air and the space air mix within the terminal as thermal conditioning of the mixed air occurs. For this strategy the supply duct will be connected directly to the fan-coil terminal. A third operational protocol has the fan-coil terminal placed along the perimeter of the building. The fan-coil terminal draws in outside air through an opening in the building envelope, and this outside air is then mixed with space air (that can be a mix of air from the space and air supplied by a central distribution system). A sub-alternative for this third protocol

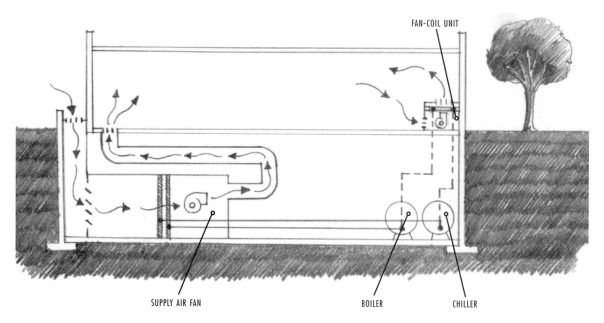

FAN-COIL UNIT

SUPPLY AIR FAN   BOILER   CHILLER

Figure A.42 An air-water system utilizing fan-coil units.

Figure A.43 A typical fan-coil unit is used to provide temperature conditioning for the lobby of a building. Note that this unit has been built into the wall of the lobby. The face plate standing to the left of the embedded unit normally covers the unit: this face plate was taken off to enable taking the photograph. Also, on the wall to the upper right of the unit is a thermostat that senses the air temperature of the lobby.

is that *no* centrally-distributed air actually enters the space, and all of the fresh air comes into the space through the fan-coil terminal that overlays the envelope opening (i.e., either no central distribution of supply air will exist in the building or no centrally distributed supply air is ducted to the specific space).

Common locations for these in-the-space terminals include, for induction terminals, on perimeter walls, especially under windows or, less often, attached to ceilings. Fan-coil terminals may also be placed along perimeter walls (under windows) and attached to ceilings. Fan-coil units may also be embedded into wall assemblies with the front of the unit facing outward to the space (where the wall assembly is deep enough to enclose the unit [see Figure A.43]). Placing either induction or fan-coil terminals under windows will enable the units to warm the glazing surfaces during wintertime operations when occupant discomfort resulting from radiational cooling might otherwise be present.

A.3.4   ALL-WATER SYSTEMS

All-water systems are essentially a sub-variant of air-water systems: the all-water systems transport hot and/or cold water around buildings to in-the-space fan-coil terminals. No central air-handling is provided in this system type. Instead, fresh air is brought into occupied spaces through openings in the building envelope which furnish the air directly to fan-coil units. The entering air experiences little of the preconditioning—the careful filtration and temperature and humidity conditioning—of the all-air and air-water systems. Consequently, air quality and space temperature and humidity control are less effective than that found with the other systems types.

In some limited circumstances where building regulations permit, all-water systems may transport water to convector units (often referred to as "radiators"). In such circumstances usually only hot water will circulate, thus affording space heating. The obvious limitation of this system is that no ventilation is provided for: convectors are essentially passive devices and offer no means for the controlled introduction of air to the space. Thus, unless occupants open windows or doors, no fresh air will be admitted. Further, by relying on the admission of fresh air through doorways and windows, no conditioning or cleaning of the air will be possible.

SIDEBAR A.10 One other variant of all-water systems: radiant surfaces

Radiant surfaces can be used for either heating or cooling, although in North America they are most often applied for heating. Radiant surfaces can be attached to or embedded in floors, walls, or ceilings, or they can be hung from walls or ceilings (see Figure A.44). These surfaces rely on a line-of-sight between the surface and the occupant: in other words, for the surface to be an effective conditioning vehicle, there must be an unimpeded direct pathway between the radiant surface and the occupant.

The major advantage offered by radiant surfaces is that they can enhance occupant thermal comfort by creating a favorable radiant exchange between the surface and the occupant. The radiant surface will operate at an essentially constant temperature and will afford a beneficial mean radiant temperature for the occupied space. A second advantage is that air movement resulting from the radiant exchange will be minimal, thus minimizing occupant distress due to drafts (see Section 3.4).

The principal liability for relying on radiant surfaces as the sole means for treating a space mechanically is that no ventilation capability is automatically present. Instead, a complementary ventilation system must be integrated with the radiant surface, if the full features of a well-developed HVAC system are to be furnished for space occupants.

The range of applications for radiant surface conditioning systems is quite broad. Among such applications are outdoor restaurants and cafes, hospital patient rooms or patient interview rooms in clinics, toilet rooms (in both residential and nonresidential facilities), swimming pools, skating rinks (particularly for spectator seating areas), and garages and work areas. In numbers of these applications, an ability to thermally condition the air in the space will be inefficient because of the openness of the space. Thus, instead of treating the air (and creating a favorable air temperature in the space), the treatment choice is to enhance occupant thermal comfort by fostering beneficial radiant exchange circumstances.

Figure A.44 This coffee bar in Seattle is heated jointly by the heat expended by the espresso machine and a series of ceiling-hung electric radiant heaters. During the winter the air temperatures in the coffee bar are commonly only a bit warmer than ambient external air. So, instead of relying on means for heating the air in the coffee bar, these radiant sources—the ceiling-hung heaters and the espresso machine—furnish useful warmth for the patrons.

A.3.4.1   Building applications for all-water systems   The traditional applications for this system type are primary schools, residential buildings (hotels, motels, dormitories, and patient rooms in some hospitals), and museums where less precise ventilation provision and temperature and humidity controls are acceptable. All of these building applications will likely be composed entirely of perimeter spaces.

A.3.4.2   Equipment and its operation for all-water systems   Hot and/or chilled water is (are) produced centrally using equipment similar to that used for all-air and air-water systems (i.e., boilers or steam/hot water heat exchangers and chillers, respectively). The resulting hot and chilled water streams are pumped through piping to remote locations throughout a building where thermal conditioning is required. Either fan-coil units or convectors will be used as the heat exchanger assemblies in the occupied spaces.

Where convectors are used, no opportunity for controlled ventilation will be available. Alternatively, fan-coil terminals can take in outside air through the building envelope (see Figure A.45). In the terminal the entering air is passed through a filter to remove particulate matter. If the occupied space requires warming, hot water will pass across the coil and warm the air before it enters the space. If a chilled water supply is available, cold water can pass through a terminal coil. Air passing across the coil (with cold water present in the coil) will be cooled, thus enabling space cooling. Additionally, as air moves

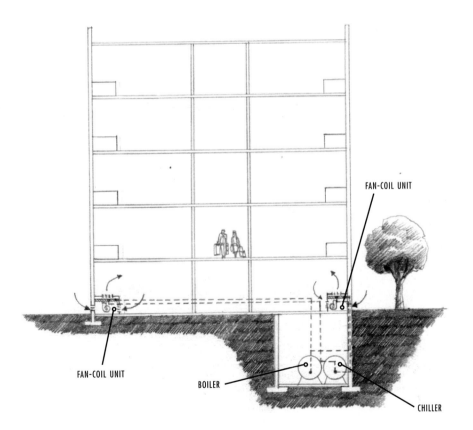

Figure A.45 A prototypical all-water system utilizing fan coil units.

across the coil (with cold water in the coil), excess water vapor entrained in the incoming air will condense and be captured by a condensate tray or run-off pipe (thereby providing humidity control).

Water distribution for all-water systems will consist of either two-pipe or four-pipe arrangements. In many of the building applications for which all-water systems are employed, only heating will be furnished by the system. In such instances two-pipe systems will be appropriate. However, if both heating and cooling of remote spaces are required, a four-pipe distribution system should be used (and two separate coils should be present in each terminal). The fan-coil terminals will be located along the building perimeter underneath windows (wherever possible to facilitate the taking in of fresh air). Thermostatic controls will be used to regulate and guide the operation of these fan-coil units. The thermostats should be placed on walls opposite to the fan-coil units.

A.3.5   DIRECT-REFRIGERANT SYSTEMS

The basic premise of the direct-refrigerant system is that a single hardware assembly (or, in some instances, two separate, but physically connected assemblies) can provide both thermal conditioning and ventilation (air-handling) for building spaces. In contrast, the all-air and air-water systems (and, to a lesser extent, all-water systems) typically consist of central heating and chilling equipment, air-handling assemblies, and remote terminals, each component of which is located in different places in a building. For the direct-refrigerant assembly, all of the necessary conditioning and air-handling components can be present in a single location within a building or immediately external to the building.

Direct-refrigerant systems are available in a number of different configurations: window air-conditioners; through-the-wall air-conditioners; unitary air-conditioners (that can be located either inside or immediately outside of a building), and heat pumps (that are either air-to-air or water-to-water units). Within the typical direct-refrigerant assembly will be a compressor and a condenser (both of which are necessary for providing cooling), heating and cooling coils, one (or more) fan(s) for moving air across the coils and into the building space (and for enhancing a return air capability for the system), a humidity controller, filters for air cleaning, and appropriate sets of controls for managing the operation of the assembly. The assembly can be directly attached to a ducting network, enabling the air handling of spaces remote from the assembly. Or the assembly can inject air directly into the space in which the assembly is located (i.e., no ducting will be needed to transport supply air.)

Many direct-refrigerant assemblies are furnished as a single unit (see Figure A.46). Alternatively, other assemblies are available as split-system arrangements (e.g., with indoor and outdoor components for the overall system)(see Figure A.47). Usually, one portion of the split system will provide for the air-handling functions (including the thermal conditioning of the air stream). This portion will be placed inside the building. The other portion of the system — placed just outside of the building — will house the compressor and condenser, which are essential for air-cooling. Air heating (with a heating coil) will be done within the indoor section.

Direct-refrigerant system assemblies are designed and constructed by an air-conditioning manufacturer. Because of the inclusive operation furnished by the assembly and the fact that a manufacturer constructs the assembly as a unit, these systems assemblies are often described as "packaged" systems. These assemblies thus are available as stock items that are identified in various manufacturers' catalogs (of commercially available

Figure A.46 A direct-refrigerant system utilizing a rooftop package unit.

products). These packaged assemblies are designed and produced to furnish specific performance levels (e.g., for cooling and heating capacities and volumetric flow rates). Thus, when an engineer determines the service amounts needed for conditioning and ventilating a building, s/he can look in a manufacturer's catalog for an assembly that will satisfy these amounts and place an order for the assembly. The ordered assembly will be constructed in the manufacturer's factory, tested there, shipped to the construction site, and lifted into place. Note that *custom*-designed and constructed direct-refrigerant assemblies also are generally available from many manufacturers. But, for the reason of the extra costs associated with in-plant designing and special construction, the application of custom-designed assemblies can usually be justified only for large-scale building projects.

The typical building applications for direct-refrigerant systems include many small buildings, particularly when the building is used either for a single function or when two or more functions have similar ventilation and conditioning requirements. Application examples include small offices, medical and dental clinics, retail stores, restaurants, small libraries, personal care and exercise centers, small churches and meeting houses, and funeral homes. These systems are widely used for ventilating and conditioning single-family and multifamily housing, as well as for guest rooms in hotels and motels.

Other building applications for which these direct-refrigerant systems are well suited include any number of different types of buildings that are being renovated (especially, buildings undergoing historic preservation). These packaged units arrive at the building site already assembled and are efficient space users. Often, for historic buildings in which space

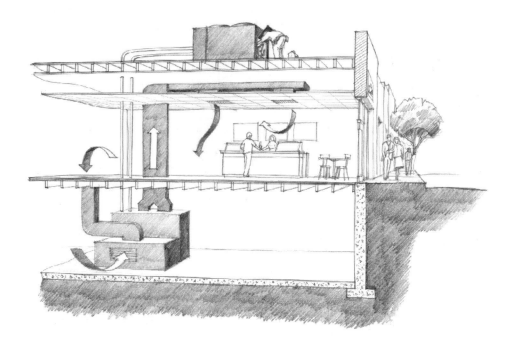

Figure A.47 A split-package direct-refrigerant system is shown here. On the roof are the compressor and condenser. In the basement is an air-handler with heat exchanging coil. A refrigerant will flow between the rooftop component and the coil.

for HVAC systems installations may be quite limited, the adoption of a split-system direct-refrigerant assembly is well advised. The indoor section containing the air-handling capabilities will occupy a relatively small floor area and volume, and the other section can be placed adjacent to this indoor section, but just outside of the building.

Two additional application strategies exist for direct-refrigerant systems. First, these assemblies can be used to service internal spaces for buildings whose perimeter spaces are being serviced by air-water systems. Because air-water systems do not offer good servicing for internal spaces, direct-refrigerant assemblies can be located just external to a building (on the roof or next to a perimeter wall at grade level). Such an assembly can then be connected to ducting that will transport air into the building interior. Whereas air-water systems rely on perimeter-located terminals for the principal thermal conditioning for individual spaces, the principal thermal conditioning offered by the direct-refrigerant systems occurs in the packaged unit itself. Thus, the supply air leaving the packaged unit will be adequately cooled (or heated) to satisfy the conditioning need for the building interior.

Second, these packaged assemblies can be installed and operated in tandem to enable the conditioning and ventilation of larger spaces. In this situation modular direct-refrigerant units will be organized to serve fractions of a larger space. The modular units may be regulated by a common control device, or each unit module may operate independently, thereby offering flexibility for the thermal conditioning of each fraction of the larger space (e.g., if a large space has north, east, and south-facing elevations, a packaged unit on the south may need to offer cooling while a unit on the north provides heating).

Further discussion about the use of a direct-refrigerant system appears in Section B.3.

Section A.4 | RULES-OF-THUMB AND OTHER PLANNING GUIDELINES FOR ANTICIPATING SPATIAL REQUIREMENTS FOR NONRESIDENTIAL HVAC SYSTEMS

A guiding premise of this text is the belief that if architects can make proper accommodations for the inclusion of HVAC systems during the early phases of building planning (i.e., while performing schematic designing), the design process will proceed more efficiently,

---

SIDEBAR A.11 Criteria for selecting from among HVAC system types

A. Service characteristics
1. Overall quality of service: ability to provide good temperature conditioning and ventilation to a space or numbers of spaces.
2. Flexibility: ability to alter service capabilities when conditioning and ventilation requirements change during occupancy.
3. Ventilation quality: air cleanliness, appropriate air temperature range, adequate volumetric airflow rates, comfortable air velocities around occupants.
4. Ability to maintain uniform or variable air temperatures or radiant exchange conditions in occupied spaces.
5. Humidity control: ability to humidify or dehumidify space(s).
6. Fire event management: beneficial control in a fire event (localized or building-wide).

B. Nature of system equipment
1. Complexity of system equipment.
2. Spatial requirements for housing equipment.
3. Locations where system equipment would be most beneficially placed (to achieve good operation).
4. How readily system equipment can be integrated with other building systems and with the overall architecture.

5. Appearance of equipment when it is present in occupied spaces.
6. Intrusiveness of equipment (in the event that it must be placed in occupied spaces to achieve good operation).

C. Operation characteristics
1. Energy-efficiency of system operations.
2. Noise levels commonly present during system operation.

D. Costs
1. First costs (for installation and start-up activities).
2. Operating costs.

E. Care requirements
1. Requirements of maintenance, repair, and component (or system) replacement.
2. Useful lifetime for main system assembly (assemblies) hardware.
3. Effect on building operation—occupant functioning—when system (or components) are being maintained, repaired, or replaced.

and functionally superior buildings will result. To facilitate inclusion of these systems in the early design proposals, planning information must be available that describes the likely spatial requirements for placing the systems. This information should include guidelines about system selection, equipment identification (for use after system selection has occurred), space-sizing (for predicting spatial needs after equipment identification has occurred), equipment-locating, and other advisory notes useful for making needed accommodations.

Consulting engineers working in cooperation with architects will most often make system selection decisions for a building. A number of selection criteria—used by engineers—are well-established; these criteria are itemized in Sidebar A.11. The criteria address the functionality and costs of alternative systems.

In Table A.1 service properties—considering the functionality and costs of the several system types and subtypes described in Section A.3—have been cataloged. Thus, using these criteria and factoring in historical experience, recommendations can be generally categorized for identifying those systems that are most often appropriate for specific building applications. These recommendations are presented in Table A.2.

Once a system type has been selected for a specific application, then identifying which equipment components will comprise the system can be undertaken. At the same time prediction of where these components will likely be located is possible. Table A.3 identifies which components are likely to be placed in the five conventional system locations for each system type: mechanical (or fan) rooms, vertical accessways, ceiling plenums, in the occupied room(s), and on the rooftop (or at the building exterior).

TABLE A.1
HVAC SYSTEM TYPES AND SUBTYPES: SERVICE PROPERTIES

MAJOR PROPERTIES

SYSTEM TYPE	COMPREHENSIVE SERVICE? Heating & cooling capabilities; range of volumetric flow rates; thermal comfort promise; indoor air quality assurance?	OPERATIONAL FLEXIBILITY? Ability to condition multiple zones; use of economizer-cycle cooling; heat recovery on return air service?	SPACE CONSUMPTIVE? Size of system throughout building & in occupied rooms?
ALL-AIR	Can supply high airflow rates; can vary airflow rates; best means to assure thermal comfort; best opportunity to clean air & control humidity	High potential for heating or cooling alternative zones simultaneously; ready use of economizer cycle for cooling; fully developed supply & return airflow looping	Fully developed systems require *greatest amount of space*: space needs accentuated by large air-handling capabilities (for supply & return air streams)
Terminal reheat	Consistent with ALL-AIR summary above (except air-flow rate is consistent)	Consistent with ALL-AIR summary above (varying supply temperatures made possible with in-the-ceiling terminals	Consistent with ALL-AIR summary above
Variable air volume	Consistent with ALL-AIR summary above, but can experience indoor air quality problems if volumetric flow rates are low	Consistent with ALL-AIR summary above (constant temperature supply; but can be altered with in-duct heaters)	Consistent with ALL-AIR summary above

TABLE A.1 (continued)
HVAC SYSTEM TYPES AND SUBTYPES: SERVICE PROPERTIES

MAJOR PROPERTIES

SYSTEM TYPE	COMPREHENSIVE SERVICE?	OPERATIONAL FLEXIBILITY?	SPACE CONSUMPTIVE?
ALL-AIR **Multizone**	Consistent with ALL-AIR summary above (plus offers very good control for individual spaces)	Consistent with ALL-AIR summary above (supply temperatures set at air-handler for specific zones; use of zone-specific ducting)	Consistent with ALL-AIR summary above
Dual duct	Consistent with ALL-AIR summary above (plus provides the best of all means for thermal-conditioning and setting of airflow amounts)	Consistent with ALL-AIR summary above (separate warm & cold supply air streams run to in-the-ceiling mixing terminal; variable or constant airflow rates possible)	Consistent with ALL-AIR summary above (requires additional space for running separate, parallel warm & cold air ducts)
AIR-WATER	Low & constant airflow rates with conditioning dependent on remote terminals; indoor air quality marginalized by low airflow rates; thermal comfort dependent on terminal operation	Useful for perimeter zones only (need other system type for interior zones); can use economizer-cycle for air cooling; return air system may or may not be present	Central air-handling system requires less space than for ALL-AIR types; return air capability also smaller or not present at all; terminals required in occupied spaces
Induction unit	Consistent with AIR-WATER summary above	Consistent with AIR-WATER summary above	Consistent with AIR-WATER summary above
Fan-coil unit	Consistent with AIR-WATER summary above	Consistent with AIR-WATER summary above	Consistent with AIR-WATER summary above
ALL-WATER	No central air-handling: air supplied through-the-wall; minimal control on air quality (via fan-coil operation); thermal comfort dependent on fan-coil unit and often limited; marginal humidity control	Water distribution to fan-coil unit: perimeter zones only; fan-coil unit conditions and provides air for single zone; limited space area that can be effectively conditioned and ventilated by fan-coil unit; no return air-handling (exhausting to perimeter)	Little central space needed: for boiler or hot water/heat exchanger & chiller; no central air-handling; no in-the-ceiling-terminals; perimeter fan-coil units; can be least space consumptive systems alternative
Two-pipe	Consistent with ALL-WATER summary above (but provides only heating or cooling; thermal comfort dependent on fan-coil unit & often limited; marginal humidity control)	Consistent with ALL-WATER summary above (plus zonal limitations when heating required on some elevations, while cooling needed on others)	Consistent with ALL-WATER summary above
Four-pipe	Consistent with ALL-WATER summary above (plus provides both heating & cooling at same time across building)	Consistent with ALL-WATER summary above	Consistent with ALL-WATER summary above
DIRECT REFRIGERANT	Usually provides single-temperature airflow with fixed volumetric rate; air cleaning & humidity control less good than with ALL-AIR systems; units available only with factory-set capacities	Most often, single-zone capability; return-air looping readily available; economizer cycle may be available; two more units can be used modularly for larger spaces or for adjacent spaces requiring zone-by-zone control	Most often, minimized central air distribution; no water distribution; but need machine space in or close to occupied room; also, can install on rooftop with ducting down to one or several floors

TABLE A.1 (continued)
HVAC SYSTEM TYPES AND SUBTYPES: SERVICE PROPERTIES

MAJOR PROPERTIES

SYSTEM TYPE	DEGREE OF INTRUSIVENESS? Components in occupied spaces; noise problems?	DESIGN & CONSTRUCTION EASE? Difficulty of incorporating components into a building?	POTENTIAL COSTS: FIRST & OPERATING? Costs of acquisition and installation; likely maintenance & repair needs; operational energy-efficiency?
ALL-AIR	Central system components are remote from occupied spaces; in-the-ceiling terminals adjacent to occupied spaces; *occupied spaces free of system components*	Locating air-handling capabilities (air-handlers, ducts, & in-the-ceiling terminals) requires careful planning & integration with other building features	First costs large because of system comprehensiveness; most components long lasting; maintenance & repair costs low; modest energy costs (especially with use of economizer cycle)
Terminal reheat	Consistent with ALL-AIR summary above	Consistent with ALL-AIR summary above	Consistent with ALL-AIR summary above
Variable air volume	Consistent with ALL-AIR summary above	Consistent with ALL-AIR summary above	Consistent with ALL-AIR summary above; offers very good energy efficient operations
Multizone	Consistent with ALL-AIR summary above	Consistent with ALL-AIR summary above (& requires laying out of finger ducts to each of the zones supplied)	Consistent with ALL-AIR summary above
Dual duct	Consistent with ALL-AIR summary above	Consistent with ALL-AIR summary above (plus accommodation needed for running separate, parallel duct pairs)	Consistent with ALL-AIR summary above
AIR-WATER	Central air-handler & ducting remote from occupied spaces; terminals in occupied spaces; volumes for ducting smaller	Planning for air-handling still required; accommodations needed for terminals in occupied spaces; volumes for ducting smaller	Less-developed central air-handling equipment (thus, lower first costs than ALL-AIR systems); more maintenance & repair required for terminals; less energy efficient than ALL-AIR systems
Induction unit	Consistent with AIR-WATER summary above	Consistent with AIR-WATER summary above	Consistent with AIR-WATER summary above
Fan-coil unit	Consistent with AIR-WATER summary above (plus the fan operation often produces significant noise levels)	Consistent with AIR-WATER summary above	Consistent with AIR-WATER summary above, except that, with four-pipe water distribution, first cost will be substantially greater

TABLE A.1 (continued)
HVAC SYSTEM TYPES AND SUBTYPES: SERVICE PROPERTIES

MAJOR PROPERTIES

SYSTEM TYPE	DEGREE OF INTRUSIVENESS?	DESIGN & CONSTRUCTION EASE?	POTENTIAL COSTS: FIRST & OPERATING?
ALL-WATER **Two-pipe**	Consistent with ALL-WATER summary above	Consistent with ALL-WATER summary above	Consistent with ALL-WATER summary above
Four-pipe	Consistent with ALL-WATER summary above	Consistent with ALL-WATER summary above	Consistent with ALL-WATER summary above (except four-pipe systems can be as expensive as ALL-AIR systems)
DIRECT REFRIGERANT	Unit in or immediately adjacent to occupied space; compressor & fans generally cause significant noise problems	Units are factory pre-assembled & tested; often can be easily installed (particularly if rooftop application)	First costs low; maintenance & repair needs usually greater than with ALL-AIR systems (especially, if exposed to weather, as on rooftops); equipment lifetimes typically shorter than for other systems; energy-efficiency less good than ALL-AIR systems
Unitary-packaged systems	Consistent with DIRECT REFRIGERANT summary above; noise levels as high as 70 dB(A) when unit in occupied space	Consistent with DIRECT REFRIGERANT summary above	Consistent with DIRECT REFRIGERANT summary above; lifetimes no more than 10 years (especially if weather-exposed)
Split-system package	Consistent with DIRECT REFRIGERANT summary above; if compressor outside of occupied space, noise levels reduced	Consistent with DIRECT REFRIGERANT summary above	Consistent with DIRECT REFRIGERANT summary above (except indoor component of split system usually will have longer lifetime)

TABLE A.2
ALTERNATIVE SYSTEMS FOR BUILDING APPLICATIONS

	DIR REFRIG		ALL-WATER	AIR-WATER		ALL-AIR			
	Unitary	Split-System	with Fan-Coil Unit and Outside Air	with Induction Terminal	with Fan-Coil Terminal	Variable Air Volume	Reheat Terminal	Multizone	Dual Duct
RESIDENTIAL									
Single-family	yes	yes							
Apartment	yes	yes	yes						
Dormitory rooms	yes		yes		yes				
HOTELS & MOTELS									
Guest rooms	yes	yes	yes	yes	yes	less often			
Common spaces	yes	yes	yes			yes	yes	yes	
RETAIL COMMERCIAL									
Stores	yes	yes				yes	yes		
Restaurants	yes	yes	not recomm.	not recomm.	not recomm.		yes	yes	
Department stores						yes	yes	yes	
Shopping malls	yes	yes				yes	yes	yes	
GATHERING PLACES									
Churches	yes	yes				yes			yes
Theaters						yes		yes	
Auditoriums						yes		yes	
Libraries—branch	yes	yes	yes	yes	yes	yes			
Libraries—archival	yes	yes		yes			yes	yes	yes
Museums				yes			yes	yes	yes
Recreational	yes	yes				yes	yes	yes	
EDUCATIONAL BUILDINGS									
Primary schools		yes	yes						
Secondary schools		yes	yes	yes	yes	yes	yes	yes	
Colleges / universities						yes	yes	yes	yes
OFFICE BUILDINGS									
Small	yes	yes	yes	yes	yes	yes			
High-rise (towers)	yes	yes		yes	yes	yes	yes	yes	yes
MEDICAL FACILITIES									
Medical / dental clinics	yes	yes	yes			yes			
Hospitals			yes	yes	yes	yes			
LABORATORIES	yes	yes		yes	yes	yes	yes	yes	yes

This table has been reproduced from *The ABC's of Air-Conditioning*, (Syracuse, New York: Carrier Corporation, 1975), pages 16–17. Permission to reproduce this table has been granted by the Carrier Corporation. Courtesy of Carrier Corporation.

TABLE A.3
COMMON LOCATIONS FOR SYSTEM COMPONENTS

	MECHANICAL (or FAN) ROOM(s)	VERTICAL ACCESSWAY(s)	CEILING PLENUM(s)	IN-THE-OCCUPIED-ROOM	ROOFTOP or BUILDING EXTERIOR
ALL-AIR	Boiler or steam/hot water heat exchanger and/or chiller present or located in remote location (some dedicated room or external to building); supply air-handler; return air fan (probable); possibly, special exhaust fan(s)	One (or more) large vertical duct(s) or a few or several small vertical ducts; shaftway can serve as return air passageway (without discreet RA ducting); conditioning (and/or condensing) water piping can be present	Horizontal branch supply air ducting, terminals for distributing (for reheating systems), finger ducting running from terminals to ceiling-mounted diffusers, will all be present; ceiling plenums (or return ducting) will work as return air passageways to vertical shafts	A thermostat (and/or humidistat) should be present	If a chiller operates for the building, then a cooling tower will likely also be present
AIR-WATER	Boiler or steam/hot water heat exchanger and/or chiller present or located in remote location (some dedicated room or external to building); supply air-handler; return air fan (possibly)	Vertical ducting for air supply (and, possibly, air return); conditioning (and/or condensing) water piping can be present	Horizontal branch supply air ducting will be present; possibly, ceiling plenums (or return ducting) will work as return air passageways to vertical shafts	Induction unit or fan-coil unit will be present, either with floor-mounted or ceiling-mounted (above or below the ceiling plane); a thermostat can be present, separate from the unit (or as part of the unit)	If a chiller operates for the building, then a cooling tower will likely also be present
ALL-WATER	Boiler or steam/hot water heat exchanger and/or chiller present or located in remote location (some dedicated room, or even, external to the building)	Conditioning (and/or condensing) water piping will likely be present	Ceiling-mounted fan-coil unit may be present; otherwise, no other system component is likely in this volume	Fan-coil unit will be present, most likely with a floor-mounting; a thermostat can be present, separate from the unit (or as part of the unit)	If a chiller operates for the building, then a cooling tower will likely also be present
DIRECT REFRIGERANT	Likely, no mechanical (or fan) room will be present in the building	Vertical ducting for air supply — and, possibly, for air return — may be present (for example, when a packaged unit is employed to condition two or more floors)	Ceiling-mounted unit (or section for a packaged split-system) can be present; ducting from a packaged unit can run in ceiling plenum; refrigerant piping can be present; even, some supply air ducting to carry outside air from envelope to unit; return air ducting can pass from space to exterior; variable volume terminals may also be present	Floor or wall-mounted unit (or section for a packaged split system) is likely to be present; a thermostat can be present, separate from the unit (or as part of the unit)	Packaged rooftop unit may be main feature of system; condenser may be present on rooftop or external to sidewall (as external part of split-system)

A.4.1 SPACE-DEFINING RULES-OF-THUMB FOR ALL-AIR AND AIR-WATER SYSTEMS

For *all-air systems* and — to a lesser extent — for *air-water systems,* major HVAC equipment is spread throughout buildings served by these systems. The equipment is large and space consuming. Further, because the equipment must be located to fulfill specific functional goals and must be organized to accommodate these required functions, the equipment will have to be carefully integrated with other important building assemblies (e.g., elements of the structural system, the electric illumination system, the surface finishes and furnishings in the occupied spaces, and so forth). Thus, during the schematic designing for a building, spaces to house this equipment must be planned for.

This planning should include establishing reasonable locations for placing equipment and satisfying likely areal and volumetric requirements for its housing. It is not necessary to know precisely what individual equipment pieces will, in fact, be employed in the building. Rather, the architect's goal should be to have approximate ideas of what system type will likely be proposed by the engineer, of what that system will be composed, and where the probable equipment pieces are commonly located. Information for addressing these issues has been presented in Tables A.1 and A.2 in this section. Using the following space-locating and estimating rules-of-thumb, an architect should be able to make suitable accommodations for an all-air or air-water HVAC system.

A.4.1.1 Spatial guidelines for heating and refrigeration equipment

In Section A.3 we have written that fuel-fired boilers should be located in close proximity to the storage facilities provided for the fuel (e.g., oil or coal) or to a municipal natural gas supply piping line. Alternatively, boilers operating with electric resistance are essentially free of any space-locating constraints. Steam-to-hot water heat exchangers should be located in a space where the steam supply can readily be piped into the space.

Chillers — refrigeration machines — can generally be placed wherever space can be made available for housing them. However, if an absorption chiller is to be employed in a building, the chiller should be located so that there is a ready connection to a steam source (i.e., either supplied from a boiler or a municipal or campus-central steam-producing plant). Noting this one exception, there are no other operation requirements for a chiller and a boiler (or heat exchanger) to be located in the same space. For instance, if an electric chiller and a gas-fired boiler are to be applied to satisfy the hot water and chilled water source needs of a building, these two devices can indeed be placed in spaces that are widely separated (or they can be located in the same space).

In both instances — when placing and operating boilers and chillers — accommodations will need to be made for delivering the hot and chilled water to air-handlers and remote terminals (i.e., terminals located away from the air-handler). Such deliveries are accomplished by using pumps to propel and piping to transport the water streams to the requisite locations. Whether the pumps are used in association with hot water from boilers or with chilled water from chillers, the pumps will need to be located in close proximity to the boilers and the chillers.

A general rule-of-thumb for sizing a space that can house both a boiler and a chiller stipulates that the floor area of the space should be approximately 2 percent of the gross floor area of the building served by the boiler and chiller. Thus, if an office tower will have a floor area of 400,000 square feet (37,200 m²), then the floor area required for housing boilers and refrigeration machines (chillers) will be 8,000 square feet (744 m²). Whereas boilers may fit within common floor-to-floor dimensions of 12 feet (3.7 m), many chillers will require space heights of one-floor-and-a-half or, even, double-floors.

Some qualifications to this general 2 percent approximation include the following conditions. First, if boilers and chillers are separately placed in a building or the HVAC system in a building only furnishes heating or cooling, then estimate the floor area needed for the boiler(s) or the chiller(s) as about 1 percent of gross floor area of the building served by each source unit (or sets of modular units where, for instance, multiple small boilers are employed). Second, if a steam-to-water heat exchanger is used as an alternative to a boiler, then the floor area and height requirements for the heat exchanger will be similar to those of the boiler. And, third, all of these percentage-area rules include adequate floor area spaces for housing the pumps needed for propelling the hot or chilled water that will pass out of the boiler (or heat exchanger) or chiller.

When planning where to house boilers and chillers some further caveats should be borne in mind. First, because these devices are noisy, often dirty, and may produce substantial vibrations (if not properly mounted), these units should be located away, or even remote, from occupied spaces. Second, as these units will require periodic maintenance, repair, and, occasionally, component replacement, adequate space around these boilers and chillers should be provided (so that these remedial functions can be accommodated). And, third, because these units are indeed large, forethought must be given to how they can be installed during building construction and how replacement components can be brought in (and defective parts removed) during building operation (e.g., if a boiler is located in a sub-basement or a chiller is placed on the top floor of an office tower, how the devices can be installed initially and how old parts and their replacements can be moved through the building should be considered during building design).

A.4.1.2 Spatial guidelines for air-handling equipment Supply air-handlers—the assemblege of mixing plenums, heating and cooling coils, filters, and fans—can be placed centrally or modularly in buildings. Single supply air-handlers can be employed in small buildings or in reasonably large buildings (e.g., those having perhaps up to 60,000 to 80,000 square feet (5500 to 7500 m²) of floor area served by the single air-handler). Alternatively, in both small and large buildings, multiple supply air-handlers can be employed. How many air-handlers need to be employed in a building can depend on a number of factors including zonal (separate conditioning) requirements, use schedules, occupant preferences (wishes for independent control), the sizes of occupied spaces, and so forth.

In many high-rise office buildings supply air-handlers will be installed to service about 20 floors each (e.g., an air-handler at an intermediate floor of a tower—perhaps located at floors 30–31—will serve floors 21–30 and 31–40). Additionally, if the occupied area of each floor exceeds about 10,000 square feet (930 m²), two main air-handlers will often be employed to serve the 20-story increment with one air-handler supplying air to the perimeter zone of each floor and the other air-handler supplying air to the internal zone of each floor. A parallel planning strategy that is employed for buildings covering substantial ground areas (e.g., for manufacturing plants, shopping malls, large suburban high schools) is to employ several supply air-handlers with each one being responsible for conditioning some fraction of the floor area. Thus, instead of dividing the building vertically as is done with office towers, these sprawling buildings are divided horizontally into a number of independent zones.

At the other end of the planning spectrum is the approach of using modular supply air-handlers. For an office tower, each floor may have a single air-handler located on that floor and dedicated to ventilating and conditioning that floor. A similar planning strategy would be to set up each store in a shopping mall with its own supply air-handler (e.g., this protocol is used in numbers of merchandise marts where large numbers of similarly sized showrooms or retail stores occur in a single building; each showroom or store will be treated by a single independent air-handler).

The natures of the supply air-handlers applied to these alternative occupancies and floor-area magnitudes will differ. Most often, when supply air-handlers service large floor areas, the units will be *built-up* devices that are designed as *one-off* units specifically for the building. When modular air-handlers are used in large buildings—such as office towers or suburban high schools — these devices can be designed and assembled particularly for the building, or they can, in fact, be *packaged* assemblies that satisfy the ventilation and conditioning needs of the modularly defined spaces. For numbers of such modularly organized systems the distinction blurs between employing specially designed and fabricated air-handlers and using packaged air-handlers (the former units thus becoming devices that are virtually standardized, if sufficient numbers are produced).

Offering space-sizing rules-of-thumb for air-handlers raises the issue of how comprehensive any air-handling system will be. For instance, in a well-developed all-air system the floor area required for placing the supply air-handler will generally be 4 to 5 percent of the gross floor area of the building served by this air-handler. If this air-handler is a central unit serving perhaps 10 floors of an office tower, then the floor area required to house this unit will be 4 to 5 percent of the total area of those 10 floors. Alternatively, if the air-handler is one module serving a specific floor of an office tower, then to house this modular air-handler an area of 4 to 5 percent of the area of the specific floor will be required. For each of the other floors served by similar modular air-handlers, there must be areas set aside on each of these floors equal to the area needed for the first of these modules (i.e., the fan rooms housing these modular air-handlers are essentially modular fan rooms).

The magnitude of the floor area required for housing an air-handler is as large as it is because of the various components of the air-handler that must be present to furnish the necessary services. In addition to the air-propelling fan and its motor, there must be a fresh air-return air mixing plenum (or chamber), filters, hot water and cold water coils, and a humidity-controlling section. To regulate the percentages of fresh air and "used" air mixed in the mixing plenum, there will need to be a damper separating each air stream from the mixing plenum. Some ducting may be needed to transport air from the outdoor (fresh) air intake into the mixing plenum. And ducting will certainly be required to transport the supply air from the air-handler to the vertical and/or horizontal pathways along which this supply air will pass to the occupied spaces.

For all-air systems used air from the occupied spaces must be collected and returned. Most of this air will be transported by the return air portion of the air-handling system, but some of this air, which has been used in toilet rooms will be exhausted to the building exterior by a toilet-exhaust fan assembly (or subsystem). For the main return air-handling, a return air fan and its motor will be required. Additionally, ducting must be provided to transport the used air from the various horizontal and/or vertical pathways that return this air back to the return air fan. Then, ducting will be required to provide pathways both to transport the used air to the mixing plenum and to the building exterior (where the unrecirculated used air is expelled to the atmosphere). Essentially, these two pathways leading from the return air fan appear in a T form, with one leg passing to the mixing plenum and the other to the building exterior. A rule-of-thumb that can be used to estimate the floor area needed for housing the return air fan, its motor, and the ducting is that an area equal to 2 percent of the gross floor area served by this return air fan should be made available in the schematic plan for the return air subsystem. This floor area accommodation should also be adequate for housing the toilet-exhaust fan(s) and the related ducting.

For some buildings additional fans will be required for various specialized services. For instance, if some activities in a building render the used air from those spaces not suitable for recirculation, then this contaminated air will have to be passed directly to the exterior (unless special filtering or chemical cleaning of this air is mandatory). Otherwise, for relatively conventional contaminated air streams, exhausting fans and associated ducting will be needed. Common examples of where such special exhausting is standard practice are the venting to the exterior of air from kitchens in restaurants; from commercial operations in which chemicals are used (e.g., photographic and printing processing, beauty salons, mortuary facilities, and a range of different industrial applications); or from wood-working shops.

Another set of air-handling devices that are being applied increasingly more frequently are heat recovery devices. These devices capture some of the heat embedded in used air before the air is exhausted to the exterior. This captured heat is transferred to incoming fresh air, thereby reducing the amount of energy that must be consumed to warm the cold fresh air. A variety of mechanisms and scales are available for performing the heat recovery function. These devices are commonly located in mechanical (or fan) rooms, and they occupy space (i.e., some floor area must be made available in the rooms for housing these devices).

Offering a generally useful rule-of-thumb for accommodating extra air-exhausting fans and heat recovery devices is problematic because of the variety of devices and the range of circumstances for which this equipment can be applied. If such equipment will be present in a proposed building, then allowing for at least an additional 1 to 2 percent of the gross floor area served by the equipment will be prudent when planning the space housing the equipment (i.e., this accommodation should be an extra one and should be added after the supply and return air-handling equipment are accounted for). Otherwise, the designer should seek direct advice from an HVAC engineer when the need arises for housing such equipment.

Satisfactorily anticipating the necessary vertical dimensions for housing air-handling equipment is also an important design issue. For *modular* air-handlers that are utilized as components of all-air systems, the height of the space required for placing the air-handler and the related ducting will likely match the clear height afforded by the conventional floor-to-floor dimensions of many contemporary office, school, and retail commercial buildings. Thus, if the floor-to-floor dimension is about 12'-6" to 13'-0" (3.8 to 4.0 m), then a clear vertical span from the floor to the structural grid above would probably be about 9 to 10 feet (2.7 to 3.1 m). Requiring more height — greater than conventional floor-to-floor dimensions — for housing a modular air-handler could become a significant cost increment if these modular air-handlers are to be used on each floor of a 40 or 50-story highrise tower.

For *central* supply air-handlers — those employed to ventilate and condition either an entire building or 10 or 20 stories of a highrise tower — the height requirements of the mechanical (or fan) rooms will generally be anywhere from about 16 to perhaps 25 feet (4.9 to 7.6 m) (i.e., the clear dimension from the floor to the bottom of the structural grid above). This clear dimension will enable the placement of the air-handler as well as the ducting that runs from the air-handler out of the mechanical (or fan) room to the occupied spaces of the building. These height guidelines will also permit the return air fans to be placed in the mechanical (or fan) room.

One further qualification about sizing spaces for housing air-handlers — particularly for central air-handlers — is that if the mechanical (or fan) room containing an air-handler

SIDEBAR A.12 Fresh air intakes and security issues

Contemporary events involving the potential introduction of hazardous biological and/or chemical
agents into workplaces and other enclosed spaces
have raised concerns about the safety of building
environments. As many of the hazardous substances
can be transmitted by airborne means, particular
attention must now be directed at how ventilation systems are designed (i.e., to ensure occupant safety and
health). Two strategies for designing safe ventilation
systems seem most fundamental. First, fresh air
intakes must be placed so that no hazardous substances can be passed into the supply air system.

Thus, these intakes should be located in places
removed from public access (see Figure A.48). For
example, placing these intakes at roof locations facing away from building perimeters would be
warranted. Second, air-handling equipment in buildings — including the air-handlers and ducting,
especially — should be located in equipment rooms
(and enclosed volumes elsewhere in buildings) that
can be maintained with appropriate security devices.
Thus, opportunities should be strictly prohibited for
people other than systems-operating staff to gain
access to air-handling systems within buildings.

FRESH AIR INTAKE (VIA GRILLE)

Figure A.48 The fresh air intake grille for this building occurs along the walkway in the center of this photograph (i.e., at grade and along the concrete walk). The air-handler is located two stories below grade, but fresh
air for it is gathered through this at-grade grille and passed downward through a vertical chimney that connects
the grille and the air-handler. Placing the air intake grille at grade and exposed to passers-by compromises the
security of the building air-handling system.

is located below grade (in a basement or sub-basement), then some additional floor area must be set aside to enable bringing fresh air into the building. A rule-of-thumb suggested for accommodating the fresh air intake and a passageway into a mixing air plenum states that the floor area provided for the central supply air-handler should be increased by an additional 20 percent (i.e., that the floor area estimated for the supply air-handler alone be multiplied by a factor of 1.2).

Besides these space-sizing approximations some guidelines can be offered about where mechanical (or fan) rooms should be located. First, whereas a boiler (or heat exchanger) and/or a chiller can be located in an enclosed space outside of the building served by these heat and coolth sources, central or modular air-handlers essentially must be located within the building served by the air-handler(s). Second, a mechanical (or fan) room housing an air-handler should be placed along the perimeter of the building (rather than be an internal room): because fresh air must be supplied to the air-handler, passing the fresh air to an internalized room becomes appreciably more difficult. Third, as noted above, if the mechanical (or fan) room is located below grade, then the floor area required for the room will need to be increased, specifically to enable the intake of fresh air and its passage to the supply air-handler. And, fourth, because fresh air and used (and exhausted) air streams should not mix at their respective entry and exit points at the building perimeter, the fresh air intake location and the used (and exhausted) air outlets should be separated by a distance of at least 30 feet (9.2 m) when the intake and outlet locations occur on the same building elevation. A better planning strategy for locating intakes and outlets is to place them on opposite elevations. Or, instead, take the fresh air in at grade level and dump the used (and exhausted) air streams at the building roof. Or, even, take air in at the roof and expel the used (and exhausted) air streams at the grade level.

So far in this section the rules-of-thumb offered for sizing spaces to accommodate air-handlers apply preferentially for all-air systems. For air-water systems some of these guidelines require modification. Air-water systems operate by furnishing lesser quantities of supply air to occupied spaces (in comparison to the amount of air transported by all-air systems). The amounts for typical air-water systems will be less because the occupant densities in buildings ventilated by these systems are smaller. Further, because air-water systems include terminals that are placed in occupied spaces and these terminals are present specifically to finalize the thermal conditioning of the supply air, there is a reduced need for the central air supply to fully condition the occupied spaces. Thus, less air is needed to transport the necessary heat and/or coolth throughout the building. Consequently, the floor area and height needs for air-water equipment spaces are reduced. For instance, instead of providing floor area in a mechanical (or fan) room equivalent to 4 to 5 percent of the gross floor area served for the supply air-handler (that is recommended for all-air systems), the necessary floor area for an air-handler for an air-water system should likely be about 2 to 3 percent of gross floor area served.

Return air fans may or may not be included as components in air-water systems. If they are, then these fans will also have smaller capacities than those used for all-air systems. If return air fans are not employed at all (to transport used air), then no space accommodation will be necessary. Exhaust fans for removing toilet air, kitchen air, or other such facilities will be essential. But, because occupant densities in buildings serviced by air-water systems are generally small, fewer toilet rooms or other personal care facilities will likely be present in the buildings (and air-handling services necessary for these facilities are less developed). Thus, the floor areas devoted to housing the requisite air-handling equipment for air-water systems will be smaller.

A.4.1.3   Spatial guidelines for vertical accessways   When central supply air-handlers are used to ventilate and to condition a number of floors in a building — as opposed to modular air-handlers that serve single floors — there will be a need to run ducting vertically from the floor on which the central air-handler is placed to other floors with occupied rooms. For reasons of fire protection and appearance, vertical ducting is most often enclosed in shafts. The vertical ducting in the shafts may consist of parallel supply air and return air ducts. Or the shaft may simply have supply air ducting, and the shaft enclosure will serve as the return air passageway (i.e., there is no vertical return air ducting). Note that if an all-air system with dual-duct or multizone distribution is employed for a building, then more than one vertical supply air duct will generally be present in the vertical shaft(s). These shafts can also furnish pathways for running water piping vertically throughout a building (e.g., hot water for heating; chilled water for cooling; condenser water running from a chiller to a cooling tower and back again; and so forth). Additionally, electrical power conduit often will be run vertically in the shafts, as well as communication cable conduit, fire protection services, and even sometimes plumbing water supply and waste piping.

How many vertical shafts should be employed in a building is an issue subject to a number of qualifications. First, the number depends on the geometry of the building (e.g., how is the floor plan of the building organized, and how many floors will be served by a shaft?). The complexity and the size of the needed ducting are also important factors. And, third, how readily shafts can be integrated into the overall building organization can be a significant determinant.

In buildings with a nearly square floor plan and a limited number of stories a single shaft may be adequate. In many conventional highrise towers, with air-handlers serving many floors, a conventional solution is to use two shafts: the first provides air-handling for the perimeter zone of several floors, and the second offers air-handling for the interior zone of these floors. In the Gould Hall example presented in Section A.2, the designers chose to apply four shafts, each near the centroid of the northeast, northwest, southwest, and southeast quadrants of the building floor plan. General guidelines for determining a reasonable number and suitable locations for vertical shafts include the following recommendations. First, vertical air ducting, and thus the shafts enclosing them, should be organized to simplify the horizontal ducting needed to transport air to occupied spaces (and from the occupied spaces back to the shafts). Often, the shorter such horizontal ducting can be, the better functionally and cost-wise the solution will be. Second, multiple, smaller, localized shafts are almost always preferable to employing a single large central shaft. And, third, running smaller, modular vertical ducting and shafts can be made feasible and efficient by laying out large horizontal trunk ducts at the same story where the central air-handler occurs (i.e., by placing large trunk ducts at the story where the floor-to-floor dimension is already large so as to accommodate the spatial requirements of the air-handler, a number of small vertical ducts can be run from these trunk ducts near or directly to occupied spaces.

A rule-of-thumb for sizing the floor area required for passing shafts vertically through a building is that the *total* floor area for these shafts — whether single or multiple in number — should be 0.8 to 1.0 percent of the gross floor area served by the shafts. Thus, if four shafts are to be laid out on a quadrant basis, the floor area for each should be 0.8 to 1.0 percent of the floor area served by each shaft. This total area guideline will furnish adequate space for accommodating supply air ducting, the return air stream (whether in a separate duct or enclosed by the shaft walls), and the other service devices identified above (e.g., conditioning water, electrical, fire protection, and plumbing utilities). Two further guidelines for organizing the shafts are that their footprints should be rectangular (instead of square) with length-to-width ratios of from 2:1 to, perhaps, 4:1 and that any horizontal ducting running from each shaft should emanate from either of any two adjacent sides of a shaft (i.e., for this latter guideline the two sides should be free of having the other utility pipes and conduits run along these sides of the shaft).

A.4.1.4 Spatial guidelines for ceiling plenums

Ceiling plenums are generally the volumes above finished ceilings and beneath the structural members and flooring (or roofing) above. The plenums house the various environmental control systems that are needed to make occupied spaces suitably habitable. In situations where finished ceilings are not used, systems equipment will still likely be present and adequate space for housing the equipment will still be required.

SIDEBAR A.13 A procedure for estimating duct sizes

Being able to predict the likely size of ducting can be useful when considering what depths are needed for ceiling plenum spaces. In addition to the guidelines offered in Section A.4.1.4, an alternative procedure is available.

The premise for any duct layout is that the ducting will supply air to (or return air from) some space. Thus, the first step in this size-estimating procedure requires determination of what the floor area of that space is (i.e., whether the duct serves a room, a series of rooms, a whole floor of a building, or several floors of a building). Note that this area is essentially the tributary area: the area that is downstream from the duct at some specific point along the duct run.

Once the floor area can be determined—by doing areal take-offs from schematic drawings—then the area can be multiplied by a factor found in Table A.4. These factors—rendered in units of cubic feet per minute/square foot (liters per second/square meter)—are *first-approximation* estimates of likely supply air requirements for various building applications. Multiplying the tributary floor area by the appropriate factor furnishes the volumetric flow rate—in CFM (or L/s)—that will pass through the duct at the specific point along the duct run. Then, the volumetric flow rate

can be divided by the recommended (or maximum) air velocity (in ft/min or m/s)—presented in Table A.5—to arrive at the cross-sectional area (ft^2 or m^2) required for the duct to transport the volumetric flow rate. To convert the cross-sectional area to square inches (from ft^2), multiply it by 144 in^2/ft^2).

Lastly, the likely dimensions for the duct at the specific point along the duct run for which this determination was undertaken can be found by utilizing any one of the three following procedures. First, take the square root of the duct cross-sectional area (to estimate the dimensions for a square duct). Second, divide the cross-sectional area by some number to elicit the potential dimensions for a rectangular duct. Or, third, divide the cross-sectional area by P, take the square root of the dividend, and multiply the root by 2 to arrive at the diameter for a round duct.

Two qualifications apply to this procedure. First, if a rectangular duct cross-section is to be sought, the aspect ratio—the ratio of the height to the width—should be no smaller than 1:4 (i.e., 1:2 or 1:3 are suitable; 1:5 is not). Second, if the duct is to be insulated for reasons of sound absorption or to minimize heat loss, then the thickness of the insulation will need to be added to the internal dimensions.

TABLE A.4
FIRST-APPROXIMATIONS FOR ESTIMATING COOLING LOAD & VENTILATION NEEDS

	COOLING LOAD REQUIREMENTS (in sq ft/ton or in m²/kW)	GENERALIZED VENTILATION REQUIREMENTS in CFM/sq ft or in (L/s/m²)
RESIDENTIAL		
Single-family	500 (163)	1.3 (6.6)
Apartment	400 (131)	1.3 (6.6)
Dormitory rooms	300 (98)	1.4 (7.1)
HOTELS & MOTELS		
Guest rooms	300 (98)	1.4 (7.1)
Common spaces	150 (49)	1.3 (6.6)
RETAIL COMMERCIAL		
Stores	200 (65)	1.8 (9.1)
Restaurants	120 (39)	2.0 (10.2)
Department stores	275 (90)	1.2 (6.1)
Shopping malls	230 (75)	2.0 (10.2)
GATHERING PLACES		
Churches	250 (82)	2.5 (12.7)
Theaters	250 (82)	2.5 (12.7)
Auditoriums	50 (82)	2.5 (12.7)
Libraries	280 (91)	1.6 (8.1)
Museums	280 (91)	1.6 (8.1)
Recreational	180 (59)	2.0 (10.2)
EDUCATIONAL BUILDINGS	180 (59)	2.0 (10.2)
OFFICE BUILDINGS	280 (91)	1.2 (6.1)
MEDICAL FACILITIES		
Medical / dental clinics	250 (82)	1.2 (6.1)
Hospitals	220 (72)	0.6 (3.0)
LABORATORIES	200 (65)	2.0 (10.2)

This table has been reproduced from *The ABC's of Air-Conditioning,* (Syracuse, New York: Carrier Corporation, 1975), pages 18–19. Permission to reproduce this table has been granted by the Carrier Corporation. Courtesy of Carrier Corporation.

TABLE A.5
RECOMMEND & MAXIMUM VELOCITIES FOR AIR MOVEMENT IN DUCTS

RECOMMENDED VELOCITIES IN FT/MIN (M/S)

	RESIDENCIES	SCHOOLS, THEATRES PUBLIC BUILDINGS	INDUSTRIAL BUILDINGS	
Outdoor air intakes	500 (2.5)	500 (2.5)	500 (2.5)	
Main (trunk) ducts	700–900 (3.6–4.6)	1000–1300 (5.1–6.6)	1200–1800 (6.7–9.1)	
Branch (horizontal) ducts	600 (3.0)	600–900 (3.0–4.6)	800–1000 (4.1–5.1)	
Branch (vertical) risers	500 (2.5)	600–700 (3.0–3.6)	800 (4.1)	

MAXIMUM VELOCITIES IN FT/MIN (M/S)

	RESIDENCIES	SCHOOLS, THEATRES PUBLIC BUILDINGS	INDUSTRIAL BUILDINGS	
Outdoor air intakes	800 (4.1)	90 (4.6)	1200 (6.1)	
Main (trunk) ducts	800–1200 (4.1–6.1)	1100–1600 (5.6–8.1)	1300–2200 (6.6–11.2)	
Branch (horizontal) ducts	700–1000 (3.6–5.1)	800–1300 (4.1–6.6)	1000–1800 (5.1–9.1)	
Branch (vertical) risers	650–800 (3.3–4.1)	800–1200 (4.1–6.1)	1000–1600 (5.1–8.1)	

This table has been reproduced from the *1972 ASHRAE Handbook of Fundamentals,* (Atlanta: American Society of Heating, Refrigerating, and Air-Conditioning Engineers, Inc., 1972), page 481. Permission to reproduce this table has been granted by the Society (© American Society of Heating, Refrigerating, and Air-Conditioning Engineers, Inc., www.ashrae.org).

An initial distinction about ceiling plenums concerns whether the plenum is located inside an enclosed, occupied room or in some more central communal space such as a corridor or waiting area. The reason for addressing this distinction is that acceptable ceiling heights are often different in alternative locations. For occupied rooms ceiling heights in nonresidential buildings are expected to be at least 8'-6" or 9'-0" (2.6 or 2.7 m), whereas ceiling heights in communal spaces can be somewhat lower. The vertical dimension for ceiling plenums can be as little as perhaps 2'-0" to as great as 10'-0" (0.6 to 3.1 m) (or, rarely, even greater).

Necessarily, the allowable height between the finished ceiling and the structural grid and floor (or roof) above will dictate how the ceiling plenum can be utilized (or, instead, how the ceiling plenum space must be designed). A fundamental question for architects during building design is establishing what is an acceptable floor-to-floor height. The height must be great enough to provide ergonomically satisfactory space for occupancy and to enable effective placement of the various environmental control systems that are commonly located therein. But making the floor-to-floor dimension too great can add a construction cost increment for the building (i.e., especially if the building is a high-rise for which the added excessive height increment will be multiplied by 40 or 50 stories).

In terms of HVAC systems the ceiling plenum provides an enclosure for running horizontal supply air ducting from vertical shafts to occupied spaces. In-the-ceiling terminals are also placed in ceiling plenums. The supply air will then enter the occupied space passing through diffusers that are connected to the terminals. Return (used) air will be gathered through ceiling grilles. The return air may be collected into return air ducting that will run to the vertical shafts. Or the ceiling plenum will serve as the enclosure for transporting the return air to horizontal ducting located outside of the occupied room, where the ducting will pick up the return air and transport it to a vertical shaft.

In addition to the supply and return air stream hardware, the ceiling plenum will commonly house conditioning water pipes, electrical power and communication lines (as well as the inevitable lighting fixtures), fire protection facilities, and water supply and waste piping. Most often these various equipment systems will be organized in discrete layers within the ceiling plenum volume. One analogy for describing this organization is that it resembles a bacon, lettuce, and tomato sandwich (i.e., the plenum volume can be viewed essentially as a "ceiling sandwich").

A rough rule-of-thumb for estimating the probable vertical depth of ceiling plenums suggests that the ceiling plenum will be approximately 25 percent of the floor-to-floor dimension. Thus, for a floor-to-floor dimension of 12'-6" to 13'-0" (3.8 to 4.0 m) (which is quite common for contemporary buildings), the depth of the volume from the bottom of the finished ceiling to the top of the finished flooring above will be about 3'-0" to 3'-6" (0.9 to 1.1 m). The layering dimensions for the principal hardware components are, generally, about 14" to 20" (0.36 to 0.50 m) for horizontal branch ducting and conditioning and/or distribution terminals, about 10" to 12" (0.25 to 0.30 m) for electrical power distribution and lighting fixtures, and about 8" (0.20 m) for potable and waste water piping. The fire protection facilities — most often, sprinkler piping — can be placed in the same layer as the potable and waste water piping.

The common estimate for the depth of ceiling plenums — about 3'-0" to 3'-6" (0.9 to 1.1 m) — will be useful for many building types (e.g., educational, office, retail commercial, libraries, museums, and so forth). However, certain building applications can have ceiling plenum depth requirements that are substantially greater (e.g., selected laboratories, hospitals, and manufacturing plants). Ceiling plenum depths for some of these building applications can range from 4'-0" to as much as 12'-0" (1.2 to 3.7 m). Not all of these building types will require such substantial depths, but a few can.

A.4.1.5 Spatial guidelines for in-the-room equipment For all-air systems the only equipment in occupied rooms is usually a controlling device such as a thermostat and/or a humidistat. Supply air diffusers and return air grilles will be installed in room envelopes — most often, in the finished ceiling — but these entry and exit components are not specifically in rooms. Designating locations for thermostats and/or humidistats is normally an issue that is best confronted later in the design process (i.e., after schematic designing). As these devices are wall-mounted and require little space, establishing a mounting location usually only involves seeking a place where good and true sensing can be achieved.

For air-water systems, however, induction and fan-coil terminals will need placement in occupied rooms. Both of these terminal devices are commercially available in a variety of forms and can be installed in a variety of room locations. Both terminal types can be installed as vertical units or as horizontal units. They can be free-standing, or they can be furred into the walls or ceiling of a room. Because induction terminals require attachment to supply air ducts, the induction terminal will need to be integrated with the planned supply duct run for the room. Fan-coil terminals can be attached to supply air ducting, or they can function as stand-alone units. If the fan-coil unit requires attachment to supply air ducting, then establishing a location for the fan-coil terminal will depend on where the duct run can be placed. Otherwise, a fan-coil terminal can be placed on a wall that is adjacent or opposite to the incoming supply air stream, or a terminal can be mounted on or in the ceiling. Also possible is the situation where a fan-coil terminal is specifically placed on a perimeter wall — usually, under a window — to enable warming of the glazing surface during winter times (thus, to minimize radiational discomfort).

Induction units can be placed against a wall or furred into a wall. Or they can be attached to a ceiling or furred into the ceiling. The approximate dimensions of common vertical induction units are about 3' wide × 1.5' high × 1' deep (toward or into a wall) (0.9 m × 0.5 m × 0.3 m). Ceiling-mounted induction terminals will have similar sizes. The supply air capacities for common commercial induction terminals are about 150 CFM (71 L/s). Thus, the number of induction units required for the room can be determined by dividing the volumetric air flow rate needed for the room by the capacity of the induction terminal (likely, 150 CFM [71 L/s]).

Vertical fan-coil units for use in air-water systems are available in low-rise cabinet forms or in taller, narrow stack forms. The low-rise cabinet terminals will range in size with the largest units having dimensions of about 8' wide × 2.5' high × 1' deep (2.4 m × 0.8 m × 0.3 m). Smaller-capacity low-rise terminals will have similar heights and depths and be less wide (perhaps, about 3.5' [1.1 m]). The stack units will have dimensions of about 2' wide × 8' high × 2.5' deep (0.6 m × 2.4 m × 0.8 m). Horizontal fan-coil units have dimensions of about 6' wide × 1' high × 2.5' deep (1.8 m × 0.3 m × 0.8 m). As with the induction terminals, these fan-coil units can be placed against a wall or ceiling or furred into a wall or ceiling. The per-unit capacities of these terminals range from about 200 to 1200 CFM (94 to 566 L/s). Thus, the number of fan-coil terminals required to ventilate and condition a room can be found by dividing the volumetric air flow requirements for the room by a per-unit capacity (in CFM [L/s]).

To estimate the volumetric airflow rate required to ventilate and condition a building space, an approximate procedure involves arriving at an areal take-off for the space and multiplying that area by a factor from Table A.4. These factors in the table—with units of CFM/sq ft (or L/s/m²)—are listed in terms of building application types. If an application being planned for does not appear in this table, we suggest comparing the following parameters—occupant density, likely electrical power requirements, solar heat gain potential, and need for fresh air—for the unlisted application against those parameters for listed applications and seeking an approximate match. Then, the CFM/sq ft (L/s/m²) factor for the listed application can be used for the unlisted application.

A.4.1.6 Spatial guidelines for rooftop (or immediately adjacent external) equipment for all-air and air-water systems

Cooling towers or condensers can be located either on rooftops or in exterior areas immediately adjacent to buildings served by the units. These cooling towers (see Figure A.49) or condensers (see Figures A.29 and A.30) are essential components of the hardware assembly required to produce chilled water (i.e., they enable the exchange of heat generated by the chilling process with the atmosphere). These units create a localized warm, humid air in their immediate vicinity, can be noisy, and are not especially attractive. Therefore, their placement away from areas frequented by building occupants is warranted (i.e., on rooftops or at grade level at backs of buildings or in parking areas or in fenced-in yards). To estimate the footprint required for placing one of these units, determine the gross floor area served by the unit and multiply that area by 0.25 percent.

The other potential systems hardware that is often placed on building rooftops includes large packaged air-handling units (i.e., to provide ventilation and thermal conditioning for the buildings). These rooftop packaged air-handling units offer an alternative

Figure A.49 Here are top and side views of the cooling tower that provides the waste heat exchange for the two centrifugal chillers shown in Figure A.32. This cooling tower transfers waste heat generated by the chillers to the atmosphere external to the building.

to the use of in-the-building air-handlers. The packaged units also provide reliable thermal conditioning of the supply air. These conventional rooftop air-handling units will generally be composed of supply air and return air fans, a mixing plenum, supply air stream filters, heat and coolth production, coils for heating or cooling the supply air stream, and, possibly, humidity modification capability. All of these devices will be packaged in a single unit that can be lifted into place and connected to already-installed ducting runs. To estimate the footprint area required for placing one of these rooftop air-handlers, a very rough rule-of-thumb suggests determining the gross floor area that will be served by this rooftop unit and multiplying by 7.5 percent. Note that this estimate is comparable to the rules-of-thumb suggested in Section A.4.1.2.

A.4.2   SPACE-SIZING GUIDELINES FOR ALL-WATER SYSTEMS

Three sets of components are usually present in all-water systems. First, there will be hot and/or cold water producers (e.g., a boiler or steam-to-water heat exchanger and/or a chiller). Second, pumps, storage tanks, and piping will be utilized for transporting the conditioning water to the occupied spaces. And, third, some heat exchange device will be located in the occupied space. The common heat exchange devices will either be fan-coil terminals, convectors or radiators, or baseboard strip assemblies. The hot and cold water producers can be identical in nature to those used for all-air and air-water systems (except that the capacities for these producers will likely be smaller because of the usually smaller sizes of buildings conditioned by all-water systems). Thus, the rules-of-thumb for sizing spaces to accommodate boilers or heat exchangers and chillers, that were suggested in Section A.4.1.1, still apply. If a boiler or steam-to-water heat exchanger and a chiller will both be employed in an all-water building, then set aside a floor area for these two devices equal to about 2 percent of the gross floor area served by these two units. Instead, if only one of these units is used (e.g., a boiler is provided to supply hot water, but no chiller is furnished), then include a floor area for the unit equal to 1 percent of the gross floor area served by the unit. Also, if two (or more) small modular, cascading boilers are applied (rather than using a single large boiler), the floor area requirement for the two (or more) boilers will be quite similar to that needed for housing the one large boiler.

Generally, no substantial space planning will be needed to run water piping throughout these all-water buildings. The pipes will rarely be more than 1 to 3 in (25 to 75 mm) in diameter and can be built into wall, floor, or ceiling assemblies.

Space accommodations for placing fan-coil terminals (and convectors or radiators) in occupied rooms will be similar in nature and size to those offered for air-water systems for which fan-coil terminals are employed. Fresh air supplies for buildings conditioned by all-water systems must be admitted from the building exteriors. Therefore, when fan-coil terminals are used, they must be placed at perimeter walls, either vertically or horizontally (with wall cavities provided to bring in fresh air). Or fan-coil terminals can be mounted in the ceiling or on the ceiling—away from the perimeter—but with a small duct built into the ceiling to transport fresh air from the building perimeter to the terminal. The fan-coil terminal sizes for all-water systems are identical to those cataloged in Section A.4.1.5 for air-water systems (i.e., with the largest vertical low-rise units having dimensions of about 8' wide × 2.5' high × 1' deep (2.4 m × 0.8 m × 0.3 m) and the largest horizontal units being about 6' wide × 1' high × 2.5' deep (1.8 m × 0.3 m × 0.8 m). Note also that vertical fan-coil terminals can be placed next to a wall or furred into the wall.

Determining the number of fan-coil terminals that will be required to ventilate and condition a space can be established by dividing the volumetric air flow requirement for the room by the per-unit air flow capacity. Typically, the per-unit capacities of these fan-coil terminals range from about 200 to 1200 CFM (94 to 566 L/s). Estimating the volumetric air flow requirement for a building space can be found by performing an areal take-off for the space and multiplying that floor area by a factor—suitable for the specific building application—found in Table A.4.

When convectors, radiators, or baseboard strip assemblies are used in all-water systems, no direct means for ventilating occupied spaces will be furnished. Then, fresh air must be introduced using operable windows or doors. Or the building occupant must count on the admission of fresh air by infiltration.

A.4.3   SPACE-SIZING GUIDELINES FOR DIRECT-REFRIGERANT SYSTEMS

The group of direct-refrigerant systems presents a complex array of alternative sizes, capacities, operation strategies, and placement options. This group includes units as small as window air-conditioners and unitary through-the-wall heat pumps and as large as commercial rooftop (or so-called penthouse) whole-building units. Most often, the direct-refrigerant systems exist as single comprehensive units or as two-part split-system assemblies. In the following discussion we will discuss three alternative configurations and offer planning information for each: small-capacity single units and split-system assemblies; medium-to-large-capacity single units; and medium-to-large-capacity split-system assemblies. The large-capacity rooftop whole-building units have been discussed in Section A.4.1.6.

A.4.3.1   Small-capacity single units and split-system assemblies   These devices are commonly employed in residential and small commercial applications (e.g., small retail stores, single-office buildings, or for individual offices that are grouped in a larger building). The smallest devices in terms of floor area are window air-conditioners and floor-mounted through-the-wall units. Each such unit commonly operates to condition and ventilate a single room. Some of these units will only provide cooling, whereas others will furnish both heating and cooling. The basic parts inside these units consist of a compressor and condenser, a fan, a conditioning coil, an air intake (drawing air in from the building exterior), an air filter, and an output (for discharging air into the room). The cooling capacities of these units are usually about 0.5 to 2.5 tons (1.8 to 8.8 kW) for the window air-conditioners and 1 to 5 tons (3.5 to 17.6 kW) for the through-the-wall units. The sizes of the window air-conditioners are about 3' wide × 2' high × 1' deep (0.9 m × 0.6 m × 0.3 m). The sizes of the through-the-wall units are about 3' wide × 3' high × 2' deep (0.9 m × 0.9 m × 0.6 m).

The other configuration of these small-capacity systems involves inside and outside sections. The outside section will at least house a condenser, although in many outside sections a compressor and a condenser will both be present. The inside section will include a fan (for propelling supply air through ducting or, more simply, into the occupied space in which the inside unit resides) and a conditioning coil (which will temper the supply air). The inside section may include a compressor (or the compressor may be placed in some other inside space within the building, but remote from the fan-coil unit). The supply air fan will draw fresh air into the inside section using ducting connected between the building envelope and this inside unit. Used air will be expelled via exfiltration through the envelope, or it may be gathered with return air ducting and dumped to the exterior.

Whenever possible it is preferable to place these inside sections — whether fan-coil devices or fan-coils with a separate compressor — away from occupied spaces. Similarly, the outside sections — whether compressor-condenser combinations or simply a condenser — should be placed away from windows (particularly, operable windows). A common problem for all of these single-assembly or split-assembly units is that they are quite noisy (and thus can be bothersome for building occupants). The conditioning capacities for split-assembly units typically range between 1 to 5 tons (3.5 to 17.6 kW). The largest common inside section will have the dimensions of about 5' high × 2' wide × 2' deep (1.5 m × 0.6 m × 0.6 m). Outside sections usually have the approximate dimensions of 3' × 3' × 3' (0.9 m × 0.9 m × 0.9 m).

A.4.3.2 Medium-to-large-capacity single packaged units

These units typically provide conditioning capacities of between 5 to 60 tons (17.6 to 210 kW) with ventilation supply air capabilities as great as about 25,000 CFM (11,800 L/s). Single packaged units will consist of compressors, condensers, conditioning coils, and fans, all assembled in a unitary container. These units are basically indoor devices and are most often configured in vertical positions.

The vertical units can be installed with any of several organizations. First, a unit can be placed with its back to a wall to enable the exchange of air for condenser cooling (with fresh air for ventilation supplied by an alternative pathway, such as by ducting between the unit and the envelope at a different location). Second, a unit can be placed in the midst of a building with ducts provided to bring in fresh air and to carry air in and out of the building for heat exchanging for the condenser. Or, third, a vertical unit can be divided into condenser and compressor-fan coil subcomponents: in these formats the condenser subcomponent can be placed against a wall (or even on a roof above the occupied space), and the compressor-fan coil subcomponent can be located anywhere in the occupied space. In this third format, air for conditioning the occupied space is discharged from the compressor-fan coil subcomponent directly into the space. Fresh air is taken in elsewhere and ducted to the compressor-fan coil subcomponent. And the condenser and compressor-fan coil subcomponents are connected by a series of small pipe runs (for transporting the refrigerant fluid). The dimensions for the largest unitary assemblies — the first and second options above — are approximately 7' to 8' long × 2' to 2.5' deep × 7' to 8' high (2.1 to 2.4 m × 0.6 to 0.8 m × 2.1 to 2.4 m). If a discharge plenum is placed on the top of the unit (for connecting to supply air ducting, the height dimension for the assembly will be about 1.5 to 2' (0.45 to 0.6 m) taller.

Smaller horizontal units are available, although their conditioning capacities will be in the range of 1 to 5 tons (3.5 to 17.6 kW) and their supply air capabilities usually are no larger than 2000 CFM (940 L/s). These horizontal units most often are hung from structural floor (or roof) members (e.g., installed above a finished ceiling). Ducting is used to bring fresh air to the unit and to discharge supply air into the occupied space (through ceiling-installed diffusers). The common dimensions for these units are about 6' long × 4' wide × 2' high (1.8 m × 1.2 m × 0.6 m).

A.4.3.3 Medium-to-large-capacity split-system assemblies

These split-system assemblies offer magnitudes of conditioning capacities and volumetric air flow capabilities similar to those afforded by central boilers, chillers, and air-handlers. Conditioning capacities ranging from 10 to 200 tons (35 to 700 kW) are readily available, as are volumetric airflow rates of between 1,000 to 50,000 CFM (470 to 23,600 L/s). These magnitudes are commonly achieved with two sections, a compressor-condenser unit and a fan-coil or central air-handling unit. The compressor-condenser units will most often be placed on building rooftops, although they can be located at grade level in the backs of buildings, in parking areas, or in fenced-in enclosures at short distances from the buildings. Alternatively, some compressor-condenser units will be set up inside buildings and will operate in conjunction with a rooftop or grade-level cooling tower. The fan-coil or central air-handling unit will be located within a building and placed to accommodate ducting system runs.

The more common assembly type among these split-system packages involves a rooftop condenser-compressor unit paired with an inside-the-building fan-coil unit. These two units are connected with piping through which a refrigerant fluid is propelled. One variation of this basic split-system package uses a rooftop condenser with the compressor(s) located remotely inside the building. The conditioning capacities of these packages are usually about 10 to 50 tons (35 to 176 kW) with volumetric airflow rates of between 2000 to 6000 CFM (940 to 2830 L/s). The range of approximate sizes of the common rooftop units is 6' to 13' long × 4' to 7' wide × 3' to 3' high (1.8 to 4.0 m × 1.2 to 2.1 m × 0.9 to 2.1 m). The dimensions for the fan-coil units range from about 4' to 8' long × 2' to 3' wide × 6' to 8' high (1.2 to 2.4 m × 0.6 to 0.9 m × 1.8 to 2.4 m).

The other large-capacity split-system packages usually involve a condenser-compressor unit and a central air-handling unit. The conditioning capacities of these packages range from about 10 to 200 tons (35 to 700 kW), and the volumetric airflow rates can be as great as about 50,000 CFM (23,600 L/s). The compressor-condenser unit may be placed externally, either on a rooftop or at grade level, or this unit can be installed within a building and connect to a cooling tower. The central air-handling unit will be located to conform with duct run requirements (i.e., at the terminus of the duct run). The approximate dimensions for the largest external condenser-compressor units are about 20' long × 8' wide × 8' high (6.1 m × 2.4 m × 2.4 m). Dimensions for large internal condenser-compressor units are about 12' long × 3' wide × 6' high (3.7 m × 0.9 m × 1.8 m). Central air-handling units for these split-system packages range in size from 3' to 8' wide × 3' to 8' high × 11' to 15' long (0.9 to 2.4 m × 0.9 to 2.4 m × 3.4 to 4.6 m).

ENDNOTES and SELECTED ADDITIONAL COMMENTS

1. The design team for Gould Hall consisted of Daniel Streissguth and Gene Zema, principal architects, with Dale Benedict, Grant Hildebrand, and Claus Seligmann, associated architects; Robert Albrecht and Einar Svensson, structural engineers; Miskimen/Associates, mechanical engineers; Beverly A. Travis and Associates, electrical engineers; Robin M. Towne and Associates, acoustical consultants; and Talley and Associates, landscape architects.

2. The chilled water coil in the Gould Hall system is never used, following a University of Washington directive. The centralized capacity for producing chilled water is limited and does not have enough potential to furnish all of the university buildings with chilled water. Instead, only those buildings with "critical" cooling needs are permitted to use the chilled water (e.g., spaces involved in human patient care, laboratories in which animals are present, laboratories in which special research equipment exist, and so forth). The mild climate that Seattle offers generally enables and supports this practice (i.e., in contrast to buildings located in regions experiencing warmer climates).

3. One qualification that many building codes establish is that at least 20 percent of the air supplied throughout a building must be fresh air taken in from the outside. Thus, no more than 80 percent of the air supplied around a building can come from the "used" return air.

CHAPTER B

Small-Building HVAC Systems and Related Issues

Section B.1 | DIFFERENTIATING HVAC SERVICES BETWEEN LARGE- AND SMALL-SCALE BUILDINGS

IN CHAPTER A.1 the presentation focused on describing heating, ventilating, and air-conditioning (HVAC) systems used in larger buildings. Here, discussion will be offered for developing HVAC systems for smaller buildings (e.g., single and multiple-family housing, small-scale retail commercial establishments, neighborhood restaurants and taverns, community libraries, and so forth). In most of these building types the numbers of occupants are usually relatively small. Further, the ratios of building area to occupant numbers—expressed in terms of floor area per occupant—will generally be greater than that commonly experienced in larger buildings. The incidence and complexity of other service systems—for example, electrical power systems, communication network systems, plumbing systems, and the like—in these building types will often be less developed. Also, in these smaller buildings there will typically be little use of process equipment (i.e., special devices essential to the performance of tasks associated with the building purpose).

For many of these smaller-scale, less complicated buildings, the thermal conditioning requirements can most often be characterized as *envelope-load-dependent,* rather than as internal-load-dominant. One factor leading to this characteristic thermal behavior is that ratios of envelope-surface-area-to-volume will be greater than are typically found with larger buildings. A second factor is that ratios of usable floor areas to envelope-surface-areas will be smaller for these small-scale buildings. And a third factor is that the number of occupants and the presence of electrically powered devices — lighting systems, process equipment, office hardware, and so forth — will usually be less than those in larger buildings. Thus, there will be fewer heat gain sources in these small-scale buildings, and the sources that are present will commonly generate less intense heat gain rates.

For HVAC systems for these smaller-scaled buildings, the most important systems capability will be insuring that occupants will be thermally comfortable. Furnishing ventilation — for the preparation and distribution of fresh air — for these small-scale buildings will often have a lesser importance. Indeed, for some of these building types, mechanical ventilation may not even be furnished. Whether or not mechanical ventilation is supplied will depend on what is considered good design (and operations practice) and what is required by applicable building regulations.

In the following sections of this chapter we will describe how HVAC systems can be designed for these small-scale buildings. We will also discuss issues that may determine whether or not to incorporate mechanical ventilation in these buildings (e.g., as means of insuring good indoor air quality).

Section B.2 | ALTERNATIVE HVAC SYSTEMS FOR SMALL-SCALE BUILDINGS

B.2.1   ESTABLISHING WHICH HVAC SERVICES SHOULD BE PROVIDED

The fundamental issue in creating an HVAC system for any small-scale building concerns establishing how comprehensively services should be provided for the building. Thus, whether heating, cooling, ventilation, and humidity control are all required for each building or whether some smaller sub-set of these services should be rendered is a basic question that requires answering during system creation (and for the design of building spaces). A number of factors such as client wishes, building regulations, climatic influences, standards of good practice, and/or cost limitations can determine what capabilities an HVAC system should offer. Building designers and construction professionals can also impose specific expectations for the functioning of HVAC systems.

An example of how one of these factors can dictate what capabilities an HVAC system should provide arises from the differing effects of climate. In a large office building, school, or department store, there will likely be numbers of internal-load-dominant spaces. Regardless of whether such a building is located in hot, dry or cold climate — Phoenix or Calgary — air cooling and humidity control services will be required for large buildings. But single-family residences or small-scale retail commercial buildings created for these alternative climates would likely have substantially different HVAC system requirements. Certainly, building regulations and standards of good design and operations for these two locales will be similar for larger buildings and quite different for smaller-scale buildings. Thus, HVAC systems created for buildings in these locales would have to address the different circumstances presented.

Because the definition of which capabilities an HVAC system should display for small-scale buildings is less precise than for larger buildings, there is generally a greater range of system alternatives available for use in these smaller buildings. For larger buildings there is a greater tendency in building design and operation to rely strictly on mechanically driven thermal conditioning and ventilation systems. For smaller-scale buildings passive responses for thermal conditioning and ventilation can more likely be successfully incorporated into building operation. Thus, when natural ventilation or passive heating or cooling strategies can be applied to satisfy conditioning and/or ventilation requirements, then the dependence on active control systems can be lessened.

Another issue that affects HVAC system creation, particularly for small-scale buildings, is whether energy conservation guidelines for building design and operations are mandated by regulatory agencies. In locales or regions where such energy conservation regulations exist, then the permissible capacity and operational protocols for HVAC systems will be dictated. Further, these regulations will usually be more strictly defined for smaller-scale buildings than for larger buildings.

A fourth qualification concerning HVAC system selection and design arises from the availability and/or practicality of energy sources. Climate will have a marked influence on how well solar heating or cooling will function. The performance and utility of passive conditioning or ventilating devices will also be dictated by climate and other localized features (e.g., topography, vegetation, the presence of nearby built forms, and so forth). Additionally, whether conventional fuels (gases, oil, or coal), various biomass products, or other alternative (renewable) energy sources are readily and relatively cheaply available in a locale can influence the designing and selection of HVAC systems.

B.2.2   PRIMARY TYPES OF HVAC SYSTEMS FOR SMALL-SCALE BUILDINGS

B.2.2.1   Differentiating between air- and water-based systems   A catalog of common small-scale heating, ventilating, and air-conditioning system alternatives is presented in Table B.1. There are two main alternatives here — those systems that employ air to distribute heat (and coolth) throughout a building and those that employ water to distribute heat and coolth. Both sets of alternatives are widely used, and both have well-established histories of application. Because each operates using the same energy sources as the other, the ability to use one or the other of these sets is comparable. Further, each set demonstrates good thermal conditioning performances, both in terms of providing satisfactory capacities and offering relatively precise controls.

The two principal points for differentiating between air and water distribution involve the means for providing ventilation and humidity control. An air distribution system involving a central source and ducting fundamentally furnishes means for transporting fresh air around the building. Outside air is drawn in to the central source — for example, a furnace — where the air can be filtered, adequately tempered, and even have its humidity altered. Then, the air can be sent out through a ducting network to remote areas of the building.

A system that transports water around a building does not necessarily offer a similar opportunity to provide controlled ventilation throughout the building. With most water-based temperature-conditioning systems, when ventilation is furnished, it will most often be provided locally on a room-by-room basis. The localized ventilation will involve drawing in air through the building envelope. The means for bringing in outside air can be any of several alternatives: a localized mechanical device such as a fan-coil terminal can draw in air, the air can come through an open window or door (by natural ventilation), or the air can pass inward by infiltration. Of these three means the fan-coil unit alone offers any particular ability to alter the properties of the incoming air (see Figure B.1). This air can

TABLE B.1
COMMON ALTERNATIVE (ACTIVE) SPACE-CONDITIONING SYSTEMS

ENERGY SOURCE	CENTRAL CONDITIONING DEVICE	DISTRIBUTION MEDIUM	DISTRIBUTION NETWORK	TERMINAL DEVICE	HVAC "PRODUCTS"
Oil, gases, electricity	Furnace	Air	Ducting	Diffusers	Heating, ventilation
Oil, gases, electricity with electricity for A/C coils	Furnace w/air-conditioning coils	Air	Ducting	Diffusers	Heating, ventilation, cooling & humidity control
Active solar energy collection	Heat exchanger (w/some second device as back-up)	Air	Ducting	Diffusers	Heating, ventilation
Electricity	Heat pump	Air	Ducting	Diffusers	Heating, ventilation, cooling & humidity control
Oil, gases, electricity	Hot water boiler	Water	Piping	Convectors	Heating
				Baseboard radiation	Heating
				Radiant panels	Heating
				Fan-coil units	Heating & ventilation
Electricity	(not applicable)	(not applicable)	Electrical circuitry	Baseboard radiation	Heating
Electricity, oil, gases, biomass	(not applicable)	(not applicable)	(not applicable)	Fireplaces, stoves, unit heaters	Heating

Adopted from the *1999 ASHRAE Handbook: Applications,* (Atlanta: American Society of Heating, Refrigerating, and Air-Conditioning Engineers, Inc., 1999), page 1.1, and has been reprinted with the permission of the Society (© American Society of Heating, Refrigerating, and Air-Conditioning Engineers, Inc., www.ashrae.org).

COIL

FAN

Figure B.1 The principal internal components of a fan-coil unit are shown here: the fan and the coil. Air enters from the bottom (or from the exterior through a vent in the wall) and exits the unit from the top. Placing the unit underneath a window provides heating for the potentially cold window surface (to offset radiational discomfort [see Figure 3.19 for a related situation.])

be passed through a filter (present in the fan-coil unit); it can be warmed or cooled as it passes over the coil; and, if cold water is passing through the coil, some dehumidification can be accomplished. Generally, though, the quality of air tempering, cleaning, and humidity controlling achieved with fan-coil units will be inferior to that afforded by a central air-handling system.

Relying on ventilation provided by natural means — whether by intentionally operating openings (e.g., doors and windows) in the building envelope or by anticipating the action of infiltration — offers even less satisfactory control of the entering air. Neither natural ventilation nor infiltration provides means for managing the rate with which air passes into the building interior. The quality of the incoming air cannot be deliberately altered (e.g., no filtration is possible, so entering air could be dirt-laden or containing allergenic substances). There is no opportunity to directly temper the entering air. And there is certainly no means for controlling the humidity of this air. Instead, the only means for improving the properties of outside air that passes naturally through the building envelope into the building will involve running inside air subsequently through a suitable mechanical device (within the building).

Humidity control — whether for the humidification or dehumidification of air — can be readily achieved with small-scale central air distribution systems. Various types of humidifiers are available and can be easily integrated with central air distribution systems that are used for heating small buildings.[1] The dehumidification of moving air can also be attained by the inclusion of dehumidifying coils in a central air distribution system. The dehumidification coils function as an "evaporator" in a conventional refrigeration cycle (see Figure A.27). Sensible heat and latent heat present in warm, moist air will transfer to the refrigerant at the evaporator, thus cooling and drying the air as it flows past the dehumidification coils.

Achieving humidity control when working with centrally distributed water systems is at best problematical. Humidification of individual spaces that are thermally conditioned with water systems must rely on portable or room humidifiers. Generally, application of these humidifiers will offer less satisfactory performances (than are available with central air distribution). These portable or room humidifiers usually have to be filled by hand, and more maintenance is commonly required (i.e., particularly for the cleaning of the humidifiers to resist mold growth).

The dehumidification of building spaces that are thermally conditioned with distributed water systems is even less promising. Whereas water vapor in moist air will condense on the surfaces of pipes that have cold fluids passing through them, getting room air to uniformly flow past such pipes is a challenging task (when employing in-the-room devices). As we noted above, the only in-the-room device that can readily cause room air to flow over a cold coil is a fan-coil unit. The principal limitation of fan-coil units, however, is that the units provide less good performances — for tempering, cleaning, and controlling the humidity of air — than do central air distribution systems.

One other important issue concerning the choice between air- and water-based conditioning systems involves the sizes of the various components used for each system type. Air-handling furnaces and water-handling boilers usually have similar dimensions (for equal capacities)(see Figure B.2). Ducting for air distribution, however, will be substantially larger than the piping required for running water. But water-handling systems will often require an expansion tank and one (or more) pump(s) for propelling the water around the building. Diffusers (for admitting air into a building space) and grilles (for enabling the passage of "used" air from the space into the return air ducting) are usually built into the floor, walls, or ceiling of a space. Thus, the inclusion of diffusers and grilles should make them easy to incorporate with other building features. But convectors, baseboard radiation,

Figure B.2 The relative sizes of a residential warm-air furnace (on the left) and a residential hot-water boiler are displayed here.

and in-the-room fan-coil units will all require space in occupied rooms (and will need to be integrated with how a room is to be laid out).

Locating the various components of these alternative systems will require attention. In a small-scale building warm-air furnaces and hot-water boilers can generally be placed anywhere that is convenient. Thus, these central conditioning devices can be located in a basement, attic, or utility room. Running piping from a hot-water boiler to a terminal device is usually straightforward and not difficult to accomplish, as the pipe diameters will be relatively small (perhaps 1–2" [25–50 mm] at maximum) and can be readily installed in wall, ceiling, or floor assemblies. The placing of hot-water terminal devices in occupied spaces also can be uncomplicated: these devices can usually be located where they will be most effective in meeting occupant needs (or wishes), and running piping to the devices through walls, floors, or ceilings should not require any special accommodations.

Laying out ducting, however, will often be more challenging because of the much larger ducting sizes. Like piping, ducting can also be incorporated in wall, ceiling, and floor assemblies. But the shapes and cross-sectional areas of the ducting must conform to the available openings in these assemblies (unless decisions are made to express the ducting as a visible element). Thus, to run ducting vertically in a wall assembly demands that the width and depth of the ducting match or be less than the cavity between the framing members and the sheathing covering these members. Alternatively, if the vertical ducting cannot be made to fit between the components of a conventional wall assembly, then the duct could be enclosed in an assembly separate from a wall, or the duct could be embedded partially in the stud space, and the portion of the duct extending out of the stud space could be covered by furring an assembly enclosure around the rest of the duct (see Figures B.3–B.5).

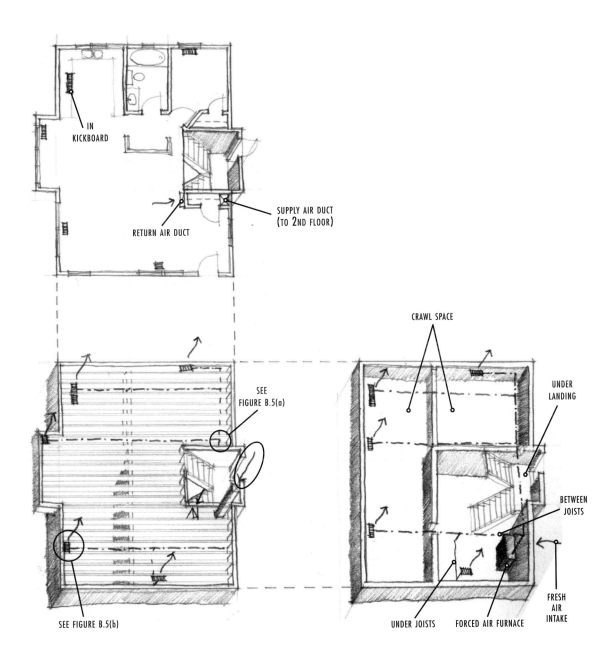

Figure B.3 The layout of a warm-air heating system is displayed here. The basic wood-framed structure for the second floor is demonstrated as well as the ducting runs for conveying air to the diffusers.

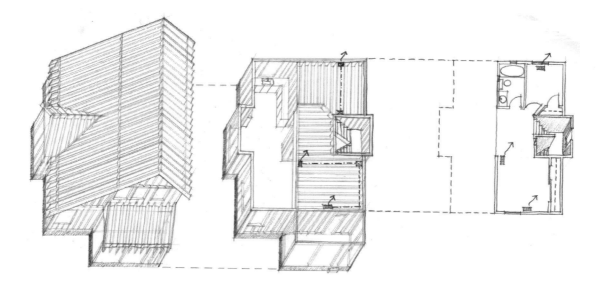

Figure B.4 A framing plan and duct run layouts are shown here for a house that is heated with a warm-air furnace system.

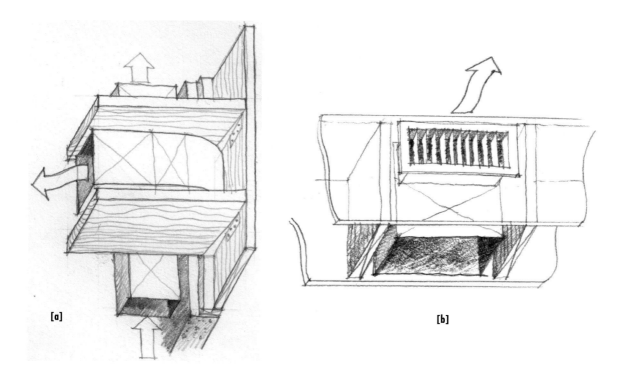

[a]   [b]

Figure B.5 These drawings show how ducting assemblies are integrated with the framing materials.

SIDEBAR B.1 Sizing vertical ducting embedded in walls

In the United States where common wood-frame wall assemblies are constructed with studding sized nominally as 2×4's and 2×6's (actually, 1 1/2" × 3 1/2" and 1 1/2" × 5 1/2" [or, 38 mm × 89 mm and 38 mm × 140 mm]) and placed at 16" (406 mm) on center, vertical ducts located in these wall assemblies can have cross-sectional dimensions of approximately 3 1/2" × 14 1/2" and 5 1/2" × 14 1/2" (89 mm × 369 mm and 140 mm × 369 mm).

Note that many municipal and state governments in the United States require that if the stud spaces in which vertical ducts pass are adjacent to unheated volumes (e.g., the stud space is part of a building envelope), then 1" (25.4 mm) of insulation must be placed between the duct and the wood member or panel adjacent to the unheated volume. Thus, the need to include insulation on one (or more) side(s) of the duct can significantly reduce the effective cross-sectional area of the ducting.

Horizontal ducting can be laid out under floor or ceiling (structural) assemblies, or the ducting can be run in between structural members (e.g., joists). Ducting can also be laid out in runs that cross over structural members and then are furred in with enclosures that are expressed outward from the principal finished surfaces in a space. Running ducting under floor or ceiling assemblies can produce either greater floor-to-floor dimensions or reduced headroom between the finished flooring and the duct bottoms (or finished ceiling assemblies hung beneath the ducting). Ducting may even be laid out above the structural flooring with a finished flooring assembly constructed above the ducting (i.e., as a *raised* flooring).

All of these planning alternatives indicate the range of strategies (and apparent complexities) for running ducting between a central conditioning device and a localized terminal device. Placing localized terminal devices (e.g., for air-handling systems, diffusers and grilles) can impose additional problems. In some instances there will be a limited number of paths for running ducting, and the placement of diffusers and grilles may have to be made to accommodate the duct run opportunities. In other instances, placing diffusers and grilles will be necessitated by performance requirements (e.g., for insuring occupant comfort) and duct runs will have to be established that get air to these diffusers and from the grilles. Please note that additional information about diffuser location (and operation) will be presented in Section B.3.4.1 below.

B.2.2.2 Alternative means for furnishing ventilation air to occupied spaces The traditional means for providing fresh air to occupied spaces—particularly in small-scale buildings—are warm-air furnaces and natural ventilation. Fan-driven warm-air furnaces have been used in buildings for somewhat longer than 100 years, whereas natural ventilation has been employed in human shelter since prehistory. Recently, some alternative air-handling devices have been introduced into small-scale building design and operation. Two of these innovations are the *air-to-air heat exchanger* and the whole-house fan.

The first of these devices—the air-to-air heat exchanger—has been incorporated into small-scale buildings as means for insuring that adequate indoor air quality can be attained. In the past decade or so, much attention by the building industry has been focused on maintaining good indoor air quality in buildings. Several reasons have led to this attention. First, buildings are being designed and constructed so that their envelopes are increasingly tighter, meaning that the rate of infiltration of fresh air through the envelopes is being reduced. Second, ever more synthetic materials are being used for finishes, furnishings, and internal building assemblies, resulting in ever-greater quantities of gaseous substances that leak out from these materials (and that can be discomforting and noxious and may even be toxic in large enough concentrations). Third, building occupants spend greater numbers of hours per day inside buildings than previous generations did. And, fourth, there is even some indication that the people today are more sensitive to airborne contaminants than their predecessors were.

The purpose of using a device such as an air-to-air heat exchanger is to increase the rate of fresh air entering buildings. The air-to-air heat exchanger is most often employed in buildings located in *cold* climates. In such climates any air infiltrating through the building envelope can lead to significant heat make-up requirements (to ensure continued occupant thermal comfort). Thus, buildings located in these climates are conventionally constructed to have very tight envelopes (i.e., so that infiltration rates will be very low). To provide for the admission of some fresh air, air-to-air heat exchangers are increasingly employed.

An air-to-air heat exchanger is a mechanical device that has two parallel, but separate, air streams, the first for drawing air into a building and the second for exhausting air out of the building (see Figure 5.51). The two streams pass in close proximity to each other (although there is no mixing of the streams). With the passage of the two streams over and around each other, the heat embedded in the exiting air is transferred to the incoming air, thus warming the entering cold air. Air-to-air heat exchangers can demonstrate efficiencies as great as about 85 percent (i.e., 85 percent of the heat carried by the exiting stream is transferred to the incoming stream). The volumetric flow rates of incoming air achieved with these air-to-air heat exchangers can be as great as about 0.5 air changes per hour (i.e., about one half of the air volume of the building will be replaced every hour). Generally, these air-to-air heat exchangers are operated continuously during the hours of occupancy for a building (see Figures B.6–B.8).

The whole-house fan is particularly well suited for use in houses located in a warm, humid climate such as that present in the southeastern United States. The purpose of the whole-house fan is to draw air through open windows and doorways into the house and up and out of vents in the attic. Thus, the whole-house fan fosters the movement of air around occupants, encouraging both evaporative and convective cooling. These whole-house fans tend to be most effective when outside air temperatures are less than or equal to 82 °F (27.8 °C). When outside air temperatures are greater than 82 °F (27.8 °C), the cooling capability of the air movement caused by the whole-house fan will be less effective. Air velocities induced by a suitably sized whole-house fan will usually be in the range of 30 to 40 feet/minute (0.15 to 0.20 m/s).

A whole-house fan is best located either in an attic or at least in the ceiling plane of the top floor of the building (see Figure B.9). The whole-house fan should be open to a central hallway so that it can draw air equally from all the rooms of the building. Windows in each of these rooms should be operable (and opened), or there should be louvers included in the exterior envelope to enable outside air to pass into the building. Operation of a whole-house fan can be controlled using a thermostat or a humidistat or, alternatively, simply by a manual switch. The fans used in commercially available whole-house fan assemblies usually have diameters of about 2 to 3 feet (0.6 to 0.9 m) with housings that are slightly larger. These fans are driven by motors that either are in-line or lay alongside the fans and are connected with fan belts to the fan shaft.

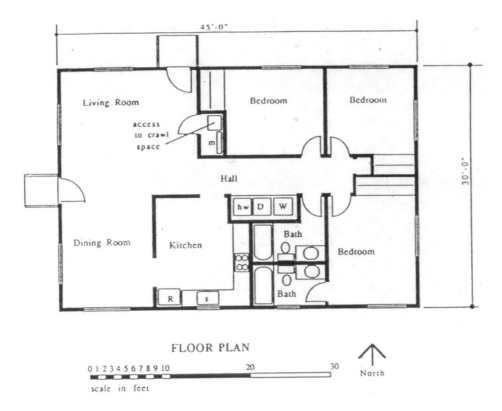

FLOOR PLAN

0 1 2 3 4 5 6 7 8 9 10   20   30   ↑
scale in feet   North

Figure B.6 The house in which an air-to-air heat exchanger has been installed (and the house floor plan) are shown here. In the following two figures the heat exchanger and the ducting for the air-to-air heat exchanger system are presented.

Figure B.7 The air-to-air heat exchanger is located in the truss space above what will be the finished ceiling.

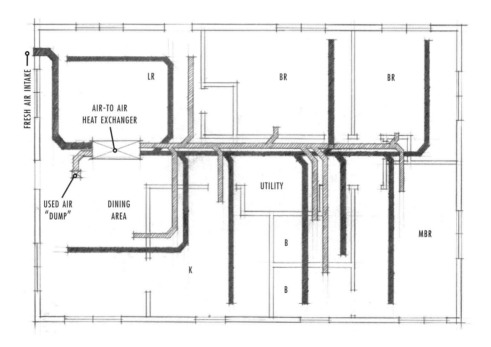

Figure B.8 A reflected ceiling plan for the ducting used with the air-to-air heat exchanger shown in Figure B.7. The black lines represent the in-coming (supply) air flow; the gray lines depict the return (out-going) air passage. The X-marked rectangle is the air-to-air heat exchanger.

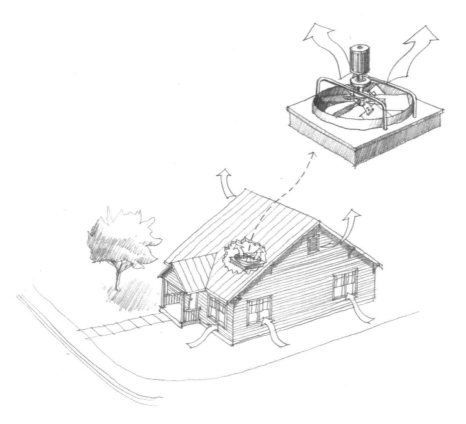

Figure B.9 A whole-house fan is installed in the attic of this house.

B.2.2.3   Active systems alternatives for space cooling   In Sections A.3.5 and A.4.3 we have described various direct-refrigerant systems. These systems are conventionally employed in smaller nonresidential building applications such as for retail commercial, small office, restaurant, district library, and related buildings. Some of the smaller direct-refrigerant systems are also used in residential buildings. The most common cooling system devices will be window air-conditioners, through-the-wall conditioners, unitary air-conditioners, split-system packages, and heat pumps. The first three of these five devices basically are composed of single packages (i.e., with all of the heating, cooling, and ventilating functions performed within the single assembly). The split-system conditioner will typically have two principal components. And the heat pump may be a single package or may instead consist of two or three separate, small components.

The types of direct-refrigerant space cooling devices described in the previous chapter and discussed here are essentially indistinguishable: they are all part of a continuum, differentiated only by the conditioning capacities and the physical sizes of the assemblies. In residential applications the primary space cooling systems alternatives are the window air-conditioner, the heat pump, and the air-conditioning coil (that will be attached and operated as part of a furnace assembly). Space cooling in other small-scale building applications will likely employ similar systems hardware, or the space cooling can be performed using other direct-refrigerant systems alternatives.

Heat pumps and air-conditioning coils attached to conventional warm-air furnaces both employ the same collection of subcomponents: an indoor section, a compressor, and an outdoor section. Both of these two devices—the heat pump and the air-conditioning coils—operate following the refrigeration cycle described in Sidebar A.6. The indoor section and the outdoor section are essentially heat exchangers. Whether each section is gaining or losing heat depends on the direction in which the refrigeration cycle is proceeding (and whether cooling or heating is sought at the indoor section).

A heat pump may be composed of three separate units: a fan with a heat exchanger (the indoor section), a compressor, and a fan with a heat exchanger (the outdoor section) (see Figure B.10). Or a heat pump may be composed of two units: a fan with heat exchanger (essentially, a fan-coil unit) and a compressor-outdoor section. In either instance the indoor section—a fan with heat exchanger—essentially operates similarly to a warm-air furnace. Air is blown past the heat exchanger by the fan, and the air is conditioned as it passes the heat exchanger. Then, the conditioned air enters a ducting system and is distributed to the occupied areas of the building. When the building requires heating, the heat exchanger (in the indoor section) will warm the air flowing past the heat exchanger. When cooling is needed, the heat exchanger will cool the passing air (i.e., by extracting heat from the passing air).

A fundamental difference between the heat pump and the warm-air furnace is that the heat pump can be used either to heat or to cool the distributed air whereas the warm-air furnace only serves to heat building spaces. The basis for this difference arises from the alternative functioning of the heat exchanger in each. For the furnace, the exchanger transfers heat to the distribution air as the heat is produced with the combustion of a fuel or with the resistance of electricity passing through a circuit. For the heat pump, the heat exchanger employs the product of the refrigeration cycle—either warmth or coolth—to condition the distribution air).

The heat pump can both heat or cool a building using its basic assembly hardware whereas a warm-air furnace—to furnish cooling—must be supplemented with an air-conditioning coil, a compressor, and an outdoor section. The air-conditioning coil will most often be installed on top of the furnace so that the furnace fan can blow air past the coil producing cool air (which will then flow into the ducting system for distribution throughout the building) (see Figure B.11). The air-conditioning coil will be connected via piping to a compressor and an outdoor section (just as the indoor section of a heat pump is connected via piping to a compressor and an outdoor section). A refrigerant fluid will flow through the piping between the three components of either the air-conditioning coil or heat pump assembly.

When designing spaces for housing heat pumps and furnaces with attached air-conditioning coils, several points should be considered. First, in small-scale buildings, the sizes of the components comprising heat pumps and the air-conditioning operation for warm-air furnaces are all relatively small: the indoor section for a heat pump and the warm-air furnace with attached air-conditioning coils will both have footprints of about 2' × 2' to 3' × 3' (0.6 m × 0.6 m to 0.9 m × 0.9 m) with a height of about 4' to 5' (1.2 m to 1.5 m). The compressors will usually have about the same footprint with a lesser height, and the outdoor section will have about the same approximate dimensions as the indoor section (or the warm-air furnace with the air-conditioning coils attached to it).

Second, for heat pumps the cross-sectional area of supply air ducting will usually need to be about twice the cross-sectional area required for warm-air furnaces (an explanation for this requirement will be offered in Section B.3.4.4). The significance of this qualification is that larger accessways will be needed for running this ducting throughout

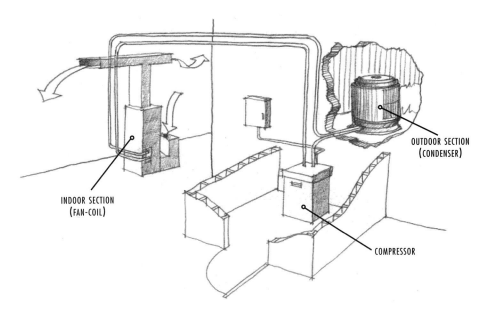

Figure B.10 The three components of a residential heat pump are the indoor section, a compressor, and an outdoor section. In many contemporary residential heat pumps, the outdoor section and the compressor will be placed in a single housing.

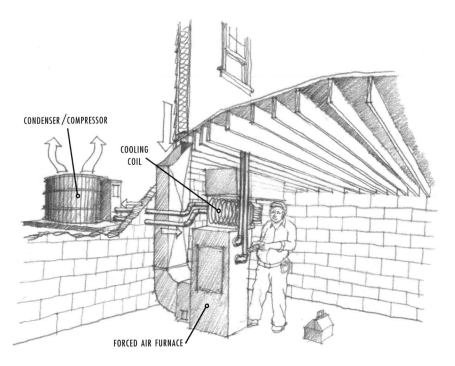

Figure B.11 The furnishing of cooling air can be accomplished by installing a cooling coil on the top of a conventional warm-air furnace. Note that an outdoor section—consisting of a compressor and a condenser—will be required, too.

buildings served by heat pumps (e.g., within wall assemblies and under or through floor and ceiling assemblies).

Third, heat pumps become progressively less effective as a heat source when the outside air temperature falls below about 40 °F (5 C). If outside air temperatures lower than this level are frequent occurrences in a given locale, then a backup heat source should be included as part of the temperature-conditioning system. One means of furnishing backup heat that is commonly employed in colder climates is the inclusion of an electric resistance coil in the air pathway of the indoor section (see Figure B.12).

Fourth, compressors and outdoor sections — for either heat pumps or air-conditioning coils mounted on furnaces — tend to be overly noisy. Compressors should be located well away from areas of buildings in which quiet backgrounds are necessary (e.g., for residential applications, bedrooms, music practice rooms, dens; for small office buildings, private offices; for community libraries, reading or study rooms; and so forth). Outdoor sections, too, are often quite noisy and should be located away from envelope assemblies with lesser noise separation capabilities (e.g., the outdoor sections should generally be located away from window assemblies, particularly large-area assemblies). These outdoor sections should also be located away from internal building spaces that contain activities requiring quiet backgrounds (e.g., the same spaces cataloged above for compressors).

Fifth, wherever a compressor is located, there should be an adequate amount of free space around the compressor to enable maintenance and repair. Failure of the compressors used in these small-scale building applications occurs much more often than for virtually

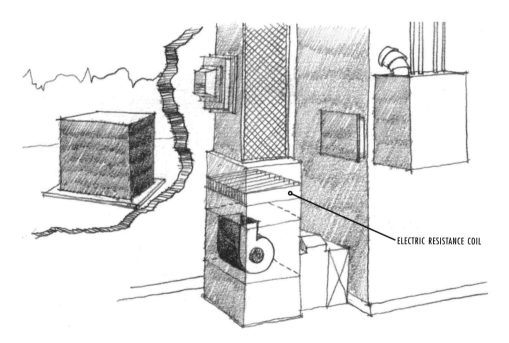

ELECTRIC RESISTANCE COIL

Figure B.12 Heat pumps generally perform less well in a heating mode when external air temperatures fall below about 40 °F (4 °C). To insure that occupants of buildings heated with heat pumps have adequate heating capacities when external temperatures do reach such levels, electric resistance heaters are added to the indoor sections of heat pumps. Thus, supply air streams can be suitably warmed to overcome greater building heat losses. The supplemental electric resistance heater is commonly placed just above the fan body in the indoor section.

any other HVAC systems component. Thus, when laying out space in which a compressor will be located, make sure that servicing (and replacement) can be readily accomplished.

Sixth, the cost of purchasing and installing a heat pump or a warm-air furnace with an attached air-conditioning coil (and its related compressor and outdoor section) will usually be two to three times as expensive as purchasing and installing a conventional warm-air furnace. Note that this estimate is independent of costs that are necessary for purchasing ducting materials and installing ducting runs.

Lastly, inspite of these several foibles or operational qualifications, heat pumps offer particularly attractive performances: they are energy-efficient; they provide both heating and cooling capabilities utilizing the same hardware; and, in locales where electrical energy costs are quite high and the climate is temperate, their operating costs can be cost-effective when compared to the costs for utilizing other small-scale heating and cooling systems.

Section B.3 | DESIGNING HVAC SYSTEMS FOR SMALL-SCALE BUILDINGS

As a preface for this section and Section B.4, let us indicate these two sections involve issues that are often taken up following the completion of schematic designing. However, we have chosen to include this material because it will offer information on the creation, composition, and operation of HVAC systems for small-scale buildings.

Subcontractors — working for general contractors — will often design HVAC systems for small-scale buildings. Less often, an engineer, a manufacturer's representative, or an architect will design the needed HVAC system. The principal issues involved in designing HVAC systems for small-scale buildings include selecting an appropriate system type, identifying the system components, developing the layout for the system, and ensuring that the several components are adequately sized and that occupants will be thermally comfortable and will have sufficient ventilation (and air quality). It will also be necessary to establish good space utilization and an effective integration of the HVAC system components with the structural system, the building envelope, and the overall architecture of the building.

Using rules-of-thumb and judicious guidelines, it is generally possible to create a good design approximation for a successful HVAC system. In the following pages the steps involved in designing an HVAC system for a small-scale building will be cataloged and explained. The principal steps in this design process are the identification of design conditions, the estimation of thermal and ventilation loads, the identification of systems alternatives and the selection of a preferred system, the laying-out and sizing of the system components, and the development of assurances that the HVAC system can be well-integrated with the other important elements of the building.

B.3.1   IDENTIFICATION OF DESIGN CONDITIONS

The purpose of identifying design conditions for a building is to define the microclimate surrounding the building, the necessary internal environment of the building, and whether any spaces or features of the building demand special attention while the HVAC system is being designed. Having information about the macroclimate — essentially, the climate for the region or community in which the building is to be placed — is a good first approximation. But further attention should be paid to investigating whether there are specific, localized climatic features that will more immediately present climatic challenges for a future building. Examples of issues that should be considered when assessing the micro-climate include estimating the potential influences of topography, townscape forms, vegetation, sun paths, wind flow patterns, and precipitation incidence.

In Chapter 3 eight parameters have been identified as those that affect a person's ability to experience thermal comfort. Four of these parameters are environmental in nature (i.e., they characterize the environment immediately surrounding a person). The other four parameters involve personal qualities (i.e., properties of a person's clothing ensemble and activity rate). Establishing the thermal conditions needed inside the building can begin with consideration of what values for the important environmental parameters should be evident and what personal parametric values will likely characterize the occupants. The environmental parameters requiring attention are the dry-bulb air temperature, the relative humidity, the radiant exchange conditions between occupants and surrounding surfaces, and the probable velocities of air flow around the occupants. These parameters should have values within the thermal comfort ranges, or specific steps should be planned to off-set any values that lie outside of normal thermally comfortable conditions (see Section 3.5 for further information about suitable ranges of these parameters for promoting thermal comfort). The two personal parameters that can markedly affect thermal sensations of comfort are the occupants' activity rates and the insulative characteristics of the occu-pants' clothing. Systems designers can predict likely values for each of these two parameters, by thinking about how people will behave and clothe themselves while they occupy individual spaces in the building.

Finally, a mental exercise that can be used effectively while assessing the conditions needed in the building involves seeking answers to the following questions. First, who will occupy the spaces in the building (i.e., how would you characterize these people)? Second, what activities will these people engage in while they occupy these spaces (e.g., how intense are the levels of activity; how many people will participate in the activities; what equipment will they need to pursue these activities; are particular environmental conditions needed to support these activities; and so forth)? Third, when are the people likely to occupy these spaces, and will their activities change over the period of occupancy (i.e., across the day, week, or, even, year)? Fourth, how might features of the building affect thermal sensations or feelings of comfort (e.g., are there large glazing surfaces that might create radiant heat-ing or cooling problems; will specific spaces need dehumidification or extra ventilation because they are likely to have high humidity levels [notably, kitchens and shower rooms]; are there specific activities present that may cause potential indoor air quality problems; and so forth)? Asking these questions and then seeking answers for them are intended to focus the collection of data that a designer can use to guide the creation of the HVAC system.

In addition to evaluating climatic properties and necessary environmental conditions within the future building, some attention should be directed at identifying ventilation requirements for the building occupants. First, an examination of the quality of the ambi-ent air at the building site should be undertaken. Issues that might be raised include whether the air is likely to be too humid or too dry, dusty, laden with potential allergens, odoriferous, carrying noxious or toxic substances created by nearby industries or trans-portation vehicles, and so forth. Second, the likely ventilation needs in the building should be identified: what air change rates are needed; at what velocities should ventilation air be introduced into internal spaces; and at what ranges of temperature and relative humidity should the supply air be passed into specific spaces? And, third, a preview of air quality requirements for building spaces and occupant activities should be performed, including determining whether there are any special indoor air quality needs (e.g., as in "clean rooms" for semiconductor manufacturing or in research laboratories); whether specific process equipment or activities will cause air quality challenges for the occupants (e.g., as in a wood-working shop, a photographic materials processing laboratory, an artist's studio, a veterinary clinic, and so forth); or whether likely occupant groups could be especially susceptible to poor indoor quality conditions (e.g., the elderly, the infirm, and those requiring neonatal care).

B.3.2   ESTIMATING THERMAL LOADS

The basic purposes of an HVAC system are to ensure that occupants will be thermally comfortable and will have suitable ventilation. Providing thermally comfortable spaces requires that the air temperature, relative humidity, the velocity of air moving around occupants, and the radiant exchange between the occupants and the surrounding surfaces be maintained within acceptable ranges (see Section 3.5 for definitions of what the acceptable ranges of these parameters should be).

The challenges to maintaining a thermally comfortable building interior involve offsetting heat losses and gains through the building envelope and internal heat gains (produced by people, lighting fixtures, electrically powered equipment, and other process equipment). The heat gains and losses through the building envelope will largely be *sensible* (i.e., occurring as a result of temperature differences between room air and external air and between internal and external objects). The specific gain and loss mechanisms will include transmission, infiltration, and ventilation gains and losses and solar heat gain. The one instance by which latent heat exchange may occur across the building envelope arises when moisture migration occurs either into or out of the building.

Internal heat production occurs in both sensible and latent forms. Occupants contribute sensible heat to the building air and to internal surfaces. In the course of their respiration and perspiration, they pass latent heat into the building air. Lighting fixtures only give off sensible heat. Electrically powered equipment can add both sensible and latent heat to the air (e.g., for clothes and dishwashing; food preparation; developing and printing photographic materials; and potable water coolers and dispensers). Additionally, other laboratory, assembly, cleaning, and general industrial processes can also give off both sensible and latent heat (e.g., burning methane or propane for space heating, cooking, or conducting laboratory work; using water-based solutions for the cleaning of building surfaces; and for many manufacturing procedures in which water is used as a lubricant).

Performing comprehensive thermal load estimates requires careful and potentially laborious analyses. These calculations can be performed using prescriptive methods described in numbers of textbooks, each of which draw upon procedures set forth by the American Society of Heating, Refrigerating, and Air-Conditioning Engineers, Inc.[2] Alternatively, comprehensive thermal load estimates can also be established by employing any of several thermal simulation computer programs to analyze and predict hourly, daily, or monthly heat loss and gain rates.

In place of these systematic calculational load-estimation methods, a variety of rules-of-thumb and design aids have been developed and disseminated. One set of design guidelines — for suggesting envelope compositions for *envelope-load-dependent* buildings — has been presented in Section 4.4. Another set of guidelines will be offered in Table B.2 for estimating heat loss rates for envelope-load-dependent buildings. Note that for these buildings the rates of heat loss by transmission and infiltration are determined by the composition of the building envelope — what assemblies are used in the envelope — and by the difference of the inside and outside air temperatures.

TABLE B.2
ESTIMATES OF TOTAL HEAT LOSS RATE (BY TRANSMISSION AND INFILTRATION)
FOR ALTERNATIVE ENVELOPE COMPOSITIONS [i,ii,iii]

Envelope composition for walls, roof, floor	Fenestration assembly composition	Heat loss estimate Btu/hr-sq ft-°F (W/m²-K)
R-11, R-19, R-11	Single-pane	0.67 (3.80)
R-11, R-30, R-11	Double-pane	0.50 (2.84)
R-19, R-30, R-19	Double-pane	0.22 (1.25)

Notes:

i. To use this table, multiply the heat loss estimate by the total floor area of the building and the temperature difference between the inside air and the outside air (for the design condition). For example, if the building has a total enclosed floor area of 2,200 square feet (204 m²) and there is an air-to-air *temperature difference* across the building envelope — for the design condition — of 45 °F (25 °C), then the total heat loss estimate for the building (with an envelope composition of R-11, R-19, R-11 with single-pane fenestration) will be 0.67 × 2200 × 45 or 66,300 Btuh (3.80 × 204 × 25 or 19,400 W).

ii. Equivalent resistance values to match R-11, R-19, and R-30 (in the Imperial units system) are, respectively, 1.94, 3.34, and 5.28 m²-K/W (in the International System of Units [SI]).

iii. The heat loss estimate coefficients shown in the right column can also be used to calculate heat gain estimates (where the heat transfer is dependent on the temperature difference between the outside air and the inside air and the heat gain is manifested by transmission and infiltration). The calculation procedure for estimating heat gain rates would be identical to that shown in Note i. Recognize, however, that neither the heat loss estimate nor the heat gain estimate accounts for any solar heat gain incident on opaque or fenestration assemblies.

In North America conventional building envelope assemblies generally include a layer of thermal insulation. This insulation will most commonly be either a mineral or glass fiber batting or a polymeric foam board, both of which impose resistance to heat transmission. The magnitudes of resistance imposed by the fiber batting and by the foam board are approximately 3.3 and 5 per inch (1.3 and 2.0 per cm) of thickness, respectively (when the batting is fully lofted). Thus, for the batt insulation, a batt that is 3 1/2 inches (8.9 cm) thick will have a resistance of R-11 (1.94 m²-K/W); a batt that is 5 1/2 inches (14.0 cm) thick will have a resistance of R-19 (3.34 m²-K/W). Note that the units for thermal resistance in the Imperial system are ft²-hr-°F/Btu.

Present-day fenestration assemblies that are used in building envelopes generally are composed of double-pane configurations (although both single-pane and triple-pane are also employed in various locales).

These heat loss estimate coefficients are derived for the winter-time design condition. Such a design condition is established, for a specific locale, by determining the hourly outside air temperatures for the coldest 1 percent of the winter-time hours and then computing the average for these temperatures. The resulting average air temperature is referred to as the 99th percentile design condition.[3] Once the outside air temperature design condition has been determined, then its magnitude can be subtracted from the desired indoor air temperature to establish the air-to-air temperature difference across the building envelope (and, subsequently, the total heat loss rate that the building will experience at the design condition air temperature).

The total heat loss rate for this design condition air temperature thus is the magnitude of the *heat make-up* that a furnace, boiler, heat pump, or other heating source must furnish to maintain the requisite indoor air temperature (when the design condition air temperature is present outside). But note that fuel-fired furnaces and boilers, particularly, do not operate at 100 percent efficiency (i.e., some of the heat produced during the combustion of the fuel will be lost to the external environment as transported there by flue gases). Typically, these comparatively small furnaces and boilers will operate at efficiencies between 70 percent to 95 percent, depending on whether heat recovery devices are built into the furnaces and boilers. So, to account for combustion inefficiencies when selecting a fuel-fired furnace or boiler, take the heat loss rate (determined above) and divide the heat loss rate by the efficiency of the furnace or boiler (as specified by the manufacturer of the unit).

Most often, furnaces, boilers, heat pumps, and other similar heating sources will not be available to match *precisely* this adjusted heat make-up requirement. In these instances, the standard practice is to select the furnace, boiler, heat pump, or other heating source with the next larger catalog-listed capacity. A further refinement to this estimation of heat make-up requirements is to establish how much heat make-up must be provided on a room-by-room basis.

B.3.3   SYSTEM SELECTION

HVAC system alternatives have been identified in Table B.1. This table shows all of the alternatives that are commonly used in small-scale buildings.

System selection criteria have been presented in Sidebar A.10. These criteria, whereas offered for larger, nonresidential building applications, can be applied usefully for small-scale HVAC systems. The most important criteria, generally, are those involving costs, the abilities to ensure occupant thermal comfort and good indoor air quality, and the need to make the system components fit readily into the overall building. Some of these criteria require reliance on objective data (e.g., first costs, air movement capability, air quality controls). Other criteria entail more subjective insights (e.g., difficulties associated with integrating HVAC system components with other building elements). Thus, the actual selection of a system by an architect, engineer, or subcontractor will likely also involve issues of preference, past experience, and client wishes (as well as the ability of the system to satisfy issues based on strictly objective data).

A further qualification leading to system selection can be that local municipal or state building regulations effectively mandate the application of particular operational capabilities. For instance, a chapter in the Washington State Building Code — *Washington State Ventilation and Indoor Air Quality Code*[4] — stipulates that certain levels of fresh air must be supplied to building spaces and that contaminant-laden air produced in rooms such as kitchens and bathrooms must be exhausted from those spaces, using HVAC equipment. Thus, if a designer in Washington State wishes to install a radiant-heating floor system or an electrically heating baseboard system, then some complementary air-handling system must also be included to satisfy these indoor air quality tenets.

B.3.4   LAYING OUT SYSTEM COMPONENTS

The principal activities involved in this step include the identification of the system components, the determination of suitable locations for placing these components, the estimation of their sizes, and the ensuring of adequate spaces for housing them (or, alternatively, that building spaces can be modified to adequately accommodate these components). From an architectural standpoint, these activities can be performed in an approximate manner. More precise definitions and solutions may then be left to subcontractors or engineers to achieve finality.

In the remainder of this section (B.3.4) our presentation will focus on discussing how a ducted air-handling system might be laid out. Numbers of the underlying principles will also apply equally well for other conventional small-scale space conditioning systems and can thus be employed during the designing of those alternatives.

For a conventional small-scale air-handling system the principal components will be a warm-air furnace (or a heat pump or a unitary direct-refrigerant device), supply air ducting, diffusers for admitting air into the occupied spaces, grilles for taking "used" air out of the spaces, return air ducting, and a thermostat (for each conditioning zone served by the system). Additional small air passageways — ducting or chimneys — will be required for bringing fresh air into the supply air-return air loop, bringing outside air in to be used in the combustion of furnace fuel (oil or natural gas), and exhausting flue gases (from the fuel combustion) to the building exterior.

B.3.4.1   Placing terminal devices   A conventional design approach for laying out system components is to place the terminal devices — here, for an air-handling system, the diffusers — and the central air-handler such as a furnace. Then, the remaining challenge is to determine acceptable pathways for running the supply and return ducting between the terminal devices and the central air-handler. The ducting can be enclosed within the building assemblies or left exposed.

The choice of where to locate terminal devices will greatly depend on whether the conditioning air is to be used for heating or cooling the building interior. If heating is required, the common practice is to place diffusers underneath fenestration units, either horizontally in the floor plane or built vertically into the baseboard (see Figure B.13). Diffusers located beneath fenestration can then deliver warm air across the potentially cold interior window surfaces, raising the surface temperature of these windows. With warmer window surfaces there will be a decreased likelihood that occupants of the space will experience radiational discomfort or convective drafts. To ensure that the warm air exiting the diffusers will adequately cover the window surfaces, the air should be dispatched from the diffusers with sufficient force and spread (remember that warm air will have a natural buoyancy, that will cause the air to rise, but fan-forced air flow will furnish a better distribution).

A second strategy to ensure that good circulation of the warm supply air will occur is to locate return air intake grilles in interior walls opposite to the window surfaces. These grilles should be placed vertically close to the floor (as a first choice) or at a higher wall elevation (as a second choice). Locating these return air grilles as close to the floor as possible will foster better air circulation throughout the conditioned space than if the grilles are located at a higher wall elevation. Avoid installing return air grilles in the floor

THE TWO DIFFUSERS ALONG THE EAST ELEVATION

Figure B.13 In keeping with the need to warm large expanses of glazing (during cold winter months), there are four diffusers installed in the top of the window seating underneath the windows (note the one just to the left of the fireplace.) The ducting that furnishes air to these diffusers is contained within the window seat assembly.

plane (i.e., the probability of small objects or spilled liquids falling through floor-mounted grilles is substantial)(see Figure B.14).

Some further guidelines for placing diffusers and intake grilles follow. First, an important design goal for any air-handling system is to furnish a uniform distribution of air (and heat or coolth) throughout occupied spaces. Thus, rather than relying on one or a few diffusers to ventilate and condition a space, designing systems with more diffusers will almost always provide better performances (and more comfortable spaces). Second, for small-scale building heating systems, the amount of heat make-up supplied by a single diffuser should generally be limited to a maximum of about 8,000 Btu/hour (2,350 W). Third, an effort should be made to ensure that air exiting a diffuser does not directly flow over an occupant. Whether the supply air is warm (so as to heat a space) or cool (to offset the overheatedness of a space), the combined effects of the air temperature and the elevated air velocity of the exiting air can cause occupants, who are directly exposed to such air streams, to be thermally uncomfortable. Air exiting a diffuser should be permitted to disperse into the space, mixing readily and thoroughly with the ambient air in the space. And, fourth, any enclosed space that receives air supplied by an air-handling system should have at least one return air intake (or should have some open pathway — such as a louver assembly in a door — that enables the passage of "used" air to exit the space and be gathered up by a return air intake operating in an immediately adjacent space).

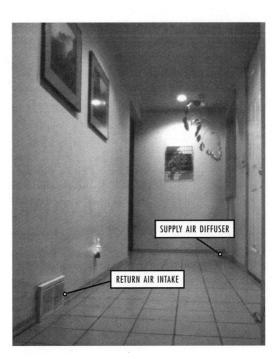

Figure B.14 Appropriate locations for supply air diffusers and return air intakes in residencies are demonstrated here. Supply air diffusers should be placed underneath windows so that the air can pass upward, warming the window surface. Return air intakes should be placed on walls opposite to the supply air diffusers. The intakes should be located either near the floor or at the upper wall (to promote satisfactory air circulation through the space.)

If cooling is the principal space-tempering need, then the air supply should be furnished from diffusers mounted on the ceiling or on walls near the ceiling. The flow of chilled air exiting diffusers will naturally be downward (as cool air descends upon entering a warmer space). But the system designer should take care to ensure that the cool air is diffused outward, thus avoiding the directing of concentrated cold air streams at occupants. When the principal space-tempering need is cooling, return air intakes should be located at lower elevations of walls (although the more conventional practice is to place return air intakes in the ceiling across the space from any ceiling-mounted diffusers). The practice of locating both supply air diffusers and return air intakes in the ceiling plane is one based on expedience (i.e., initial installation is easier and more opportunities will exist for future relocation of diffusers and intakes).[5]

B.3.4.2 Placing warm-air furnaces, heat pumps, and split-system units Warm-air furnaces can be placed in a number of locations: in basements, crawl spaces, attics, utility rooms, or even in large closets. If a furnace is oil-fired, space must be made for locating an oil storage tank and, ideally, the distance between the tank and the oil furnace should be as short as possible. The location for a gas-fired furnace can generally be established for the convenience of the building designer (as long as there is adequate means for running the gas supply line to the furnace). For these fuel-fired furnaces accommodations must be provided for transporting air to the furnace for combustion and for discharging flue (combustion) gases to the exterior of the building. When a high-combustion-efficiency furnace is employed in a small-scale building, flue gases may be discharged horizontally from the furnace at the perimeter of the building (e.g., for a basement furnace flue gases may be discharged just above the ground plane). However, for lower-combustion-efficiency furnaces, flue gases must be transported vertically and expelled above the building roof. The operation of an electric-resistance furnace does not require an air supply for combustion or the expelling of flue gases. Finally, note that for all warm-air furnaces fresh air should be brought in from the building exterior and mixed with returning "used" air to form the supply air that will be circulated throughout the building. Thus, this fresh air must be ducted in from the building perimeter to the furnace, and this ducting must be connected to the ducting transporting the returning used air. Commonly, this integration of the two air streams occurs in a mixing plenum (that will be located just up-line from the temperature-conditioning portion of the furnace).

If a heat pump or a split-system direct-refrigerant unit is to be employed as the central air-conditioning device for a small-scale building, then more than one space will most often be required for placing these central conditioning components. The indoor section — the fan-coil component — should be located following the same approach required for placing an electric-resistance furnace. If a stand-alone compressor is part of one of these systems, it should be placed in a location that affords adequate noise separation from occupied spaces and that has sufficient space surrounding the compressor to enable regular maintenance and repair. Whether the outdoor section is a stand-alone component or is packaged with the compressor, in either instance the unit should be located away from windows and doors (i.e., to minimize noise intrusion). Because indoor and outdoor sections (and stand-alone or coterminous compressors) need only to be connected with small-diameter piping (through which a refrigerant fluid will be transported), these sections may be separated by as much as about 50 feet (15.2 m).

B.3.4.3   Organizing ducting   Once supply air diffusers and a central heating or cooling source have been located in a building plan, then a ducting system can be laid out to connect the source and the diffusers. A fundamental design decision at this stage will be whether the ducting layout should be integrated within the vertical and/or horizontal structural assemblies (or wall, ceiling, or floor infill) or whether the ducting should be left exposed in occupied spaces. This decision will often involve issues of appearance, maintenance, noise separation, economics, and client and (architectural and HVAC) designer preferences. Usually, such decisions should be made on a case-by-case basis (i.e., there are no general, profound reasons to argue in favor of a blanket decision to either cover or expose ducting all of the time).

Laying out ducting — especially, in small-scale buildings — can follow the image of a tree: diffusers (leaves) are connected with small ducts (branches) that pass to larger ducts (larger branches) and on to trunk ducts (the main trunk(s) of the tree). It is usually more efficient to rely on having many ducting runs of smaller dimensions arrayed modularly and connecting to fewer larger-branch ducts. These larger-branch ducts should connect to one (or a few) main trunk duct(s). The main duct trunk(s) should be located centrally, connecting ultimately to the central air-handler.

Because diffusers for the supply air side of a *warm-air* system should be placed at the perimeter of the building, the ducting runs for the supply-air side of the system will usually require greater ingenuity and care to integrate with the other features of the building (e.g., the structural, partition, and flooring/ceiling assemblies). Alternatively, if the principal air-tempering requirement of the air-handling system is to furnish cool air, then this cooling air can be supplied from ceiling-mounted diffusers, to which ducting runs may be laid out more easily. Return-air duct runs that connect return air intakes to the central air-handler often will be simpler to lay out because the intakes tend to be aggregated toward the core of the building (i.e., in most spaces, opposite to the building perimeter). Thus, air-return ducting can be located centrally. For example, in a two or three-story building, small, short-length, horizontal return ducts could pick up used air from individual spaces and pass the air streams to a main return-air duct that could run vertically at the center of the floor plan for the building.

B.3.4.4   Approximate sizing of ducting for small-scale buildings   The approximate size of a duct run used principally for *heating* building spaces can be established by employing the following procedure. First, determine the volumetric airflow rate (in CFM

TABLE B.3
VOLUMETRIC AIR FLOW ESTIMATES BASED ON OFFSETTING THE
TOTAL ENVELOPE HEAT LOSS FOUND FROM TABLE B.2

Heat loss estimate, Btu/hr-sqft-°F (W/m²-K) (from Table B.2)	CFM/sqft (estimate) Supply air temperature = 100 °F	CFM/sqft (estimate) Supply air temperature = 120 °F	Liter/sec-m² (estimate) Supply air temperature = 38 °C	Liter/sec-m² (estimate) Supply air temperature = 48 °C
0.67 (3.80)	$0.0207 \times (T_{IA}-T_{OA})$	$0.0124 \times (T_{IA}-T_{OA})$	$0.1051 \times (T_{IA}-T_{OA})$	$0.0630 \times (T_{IA}-T_{OA})$
0.50 (2.84)	$0.0154 \times (T_{IA}-T_{OA})$	$0.0093 \times (T_{IA}-T_{OA})$	$0.0782 \times (T_{IA}-T_{OA})$	$0.0472 \times (T_{IA}-T_{OA})$
0.22 (1.25)	$0.0068 \times (T_{IA}-T_{OA})$	$0.0047 \times (T_{IA}-T_{OA})$	$0.0345 \times (T_{IA}-T_{OA})$	$0.0239 \times (T_{IA}-T_{OA})$

Note: To estimate the volumetric airflow that will be required to condition a space, first determine which heat loss estimate quantity (found from Table B.2) matches the likely building envelope assemblies for a specific building design. Then, establish what supply air temperature will be furnished by a proposed heat source (e.g., 100 °F [38 °C] for heat pumps; 120 °F [48 °C] for warm-air furnaces). Multiply the corresponding coefficient (that matches the heat loss estimate and the supply air temperature) by the temperature difference between the inside air and the outside air (for the design condition). This product will furnish an estimate of the volumetric airflow rate per unit floor area, in CFM/sqft or Liters/sec-m², that will be needed to transport adequate make-up heat to the conditioned area. Then, multiply the volumetric airflow rate per unit floor area by the floor area that is to be conditioned by this airflow.

For example, if the building envelope is to be composed of insulation quantities of R-19 batts in the walls, R-30 batts in the ceiling (or roof), and R-19 batts in the floor and of double-pane glazing assemblies, then use the 0.22 Btu/hr-sqft-°F heat loss estimate. Suppose that the building is to be temperature-conditioned by a warm air furnace providing supply airflows at about 120 °F. Then, the volumetric airflow rate per unit floor area will be $0.0047 \times (T_{IA}-T_{OA})$. If the temperature difference between the inside air and the outside air (for the design condition) is 45 °F, the volumetric airflow rate per unit floor area will be 0.21 CFM/sqft. If the floor area being served is 400 sq ft, then the volumetric air flow rate to serve this area would be 84 CFM.

One further qualifier is that the volumetric airflow rate established to transport the necessary make-up heat should be compared to the volumetric airflow rate required to ensure adequate air quality. Most often, the volumetric air flow rate needed to transport the make-up heat will be greater than the flow rate required to maintain good air quality. But, in some circumstances for which high air change rates are needed, then the volumetric airflow rate required for meeting air quality provisions may be predominant.

or liters/second) that the duct is expected to transport. The volumetric airflow rate can be estimated by applying the coefficients found in Table B.3 and multiplying by the floor area served by the duct. Second, select a suitable velocity (for air flow in ducts, in feet/minute or meters/second) for the specific building application (see Table A.5). Then, divide the volumetric airflow rate by the air flow velocity to arrive at the necessary internal cross-sectional area for the duct (in square feet or square meters).

Sizing duct runs that are used principally for *cooling* (or that are regularly used for both heating and cooling) employs a similar procedure, except that an alternative means for establishing the volumetric airflow rate per unit area should be applied. For small-scale buildings whose spaces will predominantly be cooled (or will require cooling and heating at different times of the year or even at different times of a day), a suitable coefficient — volumetric air flow rate per unit area — can be obtained from Table A.4. Multiplying the coefficient by the floor area served by a duct run will produce the requisite volumetric airflow rate (in CFM or L/s) needed for performing the cooling of the area served. Then, taking the volumetric air flow rate and dividing by the recommended velocity for air flow in the ducting (from Table A.5) will establish the internal cross-sectional area for the ducting.

The coefficients presented in Table A.4 vary according to the type of activities for which a building will be used. In some instances (e.g., for restaurants and selected retail stores) higher volumetric air flow rates per unit area are required because of heat gain contributions from the types of services provided in the buildings (e.g., the food and beverage handling and cooking in a restaurant; the elevated activity rates of the participants in recreational buildings; the higher occupant densities in educational buildings; and so forth).

In many instances the volumetric air flow rates required to perform cooling of a building space will be greater than the volumetric air flow rates needed to furnish a like amount of heat for the same space. One of the reasons why a greater air flow rate is required for cooling than for heating is that the temperature difference between the supply air and the room air will generally be larger *when heating is supplied.* In a heating mode, the supply air temperature will generally be as great as 120 °F (49 °C) with a room air temperature of about 70 °F (21 °C), resulting in a temperature difference of about 50 °F (28 °C). In a cooling mode, the supply air temperature will more often be about 55 to 60 °F (13 to 16 °C) with a desired room air temperature of perhaps 70 to 75 °F (21 to 24 °C), furnishing a temperature difference of about 10 to 20 °F (5.5 to 11 °C). Thus, a greater volumetric airflow (in CFM or L/s) will be required to enable cooling, even if the amounts of heat to be extracted (resulting from heat gain) and to be supplied (to offset heat loss) were identical.

The second factor explaining why greater volumetric air flow rates will be needed to cool building spaces is that the magnitudes of cooling loads will often be greater than the magnitudes of heating loads. For buildings *whose thermal performances are dictated by envelope-dependent-load conditions,* during summers the combination of heat gain resulting from air-to-air temperature differences and solar radiation transmission will often be greater than the heat loss rates experienced during the winter. Alternatively, for buildings whose thermal performances are based on internal-load-dominance, then the need for cooling will commonly be substantially greater than the heat loss rates experienced at the envelope of the building.

Thus, for buildings that will need heating and cooling (at different times of the year or for different times of a day), air-handling ducting will usually have to be sized to satisfy the cooling loads.

Ducting is most commonly fabricated in rectangular, square, circular, and elliptical cross-sections. Once the cross-sectional area required for a duct has been established (i.e., by following the procedure described previously), then a dimension or dimensions can be solved for (by algebraically factoring the magnitude of the cross-sectional area). For rectangular cross-sectional ducting, the aspect ratio between the two sides of the rectangle should be no less than 1:3 (i.e., for a horizontal rectangular duct, the width should be no more than three times the height of the duct). One other qualification concerns the common practice of either constructing ducts out of semirigid glass or mineral fiber boards or of sheet metal that is wrapped with an insulating assembly. In either instance the thickness of the insulating board or wrapping should be no less than one in (25 mm). Wrapping ducting with insulative blankets or constructing the ducting from semirigid boards is required in many jurisdictions in North America, particularly where the ducting passes through envelope assemblies, unheated spaces, or overheated spaces.

The sizing of the ducting runs should begin with the most out-lying runs. Then, the next most out-lying runs should be sized, working progressively closer to the central components. In the typical branch-and-trunk air supply system the out-lying ducts will be relatively smaller and the inward-progressing ducting will become increasingly larger. The central trunk(s) will be largest of all: this image of smaller components meeting up with ever-larger components follows on the metaphor of the ducting system organized like a tree.

To enable the looping of air circulation throughout a building, a complete return air system should generally be provided. The return air intakes should be placed opposite to the supply air diffusers. These intakes should connect as directly as possible with return air feeder ducts to the central return air ducting. The magnitudes of volumetric air flow rates (in CFM or L/s) present in a return air system may be somewhat less than the supply air flow rates: some air will leak out of the building envelope to the exterior both through cracks and gaps in the envelope and through the opening and closing of doors and windows. However, for expediency, the volumetric air flow rate present in the return air system can be assumed to be equivalent to the volumetric air flow rate offered by the supply air system. Thus, individual duct runs should be sized to adequately transport the volumetric airflows reaching them (both from immediately adjacent building spaces and from further-out runs that connect to closer-in runs). As the magnitudes of the volumetric air flow rates are established for the various duct runs in a return air-handling duct system, then the cross-sectional areas of these runs can be found by dividing the volumetric air flow rates by recommended velocities for the returning air. Note that the velocities of return air streams in ducts can be somewhat greater than for velocities of supply air streams. The greater return air velocities are less likely to introduce noise into occupied spaces.

B.3.5 INTEGRATING AND FINE-TUNING THE DESIGN OF HVAC SYSTEM COMPONENTS

Once duct run sizes for the supply and return air systems have been estimated, then the next step in the design process is to make sure that these ducts can fit within the available enclosed volumes that are planned for the building (e.g., in between structural members or above or beneath finished surface assemblies). If the ducts cannot readily be contained within available enclosed spaces, then can some or all of these duct runs be left exposed? Or could the ducts be enclosed in furred out volumes (located to accommodate these duct runs)? A common occurrence in seeking to integrate HVAC and structural systems and architectural forms and features is that some duct runs will be difficult to arrange: finding solutions that are both functionally and aesthetically satisfying will often be a challenge.

A second point of verifying that a system will satisfactorily meet performance requirements involves checking to identify any potential "problem areas" and ensuring that a planned system furnishes adequate conditioning and ventilation for these areas. A range of situations that can negatively affect occupant comfort include the presences of large window areas (which can cause substantial heat loss or heat gain problems), building entrances (which can cause discomfort from drafts and rapid heat loss or gain), water vapor-producing areas (bathrooms and kitchens in residences and nonresidential spaces with process equipment that use large quantities of water), odor-producing areas (toilet rooms, bathrooms, locker rooms, kitchens, laboratories), and so forth. For example, common solutions for bathrooms and kitchens dictate that each of these spaces should have exhaust fans. These exhaust fans will expel airborne odors and the high concentration of water vapor directly to the building exterior (thus minimizing opportunities for the odors and water vapor to drift into other occupied spaces in a building). So, in summary, this type of a "cautioning" checklist should be maintained and expanded as design experience is gained.

System controllers should also be considered and planned for. First, thermostats should be located so that the operation of the air-handling and temperature-conditioning system is enhanced. The number of thermostats present in a building will match the number of zones planned for the building. Zonal control provides flexible, responsive conditioning, insuring that occupant thermal comfort and ventilation quality can be well met. Thermostats are commonly best placed on walls opposite or away from supply air diffusers (and, where possible, at eye level with standing occupants). A related guideline for placing thermostats is to locate them near or in areas where occupants spend time (i.e., so that an occupant can set the thermostat to reflect the conditions the occupant wants to experience).

Other instruments that are used to sense environmental parameters include humidity or indoor air quality sensors. Humidity sensors can beneficially be provided in spaces subjected to humid ambient air or where high rates of water vapor are likely to be produced (e.g., commercial and residential kitchens, bathrooms, indoor swimming pools and other recreational facilities with hot tubs or spas). Indoor air quality sensors can be deployed in buildings either to detect ventilation adequacy or to ascertain whether harmful contaminants are present. Ventilation adequacy is often assessed using a sensor that continuously measures the concentration of carbon dioxide in room air. The detection of the presences of other potential contaminants requires use of various specialized sensors: designers should expect project clients to provide appropriate identifications for these sensors.

In addition to the presence of heating sources and fans, ducts, and diffusers and grilles, a number of other devices are regularly included in air-handling systems for small-scale buildings. Among these devices are smoke detectors, noise spread inhibitors and duct lining assemblies, supplemental in-the-duct heating coils, and dampers. The use of smoke detectors is discussed in Chapter C. Means for controlling noise are presented in Chapter 13. Lastly, dampers are incorporated in duct runs to regulate the distribution of air throughout a building (i.e., establishing what fraction of the system capacity is delivered to each zone or space). The presence of dampers will also enable the testing and balancing of an air-handling system (as a part of a commissioning process).[6]

B.3.6 FACTORS THAT MAY INFLUENCE SYSTEM DESIGNING

B.3.6.1 Energy conservation standards and codes   In the United States a majority of state governments have legislated the adoption of energy codes,[7] requiring the construction and operation of energy-conserving buildings. These codes apply to the designs for new buildings and for buildings that are undergoing renovation. And, typically, most of the states that have adopted energy conservation codes have composed their respective codes to address two alternative building types: residential buildings, with heights of three stories or less, and commercial buildings and multifamily buildings, with heights of four stories or more.

The writing of energy conservation standards and codes commenced in the early 1970s. The precursor for most of today's codes was the ASHRAE Standard 90-75, *Energy Conservation in New Building Design,* published in 1975.[8] Subsequent amendments and revisions followed, leading to the publication of a series of model energy codes during the early 1990s.[9] These model energy codes served as the bases for many of the state energy conservation codes presently in existence across the United States. The model energy codes applied principally to residential buildings with heights of three stories or less. In 1989, a Standard 90.1-1989, *Energy Efficient Design of New Buildings Except Low-Rise Residential Buildings,* was published.[10] This standard concentrated on commercial buildings and residential buildings with heights of four stories or more. Most recently, the *2000 International Energy Conservation Code* has been developed and now serves as a model standard suitable for adoption by state or municipal governments. The *2000 International Energy Conservation Code* is a product of the International Code Council.[11]

The *2000 International Energy Conservation Code* and most of its antecedents stipulate how the design and construction of four building element groups should be undertaken: building envelopes, HVAC systems, electrical lighting and motors, and service (domestic) hot water production. The code statements concerning the building envelope impose controls on allowable rates of transmission and infiltration heat loss, especially for residential buildings, and of solar radiation heat gain for commercial and other nonresidential building types. Three pathways are offered within the code for demonstrating that envelope components satisfy code statements: first, the performance of envelope assemblies can be predicted (using conventional analytic calculations that are established in ASHRAE documents) and then compared against the code statements; second, the composition of envelope assemblies can be matched prescriptively against tabulated requirements listed in the code; and, third, using any one of a variety of computer simulation programs, the performance of a proposed building design can be modeled and compared against a standardized code-complying building design.

Design issues that are treated in the *2000 International Energy Conservation Code* statements for HVAC systems include guidelines for equipment sizing, bases for establishing zoning in buildings, directives about the required efficiencies of alternative cooling systems (e.g., heat pumps and packaged unitary and split-system refrigeration units), instructions for organizing system balancing and control mechanisms, design procedures for setting up economizer cycles, and requirements for furnishing duct insulation. For the service (domestic) hot water supply and delivery systems, guidelines are stipulated for the allowable efficiencies of heating devices, for providing insulated storage tanks, and for the insulation of delivery piping. For electrical systems, required motor efficiencies are stated and allowable lighting power budgets are tabulated (e.g., identifying the numbers of watts per unit floor area that are permissible for alternative building uses).

B.3.6.2   Promoting indoor air quality   During the past two decades the maintenance of good indoor air quality has become an important subject for building operators and occupants. A number of factors have contributed to the new-found attention devoted to this subject. First, people tend to spend more time indoors now than their forebears did in previous generations. Second, building owners wishing to administer energy-conserving practices for the operation of their buildings have sought tighter building envelopes (i.e., reducing the amounts of fresh air entering buildings by means of infiltration). Some building operators have also reduced the volumetric supply airflow rates provided by HVAC systems. Further, how well air-handling systems are cared for has become a topic for increased concern: can bacteriological entities grow and be spread inside these systems; are filters changed often enough; are particulate matter or potentially noxious compounds transmitted by the moving air; and so forth? And, third, building materials and furnishings used inside buildings are increasingly fabricated with synthetic materials (e.g., plastics, adhesives, surface finishes, and fibrous products). Numbers of these synthetic materials emit gases that are often both malodorous and potentially noxious.

The types of maladies and discomforts experienced by building occupants who are exposed to problematic indoor air quality are almost as multitudinous as the likely causes of these difficulties. The more widely reported indications of poor air quality include various respiratory ailments (e.g., coughing and wheezing, nose and throat inflammation, allergies, and asthma), headaches, skin irritations, and a range of performance limitations (e.g., as caused by feelings of nausea, fatigue, sleepiness, insomnia, muscle aches, and so forth). The breadth of the difficulties that result from inadequate air quality supports the belief in the building industry that more information is needed about this subject and that better solutions are required to lessen occupant difficulties.

The major contaminant groups. There are four basic groups of contaminants whose presences contribute to problematic indoor air quality. First, a number of simple chemical elements or compounds are particularly noxious. For example, several gases produced by the combustion of fossil fuels can cause significant damage to occupants' health; amongst these are carbon monoxide, sulfur dioxide, hydrogen sulfide, nitrogen dioxide, and nitrous oxide. Other gases that are found in buildings and that can cause health problems include radon and ozone. The presence of lead — especially, in paints and gasoline — is also to be avoided.

Second, various particulates are well-known to be bothersome — such as those present in tobacco smoke and the dust, dirt, and sand that become airborne from the force of the wind. Also, asbestos particles when they enter the air of enclosed spaces can be decidedly injurious. Third, a large number of volatile organic compounds (VOC's) are well-known for producing discomfort and disease in people exposed to them. Currently, approximately 300 such compounds have been identified as likely causes of occupant difficulties. And, fourth, numbers of microbiological entities are known to instigate occupant discomfort and loss of function: mold, fungi, bacteria, viruses, plant pollen, animal and human dander, and excreta from insects (e.g., from dust mites).

Where contamination becomes evident. If we examine buildings, we can identify several means by which indoor air becomes contaminated. We have already written about the growing tightness of building envelopes. For example, housing constructed in North America over the past fifty years has been produced with ever-increasing tightness. Past measurements of common housing stock have revealed natural air change rates of about 1.0 air change per hour for houses built conventionally in the 1960s. Yet, similar housing forms constructed with practices that were becoming common in the 1980s had air change rates closer to about 0.50–0.60 air changes per hour. Now, with some superinsulated houses that are being constructed in the northern United States and Canada, natural air change rates can be as low as 0.10 air changes per hour. Such levels of envelope tightness are being achieved with the use of wrapped and sealed vapor barriers and careful attention to the caulking and sealing of envelope joints amidst the framing.

HVAC systems have been shown to function as both sources of contamination and pathways for the spread of the contaminants. The types of contamination that can develop in an HVAC system and can then be spread by the system include various biotic materials such as bacteria, viruses, molds, and fungi. The air passing through an air-handling system can possess the requisite properties to promote growth and sustenance: adequate moisture and a hospitable temperature. The outbreak of Legionnaires' Disease in a Philadelphia hotel in 1976 is but one of a number of examples of situations where a contaminating agent developed within a conditioning and ventilating system and caused significant occupant distress. Some of these biotic materials will cause occupant discomfort. Others like the Legionnaires' Disease can (and did) actually kill affected occupants.[12] It should be recognized that air-handling systems provide continuous pathways for the movement of contaminated air throughout buildings and can enable the spread of airborne biological substances into occupied spaces.

Various nonbiotic substances can also contaminate the air in a ventilating and conditioning system. One circumstance that happens somewhat frequently is the placement of a fresh air intake in some injudicious location (e.g., near a loading dock where vehicles may wait with their engines idling or next to a plaza where tobacco consumers go to smoke cigarettes). Smoke or dust from some industrial operation can also be drawn into a supply air system if the airborne concentration of these materials is sufficiently high (even if fresh air intakes are well-placed). Lastly, in many urban environments bringing clean, fresh air into an air-handling system can pose particular challenges for the system designer.

Another significant problem area for insuring good quality air is the increasing presence of synthetic materials in buildings. Instead of the reliance on natural materials for building assemblies, finishes, and furnishings, as was the case through about the 1960s, in the last 30 years there has been the introduction of many polymeric substances. These substances can be solids—such as plastics or rubbers—or they can be liquids like paints, varnishes, solvents, lubricants, adhesives, and so forth. Solid polymeric substances will tend to out-gas over several to many years after an initial application, thus posing long-term exposure problems for occupants. Liquid substances—the volatile organic compounds—will evaporate, thereby passing contaminants into the building air. How long any of these liquid substances will create poor air quality conditions is dependent on the length of time that a liquid remains in use (and can continue to volatilize).

Related contaminants are those products consisting of fibrous materials. Examples of such fibrous materials would be those composed of glass, mineral, or wood fibers, which can escape readily into the building air. Sources of these fibers can include insulation batts, duct and pipe insulation, acoustic tile, various woven cloth products, carpeting, and so forth. The difficulty posed to occupants by these fibrous materials is that fiber strands will become airborne and enter into the respiratory passages of the occupants causing irritation and discomfort.

A final grouping of building air contaminants will comprise many of the substances, materials, and other things that we bring into our buildings (or use just outside of our buildings) as part of our everyday lives. Such air contaminants will involve combustion gases from wood stoves, fireplaces, and gas cooking; exhaust from motor vehicles; gases and particulate matter produced by smoking tobacco (or other leafy materials); cleaning and other service chemical compounds; cosmetics and personal care products (including perfumes, colognes, air "fresheners"); and pesticides. One other type of indoor air contaminant includes the inevitable body odors and human (and animal)-produced gases, which are also normal life components.

Potential solutions to ensure indoor air quality. To create an environment with good air quality the primary requirements are that the air should have properties consistent with thermal comfort needs and that there should be satisfactory air circulation. Thus, the air (dry-bulb) temperature in building spaces should exist between 68 to 80 °F (20 to 27 °C), and the relative humidity should range between 25 to 55 percent (usually, approaching the higher end of this range).[13] The volumetric airflow rate should be 20 CFM/occupant (9.4 L/s-occupant). As a first-level indicator (for adequate air quality), the concentration of carbon dioxide in any building space should be less than 850 parts per million (ppm).[14]

Once the basic properties of the building air have been shown to be satisfactory, then choices of building assembly materials, finishes, and likely furnishings should be considered. A first step would be to ensure that the building is not located in an area where radon is likely to rise from the ground on which the building sits. If the building is to be constructed on a site known to experience radon exposure, then mitigation strategies must be followed to inhibit any entrance of radon into the building. Similarly, the potential exposure to other well-known hazardous materials—such as asbestos, lead, and, possibly, PCB's (polychlorinated biphenyls)—should be considered. If such hazardous materials are present in an existing building or on a proposed construction site, actions to remove them must be commenced.

A second step in seeking to promote good air quality is to minimize the presence of particulates or materials that can generate particulates. Controlling particulates can be as simple as creating few surfaces on which dirt or dust can accumulate. Alternatively, if the use of dust or dirt-collecting surfaces is inescapable, then these surfaces should be made easy to clean. Where dust and dirt particles are likely to be spread throughout a building by the HVAC system, then careful attention must be paid to incorporating good filtration means within the basic supply air handler. If, too, dust or dirt might probably accumulate on the interior surfaces of ducting, then provisions should be offered to allow the cleaning of the surfaces.

A third step is to seek to limit the amounts of fibrous segments that can become airborne. For instance, when interior surfaces of ducting are to be lined with fibrous materials—for noise mitigation—then the selection of those materials must be made such that fibrous components will not easily abrade and enter the moving air stream. Building assemblies that are composed of fibrous materials—for example, acoustic paneling, carpets, cloth fabrics, insulation batts, and the like—should be installed with sealing finishes (thereby, to prevent fiber segments from breaking off and entering the room air).

A fourth step in seeking good air quality should involve limiting the use of sources of volatile organic compounds (VOC's) within occupied building spaces. Probably, of all the various tasks required to promote good air quality, this step will prove to be the most difficult to accomplish, primarily because of the ubiquity in today's buildings of the VOC sources and the VOC's that these sources emit. Some of the more obvious sources of VOC's include common synthetic adhesives, sealants, and surface coatings; particleboard, plywood, and fiberboards; various flooring products such as carpeting, cork, and vinyl tiles; and many kinds and types of furniture. Often, the base materials in these sources do not cause poor air quality. Instead, where these sources are used in buildings, air quality is compromised by the substantial inclusion of adhesives, sealants, and surface coatings, all of which augment the base materials. Perhaps the products that most contaminate indoor air are the furniture pieces placed throughout buildings. Much of current furniture manufacturing is done using plastics as the base materials and then supplementing these base materials with synthetic adhesives, dyes, and paints and other sealants. Both the base materials and these supplementary additives will emit various VOC's into room air for sustained periods long after the introduction of these furnishings into buildings.

A fifth step in fostering the provision of good air quality requires considering whether any of a variety of microbiological contaminant sources is likely to be present in a building. Some human-produced or caused sources are perhaps inevitably present in buildings (e.g., human and animal dander and the associated dust mites and their excreta). The existence of pollen and its entrance into buildings seem inescapable (although means are available for minimizing the airborne concentration of pollen). Bacteria, mold, and fungi can be introduced into buildings in numbers of ways and from many alternative sources. Most of these ways and sources result from the occupancy and use of a building. Less often are bacteria, mold, and fungi introduced into a building during its construction (or as a result of a direct act of designing). Generally, the growth and propagation of these

SIDEBAR B.2 Selected annotated bibliography about indoor air quality

————. *Introduction to indoor air quality: a self-paced learning module* [produced by the United States Environmental Protection Agency, United States Public Health Service, and National Environmental Health Association], (Washington, D.C.: U.S. Environmental Protection Agency, Office of Air and Radiation, 1991).

The principal topics include descriptions of the contaminants causing poor air quality, potential health concerns (and human responses) for poor air quality, and the probable causes of the poor air quality. Guidelines for controlling (and solving) air quality problems are suggested. Regulatory approaches for treating air quality issues are identified.

Lee, T., D. DeBiasio, and A. Santini, *Health and The Built Environment: Indoor Air Quality* [produced as a Resource Package for the Vital Signs Curriculum Materials Project, University of California, Berkeley, 1995], available at the Web address: http://www.arch.ced.berkeley.edu/vitalsigns/res/downloads/rp/iaq/iaq.pdf.

This package describes the types of contaminants and the sources from which the contaminants enter building air. Methodologies for measuring air quality and identifying air contaminants are explained, and strategies for implementing measurement procedures are suggested.

Hays, S.M., R.V. Gobbell, and N.R. Ganick, *Indoor Air Quality: Solutions and Strategies,* (New York: McGraw-Hill, Inc., 1995)

An architect, industrial hygienist, and mechanical engineer have written this excellent book. It

consists of three main chapters entitled, "Industrial hygiene and its application to IAQ," "Mechanical engineering and IAQ," and "Architecture, construction, and operations." The book offers practical scientific explanations of the causes of poor air quality and engineering and architectural solutions for remediating air quality problems.

LeClair, K., and D. Rousseau, *Environmental by Design, Volume I: Interiors,* (Point Roberts, Washington: Hartley & Marks, Inc., 1992).

The focus of this book is to identify specific building products whose use will provide good air quality for building occupants. Detailed information is offered about sources of well-behaving and well-performing products. Thus, architects wishing to specify materials and assemblies that will afford healthy environments for their occupants can employ the information presented in this book.

————. "Air contaminants," *2001 ASHRAE Handbook of Fundamentals* [Chapter 12], (Atlanta: American Society of Heating, Refrigerating, and Air-Conditioning Engineers, Inc., 2001).

This chapter offers a brief, yet reasonably thorough, introduction for likely air contaminants, their sources, and some remedies for avoiding the problems otherwise caused by these contaminants. Chapter 13 ("Odors") discusses odors in buildings, identifies potential sources, and describes levels of sensitivities that occupants can exhibit.

biotic forms rely on the presence of greater levels of moisture in the air and/or wetness on surfaces or in building materials. Careful and regular maintenance of HVAC systems and frequent cleaning of internal building surfaces and furnishings are both essential means for limiting the presence and effects of these biotic forms.

The effects of these biotic forms on human health most frequently are to cause allergic reactions or to induce asthma. For a small number of instances the biotic forms can cause pneumonia. A final group of biotic forms encompasses the population of viruses that can infect human beings. The sources of viruses are almost always human beings and other living creatures. Viruses are virtually always spread by human contact with virus-bearing material (i.e., not by airborne means). So, seeking to design buildings or systems to prevent infection by viruses probably has little utility.

Lastly, there can be little question that designing to achieve good indoor air quality is now a relevant subject and is likely to become increasingly more important as more is learned about the causes and sources of air contamination and the solutions that can be applied to reduce it. The discussion offered here is intended to present a brief introduction to this subject. The scientific and professional literature, however, is expanding rapidly and should be consulted freely to maintain currency with the subject.

B.3.6.3 Debating the benefits and liabilities of natural ventilation Many HVAC engineers will argue against relying on natural ventilation strategies as the sole means for providing air circulation and temperature conditioning in buildings. Two principal concerns will usually be cited as the main drawbacks. First, the engineers are seldom confident that occupants will assuredly experience thermal comfort when depending on natural ventilation. Second, the engineers doubt that satisfactory air circulation patterns can be established across building spaces when air is admitted into the spaces only from the building envelope. For these reasons and others that will be identified, engineers will generally oppose design solutions based principally on the implementation of natural ventilation.

Clearly, however, there are long traditions in many regions for the use of natural ventilation strategies for the temperature conditioning and promotion of air circulation. In many locales that have periods of warm, humid weather, natural ventilation strategies have been a conventional answer for responding to the challenges imposed on occupant thermal comfort (for instance, see the discussion in Sections 5.1 and 5.4). Before the advent of air-conditioning practices that are now widely available, the admission of external air using natural ventilation strategies was the foremost method for offering evaporative and convective cooling for building occupants.

Natural ventilation strategies—as means for enabling temperature conditioning and air circulation—offer a number of important benefits for building occupants. First, the practice is energy-efficient: no active devices are required to enable conditioning and circulation. Second, natural ventilation is utilized at the discretion of the occupant: thus, s/he decides when conditioning and/or circulation is/are desirable and institutes the manual controls needed to facilitate its use. Third, natural ventilation makes possible fresh air admission and the alteration of room temperatures virtually immediately after commencing it (as well as in the near vicinity of where an occupant is in the space). And, fourth, admitting external air and permitting it to flow across a building space will often produce a diversity of experience in the space (i.e., the thermal and air movement properties of the space will vary across the space).

In contrast, a number of liabilities can also be evident when occupants rely on natural ventilation for temperature conditioning and air circulation. A principal limitation is that spaces in which intermediate partitions are present or for which the distances between air entry locations are large cannot be naturally ventilated effectively (i.e., air taken in at envelope entry locations will not flow uniformly and well throughout such spaces). Thus, for natural ventilation to function well, buildings must be laid out in single-banked floor plans and with shorter distances between entry and exit locations (see section 5.1.3.1). Second and relatedly, the admission of outside air by natural ventilation can usually be controlled only in limited fashions. Thus, where the admitted air flows and how rapidly it flows are often not subject to ready manipulation. The pattern of inward flow will be dependent on the magnitude of the pressure gradient exerted by the incoming air (i.e., the difference between the wind pressure and the ambient atmospheric pressure). The pattern will also be dependent on whether the air is principally admitted on a windward or lee-ward elevation of the building.

The incoming air will exhibit a greater pressure gradient at the building envelope. As the entering air moves into and across the floor plan of the building, this pressure gradient will dissipate and the airflow will be more diffused. So, to encourage the flow of incoming air in useful directions and with an effective spread (distribution) will require careful forethought (and may require some modification of the entry devices and directional controls following initial occupancy).

Another group of liabilities posed for natural ventilation concerns the usually limited abilities to control the nature of the incoming air. When natural ventilation is employed as a fully passive operations strategy, there will be little opportunity to modify the temperature or relative humidity of the incoming air. To get air usefully into more central areas of a building floor plan (inward from the envelope entry locations), the airflow must be driven by a sufficient pressure gradient. A particular liability with bringing in exterior air to cool the interior of a building is that if an occupant sits or works in close proximity to an entry location and the entering air flows in with substantial pressure (and velocity), the occupant may often feel thermally uncomfortable (e.g., just like being exposed to drafty conditions).

Additionally, the air entering via natural ventilation cannot be cleansed of dust, dirt, and other air contaminants such as pollen and various other biotic materials, odors, vehicular exhaust gases, and so forth. Noise admission is also a common problem when external air is brought into buildings for natural ventilation. Many cityscapes in the Third-World are as noisy as cities in the industrialized nations: complaints about the trade-offs between utilizing natural ventilation and dealing with the resulting noise intrusions are many and consistent. Also, air entry pathways must be covered with suitable insect screening to minimize opportunities for insects to invade living and work spaces. And the air entry pathways must be protected so that precipitation will not be admitted into occupied building spaces.

One final qualification about the liabilities of relying on natural ventilation is that the entry pathways for air must be adequately protected so that the personal security of occupants is not compromised. Thus, these entryways should not enable ne'er-do-wells from gaining unintended access to buildings.

In summary, natural ventilation offers powerful and useful opportunities for providing thermal conditioning and for promoting air circulation in buildings. But it must be designed for carefully (i.e., with regard to potential liabilities). Further, it is possible—although admittedly somewhat difficult—to integrate natural ventilation strategies with the operation of HVAC systems (thus, creating hybrid systems and operations). The principal difficulty is balancing the supply and return air streams of the HVAC system so that effective looping of the moving air occurs. Generally, natural ventilation strategies function better at the perimeter of buildings, whereas mechanical ventilation can work in either the interior or perimeter zones. But HVAC systems can be designed to provide principal conditioning and circulation for the building interior with the perimeter being treated by natural ventilation.

One other strategy for enhancing natural ventilation possibilities is the application of controlled channels for transporting external air further into buildings (i.e., beyond simply ventilating the perimeter zone of a building). In Section 5.2.3.2 we have described the uses of wind scoops and cool tubes as two examples of devices by which external air is admitted to the interior — more central areas — of buildings. Such devices are fundamentally passive operations techniques, as they are employed in vernacular building forms. But the performance of such devices can be enhanced by the addition of motor-driven fans into the air channels.

Section B.4 | A SAMPLE DESIGN AND INTEGRATION OF AN HVAC SYSTEM

In the following text we are going to demonstrate how an HVAC system could be designed for a representative building. The emphasis here will be on presenting a systematic problem-solving approach to the problem. The resulting solution will necessarily

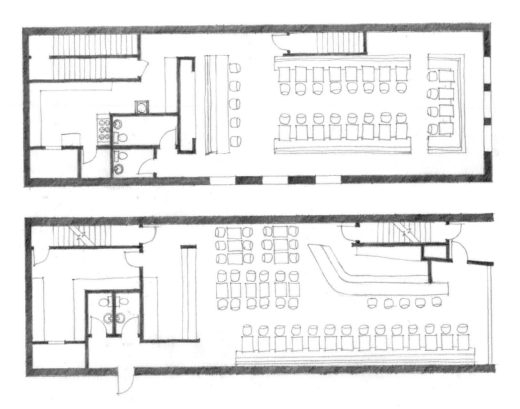

Figure B.15 Floor plans for the two stories of the restaurant are presented here. The first floor is shown in the bottom image, and the second floor appears at the top.

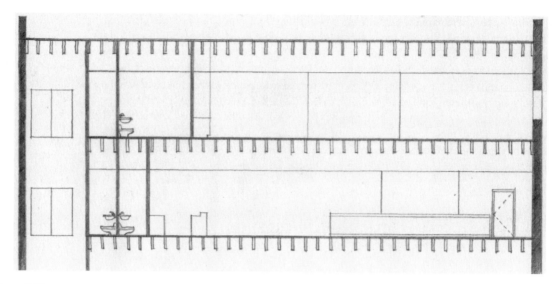

Figure B.16 A sectional drawing showing the two floors and the interstitial spaces for the restaurant building.

be approximate, relying on the information previously offered in this chapter. But the problem-solving approach and the solution should show well enough how a typical HVAC system can be arrived at.

The problem involves designing a heating, ventilating, and air-conditioning system for a restaurant. This restaurant is located in a city in the northern part of the American Midwest. The restaurant will occupy an old light-industrial building that is being remodeled to house it. The owners wish to serve contemporary cuisine focusing on providing a fine dining experience for their customers. Service will be provided for both lunches and dinners.

The main part of the restaurant — the part that is to be conditioned and ventilated by the HVAC system — consists of two stories above grade. A partial basement is present, but it can only be used for storage and dish washing. Food preparation will occur on both of the above-grade floors. Dining will also occur on both floors. Proposed architectural layouts for the first and second floors are shown in Figure B.15, and an architectural section appears in Figure B.16.

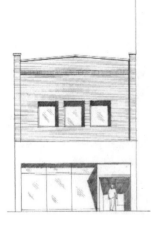

Figure B.17 The front elevation for the restaurant.

The building was initially constructed in the 1890s and is composed of masonry walls and wood-framed floors and roof. The developers of the restaurant — the future operators — wish to retain as much of these original assemblies, although they will alter the street front elevation (see Figure B.17). The building has floor-to-floor heights of 16' (4.9 m) for each of the two stories. The side wall-to-side wall dimension is 24' (7.3 m). No intermediate structural members are present between these sidewalls. Instead, the side-wall-to-side-wall dimension is spanned by joists with the *actual* sizes of 3" × 24" (76 mm × 609 mm), that are spaced at 24" (609 mm) on-center. Note that the use of such heavy-timber joists was contemporary with the initial construction of the building: large integral members were readily available in the 1890s American Midwest. On top of the joists is 2" (51 mm) thick wood-decking. The finished surfaces of the ceilings will be gypsum board. The brick surfaces of the walls will be cleaned and finished. Various tapestries will be hung from these walls. The floors will be carpeted, and appropriate furnishings will be used throughout the dining areas of both floors.

B.4.1   ORGANIZING A SYSTEMS DESIGN SOLUTION

The overall objectives of this problem are several. First, it is necessary to create a comfortable, efficient, and reasonably cost-effective HVAC system. Second, the operation of this system must satisfy the restaurant function (i.e., both diners and the staff must be provided with a pleasant environment in which to eat and work, respectively). Third, the solution to this problem should identify the components of a suitable system and the locations in the building where the components would be installed. And, fourth, the solution should offer information about how the components can be integrated with the structural system and how the desired character for the restaurant spaces can be maintained. To demonstrate systems integration (i.e., that the components of these systems will fit within available spaces), establishing the sizing of components for the HVAC system will also be useful.

Design conditions. The air temperature and humidity in the dining areas should be maintained within comfortable ranges (likely, 68–72 °F [20–22 °C] and about 40 percent relative humidity). Similarly, food preparation and service will benefit from the maintenance of acceptable thermal and humidity conditions in the kitchen areas (although wider ranges of temperature will probably be tolerable for the staff). In the dining area the thermal loads — the amount of heat contributed by the diners — will vary depending on the number of occupants present at any time (i.e., the greater the number of diners in attendance, the larger the heat gain). Note also that the thermal loads will generally reach peaks twice per day: the first during the luncheon hours, the second during dinnertime. High heat gain rates will be generated in the kitchen areas because of the number of food preparation devices used there (e.g., cooking facilities, coffee makers, food processors, refrigerators, steam tables, and even the high activity rates of the staff).

The maintenance of good air circulation will also be important. First, odors (aromas) created during the preparation of food must be kept away from the diners: if such odors reach the diners, the diners' taste buds will be desensitized, causing losses of appetite. Second, the required airflow direction must be from the dining areas toward the kitchens, and not vice versa. Thus, the dining areas should be operated at a slightly positive pressure differential (relative to atmospheric pressure), and the kitchen areas should be maintained at slightly negative pressure differentials. To enable these pressure regimes and to provide means for expelling cooking heat and odors from the kitchens, installation of exhaust hoods over the cooking areas is essential. The operation of these exhaust hoods and the careful admission of fresh air will both aid in establishing thermally comfortable conditions in the kitchen. Third, because return (used) air taken from the dining areas will be laden with food odors and because it is quite difficult to remove these odors from the air — filtering will not work adequately — this return air must be expelled to the building exterior. Heat from this used air can be recovered using commercial-sized air-to-air heat exchangers. But careful cost analyses should be performed to ascertain whether investing in such additional heat-recovery systems equipment is warranted.

Thermal load characteristics. The occupant density for dining areas in restaurants is generally estimated to be one diner per 30 square feet (per 2.8 m^2). As there are approximately 3000 square feet (279 m^2) of dining area, then about 100 diners can be expected to be in attendance when the restaurant is fully occupied.

The restaurant — both the kitchen areas and the dining areas — will operate in an *internal-load-dominant* manner when the restaurant is half to fully occupied (i.e., the rate of heat produced by the occupants, lighting systems, kitchen equipment, and so forth will exceed — even greatly — the rate of heat loss at the building envelope). Thus, the air-conditioning system will be required to provide heat removal much of the time that the restaurant staff are serving food to diners. Using Table A.4, a first-approximate basis for estimating cooling loads for restaurants is that one ton of cooling will be required for each 120 square feet of occupied space (0.31 kW/1 m²). As the total floor area for the two stories of the restaurant is about 4000 square feet (372 m²), a cooling load for the building will be about 33 tons (115 kW).

An estimate of required ventilation capacities can be obtained also from Table A.4. For restaurants, the need for supply air circulation is suggested to be 2.0 CFM/square feet of occupied floor area. Again, as the total floor area for the two stories of the restaurant is about 4000 square feet (372 m²), then the total volumetric air flow rate provided by the air-handling system should be 8000 CFM (3775 L/s).

System selection. First, the air-conditioning system for this restaurant should be capable of providing heating during the start-up times when the staff has just begun operations for the day and before the first diners arrive. Of course, if the daytime external temperatures are already warm—as during summer—then no heating would be required. When the restaurant is serving lunches or dinners and is at least half-occupied with diners, cooling will be necessary. And a well-developed ventilation capability for the system is essential.

Other issues should also be considered when selecting an air-conditioning system. As a first approximation, we will presume that the restaurant will basically operate as a single zone. Either heating will be required throughout the building (during start-up times), or cooling will be required throughout the building (during the rest of any day). There do not appear to be any circumstances where heating and cooling could be required simultaneously and in different locations in the building. The rate of heat gain in the kitchens will usually be greater than in the dining areas, but treating these different rates of heat gain can be done by supplying more cooling air to the area with the greater cooling need.

A second issue concerns the limited space on each of the two floors that would be available for installing an air-conditioning system. If we employ the rule-of-thumb suggested in Section A.4.1, then an internal floor area of about 10 percent of the 4000 square feet (372 m²) of the restaurant will be needed to house the conditioning and ventilating central devices. Thus, internal space for a fully developed air-conditioning system might require a floor area of about 400 square feet (37.2 m²). As this amount of space might otherwise be used to seat diners or for food preparation, getting the restaurant owners to agree to place the main air-conditioning equipment within the building may prove challenging. Installing the main air-conditioning equipment in the basement may require either substantially enlarging or rehabilitating the basement area to accommodate this equipment. Another concern about placing the equipment in the basement could involve questions about how to get the equipment into the basement initially and how to repair and replace equipment components during the operating lifetime of the equipment.

One further topic—relating concerns about equipment installation, maintenance, and replacement—should address a matching between the useful lifetime of any main air-conditioning equipment and the probable lifetime of the restaurant business itself. Whereas the useful operating lifetime for air-conditioning equipment can usually be predicted, how long a restaurant will remain in business is uncertain. Additionally, once the building in its original state has been converted into a restaurant, whether the building could subsequently be adapted to serve some other business function is problematic. However, recognizing that this restaurant with its present ownership might be expected to remain in business for less than one (or two) decade(s), then choosing the main air-conditioning equipment for a similar service period seems to make good economic sense.

Therefore, given these performance requirements and operating concerns, let us offer a series of recommendations. First, an *all-air system* operation should be sought for the air-conditioning system (i.e., air will be circulated by the system, both to provide temperature conditioning and to furnish ventilation). Either a constant volume, variable temperature, or a variable air volume with constant temperature operation could be successful. The variable volume operation — matching the amount of airflow to the numbers of diners present —

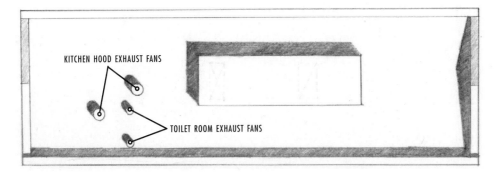

Figure B.18 A rooftop view (showing the locations of the rooftop conditioning unit and the exhaust fans).

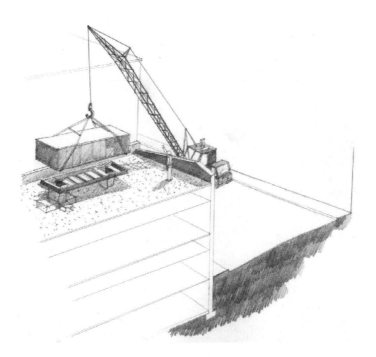

Figure B.19 Here, the direct refrigerant unit is lifted into place on the rooftop. Prior to this installation step, the mounting will have been constructed. The ducting and controls will also have been assembled. When the unit is dropped onto the mounting, it can be attached to the necessary mechanical and electrical connections and will be ready immediately for operation.

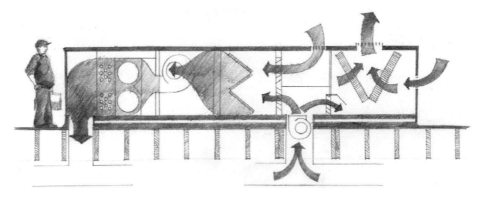

Figure B.20 The internal workings of the rooftop, unitary, direct-refrigerant, air-conditioning device are shown here. The basic components include, starting on the right and moving toward the left:

- A compressor and condenser (the slanted coils provide an air-cooling operation for the condenser).
- Fresh air and return air could be mixed in a plenum just to the left of the entries of these two air streams (but there are dampers in the passages of each of the airstreams into the mixing plenum, and the dampers for the return air would be closed for this restaurant [to negate the reuse of the odor-laden return air.])
- The air passing through the mixing plenum will flow through filters, being drawn to the left by the supply air fan.
- The two large circles divert the air flowing from the fan to make the flow more laminar.
- The supply air will then flow across a series of coils at which the air will be temperature conditioned to satisfy thermal requirements for the restaurant interior.
- Lastly, the air will enter into the supply air ducting system for distribution throughout the two floors of the restaurant.

Figure B.21 A hood would be placed above the principal cooking surface in the first-floor food preparation area. The cooking gases and odor-laden air would be exhausted from this food preparation area by an exhaust fan that is located on the roof (see Figures B.18 and B.22).

will more likely be more energy-efficient. But, with the possibility that there might be substantial heat generated in the kitchen on any day prior to the arrival of the luncheon diners, having a constant volume system might offer better means for maintaining thermal comfort for the restaurant staff. The choice of the specific operating scheme will thus require further study (that can be postponed until the design development phase).

A second recommendation is that a unitary packaged direct-refrigerant system should be employed. Several reasons for this choice can be cited. First, the packaged direct-refrigerant unit will provide full service capabilities in terms of both temperature conditioning and ventilation. This unit is ideally suited to operate for a single-zone building, and can supply either warmed or cooled air at any time. Supply and return air-handling fans are present in the unit. And constant volume or variable volume ventilation options are both available. The system also furnishes economizer-cycle operation (thereby offering the promise of achieving greater energy-efficiency during operation). In addition, depending on where the packaged unit is placed, easy installation and service access can be attained.

The location recommended for placing the direct-refrigerant unit is on the roof of the restaurant (see Figure B.18). The curb mounting and connections to the ducting system can be prepared prior to the delivery of the rooftop unit. Then, the unit can be brought to the restaurant site, easily lifted into place (see Figure B.19), and connected to the ducting system (and to the electrical power service). Once installation has been completed, the system can begin operation (see Figure B.20).

System layout. The ducting system is organized in the following manner. Horizontal supply and return ducts are run in ceiling spaces that lie between the bottom of the joists and the top of gypsum ceiling board. With a floor-to-floor dimension of 16' (4.9 m), a floor-to-finished-ceiling height of 11' (3.4 m), and a joist and decking depth of about 26" (660 mm), there will be an open vertical space in the ceiling of about 32" (812 mm) that is available for running horizontal ducting. Vertical ducting running from the rooftop unit to the horizontal ducting will be enclosed within infill surrounding the cooking area on the first floor and the bar area on the second floor. Cooking and kitchen exhaust ducting — coming off dedicated hoods — will run vertically to the roof and will be driven by a pair of rooftop exhaust fans (see Figures B.21 and B.22). The two smaller rooftop exhaust fans will remove air from the first- and second-floor bathrooms.

More specifically, the air supply ducting is organized, on a floor-by-floor basis, to furnish eight diffusers regularly placed in the dining areas and two diffusers located in the cooking and kitchen areas, for each of the two floors. A three-dimensional representation of the supply air ducting system is shown in Figure B.23. In this drawing it can be seen that the total supply air quantity leaves the rooftop unit and passes into a main horizontal duct running in the second floor ceiling volume. Half of the air passes horizontally to the second-floor air supply ducting. The other half of the air passes horizontally to a vertical duct that transports that air volume to the horizontal ducting of the first-floor supply network. Then, from the several diffusers in the ceilings of the two floors, the ventilating and conditioning air streams will pass into the occupied spaces. Using 10 supply air diffusers for each floor offers a greater likelihood that the supply air will be uniformly distributed throughout these occupied spaces. Further, choosing 10, rather than a fewer number, ensures that the supply air streams may enter the occupied spaces at relatively lower velocities. Such lowered velocities will usually provide more thermally comfortable conditions, as well as lower noise levels emanating from the supply system.

A three-dimensional drawing of the return air system is presented in Figure B.24. In the ceiling of each floor, three grilles provide return air intakes from the dining areas.

Figure B.22 A kitchen hood exhaust fan (mounted on the roof an adequate distance from the direct refrigerant unit).

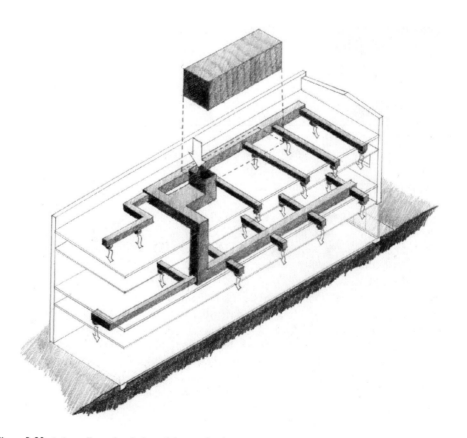

Figure B.23 A three-dimensional view of the supply air system.

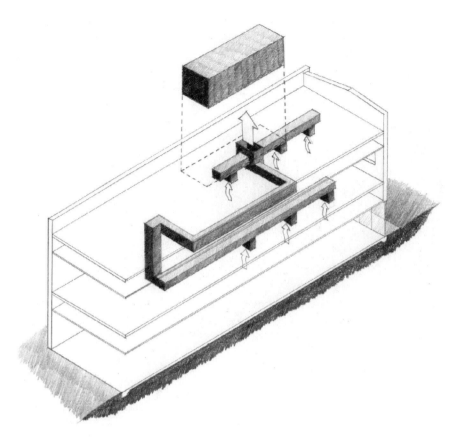

Figure B.24   A three-dimensional view of the return air system.

These grilles are connected with horizontal ducting. The returning air from the first floor ascends in a vertical volume that contains the return air ducting, as well as the ducting that transports cooking exhaust to the roof. The vertical duct containing the returning air from the first floor passes to a horizontal duct located in the second floor ceiling, which in turn connects to return air ducting that services the second-floor grilles. All of this return air from the dining areas of the two stories then runs vertically up to the rooftop unit (drawn there by the return air fan that is a component of the rooftop unit).

Note that the cooking and kitchen hoods take in the used air in these areas and pass it to vertical ducting, which run to the roof. The exhaust intake (hood) for the first floor is located over the cooking area. Alternatively, the exhaust intake (hood) for the second floor is located in the kitchen area behind the bar area. These hoods thus take over the role of the return air grilles and ducting (that serve the dining areas).

Plan views of the combined supply air and return air ducting layouts are shown in Figure B.25. In numbers of locations the supply air ducting runs and the return air ducting runs cross over each other. Each ducting run — supply and return, respectively — is accorded a specific plane, with the supply air ducts uniformly placed beneath the return air ducting.

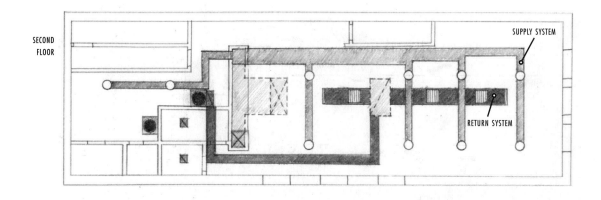

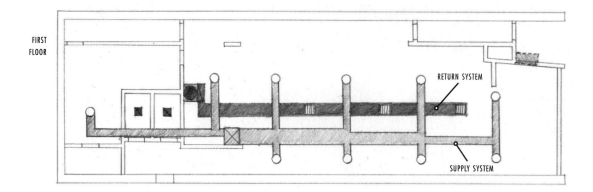

Figure B.25 Reflected ceiling plans for the supply and return air handling ducting layouts.

Integrating and fine-tuning the design of HVAC system components. A proposal for the sizing of the various supply and return ducts is offered in Figures B.26 and B.27. This proposal begins by having an equal amount of volumetric air flow exiting each supply air diffuser on each floor (400 CFM [189 L/s]). The amount of air flowing in each supply air duct segment is accumulated (working back toward the rooftop unit). The supply air duct sizing is established, first, by supposing that the velocity of air movement in the ducting is 800 feet/minute [4.06 m/s] (see Table A.5). Second, the amount of air flowing in each duct segment — in CFM or L/s — can then be divided by the air velocity — in fpm or m/s — to arrive at the necessary cross-sectional area for the duct segment (in square feet or m²).

The sizing of the return air ducting can be accomplished in the same manner, although we offer some variants to the procedure here. First, the return air velocity can be set somewhat higher than the supply air velocity. Second, rather than sizing the return air ducting on an accumulative basis (as was done with the supply air ducting), we will propose using constant cross-sectional areas for the return air ducting (a strategy that is sometimes used for return air ducting).

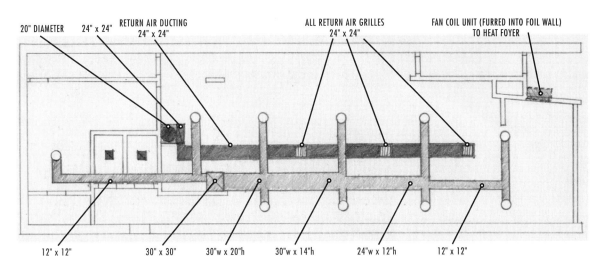

ALL BRANCH DUCTS, 6"w x 12"h   •   ALL SUPPLY AIR DIFFUSERS, 16" DIAMETER

Figure B.26 Approximate sizes for the HVAC system components for the first floor of the restaurant (as shown in a reflected ceiling plan).

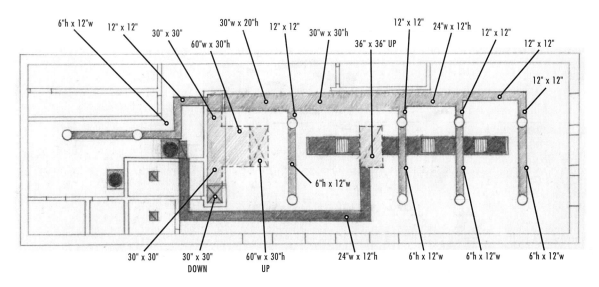

ALL SUPPLY AIR DIFFUSERS, 16" DIAMETER
EXHAUST VENT DUCT, 1ST FLOOR TO ROOF, 20" DIAMETER

ALL RETURN AIR GRILLES, 24" x 24"
EXHAUST VENT DUCT, 2ND FLOOR TO ROOF, 14" DIAMETER

Figure B.27 Approximate sizes for the HVAC system components for the second floor of the restaurant (as shown in a reflected ceiling plan).

Previously, we noted that there should be an open rectangular volume in the ceiling spaces between the bottoms of the joists and the gypsum ceiling board with a depth of about 32" (812 mm). Where the supply and return air ducts cross over each other, the combined thickness of any duct crossings will be no greater than about 22–24" (560–610 mm), allowing for duct insulation and any related joining and installation hardware. Also, the largest depth of a duct segment would be the 30" (760 mm) dimension present for the main supply air duct leaving the rooftop unit.

Two qualifications to this sizing proposal should also be noted. Often, the magnitudes of the volumetric air flow rates — in the various duct segments of the supply and return systems — that are predicted during designing will be modified when the system designers undertake the commissioning of the system. So, one goal of the systems designers is to ensure that during commissioning there can be some flexibility in the final setting of these volumetric flow rates (e.g., by sizing the ducting to enable this commissioning).

The other qualification concerns the disposition of the gathered return air, which will be laden with food odors that cannot easily be removed. To ensure that the supply air does not reintroduce these food odors into the dining areas, the return air would need to be expelled to the atmosphere (i.e., "dumped"). In this proposed solution we have not included a heat recovery device. But such a device might well be designed and installed in such a system as this one. However, before a decision could be made about the utility of a heat recovery device in this system, the system designer should conduct a careful study to assess whether the installation and use of such a device would be cost-effective.

Finally, we estimated that the rooftop unit would need a capacity of at least 33 tons. Since most manufacturers of rooftop air-conditioning units size their equipment in increments of approximately 10 tons per step increase, we will select a rooftop unit having a 40 ton (140 kW) capacity. The approximate size for such a unit will be about 26' (7.9 m) long by 8' (2.4 m) wide by 6' (1.8 m) high. An approximate weight for such a unit would be about 8000 pounds (3630 Kg), so some building-up of the roof structure would be needed to accommodate the mass of this unit.

ENDNOTES and SELECTED ADDITIONAL COMMENTS

1.   ———. Chapter 20 ("Humidifiers") of the *2000 ASHRAE Handbook: HVAC Systems and Equipment,* (Atlanta: American Society of Heating, Refrigerating, and Air-Conditioning Engineers, Inc., 2000), pages 20.1–20.10.

2.   ———. *2001 ASHRAE Handbook of Fundamentals* (Atlanta: American Society of Heating, Refrigerating, and Air-Conditioning Engineers, Inc., 2001); see Chapters 25–30.

3.   A catalog of 99th percentile (winter) design condition temperatures for many North American and world cities appears in Chapter 27, "Climatic design information," of the *2001 ASHRAE Handbook of Fundamentals* (Atlanta: American Society of Heating, Refrigerating, and Air-Conditioning Engineers, Inc., 2001).

4.   ———. *Washington State Ventilation and Indoor Air Quality Code,* Chapter 51-13 of the Washington Administrative Code, prepared by the Washington State Building Code Council (commencement date: July 1, 2001).

5.   For a further explanation about locating air-handling terminal devices and discussion about air movement in spaces, see Chapter 32, "Space air diffusion," of the *2001 ASHRAE Handbook of Fundamentals* (Atlanta: American Society of Heating, Refrigerating, and Air-Conditioning Engineers, Inc., 2001).

6. For further information about commissioning, see Chapter 41, "Building commissioning," in the *1999 ASHRAE Handbook: Heating, Ventilating, and Air-Conditioning Applications* (Atlanta: American Society of Heating, Refrigerating, and Air-Conditioning Engineers, Inc., 1999).

7. ———. "Status of State Energy Codes," May/June 2000 (published at the Web address: http://bcap-energy.org/update.html).

8. ———. *Energy Conservation in New Building Design,* ASHRAE Standard 90-75 (Atlanta: American Society of Heating, Refrigerating, and Air-Conditioning Engineers, Inc., 1975).

9. ———. *Model Energy Code,* (Falls Church, Virginia: Council of American Building Officials). Initial and subsequent versions were published in 1992, 1993, and 1995.

10. ———. *Energy Efficient Design of New Buildings Except Low-Rise Residential Buildings,* Standard 90.1-1989, jointly produced by the American Society of Heating, Refrigerating, and Air-Conditioning Engineers, Inc. and the Illuminating Engineering Society of North America, (Atlanta: American Society of Heating, Refrigerating, and Air-Conditioning Engineers, Inc., 1989). Note that a revised version of this standard, renumbered as 90.1–1999, has more recently been issued by the American Society of Heating, Refrigerating, and Air-Conditioning Engineers, Inc., the Illuminating Engineering Society of North America, and the Building Standards and Guidelines Program of the U.S. Department of Energy.

11. Turchen, S., "The latest and greatest on energy efficiency in residential building codes and standards," presented at the Excellence in Building Conference, Energy Efficient Building Association, October 1998 (published at the Web address: http://www.energycodes.org/news/98paper.htm).

12. Fraser, D.W., et al., "Legionnaires' Disease: Description of an epidemic of pneumonia," *New England Journal of Medicine, 297,* pages 1189–1203, 1977.

13. See Section 3.5 for further information about thermal comfort requirements.

14. Second-level indicators or tests for air quality could include determining whether the air in a space had elevated or lower concentrations of carbon monoxide, sulfur dioxide, nitrogen dioxide, nitrous oxide, and, potentially, other inorganic gases that were above or below specific industry standards.

Services and Systems for Achieving Fire Safety and Protection

IDEALLY, BUILDINGS SHOULD be designed to prevent fire from occurring within them. However, because many — if not, most — building fires result from materials brought into buildings after occupancy rather than from the building assemblies themselves, designers alone cannot avert the occurrence of fire, which will inevitably happen in some buildings. Therefore, the responsibility of designers is to create buildings whose characteristics minimize the potentially disastrous effects that fire can have for occupants and property.

Four fundamental issues arise when designers seek to create buildings that will offer safety and protection against fire. First, in the presence of a fire event, means must be available to ensure that the building occupants can be evacuated or otherwise rendered safe from the hazardous conditions produced by the fire. Thus, the likelihood of occupant injury or death resulting from a fire event must be reduced to as near a probability of zero as possible. Second, the protection of property in the course of a fire event is strictly important. Design efforts must be made to minimize the damage that may result. Third, initial building design work must be directed toward minimizing the amounts of money and time that would otherwise be needed for making repairs *after* a fire event does happen. And, fourth, buildings must be designed to minimize circumstances whereby buildings adjacent to one in which a fire event occurs might suffer fire-related damage.

In addition to these four general goals for designing safe and protected buildings, there are seven principal tasks that designers must deal with while seeking to create fire-safe buildings. First, building assemblies should be created—by design and construction—that will minimize the occurrence of fire events. Second, if a fire should occur, then the building assemblies should minimize the opportunities for the growth and spread of the fire *within the fire zone*. Third, systems should be present to detect the onset of a fire event and to alert building occupants of the fire. Fourth, means for evacuating occupants from the fire zone (or moving them into areas of refuge) must be well developed. Fifth, fire suppression systems must be present and should function automatically. Sixth, building assemblies must be utilized that will limit the spread of the fire *beyond the immediate fire zone*. And, seventh, ready accessibility to the fire zone and well-functioning extinguishment capabilities must be available for fire fighters.

Selected approaches to address these seven tasks will be discussed throughout the remainder of this chapter. As a means for organizing these discussions, this chapter is divided into two components. The first component will discuss building fire safety features that should be considered and should begin to be implemented during the schematic design phase. These features will largely involve a series of *passive* building elements that must be incorporated into the basic organization of the building (e.g., egress provisions, creation of fire spread barriers, facilitation of fire-fighting, and so forth).

Alternatively, attention to the placement and incorporation of *active* fire safety hardware systems is best left to later phases of the design process (with the exception of the approximate incorporation of sprinkler system hardware, which should be accounted for during schematic designing). However, in the second component of this chapter, brief explanations will be offered about the characteristics of the generic fire event along with the active control systems that are required to ensure occupant safety and property protection.

Section C.1 | PROVIDING FOR FIRE SAFETY DURING THE SCHEMATIC DESIGN PHASE

Four topics appear most likely to need attention during schematic designing; these subjects demand space planning consideration and require that specific accommodations be integrated in layout solutions from the earliest design phases. The topics include making provisions for occupant egress, taking care of fire suppression capabilities (here, specifically, using automatic sprinkler systems), supporting fire-fighting activities, and ensuring that effective fire barriers are established between building spaces (otherwise known as furnishing *compartmentation*).

C.1.1   ESTABLISHING MEANS OF EGRESS

The basic principle of providing egress from a building space in which a fire could occur involves ensuring that occupants have *continuous, unobstructed, fire-safe pathways* leading from their occupancy spaces to grade-level external areas beyond the affected building. Alternatively, if access to the exterior of a building at grade-level cannot be gained (e.g., by mobility-challenged occupants of high-rise buildings, bed-ridden patients in hospitals, or elderly occupants of nursing facilities), then these people must be provided with areas of refuge within the building. Areas of refuge must be separated from common building areas by fire-resistive construction: these areas are intended to serve as temporary staging areas while fire suppression is begun.

Means of egress for building occupants generally consist of multiple sets of three components: an exit access, the exit, and an exit discharge (see Figures C.1 and C.2). The *exit access* is the pathway leading from the occupant's usual location in the building to the exit. Thus, the exit access typically includes the walkway from an occupant's workstation (or desk, seat, and so forth) through the general circulation area of the building floor and to the exit. In the exit access are likely to be doors, corridors, unenclosed stairs or ramps, all of which comprise the walkway leading to an exit. The *exit* consists of vertical and/or horizontal walkways that are enclosed within fire-resistive construction. Common elements of a vertical exit will be the passive enclosure itself, entrance doors, stairways, landings, and a door leading either to a horizontal exit or an exit discharge (i.e., a doorway opening directly on the grade-level exterior). The horizontal exit would consist of a fire-resistive enclosed walkway leading from the stairway to an exit discharge. The *exit discharge* is generally construed as the pathway running from the exit to the building exterior. The exit discharge can be as simple as a fire door separating a stairway from the building exterior or as developed as a passageway leading from the exit to the building exterior. One limitation with exit discharges opening directly to the building exterior is that some fires may occur at grade level, thus blocking the use of the exit (and the exit discharge). Thus, a design guideline offered by the National Fire Protection Association recommends that no more than 50 percent of all exits for any building discharge directly to the exterior. The remaining exit discharges should have protected openings (e.g., where these openings are enclosed in fire-resistive constructions, are served by automatic sprinkler systems, and lead to an area away from the building perimeter).[1]

The intent in the design of egress is to create pathways that will be free of smoke, flame, and heat, for the time necessary for occupants to leave the building. The components of egress include the enclosures, the passageways, and doors separating exit accesses and exits, as well as exits and the exterior. The designing of exits and exit discharges require that they be enclosed with fire-resistive assemblies that effectively separate the spaces from the remainder of the building. In addition to these passive components, any exit that is present more than 75 ft (22.9 m) above grade level must be able to be pressurized by mechanical means — have pressurizing fans present — to minimize smoke entry into the exit.

A second design requirement is that there should be two (or more) means of egress from any space within the building. Thus, there must be two (or more) exits. The specific number of means of egress (and exits) depends on several building parameters, of which the most important are the number of occupants in the building, the distances occupants will be from these exits, the capacity of the exits (how many people can readily use an exit per unit time), and the likely amount of time that will be available for getting people to leave the building. The two (or more) exits should be adequately separated across the floor area of the building, thereby ensuring that if one exit is blocked by the presence of smoke, flame, and heat, then the other exit can function as a fire-safe means of egress.

When people occupy spaces that they cannot readily leave (because of personal physical disabilities), then areas of refuge must be provided for them. Similarly, if occupants are located in building spaces that are too distant for these occupants to easily get to the grade-level building exterior — perhaps, because they occupy an upper floor of a high-rise building — areas of refuge for these occupants must also be created. For instance, bed-ridden patients can scarcely be expected to leave a hospital ward. Also, wheelchair users cannot leave a building via stairways (and elevator usage during fire events generally is restricted). In these instances places of refuge must be created during schematic designing to enable the safe occupancy of the building by these people. These refuge areas need

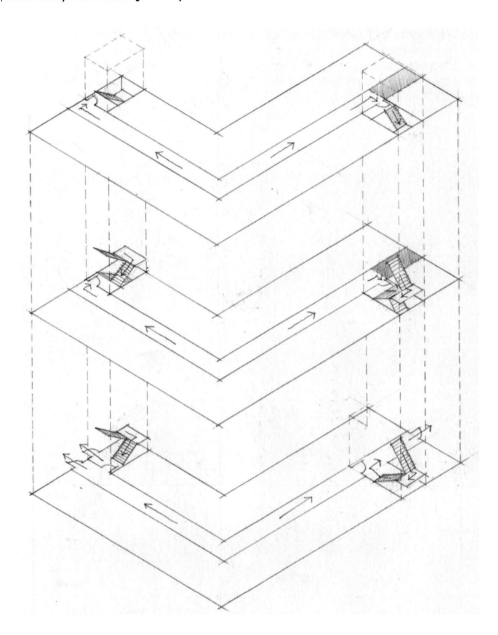

Figure C.1 For this building two sets of exits—fire stairs enclosed in fire-resistive (and smokeproof) assemblies—are present. In the event of a fire (or other emergency) occupants will leave their offices and progress along corridors enclosed with fire-resistive assemblies (exit accesses). The occupants will pass through fire-resistive (and smokeproof) doors into the fire stair enclosures—vertical exits—and descend to the grade level. At the grade level occupants using the north stairway will pass through a fire-resistive (and smokeproof) door—an exit discharge—directly to the building exterior. The occupants employing the east stairway will leave the stairway at grade level and pass along a corridor constructed with fire-resistive (and smokeproof) assemblies—a horizontal exit—to a fire-resistive (and smokeproof) door—an exit discharge—directly to the exterior. Note that on the third and second floors the portion of the east corridor that extends beyond the east fire stairway is regarded as a *dead-ended* corridor. Typically, building codes stipulate a maximum length for such dead-ended corridors. For example, the *Uniform Building Code* allows a maximum distance that a corridor may extend beyond a fire stairway as 20 ft (6.1 m). See Section 1005.3.4.6 of the *1997 Uniform Building Code,* (Whittier, California: International Conference of Building Officials, 1997), page 1–117.

Figure C.2 An exiting experience from a classroom: both doorways—one is shown in (a)—empty to the third floor balcony (exit access) presented in (b); from this balcony occupants will progress through a fire-resistive door to the fire stairs (exit) and descend the stairs (c); near grade level a fire-resistive door (an exit discharge) opens to an exterior landing that has stairs leading to the grade level. Note that a second set of fire stairs exist and can be used if the occupants leave the classroom and turn to their left.

to be enclosed with assemblies that will resist the penetration of smoke, flame, and heat for suitable lengths of time (i.e., until appropriate fire suppression actions can be taken).

A final requirement for planning exit capabilities is that means must exist to minimize any chances that smoke, flame, or heat can spread vertically by way of an exit (e.g., a stairway). Door assemblies must be selected that will minimize the entrance of smoke, flame, and/or heat. The inclusion of vestibules fronting the exits may also be required. Vertical wall (and any horizontal) assemblies that enclose the exits must be made as impenetrable to smoke, flame, and heat as possible. The passage of ducting, electrical conduit, water supply piping (other than for fire suppression), and so forth through the walls, floors, and ceilings of exit enclosures should be avoided. Lastly, fans must be present to pressurize exits whenever they extend 75 ft (22.9 m) or higher above grade level.

C.1.1.1   Design guidelines for planning means of egress   The intent of the discussion in this section is to identify issues about means of egress that require attention during schematic designing. Because different building occupancies have different requirements for egress design, no single set of numerical values or guidelines will apply as overriding directives for sizing egress components in all buildings. Instead, the provision and sizing of egress components will be governed both by a series of general principles and by numbers of directives that are written specifically for particular occupancies.

The design information that will be presented here applies specifically for new buildings. Information similar in nature but different in magnitude has also been published for existing buildings (e.g., generally in building regulations such as various codes). Note also that industry standards for designing new buildings can also be studied to gain insight about modifying existing buildings.

Laying out adequate means of egress depends on the proper consideration of a series of issues concerning how occupants move through building spaces. First, different activities will require different egress accommodations. People sitting in a movie theater and people working in an office building will have different needs for egress accommodation. The numbers of people in the building and the density with which the building spaces are occupied both should influence how means of egress must be planned (see Table C.1). Greater numbers of people or greater densities of occupants each dictate increased numbers of exits or, possibly, increased exit sizes. Further, the probable ages and physical conditions of the occupants should also be considered when planning means of egress.

A fundamental goal for egress design must be to ensure that occupants have sufficient time to escape from the fire zone (i.e., that means of egress are provided in appropriate numbers and sizes to enable occupant travel away from the fire zone in some time length). For instance, for planning U.S. federal buildings, the General Services Administration recommends that, first, occupants leaving a fire zone should be able to arrive at a fire-safe place—an exit—within 90 seconds of the moment of learning of the existence of a fire and, second, for vertical travel in a stairway, the occupants must be able to arrive at a refuge area (or a grade-level location external to the building) within 5 minutes of downward travel or 1 minute of upward travel. Travel times of greater durations are expected to cause possibly debilitating fatigue among ordinary occupants.[2] The distances along which occupants can move during these travel time estimates are dictated by walking speeds anticipated for people who are likely moving in crowds in response to a fire event (i.e., speeds attainable by groups of people attempting to travel along means of egress during an emergency will be slower than speeds achieved when an occupant moves through a building in ordinary circumstances).

Two further qualifications that govern how egress designs should be executed involve whether the building will be served by a sprinkler system or not and whether substantial quantities of hazardous materials may be present in a building. Generally, buildings that will be served by sprinkler systems can be designed following slightly relaxed egress requirements. For buildings housing the use or storage of hazardous materials (e.g., manufacturing facilities, furniture workshops, photographic processing laboratories, and so forth) requirements for means of egress are more stringent than those stipulated for most other building occupancy types. These more stringent requirements are based on the recognition that higher levels of flammable materials and the greater presence of potential

TABLE C.1
MAXIMUM FLOOR AREA ALLOWANCES PER OCCUPANT

OCCUPANCY	FLOOR AREA IN FT²/OCCUPANT (M²/OCCUPANT)	OCCUPANCY	FLOOR AREA IN FT²/OCCUPANT (M²/OCCUPANT)
Airport terminal		**Kitchens,** commercial	200 (18.59) gross
Concourse	100 (9.29) gross		
Waiting areas	15 (1.39) gross	**Libraries**	
Baggage claim	20 (1.86) gross	Reading rooms	50 (4.65) net
		Stack areas	100 (9.29) gross
Assembly without fixed seats			
Concentrated (chairs only)	7 (0.65) net	**Locker rooms**	50 (4.65) gross
Standing space	5 (0.46) net		
Unconcentrated (tables & chairs)	15 (1.39) net	**Mercantile**	
		Basement & grade floor areas	30 (2.79) gross
Dormitories	50 (4.65) gross	Areas on other floors	60 (5.58) gross
		Storage, stock, shipping areas	300 (27.88) gross
Educational			
Classroom area	20 (1.86) net	**Residential**	200 (18.59) gross
Shops & other vocational areas	50 (4.65) net		
		Stages and platforms	15 (1.39) net
Exercise rooms	50 (4.65) gross		
Institutional areas			
Inpatient treatment areas	240 (22.30) gross		
Outpatient areas	100 (9.29) gross		
Sleeping areas	120 (11.15) gross		

This table appears as Table 1003.2.2.2 of the *International Fire Code 2000,* page 99. Copyright 1999, International Code Council, Inc., Falls Church, Virginia. Reproduced with permission. All rights reserved.

ignition — fire-starting — sources are both likely to exist in these more hazard-laden facilities. Additionally, having hazardous materials and ignition sources existent in these buildings increases the probable intensity and severity of any fire that does begin, thus requiring enhanced egress opportunities for the occupants.

The principal issues dictating how buildings should be designed to accommodate means of egress requirements include the number of exits and their capacities, exit access distances, and vertical and horizontal exit sizes. Determining specific numerical guidelines for each of these issue groups can be gathered from alternative sources. The document *Life Safety Code Handbook,*[3] written by the National Fire Protection Association and based on the *Life Safety Code* (designated as NFPA 101),[4] furnishes explanations of systematic derivations of these numerical guidelines. The other principal source of design guidelines is the *International Fire Code,*[5] a joint production of the three major building-standard-writing bodies in the United States (i.e., the Building Officials and Code Administrators International, Inc. [BOCA], the International Conference of Building Officials [ICBO], and the Southern Building Code Congress International, Inc. [SBCCI]). The *International Fire Code* offers extensive prescriptive statements about how buildings should be laid out to attain fire-safe conditions. As such, the *International Fire Code* functions as a model standard that is the basis for the three principal codes used throughout the United States (i.e., those written by the three organizations identified above). Further, in many respects the authors of the *International Fire Code* have composed their prescriptive statements by drawing upon statements presented and procedures described in the *Life Safety Code.*

The placement of exits in building floor plans depends upon the minimum number of exits required for occupant egress and the exit access distances allowed between occupant locations and the exits. The *International Fire Code* stipulates that the minimum number of exits for a building should be established to match the number of occupants who would use these exits during a building fire. Thus, the minimum number of exits *per floor* should be two, for occupant loads of between one and 500; three, for occupant loads of between 501 and 1000; and four, for occupant loads of more than 1000.[6]

The guidelines for allowable travel distances for exit access address a series of different conditions: common pathways, dead-ended corridors, and exit access travel distances. Generally, permissible travel distances are determined by the nature of the building occupancy (e.g., institutional, educational, assembly, hazardous materials usage, and so forth) and by whether or not the building will be served by a sprinkler system. For buildings with sprinkler systems, allowable travel distances for exit access pathways can range from 200 to 400 feet (61 to 122 m), depending on the occupancy type and with the provision that no hazardous materials are present. Alternatively, if the building will not be served by a sprinkler system, then permissible exit access distances can range from 150 to 300 feet (46 to 92 m), also depending on occupancy type and with the provision that no hazardous materials are present. For buildings that will have hazardous materials present, the exit access pathways must be served by sprinkler systems, and the permissible travel distances can range from 75 to 200 feet (23 to 61 m), depending on the potential severity of the hazardous materials.[7]

Two qualifications exist concerning these permissible travel distances: whether common (or shared) pathways are components of the overall exit access travel distance and whether dead-ended corridors are present adjacent to the exit access pathways. Common pathways are walkway lengths that are shared by alternative exit routes (e.g., exit access pathways to different exit routes lie along the same walkway for some travel distance). The permissible lengths for common pathways range from 75 to 100 feet (23 to 30 m) depending on occupancy type, except in buildings housing hazardous materials for which the permissible common pathways can be no more than 25 feet (7.6 m). A corridor is described as dead-ended where a portion of the corridor extends beyond the entrance to an exit. In such corridors occupants can walk toward and past the entrance to the exit before realizing that they have passed by the entrance (thus, requiring them to retrace their exit access pathway). The permissible lengths for the dead-ended portion of a corridor range between 20 to 50 feet (6.1 to 15.2 m) depending on the occupancy type.

The required width of a corridor leading to one (or more) exit(s) can be established by determining the number of occupants who will use the corridor during a fire, dividing that number by the number of exits to which the corridor leads, and multiplying the resulting dividend by the occupant width factor (see Table C.2). However, the minimum width for corridors is 44" (112 cm) clear.

When executing the schematic design for vertical and horizontal exits, the designer should identify dimensions for widths and heights, floor-to-floor spacings, and stairway components. These dimensions will differ for various occupancy types, as well as for whether a building is to be served by a sprinkler system or not. Further, if the building or a specific floor or particular area is to be *accessible* (i.e., for mobility-challenged occupants), then alternative guidelines will need to be applied. A general rule for establishing widths of doorways, stairs, landings, and so forth stipulates that the width of exit components shall not be less than the product of the number of occupants to be served by the component multiplied by an occupancy width factor (from Table C.2) that ranges from 0.15 to 0.7 inch/occupant (depending on the occupancy type and whether a sprinkler system will be present).[8] Two corollaries to this first rule should be noted. First, the width

TABLE C.2
OCCUPANT WIDTH FACTORS

OCCUPANCY	WITHOUT SPRINKLER SYSTEM		WITH SPRINKLER SYSTEM	
	Stairways, in/occupant (mm/occupant)	Other egress components, in/occupant (mm/occupant)	Stairways, in/occupant (mm/occupant)	Other egress components, in/occupant (mm/occupant)
Occupancies other than those listed below	0.3 (7.62)	0.2 (5.08)	0.2 (5.08)	0.15 (3.81)
Hazardous: H-1, H-2, H-3, and H-4	0.7 (17.77)	0.4 (10.16)	0.3 (7.62)	0.2 (5.08)
Institutional: I-2	0.4 (10.16)	0.2 (5.08)	0.3 (7.62)	0.2 (5.08)

established for the largest occupancy load in a building must be maintained throughout the entire building. Second, in buildings with multiple means of egress, the blockage of any one means must not reduce the capacity of the remaining means — one or more — to less than 50 percent of the total capacity of all of the pre-fire means of egress.[9]

The *International Fire Code* stipulates that the clear minimum width of stairways shall be 44" (112 cm) above railings (that may protrude from wall surfaces no more than 3.5" [8.9 cm]). However, if the stairways are to be designated as accessible, then they must have a clear minimum width (above railings) of 48" (122 cm). Other dimensions that are set out for stairway composition include: maximum height between landings, 1' (3.7 m); ceiling heights, no less than 7 feet (2.1 m); acceptable height for stair risers, 4" to 7" (10.2 to 17.8 cm); minimum stair tread depth, 11" (27.9 cm); and landing depths at least equal to the stair width.[10] Clear minimum widths for doorways leading into and out of vertical exits generally must be at least 32" (81 cm). However, some occupancy types permit smaller doorways, whereas other occupancy types require doorways larger than 32" (81 cm).

Vertical exits can lead to exit discharges at the building perimeter (i.e., to doorways opening to the building exterior), or the vertical exits can terminate at horizontal exits. As noted previously, no more than 50 percent of the vertical exits can lead immediately to the exterior. Thus, the remaining exits should discharge into a fire-protected passageway — a horizontal exit — leading to the exterior (beyond the immediate perimeter). This protected passageway should be constructed of a fire resistance-rated construction assembly (generally, with a two-hour timed resistance to fire penetration). The horizontal passageway should also be served by an automatic sprinkler system.

Designing exit discharges must proceed from the premise that the capacity, size, and spacing adopted for the exits leading to the exit discharge will *not* be lessened at the exit discharge (e.g., widths established for the exits must be maintained). In addition — and consistent with the previous paragraph — no more than 50 percent of vertical exits can discharge directly to the building perimeter at grade-level. The remaining exit discharges must be composed of protected passageways leading out of the building, or these exit discharges must lead to vestibules that provide alternative protected means of leaving the building. If the exit discharge leads into a courtyard, it must be designed to foster safe passage out of it, thus preventing the possibility that smoke or burning materials from the fire could enter the courtyard.

C.1.2   SETTING UP AUTOMATIC SUPPRESSION SYSTEMS

A variety of fire suppression systems are used in buildings. The most common of these systems is the automatic sprinkler, which includes a water supply source (usually, either a connection to a public water main or a storage tank), a series of valves (to regulate water flow to the system), piping to transport water from the source to the individual sprinkler heads, and the sprinkler heads (see Figures C.3 and C.4). Depending on the height of the building served by the sprinkler system, pumps may be needed to raise water to elevated storage tanks.

The generic sprinkler system responds upon experiencing elevated room air temperatures — such as would be present during a building fire — and releases water into the affected building area. The distinguishing characteristics of sprinkler systems include the triggering mechanism that initiates the water release, the water release pattern, and the overall system control type.

Figure C.3 The main water supply piping and control valve for an automatic sprinkler system. These devices are located in one corner of a mechanical room occupying approximately 50 square feet (5 square meters).

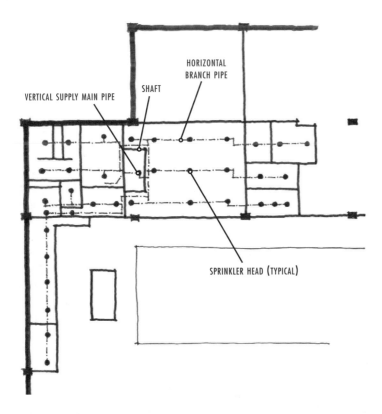

Figure C.4 This drawing presents the layout of a portion of the sprinkler system for the first floor of Gould Hall (the building whose HVAC system was described in Chapter A; for instance, Figure A.23 similarly shows the same area). The main vertical water supply pipe for this quadrant of the first floor is placed in the shaft enclosure. The horizontal pipes and sprinkler heads radiate outward from this main pipe.

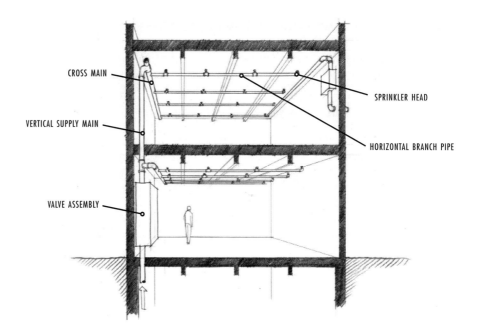

CROSS MAIN

VERTICAL SUPPLY MAIN

VALVE ASSEMBLY

SPRINKLER HEAD

HORIZONTAL BRANCH PIPE

Figure C.5 A prototypical wet-pipe sprinkler system. The principal components include a vertical supply main, a valve assembly, a cross main (at each floor), horizontal branch pipes, and regularly placed sprinkler heads. The valve assembly regulates the water pressure and, in the event of a fire occurring in one of these spaces, the water flow rate.

Four control types are widely applied for sprinkler system operation: wet-pipe, dry-pipe, preaction, and deluge. *Wet-pipe* systems operate with water present in the sprinkler system piping of a building (see Figure C.5). The sprinkler heads are maintained in a closed fashion (i.e., water is inhibited from flowing through the sprinkler heads until it is released). When a fire occurs and causes heads in the fire space to open, then water will pass out of the affected heads into the fire space. These wet-pipe sprinkler systems are the most widely applied of the four alternatives and are found in many occupancy types (e.g., office buildings, educational buildings, retail stores, factories, hospitals, and multiperson residential buildings). *Dry-pipe* sprinkler systems are most often used in buildings where the possibility exists that water could freeze in the sprinkler pipes (e.g., in unheated warehouses, concession stands at outdoor stadiums, and so forth). For dry-pipe systems the pipes are filled with pressurized air. When sprinkler heads in a fire space open (in response to the elevated air temperatures produced by the fire), the pressurized air will be released. The resultant pressure drop will induce a centralized water flow-controlling valve to open, releasing water into the system pipes. The water will pass through the piping of the sprinkler system and out of the opened heads (located above the fire).

Preaction sprinkler systems exist with normally dry pipes that are filled with pressurized air. The preaction system includes a series of detectors that, when triggered by a fire event, cause the preaction water valve to open, withdraw the pressurized air, and admit water into the sprinkler pipes. When sprinkler heads open in response to elevated air temperatures (produced by the fire), water will be released from these opened heads. Thus, once the preaction water valve opens, this system type will function similarly to the wet-pipe system. Preaction sprinkler systems are often used in facilities where ordinary water leakage from filled pipes could cause significant damage to equipment used in the building (e.g., wherever electronic equipment is used as in radio and television control rooms, computer use centers, semiconductor fabrication facilities, and so forth). The *deluge* sprinkler system exists with the sprinkler heads maintained in the open position continuously (i.e., the pipes will be filled with air at normal atmospheric pressure). A valve holds water back from entering the pipes. The valve is connected to a detection system similar to that used by the preaction system. When the detection system senses the commencement of a fire, the valve releases the water into the pipes, and water passes out of the sprinkler heads as soon as it reaches them. Thus, a large quantity of water—essentially, a deluge—can enter the fire zone quickly. Deluge sprinkler systems are employed in occupancy types involving hazardous materials and where fires can become very hot and spread rapidly.[11]

Automatic sprinkler heads are most widely available with two opening mechanisms: a fusible alloy or a breakable bulb (see Figures C.6 and C.7). Both of these heads function as a cap on top of a pipe through which water can pass. At the end of the cap will be a deflector that will direct the water when the cap opens.

The physical apparatus in a fusible alloy sprinkler head consists of a set of levers or struts that maintain the pipe cap in place. A plug consisting of a low-melting metal alloy (i.e., essentially, a solder) holds together the lever or strut set. When the air surrounding the plug reaches an elevated temperature (as the result of a fire), the metal alloy melts

Figure C.6 Three sprinkler heads are shown in this photograph. The fusible link-and-lever head on the left was obtained from a building that was constructed in about 1920. However, such fusible link-and-lever heads are still in common use today. For fusible link-and-lever heads the two levers are held together with a low melting temperature alloy. When the heat from a fire reaches the alloy—the link—it will melt letting the levers spring apart releasing water from the sprinkler piping. The other two heads in this illustration are contemporary. These two heads employ a central bar that is held in place with a low melting temperature alloy. When the alloy is heated in a fire and melts, the bar will be sprung enabling water to be released. For the purpose of establishing the sizes of these heads an American quarter dollar coin has been included in the photograph.

Figure C.7 Three typical breakable bulb sprinkler heads are shown with an American quarter dollar coin (to indi-cate the approximate sizes of these sprinkler heads). These sprinkler heads exhibit three different characteristics. First, note the different diameters of the bulbs (i.e., the bulb on the left is smaller than the other two). Second, the shapes of the crowns for the three heads are also different: the left and center heads are similar reflecting the water stream upward and outward, whereas the right head enables the water stream to flow downward and out-ward. The third difference amongst these sprinkler heads is their diameters. The larger diameter bulbs burst at higher air temperatures than the smaller diameter bulbs. Choosing which bulb diameter to employ in a building will often be based on the rapidity with which a response is desired in a fire event.

releasing the cap on the pipe and allowing water to flow freely out heads of the pipe. A variety of alternative melting-point alloys are employed for these fusible heads, ranging from temperatures as low as about 150 °F (66 °C) to as high as 650 °F (343 °C).

The breakable bulb sprinkler head has a sealed glass bulb that sits on the end of a pipe cap and between the cap and the water flow deflector. The bulb is filled with a liquid, and a gas layer is also present in the bulb above the liquid. As the air surrounding the bulb heats up from a fire, the pressure inside the bulb increases causing the bulb to break, releasing the cap, and enabling the water to flow outward (see Figure C.8).[12]

C.1.2.1 Planning guidelines for automatic sprinkler systems Water exiting the sprinkler piping will be directed outward by a deflector that distributes the water in an umbrella-like pattern (see Figure C.9). The coverage areas of alternative sprinkler heads can range from 100 to 400 square feet (9.3 to 37.2 square meters) depending on the height of the sprinkler head, the water pressure leaving the sprinkler pipe, and the physical fea-tures of the sprinkler head. Note that the sprinkler heads can be oriented either upward or downward.

Sprinkler systems usually are either integrated into a finished ceiling assembly or, more simply, hung from the structural members of the ceiling or roof and left exposed. An alternative format for sprinkler heads locates the head immediately adjacent to a sidewall (e.g., less than one foot (0.3 m) away from the wall and having a special deflector that projects the water out from the wall surface).

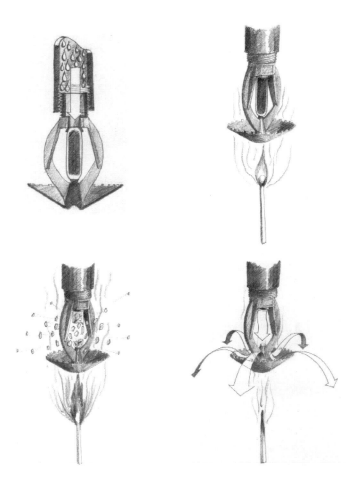

Figure C.8 Upper left, a breakable bulb sprinkler head; upper right, heat is applied to the breakable bulb sprinkler head; lower left, the bulb breaks (in response to the application of heat); lower right, water comes out of the sprinkler head.

Common practice for laying out sprinkler systems in buildings where they are required involves transporting the water vertically from the water supply source (whether municipal main or storage tank) through riser pipes. The water will be passed horizontally off of these risers in cross mains to individual spaces. Then, the horizontal branch pipelines will be modularly laid out in the spaces, and the sprinkler heads will be deployed regularly along each branch pipeline. The precise spacing required for the sprinkler heads will be dictated by the hazard level of the contents of the building space and by the potential operating characteristics of the sprinkler system (e.g., the water pressure available and the capabilities of the sprinkler heads).

For schematic designing, if the presence of the cross mains, horizontal branch pipe lines, and sprinkler heads are thought of as occupying a horizontal layer, the depth of this horizontal layer will most often be between 8 to 12 in (20 to 30 cm). Of this dimension, most of the depth is that required for the sprinkler head. The horizontal piping will have

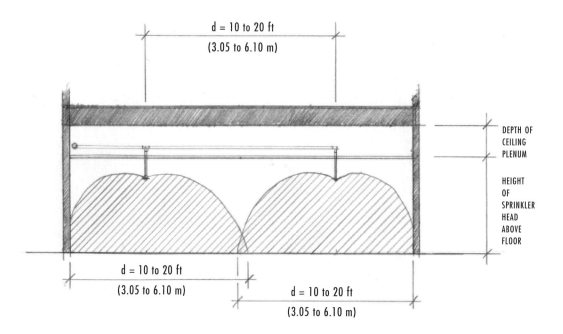

Figure C.9 A typical spread pattern for water exiting two sprinkler heads is shown here. The spread pattern will be circular with coverage diameters (at the floor) generally of about 10 to 20 ft (3.05 to 6.10 m). The coverage area will depend on the water pressure in the sprinkler pipe system, the height between the sprinkler head and the floor, and the nature of the sprinkler head itself.

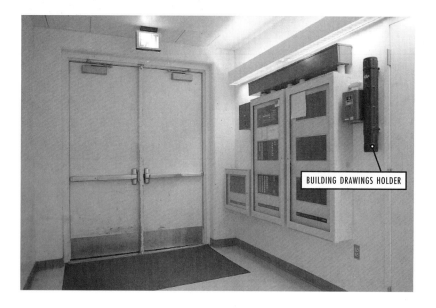

Figure C.10 An essential step for firefighters gaining access to a fire zone is finding the precise location of the fire. Upon entering a building in which a fire event is occurring the firefighters use a fire alarm control panel (as shown here) to determine which detectors have sensed the fire. To help the firefighters understand the building organization drawings of the building are included in the vertical holder at the right end of the control panel.

diameters of about 1 in (2.5 cm). Riser pipes for transporting water vertically through a building will usually have diameters of no more than 8 in (20 cm) for high-rise buildings and lesser diameters for medium and low-rise buildings. Such vertical risers can be placed in time-rated fire-resistive mechanical shafts (that usually must have wall constructions with fire resistance ratings of at least two hours). The one limitation to running the vertical risers in the mechanical shafts is that care will have to be exercised wherever the horizontal cross mains pass out through the shaft walls (i.e., to minimize the potentiality of smoke, flame, or heat passing from a fire zone into the shaft).

The valves and pumps required for operating a sprinkler system can be located in a mechanical or fan room, particularly where such a room is located at ground level or at a below-grade level.

C.1.3 PROVIDING SUPPORT FOR POTENTIAL FIRE FIGHTING ACTIONS

In the event of a fire occurring in a building a sequence of actions will be needed to extinguish it. The initial steps will involve detecting the fire, notifying the fire department of its existence (including providing information about its nature and location in the building), and having the fire department travel to the building. Once the fire fighters arrive, they will need to park their vehicles as close to the building as practicable and safe (often, a nontrivial task in suburban and urban settings). Then, they will have to gain access to the fire zone, bringing fire-fighting equipment with them (e.g., portable breathing apparatus for life sustenance, appropriate hand tools, and water hoses for extinguishing the fire). The hoses will require connection to the standpipe system, and then will have to be laid out from the standpipes through the building to reach the fire zone. Once the hoses are in proximity to the fire, the flow of water onto the fire can commence so that the actual fire fighting can begin.

Each of the several steps in this process is essential to the success of the overall operation. But the two steps that are most influenced by building design are the ability of the fire fighters to gain close access to the fire zone (see Figure C.10) and have a readily available water supply for fire extinguishment. Getting to the fire zone usually involves traveling along the same egress pathways that occupants use to exit the building (or the fire zone), except that the fire fighters will be moving in the opposite direction. If the building is a high-rise and the fire zone occurs on an upper floor, then the fire-fighters generally can utilize the elevator system rising to a floor below the fire zone and walking up the last story or two using the exit stairways. Whether in a high-rise or other building, horizontal travel to the fire zone should be able to occur along exit and/or exit access pathways. Once the fire fighters reach the proximity of the fire zone, they will seek to connect hoses to the standpipe system to gain use of pressurized water supplies.

Standpipe systems consist principally of fixed-in-place piping for transporting water through buildings during a fire. Other components will likely include water supplies, flow-controlling valves, pumps, pressure gauges, and hose connections (see Figures C.11–C.13).

Standpipe systems are designated as Class I, Class II, or Class III. What distinguishes these three classes are the sizes of the standpipes and the associated hose connections. Class I systems will generally have larger diameter pipes — usually 4 to 6 in (10 to 15 cm) (depending on the building height) — and 2 1/2 in (6.3 cm) hose connections. Class II systems will have smaller diameter pipes — most often about 2 to 2 1/2 in (5 to 6.3 cm) — and 1 1/2 in (3.8 cm) hose connections. Class III systems are basically combinations of Classes I and II systems: the standpipes will use the same diameter piping as Class I and will provide *both* 1 1/2 in (3.8 cm) and 2 1/2 in (6.3 cm) hose connections.

Figure C.11 The (automatic sprinkler and) standpipe hose connections are present on the exterior wall of this building. These standpipe hose connections enable fire fighters to run hoses between nearby water hydrants and the standpipe connectors (see Figure C.12). If water pressure from the hydrant is insufficient, then the fire fighters can connect hoses between the hydrant and their truck and between their truck and the standpipe connections and use the truck pumps to increase the flow pressure of the water.

The intentions behind these three classes of standpipe systems are, first, that Class I systems will be used only by professional fire fighters. Second, Class II systems can be used by building occupants in the time interval before the professional fire fighters arrive at a fire. And, third, Class III systems can be employed by either group: the 1 1/2 in (3.8 cm) connections can be employed until the professional fire fighters arrive, then the professional fire fighters can switch connections over to the 2 1/2 in (6.3 cm) water supply to gain a greater flow rate for extinguishment. The major reason why the smaller diameter connection is made available for building occupants is because of the difficulty associated with handling and controlling the greater water flow rates that are present with the larger pipes and hoses. It is widely thought by fire industry professionals that ordinary occupants are not prepared to control the greater flow rates and thus could be injured while trying to employ them (i.e., it requires considerable physical strength to manage hoses that operate at the higher flow rates).

In concert with these three classes of systems, five operating strategies are used for standpipe systems: automatic wet, automatic dry, semiautomatic wet, manual wet, and manual dry. Wet systems—automatic, semi-automatic, and manual—all are filled with water. Dry systems are filled with pressurized air (with flow valves holding water back from entering these dry pipes). Opening the hose valve controls both wet and dry automatic systems (e.g., the opening of the hose valve for an automatic dry system will liberate the pressurized air causing the water flow valve to open and to release the water into and out of the hose). Semiautomatic wet systems are connected to a water supply source. But, to operate and release water, a switch must be thrown (in addition to opening the hose valve). Manual systems require that water be provided via connections to water supplies that will be instituted by the fire fighters upon arrival at a building fire.[13]

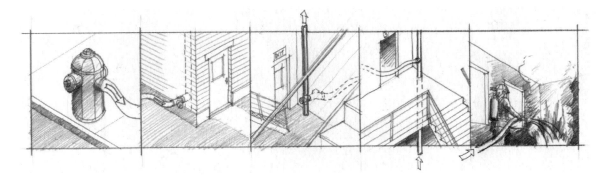

Figure C.12 This vignette demonstrates how water for fire fighting passes from a public water supply — a hydrant — to the site of the fire event. Hosing supplied by the fire fighters connects the hydrant to standpipe hose connection enabling water to enter the standpipe and travel upward. More hosing supplied by the fire fighters connects to the standpipe at the appropriate height (for reaching the fire event site) and is laid out into the site where fire suppression can proceed.

Figure C.13 A standpipe and fire sprinkler piping control assembly is shown here. The valve components — the horizontal devices to the left of the vertical standpipe — automatically control the flow rate and pressure of the water that would pass through the sprinkler and standpipe in a fire event.

Water supply requirements are dictated by the size and height of the building served by the standpipe system. Alternative water supply sources can include a municipal main with piping leading directly to the building, storage tanks in the building, and water pumped from some auxiliary source (e.g., from a public hydrant or a nearby body of water like a pond or river). For most buildings operating with automatic or semiautomatic controls an established connection must exist between the standpipe system and one of these water supply sources. Additionally, a backup, alternative source must be available. For high-rise and/or large floor-area buildings two backup, alternative water supply sources are required.

The number and location of hose connections (and, thus, the number of standpipes required for building fire protection) are also dictated by building size and height. First, the *International Fire Code* stipulates that *new* buildings shall be provided with standpipe systems.[14] Further, it states that standpipe systems and automatic sprinkler systems may be combined (i.e., thus, the vertical supply risers integral to each system can be shared). For buildings that have occupied floors that are more than 30 ft (9.1 m) above (or below) the grade level on which fire department vehicles can park, Class III standpipe systems must be employed. However, if the building will also be provided with an automatic sprinkler system, then Class I standpipe systems can be used instead. Additionally, if the building serviced by a standpipe system has a floor area larger than 10,000 ft² (929 m²) per story, then Class I systems — with automatic wet or manual wet operations — must be used wherever interior spaces are more than 200 ft (60.9 m), by any combination of horizontal and vertical pathways, from the nearest fire department vehicle.

The *International Fire Code* also states that, where Class I standpipes are required, hose connections must be placed in each of the following several locations. First, in each required (exit) stairway, a hose connection shall be provided for each floor above or below grade, with the connection at the landing level between floors. Second, hose connections shall be available on both sides of a wall "adjacent to the exit opening of a horizontal exit." Third, hose connections shall be present "in every exit passageway at the entrance from the exit passageway to other areas of a building." And, fourth, additional hose connections shall be supplied "where the most remote portion of a nonsprinklered floor or story is more than 150 ft (45,720 mm) from a hose connection or the most remote portion of a sprinklered floor or story is more than 200 ft (60,960 mm) from a hose connection."[15]

Class II standpipes and standpipe hose connections must be located so that all areas of a building serviced with these systems are no more than 130 ft (39.6 m) of a Class II hose connection (i.e., any area must be able to have extinguishing water reach it by extending the hose 100 ft (30.5 m) and then directing water 30 ft (9.2 m) outward from the nozzle). Class III standpipes and standpipe hose connections should be located in accordance with the stipulations for Class I systems. Note, again, that Class III systems should be provided with both Class I and Class II hose connections.

Lastly, during renovation, existing buildings with occupied floors more than 50 ft (15.2 m) above the level of fire department vehicle access will need the installation of standpipe systems matching the stipulations cited above.[16]

C.1.4   PROVIDING BARRIERS TO PREVENT FIRE SPREAD

Fire initiation in buildings almost always occurs in a single localized area (perhaps with the exception of when multiple fire spots are created by arson). Thus, walls, floor, and ceiling or roof assemblies will enclose the localized fire. If these building assemblies consist of fire-resistive materials and the enclosure planes are not weakened by the presence of uncontrolled penetrations, then the fire will be inhibited from spreading to other areas of the building. The strategy of creating fire-resistive enclosures around each occupied space in a building is known as *compartmentation*. The goal of establishing compartmentation during building design is to prevent the spread of smoke, flames, and heat from a fire zone into adjacent areas of the building. The dual purposes of inhibiting the fire spread are to afford occupants adequate time to leave the fire zone and to limit the property destruction caused by the fire to the immediate, localized fire zone (see Figure C.14).

The creation of separate compartments throughout a building involves developing wall, floor, and ceiling or roof assemblies that exhibit adequate time-rated fire-spread resistances. Fire spread seldom occurs strictly as a result of heat transfer through building assemblies (i.e., the heat produced by a fire in one space rarely passes through a horizontal or vertical assembly and induces combustible materials in the next space to ignite). Much more often fire spread happens because of the existence of discontinuities — intentional or not — in walls, floors, or ceilings (or roofs). Typical examples of situations that enable fire spread include having fire doors left open (by occupants), unenclosed stairways or vertical shafts, unprotected penetrations (where ducts, pipes, electrical conduit or raceways, and horizontal and vertical conveyances such as dumbwaiters and pneumatic tubes pass through fire-resistive assemblies), and nonfirestopped concealed spaces.

For many fire events that have occurred in well-compartmented buildings, once the fuel in the enclosed fire zone — furnishings, internal surface finishes, work materials, and the like — has been expended by burning, the fire will self-extinguish. And the fire damage will be limited to the single localized fire zone. Thus, a first design task in laying out buildings — while thinking about the potentialities of fire events — is to incorporate fire-resistive and fire-enclosing walls, floors, and ceilings (or roofs) throughout the building.

At what spacings walls should be placed to create appropriate sizes for potential fire zones has not been established through industry standards. Allowable floor areas are stated

Figure C.14 During the evening of May 18, 1997 a fire occurred in a laboratory on the fifth floor of Kincaid Hall at the University of Washington. The fire proceeded to flashover and consumed virtually all combustible material in the laboratory space. As Kincaid Hall was constructed with concrete walls, floors, and roof, the building was thoroughly compartmented, and the ravages of the fire event were contained in the one laboratory space. The second photograph here was taken the next morning in the laboratory space one floor directly below the laboratory in which the fire occurred.

These photographs are images captured from a videotape recording of a newscast presented by KING5-TV, a Seattle television station, on May 19, 1997. Permission to employ these images has been granted by KING5-TV.

in regional standards such as the *Uniform Building Code* and depend on both the occupancy use group and the type of construction with which the building is to be assembled. But such standards do not stipulate what spacings should be applied to achieve optimum constraints against fire spread. Nevertheless, anecdotal reports indicate that in a number of buildings in which each room was designed as a separate compartment and in which a fire then occurred in one of these compartmented rooms during occupancy, the fire in each instance was confined to the single room (i.e., no fire spread beyond the localized fire zones). Finally, one rule-of-thumb that is sometimes offered for medium-to-large open-planned floor areas suggests that to attain good fire zone compartmentation (for these open-planned areas) the distance between fire-resistive walls should be no more than eight times the room height.

MAGNETIC WALL CONTACT

Figure C.15 Building codes require that elevators on all floors must open on to elevator lobbies that are separated from the remainder of the building. This requirement also applies when elevators open on to corridors. Wall assemblies for lobbies must extend from the floor to the fire-resistive ceiling or roof above and must furnish a one-hour fire separation. Doors between a lobby and a corridor must be tight fitting and furnish a fire-protection time of at least 20 minutes. The doors must either be self-closing or have an automatic closing mechanism (that is activated by a smoke detector). For the doors shown here the automatic closing mechanism includes the metal door stop that—when the door is open—is held in place by the magnetic contact on the wall. When a smoke detector is activated, the magnetism in the contact ceases, releasing the door and allowing the closing mechanism to shut the door. See Sections 403.7 and 1004.3.4.3.2 in the *Uniform Building Code,* (Whittier, California: International Conference of Building Officials, 1997), pages 1–43 and 1–115, respectively.

The other important issue about the creation of building compartmentation concerns the handling of penetrations in these fire-resistive planes (e.g., certainly when doorways and windows will be integrated into fire-resistive walls and particularly when ducts, piping, electrical connections, and conveyances pass through walls, floors, ceilings, or roofs) (see Figures C.15 and C.16). Design practices for selecting doorway and window assemblies that will provide good service are readily available (and will not be discussed here).[17] Alternatively, identifying means of solving the problems that arise when fire-resistive planes are penetrated by these various environmental control services is more difficult. When penetrations through fire-resistive planes are suggested, either of two alternative approaches may be employed. First, and probably better, would be the search for and discovery of alternative pathways for running these control services. Second, when the penetrations cannot readily be avoided, then means for closing off the resulting openings must be incorporated in the building design. For example, ducts passing through fire-resistive assemblies — whether walls, floors, or ceilings — should have automatic fire dampers present at the points of penetration. Pipes and electrical conduit and raceways can be encapsulated with fire-resistive enclosures of their own as they pass through fire-resistive walls, floors, and ceilings (or roofs). Choosing piping and conduit materials that can resist fire damage are also good design practices.

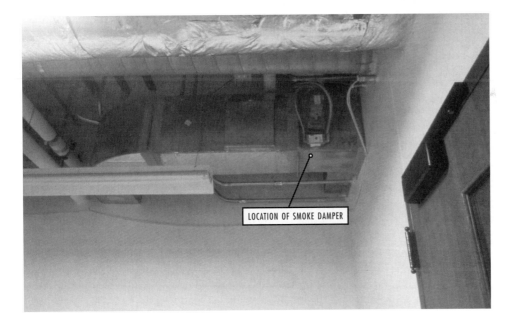

Figure C.16 To the left of where the duct penetrates the wall, a smoke damper has been included in the duct assembly. The damper is connected to a smoke detector that would sense the presence of smoke in the ducting and signal the damper to close off airflow in the duct. Where a duct passes through a smoke barrier (partition), a smoke damper must be included in the ducting.

Section C.2 | FIRE BEHAVIOR AND THE ACTIVE SYSTEMS USED TO CONTROL FIRE IN BUILDINGS

In this section we will describe the components involved in starting a fire and the active control systems that should be available in buildings for dealing with fires. Fire control systems are included in buildings to minimize occupant injury and death as well as to reduce the potential damage and lost use time in the event of a fire. The principal systems we will discuss will be those applied for fire detection, occupant alarm (warning), occupant evacuation, and fire suppression.

C.2.1   PROPERTIES AND CHARACTERISTICS OF FIRE

C.2.1.1   Contributions to combustion   Basically, fire is a rapid chemical reaction that releases great quantities of heat. This chemical reaction nearly always involves the oxidation of some fuel (i.e., the fuel reacts with oxygen or some chemical containing oxygen). To initiate the chemical reaction an ignition source must heat the fuel to a temperature hot enough to sustain the reaction. The main products of the chemical reaction are smoke and heat. The heat generation will virtually always be sufficient to maintain the high temperatures of the fuel and the oxidant, thus continuing the reaction (i.e., keeping the fire going). Flame is present in most fires and is essentially a gaseous zone in which the oxidation of fuel occurs and from which light is emitted.

Fuel is a generic term that refers to anything that can burn (e.g., many gases, many liquids, paper, wood, cloth, plastics, adhesives, sealants, and many other materials too numerous to catalog). Nearly always, fuel will be organic in nature: it will be composed of carbon atoms and atoms of other common elements such as hydrogen, oxygen, nitrogen, sulfur, and the halogen group. The two types of carbonaceous materials that comprise organic fuel are hydrocarbons and cellulose. Hydrocarbons are compounds based on the molecular format of $-CH_2-$ where one atom of carbon is bonded with two hydrogen atoms. Common examples of hydrocarbon compounds are plastics, rubber, oil, tar, many solvents and other organic liquids, and common gases such as methane, propane, and butane. Cellulosic compounds are based on a molecular format of $-CH(OH)-$ where one carbon atom is bonded with one hydrogen atom and an hydroxyl ion. Examples of cellulosic compounds are wood, paper, and cloths.

Fuels can be in gaseous, liquid, or solid forms. However, for combustion — the process of burning — to occur, a fuel must exist in or be converted to a gaseous state to enable thorough mixing of the fuel and oxygen. With a liquid fuel, heat from combustion will cause the evaporation of some of the liquid and the resultant mixing of the fuel vapor with oxygen. Thus, combustion of the liquid fuel involves vaporization of the fuel so that the vapor can burn. Heat applied to the surface of the liquid is the first step in the combustion process; vaporization of the fuel is the second; mixing of the vapor and atmospheric oxygen is the third; and combustion of the mixture occurs as the fourth step.

Alternatively, for combustion of solid fuels, heat applied to the surface of the solid will cause the release of gases from the solid (and the usual formation of a layer of charred material at the surface). The released gases then mix with atmospheric oxygen. The resulting gaseous mixture can burn, thereby forming an ever-deeper char layer or, instead, leading to the more complete combustion of the charred material.

The role of ignition in the combustion process is to create enough heat to initiate the chemical reaction between the fuel and the oxidant. The application of this heat to the fuel and the oxidant can be gradual, occurring over many minutes, hours, or even days. As the heat is applied, the creation of a mix of gases (from the fuel) and oxygen will be happening. When sufficient quantities of mixed gases and heat are present, then combustion will begin. If enough heat is generated by the chemical reaction, then the reaction will be self-sustaining.

C.2.1.2   The combustion process   When self-sustaining combustion occurs, the heat produced will essentially create a *feedback* condition, which causes the released heat to induce further vaporization of a liquid fuel and/or the production of flammable gases from solid materials. These vapors or gases then mix with oxygen and burn, spreading the fire beyond its point of origin. The combustion process will thus continue for as long as adequate fuel and oxidant are present and the heat of combustion is maintained.

However, any one (or more) of the following actions can lead to the extinguishment of the fire. First, the fuel is totally consumed by the fire. Second, the oxidant is totally consumed by the fire. Third, by some means the heat generation by the fire is reduced sufficiently so that the temperature of the reaction falls below self-sustenance. Or, fourth, the combustion process is inhibited by the addition of some chemical or physical agent that reduces the reaction rate. These four actions constitute the range of the principal solutions for fighting fires in buildings: further discussion about suppression techniques and systems will be presented below.

The range of potential ignition sources for initiating building fires is large. The most ubiquitous ignition sources are heating systems, electrical systems (either involving errors in installation, system failures resulting from misuse, or product failures), cooking of foods, smoking, and arson. All of these sources have a fundamentally human component: for most building fires, actions (or inaction) of people cause the ignition of the fire. Indeed, an unfortunate, common ingredient in far too many building fires is human error.[18]

The process of combustion involves a number of stages, which are not necessarily sequential. Further, these stages can be brief or lengthy. The earliest stage is a precombustion phase during which fuel is being heated by an ignition source. A result of heating the fuel will be the production of a flammable vapor that could burn in a future fire event. How long a precombustion phase could endure depends on a variety of factors: for instance, the nature of the fuel — its chemical composition and its physical form; the amount of the fuel present in the space; the rate with which oxygen flows around the fuel; the speed with which heat from the potential igniter is applied to the fuel and the gaseous mixture of fuel products and oxygen; the environmental conditions in the vicinity of this precombustion; and so forth.

A second combustion stage is the process of smoldering, in which fuel will burn more slowly and less completely than when combustion with an observable flame occurs. Smoldering will usually happen very close to the surface of the fuel. An apparent glowing will often be present. Smoke and heat will be produced, although the rate of heat generation and the resulting atmospheric temperature immediately away from the surface of the fuel will be lower than what would be evident with flaming combustion (e.g., temperatures in the range of 1000 to 1500 °F (538 to 816 °C) usually result from smoldering combustion, whereas temperatures of as high as 2700 °F (1482 °C) are produced with flaming combustion). Smoldering is basically a limited form of combustion. It may lead to complete combustion — flaming — or not, depending on whether the heat generated by the reaction of fuel and oxidant (oxygen) increases sufficiently to sustain complete combustion.

Flaming combustion results when the reaction between the fuel (in a vaporous state) and oxygen releases enough heat so that a flame can be maintained. The combustion will be rapid and vigorous. Unless confined by its enclosure or limited by the amount of fuel or oxidant, a flaming fire will spread readily to any adjacent unburned materials. Note that the spreading action involves the continuing conversion of fuel into a vaporous state (that can mix with atmospheric oxygen). The temperatures in the vicinity of the flames will increase as the combustion spreads outward from its initial location.

In a fire event in a building (i.e., particularly in an enclosed space with sufficient quantities of fuel and oxidant and if the process continues without interruption), the flaming combustion will produce very hot smoke that will rise, fill the space, and contribute to the heating of everything in the space. Thus, the spreading fire will raise the temperatures of surrounding surfaces and materials, thereby promoting the production of flammable gases that emanate from all of these surfaces and materials. As ever more surfaces and materials participate in the fire event, the temperature in the space will approach uniformity. At some point *flashover* will occur, when essentially everything that is combustible in the space will become involved in the combustion process. At flashover the temperature throughout the space will peak. After some time — determined by the quantities of fuel and oxidant in the space — the rate and intensity of combustion will decrease. Concomitantly, the temperatures of the atmosphere and surfaces in the space will begin to descend.

After a period with the reduced rate and intensity of combustion (during which nearly all the combustible surfaces and materials in the space will have been consumed), the flames will burn out and some amount of smoldering combustion will be left in various locations throughout the space. Subsequently, the smoldering combustion will die out as the temperatures of the "hot spots" will descend below ignition levels, and the fire will basically have self-extinguished. Then, the elevated temperatures remaining in the air and the combusted surfaces and materials will gradually decrease to near ambient conditions. The time required to enable a fire to self-extinguish — unforced by automatic intervention or intentional human action — will vary depending on many parameters.

In this discussion we have followed the combustion process from a beginning to a conclusion. One qualification about this description would state that it is essentially prototypical: many fire events will proceed through other phases and lead to different results. A number of circumstances could affect this prototypical behavior and could lead to alternative results. A first qualifier concerns whether the fire is able to spread beyond its enclosed space: was compartmentation existent between spaces and did it protect and separate adjacent spaces? Second, are automatic or manual suppression systems — for example, a sprinkler system — in place and could they act to extinguish the fire? Third, will human intervention — firefighters — be able to extinguish the fire? Fourth, is the amount of fuel sufficient to enable the combustion to burn hot and long enough to reach flashover? And, fifth, is there enough atmospheric oxygen in the space and can it participate readily in the combustion process? Each of these circumstances could create a much less damaging and potentially less injurious result. To gain the positive intervention that any or all of these inhibitors offer thus will require informed and careful designing and the subsequent good management of any building.

C.2.1.3 Fire products   The combustion of fuel in the presence of oxygen produces smoke and heat. The levels of heat production are substantial and, when fire events are not constrained by automatic or human intervention, combustion occurring in an enclosure will proceed to flashover. Both smoldering and flame combustion often will yield copious amounts of smoke, thus causing difficulties for occupants as they evacuate the fire-ridden building. For those occupants who are unable to escape from the fire, the likely results will be injury and even death.

Smoke is a combination of hot gases, particulate matter, and aerosols, all of which are produced by the combustion of fuel. The hot gases result from the decomposition of the fuel as it oxidizes. As combustion is rarely complete, unburned or partially burned particles of the fuel will become suspended in these gases. Similarly, fine droplets of liquid — aerosols — will also enter into the smoke. The heat energy entrained in the smoke causes it to roil and expand outward rapidly. If the smoke is not enclosed, it will rise upward into the sky. If the smoke is enclosed within a building, then it will expand to fill the space, mixing with the atmospheric air and transferring its heat to the surfaces and materials in the space. For occupants still present in a smoke-filled space, the smoke will irritate the eyes and obscure vision (because of the suspended particulate matter and aerosols, both of which restrict light transmission through the smoke). The smoke will also make breathing difficult, as it affects the linings of the respiratory tract and lungs. And, most seriously, the smoke will induce narcosis, in which, first, muscle coordination and ordinary mental functions will begin to fail and, soon after, unconsciousness will occur. If an occupant continues to stay in the smoke-filled space — the occupant is rendered unable to leave — then death will follow the loss of consciousness.

What the more specific composition of smoke will be — what gases particularly will be present — depends on the nature of the fuel that is burning. The gas make-up of the smoke will also be determined by whether combustion is smoldering or flaming and by how readily oxygen is available to foster combustion. The rate at which the temperature in the burning zone increases and the temperature in the near vicinity of the fire further affect the composition of the smoke.

Until the 1960s the principal organic materials in buildings were based on cellulose. Thus, paper, wood products (usually, solid wood without the now-common polymeric adhesives and finishes), cloths, and other natural fibers were used. When these cellulosic materials burned, the principal gaseous components of smoke would be carbon dioxide, carbon monoxide, and water vapor. However, since the 1960s there has been widespread development of synthetic materials and their rampant incorporation into buildings as construction assemblies, surface finishes, and furnishings. The ever-increasing usage of synthetic materials has brought more hydrocarbon-based materials into buildings. When these hydrocarbon-based materials burn, the gas products are comparatively more dangerous. Now, in addition to the presence of carbon dioxide, carbon monoxide, and water vapor, combustion of building materials will create a range of other gases such as hydrogen cyanide; the oxides of sulfur, nitrogen, and phosphorus; halogen acids; and a plethora of organic compounds.

All of these gases — except for water vapor — are either toxic or serious irritants to human respiration. Gases like carbon monoxide and hydrogen cyanide are asphyxiants, causing the shutting down of the central nervous system and leading to unconsciousness and death. The concentrations required for these two gases to adversely affect human health are quite small. Carbon dioxide is not strictly toxic, but in high enough concentrations it can induce rapid breathing, thus enhancing the entries of carbon monoxide and hydrogen cyanide — when these gases are created in fires — into the respiratory system. Sufficient concentrations of nitrogen and sulfur oxides can cause respiratory distress and, if exposure is sustained long enough, severe respiratory irritation can result (leading eventually to respiratory failure and death). So, too, can many of the gaseous organic compounds cause respiratory irritation and subsequent respiratory failure.

Lastly, one further consequence of the combustion of surfaces and materials in building spaces is that the oxidation of these building products will lead to a depletion of oxygen in the space. As a fire continues, ever more of the atmospheric oxygen in the space is consumed by combustion. Thus, if building occupants (or fire-fighters without portable breathing equipment) are present for a sustained period in a fire space, the oxygen depletion in the space can also be life-threatening.[19]

The quantity of smoke produced by a fire can vary widely. The parameters of the fire that determine the quantity include whether smoldering or flaming combustion is occurring, how much oxidant is present (and even whether the oxidant is atmospheric oxygen or oxygen that is an element in some chemical that exists in the space), how rapidly the fire grew to some level, and even what the temperature of the fire became when partial or fully-developed combustion was reached. Thus, predicting the amount of smoke that will be created by a fire is problematic. Instead, anticipating that a substantial quantity will exist when a fire occurs seems prudent.

Four goals of smoke management and control are paramount. First, occupants should be able to rapidly leave the fire zone or gain access to smoke-free areas of refuge. Second, smoke barriers should be present so that smoke will be prevented from passing out of the immediate fire zone (into other spaces in the building). Third, smoke should be released from the fire-ridden space so that fire fighters can readily gain access and can more expeditiously seek to extinguish the fire. And, fourth, making it possible to reduce the amount of smoke that may be produced by a fire event will likely reduce the magnitude of building damage caused by the fire. Thus, planning for smoke management and control is an essential task. In the following sections we will describe alternative smoke management systems.

C.2.2   DETECTION SYSTEMS[20]

C.2.2.1   Fire detector operations
Detection systems are placed in building spaces to sense the presence of some fire product. Once a detector has sensed that a fire event is occurring, then the detector will furnish a signal to an alarm device or system, or the detector will emit an aural or visual signal directly to occupants. Thus, the detector may have an alarm capability as a component, or the detector may be connected electronically to an alarm device or system. In most building applications the design, selection, placement, and installation of the detection and alarm systems should be accomplished by fire protection engineers. But to ensure the successful integration of detection and alarm systems with the other environmental control systems, architects should carefully oversee decision-making about these systems.

A range of alternative detectors is available. First, automatic and manual detectors are used in buildings: automatic systems operate continuously without direct human intervention, whereas manual systems depend entirely on human initiation (see Figure C.17). Second, any of three fire products can be the phenomenon that the detector will sense: heat convected from a fire, smoke, or heat radiated by a fire. Third, the operation of detectors can be set to sense when some level of the phenomenon has been reached (e.g., a specific air temperature, a gas concentration, a smoke density, and so forth). Or the detectors can be made to sense the rate of change of some phenomenon. For this latter circumstance, one type of detectors is able to sense the rapidity with which the air temperature in the vicinity of the detector changes. Thus, essentially, these detectors are programmed to respond when some increment of temperature increase per unit time occurs in the vicinity of a detector.

Figure C.17 Manual fire alarm pull stations must be installed in close proximity to the entrance to each exit. When pulled the building fire alarm system will be activated alerting occupants that a fire event is occurring. See Section 907.4 of *The 2000 International Fire Code,* (Falls Church, Virginia: International Code Council, 1999), page 82.

Fourth, detectors can be applied to operate on a *spot* basis (where each detector senses conditions for a portion of floor area or of a volume in a space). Or the detector can be deployed in a *lineal* fashion (i.e., basically, the sensor is a wire cable laid out modularly across a floor area). Fifth, one other detector type operates by continuously sampling the air in building spaces. Thus, the detector regularly and frequently draws into an internal chamber some volume of air and tests the properties of the air to see if products of a fire event are evident.

C.2.2.2   Alternative fire detector types   The more commonly used *heat* detectors sense either that some elevated air temperature has been reached in a building space or that some incremental increase in the air temperature per unit time has occurred. Thus, a fusible-link sprinkler head is basically a heat detector: the fusible-link will melt at some elevated temperature and release the available suppressant. Another heat detector type is a two-wire cable with the wires separated by low-melting-temperature insulation. Electrical current is passed through a circuit encompassing the two wires. When a fire occurs causing the insulation to melt, the wires come in contact, producing a shorting in the circuit. As the shorted circuit occurs, an annunciation unit in the detector will send out a signal.

Smoke detectors sense the presence of suspended particulate matter and aerosols in the hot gases emitted by a fire (see Figure C.18). The two most common smoke detectors are the ionization chamber and the photoelectric sensor. The ionization chamber operates by using a small bit of radioactive material to ionize air molecules in close proximity to the chamber, thus making the air electrically conductive (see Figure C.19). Electrodes are present on either side of the chamber and a current passes between the electrodes through

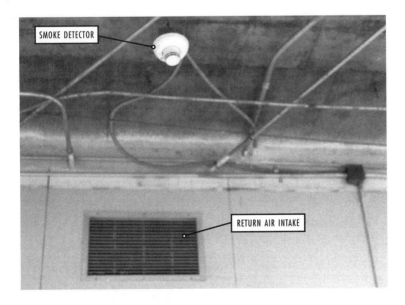

Figure C.18 A common smoke detector is installed in close proximity to a return air intake. As used air in this space is drawn inward by the return air fan downstream from this intake, any smoke that would be created by a fire event in this space could be sensed by the smoke detector.

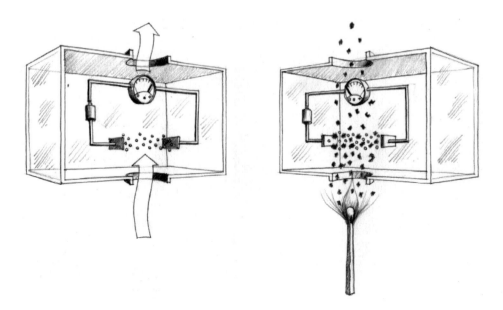

Figure C.19 An ionization chamber is shown — in its unexcited state — on the left. The ionized air between the electrodes is not disrupted by the ordinary flow of air between these electrodes. But when smoke particles — as indicated in the right image — disrupt the ionized air, then the circuit is broken and a signal will be sent to an alarm system to notify the occupants of the space (or building).

the ionized air. When smoke particles or aerosol enters the air space between the electrodes, the particles or aerosol disrupt the conductivity of the air, and the current flow between the electrodes is inhibited causing the detector to emit a signal.

There are two types of photoelectric sensors. In one type a beam of light shines across an air space onto a photoreceptor. When smoke particles or aerosols impede the light gathering by the photoreceptor, the detector emits a signal (see Figure C.20). In the other type, a beam of light shines outward. The photoreceptor is placed away from the line of sight of the beam. But, when smoke particles or aerosols enter the air space in the vicinity of the beam, they scatter the light, thereby enabling the photoreceptor to gather some of the scattered light and causing the detector to emit a signal (see Figure C.21).

One other group of building smoke detectors applies gas sampling units. These detectors take in samples of air discretely or continuously and test the air for certain contaminants. A variety of alternative sensing mechanisms are employed for testing the samples. These gas sampling detectors can be used on a spot basis (i.e., serving a localized area), or they can draw air in through a network of tubing deployed over a much wider area.

Flame detectors operate by sensing either ultraviolet or infrared radiation. These flame detectors use camera-like devices that include a lens and an element that is sensitive to some particular radiation bandwidth. Combinations of ultraviolet and infrared radiation sensors are sometimes used (i.e., where they are paired together in the detector assembly).

C.2.2.3 Guidelines for placing detectors A first principle for installing detectors requires that they be placed in the vicinity of wherever potential fuel will be located.

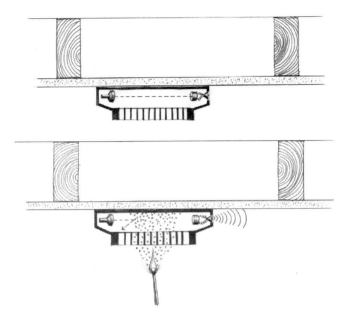

Figure C.20 A photoelectric detector is shown in the top image. With no smoke particles in the air that enters into the detector, the passage of light from the source to the receiver is unimpeded. But when smoke particles enter the detector and disrupt the light beam (as shown in the right image), an alarm will sound, warning the occupants of the space.

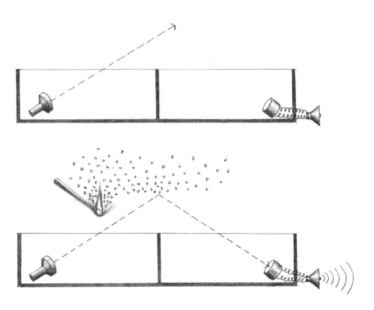

Figure C.21 The second type of photoelectric detector is demonstrated here. For this type in the unexcited state—shown in the upper image—a light beam shines outward and is not impeded. But when smoke particles enter the air and cause the reflection of light off of the particles, some of the light will fall on the receiver (shown in the lower image). When the receiver acquires the reflected light, it initiates an alarm for the occupants of the space.

A second principle suggests that detectors should be placed so that there is a clear passage of air and/or a line-of-sight between the detector and potential fire event areas in the space. Thus, if flame detectors are to be employed in a space, there should not be solid structural members or intermediate-height partitions that might block the line-of-sight between the detectors and the potential fuel materials. Or, if smoke detectors are established to sense potential fire events, ready air movement around each detector is necessary for the detector to sense the nature of the air.

When spot detectors are used, most often these units will be deployed in a regular modular fashion so that each unit may sense conditions for some area (e.g., perhaps 100 to 200 ft² [9.3 to 18.6 m²] as dictated by the capacity of the unit). Generally, these spot detectors will be placed on ceilings and upper walls. Spot detectors commonly operate as flame sensors (i.e., searching for abnormal radiation forms in the ultraviolet or infrared spectra). Thus, when flame detectors are applied, they should be placed, first, to minimize the chances that any building component or furnishing might block their sight lines with potential fuel sources. Second, flame detectors will usually be placed on a modular basis when a large floor area is to be protected. Flame detectors must be located so that solar radiation or radiation from various artificial sources does not reach the sensing surfaces, so the detectors do not initiate false alarms.

Lastly, linear cable (heat) detectors are usually laid out in parallel strips that are separated by distances specified by the cable manufacturer.

One additional set of guidelines for locating detectors concerns their placement relative to the operation of air-handling systems components. If detectors—especially, smoke detectors—are placed in front of supply air diffusers, then the air moving across the detectors will provide inaccurate information about the state of the ambient room atmosphere. Alternatively, positioning detectors near return air intakes can provide the detectors with better opportunities to sense the ambient air conditions. One other suitable location for placing detectors—again, smoke detectors—is within return air ducting. Thereby, the used room air—that could contain fire event products—would flow across the detector providing a ready opportunity for the detector to test the room air composition.

Finally, regarding the placement and spacing of detectors—heat, smoke, or flame—industry standards such as the *National Fire Alarm Code* (NFPA 72) provide extensive guidelines and calculation procedures for installing these devices.[21] The choice of which detector type and operating strategy to employ in a building should be based on a series of factors. One factor of major importance concerns expectations—by designer and client—about what sort of a fire event could possibly occur in a building. For instance, if large quantities of flammable materials—fuel—are to be stored in the building or if many ignition sources are present (e.g., in a manufacturing facility that uses high temperature production techniques), detectors will be required whose capabilities are well matched to the likely products of fires created by such fuels or ignition sources. Further, various combinations of fuels and ignition sources are more or less likely to promote smoldering or flaming combustion. Therefore, the type of combustion that might more likely occur with a specific fuel or ignition source should dictate the choice of appropriate detectors. Some detectors—usually, ionization chamber detectors—can sense gas emissions from a preignition fire stage. When such emissions are anticipated to be potential products of some process that will be housed within a building, then deploying these detectors is a prudent decision. Thus, the detector performance must match the fire properties that could be expected from the fuels or ignition sources.

A second selection criterion requires the detector be reliable (i.e., that the sensitivity of the detector is dependable over time and for any of a variety of environmental conditions).

One important aspect of reliability is that the detector will not respond falsely—initiate false alarms—when environmental conditions vary. A third selection issue concerns how rapidly the detector can sense the presence of a fire. For instance, ceiling-mounted heat detectors—especially fusible-link units—can be quite slow in sensing a fire because the heat produced by the fire may rise slowly to the elevation where the unit has been installed.

A fourth selection issue concerns the cost of the detection system. Fusible-link heat detectors are components of sprinkler systems. Thus, no further cost is involved in their usage. Photoelectric sensors based on the light beam obscuration mechanism are relatively inexpensive. Ionization chamber detectors are often several times more expensive than photoelectric detectors. And the various gas-sampling units—particularly those capable of sampling over a larger floor area—can be even more expensive than the ionization chambers.

C.2.3   FIRE ALARMS

Alarm systems are installed in buildings in a number of different configurations. First, the alarms can be physical parts of detector systems. For instance, a detector-alarm unitary device senses products of a fire event and triggers an alarm signal (see Figure C.22). Second, the alarms can be separate from, but connected electronically to, the detector systems. So, a localized detector senses fire products and sends an electronic signal to a

Figure C.22 A unitary alarm device has both sound and blinking light signal components.

remote alarm (or perhaps a series of alarms throughout a building). Or, third, alarms can be entirely separate from the detector systems, and the operation of the alarm will depend on some sort of human intervention (i.e., an occupant senses a fire and activates an alarm). Thus, an alarm system can operate automatically or manually.

The nature and composition of the signal emanating from an alarm can be auditory or visual, and it can contain coded or uncoded information. The conventional fire alarm is one that emits a loud noise (or series of noises). This auditory alarm can be based on a siren, a horn, a buzzer, or some prerecorded combination of sounds. Alternatively, the sounds can involve spoken messages relayed over a loudspeaker system. Thus, a fire official who is centrally located in a fire command center can announce the initiation of a fire event, or spoken messages can be recorded (in anticipation of future fire event) and played back when a fire is detected.

When the auditory message is simply a loud warning noise, the message offers no information about where the fire event is located, its severity, what paths of egress will be most useful, what areas of refuge should be sought, and so forth. Thus, such a message is uncoded (i.e., it provides no direct information about the fire other than to warn the occupants that a fire event is in progress somewhere in the building). In contrast, a spoken message relayed from a fire command center through a building-wide loudspeaker system offers a coded message: it can provide detailed information about the nature and location of the fire event and about means for dealing with evacuation and fighting the fire. These are two extremes of audible messages—the simple uncoded noise versus the coded message consisting of detailed information. In between these two extremes is a range of forms of partially coded messages that will contain some useful information.

The alternative fire alarm message form is a visual one. Typically, the visual form will consist of lights that flash or that vary repetitively in brightness (as when a beacon turns). For example, strobe lighting is gaining in frequency of application in buildings. The usage of visual alarms is predicated on the probability that some percentage of building occupants will be hearing-impaired and thus will be unable to recognize an auditory signal. Another situation in which visual alarms are useful occurs when the background noise level in the building is high and recognizing auditory signals would be problematic (e.g., in a factory, night club, health club, recreational facility, automobile repair shop, and so forth).

When visual alarm sources are used in buildings, design attention must be given to assure that clear lines-of-sight will be readily available from the source into occupied areas. A second design concern for placing visual alarm sources is whether occupants will be facing in the direction of the source or will be facing away. Thus, visual sources that are in the direct view field of the occupants will be preferable. But if such source locations are not readily available, then higher-brightness sources should be employed to accomplish indirect signaling. In spaces with large floor areas (e.g., warehouses, convention centers, recreational facilities, and so forth) either multiple sources or especially bright single sources should be employed.

Alarm devices that produce both auditory and visual signals are increasingly being installed in buildings.

C.2.4   FIRE EXTINGUISHMENT ALTERNATIVES

As described in Section C.2.1, fire occurs when a fuel and an oxidizer react in an uncontrolled and very rapid fashion. The initiation of a fire—whether in a smoldering or flaming form—

requires an igniter that heats the fuel and oxidizer to a temperature at which combustion begins. And as long as there is sufficient heat generation by the fire event to sustain combustion, the fire will proceed. Thus, the basic components of fire are the fuel, the oxidizer, the ignition source, and the generation of heat sufficient to sustain combustion.

The practice of fire extinguishment involves the removal or overcoming of some one or more of these basic components. There are a series of alternative mechanisms for achieving extinguishment. First, *cooling of the fire* can be sought. Second, *removing unburned fuel* from the combustion zone or even *diluting the fuel* can be carried out. Third, *separating the oxidizer from the fuel* can be performed. Fourth, *excluding the oxidizer from the combustion zone* can be attained. And, fifth, *some other material or substance that affects the combustion reaction can be added* to the fire event.

For example, casting water on a fire can separate the fuel from the oxidizer and will alter the fuel, thus cooling the reaction. Additionally, water poured on the fire will likely form steam that can interfere with atmospheric oxygen reaching the fuel surface. A second example involves the introduction of carbon dioxide into a fire zone. Carbon dioxide is virtually inert and will not participate in the fire reaction. The gas will displace oxygen, carbon dioxide being a more massive molecule. By displacing the oxygen, carbon dioxide also separates the fuel from the atmospheric oxygen. Third, a variety of inorganic salts — for example, sodium bicarbonate and potassium bicarbonate (this latter substance is known in the fire protection industry as *Purple K*) — are used for extinguishing fires with hydrocarbon fuels (e.g., oil, gasoline, organic solvents, paints, and so forth). These inorganic salts are usually cast upon the burning fuel as part of gaseous slurry. The salt coats the fuel, separating it from the flame and also inhibiting the mixing of the combustible vapors produced by the fuel and the atmospheric oxygen. In each of these three examples, extinguishment occurs by more than one mechanism: such multidirected performances are typical of the majority of extinguishing agents used for fighting building fires.

The agents used for extinguishing building fires are water, foams, dry chemicals, and inert gases. Water is most often employed because in many respects it offers the best overall performance. It is readily available, can be stored easily, and can be discharged onto a fire using a variety of techniques (e.g., from wet or dry sprinkler systems and with standpipe and hose deliveries). Water functions well as an extinguishing agent, acting to separate the fuel and oxidizer, to displace atmospheric oxygen from the vicinity of the fuel, and to cool the reaction. Additionally, water is effective in extinguishing fires based on most of the combustible materials found in buildings. The distribution of water and its injection into building spaces are accomplished either with sprinkler or hose systems. Both have been discussed earlier in this chapter.

However, when certain highly flammable liquids or gases are present in buildings or when the use of water as the extinguishing agent could cause additional damage (beyond what a fire event might cause), then alternative extinguishing agents should be applied. Foams are employed particularly for extinguishing fires in which the fuel is some flammable liquid (e.g., petroleum products, vegetable oils, and animal fatty oils). The mechanism by which these liquids burn involves the formation of a fuel vapor layer above the liquid. The fuel vapor mixes with atmospheric oxygen, and the resulting mixture promotes continued combustion. Foaming agents are typically mixtures of a foaming product and water, where the product and the water interact to form a low-density suspension. Such suspensions behave like quite viscous gases that can be spread over the surface of a burning liquid. The foam suspension inhibits the ability of the liquid to vaporize and also prevents atmospheric oxygen from reaching whatever fuel vapors that can form. The foaming products that are used include protein-based chemicals, soapy detergents, and synthetic organic surfactants. These various products are employed because they create foams that remain stable despite the high temperatures generated by the fires.

Distribution of a foam and its injection into a building space can be achieved relying on either a centralized system or by local means. In a centralized supply a foam is delivered to a fire zone through a piping system similar to that used for a water-based system. Thus, a central tank (in which the foam is produced) is connected to vertical and horizontal piping, and the foam is injected into fire event spaces through ceiling-mounted sprinkler heads. Central foam distribution can be operated as either a wet-pipe or dry-pipe system, although dry-pipe operations — with foam produced on demand — are more commonly employed. Localized versions of these central systems are also constructed, although their applications tend to be limited to large buildings with just a few main spaces.

Water and foams are the two most widely used "wet" extinguishment agents. "Dry" extinguishment agents are also employed for fire protection, particularly for buildings where the use of wet agents could cause damage in addition to what is produced by the fire event. Likely applications for dry agents will include facilities in which electrical equipment is extensive (e.g., computer rooms, semiconductor fabrication plants, electrical power-handling services, and so forth), commercial kitchens, and paper-based record-keeping storage. Two generic types of dry agents are most often employed: inert gases and inorganic salts.

The principal inert gas used for fire extinguishment is carbon dioxide. Other gases that are occasionally employed are nitrogen and steam. Building applications for which inert gases, generally, and carbon dioxide, particularly, are well suited include spaces with significant presences of electrically powered equipment. Thus, facilities used for electrical power handling (electrical vaults and closets), for communications systems, and for computer devices (servers, printers, and central data storage devices) are often protected with inert gas extinguishment systems. Carbon dioxide functions as an extinguishment agent by replacing atmospheric oxygen, thus separating the fuel from its oxidant. As an extinguishing agent carbon dioxide can be used to puddle across the floor area of a room (as carbon dioxide is heavier than atmospheric oxygen or air), thus separating burning materials from the atmospheric oxygen. Or the carbon dioxide can be supplied to and around a small fire, essentially surrounding the burning material and shutting off its supply of oxygen.

Distribution of carbon dioxide and its injection into potential fire zones can be accomplished with either a centralized, localized, or portable system. Central systems are available either as high-pressure or low-pressure organizations. The high-pressure systems use numbers of carbon dioxide storage canisters connected to a distribution network composed of flow controls, piping, and outlet heads. The heads may be fixed-in-place (usually at the level of the ceiling), or a hose may be attached to a distribution pipe with the head at the end of the hose. With this latter arrangement the movable head can be directed specifically at a localized fire. Low-pressure central distribution is commonly used when large floor area facilities are to be protected with carbon dioxide extinguishment (e.g., for the assembly area of an electric products fabrication plant). For the low-pressure system, the carbon dioxide is obtained from a commercial supplier and stored in liquid form in a large insulated and refrigerated tank. Distribution is performed in manners similar to those used for high-pressure systems. Localized and portable carbon dioxide extinguishers are intended for single-room and small-fire extinguishment, respectively. Localized carbon dioxide extinguishment typically involves having a small storage tank placed in a room. The tank is connected to a hose and is operated with a directional head. Portable carbon dioxide extinguishers are usually small cylindrical tanks with a release valve and a nozzle that can be directed at a small fire.

One other group of dry gases that, until relatively recently, have been used for fire extinguishment is the Halon group. But these Halon gases are various chlorofluorocarbon compounds and are presently banned from general commercial production (because when released into the atmosphere they damage the radiation-shielding capability of the upper atmosphere). These halogenated gases were developed for the U.S. Air Force for use in buildings in which airplane fuels were handled (e.g., aircraft hangars). Their extinguishment capabilities are superior to carbon dioxide and have the added benefit of not being hazardous to the health and well-being of human beings (who can be involved in the manual release of these agents during fire fighting). Carbon dioxide, used in quantity, causes human beings to lose consciousness. If human beings are exposed to higher concentrations of carbon dioxide and for sufficiently long exposures, this combination can eventually cause the death of the occupants. Presently, scientific research is underway seeking less atmosphere-damaging halogenated agents, but no new products are yet available.

The final group of dry extinguishment agents is a series of inorganic salts. The most widely used is sodium bicarbonate. Potassium bicarbonate ("Purple K") and monoammonium phosphate are also employed. The phosphate is used in residential-scaled fire extinguishers. The two bicarbonates are commonly mixed with a variety of gases that serve as transporting media for these salts. The mixing of gas and salts occurs in tanks upon receipt of signals from a detector system. The gas-entrained salts can then be passed, under pressure, through piping or hoses to a fire zone. The salts will then be released through directional heads into the zone.

C.2.5   OTHER FIRE PROTECTION SYSTEMS

Two other systems are especially deserving of attention: emergency electrical power supply and smoke venting. An emergency power supply system furnishes electricity in the instance when the main electrical system of a building fails during a fire event. A number of services thus would be supported and maintained with this backup source of electrical power. The most common consumption of emergency power is the running of emergency lighting systems. These lighting systems assist occupants while they evacuate a building during a fire event. Note also that the emergency lighting system will likely better enable fire-fighting activities after the everyday occupants have exited the building. The emergency lighting system will work independently from the main lighting system (although both systems may function simultaneously, if the conventional electrical power system remains active during the fire event).

A second application for emergency electricity is the provision of power for the continued operation of critical patient health care services in hospitals and clinics (e.g., for life-support and during surgery). A health care industry guideline stipulates that the time gap between a shutdown of primary electrical service and the commencement of emergency electrical service should be no more than 10 seconds.

A third requirement for emergency power is that it provides the energy for the automatic closing of fire doors (see Figure C.23) and the operation of stairwell pressurization systems and other smoke management facilities.

Three alternative sources of emergency electricity are all commonly used in buildings. For relatively simple buildings (or buildings with low occupancy numbers) that have comparatively small electrical consumption rates and short duration requirements for

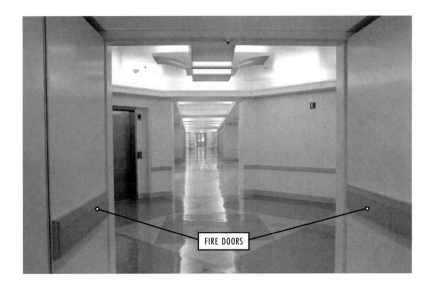

Figure C.23 In a laboratory building a set of fire doors automatically close if a fire event occurs. These fire doors would separate this lobby area from the fire stairs that are just behind this opening.

Figure C.24 This diesel generator is one of three units in this application that operate to produce electricity in the event that an emergency causes the failure of the municipal power network. During operation these generators produce considerable heat and are very noisy. In planning for the placement of diesel generators remember to provide space to accommodate a suitably large fuel storage tank. The capacity of the tank should be determined by the rate with which each generator consumes fuel and the length of time that the generator should be kept running.

emergency electricity, a power supply can be furnished with a series of batteries. The batteries should at least be capable of powering the emergency lighting system, the detection system, and the alarm system. Sufficient electrical energy storage capacity should be available to last up to 24 hours (although some municipalities or building operators may require shorter duration storage capabilities).

For larger buildings and for building applications where the emergency electrical supply must last for longer durations and provide more elaborate services (e.g., patient care equipment in a hospital), one or more electrical generators must be provided to ensure an adequate and suitably long-lasting capacity (see Figure C.24). Such generators are often driven by the combustion of a fossil fuel (e.g., No. 2 diesel oil). Thus, where one or more generators are included, a tank will be needed to store fuel used to operate them. This tank must be located so that the resupply of fuel can be readily conducted. Additionally, air intake (to enable combustion of the fuel) and an exhaust passageway (from each generator to the exterior) will be required. Indeed, the amount of floor space required to house one or more emergency generators can generally be as much as approximately 1 percent of the gross floor area served by the generators. Floor-to-ceiling dimensions for housing generators and associated piping, air intake ducting, and exhaust gas dumping should likely be at least 10 to 12 ft (3.1 to 3.7 m).

A third alternative source of emergency power can be another main power supply line that is entirely independent and physically well-separated from the primary electrical power line. Providing such an independent, alternative power line requires that there be not only sufficient distance between the two different supplies, but also that there are adequate fire-construction-rated building enclosures present to separate the alternative supply lines. Thus, there must be assurance that if one line should be rendered unusable during a fire event, the alternative line would likely be well-protected and safe from damage.

The other additional equipment group is a smoke management and control system. This system is a necessary component of the overall plan for enabling occupant evacuation during a fire event. The smoke management and control system is also essential in allowing fire-fighting professionals to get to the fire zone.

A first requirement for smoke management is that the means of egress — the pathways for occupant evacuation and fire-fighter admission — be kept smoke-free. Thus, to ensure that smoke from a fire zone does not pass into and along egress pathways, the pathways must be positively pressurized. Such pressurization is commonly achieved with the operation of a fan that is dedicated specifically for this task. These fans are most often used for pressurizing stairwells. The fans can be located at the top of the stairwell or at the outside grade level. A basic design question (usually resolved by fire engineers) is whether the pressurizing air from the fan should be supplied to a stairwell from a single location (e.g., from the top of the stairwell or from a near grade level) or from a series of locations along the stairwell height)(see Figure C.25). Choosing to rely on one or more locations for passing pressurized air into a stairwell can depend on the nature of the building occupancy, the number of floors served by the stairwell, and the types of door assemblies used by occupants to enter the stairwell. One potential problem that fire engineers must consider when deciding where to locate pressurizing fans involves ensuring that smoke from a fire event, that is escaping from the building, cannot be drawn into a stairwell (or other egress component) by the pressurizing fan. Thus, where smoke might exit a burning building must be anticipated when locating a pressurizing fan.

A second component group for a smoke management and control system is a venting system. A venting system enables the release of smoke from a building fire event to the atmosphere. Smoke venting commonly occurs at the roof plane of a building and involves

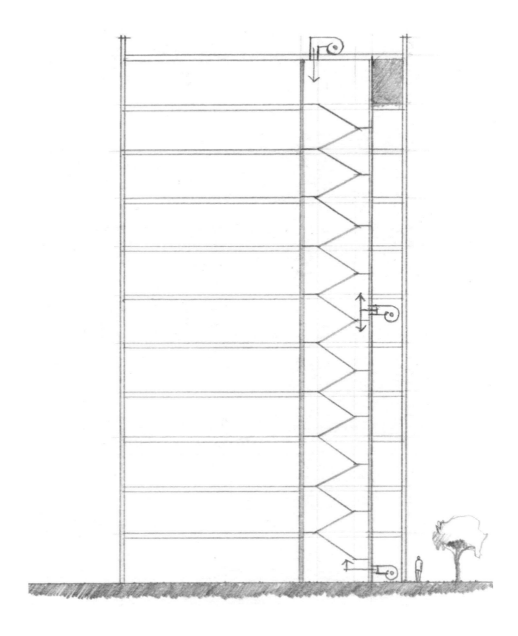

Figure C.25 American building codes generally stipulate that any vertical exits having heights greater than 75 ft (22.9 m) above grade must be positively pressurized. The placement of pressurizing fans is, however, not dictated. Thus, pressurizing fans can be placed at the top or bottom or in intermediate locations of the exit enclosure. Indeed, one or more fans may be devoted to providing adequate pressurization. For an example of this code requirement, see Statement 1005.3.3.7 in the *Uniform Building Code,* (Whittier, California: International Conference of Building Officials, 1997), pages 1–116.

a few large operable vents or many small modular vents (see Figure C.26). Because such venting most often is organized at the roof plane, this strategy works best with low-rise buildings (e.g., a factory, warehouse, shopping mall, or even a high school). The provision of an organized venting system is particularly important for buildings with large open floor plans such as factories, warehouses, and shopping malls. If a building includes an atrium, then venting of the atrium space should be made possible. Both sizing individual

Figure C.26 For this atrium space, along the topmost wall on the right hand side there is a series of smoke release vents. In the event that smoke enters the atrium the vent doors will swing open allowing the smoke to escape to the atmosphere.

or multiple roof vents and establishing adequate spacings for the vents are engineering decisions and should be treated on a case-by-case basis. One additional qualification about venting systems concerns the integration of a venting system with a sprinkler system. Currently, contrasting opinions exist in the fire protection profession as to whether the operation of sprinklers will support or degrade the performance of a venting system. This dispute is long-standing and remains unresolved.

ENDNOTES and SELECTED ADDITIONAL COMMENTS

1. Lathrop, J.K., "Concepts of egress design," (Section 8, Chapter 2), pages 8-31 to 8-50, in Cote, A.E. (editor), *Fire Protection Handbook,* 18th edition, (Quincy, Massachusetts: National Fire Protection Association, 1997).
2. Bryan, J.L., "Human behavior and fire," (Section 8, Chapter 1), pages 8-3 to 8-30, in Cote, A.E. (editor), *Fire Protection Handbook,* 18th edition, (Quincy, Massachusetts: National Fire Protection Association, 1997).
3. Cote, R. (editor), *Life Safety Code Handbook,* 7th edition, (Quincy, Massachusetts: National Fire Protection Association, 1997).
4. ———. *Life Safety Code* [identified as NFPA 101], (Quincy, Massachusetts: National Fire Protection Association, 1997).
5. ———. *The 2000 International Fire Code,* (Falls Church, Virginia: International Code Council, 1999).
6. Statement 1005.2.1 of *The 2000 International Fire Code,* (Falls Church, Virginia: International Code Council, 1999).
7. Exit access travel distance lengths for specific occupancy types can be found in Section 1004 of *The 2000 International Fire Code,* (Falls Church, Virginia: International Code Council, 1999), page 115.
8. Table 1003.2.3 of *The 2000 International Fire Code,* (Falls Church, Virginia: International Code Council, 1999), page 100. Also, Section 5-3.3 in Cote, R. (editor), *Life Safety Code Handbook,* 7th edition, (Quincy, Massachusetts: National Fire Protection Association, 1997), page 130.
9. Statement 1003.2.3 of *The 2000 International Fire Code,* (Falls Church, Virginia: International Code Council, 1999). Note that specific occupancy load width factors can be found in Table 1003.2.3 of *The 2000 International Fire Code,* (Falls Church, Virginia: International Code Council, 1999), page 100.
10 Table 5-2.2.2.1(a) in Cote, R. (editor), *Life Safety Code Handbook,* 7th edition, (Quincy, Massachusetts: National Fire Protection Association, 1997), page 78; and Section 1003 of *The 2000 International Fire Code,* (Falls Church, Virginia: International Code Council, 1999).
11. Solomon, R.E., "Automatic sprinkler systems," (Section 6, Chapter 10), pages 6–136 to 6–164, in Cote, A.E. (editor), *Fire Protection Handbook,* 18th edition, (Quincy, Massachusetts: National Fire Protection Association, 1997).
12. Isman, K.E., "Automatic sprinklers," (Section 6, Chapter 9), pages 6-124 to 6-135, in Cote, A.E. (editor), *Fire Protection Handbook,* 18th edition, (Quincy, Massachusetts: National Fire Protection Association, 1997).
13. Shapiro, J.M., "Standpipe and hose systems," (Section 6, Chapter 16), pages 6-249 to 6-263, in Cote, A.E. (editor), *Fire Protection Handbook,* 18th edition, (Quincy, Massachusetts: National Fire Protection Association, 1997).
14. Statement 905 of *The 2000 International Fire Code,* (Falls Church, Virginia: International Code Council, 1999).
15. All three of these quotations appear in Statement 905.4 of *The 2000 International Fire Code,* (Falls Church, Virginia: International Code Council, 1999), page 72.

16.   Statement 905.11 of *The 2000 International Fire Code,* (Falls Church, Virginia: International Code Council, 1999), page 73.

17.   See, for example, Campbell, J.A., "Confinement of fire in buildings," (Section 7, Chapter 5), pages 7-77 to 7-92, in Cote, A.E. (editor), *Fire Protection Handbook,* 18th edition, (Quincy, Massachusetts: National Fire Protection Association, 1997); or NFPA 80, *Standard for Fire Doors and Fire Windows,* (Quincy, Massachusetts: National Fire Protection Association, 1995).

18.   Hall, J.R., Jr., and A.E. Cote, "America's fire problem and fire protection," (Section 1, Chapter 1), pages 1-3 to 1-25, in Cote, A.E. (editor), *Fire Protection Handbook,* 18th edition, (Quincy, Massachusetts: National Fire Protection Association, 1997).

19.   Hartzell, G.E., "Combustion products and their effects on life safety," (Section 4, Chapter 2), pages 4-10 to 4–21, in Cote, A.E. (editor), *Fire Protection Handbook,* 18th edition, (Quincy, Massachusetts: National Fire Protection Association, 1997).

20.   Moore, W.D., "Automatic fire detectors," (Section 5, Chapter 2), pages 5-12 to 5-23, in Cote, A.E. (editor), *Fire Protection Handbook,* 18th edition, (Quincy, Massachusetts: National Fire Protection Association, 1997).

21.   ———. *National Fire Alarm Code,* NFPA 72, (Quincy, Massachusetts: National Fire Protection Association, 1993).

Electrical Systems for Buildings

ELECTRICAL SYSTEMS PROVIDE two services for building occupants. First, electrical systems supply power that enables the operation of the many electrical task devices that exist in buildings. Second, electrical systems serve as the foundation for the various communication and signaling devices that are used in buildings. In this chapter we will first discuss power systems. Subsequently, we will treat communication and signaling systems.

Section D.1 | BASIC PREMISES OF ELECTRICAL POWER SYSTEMS

Electrical systems furnish a means for transporting energy from one location to another. The source of the energy can be near or far removed from where the energy is to be consumed. Indeed, electrical systems enable energy to be transported over distances of many hundreds of miles so that the location of the source is determined by the nature of the source, rather than by the location of the consumer. For example, if a source is a wind farm or solar photovoltaic cell array, then these sources can be set up where the wind is strong and constant or the sky conditions are nearly always clear and the solar radiation is intense.

Sources of electricity include energy derived from the combustion of fossil fuels or biomass, the fission of nuclear materials, the reaction of chemicals, falling water, solar

Figure D.1 The process by which solar energy is converted to electricity is shown here. The radiation from the sun is received by photovoltaic cells (that are mounted on the roof of the building.) The solar radiation causes a flow of electrons through and out of these PV cells. The electrical energy — manifested by the current flow — can then be stored in the battery. Subsequently, the electrical energy stored in the battery can be used to power the electric lamp. Note the similarity between this thermoelectric energy conversion and the energy conversion demonstrated in Figure 2.1.

radiation, wind, geothermal energy releases, and tidal flows. Note also that each of these sources functions by converting energy of some sort into electricity. For example, falling water drives turbines, converting mechanical energy to electrical energy. Alternatively, burning biomass produces thermal energy that is used to heat water to create steam. Then, the steam passes to a turbine where the thermal energy is converted to electrical energy, and so forth (see Figure D.1).

The consumer can be virtually independent from the energy source. The only requirement for the consumer to benefit from a remote energy source is that the consumer must be able to operate by using electricity. Thus, this electrical energy can be used to heat or illuminate a space, operate an elevator motor, drive a water pump, power a computer, or cook a meal. The consumption of the electricity in the performance of each of these tasks does not depend on how the electricity was generated. Instead, enabling the performances of these tasks simply requires that the electricity reaching the task device via the transporting system will match the rate and form of the electrical energy that the device requires for operation.

Electrical systems are composed of numbers of interconnecting elements beginning at the location where the generation of electricity occurs and ending at the wiring that transports the electricity to the task device. The elements of electrical systems have been developed to relate to each other and to function as components of a whole. These elements thus are integrated, ensures good performance by the whole system. From the earliest days of the electrical systems industry — beginning with Edison and the development of a commercially viable light bulb — the focus has been on creating complete systems that include the generation of electricity, the transporting of the electricity to the user, and the manufacture and selling of devices that consume electricity as the basis for their operation. Thus, from about 1880 to the present, the industry has proceeded, first, with the development of whole systems and, second, with successive searches for improvements of the systems and the many components used in the systems. Further, the ready acceptance of the industry by both individuals and businesses (and the resultant growth of the industry) have occurred, at least partially, because of the establishment within the industry of standardized definitions of products and services.

Section D.2 | CIRCUITS, SYSTEMS, AND COMPONENTS

D.2.1   INTRODUCING CIRCUIT TERMINOLOGY

A simple, complete electrical system is shown in Figure D.2. A battery furnishes electrical energy through a wire circuit to a lamp. The flow of electrical energy and the operation of the lamp are controlled by the switch. When the switch is thrown to its "ON" position, the circuit is closed, and electrical energy moves throughout the circuit. Alternatively, when the switch is in its "OFF" position, the circuit is opened, and the electrical energy is stopped from moving throughout the circuit.

In this — and any other — electrical circuit, the movement of electrical energy occurs by the flow of electrons from the battery through the wire around the circuit. The electron flow is identified as the *current,* which is essentially the number of electrons moving through the circuit for a unit of time. The current flow in a circuit is expressed in terms of *amperes* (or, more simply, amps).

The battery in this circuit propels the electron flow. Using a mechanical analogy, we might say that the electron flow through the circuit is "forced" by the battery (i.e., that the battery exerts a force on the electrons). This analogy — whereas appealing as a visualization aid — is not strictly accurate. Instead, the battery imposes a *potential difference* on the circuit prompting the flow of electrons. The reference to a potential difference coincides with the notion that the battery is an energy source (or, more particularly, a potential energy source, until the battery is included in a complete circuit). The potential difference in a circuit is expressed in terms of *volts.* Also, note that the potential difference is often referred to as the *voltage.*

The third property of this circuit is that as the current flows through the circuit, the current experiences a drag, or *resistance,* to this flow. Resistance to the flow is imparted by each of the components in this circuit: the lamp, the switch, and the wiring that connects the devices into the circuit. The amount of resistance that any component in a circuit imposes on the current flow is equivalent to the potential difference (or voltage) divided by the current. The resistance thus imposed is expressed in terms of *ohms.* Generally speaking, the resistances imparted by the wiring and the switch (when closed) are both very small

Figure D.2 A simple circuit is shown with an energy source (the battery), a switch (that offers user control of the circuit), and a lamp (which is one of many alternative devices that operate with electrical energy.)

amounts, whereas the resistance of the lamp will constitute nearly all of the observed (or measured) resistance in the circuit. Note that if the resistance in the circuit can be found by dividing the voltage by the amount of current (R = V/I), then, the voltage will be equal to the current multiplied by the resistance (or, V = I × R).

A fourth property of the circuit is that the rate of electrical energy flowing through the circuit per a unit of time is described as the *power* present in the circuit. Alternatively, we might write that power is the rate with which energy is produced by the battery per a unit of time or is consumed by the remainder of the circuit per a unit of time. Thus, if we use the symbol E to represent the energy flowing in the circuit, then the power (P) is equivalent to the energy (E) divided by the amount of time (t) for which the energy flow is observed (or, expressed algebraically, P = E/t). Note that power is expressed in terms of *watts.* One other important relationship that can be used to describe the power present in this circuit is that the power is equivalent to the voltage multiplied by the current (or P = V × I). Further, because the voltage is equivalent to the current multiplied by the resistance in the circuit, power is also equivalent to the resistance multiplied by the square of the current (or P = R × I2).

The fifth property of this circuit is that the amount of energy that flows through the circuit is equivalent to the power multiplied by the amount of time for which the power is exhibited. Thus, written algebraically, E = P × t. The basic term used for quantifying electrical energy — principally, for describing the amount of energy consumed — is *watt-hour.*

One additional issue regarding these terms and quantities is that the amounts of amperes, volts, watts, and watt-hours that are produced, flow, and are consumed in electrical systems — regional and local — are generally quite large. Therefore, a number of prefixed letters are used to compress the numbers into more manageable forms. The most common of these prefixes are the letters k, M, and G (for kilo, mega, and giga, respectively). For example, electrical consumption for residential operation is generally expressed in units of kilowatt-hours (or kWh). Alternatively, the amount of power that a commercial power plant — a power generator — may produce is usually described in terms of megawatts (or MW).

D.2.2   DIRECT AND ALTERNATING CURRENTS

In the circuit shown in Figure D.2, current flows directly around the circuit from the battery to the lamp. The flow is continuous and occurs in a single direction. Thus, this current flow is identified as *direct current* (dc).

A second way to create direct current is to produce a circuit composed of some wire, the lamp, and the (closed) switch. With no battery present in the circuit, there will be no source of electrical energy and no current flow. However, if a horseshoe magnet (with its characteristic magnetic field that emanates from its two poles) is brought into the vicinity of the wire and is moved relative to the fixed-in-place wire, a current will be induced to flow through the circuit (Figure D.3). This induced current flow is similar to the current flow that was present when the battery was included in the circuit. Thus, we may describe the effect of the moving magnetic field on the circuit as inducing a voltage in the circuit (thereby, furnishing energy that causes the current flow in the circuit). The current flow created by moving the magnet (and its magnetic field) relative to the fixed-in-place wire is also *direct current.*

Suppose we construct a modified version of this battery-less circuit (Figure D.4). In this new circuit a portion of the wire is shaped into a coil, and the two ends of the coil are

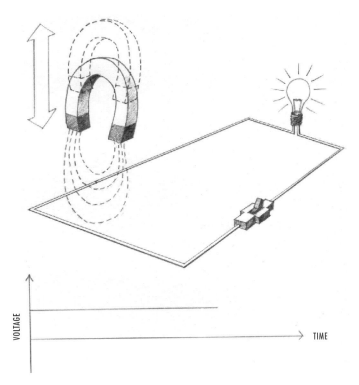

Figure D.3 Producing direct current electricity occurs by moving a magnetic field—with the magnet—up and down across the wire in this circuit. The potential difference—the voltage—thus generated is a constant positive value, as shown in the graph presented below the circuit.

each attached to slip rings that connect to the remainder of the circuit. The coil is placed in a magnetic field that exists between the two poles of a horseshoe magnet. Then the coil is rotated in this magnetic field. The resulting current flow in the circuit differs from the direct current observed previously. As the coil rotates through the magnetic field, the voltage induced in the coil will vary *sinusoidally* from a maximum (positive) strength to a zero (or neutral) strength to a maximum (negative) strength to a zero (neutral) strength to a maximum (positive) strength and so forth (Figure D.5). During the part of this cycle while the voltage is positive, the current flows in one direction through the circuit. And, when the voltage is negative, the current flows in the opposite direction. Thus, the rotation of the coil through the magnetic field produces *alternating current* (ac). Note that although the electrical energy flow is described as alternating current, the voltage in this circuit also varies in an alternating manner.

In the production of alternating current the speed of rotation of the coil (or coils) through the magnetic field is usually maintained at a constant rate. This speed of rotation is equivalent to the number of cycles that the current (or the voltage) undergoes for some unit of time (i.e., how many times a maximum positive voltage or maximum negative voltage is achieved for this amount of time). Commonly, the amount of time that is considered for this rate of rotation is one second. Thus, the number of rotations (or cycles) occurring for a second of time is identified as the frequency of the alternating current and is

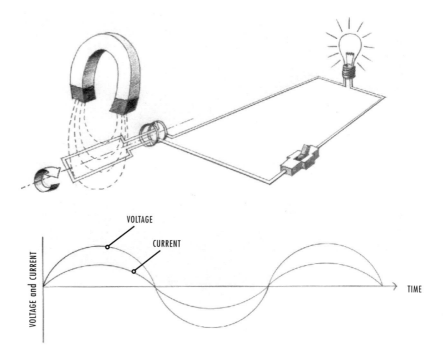

Figure D.4 Turning a coil through a magnetic field produces alternating current. The current produced by this action passes from the coil via a pair of slip rings that are connected to the wires of a circuit. When the switch is "ON," the current will cause the lamp to give off light. The alternating current and the accompanying voltage—generated by the rotating coil—are displayed in the graph. In this representation, the larger-magnitude variable is the voltage; the magnitude of the current is portrayed by the lesser-magnitude curve.

expressed in terms of Hertz (Hz). In North America, conventional alternating current electricity is supplied at 60 Hz, whereas in Europe and much of the rest of the world the electric supply frequency is set at 50 Hz.

The history of the developments of direct and alternating current for use in the commercial supply of electricity began in about 1880 with the introduction of the Edison lighting system. This system was composed of a viable electric lamp, generators for producing electrical energy, and a distribution technology for transporting the electricity from centralized generators to localized (remote) consumers. The initial deployment of a whole system was carried out in lower Manhattan (New York City). This system and numbers of other Edison-backed municipal systems that were installed in North America and Europe in that era were based on *direct current.*

Commencing only a few years later and proceeding in competition with the deployment of direct current systems, alternating current systems were being developed and marketed to other municipalities. For a period of perhaps the next two decades a "battle of the systems" continued, until gradually the adoption of alternating current systems became commonplace, and the use of direct current systems as a basis for commercial electricity supply receded. For most of the 20th century the application of alternating current systems for powering industry, commerce, and home occupancy has been nearly a

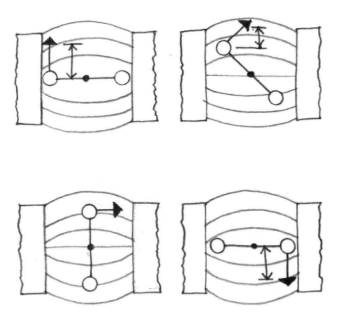

Figure D.5 This representation shows how the relative positions of the coil in the magnetic field produce the variation in the magnitudes of the voltage. In the upper left position the full strength of the magnetic field is experienced, producing the greatest voltage magnitude. In the lower-left image there is a partial effect from the magnetic field, and the voltage is greater than zero. In the upper-right image no effect on the coil is exerted by the magnetic field: the coil is in a neutral position. Thus, the voltage is zero. In the lower right image—which is opposite to the upper-left image—the voltage is at its negative maximum.

This diagram is a reproduction of a drawing in the document, *At the flick of a switch* (Seattle, Washington: City of Seattle Lighting Department, 2000.) Permission to reprint this diagram has been granted by the City of Seattle Lighting Department.

monopoly. But quite recently the implementation of direct current systems as a means for supplying large quantities of power, locally and regionally, has reemerged and is beginning to compete with alternating current systems.

Prior to recent times the fundamental drawback that limited the use of direct current as the basis for regional supply systems was the voltage losses that were experienced when direct current electricity traveled any substantial distance between its generation and its consumption. To appreciate this voltage loss, consider the resistance that any current is subjected to as it flows through a conductor (e.g., wire). The amount of resistance that the current experiences is directly proportional to the length of the conductor (i.e., the longer the conductor, the greater the total resistance). This resistance imposes a reduction, or drop, on the voltage that passes through the conductor (because voltage is equal to the product of the flowing current times the resistance [or $V = I \times R$]). Thus, when current flows over longer distances, greater resistances will be present in the circuit. The voltage reduction will increase accordingly, so that the voltages reaching more distant users will be lessened (see Figure D.6). Consequently, if a particular electrical device requires some specific voltage to operate and the supplied voltage is inadequate,

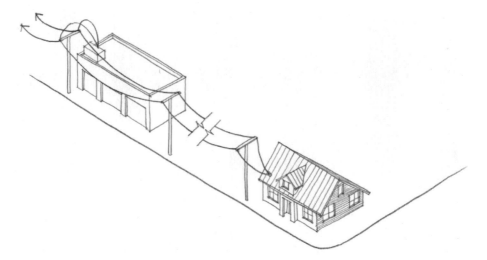

Figure D.6 Because the lack of an ability to transform voltages in a direct current transmission line, substantial electrical energy is lost when direct current electricity is transmitted over long distances. This loss occurs because of the resistance in the cables transmitting the electricity.

This drawing has been printed in a document by Liu, Franklin S., Dennis M. Gray, and Dana Backiel, *Seattle City Light Power System Engineering Information,* (Seattle: City of Seattle Lighting Department, 1998.) Permission to reprint this image has been granted by the City of Seattle Lighting Department.

The capability that enabled alternating current systems to gain and hold sway for most of the 20th century is the ability for alternating current to be *transformed.* Transformation of alternating current involves the changing of the quantities of current that flow through circuits and of the voltages that exist across circuits. This transformation process involves the use of a *transformer.*

A transformer — rendered most simply — consists of a core (a circular ring or rectangular donut), usually formed of iron with sets of circuit wires wound around the two opposite sides of the ring (or rectangular donut)(see Figure D.7). One set of circuit wire will come to the transformer from the electrical energy source. The other set of circuit wire will proceed from the transformer in the direction of the power consumer. The circuit wire running from the electrical energy source to the transformer will induce a magnetic field in the iron core. This magnetic field will, in turn, induce a current flow in the circuit wire passing from the transformer to the power consumer.

The transformation process is founded on two principles. First, in an *ideal* transformer, the amount of power reaching the transformer from the electrical energy source will be equal to the amount of power running from the transformer to the consumer. Second, the nature of the transformation process — what the "entering" and "leaving" voltage and current magnitudes will be — is determined by the number of windings of circuit wire on each side of the core (i.e., how many times each circuit wire has been wound around the core). For this second principle, the ratio of the number of windings on each of the two sides is proportional to the ratio of the voltages on the two sides of the core, thus $V_1/V_2 = N_1/N_2$. For the first principle — for the power equivalency — as power is equal to the product of the voltage in the circuit times the current, $V_1I_1 = V_2I_2$ or $V_1/V_2 = I_2/I_1$.

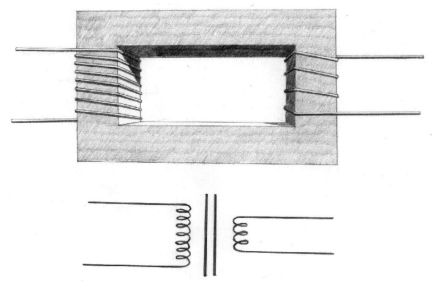

Figure D.7 An alternating current transformer, simplified. On the left side of the upper image, higher-voltage power arrives at the transformer core. This voltage creates a magnetic field around the core, inducing a voltage to be produced in the wiring leaving from the right side of the core. Because there are more wire turns on the left side than on the right, this transformer is a *step-down* transformer, and the voltage leaving the right side will be less than arriving at the left side. In the lower image a standard representational symbol for a transformer is displayed.

Using the second transformer principle—that the ratio of voltages is equal to the ratio of the numbers of windings—a voltage in an alternating current circuit can be changed from one magnitude to another by passing it through a transformer with the requisite number of windings on each side of the core. Thus, if the voltage passing from the generating source to the transformer is 100 V and we wanted to change the voltage "leaving" the transformer (and running to the consumer) to 200 V, we would employ a transformer that had twice as many windings on the "leaving" side as on the "entering" side (of the core). Further, if the current on the entering side for this core is 10 amps, then the current leaving the core (and passing toward the consumer) would be 5 amps.

Two conventions that are used to describe the actions of a transformer involve which side of the transformer core is connected to the electrical energy source—what we have been calling the "entering" side—and whether the leaving voltage is greater or less than the entering voltage. The first of these conventions concerns the direction of the electrical energy flow. The core side that receives the electrical energy (electricity) from the generating source is called the *primary*. The core side from which the electrical energy flows toward the consumer is called the *secondary*. For the second convention, if the voltage arriving at the primary (or entering) side of the core is greater than the voltage leaving the secondary side, then the device is a *step-down* transformer. Instead, if the voltage leaving the secondary side is greater than the voltage arriving at the primary side, the device is a *step-up* transformer.

Now, returning to the question of why alternating current systems supplanted direct current systems, the transformer provided that voltage reductions resulting from long-distance supply circuitry would be much smaller for the alternating current systems. The current flowing through the supply circuitry could be made relatively small by stepping-up (increasing) the voltage. Reconsidering the relationship between system voltage and current magnitudes ($V_s / V_p = I_p / I_s$), as the secondary voltage is made large relative to the primary voltage, the secondary current will be rendered small. Thus, if the secondary voltage—for long-distance transporting—can be stepped-up perhaps by a factor of 30 to 50, then the secondary current will be changed inversely to $1/30$th to $1/50$th of the primary current. The voltage losses experienced for this secondary current resulting from the resistance imposed in the conductor (using the $V = I \times R$ relationship) will be small (in contrast to losses that would be present with potentially long-distance direct current systems that did not have this transformation capability). Note also that voltage lost is energy lost: electrical energy is equivalent to the product of the power carried in a circuit multiplied by the time of supply (where power, P, is equivalent to the voltage, V, multiplied by the current, I, or $P = (IR) \times I = I^2R$; so that the magnitude of energy lost varies with the square of the magnitude of the current, making efforts to reduce current magnitudes in long-distance transporting even more greatly rewarding)(see Figure D.8).

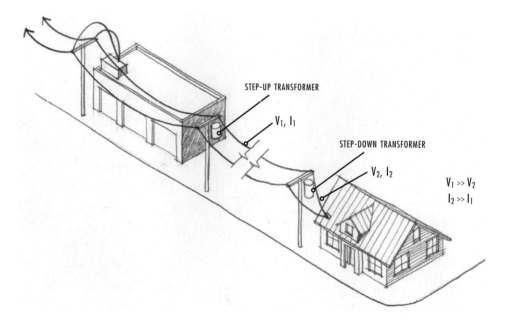

Figure D.8 In contrast to direct current transmission (as depicted in Figure D.6), alternating current transmission is more efficient. The greater efficiency results from the ability to transform the voltages used (and the amounts of current passed) when electrical energy is transmitted over considerable distances.

This drawing has been printed in a document by Liu, Franklin S., Dennis M. Gray, and Dana Backiel, *Seattle City Light Power System Engineering Information,* (Seattle: City of Seattle Lighting Department, 1998.) Permission to reprint this image has been granted by the City of Seattle Lighting Department.

D.2.3   ONE-PHASE VERSUS POLYPHASE ELECTRICITY GENERATION AND TRANSPORTING

The alternating current produced by rotating a coil through a magnetic field is described as having a *one-phase* electricity form. In contrast to this alternating current production, multiple coils may be assembled together and rotated through the magnetic field. For instance, suppose a coil assembly is fabricated to consist of three equally spaced coils. When this three-coil assembly is placed within the magnetic field, the assembly is rotated, and the voltage variations are recorded, three identical sine waves are found (see Figure D.9). As the three coils are each separated from the next by a 120° angle (when viewed in an edge-on perspective), so, too, are the sine waves separated by the same 120° displacements. Thus, a three-phase electricity form is produced. In similar fashions various other multiple-coil assemblies can be created (with suitable, regular, angular spacings), rotated in magnetic fields, and thereby used to produce *polyphase* electricity forms.

Historically, two- and four-phase electricity forms were developed and used for limited periods and applications. In recent times, six-, nine-, and twelve-phase electricity forms are being employed in special circumstances. But, for the most part, one-phase and three-phase electricity forms predominate for the generation and transportation of electrical energy.

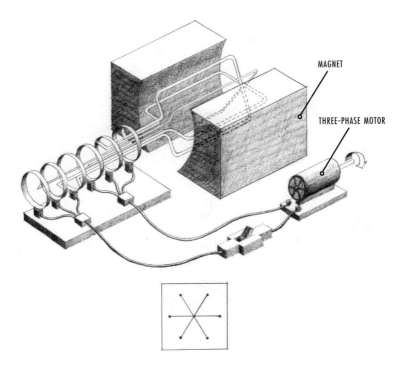

Figure D.9 Three-phase alternating-current electricity is generated by turning three coils through a magnetic field. Each arm of these coils is separated from the next by 60° (as shown in the lower diagram where the coils are viewed from one end.) The voltage variations produced by these three coils as they turn through the magnetic field are shown in Figure D.10.

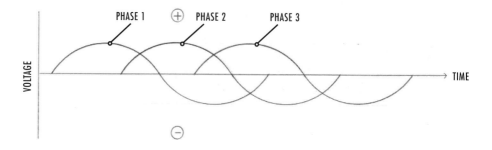

Figure D.10 The three phases of three-phase alternating current electricity are separated one from the next by 120°. The principal benefit of transmitting three-phase electricity is that a denser energy flow occurs (in comparison to one-phase electricity). A second advantage is that the instantaneous voltage magnitude of three-phase electricity remains closer to a maximum amplitude than would be present for one-phase electricity.

Most commercial generation of electricity presently occurs using a three-phase composition. In contrast to a one-phase format, three-phase electricity offers a more dense energy flow per unit time. Similarly, the three-phase format provides energy with a smoother, less-pulsating quality than one-phase does (see Figure D.10). Alternatively, if we contrast using a single three-phase circuit or three one-phase circuits to transport equal magnitudes of electrical energy, we would discover that a smaller amount of conductor material would be required to transport the three-phase energy. Further, the equipment used for controlling and manipulating the three-phase energy will be smaller in size, less massive, and more efficient than one-phase equipment (that would be required to handle a like amount of electrical energy). Therefore, electrical energy production and supply using polyphase formats, generally, and the three-phase format, particularly, has been nearly universally accepted.

Section D.3 | LARGE-SCALE PRODUCTION AND TRANSPORTATION OF ELECTRICAL POWER

The electrical energy supply system in North America and Europe largely consists of four types of components: generation, transmission, distribution, and utilization.

Any supply system commences with a generation facility that may be located relatively closely to the ultimate energy consumers or placed a considerable distance away. The basis for choosing the location for a generation facility often depends on a number of variables including whether some natural resource is to be exploited (as the energy source for driving the generators), the aggregation of sufficient numbers of consumers (to finance the required investment), an available infrastructure for dispersing the energy (from the generation facility to the places occupied by the consumers), a compliant political environment, and available land (for locating the various systems components and for the rights-of-way to enable transmission). Additionally, many electrical energy suppliers—utilities—rely on multiple generation facilities, each of which often operates independently of other such facilities.

Two basic formats are most common for generation facilities: thermal or hydroelectric. Some facilities depend on thermal energy to drive generator operation (i.e., where the thermal energy is derived either from the combustion of coal, gas, or oil or from heat produced by nuclear fission). The heat from combustion or fission forms very hot, highly pressurized steam (temperatures as high as 1000 °F [538 °C] and pressures as great as 2000 psi [13,790 kPa] are employed). The steam then drives turbines whose shafts turn the generator coils). The major alternative source is hydroelectric, where falling water provides mechanical energy to operate the generators. Presently, in the United States about 90 percent of electrical generation employs thermal energy as the empowering agent. In some of the Scandinavian countries the majority of electricity production instead is based on hydroelectric generation.

In most large-scale generators the rotating coils bear the magnetic field, and the static windings that surround the rotating coils have alternating current induced within these windings (in contrast to the simplified alternating current generator shown in Figures D.4 and D.9). The rotation of these coils results from either the force of the hot, pressurized steam or of the falling water. An approximate representation of a waterwheel generator is shown in Figure D.11. For the waterwheel, the axis of rotation of the generator is vertical to take advantage of the falling water. But, in a steam-driven generator, the axis of rotation is horizontal (see Figure D.12).

Where the generation of electricity has been performed at a remote source, such as at a hydroelectric dam, the transmission lines serve as point-to-point conductors, transporting the energy from the distant source to aggregated consumer groups. Or, where a generation facility is located in a rural area outside of an urban center (as nuclear power plants often are), the electricity will need to be brought into the population hub. The transmission of electrical power is based on the transforming of the generated electricity to very large voltage magnitudes such that comparatively small currents flow along the transmission lines (and the transmission conductors can be made smaller in cross-section). In North America alternating current systems transmission occurs at levels such as 230, 345, 500, and 765 kilovolts (kV). Thus, the transmitted electricity is transformed from more modest voltages, perhaps in a range from 12 to 24 kV produced at the generators, to these "high" or "extra high" voltages. The greatly reduced current flows — made possible by the substantial stepping-up of the voltages — are more efficient as voltage, and power losses are kept small inspite of long transmission distances. As the transmission lines running from the generation facility to distribution centers usually traverse rural areas, the tower support structures and their associated rights-of-way can be located to minimize transmission distances (excepting when topographical features inhibit rights-of-way). The tower structures used for supporting long-distance transmission lines are constructed so that the conductor lines will be placed anywhere from about 60 to 100 ft (18.3 to 30.5 m) above the ground (see Figure D.13).

At the other end of these transmission lines — usually placed on the edge of cities and suburban areas with large groups of power consumers — the high voltage (or extra high voltage) electricity will be stepped down to what are described as "medium" voltages (e.g., 69, 34.5, 26, and, possibly, about 15 kV). This step-down transformation will commonly be performed at *substation distribution* facilities (see Figure D.14). Siting criteria for determining where and how many distribution substations should be provided for urban and suburban power consumers can be complex. Often, a principal concern is matching the electrical energy supply with the voltages needed by the many, varied consumers. In other words, it is desirable to run higher-voltage distribution lines to as near the consumers as feasible — to reduce power loss and equipment costs. But most commercial and residential consumers will need to have low-voltage supplies (e.g., 600 volts or less).

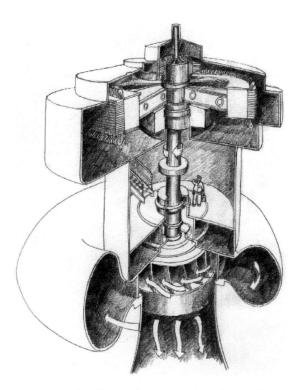

Figure D.11 The approximate interior of one of the generators located in the Ross Dam Power House is shown here. Water from behind the dam flows into the horizontal piping causing the rotor to turn. Contrary to the idealized alternating-current generators shown in Figures D.4 and D.9, at the Ross Dam the magnets rotate and the coils are held stationary. At the top of the rotor are the magnets. For an indication of the size of these rotors and the generators, note the presence of the workman (who might be called in to periodically service the rotor bearings).

This illustration is an approximate reproduction of a photograph published in a document by Liu, Franklin S., Dennis M. Gray, and Dana Backiel, *Seattle City Light Power System Engineering Information,* 1998 (Seattle: City of Seattle Lighting Department, 1998.) Permission to reprint this image has been granted by the City of Seattle Lighting Department.

Of course, other site factors are also important: the density of consumption; the availability of suitable land; the types of security needed; and so forth. For many urban and suburban areas in North America, distribution substations are organized in a pyramiding voltage step-down format (e.g., from 230 or 345 kV to perhaps 69 or 34.5 kV at the first substation; and then from about 34.5 kV to about 12.5 kV at a succeeding substation). In this fashion a cascading series of step-down substations will be arranged to bring utilizable voltages to the various consumers.

The fourth major component of the electrical energy supply system involves utilization. The utilization of electricity occurs in individual buildings, for street lighting, for public transportation (e.g., conventional and light-rail trains and buses), and for commercial and industrial activities. Utilization voltages—those *supplied to* individual buildings may be as high as 13.8 kV or as low as 120 V. But the voltages *used inside* of buildings are normally no higher than 480 V, and lower voltages will commonly be employed extensively.

Figure D.12 In the foreground is an alternating current generator that is located in the University of Washington Power Plant. Its capacity is about 5 kW. This generator is driven by high-pressure steam that is produced in a series of boilers in the power plant (see Figure A.10 for an example of these boilers). Though the physical size and capacity of the generator are relatively small—in comparison—to those generators found in municipal power plants, the form and organization of the UW generator are similar to the much larger commercial plants.

Figure D.13 Conventional high-voltage transmission power lines are shown here. Transmission lines such as these can pass voltages as high as 345 kV (or even greater voltages), as well as comparatively lower voltages (e.g., a variety of intermediate voltages, such as 69 and 34.5 kV).

Figure D.14 The major substation distribution facility for the City of Seattle Lighting Department is located in Bothell, Washington, a suburb of Seattle. At this facility high-voltage electricity (at 230 kV) is stepped down to 115 kV, and this comparatively lower-voltage electricity is distributed to approximately 15 intermediate substations across Seattle. This photograph has been prepared by the City of Seattle Lighting Department. It is reprinted here with their permission.

D.3.1 SUPPLYING ELECTRICAL POWER TO BUILDINGS ON THE UNIVERSITY OF WASHINGTON CAMPUS — A CASE EXAMPLE

Electrical energy for operating the Seattle campus of the University of Washington is supplied by a public utility, the City of Seattle Lighting Department (more familiarly known as "Seattle City Light"). The campus is composed of approximately 220 buildings with about 10,000,000 ft² (approximately 930,000 m²) of occupied space. The range of activities performed on this campus are consistent with many large universities located in North America and include teaching, research, administration, housing and food services, and a host of perhaps less primary pursuits. The need for and use of electrical energy on the University's campus are both conventional and yet diversified (perhaps more so than numbers of other single-purpose large aggregated-supply consumers such as the Boeing Corporation or the many large commercial office buildings that are present in the central business district of Seattle).

Most of the electrical energy that Seattle City Light consumers use is produced by generators located at seven dams that are owned and operated by Seattle City Light. Additional electrical energy is purchased from several sources including the Bonneville Power Administration, a series of public utility districts (PUD's), the Puget Sound Power Company, and a variety of electricity producers beyond the State of Washington. Thus, electricity reaches the City of Seattle (and the University of Washington) from many distant sources. A nationwide grid of transmission lines connect all of these sources and enable electrical energy to be transported over long distances and even from other regions of the United States (and Canada).

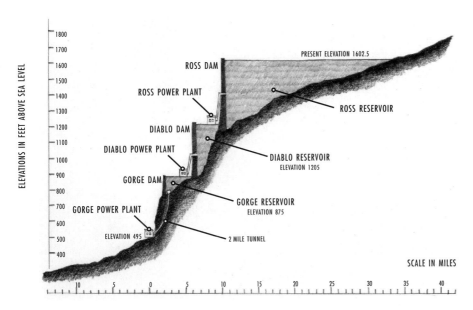

ELEVATIONS IN FEET ABOVE SEA LEVEL

PRESENT ELEVATION 1602.5

ROSS DAM

ROSS POWER PLANT

ROSS RESERVOIR

DIABLO DAM

DIABLO POWER PLANT

DIABLO RESERVOIR
ELEVATION 1205

GORGE DAM

GORGE RESERVOIR
ELEVATION 875

GORGE POWER PLANT

ELEVATION 495

2 MILE TUNNEL

SCALE IN MILES

Figure D.15 Three hydroelectric dams provide a substantial quantity of the power consumed by the Seattle City Light utility: Ross, Diablo, and Gorge. Here, their comparative elevations and head heights are shown.

This drawing has been printed in a document by Liu, Franklin S., Dennis M. Gray, and Dana Backiel, *Seattle City Light Power System Engineering Information,* (Seattle: City of Seattle Lighting Department, 1998.) Permission to reprint this image has been granted by the City of Seattle Lighting Department.

Seattle City Light has been in operation since 1904. For the past 80 years a significant fraction of the electrical energy generated by Seattle City Light—about 45 percent—has been supplied by a group of three dams, Ross, Diablo, and Gorge (see Figure D.15). These three dams are situated in the North Cascade Mountain range about 110 mi (175 km) northeast of Seattle. Each of the three dams is located on the Skagit River. The largest of these three facilities is the Ross Dam (see Figure D.16). The water stored behind Ross Dam is used to drive four generators. The power generated by each of these four units is 90,000 kW. The voltage derived from these four generators, operating in parallel, is three-phase, 60 Hz, 13.8 kV. This voltage magnitude is passed to a series of transformers where the electricity is stepped up to 230 kV for transmission.

The electricity generated at Ross Dam runs to the Diablo Dam where it joins with the electrical energy from the Diablo and Gorge Dams. This composite energy stream then is transmitted over elevated, high voltage lines 90 mi (144 km) to Bothell, a suburb of Seattle. At the Bothell distribution substation the 230 kV electricity is stepped down to 115 kV. Then, this 115 kV electricity is transmitted using *underground* lines to a number of intermediate substations, one of which—the University Receiving Substation—is located about 1 mi (1.6 km) west of the University of Washington campus. Note that two other intermediate distribution substations also pass energy on to the University Receiving Substation, thus demonstrating the typical interconnectedness of distribution systems found in suburban and urban areas (see Figure D.17).

The 115 kV electricity that arrives at the University Receiving Substation is stepped down to 26 kV. This 26 kV electricity is sent on, again using underground lines, to two further substations—East Campus and West Campus—where the electricity is finally stepped down to 13.8 kV for its dispersal to individual classroom, laboratory, and other large power-consuming buildings on the campus. Distribution of the 13.8 kV electricity occurs across the campus with the electrical energy running in cables that are passed through a network of tunnels that exist under the University of Washington campus (i.e., the same tunnels that provide pathways for piping that transports steam and chilled water for the thermal conditioning of university buildings [see Figures A.12 and A.13]).

Figure D.16 Ross Dam is located in the North Cascade Mountain range about 110 miles (175 km) from Seattle. This dam is a principal source of electrical energy for the City of Seattle Lighting Department (the electric utility for the city). This photograph has been prepared by the City of Seattle Lighting Department. It is reprinted here with their permission.

Figure D.17 The University District intermediate substation receives electrical power from the Bothell substation (see Figure D.14) and two other intermediate substations. At the University District substation electricity is stepped down from 115 kV to 26 kV. This intermediate-voltage electricity then is distributed throughout the district, but principally to the University of Washington campus. This photograph has been prepared by the City of Seattle Lighting Department. It is reprinted here with their permission.

Section D.4 | DISPERSION AND UTILIZATION OF ELECTRICAL ENERGY IN BUILDINGS

D.4.1 EQUIPMENT FOR ENERGY CONTROL AND MANIPULATION

The function of electricity distribution is to transport electrical energy from regional substations to individual buildings. This distribution is coordinated by public power utilities and is generally transported at medium voltages, in the range of 13 to 35 kV (i.e., at levels below the high- or extra-high voltages used for long-distance transmission). As with the use of high voltages for transmission, the use of medium voltages for distributing electricity in municipal locales is supported by the search for higher operating efficiencies (e.g., to reduce energy losses resulting from conductor resistances). Note that the municipal distribution will commonly involve three-phase electricity only.

For many nonresidential buildings the first responsibility of a building electrical system will be to connect to the public utility. This connection will usually include some level of control and protection for the building system. Standard components of the connecting equipment will be a main service switch, fusing, and metering. The service switch enables the building to be isolated from the utility system (e.g., if maintenance or repair needs to be performed on the main electrical system components in the building). Fusing protects the building electrical system from power surges on the utility system or limits possibilities of excessive service consumption by the building occupants. Metering registers energy consumed over time, as well as indicating "demand" requirements (i.e., demand identifies the greatest energy need for some short duration; commonly, the measure will be the number of kilowatts (of power) required for any one hour (or any quarter hour) period of building operation.

The second major electrical system function in the building will be to step down the medium voltage supplied by the power utility. The voltages that will be required in buildings will normally be 600 V or less (unless a building has a very large floor area and voltages in the range of 2.4 to 13.8 kV may be transported in the building and stepped down at a number of locations). This stepping-down of the utility-supplied medium voltage will be achieved with a main transformer. The stepping-down process may involve transformation from the medium voltage to a single low voltage level or to a combination of two low voltages (e.g., 13.8 kV–480/277 V, where the 13.8 kV level arrives at the primary side of the transformer and 480 V and 277 V can each be obtained from the secondary side of the transformer).

Most electrical utilization devices operate according to standardized voltage needs. For example, many motors — that drive fans, pumps, elevator cars, and so forth — require 460 V (so that 480 V will normally be supplied to these motors). Other smaller motors may operate at 240, 208, or 120 V. Fluorescent or high-intensity discharge light fixtures are conventionally powered at 277 V, particularly for buildings where lighting system energy requirements are substantial (e.g., a many-story office tower). Incandescent lamps—whether present in built-in assemblies or used in personalized desktop lamps—operate at 120 V. Computers, related office equipment, and any other appliances that connect directly to the usual wall-mounted receptacles will also operate at 120 V. Yet other generally specialized office or laboratory-bench equipment will likely have different voltage needs.

If the utilization voltages required for operating equipment are limited to some combination of low voltages (e.g., 480 V and 277 V) that can be obtained by the stepping-down process performed at the main transformer, then no additional (secondary) transformers will be needed in the building. But, more likely, where other combinations of voltages are also required for powering utilization equipment (e.g., 120 V used in addition to 480 V and 277 V), then one (or more) secondary transformer(s) will be required. Whether a secondary transformer is located in close proximity to the main transformer or whether a number of secondary transformers are strategically placed throughout a building will depend on how much electrical power will be needed in the building.

The third major function of the building electrical system will be to disperse the power that has been formed at the main transformer. This third function will be performed at a main dispersion panel. The electrical energy passing through this main dispersion panel will likely be spread out to such control devices as motor control centers, branch-circuit panelboards, various safety switches, secondary transformers, emergency power equipment, and so forth). The voltages that will be in operation at the main dispersion panel will be those produced by the main transformer.

The electrical energy that passes through this main dispersion panel will enable a variety of fourth-level functions. Electrical energy that flows to a motor control center can be used to operate each of the motors that may be present in a building. For instance, such motors can drive air-handling systems equipment, elevator equipment, or potentially any devices engaged in process activities (e.g., for manufacturing or product servicing). Other electrical energy streams may flow to branch-circuit panelboards that in turn supply electricity to utilization equipment that requires a voltage available from the main dispersion panel: for example, fluorescent light fixtures, as described above, are usually operated at 277 V in buildings where these fixtures constitute a significant fraction of the overall electrical energy load. Another energy stream that could likely flow from the main dispersion panel would be sent to a secondary transformer, where utilization voltages could be stepped down yet again (e.g., taking 480/277 V and stepping the power streams down to 208/120 V).

Then, these voltages produced at a secondary transformer would be passed to further branch-circuit panelboards (i.e., the fifth layer of equipment in the electrical system for a typical building). At these panelboards short branch circuits would be run to the various items of utilization equipment that would be present near these panelboards. As these panelboards utilized electrical energy at voltages produced at the secondary transformer—for instance, 120 V (which is the lower amount from the secondary side of a 480 V–208/120 V transformer)—this power could be used to operate incandescent lamps, computers and other small office equipment, small space heaters, handheld kitchen appliances, devices for personal grooming, and so forth (all of which are essentially a sixth-level of electrical equipment).

D.4.2 EQUIPMENT FOR TRANSPORTING ELECTRICAL ENERGY THROUGHOUT BUILDINGS

In addition to these six layers of electrical equipment (that enable energy handling, manipulation, and consumption), other equipment is used to transport (conduct) the electrical energy between these layers of equipment. In most nonresidential buildings three types of conductor devices will transport: cable, busways, and raceways. Note that these three types are listed here in a descending order of the voltage typically carried by these conductors.

Cable is conventionally employed to transport electricity at medium voltages (e.g., in the range between 13 to 35 kV). Thus, cable will be used to connect the utility service—supplied by the municipal power utility—through the service switch and fusing to the main transformer. Additionally, if electrical energy at these medium voltages (usually, any level above 1000 V) is transported in a building, then cable will be used as the conductor for such transportation. Employing cable as the conducting device at these medium voltages is practical because the amount of current that will flow through the cable will be comparatively small. Thus, cable can perform adequately with small cross-sectional areas.

The second principal means for conducting electricity in buildings is with *busways* (see Figure D.18). A busway is a metal enclosure that contains a number of busbars. These busbars are bars of either copper or aluminum that are arranged in layers of conducting metal sandwiched between and surrounded by insulation. Busbars and busways both have rectangular cross-sections. Generally, busways are constructed of modular lengths that can be fitted together. The busways also are composed of various elbows and tee sections that enable them to run in multiple directions. An additional, important feature of busway design is that numbers of plug-in devices can be mounted on the basic busway assembly, thus allowing connections between a busway and other electrical devices (e.g., branch-circuit panelboards, particular electrical utilization equipment such as motors, secondary transformers, and so forth).

The principal reason for the use of busways is that they enable the transportation of large amounts of current, either inside or outside of a building, using space-efficient assemblies. Generally, the voltages present in busway circuits are less than 600 V and are more often no higher than 480 V. Current densities in the busway circuits will be large. To

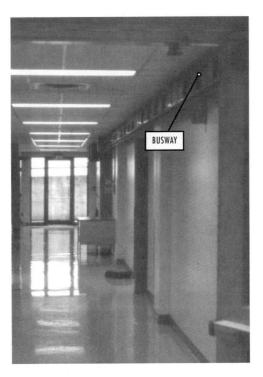

Figure D.18 A busway is present in the right-hand junction between the corridor wall and the ceiling. The building in which this busway is used is a laboratory building. As in many buildings that house laboratories, the considerable quantities of scientific equipment require large amount of electrical energy for operation.

transport equal amounts of current using cabling would require a much larger array of cables. Also, because busways are usually assembled of modular components, the construction of busways — versus the use of cabling with equal current-carrying capacities — offers substantial labor savings.

Major applications of busways can occur in central electrical vaults for the transportation of large current amounts between main transformers and secondary transformers and between transformers and switchboards (see Figure D.19). Other applications can include where large current amounts are transported in large buildings from a central electrical vault to remote secondary electrical room (closet) spaces. For example, in numbers of high-rise office buildings, busways can be used to transport current from a central electrical vault (where connection to the public power utility occurs) to electrical closets located on each of the many floors of the office tower. Alternatively, another use of busways can occur in large manufacturing plants where large amounts of current must be transported from a central electrical vault to the many machines that are spread out across a large floor area.

The third principal means for transporting electrical energy throughout buildings is via *raceways*. Raceways are, collectively, enclosures in which insulated wires are run. Raceways are typically used between branch-circuit panelboards and the utilization equipment that is powered by these circuits. The main functions of raceways are to provide physical protection for the enclosed wires and, on numbers of occasions, to establish grounding pathways.

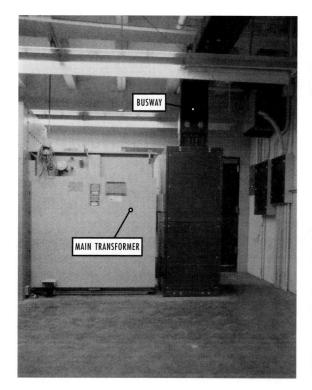

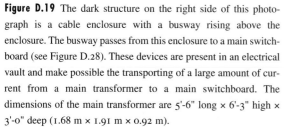

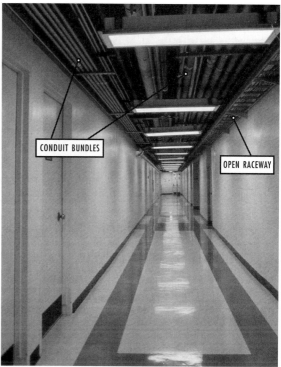

Figure D.19 The dark structure on the right side of this photograph is a cable enclosure with a busway rising above the enclosure. The busway passes from this enclosure to a main switchboard (see Figure D.28). These devices are present in an electrical vault and make possible the transporting of a large amount of current from a main transformer to a main switchboard. The dimensions of the main transformer are 5'-6" long × 6'-3" high × 3'-0" deep (1.68 m × 1.91 m × 0.92 m).

Figure D.20 This basement hallway is located in a building that consists of a number of large (200–700 person) classrooms. Power and communications wiring have been run from basement control spaces to these classrooms. The wiring passes through the extensive circular conduit assemblies in a plane above the fluorescent lamp fixtures. Also note the open raceway that runs along the right side of the hallway wall. Piping for water supply and waterborne waste handling is present, too, in the volume above the fixtures.

The term *raceway* comprises several alternative types of enclosures, most notably circular conduit (see Figure D.20) and rectangular cross-section channels (see Figure D.21). The materials that may be employed in the construction of raceways include metals (steel and aluminum, principally) and polymeric compounds. Conduit can be rigid, or it can be composed of flexible-wall assemblies. Rigid conduit can have thin-gauge or standard gauge walls. Various raceways can be used in underground applications, or they can be embedded in concrete slabs (or concrete decking). Raceways can also be used in built-up floor assemblies, in ceiling plenum spaces, and in vertical configurations where pole-like assemblies are "dropped" from overhead horizontal raceways (see Figure D.22). Raceways may be used in occupied spaces mounted on floor or various wall surfaces.

Raceways generally traverse the distances from panelboards to utilization equipment. Ideally, these distances will be short. But, where the distances are longer, where the pathways are indirect, or where the pathways of some raceways lead to utilization equipment, then a variety of intermediate or terminal devices will be built into the raceway pathways.

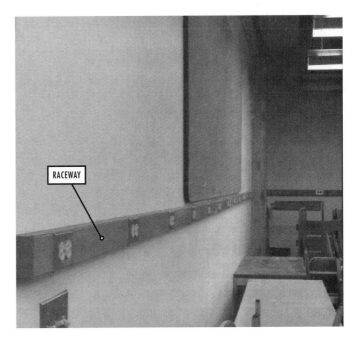

Figure D.21 A conventional closed rectangular raceway is pictured here in this laboratory space. This raceway is used to house wiring for a series of receptacles that are placed around the room perimeter.

Figure D.22 A pole raceway is used in this library to bring in new wiring for the desktop computers and connections to the various computer networks. The use of the pole raceway is a retrofit: when the building was constructed in the early 1970s no accommodations were made for installing personal computers.

Figure D.23 Here are two open pull boxes, which are used to bring wire runs together and to enable the joining of the wires.

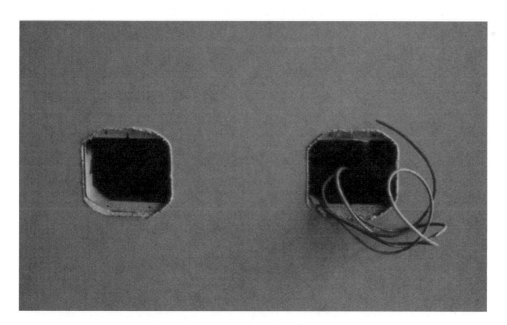

Figure D.24 In an office building two outlet boxes are placed side-by-side in the wall behind where a workstation will be located. The left box will provide connections to the computer network for the building; the right box will house receptacles furnishing 120 V alternating current.

Examples of these intermediate or terminal devices include pull boxes (that are used to thread wires between power-handling and utilization equipment), junction boxes (where alternative strands of wire cross or are to be joined), device boxes (where wiring is connected to devices such as switches and receptacles), and outlet boxes (where devices such as lighting fixtures and ceiling-suspended fans are installed and connected to wiring)(see Figures D.23 and D.24). These intermediate or terminal boxes commonly must be located and installed so that they are accessible during the lifetime of the building, *without having to remove fixed-in-place building assemblies* (i.e., finishing surfaces used to cover these boxes must always be temporary).

Section D.5 | ELECTRICITY DISPERSION AND UTILIZATION IN A CONVENTIONAL UNIVERSITY OF WASHINGTON BUILDING — GOULD HALL

D.5.1   MAJOR POWER SYSTEM COMPONENTS

Gould Hall is a typical University of Washington building, providing classrooms, laboratories, offices, and administrative centers (see Figure A.5). Its gross floor area is 62,000 ft² (5760 m²), and it has six stories, four above ground and two below grade. The principal electrical energy (power) needs for Gould Hall are to operate lighting systems (fluorescent and incandescent), motors (fans and pumps for HVAC systems and an elevator), and assorted hardware devices (particularly for classroom support, computers, and wood shop machinery).

Just as Gould Hall is a typical university classroom building, so, too, its electrical system can be considered as relatively typical for a building of its size and range of occupant services. The overall organization of the electrical system in Gould Hall involves a central service facility where utility power is brought into the building and is then stepped down. The reduced-voltage power is dispersed to a series of more localized dispersal satellites that are arrayed on a floor-by-floor basis. Then, at these dispersal satellites, conductors branch out to carry electrical energy to lighting fixtures and receptacles in individual rooms.

The central service facility includes a main service switch and fusing, metering, a main transformer, and switchgear (see Figure D.25). The main service switch permits disconnecting the building from the utility service. The main fusing provides protection against utility system power surges or excessive power demand from within the building. The main transformer steps the utility service voltage down to a range that can be distributed around the building. The switchboard takes the stepped-down electricity and sends the power out to the principal electrical equipment groups and panelboards throughout the building (where the panelboards function as intermediate connection and control facilities that are placed regularly and strategically).

So, for Gould Hall, utility service is provided to the building in the form of three-phase, 13.8 kV electricity (that arrives in the building, via the University tunnel network, from the West Campus distribution substation). The main transformer steps the 13.8 kV service down to a secondary service of 480/277 volts (i.e., from the secondary side of the transformer, supply lines can provide either 480 volts or 277 volts). Most of the resulting power passes to the main switchboard (see Figure D.26). A small fraction of the power flows instead to an emergency power system. In the main switchboard 480-volt electricity

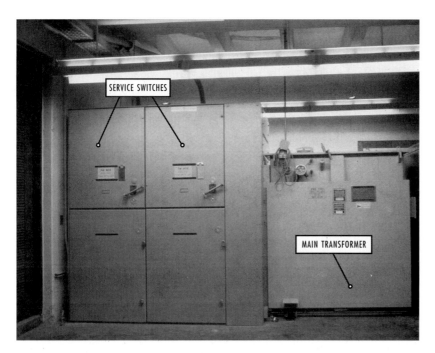

Figure D.25 The service switches and main transformer for Gould Hall are shown. The service switches are connected to utility power cables that furnish electrical power for the building. The main transformer steps down the service power from 13.8 kV to 480/277 V electricity. Note that this transformer also appears in Figure D.19. The combined dimensions for these two service switch modules are 7'-4" long × 8'-0" high × 4'-8" deep (2.24 m × 2.44 m × 1.42 m).

Figure D.26 The main switchboard for Gould Hall is shown here. The dimensions of this switchboard are 14'-2" long × 7'-6" high × 3'-9" deep (4.32 m × 2.29 m × 1.14 m).

is sent by one circuit to operate an elevator motor. A second circuit disperses 480-volt electricity to a series of fan motors and pumps that operate the HVAC system. Electrical power at the 277-volt level is dispersed from the main switchboard to a series of lighting panelboards. These lighting panelboards furnish 277-volt electricity for operating the fluorescent fixtures that are present throughout the building. Lastly for the 480/277 V power, some of the electrical energy is sent on to a secondary transformer that steps the electricity down further to a level of 208/120 volts. This 208/120-voltage service then passes through a secondary switchboard and on to a series of power panelboards that are arrayed throughout the building. The 120-volt power is consumed for operating incandescent fixtures, conventional classroom support equipment, computers and their peripheral equipment, and any devices that can be operated by plugging their power cords into ordinary wall and floor receptacles.

In Gould Hall, the central system components — the utility service connection, the main switch and fusing, the main transformer, the main switchboard, the emergency power panels (and a secondary transformer), the secondary transformer, and the 208/120-volt switchboard — are all located in a basement electrical vault (see Figures D.27 and D.28). The lighting panelboards — for exercising intermediate control of the fluorescent fixtures (at 277 volts) — are located on the basis of two lighting panelboards per above-ground floor. A ninth, similar lighting panelboard offers control of fluorescent fixtures

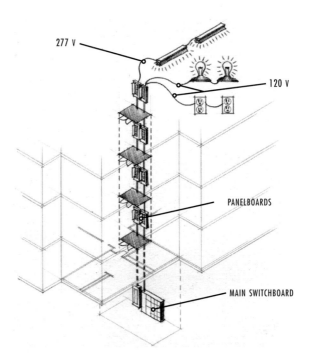

Figure D.27 An approximate layout of the Gould Hall electrical system is shown here. Electricity arrives in the building through service cables from the public power utility. It is stepped down at the main transformer. The main switchboard distributes the electricity to serve the needed operations. Some of the electricity (at 480/277 V) is distributed selectively. The remainder (mostly at 120 V) is distributed generally. The distributions of the 277 V and 120 V services occur through the panelboards that are regularly placed throughout the building.

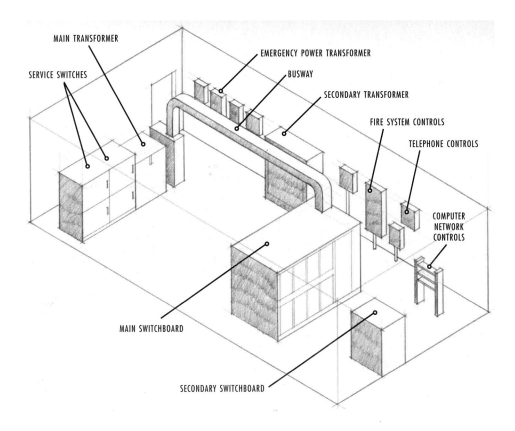

Figure D.28 The main components of the Gould Hall electrical vault are identified here. These components include the service switches, main transformer, the busway that connects the main transformer to the main switchboard, a secondary transformer, a secondary switchboard, an emergency transformer, panelboards (regular and emergency), fire detection and alarm controls (for the building), telephone and computer network control assemblies, and an assortment of cables and conduits.

present in the two below-grade floors. The two lighting panelboards for each floor are placed in electrical closets that exist in diagonally opposite corners and that are vertically cored up through the building.

The power panelboards — most of which are used to provide 120-volt electricity — are laid out so that four panelboards are placed on each above-ground floor and two panelboards are located in the basement. All of these power panelboards are located in electrical closets, each one of which is placed at a corner of the building (see Figure D.29). On each of the four above-ground floors, one power panelboard is placed at each of the four corners of the building. A nineteenth power panelboard is located in the wood shop. 208V electricity is provided for the operation of the various floor-mounted power tools that are used for working with woods and metals. This panelboard also furnishes 120-volt electricity for powering hand tools (e.g., sanders, drills, and so forth).

Figure D.29 Two panelboards are present in this electrical closet: one provides circuit breakers for fluorescent lighting fixtures (at 277 V); the other has circuit breakers for incandescent lamps, receptacles, and related 120 V equipment.

Section D.6 | SPACE PLANNING GUIDELINES FOR ELECTRICAL (POWER) EQUIPMENT IN BUILDINGS

The following discussion will concentrate on organizing building spaces for power handling in nonresidential buildings. Further, the focus of this discussion will be on larger buildings for which greater electricity loads are present. For single-family residential and small commercial buildings, creating separate, discrete spaces for power-handling equipment is generally not warranted (or required by regulation). However, for multifamily residential buildings — particularly, high-rise apartment and condominium buildings — the need for well-organized spaces devoted to power-handling equipment will be similar to requirements for larger, nonresidential buildings.

In larger nonresidential buildings there will usually be four groups of spaces in which power-handling equipment will be present: a *service entrance room;* commonly, several *electrical closets* and the vertical (or horizontal) pathways that connect these closets with the service entrance room; *horizontal pathways* connecting the electrical closets with the utilization equipment (e.g., motors, light fixtures, receptacles, and so forth); and *volumes in rooms* that contain the various utilization equipment (e.g., fixtures incorporated in ceiling plenum assemblies, mounted on walls, or floor-standing).

The principal goals that space (and systems) designers should bear in mind when creating spaces for housing the power-handling equipment are perhaps three-fold: to provide good electrical supplies throughout the building; to promote the efficient use of equipment and the efficient consumption of electrical energy; and to ensure ready and safe access to all of the equipment for those qualified persons who are responsible for its operation and maintenance. The space planning recommendations that will be offered below are based on adherence toward satisfying these goals.

D.6.1   SERVICE ENTRANCE ROOMS

D.6.1.1   Principal components and their functions   The major equipment pieces that will normally be present in these service entrance rooms include cables bearing electricity supplied at a voltage set by the source utility, one (or more) service transformer(s), protective equipment (including fusing and service switches), associated switchgear (for the central dispersion of the electricity throughout the building), an emergency power source (including related emergency switchgear), and, possibly, one (or more) lower-voltage transformer(s) and dedicated switchgear for lower-voltage transformer(s). The tasks for this collection of equipment are to take in the electrical energy supply (furnished at a voltage offered by the utility provider), to reduce the service voltage to voltages that match what the utilization equipment requires for good operation, and to disperse the electrical energy (power) throughout the building. Additional requirements will include ensuring safety for the building occupants who use the electricity and ensuring that the operations of these central electrical devices will not interfere with ordinary occupant activities elsewhere in the building.

D.6.1.2   Planning considerations for service entrance rooms   Generally, service entrance rooms that house one (or more) transformer(s) will be overly warm, noisy, and requiring strictly limited access (so that only qualified persons can gain access to the rooms). The heat is a by-product of the transformation process. Building regulations — codes — are commonly written to exclude the presence of conventional air-handling systems equipment in electrical service entrance rooms, instead requiring that the rooms be ventilated by passive means. Note, however, that ducting *that is independent from conventional air-handling systems* can be installed to connect service entrance rooms with the building exterior, thus enhancing the cooling of these rooms. Such independent ducting can pass air horizontally or vertically from a service entrance room, and fans can be incorporated within this ducting to enhance airflow through the ducting.

Service entrance rooms containing one (or more) transformer(s) will usually have noise levels ranging from, perhaps, 55 to 75 dB(A), depending on the capacity and size of the transformer(s). And, because of the need to guarantee building occupant safety, these electrical service entrance rooms should be secured against entry by anyone who is not authorized.

Basic requirements for the planning of service entrance rooms include the following recommendations. First, service entrance rooms should be isolated from spaces commonly used by conventional building occupants (to offset the attendant heat, noise, and security issues). Second, because the heat generated in these rooms will most often need to be diluted by relying on passive means (i.e., using natural ventilation), the rooms should be located along the building perimeter. Note that if a service entrance room is to be placed in a basement, then some external pathway must be furnished to enable outside air to enter through a perimeter wall of the room (e.g., using ducting independent of conventional air-handling systems for the building). Third, the space must be well lighted to enable service workers to clearly see the equipment. Fourth, service entrance rooms should be kept dry, allowing no water to accumulate on room surfaces. And, fifth, fire stops and envelope assemblies with sufficient fire delay durations must be provided for these rooms (according to the type and capacity of the transformers housed in them; see Sidebar D.1 for further information about such fire restriction requirements).

SIDEBAR D.1 Describing transformers

A. The need for transformation

Whether transformation equipment will be required in a building depends upon three factors: what service voltage the utility can (or will) furnish to the building; whether a single utilization voltage is required for building operation or whether some combination of utilization voltages are required; and what power density is needed for occupant activities.

Increasingly, utilities in North America are offering medium voltage services throughout their customer regions. Service voltages that are made available can extend from a low of 2.4 kV to a high of 34.5 kV, with voltages in the 12–15 kV range the most often furnished. These services will nearly always be supplied as three-phase electricity. Concomitantly, the utilization voltages in nonresidential buildings — the voltages required for the operation of the various electrically powered equipment devices — will normally be 600 V or less. Multiple utilization voltages will generally be required: for example, 480 V power will be needed for motors (for air-handling fans, pumps, and elevators); 277 V power is used to operate fluorescent and high-intensity discharge fixtures (when a substantial number of these fixtures are present in the building); 120 V power will be provided for incandescent fixtures and for common receptacles; and 208 V power may be used for selected other electrical devices. And, in buildings where power densities are high (because of large numbers of electricity-consuming devices or a smaller number of devices that each draws considerable energy for operation), it will be more efficient to bring into such buildings higher service voltages. It may even be more efficient to disperse higher voltages around the building (e.g., instead of dispersing 480 V power around a building, perhaps 2.4 kV power will be dispersed and then stepped down at small transformers that are placed on a floor-by-floor basis, as in a high-rise office tower, or on a floor area basis, where a building is laid out over a large horizontal distance, as is the case with many manufacturing plants).

In residential areas of urban and suburban communities public utilities will often send electrical power throughout neighborhoods at a medium voltage and provide transformers placed on poles or at grade that step the medium voltage down to a level that can be utilized in individual housing units (e.g., 240/120 V). These residential neighborhood transformers will usually be arrayed so that each serves some small number of housing units such as four to eight. Similarly, where small commercial buildings are placed in low-density settings (perhaps along secondary roads), a public utility will also send the power out at a medium voltage and will furnish transformers along the road (for stepping the voltage down to accommodate the individual commercial establishments). In rural areas, whether for residential or small commercial buildings, a variety of voltage and transformation strategies are employed.

B. Common types of in-building transformers

Three types of transformers are used in buildings: liquid-filled, ventilated-dry, and sealed-dry. The feature

SIDEBAR D.1 (continued)

that distinguishes these three types is how the iron core is cooled as the transformation proceeds (i.e., whether a liquid or gas is used as the heat dissipating medium and whether the dissipation process involves a sealed or open enclosure). Note that these media—liquids or gases—are all *dielectrics* (i.e., substances that do not conduct electricity). For liquid-filled transformers the liquid circulates across the core and passes through a series of cooling fins (for the exchange of heat to the room air surrounding the transformer and its fins). This heat exchange may be hastened by incorporating one (or more) fan(s) placed in front of the fins. Historically, the liquid that was most often used in liquid-filled transformers was a synthetic hydrocarbon (identified as *askarel*). But, as this liquid was found to contain polychlorinated biphenyls (PCB's)—which are injurious to occupant health should they leak from the transformer—its use has been discontinued. Instead, the principal replacement liquid is a silicone that furnishes similar insulating, heat transfer, and inflammability characteristics.

Ventilated, dry transformers use air as the insulating and heat exchanging medium. For most dry transformers that take in medium-voltage power and step the power down to utilizable voltages, the core and the winding coils are usually enclosed inside a heavy screened metal enclosure. Air passes over the core and coils passively by convection, and the heated air mixes with the ambient air.

Sealed, dry transformers have a metal tank that entirely surrounds and encloses the transformer core and coils. The tank is filled with some dielectric gas such as nitrogen or a fluorocarbon compound. This gas is maintained under a positive pressure, and leakage of the gas is minimal. Heat produced during transformer operation convects passively from the outer surface of the metal tank to the surrounding room air.[1]

C. Transformer ratings

Transformers are categorized in terms of their apparent power capacities, the primary and secondary side voltages, the number of phases, and the frequency (as well as the type of the dielectric medium that surrounds the core and winding coils). Apparent power is described in terms of volt-amperes (or, more commonly, kilovolt-amperes [kVA]). The apparent power is differentiated from real power, the latter being the magnitude of the load (or the rate with which electrical energy is consumed to operate all of the utilization equipment that receives energy from the transformer). Note that the real power—the (utilization) load—is expressed in watts (or, more likely, in kilowatts [kW]). So, for example, some typical dry transformer might be described as offering three-phase, 500 kVA, 480–208/120, 60 Hz performance. For reference, *representative* physical dimensions for such a transformer would approximately be 75 in high × 60 in wide × 50 in deep (1930 mm h × 1525 mm w × 1270 mm d). The approximate weight (mass) for such a representative transformer would be 4190 pounds (1904 kilograms).

D. Fire safety issues and room envelope composition requirements

Because the operation of transformers involves significant, concentrated energy flows and heat production, there is the constant threat of failure for a transformer and its related controlling equipment (e.g., switchgear, fuses, and so forth). Although the principal dielectric liquids that are used today in liquid-filled transformers are largely inflammable, earlier generations of dielectric liquids occasionally demonstrated explosive behaviors and also caused tank ruptures and fires. Comparably, ventilated, dry transformers exhibit some possibilities to form smoke and even, in limited occurrences, to commence fires within the transformer. On the other hand, sealed, dry transformers in operation are generally not hazardous.

The consequences of these potentially dangerous behaviors are that the envelopes of rooms in which transformers are present in buildings must be able to withstand such behaviors. Thus, room envelopes in which one (or more) liquid-filled transformer(s) is (are) present are required to display three-hour fire-resistance ratings. Envelopes that satisfy this requirement should be composed of 8 in (203 mm) of reinforced concrete and have doors rated to be fire resistant for three hours duration. A further requirement for rooms containing liquid-filled transformers is that each transformer must be surrounded with a 6 in (152 mm) high floor-mounted

SIDEBAR D.1 (continued)

dam that can retain any liquid that might leak from the transformer.

Room envelope requirements for ventilated, dry transformers are less stringent and are based on the capacity (and primary voltage) of the transformer. For ventilated, dry transformers that have capacities less than 112 1/2 kVA, there is no minimum envelope composition stated (i.e., in terms of resisting some potentially calamitous failure). Instead, the room envelope should provide an adequately secure, dry, and sound-transmission-resistant barrier. For these smaller-capacity ventilated, dry transformers it is also required that no other service entrance equipment be placed within 12 in (305 mm) of a transformer. For ventilated, dry transformers with capacities greater than 112 1/2 kVA, these transformers must be installed in rooms with envelopes having at least a one-hour fire-resistance rating. Lastly, for ventilated, dry transformers with primary voltages greater than 35 kV, such transformers must be enclosed in rooms with envelopes having a three-hour fire-resistance rating (i.e., matching the requirements set for liquid-filled transformers).

Room envelope requirements for sealed, dry transformers are similar to those set for the lower-capacity ventilated, dry transformers (i.e., that they must be placed in rooms that are dry, secure, and resistant to noise transmission).

E. Preliminary bases for selecting any one type of transformer

Liquid-filled transformers and ventilated, dry transformers are each readily available in the ranges of power capacities and primary voltages that are commonly required for building operation. A major reason why liquid-filled transformers may be preferred over ventilated, dry transformers is that liquid-filled transformers exhibit much better *overload* capabilities than like-capacity ventilated, dry transformers. The ability to take on an overload enables a transformer to continue to perform safely and well despite being subjected to greater-than-designed demand capacities, as may happen when an aggregated demand by utilization equipment exceeds designed conditions. For example, a transformer may be designed to have a normally full

capacity when, perhaps, 80 percent of the utilization equipment is in operation (i.e., a common basis for electrical service designing). But on some occasions the demand for electrical energy may exceed the designed full capacity. For these times it is desirable for affected transformers to be capable of continuing to operate safely and well in these overloaded circumstances. A second reason for preferring liquid-filled transformers over like-capacity ventilated, dry transformers is that the liquid-filled units tend to have smaller footprints than the ventilated, dry units.

Alternatively, ventilated, dry transformers will have lower first costs than liquid-filled transformers of like capacities. Additionally, because of the requirements for more fire-resistive envelopes for a room housing any liquid-filled transformer, there will be greater envelope costs for housing liquid-filled transformers. Other criteria such as heat gain rates, noise production levels, mass loading (dictating structural system requirements), and so forth will likely be relevant in various choice situations, but these other criteria should be examined on a case-by-case basis.

Generally, sealed, dry transformers will be available only for ranges of lower power capacities and, thus, cannot as readily be applied for the wider variety of building situations for which the other two transformers types can be employed. However, when smaller power capacities are required for the operation of a building, the selection of sealed, dry transformers offers an attractive alternative to the other transformer types.

1. Earley, M.W., J.V. Sheehan, and J.M. Caloggero, *National Electrical Code Handbook, 8th edition,* (Quincy, Massachusetts: National Fire Protection Association, 1999), Article 450 ("Transformers and Transformer Vaults [Including Secondary Ties]"), pages 512–529. Note page 524, specifically.

One further consideration is that if the floor area of the building powered from the service entrance room is quite large (e.g., for an office tower or a manufacturing plant), additional main transformer rooms will likely be necessary. Rooms housing main transformers may thus be included in the building scheme relying on a modular format. For example, for an office tower, a service entrance room housing a main transformer could be placed in the basement of the building. Then, similar main transformer rooms might be placed at the 20th, 40th, 60th (and so on) floors. Each of these main transformers would likely operate with its primary side dealing with a medium voltage (e.g., somewhere in the range of 13 to 35 kV).

D.6.1.3   Spatial guidelines for service entrance rooms

Essential criteria that must be satisfied when sizing service entrance rooms include providing adequate space in front of (and, possibly, behind) transformers and switchgear equipment, offering adequate vertical clearances for running busways between equipment, and ensuring space for service expansion. The expected lifetimes of service entrance equipment usually range between 20 to 40 years. Thus, replacement of this equipment or components of the equipment will likely occur sometime during the often much longer building lifetime. Maintenance and repair will be required on a more regular and shorter time frame. Code-stipulated *horizontal separations* between adjacent equipment items range from 3 to 12 ft (0.9 to 3.7 m) depending on the nature and capacities of the equipment items. Also, guidelines state that two-way travel — being able to walk around either end of the equipment — must be possible when working on the equipment. Similarly, *clear vertical distances* of up to 9 feet (2.7 m) above the top of the cabinetry housing the equipment are stated in the *National Electrical Code* (i.e., this vertical distance above the cabinetry is supposed to be clear of nonelectrical system equipment, so that electrical system equipment such as busways can be placed there).[1]

Entrances — doorways — into service entrance rooms must be sized adequately so that repair tools can be brought into these rooms and failed equipment can be removed from (and new equipment brought into) the rooms. Also, because the weights (masses) of equipment items can be substantial, accommodations must often be available for introducing mobile lifting devices (portable hoists) into the rooms. Other related requirements — for repairing or removing equipment items — can be instituted and observed not by regulatory bodies, but rather by the public utilities. For example, the City of Seattle Lighting Department — the public electrical utility for the City of Seattle — requires that if a transformer or some switchgear assembly requires handling by their engineers or other repair staff, the item must be delivered to a ground floor entrance of the building powered by the item. Thus, if the equipment item happens to be located on an upper floor of an office tower, accommodations must be included in the building design to enable the movement of the item between its operating space to a building entrance. These accommodations usually include having suitably large doorways from an equipment room leading to a corridor of sufficient width that, in turn, leads to a freight elevator with adequate lifting capacity.

Another important consideration when sizing service equipment rooms (and all other electrical systems spaces in buildings) is the need to plan for the possible expansion of capabilities. The demand for electrical energy resources in buildings has increased significantly in the past few decades. The wide-spread introduction of personal computers and associated peripheral support devices into workplaces is one indication of this growth tendency. Another example occurs in college dormitory rooms. Prior to about 1990 college students typically would use, as electrical equipment, desk lamps, stereo sets, electric shavers, and electric blankets. Now, additional dormitory room equipment includes computers, printers, scanners, CD burners, televisions, refrigerators, microwave ovens, small space heaters (to provide room heating during the swing seasons when the main heating system is likely to be dormant), more advanced stereo systems, and so forth. Considering that the typical college dormitory will have up to a few hundred rooms, and most will have all of these recently employed electrical devices, it is little wonder that the needs for expanding electrical energy resources and for spaces for supplying and controlling these resources have increased even drastically.

Finally, a rule-of-thumb to predict areas for service entrance rooms suggests that the floor area of the room should be equal to 0.5 percent of the gross floor area of the building served by this room. If multiple rooms in a building contain main service transformers and related switchgear (as in an office tower), then the total floor area of these rooms should be equal to this quantity of 0.5 percent of the gross floor area of the building. No rule-of-thumb is widely recognized for predicting service entrance room heights. But, generally, a floor-to-bottom-of-the-structural-grid dimension of about 12 ft (3.7 m) should be a good first approximation to work with.

D.6.2   ELECTRICAL CLOSETS (AND INTERMEDIATE ELECTRICAL ROOMS)

D.6.2.1   Principal components and their functions   The power-handling components that are most likely to be present in electrical closets (and intermediate electrical rooms) will be panelboards, conduit for transporting wiring from service entrance room equipment to electrical closets, pull and junction boxes, and, possibly, lower-voltage transformers (see Figures D.29 and D.31). Also, if a large quantity of electrical energy needs to be transported from a service entrance room to intermediate floors or spaces in a large building, busways can be used as power-handling equipment. Whether conduit-encased wiring or busways are used in tall buildings, by necessity each will pass upward through the building in riser volumes (that will require dedicated floor areas in electrical closets or electrical rooms).

Generally, what differentiates an electrical closet and an intermediate electrical room is whether a lower-voltage transformer is present: when a transformer is included, the enclosed space is considered to be an electrical room. In larger buildings, where medium voltages (at levels from 2.4 to 13.8 kV) may be transported within the building, there may be numbers of lower-voltage transformers—providing voltage step-downs to voltage levels below those produced in main transformer rooms. These lower-voltage transformers (e.g., 4.16 kV–480/277 V, 2.4 kV–208/120 V, and so forth) may be present in electrical rooms that are arranged on a floor-by-floor basis for an office tower or in a number of localized, modular electrical rooms that may be laid out across the large floor area of a manufacturing assembly plant. The electrical rooms that will house these lower-voltage transformers will need to be larger than electrical closets. These intermediate electrical rooms will often have to be composed of more substantial room envelope assemblies than would be expected for electrical closets that simply contain panelboards and wire-carrying hardware.

Panelboards are fundamental components of any power-handling dispersion system in buildings. The panelboards provide control of branch circuits and offer overcurrent protection (i.e., inhibiting any excessive demand for electrical energy on a given circuit). Panelboards are typically cabinets that contain a collection of switches, overcurrent protective devices (fuses or circuit breakers), and buses (for conducting power within the

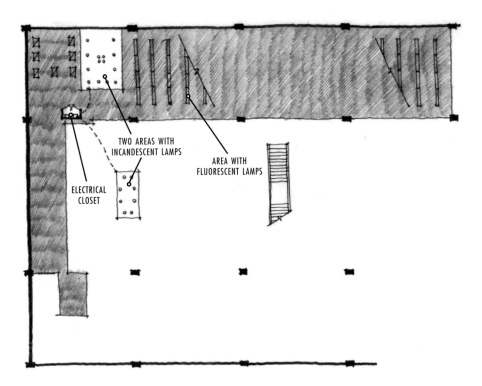

Figure D.30 This is the tributary load area that is served by the electrical closet shown in Figure D.29. Most of the electricity consumed across this area powers the banks of fluorescent lamps (at 277 V). Additionally, electricity is consumed at 120V by incandescent lamps and at numerous wall receptacles.

panel). These panelboard cabinets are most often metal-enclosed, are either surface-mounted on walls or embedded in wall assemblies, and are always accessible only from their fronts. Typical dimensions are about 4 to 10 in (102 to 254 mm) deep by 20 to 40 in wide (0.5 to 1.0 m) wide by 4 to 6 ft (1.2 to 1.8 m) high. Panelboards in the United States may have up to 42 circuit breakers per board. If more than 42 branch circuits are to be controlled in an electrical closet, then more than one panelboard must be present in the closet. Also included in panelboards can be main circuit breakers or fusible switches that will furnish control of the entire board.

The two categories of panelboards used in buildings are lighting and appliance panelboards and power-handling panelboards. The distinction between these two categories is that, for lighting and appliance panelboards, more than 10 percent of the number of overcurrent devices will be devoted to protecting circuits involved with lighting and appliance hardware. Power-handling panelboards are those having less than 10 percent of their overcurrent devices responsible for lighting fixtures and appliances.

D.6.2.2 Planning guidelines   Panelboards should always be placed in electrical closets or intermediate electrical rooms (except where highly concentrated electrical loads occur in specific spaces). Panelboards should never be located in custodians' closets or in bathroom entries.

In rooms in which highly concentrated electrical loads are present — for example, in laboratories or in manufacturing plants — panelboards devoted to the activities undertaken in these rooms will often need to be made directly accessible in these areas. For these in-room panelboards, they should be embedded in wall assemblies. These in-room panelboards should be mounted as close to columns or other permanent structural members and assemblies as possible (to minimize any future need for the relocation of the panelboards).

For most other building applications surface-mounted panelboards are preferable to embedded panelboards (because surface-mounted panelboards are easier to work on). Lastly, electrical closets and intermediate electrical rooms should be kept free of any other control system equipment. Thus, no ducting or piping — whether for HVAC systems or for plumbing — should pass through electrical closets or intermediate electrical rooms.

A minimum floor area for an electrical closet is likely to be about 2 ft (0.61 m) deep by 6 ft (1.83 m) wide. The ceiling height should be at least 6 1/2 ft (1.98 m) high, although there should be a distance of 3 ft (0.91 m) from the top of any panelboard to the ceiling. Two criteria are critical when establishing the depth of an electrical closet. First, workers must be able to open panelboard doors so that any door can establish an angle of 90° with the front of the panelboard. Second, there must be adequate space in the electrical closet so that a worker can safely work on the panelboard. Further, the *1999 National Electrical Code* stipulates that the minimum width of the space in front of a panelboard must be the width of the panelboard or 30 in (0.76 m), *whichever is greater.*[2] A doorway for an electrical closet does not need to be centered in front of the panelboard, as long as there is adequate space for a worker to manipulate the panelboard and its components. Alternatively, when an electrical closet contains two (or more) panelboards aligned side-by-side, it is recommended that side-by-side doors of at least standard width be used at the entrance to the electrical closet. The doors to an electrical closet should open on to a corridor or lobby area.

Providing a quick, rough estimate of the number and locations of electrical closets that a building should have is a somewhat imprecise process. A general guideline that electrical system designers employ is to seek to make branch circuits — running conductors from a panelboard to the utilization equipment — as short as possible (without having to rely on an excessive number of panelboards). Thus, the process normally involves identifying the likely locations for utilization equipment. Then, these locations can be approximately aggregated into a small number of groups. Centers of gravity for the groups are determined, and these centers are proposed as likely panelboard locations.

In a building having several stories, several electrical closets will likely be needed. Where several electrical closets are required, the designers will usually seek to vertically stack the panelboard locations (and the placement of the electrical closets). For a building having a number of floors, most often at least one electrical closet should be present on each floor. Of course, if the size of the story-by-story floor plan is large or there are substantial power density requirements for each floor, then two (or more) electrical closets will be needed for each floor. One other important planning guideline that merits careful attention is that ample space in electrical closets should be left for the expansion in the number of panelboards. Also, rather than filling all circuit breaker slots during the initial construction of a building, foresight dictates that, for any panelboard, perhaps about 30 percent of the available circuit breaker slots should be reserved for the future expansion of electrical energy dispersion.

Estimating whether intermediate electrical rooms — those containing transformers that form lower-voltage electricity — will be needed in a building is also an imprecise process. One rule-of-thumb that is used for electrical systems designing suggests that an intermediate electrical room will be needed for every 15,000 to 20,000 ft² (1394 to 1859 m²) of gross floor area. This floor area range is based on the convenient sizes of small ventilated, dry transformers (which are the principal type of transformers that are appropriate for modular placement throughout a large building).

A sample floor plan for an intermediate electrical room is shown in Figure D.31. In a many-story office tower with a large floor area per story, an intermediate electrical room may be needed for each floor. In that instance the intermediate electrical rooms throughout the tower should be stacked vertically.

Other design considerations for intermediate electrical rooms arise because building spaces containing transformers can become over-warm and will generally be noisy (i.e., transformers generate heat and noise as by-products of their operation). Thus, some means

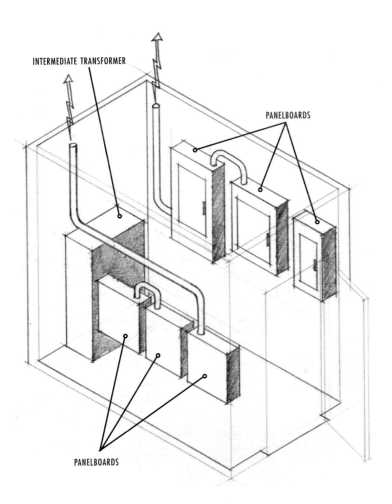

INTERMEDIATE TRANSFORMER

PANELBOARDS

PANELBOARDS

Figure D.31 A prototypical intermediate electrical room is displayed here. The principal components in this modular facility are likely to be a secondary transformer and a series of panelboards (most likely at 277 V and 120 V power levels).

for heat dilution will be warranted for intermediate electrical rooms. The magnitudes of noise levels that may be anticipated for ventilated, dry transformers with capacities likely to be needed in intermediate electrical rooms will perhaps be 50 to 55 dB(A). With these noise level magnitudes, well-assembled stud walls (with wood or metal studding) should provide adequate noise separation. But care should be taken in selecting door assemblies (that often display less good noise separation capabilities).

Further issues concerning doors and doorways include being able to remove and replace a failed transformer and providing adequate security for intermediate electrical rooms. Because transformers will occasionally fail during operation, it is essential that a pathway for removal (and replacement) be designed for every transformer in a building. Thus, doorways, corridors, and at least one elevator (in a multiple-story building) must be sized to enable the movement of any transformer through the building and out to the building perimeter. Further, entrance doors to intermediate electrical rooms should be designed so that they can be locked (i.e., to maintain security).

D.6.3   BRANCH CIRCUIT LAYOUT AND PLANNING

Branch circuits that connect panelboards to individual utilization equipment commonly are run in either one of two types of raceway assemblies: circular conduits and surface-mounted metal raceways. Circular conduit is available in sizes ranging from $1/2$ to 6 in in diameter (note that the metric sizes of conduit will not exactly match the *Imperial* dimensions used in the United States). Which size will be appropriate for any application depends on the number and size of the conductors (and their insulation) that will be enclosed within the conduit. A second issue that can determine the necessary size of a conduit cross-section concerns whether wiring can readily be pulled through the conduit (i.e., if the force needed to pull wiring is too great, the wiring can be damaged resulting in the failure of the branch circuit). Conduit is composed of either a metal—usually, an alloy of iron or aluminum—or a polymeric material (most often, polyvinyl chloride). The conduit can be either rigid or flexible. Conduit runs can thus be linear or curvilinear: for the latter, if rigid forms are used, the conduit will be bent to comply with design requirements. Conduit runs can be embedded in walls or concrete floors. They can be attached to wall, floor, or ceiling surfaces, using clips. Conduit runs can also be suspended in ceiling plenums, and they can be supported above the floor in raised-floor assemblies. Where multiple conduits are to be run in the same direction, they can be run in parallel, either side-by-side or in an over-under format.

Where conduit in buildings can be placed is limitless: conduit can be run wherever it is needed and where its presence is tolerable. Ideally, conduit should be run so that the pathway between a panelboard and any piece of utilization equipment is as direct as possible. But, because some designers and/or occupants may regard conduit as unsightly, it is certainly possible to hide conduit by embedding it in walls and in ceiling or floor assemblies. The principal limitation to embedding conduit is that it will be inaccessible if alterations of branch circuits are needed sometime in the future. When changes in branch circuits are required, it may be simpler to leave old conduit in place, seal the ends of the old conduit, and run new conduit for new branch circuits (i.e., because the cost of conduit material is often relatively insignificant). Similarly, placement of junction and pull boxes should be established where needed for systems assembly (e.g., to ensure ready accessibility should future modifications be required). But, often, it is possible to select locations for junction and pull boxes so that the boxes will not be visually intrusive. Lastly, grouping conduit runs — running conduit in parallel — often makes good sense because this strategy offers an organization for these systems assemblies, as well as offering installation efficiency.

Rectangular cross-section raceways are used principally to run wiring in occupied spaces. The wiring can offer electrical power for operating conventional utilization equipment (e.g., portable lamps, computers and related peripheral devices, audio-visual units, coffee makers, and so forth). Most often, connections between the raceway wiring and the utilization equipment are established using plugged connections with conventional receptacles. Alternatively, wiring can enable a range of communications including for telephones, computer networks, radio and television signals, and so forth.

These rectangular cross-section raceways can be surface-mounted, or they can be installed within wall, floor, or ceiling assemblies. Surface-mounted raceways are usually composed of galvanized steel. Common dimensions for these surface-mounted raceways are about 4 to 6 in (102 to 152 mm) high by 2 to 3 in (51 to 76 mm) deep. The surface-mounted raceways are manufactured in a wide variety of fitting options that allow the raceways to conform to room and surface geometries. These raceways are also produced with many different faceplates, numbers of which are configured for mounting various receptacle or jack assemblies (i.e., the latter, for communications devices).

Rectangular cross-section raceways are also used in ceiling plenums and in built-up floor assemblies. When these rectangular cross-section raceways are deployed in ceiling plenums, the conventional means for bringing wirings down to occupant levels is by means of vertical poles (see Figure D.24). These poles attach directly to in-the-plenum raceways and usually terminate at the floor. Vertical poles can furnish connections to power or for communication devices (e.g., telephones or computer networks). The use of in-the-plenum raceways and vertical poles is especially suitable for the renovation of older buildings, particularly those which were originally constructed with power and communication systems that are deficient by today's standards and needs. In built-up floor assemblies the raceways can be run under the finished floor surface. Where power or communication capabilities are required (e.g., at workstations or where various process equipment will be located), vertical riser raceways are installed to carry wiring from the raceway to the specific work surface or machine. Both of these raceway assemblies offer considerable flexibility when the locations of workstations and machines are first being determined. Also, when it is anticipated that future workstations and office machines may need to be relocated, using these ceiling and floor raceways should enable subsequent electrical system service requirements to be readily satisfied.

D.6.3.1   Spatial accommodations for lighting fixtures   The sizes of rectangular cross-section raceways passing through ceiling plenums and built-up flooring are similar to surface-mounted rectangular cross-section raceways (e.g., about 4 to 6 in [102 to 152 mm] by 2 to 3 in [51 to 76 mm]). As written above, circular conduit will be used in diameters from 1/2 to 6 in (13 to 152 mm). Thus, making spatial accommodations for rectangular raceways and circular conduit usually should not pose particular challenges during building planning

Alternatively, providing suitable spaces for lighting fixtures is an important design requirement. Typically, in ceiling plenums fluorescent lamp fixtures and incandescent lamp cans will occupy a layer with a depth of between 8 to 12 in (203 to 305 mm). This lighting layer will normally include whatever conduit or rectangular raceways that are used for branch circuit power (and communication systems) dispersion. Most often, the lighting layer will be located beneath the HVAC systems layer, both of which are suspended from the structural system materials above. The bottom of the lighting layer will coincide with the finished ceiling materials (e.g., acoustic tile assemblies or gypsum plaster board).

Lighting fixtures—whether fluorescent, incandescent, or high-intensity discharge—that are mounted on walls will require spatial accommodations for the fixtures themselves. But spatial accommodations for the branch circuit running to the fixture should be minimal. Wiring for the fixture will likely be run in conduit. And the conduit can be embedded in the wall, or it can be surface-mounted (running down from the ceiling or up from the floor to the fixture).

D.6.4   ELECTRICAL EQUIPMENT PLANNING FOR BUILDINGS WITH SMALLER POWER DEMANDS

D.6.4.1   Electrical equipment components Many small buildings—single-family residential, multifamily residential, and some commercial—generally will not require the presence of transformers in the buildings themselves. Electrical energy will be utilized in these buildings at one (or two) voltage(s). For example, most single-family houses in the United States will be furnished by their local (or regional) electrical utility with one-phase, 240/120 V service. In Seattle, for instance, Seattle City Light—the public electrical utility—distributes electrical energy at three-phase, 15 kV throughout most residential neighborhoods. This 15 kV power is stepped down by transformers that are hung on the power/telephone poles (i.e., the transformers are designated as 15.0 kV–240/120 V). Thus, the service provided to the individual housing units is 240/120 V.

For these smaller buildings the service connections will usually involve wiring running from a utility device: either via overhead wires that are supported by a network of poles or via wires encased in buried underground raceways. Service entrance conductors will pass from the utility device to an electric meter. This meter will usually record consumption (most often in kilowatt-hours [kWh], although the meter may also record peak power demand for some length of time [e.g., to identify maximum kW demand for some short period of time—for an hour or 15 minutes—for the past month.]) Wires will then run from the meter to a main service panelboard.

The panelboard will consist of a service switch and a number of circuit breakers (overcurrent protectors). Each circuit breaker will function as the origin of a branch circuit. Some branch circuits will run to the various large appliances and lighting fixtures that

---

SIDEBAR D.2 Power usage in single-family residences

In newer housing units electrical energy will usually be furnished at both 240 and 120 V. These two voltages are supplied in order to power a variety of different appliances and electrical devices. A number of larger appliances will utilize 240 V power: electric ranges, electric ovens, central air-conditioning units, water heaters, water pumps, clothes dryers, hot tubs and spas, and so forth. These several devices all require larger amounts of power for operation. Alternatively, a number of other electrical devices have smaller power needs and operate at 120 V: countertop appliances (such as microwave ranges, food processors and blenders, toasters, can openers, garbage disposals, and so forth), lighting fixtures, and common receptacles (sometimes called "convenience outlets").

are hard-wired (i.e., where the utilization device is connected directly to a branch circuit). Other branch circuits will connect to receptacles (where perhaps as many as 10—or more—receptacles might be connected along a single branch circuit).

The wiring that runs from the panelboard to utilization devices may consist of either nonmetallic-sheathed cables (with two or three conductors present) or individual (insulated) conductors contained within conduit (usually, electrical nonmetallic tubing). Both of these wiring alternatives can be embedded within wall, floor, or ceiling assemblies. Most often, the wiring alternatives will run in parallel with framing members. When they pass through framing members, bushings or grommets may be needed to protect the wiring. Further, when nails or screws may be inserted into the envelope assemblies where these wiring alternatives are embedded, then steel sleeves or plates should be used as covers for the wiring alternatives.

D.6.4.2 Design guidelines   There are no prescribed requirements for locating the service entrance, the meter for recording use, and the main service panelboard(s). Usually, these components are located for the sake of convenience and, perhaps, for proximity to the public utility service. However, the use meter is commonly installed external to the building to permit easy access for a meter reader (who works for the public utility).

In commercial and other small nonresidential buildings, the service entrance and the main panelboard(s) are often located in the same room that contains the central air-handling equipment for the HVAC system. The principal design suggestions for such a room would be that it is well-lighted and secure and that there should be adequate space in the room to enable maintenance and repair work for all of the various service systems components present in the room. The panelboard(s) can be surface-mounted on a wall, and there must be adequate space in front of the panelboard(s) to allow the panelboard door(s) to swing freely out so that any door can be at least perpendicular to the surface bearing the service switch and circuit breakers (e.g., for planning, inclusion of a working space measuring 30 in [760 mm] wide by 30 in [760 mm] deep in front of each panelboard would be beneficial).

In single-family residences the service entrance and the panelboard can be located in a basement, in a furnace room, or even in a closet. Installing a panelboard in a laundry room is seldom a good practice because of the high humidities that often exist in such rooms. In any of these spaces the panelboard should be surface-mounted (to permit easy working on the branch circuitry). Wherever installation of the panelboard is accomplished, it is essential that the panelboard door can swing out perpendicular to the front of the panelboard. Again, as with other small buildings, the space containing the panelboard should be well-lighted (and secured against interventions by children).

Consistent with suggestions offered when large buildings were discussed, it is good (and thoughtful) practice to anticipate that any initially designed and installed electrical system for a small building will likely have need for future modification and, possibly, expansion. Thus, when laying out spaces for these electrical system components, it makes great good sense to provide extra space both for locating the central equipment and for running branch circuitry throughout the building.

Section D.7 | COMMUNICATION AND SIGNALING SYSTEMS: COMPONENTS AND SPACE PLANNING

As we stated in the introduction to this chapter, electrical systems offer two services for building occupants. First, electrical systems supply electrical energy for the operation of all the electrical task devices present in buildings. And, second, electrical systems are the foundation for a host of communication and signaling systems that occupants use to gather and disperse information around a building and between a building and the external world. The principal communication and signaling systems afford contact by voice and video, with data systems, and via a series of other automated (intelligent) building systems. Voice and video systems include telephony, public address, intercom, assisted listening (for schools and conference rooms), closed-circuit television, commercial television services, and a variety of localized audio-visual and room services equipment. Data systems encompass all of the various services that are based on computers and especially concern local area networks and connections to the Internet. Other automated (or, even, intelligent) signaling systems involve fire detection and alarm, security assessment, clock and bell control (for educational institutions), electrically operated window and shading control, and patient care (for medical and assisted-living centers).

The common elements of all of these various communication and signaling systems are connections to relevant external communication and signaling centers, a central control facility within a building, a network of messaging distribution equipment spread throughout the building, and a plethora of dedicated devices that are present in virtually every occupied space in a building. It is common practice when constructing a building to provide service connections — hook-up capabilities — for nearly every occupy-able room in a building (even if some of these spaces will not be immediately occupied or if the functions of occupants in these spaces have not been determined). It is easier to provide comprehensive service capabilities for every space initially, than to have to make service adjustments at some future time.

The two major communications and signaling services that are present in most buildings are for telephony and data transfer (i.e., via computer networks, both local and with the Internet). In the following subsections we will describe planning issues and guidelines for these two services.

D.7.1   TELEPHONY FACILITIES

For larger buildings — perhaps those having floor areas exceeding 10,000 square feet (930 m²) — the principal components of a fully developed telephony service will usually be a main equipment room, riser systems, equipment closets, possibly auxiliary equipment rooms, horizontal distribution pathways, and suitable desktop hand-ear sets.

The main, or central, equipment room will function as the service entrance for all telephone cables coming into a building from the public utility. This central room may contain a main terminal through which all of the entering telephone cables will pass or, instead, the room can have a main distribution panel that links the entering cables and the wiring that passes around the building (see Figure D.32). Environmental requirements for this main room include that the room should be secure, well-lighted, ventilated and cooled, and should have adequate electrical power. Guidelines for predicting the necessary sizes for main equipment rooms are at best approximate. For medium-sized to larger buildings — those with floor areas up to 100,000 ft² (9300 m²) — a minimum floor area for a main equipment room might be about 200 to 300 ft² (18.6 to 27.9 m²). For smaller buildings — perhaps with floor areas between 10,000 to 25,000 ft² (930 to 2320 m²) — a main equipment room can likely be as small as a large walk-in closet (perhaps 50 to 100 ft² [4.7 to 9.3 m²]. Finally, in some building applications, the central telephone connection equipment will be included in a portion of the main electrical room or vault (i.e., where the utility service enters the building).

Figure D.32 Here, communication networks for three services are organized. The free-standing rack in the foreground provides hardware for a building-wide local area network for computer services. The wall-mounted boxes on the left are for the central fire alarm and detection equipment for the building. The assemblies on the wall behind the computer rack are the central relays for the telephone service in the building.

The cabling leaving the main telephone equipment room will pass upward through a building in conduits or riser shafts. Often, telephone cables will be bundled and run in conduits that are sized to have at least 4 in diameters (note that this approach is a common practice in the United States; other solutions may be employed elsewhere). Where these large-diameter conduits are used for carrying telephone cables vertically, the number of these conduits will be directly related to the floor area of the building (e.g., for buildings with floor areas up to 50,000 ft² [4650 m²], two conduits with at least 4 in diameters are required; for floor areas between 100,000 to 200,000 ft² [9290 to 18590 m²], four conduits with at least 4 in diameters are required).[3] The alternative to running telephone cabling through conduits is to use enclosed riser shafts that pass vertically upward. In either instance — using conduit or enclosed riser shafts — the most efficient space planning and subsequent installation of telephone cabling will be achieved when these devices are directly aligned vertically.

Equipment closets are used as intermediate connection facilities in which cabling from the main equipment room connects to wall-mounted circuit boards, and cabling from these boards passes out to specific, localized telephone devices (see Figure D.33). Optimally, equipment closets will be established on a floor-by-floor basis (except where the floor areas of individual building floors are large and more than one electrical closet per

Figure D.33 Here is an electrical closet for telephone and computer services and a panelboard with circuit breakers for 120 V electricity.

floor is needed). These equipment closets should be designed as "walk-in" closets with recommended minimum internal dimensions of 5 ft (1.5 m) width by 3 ft (0.9 m) depth by 8 ft (2.4 m) height. For planning purposes it is suggested that at least one equipment room be present on each floor of a multiple-story building. Where the floor areas of individual stories are large, there should be about one equipment room for every 10,000 ft² (930 m²) of occupied area.

For the horizontal distribution of telephone cabling (i.e., from equipment rooms to specific localized telephone devices), two alternative approaches are available. The most commonly applied technique is to pass the cabling through ceiling volumes — usually, ceiling plenums. Then, the cabling can be directed downward by any of three methods: in wall assemblies to wall-mounted plug-in jacks; with surface-mounted raceways that lead to room-perimeter workstations; or via utility poles (when connections are sought in the midst of rooms [see Figure D.24]). When the cabling is run through these ceiling volumes, the cabling will be confined in raceways. The alternative approach uses built-up floor assemblies with the cabling enclosed in raceways and brought up through the floor at individual workstations. A third approach for running telephone cabling that has been much used previously is to enclose the cabling in raceways and to embed these raceways in poured-in-place concrete flooring. Before the concrete is poured, specific up-feed mounts are attached to the raceways at locations where workstations will be placed subsequently. Later, after the flooring has been finished, covering assemblies are attached to the up-feed mounts, and cabling from workstation telephone devices are connected to the covering assemblies. The limitation to this third approach is that the flexibility for changing the location of workplaces any time after initial occupancy is sacrificed.

In some buildings more complex telephony services are employed (e.g., using switchboards based on private branch exchanges [PBX] or central exchanges [Centrex]). Where these services are applied, additional spaces will be required to accommodate the increased amounts of equipment (i.e., necessitating the presence of auxiliary telephone equipment rooms). Predicting spatial needs and sizing for these specialized services is not useful, given the individual features generally afforded by the services.

D.7.2   DATA TRANSFER SYSTEMS FACILITIES

Data transfer generally involves communications between computers within a specific building and between computers in a building with computers and systems well beyond the local building. For the intra-building communications the development of local area networks (LAN's) is commonly the basis for data transfer. Alternatively, for connections between computer users in a specific building and computers beyond the building, either company-wide or campus-wide networks may be used for communications or, instead, data transfer may depend on communications with the Internet.

For a building with a well-developed localized computer network (that also communicates with the Internet) four types of spaces will need to be provided during building designing. These spaces include central communications rooms, cable connection closets, vertical and horizontal cabling pathways throughout the building, and individual workstations. These spaces and the functions they support for data transfer systems are quite similar to the principal service spaces that are used for telephony systems. Indeed, in many buildings, when planning for these two services — telephony and data transfer systems — a designer can lay out space for one service and then simply expand the space to also accommodate the other service (to, perhaps, double the size required for the first service).

For data transfer systems, the central communications room furnishes space for placing local network servers and computers for controlling the servers, staff workstations, and the dedicated peripheral equipment that supports a local area network (e.g., printers, plotters, scanners, centralized data storage units, and so forth). Related environmental control issues for a central communications room consist of ensuring that the room is well-lighted (including minimizing the potential for glare on video display screens), ventilated, cooled, and secure. The sizes for these rooms are greatly variable depending on the amount of computer equipment that will be needed for any given building application. Central communications rooms can be as small as 200 to 300 ft^2 (approximately 20 to 30 m^2) or could be several thousand square feet (about several hundred square meters). Again, the likely size for any central communications room will be conditional on the overall size of the building, the number of occupants present in the building, and the types of activities these occupants engage in). Some computer industry personnel suggest that a central communications room should be sized to be somewhat larger than the main telephone equipment room (i.e., with this central computer room being perhaps 125 to 150 percent of the floor area of the main telephone equipment room).

Equipment closets for computer cabling serve the same function as the equipment closets for the telephone services: the closets provide intermediate connection points for cabling coming from the central communications room and going to individual workstations. As with the telephone equipment closets, a computer equipment closet should best be placed on each floor of any multiple-floor building. Preferably, computer equipment closets should be stacked — aligned vertically — in these buildings. The computer equipment closets can be the same size as the telephone equipment closets. Furthermore, the two closets are often combined into a single, somewhat larger closet that provides for both services.

Cables for computer services tend to involve wiring sets that are slightly larger in diameter than the cables used for telephone services. But, as a good approximation, the numbers and cross-sectional areas of vertical pathways for computer cabling equipment — whether run in conduits or riser shafts — can be matched to those suggested for telephone services. Aligning the computer cabling pathways vertically generally offers the most efficient applications of materials and labor (during installation). Horizontal distribution of computer cabling can be accomplished using all of the same options described for telephone cabling. When creating a new building or working on a building that is to be substantially renovated, computer industry professionals prefer to use built-up flooring to create pathways for running horizontal cabling. The benefits afforded by built-up flooring are that flexibility is maximized for altering workplace location during the lifetime of the building and that running new cabling is easiest as applications change.

Section D.8 | SUGGESTED REFERENCES FOR GAINING FURTHER INFORMATION ABOUT BUILDING ELECTRICAL SYSTEMS

For information about the historical development of electrical systems — both concerning the generation and the distribution of electricity — see the book by Hughes, T.P., *Networks of Power: Electrification in Western Society, 1880–1930,* (Baltimore: Johns Hopkins University Press, 1983).

For descriptions of contemporary large-scale generation and distribution methods of electricity, see the book by Faulkenberry, L.M., and W. Coffer, *Electrical Power Distribution and Transmission,* (Upper Saddle River, New Jersey: Prentice-Hall, Inc., 1996). Also, two very informative documents have been written by engineers working for the City of Seattle Lighting Department. The first document has been written by Liu, F.S., D.M. Gray, and D. Backiel, *Seattle City Light Power System Engineering Information,* 1998 (Seattle: City of Seattle Lighting Department, 1998). The second document is by Mithoug, R. E., *At the Flick of a Switch,* (Seattle: City of Seattle Lighting Department, 1998).

For a simplified treatment of basic electrical concepts, see the book by Gussow, M., *Schaum's Outline of Theory and Principles of Basic Electricity,* (New York: The McGraw-Hill Companies, Inc., 1983).

For identifications, descriptions, elaborations, and further information about electrical systems in buildings, we recommend the following documents:

Earley, M.W., J.V. Sheehan, and J.M. Caloggero, *National Electrical Code Handbook, 8th edition,* (Quincy, Massachusetts: National Fire Protection Association, 1999).

Hettema, R.M., *Mechanical and Electrical Building Construction,* (Englewood Cliffs, New Jersey, Prentice-Hall, Inc., 1984).

Stein, B., and J.R. Reynolds, *Mechanical and Electrical Equipment for Buildings, 9th edition,* (New York: J. Wiley & Sons, 2000).

"Facility Design Information, 2001" (an unpublished manuscript prepared by the Engineering Services Department, University of Washington, Seattle, Washington).

ENDNOTES and SELECTED ADDITIONAL COMMENTS

1. Earley, M.W., J.V. Sheehan, and J.M. Caloggero, *National Electrical Code Handbook, 8th edition,* (Quincy, Massachusetts: National Fire Protection Association, 1999), Article 110 ("Requirements for Electrical Installations"), pages 30–56. Note Sections B and C.
2. Ibid., Article 110.B.(2), page 48.
3. *IEEE Recommended Practice for Electric Power Systems in Commercial Buildings* (IEEE Standard 241-1990), (Piscataway, New Jersey: Institute of Electrical and Electronic Engineers, 1990), page 590.

Plumbing Systems in Buildings

E

PLUMBING SYSTEMS SERVE building occupants by furnishing water for both living and work activities and by providing means for ridding buildings of liquid and liquid-bearable wastes. In this chapter we will describe the organizations and components that comprise plumbing systems, both the water supply system and the liquid-waste handling system. We will also offer guidelines for the planning and layout of plumbing fixtures, focusing especially on those fixtures employed in bathrooms (or toilet rooms). This chapter will not offer design guidelines for kitchen planning (as a number of kitchen appliances do not truly serve as plumbing fixtures).

Fundamentally, plumbing systems are entrusted with three functions: supplying sufficient amounts of water to building locations where the water will be used; enabling occupants to use the water efficiently in their living and working pursuits; and, then, getting rid of the used water, other liquids, and liquid-borne wastes in expeditious fashions. Plumbing systems should therefore be designed, installed, and operated to support occupant usage and to ensure occupant comfort and safety.

Section E.1 | PLUMBING SYSTEM FUNCTIONS AND SERVICES

Plumbing systems in buildings offer two main services for building occupants. First, plumbing systems provide potable water that occupants can consume, use to prepare food, and use to cleanse their bodies. Potable water should be free of biological and excessive mineral contaminants, should be reasonably clear, should have an acceptable taste, and should be supplied at appropriate temperatures. Potable water supplies should also operate with adequate pressures and volumetric flow rates. Potable water should be furnished in each of the locations in buildings where water with these qualities is expected.

In addition to the provision of potable water, nonpotable water supplies can be required for numbers of activities and procedures that occur in buildings. Examples of applications for which nonpotable water can be employed include in photographic materials processing, in any of a number of manufacturing and assembly facilities, and in various laboratories. For instance, laboratories in which marine life and the marine environment are studied will typically require a regular supply of saltwater. Or in manufacturing or minerals-processing facilities, nonpotable water can be used for the cleaning of components, lubrication, and the cooling of goods and machinery during fabrication activities. For these alternative situations, what differentiates the nonpotable water from potable water is that either less processing of the water has been rendered (e.g., for the manufacturing activities) or that a water source other than one providing fresh water was the starting point for the water supply (e.g., furnishing saltwater for the marine studies).

The second main service that plumbing systems afford is the transporting away of used liquids and wasted substances that can be borne by the liquids. The used liquids can be those produced by human beings (e.g., urine) or those employed by human beings as integral components of their living and work activities (e.g., water used to wash dishes or clothes or one's body; water used in food preparation in a restaurant; or water used to wash a vehicle). In many instances the used liquid can be something other than water or an aqueous solution. For instance, in some laboratories various chemicals might need to be wasted. Whether these chemicals can be dumped into a common drainage line leading to a public sewer without causing damage to the drainage assembly or a later repository may be important concerns for the design and operation of the waste-handling system. Indeed, in such laboratories it may be necessary to create separate waste-handling facilities: one to transport ordinary liquids consisting principally of water and one (or more) pathway(s) for the transporting (and, possibly, treatment) of other more damaging or dangerous chemicals.

Waste-handling systems will also provide transport for solid materials that can be borne by liquids. These solids can be the fecal matter excreted by human beings or remnants of many different activities performed by human beings (e.g., food products discarded during preparation, solids rinsed off of tools during building assembly, dirt washed from an athletic uniform, and so forth). Some of these wasted solids could, no doubt, be exchanged to the environment beyond the building by other means. But waste-handling plumbing systems are generally employed because of the ease with which they can be applied.

In the following sections, we will first discuss fixtures and various planning guidelines and requirements associated with their installation in buildings. Second, we will describe water supply systems and their standard components. Third, we will identify and explain the organizations of drainage, waste, and venting systems, as well as their components.

Lastly, we will suggest a variety of planning guidelines for the laying out of spaces that house these plumbing system devices.

Section E.2 | ACCOMMODATING FIXTURES — REQUIREMENTS AND GUIDELINES

A fixture is fundamentally a device that enables a human being to perform some bodily or life function. Thus, plumbing fixtures are those devices that involve the consumption of water and the purging of used water, other liquids, and water- or liquid-borne solids. The fundamental types of fixtures are those that supply water for consumption (e.g., to slake one's thirst and in preparation of food), for cleansing (e.g., for washing one's body, food, clothes, dishes, and any of a myriad other human devices), and for the elimination of human bodily and other wastes.

E.2.1   FIXTURE TYPES AND NUMBERS REQUIRED FOR OCCUPANCY TYPES

The number of different types of plumbing fixtures used in buildings is quite large. But a few types of fixtures will be found in virtually any building. The most common fixtures are toilets (water closets), urinals, lavatories (bathroom sinks), any of a variety of other sinks (kitchen, laundry, mop, equipment, and so forth), showers and bathing tubs, floor drains, water heaters, and a range of washing machines (particularly, for clothes and dishes, but also for commercial and industrial processes) (see Figures E.1–E.6). Other widely included fixtures are garbage and waste disposals; drinking water coolers and fountains; ice makers; spas, hot tubs, and soaking and whirlpool tubs; conventional swimming pools and stationary lap pools; and church baptistries. All of these many fixtures require that water be brought to each and that there be means for removing water from the fixture.

Figure E.1 An unconventional water closet (i.e., a conventional toilet with a masking cover).

E.2.1.1   Provisions for conventional fixtures   In a residence the basic fixtures are a kitchen sink, a toilet (water closet), a lavatory (bathroom sink), a bathtub or shower, and one lavatory tray (connection) for an automatic clothes washer. Each of these fixtures must be furnished in a single-family dwelling unit to satisfy most building codes. Additional fixtures — such as a second toilet, a connection for an automatic dishwasher, an outside hose bibb, or any other fixtures — can, of course, be incorporated in a building design. But these additional fixtures will be furnished as optional equipment. The exact locations — which spaces in a house — that these basic (and additional) fixtures are placed are not dictated by building codes. Indeed, only the spacings between selected fixtures are stated in most codes (e.g., the lateral separation between a toilet and a bathtub).

In nonresidential building occupancies such as assembly places, office buildings, commercial facilities, educational buildings, and so forth, alternative fixture requirements are stipulated in building codes. For these nonresidential buildings the most basic fixture grouping will include the presence of water closets, lavatories, urinals (for male toilet rooms) and drinking fountains. Bathtubs and/or showers may not be required, depending on the occupancy type of any given building. Similarly, whether kitchen sinks and automatic clothes washing connections are required will also be conditional on the nature of the building occupancy.

Figure E.2 Urinals and water closet stalls in a men's toilet room in an institutional building. Note that the urinals require no water supply. Two of the toilet stalls are for conventional toilets. The third is a wheelchair-accessible toilet stall (WATS).

WHEELCHAIR-ACCESSIBLE LAVATORY

Figure E.3 In the same toilet room as the one shown in Figure E.2, a series of conventional lavatories and one wheelchair-accessible lavatory exist on the wall opposite the toilets and urinals. Also, note the alternative heights for the two paper towel dispensers: the lower one is provided for wheelchair users.

Figure E.4 The fixture mounts, supply piping for the fixtures, and the vent piping are displayed for a toilet room.

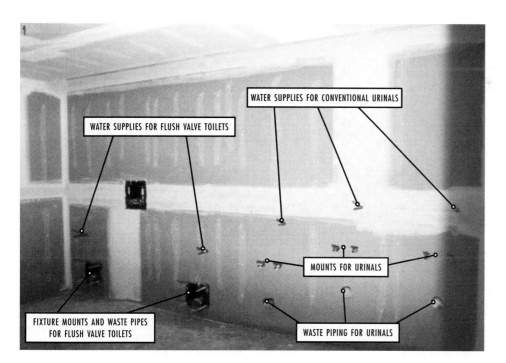

Figure E.5 For the same bathroom shown in Figure E.4, gypsum wallboard has been installed (in preparation for the mounting of the fixtures).

Figure E.6 For the same bathroom shown in Figures E.4 and E.5 the fixtures and stalls have been installed. The photograph on the left shows the toilet stalls. The photograph on the right presents the urinals: note that the left urinal is placed to enable usage by a wheelchair-bound person.

TABLE E.1
MINIMUM PLUMBING FACILITIES (ABRIDGED)

TYPE OF BUILDING OR OCCUPANCY	WATER CLOSETS FIXTURES/PERSON MALE FEMALE	URINALS FIXTURES/PERSON MALE	LAVATORIES FIXTURES/PERSON MALE FEMALE	BATHTUBS OR SHOWERS FIXTURES/PERSON	DRINKING FOUNTAINS FIXTURES/PERSON
Assembly places — Theatres, Auditoriums, Convention Halls, etc. — for permanent employee	1: 1–15 1: 1–15 2: 16–35 3: 16–35 3: 36–55 4: 36–55 Over 55, add 1 fixture for each additional 40 persons	0: 1–9 1: 10–50 Add one fixture for each additional 50 males	1 per 40 1 per 40		
Assembly places — Theatres, Auditoriums, Convention Halls, etc. — for public use	1: 1–100 3: 1–50 2: 101–200 4: 51–100 3: 201–400 8: 101–200 11: 201–400	1: 1–100 2: 101–200 3: 201–400 4: 401–600	1: 1–200 1: 1–200 2: 201–400 2: 210–400 3: 410–750 3: 401–750 Over 750, add 1 fixture for each additional 500 persons		1: 1–150 2: 151–400 3: 401–750 Over 750, add 1 fixture for each additional 500 persons
Dormitories School or Labor	1 per 10 1 per 8 Add 1 fixture for each additional 25 males (over 10) & 1 for each additional 20 females (over 8)	1 per 25 Over 150, add 1 fixture for each add'l 50 males	1 per 12 1 per 12 Over 12 add 1 fixture for each additional 20 males and 1 for each 15 add'l females	1 per 8 For females, add 1 bathtub per 30. Over 150, add 1 per 20.	1 per 150
Dormitories for staff use	1: 1–15 1: 1–15 2: 16–35 3: 16–35 3: 36–55 4: 36–55 Over 55, add 1 fixture for each additional 40 persons	1 per 50	1 per 40 1 per 40	1 per 8	

TABLE E.1
MINIMUM PLUMBING FACILITIES (ABRIDGED)

TYPE OF BUILDING OR OCCUPANCY	WATER CLOSETS FIXTURES/PERSON MALE	FEMALE	URINALS FIXTURES/PERSON MALE	LAVATORIES FIXTURES/PERSON MALE	FEMALE	BATHTUBS OR SHOWERS FIXTURES/PERSON	DRINKING FOUNTAINS FIXTURES/PERSON
Dwellings							
Single dwelling	One per dwelling			One per dwelling		One per dwelling	
Multiple dwelling or Apartment House	One per dwelling or apartment unit			One per dwelling or apartment unit		One per dwelling or apartment unit	
Office or Public Buildings	1: 1–100　3: 1–50 2: 101–200　4: 51–100 3: 201–400　8: 101–200 　　　　　11: 201–400 Over 400, add 1 fixture for each add'l 500 males and 1 for each add'l 150 females		1: 1–100 2: 101–200 3: 201–400 4: 401–600 Over 600, add 1 fixture for each add'l 300 males	1: 1–200　1: 1–200 2: 201–400　2: 201–400 3: 401–750　3: 401–750 Over 750, add 1 fixture for each additional 500 persons			1 per 150
Office or Public Buildings for employee use	1: 1–15　1: 1–15 2: 16–35　3: 16–35 3: 36–55　4: 36–55		0: 1–9 1: 1–50 Add one fixture for each additional 50 males	1 per 40		1 per 40	
Restaurants, Pubs, and Lounges	1: 1–50　1: 1–50 2: 51–150　2: 51–150		1: 1–50 Over 150, add 1 fixture for each add'l 150 males	1: 1–150　1: 1–150 2: 151–200　2: 151–200 3: 201–400　3: 201–400		1: 1–150 2: 151–200	
Schools — for staff use All schools	1: 1–15　1: 1–15 2: 16–35　2: 16–35 3: 36–55　3: 36–55 Over 55, add 1 fixture for each additional 40 persons		1 per 50	1 per 40　1 per 40			
Schools: for student use							
Nursery	1: 1–20　1: 1–20 2: 21–50　2: 21–50 Over 50, add 1 fixture for each additional 50 persons			1: 1–25　1: 1–25 2: 26–50　2: 26–50 Over 50, add 1 fixture for each additional 50 persons		1 per 150	
Elementary	1 per 30　1 per 25		1 per 75	1 per 35　1 per 35			1 per 150
Secondary	1 per 40　1 per 30		1 per 35	1 per 40　1 per 40			1 per 150
Others (colleges, universities, adult centers)	1 per 40　1 per 30		1 per 25	1 per 40　1 per 40			1 per 150
Worship Places							
Education & Activities	1per 150　1 per 75		1 per 150	1 per 2 water closets			1 per 150
Principal Assembly	1per 150　1 per 75		1 per 150	1 per 2 water closets			1 per 150

This table is a portion of Table 4-1 of the *Uniform Plumbing Code,* 2000 Edition, pages 30–32. Permission to reproduce the material in Table E.1 from the 2000 Edition of the *Uniform Plumbing Code,* copyright 1999, has been granted by the publishers, the International Association of Plumbing and Mechanical Officials, 5001 East Philadelphia Street, Ontario, California 91761-2816. All rights reserved. Please note that Table E.1 as printed above is an abridgement of the Table 4-1 in the *Uniform Plumbing Code,* 2000 Edition. See the *Uniform Plumbing Code,* 2000 Edition, for the entire table.

The number of a specific type of fixture—toilets, lavatories, drinking fountains, and so forth—that must be furnished for any building will be determined by the number of occupants, either in the entire building or in some areal fraction of a building (where the areal fraction likely is defined by how far an occupant may have to traverse to reach a specific fixture). Fixture requirements will differ for buildings that shelter multiple types of occupants (e.g., in department stores where codes distinguish between customers and the sales staff, or for penal institutions where services for the prisoners and the institutional staff are differentiated). Also, in most nonresidential toilet rooms for male occupants, some ratio of toilets-to-urinals will usually be dictated (where the urinals will substitute for toilets).

The types and numbers of fixtures that are required for various building occupancies are stated in the 2000 *Uniform Plumbing Code* and are identified here in Table E.1. Note that the types and numbers of fixtures that are set forth in this table represent a catalogue of minimum requirements (i.e., larger numbers of fixtures and potentially other fixtures will likely enhance occupancy of any building). These requirements are distinguished between public and employee use, resident and employee use, and student and staff use in the various categories of occupancy types.

Other distinctions in the provision of minimally acceptable fixtures concern what vertical separations between occupants and facilities (restrooms) are permissible, whether separate or unisex facilities can be furnished, what facilities must be made available in retail commercial and food service occupancies, and what accommodations must be offered for the physically handicapped. For instance, in buildings consisting of multiple floors, the physical distance between any occupant's station and required plumbing facilities should not exceed one vertical story.[1]

Separate plumbing facilities must be provided for both genders except for residential occupancies and for other occupancies when 10 or fewer people will be served by the facility. Alternatively, for business and mercantile occupancies having floor areas equal to

---

SIDEBAR E.1 Choices of fixtures

Choosing which types of fixtures should be present is dictated, first, by building code; second, by good or common design practice; third, by client needs or wishes; and, fourth, by budgetary constraints. However, once the fixture types have been identified, then the selection of specific fixtures—in terms of style, capacity, or other attribute—can require substantial time investment.

Presently, some basic criteria must be observed. For instance, most model plumbing codes require the choice of *water-conserving* fixtures. For such fixtures, rates of water consumption per use and/or rates of water flow during use are stipulated. Specific fixture dimensions and forms can also be prescribed, particularly for buildings and other facilities that are designed and constructed to be *accessible*. The spaces between fixtures and the spaces in which fixtures are enclosed (as in toilet stalls) are also established in building standards and codes. Also, numbers of different installation and operation practices will be set forth in building guidelines and regulations.

Determining which fixture types and the numbers of each fixture type are required should ideally be established during the programming phase. Designing to accommodate fixture placement should be executed during the preliminary schematic phase. But most of the decisions concerning the selection of specific fixtures—again, in terms of style, capacity, or other attribute—can be delayed until the design development phase. Thus, during schematic designing it is important to provide adequate sizing for the spaces that surround and separate the various fixtures.

or less than 1500 ft² (139.5 m²), a single toilet with an accompanying single lavatory can serve both genders (with the qualification that no more than one person may occupy the facility at a time).[2] Where buildings used for business and mercantile occupancies have larger floor areas, then increased numbers of facilities — accommodating each gender separately — will be required. However, there do not need to be alternative facilities for customers and employees, as both customers and employees can employ single sets of facilities. The total number of fixtures required in these instances will be derived to satisfy the greater number of people, whether customers or employees. Additionally, where the business and mercantile occupancies are laid out as parts of a cluster of commercial

---

SIDEBAR E.2 The auspices of the *2000 Uniform Plumbing Code*

The *2000 Uniform Plumbing Code* is a product of a collaboration and sponsorship between several different plumbing industry organizations. These organizations represent both professional and skilled-trade groups, all of whom participate in the creation of plumbing systems for buildings. These organizations include the International Association of Plumbing and Mechanical Officials (IAPMO), the National Association of Plumbing-Heating-Cooling Contractors (NAPHCC), the Mechanical Contractors Association of America (MCAA), the American Society of Sanitary Engineers (ASSE), the United Association of Journeyman and Apprentices of the Plumbing and Pipe Fitting Industry of the United States (UA), and the Western Fire Chiefs Association (WFCA).

Further, in 1999, the International Association of Plumbing and Mechanical Officials (IAPMO) and the National Fire Protection Association (NFPA) resolved that they would jointly work together to produce a consensus model code by 2003. This consensus model code would thus coordinate the contents of the *Uniform Plumbing Code* and the *Uniform Mechanical Code* and all standards written by the National Fire Protection Association.[1]

Note that the copyright for the 2000 Uniform Plumbing Code is held by the International Association of Plumbing and Mechanical Officials (IAPMO).

1. *Uniform Plumbing Code, 2000 Edition,* (Walnut, California: International Association of Plumbing and Mechanical Officials, 2000), page iii.

SIDEBAR E.3 Water closets — flush tanks and flushometer valves

To promote the effective and thorough cleansing of the toilet bowl after its use, water must be flushed into the bowl under sufficient pressure. Two alternative mechanisms are commonly available for providing the necessary water flow: the flush tank and the flushometer valve (see Figure E.6). The flush tank most often sits above the bowl. When the tank is flushed, water is released downward into the bowl providing the cleansing action. Alternatively, the flushometer valve mechanism involves the release of water that is held in check within the supply system. The water in the sup-

ply system behind the flushometer valve is maintained at some elevated pressure that is adequate for providing sufficient water flow into the toilet bowl (when the valve is opened).

Until recently, the flush tank toilet had a conventional water usage rate of about 5 gallons (18.9 liters) per flush. Currently, many jurisdictions in the United States now require the installation of toilets operating with 1.6 gallons (6.1 liters) per flush. This use reduction has been undertaken to promote fresh water conservation.

establishments (as in a shopping mall), the maximum distance between any establishment and the restroom facility must be less than 500 ft (152.4 m). A further stipulation is that if the commercial establishments are stores and the floor areas of these stores are 150 ft² (13.9 m²) or less, then the maximum distance between any store entry and the facility must be 300 ft (91.4 m) or less.[3] Lastly, in food service enterprises when the occupant load exceeds 100 people, then separate facilities must be furnished for customers and employees. If fewer than 100 occupants are present in a food service enterprise, then customers and employees may share single sets of facilities that are separated by gender.[4]

Lastly, when toilet rooms are provided for both genders in a nonresidential building or facility, a general minimum set of toilet room fixtures can be defined. Thus, for males, the toilet room set will include one water closet (toilet), one urinal, and one lavatory. For females, the set will consist of one water closet (toilet) and one lavatory.

E.2.1.2   Providing accessible fixtures

The Americans with Disabilities Act (ADA) was first passed as a U.S. federal law in 1990. Its goal is to ensure that individuals with physical or mental disabilities are able to function successfully in the various environments that otherwise have been designed and constructed for the able-bodied. The ADA seeks to remove barriers that might inhibit or prevent accessibility in the environment to any occupants. Thus, the ADA "prohibits discrimination on the basis of disability."[5]

The accessibility guidelines established by the ADA apply to buildings and other facilities that may be occupied by people with disabilities. These guidelines are to be used during the design, construction, and alteration of places of public accommodation and commercial facilities. Public accommodations are those facilities, services, privileges, goods, and so forth that are furnished for the general public. Commercial facilities are built spaces that are involved in commerce or are employed for nonresidential use by a private entity.

The ADA guidelines stipulate physical conditions that must be maintained for pathways between buildings, entrance and egress means for buildings, horizontal passageways in buildings, vertical movement between building floors, windows and doors, plumbing fixtures, fixed or built-in seating and tables, assembly areas, telephones, signage, alarms, and warning devices. The plumbing fixtures for which particular guidelines are furnished include drinking fountains, water closets (toilets) and toilet stalls, urinals, lavatories and mirrors, and bathrooms, bathing facilities, and shower rooms (noting, specifically, bathtubs,

---

SIDEBAR E.4   Common use and public use spaces

These two terms—*common use* and *public use*—are defined in the ADA Accessibility Guidelines for Buildings and Facilities in the following manners:

Common use "refers to those interior and exterior rooms, spaces, or elements that are made available for the use of a restricted group of people (for example, occupants of a homeless shelter, the occupants of an office building, or the guests of such occupants)."

Public use "describes interior or exterior rooms or spaces that are made available to the general public.

Public use may be provided at a building that is privately or publicly owned."

(Source: Appendix A ("ADA Accessibility Guidelines for Buildings and Facilities") in "Nondiscrimination on the basis of disability by public accommodation and commercial facilities," *Code of Federal Register, Title 28, Part 36.101*, (Washington, D.C.: Office of the Federal Register, National Archives and Records Administration, July 1, 2000), pages 530–531.

shower stalls, storage facilities, sinks, and accessing equipment such as tub and shower seats and grab bars and handrails). The minimum number and the required dimensions of these plumbing fixtures and accessing equipment are identified in "Standards for Accessible Design."[6]

Drinking fountains and water coolers. In a building that must be accessible these units should be designed with sizes that satisfy accessibility needs.

Toilet rooms. Where toilet rooms are provided—in buildings that are required to be accessible—each toilet room that is furnished for *common use* or *public use* must be made accessible.

The specific conditions that render the toilet room accessible follow. First, if toilet stalls are included in the design of the room, at least one stall must conform to a standard, accessible sizing (which will be identified in Section E.2.2.2) (see Figure E.7). Second, if six or more stalls are included in the toilet room design, then—in addition to the standard, accessible stall—at least one further stall must match the following guideline: the stall

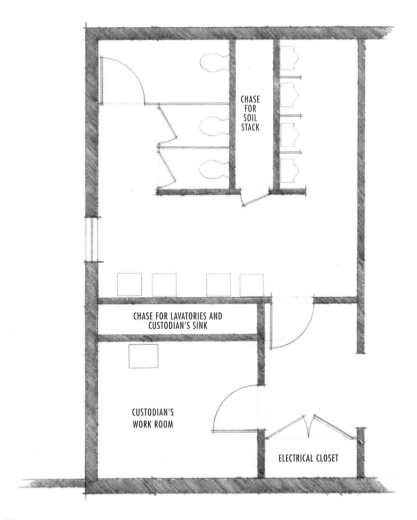

Figure E.7 A layout is displayed for a toilet room having both conventional and wheelchair-accessible fixtures.

must be 36 in (915 mm) wide, have an outward-swinging door, and have suitable parallel grab bars (see Figure E.8). Third, the water closets in the standard, accessible stall and any additional accessible stall(s) must match accessibility sizing and accommodations (see Section E.2.2.2). And, fourth, if stalls are not to be used in the toilet room, then at least one water closet must have accessibility sizing and accommodations.

Urinals. When urinals are provided in accessible toilet rooms, at least one must match accessibility sizing and accommodations (see Section E.2.2.2).

Lavatories and mirrors. In any toilet room that is accessible, at least one lavatory and mirror must be rendered accessible (see Section E.2.2.2 for sizing guidelines).

Bathrooms, bathing rooms, and shower rooms. First, if water closets, urinals, and lavatories and mirrors are included in these rooms — that are designed to be accessible — then the numbers guidelines in the paragraphs above must be satisfied. Second, if bath tubs or showers are provided in these rooms, then at least one accessible bath tub or at least one accessible shower must be provided (see Section E.2.2.2 for sizing guidelines for tubs and showers).

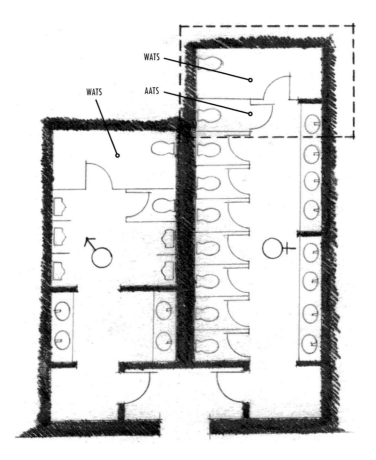

Figure E.8 The toilet room on the left — for women — contains one WATS (wheelchair-accessible toilet stall) and one AATS (ambulatory-accessible toilet stall.) The WATS facility complies with the need for a "standard" accessible stall. Inclusion of the AATS facility satisfies the requirement that when toilet rooms contain six or more stalls, one must be an AATS.

A number of qualifications exist for the designing of accessible facilities. First and most important, all of these fixtures and the spaces housing them must be able to be reached along an accessible route (i.e., the corridor or other space that leads up to the accessible toilet room, bath room, shower room, and so forth must be readily accessible for users of these rooms). Second, when children are the principal users of a toilet room, bath room, shower room, and so forth, then the same number of accessible devices (as for rooms used primarily by adults) applies. But the sizing of the accessible fixtures should match the smaller stature of the children (see Section E.2.2.2). And, third, where various dispensers, electrical receptacles, and other equipment are present in these rooms, at least one of each device must be accessible (i.e., by having the appropriate sizing and placement).

Further qualifications concern accessibility features that must be accommodated whether an addition is being made to an existing building (or facility) or whether some portion of an existing building (or facility) is being altered. Additions to existing buildings (or facilities) that are being made accessible must comply with the same accessibility requirements stipulated for the design and construction of new buildings (or facilities). Thus, for plumbing fixtures, the guidelines identified above (for new buildings and facilities) must be applied for the design and construction of additions to existing buildings (and facilities).

For any portion of a building or facility that is being altered, that portion must be made accessible according to the guidelines described above for new buildings or facilities. An exception is offered, however, when it is deemed to be technically infeasible to make the building or facility portion accessible. Bases for technical infeasibility include structural system limitations or other physical or site constraints that prohibit the ready and practical modification of building or facility elements that would otherwise have to be altered to achieve accessibility. When technical infeasibility makes compliance with the guidelines for new construction unachievable specifically for toilet rooms, then the design and construction of at least one unisex accessible toilet or bathroom must be provided per floor. This unisex toilet or bathroom must have a water closet and a lavatory that satisfy accessibility requirements. There must also be a suitable privacy latch on the entry door for this toilet or bathroom. Alternatively, if toilet room stalls already exist in a toilet room that is to be altered and a standard accessibility stall cannot be furnished in the newly altered room, then an alternately-sized accessibility stall must be furnished. Lastly, when no accessible toilet or bathroom can be furnished in the altered portion of a building or facility, then signage must be supplied indicating the location of the nearest accessible toilet or bathroom within the building or facility.[7]

E.2.2   SPATIAL SIZING TO ACCOMMODATE PLUMBING FIXTURES

E.2.2.1   Sizing for spaces to provide for conventional fixtures   The sizes of spaces designed to house *conventional* bathroom and shower room fixtures are all identified in the document, *Safety Requirements for Plumbing.*[8] This document has been composed by a Joint Task Force of the Mechanical Contractors Association of America (MCAA) and the National Association of Plumbing-Heating-Cooling Contractors (NAPHCC). In the document, spaces between adjoining fixtures, spaces between specific fixtures and surrounding wall surfaces, and clearance distances in front of the various fixtures are set forth.

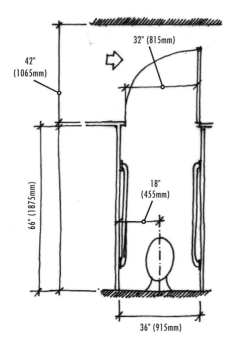

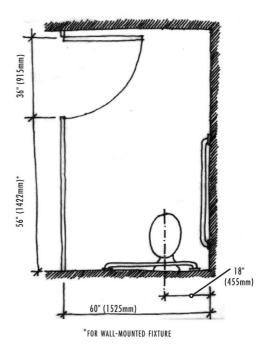

*FOR WALL-MOUNTED FIXTURE

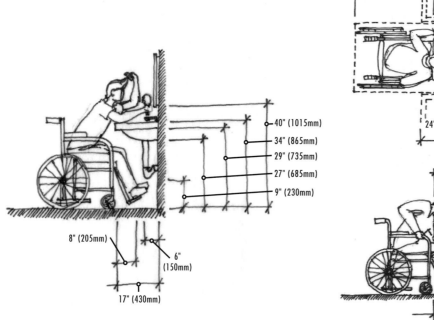

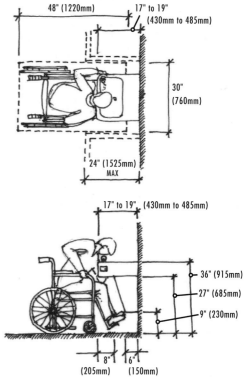

Figure E.9 Examples of spatial allowances for accessible bathroom fixtures. Source: http://www.access-board.gov/adaag/html/adag.htm

E.2.2.2 Sizing for accessible spaces Spacing guidelines for *accessible* buildings and facilities appear in Appendix A of Part 36 ("Nondiscrimination on the Basis of Disability by Public Accommodations and in Commercial Facilities") of Title 28 of the Code of Federal Regulations. This Appendix A is entitled *Standards for Accessible Design.*[9] These standards lay out spacing guidelines for all of the various building elements and spaces that can be occupied by persons experiencing disabilities. Of note for the purposes of this chapter, spacing guidelines are provided for drinking fountains and water coolers, toilet rooms (and their fixtures), bathing rooms (and their fixtures), and related other accessories and services (e.g., storage, signage, and accessible routes). Examples of particular accessible fixture spaces and these spacing guidelines are presented in Figures E.9–E.11.

Figure E.10 A wheelchair-accessible toilet stall.

Figure E.11 This standard wheelchair-accessible shower stall is located in the shower room of a recreational sports facility. Note that a retractable bench is hidden from view behind the shower curtain (i.e., the bench can be rotated downward to a horizontal position).

Section E.3 | WATER SUPPLY SYSTEMS

Water supply systems are organized to deliver water to the various plumbing fixtures that serve building occupants. Supply systems also furnish water for a wide variety of commercial, institutional, and industrial uses and processes. Water that is distributed to conventional fixtures is most often *potable* (i.e., that is safe for human consumption, such as for drinking and food preparation).

In some instances where water will not be used for drinking or food preparation, the water conveyed to fixtures—shower and bathing facilities, clothes washers, and so forth—may be of a *recycled* nature. Such recycled water can be derived from wastage from food preparation activities including dishwashing. Or the recycled water may previously have been used in shower and bathing activities or for clothes washing. Note that no treatment of this recycled water is required. Instead, the sole requirement permitting the recycling of water is that the water must remain free of human waste (e.g., urine and feces). In some situations recycled water may be reused for selected applications as many as eight to ten times before it will be wasted to a sewage system. Even then, before the recycled water is wasted, it may be used as a flushing medium for toilets or urinals.

Alternatively, water that is supplied for many commercial, institutional, and industrial applications may be, as likely as not, *nonpotable,* or it may even be *reclaimed.* Nonpotable water will generally match most of the qualities of potable water, but the overall health and safety of the water cannot be assured (and, thus, is not fit for human consumption). Reclaimed water is most often a product of a wastewater treatment plant that processes human and/or industrial sewage. The reclamation process involves removal of harmful pathogens, organic materials, and heavy metals. However, because the reclamation process is rarely complete, the reclaimed product lacks adequate safety for human consumption.

Water supply systems can be organized to transport and deliver any of these four water forms. Where more than one water supply product is furnished in buildings, it is important for designers and contractors to accurately and faithfully label what product flows in which

SIDEBAR E.5 Standards for water quality

In the United States the principal force for defining water quality standards has been the Safe Drinking Water Act that was enacted by Congress in 1974 and which has twice been amended in 1986 and 1996. The goal of this act is to regulate public water systems and to ensure the safety of the American public through the promotion of healthful drinking water. The original act specified suitable treatment procedures for water supply systems. The subsequent amendments promoted enhanced water quality standards and treatment procedures.

For information about the Safe Drinking Water Act, see the Web page http://www.epa.gov/safewater/ sdwa/sdwa.html. For definitions of the quality standards for drinking water, see the document *2002 Edition of the Drinking Water Standards and Health Advisories* (EPA 822-R-02-038) that is issued by the U.S. Environmental Protection Agency. This document identifies the many organic and inorganic contaminants that can be present in water supplies and that can cause harm to human consumers. Maximum safe consumption rates for these various substances are cataloged. The Chemical Abstracts Service Registry Numbers (CASRN) for each of these substances are also cited. The Web address for this document is http://www.epa. gov/waterscience/human health/.

supply system (see Figure E.12). Care must also be taken to assure that only potable water is supplied to fixtures for which human consumption will occur. Similarly, recycled water must only be supplied to fixtures where it is safe to employ the recycled water.

The sources of potable water are several. Some sources will be located below grade (i.e., they will be ground—or subsurface—water sources). Examples of ground water sources include wells, springs, aquifers, and underground rivers. Alternatively, the other major category of water sources is surface water. Examples of surface water sources include (above-grade) rivers, streams, lakes, and so forth. One other distinction about sources that is relevant is whether any source is privately or publicly owned. Virtually any combination of ground or surface water, private or public source, exists, and most combinations occur widely.

To ensure that a source can furnish potable water the source must be tested against well-established standards to demonstrate that the water is safe for human consumption. Whether a water source readily passes such testing or the source requires some treatment, it is often common practice to conduct yet-further treatment for the water source. Examples of treatments may include chlorination, fluoridation, sedimentation, flocculation, and the addition of a variety of other chemicals, any or all of which are used to create a safer, better-tasting, more attractive product (i.e., one that people will willingly drink and use in food preparation).

Potable water that is furnished by public utilities in urban and suburban localities commonly is distributed throughout the supply area in community mains. These mains are

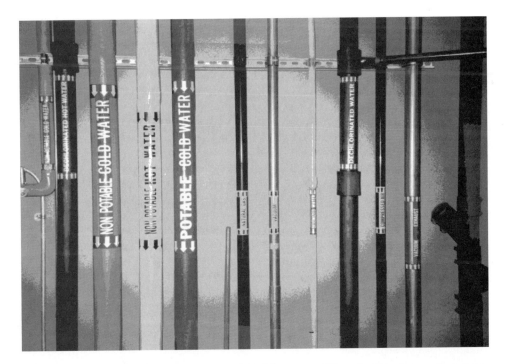

Figure E.12 In laboratory, health care, and/or industrial buildings many different liquid (and gaseous) substances will often be supplied and wasted. This collection of pipes demonstrates the range of substances needed to service a fisheries science laboratory building.

pipes that are laid below grade — usually, beneath community thoroughfares. The water passing through these public (main) supply pipes will be propelled at elevated pressures and with large enough flow rates to furnish adequate water supplies to subscribers.

One alternative to this conventional public service model is the use of private wells by inhabitants of rural or unincorporated areas. In these rural areas building occupants will create wells, usually by drilling, digging, or boring into subsurface land in search for adequate quantities of water. Once a suitable subsurface source — that furnishes good-quality water with an adequate quantity — has been identified, then the water can be extracted with a pump.

SIDEBAR E.6 Water contaminants and treatment practices

Both subsurface water and groundwater sources will likely have present at least small concentrations of any of a range of contaminants (i.e., substances that, in sufficient quantities, can be injurious to human health). These contaminants can include microbial substances (various bacteria such as fecal coliform and E. coli and parasites such as cryptosporidium and giardia lambila), radionucleides (materials that emit radioactivity), inorganic substances (a variety of metals, salts, and compounds such as asbestos), synthetic organic compounds (such as pesticides and herbicides), and volatile organic compounds (that are products of industrial and other work-related processes). The U.S. Environmental Protection Agency identifies approximately 90 contaminants in its drinking water standards and sets maximum permissible human consumption levels for each of these contaminants.

A number of treatment techniques are widely employed. The selection of which techniques to use is dependent on which contaminants are present in the water source. The goal for any treatment technique is to produce clean, healthful water that is visually appealing and has an acceptable taste.

Treatment techniques are usually applied in combinations. Coagulation and flocculation procedures are employed if a source water is turbid and contains entrained solid particles. The coagulation process will cause the particles to bunch together, whereas flocculation will hasten the aggregation of the particles by slowly agitating the water with a stirring action. As the particles clump together, then these particles will pass to the bottom of the treatment containers and can be removed as a residual sediment. Alternatively, the water can be filtered — by passing it through sand beds — if the entrained particles are too small to be effectively removed by the sedimentation process. When the source water has embedded gases (usually present because the water has been in contact with mineral compounds), these gases can be removed by oxidizing the water. Oxidation of the water will also be useful for reducing the potential concentrations of water-borne ions of such metals as iron and manganese. Lastly, when source water has unacceptable quantities of potentially harmful organisms, then the water will need to be disinfected. Disinfection can be accomplished by adding any of several substances such as chlorine (as an elemental gas or as part of a chemical compound), chloramine (a mixture of chlorine and ammonia), chlorine dioxide, and/or ozone.

Further information on this subject can be found on the U.S. Environmental Protection Agency Web site (at http://www.epa.gov/safewater/hfacts.html). Also, see the books by Ray, B.T., *Environmental Engineering*, (Boston, Massachusetts: PWS Publishing Company, 1995) and Vesilind, P.A., *Introduction to Environmental Engineering*, (Boston, Massachusetts: PWS Publishing Company, 1997).

E.3.1   COMMON COMPONENTS OF BUILDING WATER SUPPLY SYSTEMS

Whether water is furnished to a building from a community main or a private source such as a well, the water service pipe entering the building almost always is located beneath grade level. Thus, the piping connection between the source—the community main or a well—and the building will be buried some few to several feet (perhaps, 1 m to a few meters) beneath the existing grade. Burying the water service pipe offers protection against damage from any property use by the building occupants and from the climate (i.e., passing the piping below grade both provides a cooling mechanism for the water, as well as insulation against freezing). How deep the water service pipe needs to be located to protect it from climatic features depends on the severity of the climate.

The principal components of a water supply system in a building are the piping and a series of regulating, treatment, and storage devices. Most commonly, piping is acquired in standardized lengths. Then, a water supply system is assembled by joining alternative segments that are cut from these standardized lengths. The assembly of piping is accomplished with any of a group of fittings. The variety of fittings includes unions (couplings), tees, wyes, elbows, and caps (see Figure E.13).

Regulating devices include usage meters, pumps, valves, flow restrictors, and backflow prevention devices. The usage meters will generally record consumption of water (e.g., for water obtained from a public source, how much water is used over a billing period). But

---

SIDEBAR E.7 Water consumption rates

Describing the amount of water consumed by people in their daily lives is made difficult because of the lack of standardization among reporting bodies. For instance, the amount of drinking water *ingested* by the average adult inhabitant of the United States is estimated to be 1.2 l (0.26 gal)/day.[1] Alternatively, the amount of water consumed by an average household of four persons in the United States is stated to be about 350 g/day (1325 l/day), for people who obtain water from a public water supply system.[2] For people in the United States who obtain their water from a private system, the daily consumption rate is estimated to be about 200 g/day (757 l/day) for a family of four. The average water consumption in countries of the European Union is estimated to be about 150 l/capita/day (39.6 g/capita/day).[3] Daily water usage in the average European Union residence is divided among the following activities: for personal hygiene, 33 percent; for clothes and dish washing, 33 percent; for food preparation and drinking, 5 percent; and for toilet flushing, 28 percent.[4]

From the reports cited below—both in the United States and the European Union—water

consumption in residences is stated to be about 10 percent of all water used. The other 90 percent is used for industry and agriculture.

1. "Estimated Per Capita Water Ingestion in the United States," *Drinking Water and Health Advisories*, prepared by the U.S. Environmental Protection Agency, 2002. See http://www.epa.gov/water science/drinking/percapita/.

2. "How Much Drinking Water Do We Use in Our Homes?" *Water on Tap: A Consumer's Guide to the Nation's Drinking Water*, prepared by the U.S. Environmental Protection Agency, 2002. See http://www.epa.gov/OGWDW/wot/howmuch.html.

3. "Household water consumption," *Indicator Fact Sheet Signals 2001—Chapter Households* (Report No. YIR01HH07), prepared by the European Environment Agency, 2001. See http://themes.eea.eu.int/Sectors_and_activities/households/indicators/energy/hh07household.pdf.

4. Ibid.

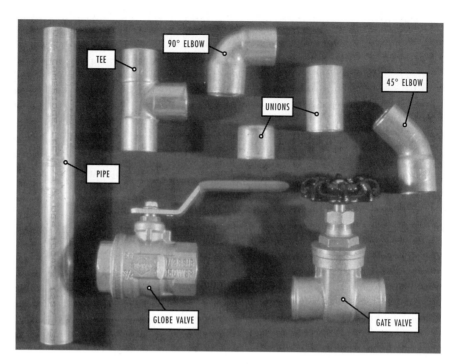

Figure E.13 A collection of pipe fittings that are commonly employed in residential water supply systems.

some meters will record demand utilization, where usage will be measured for some short period of time like an hour or a day. Demand meters are sometimes required by municipal water utilities as a means of determining the short-terms rates with which customers consume water. Pumps are employed to propel water through a supply system principally by increasing the pressure of the flowing water. Therefore, pumps are generally used to overcome the effects of gravity or to ensure that there is sufficient pressure in a water supply pipe to enable the operation of some fixture. Valves are used to regulate the pressure of the water flowing into a building or through the building supply system (see Figure E.14). Valves are also employed to shut off flow to a fixture (e.g., to a toilet) or to shut off flow from a fixture (e.g., from a lavatory faucet). Flow restrictors control the rate of water flowing through some length of piping or through a fixture (e.g., to regulate the rate of water flowing through a shower head). Finally, backflow prevention devices stop the backward flow of water in a supply system (i.e., to ensure that the flow of water in a supply system will only be directed from the source to and through the fixtures).

Common treatment devices range from water heaters and coolers to water softeners and purifiers to simple filters. The heaters and coolers alter the temperature at which water is supplied to one or several fixtures. Water softeners modify the mineral content of the water arriving from a public or private source. Water purifiers can change the chemical or biological composition of arriving water. These softeners and purifiers usually operate by adding various chemical reagents to the incoming water. Alternatively, simple filters function by having the arriving water pass through some sort of filtration device or system that causes a *physical* separation of the water and the offending material.

Figure E.14 A pressure reducing valve assembly is employed when the water supply pressure is excessive. The need for the assembly shown in this photograph arises because the pressure of the water entering the building exceeds 100 psi (690 kPa). The pressure reducing valve assembly decreases supply pressure to 80 psi (552 kPa) or less.

Storage devices are basically retention means that enable supply water to be held inertly until there is need for the water at some fixture. In private supply systems a well can serve as a storage device, water can be stored in a cistern, or a tank can be a repository (see Figure E.15). Most often, when water is stored in any of these locations, the water will have no pressure acting on it and will essentially be a *passive* medium. To initiate water flow from the tank, either pressure will have to be exerted on the water with the action of a pump or the water must be allowed to flow downward from the tank, thus gaining momentum (and pressure) as the flow is affected by gravity.

E.3.2   ORGANIZATION OF BUILDING WATER SUPPLY SYSTEMS

The piping that runs from a community main or a well into a building is generally identified as the water service pipe. The service pipe will connect to a consumption (and/or demand) meter. Then, on the other side of the meter the water distribution pipe system will commence. This distribution pipe system will consist of various horizontal and vertical (riser) lengths of pipe (and their associated fittings, treatment and flow-regulating devices, and storage tanks). From this distribution pipe system, fixture branch pipes will split off and run toward the fixtures that will be served by any branch (i.e., usually, no more than two fixtures may be served by a single branch pipe). Lastly, fixture supply pipes will run to individual fixtures from the fixture branch pipes (see Figure E.16).

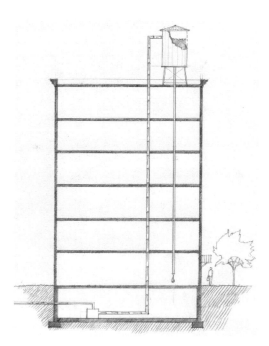

Figure E.15 Storage tanks on roofs have been used in many older urban buildings. The heights of these tanks above the roof level will be established to acquire sufficient downward pressure to operate the highest fixtures within the building.

E.3.2.1   Materials choices for water supply systems   These components—both the piping and all of the other associated parts of the supply system—are available in a variety of materials. Materials that are identified by the *Uniform Plumbing Code, 2000 Edition,*[10] as suitable for water supply system components are copper, brass, cast iron, galvanized malleable iron, galvanized wrought iron, and galvanized steel. Further, asbestos-cement, chlorinated polyvinyl chloride (CPVC), polyethylene (PE), polyvinyl chloride (PVC), and cross-linked polyethylene (PEX) have all been identified as acceptable materials for *cold-water* supply system components. Chlorinated polyvinyl chloride (CPVC) and cross-linked polyethylene (PEX) are identified as suitable for *hot-water* supply system components. Lastly, the code stipulates that "all materials used in the water supply system, except valves and similar devices, shall be of a like material, except where otherwise approved by the Administrative Authority"[11] (where the *Administrative Authority* is the regulatory official or agency for the jurisdiction in which a building is being designed and constructed).

E.3.2.2   Pressure relationships in water supply systems   The basic goals in organizing a water supply system are to ensure the maintenance of adequate pressure and a stable flow rate. To obtain satisfactory operation from most fixtures, sufficient water pressure must be present up line from the fixture in the supply system. Water pressure in most supply systems is furnished from the pressure that is present in the community main (or that is created by a pump in a private well system). Thus, the community main pressure (or pressure established by a localized pump in a private system) will drive the flow of water in a building supply system.

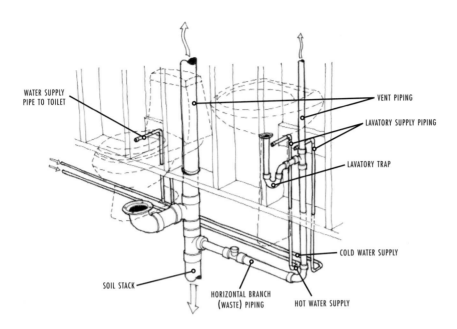

WATER SUPPLY
PIPE TO TOILET

VENT PIPING

LAVATORY SUPPLY PIPING

LAVATORY TRAP

COLD WATER SUPPLY

SOIL STACK

HORIZONTAL BRANCH
(WASTE) PIPING

HOT WATER SUPPLY

Figure E.16 Supply system piping and drainage, waste, and vent (DWV) system components are shown here for a highest-floor toilet room (i.e., no toilet rooms are above this one; thus, the soil stack functions as a stack vent above this toilet; see Figure E.22). The water supply piping furnishes cold water to the toilet and the lavatory; hot water is piped to the lavatory.

The community main pressure essentially serves as a resource that can be used to operate a water supply system in a building. This available pressure will act to offset resistance from three different factors that are present in building supply systems. First, resistance to water flow occurs due to friction from the pipe surfaces. Similarly, friction will be experienced as water flows through the several fittings, meters, and regulating devices, all of which are components in a supply system. So, as the water flows along piping and through these various components, frictional resistance occurs. Second, because the supply water enters a building through a service water line that is located below-grade and most of the building fixtures will be placed above-grade, the water will have to flow upward moving against the force of gravity. Thus, flow resistance results from the need to overcome gravity. And, third, the fixtures will all impart resistance to water flow as they operate. The water flowing in the water supply system must have enough available pressure at each specific fixture to enable the operation and flow of water through the fixture (i.e., to surmount the flow resistance caused by the fixture).

These three flow resistances are cumulative in a building water supply system. To enable water flow in the system and to ensure the operation of each of the several fixtures, the pressure of water flow in the community main must equal these summed resistances. Thus, the available pressure in the community main can be thought of as enabling the operation of the overall supply system.

E.3.2.3 Designing building water supply systems Now, let's consider this resource—the pressure available in a community main—from a design and operational standpoint.

An important issue in the designing of a water supply system—by either a plumbing engineer or subcontractor—is to establish the appropriate cross-sectional sizes for the piping and other various components of the supply system (i.e., the fittings, meters, and regulating devices). The amount of frictional resistance caused by the piping and the other various components will be determined by the cross-sectional sizing of the piping and components. When the piping and components are adequately sized, then effectively the frictional resistance to water flow will be optimized (in relation to pressure availability and water flow stability). Alternatively, the amount of flow resistance imposed by any fixture is established with the choice of the fixture (e.g., whether flush tank or flushometer toilets will be used in a supply system). When these two flow resistances—for pipe and system component friction and fixture operation—are summed and then subtracted from the pressure available in the community main, the remaining pressure amount is what is left to overcome the force of gravity. The greater this remainder is, the higher the water in the supply system can be pushed upward in a building (relying simply on the community main pressure).

Community main pressures in many urban and suburban locales in North America range from perhaps as low as 20–30 pounds per square inch (psi) (138–207 kPa) to as great as 110–120 psi (759–828 kPa). A most common—median—pressure value is probably about 50–60 psi (345–414 kPa). Using conventional fixtures and laying out buildings with ordinary floor-to-floor dimensions, community main pressures of 50–60 psi (345–414 kPa) can enable successful fixture operation perhaps as high as the 5th or 6th floor of a building. Alternatively, utilizing main pressures in the range of 110–120 psi (759–828 kPa) can allow the upward water flow and fixture operation on about the 15th story of a building (without relying on a supplemental pump).

As a further design issue, water supply systems are organized in terms of *pressure zones*. A pressure zone is an area of a building that uses a common pressure source (e.g., from the community main, from the action of a pump, from pressure established by water flowing through a pressure-reducing valve, and so forth). An entire building can have a single pressure zone, or a building may be operated with two or more pressure zones. The importance of the pressure zone as a design and operational directive is that there is a need to limit the maximum pressure that might act upon any fixture. The specific maximum pressure is 80 psi (552 kPa) (i.e., no fixture should be subjected to water supply pressures in excess of this magnitude). Water supply pressures higher than 80 psi (552 kPa) acting upon conventional fixtures will cause the fixtures to fail or to produce poor and/or uncontrollable performances.[12]

Suppose a building obtains its water from a community main that supplies water at pressures greater than 80 psi (552 kPa). Some portion of the building near the ground will need to use a pressure-reducing valve to decrease the available pressure for operating the fixtures on the floors near the ground (for example, see Figure E.17). Higher floors of the building can be serviced by the greater than 80 psi (552 kPa) water pressure because some of the available pressure will be dissipated in pushing the water to these upper floors. For example, in a 12-story building that is serviced by a community main providing a water supply pressure of 100 psi (690 kPa), water for the lower floors—perhaps, the first 6 stories—would pass through a pressure-reducing valve and flow to the fixtures on these first 6 stories. Another supply pipe would carry water from the community main (at 100 psi [690 kPa]) upward to the 7th through the 12th stories of the building. After overcoming the effects of gravity by pushing the water to the base of the 7th floor, the water supply pressure that could act on the upper floors would have been reduced sufficiently so that the fixtures on these upper floors would perform well.

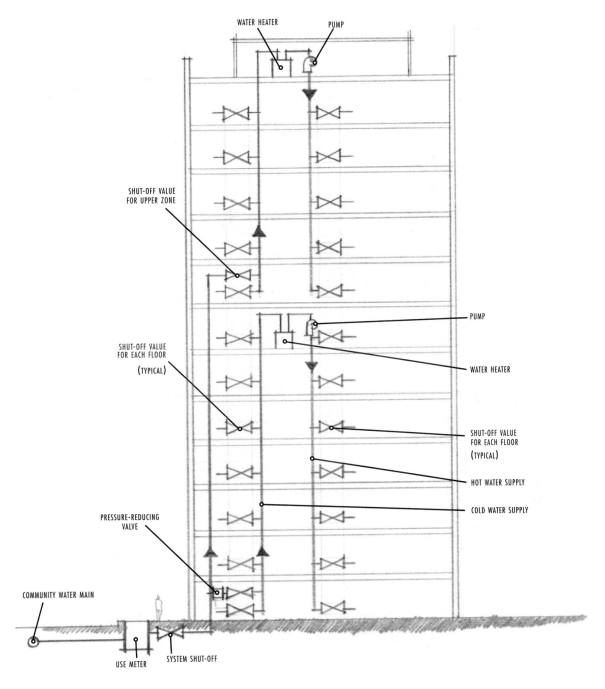

Figure E.17 A water supply system that furnishes cold and hot water is shown for this 12-story building. The cold water supply system consists of two zones: floors 1–7 and floors 8–12. As the community main pressure is sufficient to propel water to the roof of the 12th story, the water entering the lower zone will have to pass through a pressure reducing valve assembly to bring the pressure for this lower zone to a maximum magnitude of 80 psi (552 kPa). On the 7th floor and in the roof enclosure are tanks in which cold water is heated by heating coils producing the hot water for the supply system. To provide sufficient pressure for fixtures using the hot water, pumps at the 7th floor and in the roof enclosure will be utilized to propel the hot water downward. In summary, cold water is supplied in an upfeed manner, whereas hot water is supplied in a downfeed manner.

The upper limit for pushing a water supply using the available pressure from a community main is approximately 15 stories when the stories have conventional floor-to-floor dimensions (i.e., when the community main pressure has a maximum value of about 120 psi [828 kPa]). When the community main pressure is less (as it most often will be), then the maximum water supply height relying only on the pressure available in the community main will be many floors lower than the 15 stories suggested here. In any case, for buildings with heights greater than 15 stories, pushing supply water above whatever height the community main pressure will enable will require usage of pumps (see Figure E.18). Thus, the function of these pumps is to supplement the available community main pressure, creating enough pressure to overcome the greater gravity forces that exist for having more stories in a building.

Note that when these greater water pressures are created (for pushing water to yet-higher elevations), the fixtures on the lower floors of such buildings will still have to be supplied with water at pressures less than 80 psi (552 kPa). To ensure that this 80 psi (552 kPa) pressure limit is maintained throughout a tall building, multiple pressure-reducing valves will need to be included in the water supply system, thereby creating multiple pressure zones in the building. Commonly, in tall buildings such as those with 40, 60, or more stories, succeeding pressure zones will be established in increments of about 7 to 8 floors each. In each pressure zone the maximum water supply pressure reaching any fixture will be less than 80 psi (552 kPa).

Perhaps the final major element in the design and operation of water supply systems, particularly for taller buildings, concerns the use of *gravity tanks*. For upper floors of taller buildings — whether medium or high-rise — supply water can be pumped to upper pressure zones and then to individual stories of the pressure zone. In other words, pumping action will create sufficient pressure to push supply water to the highest floor elevations in a building. To service an intermediate pressure zone some of the high-pressure supply water will be passed through a pressure-reducing valve admitting the supply water for this intermediate pressure zone at no more than the allowable 80 psi (552 kPa) pressure. Supply water under this allowable pressure will then pass upward through distribution risers and fixture branches to service ever-higher fixtures in this intermediate pressure zone. So, the maximum pressure entering this intermediate pressure zone might be about 80 psi (552 kPa). At each succeeding higher story of the pressure zone, the supply water pressure will be reduced in accordance with the increasing height and the increasing gravity load that resists water flow.

Figure E.18 A cold water supply system for a 21-story building is presented here (note that hot water could be furnished in a manner similar to that shown in Figure E.19 using tanks and assisting pumps placed at appropriate intermediate floors). The cold water supply system for this building is organized in four zones. The lowest zone — serving floors 1–5 — is supplied utilizing the pressure in the community main. Water for the three higher zones is propelled to these zones by one (or more) pump(s) placed in the basement of the building. Water streams entering the second zone (for floors 6–12) and the third zone (for floors 13–17), respectively, will pass through pressure reducing valve assemblies ensuring that the entering pressures will be no more than 80 psi (552 kPa). Water for the fourth (highest) zone (for floors 18–21) will pass into a storage tank in the roof enclosure. At this level a pump will furnish sufficient pressure for the water that flows downward to fixtures on floors 18–21. For further information about organizing water supply systems and also about alternative system organization practices, see the chapter, "Water distribution systems in buildings," by T. Musialowski, in the book edited by C.M. Harris, *Practical Plumbing Engineering,* (New York: McGraw-Hill, Inc., 1991), pages 3.1–3.18.

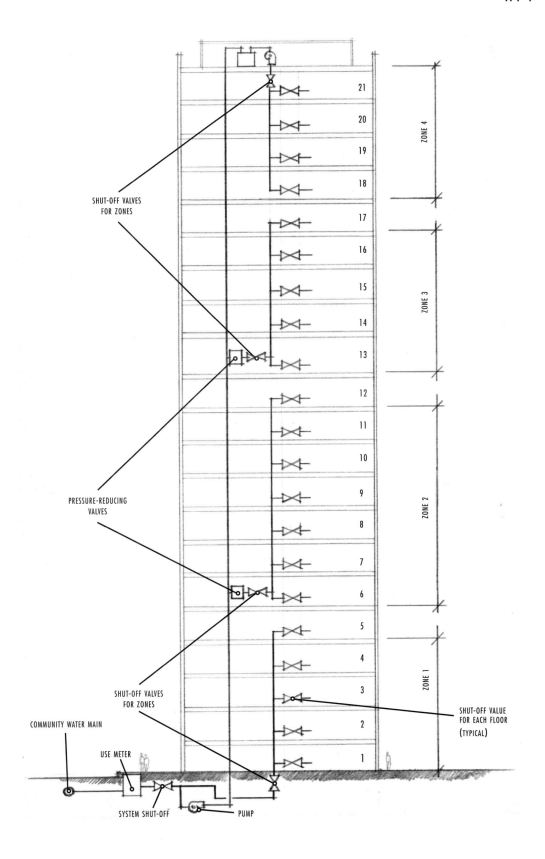

SHUT-OFF VALVES
FOR ZONES

PRESSURE-REDUCING
VALVES

SHUT-OFF VALVES
FOR ZONES

COMMUNITY WATER MAIN

USE METER

SYSTEM SHUT-OFF

PUMP

SHUT-OFF VALUE
FOR EACH FLOOR
(TYPICAL)

ZONE 4

ZONE 3

ZONE 2

ZONE 1

21
20
19
18
17
16
15
14
13
12
11
10
9
8
7
6
5
4
3
2
1

An alternative design and operational strategy is to pump supply water to the top of the building or to the top of a pressure zone and to have it settle into a storage (gravity) tank. In such a tank the supply water can be held until it is needed for fixture operation at some distance below. Note that when the water resides in an elevated storage tank, this water essentially exerts no pressure (i.e., it has a pressure of zero psi [o kPa]). But, as the supply water descends from the storage tank to enable the operation of a fixture, the supply water gains pressure. The magnitude of the pressure for the supply water will thus grow larger as the water moves further downward from the storage tank.

The water supply must gain enough pressure before the flowing water can enable the operation of any fixture. To gain enough pressure, then, there must be a sufficient vertical distance between the storage tank and any particular fixture. So, if a flushometer toilet requires twice the water pressure to operate compared to a flush tank toilet, then the distance between the storage tank and the flushometer toilet will have to be twice as great as the distance between the storage tank and the flush tank toilet. In any case, the fact that the water flow from the storage tank gains pressure by virtue of the force of gravity has lead to the identification of these tanks as *gravity tanks*.

For high-rise buildings with their large heights, multiple gravity tanks may be employed. For buildings that are composed of 40, 60, or more floors, two or more gravity tanks may be present. Normally, a high-rise building will be composed of several pressure zones. So, for example, for a building having perhaps 60 stories and eight successive pressure zones from top to bottom, one gravity tank might supply the top four zones, a lower gravity tank (on perhaps about the 30th floor) might supply the next three lower zones, and the bottom zone would be supplied by water flowing upward from the pressure in community main. For the top gravity tank, as the water flowed downward to supply the four zones, water entering the three lower zones — the 5th, 6th, and 7th from the ground — pressure-reducing valves would have to be installed to keep the maximum water pressure reaching any fixture in these zones below 80 psi (552 kPa).

So, summarizing these operational strategies and design options, the use of supply pressure made available from water flowing in a community main is often described as an *upfeed* operation or system. How high water can be pushed in an upfeed system is dictated largely by the magnitude of the pressure exerted by the community main. The flow resistances produced by, first, the pressure losses due to the friction in the piping and the other equipment in the supply system and, second, by the pressure required to operate any fixture each have less relative influence on how high water can be pushed in a supply system. As an alternative to the upfeed system, water that is pumped to the top of a building or to the top of a pressure zone and then is allowed to flow downward to gain pressure for operating fixtures is identified as a *downfeed* system. Downfeed systems will usually be organized into two or more pressure zones. Downfeed systems will also generally employ a series of pumps, storage (gravity) tanks, and pressure-reducing valves. Upfeed systems will usually be present in low-rise buildings and the lower stories of medium- and high-rise buildings. Downfeed systems will commonly be employed in medium- and high-rise buildings. But the water supply systems in some medium- and high-rise buildings can be organized with combinations of pumps and pressure-reducing valves so that water is always brought into the lowest floor of each pressure zone and pushed upward through that zone by pressure applied from below the zone.

E.3.2.4 Hot water supply systems   The previous discussion concerning the operation of water supply systems best describes how *cold* water is moved through buildings. Supply systems for distributing hot water follow slightly different strategies. Conventionally, water entering a building from a community main (or a private well) is at a subsurface temperature and thus can directly be employed as cold water. The flow of the cold water will typically be divided just after it enters the building and a fraction of this flow will be distributed through the building as cold water. The other flow fraction will pass into the hot water system.

One major difference between cold and hot water supply systems is the inclusion of one (or more) water heater(s) in the hot water supply system. Generally, two principal types of hot water heaters are employed in buildings (producing in either case what is labeled as *domestic hot water* (DHW) and which is differentiated from the hot water that may be used in HVAC system operation). One type of water heater combines a heating assembly and a storage tank (and is described as a *storage-tank heating* arrangement). Water is heated and maintained at elevated temperatures within the tank and is available whenever hot water is needed. The other type heats water flowing through the heater on an instantaneous basis (i.e., the water is heated on demand as it flows across the heating assembly). Water supply systems that apply instantaneous heating do not require a storage tank for holding the hot water (and are described as "instantaneous" and "tankless"). The major distinction between these two principal types of water heaters is the amount of hot water that each can furnish at a given time. The storage-tank heater can furnish a large volume of hot water when it is needed. Alternatively, the tankless, instantaneous water heater can furnish smaller quantities of hot water at any moment. The storage-tank heater often will expend more thermal energy (and consume more fuel) to heat and maintain the elevated temperature of the stored hot water than the instantaneous hot water heater that only has to heat the water. But, when a larger hot water flow rate is needed and this flow rate exceeds the operational capacity of the instantaneous heater, the water flowing out of the instantaneous heater will be at a lower temperature than would be produced at normal flow rates (i.e., the hot water would likely be only tepid or lukewarm).

Building types in which storage-tank heaters might reasonably be used include athletic centers with the associated shower rooms, eating establishments where diners eat on regular bases (corporate dining rooms or school cafeterias), or college dormitories. Alternatively, instantaneous, tankless heaters will be found in buildings where hot water needs are spread out somewhat uniformly across a work day (e.g., in an office building, a shopping mall, or in restaurant bathrooms).

Lastly, providing hot water supplies for low-rise and higher-rise buildings will usually show differences. In low-rise buildings hot water heaters will usually be located at levels proximate to where the cold water enters the building. If hot water is produced with an instantaneous, tankless heater, then the pressure supplied by the community main can be used to push the hot water upward to the several fixtures. If, instead, hot water is generated by a storage-tank heater and the hot water resides in the tank for some period of time until needed, then the hot water will have to be propelled upward with the action of a pump.

For medium- and higher-rise buildings, particularly when larger hot water flow rates are required, the most used practice is to place storage-tank heaters at the top floor of the building or, secondarily, at the top floor of a pressure zone. Cold water is pumped upward to these tanks. In these storage tanks water is heated and stored for subsequent demand. As the hot water is needed, it is released to flow downward, gaining the pressure necessary to operate various fixtures.

Section E.4 | PLUMBING DRAINAGE SYSTEMS

Drainage systems are means for conveying wastewater, other liquid wastes, and water-borne solid wastes from fixtures to public sewers or private septic systems (see Figure E.19). Generally, drainage systems operate strictly under the force of gravity. But pumps and other lifting equipment may be included in specific drainage systems where the positioning of fixtures, waste-holding tanks, and sewers or septic systems do not permit reliance on gravity.

Drainage systems are intended to operate in a closed fashion (i.e., the operation and maintenance of these systems by building occupants are expected to be minimal). However, in anticipation that drainage flow may become inhibited, cleanout plugs can be utilized for gaining access to the system. Ideally, drainage systems will operate in safe and sanitary fashion. Because a fundamental purpose of drainage system is to transport human waste—urine and fecal matter—out of buildings and because fecal matter is infested with bacteria that can be unhealthy, the need for the system to perform in a sanitary fashion is manifest. Thus, it is essential that drainage systems function hygienically, keeping building occupants from contact with any of the substances that flow through the systems. Other important, generic performance requirements for drainage systems include that no opportunities for the clogging of flow pathways or for solids build-up be present and that no circumstances enabling backflow exist. Note that backflow occurs when drainage materials exiting from a fixture at a higher elevation are able to reenter a fixture at a lower

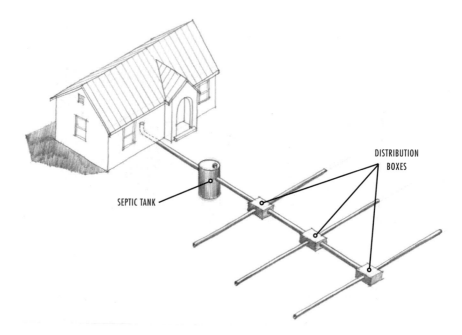

Figure E.19 A septic system will usually consist of a septic tank, distribution boxes, and drainage pipes. The extent of the drainage field—including the distribution boxes and the drainage piping—will depend on the percolation capability of the ground in which the system has been constructed.

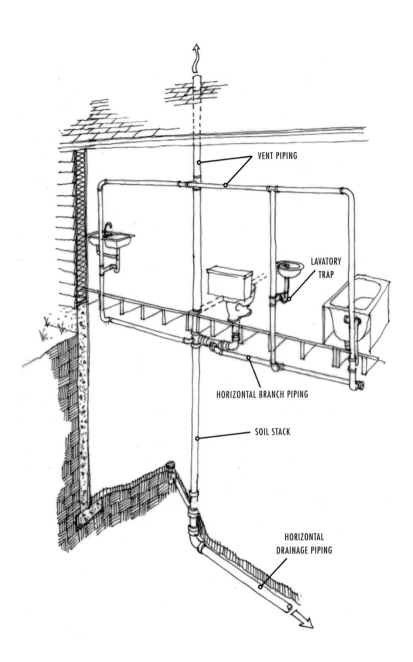

Figure E.20 A conventional drainage, waste, and venting system for a single-family residence is shown here.

elevation. To ensure good flow of drainage materials out of a building the drainage system must be appropriately configured and sized (and occupants must use the system sensibly).

Drainage systems are often referred to in the industry or in professional literature as "drainage, waste, and venting" (DWV) systems. This latter appellation is used to identify three of the basic components of these systems. Indeed, there are five major sets of components that comprise most drainage systems in buildings. These components are traps, horizontal branch piping, stacks, vents, and building (horizontal) drainage piping (see Figure E.20). Some of these components—stacks and vents—are used in a variety of different formats. In the following sections we will describe their forms and applications.

E.4.1   BASIC DRAINAGE SYSTEM COMPONENTS: FORMS AND FUNCTIONS

Traps. For most fixtures, a trap is attached at the fixture outlet. The standard trap is a P-shaped pipe, where the approximately half-circular end of the pipe is connected to the fixture outlet. The straight end of the trap will usually be connected to a horizontal branch pipe that, in turn, will be connected to a vertical stack pipe (see Figure E.21).

When a fixture releases whatever water or other liquid that has been used in the fixture, some of the wasted liquid will remain within the half-circular end creating a *liquid seal* between the fixture outlet and the rest of the drainage system. The presence of this liquid seal will prevent unpleasant gases and odors that exist in the drainage system, from passing from the drainage system back out of the fixture outlet and into the ambient air of the occupied space. To ensure the continued presence of a liquid seal between the fixture outlet and the drainage system, evaporation of the entrapped liquid will need to be minimized.

Some fixtures—particularly, water closets—are constructed with an integral trap (i.e., a trap-shaped pathway for wastewater flow is built into the fixture). But most other fixtures do not have integral traps and must be served by a separate trap device. Thus, such fixtures as bathtubs, showers, lavatories, sinks, laundry tubs, floor drains, urinals, drinking fountains, and so forth must have traps installed in their connections to a drainage system. Note also that some small numbers of fixtures such as adjacent lavatories or laundry tubs may be served by a single trap, as long as these fixtures are quite close together.[13]

Specific spatial requirements that are mandated for trap installations include that the depth of the water seal must be equal to at least 2 in (51 mm) and less than 4 in (102 mm) and that the vertical distance between the fixture outlet and the bend in the trap should be as short as possible, but no more than 24 in (609 mm). Additionally, most traps are required to have a cleanout plug incorporated into the bottom of the trap bend.

Horizontal branch piping. This piping is used to connect the end of the trap at its terminus away from the fixture outlet to the vertical drainage stack. In many applications, single fixtures will be connected with single branches to stacks. But when multiple fixtures are placed close together, then a single branch may connect more than one fixture to the stack.

Drainage stacks. A stack is a vertical pipe that starts at the horizontal drainage piping (the pipe that connects the drainage system of a building with the sewer or septic system) and runs vertically to the level of the highest fixture in the building (that is being served by this stack). Two types of stacks are commonly employed in buildings. One type is the *waste stack,* which is a stack that serves a series of fixtures that do not yield human waste (urine and fecal matter). Thus, a waste stack could serve combinations or single groups of lavatories, bathtubs, showers, kitchen sinks, clothes washers, and so forth. Alternatively, the other type is the *soil stack,* which is a stack that is connected to fixtures bearing

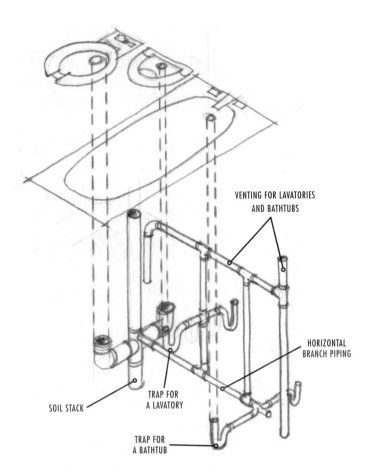

VENTING FOR LAVATORIES
AND BATHTUBS

HORIZONTAL
BRANCH PIPING

SOIL STACK

TRAP FOR
A LAVATORY

TRAP FOR
A BATHTUB

Figure E.21 Drainage equipment is shown for two residential bathrooms that are laid out back-to-back. Note that this image presents back-to-back bathrooms for one floor (of a building that may have more than one floor.) Thus, the hardware shown could be one module of the plumbing system for the building.

human waste (urine and fecal matter). Note that a soil stack may also serve fixtures at which no human waste is produced, but, wherever human waste enters a stack, the stack functions as a soil stack.

Vents. The basic purpose for vent pipes in a drainage system is to enable gas transport throughout the system. Gases produced in the system or passed from fixtures into the system can be carried upward and expelled to the atmosphere. The venting component of a drainage system thus typically runs, as a combination of horizontal and vertical pipes, from the horizontal drainage pipe (at the bottom of the drainage system) to above the roof of a building.

Gas transport in the series of venting pipes in any drainage system serves three functions. First, ventilation of the entire drainage system—the circulation of air—is enabled by the connection of venting pipes to the other components of the drainage system. Second, the venting piping provides an air-moving pathway that is an alternative to air movement in the vertical stacks. The venting piping prevents siphonage and back pressure to develop in the vertical stacks when waste and soil materials flow downward in the drainage system. Siphonage is a "condition in piping where suction is created by reducing the pressure in a certain section [of the piping] below atmospheric pressure."[14] Thus, siphonage occurs when liquid or solid matter flows through piping leaving a reduced air pressure in the wake of this flow. The greater the flow rate or the more completely the cross-sectional area of the pipe is closed off by the flowing matter, the greater the reduction in air pressure will be in the wake of the flow. The availability of air, circulated by venting pipes, negates the creation of siphonage and back pressure (and backflow) in the stacks. Third, because air circulation is enabled and air pressure differences are minimized, there can be a free and quiet flow of liquid and solid matter through the drainage system.

Typical venting systems consist of several standard components: individual vents, common vents, branch vents, vent stacks, and stack vents. An individual vent is simply a pipe that connects a waste or soil-carrying drainage pipe (after the drainage pipe exits a fixture) with a branch vent or a stack vent. A common vent is a vent pipe that serves two (or more) fixtures, running from these fixtures to a stack vent. A branch vent is piping that connects one (or more) individual vent pipe(s) with a vent stack, thus enabling the circulation of gases between the fixture(s) served and the vent stack. Vent stacks are the vertical vent piping that run from the horizontal drainage piping (at the bottom of a drainage system) to the highest-elevation fixture served by the stack. A stack vent is an extension of a vent stack

---

SIDEBAR E.8 Sizing drainage system components

The sizing of the components of a drainage system involves estimating the amount of drainage matter that is likely to pass through any component. First, each fixture in a building is identified. Second, the various fixtures are each assigned a number of drainage fixture units relying on a standardized table. Third, each component in the drainage system is analyzed to determine how many drainage fixture units that the component will serve. Then, the number of drainage fixture units

serviced by the component can be matched against tabulated sizing guidelines for that component type.

Generally, the number of drainage fixture units assigned a drainage system component is directly related to the amount of waste or soil matter that will likely flow through the component per unit time (i.e., as measured in gallons/minute or liters/second). For example, in the following abbreviated table, typical fixtures and their assigned drainage fixture units are noted.

FIXTURE	NUMBER OF DRAINAGE FIXTURE UNITS
Kitchen sink	2
Bathroom shower	1
Lavatory (bathroom sink)	2
Urinal (for both private and public uses)	2
Water closet, flush tank	Private building, 3; public building, 4
Water closet, flushometer (1.6 gpf [6.1 lpf])*	Private building, 3; public building, 4
Water closet, flushometer (>1.6 gpf [6.1 lpf])*	Private building, 4; public building, 6

* gpf = gallons per flush; lpf = liters per flush

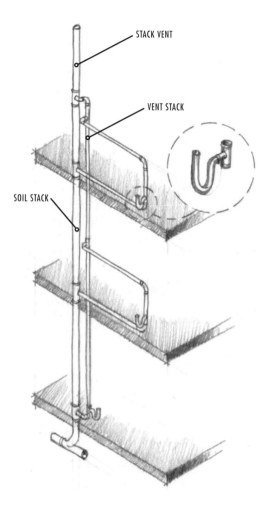

STACK VENT

VENT STACK

SOIL STACK

Figure E.22 A vent stack becomes a stack vent above the highest fixtures served by the stack. The function of this continuation of the vent stack upward — the stack vent — is to enable off-gassing of the drainage system to the atmosphere (and to enable the entrance of ambient air into the system.)

from the position where the branch vent from the highest-elevation fixture connects with the vent stack (see Figure E.22). This pipe extension — the stack vent — runs vertically to some elevation above the roof of the building. Requirements for stack vents include that the stack vent piping terminate at least 6 in (152 mm) above any roof surface and at least 12 in (305 mm) from any vertical surface. Additionally, a stack vent pipe should end no closer than a horizontal distance of 10 ft (3.05 m) from or a vertical distance of at least 3 ft (0.91 m) above any operable window, door, the opening of an air intake, or other vent piping. Further, no stack vent should have a horizontal distance closer than 3 ft (0.91 m) from a property lot line.[15] Note also that a vent stack for a "tall" building — here, whenever a drainage stack has a vertical distance more than 10 stories above the horizontal drainage piping — shall have a parallel vent stack that is of the same vertical length as the principal vent stack and that is connected to the principal vent stack at five-story intervals.[16]

Horizontal drainage piping. This piping runs from the bottom of the vent stacks out of a building to either a public sewage system (most often, simply a sewer) or a private septic system. A principal requirement concerning drainage piping is that it be laid with a uniform slope that is not less than $1/4$ in of downward direction per foot of pipe run (or, 20.9 mm of drop per 1 m of pipe length). Alternatively, the downward orientation for drainage pipe run may be set as a 2 percent slope. The one qualification to this requirement offers that where satisfying this slope condition is inhibited by site conditions and the drainage pipe has a diameter of at least 4 in (100 mm), then a slope of $1/8$ in per foot of pipe run may be employed (10.5 mm of drop per 1 m of pipe length). The second significant requirement for drainage piping is that cleanout fittings — removable plugs that are otherwise gastight and watertight — must be included at the base of the drainage piping where the drainage stack connects to the drainage piping and then, along the drainage pipe run, regularly, at 100 ft (30.5 m) intervals or at any fraction of a 100 ft (30.5 m) interval (when a lesser run distance than 100 ft (30.5 m) is employed).

When a drainage system inside a building ends — for instance, at the bottom of a drainage stack — beneath the level of the responsible sewage system, then accommodations must be included to pass the building drainage products into the sewage system. A standard approach is to pass the drainage products through a drainage pipeline into a watertight sump or receiving tank. Then, the matter collected in the sump or tank should be raised by some sort of ejector, pump, or other lifting equipment to the level of the sewage system. Note that the drainage piping leading from the building drainage system to the sump or tank should be constructed with appropriate valves to prevent backflow from the sump or tank to the building drainage system.

E.4.2   MATERIALS AND SIZING FOR DRAINAGE SYSTEM COMPONENTS

A range of materials may be used in drainage systems in buildings. The *Uniform Plumbing Code, 2000 Edition,* stipulates which materials are permissible for the various component groups.[17] For horizontal and vertical piping as in stacks, horizontal branches, and horizontal drainage pipes, materials that are acceptable include cast iron, galvanized steel, galvanized wrought iron, copper, brass, Schedule 40 ABS (acrylonitrile-butadiene-styrene) DWV, and Schedule 40 PVC (polyvinyl chloride) DWV. Lead may also be used in vertical drainage stacks. Vitrified clay pipe (extra strength) may be used for drainage system applications, as long as it is only employed below ground. Alternatively, galvanized steel and galvanized wrought iron may only be used above ground. Materials permitted for use in trap construction are cast iron, brass, Schedule 40 ABS DWV, Schedule 40 PVC DWV, lead, and polypropylene. Acceptable materials for cleanout plugs depend upon into what materials the plugs are being inserted. For example, for cast iron piping, a cast iron or brass plug should be used; brass plugs should be used when piping is composed of galvanized steel, galvanized wrought iron, copper, or brass. When ABS pipe is used, the plugs should also be fabricated of ABS. So, too, PVC plugs should be used with PVC piping.

One qualification arises about the applicability of various materials for drainage system application: the combustibility of the various materials must be noted, as well as whether drainage system components pass through fire resistance-rated building assemblies. Thus, the two predominant plastic materials ABS and PVC are regarded as combustible, whereas the metals are not. The application of these plastic materials must comply with fire resistance requirements stipulated in building code regulations (so that the use of these materials matches what is allowed for various occupancy groups, building heights and areas, and types of construction). Similarly, where the pipes of these plastic materials and metals pass through fire resistance-rated building assemblies, then appropriate fire-stops must be installed around the pipes to inhibit fire spread between the piping and the assembly through which the piping passes.[18]

The sizes of the various components of a drainage system are determined by the amounts of drainage matter that will likely flow through these components. Additionally, most components in a drainage system are directly linked to other components in a tributary manner (i.e., the flow loads handled by higher-elevation components pass, in a cascading or accumulative fashion, to lower-elevation components). The sizes of components established for the higher-elevation components become practicable minimums for the lower-elevation components: thus, lower-elevation components cannot be smaller than higher-elevation components that are served by the lower-elevation components. Minimum sizes of traps and horizontal branch drainage piping are $1\,1/4$ in (32 mm) diameter for such fixtures as lavatories and drinking fountains. Alternatively, a standard size for traps and horizontal branch drainage piping serving a water closet will be a 3 in (76 mm) diameter.

The number and types of fixtures that are served by any drainage stack determine the size of the stack. A stack that serves a simple bathroom—consisting of a lavatory, a combination bathtub/shower, and a water closet—will need to have a 3 in diameter (to match the trap and horizontal branch drainage piping served by this soil stack). Alternatively, if a two-story residence has a second-story laundry room (with clothes washer and dryer and laundry tub) and the fixtures are served by a waste stack—no human waste (soil) passes down from the second story to the first story through this stack—then the diameter of this waste stack would need to be only 2 in (50 mm).

In larger buildings—such as urban high-rise office towers and large floor-area commercial and industrial centers—the accumulated drainage loads can become substantial. In such buildings the diameters of drainage stacks at the bottoms of these buildings can be as large as 8 to 12 in (200 to 300 mm). For example, in a 50-story office tower having a floor area of perhaps 1,000,000 ft² (about 93,000 m²), the diameter of a drainage stack at its base will likely be about 8 in (200 mm).

The sizing of vent piping—whether horizontal or vertical—is also determined by the number and type of fixtures served by each vent. Generally, the diameter of a vent will be similar to the diameter of a stack that is served by the vent. Thus, for the simple bathroom described in the previous paragraph—consisting of a lavatory, a combination bathtub/shower, and a water closet—the vent diameter would need to be $1\,1/2$ in (to comply with the code requirement that vents must be at least one-half the diameter of the soil stack [drainage piping] served by the vent).[19] For other similarly small buildings having relatively limited numbers of conventional fixtures, the diameters of vent piping can often be smaller than the drainage stacks served by the vent piping. But, in larger buildings with their attendant larger numbers and range of types of fixtures, main vent piping diameters will be identical to the main drainage stacks that are served by the vent piping.

E.4.3   STORM WATER DRAINAGE

In addition to providing means for removing wastewater and sanitary waste from buildings, accommodations must be provided for draining storm water from roofs, paved areas, yards, and courtyards. The storm water must be conveyed into storm sewers (when they are present separately from sanitary sewers), combination sanitary/storm water sewers (when separate storm sewers are not available), or some other means of runoff control such as a catch basin or a drainage route emptying into a natural repository like a river or lake. Note that for one and two-family housing storm water can simply be discharged to flat areas adjoining the housing (e.g., paved areas or lawns) as long as the storm water flows away from the building.

A storm water drainage system is typically composed of either one of two alternative drainage options. First, water can be gathered by rooftop drains and fed to conductors where the water passes downward within the building. Alternatively, storm water may run off of roof surfaces to gutters that are hung at the edges of a roof. Then, the gutter-collected water runs downward through leaders (or downspouts) that are mounted on the exterior of the building. When rooftop drains are used, then strainers should be included to cover the drains, thereby blocking leaves and other materials from entering the conductors and clogging them. Strainers can sit up above the roof plane, or strainers can be built in flush with the plane of the roof. Also, overflow drains or scuppers (provided in parapet walls) should be included as protection against storm water forming ponds on roof surfaces around rooftop drains.

When conductors or leaders connect to a combined sewer system (that transports both storm water and sanitary waste), a trap must be placed at the base of the conductor or leader, before either connects with the combined sewer. Conductors and leaders connecting to storm sewers are not required to have a trap installed in the storm drainage system.

Subsoil drains are necessary and should be installed at the perimeters of buildings when those buildings include basements, cellars, crawl spaces, or other floors located below grade. These subsoil drains should consist of open-jointed or perforated clay tile piping. Storm water collected by these subsoil drains should be discharged into storm sewers or other catchments such as sumps or approved water courses.[20]

When roof drains and conductors are used for storm water drainage systems, then the approved materials for drains are "cast iron, copper or copper alloy, lead, or plastic."[21] Approved materials for conductors are cast iron, galvanized steel, wrought iron, brass, copper, lead, Schedule 40 ABS DWV, and Schedule 40 PVC DWV. And approved materials for gutters and leaders include nearly all of the materials identified for conductors as well as several others.[22]

Sizing *vertical* storm water drainage system components depends on three parameters: the tributary roof area served by any component; a rainfall rate identified as the maximum amount of rain that would fall during 60 minutes for a once-in-100-years event rainfall (for a specific locale); and the diameter of the component. Thus, having information about any two of these three parameters enables determination of the third parameter by employing tables presented in the *Uniform Plumbing Code, 2000 Edition*.[23] Similarly, sizing of horizontal drainage piping and gutters may be performed using these three parameters, plus a fourth parameter—the slope of the component.[24]

Section E.5 | GUIDELINES FOR PLANNING PLUMBING SYSTEM LAYOUTS

In Section E.2 guidelines for accommodating fixtures in bathrooms were set forth. Here, guidelines for placing bathrooms in buildings will be suggested. Initially, planning directives will be offered for nonresidential buildings. Later, suggestions will also be presented for residential buildings.

Location guidelines. For nonresidential buildings any toilet room should be located on the same floor as the people who will be served by it. Occupants should not have to ascend or descend stairs to reach a serviceable toilet room (or, in the case of a mobility-challenged person, use an elevator). Second, a toilet room should be located within 75 ft (22.9 m) of any workstation that is to be served by the toilet room. Third, the locations of toilet rooms in buildings should be readily evident and visible to the occupants of buildings (and guests who visit the buildings). And, fourth, toilet rooms should be located so that these rooms are both convenient and accessible to the entire building population and all visitors to the building.[25]

Guidelines for numbers of toilet rooms. Minimum standards for numbers of toilets, urinals, lavatories, bathtubs or showers, and drinking fountains have been identified in Section E.2.1.1 and Table E.1. Here, we will suggest some further guidelines. First, when considering the likely occupant population for nonresidential buildings — and, particularly, educational, assembly, commercial, and other institutional buildings — we suggest that, for the purposes of planning the numbers of toilet rooms, an occupancy ratio of 60 percent female occupants to 40 percent male occupants be implemented. Secondly, when establishing the numbers of toilets (and urinals), we recommend applying a design ratio of at least three women's toilets for every two men's toilets and urinals. Also, in Section E.2.1.1, we stipulated that the basic minimum fixture sets for toilet rooms should be, for men, one toilet, one urinal, and one lavatory and, for women, one toilet and one lavatory. Further, generally, any unisex toilet room should be accessible for all occupants.

Layout guidelines. When designing multiple-story buildings, toilet rooms should be located on each floor (as stated in the paragraphs above). *Coring* toilet rooms — stacking them with a second-floor toilet room placed immediately above the first-floor toilet room and so forth ascending up through the building — will generally present an easier design scheme to execute. Additionally, the use of water supply system and drainage system components for cored toilet rooms will be more efficient (i.e., the amount of piping and other fittings can essentially be minimized) (see Figure E.23). Also, when planning multiple-floor buildings with toilet rooms for each gender located on each floor, placing the men's and women's toilet rooms back-to-back enables the use of a common chase for running

SIDEBAR E.9 Planning bathrooms and kitchens for single-family housing

The basic set of bathroom fixtures for a single-family house consists of a water closet (toilet), a lavatory, and a bathtub (with or without a shower spigot). This combination is labeled as a "full" bathroom. Alternatively, a bathroom that has a water closet, a lavatory, and a shower stall (with no bathtub) is identified as a "three-quarters" bathroom. And a residential bathroom with simply a water closet and a lavatory is listed as a "half bathroom." Determining the minimum floor area requirements for each of these bathroom organizations will necessarily depend on the sizes of individual fixtures and the required spacings between and in front of the fixtures. The spacing requirements for conventional fixtures are identified in the document, *Safety Requirements for Plumbing.*[26]

What is perhaps the most useful kitchen planning guideline suggests that, first, the refrigerator, the stove top (cooktop), and the kitchen sink should be regarded as the three corners of a triangle; second, no other appliance should lie along a direct line between any two of these three appliances; and, third, the total perimeter for the triangle should be equal to or less than 25 ft (7.62 m). The premise behind this planning guideline is that these three appliances are most basic to kitchen use and that they should be contiguous and reasonably close to each other for comfort and efficiency.

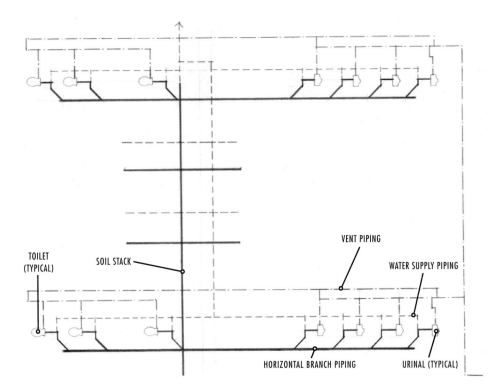

Figure E.23 A plumbing riser diagram for a series of cored toilet rooms in a four-story institutional building is shown here. The soil stack, venting, and water supply lines are included in this riser diagram. Note that the fixtures and related plumbing systems for the second and third floors are not included here (but they would be essentially identical to those for the first and fourth floors).

supply and drainage piping to each toilet room on each floor. When laying out chases that will serve back-to-back toilet rooms, figure that the clear width inside the chase should be about 2 ft (0.6 m).

In multifamily residential buildings — apartments, condominiums, residence hotels and so forth — the use of coring for bathroom planning can simplify floor layouts and the subsequent installation of water supply and drainage systems equipment. Further, for multiple-story residential buildings, laying out bathrooms and kitchens on a back-to-back basis can offer plan and plumbing system equipment efficiencies.

But, for single-family housing, whereas the use of coring as a planning mechanism makes good and practical sense, it is still quite reasonable to layout bathrooms and kitchens to accommodate client and designer wishes. In single-family housing piping sizes will be comparatively small (e.g., for water supply systems, pipes will usually be 3/4 or 1 in (19 mm or 25 mm) in diameter; for drainage systems, vent and stack piping should be no more than 3 in — or, possibly, 4 in — (76 or 102 mm) in diameter. Thus, it is readily practical to run supply and drainage pipes in walls and above finished ceilings without introducing unfortunate design complications. Perhaps the only concerns for laying out spaces for plumbing systems in single-family housing are to ensure ready access to clean-outs, to keep water supply pipes out of perimeter walls (to minimize chances for water freezing in the pipes), and to provide adequate noise separation where supply and drainage piping are located in walls, floors, or ceilings immediately adjacent to occupied spaces.

ENDNOTES and SELECTED ADDITIONAL COMMENTS

1. *Uniform Plumbing Code, 2000 Edition.* (Walnut, California: International Association of Plumbing and Mechanical Officials, 2000). Section 413.2.1.

2. Ibid., Section 413.3.

3. Ibid., Section 413.5.

4. Ibid., Section 413.6.

5. "Nondiscrimination on the Basis of Disability by Public Accommodation and Commercial Facilities," *Code of Federal Register, Title 28, Part 36.101,* (Washington, D.C.: Office of the Federal Register, National Archives and Records Administration, July 1, 2000), page 504.

6. Op. cit., Appendix A to Part 36, pages 526–616.

7. Op. cit., Appendix A to Part 36, Section 4.1.6, pages 539–540.

8. *Safety Requirements for Plumbing* (American National Standard [ANSI] A40-1993), (Rockville, Maryland: Joint Task Force of MCAA/NAPHCC, 1994).

9. *Standards for Accessible Design* (Appendix A) to "Nondiscrimination on the Basis of Disability by Public Accommodation and Commercial Facilities," *Code of Federal Register, Title 28, Part 36.101,* (Washington, D.C.: Office of the Federal Register, National Archives and Records Administration, July 1, 2000).

10. Ibid., *Uniform Plumbing Code, 2000 Edition.* (Walnut, California: International Association of Plumbing and Mechanical Officials, 2000). Section 604.1.

11. Ibid.

12. *Uniform Plumbing Code, 2000 Edition.* (Walnut, California: International Association of Plumbing and Mechanical Officials, 2000). Section 608.2.

13. Op. cit., Section 1002.2.

14. *Uniform Plumbing Code Training Manual, 2000 Edition.* (Walnut, California: International Association of Plumbing and Mechanical Officials, 2000); page 66.

15. *Uniform Plumbing Code, 2000 Edition.* (Walnut, California: International Association of Plumbing and Mechanical Officials, 2000). Sections 906.1 and 906.2.

16. Op. cit., Section 907.

17. *Uniform Plumbing Code, 2000 Edition.* (Walnut, California: International Association of Plumbing and Mechanical Officials, 2000). Sections 701.1, 701.2, 707.1, 903.1, and 1003.1.

18. *Uniform Plumbing Code, 2000 Edition.* (Walnut, California: International Association of Plumbing and Mechanical Officials, 2000). Chapter 15.

19. *Uniform Plumbing Code, 2000 Edition.* (Walnut, California: International Association of Plumbing and Mechanical Officials, 2000). Section 703 and Table 7.5.

20. *Uniform Plumbing Code, 2000 Edition.* (Walnut, California: International Association of Plumbing and Mechanical Officials, 2000). Section 1101.5.

21. *Uniform Plumbing Code, 2000 Edition.* (Walnut, California: International Association of Plumbing and Mechanical Officials, 2000). Section 1105.1.2.

22. *Uniform Plumbing Code, 2000 Edition.* (Walnut, California: International Association of Plumbing and Mechanical Officials, 2000). Section 1102.

23. *Uniform Plumbing Code, 2000 Edition.* (Walnut, California: International Association of Plumbing and Mechanical Officials, 2000). Section 1106 and Table 11-1.

24. *Uniform Plumbing Code, 2000 Edition.* (Walnut, California: International Association of Plumbing and Mechanical Officials, 2000). Section 1106 and Tables 11-2 and 11-3.

25. *Facility Design Information, 2001* (prepared by the Engineering Services Department, University of Washington), (Seattle: University of Washington, 2001).

26. *Safety Requirements for Plumbing* (American National Standard [ANSI] A40-1993), (Rockville, Maryland: Joint Task Force of MCAA/NAPHCC, 1994).

CHAPTER F

Systems for Conveying
People in Buildings

IN THIS CHAPTER we will present information about elevators, escalators, and horizontal/ sloped people movers. Emphasis will be placed on describing the principal components of each of these systems and offering planning guidelines for use during schematic designing. Elevators and escalators have made possible the ready occupancy of medium and high-rise buildings. Further, the use of elevators especially has enabled dense settlement patterns to be achieved in cities, as buildings with large total floor areas can be constructed on relatively small property lots. The main utility of escalators is that they provide stairs that move. Whereas a building occupant using an escalator cannot move up and down a building as quickly as with an elevator, more people can move up and down from story to story using an escalator. Horizontal people movers are most often used to shorten walking times experienced when occupants have to travel along relatively long distances in building concourses and on walkways.

Section F.1 | CREATING BUILDING SPACES FOR ELEVATORS

F.1.1   A BRIEF HISTORY OF THE DEVELOPMENT OF ELEVATORS

The use of assemblies to lift commodities can be traced as far back in time as the Roman Empire. In those days lifts were employed to raise goods and materials, but seldom people. The power to lift such objects was provided either by humans or domesticated animals. Generally, these lifting assemblies consisted of ropes, pulleys, and small platforms. The goods and materials would lie on the platform. The platform would be suspended from the pulley by a rope. The other end of the rope would be pulled or gradually released by people or animals, enabling the platform to be raised or lowered.

The level of lifting technology that was developed by the Romans persisted for the next 1,500 years. Not until the beginning of the 19th century was an alternative power source developed and applied to lifting assemblies. About 1800, machines driven by steam began to be used to lift objects, but still not people.

Prior to the middle of the 19th century, the problem that prevented the use of lifting assemblies for transporting people was the general lack of safety. If a lifting rope failed, as many did because of the relatively poor quality of ropes, the lifting platform would plunge to the bottom of the lifting channel. Elisha Graves Otis developed the first suitable safety device in 1853. His technique incorporated a pair of wedges that were placed beneath the lifting platform and two vertical racks with jagged teeth that were stationed at opposite sides of the lifting channel. In the event that a lifting rope failed, these wedges would be propelled by a spring into the jagged teeth of the vertical racks preventing the platform from descending.

Almost immediately, passenger elevators began to be installed in buildings. The first recorded application of a lifting platform that was fitted with Otis's safety device was in the Haughwout & Company Department Store in New York City in 1857. For these early elevators steam-powered machines provided the energy to raise and lower the elevator platforms. In 1889 a first application of a machine powered by electricity occurred, also in New York City. Subsequently, in 1903, a high-speed elevator was introduced. Over the 100 years since this introduction of the high-speed elevator, lifting technologies have been enhanced by faster lifting assemblies, better controls, improved safety devices, and better passenger service.

F.1.2   THE BASIC TYPES OF ELEVATORS

There are two main types of elevators in wide usage today: hydraulic and traction. In *hydraulic* elevators the lifting platform is pushed upward or pulled downward by the action of either a single plunger or a pair of plungers (see Figure F.1). The plungers—whether used singly or in pairs—are incorporated with cylinders into which the plunger is (or plungers are) inserted. A hydraulic liquid—usually, an oil—is forced into or withdrawn from the cylinder(s). Forcing the liquid into the single (or double) cylinder(s) causes the plunger(s) to rise and lift the platform. Withdrawing the liquid from the cylinder(s) causes the plunger(s) to descend, driving the platform downward. The hydraulic liquid is forced into or withdrawn from the cylinder(s) by a pump. A tank to contain the hydraulic liquid is also a principal system component (see Figure F.2). When the liquid is withdrawn from the cylinder(s), it is stored in the tank. Alternatively, when the platform

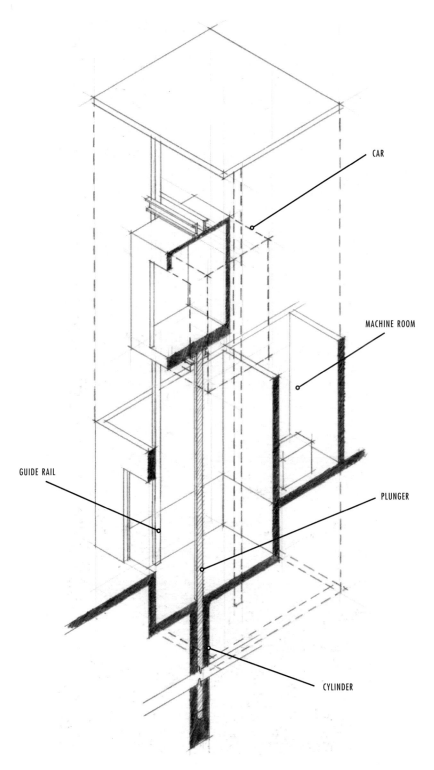

CAR

MACHINE ROOM

GUIDE RAIL

PLUNGER

CYLINDER

Figure F.1 A sectional view of a *holed* hydraulic elevator: the principal components are the hoistway, the car, the plunger and its cylinder, the guide rails, and the machine room (shown here behind the hoistway).

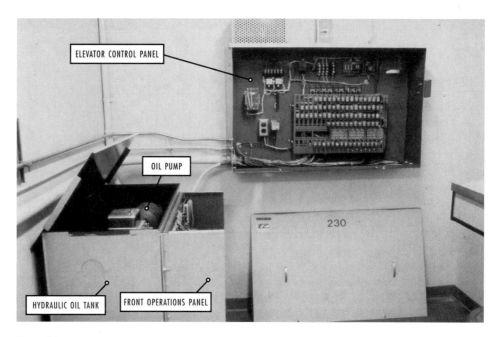

Figure F.2 In this photograph the hydraulic oil tank and control panel for a conventional hydraulic elevator are shown. The covers for the tank and the control panel have been removed so that the internal assemblies in each can be seen. The dimensions of the tank and its front operations panel are approximately 30 in deep x 36 in wide x 36 in high (762 mm x 914 mm x 914 mm). The dimensions of the elevator control panel are approximately 36 in wide x 24 in high x 8 in deep (914 mm x 609 mm x 203 mm). Note also that the operation of the mechanisms in a hydraulic elevator machine room is noisy with common sound pressure levels of about 80–85 dB(A).

TABLE F.1
PERFORMANCE CAPABILITIES OF CONVENTIONAL HYDRAULIC ELEVATORS

	HEIGHT OF ASCENT, IN FEET (M)	NUMBER OF STOPS POSSIBLE	SPEED IN FEET/MINUTE (M/S)	STANDARD LIFTING CAPACITY, LBS (KG)
Holed	60 (18.3)	7	150 (0.76)	2000–5000 (907–2269)
Holeless	20 (6.1)	3	150 (0.76)	2000–5000 (907–2269)
Telescoping holeless	26 (7.9)	3	150 (0.76)	2000–5000 (907–2269)
Roped	60 (18.3)	7	150 (0.76)	2000–5000 (907–2269)

is to ascend, then the pump will force the liquid out of the tank and into the cylinder(s). In many contemporary hydraulic elevators the pump will be enclosed within the liquid storage tank.

For hydraulic elevators there are four system variants: holed, holeless, telescopic holeless, and roped. The holed hydraulic elevator has a single cylinder that is bored into the ground. This cylinder will have a depth that matches the height the plunger and lifting platform will ascend. The holeless hydraulic elevator utilizes no in-the-ground hole. Instead, it employs a pair of above-ground cylinders placed on two opposite sides of the platform with a plunger inserted into each of these cylinders. The telescopic holeless hydraulic elevator is a subvariant of the holeless hydraulic elevator. For the telescopic version, the plungers in the above-ground cylinders can extend further upward by utilizing a telescoping format. The roped hydraulic elevator also employs above-ground cylinders and plungers on two opposite sides of the lifting platform. But this roped hydraulic elevator has rope attachments running from the plungers to winding spools that are affixed to the frame of the lifting platform.

The utilization characteristics for these hydraulic elevators include the heights that the lifting platform can be raised, the number of stops that the platform can have in its ascent, the speed with which the platform rises, and the lifting capacity that the platform can raise. These characteristics are listed in Table F.1.

The principal components of a conventional *traction* elevator are a lifting platform, lifting machinery, a counterweight, and cables (see Figures F.3–F.5). The lifting platform includes a frame that is an integral part of the platform. The lifting cables are thus attached to this frame, pass across the lifting machinery, and are connected at their other ends to the counterweight assembly. To raise a traction elevator platform and frame, the lifting machinery draws up the cable set allowing the counterweights to descend. Alternatively, for the platform and frame to travel downward, the counterweight is drawn upward. Thus, the platform and frame move in the opposite direction to the counterweight.

There are two major types of traction elevators: geared and gearless. What distinguishes the two is the use of a gear assembly—for the geared elevators—that is placed between the lifting motor and the drive sheave over which the cables pass (see Figure F.6). The gear assembly provides beneficial gear reduction ratios so that smaller lifting motors can be utilized to ensure efficient and comfortable operation.

Generally, geared traction elevators are employed for medium speed and medium height applications. Alternatively, gearless traction elevators are used in buildings with greater heights and for which greater lifting speeds are necessary. The major performance differences between geared and gearless elevators are catalogued in Table F.2.

TABLE F.2
PERFORMANCE CHARACTERISTICS OF CONVENTIONAL TRACTION ELEVATORS

	HEIGHT OF ASCENT, IN FEET (M)	NUMBER OF STOPS POSSIBLE	SPEED IN FEET/MINUTE (M/S)	STANDARD LIFTING CAPACITY, LBS (KG)
Geared	To 300 (91)	30	300–500 (1.52–2.54)	2000–4000 (907–1815)
Gearless	To 500–750+ (152–229+)	30–80	500–1200+ (2.54–6.10+)	2000–4000 (907–1815)

Figure F.3 The Space Needle, a landmark in Seattle, Washington, stands 605 ft (184 m) tall. Its principal facilities are restaurants at approximately the 100 ft (33 m) elevation and at the top. Both are served by three traction elevators, one of which is visible here.

Note that gearless traction elevators effectively can ascend to heights that are limited only by what may be regarded as technologically feasible (and economic) building designs. Generally, as elevator services in very tall buildings are zoned (so that any elevator only serves some fraction of the overall height of the building), the net ascent distance will be limited by factors other than strict mechanical performance capabilities. Similarly, whereas the maximum speeds cited in Table F.2 are suggested to be about 1200 ft/min (6.10 m/s), some commercially available gearless elevators can ascend at rates as great as 2000 ft/min (10.2 m/s).

Figure F.4A Three open hoistways for traction elevators are shown here (with the car for one of these hoistways). The car and its structural frame are visible as well as the guide rails at the sides of the hoistways.

Figure F.4B A close-up view of the elevator car shown in Figure F.4A.

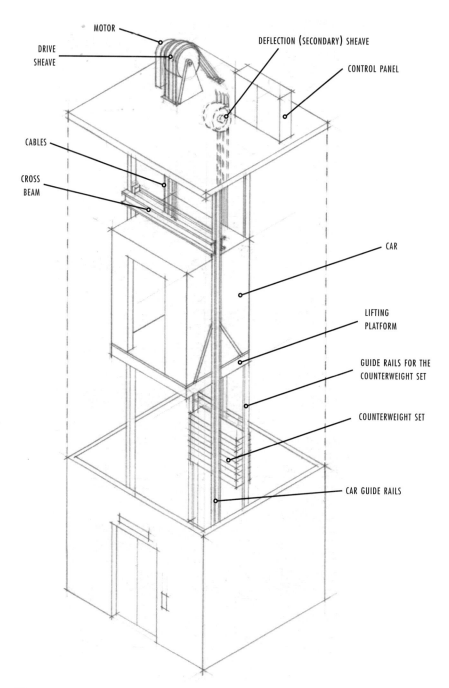

MOTOR

DRIVE SHEAVE

DEFLECTION (SECONDARY) SHEAVE

CONTROL PANEL

CABLES

CROSS BEAM

CAR

LIFTING PLATFORM

GUIDE RAILS FOR THE COUNTERWEIGHT SET

COUNTERWEIGHT SET

CAR GUIDE RAILS

Figure F.5 For a traction elevator, the principal components are shown: its hoistway, the car and its structural frame (including the platform and the cross-beam above the car enclosure), the counterweight assembly, the cables (running from the cross-beam to the counterweight), the drive (and secondary) sheaves, the motor, and the control panel. Additionally, the lobby doors, the call buttons, and the floor indicator are also displayed. This drawing has previously been published in an advertisement for the G.A.L. Manufacturing Company, Bronx, New York, that appeared in the November 1998 issue of Elevator World. Permission to reprint this drawing has been granted by the G.A.L. Manufacturing Company.

Figure F.6 This lifting assembly for a *geared traction* elevator consists of a motor, a gear set, the drive sheave, a deflecting sheave, and the cables.

F.1.3   THE PRINCIPAL COMPONENTS OF ELEVATORS

All elevators are comprised of a hoistway, a pit, a machine room, a car, guide rails, safety devices, doors, lobbies, traveling cables, and communication panels and displays. Hydraulic elevators employ plungers, cylinders, pumps, and tanks (see Figures F.1 and F.2). Traction elevators utilize hoist (or lifting) cables, sheaves, and a counterweight assembly (see Figure F.5). Note that some of these various components are building spaces, whereas other components are pieces of system hardware and machinery.

Perhaps the most fundamental *spatial* components of any elevator are the hoistway and the machine room. The hoistway is a vertical enclosure in which the elevator car ascends and descends. When the hoistway is constructed within a building (as opposed to being placed external to the building), the enclosure must be constructed of fire-resistive assemblies. The specific fire ratings required for hoistways differ according to the natures of the occupancy group(s) present in the building and the types of construction applied for the building.

At the bottom of the hoistway is a pit that extends down beneath the lowest floor level served by the car. For a hydraulic elevator the hoistway runs from the pit to the building roof (or the ceiling of the top floor served by the elevator, in the event that the elevator travel terminates beneath the highest occupied floor of a building). For most traction elevators the hoistway extends from the pit to a rooftop machine room. In the circumstance where the machine room is located elsewhere in the building, then for those traction elevators the hoistway would terminate some modest distance above the highest elevation to which the elevator car can ascend.

The pit is the bottom portion of the hoistway and may extend almost a full story height below the lowest floor served by the elevator car. The components normally placed in the pit include one (or more) buffer(s), an emergency stop switch, and secondary rope or cable equipment (that is present mostly for traction elevators). The guide rails for the car (and, also, for the counterweight assembly for traction elevators) reach to the bottom of the pit. All elevators will have a car buffer that acts as a mechanical shock absorber in the event that a car descends too rapidly. This buffer may consist principally of a spring or a liquid-filled reservoir. Traction elevators will also have a counterweight buffer placed at the bottom of the guide rails for the counterweight assembly. A wall-mounted vertical ladder will usually be present to enable maintenance workers to gain access to the pit floor (to work under a car).

Machine rooms serve different purposes and are located in different locations depending upon whether the elevator is a hydraulic or traction type. For hydraulic elevators the machine room will contain a motor, a pump (for pumping the hydraulic liquid into and out of the cylinder[s]), a tank for holding the hydraulic liquid, valve assemblies, piping for the distribution of the hydraulic liquid, and controls for managing the liquid flow and the overall operation of the elevator (see Figure F.2). Commonly, the motor, pump, and valve assembly will be housed within the hydraulic liquid tank, and the piping will run from this tank to the cylinder(s). For most hydraulic elevators the machine room will be located near or at the same level as the bottom of the hoistway and next to the pit.

Machine rooms for traction elevators will house the lifting (or drive) motor, gears (for geared traction elevators), sheaves, brakes, and control panels (see Figure F.7). Most often, a machine room for a traction elevator will be located at the roof level or, at least, above the highest floor served by the elevator car. In some circumstances the machine room for a traction elevator can be placed at some intermediate floor along the hoistway or even at the bottom level of the hoistway.

The elevator car is a built-up assembly. First, a frame is established consisting of an under-car beam and plank construction, vertical stiles (essentially, side columns), and a horizontal, overhead cross beam (that spans between the two stiles). On top of the beam and planking a platform is attached. Then, the walls of the car (or cab, as in *cabinet*) are attached to the frame and platform. As these walls are inherently not load-bearing, there is a great deal of design freedom in the choice of materials, finishes, and accessories, both for the car enclosure and the car interior. Signaling and motion indicators and control panels are necessary components for integration with the car interior. Finally, a car door assembly will offer admission to and exiting from the car. The operation of the door assembly will be coordinated with the operation of the lobby doors (at each floor level that the elevator serves).

For hydraulic elevators, the plunger is attached to the under-car beam and plank construction. The upward and downward motion of the hydraulic elevator car thus is integral

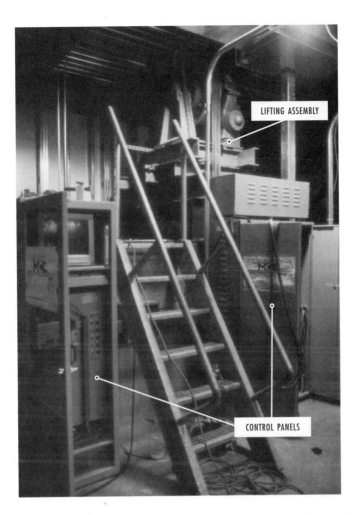

Figure F.7 One half of a machine room for two geared traction elevators appears here. The control panel cabinets are on the lower level of this room. The lifting assembly (as shown in Figure F.6) is located on an upper level.

with the ascension and descent of the plunger. For the traction elevator car, the hoisting cables are attached to the overhead cross beam of the car frame. As the cables are pulled up or let down by the lifting motor, the car rises or descends.

The cables used in traction elevator are strung from the overhead cross beam of the car frame up to the drive sheave of the lifting motor assembly (in the overhead machine room). The cables pass over a secondary or deflecting sheave and run down to and connect with the counterweight assembly. These sheaves function as pulleys. The sheaves are basically wheels with grooved channels through which the cables pass. The contact between the cables and the grooved channels produces friction so that as the sheave turns the cable will move in the same direction.

For a geared traction elevator, the drive motor is connected to a gear assembly, and the gear assembly is attached to the drive sheave (see Figure F.6). One end of the lifting cables passes across the drive sheave and down to the car frame. The other end of the lifting cables is strung from the drive sheave, over a deflecting sheave, and down to the counterweight assembly. Alternatively, for gearless traction elevator, the drive motor is connected directly to the drive sheave. The lifting cables pass upward from the car frame, across the drive sheave to a secondary sheave, and down to the counterweight assembly. Note that the deflector and secondary sheaves function as spacing agents, providing adequate horizontal separation at the level of the machine room (between the cables attached to the elevator car and the counterweight assembly). These deflector and secondary sheaves do not contribute lifting force.

The counterweight assembly that is fundamental to the operation of traction elevators serves two functions. First, the downward force exerted by the assembly provides the needed friction between the lifting cables and the drive sheave. And, second, the counterweight assembly offers a counterbalance against the mass (weight) of the car and its occupants. Generally, the quantity of mass provided by the counterweight assembly will be approximately equal to the mass of the car plus 40–50 percent of the estimated mass of occupants (or freight) when the car is filled to its recommended capacity.[1]

In both hydraulic and traction elevators each car travels up and down its hoistway along a pair of guide rails. These guide rails are placed at the sides of the hoistway (as opposed to the front and back) and run from the bottom of the hoistway pit to the highest floor that is serviced by the car (see Figures F.1 and F.5). Typically, the rails will have a tee-shape, will be composed of steel, and will be fixed to the sidewalls or horizontal floor-by-floor braces in a hoistway. Each car will contact its set of guide rails with a set of wheels on each side of the car: this contact resembles how the wheels of a train ride on tracks. The principal function of these guide rails is to ensure that the travel of the car is stabilized and free of wobble or lateral drifting.

For traction elevators, a pair of guide rails will be furnished for the counterweight assembly for each car. These guide rails will be placed on either side of the assembly and will also run from the bottom of the hoistway pit to the highest floor serviced by the car. Typically, these guide rails and the counterweight assembly will be placed along the back of the elevator car. However, when the car has operable doors on both its front and back sides, the guide rails and the counterweight assembly will be located on one side of the car (separated from the car by the intervening car guide rail).

The hoist (lifting) cables in a traction elevator that run from the car frame over the drive and spacing sheaves to the counterweight assembly are composed of mild or high-carbon steel wire. A conventional cable is an assembly of wound and stranded wire. First, 19 to 27 wires are wound into a strand. Then, six to eight strands are wound around a core consisting of hemp or a vegetable fiber.[2] Generally, each traction elevator car will be suspended from a multiple number of such cables where each cable has sufficient tensile strength to support a loaded car in the event that the other cables were to fail.

The well-being of elevator car occupants is maintained with combinations of governors and safeties (see Figure F.8). The governor is used in traction elevators and is basically a velocity-controlling device. It involves a wire cable that runs from a sheave in the machine room to a tensioning sheave in the hoistway pit. The elevator car moves alongside the wire cable. If the governor senses that the car is traveling downward too rapidly, then the governor grips on to the wire cable commencing the deceleration of the car. Simultaneously with the operation of the governor, the safeties are activated. In normal operation the safeties travel along the guide rails exerting minimal pressure. But when the governor is triggered, then the safeties greatly increase their pressure against the guide rails, utilizing this friction to slow and stop the descent of the car.[3]

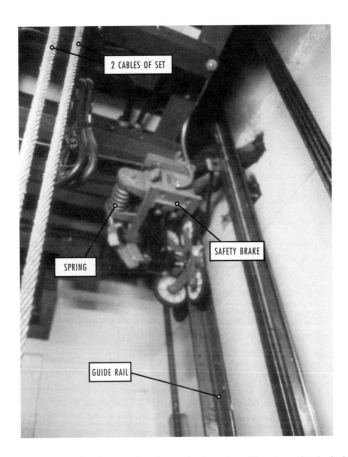

Figure F.8 One of two safety brakes for a traction elevator is shown here (the other safety brake is present on the opposite side of the car.) The safety brake is attached to the underside of the lifting platform. The brake travels along the guide rail. In the event of a failure with the cable set a brake shoe is forced against the guide rail by the spring mechanism, which exerts substantial friction between the brake shoe and the guide rail, slowing the car and causing it to stop.

In addition to these lifting cables, another set of cables is typically present for both hydraulic and traction elevators. This alternative cable set is identified as *traveling* cables and is used for passing communication signals between the car and the machine room. These traveling cables are generally tied to the bottom of the car and are attached to the in-car operations panel. The traveling cables then run to the car controller in the machine room.

A car controller is used to manage the operation of each elevator car in a building. The car controller will be located in the machine room and will regulate both the movement of the car and the requests for service (from building occupants). Additionally, the car controller manages the elevator doors. In buildings where there are multiple traction elevator cars, a group controller will also be present in the machine room. The function of the group controller is to organize and direct the responses to requests for service when two or more cars serve a given floor. The group controller identifies which car in a group of cars will answer an occupant's service request. A positioning device for each car senses the location of each car in its respective hoistway and communicates that information directly to the controllers. Thus, in each machine room that has lifting equipment—motors, sheaves, gear assemblies, and so forth—for more than one traction elevator car, there will be one car controller per car and one group controller for all the cars serving the same zone of floors.[4,5]

Both in each elevator car and in the hallway lobbies on each floor served by an elevator are collections of operation panels, call buttons, directional indicators, floor identifiers, and door controls.[6] These various signaling and display devices are connected to the car controller (and group controller, when more than one car is involved for a particular zone of service). The connections between the signaling and display devices and the car controller are maintained through the traveling cables.

Lastly, car and hoistway doors operate in tandem. At each floor that is serviced by an elevator car, the set of hoistway doors will open and close in response to the operation of the car doors. Generally, the doors on an elevator car will either be positioned in the center of the entrance side or off-center. For center doors two halves of the car door will meet at the center of the doorway (when closed), and the two halves will open by retracting to their respective sides. For off-center doors the car door will be composed of one (or two) panel(s). The single (or double) panel(s) will open by retracting into the remainder of the entrance side of the car. A motor placed on the roof of the elevator car will open and close the car doors. The hoistway doors on each floor will be positioned to match the location of the car doors. Similarly, the operation of the hoistway doors on each floor will occur simultaneously with the action of the car doors. A mechanical triggering device that is a component of the elevator car door assembly initiates the opening and closing of the hoistway doors at each floor. Alternatively, the car controller manages the operation of the car doors whenever the elevator car reaches a floor to discharge and pick up passengers (or freight).[7]

F.1.4   DESIGNING TO ACCOMMODATE ELEVATOR SYSTEMS

F.1.4.1   Major system organization issues
Planning for elevators in a building involves confronting some basic questions. First, how many elevators are required to accommodate occupant travel within the building? Second, what capacities and sizes should the elevator cars possess? Third, what floor areas and volumes are needed to provide adequate space for such components as hoistways and their enclosures, lobbies, and machine rooms? Fourth, where should these spaces be placed in a building?

Generally, there are two guiding forces that govern how these questions should be answered. One of the guiding forces concerns *time*-based operation requirements: building occupants commonly expect certain service qualities from elevator systems (i.e., qualities that are defined in terms of acceptable lengths of time for various aspects of the service). The second guiding force involves an industry standard that dictates how the hardware components of elevator assemblies should be organized, operated, and maintained.

A variety of temporal issues must be considered when designing elevator systems. For any elevator operation, numbers of individual events occur and determine how readily the elevator satisfies the need of occupants for time-efficient service. For instance, each step in the use of an elevator consumes time: an elevator arrives at a floor; the doors open; passengers disembark; new passengers board; the doors close; the car lifts or descends some distance; passengers get on or off; and so forth.

Three temporal properties are often cited as important performance measures: the time required for a round trip; the length of time, or interval, between an occupant pushing a call button and the moment when a car reaches the occupant's floor; and the ability of the elevator system in a building to transport some specific fraction of the total occupancy of the building over a particular length of time. One temporal guideline that is widely accepted for elevator operations suggests that the time for elevator car round trips — basically, up to the highest level requested by an entering passenger (or called by an occupant at some elevated floor) and down to the ground level — should be no longer than two to three minutes. Secondly, the time interval — between requesting an elevator car and its arrival — should be less than or equal to 30 seconds. And, thirdly, a principal operations goal for an elevator system is that about 12–15 percent of the total occupancy of a building should be able to use the system during any *five-minute-long* period. This third guideline proposes that such a number of occupants would be able to ascend to their workplaces at the beginning of the workday or to descend at the close of the business day, the two peak periods of daily elevator usage.

Consideration of these temporal parameters and related service issues — selecting car sizes and passenger capacities, numbers of floors served by a group of elevators, car speed — can be explored systematically using pencil-and-paper calculations that involve trial-and-error procedures. Generally, such calculations are most advantageously performed during later design phases after schematic designing. In subsection F.1.4.2 we will offer a series of guidelines and rules-of-thumb that can be used to generate approximate definitions of elevator system compositions for buildings. These pencil-and-paper calculations are described in textbooks by Strakosch and Stein and Reynolds.[8] Alternatively, a number of computer simulation programs are available for studying elevator behaviors and for making decisions about numbers, sizes, speeds, and so forth. Application of these computer programs is also best left to design phases after schematic designing.

The elevator industry standard that provides considerable detail about elevator hardware, both for its organization and operation, is the *Safety Code for Elevators and Escalators.* The opening paragraph of this standard states its scope: "This Code of safety standards covers the design, construction, operation, inspection, testing, maintenance, alteration, and repair of the following equipment, its associated parts, and its hoistways, where located in or adjacent to a building or structure…."[9] The "following equipment" are identified as hoisting and lowering mechanisms, including elevators and wheelchair and stairway chairlifts; power-driven stairways and walkways for carrying persons between landings, including escalators and moving walks; and hoisting and lowering mechanisms, including dumbwaiters and material lifts and dumbwaiters with automatic transfer devices.

Principal building codes[10] stipulate that *new* elevators, escalators, dumbwaiters, and moving walkways be designed and operated to conform to this standard and its supplements. For existing elevators and escalators the building codes refer instead to the document, *Safety Code for Existing Elevators and Escalators.*[11]

Either Safety Code provides considerable detail about the hardware components of elevator, escalator, and related systems. Its directives do not specifically furnish architectural design guidelines. Instead, the directives effectively define the hardware components in such manners that design guidelines may be inferred from the code.

F.1.4.2 Guidelines for designing for elevator systems

Establishing the number of elevators needed. Elevator industry officials suggest that when beginning planning for an elevator system in a building, the wise strategy is to start with a minimum of two cars. For example, the late W.S. Lewis, who was a leading engineer and stalwart for the industry, is reputed to have said, "Two elevators are a system, one is a toy."[12] The rationale for this recommendation is that elevators are required in buildings to satisfy at least four provisions: to furnish accessibility for mobility-challenged occupants and visitors; to serve in the event of a medical emergency (for instance, when someone needs to be removed from a building on an ambulance stretcher); to move occupants up and down a building efficiently and comfortably; and to satisfy freight handling needs (for materials, goods, equipment, furnishings, and so forth).

Note that when a building is served by a single elevator, any time that that elevator is out of service for maintenance or repair, the building will be inaccessible to wheelchair-bound occupants and visitors. Having two elevators makes it likely that one will be available when the other is undergoing maintenance. Further, if an elevator car is being held from general usage while transporting freight — loading several packages, a sofa, or a custodian's cart — then a second elevator car enables occupant service to continue. The availability of two elevator cars also offers significantly greater promise that the temporal requirements for an elevator system will be fulfilled.

Determination of the number of elevator cars in a system — beyond the suggested minimum of two — depends both on the number of occupants in a building and the floor area of the building. Other issues that can strongly influence decisions about the number of cars are the floor area of specific building stories and the overall height of a building. Strakosch suggests that, beyond the minimum of two cars, the number of cars in an elevator system for a multistory commercial building should be estimated from the rule-of-thumb requiring one car per 225 to 250 occupants.[13] A variant of this rule-of-thumb stipulates that the number of cars can be based on the guideline that one car should be provided for each 30,000 ft² (2788 m²) of occupied floor area in the building. This latter guideline is based on the premise that the occupant density of many commercial office buildings is approximately 120–130 ft² (11.2–12.1 m²) per occupant. Note that Strakosch states his rule-of-thumb loses accuracy when a commercial office building has more than 20 stories. In such instances round-trip times can become too long, necessitating either the provision of more cars than the rule-of-thumb suggests or the development of more than one zone of elevator service.

Strakosch also suggests that, separate from the determination of a sufficient number of passenger elevators for commercial office buildings, one service (freight) elevator should be furnished for every 300,000 ft² (27,880 m²) of occupied space.[14] Where buildings — whether commercial offices or otherwise (e.g., libraries, educational buildings, and so forth) — are considerably smaller than 300,000 ft² (27,880 m²), then one of the passenger

---

SIDEBAR F.1 Service zones

A common practice in organizing elevator systems for tall buildings is to limit the number of floors that each elevator car serves (i.e., instead of having each car serve all floors in the building). Thus, one car, or more likely a group of cars, will serve no more than perhaps 20 or so stories. Such an increment is regarded as a single zone. Typically, these single-zone cars will end their vertical ascent at a sky lobby. At the sky lobby passengers seeking yet higher floors can transfer to cars that begin their ascent from the sky lobby and traverse a higher zone.

A principal reason for employing this organizational strategy is to control the length of travel time that passengers experience. A second important reason is that the number of hoistways can be limited, thereby reducing the amount of floor area required for elevator cars (as will be further discussed in subsection F.1.4.2).

elevators should be selected to enable the lifting of freight. Note, however, that if an elevator car is needed to transport potentially large loads (such as in a museum), then an elevator car should be principally devoted for this freight service.

One further method for preparing a quick, rough estimate of the number of elevators required to serve a building applies a correlation of the number of elevators to the number of floors in the building. This correlation has been derived from examining a sample of existing buildings and has been synthesized from data collected and published by Guise.[15]

What Table F.3 suggests is that the number of elevator cars needed to provide adequate vertical transportation in a building is dependent on the overall floor area of the building. The two parameters determining the total floor area of a building are the number of stories in the building and the floor area for each story in the building. Further, in many commercial high-rise buildings the occupant density for the whole building will be established in keeping with a ratio of the floor area required for each occupant (as in the number of square feet or square meters per occupant). Generally, as the number of occupants in a building increase, then the number of elevators required to service these occupants also increases.

Another important distinction—particularly for buildings more than about 40 stories high—is that the total number of hoistways that run upwards through a building may be less than the number of elevator cars. In taller buildings many cars in hoistways may run up only part way to the roof and end at some intermediate height, usually at a sky lobby. Then, another car in that hoistway will run from the sky lobby to the top of the building. In this manner the total number of hoistways can be as few as half or one-third of the number of elevator cars employed throughout the building. This placement of more than one car in a hoistway will be discussed further at the end of this section.

A third method that is being applied in very tall buildings—those of 80 stories and higher—to reduce the number of cars needed to provide vertical transportation for the building occupants is to use *double-deck car platforms* in traction elevator hoistways. These double-deck platforms have two cars stacked one on top of the other. Thus, with each stop as the double-deck car moves up and down the hoistway, two floors can be

TABLE F.3
ESTIMATING THE NUMBER OF TRACTION ELEVATOR CARS NEEDED
FOR SERVING HIGH-RISE COMMERCIAL OFFICE BUILDINGS

BUILDING HEIGHT, IN NUMBER OF STORIES	APPROXIMATE AREA PER STORY THROUGHOUT THE BUILDING, FT² (M²)	ESTIMATED NUMBER OF PASSENGER ELEVATOR CARS REQUIRED PER BUILDING STORY
Up to 10 stories	5000–10,000 (465–929)	0.16 to 0.25
Up to 20 stories	About 5000 (465)	0.16 to 0.20
Up to 20 stories	10,000–20,000 (929–1859)	0.33
Up to 40 stories	20,000–25,000 (1859–2323)	0.50
Up to 60 stories	To 40,000 (3717)	0.83

served simultaneously. Commonly, one deck will only serve odd-numbered floors, and the other deck will serve even-numbered floors. For example, the bottom car platform would serve odd-numbered floors, and the top platform would serve even-numbered floors. Escalators are provided at main floor lobbies and at sky lobbies to enable passengers to move to the platform for alternate-numbered floors. Therefore, to travel from the 67th floor to the 24th floor in an 80-story building, a passenger would likely descend to the 41st story (which would be the top floor of a two-story sky lobby placed at the 41st and 40th floors). Then, the passenger would take an escalator to the 40th floor and descend to the 24th floor in an elevator car that serves even-numbered floors.

The principal reasons for applying double-deck car platforms involve both space and time. First, using double-decked platforms in hoistways requires less building floor area be made available for a sufficient number of elevator hoistways. Thus, with smaller elevator cores more lease-able area is made available for occupancy. Secondly, with double-decked platforms, the cars only have to stop half as often as they move vertically (in comparison to single-decked cars). As a result, both round-trip times and waiting intervals are reduced, improving occupant satisfaction with trips requiring moving many stories.

An early use of these double-deck car platforms for very tall buildings occurred in the Sears Tower in Chicago. A number of very tall buildings that employ this technique have since been constructed in Asia (e.g., the Petronas Towers in Kuala Lumpur).[16]

Sizing elevator cars. Elevator cars should be sized, at the minimum, to accommodate the lifting of wheelchair-bound passengers. The minimum car size to accommodate an occupied wheelchair is 68 in (1727 mm) wide by 54 in (1372 mm) back wall-to-door (with the added requirement that the back wall-to-front operation panel should be 51 in (1295 mm).[17] When a building is limited to one (or two) elevator(s), then all cars should be sized to satisfy this accessibility need.

In buildings with four or more stories, at least one elevator car should be large enough to enable the vertical transporting of an ambulance stretcher. The internal car dimensions to fulfill this requirement are a width of 80 in (2032 mm) by a depth of 54 in (1372 mm) and a distance from the back wall to the operation panel of 51 in (1295 mm). The minimum doorway width should be 42 in (1066 mm). These car dimensions will allow bringing into the car an ambulance stretcher set horizontally with the dimensions of 76 in (1930 mm) in length by 24 in (610 mm) in width.[18] Generally, elevator cars that have these interior dimensions will have a minimum loading capacity of 3500 lbs (1588 kg). Cars with smaller load capacities—2000–3000 lbs (907–1361 kg)—will otherwise have too small interior dimensions.

To consider the similarity of the sizes for cars and their hoistways for hydraulic, geared traction, and gearless traction elevators, see Tables F.4–F.6 below. The dimensions of the cars, hoistways, machine room height minima (specifically for traction elevators), and pit depths have been assembled from Web-published manufacturers' product literatures. What is apparent from these comparisons is that car sizes—when the loading capacity has been held constant (here we chose 3500 lbs [1588 kg])—are virtually identical when viewed for the various types of elevators and for the alternative manufacturers. The ready explanation for this uniformity of car sizing is that all the manufacturers have sought to closely comply with building codes.

Sizing hoistways. Similarly, when the hoistway dimensions are compared for a given elevator type—holed hydraulic, geared traction, or gearless traction—the differences between various manufacturers' products are minimal. Instead, the major difference in hoistway dimensions exists when the two types of elevators—hydraulic and traction—are contrasted. This difference is exhibited in the depths of the respective hoistways:

TABLE F.4
TYPICAL HOLED HYDRAULIC ELEVATOR DIMENSIONS (FOR A 3500 LB [1588 KG] CAPACITY CAR)
(ALL FOR CARS WITH FRONT-OPENING DOORS)

MANUFACTURER	OTIS	THYSSENKRUPP	KONE
MODEL	3500 LB	SEVILLE 3500 OILDRAULIC	MX 3500 (1588 KG)
Maximum rise	60' (18.3 m)	60' (18.3 m)	45' (13.7 m)
Maximum stops	7	Data not furnished	6
Speed range	100–150 ft/min (0.50–0.76 m/s)	80–125 ft/min (0.41–0.64 m/s)	80–150 ft/min (0.41–0.76 m/s)
Hoistway width	8'-4" (2.54 m)	8'-4" (2.54 m)	8'-4" (2.54 m)
Hoistway depth	6'-11" (2.11 m)	6'-11" (2.11 m)	6'-11" (2.11 m)
Car height	8'-0" (2.44 m)	7'-11" (2.41 m)	8'-0" (2.44 m)
Car width	6'-8" (2.03 m)	6'-8" (2.03 m)	7'-0" (2.13 m)
Car depth	5'-5" (1.65 m)	5'-5" (1.65 m)	5'-5" (1.65 m)
Car door width	3'-6" (1.07 m)	3'-6" (1.07 m)	3'-6" (1.07 m)
Car door opening (clear)	7'-0" (2.13 m)	7'-0" (2.13 m)	7'-0" (2.13 m)
Passenger capacity	23 (in USA)	Data not furnished	Data not furnished
Minimum pit depth	4'-0" (1.22 m)	4'-0" (1.22 m)	4'-0" (1.22 m)
Height of highest floor elevation to top of hoistway (clear overhead)	12'-3" (3.73 m)	12'-0" to 12'-3" (3.66 to 3.73 m)	12'-0" to 12'-4" (3.66 to 3.76 m)

Web addresses for data acquisition:

Otis: http://www.otis.com/products/detail/0,1355,CLi1_PRD245_PRT30_PST46_RES1,00.html

ThyssenKrupp: http://www.thyssenkruppelevator.com/oildraulicmain.asp

KONE: http://www.kone.com/static/Imagebank/GetFile_pdf/0,,fileID=60263,00.pdf

TABLE F.5

TYPICAL GEARED TRACTION ELEVATOR DIMENSIONS (FOR A 3500 LB [1588 KG] CAPACITY CAR)

(ALL FOR CARS WITH FRONT-OPENING DOORS)

MANUFACTURER	OTIS	THYSSENKRUPP	SCHINDLER
MODEL	GEARED ELEVONIC 3500 LBS	SPF 35 (3500 LBS)	MICONIX TX 3500 LBS
Maximum rise	300 ft (91 m)	Data not furnished	Data not furnished
Maximum stops	Data not furnished	27	Data not furnished
Speed range	350–500 ft/min (1.78–2.54 m/s)	200–500 ft/min (1.01–2.54 m/s)	350–500 ft/min (1.78–2.54 m/s)
Hoistway depth	7'-10" (2.39 m)	7'-10 3/4" (2.41 m)	7'-9 1/2" (2.37 m)
Hoistway width (one car)	8'-4" (2.54 m)	8'-4" (2.54 m)	8'-4" (2.54 m)
(two cars)	17'-0" (5.18 m)	17'-0" to 18'-8" (5.18 to 5.69 m)	Data not furnished
(three cars)	25'-8" (7.82 m)	Data not furnished	Data not furnished
Car height	8'-0" (2.44 m)	7'-11" (2.41 m)	8'-0" (2.44 m)
Car width	6'-8" (2.03 m)	6'-8" (2.03 m)	6'-8" (2.03 m)
Car depth	5'-5" (1.65 m)	5'-5 1/2" (1.66 m)	5'-5" (1.65 m)
Car door width	3'-6" (1.07 m)	3'-6" (1.07 m)	3'-6" (1.07 m)
Car door opening (clear)	7'-0" (2.13 m)	7'-0" (2.13 m)	7'-0" (2.13 m)
Passenger capacity	23**	Data not furnished	Data not furnished
Minimum pit depth*	5'-2" to 6'-4" (1.57 to 1.93 m)**	5'-0" to 6'-6" (1.52 to 1.98 m)	5'-0" to 5'-10" (1.52 to 1.78 m)
Height of highest floor elevation to top of hoistway (clear overhead)*	16'-5" to 19'-1" (5.00 to 5.81)	15'-4" to 17'-6" (4.67 to 5.33 m)	15'-4" to 16'-0" (4.67 to 4.87 m)
Minimum machine room height	7'-6" (2.29 m)	7'-6" (2.29 m)	Data not furnished

Notes: * magnitude depends on the speed of the car
　　　** in the U.S.A.

Web addresses for data acquisition:
　Otis: http://www.otis.com/products/dimensions/0,1356,CLI1_PRD738_PRT30_PST47_RES1,00.html
　ThyssenKrupp: http://www.thyssenkruppelevator.com/tractionmain.asp
　Schindler: http://www.us.schindler.com/SEC/webscan.nsf/pages/elev-apptables-TractionGP-01

TABLE F.6
TYPICAL GEARLESS TRACTION ELEVATOR DIMENSIONS (FOR A 3500 LB [1588 KG] CAPACITY CAR)
(ALL FOR CARS WITH FRONT-OPENING DOORS)

MANUFACTURER	OTIS	OTIS	THYSSENKRUPP	SCHINDLER
MODEL	ELEVONIC 3500 LBS	ELEVONIC 3500 LBS		MICONIX TX 3500 LBS
Maximum rise	300 ft (91 m)	420 ft (128 m)	Data not furnished	Data not furnished
Maximum stops	36	50	27	Data not furnished
Speed range	500 ft/min (2.54 m/s)	700 ft/min (3.56 m/s)	250–500 ft/min (1.01–2.54 m/s)	350–500 ft/min (1.78–2.54 m/s)
Hoistway depth	7'-10" (2.39 m)	7'-10" (2.39 m)	7'-10 3/4" (2.41 m)	7'-9 1/2" (2.37 m)
Hoistway width (one car)	8'-4" (2.54 m)	8'-4" (2.54 m)	8'-4" (2.54 m)	8'-4" (2.54 m)
(two cars)	17'-0" (5.18 m)	17'-0" (5.18 m)	17'-0" to 18'-8" (5.18 to 5.69 m)	Data not furnished
(three cars)	25'-8" (7.82 m)	25'-8" (7.82 m)	Data not furnished	Data not furnished
Car height	8'-0" (2.44 m)	8'-0" (2.44 m)	7'-11" (2.41 m)	8'-0" (2.44 m)
Car width	6'-8" (2.03 m)	6'-8" (2.03 m)	6'-8" (2.03 m)	6'-8" (2.03 m)
Car depth	5'-5" (1.65 m)	5'-5" (1.65 m)	5'-5 1/2" (1.66 m)	5'-5" (1.65 m)
Car door width	3'-6" (1.07 m)	3'-6" (1.07 m)	3'-6" (1.07 m)	3'-6" (1.07 m)
Car door opening (clear)	7'-0" (2.13 m)	7'-0" (2.13 m)	7'-0" (2.13 m)	7'-0" (2.13 m)
Passenger capacity	23 (in USA)	23 (in USA)	Data not furnished	Data not furnished
Minimum pit depth*	6'-5" (1.96 m)	9'-8" (2.95 m)	5'-0" to 6'6" (1.52 to 1.98 m)	5'-0" to 6'-6" (1.52 to 1.98 m)
Height of highest floor elevation to top of hoistway (clear overhead)*	18'-11" (5.76 m)	24'-9" (7.54 m)	15'-4" to 17'-6" (4.67 to 5.33 m)	15'-4" to 16'-0" (4.67 to 4.87 m)
Minimum machine room height	7'-6" (2.29 m)	7'-6" (2.29 m)	7'-6" (2.29 m)	Data not furnished

Notes: For the Otis Elevonic Class, elevators are available with speeds of 800–1200 ft/min (4.07–6.10 m/s), 60–87 stops, and maximum rises of 500–720 ft (152–220 m).

Web addresses for data acquisition:
   Otis: http://www.otis.com/file/display/0,1394,6482,00.pdf
   ThyssenKrupp: http://www.thyssenkruppelevator.com/tractionmain.asp
   Schindler: http://www.us.schindler.com/SEC/websecen.nsf/files/cat9-BRS-1034_MTX.pdf/Sfile/BRS-1034_MTX.pdf

traction elevators require a depth that is greater by approximately 12 in (305 mm). This greater depth is made necessary by the presence of the counterweight assembly. The counterweight assembly for traction elevators *with front-opening doors* will conventionally be located behind the car (between the back of the car and the hoistway wall). Note that when a traction elevator car with both front- and back-opening doors is employed, then the counterweight assembly must be located along one side of the car. For traction elevator cars with front- and back-opening doors, the depth of the hoistway can be made similar to what is required for a hydraulic elevator. But the width of the hoistway will have to be increased to make space for the counterweight assembly.

Differences in performance capabilities are present between hydraulic, geared traction, and gearless traction elevators. The gearless traction elevator offers the highest rise capability, the greatest number of stops permissible, and the most rapid movement. Rise potentials as great as 720 ft (220 m) are readily available, and speeds as fast as 1200 ft/min (6.1 m/s) can commonly be obtained (although, in particular situations, speeds as great as 2000 ft/min [10.2 m/s] have been applied). Geared traction cars usually have a service height limit of 300 ft (91 m) and display speeds no greater than 500 ft/min (2.54 m/s). The number of floors that can be served by a geared traction elevator is normally less than 30. Alternatively, for hydraulic elevators, rise distances seldom exceed 60 ft (18.3 m), and car speeds of 150 ft/min (0.76 m/s) are the maximum.

This range of speeds amongst the various traction elevators leads to different needs for the depth of the pit and the height of the hoistway above the highest floor that is serviced by a traction elevator car. As the car speed increases, so, too, do the needs for greater pit depth and increased hoistway heights above the car travel termination. For example, for the faster elevator cars, the hoistway extensions require nearly two full-story heights above the top of the car. Thus, a hidden cost for elevators displaying faster speeds will be the need for more building height to enclose the hoistways (and the machine room above the hoistways).

Sizing lobbies (in relation to cars and hoistways). Designing elevator systems in buildings requires space accommodation for the elevator cars, the hoistway enclosures that surround the cars, and the lobbies that passengers occupy while waiting for or exiting from an elevator car (see Figure F.9). We have already offered design guidelines for sizing cars and hoistways. Here we will offer suggestions for lobby sizing, relying on suggestions offered by two elevator industry authorities.

First, Strakosch recommends that, for side-by-side elevators, lobbies present on upper floors — above ground-level building entries — should have a free distance away from the elevator that is similar to the depth of the elevator car. For example, for an elevator car that has a lifting capacity of 3500 lbs (1588 kg), its depth — the distance from the back wall to the elevator car doors — will routinely be 65 in (1650 mm) (for verification of this depth, see Tables F.4–F.6). Thus, the free distance outward from the lobby wall of the hoistway should at least match this 65 in (1650 mm) dimension. Strakosch further offers that when elevator cars are placed facing each other, then the preferred free distance between lobby walls of the hoistways should be 1.5 to 2 times the depth of the elevator cars. For cars with the lifting capacity of 3500 lbs (1588 kg) and a depth of 65 in (1650 mm), then the free distance between the opposite hoistway walls should be at least 98 in (2480 mm) to 130 in (3300 mm).[19]

Figure F.9 The lobby for three side-by-side traction elevators.

TABLE F.7
RECOMMENDED FLOOR AREAS FOR LOBBIES, CAR EQUIPMENT, AND HOISTWAY ENCLOSURES FOR A TRACTION ELEVATOR (FOR EACH FLOOR LEVEL SERVED)

CAR LIFT CAPACITIES AND NUMBERS	FLOOR AREA FOR EACH LEVEL SERVED	LIFT LOBBY	CAR, GUIDE RAILS, & COUNTERWEIGHT	THE ENCLOSURE SURROUNDING THE HOISTWAY
One 1000 kg (2200 lbs) car	13.5 m² (145 ft²)	44%	41%	15%
1600 kg (3500 lbs) cars (8 total) arranged with 4 cars facing 4 cars	86 m² (925 ft²)	34%	54%	12%
1600 kg (3500 lbs) cars (8 total) arranged 8 in a row	64 m² (689 ft²)	47%	40%	13%

An alternative set of guidelines for lobby dimensions has been set forth by Howkins.[20] Table F.7 summarizes the series of data presented by this industry engineer for conventional high-rise commercial office buildings.

Table F.7 suggests—for example—that for a single 1000 kg (2200 lbs) car, the total floor area required for the car and counterweight assembly and their pairs of guide rails, the hoistway enclosure, and the requisite lobby is typically about 13.5 m² (145 ft²). Of this total area, 56 percent (or 7.6 m² [81 ft²]) is needed for the hoistway and car equipment. The remaining 44 percent (or 5.9 m² [64 ft²]) will be an appropriate floor area for the lobby space in front of the hoistway enclosure.

Note also from this table that the floor area required for a car, counterweight assembly, and their guide rails, the hoistway enclosure, and the associated lobby, *on a car-by-car basis,* decreases from 13.5 m² (145 ft²) per car to 10.8 m² (116 ft²) per car to 8.0 m² (86 ft²) per car, as one progresses from consideration of a single traction elevator to these two eight-car arrangements. From this comparison of the three alternative arrangements the placement of eight elevators in a single row is most space-efficient. But whether any eight-elevator row would be most effective for passenger transportation throughout a building could likely depend on other issues (e.g., how the elevators should best be grouped, how such a row might affect lobby space utilization, and so forth).

One further concern about lobby planning involves providing wall and door assemblies that separate any elevator lobby area and the remainder of the building, such as corridors, other means of egress, and office areas. A number of standards and codes stipulate that these wall and door assemblies should present at least a one-hour fire resistance. Further, the walls should run from the structural floor assembly to the bottom of the structural ceiling or roof assembly above.[21]

An additional, quite approximate set of estimates suggests the area per building story required to place necessary hoistways and lobbies for elevator service for high-rise commercial buildings (see Table F.8). This set has been developed from observation of numbers of buildings. These estimates are intended mostly as quick-and-dirty indications of how much floor area per story should be provided early during plan layouts to ensure that adequate space is made available for the hoistways and lobbies (that can then be more specifically defined later in the design process).

Locating elevators in buildings. In many buildings, elevators will be incorporated into a service core. The conventional service core will be composed of HVAC, electrical, and plumbing systems equipment and toilet rooms, fire stairs, and elevator hoistways and lobbies. Such service cores will generally comprise between 20 to 25 percent of the overall floor area of each floor. Placement of these cores—on a story-by-story basis up and down through the building—most often will be set at the center of the floor plan. Another

TABLE F.8
RECOMMENDED AREAS PER FLOOR FOR HOISTWAYS AND LOBBIES FOR BUILDINGS OF VARIOUS HEIGHTS

BUILDING HEIGHT	10–20 STORIES	40–60 STORIES	100 STORIES
Fraction of floor area for hoistways & lobbies	3 to 6%	12 to 15%	20%[22]

location includes placing the core in an off-center position, perhaps along a long side of the building perimeter. A third strategy is to divide the service core into two distinct areas and to place each of these two halves at opposite ends of a rectangular floor plan. For this third strategy the rectangular footprint of the building may have a length-to-width ratio as large as 3:1 or 4:1. Using a central core for a building with this type of footprint could mean relying on extensive horizontal ductwork (with concomitantly deep ducting), on occupied building stories. Also, occupants may have to walk too far to gain access to elevator service. Both to reduce the need to run large ducting and to make gaining access to elevators easier, setting up service cores at the two ends of buildings with long rectangular footprints can enhance system services.

Wherever elevators are placed in a building, it is desirable to minimize the distance that a person must traverse from any building entrance to the elevator(s). Distances should perhaps be in the range of 50–100 ft (15–30 m) from a building entrance to the appropriate elevator. In buildings with perhaps as many as three or four elevators servicing a specific elevation zone (e.g., floors 25–38 in a 50-story building), all the elevators servicing such a zone should be grouped. Grouping elevators — whether by laying them out in a single row or immediately across from one another — assures that passengers will have a ready opportunity to gain access to the next available car. Additionally, by enabling the prospective passenger easy access to that car, the process of loading the elevator car is hastened making for a more time-efficient round trip.

Laying out multiple elevators. When more than one elevator will be used in a building, the elevators should be arranged side-by-side, rather than across from each other. However, when six or eight or more elevators are required to provide lifting service, then the elevators should be arranged in groups of three or four with such groups paired and facing each other (see Figure F.10). When more than about eight elevators are employed, multiple groupings will be needed with groups of three or four elevators facing each other, and then such pairs of groups will be replicated back-to-back as often as needed to provide the total number required. For example, in a building requiring sixteen elevators, four groups of four elevators can be employed. Each group might have four elevators arranged side-by-side. The first two four-car groups would face each other. The second and third groups would be placed back-to-back. The fourth group would then face the third group.

Arranging two or more elevator cars in a side-by-side fashion allows the cars to have adjacent hoistways that are not separated. Such possible interconnections of hoistways are specifically addressed in many industry standards and building codes.[23] A first directive stipulates that up to three cars can share the same hoistway enclosure. If four cars will be used and arranged side-by-side in one grouping, then the four must be divided so that there are two separate, enclosed hoistways. This separation of the hoistways is mandated to provide an alternative hoistway enclosure in the event that one fills with fire and/or smoke, rendering it unusable. If more than four cars are to be used in a building, then up to four cars can be located in a single interconnected hoistway enclosure (because the remaining elevator cars would be placed in a separate hoistway enclosure). So, if eight cars are to be used in a building, then they could be arranged in groups of four each in two separate hoistway enclosures, presumably with the two groups opposite and facing each other. One other layout guideline becomes relevant when planning elevator organization for a very tall building (e.g., perhaps for more than 40 stories). In such an instance, elevator service should be divided into modules (or zones), with the first module providing vertical transportation for building occupants as high as the first one-third or one-half of the building, a second module lifting occupants to the second one-third or the second one-half, and a third module used if the first two offered transportation for just two-thirds of the building height.

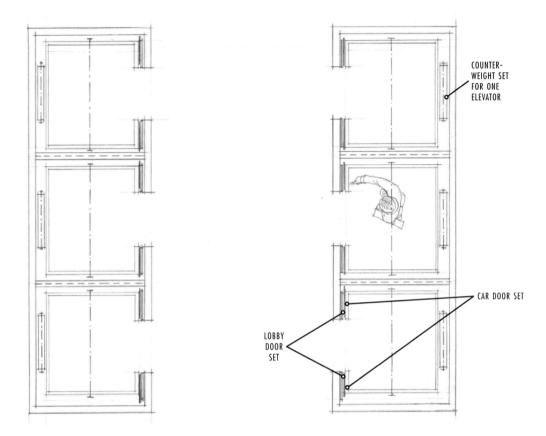

Figure F.10 Six traction elevators arranged in a three-by-three grouping (as might be found in a high-rise office building) are shown here. Note the presence of a counterweight assembly behind each car. This illustration has been drawn to scale to demonstrate the relative depths of the hoistways, cars, and lobby that are appropriate for elevator layouts. This drawing has previously been published in a technical data brochure for the Elevonic 411/4050 elevator by the Otis Elevator Company, © 1990. "Elevonic" is a registered trademark of the Otis Elevator Company. Permission to reprint this drawing has been granted by the Otis Elevator Company.

Vertical transportation in these very tall buildings usually will involve elevator shuttles—basically, expresses—that run from the bottom of a module to its top without stopping at any intermediate floors. The top floor of each module will function as a sky lobby at which occupants can transfer to the next elevator shuttle if they are ascending to the top of this module. In addition to the various express shuttles that pass from the bottom to the top of each module, there will be a series of elevators that serve the intermediate floors of the module, commencing at a sky lobby. These local elevators will provide transportation for increments of about 15 to 20 stories.

Finally, two principal arguments justify this modular organization with the combination of express shuttles, local short-rise elevators, and the various sky lobbies. First, employing a mixture of shuttle and local service elevators is the most time-efficient means for lifting the building occupant population. And, second and more important from a building layout standpoint, the application of planning modules—each with its assortment of local elevators — enables the various local elevator hoistways for an upper module to be stacked on top of a local elevator hoistway from the next lower module. Thus, the amount of building floor area devoted to elevator hoistways is moderated.[24]

Locating and sizing machine rooms. Generally, machine rooms for hydraulic elevators are placed near or at about the same level as the bottom of the hoistway and next to the pit. Alternatively, the most often used placement for machine rooms for traction elevators is immediately above the hoistways. On some occasions, however, the machine room for traction elevators can be placed at levels below the top of the hoistways.

The machine room for a hydraulic elevator will mainly contain a hydraulic liquid tank in which a pump, its motor, a valve assembly, and the oil will be housed. Piping from the hydraulic liquid tank to the elevator plunger will also be present. The floor area for a machine room for a hydraulic elevator should be perhaps 50 percent larger than the hoistway dimensions (width and depth) for the elevator served by this machine room. Extra space beyond what is needed for the hydraulic liquid tank and piping will be beneficial when maintenance and repair of the pump and motor are required. The minimum height for such machine rooms should be 90 in (2290 mm).

Machine rooms for traction elevators will provide space for the lifting motor, gear assemblies (where used for geared elevators), sheaves, brakes, and control panels. In

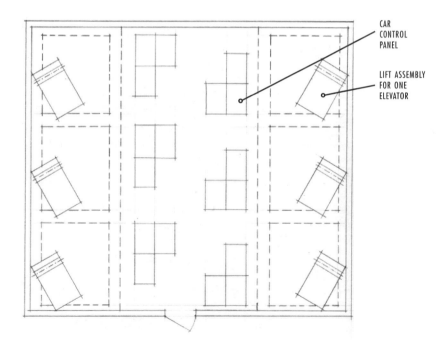

Figure F.11 A typical layout for the machine room for six traction elevators. Each elevator requires a lift assembly and a car controller, and the six elevators will need a group controller. This drawing has been drawn to a scale to show the relationships of the individual elements to each other. This drawing has previously been published in a technical data brochure for the Elevonic 411/4050 elevator by the Otis Elevator Company, © 1990. "Elevonic" is a registered trademark of the Otis Elevator Company. Permission to reprint this drawing has been granted by the Otis Elevator Company.

machine rooms located above one (or more) hoistway(s), the lifting motor, gear assembly (where used), sheaves, and brake for each traction elevator will be placed over the hoistway served by this equipment. Thus, the floor area required for the lift equipment—the motor, gearing (when used), sheaves, and brake—will closely match the hoistway width and depth. Similarly, where two or more hoistways are placed side-by-side in one extended hoistway enclosure, then the lift equipment for each car in the hoistway enclosure would be placed above the hoistway for the car and side-by-side with the other lift equipment machinery (see Figure F.11). The total floor area to accommodate the lift equipment sets for two or more traction elevator cars would match the total width and depth needed for the adjacent hoistways.

Floor area in machine rooms for traction elevators must also be made available for the car and group controllers. Each car will have its own car controller, and the group will have a single group controller. The extra floor area needed for these individual car controllers and a group controller should approximately match the floor area required for the lift equipment sets. Indeed, one way to establish first-approximation machine room dimensions is to employ the width of the multiple hoistways and to double the depth of the hoistway. When groups of hoistways are employed—for example, when perhaps four groups of four adjacent hoistways are to be used—then the floor area for the machine room for such a group should be similar to the total areas for the hoistways and the lobbies on the floors below the machine room.

The minimum height for a machine room for traction elevators should be 90 in (2290 mm).

Section F.2 | CREATING BUILDING SPACES FOR ESCALATORS

Escalators are inclined moving staircases that can transport occupants from one floor to the next, either upward or downward. Transportation by escalators occurs by the movement of steps that typically operate continuously during the hours of building occupancy. Note that the steps of an escalator move at a constant speed: there is no acceleration or deceleration in the motion of these steps as there is with elevator cars. Escalators are mostly deployed in pairs with one unit furnished to move people upward from one floor to the next higher floor and a second unit to transport people downward from the higher floor to the next lower floor.

Escalators offer a series of benefits for the building owner and occupants. First, because of the continuous operation of the steps, an escalator can transport many more people during a given period than can an elevator. Second, the use of an escalator involves no waiting interval such is often experienced while an occupant waits for an elevator car to arrive at the occupant's floor. And, third, because the escalator is basically open, allowing its passengers to see where they are being transported, the escalator can be used as a device to communicate—to highlight—what is present at the floor being reached (by carefully displaying goods in the view field of the arriving passenger).

When building occupants have the choice of whether to employ an elevator or an escalator to move vertically through a building, the decision-making will often involve the number of floors that the occupant wishes to move. Observations by vertical transportation engineers show that when occupants indeed have the choice of using an elevator or an escalator and these occupants wish to vertically move a small number of floors, the occupants are more likely to select movement by escalator. Alternatively, when the occupants wish to

TABLE F.9
OCCUPANTS' PREFERENCES FOR VERTICAL MOVEMENT BY ELEVATOR OR ESCALATOR
(WHEN BOTH MEANS ARE AVAILABLE)[25]

FLOORS TO BE TRAVELED	CHOICE OF ESCALATOR	CHOICE OF ELEVATOR
1	90%	10%
2	75%	25%
3	50%	50%
4	25%	75%
5	10%	90%

This table has previously been published in a chapter by Turner, D.L., "Escalators and moving walks," in the book by Strakosch, G.R. (ed.), *The Vertical Transportation Handbook,* (New York: J, Wiley & Sons, Inc., 1998), page 243. Permission to reproduce this table has been granted by Mr. Turner and John Wiley & Sons, Inc.

move four or more floors, then they are more likely to choose to travel by elevator. These observations have been summarized in Table F.9.

However, just as escalators offer benefits to their passengers, escalators also bear liabilities in comparison to travel by elevator. Once an elevator car has been accessed, travel between floors can occur much more rapidly. Travel by elevator up or down a medium- or high-rise building is much more practical than by escalator: seldom will combinations of escalators be deployed higher than six or eight stories above ground and, where six or eight stories of escalators do exist, travel from the top of the building to the ground or from the ground to the top by escalator will require substantially more time than by elevator. Third, elevator assemblies occupy less space on a floor-by-floor basis than do escalators. Fourth, elevators enable movement up or down through buildings by wheelchair-bound occupants. Fifth, in an emergency, moving a person by horizontal stretcher is considerably easier by elevator than by escalator. And, sixth, elevators are far more efficient for the movement of freight.

The Elevator Escalator Safety Foundation reports that there are 30,000 escalators in current use in the United States (in contrast to 600,000 elevators.[26] The most common applications for escalators are in commercial, transportation, recreational, and entertainment buildings. Widespread examples of uses of escalators include in department stores and shopping malls, for subway and elevated train stations, airports, and bus terminals, and in sports arenas, auditoriums, and convention centers.

The history of escalator invention, development, and first installations commenced in the 1890s, although an earlier "revolving stair" unit was proposed and patented in the United States in 1859. This earlier unit and its patent—obtained by Nathan Ames—largely passed into a technological dead-end because electricity to power the assembly was unavailable: distribution systems for electrical energy were not developed until the 1880s. Additionally, the "revolving stair" assembly was unsatisfactory because of the difficulty of people mounting and getting off the revolving stair units.

The commercial development and installation of escalators began with a series of inventions and refinements that were proposed in the 1890s in the United States and the United Kingdom.[27] The principal inventors were Jesse Reno, Charles Seeburger, and George Wheeler, all of whom were instrumental in creating continuously lifting stairways and human conveyance systems. These inventors continued through the next decade with the further development of the escalator concept and the hardware systems that were derived from the concept. In the late 1890s the Otis Elevator Company acquired parts of the basic patents held by Wheeler and Seeburger and began commercial production of escalators. These Otis escalators were initially installed in New York and Philadelphia department stores. At about the same time Reno was building and installing escalators in New York and London, both for other department stores and for the London Underground (subway) system. In 1911, the Otis Elevator Company acquired the Reno patents, consolidating its leadership in the development and marketing of escalators. Over the past 90 years other manufacturers have entered the escalator manufacturing industry so that now there are perhaps 10 to 20 major escalator manufacturers worldwide.

F.2.1   PRINCIPAL COMPONENTS OF AN ESCALATOR UNIT

Any escalator consists of an open — visible to its passengers — portion of the unit, and a closed (or hidden) portion that resides below the open, visible components (see Figure F.12). The open, visible components include the moving stairs, the landings at the two ends of the moving stairway, the balustrades, and the moving handrails. The hidden parts consist of a supporting truss, the drive assembly, and the drive chain.

A steel truss carries the entire load — both the deadweight and passengers — of an escalator unit. The truss is typically supported at top and bottom load points, although for long spans the truss may also have a mid-span load point. Conventionally, the truss will be enclosed within the hidden (or lower) portion of the escalator unit. Extension posts will project upward from the top chord of the truss furnishing support for the upper track for the handrail.

The main drive motor usually resides at the higher end of the hidden portion of the escalator (see Figure F.13). This drive motor is connected to a drive shaft that turns a drive chain. Sprockets on the drive chain are attached to individual steps on the moving stairway. Thus, as the drive shaft turns the drive chain, the steps move. The drive chain runs on steel tracks and is uniformly supported by these tracks. Tension on the drive chain is maintained as the chain wraps around a carriage wheel that is present at the lower end of hidden portion of the escalator. Commonly, the upper end of this hidden portion is identified as the machine room for the escalator, whereas the lower end is the pit. The drive chain runs parallel to the truss and is fully encased within the hidden portion. Note that this combination of drive shaft, drive chain, and tensioning arrangement is analogous to the operation of a bicycle propulsion system. Also, in the vicinity of the drive shaft and functioning as part of the drive apparatus, an emergency brake assembly is present.

The moving steps are located between balustrades placed on both sides of the upper (visible) part of the escalator unit (see Figure F.14). These steps are typically composed of parallel and slotted aluminum cleats, organized in a comb-like fashion. The widths of these steps have been standardized across the escalator industry and may either be 24 in (600 mm), 32 in (800 mm), or 40 in (1000 mm). The depths of the steps shall be not less than 15 3/4 in (400 mm), and the risers will be not more than 8 1/8 in (216 mm).[28]

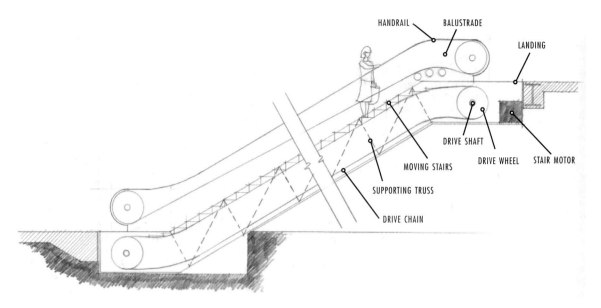

Figure F.12 The visible and hidden components of a conventional escalator assembly appear here. The moving stairs, landings, balustrades, and handrails are essential parts of the visible portion of the escalator assembly. The supporting truss, stair motor, drive shaft and wheel, and drive chain are present in the hidden portion.

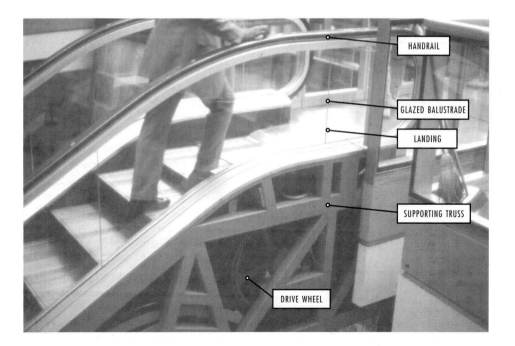

Figure F.13 At the top end of an escalator a number of important components are visible. The supporting truss and the drive shaft and wheel are underneath the moving stairs. The top landing, the glazed balustrades, and the handrails are also evident.

Figure F.14 The upper landings for a series of escalators appear here. These escalators are present in an airport concourse and lead downward to the set of horizontal people movers that are shown in Figure F.18.

The balustrades on either side of the moving stairs are low-rise walls that bound the stairway. These walls are approximately 39 in (990 mm) high at the two ends of the stairway. The balustrades must be totally closed and may be composed of opaque or transparent materials.[29] A handrail runs on a track placed on the top of each balustrade, moving at a speed that matches the stairway. The handrail should have a minimum width of 4 in (102 mm) and is typically composed of synthetic rubber that is reinforced.

The landings — or entrance and exit — for an escalator should have at least two and not more than four flat steps. A flat step is defined as 30 in (760 mm) in length, essentially matching the stride length of an adult male. A second requirement for these entrances and exits is that they must be at least as long as two times the distance between the centerlines of the handrails. The widths of the entrances and exits must be not less than the distance between the centerlines of the handrails plus 8 in (203 mm).[30]

F.2.2   GUIDELINES FOR DESIGNING FOR ESCALATORS

Estimating how many escalators may be needed. The speed and width of the unit and some likely personal idiosyncrasies of the passengers determine the capacity of an escalator. A *nominal* capacity can readily be estimated by considering the speed and width of the escalator unit. In the United States the speed of escalators is widely set at 100 ft/min (0.51 m/s), although industry standards suggest that speeds can vary between 90–125 ft/min (0.46–0.64 m/s). Second, the standard widths for escalator steps are 24 in (600 mm), 32 in (800 mm), and 40 in (1000 mm). And, third, members of the escalator industry generally agree that one person can comfortably occupy a 24 in (600 mm) step and two people *can* stand side-by-side on a 40 in (1000 mm) wide step. Utilizing these facts, product data published by the Otis Elevator Company states that the *nominal* capacities for escalators with the step widths of 24 in (600 mm), 32 in (800 mm), and 40 in (1000 mm) are, respectively, 2250, 3375, and 4500 passengers per hour (for escalators with a maximum rise of 20 ft [6.1 m]).[31] Note that these nominal capacity projections by the Otis Elevator Company match forecasts that are offered by other escalator manufacturers.

The *actual* number of passengers that will ride on an escalator per unit time is, however, somewhat less than these nominal capacities. The cause of the differentiation between the nominal and actual number of passengers is a factor identified by Fruin as the "human buffer zone."[32] This zone is essentially a space (or volume) that people seek to maintain about themselves, separating themselves physically from other people. This zone also provides accommodation for the time required for a passenger to get set to board the escalator (accounting for any hesitancy a person might experience stepping on a moving stair). For example—in the first instance—whereas two people can theoretically stand next to each other on a 40 in (1000 mm) wide step, most often passengers will stand one person to a step. Or, on an escalator with 24 in (600 mm) wide steps, passengers will commonly board the escalator on every other step thus leaving the intervening steps unused. Thus, the number of passengers who actually ride on an escalator per unit time is considerably less than the nominal projection. A realistic estimate of actual passengers is probably closer to 50–60 percent of the nominal capacity.

Placement locations for escalators. When escalators are used in retail commercial facilities, such as department stores and malls, the escalators should be placed in the center of floor areas or at the juncture of main pedestrian pathways. In either instance the escalator becomes a space-organizing device, better enabling occupants to conceptualize how the facility is laid out. Also, in the case of placing escalators in department stores, the ride itself can be a significant opportunity for the sellers to display important products or wares to the potential purchasers.

For sporting venues, auditoria, and convention centers, escalators can ease and speed the passage of the audience from the places of entry to people's seats or observation areas. The placement and movement of the escalators indicate to the participants in what directions they should be moving to gain access to the event they have come to view. Thus, the escalators should be placed as close to the entries as possible and should transport the participants as near as possible to their seating or viewing areas. Similarly, escalators can also be effective means for enabling the participants to exit the seating or viewing areas after the conclusion of the event.

For transportations facilities, escalators offer an important means to transport passengers from arriving vehicles—subways, trains, airplanes, and so forth—into main terminals or to street levels. Other escalators can be used to carry passengers to their departing vehicles. Because many transportation facilities are organized via multiple use levels—for boarding and disembarking, for ticketing, for baggage pick-up and making connections with street transportation—escalators are essential means for easing passenger traffic between levels (and for guiding such traffic).

Placement formats for escalators. There are perhaps four primary ways to organize and stack escalators when they are employed for buildings of several stories. These four variations are the parallel, criss-cross, stacked, and in-line (see Figures F.15–F.17). What distinguishes each of these from the others are the basic layout of the multiple escalator units in the overall system and the pathways between units that passengers must traverse in a trip upward or downward.

Figure F.15 Here are two pairs of criss-cross escalators. Commonly, criss-cross escalators will be organized so that the landings (or the ending of one run and the beginning of the next) are coincident. Thus, no walking around from one run to the next is necessary. However, these pairs of criss-cross escalators—located in an urban shopping mall—are atypical and the end of one run and the beginning of the next are at opposite sides of the escalator space. Encouraging riders to walk around the escalator assemblies is a useful practice for retail malls and shopping centers. The walk-around enables the riders to see what activities are present on each floor that the riders traverse.

Other formats are occasionally utilized. For example, one of these four arrangements will be employed to go from floor-to-floor in a common format. In addition, a longer multiple-story escalator can be incorporated into the system to provide immediate transportation from a higher floor to some lower floor, essentially as an express. Another arrangement that is applied when there are regularly scheduled high volumes of traffic in one or the other direction (e.g., commuters entering a central business district by subway or train; fans coming into a sports stadium before the start of a game; the audience arriving at an entertainment center; and so forth) enables changing of the direction that the escalators move. In such instances a bank of parallel escalators might be set—at the beginning of the event—to mostly take people inward. Then, at the end of the event, the prevailing direction of the escalator bank could be reversed to enable the exiting of the occupants.[33]

Figure F.16 These escalators are described as "stacked." Conventionally, for stacked escalators, the end of one run and the beginning of the next run—ascending or descending—are at the opposite sides of the escalator space. Thus, to get from one run to the next during an ascent or descent, the rider must walk around the escalator space. Similar to the escalator pairs in Figure F.15, the specific stacked escalators in this photograph are located in an urban shopping mall.

Sizing issues for placing escalators. The major dimensions for escalators concern the incline angle, the horizontal lengths, the overall widths, the opening in a floor to accommodate insertion of the pit volume, and the necessary headroom between units when one unit is placed directly above another.

The maximum inclination angle for escalators is 30° (where the inclination angle is bounded by the centerline of the escalator steps and the floor at the lower landing).[34] Indeed, this 30° angle is commonly regarded as the standard inclination angle for escalator placements.

Figure F.17 Pairs of inline (parallel) escalators are present in this convention center. For each pair of escalators, one ascends and the other descends. As riders traverse the escalators, they may continue upward or downward, or they may stop at any landing and sample the displays and activities on that floor. There is no need for walk-around space (i.e., to get from one escalator run to the next in the journey upward or downward). The potential space penalty in employing this organization is that there must be substantial length to the building to enable laying out inline escalators.

The *horizontal* length of an escalator depends on the height between floors that an escalator traverses and the number of flat steps incorporated at landings of the escalator. The maximum floor-to-floor dimensions for escalator units will be about 20–25 ft (6100–7600 mm), depending on manufacturer. Escalators for floor heights greater than these common height limits can usually be obtained upon the placement of special orders with any of the various manufacturers. Formulae for determining the horizontal length of an escalator unit are as follows:[35]

For escalators with two flat steps at the landings,

Length = (1.732 × Floor height) + 185 in (4700 mm)

For escalators with three flat steps at the landings,

Length = (1.732 × Floor height) + 215 in (5460 mm)

The overall widths of escalators are basically determined by the widths of the moving stairs: the wider the stairs, the wider the overall escalator unit. So, if the standard stair widths are 24 in (600 mm), 32 in (800 mm), and 40 in (1000 mm), the widths for the over-all escalator units are, respectively, 45 in (1150 mm), 53 in (1350 mm), and 61 in (1550 mm). These overall widths represent the dimensions for the upper (visible) part of the escalator unit. The overall widths for the lower (hidden) part of the unit will be an additional 4 in (100 mm) greater. Thus, an escalator with a stair width of 24 in (600 mm) will have an overall width for the upper (visible) part of 45 in (1150 mm) and an overall width for the lower (hidden) part of 49 in (1250 mm). The overall width for the lower (hidden) part of an escalator unit is therefore the width of the pit (i.e., the width of the opening in the floor that must be provided to enable the insertion of the escalator pit).

The horizontal length of the opening in the floor to permit insertion of the pit volume should be 14'-8" (4470 mm); this dimension is the same for all three unit widths. The depth—the distance from the level of the finished floor downward—for the pit volume will typically be 3'-6" (1070 mm). The opening in the higher floor for an escalator unit first will have to be wide enough to accommodate the insertion of the machine room volume that generally has the same width as the pit. And, second, the horizontal length of the ceiling opening will be dictated by the provision of adequate headroom for an ascending or descending passenger. The clear height for a passenger is measured from the level of an escalator step to the bottom edge of the ceiling plane. The minimum acceptable clear height—headroom—is 7 ft (2130 mm).[36] In a similar fashion, when two escalator units are stacked vertically, then the clear headroom between these units must also be 7 ft (2130 mm).

Section F.3 | DESIGN PRINCIPLES FOR MOVING WALKWAYS

In a number of respects moving walkways closely resemble the forms and functions of escalators. The principal function of a moving walkway is to offer building occupants a means of traveling more quickly and with relatively little personal effort over long pathways (see Figure F.18). Moving walkways may either traverse a horizontal concourse or provide a gentle ascent (or descent) from one floor to another. These moving walkways are most often employed in transportation terminals such as airports and railroad stations. They may also be applied in large shopping malls.

The basic form of a moving walkway unit is indeed similar to that of the escalator (see Figure F.19). For the moving walkway, there are an upper (visible) part and a lower (hidden) part. For a horizontal moving walkway, the lower (hidden) part is incorporated into the floor assembly, whereas the upper (visible) part stands above the floor. Alternatively, for an inclined moving walkway much of the unit will exist above floor level. For such an inclined moving walkway the two ends will be embedded in the respective floors of the two levels served by the unit.

The lower (hidden) part of a moving walkway unit will contain at one end of the unit a drive motor, a drive shaft, and a wheel (that is turned by the drive shaft). At the other end a tensioning wheel will be present. Between these two wheels a pallet chain runs. This chain attaches to the bottoms of the pallets that comprise the moving treadway surface of the upper (visible) part of the walkway unit. As the chain moves, so too does the treadway, thereby transporting the passengers along the walkway. One further major component of the lower (hidden) part is a truss that furnishes the structural integrity for the overall moving walkway unit.

Figure F.18 A horizontal people mover offers a convenient means for traversing long distances in airport concourses. People may either stand or walk on the moving walkway surface.

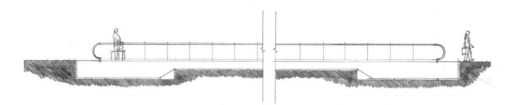

Figure F.19 A longitudinal section of a horizontal people mover assembly shows the basic spatial requirements for the installation of a people mover. The upper (or visible) portion of the assembly consists of landings, moving walkway surfaces, balustrades, and handrails. The lower (or hidden) portion contains the structural truss, drive motor, drive and tensioning wheels, and the pallet chain.

The upper (visible) part of the moving walkway unit encompasses the surface of the moving treadway, the balustrades, and handrails. Balustrades are placed on both sides of the moving treadway and separate the moving treadway from surrounding pedestrian surfaces. Handrails are included on the tops of the balustrades; these handrails will move in the same direction and at the same velocity as the moving treadway surface.

F.3.1 GUIDELINES FOR ACCOMMODATING MOVING WALKWAY UNITS IN BUILDING DESIGNS

The allowable widths for the moving treadway depend upon the speed of the treadway and the inclination intended for the moving walkway unit. For relatively slow treadway speeds (up to 140 ft/min [0.91 m/s]) and flat or slightly inclined (up to 4° slope) the maximum allowable width for treadways will be 60 in (1520 mm). For greater speeds and/or greater slopes the maximum allowable width for treadways is 40 in (1020 mm). Note that combinations of treadway speeds greater than 140 ft/min (0.91 m/s) and slopes greater than 8° are not permitted.[37]

The standard treadway widths utilized by many moving walkway manufacturers for their units are 32 in (800 mm) and 40 in (1000 mm). The 40 in (1000 mm) treadway unit has sufficient width so that two riders can stand side-by-side comfortably. Alternatively, with this 40 in (1000 mm) width, one rider can stand at one side of the treadway and other riders can readily walk past. The overall single-unit widths for these two treadway sizes are, respectively, 55 in (1400 mm) and 63 in (1600 mm). The minimum rough opening widths for the installation of these single units then are 58 in (1480 mm) and 66 in (1680 mm). When two units are installed side-by-side, the required rough opening width for two units, each with 32 in (800 mm) wide treadways, should be 9'-4" (2840 mm). Similarly, when two units with 40 in (1000 mm) wide treadways are placed side-by-side, the rough opening widths should be 10'-8" (3250 mm).

The lengths of commercially available horizontal moving walkways are largely variable and dependent on the need for a given building. For instance, Schindler USA offers moving walkways with a maximum length of 328 ft (100 m). However, a practice that is employed for long airport concourses is to install two or more consecutive moving walkways with ordinary (nonmoving) pedestrian surfaces between the moving walkway lengths. Such ordinary, intermediate surfaces allow walkway riders to exit from the walkway or, where parallel units are present, to change from one to the other (e.g., where parallel moving walkways are present and moving in the same direction, riders on one unit will simply stand and the riders on the other unit will walk, increasing the speed with which they can move along the concourse).

The volumes required for moving walkways pits—whether containing the machine drive unit or not—usually have rough depths of about 42 in (1070 mm) and lengths of about 18 ft (5.50 m). For inclined moving walkways these pits will be embedded into floor assemblies at the respective ends of the walkway unit. The lower (hidden) volume of an inclined moving walkway—spanning from the pit at one end of the unit to the pit at the other end—will be enclosed and contain the pallet chain. For horizontal moving walkways the entire lower (hidden) volume—both pits and the intermediate space containing the pallet chain—will be incorporated into the floor assembly.

Balustrades are required on both sides of the treadway of a moving walkway and can be between 30 to 42 in (760 to 1070 mm) high.[38] The balustrade height preferred by a number of manufacturers is 40 in (1000 mm). Handrails on top of these balustrades should be 4 in wide and should move in the same direction and at the same velocity as the treadway.[39]

The minimum headroom above the moving treadway surface should be 7 ft (2130 mm).

Section F.4 | BIBLIOGRAPHY FOR HUMAN CONVEYANCE SYSTEMS

The standard, comprehensive textbook for vertical and horizontal people-moving systems has been composed by Strakosch, G.R. (ed.), *The Vertical Transportation Handbook,* 3rd edition, (New York: J. Wiley & Sons, Inc., 1998). Other texts present briefer treatments of this subject. Among these texts are Stein, B., and J.R. Reynolds, *Mechanical and Electrical Equipment for Buildings,* 9th edition, (New York: J. Wiley & Sons, 2000); Janovsky, L., *Elevator Mechanical Design,* 2nd edition, (New York: Ellis Horwood, 1993); and Barney, G.C., and S.M. Dos Santos, *Lift Traffic Analysis Design and Control,* (London: Peter Peregrinus Ltd., 1977). Also, another book that offers an interesting and provocative treatment of vertical transportation systems has been composed by Lampugnani, V.M., and L. Hartwig (eds.), *Vertical: A Cultural History of Vertical Transport,* (Berlin: Ernest & Sohn, 1994).

The principal journal that describes vertical and horizontal people-moving systems and their applications is *Elevator World.* Information about this journal can be found at the Web address, http://www.elevator-world.com.

ENDNOTES and SELECTED ADDITIONAL COMMENTS

1. "Cars & Counterweights," *Inside the World of Elevators,* (Farmington, Connecticut: Otis Elevator Corporation, 1986), page 4.

2. "Machines, Brakes, & Roping," *Inside the World of Elevators,* (Farmington, Connecticut: Otis Elevator Corporation, 1986), page 6.

3. "Governors & Safeties," *Inside the World of Elevators,* (Farmington, Connecticut: Otis Elevator Corporation, 1986), pages 2–3.

4. "The Machine Room," *Inside the World of Elevators,* (Farmington, Connecticut: Otis Elevator Corporation, 1986).

5. "Control & Signaling Equipment," *Inside the World of Elevators,* (Farmington, Connecticut: Otis Elevator Corporation, 1986).

6. Ibid, pages 6–7.

7. "Cars & Counterweights," *Inside the World of Elevators,* (Farmington, Connecticut: Otis Elevator Corporation, 1986), pages 12–15.

8. Strakosch, G.R., "Incoming traffic," in Strakosch, G.R. (ed.), *The Vertical Transportation Handbook,* 3rd edition, (New York: J. Wiley & Sons, Inc., 1998), pages 71–96; and Stein, B., and J.R. Reynolds, *Mechanical and Electrical Equipment for Buildings,* 9th edition, (New York: J. Wiley & Sons, Inc., 2000).

9. *Safety Code for Elevators and Escalators,* ASME/ANSI A17.1-1996, (New York: American National Standards Institute, 1996).

10. For example, see Section 3012, "ANSI Code Adopted," in Appendix Chapter 30 ("Elevators, Dumbwaiters, Escalators, and Moving Walks") of the *Uniform Building Code,* (Whittier, California: International Conference of Building Officials, 1997), pages 1–399.

11. *Safety Code for Existing Elevators and Escalators,* ASME/ANSI A17.3-1996 (New York: American National Standards Institute, 2001).

12. This quotation appears in an article by J.W. Brannon, "Elevator traffic: analysis and selection for smaller buildings," *Elevator World,* 46(5), May 1998, pages 86–87. Note the quotation also is cited in Strakosch, G.R. (ed.), *The Vertical Transportation Handbook,* 3rd edition, (New York: J. Wiley & Sons, Inc., 1998), page 47.

13. Strakosch, G.R. (ed.), *The Vertical Transportation Handbook,* 3rd edition, (New York: J. Wiley & Sons, Inc., 1998), page 271.

14. Ibid, page 272.

15. Guise, D., *Design and Technology in Architecture,* (New York: J. Wiley & Sons, 1985). Note pages 231–265.

16. Siikonen, M-L., "Double-deck elevators: savings in time and space," *Elevator World,* 46(7), July 1998; and Fortune, J.W., "Mega-high-rise elevatoring," *Elevator World,* 45(12), December 1997. (The first paper is available at http://www.elevator-world.com/magazine/archive01/9807-001.html-ssi, and the second paper can be found at http://www.elevator-world.com/magazine/archive01/9712-003.html-ssi.)

17. For instance, this car size requirement is stipulated in Section 3003.4.1 of the *Uniform Building Code,* (Whittier, California: International Conference of Building Officials, 1997), pages 1–285.

18. The car size to enable vertical transportation of an ambulance stretcher is set forth in Statement 3003.5 of the *Uniform Building Code,* (Whittier, California: International Conference of Building Officials, 1997), pages 1–286.

19. Strakosch, G.R. (editor), *The Vertical Transportation Handbook,* 3rd edition, (New York: J. Wiley & Sons, Inc., 1998), page 53.

20. Howkins, R., "Elevator core areas," *Elevator World,* 46(11), November 1998, pages 58–64.

21. See either Section 6-2.4.5 of the *Life Safety Code Handbook,* 7th edition, R. Cote (ed.), (Quincy, Massachusetts: National Fire Protection Association, Inc., 1997), page 185; or Section 403.7 #1 of the *Uniform Building Code,* (Whittier, California: International Conference of Building Officials, 1997), pages 1–43.

22. This one value has been taken from page 62 of Strakosch, G.R. (editor), *The Vertical Transportation Handbook,* 3rd edition, (New York: J. Wiley & Sons, Inc., 1998).

23. For example, see Section 6-2.4.9 of the *Life Safety Code Handbook,* 7th edition, R. Cote (ed.), (Quincy, Massachusetts: National Fire Protection Association, Inc., 1997).

24. Fortune, J.W., op.cit.

25. Turner, D.L., "Escalators and moving walks," in Strakosch, G.R. (ed.), *The Vertical Transportation Handbook,* 3rd edition, (New York: J. Wiley & Sons, Inc., 1998), page 243.

26. "U.S. Fact Sheet," The Elevator Escalator Safety Foundation (as found at the Web address: http://www.eesf.com/fact.htm).

27. Cooper, D.A., "The history of the escalator," *Elevator World,* 47(4), April 1999, pages 84–90.

28. *Safety Code for Elevators and Escalators,* ASME/ANSI A17.1-1996, Section 802.5b.

29. Ibid, Section 802.3a.

30. Ibid, Section 802.6d.

31. *Otis Escalators/Escal-Aires* (Farmington, Connecticut: Otis Elevator Company, 1986), page 3. Or see: http://www.otis.com/products/detail/0,1355,CLI1_PRD765_PRT44_PST69_RES1,00.html.

32. This finding by J.J. Fruin is cited in the article by Al-Sharif, L., "Escalator handling capacity," *Elevator World,* 44(12), December 1996.

33. Turner, D.L., "Escalators and moving walks," in Strakosch, G.R. (ed.), *The Vertical Transportation Handbook,* 3rd edition, (New York: J. Wiley & Sons, Inc., 1998), pages 219–244.

34. *Safety Code for Elevators and Escalators,* ASME/ANSI A17.1-1996, Section 802.1.

35. "Escalator planning data sheet," furnished by the ThyssenKrupp Elevator Corporation at the Web address, http://www.thyssenkruppelevator.com/escalatorsmain.asp.

36. *Safety Code for Elevators and Escalators,* ASME/ANSI A17.1-1996, Section 802.12.

37. *Safety Code for Elevators and Escalators,* ASME/ANSI A17.1-1996, Section 902.7.

38. *Safety Code for Elevators and Escalators,* ASME/ANSI A17.1-1996, Section 902.2.

39. *Safety Code for Elevators and Escalators,* ASME/ANSI A17.1-1996, Section 902.4.

Illustration Credits

A number of the photographs identified below have been adopted, with permission, from the Slide Collection of the College of Architecture and Urban Planning (CAUP), University of Washington. Permission to use these slides was granted by Gordon Varey, late Dean of the College. The photographers who donated slides to the collection and whose slides have been used in this text will be identified in the following catalog.

CHAPTER 2
Figures 2.1–2.7 and 2.9–2.14 drawn by Lisa Kirkendall. Figure 2.8 photographed by Dean Heerwagen.

CHAPTER 3
Figures 3.1–3.5, 3.8–3.14, 3.19 drawn by Lisa Kirkendall. Figures 3.6–3.7 drawn by Kate Sweeney. Figure 3.15 photographed by Elizabeth McCullough, Kansas State University. Figures 3.16–3.18 drawn by David Hudacek.

CHAPTER 4
All figures drawn by David Hudacek.

CHAPTER 5
All drawings done by David Hudacek. Figures 5.2, 5.5, 5.6, 5.45, 5.47–5.49, 5.63, 5.66, photographed by Gordon Orians (CAUP collection). Figures 5.11, photographed by Floyd Naramore (CAUP collection). Figures 5.16, 5.19, 5.24, 5.25, 5.53, 5.54, 5.58, 5.60, 5.62, 5.75, photographed by Dean Heerwagen. Figure 5.28, photographed by Tarik Khiati (gift to D. Heerwagen). Figure 5.31, photographed by John Johansen (CAUP collection). Figure 5.36, photographed by Norman Johnston (CAUP collection). Figure 5.77,

photographed by Earl Bell (gift to D. Heerwagen). Figure 5.15, 5.32–5.34, by unidentified photographers (CAUP collection).

CHAPTER 6
Figure 6.1, 6.3–6.6, 6.9, 6.11, 6.17–6.19, drawn by Lisa Kirkendall. Figure 6.2, 6.7–6.8, 6.10, 6.12–6.16, drawn by David Hudacek. Figures 6.20–6.23 photographed by Dean Heerwagen.

CHAPTER 7
Figures 7.1, 7.3–7.5, drawn by Kate Sweeney. Figures 7.6–7.7, 7.9–7.10, 7.12, 7.14, drawn by David Hudacek. Figures 7.26, 7.28, drawn by Lisa Kirkendall. Figures 7.2, 7.8, 7.16, 7.18–7.25, 7.27, photographed by Dean Heerwagen. Figure 7.13, 7.15, assembled by Dean Heerwagen. Figure 7.11, photographed by Sue Slatkin (CAUP collection). Figure 7.17, photographed by John Barnes (from a CAUP research project).

CHAPTER 8
Figures 8.1, 8.3–8.4, 8.18, photographed by Dean Heerwagen. Figure 8.2, photographed by Robert O'Neal (gift to D. Heerwagen). Figures 8.5–8.6, by unidentified photographers (CAUP collection) Figures 8.7, 8.15–8.17, 8.19, drawn by Lisa Kirkendall. Figures 8.8, 8.27–8.28, 8.30, 8.34–8.35, 8.38, 8.40, 8.43, drawn by Brendan Connolly. Figures 8.9–8.12, 8.14, 8.20–8.22, 8.24–8.26, 8.31, drawn by David Hudacek. Figure 8.13, photographed by T. Cannon, Solar Energy Research Insitute. Figures 8.23, 8.29, 8.32, 8.33, 8.36, 8.39, 8.41, taken from the *Graphic Daylighting Design Manual*. Figures 8.37, 8.42, assembled by Dean Heerwagen.

CHAPTER 9

All drawings prepared by David Hudacek. Figures 9.3, 9.7, 9.13, 9.17–9.18, 9.23–9.24, 9.42, 9.45, 9.48, photographed by Dean Heerwagen. Figure 9.4, produced by Libbey-Owens-Ford Company. Figure 9.8, photographed by unidentified photographer (CAUP collection). Figures 9.14, 9.26, 9.36, 9.50, photographed by Marietta Millet (CAUP collection). Figure 9.25, 9.29, photographed by Norman Johnston (CAUP collection). Figure 9.34, 9.38, photographed by John Barnes (from a CAUP research project). Figure 9.41, photographed by Lee Copeland (CAUP collection). Figures 9.43–9.44, photographed by Dick Alden (CAUP collection). Figure 9.46, photographed by Floyd Naramore (CAUP collection).

CHAPTER 10

Figures 10.1–10.17, drawn by Lisa Kirkendall. Figures 10.18–10.19, 10.21, drawn by David Hudacek. Figures 10.20, 10.22–10.23, photographed by Dean Heerwagen.

CHAPTER 11

Figures 11.1–11.3, 11.6–11.13, drawn by David Hudacek. Figures 11.4–11.5, drawn by Kate Sweeney.

CHAPTER 12

All figures drawn by David Hudacek.

CHAPTER 13

All drawings prepared by David Hudacek. Figures 13.3, 13.11, 13.19, 13.29–13.30, 13.45–13.46, 13.50–13.52, photographed by Dean Heerwagen. Figure 13.27–3.28, photographed by Norman Johnston (CAUP collection). Figure 13.34, photographed by Neal Middleton (CAUP collection). Figure 13.47, 13.53, photographed by John Barnes (from a CAUP research project).

CHAPTER A

All drawings prepared by Brendan Connolly. All photographs produced by Dean Heerwagen.

CHAPTER B

All drawings prepared by Brendan Connolly. Figure B.17 photographed by Christian Staub (CAUP collection). Figure B.18 photographed by Dean Heerwagen.

CHAPTER C

All drawings prepared by Brendan Connolly. All photographs (except for Figure C.14) produced by Dean Heerwagen. The Figure C.14 photographs were produced by KING5-TV, Seattle.

CHAPTER D

All drawings prepared by Brendan Connolly. All photographs produced by Dean Heerwagen (except for those identified on the next line). Figures D.14, D.16–D.17, produced by the City of Seattle Lighting Department.

CHAPTER E

All drawings prepared by Brendan Connolly. All photographs produced by Dean Heerwagen.

CHAPTER F

All drawings prepared by Brendan Connolly. All photographs (except for Figures F.14 and F.18) produced by Dean Heerwagen. Figures F.14 and F.18 were photographed by Norman Johnston (CAUP collection).

Index

Human body
  hearing. *See* Hearing
  heat balance with environment, 36–38, 40. *See also* Thermal comfort
  heat production within, 34–36
  metabolic rate, 35, 43, 46, 51
  net radiant exchange rate, 43, 44
  sensory system, 246–248
  sight. *See* Vision
  speech. *See* Speech
  thermoregulatory system in, 38–41
HVAC systems, 619–620
  air-water. *See* Air-water HVAC systems
  all-air. *See* All-air HVAC systems
  all-water. *See* All-water HVAC systems
  basic components of, 620–623
  chilled water production, 651–655
  direct-refrigerant. *See* Direct-refrigerant HVAC systems
  hot water production, 647–649
  location of, 623–625
  refrigeration cycle, 650–651
  small-building. *See* Small-building HVAC systems
  thermal-conditioning equipment, 647–655
  for university classroom buildings. *See* Gould Hall HVAC system
Hydraulic elevators, 886–889, 893. *See also* Elevators
  components of, 893–898
Hydroelectric dams, 2

I

Ice cap climates, 165. *See also* Cool/cold climates
Illuminance, 235. *See also* Sky illuminance
  diffuse, 311, 313
  direct-beam, 127, 196, 311, 312f, 313
Illumination. *See* Light
Incandescence, 209–210
Infrared radiation, 208
Internal-load-dominant buildings, 86
Internally-Reflected Component (IRC), 323–324
  worked example using, 349, 349f
Inverse-Square Law, 236–237, 447f
Irradiance measures, 313–314, 317
Isolux contour, 328, 329f

K

Kimbell Art Museum, 386
Köppen's climate classification system, 76, 78f

L

Land-sea breezes, 121

Language
  components of, 482
  speech. *See* Speech
Laser light, 212
Latent heat, 27–29
Li-Cor datalogger, 240f, 241
Li-Cor Photometric Sensors, 240f, 241
Light
  absorption of, 219–220, 224, 225
  beams. *See* Light beams
  brightness of, 236–238, 318. *See also* Luminance
  color. *See* Color(s)
  daylight. *See* Daylight(ing)
  efficiency of, 213
  electromagnetic radiation and, 208–209, 214–217
  emission rate, 234–235
  laser, 212
  measuring, 238–241
  media interaction, 217–222
  properties of, 214–222
  quantifying, 234–238
  reflection of. *See* Reflection/reflectance (light)
  sources of, 208–212
  surface(s) interaction, 213–214, 217–222, 235, 236–238. *See* Reflection/reflectance (light)
  transmission of, 217–219
  transverse waves, 216
  vision. *See* Vision
Light beams, 216–217
  how seen, 213–214
Lighting, 207–208. *See also* Daylight(ing)
  codes, 336
  and color, 226
  comfort/discomfort. *See* Visual comfort/discomfort
  designing for, 207–208, 419–422
  fixtures, accommodation of, 421–422, 833–834
  flicker, 294, 296
  glare. *See* Glare
  lamp filaments, heating of, 209
  levels, 284–286, 336–347
  role(s) of, 419–420
  standards, 336–346
  studies, 338–340
  surface(s) interaction, 213–214, 217–222, 235, 236–238. *See* Reflection/reflectance (light)
  veiling reflections, 293–294
Light shelves, 401–402
"Lines of defense," 4–5, 32
  for climactic challenges, 32
Listening. *See* Hearing